Winner's Electoral College Vote %	Winner's Popular Vote %	Congress	House		Senate	
			Majority Party	Minority Party	Majority Party	Minority Party
**	No popular	1st	38 Admin †	26 Opp	17 Admin	9 Opp
	vote	2nd	37 Fed ††	33 Fed ††	16 Fed	13 Dem-R
**	No popular	3rd	57 Dem-R	48 Fed	17 Fed	13 Dem-R
	vote	4th	54 Fed	52 Dem-R	19 Fed	13 Dem-R
**	No popular	5th	58 Fed	48 Dem-R	20 Fed	12 Dem-R
	vote	6th	64 Fed	42 Dem-R	19 Fed	13 Dem-R
HR**	No popular	7th	69 Dem-R	36 Fed	18 Dem-R	13 Fed
	vote	8th	402 Dem-R	39 Fed	25 Dem-R	9 Fed
92.0	No popular	9th	116 Dem-R	25 Fed	27 Dem-R	7 Fed
	vote	10th	118 Dem-R	24 Fed	28 Dem-R	6 Fed
69.7	No popular	11th	94 Dem-R	48 Fed	28 Dem-R	6 Fed
	vote	12th	108 Dem-R	36 Fed	30 Dem-R	6 Fed
59.0	No popular	13th	112 Dem-R	68 Fed	27 Dem-R	9 Fed
	vote	14th	117 Dem-R	65 Fed	25 Dem-R	11 Fed
84.3	No popular	15th	141 Dem-R	42 Fed	34 Dem-R	10 Fed
	vote	16th	156 Dem-R	27 Fed	35 Dem-R	7 Fed
99.5	No popular	17th	158 Dem-R	25 Fed	44 Dem-R	4 Fed
	vote	18th	187 Dem-R	26 Fed	44 Dem-R	4 Fed
HR	39.1 †††	19th	105 Admin	97 Dem-J	26 Admin	20 Dem-J
		20th	119 Dem-J	94 Admin	28 Dem-J	20 Admin
68.2	56.0	21st	139 Dem	74 Nat R	26 Dem	22 Nat R
		22nd	141 Dem	58 Nat R	25 Dem	21 Nat R
76.6	54.5	23rd	147 Dem	53 AntiMas	20 Dem	20 Nat R
		24th	145 Dem	98 Whig	27 Dem	25 Whig
57.8	50.9	25th	108 Dem	107 Whig	30 Dem	18 Whig
		26th	124 Dem	118 Whig	28 Dem	22 Whig
79.6	52.9					
–	52.9	27th	133 Whig	102 Dem	28 Whig	22 Dem
		28th	142 Dem	79 Whig	28 Whig	25 Dem
61.8	49.6	29th	143 Dem	77 Whig	31 Dem	25 Whig
		30th	115 Whig	108 Dem	36 Dem	21 Whig
56.2	47.3	31st	112 Dem	109 Whig	35 Dem	25 Whig
–	–	32nd	140 Dem	88 Whig	35 Dem	24 Whig
85.8	50.9	33rd	159 Dem	71 Whig	38 Dem	22 Whig
		34th	108 Rep	83 Dem	40 Dem	15 Rep
58.8	45.6	35th	118 Dem	92 Rep	36 Dem	20 Rep
		36th	114 Rep	92 Dem	36 Dem	26 Rep
59.4	39.8	37th	105 Rep	43 Dem	31 Rep	10 Dem
		38th	102 Rep	75 Dem	36 Rep	9 Dem
91.0	55.2					
–	–	39th	149 Union	42 Dem	42 Union	10 Dem
		40th	143 Rep	49 Dem	42 Rep	11 Dem
72.8	52.7	41st	149 Rep	63 Dem	56 Rep	11 Dem
		42nd	134 Rep	104 Dem	52 Rep	17 Dem
81.9	55.6	43rd	194 Rep	92 Dem	49 Rep	19 Dem
		44th	169 Rep	109 Dem	45 Rep	29 Dem
50.1	47.9 †††	45th	153 Dem	140 Rep	39 Rep	36 Dem
		46th	149 Dem	130 Rep	42 Dem	33 Rep
58.0	48.3	47th	147 Rep	135 Dem	37 Rep	37 Dem
–	–	48th	197 Dem	118 Rep	38 Rep	36 Dem
54.6	48.5	49th	183 Dem	140 Rep	43 Rep	34 Dem
		50th	169 Dem	152 Rep	39 Rep	37 Dem

Source for election data: Svend Peterson, *A Statistical History of American Presidential Elections*. New York: Frederick Ungar Publishing, 1963. Updates: Richard Scammon, *America Votes* 19. Washington D.C.: Congressional Quarterly, 1991; *Congressional Quarterly Weekly Report*, Nov. 7, 1992, p. 3552.

Abbreviations:

Admin = Administration supporters
AntiMas = Anti-Masonic
Dem = Democratic
Dem-R = Democratic-Republican
Fed = Federalist

Dem-J = Jacksonian Democrats
Nat R = National Republican
Opp = Opponents of administration
Rep = Republican
Union = Unionist

UNDERSTANDING AMERICAN GOVERNMENT

ELEVENTH EDITION

UNDERSTANDING AMERICAN GOVERNMENT

SUSAN WELCH
The Pennsylvania State University

JOHN GRUHL
University of Nebraska–Lincoln

JOHN COMER
University of Nebraska–Lincoln

SUSAN M. RIGDON
University of Illinois at Urbana–Champaign

THOMSON

WADSWORTH

Australia • Brazil • Canada • Mexico • Singapore
Spain • United Kingdom • United States

Understanding American Government, Eleventh Edition

Susan Welch, John Gruhl, John Comer, Susan M. Rigdon

Publisher: *Clark Baxter*
Acquisitions Editor: *Carolyn Merrill*
Development Editor: *Rebecca Green*
Editorial Assistant: *Patrick Rheume*
Technology Project Manager: *Gene Ioffe*
Marketing Manager: *Janise Frye*
Marketing Assistant: *Kathleen Tosiello*
Marketing Communications Manager: *Tami Strang*
Project Manager, Editorial Production: *Paul Wells*
Creative Director: *Rob Hugel*
Art Director: *Maria Epes*

Print Buyer: *Rebecca Cross*
Permissions Editor: *Roberta Broyer*
Production Service: *The Book Company*
Text Designer: *Carolyn Deacy*
Photo Researcher: *Kate Cebik*
Copy Editor: *Jane Loftus*
Cover Designer: *Carolyn Deacy*
Cover Image: *©Wally McNamee/CORBIS*
Compositor/Production Service: *Lachina Publishing Services*
Printer: *Courier Corporation/Kendallville*

For more information about our products, contact us at:
Thomson Learning Academic Resource Center
1-800-423-0563

For permission to use material from this text or product, submit a request online at **http://www.thomsonrights.com**. Any additional questions about permissions can be submitted by e-mail to **thomsonrights@thomson.com**.

Library of Congress Control Number: 2006940759

ISBN-13: 978-0-495-09869-0
ISBN-10: 0-495-09869-8

Thomson Higher Education
10 Davis Drive
Belmont, CA 94002-3098
USA

Asia (including India)
Thomson Learning
5 Shenton Way
#01-01 UIC Building
Singapore 068808

Australia/New Zealand
Thomson Learning Australia
102 Dodds Street
Southbank, Victoria 3006
Australia

Canada
Thomson Nelson
1120 Birchmount Road
Toronto, Ontario M1K 5G4
Canada

UK/Europe/Middle East/Africa
Thomson Learning
High Holborn House
50–51 Bedford Row
London WC1R 4LR
United Kingdom

Latin America
Thomson Learning
Seneca, 53
Colonia Polanco
11560 Mexico
D.F. Mexico

Spain (including Portugal)
Thomson Paraninfo
Calle Magallanes, 25
28015 Madrid, Spain

BRIEF CONTENTS

PART ONE

The American System

1 The American People 2

2 The Constitution 26

3 Federalism 56

PART TWO

Links between People and Government

4 Public Opinion 88

5 News Media 118

6 Interest Groups 164

7 Political Parties 202

8 Elections 236

9 Money and Politics 284

PART THREE

Institutions

10 Congress 316

11 The Presidency 360

12 The Bureaucracy 402

13 The Judiciary 434

PART FOUR

Civil Liberties and Rights

14 Civil Liberties 468

15 Civil Rights 518

PART FIVE

Public Policies

16 Economic Policy 568

17 Social Welfare and Health Policy 604

18 Foreign Policy 632

CONTENTS

Preface xv

About the Authors 1

PART ONE

The American System

CHAPTER 1

The American People 2

YOU ARE THERE *What Is Your Civic I.Q.? 3*

A Demographic Profile 5
  Immigration and Ethnic Diversity 5
  Immigration and Political Cleavage 9
  Religious Diversity 9
  Economic and Demographic Diversity 10
  Diversity and Identity Politics 10

Political Culture 12
  AMERICAN DIVERSITY *Identity in the Age of DNA 13*
  The Significance of Political Culture 14
  Learning Political Culture 14

The Core Values 17
  Individual Liberty 17
  Political Equality 18
  Majority Rule 19
  Minority Rights 19
  Economic Rights 19

The American Citizen 20
  Democracy in a Republic 20
  Political Participation 20
  Who Has the Power? 22

Conclusion: Is Government Responsive? 23

EPILOGUE: YOU ARE THERE *Score Your Civic I.Q. 24*
Key Terms 24
Further Reading 24
For Viewing 25
Electronic Resources 25
ThomsonNOW 25

CHAPTER 2

The Constitution 26

YOU ARE THERE *The Case of the Confidential Tapes 27*

The Articles of Confederation 29
  National Government Problems 29
  BOX: *The Black Flag on the High Seas 30*
  State Government Problems 31

The Constitution 31
  The Constitutional Convention 31
  AMERICAN DIVERSITY *Founding Mothers 32*
  Features of the Constitution 36
  BOX: *The Undemocratic Senate 38*
  Motives of the Founders 41
  Ratification of the Constitution 43
  Changing the Constitution 43

Impact of the Civil War and the Great Depression 46
  The Civil War and Reconstruction 46
  The Great Depression and the New Deal 49
  A Combination of Constitutions 51

Conclusion: Does the Constitution Make the Government Responsive? 51

    EPILOGUE: YOU ARE THERE *The President Complies in the Case of the Confidential Tapes 53*

Key Terms 55
Further Reading 55
For Viewing 55
Electronic Resources 55
ThomsonNOW 55

CHAPTER 3

Federalism 56

YOU ARE THERE *Sign the Bill or Bill the Feds? 57*

Federal and Unitary Systems 59
    Federal Systems 59
    Unitary Systems 59
    Why Choose Federalism? 60

The Political Bases of American Federalism 60
    Political Benefits of Federalism 60
    Political Costs of Federalism 61
    AMERICAN DIVERSITY *Political Culture and Federalism 62*

The Constitutional Bases of Federalism 64
    Major Features of American Federalism 64
    Interpretations of the Constitutional Provisions 65

The Changing Division of Powers 66
    Growth of Government and the Division of Powers 66
    Resetting the Balance 70

Everyday Federalism 71
    Presidential Management of the Federal-State Relationship 72
    Cooperative Federalism 73
    Conflict in the Federal Relationship 73
    States and Localities as Lobbyists 75
    GOVERNMENT RESPONSIVENESS *Hurricane Katrina: A Failure to Communicate 76*
    Relations between the States 78
    State-Local Relations 79
    People, States, and the Federal Government 79

A Return to State-Centered Federalism? 81
    The Bush Administration 81
    Congress 81
    The States 81
    The Supreme Court 82

Conclusion: Does Federalism Make Government More Responsive? 84
    EPILOGUE: YOU ARE THERE *Napolitano Vetoes the Bill and Bills the Feds 85*
    Key Terms 86
    Further Reading 86
    For Viewing 86
    Electronic Resources 87
    ThomsonNOW 87

PART TWO

Links between People and Government

CHAPTER 4

Public Opinion 88

YOU ARE THERE *Should You Intervene in a Life or Death Decision? 89*

Nature of Public Opinion 90

Formation of Public Opinion 91
    BOX: *Opinions on Same-Sex Marriage 93*
    Agents of Political Socialization 94
    Impact of Political Socialization 97

Measuring Public Opinion 97
    Early Polling Efforts 97
    Emergence of Scientific Polling 98
    BOX: *The Short-Term Impact of 9/11 on Public Opinion 99*
    Use of Polls 100

BOX: *Doubting the Holocaust? 104*

Knowledge and Information 104

Ideology 105

Public Opinion in Red States and Blue States 107

Public Opinion toward Race 111
    GOVERNMENT RESPONSIVENESS *A Government Rebate as a Failed Panacea 112*

Conclusion: Is Government Responsive to Public Opinion? 114
    EPILOGUE: YOU ARE THERE *Senator Frist Provided Another Diagnosis 115*
    Key Terms 116
    Further Reading 116
    For Viewing 116
    Electronic Resources 116
    ThomsonNOW 117

CHAPTER 5

News Media 118

YOU ARE THERE *Should You Torpedo the Admiral?* 119

The Media State 120
  Dominance of the Media 121
  Concentration of the Media 122
  Atomization of the Media 124

Relationship between the Media and Politicians 128
  Symbiotic Relationship 128
  Adversarial Relationship 132
  Relationship between the Media and Recent
    Administrations 135
  Relationship between the Media and Congress 138
  Relationship between the Media and the Supreme Court
    138
  Relationship between the Media and the Military 139
  BOX: *Reporting from Iraq* 140

Bias of the Media 141
  Political Bias 141
  GOVERNMENT RESPONSIVENESS *What You Watch*
    Affects What You Believe 146
  Commercial Bias 148
  AMERICAN DIVERSITY *Color and the Clicker* 149

Impact of the Media on Politics 153
  Impact on the Public Agenda 153
  Impact on Political Parties and Elections 154
  GOVERNMENT RESPONSIVENESS *Cartoons Kill,*
    Media and Government Chill 156
  Impact on Public Opinion 158

Conclusion: Are the Media Responsive? 159
  EPILOGUE: YOU ARE THERE *Evans Pursued the*
    Admiral 161
  Key Terms 162
  Further Reading 162
  For Viewing 162
  Electronic Resources 163
  ThomsonNOW 163

CHAPTER 6

Interest Groups 164

  YOU ARE THERE *Do You Support the "Day without*
    Immigrants?" 165

Group Formation 167
  Why Interest Groups Form 167
  Why People Join 168
  Which People Join 168
  Have Americans Stopped Joining? 168

Types of Interest Groups 169
  Private Interest Groups 169
  BOX: *Interest Group Responsiveness to a National*
    Crisis 174
  Public Interest Groups 176
  AMERICAN DIVERSITY *The Origin of Gay and*
    Lesbian Rights Groups 178
  BOX: *Hey, Kid! Have I Got a Deal for You* 181

Strategies of Interest Groups 184

Tactics of Interest Groups 184
  BOX: *Earmarking, Better Than Hitting the Lottery* 185
  Direct Lobbying Techniques 185
  Indirect Lobbying Techniques: Going Public 189
  Building Coalitions 193
  AMERICAN DIVERSITY *Organizing Protest: The*
    Montgomery Bus Boycott 194

Success of Interest Groups 196
  Resources 196
  Competition and Goals 197

Interest Groups and Democracy 197

Conclusion: Do Interest Groups Help Make
Government Responsive? 198

  EPILOGUE: YOU ARE THERE *Father Mahony Advises*
    against Workers Staying Away from Work and
    Students Staying Away from School 200

  Key Terms 200
  Further Reading 200
  For Viewing 201
  Electronic Resources 201
  ThomsonNOW 201

CHAPTER 7

Political Parties 202

YOU ARE THERE *Do You Follow a 50-State Strategy?*
  203

Political Parties and Popular Control of Government
204

The American Party System 206
  Two Parties 206
  Fragmentation 207
  Moderation 207
  Minor Parties in American Politics 208

The Rise of American Political Parties 210
  The Founders and Political Parties 210
  Birth of Political Parties 211
  Development of Mass Parties 211

Party Realignments 212
   Rise of the Republicans and the Golden Age
    of Parties 213
   BOX: *A Day in the Life of a Machine Politician 214*
   Progressive Politics and the Weakening of Parties 214
   Rise of the Democratic Party 215
   Party Identification Today 216

Decline of Parties 222
   Diminution of Party Functions 222
   Erosion of Popular Support for Parties 224

Resurgence of Parties 224
   Continuing Importance of Political Parties 225
   Party Influence on Policy Making 226

Party Organization 226
   National Party Organization 227
   State and Local Party Organizations 227
   BOX: *Party Responsiveness in a National Crisis:*
    Bipartisanship for a While 228

Parties and Voting 228
   Party Identification 230
   Candidate Evaluations 231
   Issues 231
   Parties, Candidates, and Issues 232

Conclusion: Do Political Parties Make Government
More Responsive? 232

   EPILOGUE: YOU ARE THERE *234*

   Key Terms 234
   Further Reading 234
   For Viewing 235
   Electronic Resources 235
   ThomsonNOW 235

CHAPTER 8

Elections 236

YOU ARE THERE *Should You Run on the War? 237*

The American Electorate 240
   Early Limits on Voting Rights 240
   Blacks and the Right to Vote 240
   The Voting Rights Act and Redistricting 241
   BOX: *Racial Gerrymandering 243*
   AMERICAN DIVERSITY *Blacks and Hispanics in*
    Office 244
   Women and the Right to Vote 245
   Young People and the Right to Vote 246
   Felons and the Right to Vote 246
   Election Reform and New Threats to Voting Rights 246
   AMERICAN DIVERSITY *Women in Office 247*

Voter Turnout 248
   Political Activism in the Nineteenth Century 248
   Progressive Reforms 248
   Recent Turnout 249
   Who Does Not Vote? 249
   BOX: *Rock the Vote or Mock the Vote? 250*
   Why Turnout Is Low 252

Presidential Nominating Campaigns 256
   Who Runs for President and Why? 256
   How a Candidate Wins the Nomination 256
   AMERICAN DIVERSITY *Can an African American Be*
    Elected President? 258
   Presidential Caucuses and Conventions 259
   Presidential Primaries 260
   Reforming the Nomination Process 261
   The National Conventions 262
   Independent and Third-Party Nominees 264

The General Election Campaign 264
   Campaign Organization 265
   Campaign Strategies 266
   Campaign Communication 266
   GOVERNMENT RESPONSIVENESS *Voting in the*
    Shadow of Terrorism 267
   Campaign Funding 271
You've Got Mail 272
   The Electoral College 272
   The 2000 Election: A Perfect Storm 274
   Voting Patterns in the 2004 Election 276

The Permanent Campaign 276

Congressional Campaigns 277
   Incumbents: Unsafe at Any Margin? 277
   Challengers 278
   Campaigns 278
   Voting for Congress 279

Conclusion: Do Elections Make Government
Responsive? 280
   EPILOGUE: YOU ARE THERE *281*
   Key Terms 282
   Further Reading 282
   For Viewing 282
   Electronic Resources 283
   ThomsonNOW 283

CHAPTER 9

Money and Politics 284

YOU ARE THERE *Should You Make a Deal? 285*

Money and Politics in America's Past 287

BOX: *Honest Graft 287*
Money in Nineteenth-Century American Politics 288
Early Reforms 288
Reforms of the 1970s 289

Fundraising in Today's Campaigns 289
The President as Chief Fundraiser 290
Members of Congress as Fundraisers 291

Regulating Money in Modern Campaigns 292
*Recent Attempts at Reform: The McCain-Feingold
Act 292*
Disclosure 292
Regluating Campaign Spending 292
BOX: *How the Swift Boat Ad Became a National
News Story 294*
Contribution Limits and Ways to Avoid Them 294

Reforming Campaign Finance 297
Is Real Reform Possible? 297
Opposition to Reform 297
Ideas for Reform 297
BOX: *Congress as a Bad Neighborhood 300*

The Impact of Campaign Money 300
*Does the Campaign Finance System Deter Good
Candidates? 301*
Does Money Win Elections? 301

Does Money Buy Favorable Policies? 302
*Does Our Campaign Finance System Widen Class
Differences? 303*
BOX: *Buying Energy and Influence 304*
*Does Our Campaign Finance System Encourage
Extortion? 306*
*Does Our Campaign Finance System Lead to Money
and Public Cynicism? 307*
AMERICAN DIVERSITY *Campaign Donors 308*

Conflicts of Interest 308
The Abramoff Scandal and Concierge Politics 309
Regulating Ethical Behavior 310

Democratic and Republican Corruption 311

**Conclusion: Does the Influence of Money Make
Government Less Responsive? 312**

EPILOGUE: YOU ARE THERE *Reed Took the
Deal 314*

Key Terms 314
Further Reading 314
For Viewing 315
Electronic Resources 315
ThomsonNOW 315

PART THREE

Institutions

CHAPTER 10

Congress 316

YOU ARE THERE *Bipartisanship or More Partisanship? 317*

Members and Constituencies 319
Members 319
Constituencies 321
Congress as a Representative Body 322
AMERICAN DIVERSITY *Congress Is Not a Cross
Section of America 324*
BOX: *Pay and Perks of Office 327*
The Advantages of Incumbency 327

How Congress Is Organized 329
The Evolution of Congressional Organization 330
Contemporary Leadership Positions 331
Committees 334
Staff and Support Agencies 338

What Congress Does 338
Lawmaking 338

Oversight 343
Budget Making 344
GOVERNMENT RESPONSIVENESS *Must All Politics
Be Local? 346*

Members on the Job 348
Negotiating the Informal System 348
Making Alliances 350
Using the Media 351
Balancing the Work 353

Congress and the Public 353
BOX: *A Day in the Life of a U.S. Senator 354*

Conclusion: Is Congress Responsive? 356
EPILOGUE—YOU ARE THERE *Sen. Roberts Chooses
Party Loyalty 358*
Key Terms 359
Further Reading 359
For Viewing 359
Electronic Resources 359
ThomsonNOW 359

CHAPTER 11

The Presidency 360

YOU ARE THERE *How Should You Spend Your Political Capital? 361*

Development and Growth of the Presidency 364
  Eligibility 365
  Pay and Perks 365
  Tenure and Succession 366

Power and Leadership 367
  Head of State 368
  Chief Executive 369
  Fiscal Leader 372
  Legislative Leader 373
  Diplomatic and Military Leader 376
  GOVERNMENT RESPONSIVENESS *A Return of the Imperial Presidency 380*
  Party Leader 382
  The Ebb and Flow of Presidential Power 383

Presidential Staff 385
  Executive Office of the President 385
  White House Office 386
  Office of the Vice President 387
  BOX: *The First Lady: A Twofer? 388*

Personal Presidency 390
  Going Public 392
  Spectacle Presidency 393
  The President and Public Opinion 394

Presidential Reputation 395
  President as Persuader 395
  Presidential Character 396
  Goals and Vision 397
  BOX: *Rating the Presidents 397*

Conclusion: Is the Presidency Responsive? 398

  EPILOGUE: YOU ARE THERE *Bush Spends Some Capital on Social Security 399*

  Key Terms 400
  Further Reading 400
  For Viewing 400
  Electronic Resources 401
  ThompsonNOW 401

CHAPTER 12

The Bureaucracy 402

YOU ARE THERE *Should You Blow the Whistle on the U.S. Army Corps of Engineers? 403*

AMERICAN DIVERSITY *Women and Minorities in the Civil Service 406*

The Nature of Bureaucracies 407
  Goals 408
  Performance Standards 408
  Openness 410

Growth of the Federal Bureaucracy 412
  Why the Bureaucracy Has Grown 413
  Controlling Growth 414
  Agencies within the Federal Bureaucracy 415
  BOX: *What Do Bureaucrats Want, Anyway? 417*

What Bureaucracies Do 418
  Administering Policy 418
  Making Policy 418
  Regulation 419
  Data Collection and Analysis 420

Politics and Professional Standards 421
  The Merit System 421
  Neutral Competence 421

Overseeing the Bureaucracy 423
  President 423
  GOVERNMENT RESPONSIVENESS *Who Does the Bureaucracy Serve? 424*
  Congress 428
  Courts 428
  Interest Groups and Individuals 429

Conclusion: Is the Bureaucracy Responsive? 431

  EPILOGUE: YOU ARE THERE *Mrs. Greenhouse Blows the Whistle 432*

  Key Terms 432
  Further Reading 432
  For Viewing 433
  Electronic Resources 433
  ThomsonNOW 433

CHAPTER 13

The Judiciary 434

YOU ARE THERE *Should You Be Candid? 435*
  Development of the Court's Role in Government 438
  Founding to the Civil War 438
  Civil War to the Great Depression 440
  Great Depression to the Present 441
  The Next Era 443

Courts 444
  Structure of the Courts 444
  Jurisdiction of the Courts 444

Judges 445
  Selection of Judges 445
  GOVERNMENT RESPONSIVENESS *Surveillance Court 446*
  AMERICAN DIVERSITY *Do Women Judges Make a Difference? 449*
  Tenure of Judges 450
  Qualifications of Judges 450
  Independence of Judges 451
  BOX: *Rubbing Elbows with Powerful Politicians 452*

Access to the Courts 453
  Wealth Discrimination in Access 453
  Interest Groups Help in Access 453
  Proceeding through the Courts 454

Deciding Cases 454
  Interpreting Statutes 454
  Interpreting the Constitution 455

Restraint and Activism 456
  BOX: *Who are the Activists? 457*
  Following Precedents 457
  Making Law 458
  Deciding Cases at the Supreme Court 459

Power of the Courts 461
  BOX: *The Funniest Justices 462*
  Use of Judicial Review 462
  Use of Political Checks against the Courts 463

Conclusion: Are the Courts Responsive? 463

  EPILOGUE:YOU ARE THERE *Alito Refuses to be Candid 465*

  Key Terms 466
  Further Reading 466
  For Viewing 466
  Electronic Resources 467
  ThomsonNOW 467

PART FOUR

Civil Liberties and Rights

CHAPTER 14
Civil Liberties 468

YOU ARE THERE *Do You Challenge the President in Wartime? 469*

The Constitution and the Bill of Rights 471
  Individual Rights in the Constitution 471
  The Bill of Rights 471
  BOX: *Civil Liberties in the Bill of Rights 472*

Freedom of Expression 473
  Freedom of Speech 473
  Freedom of Association 480
  Freedom of the Press 481
  Libel and Obscenity 483

Freedom of Religion 485
  Free Exercise of Religion 486
  Establishment of Religion 488

Rights of Criminal Defendants 492
  Search and Seizure 492
  BOX: *What about the Second Amendment? 493*
  BOX: *When a Court Reverses a Conviction 494*
  Self-Incrimination 494
  Counsel 495
  Jury Trial 496
  Cruel and Unusual Punishment 497

Rights in Theory and in Practice 498

Right to Privacy 498
  Birth Control 498
  Abortion 498
  BOX: *Teen Pregnancies and Abortions 502*
  Birth Control, Revisited 503
  Homosexuality 504
  Right to Die 507

Implications for Civil Liberties from the War on Terrorism 508
  Interrogations 508
  Surveillance 510
  GOVERNMENT RESPONSIVENESS *The USA Patriot Act 512*

Conclusion: Are the Courts Responsive in Interpreting Civil Liberties? 514

  EPILOGUE: YOU ARE THERE *Federal Courts Can Hear Detention Suits—for Now 515*

  Key Terms 516
  Further Reading 516
  For Viewing 517
  Electronic Resources 517
  ThomsonNOW 517

CHAPTER 15

Civil Rights 518

YOU ARE THERE *Friend or Foe? 519*

Race Discrimination 521
  Discrimination against African Americans 521
  AMERICAN DIVERSITY *Black Masters 522*
  *Overcoming Discrimination against African
    Americans 526*
  BOX: *Passing the "Brown Bag Test" 528*
  *Continuing Discrimination against African
    Americans 535*
  Improving Conditions for African Americans 541
  Discrimination against Hispanics 542
  Discrimination against American Indians 547

Sex Discrimination 550

Discrimination against Women 550
The Women's Movement 551
BOX: *Sexual Harassment at Work 557*
Discrimination against Men 559

Affirmative Action 560
  In Employment 560
  In College Admissions 562

Conclusion: Is Government Responsive in Granting
Civil Rights? 563

  EPILOGUE: YOU ARE THERE *Exclusion of Japanese Is
    Upheld 565*

  Key Terms 566
  Further Reading 566
  For Viewing 567
  Electronic Resources 567
  ThomsonNOW 567

PART FIVE

Public Policies

CHAPTER 16

Economic Policy 568

YOU ARE THERE *Should You Play the Trifecta? 569*

Democracy and Capitalism 571

Government and the Economy 573
  Economic Problems 573
  Economic Tools 574
  Economic Policy and the Election Cycle 580

Current Issues 582
  Tax Reform 582
  Deficit and Debt 586
  The U.S. in the Global Economy 591
  Immigration 592
  GOVERNMENT RESPONSIVENESS *How Much
    Protection Can Government Offer Workers? 593*
  Income Distribution 597

Conclusion: Is Our Economic Policy Responsive? 600

  EPILOGUE: YOU ARE THERE *Murray Says No to the
    Trifecta 601*

  Key Terms 601
  Further Reading 602
  For Viewing 602
  Electronic Resources 603
  ThomsonNOW 603

CHAPTER 17

Social Welfare and Health Policy 604

YOU ARE THERE *Should a Conservative Say Yes to
Mandatory Health Insurance? 605*

The Political and Legal Basis of Social Welfare
Policies 607

The Evolution of Social Welfare Policies 608

Income Support Programs 609
  Retirees and Their Dependents 609
  The Poor 611
  Farmers 614
  Veterans 616
  The Impact of Income Support Programs 616

Health Care Programs 616
  Health Care for Seniors 616
  Health Care for the Poor and Disabled 617
  Health Care for Veterans 617

Subsidized Services 617
  Education 617
  GOVERNMENT RESPONSIVENESS *The GI Bill
    of Rights 618*
  Housing 619
  Agriculture 620

Tax Subsidies 620

Corporations 621
Families and Homeowners 622

Current Issues 622
Health Care 622
Social Security 625
Reforming Aid to the Poor 627

Conclusion: Are Social Welfare Programs Responsive? 629

EPILOGUE: YOU ARE THERE *Romney Says Yes and No 30*

Key Terms 630
Further Reading 630
For Viewing 631
Electronic Resources 631
ThomsonNOW 631

CHAPTER 18

Foreign Policy 632

YOU ARE THERE *Should You Attack the President's War Policy? 633*

Foreign Policy Goals 635

Making Foreign Policy in a Democracy 636
The President and His Inner Circle 637
Specialists 639
Congress 640
Interest Groups and Lobbyists 642
Public Opinion 643

Changing Approaches to U.S. Foreign Policy 645
Isolationism 645
Containment 646
Détente 651
Cold War Revival and Death 652
Merchant Diplomacy and Multilateralism 653
Regime Change and Preemptive War 654
GOVERNMENT RESPONSIVENESS *Ideals and National Interest in Middle East Foreign Policy 657*

Redefining Security in the Global Age 660
Physical Security 660
Economic Security 664

Conclusion: Is Our Foreign Policy Responsive? 667

EPILOGUE: YOU ARE THERE *Murtha Goes Public 668*

Key Terms 669
Further Reading 669
For Viewing 670
Electronic Resources 671
ThomsonNOW 671

APPENDIX A

The Declaration of Independence 672

APPENDIX B

Constitution of the United States of America 674

APPENDIX C

Federalist Paper 10 683

APPENDIX D

Federalist Paper 51 686

APPENDIX E

Abraham Lincoln's Gettysburg Address 688

Notes 689

Glossary 730

Photo Credits 739

Index 741

PREFACE

The bitter midterm elections of 2006 were a strong repudiation of the Republican president and Republican dominated Congress. Participation appeared to be high for a midterm election (though official statistics are not available at this writing). To many observers, the election seemed to have been a mandate for the new Democratic majority to reshape domestic and international policy and to clean up the ethical standards of recent Congresses.

Yet, those who understand American politics know that even landslide elections are not always mandates and that change is difficult to bring about. George W. Bush thought he had won a mandate in 2004 when he was re-elected and a Republican majority returned to Congress. Yet, since that time, the Republican agenda has been stalled at every turn. The presidential response to the Katrina hurricane disaster led to a perception of incompetence and disarray in the administration. And instead of basking in the aftermath of a successful Iraqi war, the president found the war increasingly unpopular and the probabilities for success sinking by the month. Thus, instead of moving ahead with a mandate on the basis of his reputation for strong leadership, the president's sinking popularity emboldened those opposing his agenda.

We hope the students reading this book will come to understand how the everyday practice of politics, including the dwindling of a perceived electoral presidential mandate, is rooted in the larger principles of government and political culture. We want to convey to students, whether they are taking this course as an elective or a requirement, why it is important for every American to understand how our government functions. We hope they find that it is also an interesting and often exciting subject that has relevance to almost every aspect of their lives. We believe an introductory course succeeds if most students develop an understanding of the major concepts of our form of government, an interest in learning more about politics, and an ability to analyze political issues and evaluate the news they hear about them.

Students should come out of an introductory course with a firm grounding in the essential "nuts and bolts" of American government, but it is also crucial that they understand the political environment in which government functions. We offer the essentials of American government, but we also want the student to understand why (and sometimes how) these important features have evolved, their impact on government and individuals, and why they are controversial (if they are) and worth learning about. For example, we prefer that students leave the course remembering why government tries to regulate corporations, how it does so, and the political factors that lead to stronger or weaker regulations rather than memorizing specific regulatory acts. The latter will change or soon be forgotten, but understanding the "whys" will help the student understand the issues long after the course is over.

We have also tried to interest students by describing and discussing the impact of various features of government. For example, students who do not understand why learning about voter registration laws is important may "see the light" when they understand the link between such laws and low voter turnout.

Therefore, a particular emphasis throughout the book is on the *impact* of government: how individual features of government affect its responsiveness to different groups (in Lasswell's terms, "Who gets what and why?"). We realize that nothing in American politics is simple; rarely does one feature of government produce, by itself, a clear outcome. Nevertheless, we think that students will be more willing to learn about government if they see some relationships between how government operates and the impact it has on them as American citizens.

We hope a greater understanding of and appreciation for American government may encourage those not already engaged in civic and political activities to become more active citizens. Though students did vote at a higher rate in 2004 than they have in decades, a 2006 survey by the National Constitution Center found that more teenagers could identify the Three Stooges (59%) than could name the three branches of government, six times as many knew the hometown of Bart Simpson than knew where Abraham Lincoln came from, and not even 2% could correctly identify James Madison.

The Organization and Contents of the Book

Although the basic organization of American government books is fairly standard, our text has a unique chapter on money and politics. Other features include a civil rights chapter that integrates a thorough treatment of constitutional issues concerning minorities and women, a discussion of the civil rights and women's rights movements, and contemporary research on the political status of these groups. We include in this chapter the special legal problems of Hispanics and Native Americans.

Substantive policy chapters reinforce the emphasis on the impact of government action. The chapter on social welfare and health policy now includes major sections on types of policies: income support programs, health care programs, other subsidized services (including education, insurance, mortgages, and agriculture), and tax subsidies. A chapter on economic policy making complements the section on budgeting found in the chapter on Congress. The treatment of economic policy highlights the relationship between politics and the economy, and it should help the student better understand issues such as the deficit, inflation, and unemployment. This chapter gives attention to economic policy choices that bedevil our policy makers in the areas of tax reform, the deficit, income redistribution, and economic growth. The chapter on foreign policy places current foreign policy issues in the context of the history of our foreign policy aims, especially since World War II, and features new issues arising from the post–9/11 world.

Some instructors will prefer not to use any of the policy chapters. The book stands as a whole without them, because many policy examples are integrated into the rest of the text. Or different combinations of the policy chapters may be used because each chapter is independent.

The organization of the book is straightforward. After material on democracy, the Constitution, and federalism, the book covers linkages, including money and politics,

then institutions. Civil liberties and rights are treated after the chapter on the judiciary.

But the book is flexible enough that instructors can modify the order of the chapters. Some instructors will prefer to cover institutions before process. Others may prefer to discuss civil liberties and rights when discussing the Constitution.

Changes in the Eleventh Edition

The marked erosion of presidential popularity, the continuing war on Iraq, the political and policy impact of the "war on terror," and the run up to the 2006 congressional elections provide new issues of interest for analysts of American government. The 2006 elections are covered in several chapters, although the book went to press before a full discussion of their implications was possible.

The text of every chapter has been substantially revised. We have comprehensively revised and reorganized Chapter 4 on public opinion and added new discussions of red and blue states in that chapter. Discussions of increasing concerns over voting rights and irregularities in the 2004 elections are expanded in Chapter 8. The Abramoff and other congressional ethics scandals are integrated into the money and politics chapter. Throughout we have also replaced photos and cartoons to complement the new material and to give students a chance to learn through graphic as well as textual material. As always, we have updated the judiciary, civil liberties, and civil rights chapters to incorporate new Supreme Court decisions. Expanded treatment of gay rights appears in the chapters on interest groups and civil rights. Of course, all the policy chapters have been revised to reflect new public policy developments.

The new "Governmental Responsiveness" boxes bring the book's central theme into sharper focus in each chapter. We examine who the government is responding to and why, or why not, on issues including the PATRIOT Act, tax policy, presidential powers, disaster aid, and health insurance, for example.

Many of these issues sprang from the post–9/11 need for tightened security, and the intertwining of the war on terror with domestic issues is addressed in several chapters. The war on terrorism has also buttressed governmental and presidential power, and we explore this in most chapters, including those on the presidency, the courts, and civil liberties.

We are delighted to have the opportunity to write this eleventh edition and to improve the text further in ways suggested by our students and readers. We have been extremely pleased by the reaction of instructors and students to our first ten editions. We were especially gratified to have won three times the American Government Textbook Award from the Women's Caucus for Political Science of the American Political Science Association.

Special Features

Student interest and analytic abilities grow when confronted with a clash of views about important issues. Today there is much discussion about how to stimulate the critical thinking abilities of students. Beginning with the first edition, our text has provided features especially designed to do this by involving students in the controversies—and excitement—of American politics.

You Are There

Each chapter opens with a scenario called "You Are There." In a page or two, the student reads about a real-life political dilemma faced by a public official or a private citizen involved in a controversial issue. Students are asked to put themselves in that individual's shoes, to weigh the pros and cons, and to decide what should be done. The purpose of this feature is to stimulate thinking on the various complex factors that weigh on decision makers when faced with significant policy choices. The instructor may want to poll the entire class and use the "You Are There" pages as a basis for class discussion. In the "Epilogue" section at the end of the chapter, we reveal the actual decision and discuss it in light of the ideas presented in the chapter.

Three-quarters of the "You Are There" features in this edition are new. They focus on contemporary topics such as the Republican chair of the Senate intelligence committee deciding whether to investigate pre-Iraq intelligence analyses (Chapter 10), a Supreme Court justice's decision in the Guantanamo Bay detainees' cases (Chapter 14), Karl Rove's decisions about the Republican's 2006 midyear election strategy (Chapter 8), Howard Dean's 50-state organizing strategy for the Democratic Party (Chapter 7), and the president's decision to use his 2004 election victory to push for Social Security reform (Chapter 11).

American Diversity

In many chapters, "American Diversity" boxes illustrate the impact of the social diversity of the American population on political life. These boxes help students understand how a variety of backgrounds and attitudes shape views of politics and positions on issues.

Boxes

In each chapter, boxes highlighting interesting aspects of American politics draw the students into the material. Many illustrate how government and politics really work in a particular situation—how a corporation lobbies for government benefits, how a seemingly powerless group is able to organize for political action, how interest groups solicit money by mail, and how political polls are done. Others highlight features of government that may be of particular interest to students—how ethnicity shapes voting behavior and how teen pregnancies and abortions affect the abortion debate.

Other Features

Several other features also help students organize their study.

Key Terms

Key terms are boldfaced within the text and listed at the end of each chapter and in the glossary.

Further Reading

A brief, annotated list of further readings contains works that might be useful to a student doing research or looking for additional material.

For Viewing

The endmatter for each chapter also includes an annotated list of selected films, both commercial and documentary, that deal with topics discussed in the chapter.

Electronic Resources

Each chapter provides the URLs for particularly interesting or useful Internet sites that relate directly to the topics covered in the chapter.

ThomsonNOW

A reminder for students to visit ThomsonNOW, with its many helpful tools, appears at the end of each chapter.

Ancillaries for Instructors

For details, please contact your Thomson representative or visit www.thomsonedu.com/tlc/.

Multimedia Manager with Instructor Resources CD-ROM: A Microsoft® PowerPoint® Link Tool

An advanced PowerPoint presentation tool containing text-specific lecture outlines, figures, and tables allows instructors to deliver dynamic lectures quickly. In addition, it provides the flexibility to customize each presentation by editing what we have provided or by adding a personal collection of slides, videos, and animations. This instructor's resource provides a wealth of materials available electronically, including the full Instructor's Manual, Test Bank in ExamView and Word, a Resource Integration Guide, video clips from ABC News, and additional American Government tables and figures to incorporate into your lectures.

JoinIn on TurningPoint for *Understanding American Government*

JoinIn quiz questions derived from this book as well as political polling questions add useful pedagogical tools and high-interest feedback during your lecture. Save the data from your students' responses all semester—track their progress and show them how political science works by incorporating this exciting new tool into your classroom. *For college and university adopters only. Contact your Thomson representative for more information about* **JoinIn on TurningPoint** *and our exclusive infrared or radio frequency hardware solutions.*

Political Theatre DVD

Video and audio clips drawn from key political events from the last seventy-five years: presidential speeches, campaign ads, debates, news reports, national convention coverage, demonstrations, speeches by civil rights leaders, and more.

JoinIn on TurningPoint for Political Theatre

For even more interaction, combine **Political Theatre** with the innovative teaching tool of a classroom response system through **JoinIn™**. Poll your students with questions we've created for you or create your own. Built within the Microsoft® PowerPoint® software, it's easy to integrate into your current lectures, in conjunction with the "clicker" hardware of your choice.

ABC News Videos for American Government

A collection of three- to six-minute video clips on relevant political issues. They serve as great lecture or discussion launchers. On VHS or DVD.

Video Case Studies for American Government

Free to adopters, this award-winning video contains twelve case studies on the debate on recent policy issues, such as affirmative action. Each case ends with questions designed to spark classroom discussion.

Wadsworth Political Science Video Library

So many exciting new videos . . . so many great ways to enrich your lectures and spark discussion of the material in this text. Your Wadsworth/Thomson representative will be happy to provide details on our video policy by adoption size.

WebTutor™

Takes your course beyond classroom boundaries! Rich with content for your American government course, this Web-based teaching and learning tool includes course management, study/mastery, and communication tools. Use WebTutor to provide virtual office hours, post your syllabus, and track student progress with WebTutor's quizzing material. For students, WebTutor offers real-time access to interactive online tutorials and simulations, practice quizzes, and Web links—all correlated to *Understanding American Government*. Available in WebCT and Blackboard.

Building Democracy: Readings in American Government

This extraordinary collection provides access to over 500 readings to create the ideal supplement for any American government course. Thomson Custom Solutions' intuitive **TextChoice** website at http://www.textchoice.com/democracy/ allows you to quickly browse the collection, preview selections, arrange your table of contents, and create a custom cover that will include your own course information. Or if you prefer, your local Thomson representative will be happy to guide you through the process.

Ancillaries for Instructors and Students

Thomson Wadsworth is proud to offer both discipline- and book-specific web resources for both instructors and students.

Visit http://www.thomsonedu.com/politicalscience/ for access to:

Open and available to any user! **Political Science Homepage,** containing:
- Online catalog for our titles
- Information about our wealth of resources to help with your class
- PoliSci careers
- Web links
- Midterm elections update.

Visit http://www.thomsonedu.com/politicalscience/ welch/ for access to:

Open and available to any user! ***Understanding American Government* Companion Website,** containing:

- Learning objectives
- Interactive quizzes
- Online chapter for regulation and environmental policy
- Chapter glossaries
- Flash cards
- Crossword puzzles
- Internet activities linked with the boxed features in this book

Adopting Instructors Only receive password-protected access to:

- Electronic version of the Instructor's Manual
- Microsoft PowerPoint lecture presentations

Visit http://www.thomsonedu.com/thomsonnow/ for access to:

Sign-in for those who purchased a book with ThomsonNOW or the chance to purchase access. ThomsonNOW will generate a personalized study plan for each student and direct them to the appropriate premium resources, including:

- Integrated online E-book
- Interactive simulations
- Video case studies
- MicroCase exercises
- Timelines
- InfoTrac readers and exercises

Adopting Instructors Only receive password-protected access to:

- Management tools and Gradebook to assign and supervise your students' use of ThomsonNOW, if you wish to do so.

Additional Student Resources

Critical Thinking and American Government, Third Edition

By Kent M. Brudney and Mark E. Weber.

Information and exercises provided here help students hone the skills necessary for interpreting and analyzing American government issues.

Election 2006: An American Government Supplement

By John A. Clark and Brian Schaffner.

The use of real examples in this election booklet, which will address both the 2006 congressional and gubernatorial races, makes the concepts covered come alive for students.

9/11: Aftershocks of the Attack

By Jeremy Meyer.

This resource focuses on how the American political system is responding to the challenges posed by the 9/11 attacks.

Battle Supreme: The Confirmation of Chief Justice John Roberts and the Future of the Supreme Court

By David W. Neubauer and Stephen S. Meinhold.

An inside look at the Supreme Court nomination process examines the confrontation over the replacements of Sandra Day O'Connor and William Rehnquist, which involves every aspect of the American political system.

American Government: Using MicroCase ExplorIt, Ninth Edition

By Barbara Norrander.

This Windows-compatible package includes access to MicroCase datasets and workbook. Students make their own decisions about the issues as they analyze and interpret current NES and GSS data.

Classics in American Government, Third Edition

By Jay M. Shafritz and Lee S. Weinberg.

The authors provide a collection of many of the most important readings in American government.

Thinking Globally, Acting Locally

By John Soares.

Designed to help students get involved and become active citizens, topics include tips for writing letters to the editor, volunteering, how to change laws, and registering to vote.

InfoTrac College Edition Student Guide for Political Science

This resource helps students make the most of the InfoTrac database available with their textbook, including suggested keyword search terms for political science.

The Handbook of Selected Court Cases

More than thirty key Supreme Court cases are included.

The Handbook of Selected Legislation and Other Documents

Excerpts from twelve laws passed by the U.S. Congress that have had a significant impact on American politics are featured.

Acknowledgments

We would like to thank the many people who have aided and sustained us during the lengthy course of this project.

We first want to thank Michael Steinman, our original coauthor and original primary author of Chapters 1, 11, and 12, who helped plan this book and continued his coauthorship for several editions. The shape of the book still reflects his insights and efforts. Then, we thank Margery Ambrosius and Jan Vermeer for their intellectual contributions to this book through their coauthorship in previous editions. Our current and former University of Nebraska and Penn State colleagues have been most tolerant and helpful. We thank them all. In particular, we appreciate the assistance of Philip Dyer, David Forsythe, John Hibbing, Robert Miewald, John Peters, David Rapkin, and Beth Thiess-Morse, who provided us with data, bibliographic information, and other insights that we have used here. Susan Welch's Penn State colleagues Ron Filippelli and Ray Lombra have been a source of encouragement, support, and many interesting political insights.

We are also grateful to the many other readers of our manuscript and earlier editions of the book, as listed here. Without their assistance the book would have been less accurate, less complete, and less lively. And thanks too to those instructors who have used the book and relayed their comments and suggestions to us. Our students at the University of Nebraska have also provided invaluable reactions to previous editions.

Our editors at Wadsworth Publishing also deserve our thanks. Clark Baxter was a continual source of encouragement and optimism from the beginning of the first edition through the beginning of the ninth edition. Carolyn Merrill has been an able replacement for this new edition. Also for this new edition, special thanks go to our terrific production team of Dusty Friedman, our super-efficient production editor, and Kate Cibek, our tireless and creative photo researcher. They were always willing to do a little more.

REVIEWERS OF THE NEW EDITION

Melinda K. Blade, *Academy of Our Lady of Peace;* Bert C. Buzan, *California State University–Fullerton;* Stefanie Chambers, *Trinity College;* David V. Edwards, *University of Texas at Austin;* Robert Glen Findley, *Odessa College;* Bernard-Thompson Ikegwuoha, *Green River Community College;* Terri Johnson, *University of Wisconsin–Green Bay;* Michael K. Moore, *University of Texas at Arlington;* Catherine C. Reese, *Arkansas State University;* K.L. Scott, *University of Central Florida;* Richard S. Unruh, *Fresno Pacific University;* Alex H. Xiao, *Sacramento City College.*

REVIEWERS OF PREVIOUS EDITONS

Alan Abramowitz, *State University of New York at Stony Brook;* Larry Adams, *Baruch College–City University of New York;* Danny M. Adkison, *Oklahoma State University;* James Alt, *Harvard University;* Margery Marzahn Ambrosius, *Kansas State University;* Kevin Bailey, *North Harris Community College;* Bethany Barratt, *Roosevelt University;* Kennette M. Benedict, *Northwestern University;* James Benze, *Washington and Jefferson College;* Timothy Bledsoe, *Wayne State University;* Jon Bond, *Texas A&M University;* Paul R. Brace, *New York University;* Joseph V. Brogan, *La Salle University;* James R. Brown Jr., *Central Washington University;* Kent M. Brudney, *Cuesta Community College;* Chalmers Brumbaugh, *Elon College;* Alan D. Buckley, *Santa Monica College;* Richard G. Buckner Jr., *Santa Fe Community College;* Ronald Busch, *Cleveland State University;* Carl D. Cavalli, *Memphis State University;* Richard A. Champagne, *University of Wisconsin, Madison;* Mark A. Cichock, *University of Texas at Arlington;* Michael Connelly, *Southwestern Oklahoma State University;* Gary Copeland, *University of Oklahoma;* George H. Cox Jr., *Georgia Southern College;* Paige Cubbison, *Miami-Dade University;* Landon Curry, *Southwest Texas State University;* Jack DeSario, *Case Western Reserve University;* Robert E. DiClerico, *West Virginia University;* Ernest A. Dover Jr., *Midwestern State University;* Georgia Duerst-Lahti, *Beloit College;* Ann H. Elder, *Illinois State University;* Ghassan E. El-Eid, *Butler University;* C. Lawrence Evans, *College of William and Mary;* Rhodell J. Fields, *St. Petersburg College;* Murray Fischel, *Kent State University;* Bobbe Fitzhugh, *Eastern Wyoming College;* Jeff Fox, *Catawba College;* Stephen I. Frank, *St. Cloud State University;* Marianne Fraser, *University of Utah;* Jarvis Gamble, *Owens Community College;* Sonia R. Garcia, *St. Mary's University;* David Garrison, *Collin County Community College;* Phillip L. Gianos, *California State University–Fullerton;* Doris A. Graber, *University of Illinois–Chicago;* Michael Graham, *San Francisco State University;* Ruth M. Grubel, *University of Wisconsin–Whitewater;* Stefan D. Haag, *Austin Community College;* Larry M. Hall, *Belmont University;* Edward Hapham, *University of Texas–Dallas;* Peter O. Haslund, *Santa Barbara City College;* Richard P. Heil, *Fort Hays State University;* Peggy Heilig, *University of Illinois at Urbana;* Craig Hendricks, *Long Beach City College;* Marjorie Hershey, *Indiana University;* Kay Hofer, *Southwest Texas State University;* Samuel B. Hoff, *Delaware State College;* Robert D. Holsworth, *Virginia Commonwealth University;* Jesse C. Horton, *San Antonio College;* Gerald Houseman, *Indiana University;* Timothy Howard, *North Harris College;* Peter G. Howse, *American River College;* David W. Hunt, *Triton College;* Pamela Imperato, *University of North Dakota;* Jerald Johnson, *University* of Vermont; Loch Johnson, *University of Georgia;* Evan M. Jones, *St. Cloud State University;* Joseph F. Jozwiak Jr., *Texas A&M University–Kingsville;* Matt Kerbel, *Villanova University;* Marshall R. King, *Maryville College;* Orma Lindford, *Kansas State University;* Peter J. Longo, *University of Nebraska–Kearney;* Roger C. Lowery, *University of North Carolina–Wilmington;* H. R. Mahood, *Memphis State University;* Kenneth M. Mash, *East Stroudsburg University;* Alan C. Melchior, *Florida International University;* A. Nick Minton, *University of Massachusetts–Lowell;* Matthew Moen, *University of Maine;* Michael K. Moore, *University of Texas at Arlington;* Michael Nelson, *Vanderbilt University;* Bruce Nesmith, *Coe College;* Walter Noelke, *Angelo State University;* Thomas Payette, *Henry Ford Community College;* Theodore B. Pedeliski, *University of North Dakota;* Jerry Perkins, *Texas Tech University;* Toni Phillips, *University of Arkansas;* C. Herman Pritchett, *University of California–Santa Barbara;* Charles Prysby, *University of North Carolina–Greensboro;* Sandra L. Quinn-Musgrove, *Our Lady of the Lake University;* Donald R. Ranish, *Antelope Valley Community College;* Linda Richter, *Kansas State University;* Jerry Sandvick, *North Hennepin Community College;* James Richard Sauder, *University of New Mexico;* Eleanor A. Schwab, *South Dakota State University;* Earl Sheridan, *University of North Carolina–Wilmington;* Edward Sidlow, *Northwestern University;* Cynthia Slaughter, *Angelo State University;* John Squibb, *Lincolnland Community College;* Glen Sussman, *Old Dominion University;* M. H. Tajalli-Tehrani, *Southwest Texas State University;* Kristine A. Thompson, *Moorehead State University;* R. Mark Tiller, *Austin Community College;* Gordon J. Tolle, *South Dakota State University;* Susan Tolleson-Rinehart, *Texas Tech University;* Bernadyne Weatherford, *Rowan College of New Jersey;* Richard Unruh, *Fresno Pacific College;* Jay Van Bruggen, *Clarion University of Pennsylvania;* David Van Heemst, *Olivet Nazarene University;* Kenny Whitby, *University of South Carolina;* Donald C. Williams, *Western New England College;* James Matthew Wilson, *Southern Methodist University;* John H. Wilson Jr., *Itawamba Community College;* Clifford J. Wirth, *University of New Hampshire;* Ann Wynia, *North Hennepin Community College;* Mary D. Young, *Southwestern Michigan College.*

SUSAN WELCH received her A.B. and Ph.D. degrees from the University of Illinois at Urbana-Champaign. She is currently Dean of the College of Liberal Arts and Professor of Political Science at The Pennsylvania State University. Her teaching and research areas include legislatures, state and urban politics, and women and minorities in politics. She has edited the *American Politics Quarterly.*

JOHN GRUHL, a Professor of Political Science, received his A.B. from DePauw University in Greencastle, Indiana, and his Ph.D. from the University of California at Santa Barbara. Since joining the University of Nebraska faculty in 1976, he has taught and researched in the areas of judicial process, criminal justice, and civil rights and liberties. He has won University of Nebraska campus-wide and system-wide distinguished teaching awards and has become a charter member of the University's Academy of Distinguished Teachers.

JOHN COMER is a Professor of Political Science at the University of Nebraska. He received his A.B. in political science from Miami University of Ohio in 1965 and his Ph.D. from the Ohio State University in 1971. His teaching and research focus on interest groups, public opinion, voting behavior, and political parties.

SUSAN RIGDON received A.B. and Ph.D. degrees in political science from the University of Illinois in 1966 and 1971. She has taught American government at several institutions in the United States and China and has other teaching and research interests in comparative government, poverty and development, and culture and politics. She is a Research Associate in Anthropology at the University of Illinois at Urbana-Champaign.

A Demographic Profile

Immigration and Ethnic Diversity

Immigration and Political Cleavage

Religious Diversity

Economic and Demographic Diversity

Diversity and Identity Politics

Political Culture

The Significance of Political Culture

Learning Political Culture

The Core Values

Individual Liberty

Political Equality

Majority Rule

Minority Rights

Economic Rights

The American Citizen

Democracy in a Republic

Political Participation

Who Has the Power?

Conclusion: Is Government Responsive?

What Is Your Civic IQ?

In the opening section of each chapter in this book, you will be asked to step into the shoes of decision makers and to analyze, based on the circumstances, what the person would have done in the given circumstance. The *Epilogue* to each chapter provides the actual outcome of the decision-maker's dilemma.

We begin this first chapter on the American people with a slightly different kind of question because it is addressed to you, and it is not about what you would do but how much you know. This is an exercise in self-awareness, not a quiz. It is to prod you to think about how much you know about the workings of the American political system and the structure of government. We ask you to evaluate yourself as a citizen as well as a student of American government.

Every democracy—*every government* in the American way of thinking—should begin with the people. Our indirect, or republican, form of democracy is premised on citizen participation, even though elected officials make almost all major policy decisions for us. Views on how much participation is necessary and what portion of the population should have participatory responsibilities have varied over time. But today, even as the United States tries to export democracy to other parts of the world, only a small percentage of Americans are politically active. The majority do not even vote in most elections. The 63 percent voter turnout in the 2006 Israeli parliamentary elections was a historic low for that country, but it would have been a stellar show of voter interest in a U.S. election.

Young adults are among the least likely to participate, despite the fact that many are involved in volunteer and community activities. Some voting rights activists have recommended a "No Voter Left Behind" program, which would get every eligible student registered by the time of high school graduation. They advocate granting high school credit for volunteer work in election offices to give students the opportunity to learn about the election process and how to register. Some schools have already moved in this direction; in New York City's public schools, for example, high school graduates get registration forms with their diplomas. Vermont's high schools have a voter registration week, and Hawaii allows preregistration at age sixteen.[1]

But getting people registered does not get people to turn out at the polls nor does it inform them about the candidates and issues at stake. Some researchers connect low voting and participation levels to lack of knowledge about politics and government and to not caring about politics, on the assumption that government and politicians do not address the issues that most concern young adults.[2] According to an MTV poll, one-quarter of eighteen- to twenty-four-year-olds could not identify the two presidential candidates in the 2000 election, and 70 percent could not name their running mates.[3] One study classifies at least one-third of the public as uninformed about the structure and functions of their government.[4] The low level of knowledge of American history and government among students led Senator Lamar Alexander (R-Tenn.) and Edward Kennedy (D-Mass.) to introduce the American History Achievement Act in the Senate in 2005 to establish a pilot program to assess the teaching of history and civics in public schools.

The job of a textbook is to inform but also to make people *want* to learn, and the more aware students are of holes in their knowledge, the more they may want to learn. Here are some basic questions that test rudimentary knowledge of American government. How many can you answer correctly?

By no means are these questions meant to encapsulate the most important information needed for a citizen to vote or participate in American politics. They are simply tools to get you to think about how well you understand some of the fundamentals of the structure of American government and how familiar you are with contemporary policy makers so that you may want to learn more.

Based on this sampler, how do you score your civic IQ?

1. The Bill of Rights is
   a. legislation passed by Congress that grants certain rights and liberties that are subject to change by other congressional legislation.
   b. a series of amendments to the Constitution that can be altered only by amending the Constitution.
   c. a list of ideals appended to the Declaration of Independence that do not have the weight of constitutional statutes or congressional legislation.
2. Name the member of the House of Representatives from your home district and the two U.S. senators from your state.
3. True or false: Congress determines the limits of free speech.
4. Who is the chief justice of the United States Supreme Court?
5. True or false: The federal government can censor the Internet.
6. Voting rights
   a. were defined by the Founders in Article 1 of the Constitution.
   b. were left by the Founders to the states to determine as they saw fit.
   c. were redefined by amendments to the U.S. Constitution and congressional legislation.
7. True or false: It is illegal to burn or mutilate the flag of the United States.
8. The U.S. Constitution assigns the power to declare war to
   a. Congress.
   b. the president.
   c. the president, with Senate ratification.
9. True or false: Every state in the United States has its own constitution and a republican form of government.
10. True or false: Congress has the power to change the structure and size of the federal courts.

Check the You Are There: Epilogue for answers and to see how you measure up against other Americans who have responded to some of the questions.

Americans take pride in their form of government but express ambivalence toward the political process. We cherish the Declaration of Independence and the Constitution and love the symbols of democracy. We visit Washington, D.C. to marvel at the Washington Monument, the Jefferson and Lincoln memorials, the Capitol, and the White House. We show these symbols of our democracy to our children, hoping they will learn to revere them too.

But at the same time that we point with pride to the documents and symbols of American democracy, we often seem unwilling to accept the realities of democratic practice or to spend the time it takes to familiarize ourselves with candidates and issues.[5] We are impatient with the slow pace at which government deals with the nation's problems. We refer to debates over issues as quarrels or bickering; we call compromises "selling out"; we too readily label conflict as mere self-interest and tag interest groups and political parties as *special* interests. In other words, we love the concept of democracy but hate the rough and tumble, the give and take, and the conflict of democracy in action.[6]

Despite the conflict in our political life, Americans are members of one community. We are parties to a single legal contract, the Constitution, and are all equally subject to the protections and obligations of a common set of laws. We also share an economic system, and although the Constitution has little to say about its nature, our government is deeply implicated in its successes and failures. In fact, government's role in managing the economy is sufficient to link the level of confidence we have in government to how well the economy is doing or, at minimum, to how well we are doing. Our economic well-being also affects how much we participate and how much access we have to policymakers.

It is part of the American political character to fear any concentration of power that threatens individual liberty and hence to be suspicious of government for its potential to concentrate and misuse power. Yet in arguing for the ratification of the Constitution in 1789, John Jay wrote, "Nothing is more certain than the indispensable necessity of Government."[7] Why is government indispensable? Because even though government *can* be a threat to individual liberty, there is no way to guarantee liberty without the protections and constraints that government and the rule of law can provide. The Preamble to the Constitution identifies other governmental functions—to form a union among the disparate states, to establish a system of justice, to maintain social order, to promote the general welfare of the people, and to defend against external threats. How far its authority extends in fulfilling any of these tasks is the topic of an eternal debate about the proper role of government in a system of constitutionally restricted powers. This debate in turn encompasses much of what is at stake in the political process.

If government is the instrument for forging one interest out of many in order to legislate and to speak for the country as a whole in matters of national interest, then **politics** is a means through which individual and group interests compete to shape government's impact on society's problems and goals. In political science, the term *politics* encompasses a much wider spectrum than actions directed toward government policy; it applies to all power relationships and to attempts to influence the distribution of resources in the private sphere as well as the public. But in this text we are concerned with politics as it affects competition for and performance in government office and efforts to influence policy made by government officials.

In their attempts to shape policy, individuals and groups compete through political parties and many other extragovernmental organizations, but politics is more than competition. Though private organizations such as parties and interest groups do exist primarily to give voice to competing interests, government's role is to mediate among them, resolve conflicting points of view, and formulate policies that represent a collective view. Thus politics is essential to the art of governing. This is why more than two thousand years ago, Aristotle wrote that politics is the most noble endeavor in which people can engage, partly because it helps individuals know themselves and partly because it forces individuals to relate to others. Through political participation, individuals pursue their own needs and interests, but not without consideration for the needs of other citizens. In other words, it is through politics that we learn to balance our own needs and interests against the good of the political community as a whole.

Today, Americans are less inclined to share Aristotle's conception of politics than they are the cynical view of novelist Gore Vidal: "Who collects what money from whom in order to spend on what is all there is to politics."[8] Yet the high ideals of our founders and the beliefs in democracy that we claim to cherish are about far more than who collects what to spend where. This book describes how people, politics, government, and the economy come together to form the American system. We discuss how these relationships might change as we move through a century that is being transformed by technology, restructuring to adapt to a globalized economy, and new kinds of threats to our national security.

This chapter begins the discussion by profiling the American people, identifying the political values we share, and describing how they are expressed in our form of government. It also briefly describes how democracy, when practiced by people who are ethnically, economically, and religiously diverse and scattered across a vast and varied landscape, is destined to be characterized as much by competition and conflict as by cooperation and community. All of these topics will be developed in greater detail in later chapters.

A Demographic Profile

When the poet Walt Whitman wrote, "Here is not merely a nation but a teeming Nation of nations," he said a lot about our country and its politics.[9] It is a cliché, yet true, that the United States is a land of immigrants, peopled by individuals from all over the world. Americans are a conglomeration of religions, races, ethnicities, cultural traditions, and socioeconomic groups—what one historian calls "a collision of histories."[10]

Immigration and Ethnic Diversity

Long before Europeans arrived, the population of North America was characterized by cultural diversity. Anthropologists are still debating the timing and points of origin of the first inhabitants, but many probably arrived by crossing a land bridge from Asia thousands of years ago, and others may have entered South America by sea and migrated north. Although sometimes characterized by a single term such as *Indians* or *Native Americans*, the first immigrants went on to found many different civilizations, both agricultural and hunting-gathering. Their nations were competitive and at times at war, and their differences were substantial enough to doom eighteenth-century efforts to

Immigrants crowd a New York City neighborhood in 1890.

form pan-Indian alliances against European colonization.[11] Today, the U.S. Census Bureau recognizes 562 different tribes, many fewer than three hundred years ago, but still suggestive of the wide array of cultures that predated European settlement.

The umbrella term *European* is itself somewhat deceptive in that European settlers emigrated from countries that not only differed linguistically, religiously, and politically but also had often been at war with one another. Migrants carried some of these conflicts with them to America. Because the colonies were ruled from England, and its language and culture were dominant, we tend to think of early Americans as Anglos and Protestants. But the earliest European settlers of the southeastern and southwestern territories were more likely to be Roman Catholics from France and Spain than Anglo-Protestants. In fact much of what are now Arizona, New Mexico, California, and Texas were populated by Mexican Catholics of mixed Spanish and Indian

descent. Over time, Germany, a distinctly non-Anglo country and one evenly split between Catholics and Protestants, provided more immigrants to America than England. By preference, or to avoid discrimination by earlier-arriving or more dominant settlers, immigrants often self-segregated into territories (Puritans in Massachusetts, Quakers in Pennsylvania and Rhode Island, Catholics in Maryland), which later became states. These different beliefs and traditions contributed to the rise of distinctive local cultures and to the varying character of state governments and politics.

Like Europeans, Africans, too, came from a huge continent that encompassed many languages, cultures, and religions. Even though the European slave trade was concentrated in coastal areas of Africa, the men and women forcibly removed to the Americas did not share a common tradition. But their experience in the American colonies united most in a common condition as noncitizens lacking all political and economic rights.

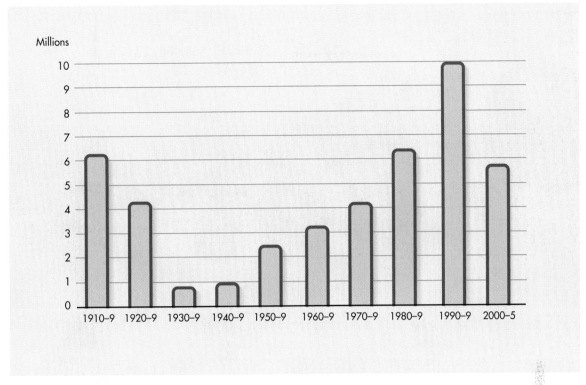

FIGURE 1.1 ■ Legal Immigrants in Each Decade, 1900–present

Source: *Yearbook of Immigration Statistics*, 2005, Table 1. (www.usics.gov)

After the Revolution and the formation of the United States, the new government began to articulate an immigration policy, removing it from the hands of state governments. Ever since there have been disagreements over the standards for regulating admission, some giving priority to economic needs, others to cultural considerations. Congress began restricting immigration in 1798, when it gave the president power to deport people he deemed "dangerous to the peace and safety" of the country. An 1807 law prohibited the migration or "importation" of people for purposes of slavery. But the ethnic and racial composition of the American population broadened in the mid- to late-nineteenth century as new waves of settlers came from southern and eastern Europe, China, and Japan, as well as Ireland and Germany. They included large numbers of Roman, Eastern, and Russian Orthodox Catholics; Jews; and some Buddhists until an 1882 law prohibited further immigration from China. The 1907 "gentleman's agreement" with the Japanese government restricted Japanese entries to the Hawaiian Islands. But immigration continued at high levels into the twentieth century before peaking in the decade 1905–1914, when more than ten million immigrants entered the country.

This surge led to efforts to slow the number of admissions. Between the 1920s and 1960s, immigration was open mainly to the European countries represented in the American population at the time of the 1910 census, thereby favoring British, German, and northern Europeans and penalizing southern and eastern Europeans. Laws passed through the end of World War II added new categories of people prohibited entry, including anarchists and revolutionaries, members of communist parties, alcoholics, individuals with contagious diseases, and others deemed undesirable.

Not all immigrants who came, stayed. In addition to deportations, about 30 percent of those who arrived between 1900 and 1990 returned voluntarily to their home countries. For a few years during the Great Depression of the 1930s, more people left the United States than entered.[12] Then, following the peak years of the second decade through the end of World War II, a deliberate effort was made to slow the rate of new arrivals. (see Figure 1.1)

In 1965 the civil rights movement led to the end of the nationality restrictions on immigration that had been in place since the 1920s. With the removal of the old quota system, the door opened to people of every race, religion, and nationality. To ensure that people

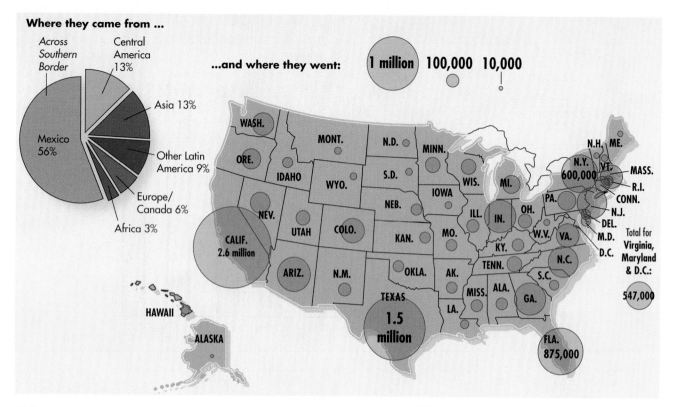

FIGURE 1.2 ■ Illegal Immigrants *These numbers are estimates of all illegal immigrants in the United States as of 2005.*
SOURCE: *Washington Post, National Weekly Edition,* May 29–June 4, 2006, 8. Copyright © 2006, The Washington Post, reprinted with permission.

from all parts of the world have a chance to apply, the U.S. Citizenship and Immigration Services division of the Department of Homeland Security (formerly known as the Immigration and Naturalization Service) divides the world into regions and assigns annual quotas to countries within each region. Applicants who fit into newly created political categories were also singled out for preferential treatment. During the Cold War, for example, virtually everyone fleeing a communist country, including several million Cubans, Russians, Eastern Europeans, Vietnamese, Cambodians, and Laotians, were allowed in. Thousands of Chinese students were granted permanent residency under an amnesty following the 1989 Tiananmen Square massacre in Beijing. Other rule changes led to a wave of immigrants between 1987 and 1996 that surpassed the peak years of the early twentieth century.

Rivaling the surge in legal immigration in the 1990s are the millions of people who arrived without papers since 2000, most of whom entered the country by crossing the Mexican border into the southwestern United States. In 2006, nearly twelve million undocumented people lived in the United States, with the number increasing annually at almost the same rate as legal immigration (see Figure 1.2). The United States has more than thirty-four million foreign-born residents,

the largest number since the U.S. Census Bureau started keeping such statistics in 1850. Foreign-born residents were 11.9 percent of the population, below 15 percent in the peak year of 1910, but three times as many as in 1970.[13]

When permanent residents become citizens—and one-third of all Americans who are foreign-born *are* naturalized U.S. citizens—all immediate members of their families living outside the United States automatically qualify for residency visas. This is part of a preference system put in place as part of the 1960s reforms; it gives priority to family reunification and to those with specific job skills. This system has undergone considerable tinkering, including an amnesty that gave permanent residency to 2.6 million illegal residents between 1989 and 1992, but the priority system remains in place despite post–9/11 policy changes.

In 2004 immigrants were admitted from 188 countries. More new arrivals were born in Mexico than any other country, followed by persons born in India and China.[14] This ensures that current trends in the ethnic diversification of the American population will continue and explains why Hispanics, who accounted for less than 7 percent of the population in the 1990 census, are now more than 14 percent of the population and America's largest ethnic minority.

Immigration and Political Cleavage

Antiforeign, or nativist, sentiments have been common throughout our history; there have always been some native-born Americans who fear economic competition from newcomers or perceive non-English-speaking people or anyone with different traditions and religious practices as a cultural threat. These sentiments usually are greatest when immigration levels are high, which is why strong nativist sentiments influenced the politics of the mid-1800s, the 1920s, the 1990s, and why they are again a force at the beginning of this century. Some of the most intense political cleavages have arisen between older and newer immigrants.

The wave of immigration produced by Ireland's potato famine in the 1840s created a fever of anti-Irish and anti-Catholic sentiment, which found expression in the Know-Nothing Party. Patriotic fervor during World War I produced hostility toward Americans of German ancestry, and the Russian Revolution led to the Red Scare of the 1920s and the deportation of many Russian and Eastern European immigrants. During World War II, Japanese Americans were targeted as potential collaborators with Japan, had their property confiscated, and were imprisoned in camps under military guard (discussed further in Chapter 14).

Although each generation of immigrants has faced resentment from preceding generations, each has contributed to the building of America. Early European immigrants settled the eastern seaboard and pushed west to open the frontier. Africans' slave labor helped build the South's economy. Germans and Scandinavians developed the Midwest into an agricultural heartland, and free Blacks and Irish, Italian, Polish, and Russian newcomers provided labor for America's industrial revolution and turned many cities into huge metropolises. Chinese immigrants helped build the transcontinental railroad linking East and West, and Japanese and Hispanics helped California become our top food producer. More recently, young Chinese and Indian immigrants have figured prominently in high-tech industries, and older Indian immigrants dominate the motel business in the United States. All immigrant groups have gone on from their initial roles to play a fuller part in American life.

Religious Diversity

Voltaire, the great French philosopher, once wrote that a nation with one church will have oppression; with two, civil war; with a hundred, freedom.[15] We know that many of our earliest settlers—French Huguenots, German Anabaptists, British Methodists, Catholics, and Quakers—came here to escape religious intolerance in Europe. Nevertheless, few who emigrated to the Americas expected to live in an areligious state. Once here, however, many found it necessary to establish separate communities to ensure freedom for their form of religious practice. New Jersey, Pennsylvania, and Maryland were conceived and established as "plantations of religion" that gave state protection to specific religious groups.[16] Rhode Island was founded by the religious dissident Roger Williams, who, after being expelled from Massachusetts's Puritan society, bought land from the Narragansett Indians and founded a colony for other religious outcasts.[17]

With independence, the United States disassociated itself not just from the government of England but from its state religion, the Church of England (or Anglican church), which was, and is today, headed by the monarch. Some at the Constitutional Convention wanted to name the Episcopalian church, the newly independent Anglican church in the United States, as the state religion, but most knew that in a country of wide religious diversity, a Constitution with such a provision would never be ratified. But six of the thirteen original states did establish an official religion, and some levied a religious tax, leaving it to individual taxpayers to designate which church would receive their tax payments. State religions were not disestablished in Connecticut, Massachusetts, or New Jersey

The Library Company of Philadelphia

A Catholic church aflame in the Philadelphia church burnings of 1843. Insistence that Catholic children read the Protestant King James version of the Bible, coupled with anti-Catholic material in some schools and Protestant fears of increasing numbers of Catholic immigrants, led to violence. Both Protestants and Catholics were killed.

until the nineteenth century, and even then, some courts considered Christian teachings an integral part of common law.[18]

Despite the diversity in religious practice, instruction and textbooks in public schools drew much of their content from the Protestant Bible. School officials maintained that instruction was "nonsectarian," but their reluctance to remove blatantly anti-Catholic material led to the creation of Catholic church-run schools, which remain today a major alternative to public schools. Occasionally, religious differences led to violence, as in Philadelphia's Bible riots of 1843, when Protestants burned down a Catholic school and thirteen people were killed.[19] The Philadelphia church burnings targeted only Irish Catholic churches, not those of the older American German Catholic population.

The Know-Nothing Party won popularity during this period by spreading fear of a Catholic takeover. Catholic-Protestant conflict lasted well into the twentieth century, could be intense, and sometimes trumped ethnicity. In the small farm community of Carroll, Iowa, for example, German and other Protestants joined forces against allied German and Irish Catholics, passing "puritan Sunday" laws that prohibited Catholic church dances, singing parties, and serving alcohol on the Sabbath.[20]

These anecdotes from the distant past are a reminder that being all white and all Christian did not spare communities from exclusionary or repressive assimilationist tactics or violence against those of a different ancestry or religion. Claims that our political unity is being undermined by ethnic and religious diversity are hardly new.

America's religious profile is changing along with its ethnic makeup. Although a large majority (83 percent) still identify as Christians, Americans now claim affiliation with an estimated sixteen hundred different religions and denominations, including three million Jews, one million Buddhists, three-quarters of a million Hindus, and one to three million Muslims.[21] To some observers, these figures represent the potential for social fragmentation; but a proliferation of religious affiliations may both bolster liberty and serve as its measure.

Economic and Demographic Diversity

Diversity involves more than differences in national origin and religious affiliation. Where people settle, what they do for a living, how much they earn, when they were born, and how long they have been here are all potential bases for political difference, and over time these factors are probably more important than religion or country of origin.

Although racial and ethnic cleavages have garnered much of the attention throughout our history, economic diversity is at least as important. We may think of America as a land of opportunity, but most people who are born poor in the United States stay poor. Opportunities knock harder and more often for those who are born into the upper and middle classes. And although our society is not as class conscious as many others, our personal economic situations play an important part in shaping our views toward politics and our role in the process. Most people who are poor, for example, do not vote, but those who do vote tend to vote Democratic. Most well-off Americans do vote, and they vote in larger numbers for Republicans than for Democrats.

Regional and residential differences can also be important, especially since they often intertwine with economic interests. Farmers in California and the Midwest, for example, are more likely than city dwellers to be supportive of farm subsidy legislation. City dwellers may be far more enthusiastic about federal laws creating national parks or wilderness areas than the western ranchers who use the land to graze their livestock. The classic and most costly example of regional conflict in our history was the division between South and North over the right of southern states to secede from the Union in order to maintain a regional economic system rooted in slavery. Although in that case, economic and political disparities led to the bloodiest conflict in our history, regional diversity usually results in no more than political difference. However, in the face of growing income inequality and the residential segregation of gated communities, there is the danger that residential separation will lead to the political indifference of the well-off to the needs of poor neighborhoods.

Age differences, too, can affect political orientation. The needs and interests of older citizens are substantially different from those of young adults. The United States, like Canada and Western Europe, has an aging population; in 2006, one in eight Americans was sixty-five or older.[22] A greater percentage of Americans in this age bracket than in any other age group voted in the 2004 election, and their interest groups are among the most powerful in the country. This fact has made economic security and health care for senior citizens high-priority policy issues, even while the number of children living in poverty is increasing.

Diversity and Identity Politics

There is nothing new or strange about organizing around difference. Up to a point, it is common sense. How we are situated in the world in terms of power,

The middle of the middle class: This family in West Fargo, North Dakota, has the median income in the United States. The man is a computer programmer, and the woman is a stay-at-home mother. Their house has four bedrooms, two baths, and a two-car garage.

money, geography, race, ethnicity, age, and religion affects our perceptions of the world. As a result, people tend to define society's problems differently and have conflicting views about what government should do about them. Reconciling differences is what the political process is for.

Why, when the American population has always been so heterogeneous, does diversity seem to have so much more meaning in contemporary political life? The reason in part is that although society was diverse in the early decades of the Republic, the political spectrum was narrow, and the majority of citizens were excluded from participation. Those granted full rights of participation varied from state to state, but two groups—women and African American men, with the exception of a small number of free black men living in the North—were comprehensively shut out after the ratification of the Constitution, as were some white men who did not own property.

Diversity's scope for expression has been greatly broadened through the slow expansion of the electorate and the opening up of the political system. This process (discussed in Chapter 8) included the extension of voting rights to African American men and, almost fifty years later, to all women. About the same time, citizenship was granted to American Indians and to residents of Puerto Rico, whose country had been incorporated as a U.S. territory after the Spanish-American

War in 1898. Due to restrictions in state voting laws, full Native American suffrage was not achieved until 1948 and full black suffrage not until the 1960s, but the voting and politically active public has become steadily more heterogeneous since the 1920s.

Two later developments—the federal government's adoption of race, gender, and ethnic preference programs, beginning in the Nixon administration, and the wave of immigration from Asia and Latin America in the 1980s and 1990s—have increased the importance of diversity in American politics.

As government adopted affirmative action policies to compensate for historical discrimination (see Chapter 15), an individual's race, gender, or ethnicity took on added political importance. The use of such factors to influence the division of public resources has given rise to **identity politics.** This is the practice of organizing on the basis of one's ethnic or racial identity, sex, or sexual orientation to compete for public resources and to influence public policy.[23]

Paradoxically, identity politics has intensified during a period in which racial and ethnic boundaries are beginning to blur (see the box "Identity in the Age of DNA"). DNA testing has shown how problematic the concept of race is when used as a census category in the United States, but the ways we group by ethnicity or cultural heritage are just as slippery. The categories Hispanic, African, Asian, Christian, and Muslim are all

The new National Museum of the American Indian on the Washington Mall reflects identity politics. Native Americans lobbied for the museum, consulted on its design, and here participated in opening ceremonies.

simplistic when used as markers in the arena of identity politics. Hispanic is a catch-all term for Mexicans, Puerto Ricans, Cubans, and others with national origins in Central and South America and the Caribbean. Americans of Spanish ancestry tend to reject the Hispanic label altogether as a means of self-identification, and more than 40 percent of Hispanics would choose a racial category other than what is offered on the Census.[24] These are culturally and linguistically distinct groups of people, very mixed racially, and with different legal status within the United States: All people born in Puerto Rico are citizens by birth, for example, and Cuban immigrants enter the country under rules that do not apply to other Hispanics seeking entry. The "African" category might include an African American whose ancestors have been in the country since the seventeenth century, or it may include first generation Americans who emigrated after laws restricting immigration from Africa were lifted in the 1960s. Since that change more Africans have come to the United States than were brought here against their will during all the years of slavery.[25]

Similar variance can be found in religious categories. No one today would suggest that "Christian," as an unmodified category, is a predictor of political views or voting behavior, but this is also true for "Muslim." American Muslims are among the most diverse in the Islamic world. Twenty percent are African American, about one-quarter have Middle Eastern Arab ancestry, more than a third are South Asian, while the remainder came from Africa and other regions.[26]

The decidedly mixed ancestry of Americans is steadily becoming more complex through intermarriage. So much racial and ethnic mixing occurs that by the 1990 census, one hundred million Americans could name no specific ancestry, or they reported multiple ancestries.[27] Although 93 percent of whites and 87 percent of blacks still marry within-group, a third of all Hispanic and Asian marriages are mixed.[28] Among third-generation Hispanics and Asians, over half of their marriages are mixed.[29] Furthermore, 23 percent of all births in the United States in 2005 were to foreign-born women, an overwhelmingly Hispanic and Asian group. Should this pattern continue, the majority of residents in the United States by 2050 will be of mixed race.[30]

Political Culture

In recent years, *diversity* has become a political catchword and has been raised to the level of a civic virtue. Yet our national motto is *E Pluribus Unum* (Out of Many, One) referring to the union of many states and the molding of one people from many traditions. There is a popular saying that Americans are people of many cultures united by a single idea. But what is that single idea, and is it, however fundamental, sufficient to form a political culture? A **political culture** is a shared body of values and beliefs that shapes perception and attitudes toward politics and government and in turn influences political behavior.

In the 1970s, after the TV series *Roots*, inspired by Alex Haley's book of the same name, sent millions of Americans in search of their ancestors, it became increasingly common for people to assume a hyphenated identity, that is to identify themselves both by citizenship and family heritage. Today the hyphen has been dropped, but many of us cling to two-, three-, and even four-part identities as African, Chinese, Cuban, Irish, Arab, Mexican or—fill in the blank—Americans. This distinguishes contemporary Americans from earlier generations of immigrants, whose children were eager not to be taken for greenhorns (new arrivals) who were still attached to the old countries. And those Americans who had already been here for generations were unlikely to call themselves, German, Anglo, Spanish, Dutch, or Swedish Americans. If asked about their heritage, they may well have responded as Theodore Roosevelt, the descendant of Dutch immigrants, did when he declared himself an "American-American."[1]

What has claiming a tie to the cultures and countries of one's ancestors to do with government? Ancestry affects opportunity, just as being of Protestant European descent had a de facto impact for generations. Since the 1970s, public institutions in the United States—schools, government agencies, the armed forces—as well as private institutions and businesses that receive federal money, have been striving to look more like a cross section of the American people. In fact it is the law that they try to do so (see the section "Diversity and Identity Politics").

Enforcement of these laws requires that we know the racial and ethnic composition of the country. We get this information from the census that Article I of the Constitution authorizes the U.S. government to take every ten years. Its primary purpose is to determine the distribution of seats in the House of Representatives, but racial categories have been used in census counts since the first one was taken in 1790. Today, however, unlike the past, the collection of information on the racial heritage of Americans has greater significance for inclusion than for exclusion. Laws guaranteeing equal access and representation have meant, in practice, that the racial or ethnic composition of the population affects who is admitted to universities, how the boundaries of legislative districts are drawn, whether school districts need to submit desegregation plans, and whether minorities are adequately represented among workers hired on federally funded projects and among business owners receiving federal contracts.

Over time little has been fixed about how census takers define race and ethnicity. Whites, slaves (assumed to be black), and free blacks (beginning in 1820) were the pre–Civil War categories.[2] In the late nineteenth century, the census developed multiracial categories for those of black and white heritage, terming them *mulatto* or even categorizing further into *quadroon* or *octoroon* for those with one-fourth or one-eighth African American ancestry. Asians were classified as Chinese or Japanese, then in the early twentieth century, Filipinos, Koreans, and Hindu (confusing religion with race) appeared. Mexicans, who had been counted as white, in 1930 were labeled as a race, but the category was dropped after a protest by the Mexican government.

After the U.S. Census Bureau dropped the mulatto categories, those of mixed white and other ancestry were usually counted as "other" and judged by the Census taker. It was not until the 1980 census that an individual's ethnicity and race were determined entirely by self-classification.[3] In the 1990 census the choice was limited to one of four racial groups: black, white, American Indian or Native Alaskan, Asian or Pacific Islander. In addition to a racial group, one could claim Hispanic/Latino ethnic heritage. These limited options simply didn't jibe with the multiethnic composition of the population or our more sophisticated understanding of genetics. So Census 2000 offered five racial categories (Native Hawaiians and Pacific Islanders were split off from Asians), while retaining the Hispanic ethnic designation. It allowed every individual to check as many boxes as applicable. This made better sense to golf pro Tiger Woods, who describes himself as a "Cablinasian," a person of white, African, American Indian, and Asian ancestry. Former Secretary of State Colin Powell, a first generation American whom President Clinton often held up as a model for affirmative action, is another prominent example. We do not know which box or boxes Mr. Powell checked on his census form, but his maternal grandparents were Scots, and on petitioning in 2004, he was issued a Scots heraldic crest.[4]

The new method of self-identification permits up to sixty-three variations in reporting race and ethnicity, but the multiresponse option creates new problems. In the analysis of the 2000 census data someone had to decide whether to count the multiple-box checkers more than once, divide them into fractions, or just assign them to a single racial category.[5] This may sound ridiculous, but it is a very real problem to the Census Bureau as well as for minority interest groups, one of whose leaders said, "If you can't tabulate it, you've undermined the ability of the federal government to provide information that will help set policy and

Wayne Joseph grew up as a black American. His race influenced his choice of a high school and the girls he dated and the woman he married. He cultivated an interest in African American literature. He wrote about Black History Month. All along, he assumed his ancestry was approximately 70 percent African. According to his DNA, however, his ancestry is actually 57 percent European, 39 percent Native American, 4 percent Asian—and 0 percent African. He was floored, but he eventually concluded, "Now I'm a metaphor for America."

help ensure that the civil rights laws are effectively enforced. That is the bottom line."[6] Or, as more bluntly put by a member of the House committee that oversees the Census Bureau, "The numbers drive the dollars."[7]

That notions of "race"—African, Caucasian, Native American, or Asian—reflect common or social usage rather than scientifically determined biological differences has become ever more clear with advances in genetic research. Now the commercial availability of DNA testing has brought a new twist to racial and ethnic self-identification by providing a scientific basis for claiming ancestry in groups covered by minority preference programs. "Naturally when you're applying to college you're looking at how your genetic status might help you," said a man who had adopted twin boys whose skin was a tannish color. DNA testing showed his sons, whose biological parents were "white," were 9 percent Native American and 11 percent northern African. The father said he learned the results too late for the admissions process but thought it might help get financial aid.[8]

In a recent Public Broadcasting System series, the noted African

American scholar, Henry Louis Gates, led nine prominent African Americans through a search for their ancestors, including DNA tests.[9] Gates himself was amazed to find out that 50 percent of his genetic heritage was European, including an Ashkenazi (Jewish) woman. Others, too, were surprised that their ancestors included Asians, American Indians, and, of course, whites. Students in a race and ethnicity class at Pennsylvania State University, who can have their DNA tested as part of a class, often discover mixed race ancestry they knew nothing about.

DNA testing has also brought about legal claims for group membership. A group of African Americans has demanded membership in Native American tribes who owned their ancestors until a nineteenth-century treaty with the United States forced their emancipation.[10] DNA testing has supported their claim of partial Indian ancestry, undoubtedly through intermarriage or the sexual contact between slaves and owners that was also common in black/white slave/owner relationships. But the tribes have rejected their request for the health benefits and other services

The Significance of Political Culture

Governments rely for their stability and vitality on the support of citizens: their identification with the country and its method of governing and their adoption of the political values and behavior necessary to sustain the system. The alternatives are for government to be ineffective or to gain obedience through force or coercion.

In a democracy, sharing a political culture does not mean that citizens must agree on specific issues or even generally on what government's role should be in dealing with the country's problems. Democracy embraces conflict and competition just as it requires cooperation and a sense of community. A basic function of government is to establish the rules under which interests can compete. Thus, the essence of po-

litical culture is not agreement on issues but on fundamental principles and on a common perception of the *rights* and *obligations* of citizenship and the rules for participating in the political process. These shared values reduce the strains produced by our differences and allow us to compete intensely on some issues while cooperating on others.

Learning Political Culture

Whether the newly created United States of America came about by "design of Providence," was a "lucky accident," or was the result of the Founders' skill in shaping a workable Constitution, it faced a problem common to all political systems: how to create a national identity among the citizenry.[31] Although American society has often been characterized as a melting

offered to tribal members, saying their Indian ancestry is not genuine.

So many Americans are now claiming Native American ancestry that a once dwindling minority population is burgeoning. The numbers began increasing rapidly with the civil rights movements of the 1960s when some Indians who had left reservations began reclaiming their heritage. But the enactment of affirmative actions programs and the growth of the gambling industry on reservation land have undoubtedly motivated some of the more recent claims. Although the 1960 census registered only a few hundred thousand Native Americans, by the 2000 census their numbers stood at more than four million.[11] Today some federally recognized tribes are authorized to issue a Certificate of Degree of Indian Blood, or "white card," that certifies the carrier has a specified Indian "blood quantum."[12]

What percentage of genetic inheritance does one have to have to claim identity as a minority? And what counts most in qualifying for a preference program—one's genes or one's culture and life experience? Diversity programs were designed to right historical discrimination. If a person was unaware of minority ancestry, never experienced their culture, and was never subject to discrimination targeting the minority, can genes alone define group membership? Those who say genetic heritage is not enough fear that the tests could undermine programs meant to compensate those denied opportunity because of their race or ethnicity.

Only 6.8 million, or 2.4 percent, of all Americans self-identified as multiracial in the 2000 census, slightly higher than predicted but way below the actual numbers of Americans with multiracial heritage. DNA testing may force us to rethink the categorization of people by race and ethnicity in an increasingly multiracial/multiethnic society. Almost half of both black and white respondents to a poll said that the U.S. Census, like Canada's, should not collect information on race at all.[13]

[1]In a copy of his 1915 book, "America and the World War," presented to the great American novelist, Roosevelt wrote: "To Edith Wharton from an American-American." Quoted in Alan Cowell, "After a Century, an American Writer's Library Will Go to America," *The New York Times,* December 15, 2005.
[2]The material in this paragraph is drawn from Kenneth Prewitt, "Does Ethno-Racial Classification have a Place in Policy Making?," *Public Affairs Report* 44 (Spring, 2003) (http://www.igs .berkeley.edu/publications/par/spring2003/classification.htm).
[3]Campbell J. Gibson and Emily Lennon, "Historical Census Statistics on the Foreign-Born Population of the United States: 1850–1990," Census Bureau, Population Division Working Paper, no.29 (February 1999), p. 9.
[4]The Scotsman Website (thescottsman. scotsman.com/index.cfm?id=535722004).
[5]To see how this problem was resolved for one census category see U.S. Census Bureau, Census 2000 Special Reports, "We the People: American Indians and Alaska Natives in the United States," February 2006, 2–4.
[6]Ibid., 2355.
[7]Representative Thomas C. Sawyer (D-Ohio) quoted in Wright, "One Drop of Blood," 47.
[8]Amy Harmon, "The DNA Age: Seeking Ancestry in DNA Ties Uncovered by Tests," *The New York Times,* April 12, 2006.
[9]See African American Lives, cited in "For Viewing."
[10]Ibid.
[11]"We the People: American Indians and Alaska Natives in the United States," 1.
[12]Jack Hitt, "The Newest Indians," The *New York Times Magazine,* August 21, 2005, 36.
[13]Tom Morganthau, "What Color Is Black?" *Newsweek,* February 13, 1995, 64.

pot, it has been a slow melt, and it has not happened by luck or accident. The Founders spoke of a united country, a people with common ancestry, a shared language, the same religion, and a commitment to the same political principles. From what you have read earlier in this chapter, you know this view was in some part wishful thinking. One of the most significant challenges to establishing a national political culture was the division of Americans among sovereign states. It is easy to forget that not long ago, people's identity as Virginians or Pennsylvanians was much more important to them than being American. And it was not until the Civil War, under the influence of Abraham Lincoln's powerful reference at Gettysburg to the "unfinished work" of preserving the Union, that Americans began referring to the United States with the singular *is* rather than the plural *are.*[32]

Most of the Founders believed that an educated citizenry was essential to the survival of the new republic, and advocates of public education such as Daniel Webster and Thomas Jefferson argued that only educated citizens would be able to understand public issues, elect virtuous leaders, and "sustain the delicate balance between liberty and order in the new political system."[33] As the public school system emerged, increasing emphasis was placed on the "training of citizens in patriotism, political knowledge and public affairs."[34] Although schools were then (as they are now) under local control, there was some common content in civic education around the country. By the mid–twentieth century, most elementary school children were studying current events in their *Weekly Reader* and beginning each day by reciting the Pledge of Allegiance to the flag. Many high school students are required to pass an exam on the U.S. Constitution, and perhaps their state's constitution as well, to graduate. However, civics is not one of the subject areas in which students must show proficiency under the new federal system of mandatory testing, and there is evidence that it is being increasingly neglected in favor of math, science, and English, courses that *are* subject to proficiency standards.[35]

Elementary and secondary schools are not the only purveyors of political culture. Much is absorbed simply by living in the country and participating in the political process. Television and newspapers also transmit a great deal of information on the rules of the game and how government and politics work in the United States.

Today, one of the most controversial issues in the debate over what is required to sustain a political culture is whether all citizens should speak a common language. But the Founders took it for granted that English would be the national language, and Noah Webster's 1783 textbook promoting "a new national language to be spelled and pronounced differently from British English" was one of the first attempts to create an American national identity.[36] Webster, a Connecticut school teacher, wanted British textbooks banned from the classroom, saying that the wiping out of old world maxims had to begin in infancy: "Let the first word he lisps be Washington."[37] In 1828 Webster published the *Dictionary of American English*—a dictionary "suited to the needs of the American people"—because, he argued, Americans could never accept the British definitions of senate, congress, assembly and courts.[38] Another objective was to standardize the multitude of dialects, some mutually unintelligible, spoken by Americans of the time.[39] Today the United States has fewer spoken dialects than any other of the world's largest countries, a considerable accomplishment given the diversity of our collective heritage and strong regional cultures.

Webster's belief that a single language was essential to developing a common political culture has been an abiding issue in American politics. Fear of German-speaking immigrants in the early part of the twentieth century led Iowa to pass a law requiring all groups of two or more people to speak in English, even when using the telephone.[40] In the current era, when most immigration has come from non-English-speaking countries and some urban school districts teach in a hundred or more languages, twenty-seven states have passed laws establishing English as the official language. And proof of minimal competency in English is part of the civics test given to those applying for U.S. citizenship.

The significance of political culture—even its definition—has long been and will continue to be a topic of debate. Some people argue that Americans are too diverse to share a common set of political values and that every country in the world, regardless of its level of development, is composed of "competing political cultures, not a single political

Assimilation can take awhile. These children of Asian immigrants—from Taiwan, India, the Philippines, Bangladesh, and Korea—have grown up in America but feel, one said, "like the hyphen" in Asian-American—that is, between Asian and American.

Our ideal is that all Americans, regardless of their origins and their diversity, will unite under one flag and one set of core values.

culture."[41] Although government provides rules and venues for these interests to compete, this is not the reason government exists. Unless there is some overarching commitment, some principles that take precedence over group interests, there will be no basis for political unity.

The Core Values

Our "nation of nations" is crosscut with cultural, political, and economic cleavages, but despite our sometimes overwhelming diversity, most Americans do share some basic goals and values. The words Americans use to characterize their form of government are less likely to come from the Constitution than from the second paragraph of the Declaration of Independence: "We hold these Truths to be self-evident, that all Men are created equal, that they are endowed by the Creator with certain unalienable Rights, that among these are Life, Liberty, and the Pursuit of Happiness."

These words suggest the basic assumptions, or core beliefs, on which the American system was founded: universal truths that can be known and acted on, equality before the law, belief in a higher power that transcends human law, and rights that are entitlements at birth and therefore can be neither granted nor taken away by government. The fundamental concept is liberty, especially the freedom to pursue one's livelihood and other personal goals that lead to a "happy" life.

The Declaration was primarily a political argument for separation from Great Britain, so it was concerned with the basic principles and philosophy of government.[42] Guaranteeing the rights of individuals, the Declaration postulated, was the primary reason for government to exist. Later, the Constitution reinforced the Declaration's emphasis on equality while specifying other core principles of American democracy: majority rule exercised through elected representatives and minority rights (a reference to political and religious minorities, not to racial and ethnic minorities). But unlike the Declaration, the Constitution had to deal with the practical problems of governing and of creating institutions that would protect the rights and pursuits of the individual while balancing them against the public interest. Thus, whereas the Declaration is all principle, the Constitution is, of necessity, founded on political compromise.

Here we look briefly at each of the core principles of American democracy. Chapter 2 provides a more detailed description of how they are expressed in the Constitution.

Individual Liberty

Our belief in individual liberty has roots in the Judeo-Christian belief that every individual is equal and has worth before God. It has also been shaped by the works of the English philosophers Thomas Hobbes and John Locke. Briefly, they wrote that individuals give some of their rights to the government so that it can protect them from each other. Individuals then use their remaining liberties to pursue their individually defined visions of the good life. These ideas are part of social contract theory, which we discuss in Chapter 2.

"We can't come to an agreement about how to fix your car, Mr. Simons. Sometimes that's the way things happen in a democracy."

Influenced by these ideas, early Americans emphasized individual liberty over other goals of government. James Madison, for example, justified the Constitution by writing that the government's job is to protect the diversity of interests and abilities that exists among individuals. Liberty is also reflected in our long tradition of rights, deriving from Great Britain's. Usually, these rights are framed as powers *denied* to the government—for example, the government shall not deny freedom of assembly or engage in unreasonable searches and seizures. Essentially, this means the overall right to be left alone by the government. Such individualistic values have molded popular expectations. Immigrants often came and still come to America to be their own bosses. The other side of this coin is that we are also at liberty to fail and accept the consequences. Although the opportunities for many individuals to get ahead in America are limited by prejudice and poverty, living in a society with an explicit commitment to individual liberty can be exciting and liberating.

The commitment to liberty is not absolute however; that is, it cannot be exercised free of restrictions. This is what it means to live under a constitutional government and in society with other citizens: we give up some rights for the good of all and to achieve the purpose for which the government was created in the first place. The kinds of restrictions that can be placed on our exercise of individual rights and liberties is another subject of those ongoing debates about what American democracy was intended to be and should be.

One of the liveliest debates in the past few decades has been that between advocates of broadening individual liberty and those who believe there has been an overemphasis on individual freedom at the expense of community interests. Many believe that our fixation on individual rights has led to declining community consciousness and a general lack of civility. They advocate revitalizing the concept of citizenship, including the responsibilities to participate in public life and renewed emphasis on "shaping the qualities of character that self-government requires."[43] They call their program *communitarianism* and claim that it is much closer to the Founders' republican conception of freedom than is the modern liberal celebration of the unencumbered individual.

Political Equality

The Judeo-Christian belief that all people are equal in the eyes of God led logically to other types of equality, such as political equality. The ancient Greek emphasis on the opportunity and responsibility of all citizens to participate in ruling their city-states also contributed to our notion of political equality. Thus, the Declaration of Independence proclaims that "all Men are created equal." This does not mean that all people are born with equal talents or abilities. It means that all citizens are born with equal standing before government and are entitled to equal rights.

In the early years of our country, however, as in the ancient Greek city-states, full rights of citizenship were conferred only on those thought to have the intellectual and moral judgment to act in the public interest. This wisdom could be acquired from experience in the public arena, such as through one's work, not just by formal education. In both Greece and the United States, such thinking denied political rights to slaves, who were believed incapable of independent judgment, and to women, whose knowledge was seen as limited to the private or domestic sphere. This left a deep tension between the religious view that sees each individual as equal before God and the secular concept of differential political rights. Over time, this conflict was resolved in favor of the inherent worth of every individual and hence the political equality of all. The conscious closing of this gap was noted by Lyndon Johnson when signing the 1964 Civil Rights Act into law: "those who are equal before God shall now also be equal in the polling places, in the classrooms, in the factories . . ."[44]

Long before the Civil Rights Act was passed, most Americans considered themselves relatively equal politically and socially, if not economically. At minimum, Americans tend to believe that they are *inherently* equal, even when equality cannot be realized in the political arena. Alexis de Tocqueville, a perceptive Frenchman who traveled through the United States in the 1830s, observed that Americans felt more equal to one another than Europeans did. He attributed this feeling to the absence of a hereditary monarchy and aristocracy in this country. There was no tradition in America of looking up to royalty and aristocrats as one's "betters."[45]

A belief in political equality leads to **popular sovereignty,** or rule by the people. Lincoln expressed this concept when he spoke of "government of the people, by the people and for the people." If individuals are equal, no one person or small group has the right to rule others. Instead, the people collectively rule themselves; and so we arrive at our form of government, a **democracy.**

The word *democracy,* derived from the Greek, means "authority of the people." If all political authority resides in the people, then the people have the right to govern themselves.

Majority Rule

If political authority rests in the people collectively, and if all people are equal, then the majority should rule. That is, when there are disagreements over policies, majorities rather than minorities should decide. If individuals are equal, then policies should be determined according to the desires of the greater number. Otherwise, some individuals would be bestowed with more authority than others.

Majority rule helps provide the support necessary to control the governed. Those in the minority go along because they accept this principle and expect to be in the majority on other issues. At a minimum, the minority expects those in the majority to respect their basic rights. If these expectations are not fulfilled, the minority is less likely to accept majority rule and to tolerate majority decisions. Thus majority rule normally entails minority rights.

Minority Rights

Although majority rule is important, it sometimes conflicts with minority rights. Majorities make decisions *for* "the people" but in doing so do not *become* "the people." *The people* is inclusive, encompassing members of the majority *and* members of the minority. As a result, majorities that harm minority rights diminish everyone's rights.

Sadly, as James Madison and other writers of the Constitution feared, majorities in the United States have sometimes forgotten this principle, the most egregious example being the enslavement of African Americans. At various times in our history, women and ethnic, political, and religious minorities have been denied basic rights. The idea that everyone loses when minority rights are trampled is a lesson that does not stay learned.

Economic Rights

Everyone is familiar with the idea that the American Revolution was triggered by what the colonists saw as unfair taxation and other economic burdens placed on them by the British Parliament. To a certain extent, Americans fought the Revolution to be left alone to pursue their livelihoods and to ensure that they would not have to give up any part of their wealth without their consent.

Economic freedom, specifically the right to own property, is an adjunct to our concepts of individual liberty and the "pursuit of happiness." But just as tension exists between majority and minority rights and between individual liberty and the good of all, there is also potential conflict between the political equality the Declaration avows and the property rights the Constitution protects. Inevitably, some people, through inheritance, luck, or initiative, amass more wealth and power than others and come to exercise more influence over government. The ancient Greeks feared that democracy could not tolerate extremes of wealth and poverty. They thought that a wealthy minority, out of smugness, and an impoverished minority, out of desperation, would try to act independently of the rest of the people and consequently would disregard the public interest.

Early Americans worried less about this. They thought they could create a government that would protect individual diversity, including economic disparity, and still survive. But the pursuit of political equality in a real world of great economic inequities has led government to a much greater role in regulating economic activity than the Founders anticipated.

We can see that democratic principles sometimes contradict each other. Americans have struggled for more than two centuries to reconcile practice with democratic aims and to perfect a system of government that was revolutionary for its time. We will see these contradictions many times in this book as we explore how government actually works.

The American Citizen

Supreme Court Justice Louis Brandeis once said, "The most important office in a democracy is the office of citizen."[46] That democratic principles come alive only when people participate in government is a commonly held view. This raises two basic questions: how do rules for participation affect the level of participation, and how willing and prepared to participate is the average citizen?

Democracy in a Republic

One fundamental given that sets limits on citizen participation is that our form of government is an **indirect democracy**, also known as a **republic.** Citizens do not pass laws or make policy; they select policy makers to make decisions for them. It is members of Congress, not individual citizens, who vote bills into law. These officials are not rulers or independent agents but representatives of the people who draw their authority from a constitution sanctioned by the people.

This contrasts with a **direct democracy**, in which citizens vote on most issues and legislate for themselves. In the United States, forms of direct democracy exist only at the state and local levels. The best example is the town meeting, which has been the form of governance of many New England towns for over 350 years. Although town meetings today are often attended by relatively small numbers of citizens, they still offer one of the few opportunities people have to govern themselves directly. Citizens attending town meetings make their own decisions (for example, whether to put parking meters on the main street) and elect officers to enforce them (such as the police chief and city clerk). Another form of direct democracy, the initiative, allows proposed legislation that has been initiated by members of the public (either individuals or interest groups) to be placed on a statewide election ballot if enough voters sign petitions supporting the proposal. If an initiative receives a majority of votes, it can, under some state constitutions, become law, allowing citizens to legislate directly. (More information on the initiative can be found in Chapter 3.)

As with many provisions in the U.S. Constitution, there are different ways to interpret what the Founders intended in choosing the republican form of government. Some people emphasize the impracticality of a direct democracy for any but a small citizenry, such as a town or a city-state. How could people from thirteen states meet to legislate for the country as a whole? Or how could so many individuals ever reach the compromises reflected in the final wording of most legislation? In this interpretation, the Founders never considered direct democracy because it was impracticable. Other interpreters of the Founders' intentions place more emphasis on the fear of popular rule, and there is no doubt that some Founders thought of direct democracy as something closer to mob rule. Specific provisions in the Constitution, such as those for suffrage, which was deferred to the states, and selection of government officials, allowing only House members to be directly elected, suggests that fear of direct democracy was a significant, if not primary, reason for selection of the republican form.

Given that the republican form of government does delegate decision-making authority to a limited group of officials, what must citizens contribute to the political process to make our government function democratically? The Founders did not leave many instructions for citizens. Obviously, they expected that some of the citizens ruled eligible by their states would vote, expected that some would stand for office, and expected that most would come to the defense of the country in emergencies (although service was not compulsory). We can also deduce that they expected that the small part of the electorate who voted would need to spend some time becoming acquainted with issues, which explains the Founders' support for education. Beyond that, however, little was said.

Political Participation

If you rented one of the classic movies about American government, you would likely see a story about a handful of idealistic elected officials who, with backing from the mass of equally idealistic citizens, triumph over complacent, jaded, or corrupt politicians. These stories reflect what is sometimes called our *self-belief*, our belief in the efficacy of our system of government and our fitness to govern ourselves. If our political process worked the way moviemakers, philosophers, and model builders think it should—and many Americans think it does—the majority of the public would be well informed, would discuss public affairs regularly, would let public officials know what we think, and would vote. In other words, most citizens would be committed to learning about and participating in government. And if you were to read most American government textbooks written before World War II, that is how the functioning of our democracy would have been described.

However, as more rigorous methods were applied to polling and survey studies, researchers discovered that far fewer citizens take advantage of their democratic rights

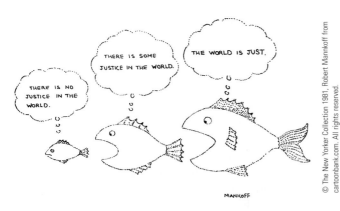

than old theories and models predicted. For example, voting is the easiest way to participate in politics and the least costly in terms of time and energy. Yet slightly more than half of all eligible Americans vote in presidential elections, far fewer in non-presidential-year elections, and fewer still in local elections. Instead of being motivated to participate in politics as in a model democracy, most Americans are little involved. Only a tiny minority are activists who take full advantage of opportunities to participate. In fact, one-fifth of the electorate do nothing at all political; they do not even discuss politics.[47]

Why Don't Americans Participate?

Why does the reality of political participation fall short of theorists' expectations, popular views of democracy, and our own self-belief? One explanation is that many Americans do not participate because they are turned off by, among other things, long political campaigns in which sound bites and negative campaigning replace meaningful dialogue about issues.[48] The author of a recent book, *Bowling Alone,* argued that many Americans are no longer the social animals they once were because technology has allowed us to build little islands of self-sufficiency for ourselves in our homes. We do not join teams or clubs and are no longer dependent on public events or group activities, including participation in civic life. In short, we still bowl, but we bowl alone.[49]

Education and income predict civic participation. Those who participate tend to be better educated and to have more money and more leisure time. Many poor adults are single heads of families with little spare time for political activity or money for transportation and babysitters. As a result, they have fewer opportunities to be drawn into political action through such associations and in turn have no strong organizations to promote their political participation. It is a paradox, though, that as levels of education and income rise, participation in civic life has fallen.

Race and ethnicity explain political participation, too, but not as well. Overall, African Americans and Hispanics participate less than others, but this is due primarily to average lower education and income levels. At each education and income level, African Americans and Hispanics participate at about the same rates as non-Hispanic whites.

Age also explains participation in politics. Young people participate much less than their elders. The middle-aged are more likely to be established in a career and family life and have more time and money to devote to political activities, and seniors are likely to be retired, have more leisure time, and be better informed than young adults.

Can We Be Democratic without Participation?

The overall low participation level and the different rates of participation by people of various incomes, races, and ethnicities throw some kinks into our image of how a democracy should function. Majorities cannot rule, minority rights may go unprotected, and the plurality of interests across income, racial, ethnic, and regional lines may not be reflected in policy when most people do not take advantage of their right to vote or try to influence government by other means.[50] What it comes down to is that elected officials are increasingly being chosen by wealthier and better-educated Americans. It should not surprise us then that these officials are more likely to share the perspectives of those who elect them than the views of the less well-off and less educated who do not vote.

The fundamental need for our form of democracy to prevail is that each of us should win some of the time and no one should be a "permanent loser."[51] But can this happen if we do not participate? Some say yes, because our country has thousands of interest groups organized around the broadest range of issues, and their leaders and paid staff carry the membership's views to decision makers. Even if many do not participate individually, enough Americans belong to politically relevant groups (called interest groups) to ensure that government ultimately hears everyone.[52] In this view, democracy works because the constant competition among interest groups produces a kind of balance in which no group loses so often that it stops competing. As long as individuals continue to believe that they will win a future election or policy debate, they continue to participate and to accept compromise. But this multiplicity of interests can also encourage elected officials to avoid making major policy changes for fear of upsetting the existing balance of interests and their political bases of support.

Is Interest Group Democracy Really Democracy?

Interest group democracy is a kind of indirect participation, with citizens essentially hiring private representatives to take their interests to their elected representatives. Some scholars argue that this is one explanation for lower citizen participation: If interest group leaders can do a better job of getting what they want for them than they could do themselves, why does the average person need to participate?[53] But this assumes that democracy can be measured just as well by policy outcomes (who gets what, when, and how) as by the quality and levels of citizen participation.

This idea that groups represent us is sometimes called the pluralist model of democracy. Just as private businesses compete against each other for our business, some would argue that, in our democracy, groups can be seen as competing in a marketplace of ideas, interests, and political objectives under rules that ensure a distribution of policy victories across the great majority of the electorate, thus preventing any one group from becoming permanent losers. If policies *were* made in this way, it would allow the greater good to be served with an economy of participation.

As Chapter 6 will show, however, many people and issues do fall through the cracks of interest group representation. The poor are especially unlikely to be organized or to have sufficient resources to fight political battles. As unions have shrunk in influence, and as the gap in participation between the wealthy and working class widens, working-class Americans also have less of a voice in government than before. In addition, there is no guarantee that every issue can be resolved through competition to influence decision makers. Thus, there are groups and classes of individuals—those with little or no access to decision makers in the public or private sector—who usually lose.

Some argue, however, that this is not always bad or antidemocratic. Some point out that members of the wealthy or highly educated groups can sometimes represent the interests of those less well-off. For example, without the Ivy League academics and intellectuals, think tanks, and foundations such as the Brookings Institution and the Ford Foundation, we would not have had the sweeping social welfare and redistributive policies of Franklin Roosevelt's New Deal or the War on Poverty legislation of the Kennedy and Johnson administrations. But, most of the time corporate America and the wealthy are looking out after their own interests, not those of their employees.

Who Has the Power?

These debates might be summarized in the most central question in the study of government: Who has the power? In what offices or institutions, and in which people, is power vested?

The argument that our government is run by the few rather than the many continues to find credibility with the public. Opinion polls that ask whether government is "run by a few big interests looking out for themselves or run for the benefit of all" invariably find only a minority of the public who believe it is being run for the benefit of all. As one newspaper columnist put it, "All the evidence suggests that when Americans look at Washington they see a conniving bunch of hustlers playing an insider's game at the expense of the nation."[54] This may be due in part to the very real role that big money plays in elections and the legislative process. But it is also a fact that it is often hard to know what *really* is going on in Washington and easy to be frustrated when the process yields outcomes we do not like.

It is misleading, however, to think that a few powerful people determine everything. America's diversity produces too many different interests and opinions to permit this. Both governmental authority and political power are dispersed among local, state, and federal decision makers as well as across the private sector in corporate boardrooms and the leadership councils of interest groups and trade unions. And today, with electronic media—e-mail, the Internet, and blogs in particular—it is very difficult for any handful of decision makers to control access to information. Furthermore, there is abundant evidence that these decision makers are often in competition with one another so that getting legislation passed requires compromises that give each group some of what it wants.

In the government the Founders designed, power was dispersed across branches and levels of government and between the voting public (at the time a small minority) and their representatives. They did not concern themselves with power exercised through the private sector, and in an overwhelmingly agrarian country, economic power did not rest in the hands of a small number of corporate leaders. Today, with universal suffrage and many more officials subject to direct election, there is more power to be exercised directly by the people than at the end of the eighteenth century. To say that many choose not to exercise their power is not the same as saying that a group of powerful people has wrested it from them.

Just as the Founders disagreed over how much participation was needed in a republic, so scholars of government argue over how much it really matters whether most people participate. The most important factor, some argue, is not the number of voters or the quality of participation but that elections for government office should be truly competitive.[55] Others say that the essence of democracy is having political and governmental leaders who deliberate on public policy in such a way as to make it possible for the public to participate in decision making.[56] From these different ideas about what it means to be democratic, it is clear that it is difficult at times not only to see who has the power but also to agree on who should have it.

Clearly, the question of who has the power is a complex one with no easy answer. In Chapter 6, we will examine in more detail the role that organized groups play in sustaining or undermining American democracy.

Conclusion: Is Government Responsive?

Our Constitution created a republic, a form of government in which the people rule indirectly and are dependent on representatives to meet their policy demands as well as the country's most fundamental needs (national security and an infrastructure to support the economy, for example). This book is organized around the theme of government responsiveness: evaluations of how effectively, and on what bases, elected representatives and other officials act on popular demands and fulfill basic government functions. But in this first chapter, we have looked at the people's relation to and responsibility for government. So perhaps it is fair to ask ourselves how we measure up as citizens.

Americans love the idea that the average person has a say in government, yet half of us do not vote, even in presidential elections. Even for a short time after 9/11, when Americans were expressing a somewhat more favorable view of government, there was no increase in participation. And neither the Bush administration nor Congress asked for any sacrifice from most Americans. Flag waving and support for military efforts abroad may be essential to national survival and personal identifications, but they have little to do with what makes the country a democracy.

Collectively, Americans have been accused of practicing "couch potato politics," refusing to accept the responsibilities of national citizenship.[57] In fact, a majority of Americans think it is possible to be patriotic without getting involved in political or civic life.[58] Why do Americans like their government on paper but act as if they dislike participating in it? Has government failed? Are the laws it enacts not what the people want? Is it the fault of the media, emphasizing mostly the negative side of government? Are average citizens actually shut out of the process? Or is the problem really the fault of citizens and not government at all? When asked, "What's wrong with government?" most Americans typically cite special interests, the media, elected officials, and

Americans, such as this man in St. Petersburg, Florida, are very patriotic, but many don't participate in our democracy.

political parties. Rarely do they blame the voters, or the public in general. Dropping out of the political process because we think it is futile or controlled by special interests is like cutting off our noses to spite our faces.

About their unwillingness to get involved in issue debates or the electoral process, Americans often say, "It's all politics." *Of course it is!* Issue debates and elections are political because the competition to determine what policy will be is essential to government. Politics is inescapable because divergence of interests is unavoidable. Ignoring politics and the institutions that represent the people to government, such as political parties and interest groups, will not eliminate politics. Rather, it would eliminate the most effective way yet developed for the public to influence government's decisions.

Although each person is not equally well situated to influence policy makers, more avenues for political participation are available now than ever before. The number of organized interests and their effectiveness in making their views known have multiplied so dramatically that government officials are besieged by a cacophony of views. We have argued that this is a necessary component of an indirect democracy serving a large and diverse nation. American government is characterized by conflict and compromise because Americans do not agree on either the nature of the problems we face or the solutions to them. If we all agreed, there would be no need for debate, bargaining, compromise, or delays.

In the coming chapters, we will examine the major institutions and processes of our republic, describe their evolution since the Founding, and take up some of the arguments on how they might be reformed to make government more efficient, more just, and more democratic.

Score Your Civic I.Q.

Here are the answers to the questions in the chapter opener. Scoring is on the honor system.

1. Choice b is correct. Forty-six percent of Americans know what the Bill of Rights are.[59]

2. If you cannot identify your representative or one or both of your senators, go to thomas.loc. gov and link to the House and Senate website to find their names. About 45 percent of Americans claim to know the name of their representative, about 30 percent can give the name. Fifty-five percent can identify one of their U. S. senators, and 30 percent can name both.

3. False. Freedom of speech is guaranteed by the First Amendment to the Constitution. Challenges to the limits of that freedom are decided by the federal courts, not Congress. Fifty-nine percent of Americans know the Supreme Court has the final say on what is constitutional,[60] but only 9 percent of Americans can identify the three First Amendment rights.

4. John Roberts was sworn in as Chief Justice of the United States in 2005 and was serving at the time this book went to press. About 55 percent of Americans with some college education could identify the Chief Justice who preceded Roberts.

5. False. Law enforcement officials can bring charges against those who use the Internet for illegal activity, and the federal government can remove material from its own and affiliated websites for reasons of national security, but it cannot censor the content of Internet users. Fifty percent of high school students believe the government can censor the Internet.[61]

6. Both b and c are correct. Amendments to the Constitution now prohibit the states from restricting voting by race or gender, property ownership or literacy, as the Founders had allowed them to do. States also cannot set a voting age higher than 18 years; however, state and local governments do still establish and administer election procedures, and states can place restrictions on voting if they are not prohibited by the Constitution. For example, a number of states do not allow ex-felons to vote.

7. False. The federal courts have ruled that burning or defacing the flag of the United States is a protected form of free speech. Three-quarters of all high school students in a national survey got this wrong, and 62 percent of their teachers thought flag-burning *should* be illegal.[62]

8. Choice a is correct. Only Congress can declare war. Thirty-four pecent of Americans knew the answer.

9. True. The Constitution gives each state the right to draft its own constitution, but the form of government created must be compatible with that of the national government, that is, a republic or indirect democracy.

10. True. Article III of the Constitution specifies there must be a Supreme Court at the top of a federal system of courts and defines part of its jurisdiction, but it gives Congress the power to determine its size, as well as to create the lower system of federal courts, their size, and jurisdictions.

Here are a few final questions. Are you registered to vote? According to the Census Bureau, 58 percent of eighteen- to twenty-four-year-olds were registered to vote in the 2004 presidential election, but only 17 percent of under-30s turned out to vote. The comparable figures for all eligible citizens in the 2004 election were 72 percent registered and 59 percent voting. Americans still trail other major democracies in voter turnout, and young people still lag behind older adults.

Would you be willing to participate in a political campaign? Since 1975 the number of adolescents answering "yes" has dropped by half.[63] How long can a democracy last if people do not participate?

To learn more about the U.S. Constitution, go to "you are there" exercises for this chapter on the text website.

Key Terms

politics	popular sovereignty	republic
identity politics	democracy	direct democracy
political culture	indirect democracy	

Further Reading

Joyce Appleby, *Inheriting the Revolution* (Cambridge, Mass.: Harvard University Press, 2000). A historian looks at what the first generation of Americans made of their new government and how they invented a new culture and identity.

Neil Baldwin, *The American Revelation: Ten Ideals that Shaped Our Country from the Puritans to the Cold War* (New York: St. Martin's Press, 2005). Written in a period when the country seemed polarized, this book discusses ten "galvanizing beliefs" that helped unify Americans in the past and argues that they could do so again.

Harold Lasswell, *Politics: Who Gets What, When, How* (New York: New World, 1958). This is a classic treatment of some very practical political problems.

Stephen Macedo, et al., *Democracy at Risk: How Political Choices Undermine Citizen Participation, and What We Can Do About It* (Washington, D.C.: The Brookings Institution, 2005). This report, commissioned by the American Political Science Association and written by a panel of political scientists, examines the "democracy deficit" in the United States, brought about by citizen disengagement. It looks at reasons for and consequences of declining levels of political involvement and suggests some remedial measures.

Charles C. Mann, *1491: New Revelations of the America Before Columbus* (New York: Alfred A. Knopf, 2005). A science writer examines new research on migration and settlement patterns in North America and gives a revelatory picture of what the continent looked like in the year before Columbus's arrival. You will be surprised.

Sean Wilensz, *The Rise of American Democracy: Jefferson to Lincoln* (New York: Alfred A. Knopf, 2005). In this award-winning book a historian focuses on how the debate over the appropriate role for citizens in a democracy evolved during the first hundred years of the republic.

For Viewing

There are many documentaries available, most made for public and cable television, that trace the history of America's ethnic minorities. Here are just four:

African American Lives (2006). In this four-part series made for PBS, Henry Louis Gates, using archival records, family documents, and genetic testing, traces his own ancestry and that of eight other prominent African Americans including Oprah Winfrey, Quincy Jones, and Whoopi Goldberg. Their family histories cover the span of United States history and reveal the ambiguity of the racial and ethnic categories used to identify Americans by ancestry.

The Native Americans (1994). This is a five-volume video series produced by the Turner Broadcasting System for television. Each fifty-minute video deals with the peoples of a specific region of the country: the Plains, the Southwest, Southeast, the Northwest and Northeast.

The Irish Americans (1998). A four-volume video series made by Disney Studios for television, this history of the Irish in America is traced from the first wave of emigration during the potato famine of the 1840s to the present.

Italians in America (1998). This two-volume video series made for A&E's History Channel traces Italian American history from the first period of heavy immigration in the late nineteenth century to recent years.

There are many contemporary films that explore race and ethnicity in America sometimes in more realistic ways than documentaries.

The Learning Tree (1969). Gordon Park's autobiographical film about growing up black in Depression-era Kansas (1969).

Do The Right Thing (1989). Spike Lee's movie about race relations in 1989 Brooklyn.

Smoke Signals (1998). This Sundance Film Festival hit is set on an Idaho reservation.

Hester Street (1974). Set in 1896 New York, and filmed in grainy black and white, with great period atmosphere, the 1974 Oscar-nominated film *Hester Street* offers a portrait of life for Orthodox Jewish immigrants, especially women.

Gentlemen's Agreement (1947). Starring Gregory Peck, this film illustrates the so-called polite anti-Semitism prevalent in the United States prior to the Civil Rights era (compare with *Hester Street*). The fact that the hero of this film had to be a non-Jew, pretending to be Jewish, is indicative of how cautiously treatment of anti-Semitism had to be handled in any mass entertainment of the time. Its director, Eliza Kazan, later dismissed the film for its faux candor, but it won three Oscars, including best film.

 ## Electronic Resources

In each chapter, we will provide a few Internet addresses for particularly useful or interesting sites relevant to the chapter.

http://www.firstgov.gov
This is a central federal government site providing comprehensive links to government webpages, including those for all branches of government, federal agencies and commissions, and important policy areas.

http://www.c-span.org
Feeling not in the know? By using the Blogs link at C-SPAN's home page you can connect to seventy of the major political bloggers, as well as to blogs on Iraq and other specialized topics.

http://www.census.gov
This is the primary source for results of the 2000 census and updates.

http://www.uscis.gov
This site of the U.S. Citizenship and Immigration Services leads you to the text of immigration law, official statistics on legal and illegal immigration flows to the United States, and analytical reports on immigration trends.

http://www.lcweb.loc.gov/exhibits/religion
This source provides a wealth of information on the role of religion in the founding of the American republic and on the relationship between organized religion and the state governments.

ThomsonNOW™

Enter ThomsonNOW™ using the access card that is available with this text or through www.thomsonedu.com/thomsnnow. ThomsonNOW™ will assist you in understanding the content in this chapter with a personalized study plan generated for your needs. A practice test will assess the areas you need to review and provide the tools to fully comprehend those concepts, including an integrated digital eBook, interactive simulations, timelines, video case studies, MicroCase exercises, and InfoTrac College Edition readers and exercises. You'll also be connected to the learning objectives, chapter outline, chapter glossary, flash cards, crossword puzzles, Internet activities, and interactive quizzes found on the companion website.

CHAPTER 2

THE CONSTITUTION

Courtesy of Winterthur Museum.

Soon after their deaths, the Founders were venerated by the people. Here George Washington is pictured ascending to heaven.

The Articles of Confederation

  National Government Problems

  State Government Problems

The Constitution

  The Constitutional Convention

  Features of the Constitution

  Motives of the Founders

  Ratification of the Constitution

  Changing the Constitution

Impact of the Civil War and the Great Depression

  The Civil War and Reconstruction

  The Great Depression and the New Deal

  A Combination of Constitutions

Conclusion: Does the Constitution Make the Government Responsive?

YOU ARE THERE

The Case of the Confidential Tapes

In June 1972, a security guard for the Watergate building in Washington, D.C. noticed that tape had been placed across the latch of a door to keep it from locking. The guard peeled off the tape. When he made his rounds later, he noticed that more tape had been placed across the latch. He called the police.

The police encountered five burglars in the headquarters of the Democratic National Committee. Wearing surgical gloves and carrying tear gas guns, photographic equipment, and electronic gear, they had been installing wiretaps on the Democratic Party's phones.

No one expected this break-in to lead to the White House. The *Washington Post* assigned two young reporters who usually covered local matters to the story. But the unlikely pair—Bob Woodward, a Yale graduate, and Carl Bernstein, a college dropout—were ambitious, and they uncovered a series of bizarre connections. The burglars had links to President Richard Nixon's Committee to Reelect the President.

The administration dismissed the break-in as the work of overzealous underlings. Even the press called it a "caper." Indeed, it was hard to imagine that high officials in the administration could be responsible. In public opinion polls, Nixon enjoyed an enormous lead, almost 20 percent, over the various Democrats vying for their party's nomination to challenge him in the fall election. Risky tactics seemed unnecessary.

But Woodward and Bernstein discovered that White House staff members had engaged in other criminal and unethical actions to sabotage the Democrats' campaign. They had forged letters accusing some Democratic candidates of homosexual acts. They had obtained and publicized psychiatric records, causing the Democratic vice presidential nominee to resign.

In the November election, Nixon won handily, but the revelations forced his two top aides to resign and prompted the Senate to establish a special committee to investigate what was being called the **Watergate scandal.** When investigators happened to ask a lower-level aide to the president whether there was a taping device in the Oval Office, he said, "I was hoping you fellows wouldn't ask me about that." Then he revealed what only a handful of aides had known—that Nixon had secretly tape-recorded conversations in nine locations in the White House, the Executive Office Building across the street, and Camp David in Maryland. Nixon had intended to create a comprehensive record of his presidency to demonstrate his greatness.[1]

The tapes could confirm or refute charges of White House complicity in the break-in and cover-up,

Washington Post *reporters Carl Bernstein (left) and Bob Woodward uncovered the Watergate scandal.*

but Nixon refused to release them. The special prosecutor filed suit to force Nixon to do so, and a federal trial court ordered him to do so. After the federal appeals court affirmed the trial court's decision, Nixon demanded that his attorney general fire the special prosecutor. The attorney general and deputy attorney general both refused and resigned in protest. Then the third-ranking official in the Justice Department, Robert Bork, fired the special prosecutor. (Bork would later be nominated to the Supreme Court—unsuccessfully, as it turned out—by President Reagan.)

The public furor over this so-called Saturday Night Massacre was so intense that Nixon finally did release some tapes. But one crucial tape contained a mysterious eighteen-minute gap that a presidential aide speculated was caused by "some sinister force."

To mollify critics, Nixon appointed a new special prosecutor, Leon Jaworski. After his investigation, Jaworski presented evidence to a grand jury that indicted seven of the president's aides for the cover-up, specifically for

obstruction of justice, and even named the president as an "unindicted coconspirator."

The House Judiciary Committee considered impeaching the president, and Jaworski subpoenaed more tapes. Nixon issued edited transcripts of the conversations but not the tapes themselves. As a compromise, he proposed that one person listen to the tapes—a senator who was seventy-two years old and hard of hearing. Frustrated, Jaworski went to the court, which ordered Nixon to release the tapes. When Nixon refused, Jaworski appealed directly to the Supreme Court.

You are Chief Justice Warren Burger, appointed to the Court by President Nixon in 1969 partly because of your calls for more law and order. Three of your brethren were also appointed by Nixon. In the case of *United States* v. *Nixon*, the question you face could lead to a grave constitutional showdown with the president. Special Prosecutor Jaworski claims that he needs the tapes because they contain evidence pertaining to the upcoming trial of the presi-

dent's aides indicted for the cover-up. Without all relevant evidence, which possibly could vindicate the aides, the trial court might not convict them.

President Nixon claims he has **executive privilege**—authority to withhold information from the courts and Congress. Although the Constitution does not mention such a privilege, Nixon contends that the privilege is inherent in the powers of the presidency. Without it, presidents could not guarantee confidentiality in conversations with other officials or even foreign leaders. This could make it difficult for them to govern.

You have few precedents to guide you. Many past presidents exercised executive privilege when pressed for information by Congress. In these instances, Congress ordinarily acquiesced rather than sued for the information, so the courts did not rule on the existence of the privilege. Once, in 1953, the Eisenhower administration invoked the privilege, and the Supreme Court upheld the claim. However, that case involved national security.[2]

In addition to considering the merits of the opposing sides, you also need to consider the extent of the Supreme Court's power. The Court lacks strong means to enforce its rulings. It has to rely on its authority as the highest interpreter of the law in the country. Therefore, if the Court orders Nixon to relinquish the tapes and Nixon refuses, there would be little the Court could do. His refusal would show future officials they could disregard your orders with impunity.

In this high-stakes contest, do you and your brethren on the Court order Nixon to turn over the tapes, or do you accept his claim of executive privilege?

Early settlers came to America for different reasons. Some came to escape religious persecution, others to establish their own religious orthodoxy. Some came to get rich, others to avoid debtors' prison. Some came to make money for their families or employers in the Old World, others to flee the closed society of that world. Some came as free persons, others as indentured servants or slaves. Few came to practice self-government. Yet the desire for self-government was evident from the beginning.[3] The settlers who arrived in Jamestown in 1607 established the first representative assembly in America. The Pilgrims, who reached Plymouth in

1620, drew up the Mayflower Compact in which they vowed to "solemnly & mutually in the presence of God, and one of another, covenant and combine our selves together into a civill body politick." They pledged to establish laws for "the generall good of the colonie" and in return promised "all due submission and obedience."[4]

During the next century and a half, the colonies adopted constitutions and elected representative assemblies. Of course, the colonies lived under British rule; they had to accept the appointment of royal governors and the presence of British troops. But a vast ocean separated the two continents. At such distance, Britain could not wield the control it might at closer reach. Consequently, it granted the colonies a measure of autonomy, with which they practiced a degree of self-government.

These early efforts toward self-government led to conflict with the mother government. In 1774, the colonies established the Continental Congress to coordinate their actions. Within months, the conflict reached flash point, and the Congress urged the colonies to form their own governments. In 1776, the Congress adopted the Declaration of Independence.

After six years of war, the Americans accepted the British surrender. At the time it seemed they had met their biggest test. Yet they would find fomenting a revolution easier than fashioning a government and drafting a declaration of independence easier than crafting a constitution.

The Articles of Confederation

Even before the war ended, the Continental Congress passed a constitution, and in 1781 the states ratified it. This first constitution, the **Articles of Confederation,** formed a "league of friendship" among the states. As a confederation, it allowed each state to retain its "sovereignty" and "independence." That is, it made the states supreme over the federal government.

Under the Articles, however, Americans would face problems with both their national and state governments.

National Government Problems

The Articles of Confederation established a Congress, a legislative body with one house in which each state had one vote. But they strictly limited the powers that Congress could exercise, and they provided no executive or judicial branch.

The Articles reflected the colonial experience under the British government. The leaders feared a powerful central government with a powerful executive like a king. They thought such a government would be too strong and too distant to guarantee individual liberty. Furthermore, the Articles reflected a lack of national identity among the people. Most did not yet view themselves as Americans. As Edmund Randolph remarked, "I am not really an American, I am a Virginian."[5] (And George Washington worried that Kentuckians would join Spain.[6]) Consequently, the leaders established a very decentralized government that left most authority to the states.

The Articles satisfied many people. Most residents worked small farms, and although many of them sank into debt during the depression that followed the war, they felt they could get the state governments to help them. They realized they could not influence a distant central government as readily.

But the Articles frustrated bankers, merchants, manufacturers, and others in the upper classes. They

© Bettmann/Corbis

Although the Articles of Confederation gave the federal government authority to print money, the states circulated their own currencies as well.

envisioned a great commercial empire replacing the agricultural society that existed in the late eighteenth century. More than local trade, they wanted national and even international trade. For this they needed uniform laws, stable money, sound credit, and enforceable debt collection. They needed a strong central government that could protect them against debtors and against state governments sympathetic to debtors. The Articles provided neither the foreign security nor the domestic climate necessary to nourish these requisites of a commercial empire.

After the war, the army disbanded, leaving the country vulnerable to hostile forces surrounding it. Britain maintained outposts with troops in the Northwest Territory (today's Midwest), in violation of the peace treaty, and an army in Canada. Spain, which had occupied Florida and California for a long time and had claimed the Mississippi River valley as a result of a treaty before the war, posed a threat. Barbary pirates from North Africa seized American ships and sailors.

Congress could not raise an army, because it could not draft individuals directly, or finance an army, because it could not tax individuals directly. Instead, it had to ask the states for soldiers and money. The states, however, were not always sympathetic to the problems of the distant government. And although Congress could make treaties with foreign countries, the states made (and broke) treaties independently of Congress. Without the ability to establish a credible army or negotiate a binding treaty, the government could not get the British troops to leave American soil. Nor could it get the British government to ease restrictions on shipping or the Spanish government to permit navigation on the Mississippi River.[7] (See box "The Black Flag on the High Seas.")

In addition to an inability to confront foreign threats, the Articles demonstrated an inability to cope with domestic crises. The country bore a heavy war debt that brought the government close to bankruptcy. Since Congress could not tax individuals directly, it could not shore up the shaky government.

The states competed with each other for commercial advantage. As independent governments, they imposed tariffs on goods from other states. The tariffs slowed the growth of businesses.

In short, the government under the Articles of Confederation seemed too decentralized to ensure either peace or prosperity. The Articles, one leader concluded, gave Congress the privilege of asking for everything while reserving to each state the prerogative of granting nothing.[8] A similar situation exists today in the United Nations, which must rely on the goodwill of member countries to furnish troops for its peacekeeping forces and dues for its operating expenses.[9]

The Black Flag on the High Seas

Americans faced attacks from pirates as well as threats from foreign powers. As many as a hundred merchant ships sailed from American ports to Mediterranean cities each year, bringing salted fish, flour, sugar, and lumber and returning with figs, lemons, oranges, olive oil, and opium. Barbary pirates from North Africa—Tripoli (now Libya), Tunis (Tunisia), Algeria, and Morocco— preyed upon ships in the Mediterranean Sea, seizing sailors, holding them for ransom or pressing them into slavery, and extorting money from shippers and governments.[1] Historians estimate that a million Europeans and Americans were kidnapped or enslaved by these pirates in the seventeenth and eighteenth centuries.

Although American ships were protected by the British navy (and by the British government's willingness to pay tribute) during colonial times, they were not shielded after independence. The weakness of the government under the Articles of Confederation left the ships' crews to fend for themselves. The marauding pirates were not only a nasty rebuke to American merchants' desire for international trade but also to our citizens' belief in free trade on the seas, without acts of violence or demands for payments.

The conflict was mostly over riches—the Barbary states used piracy to finance their governments—but it also reflected religious views. The Barbary states, which except for Morocco were under Turkish rule, were Muslim. Although their societies would not be called fundamentalist or Islamist today—in fact, they treated their Jewish residents better than most European societies did at the time—their leaders told American officials that the Koran gave them the right to enslave infidels.[2]

The piracy would not cease until the new government under the Constitution created a strong navy and fought the Barbary Wars (1801–1805)—the first deployment of the American military overseas.[3]

[1]Other pirates patrolled the Caribbean, with some operating out of New Orleans.
[2]Previously, European states had held Muslim slaves.
[3]This led to the line in the Marines Corps anthem, "to the shores of Tripoli." The piracy did flare up again, as a result of British instigation during the War of 1812.

Sources: Christopher Hitchens, "Black Flag," *New York Times Book Review*, August 21, 2005, 7–8; Max Boot, *The Savage Wars of Peace* (New York: Basic Books, 2002), 3–29.

State Government Problems

Other conflicts arose closer to home. State constitutions adopted during the American Revolution made the state legislatures more representative than the colonial legislatures had been. Most state legislatures also began to hold elections every year. The result was heightened interest among candidates and turnover among legislators. In the eyes of national leaders, there was much pandering to voters and horse trading by politicians as various factions vied for control. The process seemed up for grabs. According to the Vermont Council of Censors, laws were "altered—realtered—made better—made worse; and kept in such a fluctuating position that persons in civil commission scarce know what is law."[10] In short, state governments were experiencing more democracy than any other governments in the world at the time. National leaders, stunned by the changes in the few years since the Revolution, considered this development an "excess of democracy."

Moreover, state constitutions made the legislative branch the most powerful. Some state legislatures began to dominate the other branches, and national leaders called them "tyrannical."

The national leaders, most of whom were wealthy and many of whom were creditors, pointed to the laws passed in some states that relieved debtors of some of their obligations. The farmers who were in debt pressed the legislatures for relief that would slow or shrink the payments owed to their creditors. Some legislatures granted such relief.

Although these laws worried the leaders, **Shays's Rebellion** in western Massachusetts in 1786 and 1787 frightened them. Boston merchants who had loaned Massachusetts money during the war insisted on being repaid in full so they could trade with foreign merchants. The state levied steep taxes that many farmers could not pay during the hard times. The law authorized foreclosure—sale of the farmers' property to recover unpaid taxes—and jail for the debtors. The law essentially transferred wealth from the farmers to the merchants. The farmers protested the legislature's refusal to grant any relief from the law. Bands of farmers blocked the entrances to courthouses where judges were scheduled to hear cases calling for foreclosure and jail. Led by Daniel Shays, some marched to the Springfield arsenal to seize weapons. Although they were defeated by the militia, their sympathizers were victorious in the next election, and the legislature did provide some relief from the law.

Both the revolt and the legislature's change in policy scared the wealthy. To them it raised the specter of mob rule. Nathaniel Gorham, the president of the Continental Congress and a prominent merchant, wrote Prince Henry of Prussia, announcing "the failure of our free institutions" and asking whether the prince would agree to become king of America (the prince declined).[11] Just months after the uprising, Congress approved a convention for "the sole and express purpose of revising the Articles of Confederation."

To a significant extent, then, the debate at the time reflected a conflict between two competing visions of the future American political economy—agricultural or commercial.[12] Most leaders espoused the latter, and the combination of national problems and state problems prompted them to push for a new government.[13]

The Constitution

The Constitutional Convention

The Setting

The **Constitutional Convention** convened in Philadelphia, then the country's largest city, in 1787. The Industrial Revolution was sweeping Europe and beginning to reach this continent. The first American cotton mill opened in Massachusetts, and the first American steamboat plied the Delaware River.

State legislatures chose seventy-four delegates to the convention; fifty-five attended. They met at the Pennsylvania State House—now Independence Hall—in the same room where many of them had signed the Declaration of Independence eleven years earlier. Delegates came from every state except Rhode Island, whose farmers and debtors feared that the convention would weaken states' powers to relieve debtors of their debts. All the delegates were men (see the box "Founding Mothers").

The delegates were distinguished by their education, experience, and enlightenment. Benjamin Franklin, of Pennsylvania, was the best-known American in the world. He had been a printer, scientist, and diplomat. At eighty-one, he was also the oldest delegate. George Washington, of Virginia, was the most respected American in the country. As the commander of the revolutionary army, he was a national hero. He was chosen to preside over the convention. The presence of men like Franklin and Washington gave the convention legitimacy.

The delegates quickly determined that the Articles of Confederation were beyond repair. Rather than revise them, as instructed by Congress, the delegates decided to draft a new constitution.[14]

The Predicament

The delegates came to the convention because they complained about a government that was too weak.

FOUNDING MOTHERS

Charles Francis Adams, a grandson of President John Adams and Abigail Adams, declared in 1840, "The heroism of the females of the Revolution has gone from memory with the generation that witnessed it, and nothing, absolutely nothing remains upon the ear of the young of the present day."[1] That statement remains true today; in the volumes written about the revolutionary and Constitution-making era, much is said of the "Founding Fathers" but little about the "Founding Mothers." Although no women were delegates to the Constitutional Convention, in various ways besides birthing and rearing the children and maintaining the homes women contributed significantly to the founding of the country. Many contributed directly to the political ferment of the time. Their political role during the revolutionary and Constitution-making era was probably greater than it would be again for a century.

Before the Revolutionary War, women were active in encouraging opposition to British rule. Groups of women, some formed as the "Daughters of Liberty," organized resistance to British taxes by leading boycotts of British goods such as cloth and tea; they made their own cloth, hosting spinning bees, and their own drinks from native herbs and flowers.

A few women were political pamphleteers, helping increase public sentiment for independence. One of those pamphlet writers, Mercy Otis Warren, from Boston, was thought to be the first person to urge the Massachusetts delegates to the Continental Congress to vote for separation from Britain.[2] She also wrote poems advocating independence and plays satirizing British officials and sympathizers among the colonists (although the plays could only be read, not staged, because Puritan Boston forbade theater). Throughout the period before and after the Revolution, Warren shared her political ideas in personal correspondence with leading statesmen of the time, such as John Adams and Thomas Jefferson. Later she wrote a three-volume history of the American Revolution.

When the Declaration of Independence was drafted, the printer—a publisher in Maryland named Mary Katherine Goddard—printed her own name at the bottom of the Declaration in support of the signers who were in hiding from the British.

Because the Continental Army lacked money to pay, feed, and clothe the troops, women raised funds, canvassing door to door, and also made clothes for the soldiers. One group of women in Philadelphia made 2200 shirts.

During the Revolutionary War many women followed their husbands into battle. As part of the American army, most filled traditional women's roles as cooks, seamstresses, and nurses, but there are reports of women swabbing cannons with water to cool them and firing cannons when their husbands were wounded. After Margaret Corbin's husband was killed, she manned his artillery piece and was wounded three times. Later she received pay as a disabled soldier, including the ration for rum or

---

Yet the Americans had fought their revolution because they chafed under a government that was too strong. "The nation lived in a nearly constant alternation of fears that it would cease being a nation altogether or become too much of one."[15] People feared both anarchy and tyranny.

This predicament was made clear by the diversity of opinions among the leaders. At one extreme was Patrick Henry, of Virginia, who had been a firebrand of the Revolution. He feared that the government would become too strong, perhaps even become a monarchy, in reaction to the problems with the Articles. He said he "smelt a rat" and did not attend the convention. At the other extreme was Alexander Hamilton, of New York, who had been an aide to General Washington during the war and had seen the government's inability to supply and pay its own troops. Ever since, he had called for a stronger national government. He wanted one that could veto the laws of the state governments. He also wanted one person to serve as chief executive for life and others to serve as senators for life. He did attend the convention but, finding little agreement with his proposals, participated infrequently.

In between were the likes of James Madison, of Virginia. Small and frail, timid and self-conscious as a speaker, he was nonetheless an intelligent and savvy politician. He had operated behind the scenes to organize the convention and to secure Washington's attendance. (He announced that Washington would attend without asking Washington first. Washington, who was in retirement, had not planned to attend and only reluctantly agreed to do so because of the expectation that he would.[16]) Madison, who had studied other countries' governments, had secretly drafted a plan for a new government, one that was a total departure from the government under the Articles and one that would set the agenda for the convention. During the

This English political cartoon satirizes a gathering of leading women of North Carolina who drew up a resolution to boycott taxed English goods.

whiskey. (Many years later she was reburied at West Point.) Some women disguised themselves as men (this was before a military bureaucracy mandated preenlistment physicals) and fought in battle. One wrapped tight bandages around her breasts and served three years and survived two wounds. Fellow soldiers, thinking she was a young man slow to grow a beard, nicknamed her "Molly."[3] Still other women fought to defend their homes using hatchets, farm implements, and pots of boiling lye in addition to muskets.

Women also served as spies. When British soldiers commandeered one house for their quarters, the mother asked if she and her children could remain. One night she overheard the officers plotting a surprise attack on Washington's camp, and she sneaked out of town to warn the camp. A sixteen-year-old girl rode forty miles to warn a militia of another pending attack.[4]

Women were so prominent in the war that British general Lord Cornwallis said, "We may destroy all the men in America, and we shall still have all we can do to defeat the women."[5]

Following independence, a few women continued an active political role. Mercy Otis Warren campaigned against the proposed Constitution because she felt it was not democratic enough. Abigail Adams called for new laws, unlike English laws which gave all power to husbands, that would provide some equality between husbands and wives. She also called for formal education for girls.

Yet independence did not bring an improvement in the political rights of women. It would be another century before the rights of women would become a full-fledged part of our national political agenda.

[1]Quoted in Linda Grant De Pauw and Conover Hunt, *Remember the Ladies* (New York: Viking, 1976), 9.
[2]Alice Felt Tyler, *Freedom's Ferment* (New York: Harper & Row), 1962.
[3]Cokie Roberts, *Founding Mothers* (New York: HarperCollins, 2004), 79–82.
[4]Mrs. Betsey Loring also made a heroic contribution to the cause by keeping a British general so "lustily occupied" in Philadelphia that he failed to move his troops to Valley Forge, where he could have destroyed the Continental Army. Alas, her motive was not patriotism; she sought a position in the British army for her husband. Roberts, *Founding Mothers*, xviii.
[5]Ibid., xix.

convention, Madison was "up to his ears in politics, advising, persuading, softening the harsh word, playing down this difficulty and exaggerating that, engaging in debate, harsh controversy, polemics, and sly maneuver."[17] In the end, his views more than anyone else's would prevail, and he would be known as the Father of the Constitution.[18] Even today, he is esteemed as "our greatest political scientist" by the dean of American political scientists, Robert Dahl.[19]

Consensus

Despite disagreements, the delegates did see eye to eye on the most fundamental issues. They agreed that the government should be a **republic**—a form of government that derives its power from the people and whose officials are accountable to the people. The term more specifically refers to an indirect democracy in which the people vote for at least some of the officials who represent them. The delegates did not seriously consider any other form of government. Only Hamilton suggested a monarchy, and only one delegate suggested an aristocracy.[20]

They also agreed that the national government should be stronger than before. At the same time, they thought the government should be limited, with checks to prevent it from exercising too much power. They agreed that the national government should have three separate branches—legislative, executive, and judicial—to exercise separate powers. They thought that both the legislative and executive branches should be strong.

Conflict

Although there was considerable agreement over the fundamental principles and elemental structure of the new government, the delegates quarreled about the specific provisions concerning representation, slavery, and trade.

Representation Sharp conflict was expressed between delegates from large states and those from small states regarding representation. Large states sought a strong government that they would control; small states feared a strong government that would control them.

When the convention began, Edmund Randolph introduced the Virginia Plan, drafted by Madison. According to this plan, the central government would be strong. The legislature would have more power than under the Articles of Confederation, and a national executive and national judiciary also would have considerable power. The legislature would be divided into two houses, with representation based on population in each.

But delegates from the small states calculated that the three largest states—Pennsylvania, Virginia, and Massachusetts—would have a majority of the representatives and could control the legislature. These delegates countered with the New Jersey Plan, introduced by William Paterson. According to this plan, the legislature would consist of one house, with representation by states, which would have one vote each. This was exactly the same as the structure of Congress under the Articles, also designed to prevent the largest states from controlling the legislature.

To complicate matters, some states claimed vast territories to their west, increasing the fears of other states that such expansion would make the frontier states even larger.

James Wilson, of Pennsylvania, asked for whom they were forming a government—"for men, or for the imaginary beings called states?"[21] But delegates from the small states would not budge. Gunning Bedford, of Delaware, threatened that the small states would leave the government and align themselves with a European country instead. "If the large states insist on representation according to population, the small ones will find some foreign ally of more honor and good faith, who will take them by the hand and do them justice."[22]

The convention deadlocked, and some delegates left for home. George Washington wrote that he almost despaired of reaching agreement. To ease tensions, Benjamin Franklin suggested that the delegates begin each day with a prayer, but they could not agree on this either; Alexander Hamilton insisted they did not need "foreign aid."

Faced with the possibility that the convention would disband without a constitution, the delegates, after weeks of frustrating debate, compromised. Delegates from Connecticut and other states proposed a plan in which the legislature, Congress, would have two houses. In one, the House of Representatives, representation would be based on population, and members would be elected by voters. In the other, the Senate, representation would be by states, and members would be selected by state legislatures. Presumably, the large states would dominate the former, the small states the latter. The delegates narrowly approved this **Great Compromise,** or Connecticut Compromise. Delegates from the large states still objected, but those from the small states made it clear that a compromise was necessary for their agreement and, in turn, their states' ratification. (The large states, though, did extract a concession that all taxing and spending bills must originate in the house in which representation was based on population. This provision would allow the large states to take the initiative on these important measures.) The compromise has been called "great" because it not only resolved this critical issue but paved the way for resolution of other issues.

This decision began a pattern that continues to this day. When officials face implacable differences, they try to compromise, but the process is not easy, and a resolution is not inevitable. It is an apt choice of words to say that officials "hammer out" a compromise; it is not a coincidence that we use *hammer* rather than a softer metaphor.

Slavery In addition to conflict between large states and small states over representation, conflict emerged between northern states and southern states over slavery, trade, and taxation.

With representation in one house based on population, the delegates had to decide how to apportion the seats. They agreed that Indians would not count as part of the population but differed about slaves. Delegates from the South, where slaves made up one-third of the population, wanted slaves to count fully in order to boost the number of their representatives. Although slaves had not been counted at all under the Articles of Confederation or under any state constitution, southerners argued that their use of slaves produced wealth that benefited the entire nation. Delegates from the North, where most states had outlawed slavery or at least the slave trade after the Revolution, did not want slaves to count at all. Gouverneur Morris, of Pennsylvania, said the southerners' position

comes to this: that the inhabitant of Georgia and South Carolina who goes to the coast of Africa, and in defiance of the most sacred laws of humanity tears away his fellow creatures from their dearest connections and damns them to the most cruel bondages, shall have more votes in a government instituted for the protection of the rights of mankind than the citizen of Pennsylvania or New Jersey who views with a laudable horror so nefarious a practice.[23]

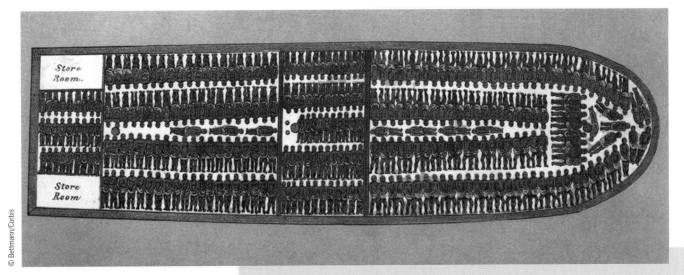

This plan of a slave ship shows the overcrowding that led to inhumane conditions, rampant disease, and high mortality.

Others pointed out that slaves were not considered persons when it came to rights such as voting. Nevertheless, southerners asserted that they would not support the constitution if slaves were not counted at least partially. In the **Three-fifths Compromise,** the delegates agreed that three-fifths of the slaves would be counted in apportioning the seats.

This compromise expanded the political power of the people who were oppressing the slaves. The votes of southern whites became worth more than those of northerners in electing members to the House of Representatives and also in electing presidents (because the number of presidential electors for each state was based on the number of members in Congress from the state). By 1860, nine of the fifteen presidents, including all five who served two terms, were slave owners.[24] Ultimately, twelve presidents were slave owners.

Southerners pushed through two other provisions addressing slavery. One forbade Congress from banning the importation of slaves before 1808; another required free states to return escaped slaves to their owners in slave states. In these provisions, southerners won most of what they wanted; even the provision permitting Congress to ban the importation of slaves in 1808 was little limitation because by then planters would have enough slaves to fulfill their needs by natural population increases rather than importation. In return, northerners, who represented shippers, got authority for Congress to regulate commerce by a simple majority rather than a two-thirds majority. Thus northerners conceded these two provisions reinforcing slavery in order to benefit shippers.[25]

Yet the framers were embarrassed by the hypocrisy of claiming to have been enslaved by the British while allowing enslavement of African Americans. Their embarrassment is reflected in their language. The three provisions reinforcing slavery never mention "slavery" or "slaves"; one gingerly refers to "free persons" and "other persons."

Slavery was the most divisive issue at the convention. As Madison noted, "The real difference of interests lay, not between the large and small, but between the northern and southern states. The institution of slavery and its consequences formed the line of discrimination."[26] The unwillingness to tackle the slavery issue more directly has been called the "Greatest Compromise" by one political scientist.[27] But an attempt to abolish slavery would have caused the five southern states to refuse to ratify the Constitution.

Trade and taxation Slavery also underlay a compromise on trade and taxation. With a manufacturing economy, northerners sought protection for their businesses. In particular, they wanted a tax on manufactured goods imported from Britain. Without a tax, these goods would be cheaper than northern goods; but with a tax, northern goods would be more competitive—and prices for southern consumers more expensive. With an agricultural economy, southerners sought free trade for their plantations. They wanted a guarantee that no tax would be levied on agricultural products exported to Britain. Such a tax would make their products less competitive abroad and, they worried, amount to an indirect tax on slavery—the labor responsible for the products. The delegates compromised by allowing Congress to tax imported goods but not exported ones. Tariffs on imported goods would become a point of controversy between the North and South in the years leading up to the Civil War.

After seventeen weeks of debate, the Constitution was ready. On September 17, 1787, thirty-nine of the original fifty-five delegates signed it. Some delegates had left when they saw the direction the convention was taking, and three others refused to sign, feeling that the Constitution gave too much authority to the national government. Most of the rest were not entirely happy with the result (even Madison, who was most responsible for the content of the document, was despondent that his plan for a national legislature was compromised by having one house with representation by states), but they thought it was the best they could do.

Features of the Constitution

William Gladstone, a British prime minister in the nineteenth century, said the American Constitution was "the most wonderful work ever struck off at a given time by the brain and purpose of man."[28] To see why it was unique, it is necessary to examine its major features.

A Republic

The Founders distinguished between a democracy and a republic. For them, a *democracy* meant a **direct democracy,** which permits citizens to vote on most issues, and a *republic* meant an **indirect democracy,** which allows citizens to vote for their representatives, who make governmental policies.

The Founders opposed a direct democracy for the whole country. Many individual towns in New England had a direct democracy (and some still do), but these communities were small and manageable. Some city-states of ancient Greece and medieval Europe had a direct democracy, but they could not sustain it. The Founders thought a large country would have even less ability to do so because people could not be brought together in one place to act. They also believed that human nature was such that people could not withstand the passions of the moment and would be swayed by a demagogue to take unwise action. Eventually, democracy would collapse into tyranny. "Remember," John Adams wrote, "democracy never lasts long. It soon wastes, exhausts, and murders itself. There never was a democracy yet that did not commit suicide."[29]

The Founders favored a republic because they believed that the government should be based on the consent of the people, and in particular, an indirect democracy, because they believed that the people should have some voice in choosing their officials. So the Founders provided that the people would elect

representatives to the House. They also provided that the state legislators, themselves elected by the people, would select senators from their state as well as their state's electors of the Electoral College, who choose the president. In this way, the people would have a voice but one partially filtered through their presumably wiser representatives.

The Founders' views reflect their ambivalence about the people. Rationally, they believed in popular sovereignty, but emotionally, they feared it. New England clergyman Jeremy Belknap voiced their ambivalence when he declared, "Let it stand as a principle that government originates from the people; but let the people be taught . . . that they are not able to govern themselves."[30]

The Founders would have been aghast at the recent proliferation of such experiments in democracy as initiatives and referenda, which allow voters to adopt public policies, or recall elections, which allow voters to replace elected officials with new officials before their terms expire. The Founders distrusted mass popularity as a means to good government.

The Founders considered a democracy radical and a republic only slightly less radical. Because they believed that the country could not maintain a democracy, they worried that it might not be able to maintain a republic either. It is said that when the Constitutional Convention ended, Benjamin Franklin was approached by a woman who asked, "Well, Doctor, what have we got, a republic or a monarchy?" Franklin responded, "A republic, Madam, if you can keep it."

During the Constitutional Convention, Benjamin Franklin wondered whether the carving on the back of George Washington's chair showed the sun coming up or going down. After the delegates agreed to the Constitution, he observed, "Now . . . I have the happiness to know that it is a rising and not a setting sun."

Fragmentation of Power

Other countries assumed that a government must have a concentration of power to be strong enough to govern. However, when the Founders made our national government more powerful than it had been under the Articles of Confederation, they feared that they also had made it more capable of oppression, so they fragmented its power.

The Founders believed that people were selfish, always coveting more property, and that leaders always lusted after more power. They assumed that this human nature was unchangeable. Madison speculated, "If men were angels, no government would be necessary." "Alas," he added, "men are not angels." Therefore, "in framing a government which is to be administered by men over men, the great difficulty lies in this: you must first enable the government to control the governed; and in the next place oblige it to control itself."[31] (Madison's views are reflected in *Federalist Papers* 10 and 51, reprinted in the appendix.) The Founders decided that the way to oblige the government to control itself was to structure it so as to prevent any one leader, group of leaders, or factions of people from exercising power over more than a small part of it. Thus, the Founders fragmented government's power. This is reflected in three concepts they built into the structure of government: federalism, separation of powers, and checks and balances.

Federalism The first division of power was between the national government and the state governments. This division of power is called **federalism.** Foreign governments had been "unitary"; that is, the central government wielded all authority. At the other extreme, the U.S. government under the Articles of Confederation had been *confederal*; the state governments wielded almost all authority. The Founders wanted a strong national government, but they also wanted, or at least realized they would have to accept, reasonably strong state governments as well. They invented a federal system as a compromise between the unitary and confederal systems. (Chapter 3 explains these types of government further.)

They even incorporated federalism into the national government by stipulating that one house of Congress, the Senate, would be based on the states. It would have two senators from each state regardless of the state's population. This system of representation would protect the interests of the states—especially the small states, which would be dwarfed in a house based on population. Thus small states have power disproportionate to their population.

Separation of powers The second division of power was within the national government. The power to make, administer, and judge the laws was split into three branches: legislative, executive, and judicial (see Figure 2.1). In the legislative branch, the power was split further into two houses. This **separation of powers** contrasts with the parliamentary system in most developed democracies, in which the legislature is supreme. In parliamentary systems, both executive and judicial officials are drawn from the legislature and are responsible to it. There is no separation of powers. Madison expressed the American view of such an arrangement when he said that "the accumulation of all powers, legislative, executive, and judiciary, in the same hands . . . may justly be pronounced the very definition of tyranny."[32] (Today, however, parliamentary systems are no more tyrannous than other systems.)

To reinforce the separation of powers, officials of the three branches were chosen by different means. Representatives were elected by the people (at that time mostly white men who owned property), senators were selected by the state legislatures, and the president was selected by the Electoral College, whose members were selected by the states. Only federal judges were chosen by officials in the other branches. They were nominated by the president and confirmed by the Senate. Once appointed, however, they were allowed to serve for "good behavior"— essentially life—so they had much independence. (Since the Constitution was written, the Seventeenth Amendment has provided for election of senators by the people, and the state legislatures have provided for election of members of the Electoral College by the people.)

Officials of the branches were also chosen at different times. Representatives were given a two-year term, senators a six-year term (with one-third of them up for reelection every two years), and the president a four-year term. These staggered terms would make it less likely that temporary passions in society would bring about a massive switch of officials or policies.

The Senate was designed to act as a conservative brake on the House, due to senators' selection by state legislatures and their longer terms. After returning from France, Thomas Jefferson met with George Washington over breakfast. Jefferson protested the establishment of a legislature with two houses. Washington supposedly asked, "Why did you pour that coffee into your saucer?" "To cool it," Jefferson replied. Similarly, Washington explained, "We pour legislation into the senatorial saucer to cool it."[33]

Separation of powers creates the opportunity for **divided government.** Rather than one political party controlling both elected branches, one party might win the presidency while the other party wins a majority of seats in one or both houses of Congress. Divided government has been common throughout

After slavery was abolished and the right to vote was extended to racial minorities and women, the equal representation of states in the Senate is perhaps the most undemocratic aspect left in the Constitution.[1]

Because each state gets two senators regardless of its population, small or sparsely populated rural states enjoy disproportionate representation relative to their size. California, the most populous state, and Wyoming, the least populous state, have equal representation, although California has seventy times more people. Therefore, voters in California have one-seventieth as much representation, or power, in the Senate as voters in Wyoming have.

The equal representation of states in the Senate is not the result of some grand theory of government. As explained in the text, it was a major concession to the small states to maintain their allegiance to the country and to obtain their support for the Constitution. At that time, people identified more closely with their state than with the nation as a whole. Today, our mass society, mass media, and transportation networks weaken these ties and strengthen our sense of national identity.

Do the people in small states have special needs to protect that would justify their greater representation? The Constitution, including the Bill of Rights and later amendments, guarantees fundamental rights. Federal laws and court decisions preserve various rights. Federalism, which splits power between the national government and the state governments, provides states with more authority than they would have in nonfederal systems. Do the people in small states have additional needs to protect beyond these? If so, what are they? And are these needs greater than the needs of other people who do not get extra representation, such as the people who are short or fat or disabled, or the people who have been the victims of widespread discrimination, such as African Americans or Native Americans?

What if a similar rationale were applied to African Americans? If the 12 percent of Americans who are black had as many senators representing them as the 12 percent of Americans who live in our smallest states have representing them, the Senate would include forty-four black senators. Would this seem fair?

Yet even if most Americans decide that the equal representation in the Senate is unfair and undemocratic, it is unlikely they could change it. The Constitution stipulates, "No state, without its consent, shall be deprived of its equal suffrage in the Senate."[2] Furthermore, Article 5, which addresses amendments, limits amendments in two categories. The provision regarding the importation of slaves could not be amended until 1808, and the provision regarding the representation in the Senate cannot be amended ever.

Some constitutional scholars suggest that an amendment repealing this provision could be adopted first and an amendment altering the representation itself could be adopted next. Other scholars think the courts would not tolerate this obvious subterfuge of the Founders' intentions.[3] Regardless, it is a moot point, because amendment of the Constitution requires ratification by

Branch:	Legislative Congress		Executive Presidency	Judicial Federal Courts
	House	Senate	President	Judges
Officials chosen by:	People	People, (originally, state legislatures)	Electoral College, whose members are chosen by the people (originally, by state legislatures)	President, with advice and consent of Senate
For term of:	2 years	6 years	4 years	Life
To represent primarily:	Common people	Wealthy people	All people	Constitution
	Large states	Small states		

FIGURE 2.1 ■ Separation of Powers *Separation of powers, as envisioned by the Founders, means not only that government functions are to be performed by different branches but also that officials of these branches are to be chosen by different people, for different terms, and to represent different constituencies.*

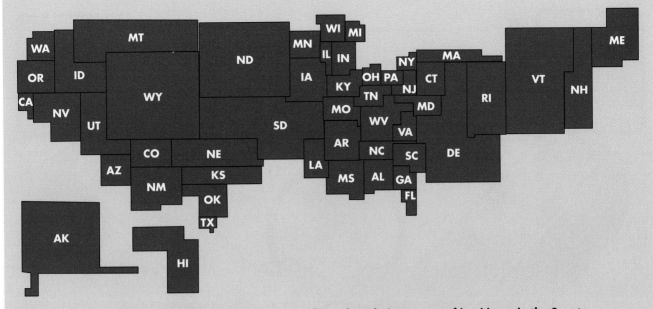

The size of each state in this map reflects the relative power of its citizens in the Senate.

FIGURE 2.2 ■

SOURCE: Michael Lind, "75 Stars," *Mother Jones* (January–February 1998), p. 130. Reprinted with permission.

three-fourths of the states. Just thirteen states can block an amendment favored by the rest of the country. The thirteen smallest states, with only 5 percent of the nation's population, thus can thwart the wishes of the thirty-seven largest states, with 95 percent of the nation's people.

[1]Most information in this box is from Robert A. Dahl, *How Democratic Is the American Constitution?* (New Haven, Conn.: Yale University Press, 2001).
[2]This provision is reinforced by Article 4, which stipulates that "no . . . state shall be formed by the junction of two or more states, or parts of states, without the consent of . . . the states concerned." Thus small states cannot be forced to combine as a way to reduce their representation.

[3]J. W. Peltason, *Corwin and Peltason's Understanding the Constitution*, 9th ed. (New York: Holt, Rinehart and Winston, 1982), 113. For a creative alternative, see Michael Lind, "75 Stars," *Mother Jones* (January–February 1998), 44–49.

the nation's history. Since the emergence of the Democratic and Republican party system (1856), it has occurred as a result of two of every five elections.[34] Since World War II, it has been the dominant mode of government.[35] In this way, American voters have added another element to Madison's concept of separation of powers.

Checks and balances To guarantee separation of powers, the Founders built in overlapping powers called **checks and balances** (see Figure 2.3). Madison suggested that "the great security against a gradual concentration of the several powers in the same department consists in giving those who administer each department the necessary constitutional means and personal motives to resist encroachments by the others. . . . *Ambition must be made to counteract ambition*."[36] To that end, each branch was given some authority over the others. If one branch abuses its power, the others could use their checks to thwart it.

Thus rather than a simple system of separation of powers, ours is a complex, even contradictory, system of both separation of powers and checks and balances. The principle of separation of powers gives each branch its own sphere of authority, but the system of checks and balances allows each branch to intrude into the other branches' spheres. For example, because of separation of powers, Congress makes the laws; but due to checks and balances, the president can veto them, and the courts can rule them unconstitutional. In these ways, all three branches are involved in legislating. One political scientist calls ours "a government of separated institutions competing for shared powers."[37]

With federalism, separation of powers, and checks and balances, the Founders expected conflict. They invited the parts of government to struggle against each other to limit any part's ability to dominate the rest. The Founders hoped for "balanced government." The national and state governments would represent different

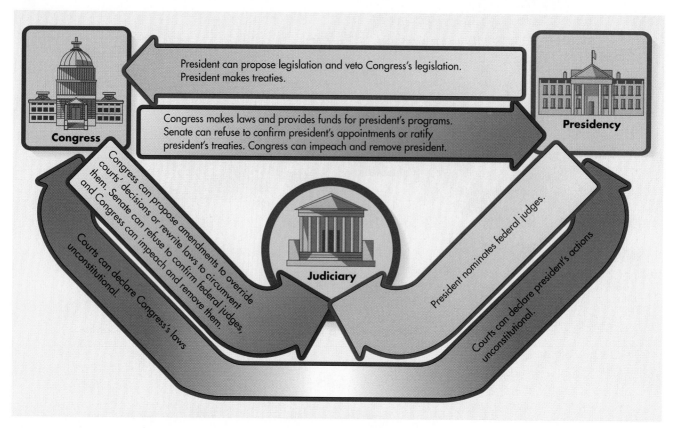

FIGURE 2.3 ■ Checks and Balances *Most of the major checks and balances between the three branches are explicit in the Constitution, although some are not. For example, the courts' power to declare congressional laws or presidential actions unconstitutional—their power of "judicial review"—is not mentioned.*

Within the figure:

President can propose legislation and veto Congress's legislation. President makes treaties.

Congress makes laws and provides funds for president's programs. Senate can refuse to confirm president's appointments or ratify president's treaties. Congress can impeach and remove president.

Congress

Presidency

Congress can propose amendments to overturn courts' decisions or rewrite laws to circumvent them. Senate can refuse to confirm federal judges, and Congress can impeach and remove them.

President nominates federal judges.

Judiciary

Courts can declare Congress's laws unconstitutional.

Courts can declare president's actions unconstitutional.

---

interests, as would the branches within the national government. The House would represent the "common" people and the large states; the Senate, the wealthy people and the small states; the president, all the people; and the Supreme Court, the Constitution. The parts of government would have to compromise to get anything accomplished. Although each part would struggle for more power, it could not accumulate enough to dominate the others. Eventually, it would have to compromise and accept policies that would be in the interest of all of the parts and their constituencies.

Paradoxically, then, the Founders expected narrow conflict to produce broader harmony.

Undemocratic Features

The Founders left undemocratic features in the Constitution that later generations would have to deal with.[38] They denied some people the right to participate in their government and denied some groups equal treatment by their government. As explained, the Constitution did not forbid slavery. It did not even permit Congress to forbid the slave trade for over two decades. The Three-Fifths Compromise actually institutionalized slavery and increased the political power of slaveholders. Furthermore, the Constitution did not

guarantee the right to vote, allowing states to exclude African Americans, Native Americans, other minorities, and women. For some years, states even excluded white men who did not own property from voting. Some states also excluded white men who were not members of the established church from voting. The Founders created the Electoral College to prevent the people from choosing the president. Despite the advent of popular election of the electors, the Electoral College still allows the election of a presidential candidate who did not receive the most popular votes. The Founders stipulated that state legislatures would choose the senators to prevent the people from choosing them. By giving each state two seats in the Senate, the Founders gave disproportionate power to the people who happen to live in small states (as explained in the box "The Undemocratic Senate").

The Founders included these features partly because of the need for political compromise and partly because of their view that the people could not be trusted. The people were seen as an unruly mob threatening stable, orderly government. As later history would show, however, the Founders exaggerated the dangers of popular majorities. When Americans became more egalitarian in the decades following the adoption of the Constitution, they demanded a greater role for the average person. One political scientist concluded that if the Constitution had been written in 1820 instead of 1787, it would have been a very different, and more democratic, document.[39]

Motives of the Founders

To understand the Constitution better, it is useful to consider the motives of the Founders. Were they selfless patriots, sharing their wisdom and experience? Or were they selfish property owners, protecting their interests?

First consider the people who migrated to America. Some came for religious reasons. Their religious beliefs put them at odds with many people in their native country. They were denied privileges or penalized or, occasionally, persecuted. Usually they were adherents of Protestant sects rather than members of established churches such as the Church of England or the Roman Catholic church. As such, they were more suspicious of governmental authority and religious authority than those who remained in the Old World. They were "runaways from authority."[40] Others came for economic reasons. Whether poor or well-to-do, they saw America as the land of economic opportunity. They sought to improve their status, acquiring property and perhaps even becoming wealthy. Although they were not as suspicious of established authority, they were opposed to active government. More government meant more taxes, which meant less money in their pockets. So both groups of people who migrated to America had reasons to prefer limited government.[41] They would pass down their beliefs to their descendants.

Now consider the philosophical ideas, political experience, and economic interests that more directly influenced the Founders.

Philosophical Ideas

The Founders were well-educated intellectuals who incorporated philosophical ideas into the Constitution. At a time when the average person did not dream of going to college, a majority of the Founders were college graduates. As learned men, they shared a common library of writers and philosophers.

The Founders reflected the ideals of the Enlightenment, a pattern of thought emphasizing the use of reason, rather than tradition or religion, to solve problems. They studied past governments to determine why the governments had failed in the hope that they could apply these lessons to the present.

From all accounts, they engaged in a level of debate at the convention that was rare in politics, citing philosophers ranging from the ancient Greeks to the modern British and French.

The views of John Locke, a seventeenth-century English philosopher, underlay many of the ideas of the Founders. In fact, his views permeate the Declaration of Independence and the Constitution more than those of any other person. Locke believed that people have **natural rights.** These rights are inherent; they exist from the moment people are born. They are unalienable; they are given by God, so they cannot be taken away by rulers.

The right to property, according to Locke, is one of the most important natural rights. When people work the land, clearing it and planting it, they mix their labor with it. This act makes the land their property. Although Americans had gotten their land through theft from the Indians or through luck from their ancestors (who had gotten it for little or nothing by a royal grant in colonial times), in this view the important thing is what they do with their land. Farmers start with dirt and grasses and trees, and they create productive land. Some, due to greater effort or better luck, accumulate more property and create more wealth than others. Thus the right to property results in significant inequality of wealth. Yet Locke thought it would lead to greater productivity for society.[42] This view of property appealed to Americans, who saw such abundant land in the new country.

In addition to his views on the rights of the people, Locke wrote about the relationship between the people and their government. He maintained that the people come together to form a government through a **social contract**—an implied agreement between the people and their government—that establishes a **limited government,** strong enough to protect their rights but not so strong as to threaten these rights. This government should not act without the consent of the governed. To make its decisions, this government should follow majority rule. (Locke never resolved the conflict between majority rule and natural rights—that is, between majority rule and the rights of those who disagree with the majority.)

The views of Charles de Montesquieu, an eighteenth-century French philosopher, also influenced the debate at the convention and the provisions of the Constitution. Although others had suggested separation of powers before, Montesquieu refined the concept and added that of checks and balances. Referring to him as "the celebrated Montesquieu," the Founders cited him more than any other thinker.[43] (Presumably, they cited him more than Locke because by this time Locke's views had so permeated American society that the Founders considered them just "common sense."[44])

The principles of the system of mechanics formulated by Isaac Newton, a late seventeenth- and early eighteenth-century English mathematician, also pervaded the provisions of the Constitution. As Newton viewed nature as a machine, so the Founders saw the constitutional structure as a machine, with different parts having different functions and balancing each other. Newton's principle of action and reaction is manifested in the Founders' system of checks and balances. Both the natural environment and the constitutional structure were viewed as self-regulating systems.[45]

Political Experience

Although the Founders were intellectuals, they were also practical politicians. According to one interpretation, they were "superb democratic politicians," and the convention was "a nationalist reform caucus which had to operate with great delicacy and skill in a political cosmos full of enemies."[46]

The Founders brought extensive political experience to the convention: eight had signed the Declaration of Independence; thirty-nine had served in Congress; seven had been governors; many had held other state offices; some had helped write their state constitutions. The framers drew on this experience. For example, although they cited Montesquieu in discussing separation of powers, they also referred to the experience of colonial and state governments that already had some separation of powers.[47]

As practical politicians, "no matter what their private dreams might be, they had to take home an acceptable package and defend it—and their own political futures—against predictable attack."[48] So, they

"Religious freedom is my immediate goal, but my long-range plan is to go into real estate."

compromised the difficult issues and ducked the stickiest ones. Ultimately, they pieced together a document that allowed each delegate to return home and announce that his state had won something.

Economic Interests

Although the Founders were intellectuals and practical politicians, they also represented an elite that sought to protect its property from the masses. The delegates to the Constitutional Convention were an elite. They included prosperous planters, manufacturers, shippers, and lawyers. About one-third were slave owners. Most came from families of prominence and married into other families of prominence. Not all were wealthy, but most were at least well-to-do. Only one, a delegate from Georgia, was a yeoman farmer like most men in the country. In short, "this was a convention of the well-bred, the well-fed, the well-read, and the well-wed."[49]

The Founders championed the right to property. The promise of land and perhaps riches enticed many immigrants to come to America.[50] A desire for freedom from arbitrary taxes and trade restrictions spurred some colonists to fight in the Revolution.[51] And the inability of the government under the Articles of Confederation to provide a healthy economy prompted the Founders to convene the Constitutional Convention. They apparently agreed with Madison that "the first object of government" is to protect property.[52]

They worried that a democratic government, responding to popular pressures, might appropriate their property or impose high taxes to help less wealthy people. They wanted a government that could resist such populism. Yet the Founders' emphasis on property was not as elitist as it might seem. Land was plentiful, and with westward expansion, even more would be available. Already most men were middle-class farmers who owned some property. Many who owned no property could foresee the day when they would, so most wanted to protect property.

The Founders diverged from the farmers in their vision to create a national commercial economy in place of the small-scale agricultural economy. Toward this end, the Founders desired to protect other property in addition to land, such as wealth and credit. Of the fifty-five delegates, forty were owners of government bonds that had depreciated under the Articles, and twenty-four were moneylenders.[53] So the delegates included provisions to protect commerce, including imports and exports, contracts, and debts, and provisions to regulate currency, bankruptcy, and taxes.[54] (See the box "Constitutional Provisions Protecting Property," p. 44.)

Political scientists and historians disagree about which of these three influences on the Founders—philosophical, political, or economic—was most impor-

tant. Actually, the influences are difficult to separate because they reinforce each other; the framers' ideas point to the same sort of constitution that their political experience and economic interests do.[55]

Ratification of the Constitution

The Constitution specified that ratification would occur through conventions in the states and that the document would take effect with the approval of just nine states. These procedures were illegal. According to the Articles of Confederation, which was still in effect, any changes had to be approved by all thirteen states. However, the framers feared that the Constitution would not be supported in some states.

Indeed, ratification was uncertain. Many people opposed the Constitution, and a lively campaign against it appeared in newspapers, pamphlets, and mass meetings.

Knowing opponents would charge them with setting up a national government to dominate the state governments, those who supported the Constitution ingeniously adopted the name **Federalists** to emphasize a real division of power between the national and state governments. They dubbed their opponents **Anti-Federalists** to imply that their opponents did not want a division of power between the governments. (See the box "*The Federalist Papers*," p. 45.)

The Anti-Federalists faulted the Constitution for lacking a bill of rights. The Constitution did contain some protection for individual rights, such as the provision that the writ of habeas corpus, which protects against arbitrary arrest and detention, cannot be suspended except during rebellion or invasion, and the provision that a criminal defendant has a right to a jury trial. But the framers made no effort to include most rights that the people believed they had because most states already included a bill of rights in their constitutions. The framers also thought that by fragmenting power, no branch could become strong enough to deny individual rights. Yet critics demanded provisions protecting various rights of criminal defendants and freedom of the press. In response, the Federalists promised to propose amendments guaranteeing these rights as soon as the government began.

The Anti-Federalists also criticized the Constitution for other reasons. Localists at heart, they were wary of entrusting power to officials far away. They correctly claimed that republics historically worked only in small geographical areas where the population was more homogeneous and the officials were closer to the people. They worried that the central government, to function effectively, would accumulate too much power and the presidency would become a monarchy or Congress an aristocracy. One delegate to the Massachusetts convention blasted the Federalists:

> These lawyers, and men of learning and moneyed men, that talk so finely, and gloss over matters so smoothly, to make us poor illiterate people swallow down the pill, expect to get into Congress themselves; they expect to . . . get all the power and all the money into their own hands, and then they will swallow up all us little folks . . . just as the whale swallowed up Jonah![56]

But the Anti-Federalists had no alternative plan. They were divided; some wanted to amend the Articles of Confederation, whereas others wanted to reject both the Articles and the Constitution in favor of some yet undetermined form of government. Their lack of unity on an alternative was instrumental in their inability to win support.[57]

Within six months, nine states had ratified the new Constitution, allowing the new government, with George Washington as president, to begin in 1788. Within one year, the four remaining states approved the Constitution.

Although this process might seem unremarkable today, this marked the first time that a nation had proposed a new government and then asked the people to approve or reject it. And the process occurred with little violence or coercion. As a constitutional historian observed, "The losers were not jailed, hanged, or politically disabled. They did not boycott, take up arms, or go into exile. They continued, as before, to be full and free citizens, but now living in a new republic."[58]

Changing the Constitution

The framers expected their document to last; Madison wrote, "We have framed a constitution that will probably be still around when there are 196 million people."[59] Yet, because the framers realized it would

Constitutional Provisions Protecting Property

Numerous constitutional provisions, some obvious and others not, were designed to protect property:

Provision	Effect
"The Times, Places and Manner of holding Elections for Senators and Representatives, shall be prescribed in each State by the Legislature thereof."	Allows states to set property qualifications to vote.
"The Congress shall have Power . . . To coin Money."	Centralizes currency.
"No State shall . . . emit bills of credit."	Prevents states from printing paper money.
"Congress shall have Power . . . To establish uniform Laws on the subject of Bankruptcies."	Prevents states from relieving debtors of the obligation to pay.
"The Congress shall have Power . . . To regulate Commerce . . . among the several States."	Centralizes commerce regulation and thereby establishes a national economy.
"No State shall . . . pass any . . . Law impairing the Obligation of Contracts."	Prevents states from relieving debtors of the obligation to pay and thereby establishes stable business arrangements.
"The United States shall guarantee to every State [protection] against domestic Violence."	Protects states from debtor uprisings.
"The Congress shall have Power . . . To provide for calling forth the Militia to execute the Laws of the Union, suppress insurrections."	Protects creditors from debtor uprisings.

need some changes, they drafted a Constitution that can be changed either formally by amendment or informally by judicial interpretation or political practice. In doing so, they left a legacy for later governments. "The example of changing a Constitution, by assembling the wise men of the state, instead of assembling armies," Jefferson noted, "will be worth as much to the world as the former examples we had given them."[60]

By Constitutional Amendment

That the Articles of Confederation could be amended only by a unanimous vote of the states posed an almost insurmountable barrier to any change at all. The framers of the Constitution made sure that this experience would not repeat itself. Yet they did not make amendment easy; the procedures, although not requiring unanimity, do require widespread agreement. More than nine thousand amendments have been proposed in Congress, but only twenty-seven (including the ten in the Bill of Rights) have been adopted.[61]

Procedures The procedures for amendment entail action by both the national government and the state governments. Amendments can be proposed in either of two ways: by a two-thirds vote of both houses of Congress or by a national convention called by Congress at the request of two-thirds of the state legislatures. Congress then specifies which way amendments must be ratified—either by three-fourths of the state legislatures or by ratifying conventions in three-fourths of the states. Among these avenues, the usual route has been proposal by Congress and ratification by state legislatures.

Amendments In the first Congress under the Constitution, the Federalists fulfilled their promise to support a bill of rights. Madison drafted twelve amendments, Congress proposed them, and the states ratified ten of them in 1791. This **Bill of Rights** includes freedom of expression and conviction—speech, press, assembly, and religion (First Amendment). It also includes numerous rights for those accused of crimes—protection against unreasonable searches and seizures (Fourth), protection against compulsory self-incrimination (Fifth), guarantee of due process of law (Fifth), the right to counsel and a jury trial in criminal cases (Sixth), and protection against excessive bail and fines and against cruel and unusual punishment (Eighth). It also includes the right to a jury trial in civil cases (Seventh).

Two amendments in the Bill of Rights grew out of the colonial experience with Great Britain—the right to bear arms to form a militia (Second) and the right not to have soldiers quartered in homes during peacetime (Third). The Bill of Rights also includes two general amendments—a statement allowing for additional rights beyond the ones in the first eight amendments (Ninth) and a statement reserving powers to the states that are not given to the national government (Tenth).

Among the other seventeen amendments to the Constitution, the strongest theme is the expansion of citizenship rights:[62]

Out of the great debate over ratification came a series of essays considered the premier example of American political philosophy. Known collectively as **The Federalist Papers,** these essays were written by Alexander Hamilton, James Madison, and John Jay. At the urging of Hamilton,[1] the authors wrote eighty-five essays that appeared in New York newspapers during the ratification debates there. The authors tried to convince delegates to the convention to vote for ratification.

In the fashion of the time, the essays were published anonymously—using the pseudonym Publius (Latin for *Public Man*). The papers were so unified in their language and arguments that few of the authors' contemporaries could identify whose pens were at work. Given the debates and compromises at the Constitutional Convention, one political scientist speculated that the framers who read the essays "must have discovered with some surprise what a coherent and well-thought-out document they had prepared."[2] Despite the unity of the papers, political scientists have identified the authors of individual ones. Hamilton wrote most of those describing the defects of the Articles of Confederation, and Madison wrote most of those explaining the structure of the new government, including the famous essays 10 and 51 (reprinted in the appendix). Before he fell ill, Jay, who was secretary of foreign affairs, wrote a few concerning foreign policy.

Actually, there is little evidence that the essays swayed any delegates. Yet they have endured because readers see them as an original source of political thinking and as a useful guide to the intentions of the framers. Judges consult them when they interpret various provisions of the Constitution.

[1]Although Hamilton worried that the Constitution would not establish a strong enough government—he called it "a frail and worthless fabric"—he thought it was preferable to the Articles, which he despised. Thus he saw his role like that of "a lawyer obliged to mount his most brilliant defense on behalf of a dubious client." Joseph J. Ellis, "The Big Man," *The New Yorker*, October 29, 2001, 80.
[2]John P. Roche, ed., *Origins of American Political Thought* (New York: Harper & Row, 1967), 163.

- Abolition of slavery (Thirteenth, 1865)
- Equal protection, due process of law (Fourteenth, 1868)
- Right to vote for black men (Fifteenth, 1870)
- Direct election of senators (Seventeenth, 1913)
- Right to vote for women (Nineteenth, 1920)
- Right to vote in presidential elections for District of Columbia residents (Twenty-third, 1960)
- Abolition of poll tax in federal elections (Twenty-fourth, 1964)
- Right to vote for persons eighteen and older (Twenty-sixth, 1971)

In recent decades, two amendments proposed by Congress were not ratified by the states. One would have provided equal rights for women (this amendment is discussed in Chapter 15), and the other would have given congressional representation to the District of Columbia, as though it were a state.

These and other recent amendments have had time limits for ratification—usually seven years—set by Congress. But an amendment preventing members of Congress from giving themselves a midterm pay raise, written by Madison and passed by Congress in 1789, had no time limit. When Michigan ratified it in 1992, it reached the three-fourths mark and became the Twenty-seventh Amendment.

Although the Constitution expressly provides for change by amendment, its ambiguity about some subjects and silence about others virtually guarantee change by interpretation and practice as well.

By Judicial Interpretation

If there is disagreement about what the Constitution means, who is to interpret it? Although the Constitution does not say, the judicial branch has taken on this role. To decide disputes before them, the courts must determine what the relevant provisions of the Constitution mean. By saying that the provisions mean one thing rather than another, the courts can, in effect, change the Constitution. Woodrow Wilson called the Supreme Court "a constitutional convention in continuous session." The Court has interpreted the Constitution in ways that bring about the same results as new amendments. (Chapters 13, 14, and 15 provide many examples.)

By Political Practice

Political practice has accounted for some very important changes. These include the rise of political parties and the demise of the Electoral College as an independent body. They also include the development of the cabinet to advise the president and the development of the committee system to operate the two houses of Congress. (Chapters 7, 8, and 10 explain these changes.)

The Founders would be surprised to learn that only seventeen amendments, aside from the Bill of Rights, have been adopted in over two hundred years. In part this is due to their wisdom, but in part it is due to changes in judicial interpretation and political practice, which have combined to create a "living Constitution."

Authorities empty barrels of beer after the Eighteenth Amendment, which prohibited alcohol, was adopted in 1919. The Twenty-first Amendment repealed the Eighteenth in 1933.

Impact of the Civil War and the Great Depression

The two most significant events in the history of the United States since its founding were the Civil War in the 1860s and the Great Depression in the 1930s. These two events had such an important impact on the Constitution that it would be inadequate, even inaccurate, for us to refer only to the Founders when we explain the Constitution.[63]

Here we will briefly sketch the impact of the Civil War and the Great Depression on the Constitution. Later chapters will further elaborate on these developments.

The Civil War and Reconstruction

The Civil War, from 1861 through 1865, and Reconstruction, from the end of the war through 1876, constituted a "second American Revolution."[64] After all the bloodletting and scorched earth, more than six hundred thousand soldiers lay in graves—one of every seven men between the ages of fifteen and thirty—and parts of the South lay in waste. The North's victory

preserved the Union, but it did far more than this: it also altered the Constitution—in the minds of the people and in formal amendments to the document.

Although the North's leader, President Abraham Lincoln, a Republican, held views that would be considered racist today (he believed that black people were inherently inferior and that they should emigrate from the United States),[65] he despised slavery because it deprived persons of their unalienable rights to life, liberty, and the pursuit of happiness promised by the Declaration of Independence. But efforts to abolish slavery were constrained by the political climate, and Lincoln was a practical politician. Before the war, he was willing to allow slavery in the southern states as long as the Union was preserved. But one year into the war, he found this goal too limited.[66] Abolitionist sentiment was spreading in the North, providing Lincoln the opportunity to lead efforts to abolish slavery as well as preserve the Union. In the process, he helped reinvent America.

The Emancipation Proclamation

The **Emancipation Proclamation** offered the promise of a new constitution. President Lincoln announced it in September 1862 and ordered it to take effect in January 1863. The document proclaimed that the slaves "shall be . . . forever free" in the Confederate states where the Union army was not in control. Its language limited its sweep, for it exempted those parts of the Confederate states where the Union army was in control and also the slave states that remained loyal to the Union (Delaware, Kentucky, Maryland, and Missouri). And despite its language, it could not be enforced in the parts of the Confederate states where the Union army was not in control. Thus, as a legal document, the proclamation was problematic. However, as a symbolic measure, it was successful. The proclamation made clear that the war was not just to preserve the Union anymore but to abolish slavery as well. The announcement captured people's imagination. Between the announcement and the date it was to take effect, the proclamation created so much suspense, according to one historian, that "it had assumed the significance of one of the great documents of all times."[67] When slaves heard about it, many left their plantations, and some joined the Union army. The result sowed confusion in the South and denied a reliable labor force for the region.[68]

The Gettysburg Address

President Lincoln's **Gettysburg Address** became the preamble of the new constitution.[69] The battle at Gettysburg, Pennsylvania, in 1863, was a Union victory and the turning point in the Civil War. Lincoln was invited to deliver "a few appropriate remarks" during the dedication of the battlefield where many had fallen. Lincoln was not the main speaker, and his speech was not long. While the main speaker took two hours, recounting the battle and reciting the names of the generals and even some of their soldiers, Lincoln took two minutes to give a 268-word speech. (He spoke so briefly that the photographer, with his clumsy equipment and its slow exposure, failed to get a single photograph.) Lincoln used the occasion to advance his ideal of equality.

He began: "Four score and seven [eighty-seven] years ago our fathers brought forth on this continent a new nation, conceived in liberty and dedicated to the proposition that all men are created equal." Here Lincoln referred not to the Constitution of 1787 but to the Declaration of Independence of 1776. For Lincoln, the Constitution had abandoned the principle of equality that the Declaration had promised. He sought to resurrect this principle. Lincoln did not mention slavery or the Emancipation Proclamation, which were divisive. A shrewd politician, he wanted people to focus on the Declaration, which was revered.

© Bettmann/Corbis

This view of the remains of Richmond, Virginia, conveys the destruction of the Civil War.

Lincoln concluded by addressing "the great task remaining before us . . . that we here highly resolve that these dead shall not have died in vain, that this nation, under God, shall have a new birth of freedom, and that government of the people, by the people, for the people shall not perish from the earth." This phrase, which Lincoln made famous, was borrowed from a speaker at an antislavery convention.[70] It depicted a government elected by all the people, to serve all the people.[71] Lincoln's conclusion reinforced his introduction; both emphasized equality.

Although his speech was brief, Lincoln used the word *nation* five times, including the phrase "a new nation." His purpose was not to encourage support for the Union but to urge people to think of the nation as a whole, its identity now forged in a bloody war of brother against brother, rather than as simply a collection of individual states with their own interests.[72]

Thus the president essentially added the Declaration's promise of equality to the Constitution, and he substituted his vision of a unified nation for the Founders' precarious arrangement of a balance of power between the nation and the states. According to one historian, "He performed one of the most daring acts of open-air sleight-of-hand ever witnessed by the unsuspecting. . . . The crowd departed with a new thing in its ideological luggage, that new constitution Lincoln had substituted for the one they brought with them."[73]

The Gettysburg Address was heard by an audience of perhaps fifteen thousand, but its language was spread through word of mouth and newspapers and eventually by politicians and teachers. It was read and repeated, and sometimes memorized, by generations of schoolchildren. Although some critics at the time perceived what Lincoln was attempting—the *Chicago Times* quoted the Constitution to the president and charged him with betraying the document he swore to uphold—most citizens came to accept Lincoln's addition. His speech, which has been called "the best political address" in the country's history, thus became "the secular prayer of the postbellum American Republic."[74] (The speech is reprinted in the appendix.)

The Reconstruction Amendments

If the Gettysburg Address became the preamble of the new constitution, the **Reconstruction Amendments** became its body. These three amendments, adopted from 1865 through 1870, began to implement the promise of equality and the vision of a unified nation rather than a collection of individual states.

The Thirteenth Amendment abolished slavery, essentially constitutionalizing the Emancipation Proclamation. This amendment focused on the wrongs committed by private persons. As such, it reflected a new perspective toward government—not as a threat to

people's liberties, as in the original Constitution and the Bill of Rights, but as a guarantor of people's freedom. Whereas the original Constitution and the Bill of Rights are preoccupied with freedom from government, the Thirteenth Amendment is concerned with freedom from exploitation by other persons.

The Fourteenth Amendment declared that all persons born or naturalized in the United States are citizens, overturning the Supreme Court's ruling before the Civil War that blacks, whether slave or free, could not be citizens.[75] The Fourteenth Amendment also included the equal protection clause, which requires states to treat persons equally, and the due process clause, which requires states to treat persons fairly. The equal protection clause would become the primary legal means to end discrimination, and the due process clause would become the primary legal means to give persons the full benefit of the Bill of Rights.[76] This amendment, one legal scholar observes, was "a revolutionary change. The states were no longer the autonomous sovereigns that they thought they were when they claimed the right of secession. They were now, in fact, servants of their people. [They] existed to guarantee due process and equal justice for all."[77]

The Fifteenth Amendment extended the right to vote to blacks. Because women could not vote at the time, the amendment essentially provided the right to vote to black men. This amendment initiated a trend of democratizing the Constitution by extending the right to vote.

As important as the substantive content of these amendments was a procedural provision authorizing Congress to enforce them. ("Congress shall have power to enforce this article by appropriate legislation.") That is, the amendments gave Congress broad power, beyond that granted in the original Constitution, to pass new laws to implement the amendments. Consequently, the federal government would come to oversee and even intervene in the policies of state and local governments to make sure that these governments did not disregard the guarantees of the amendments. These amendments thus marked the start of a trend of federalizing the Constitution by increasing the power of Congress.[78] Five later amendments also included this provision.

President Lincoln initiated the Thirteenth Amendment, and the Radical Republicans who controlled Congress after Lincoln's assassination initiated the Fourteenth and Fifteenth Amendments. There was a passionate national debate. Ultimately, the public supported the amendments. Although most Americans, northerners as well as southerners, were racists, many were inspired by Lincoln or propelled by the war to support greater equality. They elected and reelected supporters of the amendments to Congress.[79]

The net results of the Reconstruction Amendments were to promote equality and to shift power from the states to the federal government.

During Reconstruction, the Union army occupied the South and enforced the amendments and congressional laws implementing them. But white southerners resisted, and eventually white northerners grew weary of the struggle. At the same time, there was a desire for healing between the two regions and lingering feelings for continuity with the past. In 1876, the two national political parties, the Democrats and the Republicans, struck a deal to withdraw the Union army and to allow the southern states to govern themselves again. The entrenched attitudes of white southerners prompted them to establish segregation and discrimination in place of slavery, thus preventing blacks from enjoying their new rights. As a result, the new constitution would not really be enforced until the 1950s and 1960s, when the civil rights movement, Supreme Court rulings, presidential initiatives, and congressional acts would converge to give effect to the ideal of racial equality. In the meantime, the new constitution would lay, in our collective conscious, as an unfulfilled promise, occasionally emerging to foster greater equality.[80]

The Great Depression and the New Deal

The Great Depression began when the stock market crashed in 1929. Wealthy people lost their investments, and business activity declined. Ordinary people lost their jobs, with a quarter of them becoming unemployed. Investors lost their savings when many banks collapsed. President Franklin Roosevelt, a Democrat, was elected in 1932. He initiated an ambitious program, heralded as "a new deal for the American people," to stimulate the economy and to help the people who were suffering. His program and his administration came to be known as the **New Deal.**

This era also altered the Constitution—not by formal amendments but through Supreme Court rulings and political practice. In the process, it changed the minds of the people.[81] As a result, we replaced our small, limited government, as envisioned by the Founders, with a big, activist government.

Supreme Court Rulings

In the late nineteenth and early twentieth centuries, a *laissez-faire* economic philosophy was popular in this country and was reflected in governmental policies. According to this philosophy, government should not interfere in the economy (*laissez-faire* is French for "leave it alone"). Although government could *aid* businesses, it should not *regulate* them.[82] People who believed this philosophy thought it would create a robust and efficient economy. Indeed, the industrialization of the time, producing an array of new products for consumers and an increase in personal wealth for owners, seemed to confirm their expectations. But it also led to negative consequences, especially for employees, who were forced to labor in harsh, even dangerous, conditions for long hours and little pay. Many pressed government to address these problems. But when Congress and state legislatures passed laws to regulate child labor, maximum hours of work, and minimum wages for work, the Supreme Court, following the traditional philosophy, usually declared the laws unconstitutional. When Congress passed laws to implement President Roosevelt's recovery program, a majority of the Court often declared these laws unconstitutional as well. The impasse reached a climax in 1935 and 1936 when the Court invalidated twelve laws proposed by the president and passed by Congress. The Court's resistance made clear that the New Deal reforms were not simply fine-tuning governmental policy toward the economy but were overhauling it.[83] In response to the Court's resistance, members of Congress introduced thirty-nine constitutional amendments to reverse the Court's rulings.

After Roosevelt was resoundingly reelected in 1936, intense pressure from the president, Congress, and the public prompted two justices who had voted against government regulation of business to switch sides and vote for such regulation in 1937.[84] One

The David J. and Janice L. Frent Collection

VOTE FOR HERBERT HOOVER and CHARLES CURTIS for the Prosperity of your Country and the Happiness and your home....

In the 1920s the economy and stock market were booming. Herbert Hoover capitalized on the country's prosperity in the 1928 election.

case clearly illustrates the Court's about-face. Farmers had produced crop surpluses, which drove down the prices. The government sought to reduce the surpluses in order to drive up the prices. One small farmer in Ohio was allowed by the Department of Agriculture, under a law passed by Congress, to plant eleven acres of wheat, but he chose to plant twenty-three acres. When he was cited for violating the law, he said that it should not apply to him because his farm was very small. He did not sell much of the wheat—his family and farm animals consumed most of it—so he said he did not affect market prices. But now, after the switch in 1937, the Court ruled unanimously against him.[85] Thus the Court allowed the government to extend its reach far beyond what was thought permissible just a few years before.

These transformative rulings created a "constitutional revolution."[86] They took the place of formal amendments to the Constitution, which were no longer necessary once the Court acquiesced to the policies of the president and Congress. As a result, government could regulate businesses when the public believed that regulation would be beneficial.

Political Practice

Before the Depression, Washington, D.C. had been "a sleepy southern town," in the eyes of reporters.[87] When Roosevelt took office, he was uncertain exactly what to do, but he was willing to experiment, and he did believe he had a mandate from the people, who had rejected the incumbent president, Herbert Hoover, and his administration. Roosevelt's personality and his ambitious ideas attracted many more people—hundreds of thousands of people—some simply relieved to find a job, but others excited to work for the government. These reformers brought new ideas, even radical ideas, that would receive consideration and perhaps acceptance in the depths of the Depression. As federal efforts to provide relief and regulation spread throughout the country, many other people got jobs in federal offices outside Washington.

Within six years of Roosevelt's taking office, the number of federal workers in the District of Columbia had more than doubled,[88] the number of federal workers in the country had almost doubled, and the size of the federal budget had almost doubled.[89] In the process, the scope of the federal government had expanded

During the Depression, many people who lost their job lost their ability to put food on the table. Breadlines and soup kitchens were common. Here the unemployed wait for coffee and doughnuts at one of fifty-two relief kitchens in New York City in 1934.

Ap/Wide World Photos

tremendously. In short, we got big government and activist government in less than a decade. These changes were so dramatic that one political scientist has said they created a "second American republic."[90]

Roosevelt's exuberance and experimentation had given people hope. As the country gradually pulled out of the Depression (though the country would not fully recover until the economic activity generated by World War II provided the final boost), people gave Roosevelt credit, electing him to an unprecedented four terms and returning Democrats to Congress to support him.[91] Ever since, Americans, albeit to different degrees, have expected the government to tackle society's problems. While sometimes mouthing the language of the Founders—for example, Thomas Jefferson's assertion, "That government is best which governs least"—they have for the most part accepted the reality of the government that was expanded during the Depression.[92]

These changes during the Depression would lay the foundation for the government of the 1960s, which would promote the equality advanced during the Civil War. Without a powerful government pushing for change, the entrenched attitudes supporting segregation and discrimination would not have been overcome.

A Combination of Constitutions

As a result of President Lincoln and the Radical Republicans in the 1860s and 1870s and President Roosevelt and the New Deal Democrats in the 1930s and 1940s, our government is very different from the one the Founders bequeathed us.[93] Later generations of Americans made the eighteenth-century Constitution work in the nineteenth century, and then they made it work in the twentieth century—by remaking that Constitution. Changes in the nineteenth century added the concept of equality and elevated the national government over the state governments. Changes in the twentieth century transformed a relatively small, limited government into a very large, activist government.

The original Constitution and the remade Constitution reflect competing visions. Should we emphasize liberty or equality? Should we demand that individuals solve their own problems or ask government to help them? Americans have not reconciled these visions. Sometimes we cling to the Founders' Constitution; other times we embrace the post–Civil War and post-Depression Constitution. In political debates, politicians, commentators, or citizens take positions without articulating, perhaps without even realizing, that these positions hark back to the Founders' Constitution, whereas opponents espouse views that rely on the post–Civil War and post-Depression Constitution. Thus the two constitutions coexist, sometimes uneasily, in our minds and in government policies.[94] As a consequence of our history, then, we actually have a combination of constitutions.

Conclusion: Does the Constitution Make the Government Responsive?

The Constitution established a government that has survived for over two centuries. Although the United States is considered a relatively young country, it has one of the oldest constitutions in the world. As a result, the United States has the oldest democracy, oldest republic, and oldest federal system in the world.[95]

In the Constitution, the Founders set forth a mechanism to govern a vast territory and to provide for majority rule while allowing minority rights. This government has enabled more people to live in liberty and in prosperity than the people of any nation before or since.[96]

Americans have been grateful, venerating the Founders and embracing the Constitution as a secular Bible. Citizens consult it for guidance and cite it for support at the same time they debate the meaning of its provisions.

Despite its status as a political icon, however, the Constitution has been copied by few countries.[97] Although provisions of the Bill of Rights, such as freedom of speech, and of the Fourteenth Amendment, such as the equal protection clause, have been adopted by other countries,[98] the structure of our government has been less popular. Among the twenty-two democratic countries that have remained stable since 1950,[99] only five others have a federal system with significant power at the state level, only three others have a bicameral legislature with significant power in both houses, and only four others have one house with equal representation for the states regardless of their population. No others have a presidential system, and only two others have a judicial system that exercises judicial review of national legislation.[100] Our Constitution and governmental structure are seen more as a reflection of historical factors and political compromises than as a desirable form of government.

The Founders left important problems unresolved for succeeding generations. Most notable was slavery and the treatment of African Americans. Also troublesome was the uncertain relationship between the nation and the states. As we have seen, later Americans would have to resolve these problems, and in the process they, too, would contribute to the Constitution. Succeeding generations remade the Constitution most noticeably in the wake of the Civil War and the Great Depression, and they remade it more than many Americans realize.

But most of the original Constitution remains. We have retained the basic structure of government and the underlying fragmentation of power. The combination of federalism, separation of powers, and checks and balances, along with the unique method for choosing the president, make our government perhaps "the most intricate ever devised."[101] It is also perhaps "the most opaque . . . , confusing, and difficult to understand."[102]

The structure of government and fragmentation of power challenge citizens to hold their leaders accountable. If you disapprove of some policy, whom do you hold accountable in the next election—the president, the Senate, the House of Representatives, the unelected judges, or the state governments? Usually there is divided responsibility, resulting in less accountability.

Of course, the Founders sought a government that would be responsive to the people only to a limited extent. The Constitution created a republic, which granted the people the right to elect some representatives who would make their laws. In this way, the people had more say in government than the people in other countries at the time. Yet the Constitution was expected to filter the public's passions and purify their selfish desires. Thus the original Constitution allowed citizens to vote only for members of the House of Representatives—not for members of the Senate or the president. Furthermore, it fragmented power, so a single group could not control the entire government. Various changes to the Constitution have expanded opportunities for citizens to participate in the government, but the changes have done little to modify the structure of the government or its fragmentation of power.

This configuration has prevented many abuses of power, although it has not always worked. During the Vietnam War and the Iraq War, for example, one branch—the presidency—exercised vast power whereas the others acquiesced.

This configuration has also provided the opportunity for one branch to pick up the slack when the others became sluggish. The overlapping of powers ensured by checks and balances allows every branch to act on virtually every issue it wants to. In the 1950s, President Eisenhower and Congress were reluctant to push for civil rights, but the Supreme Court did so by declaring segregation unconstitutional.

But the system's very advantage has become its primary disadvantage. In their efforts to fragment power so that no branch could accumulate too much, the Founders divided power to the point where the branches sometimes cannot wield enough. In their efforts to build a government that requires a national majority to act, they built one that allows a small minority to block action.

This problem has become increasingly acute as society has become increasingly complex. Like a mechanical device that operates only when all of its parts function in harmony, the system moves only when there is consensus or compromise. Consensus is rare in a large, heterogeneous society; compromise is common, but it requires more time as well as the realization by competing interests that they cannot achieve much without it. Even then, compromise often results in only a partial solution.

At best, the system moves inefficiently and incrementally; at worst, it moves hardly at all. The Constitution has established a government that is slow to respond to change. "By intent," one political scientist noted, "the U.S. government works within a set of limits designed to prevent it from working too well."[103] Thus the system tends to preserve the status quo and to respond to the groups that benefit from the status quo.

Although the changes made in the wake of the Depression brought us big, activist government, they did not negate all of our historical aversion to such government. We still have a more limited government than other advanced industrialized countries. Contrary to what many Americans believe, our taxes are lower and governmental policies in numerous areas, such as health care, welfare, and transportation, are less ambitious.[104] This, of course, limits our ability to address our problems.

Yet some political scientists believe the American people actually prefer a system that is hard to move. Because the people are suspicious of government, they may be reluctant to let one party dominate it and use it to advance that party's policies. In surveys, many people—a quarter to a third of those polled—say they think it is good for one party to control the presidency and the other to control Congress.[105] In presidential and congressional elections, more than a quarter of the voters often split their ticket between the two parties.[106] As a result, between 1968 and 2002, opposing parties controlled the executive branch and at least one house in the legislative branch for all but six years.

Such divided government reinforces the fragmentation of power in a way that makes it difficult, if not impossible, for citizens to pin responsibility on particular officials and parties for the decisions and policies of government. "If no individual or institution possesses the authority to act without the consent of everybody else in the room, then nobody is ever at fault if anything goes wrong. Congress can blame the president, the president can blame the Congress or the Supreme Court, the Supreme Court can blame the Mexicans or the weather in Ohio."[107] If citizens cannot determine who is responsible for what, they cannot hold those individuals accountable and make them responsive.

The President Complies in the Case of the Confidential Tapes

hief Justice Warren Burger announced the unanimous decision in the case of *United States* v. *Nixon:* the president must turn over the tapes.[108] The Court acknowledged the existence of executive privilege in general but rejected it in this situation because another court needed the information for an upcoming trial and because the information did not relate to national security.

The Court emphasized that courts would determine the legitimacy of claims of executive privilege,[109] not presidents, as Nixon wanted. Because of the separation of powers, Nixon argued, neither the judicial nor the legislative branch should involve itself in this executive decision.

However, this president, who as a high school student in Whittier, California, had won a prize from the Kiwanis Club for the best oration on the Constitution, ignored the system of checks and balances, which limits the separation of powers. In this case, checks and balances authorized the courts to conduct criminal trials of the president's aides and Congress to conduct impeachment proceedings against the president. To do so, the courts and Congress needed the information on the tapes.

Within days of the Court's decision, the House Judiciary Committee passed three articles of impeachment. These charged Nixon with obstruction of justice, by covering up a crime; defiance of the committee's subpoenas for the tapes; and abuse of power. (The committee also considered an article of impeachment for cheating on his income taxes, but members decided that this was a personal matter, rather than a governmental matter, and as such not appropriate for impeachment.[110])

Despite the charges, some Republicans maintained that there was no "smoking gun"—no clear evidence of crimes. They branded the impeachment effort strictly political.

Regardless, Nixon's support in Congress dwindled, and he found himself caught between a rock and a hard place: Releasing the tapes would furnish more evidence for impeachment, but not releasing them would spur impeachment. He considered disregarding the decision, but after twelve days of weighing his options, he complied with the order.

Releasing the tapes did reveal a smoking gun. Although the tapes did not show that Nixon had participated in planning the break-in, they did show that he had participated in covering it up. When the burglars blackmailed the administration, Nixon approved paying them hush money. He ordered the head of his reelection committee to "stonewall it" and "cover up." He and an aide formulated a plan to have the CIA thwart the FBI in its investigation of the scandal. When his top aides were subpoenaed to appear before the grand jury, he encouraged them to lie. (Years later, one aide to Nixon claimed that the president himself had ordered the break-in.[111])

In addition to this evidence of crimes, the tapes revealed profanity, vulgarity, and derogatory remarks about women, Catholics, Jews, blacks, Hispanics, and various other ethnic groups. ("The Italians . . . they're not like us . . . they smell different, they look different, act different. . . . Of course, the trouble is . . . you

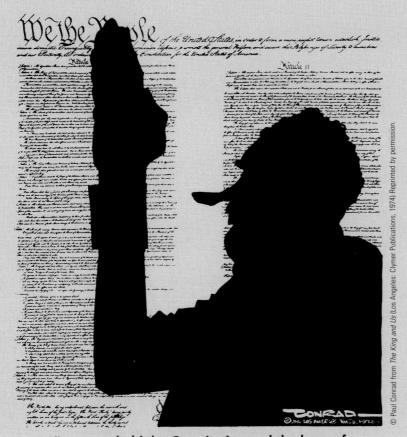

© Paul Conrad from *The King and Us* (Los Angeles: Clymer Publications, 1974) Reprinted by permission.

". . . to uphold the Constitution and the laws of the United States—as I see them . . ."

can't find one that is honest."[112]) Such language repelled the public and undercut the image Nixon had tried to project.

As his presidency came collapsing around him, White House insiders began telling people privately that Nixon was dazed, like a "wind-up doll" or a "madman." They said that he was drinking heavily, "going bananas," talking to portraits of past presidents, and showing other signs of cracking under the strain. Some worried that he was considering suicide. One day, he said to his chief of staff, General Alexander Haig, "You fellows, in your business [the army], you have a way of handling problems like this. Somebody leaves a pistol in the drawer." He paused and then added sadly, "I don't have a pistol." Afterward, Haig notified Nixon's doctors and had Nixon's sleeping pills and tranquilizers taken away.[113]

When it became clear that public opinion would force the House to impeach him and the Senate to remove him, Nixon decided to resign. On August 9, 1974—just seventeen days after the Supreme Court's ruling—he became the first American president to do so. Vice President Gerald Ford became the new president.

Although the smoking gun had been found, some people thought Nixon should not have been driven from office. But Watergate was not just a break-in. It was a series of acts, more than can be detailed here, to subvert the Constitution and democratic elections. As the magnitude of these acts came to light, Nixon lost some support. Then, as the cover-up of these acts came to light, he lost even more support. He had campaigned for the presidency on a platform calling for "law and order" and had sworn an oath promising to "take care that the laws be faithfully executed." When Watergate revelations appeared in the media, he

had proclaimed his innocence. Ultimately, the hypocrisy and the lying became too much for the public to stomach. Nixon could no longer lead the public he had misled for so long.

Despite depression and cynicism about the scandal, many people saw that the system had worked as it was supposed to. The Founders had divided power to make it difficult for any one branch to amass too much. In the face of the president's efforts to exercise vast power, the courts, with their orders to turn over the tapes, and Congress, with its Senate Watergate Committee hearings and House Judiciary Committee impeachment proceedings, checked the president's abuse of power. In addition, the media, through extensive publicity, first prompted and then reinforced the actions of the courts and Congress. However, although the system worked, it worked slowly. More than two years, more than half of the president's term in office, lapsed between the break-in and the resignation.

When the affair was over, twenty-one of the president's men were convicted and sentenced to prison for their Watergate crimes. Except for one, a burglar who was most uncooperative and who served fifty-two months (G. Gordon Liddy, who now hosts a radio talk show), the men served from four to twelve months. Nixon, who could have and probably would have been prosecuted after leaving office, received a pardon from President Ford before any prosecution could begin.

Nine years after the resignation, the security guard who had discovered the break-in was convicted for shoplifting in Augusta, Georgia. Unemployed, he had stolen a pair of shoes for his son. Unlike the president's men, he received the maximum sentence—twelve months for the $12 shoes.

Congress passed a law mandating that other, unreleased tapes and documents be turned over to the National Archives, which was to make public any that related to Watergate or had "general historic significance."

The archives has slowly released these materials. On one tape, Nixon is heard remarking to his chief of staff, "I always wondered about that taping equipment, but I'm damn glad we have it, aren't you?"[114]

Not only does Nixon's voice remain, but the effects of Watergate linger. The public has become less trusting of government officials, and the media have become more suspicious of them. The parties have become more aware of the benefits of a scandal involving their opponents. In the wake of Watergate, the Democrats captured the White House and gained many seats in Congress. These results have prompted both parties to point accusing fingers and to launch congressional investigations—though only against members of the other party—even when the alleged transgressions have been far less serious than those in Watergate. Thus Watergate contributed to the culture of scandal that afflicts American politics today.

And although the case of *United States* v. *Nixon* appeared to resolve the controversy over executive privilege, the controversy has reemerged, with President George W. Bush asserting executive privilege frequently as part of his effort to expand presidential power and administrative secrecy. This effort will be addressed in Chapter 11.

To learn more about the Watergate scandal, go to "you are there" exercises for this chapter on the text website.

Key Terms

Watergate scandal
executive privilege
Articles of Confederation
Shays's Rebellion
Constitutional Convention
republic
Great Compromise
Three-Fifths Compromise
direct democracy
indirect democracy
federalism
separation of powers
divided government

checks and balances
natural rights
social contract
limited government
Federalists
Anti-Federalists
Federalist Papers
Bill of Rights
Emancipation Proclamation
Gettysburg Address
Reconstruction Amendments
New Deal

Further Reading

Joseph J. Ellis, *His Excellency: George Washington* (New York: Knopf, 2004); *Founding Brothers: the Revolutionary Generation* (New York: Knopf, 2000), this book focuses on the interactions among the major figures; and *American Sphinx: the Character of Thomas Jefferson* (New York: Knopf, 1997). All are graceful biographies.

Leonard W. Levy, ed., *Essays on the Making of the Constitution* (New York: Oxford University Press, 1969). These essays address the question "Was the Constitution an undemocratic document framed and ratified by an undemocratic minority for an undemocratic society?"

David McCullough, *1776* (New York: Simon & Schuster, 2005). This book presents the drama of the first year of the Revolutionary War between the British redcoats and the American "rabble in arms."

Clinton Rossiter, *1787: The Grand Convention* (New York: Macmillan, 1966). This is a lively account of the Constitutional Convention and the ratification campaign.

Theodore H. White, *Breach of Faith* (New York: Atheneum, 1975). White presents a chronicle of the Watergate scandal as a Greek tragedy in which actors on both sides behaved in such ways as to fulfill their destinies.

Bob Woodward and Carl Bernstein, *All the President's Men* (New York: Simon & Schuster, 1974). This is a riveting account of journalistic sleuthing by the two reporters who broke the Watergate story.

For Viewing

All the President's Men (1976). Robert Redford and Dustin Hoffman play Woodward and Bernstein.

Amistad (1997), directed by Steven Spielberg. A shipload of Africans headed for slavery are freed by abolitionists, including John Quincy Adams.

Ken Burns' Civil War (1990). This is PBS's most watched documentary series. Compare this portrayal of the war with the romanticized treatment in *Gone with the Wind* (1939).

Glory (1989). Historically accurate, this movie presents the story of the first all-black regiment to fight in the Civil War and the white officer who led them. Starring Denzel Washington and Matthew Broderick.

 **Electronic Resources**

http://www.lcweb.loc.gov/exhibits/declara/declara4.html
The Library of Congress presents original drafts and other documents pertaining to the Declaration of Independence.

http://www.nwbuildnet.com/nwbn/usconstitution-search.html
Even the Constitution has a home page.

http://www.usconstitution.net
This Constitution page with numerous links was originally created by a political science student as a class project.

ThomsonNOW™

Enter ThomsonNOW™ using the access card that is available with this text or through www.thomsonedu.com/thomsonnow. ThomsonNOW™ will assist you in understanding the content in this chapter with a personalized study plan generated for your needs. A practice test will assess the areas you need to review and provide the tools to fully comprehend those concepts, including an integrated digital eBook, interactive simulations, timelines, video case studies, MicroCase exercises, and InfoTrac College Edition readers and exercises. You'll also be connected to the learning objectives, chapter outline, chapter glossary, flash cards, crossword puzzles, Internet activities, and interactive quizzes found on the companion website.

Illegal immigrants cross Arizona's desert.

Federal and Unitary Systems
   Federal Systems
   Unitary Systems
   Why Choose Federalism?

The Political Bases of American Federalism
   Political Benefits of Federalism
   Political Costs of Federalism

The Constitutional Bases of Federalism
   Major Features of American Federalism
   Interpretations of Constitutional Provisions

The Changing Division of Powers
   Growth of Government and the Division of Powers
   Resetting the Balance

Everyday Federalism
   Presidential Management of Federal-State Relations
   Cooperative Federalism
   Conflict in State-Federal Relations
   States and Localities as Lobbyists
   Relations Between the States
   State-Local Relations
   People, States, and the Federal Government

A Return to State-Centered Federalism?
   The Bush Administration
   Congress
   The States
   The Supreme Court

Conclusion: Does Federalism Make Government More Responsive?

YOU ARE THERE

Sign the Bill or Bill the Feds?

You are Janet Napolitano, the first-term governor of Arizona. It is May 2005, and your state is facing an historic influx of undocumented migrants. More than a million people a year are crossing along Mexico's border with Arizona, New Mexico, and California without entry papers. Immigration policy is a federal responsibility, and the ultimate resolution is out of your hands. But as a governor you have to deal with the day-to-day problems of human smuggling, drug trafficking, crime, and increased costs of education and health care.

Even if you were not already running for a second term, you could not ignore the issue because your policy agenda and the state's finances are deeply affected by the influx. Citizen anger over uncontrolled borders, migrant deaths from heat prostration and dehydration, and employers' frustration over their inability to get legal status for undocumented workers have led to a flurry of bills in the state legislature dealing with everything from border enforcement, to access to social services, to issuance of identity cards. Each time one of these bills passes you have to make a decision on whether to sign or veto.

Now you, a Democrat, have on your desk a bill passed by the Republican-led legislature that authorizes, but does not require, state and local law enforcement agencies to enforce federal immigration laws. You have already vetoed several immigration control bills, but you know something has to be done to address the anger and frustration over the inadequacy of the federal government's response. Should you veto another attempt by the state to act, or should you sign the bill and authorize a larger role for state and local agencies in enforcing federal immigration law?

You call yourself a moderate Democrat and have experience attractive to both parties. You started out as a corporate lawyer but also served on Anita Hill's legal team during the heated partisan hearings on Clarence Thomas's nomination to the Supreme Court.[1] After serving as a Clinton-appointed U.S. district attorney for Arizona, you won your race for state attorney general and became known for consumer advocacy work. Running for governor, you counted on crossover support at the polls and in office have needed Republicans to gain passage of your legislative agenda. Both of your legislative priorities, early childhood education and health care, are affected by illegal immigration. Republicans have made it plain they will make immigration an issue in your re-election campaign.

Even before you became governor in 2002, Arizona had become

The "Minutemen" are self-appointed border guards who try to prevent illegal entries from Mexico. Such action by private citizens, and its potential for violence, have prompted governors to demand that the federal government meet its responsibilities for border enforcement.

the "crossing point of choice" for those entering the country illegally due to much stronger border enforcement policies in Texas and California. Over 2000 arrests a day were being made along the Arizona border; people were dying trying to cross the desert, and almost 1500 people a year were in need of rescue. Meanwhile smugglers (*coyotes*) were making money from human and drug trafficking.[2] In addition, those crossing on foot have local ranchers and some environmentalists up in arms because of property, livestock, and environmental damage. The Arizona Homeland Security department is worried that terrorists could be among those crossing the border, finding it easier to cross on foot than to gain entry by air. And people entering the country with no papers, little money, and no transport have caused a spike in certain crimes, especially car thefts. The Arizona Corrections system is housing more than 4000 undocumented workers.[3] Border posses are forming, and some local law enforcement officers, not empowered to enforce federal laws, are looking for any kind of local statute, such as trespassing or loitering laws, to detain people in the state illegally.

Arizonans were so angry in 2004 that they passed Proposition 200, which restricted access of illegal immigrants to state-provided social services. Although there is overwhelming agreement on the need for better control of the borders, Arizonans are narrowly split on how to handle the problem of residency, with Democrats tending to prefer legalization through a guest worker program and Republicans tending to favor stronger border enforcement. But it is only a tendency; both parties are split within themselves, as are Mexican Americans and Arizona's two Republican senators. Sen. Jon Kyle favors strong enforcement laws and deportation, and Sen. John McCain favors creation of a guest worker program that will allow those who entered illegally to gain legal residence and eventual citizenship.

Illegal residents now make up 9 percent of Arizona's population; only California has a higher percentage. Arizona is already the nation's second fastest growing state, and its boom has been driven by the development of high-tech industry. In contrast, farm land and agricultural industries have been shrinking. Most of those entering the country illegally are low-skill workers who might have difficulty finding year-round employment in Arizona's high-tech economy.

You know that immigration enforcement is without question a federal responsibility, but Washington has done far too little, leaving it to the states to pick up the slack. There are thousands of children to educate and health problems to treat. Federal law mandates that children be educated, without respect to their immigration status. States can legislate who is eligible for public health benefits, but federal law does not allow hospitals to turn away emergency cases. One federal court ruled that a pregnant woman in the country cannot be deported because her fetus is already a citizen. None of these rulings is in your hands or those of the Arizona legislature. States must obey federal rulings and find a way to pay for compliance, or for that portion of costs that federal grants do not cover.

Now you have a bill that would give state and local agencies greater authority to enforce immigration law, by arresting and deporting those who have entered the state illegally. If you sign it, you believe that Arizona police officials could help curb the uncontrolled flow of immigrants over the border. You also think that this would be a politically popular move. On the other hand, you know that controlling borders is a federal responsibility. You would be committing the state to costs that are the obligation of the federal government. And, these costs would be steep. Moreover, the bill stresses enforcement whereas both your Democratic base and the state's business community support a balanced approach that would strengthen enforcement but also resolve the residency status of the thousands of illegal immigrants already within the state. What do you do? Do you sign it or veto it?

The victory of the Union over secessionist states in the Civil War (1861–1865) determined that the Union was indivisible and that the states could not nullify federal law or the Constitution. The war settled little else about the federal relationship, but war, economic crises, and the varying political philosophies of presidents, members of Congress, and Supreme Court justices have all contributed to our transformation from a small agrarian to a large, complex nation and inevitably to change in the way our federal system functions.

Today, because of the sheer size and complexity of our country, its role in world affairs, and our expanded expectations of government, we live in a nation with a strong central government. One indication of how dominant the national government has become in the public consciousness is the conflation of *federal* with *national*. It is a confusing but now common usage to say *federal government* when referring to the national government. In just over two hundred years, the national government grew from a few hundred people with relatively limited impact on the residents of thirteen small states to a government employing several millions, affecting the daily lives of more than three hundred million people in fifty states and billions of people beyond our borders. Yet we continue to disagree about just how big and how strong our national government should be.

In this chapter, we look at the politics behind the choice of federalism as our form of government, the constitutional provisions that define it, and how the federal distribution of power has changed over time through federal court rulings, territorial expansion, national crises, and the political philosophies of presidents, governors, and legislators. Finally, we look at the current division of power between the national and state governments and discuss why that balance continues to shift.

Federal and Unitary Systems

Federal Systems

The term **federalism** describes a system in which power is constitutionally divided between a central government and subnational or local governments. In the United States, the subnational governments are the states. All federal systems are not alike: nations that have them, Germany, Canada, India, Brazil, and Mexico, for example, vary greatly in their basic economic and political characteristics. They are similar only in that each has a written constitution allocating some powers to the national and some to the subnational governments.

In American federalism, both levels of government receive their grants of power from a higher authority, the will of the people (popular sovereignty) as expressed in the Constitution. In other words, federalism divides something—sovereignty—that is theoretically indivisible. This is the source of some of the conflict over jurisdiction that inevitably arises between levels of government. Making arrangements even more complex, the powers granted to each level are not necessarily exclusive. Both national and state governments have the power to tax, regulate, and provide benefits. And because each level of government is sovereign in its own right, neither can dissolve the other.

In contrast, in a **confederal system**, the central government has only those powers given to it by the subnational governments; it cannot act directly on citizens, and it can be dissolved by the states that created it. The first American government, established by the Articles of Confederation, was a confederal system in which all sovereignty was vested in the states. The national government was the creation of the states—not the people—and it existed only at their pleasure. Like the first government of the United States, the United Nations is an example of a confederal system. The lack of central authority in such systems makes them basically unworkable as governmental arrangements for modern nations.

Unitary Systems

In contrast to federalism, the national government in a **unitary system** creates subnational governments and gives them only those powers it wants them to have. Thus the national government is supreme. In Britain, for example, the national government can give or take away any power previously delegated to the subnational governments, and it can even abolish them, as it did with some city governments in the 1980s. In unitary Sweden, the national parliament abolished 90 percent of its local governments between 1952 and 1975.

In the United States, the fifty states are each unitary with respect to their local governments. Cities, counties, townships, and school districts can be altered or even eliminated by state governments. Yet every state is (and is required to be by the U.S. Constitution) a republic—that is, a representative democracy. It follows then that the difference between unitary and federal systems is not at all related to the distinction between democracy and authoritarianism. Some unitary systems are among the most democratic in the world (Britain and Sweden); others are authoritarian (Egypt and China). And though some federal systems are democracies (Canada, Mexico, Germany, India), others are authoritarian (the former Soviet Union and the former Yugoslavia) and still others, like Nigeria, have elements of both.

It is also inaccurate to classify federal systems as decentralized and unitary systems as centralized. All modern governments have to delegate some power because a central government, even in a unitary system, cannot run every local service or deal directly with every local problem. Moreover, it is inaccurate to think of federalism as a static system, with powers divided for all time. The balance of power in the United States is constantly evolving and the competition for that power unending.

Why Choose Federalism?

Except for a few loosely organized leagues of states, there were no federal governments before the United States was created. Yet by the 1960s, as much as half the world's territory was governed by federalism.[4] Some new nations created after World War II chose federalism because they, like the American colonies, were trying to unite diverse states or territories into a single country. Federal systems are often ethnically, linguistically, religiously, or racially diverse, though not always. Germany is relatively homogeneous ethnically, but it will become less so if guest workers from Turkey and North Africa gain citizenship. In 2005 Iraqis wrote a constitution with a federal division of power among Shia and Sunni Muslims, and the mostly Muslim but ethnically distinct Kurds, to get the bitterly divided factions to accept the new government. Agreeing to divide power among levels of government may be the only way to unite people who have strong motivation to live apart.

The power-sharing arrangements in federal governments often do not work, and many have failed. In some cases, there were not enough shared values to hold a nation together. Muslims left predominantly Hindu India to create Pakistan, and the Bengali people split from Pakistan to create Bangladesh. Sometimes too much power was invested in the central government, and sometimes too little. Federal systems that were not created by popular will are likely to fail when the authoritarian center collapses. Yugoslavia, the Soviet Union, and Czechoslovakia ceased to exist, and their constituent republics became independent countries. There have been failed secessionist movements in Nigeria, Canada, Mexico, the United States, and many other federalist nations.

The Political Bases of American Federalism

The Founders of the United States did not choose federalism as an ideal form of government or as a principle in itself; the few historical examples held little to recommend it as a form appropriate to the American situation. They had to write from scratch a document that would accommodate the political reality of their loose compact of states. Although at least one delegate to the Constitutional Convention proposed abolishing the states to create a unitary system, few took this option seriously.[5] But it was necessary to find a compromise that could satisfy those who thought only a strong central government could work and those who thought the union could be preserved only if the individual state governments retained most of the authority they had under the Articles of Confederation. The Founders proposed a dual form of government, a hybrid to be created by mixing the *national* form with a strong central government favored by some delegates and the *confederal*, or league of states, form favored by others. In arguing for its ratification, James Madison defended the Constitution in just this way, saying it would create a government that was partly national and partly federal.[6] Although today we refer to the government in Washington as the "federal" government, the Founders referred to the government they created by the type of democracy it was—a republic. The word *federal* does not appear in the Constitution.

Political Benefits of Federalism

The division of power between the national and state governments was one politically attractive feature of federalism for those delegates who worried about the center gaining advantage over the states. But with federalism's provisions for accommodating national diversity also came a means for limiting the authority of government in general. Madison explained how this would work. In *Federalist Paper* 10, he asserted that it is inevitable that "factions"—groups of citizens seeking some goal contrary to the rights of other citizens or to the well-being of the whole country—would threaten national stability. To restrain the destructive or obstructionist effects of unchecked competition—what Madison called the **"mischiefs of faction"**—government must either remove the causes of factionalism or control its effects. The first option, Madison believed, was unrealistic because it would require the impossible: changing human nature. It also would require taking away freedom by outlawing opinions and strictly regulating behavior. People inevitably have different ideas and beliefs, and government, he thought, should not try to prevent this.

Because the causes of faction could not be removed without placing too many restrictions on freedom, its effects had to be controlled by a properly constructed government. If a faction were less than a majority, Madison believed it could be controlled through majority rule, the majority defeating the minority faction. If the faction were a majority, however, a greater problem arose, but one for which Madison had an answer: one had only to limit the ability of a majority to carry out its wishes. Madison believed this was impossible in a small democracy, where there is little to check a majority determined to do something. But in a large federalist system, there are many checks on a majority faction—more interests competing with each other and large distances to separate those who might scheme to deprive others of liberty. As Madison noted, "The influence of factious leaders may kindle a flame within their particular States, but will be unable to spread a general conflagration through the other States."

Having many states and having them spread over a large territory would serve as major checks against majority tyranny. Madison's argument in *Federalist Paper* 10 (reprinted in Appendix C at the back of this book) remains among the most influential works of American political theory.

Perhaps the benefit of the federal arrangement for the American colonies can be best understood by the adage "politics is the art of the possible." The division of power made the Union possible. It allowed states their differences, ceded control over local affairs, and in the process protected against both an abusive central government and the tyranny of factions.

Political Costs of Federalism

If the division of power made the Union possible, what are the drawbacks of such division? One disadvantage is that allegiance to the Union can falter if too much value is placed on accommodation of state or regional differences. The Union can also erode if the differences among the states become more important than their commitment to common principles. The United States faced secessionist threats almost immedi-

James Madison

ately after its creation—by southern states when the Federalists (under John Adams) were in power and by New England states when the anti-federalists (under Jefferson) were in power. Secession was averted (until the Civil War, more than seventy years after the Constitution) in part by the fear of external threats but mainly by key political leaders' commitment to make the Union work.

The constitutional provisions protecting the rights and individuality of the states were meant to accommodate what has been called our "psychology of localism."[7] (See the American Diversity box "Political Culture and Federalism.") Although we are now a more mobile and a more nation-oriented people than we were in the eighteenth and nineteenth centuries, we retain enough local allegiance and commitment to individualism to tilt our federal system toward decentralization and fragmentation. Indeed, federalism "creates separate, self-sustaining centers of power, privilege and profit which may be sought and defended as desirable in themselves."[8] In part, federalism is *intended* to do this, but if taken too far, it can prevent coherence and unity on major policy issues. Even when there is need for national policy—whether on energy, the environment, health care, or defense spending—members of Congress may still base their votes primarily on local interests (see Chapter 10).

When we refer to the Midwest, the Southwest, New England, or the Deep South, certain images still come to mind, not just of geographical areas but of lifestyles, partisan preferences, ideology, and local economies. Our nicknames—Bible Belt, Lala Land, the Corn, Sun, and Rust Belts—reflect this. Individual states have developed sufficiently different political styles and attitudes that campaign strategists would never design the same electoral strategy for a candidate in New York as they would for one in Idaho. For the same reason, candidates for national office change the points of emphasis in their stump speeches as they move from state to state. States want to be different from one another. Each has its own constitution, flag, motto, and symbols of state, not to mention its very own official state bird and flower. Each state is basically a political actor competing for a share of the nation's resources. Just as individuals organize around identity issues, states compete with one another on the basis of their distinctive profiles.

In Chapter 1 we defined political culture as a shared body of values and beliefs that shapes perceptions and attitudes toward politics and government and that influences behavior. For much of the twentieth century, the United States was said to have three geographically based political subcultures—three distinctive ways of looking at and participating in politics.[1] The tendency of people in New England and the upper Midwest to view politics as a way of improving life and to believe in their obligation to participate was labeled a *moralistic* political culture. In the *individualistic* political culture, said to be typical of the industrial Midwest and the East, the ultimate objective of politics was not to create a better life for all but to get benefits for oneself and one's group. In the *tradi-tionalistic* political culture, associated with the states of the Deep South, politics was seen not as a way to further the public good but as a way to maintain the status quo, and little value was placed on participation. Today, traces of these patterns remain, but much has changed.

The Deep South, for example, having been the site of intense political mobilization during the modern civil rights movement, is now a center of significant grassroots activity, especially among religious conservatives. The outmigration of African Americans during the decades of segregation has been reversed, with a significant impact on electoral politics in the region.

The transformation of the United States from an industry- and agriculture-based economy to a high-tech and service economy also has had an inevitable impact on regional political cultures. The mobility of the American population makes it less likely that people will have political orientations as strongly rooted in a state or regional identity as in earlier decades. Every year, about one in seven Americans move, one-third of those from one state to another.[2] Only 25 percent of Nevadans were born in Nevada, for example. Mass media, especially television and the Internet; franchises and chains bringing the same products to all parts of the country; and transportation systems that can carry us across the nation in a few hours have all had a leveling effect on some of our regional differences.

Yet the country is just as diverse as ever; indeed, it is ethnically and racially more diverse. Patterns of dispersion of African Americans, Hispanics, and Asians, and the fact that immigrants tend to settle in clusters by country of origin in a handful of states and big cities, contributes to the retention of regional differences and distinctive state profiles. In New Mexico, 43 percent of the population is of Hispanic origin, compared with less than 1 percent in Maine. In Mississippi, African Americans make up over 36 percent of the population; in Vermont, 0.5 percent. Minorities, collectively, now form the majority of the population in four states, including Texas. In Florida, almost as many people are over age sixty-five (18 percent of the population) as are under seventeen (21 percent), but in Utah, young people outnumber senior citizens more than 3.5 to 1. In Mississippi, annual per capita income is only 54 percent of what it is in Connecticut ($22,861 versus $42,104).[3]

These disparities make for different politics in the states. The priorities of older people (health care, for instance) are different from those of younger people (financial aid for education, for example). In states with larger numbers of Hispanics and African Americans, civil rights issues are more salient than in states with predominantly white populations. Southern Baptists, who comprise 11 percent of all American Christians, live predominantly in southern states and vote overwhelmingly Republican. Jewish Americans, who tend to be more liberal and vote Democratic, are concentrated in a handful of states, including New York, Florida, and California. And Mississippi, West Virginia, and Arkansas, whose citizens are poorer than those in the rest of the country, face greater demands for services and have correspondingly fewer resources to provide them.

Although state and regional differences have not been homogenized, the three old archetypes have morphed into the two more comprehensive categories now familiar to everyone as red states and blue states. Another scheme labels them retro (red) and metro (blue), but the basic distinction is between conservative and liberal policies and lifestyles.[4]

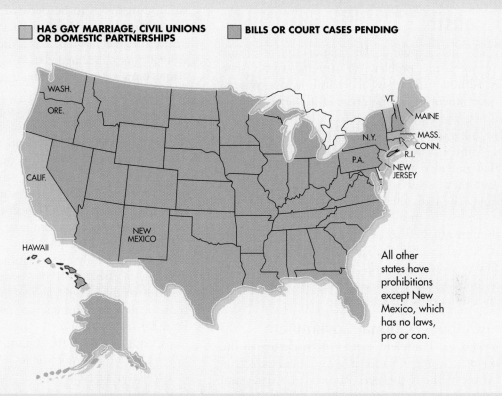

■ HAS GAY MARRIAGE, CIVIL UNIONS OR DOMESTIC PARTNERSHIPS   ■ BILLS OR COURT CASES PENDING

WASH.
ORE.
CALIF.
HAWAII
NEW MEXICO
VT.
MAINE
N.Y.
MASS.
CONN.
R.I.
P.A.
NEW JERSEY

All other states have prohibitions except New Mexico, which has no laws, pro or con.

FIGURE 3.1 ■ Political Culture Is Reflected in States' Policies *States tend to have a more liberal or more conservative political culture, which is reflected in their policies, whether for moral issues or other issues.*
SOURCE: *New York Times*, April 23, 2006, 16.

The politically conservative/moralistic/red/retro label is now attached to the South, plains states, lower Midwest and near West. The liberal/nontraditional/blue/metro state label lumps together the Northeast, upper Midwest, northwestern coastal states, and California. In fact the division of states into such broad categories masks the diversity within the two groups and is misleading in suggesting a consonance of lifestyles and political orientation within them. The divorce rate in the Bible Belt states is 50 percent higher than the national average, whereas the nation's lowest divorce rate is in Massachusetts, the bluest of blue states.[5] The wealthiest states are all in the blue column and the poorest in the red column, which means that the citizens of conservative states who are most likely to oppose social welfare policies and government programs receive substantially more per capita in government benefits than they pay in taxes.[6]

State boundaries do still mean something beyond identifying the place where you register to vote. In policy areas as diverse as economic development, taxation, welfare, and regulation of personal morality, states vary widely. (See Figure 3.1.) Nevada is the only state in the nation where prostitution is legal; Utah the only state where polygamy has been tolerated (even though illegal). South Dakota passed a law banning abortions that would never make it through the Massachusetts legislature, whereas Massachusetts and Vermont passed laws allowing same-sex marriages that would never have been passed in South Dakota. Federalism, even with a strong national government, provides sufficient autonomy for states to adopt and maintain policies consistent with their own political cultures.

[1]Daniel Elazar, *American Federalism: A View from the States*, 3rd ed. (New York: Harper & Row, 1984).
[2]U.S. Census Bureau, *Statistical Abstract of the United States, 2006* (Washington, D.C.: Government Printing Office, 2005), tab. 30, p. 36.
[3]All figures in this paragraph from *Statistical Abstract of the United States, 2006*, tabs. 23, 22, and 662. Income is in constant 2000 dollars.
[4]John Sperling, et al., *The Great Divide: Retro vs. Metro America* (Sausalito, CA: PoliPoint Press, 2004).
[5]Jim Holt, "States' Rights Left?" *New York Times Magazine*, November 21, 2004, 27.
[6]Sperling, *The Great Divide*, 34.

The Constitutional Bases of Federalism

Major Features of American Federalism

As we saw in Chapter 2, the Founders were unsure how to solve the problem of national versus state powers. Although they saw federalism as one way to limit government power by dividing it, they were creating a new form of federalism.

One thing almost all delegates could agree on was the need for a central government that was stronger than that provided for in the Articles of Confederation. But they never agreed on how much of their sovereignty the individual states would have to surrender to achieve a stronger national government. The Constitution assigned some powers, set limits on the exercise of others, but did so with an ambiguity and economy of wording that made the document acceptable to both advocates of a strong national government and supporters of states' rights.

Strengthening National Government

Two powers the Founders knew were necessary to the creation of a stronger national government were the right to tax without the permission of the states and the authority to make foreign and domestic policy without the states' consent. Granting Congress the authority to tax and to regulate interstate commerce gave tremendous power to the national government and made it far more independent of the will of the state governments than it had been under the Articles. But the Constitution also assigned Congress many general duties, granting it authority to make all laws **"necessary and proper"** for carrying out its specific powers. This is sometimes called the **implied powers clause** because the federal courts soon interpreted its vague wording to mean that Congress could legislate in almost any area it wished. This greatly expanded the reach of the national government.

The Founders' decision to create separate legislative and executive branches and make the selection of the president independent of Congress (unlike England, for example, where the head of government is chosen by and from within Parliament) also strengthened the federal government by giving the president a base from which to exercise independent national leadership. The president's role as commander in chief and principal executor of the laws of the United States further enlarged national powers.

Finally, the **supremacy clause** established the predominance of the national government over the states. It says that treaties, the Constitution, and "laws made in pursuance thereof" are to be the supreme law of the land whenever they come into conflict with state laws or state actions. Furthermore, when there is a difference of opinion as to whether state actions are in conflict with the Constitution or federal law, the matter is to be decided at the national level.[9] The Constitution did not specify the individual or institution that would make these decisions, but the federal courts assumed that role during the tenure of Chief Justice Marshall. (This is discussed at length in Chapter 13.)

The significance of the supremacy clause took some time to emerge. This was because the delegates to the Constitutional Convention were not in agreement on whether they were there as *representatives of their states* (the view of many southerners) or as *representatives of the people* of their states (the view of many New Englanders).[10] This meant there was no initial consensus on who created, and therefore who could abolish or withdraw from, the new government. Was government simply the creation of the states, as the wording of Article VII makes it seem, or was it the creation of the people, as the Preamble seems to say? Individuals may continue to disagree over what the Founders intended, but the primacy of the supremacy clause was fixed by the Union victory in the Civil War. The union was inviolable—states could not secede—and no state could nullify a law passed by Congress.

Restricting Powers of State Governments

In addition to the categorical limitation placed on state rule making by the supremacy clause, the Constitution also identifies specific actions that states cannot take because they are reserved for the national government. States cannot enter into treaties, keep standing armies or navies, make war, print or coin money, or levy import or export taxes. These prohibitions reaffirmed that with respect to foreign policy and interstate commerce, sovereignty was vested in the national government.

The Constitution also prohibits states from infringing on certain rights of individuals. For example, a state cannot pass an *ex post facto* ("after the fact") law making an action a crime and then punish citizens who committed the "crime" before it was made illegal.

Limiting Powers of the National Government

The most important general restriction on the power of the national government with respect to the states is contained in the **Tenth Amendment.** It reserves to the states and to the people those powers not granted by the Constitution to the national government. At the time it was written, the understanding of this wording was that the national government would have only those powers specifically assigned to it in the Constitution. It was added as a separate amendment in the Bill of Rights just in case this point was not clear in the body of the Constitution. But the broad construction of Congress's "necessary and proper" powers, established by many federal court rulings over the decades, weakened the Tenth Amendment. Yet the wording remains open to more restrictive interpretations, and since the 1990s, the federal courts have breathed new life into this amendment.[11]

Other limits on national powers are contained in Article IV, which prohibits the national government from abolishing existing states or altering their boundaries, and in the Ninth Amendment, which states that the enumeration of certain individual rights in the Constitution and the Bill of Rights cannot be read to mean the people do not retain other rights.

Interpretations of the Constitutional Provisions

Having reached agreement on a division of powers, the Founders left vague the details of how the nation-state relationship would work. Such was the gulf between those who thought they were creating a nation an indivisible union—and those who thought they were writing a contract between states that the Constitution might never have been ratified if it had contained specifics on the practice of federalism. These competing views are the source of what still today is the biggest disagreement about our constitutional system.[12]

Political Interpretations

Those who saw the Constitution as written by representatives of the people and ratified by the people were inclined to view the national government as the supreme power in the federal relationship. Alexander Hamilton clearly articulated this view of **nation-centered federalism** in the *Federalist Papers*. This interpretation accepts that the Constitution grants many powers to the states and recognizes that they existed before the Union and are sovereign in the sense that they cannot be dissolved by the national government. But the national government's sovereignty is seen as supreme in that its ultimate responsibility is to preserve the Union and ensure its indivisibility.[13] Nation-centered federalism was the view used by northerners to justify a war to prevent the southern states from seceding in 1861.

Opponents of the Hamiltonian interpretation, including many from the South, argued that because the Constitution recognized the states' existence as sovereign entities before the creation of the Union, the form our system was to take was **state-centered federalism**, giving precedence to state sovereignty over that of the national government or the Union. They believed the Tenth Amendment limited congressional powers to those specifically mentioned in Article I and that this view was reinforced by Madison's words in *Federalist Paper* 45: "The powers delegated . . . to the federal government are few and defined. Those which are to remain in the state governments are numerous and indefinite." In this view, any attempt by Congress to go beyond these explicitly listed powers violated state authority.

In justifying their secession from the Union, southerners held to the extreme version of state-centered federalism: that the Constitution had been written by representatives of the states, not the people. In their view, if the states had created the Union, they could dissolve it.

The Constitution can also be interpreted as having created a government in which the division of power leaves neither level dominant over the other. In this view—**dual federalism**—the Constitution created a system in which the national government and the states each have separate grants of power, with each supreme in its own sphere. In this interpretation of the division of powers, sovereignty is not just divided but divided in such a way as to leave both levels of government essentially equal. The differences between levels derive from their separate jurisdictions, not from inequality of power. Madison's description in *Federalist Paper* 39 of the government created by the Constitution as a hybrid of national and federal forms provides one basis for this interpretation.

Over the years, the dominant interpretations of power sharing in our form of federalism have shifted among the nation-centered, state-centered, and dual views. Interpretations reflect changing federal court composition, economic conditions, the philosophies of those in the executive and legislative branches, and changing public demands. Overall, there has been a general trend away from state-centered and toward nation-centered federalism, but significant shorter-term shifts have occurred back toward the states.

Early Judicial Interpretations

Very soon after the Constitution was ratified, the federal courts became the arbiters of the Constitution. John Marshall, chief justice of the United States from 1801 to 1835, was a Federalist, a firm believer in the need for a strong national government, and the decisions of his Court supported this view.

The Marshall-led Supreme Court established the legal bases for the supremacy of national authority over the states. Among the Court's most important rulings were that decisions of the state courts could be overturned by the federal courts and, in the case of **McCulloch v. Maryland**, that the implied powers given Congress in the Constitution could be broadly interpreted. The *McCulloch* decision said that the "necessary and proper" clause in Article I implied that Congress has the right to make all laws necessary to carry out its Constitutional powers.

The *McCulloch* case grew out of a dispute over the establishment of a national bank. Because the Constitution does not explicitly grant Congress the authority to charter banks, many people thought Congress may have been infringing on rights the Constitution left to the states. Ironically, it was John Calhoun, later to become the leading states' rights advocate, who introduced a bill to charter the Bank of the United States.

Once established, the bank was immediately unpopular because it competed with smaller banks operating under state laws and because some of its branches engaged in reckless and even fraudulent practices. When the government of Maryland levied a tax on the currency issued by the Baltimore branch of the bank, the constitutionality of the bank was called into question and a case was brought to the Supreme Court.

Marshall's ruling in *McCulloch* v. *Maryland* in 1819 was one of the most influential of any Supreme Court decision for the fate of the federal relationship.[14] Pronouncing the tax unconstitutional, Marshall wrote that "the power to tax involves the power to destroy." The states should not have the power to destroy the bank, he stated, because the bank was "necessary and proper" to carry out Congress's powers to collect taxes, borrow money, regulate commerce, and raise an army. Marshall argued that if the goal of the legislation is legitimate and constitutional, "all means which are appropriate, which are plainly adapted to that end, which are not prohibited, but consistent with the letter and spirit of the Constitution, are constitutional."

Thus Marshall interpreted "necessary" quite loosely. The bank was probably not necessary, but it was "useful." This interpretation of the implied powers clause allowed Congress, and thus the national government, to wield much more authority than the Constitution gave it explicitly. Although there was some negative reaction ("A deadly blow has been struck at the Sovereignty of the States," decried one Baltimore newspaper[15]), the Court maintained its strong nation-centered position as long as Marshall was chief justice.

In 1836, with a new chief justice, the Court began to interpret the Tenth Amendment as a strict limitation on federal powers, holding that powers to provide for public health, safety, and order were *exclusively* powers of the state governments, not of the national government. This dual federalism interpretation eroded some of the nation-centered federal interpretations of the Marshall Court while continuing to uphold the rights of the federal courts to interpret the Constitution.

There have since been many Court rulings on the division of power between Washington and the states, but these early rulings set the pattern for what would be shifting interpretations of how the Constitution distributes power between levels of government.

The Changing Division of Power

The first fifty years under the new constitution were characterized by the growth of nation-centered federalism in legal doctrine, by small-scale state and national government in practice, and by the beginning of intergovernmental cooperation. In the administration of George Washington the federal government had only one thousand employees, and this number had increased only to thirty-three thousand by the presidency of James Buchanan seventy years later. Little revenue was raised by any level of government; most of the funding for the national government came from import-export and excise taxes. State governments, too, were small and had limited functions. There were only a few federal-state cooperative activities. For example, the federal government gave land to the states to support education and participated in joint federal-state-private ventures, such as canal-building projects initiated by the states.

In this section we look at how territorial expansion, war, and economic crises required a greater exercise of power at the national level—raising armies, regulating trade and interstate commerce, and building infrastructure, for example—which in turn demanded an expansion of taxation authority and a larger bureaucracy. We also look at some of the forces constraining growth of national powers at the expense of the states.

Growth of Government and Division of Powers

Government has grown because, as society changes, new problems emerge, and people demand that government respond to them. Government has also grown because emergencies such as wars and depressions occur, and those in power see the need for a bigger government to cope with them. Presidents come to office with some idea of how they will use the powers of office—whether they will be maximalists or minimalists, or something in between. But a president's theoretical view of the power of the federal government can be superseded by events. How presidents respond to needs arising from war, social movements, economic crises, or natural disasters can lead to changes in the division of power, whether intended or not intended. Thomas Jefferson called his election a revolution, abolished all internal taxes, and set about making government as small, simple, and informal as possible. He tried to keep the United States out of war in Europe and closed down ports and foreign trade, but he soon found he needed federal policing to enforce his policy.[16] And despite his support for small government and state-centered federalism, when presented with the opportunity to buy the Louisiana territories from Spain, Jefferson took it, with or without formal authority. His expansionist vision instantly sent the country down the road from a small coastal nation to a vast continental empire in which his idea of a small agrarian republic would no longer be possible.

Lincoln, who was as loath as Jefferson to interfere with states' rights when it came to slavery, had no doubts about denying states the right to secede from the Union nor about using his role as a wartime commander in chief to assume extraordinary powers in domestic policy. The Civil War's outcome reaffirmed the supremacy clause, the indivisibility of the republic, and guaranteed that there would be only one national government in the continental United States. Northerners saw their Civil War victory as a severe blow to state-centered federalism, but southerners continued to see the Union, in which they were forcibly retained, as one governed by a state-centered form of federalism.

By the time Theodore Roosevelt (1901–1909) assumed the presidency, agrarian America was being replaced by a rapidly urbanizing and industrializing society. Living and working conditions for many city dwellers were appalling. Adults and children who moved into the cities often took jobs in sweatshops—factories where they worked long hours in unsafe conditions for low pay. Roosevelt's presidency was a time of tremendous government activism. He saw his office as a "bully pulpit" from which to advocate for the improvement of working conditions, environmental protection, and the regulation of big business, especially its corrupting influence on state legislatures and the U.S. Senate, which was then still elected by the legislatures. These years saw a flood of new legislation and regulatory activity as Roosevelt's concept of government as advocate for the average citizen changed the direction and purpose of government at the outset of the twentieth century.

During this period, the revenues of both the national and state governments grew. For the federal government the new revenue came through a tax on personal income, a tax Congress had power to levy

Theodore (Teddy) Roosevelt rode into the presidency determined to use government to improve working conditions, eliminate business corruption, and preserve national resources.

only after the Seventeenth Amendment to the Constitution was ratified in 1913. Many states and localities levied gasoline and cigarette taxes and raised property taxes, and some states also adopted income taxes. Federal support for state programs also grew through land and cash grants given by the federal government to the states.[17] By the late 1920s, however, the federal government still provided few direct services to individuals. States and localities were clearly the dominant partner in providing most services, from health and sanitation to police and fire protection.

As Teddy Roosevelt had expanded the federal government's role in order to curb the negative consequences of economic expansion on the individual and the environment, Franklin Delano Roosevelt (FDR; 1933–1945) expanded government power at all levels to mitigate the effects of the Great Depression, the worst economic crisis the country had experienced.

Thirty-two years after his cousin became president, Franklin Delano Roosevelt (FDR) used his unbridled confidence and public support for his New Deal to greatly expand the role of the federal government.

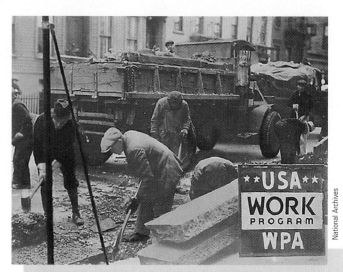

FDR took office on March 4, 1933. He immediately sent to Congress a group of legislative proposals, many of which Congress passed within the first hundred days of the new administration. FDR's program, known as the New Deal, enlarged the role of the federal government. Shown in the photo are civilians employed in the Works Progress Administration (WPA), a New Deal agency that built schools, roads, airports, bridges, and post offices throughout the country in the 1930s. The agency was successful in putting millions of unemployed Americans to work and at the same time upgrading the nation's public buildings and infrastructure.

When the stock market crashed in 1929, wealthy people became poor overnight. In the depths of the Depression, one-fourth of the workforce was unemployed, and banks failed daily. Unlike today, there was no systematic national program of relief for the unemployed—no unemployment compensation, no food stamps, no welfare, nothing to help put food on the table and pay the rent. Millions of Americans were hungry, homeless, and hopeless. States and localities, which had the responsibility for providing relief to the poor, were overwhelmed; they did not have the funds or organizational resources to cope with the millions needing help. And private charities did not have enough resources to assume the burden. FDR's predecessor, Herbert Hoover, had taken a minimalist approach, and by the time FDR came to office the dislocation and suffering of millions of Americans threatened the political stability of the country.

During his first two terms FDR formulated and Congress passed a program called the **New Deal.** Its purpose was to stimulate economic recovery and aid those who were unemployed, hungry, and in ill health. New Deal legislation regulated many activities of business and labor, set up a welfare system, and began large-scale federal-state cooperation in funding and administering programs through federal grants-in-aid. Grants-in-aid provided federal money to states (and occasionally to local governments) to initiate programs that targeted categories of needy people—the aged poor or the unemployed, for example. As Figure 3.2 indicates, the federal share of spending for domestic needs (exclusive of military spending) nearly tripled, from

17 percent in 1929, before the New Deal, to 47 percent in 1939. Local governments' share of overall spending dropped by half, reflecting the greater responsibilities assumed at the state and national level. The states' share of overall government spending stayed constant. However, even though it decreased as a proportion of all public spending, it increased dramatically in absolute terms, given the huge increase in total public sector spending. Some of that increase was from federal grants-in-aid to fund unemployment compensation, emergency welfare, and distribution of farm surpluses to the needy and for free school lunches, among other programs.

Other New Deal policies that directly affected everyday life included new regulations on banks and working conditions, federal redistributive programs designed to protect the poor (Aid to Dependent Children), and social insurance for the elderly poor, retired, and disabled (Social Security). Overall, the New Deal brought a dramatic change in the relationship between the national government and its citizens, making government more personal both because of its greater involvement in daily life and because of the closer, more interdependent relationship between the president and the people.

World War II was the other major event influencing the growth of the national government during this era. FDR, a former secretary of the navy who was well-versed in defense policy, relished his role as commander in chief. He assumed—as Lincoln had during the Civil War—extraordinary powers to meet the emergencies of wartime, including price controls, rationing, and the suspension of some civil liberties (in fact all civil liberties for Japanese Americans). Spending on armaments and the military gave a tremendous boost to the economy, and defense spending has remained an important element of many states' economies ever since.

By the 1950s, some public officials had become uneasy about the growing size of the federal government and its involvement in so many state and local programs. But the Cold War created a host of new demands for spending on national security—expansion of intelligence operations, a bigger, better equipped military with forward bases around the world, and development of a whole new arsenal of unconventional weaponry. President Dwight D. Eisenhower (1953–1961), a Republican politically inclined toward small government, had been a career military officer and leader of the Allied Forces in World War II. He went along with increased spending on many new federal programs, ranging from the massively expensive interstate highway program to college programs in science, engineering, and languages. All of these, especially interstate highway construction, were driven by defense planning and competition with the Soviet Union. Spending on grants to the states to implement these new programs nearly tripled during Eisenhower's administration. Even while accepting the United States' expanded role in world affairs, Eisenhower warned about the impact of military expenditures on the economy, and the dangers to democracy of a growing military-industrial complex.

The size of government spiked again during the tenure of Lyndon Baines Johnson (1963–1969), a Texas Democrat and experienced legislator whose concept of federalism was born in the New Deal era. This time the cause was growing pressure from the movements for social justice and racial equality. Johnson's presidency coincided with the peak activism of the modern civil rights movement whose struggle for political equality was brought into every home by television. As Americans watched protestors being beaten or attacked by police dogs, Johnson, like Eisenhower before him, had to call up, or threaten to nationalize, state militia to force state and local officials to comply with federal law. At the same time the mass media were also making the country aware of the high levels of poverty and hunger in the United States. When the movement for greater economic justice joined forces with the civil rights movement, and

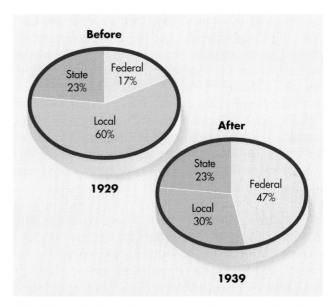

FIGURE 3.2 ■ Share of Nonmilitary Spending by the Federal, State, and Local Governments before and after the Passage of New Deal Legislation

SOURCE: Advisory Commission on Intergovernmental Relations, *Significant Features of Fiscal Federalism* (Washington, D.C.: Government Printing Office, 1979), 7.

when passive civil disobedience tactics were supplanted by riots, looting, and fires in some northern cities, there was concern that the United States might be approaching the dangerous levels of civil unrest that developed during the Great Depression.

Johnson responded to these problems by pushing through Congress voting rights legislation and a massive package of social welfare proposals. These so-called "Great Society" proposals increased the scope of government and changed the nation-state relationship in two important ways. To implement Great Society programs the federal government began funding work in domains that were formerly state and local preserves, such as law enforcement, urban mass transit, public education, and fire protection. And with federal voting rights guarantees in place, state governments no longer had the power to pass laws that denied the vote to, or restricted political participation by, African Americans. This profoundly changed the power relationship between Washington and state governments, especially those in the Deep South, because it gave federal law enforcement officials, including the FBI and the Justice Department, a strong role in monitoring state voting procedures to see they conformed to federal guidelines. Eventually these reforms also changed the distribution of power in state governments. (See Chapter 8.)

These cases illustrate that, during most of the two hundred plus years of American history, presidential leadership led to the growth of the federal government.

But most of these presidents, such as Jefferson, Lincoln, and Eisenhower, did not run as candidates advocating big government or expansion of the power of Washington at the expense of the states. Even FDR ran on a balanced budget platform. The bigger-than-life personalities of the Roosevelts and Lyndon Johnson surely affected their concepts of government activism; one can imagine them looking for problems for government to solve. But Teddy Roosevelt did not create exploitative labor practices or corrupt state legislature, any more than FDR created the Great Depression or started World War II or Lyndon Johnson the problems of inequality in American society. The expansion of federal power during their tenures came when their proclivity for activism came up against situations crying out for government response. Except for Theodore Roosevelt's support for ending the election of U.S. senators by state legislatures and Lyndon Johnson's fight to abolish the right of states to effectively nullify constitutionally guaranteed civil rights, these presidents did not attempt to curb the powers of state government.

Resetting the Balance

As federalism was designed and is practiced in the United States the locus of power is never fixed; the sometimes clear, sometimes ambiguous, division of power has meant that the struggle between the center and the lower levels of government to change the balance is constant. The competition is built into our form of government as a check on the overconcentration of power at any one level. Whenever events or presidential leadership tip the balance of power in the federal relationship too far toward Washington, there is movement to reset the balance. After years of a big-government president such as Teddy Roosevelt, a party may nominate a string of small-government candidates (Taft, Harding, Coolidge, and Hoover). Conversely, if Washington is too slow to act when a federal response is needed, the people may elect an activist president (FDR) to replace a more passive one (Hoover).

Like presidents, the federal courts swing between support for nation- and state-centered federalism, depending on the judicial philosophies of the justices. Before the Civil War, in the years of small government, the Supreme Court overturned only two congressional and sixty state laws. But beginning in the 1880s, as Congress took a larger role in regulating business and the economy, a conservative Supreme Court used the dual federalism doctrine to rule unconstitutional many federal attempts to regulate. Yet when state governments, spurred by the same revelations of unsafe and degrading conditions that led

Congress to act, passed laws against child labor and to protect workers, the federal courts often ruled that they, too, had overstepped their powers, displaying more of an antigovernment, probusiness stance than a commitment to dual federalism. From 1874 to 1937, the Supreme Court found fifty federal and four hundred state laws unconstitutional, including some of FDR's key New Deal legislation.[18] But after FDR was elected to a second term and had a chance to replace conservative justices, the Court looked on his legislative program more sympathetically. (See Chapter 13 for more on the Court and the New Deal.)

The Court decisions approving New Deal legislation were, in a sense, a return to the nation-centered federalism of John Marshall's day. But although the Supreme Court upheld much of the New Deal, it also approved more sweeping *state* regulations of business and labor than had the less activist pre–New Deal Court. Thus the change in Court philosophy did not enlarge the federal role at the expense of the powers of the states; *it enlarged the powers of both state and federal government.* In doing so, the Court was responding to the public's preference for government to play a larger role in helping people cope with the crises stemming from the Great Depression.

During the height of the civil rights movement, the federal courts struck down many state laws that restricted voting rights, criminal defendants' rights, and women's economic and educational opportunities. But since the 1990s, a federal court system dominated by Republican appointees has been reversing that trend by constricting Congress's power to overturn state laws.

Depending on its composition at any given time, Congress is more, or less, sympathetic to nation-centered federalism. The tremendous growth of government during FDR's first three terms brought a backlash from Republicans and Southern Democrats who wanted to swing the locus of power away from the center and back to the states. The growth in social welfare programs during the Johnson era eventually led to the Reagan-Republican smaller-government rebellion in the 1980s and 1990s.

Only the president and vice president have a national constituency; the power of all other elected officials is based in the states and localities. It behooves even those officials serving in the national government to cater to the localities; in fact, the Constitution invests them with this responsibility. And this is exactly what they do. Most members of the U.S. House and Senate spend far more time pursuing the interests of their districts and states than they do in defining and pursuing the national interest.

The major counterforce to nation-centered federalism is state government. Recent decades have witnessed

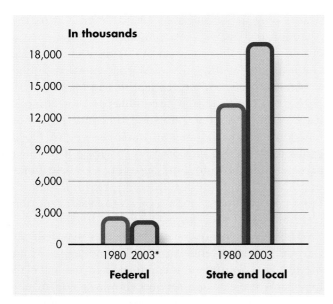

In thousands

FIGURE 3.3 ■ **Number of Full- and Part-Time Civilian Employees in the Federal and State Governments, 1980 and 2003.**

*Includes those working outside the U.S.

Source: U.S. Census Bureau, *Statistical Abstract of the United States, 2006* (Washington, D.C.: Government Printing Office, 2005), tab. 451.

increased state activism, in part because of Washington's refusal or inability to satisfy the public's expectations of government. During the Reagan years, there was an ideological commitment to reducing the scope of government in every area but national security. Yet those years of tax cutting and increased spending on defense left spiraling budget deficits and imposed fiscal restraints that made it difficult for the Clinton administration or Congress to propose new initiatives or to fund existing programs. The Vietnam War and the Watergate, Iran-Contra, and Clinton-Lewinsky scandals all contributed to increased partisanship and gridlock at the federal level and to declining trust among the public. State governments

began looking less often to Washington, instead launching their own policy initiatives.

In the 1990s, the states experimented with charter schools and vouchers for private schools, rolled back affirmative action and bilingual programs, looked at new ways to try to teach religion in schools, and adopted a variety of crime laws such as mandatory sentencing, three-strikes laws, and victims' compensation. Sixteen states have term limits for elected officials, and a few have passed tax caps and their own campaign-financing laws. Some place restrictions on gay rights, whereas others have passed laws strengthening those rights, granting health benefits to gay partners; a few states have recognized the right to same-sex marriages. After gaining control over welfare, the states experimented with many different job-training and work programs.[19] In addition, they became more bold in challenging or refusing to enforce federal regulations affecting business and the environment and in one case refused to implement federal gun laws.

Everyday Federalism

The relations between Washington and the states and localities are a mixture of cooperation and conflict. One expert calls it "competitive federalism" because states and the federal government are competing for leadership of the nation's domestic policy.[20] At the same time, given the large number of governments in the United States (see Table 3.1), cooperation in carrying out the day-to-day work of government is essential. In this section we look at the everyday practice of federalism, the main sources of cooperation and conflict between Washington and the states, and how a president's management of these relationships reflects his interpretation of the proper division of powers. We also look at cooperation and competition among states and between states and local units of government.

TABLE 3.1	**Number of Government Units in the United States**

Part of the reason that intergovernmental relations in the United States are so complex is that there are so many units of government. Though the number of school districts has decreased dramatically since World War II and the number of townships has declined slowly, the number of "special districts"—created for a single purpose, such as parks, airports, or flood control management—continues to grow.

Year	States	Counties	Municipalities	Townships and Towns	School Districts	Special Districts*
1942	48	3,050	16,220	18,919	108,579	8,299
2003†	50	3,034	19,429	16,504	13,506	35,052

* Includes natural resource, fire protection, housing, and community development districts.
† Latest figures available. The Census Bureau takes a count of governmental units every five years, in years ending in 2 and 7.
Source: U.S. Census Bureau, *Statistical Abstract of the United States, 2006* (Washington, D.C.: Government Printing Office, 2005), tab. 415.

Presidential Management of Federal-State Relations

Most presidents have not been presented with wars or domestic crises to test their interpretations of the proper division of power. Nevertheless, a large part of every president's duties as chief executive officer is the management of state-federal relationships. How expansive a role a president sees for governors and state bureaucracies in the implementation of federally mandated programs is central to understanding his views on the federal relationship. It is important to remember that governors are the chief executive officers of their states and they like to run their own shows. And, at any given time, a number of them are trying to burnish their records for a run for the presidency.

One indicator of a president's views on the federal relationship is how much control he is willing to cede to the states in administering federal programs. The return of powers to make and implement policy to subunits or lower levels of government from a higher level is called **devolution.** One important area of responsibility the president and Congress can devolve to the states is the power to determine how, and on what, the grants-in-aid Washington sends them are spent. To help pay for essential services provided by state and local governments, the federal government returns tax revenues to states for mass transit, community development projects, and to provide social welfare services and unemployment compensation, for example.

For most presidents the central issues in how Washington and the states collaborate in the administration of these grants have been administrative efficiency and political expediency (with what constituency does a president most want to curry favor), but for a few it stemmed from an ideological commitment to states' rights and a smaller federal bureaucracy. A new feature of Lyndon Johnson's Great Society era was the increasing number of grants that went directly to localities, bypassing states. City and other local officials, believing that state legislatures were unresponsive to their interests, now demanded, and got, direct federal support. And as the number of federal programs grew during the Johnson years, federal aid more than tripled, and state and local governments became increasingly dependent on federal funding.[21] The vast increase in programs and the multiplying requirements and conditions of the grants made federal aid ever more complex. State and local officials soon felt hamstrung by the increasingly burdensome regulations.

When Republican Richard Nixon (1969–1974) came into office, he wanted to make government "more effective as well as more efficient." Nixon took a managerial rather than ideological approach to streamlining the cumbersome structure created by the profusion of Great Society programs. He saw a messy bureaucratic problem and an overconcentration of decision making at the federal level, and he tried to find a solution through more efficient management.[22]

Nixon's approach did two things. First it consolidated several hundred grant programs into six major functional areas. Washington would now give block grants to the states and localities and leave it to them to determine how to fund programs in these functional areas. This greater leeway gave local officials more opportunity to target projects to local needs, and it streamlined the process at the federal level.

The second major aspect of Nixon's new federalism was general revenue sharing. Tax money paid into the federal government was returned to the states to fund local projects and services. It was a way of encouraging state activism in the hope that it would decrease the need for federal programs.

In contrast to Nixon's managerial approach, the new federalism of Republican Ronald Reagan (1981–1988) had a more ideological purpose, which he made clear in his first inaugural address: "Government is not the solution to our problems," he said. "Government is the problem." Thus his new federalism was aimed at reducing the power and influence of government rather than at improving intergovernmental management and effectiveness.

Cuts in federal funding for state and local programs had the pragmatic intent of reducing the size of the budget deficits created by Reagan's increased military spending. But even this had an ideological tinge because driving up the deficits with military spending reduced the government's domestic capabilities. Reagan's new federalism was rooted not so much in state-centered or dual federalism as it was in his opposition to government in general.[23] This approach—cutting federal spending on local and state programs to downsize government at all levels—has been called *instrumental federalism*, in contrast with Nixon's "rationalizing" approach, in which making government more efficient and effective was an end in itself.

Although Reagan had an ideological commitment to smaller government, he had no significant programmatic approach to achieve it, and he was often more preoccupied with the Cold War than with his domestic programs. In fact, the size and expenditures of the federal government grew during his administration, and states gained few new powers. Reagan took a more indirect approach to rolling back government power by slowing enforcement or blocking implementation of rules he thought were an abuse of federal power.

Like Reagan, Democrat Bill Clinton (1993–2000) came to office with a wary view of Washington and a commitment to working in partnership with governors. Clinton was a multiterm governor from a southern state (Arkansas) where the states' rights tradition held sway. Reforming state-federal relations had been a special interest when, as governor, he chaired both the National Governors Association and a reform group within the Democratic Party. Except in the area of civil rights policy, Clinton claimed to be a supporter of states' rights.

Clinton was not an advocate of state-centered federalism or smaller government for its own sake. But he was committed to the idea of the "states as laboratories" (earlier articulated by Justice Louis Brandeis)—that is, as places for policy experimentation. He used the phrase frequently, wrote it into executive orders, and eventually based his welfare, health care, and education policies around it.[24] From 1994 through the end of his administration, Clinton and congressional Republicans supported policies that delegated more powers to the states. Overall, Clinton's federalism policies were much closer to Nixon's than to Reagan's in that both Clinton and Nixon were primarily interested in "rationalizing intergovernmental relations" and making government more efficient.

Clinton's actions were shaped by both his own beliefs and the fact that during most of his term, Republicans held a majority in Congress. The Gingrich Republicans—named for the Speaker of the House, Newt Gingrich, and his conservative Republican allies—on the other hand, shared Reagan's view of government and put forward a legislative program for downsizing the federal government.

Clinton favored delegating rule implementation to state agencies, but he insisted on the right of federal agencies to set national standards, such as for clean air and water and consumer and worker safety. Bush, like Clinton, came to the presidency from the governorship of a southern state (Texas), but unlike Clinton, Bush openly advocated returning power to the states. Within months of taking office, Bush reversed Clinton-imposed regulatory standards for arsenic levels in water, pollutants in the air, and health and safety in the workplace. In addition, he issued a new order making it harder for federal officials to overrule state decisions. The rhetorical position of the Bush administration on the nation-state division of power in domestic policy might be best summarized by a close adviser's description of an ideal government as one "cut 'down to the size where we can drown it in the bathtub'."[25]

Cooperative Federalism

How a president handles the power balance helps determine whether the federal relationship is more cooperative or more conflictive. The term **cooperative**

federalism describes the day-to-day joint activities and continuing cooperation among federal, state, and local officials in carrying out the business of government: distributing payments to farmers, providing welfare services, planning highways, organizing centers for the elderly, and carrying out all the functions that the national and state governments jointly fund and organize. It also refers to informal cooperation in locating criminals, tracking down the source of contagious diseases, and many other activities.

One example of informal but intensive cooperation is the Centers for Disease Control and Prevention in Atlanta, which helps state and local governments meet health emergencies and prevent the spread of contagious diseases, such as the bird flu virus. National and state police and other crime-fighting agencies share data on crimes and criminals. The federal government and the states also jointly regulate in many areas, including occupational safety and the environment. Today, state agencies are responsible for 90 percent of all environmental enforcement actions.[26] And since the 2001 terrorist attacks, there has been increased reliance on state resources to help with national defense, especially through training programs for first responders and use of state militia to supplement regular army troops in combat zones abroad.

As discussed in the previous section, Washington and the states also work together daily to administer the programs funded by the nearly half trillion in tax dollars returned annually to the states to provide federally mandated services. (See Figure 3.4.) Despite some inefficiency, federal funding has succeeded in helping state and local governments meet real needs. Along the way, the performance standards and regulations attached to the grants have increased the professionalism of state and local bureaucrats.

States also receive indirect aid from the federal government in the form of deductions for individual taxpayers. When reporting income to the Internal Revenue Service, residents of all states are allowed to deduct the amount of income, real estate, and personal property taxes they paid to their states and localities. This is counted as aid to the states because it lowers federal revenue by hundreds of billions of dollars each year while leaving more money to be spent in the states.

Conflict in the Federal Relationship

There is always some element of conflict present in federal-state relations; it is inherent in the division of powers between the two levels of government.

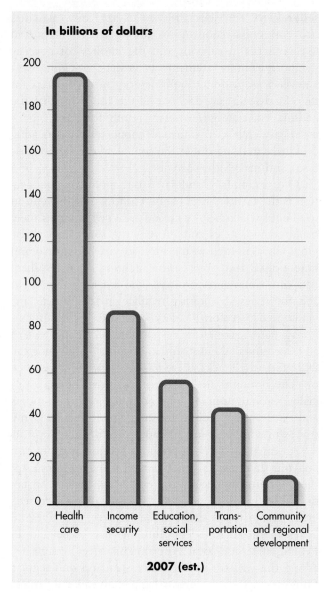

In billions of dollars

2007 (est.)

FIGURE 3.4 ■ What Does the Federal Government Give the States Money to Do? *Ninety-two percent of the estimated $459 billion the federal government is sending back to the states in 2007 is for programs in these areas. When adjusted for inflation, grants to the states and localities, other than for Medicaid, have been falling since 2005.*
Source: *Budget of the United States, Fiscal Year 2007,* "Historical Tables" (Washington, D.C.: Government Printing Office, 2006), tab.12.2.

Although few people argue that the states could do a better job than Washington providing for the national defense, there is sharp disagreement over which level of government can make other policies more efficiently and effectively. States are not bureaucracy free. Collectively, state and local governments account for 87 percent of all civilian governmental employees, and their joint revenues were just over 10 percent of

GDP in 2005, compared with 17.5 percent for the federal government.[27] The same year state and local spending from their own revenues accounted for almost 36 percent of all governmental spending; it was closer to 45 percent when federal grants are added to states' internal sources.[28] Thus state and local government is no small operation, and devolution carries no guarantee of greater efficiency or responsiveness. Voters in the fifty states elect about 7400 representatives and senators to their state legislatures who, in turn, pass more than forty thousand laws each year that reflect the policy preferences of each state's citizens.[29] They are not always in harmony with policy made in Washington.

Finances are a major source of conflict between the states and Washington. Especially controversial are the financial burdens on states from unfunded federal mandates. **Unfunded mandates** are laws or regulations imposed on the states unaccompanied by sufficient funding to implement them. Implementation of federal environmental regulations alone, for which the states now bear the greatest burden, imposes heavy costs. Other federal laws order states and localities to make alterations to public buildings, sidewalks, and transportation facilities to ensure that they are accessible to people with disabilities. States are also required to educate the children of illegal immigrants and to pay for emergency health care for them, as well as to pay for increased law enforcement costs due to failure of federal authorities to control border crossings. These costs have become so staggering in the states with the highest numbers of illegal residents that governors have sued the federal government for reimbursement. (See this chapter's "You Are There" box.)

In the 1990s the financial burden of unfunded mandates led state and local officials to join together to mount a national campaign to restrict their use. Congress passed a bill reforming procedures under which unfunded or underfunded mandates, especially regulatory mandates, are sent to the states, but it stopped short of prohibiting them. The federal government is required to provide information on the costs of implementing laws and rules before Congress or an executive branch agency, such as the Environmental Protection Agency, can adopt them. And federal agencies are required to consult with states and localities before imposing mandates and to adopt regulations that impose the smallest burden for implementation.[30]

But unfunded mandates roll on under Democrats and Republicans alike: George W. Bush's "No Child Left Behind" program imposed a testing and reporting regime on states and local school districts, and new rules for state Homeland Security departments require spending on an array of new law enforcement and disaster preparation functions. States have also had to fund many of the secondary costs of having their state militia troops called up for national service. Since the first Gulf War presidents have nationalized hundreds of thousands of state troops to serve abroad; Guard units from the fifty states have provided more than one-third of all troops who have served in the Iraq War. The federal government pays and equips them while they are under U.S. command, but the states have had to pay for social services and other assistance to the families of the wounded and dead. In addition, the states are left without the full complement of troops and equipment to deal with state emergencies such as forest fires and floods. A survey of the states' Homeland Security directors found that more than half of all states were less prepared for emergencies than before because of the demands being made on their National Guard troops by the federal government.[31]

Congress also mandated state involvement in the counterterrorism effort by passing the Real ID law in 2005. The law gave states two years to put in place standards for issuing drivers' licenses and other identity cards that will ensure that those in the country illegally cannot obtain legal means of identification. States claim their (unreimbursed) start-up costs will range from $50 million to $169 million, and cost millions to administer each year thereafter.[32] Adding to their financial burdens, states were asked in 2006 to help implement a new federal drug benefit for seniors. When the signup process went badly, leaving many patients without prescriptions or money to pay for them, state governments picked up tens of millions of dollars in costs to defuse constituent anger.

Another source of national-state economic friction is the management of federally owned land—military bases, weapons facilities, and national park and wilderness areas. Twenty-seven percent of all land within the United States is held by the federal government, the majority in western states. Few Americans are against national parks or national defense, but in those states where half or more of the land is federally owned, state governments often do not have the control they would like to have over the state's natural resources. Usually the friction is over economic exploitation of resources in park land, but sometimes states object to activities they believe put their populations at risk—radioactivity from weapons production or the testing and storage of nuclear waste. Nevada has been fighting the federal government in the courts for years to stop preparation of a national nuclear waste storage center just ninety miles from Las Vegas. The governor even threatened to stand in front of any train carrying nuclear waste into the state.

States and Localities as Lobbyists

Precisely because of conflict over use of federal money, federal administration of state lands, and the imposition of unfunded mandates, lobbying has become a crucial part of the relationship between the states and the federal government. The importance of federal money to state and local budgets and the need for coordination between federal and state bureaucracies led to the creation of interstate organizations such as the National Conference of State Legislatures (NCSL), the National League of Cities, and the American Public Welfare Association. These groups lobby for favorable legislation for states and localities and work with federal agencies to ensure that new regulations are implemented in a way that is acceptable to the states. Most of these organizations have multimillion-dollar budgets and employ sizable staffs. Many individual states and cities have their own Washington lobbyists, who have had considerable success increasing federal aid. Between 2001 and 2006 one lobbyist representing forty-four state agencies or local governments in Florida persuaded Congress to earmark $173 million for projects sought by his clients. For every dollar Floridians paid the lobbyist, they got $18 in federal spending in return.[33]

But why should states form interest groups or hire lobbyists when they are all represented by their elected representatives in the House and Senate? The members of a state's congressional delegation may belong to different parties than state leaders, or they may not agree with state leaders—as, for example, when Congress waived state sales tax on e-commerce strongly favored by most state leaders. Or a state may have an urban majority whereas its congressional delegation is closer in views to rural and suburban residents. But mainly states hire lobbyists because there is a lot at stake.

The Assembly on Federal Issues, the group that coordinates the lobbying of the National Conference of State Legislatures, monitors bills under consideration by every major committee in Congress. The group looks especially for any new provisions that would undercut state laws, have an impact on state revenue, or tie the hands of state officials in some policy area. For example, some states are concerned about the free-trade agreements Congress has approved. Many states are big exporters, and if Congress says that certain countries are exempt from

HURRICANE KATRINA:
A FAILURE TO COMMUNICATE

Sometimes problems are just too big for a city, county, or state to manage with local resources. Destruction caused by a hurricane, flood, tornado, or earthquake may be so severe and widespread that the resources of the affected states and localities are overwhelmed. When a state decides it cannot cope with the damage caused by a storm, flood, or earthquake, the governor can ask the president to declare the stricken counties a federal disaster area.

In a catastrophic event, the president can declare a national emergency without a formal request for assistance from local officials. In such emergencies the president might decide to nationalize a state's militia (National Guard), but the principal agency for coordinating relief efforts is the Federal Emergency Management Agency (FEMA). The agency was created in 1979 to cope with the effects of a nuclear attack, but before 9/11 it was called on mainly to provide financial help, temporary shelters, and other emergency aid to areas struck by natural disasters. Created for one purpose and diverted to another, the agency got off to a rough start. It was especially criticized for an inadequate response to hurricane Andrew in south Florida in 1992. It took three days for the agency to begin distributing emergency food and water, and medical help was delayed too. The widespread criticism FEMA received from both Republicans and Democrats led to some major changes. The Clinton administration set about to professionalize the agency with new appointees with significant disaster relief experience. FEMA also changed its approach, from reactive ("Let's see whether they ask for help") to proactive ("Let's see what we can do right now"). Red tape was cut, and agency response time was drastically reduced: The agency responded to the devastating floods in the Midwest in 1993, by setting up

water distribution centers and water purification systems within a day. A FEMA advance team arrived in Oklahoma City just five hours after the bombing of the Alfred P. Murrah Federal Office Building in 1995, and a search and rescue team was on the scene by 2:30 A.M. the following morning.

In the first nine months after the September 11 attacks, FEMA helped state, local, and nonprofit agencies clear debris and repair the damaged roads and sidewalks in the vicinity of the World Trade Center and provided crisis counseling and a ferry service into Manhattan to replace the subway stations destroyed by the collapse of the towers.[1] The collaboration of FEMA and other federal agencies with city and state offices, with the help of nonprofits and volunteers from around the country, resulted in one of the most remarkable intergovernmental responses to disaster the country had ever seen. The Trade Center site was cleaned up six months ahead of schedule at one-tenth of the estimated cost.

Just four years later when hurricane Katrina hit southern Mississippi and Louisiana, there was barely a hint of the federal-state cooperation that made the post-9/11 recovery so remarkable. Even though the National Hurricane Center had predicted the timing, location, and severity of the storm, President Bush had declared a national emergency prior to its landfall, and the Department of Homeland Security had predicted the day before the storm hit that the levees in New Orleans would be breached, Hurricane Katrina still turned into one of the worst natural disasters in American history.[2] Over a million people in Mississippi and Louisiana were left homeless; 100,000 New Orleaners were stranded in the city, most in the poorest neighborhoods; almost eighteen hundred died, and hundreds went missing. Just one-third of New Orleans's nursing

homes were evacuated before the storm and only the private, not the public, hospitals. Dozens of elderly and critically ill patients died, with their oxygen, IVs, and medications cut off, and in some case their attendants gone. Hundreds of bodies floated in the flooded streets with no one to recover them, and thousands were trapped in their homes or on rooftops for days waiting for rescue, without food, water, or electricity, and in some cases, medications.

Louisiana's Governor Blanco declined Bush's suggestion to put the Louisiana Guard under federal control, and neither she nor the mayor of New Orleans accepted Amtrak's proposal to evacuate people by train, the Interior Department's offer of trucks, planes, boats, and thousands of law enforcement officers, or the Governor of New Mexico's offer of National Guard troops.[3] School buses that could have transported thousands away from the storm were left in their parking lots where they were inundated by flood waters. Most of the first responders—police, firefighters, medical personnel, hazmat squads—the very people on whom such emphasis had been placed in post-9/11 homeland security training, were disabled, their stations and vehicles flooded or destroyed by high winds; and they were still plagued by the same problem that crippled first responders at the World Trade Center—incompatible communications systems.

The single greatest problem in trying to coordinate the rescue and recovery effort between local, state, and national levels was that no one seemed to know who was in charge: the mayors or governors of the affected areas, FEMA, or the Homeland Security secretary? Bush had the power to nationalize the Louisiana Guard, but he deferred to Governor Blanco. The national emergency declaration he issued before the storm's landfall gave both Homeland

During disasters, federal, state, and local rescue and recovery agencies are supposed to join forces to aid victims and organize the cleanup. Coordination failed badly when Hurricane Katrina hit Louisiana and Mississippi in 2005. In New Orleans, some residents climbed to their roofs, where they waited for days to be rescued or given water and food.

catastrophic failure of federal, state, and local collaboration? First, those responsible at the national, state, and local level, namely the president, the governor of Louisiana, and the mayor of New Orleans—the site of greatest damage— did not provide the leadership necessary to facilitate cooperation between the three levels of government. Second, the Bush administration had filled top FEMA jobs with political cronies of the president or his staff who had little if any experience in disaster management. With no competent management at the national level after 9/11, FEMA had fallen into disarray. Fifteen percent of its positions were unstaffed in the year before Katrina. Third, in the post-9/11 bureaucratic reorganization undertaken to better respond to national emergencies, FEMA was incorporated into the new Homeland Security cabinet department and lost its status as an independent agency. The added layers of bureaucracy made lines of decision making and administrative responsibility less clear.

There was not much official Washington agreed on in the highly partisan atmosphere of 2005, but Congress was unanimous in the judgment that the response to Katrina had been a failure at every level of the federal partnership. A report from the House called it a "Failure of Initiative," while the Senate committee said the failure to establish a unified command showed the country was still unprepared for a terrorist attack or other national emergency.[4]

Security Secretary Michael Chertoff and FEMA Director Michael Brown all the authority they needed to take control of the rescue and recovery effort. But when the storm hit and the New Orleans levees were breached, the president was at his ranch in Texas and Chertoff was at a conference in Atlanta. FEMA director Brown was on site, but, reluctant to communicate with Chertoff, his boss, he deferred to local and state agencies instead. With a leadership vacuum at the national level, and first responders disabled or unable to communicate with one another, a profusion of public and private agencies responded on their own with little coordination of effort. It took several days just to assign the military responsibility for distribution of food and water.

Nine months after the storm, with a new hurricane season about to begin, cleanup crews were still finding bodies in abandoned houses. With half its population gone, businesses shut down, and a gravely reduced tax base, New Orleans had to lay off half of all city employees. Thousands of homes were awaiting demolition, and millions of tons of toxic waste were still awaiting clearance. Almost 200,000 New Orleaners had still not returned to the city, having no jobs or schools to come back to and no place to live; many were still waiting for private and federal insurers to resolve damage claims so they could repair or rebuild their homes.

What happened to federal disaster relief in the four short years between 9/11 and Katrina to cause such a

[1] FEMA press release, June 3, 2002. (www.fema.gov/)
[2] Eric Lipton, "The Inquiry: White House Knew of Levee's Failure on Night of Storm," *New York Times*, February 10, 2006.
[3] Eric Lipton, "Interior Dept. Report Describes FEMA's Scant Use of Its Help," *New York Times*, January 30, 2006.
[4] "Failure of Initiative: The Final Report of the Select Bipartisan Committee to Investigate the Preparation for and Response to Hurricane Katrina" (http://katrina.house.gov); "Hurricane Katrina: A Nation Still Unprepared." (www.hsgac.senate.gov/files/katrina)

paying import taxes, it could affect the competitiveness of a state's businesses and ultimately the state's revenues. So states lobby in large part to maintain maximum control over their legislative, regulatory, and taxing authority.

The National Governors Association (NGA) and regional governors' associations exist primarily to facilitate cooperation and exchange of information among state governments, but they also lobby Washington. The NGA maintains a Center for Best Practices that studies policy and makes recommendations on improving both state and federal legislation. In 2006 the NGA wrote President Bush stating its opposition to the Department of Defense's plans to redefine the role of the National Guard in national defense planning. All fifty governors signed the letter.[34] The Western Governors Association has pressured the government to take action on illegal immigration and the price of gasoline.

Relations between the States

Dealing with Washington is not the only intergovernmental relations problem that the states face. State governments must also work with one another, and the measure of cooperation and conflict in these relations is similar to that between Washington and the states.

The U.S. Constitution laid down some of the ground rules governing interstate relationships. One important provision is the **full faith and credit clause**, which requires states to recognize contracts made in other states. The Constitution also provides that if a fugitive from justice flees from one state to another, the suspect, once captured, will be extradited (sent back) to the state with jurisdiction.

Normally, meeting full faith and credit requirements is rather routine. However, politics vary from state to state, and occasionally for one state to honor the laws of another can be controversial. A historical example is the Fugitive Slave Act, which required the authorities in every state to return escaped slaves to their owners. Abolitionists (those favoring the abolition of slavery) living in free states were loath to return escaped slaves to their owners yet were bound to do so by the Constitution.

More recently, marriage contracts have become an issue. Some opponents to gay marriage have argued that under the full faith and credit rule, a gay marriage contracted in one state would have to be recognized by every state. When Vermont became the first state to register same-sex unions, it set off a controversy in other states worried about having to extend to gay partners the same legal status and rights (health, retirement, and inheritance benefits) as married heterosexual couples. In response, Congress passed the Defense of Marriage Act, which gave every state the right not to recognize same-sex marriages conducted in other states. But when the Massachusetts Supreme Court ruled that it was unconstitutional for officials in that state to deny gay partners marriage licenses on the grounds that it was equivalent to denying a civil right granted to heterosexuals, the controversy deepened. After a few states began issuing marriage licenses to gay couples, officials in states that did not want to honor these contracts appealed to the Bush administration to support an amendment to the U.S. Constitution that would define marriage as a contract between a man and a woman. To resolve some of the interstate conflict, the Massachusetts Supreme Court ruled that out-of-state same-sex couples cannot be married in Massachusetts if their home states make such unions illegal.

The vast array of conflicting laws passed by legislatures is an ongoing problem. A national commission on uniform laws attempts to mediate, using a "conflict of laws" doctrine that lays out a framework for resolving conflicts between the laws passed in different jurisdictions.

Cooperation between states is encouraged by the fact that all governors have to deal with a set of common problems such as resource management, education, fostering economic growth, taxation, crime, and prison systems. In addition, they all have to manage a relationship with Washington. These common interests prompted the formation of the NGA and its regional counterparts.

Most state-to-state interaction is informal and voluntary; state officials consult with and borrow ideas from one another. Sometimes states enter into formal agreements, called *interstate compacts*, to deal with a shared problem—operating a port or allocating water from a river basin, for example. A common type of agreement between states is to exempt citizens from neighboring states who have taken up temporary residence from paying local income taxes. As energy demand and costs rose in 2006, fourteen states formed a new pact to cooperate in regulating electric power.

Rivalry among the states has always existed, due to cultural, political, and regional differences and because they compete for private investment and for aid from the federal government. Changing economic patterns and an overall loss of economic competitiveness by the United States in the world market have stimulated vigorous competition among the states to attract new businesses and jobs. Governors market their states to prospective new businesses by touting lower taxes, a better climate, a more skilled or better educated workforce, and less government regulation than other states competing for the same business. Most states are willing to give tax subsidies and other financial incentives to companies willing to relocate. Critics believe that these offers erode a state's tax base and have little impact on most business relocation decisions, and there is some evidence to support that view.[35] Nevertheless, without offering tax breaks or deferments or other subsidies, most states feel at a competitive disadvantage in recruiting new businesses.

Access to water is one of the most common areas of state cooperation and conflict. One certain prerequisite for business and population growth is an ample water supply, and given our shrinking resources, maintaining or increasing water flow into and out of states is a high-priority issue, especially for states that do not have large bodies of water within their boundaries. How much water should New York state officials agree to take from upstate farmers for urban dwellers or for use in New Jersey and Connecticut? The waters of the Upper Colorado are shared by four states and those of the Lower Colorado by three others. Rural residents of Colorado constantly struggle to keep ever more water from being channeled from the Colorado River to meet the needs of fast-growing metropolitan areas in other states. These are the everyday issues that governors and other state officials are continuously negotiating.

As the federal government continues to devolve responsibilities to the states, and as federal aid has grown as a percentage of state spending, competition among states to get ever larger shares of that aid has increased. Thirty-four states use "contingency fee" consultants whose job is to get as much money as possible from Washington to cover state Medicaid outlays. Because the consultants get a share of the money they bring in, they have every incentive to find any way within the law to claim additional payments to the states that employ them.[36]

States with powerful members in their congressional delegations usually fare better than others in the share of federal tax dollars returned to their home districts. And smaller states at times find common interest in voting as a bloc in the Senate to prevent the largest states from getting a share of aid in proportion to their population or to need. An egregious case was the allocation of homeland security funding, which found the more populous and higher-risk states such as New York outvoted by smaller states in attempts to win funding proportionate to their larger populations and greater chance of attack.[37] It took several years of publicity about irrelevant equipment purchases by small rural states and municipalities to reallocate funding closer to security priorities.

State-Local Relations

The relationship of states to their localities—counties, cities, and special districts—is another important feature of contemporary federalism. All but 51 of 87,576 government units in the United States exist below the level of state government (see Table 3.1). These relationships are defined by state constitutions; they are not dealt with in the federal Constitution. Although states cannot be altered or dissolved by the national government, localities are just creatures of their states. Yet some of the same problems that affect national-state relations also affect state-local relations. City and county officials often wish for more authority and fewer mandates from the state capitol. Some state constitutions grant **home rule** to local governments, giving them considerable autonomy in such matters as setting tax rates, regulating land use, and choosing their form of local government. Cities of different sizes may have different degrees of autonomy, depending on the state. And in some states, counties are given the power to create levels of government below them. In Illinois, for example, each county can decide whether to establish township governments or do without them.

Thirty-six states must also maintain working relationships with the tribal governments of Native Americans. While local units of government may be altered or abolished by the state, tribal land is sovereign territory under treaty agreements with the United States government. States have no authority to govern these areas and must negotiate any conflict over tax and environmental issues and land or other resource use with tribal councils.[38]

People, States, and the Federal Government

One of the most important elements in the federal relationship is the people. In a system with power divided among levels of government and responsibilities divided among thousands of governmental units, where do the people fit? How do they elect and communicate with all these officials and get them to be responsive?

It is often claimed that people feel closer to their state than to the national government. At the state level, the argument goes, government and its decision makers are nearby and more accessible to the voters, more likely to have a sense of their public mood, and consequently more responsive to their specific preferences. This is important because economic conditions and political culture vary from state to state, resulting in different policy preferences. Moreover, local officials may have a better grasp of local conditions and therefore be better situated to shape policy to fit these preferences.

Are state governments more responsive to the people? State governments are undeniably smaller than the national government. Yet, 42 percent of all Americans live in states with more than ten million residents, hardly small units. At the other end of the spectrum, nine states have populations under a million. If the basic premise about size and distance were correct, then people would be even closer to local government than to state government. But smaller does not make for greater familiarity; the average person is not better informed about state and local officials than national ones. Most local candidates and officeholders get far less media exposure than national candidates, partly because there are so many of them. And voter turnout rates for local and state elections suggest that there is less interest in state and local than in national government. There are layers of local government, some with taxing authority, such as townships, special districts, or planning agencies, that Americans know little about. And although most Americans know about school districts and city councils, voter turnout is much lower in elections for those bodies than for state and federal offices, and public knowledge about most of these officials is also low.

One indication that Americans neither feel especially close to state and local governments nor feel that those governments are responsive to them has been the increasing use of the ballot initiative since the 1990s. Interest groups tried to bypass not only Congress but state legislatures by getting policy questions placed on state ballots and having them decided directly by voters. Doing an end run around their state and local elected representatives, voters approved initiatives that killed state laws on affirmative action, sanctioned medical use of marijuana, imposed limits on campaign spending and contributions, expanded casino gambling, and gave adopted children the right to know the names of their biological parents. About 40 percent of all initiatives put on ballots in the 1990s became law, whereas only a tiny percentage of bills submitted to legislatures get passed into law.[39]

California remains the champion of legislating by ballot, putting so many measures before voters that one newspaper called it "government by referendum,"

and asked why California hadn't had a proposition against propositions.[40] Trying to legislate in this way can be both confusing and dangerous. One year, California's citizens had to wade through a 222-page pamphlet outlining ballot choices. In San Francisco, facing a ballot with more than one hundred items, voters passed one proposition for public financing of campaigns while simultaneously passing another measure outlawing it.[41] But the trend has strengthened in this decade, with referenda on everything from the Iraq War to prescription drug plans to tax cuts to election reforms. In 2006 Maine voters were asked to exercise a "people's veto" by voting to overturn civil rights protections for homosexuals passed by the legislature. But referenda are not a simple or clear reflection of local views. Big interests influence voting on ballot measures, with huge sums of money flowing into states from outside organizations to support or defeat them.

Lobbyists working in state capitals are at least as powerful as those working in Washington. Twenty-eight percent of state legislators who filed financial disclosure statements in 2004 sat on committees that regulated one of the entities in which they had a financial interest; 18 percent had ties to organizations that lobbied their state government. In most states these ties are far more hidden that those between federal legislators and lobbyists because the press does not cover most state legislatures as intensely as the national press covers Congress.[42]

Voters do not necessarily perceive local politicians to be more honest than members of Congress. Forty-five percent of Louisianans thought the state was so corrupt that a vote for change would not make a difference. On a scale of 1 to 10 for trustworthiness, Louisianans gave their state leaders a 5.5.[43]

Still, some see the move toward greater state autonomy and more direct democracy as taking us nearer to the Founders' ideal of a government closer to the people. But the increasing use of grassroots initiatives is *not* a move toward the kind of government the Founders envisioned. The Founders established a system of checks on popular passions.[44] Indeed, the Founders feared policy making getting too close to the people and government being too responsive to popular demands. They saw the potential for overheating the political process through too much direct democracy, which is why they chose an indirect or republican form of democracy and a federal division of power. The challenge is how to keep a balance in these divisions sufficient to prevent a tyranny of factions while maintaining a sense of national unity and purpose.

A Return to State-Centered Federalism?

The fervid support of the Gingrich Republicans for a smaller national government and more power to the states, Clinton's qualified acceptance of both, and a series of Supreme Court rulings that favored state immunity from federal rules suggested that by the time George W. Bush took office, the country was headed toward a more state-centered form of federalism. This final section on the growth of government looks at current views of the federal relationship.

The Bush Administration

The administration of George W. Bush has sent mixed signals on state-centered federalism. Although being an advocate for devolution in domestic policy making, especially regulatory policy, Bush has an expansive view of presidential powers. His support for expanding the role of the states in making and implementing welfare policy was countered by his intervention in public education to impose mandatory national testing on local school systems, and he resisted governors' demands that the distribution of electric power should be regulated at the state, not the national, level. In the area of business and environmental regulation, Bush has butted heads with governors many times, and a number of states have gone on to adopt stronger standards than those set by the federal government.

Bush *has* supported greater devolution of the responsibility for administering federal health care and social welfare programs. Consequently, increasingly greater sums of money are returned to the states to pay for these programs. However, in all other areas the amount of money sent back to the states in federal grants-in-aid "funds to support transportation, education, housing, and community development" has been falling since 2003 (when adjusted for inflation). Due to huge increases in spending for defense and medical care and massive budget deficits, the federal government is passing much of the burden for social welfare and education on to the states.

Congress

Despite its support for devolution, Congress appears to have few advocates of pure state-centered federalism. Although willing to delegate authority for administration of the biggest, costliest social insurance programs in its drive to reduce the power of those states with more liberal or activist policies than the conservative congressional majority wants, Congress continues to supersede the states in rule making whenever state laws are in conflict with its will. In recent years, bills have been introduced to supplant state laws on drunk driving with a national standard, allow property owners to bypass state courts and go directly to federal courts to protest local zoning laws, and override state laws on late-term abortions, medical use of marijuana, and assisted suicides.[45] In 2006 Congress, at the behest of lobbyists for the food industry and money lenders, was considering one bill that would supplant all state food safety regulations that are more protective than federal standards and another that would override state laws that block access to consumer credit ratings.

Congress has repeatedly used its power to regulate interstate commerce to prevent state taxation of e-commerce and other Internet activity, a prohibition that states claim has cost them billions in lost revenue.[46] Even after twenty states had negotiated interstate tax collection agreements and lobbied hard for lifting the ban, Congress renewed it in 2002 and again in 2004, a period when most states were facing serious declines in revenue and budget deficits.

One member of Congress said of his colleagues that they "don't really believe in states' rights; they believe in deciding the issue at whatever level of government they think will do it their way. They want to be Thomas Jefferson on Monday, Wednesday, and Friday and Alexander Hamilton on Tuesday and Thursday and Saturday."[47] This inconsistent approach, coupled with Bush's expansive view of presidential authority, is why—despite states' increasing authority in administering federal programs—there has been no sustained momentum toward state-centered federalism.

The States

Throughout the Bush administration, the president and Congress have been preoccupied with the wars in Iraq, Afghanistan, and on terrorism, undertaking few new domestic initiatives. With little initiative from Washington, state activism increased. While Congress was stalemated on how to handle the cloning issue, twenty-two state legislatures took up their own anti-cloning bills.[48] Four states established centers for stem cell research after the Bush administration refused to fund such work on religious grounds. After Bush appointees rolled back federal regulation, the states began re-regulating, especially in the areas of consumer and worker safety. Some state legislatures outlawed predatory lending.[49] Some passed "no call" laws limiting telemarketing, which proved so popular that Congress rushed to approve a national do-not-call register.

One lawyer called the amount of new state legislation on workplace conditions—electronic monitoring of workers, child labor laws, right to breast-feed—"mind-boggling."[50] On the use of genetic testing in hiring, for example, twenty-one states had already passed laws protecting workers from use of such tests by their employer before Congress even held hearings.[51] Thirty-four states enacted some form of equal-pay legislation, and seventeen states raised the minimum wage above the national level. Ten states adopted "clean car" standards, and several, including New York and California, adopted more stringent air quality standards than those set by the EPA. The mayors of 132 cities in thirty-five states signed on to the Kyoto protocols on global warming rejected by the Bush administration. And unhappy with Washington's inaction on illegal immigration, local law enforcement officials around the country started using local ordinances (e.g., trespassing, loitering) to detain illegal immigrants in their towns.

One of the most tangible signs of growing state power is the degree of devolution of authority over the administration of federal social welfare programs. In exchange for being delegated greater responsibility for administering and funding these programs, states have also demanded far greater control over who is eligible and what kind of services will be provided. Governors of some states have demanded and received **superwaivers**, exemptions from federally set standards for eligibility and benefits provided to clients enrolled in federal health care and welfare programs. This gives governors and state bureaucrats maximum flexibility in deciding who is eligible for a federal health care or welfare program, what services

will be provided, and the size of benefit to those enrolled. Standards for eligibility and types of services offered had been tightly controlled at the federal level until recent years.

The cost of health care is one of the areas of greatest concern to governors, because it is dominating state budgets. With no legislative initiative from the federal level—with exceptionally low approval ratings Bush was unable or unwilling to act—the states began experimenting with their own health insurance programs. Illinois established a program that covers all children and Massachusetts became the first state to adopt a mandatory universal coverage plan.

The Supreme Court

Ultimately the Supreme Court decides where the lines are drawn between what is state and what is federal authority. For fifteen years, the rulings of the Supreme Court have shown a trend toward empowering the states at the expense of the national government. In a 1995 decision, the Court ruled for the first time since the New Deal that Congress had exceeded its authority to regulate interstate commerce and in the following eight years "overturned all or parts of thirty-three federal statutes, ten of them on the grounds that Congress had exceeded its authority either to regulate interstate commerce or to enforce the constitutional guarantees of due process and equal protection."[52] Since 1992 the Court has handed down seven key decisions that restrict Congress's ability to impose rules and regulations on state governments and prevent litigants from bypassing state courts to seek remedies in federal courts.

Once the thinking of the Court's majority was known, dozens of other federalism suits were filed by those who want to limit Congress's ability to extend federal laws to state jurisdictions. These suits have been successful in preventing some disabled people from suing their employers in state courts for alleged violations of their civil rights as guaranteed under the Americans with Disabilities Act. The limitation placed on such suits by the Court has been summarized as "rights without remedies," or one that permits Congress to confer rights on citizens but not to tell the states how to enforce them. The four dissenting justices in those rulings said that decisions giving states immunity from federal rules are the "result of a fundamentally flawed understanding of the role of the states within the federal system" and that they intend to go on dissenting in all cases where this principle of state immunity is applied by the Court's majority.[53]

But the Supreme Court, like the White House and Congress, swings between support for states' rights and the exercise of federal authority. The Court's decision, during a high tide of rulings in defense of states' rights, to intervene in the Florida vote count during the 2000 presidential election, was an assertion of federal power over states' rights. (Elections, whether for national, state, or local office, are the jurisdiction of the states, not the federal government.)

When John G. Roberts joined the Supreme Court as Chief Justice in 2005 and Samuel Alito as Associate Justice in 2006, the states' rights faction on the Court was strengthened. Whereas retiring Justice Sandra Day O'Connor was a swing voter on federalism issues, Alito's record of fifteen years on the appeals court showed strong support for state-centered federalism. But his record also indicated deference to both state and federal governmental powers over individual rights. Chief Justice Roberts had ruled in few federalism cases in his short years on the appeals court, but his legal philosophy is consistent with the Scalia-Thomas rulings that have placed restrictions on Congress's power to legislate or to override state laws.

An exception to this pattern has been the Court's willingness to allow Congress to override state laws on what might be classified as conservative values issues, such as its refusal to uphold state or local laws on medical use of marijuana or gun control laws that are stronger than those passed by Congress. In a surprising departure from this trend the Court did rule in 2006 that Congress could not use federal antidrug laws to overturn an Oregon "right to die" law that allows doctors to administer, at the request of terminally ill patients, lethal doses of drugs. But it is too early to know how the Roberts Court will ultimately come down on the issue of state- versus nation-centered federalism.

The major factor in determining the balance of power between Washington and the states in the first decade of the twenty-first century was not ideological but practical. Bush's preoccupation with foreign rather than domestic issues, and his policy of combining tax cuts with huge spending increases, left the states with more budgetary flexibility than Washington. Because most states are required to have balanced budgets, governors and state legislators do not have the freedom to cut taxes while increasing spending. As federal revenues as a percentage of GDP fell throughout Bush's first term, state revenues held steady.[54]

Interest groups, seeing the trend, are shifting their efforts toward the states. Some of the largest have lobbying operations in all fifty states. This is true for both liberals and conservatives. Liberals, believing they are unlikely to win on issues fought in federal courts that are now dominated by Republican appointees or to get legislation passed in a Congress controlled by Republicans, have redirected their efforts to the state level. Conservatives pursuing a Christian-values agenda, who find attempts to gain congressional passage of bills or constitutional amendments failing because of opposition from Democrats and moderate Republicans, have also turned to state legislatures and ballot initiatives. One lobbyist for Christian conservatives said, "It is on the state level where most family issues are decided."[55]

This continues the pattern of the past seventy years: when states could not or would not respond to calls for government action, Americans have turned to Washington; when a consensus is reached that Washington is not responding to public or interest group demands, or not running programs effectively, people turn to the states. As one cynic has put it, for those times when "we have wrecked one level of government, the Founding Fathers had the foresight to provide a spare."[56]

It is important to remember that through all these policy changes, nothing has changed in the constitutional relationship between the national and state governments. Authority delegated can be taken back by the center. This is where the divergence of views occurs among contemporary supporters of devolution. Advocates of state-centered and dual federalism believe Washington has only surrendered powers that by right belong to the states, whereas the nonideological supporters of devolution see it as a practical measure to bring more efficiency to policy making and implementation.

Conclusion: Does Federalism Make Government More Responsive?

Our history suggests that most people are pragmatic, favoring policies that work by whichever level of government can make them work. In the 1990s when the public consensus was that Washington was not running welfare programs effectively, much of the responsibility was passed to the states; when state and local governments were judged to be failing at running public schools, Washington stepped in. And so it has gone for decades.

It is foolish to pretend to know how the Founders might deal with our complex federal system. However, many of them were astute politicians who would undoubtedly recognize that our system had to evolve along with population and territorial growth and social and economic change. Still, they probably did not foresee a national government that would surpass the states in power and scope of action in domestic policy. Yet one of the paradoxes of our system is that as the national government has gained extraordinary power, so have the states and localities. All levels of government are stronger than in the eighteenth century. Federal power *and* state power have grown hand in hand. It is also paradoxical that although Americans have supported the continuous growth and expansion of the country, they have continued to believe that there is something more true or sacred about small and local government. At the same time many Americans think government at every level is not sufficiently responsive and do not trust it, as indicated by the increasing use of ballot initiatives to bypass both national and local legislators.

Today, across the United States, our belief in democracy, equality, and the rule of law bind us together. But to say that Alabama is more like New York than it used to be is certainly not to say they are alike. Our federal system helps us accommodate regional differences by allowing both state and federal governments a role in policy making. Is such a complex system responsive? It is very responsive in that groups and individuals whose demands are rejected at one level of government can go to another level. The federal system creates multiple points of access, each with power to satisfy political demands by making policy that was rejected at another level.

In polls conducted in the months immediately following the 2001 terrorist attacks, Americans viewed government more favorably, but by 2006 most Americans said that government is almost always wasteful and inefficient. Trust in government had fallen to about half of what it was in 2001.[57] In some ways, that should make the Founders happy: There must be enough confidence in government for it to function and the Union to hold, yet there must be enough suspicion of government to prevent the abuse of power.

Napolitano Vetoes the Bill and Bills the Feds

Governor Napolitano vetoed the bill that would have given Arizona's state and local agencies greater power to enforce federal immigration law. In refusing to sign, she did not argue that the states should not encroach on a federal responsibility. Her veto letter said that the federal government had no right to expect the states to do its job in enforcing immigration law if it was not going to provide the funding. Napolitano said authorizing state agencies to take on additional responsibilities was a de facto unfunded mandate because of the large costs states would incur in training new personnel to take on immigration-enforcement duties.[58]

Just three months later, the Arizona legislature passed another law making smuggling people a felony and again authorizing local police to enforce immigration law.[59] In August 2005, border crossings had reached such a level that both Napolitano and Governor Bill Richardson in New Mexico declared states of emergency. Napolitano sent funds to border counties to deal with increased crime along the border, saying "ranchers are at their wits' end," and that "both federal governments [Mexico and the United States] let us down—there doesn't seem to be any sense of urgency." Governor Richardson also called the state of emergency in New Mexico "an act of desperation."[60]

Napolitano said because there is no doubt that the Constitution makes border security the responsibility of the federal government, she had sent three invoices to the U.S. Department of Justice notifying them that "they owe a staggering $217 million for the costs of incarcerating illegal immigrants who commit crimes." She claimed Arizona had received no more than pennies on the dollar from Washington in reimbursements.[61]

In December 2005, Gov. Napolitano asked Bush to send National Guard troops to the Arizona border. Governors across the nation shared her sense of urgency. State lawmakers introduced more than five hundred pieces of immigration legislation in the first half of 2006 and passed fifty-seven bills. Colorado empowered its attorney general to sue the federal government if it did not take action to enforce immigration laws.[62] Finally, in May 2006, Bush ordered a gradual transfer of six thousand National Guard troops to border areas, many of them to Arizona, to free up border agents to stem the flow of migrants across the desert. They were to be rotated out as Immigration Enforcement hired and trained additional agents. Napolitano

This couple was detained by federal officials in Nogales, Arizona, after trying to cross the border illegally.

AP Images/Gregory Bull

said, "I think the president finally has moved. . . They allowed this problem to fester for far too long." The vigilante action along the border and the millions protesting in the streets for legal status "was a cry from the country saying we want an immigration system that works and can be enforced."[63]

In February 2006, the Western Governors' Association, with Napolitano as its chair, issued its own bipartisan reform plan to address "the disproportionate financial burden on our health care, education, environmental, and criminal justice systems."[64] The governors' plan combined strong border enforcement and no amnesty with a call for a guest worker program and an overhaul of the process of applying for legal immigration.[65] The governors were trying to influence the content of final legislation being considered by Congress and also to shift the fiscal and enforcement responsibilities back to the federal government where constitutional responsibility lies. But the immigration issue gained such traction during the 2006 election campaign that Congress remained split and unable to pass new legislation. With her middle ground approach, Napolitano rolled to victory in her re-election bid, while Arizona congressional candidates supporting the Minutemen's enforcement-only policy went down to defeat.

 To learn more about immigration, go to "you are there" exercises for this chapter on the text website.

Key Terms

federalism
confederal system
unitary system
"mischiefs of faction"
"necessary and proper"
implied powers clause
supremacy clause
Tenth Amendment
nation-centered federalism
state-centered federalism

dual federalism
McCulloch v. Maryland
New Deal
cooperative federalism's causes
devolution
unfunded mandates
full faith and credit clause
home rule
superwaiver

Further Reading

Jonathan Alter, *The Defining Moment: Roosevelt's First 100 Days* (New York: Simon & Schuster, 2006). The executive editor of *Newsweek* argues that with his New Deal program Franklin Roosevelt changed forever the social contract between the federal government and the American people and in the process saved both capitalism and democracy.

David S. Broder, *Democracy Derailed: Initiative Campaigns and the Power of Money* (New York: Harcourt Brace, 2000). A senior Washington correspondent and nationally syndicated columnist takes a look at the rise in use of the ballot initiative to legislate and explains why he believes it is a threat to our republican form of government.

Federalist Papers 39 and 23–25. Read Madison's description of the relationship between state and national governments in essay 39, then compare it with Alexander Hamilton's arguments for a strong national government in essays 23–25. You will see why we are still arguing over federalism.

John W. Kingdon, *America the Unusual* (New York: St. Martin's/Worth, 1999). The essays in this slim volume summarize what American federalism looks like today and how it got that way.

Jeffrey Pressman and Aaron Wildavsky, *Implementation* (Berkeley: University of California Press, 1973). This classic looks at the difficulties of translating federal laws into working programs when dealing with a multiplicity of state and local governments.

John Sperling, et al., *The Great Divide: Retro and Metro America* (Sausalito, CA: Polipoint Press, 2004). A book and companion CD that map cultural, economic, religious and political differences between what it labels metro (liberal) and retro (conservative) states.

John Steinbeck, *The Grapes of Wrath* (New York: Viking, 1939). This celebrated novel vividly portrays the dire conditions that set the stage for the New Deal.

For Viewing

The Civil War (1990). This widely acclaimed series of documentary films took longer to make than the actual Civil War lasted. It provides great insight into the war's causes, states' rights and civil rights, and how the war created both new regional divisions and a new nation.

The Grapes of Wrath (1940). Steinbeck's novel is movingly translated to the big screen. Henry Fonda's portrayal of the everyman, Tom Joad, is one of the iconic performances of twentieth-century film.

The Storm (2005). This PBS documentary on the failure of federal, state, and local cooperation in the response to hurricane Katrina has stunning footage of the storm and flooding, and a dramatic assessment of the costs of government failure. While delivering a blistering critique of FEMA's performance, it offers a balanced account of failures at the state and local levels as well.

www Electronic Resources

http://www.ncsl.org

The National Council of State Legislatures promotes reform and increased efficiency in state legislatures, helps facilitate interstate cooperation, and lobbies for state issues. Its home page provides information about current issues of relevance to states and links to the home pages of all state legislatures.

http://www.nga.org

At this website of the National Governor's Association you can find out how federal-state relations look from the perspective of the state's fifty chief executives. You will also see a pool of likely presidential candidates for the coming decade.

http://www.publicintegrity.org

This is a very useful site monitoring ethics, money, and politics issues at the state level.

http://www.dhs.gov

At the website for the Department of Homeland Security you can read about the division of responsibility for homeland security among national, state, and local governments. It contains a link to your state's homeland security department as well as to the Federal Emergency Management Agency (FEMA).

ThomsonNOW

Enter ThomsonNOW™ using the access card that is available with this text or through www.thomsonedu.com/thomsonnow. ThomsonNOW™ will assist you in understanding the content in this chapter with a personalized study plan generated for your needs. A practice test will assess the areas you need to review and provide the tools to fully comprehend those concepts, including an integrated digital eBook, interactive simulations, timelines, video case studies, MicroCase exercises, and InfoTrac College Edition readers and exercises. You'll also be connected to the learning objectives, chapter outline, chapter glossary, flash cards, crossword puzzles, Internet activities, and interactive quizzes found on the companion website.

CHAPTER 4

PUBLIC OPINION

In this photo, Terri Schiavo looks like she is interacting with her mother, but doctors said this impression is misleading.

Nature of Public Opinion

Formation of Public Opinion

Agents of Political Socialization

Impact of Political Socialization

Measuring Public Opinion

Early Polling Efforts

Emergence of Scientific Polling

Use of Polls

Knowledge and Information

Ideology

Public Opinion in Red States and Blue States

Public Opinion toward Race

Conclusion: Is Government Responsive to Public Opinion?

YOU ARE THERE

Should You Intervene in a Life or Death Decision?

It is March 2005. You are Republican Bill Frist, senior senator from Tennessee, and majority leader of the U.S. Senate. Elected to the Senate in 1994, you said you would only serve two terms. You do plan to step down in 2006, but you hope to run for the Republican nomination for president in 2008. From a well-known family in Tennessee, you are a physician, as was your father before you. Now you are faced with a decision whether to use your medical expertise to offer advice on a case that is the subject of national controversy—whether to remove the feeding tube of a forty-one-year-old woman, Terri Schiavo, who has presumably been in a "persistent vegetative state" for fifteen years. The question now is whether Congress should intervene in this "right to die" issue that already has been addressed by numerous courts.

Terri Schiavo has become a household name. She met her future husband, Michael, as a community college student in Pennsylvania and married him in their local Catholic church. They moved to St. Petersburg, Florida, where she worked as an insurance claims clerk. In 1990, after six years of marriage, she suddenly collapsed. Paramedics found her unconscious, not breathing and with no pulse.

In the first years after her cardiac arrest, Michael attempted to get her rehabilitation, first at the University of California, then at a brain rehabilitation facility in Florida. After that, he took her to a skilled care facility in Florida where she received further testing and speech and occupational therapy. During this time, Michael began studying nursing, and eventually became an emergency room nurse. He said he wanted to learn to take care of Terri. But after four years of attempted rehabilitation and therapy, it became clear she was not responsive, and he transferred her to a nursing home. And he became concerned about the quality of her life in this condition.

She wakes and sleeps but cannot talk or move of her own volition, and she cannot perceive what people say or even where she is. She cannot eat, so she is kept alive by a feeding tube inserted into her abdomen. Numerous neurologists (brain doctors) who have examined her have diagnosed her as being in a persistent vegetative state, with irreparable brain damage. Her case raises ethical issues of when, if ever, it is appropriate to remove life support and let someone die.

The issue has become a legal and political one because Michael Schiavo wants to disconnect the feeding tube. He testified that Terri would never have wanted to be kept alive in a vegetative state. But Terri's parents, Robert and Mary Schindler, want to maintain

Senator Bill Frist addresses an evangelical assembly via video.

the feeding tube. They do not accept the diagnosis that Terri is in a persistent vegetative state; they believe that she is in a "minimally conscious state." They think that she tries to answer them and pucker her lips when they kiss her. They argue that she should be kept alive and, with further rehabilitation, could again function at least at a minimal level. And they do not believe that Michael has Terri's interests at heart. After he realized that she would not revive, he dated other women and eventually had two children with another woman, with whom he now lives.

The legal battle began seven years ago when Michael petitioned to remove Terri's feeding tube and the Schindlers fought the petition. By now,

nineteen state courts in Florida have heard the case, and all three levels of federal courts, including the Supreme Court, have refused to intervene. At each stage, Terri was examined and tested by doctors. Witnesses were heard on whether she was in a vegetative state and, if so, whether she would want to live in that state.

The Florida courts have agreed Terri is in a persistent vegetative state. And, although she did not prepare a living will indicating her wishes in the event that she were in such a state, the courts have also heard from her friends and husband that she would not have wanted to be kept alive in this condition.

When, in 2003, the Florida courts held that Michael had the right to have

the feeding tube removed, the Florida legislature sprung into action and passed "Terri's law," which enabled the governor (Jeb Bush, President George W. Bush's brother) to intervene. Governor Bush had Ms. Schiavo taken to a hospital to have the feeding tube reinserted. (The legislation also appointed a special guardian to look after the interests of Ms. Schiavo and report back to the governor. The guardian subsequently reported that there was no evidence that she was aware of her environment. He also declared that the legal basis for the decisions of the Florida courts was sound. Later "Terri's law" was found unconstitutional.)

You and your colleagues are now involved in the case because last month the courts again ordered the removal of the tube.

The Terri Schiavo case is all over the media. You cannot turn on the cable news networks—CNN, Fox, or MSNBC—which are battling each other for dominance, without hearing about it. Not surprisingly, most people have formed an opinion about it. Nearly 60 percent said that if they were her guardian they would remove the tube, but about 40 percent said they would maintain it. Large majorities, ranging from 74 to 90 percent, said that if they were in her shoes they would not want

---

Public opinion is often contradictory. The public is hostile toward political leaders for failing to respond to the public's needs, yet, at the same time, complains that leaders simply follow the latest polls. Many are angry with the government. They do not trust it; they think it is too big and spends too much money. Yet they like the services it provides, and very few are willing to cut spending to eliminate services or programs that benefit them.

This chapter explores public opinion to better understand these contradictions. It describes how public opinion is formed and measured, assesses how informed and knowledgeable the public is with respect to public affairs, discusses the role of ideology in American politics, treats some issue divisions within the population, and concludes with an assessment of the extent to which government is responsive to public opinion.

Nature of Public Opinion

Public opinion can be defined as the collection of individual opinions toward issues or objects of general interest—that is, those that concern a significant number of people. Opinion can be positive or negative about something. The distinction between positive or negative, yes or no, for or against an issue is called the direction of public opinion. Of course, there are few issues where everyone is on the same side of an issue. On any given issue or personality, some people are positive, others negative.

Intensity reflects the strength of public opinion. The public may have rather weak feelings about an issue or feel quite strongly about it. Intense opinions often drive behavior. Many people opposed the invasion of Iraq, for example, but only the most intense people protested it in the streets.

to be kept alive. And large majorities also do not think that Congress should get involved in the case.[1]

However, some of your conservative Republican base has a different view. Evangelical Protestants are almost evenly split on whether the tube should be removed.[2] Right wing bloggers and talk radio hosts are echoing the views of Terri's parents that her condition is curable and that her husband is trying to get rid of her. Right to life groups, those opposing abortion, see hers as a test case in the battle to preserve life. Pat Robertson, a televangelist, called the removal of the tube "judicial murder." Peggy Noonan, former speechwriter for President Reagan, thundered: "The Republicans are in charge. They have the power. If they can't save this women's life, they will face a reckoning from a sizable portion of their own base. And they will of course deserve it."[3]

Now Terri's parents and their supporters are appealing to Congress to pass a law that would pressure the federal courts to hear the case and overturn the state courts. They have made videos, from short snippets from many hours of film, edited to make it seem as though she is responsive to her parents and her environment. The cable networks are showing these tapes constantly, stirring the emotions of those who want to keep her alive.

As the only practicing physician in the Senate, you know that your knowledge and experience would give your views extra credibility. On health care issues, you have clout with your colleagues, both Democrats and Republicans.[4] You have worked with conservative Democrat John Breaux (D-La.) to reform Medicare and liberal Democrat Edward Kennedy (D-Mass.) to increase vaccines and training for a potential bioterrorist attack. When envelopes containing anthrax were sent to a congressional office, your colleagues appreciated your advice. (And your website received 40,000 hits a day from people worried about the anthrax threat.[5])

As the Senate's majority leader, you are in position to influence the Senate's decision. Should you urge your colleagues to intervene in the dispute? Should you follow public opinion in general or the opinion of the most conservative elements of the Republican base? This constituency will be very important in the primary elections to choose the party's nominee for president in 2008.

Should you acquiesce to the demands of the national pro-life movement by urging a congressional law to pressure the federal courts to intervene, or should you adhere to the Republicans' traditional emphasis on states' rights by allowing the Florida court decisions to stand? Republicans long have argued that the federal government should let states decide matters close to home, but social conservatives want the federal government to mandate policies reflecting their views. To intervene in this case, which involves one person and already has been adjudicated in many courts, would be almost unprecedented, and it would undermine the legitimacy of the Florida courts and turn this issue into a political football.

Of course, you are a doctor, and the medical evidence seems clear. Only a few doctors have testified on the other side, and some of them had not even seen the patient. Should you give more weight to your medical expertise or to your political future?

If you do urge your colleagues to intervene, should you use your medical expertise to buttress your argument, and risk your medical reputation, or simply make an appeal to pro-life ideology?

What do you do?

Public opinion is not very intense on most issues. A small minority may feel intensely about any issue, but a majority rarely does. Opinions also vary in stability. Some constantly change, whereas others never do. Stable opinions are often intense, grounded in a great deal of information, some of it accurate, some inaccurate.

Feelings of attachment to American political parties tend to be stable, while opinions toward candidates and public officials, particularly high profile ones like the president, fluctuate in response to changing events and circumstances. President George W. Bush began his presidency with 60 percent of the public approving the job he was doing. This rose to 90 percent shortly after 9/11 and has dropped steadily to barely more than 30 percent in mid-2006. It is not uncommon for a president's job approval to decline over the course of his term (see Figure 4.1; see also Figure 11.3). Perceived failure to deal adequately with the nation's problems reduces approval.

Opinions can fluctuate when voters know little about a candidate. Polls following the party nominating conventions in 1992 showed Clinton's margins over George H. W. Bush seesawing back and forth day to day. Most voters didn't know enough about Clinton to form a stable opinion. They would see something on television or read something in the press favorable to Clinton and report a preference for him, and then see something unfavorable and shift back to Bush.[6]

Formation of Public Opinion

People learn and develop opinions about government and politics through the process of **political socialization.** As with learning in other spheres, individuals learn about politics by being exposed to new information supplied or filtered through parents, peers, schools,

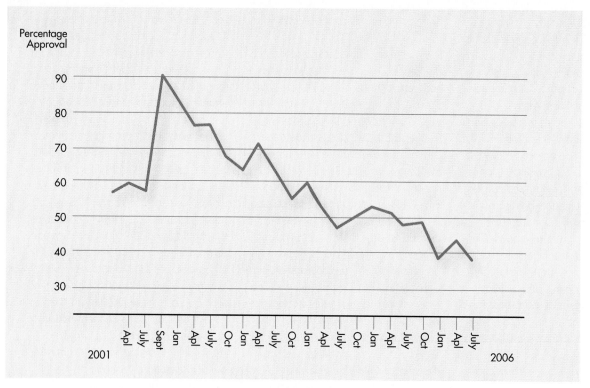

FIGURE 4.1 ■ George W. Bush's Approval Ratings Peaked after 9/11, Then Declined

SOURCE: Gallup Poll Tuesday Briefing, April 13, 2004. Update http://poll.gallup.com/content/default.aspx?ci=1723. Data are nationwide polls with sample sizes of 1,000–1,200 and a margin of error of 3 percent.

the media, political leaders, and the community. These **agents of political socialization** introduce each new generation to the rights and responsibilities of citizenship (see Chapter 1) as well as shape opinions and positions toward officeholders and political issues. Individuals, particularly adults, also learn about politics and develop opinions through personal experiences.

Political learning begins at an early age and continues throughout life. In young children, learning is influenced by reasoning capacity and expectations.[7] When parents encourage it, learning begins earlier and proceeds more quickly. Preschoolers are unable to distinguish political from nonpolitical objects. Some are unable to separate political figures from cartoon characters, and some confuse religion with politics. A significant number of five- and six-year-olds report that the president takes his orders from God.[8] By first grade, these confusions are resolved, and children begin to see government as distinct and unique.[9]

However, the inability to understand abstract concepts or complex institutions means the conception of government is limited. Most identify government with the president.[10] Children at a very early age recognize him. In a recent year, 97 percent of a group of fourth graders were able to identify the president by name,[11] a proportion that has stayed constant for several decades.[12] Many, no doubt, see him on TV and understand that he is the leader of the nation. Experiences

with parents and other adults provide children with a basis for understanding their relationship with authority figures with whom they have no contact.[13] Feelings children have toward parents are generalized to the president. Studies in the 1950s found children describing the president as good and helpful;[14] many saw him as more powerful than he really is.[15] A more recent study notes children are considerably less likely to evaluate the president as good, and this extends from fourth to eighth grade.[16] At the same time, children are more likely to describe the president as benevolent. The difference may reflect the greater capacity of children today to draw a distinction between the institutional presidency and the individual who occupies the office.

Older children are introduced to political ideas and political institutions in school and through the media. Their concept of government broadens to include Congress, the act of voting, and ideas such as freedom and democracy. The positive view of government reflected in feelings toward the president gives way to more complex and realistic images. The process can be accelerated by political events and the reaction of others to them. Children were much less positive toward the president and government in the 1970s than in the 1960s. The Watergate scandal in 1973 lowered both adults' and children's evaluations of the president.[17] The Clinton sexual scandals and the impeach-

All issues have a moral element, but those that are primarily moral have the greatest potential to divide. Slavery was a moral issue that almost destroyed the nation. In the first decades of the twentieth century, prohibition—banning the sale of alcoholic beverages—was a divisive moral issue.

Abortion emerged as a moral issue in the 1970s and remains so today. Although Americans are highly supportive of abortion when the health and safety of the mother is a concern, they are quite divided when the issue is ending an unwanted pregnancy.

In the 1990s, the rights of gays and lesbians became a moral issue. For some time, a majority of Americans have endorsed equal rights with respect to job opportunities, but it has only been in the last few years that a majority accepts that homosexual relations between consenting adults should be legal. Opinions have changed rapidly. About 60 percent accept this view today. Nearly 80 percent say that gays and lesbians should be allowed to serve in the military, an increase from less than 60 percent in 2000. Support for allowing homosexual couples to form civil unions and enjoy some of the same rights as married couples has also increased. In 1996, about one-third favored such unions; eight years later nearly two-thirds did. However, public support for same-sex marriages is considerably lower (see Figure 4.2). Only 37 percent of the public favors same-sex marriages.

Americans are increasingly willing to extend rights to gays and lesbians. Although in the short run it is unlikely that a majority of Americans will accept the term "marriage" to describe homosexual unions, the public seems willing to continue to favor the cautious extension of basic rights to homosexuals, including the right to form civil unions. Increasing acceptance of gays and lesbians is driven to a large extent by their greater visibility. Seven out of ten Americans report knowing someone who is gay or lesbian. With increased interaction and acquaintance comes tolerance.

The trend toward greater tolerance is likely to continue because younger generations are much more accepting than are older generations. Although nearly two-thirds of those over sixty-five oppose same-sex marriages, less than one-third of those between eighteen and thirty-four do. Thus, as the older generations pass from the scene, public opinion is likely to become more accepting.

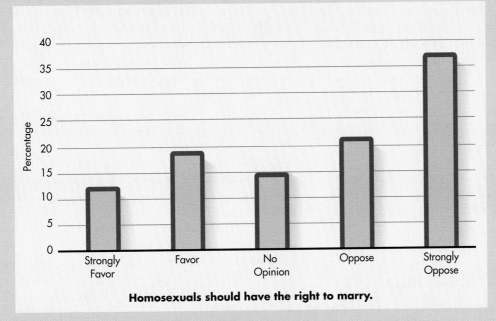

Homosexuals should have the right to marry.

FIGURE 4.2 ■ Many Feel Quite Strongly about Same-Sex Marriage

SOURCE: Gallup Poll, May 15, 2003; "Same-Sex Marriage and Civil Unions," Religious Tolerance.org, "Gays getting more acceptance as they're more open, poll says,"; *Lincoln-Journal Star*, April 11, 2004. See also "Status of Gay Marriages and Civil Unions," report prepared from Gallup and other national polling data on Ontario Consultants on Religious Tolerance, www.religioustolerance.org/hom_poll5.htm and Scott S. Greenberger, "One Year Later, Nation Divided on Gay Marriage," *Boston Globe* (May 15, 2005): A1.

ment proceedings of 1998, however, had no impact on adult evaluations of the president and government, and presumably none on children. The approval ratings of the president reached record levels, and confidence in the executive branch remained unchanged from the year before.[18]

Even when scandal lowers children's evaluations of government, the effect may not last. The negative feelings of children during Watergate diminished as they aged.[19]

In adolescence, political understanding expands still further. Children discuss politics with family and friends. By the middle teens, positions on issues develop.[20] Some fifteen- and sixteen-year-olds develop opinions that resemble those of adults. Although they begin to recognize faults in the system, they still believe the United States is the best country in the world. They rate the country low in limiting violence and fostering political morality but high in providing educational opportunities, a good standard of living, and science and technology.[21] For most, the positive feelings toward government learned earlier are reinforced.

In adulthood, opinions toward specific personalities and policies develop, and political activity becomes more serious. Although most Americans revere the country and do not want to change the system, they tend to be cynical and distrustful of political leaders. Some of this negative feeling grows out of Americans' dislike of conflict and partisanship in politics.[22] Some is caused by media coverage, which not only highlights conflict, but often exaggerates it. At the same time, the media are committed to and supportive of the American system.[23] Americans may get angry with their government, but, except for the Civil War, it has never boiled over to the point of mass violence directed toward political institutions or leaders.

Critical comments about government and political leaders sharply declined after 9/11, but that cessation was short-lived. Most Americans felt gratitude toward the brave souls—many of whom lost their lives—who courageously marched to aid those under attack. Yet, except for those who were called to serve in the armed forces or who were able to volunteer to help in the World Trade Center cleanup, Americans were not asked to translate these positive feelings into action. Though commentators on 9/11 and immediately afterward predicted that nothing would ever be the same, for most Americans life did return to normal quickly and with it, skepticism toward government.

Agents of Political Socialization

It is the agents of political socialization—principally the family and schools—that are responsible for ensuring that each new generation of Americans resembles those generations that have come before.

Family

Recent research suggests that each of us may be born with a predilection toward conservatism or liberalism and with a predilection for other political traits as well.[24] Despite that, children's party identification is strongly shaped by their family. Families are particularly important in shaping the opinions of children because of strong emotional ties and exclusive control during the early years.[25]

The family influences opinions in several ways aside from genetic ties. Parents share their opinions directly with children, who often adopt those opinions. They say or do things that children imitate. Children overhear parents' comments about the political parties and adopt them as their own. Children also transfer feelings they hold of parents to political objects. When children harbor negative feelings toward their parents, they are more likely to be negative toward the president.[26] The family shapes the personality of the child. A child who is encouraged to speak up at home is likely to do so in public. Children also inherit their social and economic position from their parents, which influences not only how they view themselves, but also how they view the world and how the world views them. A child from a wealthy family begins with advantages and opportunities that a child from a poor family can only dream about.

Children are more likely to reflect their parents' views when these views are clearly communicated and important. Parents often, if unintentionally, convey how they feel about political parties during election campaigns and children pick it up. Other opinions are less likely to be communicated to children. Seventy percent of high school seniors were able to correctly identify the party of their parents, while no more than 36 percent could identify their parents' opinion on other issues.[27]

However, even where parental influence is strong, it is not immutable. As young adults leave their parents' circle, agreement between their opinions, including party allegiance, and those of their parents, declines. New agents and experiences come into play.[28] Even among younger children, parental influence may not be as strong as in the past. Parents no longer have exclusive control during a child's preschool years, and the number of households with both parents working or with a single parent who works means less contact with parents. Others can be expected to fill this void. Today, schools often deal with problems the family dealt with in the past. While parental influence may be declining, whether or not one is raised in the traditional two-parent family or one with a single parent has little or no impact on important political opinions and political behavior.[29]

School

A child of our acquaintance who came to the United States at the age of five could not speak English and did not know the name of his new country. After a few months of kindergarten, he knew that George Washington and Abraham Lincoln were good presidents, he was able to recount stories of the pilgrims, he could draw the flag, and he felt strongly that the United States was the best country in the world. This child illustrates the importance of the school in political socialization and how values and symbols of government are explicitly taught in American schools, as they are in schools in every nation.[30]

Although we do not understand exactly which aspects of formal schooling influence political opinions, there is little doubt that education and years of formal schooling—the skills it provides and experiences it represents—make a difference. People who have more education are more interested in and knowledgeable about politics.[31] They are also more likely to participate in politics and to be politically tolerant.[32]

Yet education does not seem to lead to a greater appreciation of the real workings of democracy, that is, a form of government where there are disagreements typically resolved through bargaining and compromise.[33] Education does not prepare citizens for how democracy works in practice, or how to recognize that disagreement is fundamental to democratic processes, or how to build positive feelings toward these processes.

How do the schools influence the political opinions of children? Schools promote patriotic rituals. They often begin each day with the Pledge of Allegiance and include patriotic songs and programs in many activities. In the lower grades, children celebrate national holidays such as Presidents' Day and Thanksgiving and learn the history and symbols associated with them. Involvement in such activities fosters love and respect of country.

In the upper grades, mock elections, conventions, and student government introduce students to the operation of government. School clubs operate with democratic procedures and reinforce the concepts of voting and majority rule. The state of Illinois let the state's elementary school children vote to select the official state animal, fish, and tree, conveying the message that voting is the way issues are decided.

Textbooks often foster commitment to government and the status quo. Those used in elementary grades emphasize compliance with authority and the need to be a "good" citizen. Even textbooks in advanced grades present idealized versions of the way government works and exaggerate the role of citizens in holding public officials accountable and in shaping public policy.

Textbooks are less likely, however, to emphasize the need for citizens to uphold democratic values such as participating in politics and tolerating others' views. Nor do they help students understand that conflicts and differences of opinion are inevitable in a large and diverse society and that the role of politics is to address and resolve these disagreements.

The number of civics courses taken in high school improves students' knowledge of government and pol-

© Robin Nelson/Black Star

This boy, at a white supremacist rally, likely was socialized in these views by his parents.

itics and fosters beliefs that government pays attention to people and that elections are important in holding government responsible. Courses during the senior year are particularly important. That is when students are ready to make the transition to adulthood and when government and politics are likely to be more meaningful.[34]

Reading habits and language skills are also important to democratic citizenship. Reading, a skill learned in school but often nurtured in the home, is related to interest in politics, knowledge of public affairs, political participation, and political tolerance. Those who spend time reading are more likely to reflect attributes of democratic citizenship than those who do not.[35] Proficiency with language is important, too, as language is the mechanism for communicating and assessing information and evaluating new ideas and arguments.[36] Teachers as role models also contribute in significant ways. Perceptions that school administrators and teachers are fair are linked with expressions of trust toward other people.[37]

In sum, the major impact of kindergarten through high school seems to be that it creates "good" citizens—citizens who accept political authority and the institutions of government and who also limit their political activities to the conventional and routine such as voting in elections. In this way, elementary and secondary education serves government and the status quo in ways that the dominant interests in society prefer. Schools are not particularly effective at fostering political participation and commitment to democratic values. Nor do they provide students with the skills to critically assess social, political, and economic structures that reveal the root causes of problems and strategies for dealing with injustice and effecting political change.[38] In this regard, the failure of schools is often attributed to the "hidden curriculum."[39] Schools are not democratic institutions where students are encouraged to participate in a meaningful way. Indeed, most schools foster a climate averse to controversy. Such an environment is unlikely to produce active and engaged citizens.

The impact of college often broadens students' perspectives and leads to greater understanding of the world around them. They become more open and tolerant. They become less rigid and bound by tradition. Most students go to college to get a better job, make more money, prepare for a specific career, broaden their knowledge of the world, or learn about things that interest them. Some attend because their parents insist or because everyone else is going. Few go to college seeking to become more tolerant, but this is often the result. College students are more open and tolerant than the population as a whole, and the longer they are in college, the more open and tolerant they become, seniors more so than freshmen, and graduate students more so than undergraduates.[40]

Some recent commentators argue that college professors indoctrinate students and even suggest that state legislatures should investigate such "indoctrination."[41] In fact, a survey showed that 64 percent of the social science faculty in the nation's colleges identify themselves as liberal, and only 20 percent regard themselves as conservative. However, faculty in other fields are less liberal. For example, only 30 percent of the business faculty identify themselves as liberal.

The idea that professors are indoctrinating students seems remote, however. For example, during the height of the Vietnam War (1968–1971), students were more likely to identify themselves as liberal than students before or after the war. And after the war, fewer declared themselves liberal.[42] During the same period, the outlook of college faculty changed very little. Thus students are not simply a reflection of their college teachers. At large universities, where the largest percentage of students attend, the environment is sufficiently diverse to reinforce many points of view. Moreover, it is college that provides students with the self-confidence and independence that enables them to resist indoctrination.[43] Today, more college freshmen are moderates than liberals.[44]

On issues, college freshmen look much like the population as a whole, liberal on some issues but conservative on others. They are liberal in wanting the government to do more to control the sale of handguns, provide national health care to cover everyone's medical costs, guarantee homosexuals the right to have marital unions, and in believing that racial discrimination remains a problem. They are conservative in attitudes about crime: majorities wish to retain the death penalty and believe that the courts show too much concern for the rights of criminals. Small majorities are pro-choice, favor affirmative action, and support taxing the rich more (see Table 4.1). During the past few years, freshmen have become slightly more liberal in their opinions as well as in their self-identification.[45]

The most distinctive characteristic of college freshmen in recent years has been their low interest in politics,[46] although this may be changing. Since 2001, there has been a slight increase, but the 22 percent who report frequently talking about politics is far less than the high of 60 percent in 1968, during the Vietnam era.[47] However, in 2005 virtually all entering freshmen reported participating in an organized demonstration.[48] More than 80 percent report volunteering. Increased volunteerism reflects the growing trend of community service requirements for high school graduation (and in that sense is not really "volunteerism"). Rising levels of activism and involvement may mean increased levels of civic participation in the future.

Peers

In many instances, peers simply reinforce the opinions of the family or school. When there is a conflict between peer and parental socialization, peers sometimes win but only on issues of special relevance to youth. For example, peer influence is more important than family influence on the issue of whether eighteen-year-olds should be allowed to vote, but parental influence appears to be more significant with respect to partisanship and vote choice.[49] Peers have the most influence when the peer group is attractive to the individual and when the individual spends time with the group. With growing numbers of single-parent families and working parents, parental influence may be diminishing and friends and associates may be taking on greater importance for adults.

TABLE 4.1	Opinions of College Freshmen in 2005	
The federal government should do more to control the sale of handguns.		79%
A national health care plan is needed to cover everyone's medical costs.		74%
There is too much concern in the courts for the rights of criminals.		58%
Same-sex couples should have the right to legal marital status.		58%
Abortion should be legal.		55%
Wealthy people should pay a larger share of taxes than they do now.		58%
Marijuana should be legalized.		38%
Federal military spending should be increased.		34%
The death penalty should be abolished.		33%
It is important to have laws prohibiting homosexual relationships.		27%
Racial discrimination is no longer a major problem in America.		21%

The percentages are those agreeing strongly or somewhat with the statement.
SOURCE: "Attitudes and Characteristics of Freshmen," *Chronicle of Higher Education*, February 3, 2006. On the web at http://chronicle.com/premium/stats/freshmen/2006/data.htm#political.

Mass Media

The primary effect of the media on children is to increase their level of information about politics. The primary effect on adults is to influence what they think about—that is, the issues, events, and personalities they pay attention to.[50] The media also influence opinions about issues and individuals; in recent years, the media have reflected a high degree of cynicism and negativism toward political leaders. Research shows that changes in public opinion tend to follow sentiments expressed by television news commentators.[51] The impact of the media is explored in more detail in Chapter 5.

Adult Socialization

Not all political socialization occurs in the preadult years. Opinions develop and change throughout life as one experiences new and different things. Marriage, divorce, unemployment, a new job, or a move to a new location can affect political opinions.[52]

Economic, political, and social events have the potential to change the way Americans think about politics. Many hard hit by the Great Depression were drawn to politics seeking help. Most, voting for the first time, cast their ballot for the Democrats in 1932 and continued to vote Democratic throughout their lifetimes. World War II and the attack on Pearl Harbor shaped the opinions of a generation of Americans. The Vietnam War moved many college students to the streets in protest, whereas others moved to Canada to avoid the draft. In contrast, the short-term impact of the terrorist attacks on the Pentagon and the World Trade Center pushed the public closer to government, although the impact soon dissipated (see the box "The Short-Term Impact of 9/11 on Public Opinion," p. 99).[53]

Impact of Political Socialization

Each new generation of Americans is socialized to a large extent by those preceding it. In many ways, each new generation will look and act much like the one that came before it. In this sense, political socialization represents a stabilizing and conserving influence. Typically, it leads to support for and compliance with government and the social order. Although many disagree with particular government policies, few question the basic structure of government.

Measuring Public Opinion

Pollsters measure public opinion by asking individuals to answer questions in a survey or poll. Of course, there are other techniques used to measure opinion, and before scientific polls these techniques were all that were available. Elected officials consider the opinions of people who talk to them or write or e-mail them; journalists gauge public opinion by talking selectively to individuals; letters written to newspaper editors or newspaper editorials are a measure of public opinion. Protests and demonstrations also reflect public opinion. All of these techniques provide an incomplete picture, however. Letters or messages to public officials and newspapers are more likely to come from people with extreme opinions[54] or from those with writing skills—that is, people with more education. Nor will opinions culled from a few conversations match the pattern of opinion for the nation as a whole or even a single state. Editorial opinion is even less likely to provide an accurate picture of public opinion because most newspaper publishers tend to be conservative, and this view is often reflected in their editorials. For example, in most presidential elections in the twentieth century, newspapers favored the Republican candidate by about three to one.[55] The exception to this was that more newspapers endorsed John Kerry than George W. Bush in 2004 by a small margin.[56]

However, polling can shape public opinion as well as assess it.[57] Prior to the use of polls, people who wanted to be heard had to write letters, deliver speeches, or organize protests. Today, pollsters initiate the expression of public opinion by conducting a poll. Rather than focus on what the public is concerned about, polls concentrate on what pollsters and their sponsors are most interested in. For this reason, many issues of public importance never become subjects of a poll.

In spite of this, polling remains the only accurate way to assess what the nation as a whole thinks about political issues and public officials. In this sense, even though they are not perfect, polls are the best measure of public opinion.

Early Polling Efforts

The first attempts to measure popular sentiments on a large scale were the **straw polls** (or unscientific polls) developed by newspapers in the nineteenth century.[58] In 1824, the *Harrisburg Pennsylvanian,* in perhaps the first poll assessing candidate preferences, sent reporters to check on support for the four presidential contenders that year. The paper reported that Andrew Jackson was the popular choice over John Quincy Adams, Henry Clay, and William H. Crawford. Jackson received the most votes in the election, but John Quincy Adams was elected president after the contest was decided by the House of Representatives. Toward the end of the nineteenth century, the *New York Herald* regularly tried to forecast election outcomes in local, state, and national races. During presidential election years, the paper collected estimates from reporters and political leaders across the country and predicted the Electoral College vote by state.

Straw polls are still employed today. Some newspapers have interviewers ask adults at shopping malls and other locations for their voting preferences. Several television networks run Internet polls. CNN asks viewers of its early evening news show to register their opinions on different issues and reports the results before the broadcast ends. Major events often trigger media polls. After each presidential debate, national media invite people to cast a vote via the web on who won. Preferences are electronically recorded and tabulated. Straw polls are unlikely to reflect the opinions of the public at large, and because of this they are often labeled unscientific. They are unscien-

tific because there is no way to ensure that the sample of individuals giving opinions is representative of the larger population. Generally, straw polls are not reflective of the entire public. The famed *Literary Digest* poll is a good example. The magazine conducted polls of presidential preferences between 1916 and 1936. As many as eighteen million ballots were mailed out to persons drawn from telephone directories and automobile registration lists.

Although the purpose was less to measure public opinion than to boost subscriptions, the *Literary Digest* did have a pretty good record. It had predicted the winners in 1924, 1928, and 1932. In 1936, however, the magazine predicted Alfred Landon would win, but Franklin D. Roosevelt won by a landslide. The erroneous prediction ended the magazine's polling, and in 1938 the *Literary Digest* went out of business.

Why did the *Literary Digest* miss in 1936? The sample was biased. Owners of telephones and automobiles in the depths of the Great Depression were disproportionately middle- and upper-income people who were more likely to vote for Landon, the Republican, than lower-income Americans were.[59] Since the sample was drawn from telephone directories and auto registrations, lower-income people, and hence Democratic voters, were significantly underrepresented.

Emergence of Scientific Polling

Scientific polling began after World War I, inspired by the new field of business known as marketing research. After the war, demand for consumer goods rose, and American businesses, no longer engaged in the production of war materials, turned to satisfying consumer demand. Businesses used marketing research to identify what consumers wanted and, perhaps more important, how products should be packaged so consumers would buy them. The American Tobacco Company changed from a green to a white package during World War II because it found that a white package was more attractive to women smokers.[60]

The application of mathematical principles of probability was also important to the development of scientific polling. To determine the frequency of defects in manufactured products, inspectors made estimates on the basis of a few randomly selected items, called a *sample*. It was a simple matter to extend the practice to individuals and draw conclusions regarding a large population based on findings from a smaller, randomly selected sample.

In the early 1930s, George Gallup and several others, using probability-based sampling techniques, began polling opinions on a wide scale. In 1936, Gallup predicted that the *Literary Digest* would be wrong and that Roosevelt would be reelected with

Although the Great Depression had a long-lasting impact on American public opinion, and the Japanese attack on Pearl Harbor changed Americans' views of their role in the world conflict taking place, the influence on public opinion of the traumatic attacks of 9/11 was intense but short-lived. Before the terrorist attacks, many Americans took government for granted and considered it unimportant and irrelevant to their lives. The booming economy and surging stock market during the 1990s led to complacency. Moreover, cynicism about government was fueled by a steady stream of negative commentary about the government emanating from the media and politicians who found it useful for their careers. Reflecting this sentiment, one-third in a nationwide poll in 2001 responded that it was unimportant who was elected president, and over 80 percent believed it unimportant to listen to the president's State of the Union address.

But the smoke and devastation of 9/11 had an immediate impact on Americans' attitudes. From the ashes of the World Trade Center and Pentagon sprang a feeling of patriotism, national unity, and a willingness to help others and see the nation through a difficult crisis.

Suddenly, what the president had to say seemed important. Fifty-four percent, more than twice as many as the year before, found the president's State of the Union address in January 2002 especially important. More than 80 percent, compared with just 50 percent the year before, had a favorable view of the national government, and trust in government nearly doubled following the attacks.[1] The public standing of the president and Congress similarly surged, as government seemed necessary again. As someone remarked, "The only persons going up the stairs of the World Trade Center while everyone else was going down were government officials. The events brought home the fact that the government does important work."[2]

The changed attitudes toward government and a greater sense of national unity on the part of citizens led some to claim that America would be forever changed. After all, after the Japanese attack on Pearl Harbor in 1941, Americans rallied behind their government and mobilized for an all-out war against both the Japanese and the Germans. Perhaps the change in American attitudes after 9/11 would have been longer lasting if the nation had been called upon to sacrifice as it had in World War II. A call for mobilization and sacrifice from the president might have kept the spirit alive, but his advice to Americans was "Live your lives, hug your children."[3] "Go shopping" was the call.

Rather than use 9/11 to push for policies that would benefit the nation as a whole, the president and Republicans in Congress used 9/11 to push a narrow and partisan agenda, tax cuts for the rich, a war in Iraq, and non-competitive contracts for favored corporations doing work there. The president could have challenged the nation to use less energy to check growing U.S. dependence on foreign oil. He could have called the nation to support higher taxes to pay for the war on terror. He could have established a military draft. In the case of 9/11, asking Americans to act as if nothing had happened, the president got his wish and may have also squelched the willingness of large numbers of Americans to offer a helping hand when the nation needed it.

The legacy of 9/11 has been that public sentiments toward government have fallen back to where they were before 9/11. Perhaps the only lingering attitudinal changes will be increases in Americans afraid to fly (43 percent), enter skyscrapers (30 percent), or enter crowded public places (33 percent).

[1]Alexander Stille, "Suddenly, Americans Trust Uncle Sam," *New York Times*, November 3, 2001, online article.
[2]"Public Opinion Six Months Later," Pew Research Center for the People and the Press, news release, March 7, 2002.
[3]Benjamin Wallace-Wells, "Mourning Has Broken," *Washington Monthly*, October 2003, 16–18.

"But first our national anthem."

Harry Truman exults in incorrect headlines, based on faulty polls and early returns, the morning after he won the 1948 election.

55.7 percent of the vote. Though Gallup underestimated Roosevelt's actual vote, his accurate prediction of the outcome lent credibility to probability-based polls.

Increasingly, government used polls. In 1940, Roosevelt became the first president to use polls on a regular basis, employing a social scientist to measure trends in public opinion toward the war in Europe.

Use of Polls

Most major American universities have a unit that performs survey research, and there are hundreds of commercial marketing research firms, private pollsters, and newspaper polls. For politicians, polls almost have become what the Oracle of Delphi was to the ancient Greeks and Merlin was to King Arthur—a divine source of wisdom. During a budget debate between President Clinton and congressional Republicans, Republicans used polls that told them that promising to "put the government on a diet" would be popular in the upcoming 1996 election. Polls led Clinton to counter by accusing the Republicans of trying to cut Medicare. When the media wanted to make sense of the debate, they conducted more polls.[61]

Use by Politicians

Beginning in the 1960s, presidents increasingly turned to polls to assess the public's thinking on issues.[62] President Clinton took the use of polls to a new high. He spent more on polling than all previous administrations combined and tested every significant policy idea and the language to promote it.[63] Following the 1994 elections in which Democrats lost control of both the House and Senate, Clinton vowed never again to be out of step with the public.[64] Weekly polls shaped his centrist message, leading to his reelection in 1996. If polls showed a position to be popular, Clinton was likely to adopt it as his own. He embraced welfare reform, a Republican idea opposed by Democrats in Congress and liberals in his administration, partly because it was popular.[65] A White House poll in 1997 suggested that Americans preferred using the budget surplus to bolster Social Security rather than administer a Republican-preferred tax cut. In his State of the Union address, he called on Congress to "save Social Security first." Clinton would also quickly withdraw when polls showed an issue to be unpopular. A proposal allowing needle exchanges to check the spread of AIDS was pulled an hour before it was to be announced because a poll revealed it to be politically risky. Clinton even used polls to select a vacation spot.[66] Rather than vacation on Martha's Vineyard and play golf, Clinton went hiking in the Rockies instead, having been told by a consultant that golf was a Republican sport and that the voters he needed to win were campers.

Of course, Clinton did not always adopt positions because they were popular. He bucked public opinion and many leaders of his own party in his support for NAFTA (the North American Free Trade Agreement) and was again out of step with public opinion in his support for a multibillion-dollar bailout when the Mexican peso collapsed. He also defied public opinion in sending troops to Bosnia. To his surprise, his standing in the polls rose.[67]

George W. Bush expressed disdain for the polling done by the Clinton White House. When asked by a former Clinton press secretary at an informal luncheon what the polls showed about the administration's warnings of nonspecific terrorist threats, Bush responded, "In this White House, we don't poll on something as important as national security."[68] However, the Bush administration does poll on national security and everything else.[69]

As a result of its polling, the Bush administration has mastered the use of "crafted talk." The president proposed partial privatization of Social Security. But his pollsters learned that the word *privatization* scared the public by implying that the government would no longer guarantee a lifetime income, as Social Security does. Instead, the president opted to use such terms as *retirement security, personal accounts, choice,* and *opportunity.* The president also proposed the elimination of the inheritance tax, which was triggered when wealthy people died and left their estates to their heirs. Traditionally this tax was called the estate tax because it was imposed on the people with large estates. But the president and congressional Republicans called it the "death tax" to convey the notion that it was imposed on people when they die—that is, on everyone. In fact, it was imposed on just the wealthiest 1–2 percent. Yet the phrase *death tax* was a rhetorical success, persuading a majority of middle-class Americans to favor its elimination, even though it would never affect them.

Poll findings encouraged the administration to describe President Bush's energy plan as "balanced" and "comprehensive" and one that relies on "modern" methods to prevent environmental damage. The findings also prompted officials to call his proposal to give parents vouchers that would enable them to send their children to private schools "school choice" or "opportunity scholarships" rather than "school vouchers" or "aid to private schools."

Whereas Clinton relied on polls to identify policies with broad public support, Bush relies on them to package and camouflage policies favored by his conservative base so these policies appear more attractive to mainstream voters.[70] Crafted talk enables politicians to move from the center and cater to the views of their more extreme base—all while appearing to remain in the middle.[71]

Crafted talk often comes from the use of **focus groups,** which are small groups of average men and women brought together to share their reactions to candidates or policies or to the language used to refer to them. A focus group is not a scientific poll, and the participants might not be a cross-section of the population, but the process allows political consultants to explore participants' feelings in depth. The consultants search for the language, whether positive toward their side or negative toward the other side, that produces the desired effect on the participants. This language then can be used on the general public; it can be incorporated into speeches or commercials. The same process is employed by market researchers to sell corporations' products.

There are dozens of "word labs," but one of the most effective is run by Republican pollster Frank Luntz. In 2000, he produced a pocket-sized pamphlet called *Right Words* and a four-hundred-page loose-leaf binder called *A Conversation with America* for the Republican Party. Based on his focus groups, Luntz counseled Republicans that *Department of Defense* is preferred to *Pentagon, tax relief* to *tax cuts,* and *climate change* to *global warming.* If the goal is to turn the public away from a policy, he recommends linking it to the supernegatives *Washington* and *IRS.*

In the 2004 campaign, Luntz urged Republican candidates to link Saddam Hussein to weapons of mass destruction (WMDs) and 9/11 at every opportunity. The strategy paid off. Many Americans still believe Saddam Hussein had WMDs (although none have been found) and was involved in 9/11 (although no evidence of this has been found either). The language

does not have to be truthful to produce its desired effect. In an effort to reach women, who tend to favor Democrats, Luntz advises invoking children. In major addresses during the campaign, Bush sprinkled references to children along with *heart, love, dream,* and *hope.*

Luntz told the party faithful that by using emotional language, even without changing their policies, Republicans can have it all. "Like Pavlov's dogs, voters will come running if you ring the right verbal bells."[72]

Focus groups work if participants are similar in their race, income, education, and ideology. If they are similar, they are more comfortable, more free to express their feelings that may lie beneath the surface and rarely be expressed. Such feelings probably would not come out in public opinion polls because most respondents feel an obligation to say socially acceptable things even to their anonymous questioners. Yet such feelings do bubble up when people vote, so the consultants want to know before the campaign.

It makes one wonder whether the phrase "Real Plans for Real People" just popped into George Bush's head or was the brain child of a word lab. Did President Clinton "build the bridge to the twenty-first century" or did he have help?

Polling poses ethical dilemmas for politicians besides encouraging the use of misleading or dishonest language. It tempts some politicians to distort the results of the polls their staffs conduct. Among the pollsters who work for politicians, rather than those who work for the media or independent firms such as Gallup, many work exclusively for members of one political party. Rather than provide accurate information about public opinion, their goal is to present their client in the most favorable light.[73] They may manipulate the

This gimmick may have attracted customers, but it was not a scientific way to measure opinion about President Clinton's impeachment.

wording of questions to benefit their client. The results, when publicized, give the impression that the public thinks something that, in fact, it does not.

The **push poll** is an egregious example of misuse. Here is how push polls work. A pollster for Jones asks whether the person called supports John Jones, Mary Smith, or is undecided in the upcoming congressional election. If the answer is Smith or undecided, the voter is asked a hypothetical question that leaves a negative impression. "If you were told that Smith drives a high-powered sports car at dangerous speeds through residential neighborhoods, would it make a difference in your vote?" The voter is then asked her preference again. Naturally, the level of support for Smith falls a great deal. The goal is to see whether certain "information" can "push" voters away from a candidate or a neutral opinion and toward the candidate favored by those doing the poll.[74] Learning the weaknesses of the opposition has always been a part of politics, but push polls seek to manipulate opinion, and they often distort the facts, including candidates' records.

An even more vicious tactic is to pump thousands of calls into a district or state under the guise of conducting a poll but with the intent of spreading false information about a candidate. Senator John McCain (R-Ariz.) accused the George W. Bush campaign of spreading false information in the guise of a poll in the 2000 South Carolina primary when both were seeking the Republican presidential nomination. Rumors were spread that McCain had become mentally unstable as a result of his imprisonment by the North Vietnamese in the Vietnam War and had fathered an illegitimate black child (in fact, he and his wife had adopted a child). This phony poll halted McCain's momentum, which had been surging until this primary. Both the push poll and the phony poll are violations of polling ethics and corruptions of the political process.

Use by Media

Along with polling by candidates, polls by news organizations have also increased. The number of network-sponsored tracking polls, in which a small number of people are polled on successive evenings throughout a campaign in order to assess changes in the level of voter support, exploded in 2000. Originally used in campaigns to assess the effectiveness of political ads, ABC was the first to use tracking polls in the New Hampshire presidential primary in 1984 to assess the growing strength of Democratic presidential candidate Gary Hart. Based on small samples, no more than two hundred, networks were reluctant to air their results until CNN did so in 1988. In 2000, virtually every news organization of any size featured daily

tracking polls.[75] Tracking polls monitor the movement of candidates during the campaign, who is gaining and who is falling behind. This horse race aspect of the campaign makes a good story and attracts viewers.

The ease of conducting polls explains, in part, their increasing use. Pollsters can conduct a poll at a moment's notice and have results within hours. This ease often leads to abuse. On clearly defined issues where the public has thought about something carefully and holds strong views, such as the vote in an election taking place in a few days, a well-designed poll can provide an accurate picture of the public's views.

Recent presidential eve polls have been accurate. All eight of the election eve polls in the 1996 presidential election predicted the winner. One got it almost exactly right, finding Clinton with a 9 percent advantage over Bob Dole. The president's actual margin of victory was 8.4 percent. The average error was just 1.7 percent.[76]

In 2000, the Democratic and Republican candidates each received 48 percent of the vote, with Gore a half million votes ahead. The election proved too close to call, but all election eve polls predicted the candidates' totals within each poll's margin of error. The pre-election polls in 2004, in spite of some jumping around earlier in the campaign, also had it about right in the final week. The average of fourteen major newspaper and network commercial polls had Kerry at 47.4 percent and Bush at 48.9 percent. The actual vote was 48 percent to 51 percent.[77]

But when the public has not thought much about an issue or where the choices are less than clearly defined, polls rarely provide a meaningful guide to what the public thinks. Poll results reflecting support for candidates seeking office for the first time, or in primary elections, often jump up and down simply because voters do not know much about the candidates.

Even when issues are well defined and opinions are fairly stable, it is increasingly difficult to obtain a sample that provides a representative picture of public opinion. Many respondents refuse to be interviewed,[78] some because they don't want to be bothered, others because they fear they'll be asked to buy something or contribute money. Response rates for telephone surveys have decreased because of extensive cell phone use and call-screening technologies that allow potential respondents to avoid calls altogether.[79] Nonrespondents, those who refuse to be polled or cannot be reached, are an increasing proportion of those called and can be as high as 80 percent. Nonresponse raises concerns among pollsters that the views they record are those of stay-at-homes who are too bored, too infirm, or too lonely to hang up rather than the views of Americans as a whole.[80] However, data from five of the largest polling operations show that those who participate in polls differ little from those who do not, at least on issues that matter to pollsters.[81]

Other problems make it difficult for pollsters to get an accurate reading of public opinion. For example, there is the tendency of some respondents to express an opinion when they do not have one. No one wants to appear uninformed. Some respondents volunteer an answer even though they know little or nothing about a subject. The problem is getting worse as pollsters increasingly probe topics on which the public has no opinion and on which there is little reason to believe it should. For example, pollsters asked citizens whether the levies in New Orleans were strong enough to hold back the surge of a major hurricane and whether the U.S. military has enough troops on the ground in Iraq to win the war.

During presidential elections, **exit polls** have become ubiquitous, and controversial, features of media coverage. Since the 1960s, television networks have used exit polls to project the winners before all of the votes have been counted. Before election day, the networks identify key precincts around the nation. On election day, as voters leave these precincts, pollsters ask them how they voted. Their responses, coupled with early returns and an analysis of how these precincts voted in past elections, are used to project the winner in this election. When enough precincts in a state have been analyzed, the networks "call" the state for the winner.

To reduce costs, the networks jointly contract with one polling service, so they all receive the same data, and usually they all project the same winner about the same time. Because of fierce competition between the networks, however, each tries to beat the others, even if only by minutes.

Usually the exit polls have been accurate, but not always. At 7:50 P.M. on election night in 2000, the networks declared Democratic candidate Al Gore the winner in Florida. Because the election was very close and Florida had many electoral votes, whoever won this state probably would win the election. About 9:30 P.M., the polling service that conducted the exit polls notified the networks to pull back. Florida was "too close to call." At 2:15 A.M. the next morning, the networks declared Republican candidate George W. Bush the winner in Florida and thus the next president of the United States with 271 electoral votes, just one more than needed. They flashed their prepared graphics with a beaming Bush. But as more ballots were counted, Bush's lead in Florida eroded. About 3:30 A.M., the networks again pulled back. Florida again was "too close to call." Despite Dan Rather's assertion that if CBS called a state, "you can put it in the bank," the networks botched their calls two times in one night.

What happened? The election was so close—although Gore had a half million more popular votes, the two candidates almost evenly split the electoral votes—that any errors could affect the results. The polling sample was too small. (The networks, which had been taken over by huge corporations such as General Electric, slashed costs so much that the polling service couldn't sample enough precincts.[82]) Those who were polled were not sufficiently representative of all who voted.[83] (Absentee ballots cast before the election, which tend to be Republican votes, were not included.) And a significant number of voters in one large county who intended to vote for Gore marked their ballots, which were designed in a confusing fashion, in a way that nullified their votes. Of course, they did not realize this, and they told pollsters they voted for Gore. So they were counted as Gore voters in the exit polls but not in the actual tally.

The wrong calls were not merely an embarrassment to the networks. Because the networks initially called Florida for Gore ten minutes before polling places in the state's western panhandle closed, it is possible that a few Republicans on their way to vote might have turned around and gone home. Because the networks later called Florida for Bush, proclaiming him the "forty-third president," it is likely that many people around the country considered Bush the legitimate winner even when the networks eventually decided that the election was too close to call after all. Then in the postelection contest, when the two sides struggled for public support, Gore was put in the position of appearing to take Bush's victory, and his presidency, away from him.

Although the networks vowed to fix the polls, more problems popped up during the 2004 election. Exit polls showed John Kerry beating George Bush by a substantial margin. An aide took the president aside to tell him that he was going to lose. Of course, he did not. The pollsters may have oversampled Kerry voters or undersampled Bush voters by accident.

An alternative explanation is that the actual votes may have been tampered with. Postelection investigations showed some fraud, though not enough to change any state's election results. However, the peculiar, and difficult to explain, finding is that the difference in the Democratic vote between the exit polls and the final tally was greatest in swing states, in areas with electronic voting machines, and in states with Republican governors.[84]

Even accurate and reliable polls can affect politics in a negative way. Poor standing in the polls may discourage otherwise viable candidates from entering a race, leaving the field to others who have less chance of winning or who lack the skills necessary to govern effectively. In 2000, several potential Republican can-

Doubting the Holocaust?

A major problem for pollsters is designing questions that accurately measure opinions. Do you agree that it's not the case that a few words don't make a lot of difference in a poll question? You do, don't you? Questions with a double negative are difficult to understand. Results from such questions are unreliable. Poorly worded questions can confuse respondents and cause pollsters to draw the wrong conclusions.

The point was illustrated in a poll to discover the proportion of Americans who doubt that the *Holocaust* happened. The survey asked the following question: "As you know, the term Holocaust usually refers to the killing of millions of Jews in Nazi death camps during World War II. Does it seem possible or does it seem impossible to you that the Nazi extermination of the Jews never happened?" The results: 22 percent said it was possible that the Holocaust never happened; another 12 percent were not sure. The conclusion: About one-third of the country either doubted that the Holocaust occurred or were uncertain.

Since no reputable historian denies that the Holocaust happened, this "finding" was shocking. Commentators reflected on how the public could be so ill informed regarding a major event, not just of the twentieth century, but of recorded history.

But the wording of the question was the culprit. Another version asked, "Does it seem possible to you that the Nazi extermination of Jews never happened, or do you feel certain that it happened?" This time only 1 percent said it was possible that the Holocaust never happened. Eight percent were unsure, and 90 percent were certain that it happened.

Why the difference? A study of thirteen polls, with estimates of Holocaust doubters ranging from 1 to 46 percent, found that high estimates resulted from confusing language.

SOURCE: Richard Morin, "From Confusing Questions, Confusing Answers," *Washington Post National Weekly Edition*, July 18, 1994, 37.

showed that he could not win (he had been censured by the Senate for unethical conduct).

Additionally, polls can have a negative effect on political campaigns. Prior to polling, the purpose of campaigns was to reveal the candidates' views on the issues and their solutions to the pressing problems of the day. Instead, polls find out what the voters want, and the candidates then adopt positions and develop images to suit the voters. Too often they follow the voters rather than lead them. They consider this strategy safer than trying to educate the public about complex problems or new solutions. Former senator Daniel Patrick Moynihan (D-N.Y.) decried politicians' addiction to poll results. "We've lost our sense of ideas that we stand by, principles that are important to us," he said.[85]

As the number of polls, both good and bad, increases, their importance for the public and, perhaps, politicians may decline. The sheer number of polls may lead everyone to take them less seriously. Moreover, if politicians allow themselves to be driven by poll results and use them to manipulate the public, no one will gain an advantage from the information they provide.[86] Still, it is unlikely that ambitious politicians bent on winning at all costs will abandon something that may help them win.

In spite of problems and abuses, polls still provide a valuable service to the nation. If direct democracy, like the New England town meeting, is the ideal, the use of public opinion polls is about as close as the modern state is likely to get to it. Polls help interpret the meaning of elections. When voters cast their ballots for one candidate over another, all anyone knows for sure is that a majority preferred one candidate. Polls can help reveal what elections mean in terms of policy preferences and thus help make the government more responsive to voters. Republicans claimed their victory in the 1994 congressional elections was an indication that voters supported the party's Contract with America, a series of policies the party vowed to enact if it won a majority in the House. Polls showed that most Americans had never heard of it. While hostility of average Americans toward polls may mean that pollsters will have to work harder to get an accurate picture of public opinion, they remain the best reflection of what Americans think about politics and politicians.

didates passed up the presidential race when early polls suggested that George W. Bush was the odds-on favorite to win the Republican nomination. And, in an unprecedented move, in 2002 Senator Robert Torricelli (D-N.J.) withdrew from his reelection race just thirty-six days before the election when polls

Knowledge and Information

Asking citizens their opinions on matters of public policy, candidates for public office, and the operation and institutions of government presumes they possess sufficient knowledge and information to form opinions and that expressions of opinion reflect real preferences.

Levels of knowledge regarding some basic elements of government suggest sizable numbers of Americans do not have much information. Only one-fourth can name their two senators,[87] and only one-third can name their U.S. representative.[88] More than one-third do not know the party of their representative,[89] and 40 percent do not know which party controls Congress.[90] Prior to the 2004 election, 14 percent incorrectly identified the Democrats as controlling the House and 30 percent confessed that they did not know which party was the majority. Eleven percent incorrectly identified the Democrats as in charge in the Senate, and 38 percent acknowledged that they did not know which party was in charge.[91]

Many Americans are unable to identify prominent political personalities. Six years after he was elected vice president, 24 percent could not identify George H. W. Bush. Eighty-six percent were able to identify the more high-profile figure, Vice President Dick Cheney, prior to his and George W. Bush's re-election in 2004.[92] More people can identify television personalities than major political figures.[93] In spite of increases in education, levels of knowledge regarding politics have not changed much since the 1940s.[94]

Although Americans revere the Constitution and see it as a blueprint for democracy, many do not know what is in it. One-third think it establishes English as the country's official language, and one in six thinks it established America as a Christian nation. One-fourth cannot name a single First Amendment right, and only 6 percent can name all four.[95]

Similarly, most Americans do not keep up with what goes on in Washington, D.C. Only a small percentage of Americans can identify a single piece of legislation passed by Congress.[96]

Misperception regarding government policies is widespread, which means that many members of the public are asking to be manipulated by candidates for office. Although polls showed Americans in favor of reducing the size of the federal government, most have no idea whether the size of government is growing or shrinking.[97] Most Americans feel that the country spends too much on foreign aid and think we should cut its amount, but one-half estimate foreign aid to be about fifteen times greater than it is. Asked what an appropriate spending level would be, the average answer is eight times more than the country spends.[98] In one poll, nearly half of the public had an opinion on a nonexistent Public Affairs Act. Fearing to admit that they had never heard of it, these people gave an opinion anyway, just as they would do on real policies they had never heard of.[99]

Although many may not know the basics of American government, some argue that average citizens know what they need to know to make sound political judgments.[100] Most citizens take an active interest in politics and pay attention when they have a personal stake. Eighty percent know that Congress passed a law requiring employers to provide family leave following the birth of a child or in an emergency. With the war in Iraq and a shaky economy, six in ten Americans reported giving the 2004 presidential election a lot of thought as early as February, much earlier than in 2000. Over half reported more enthusiasm for voting, up 15 percent from 2000.[101] Greater interest and concern may translate into higher turnout.

Some suggest that average Americans rely on cues to direct them to wise decisions.[102] Are things going well or are they "screwed-up"? Is a candidate running an effective campaign? If not, can one expect him or her to run the country? Can a candidate hold his or her own in debates? All are cues reflecting whether or not a candidate can handle the job.

At the same time, lack of knowledge is an impediment to holding government accountable. Those who are less politically knowledgeable find it difficult to sort through the claims and counterclaims of politicians. Some support candidates and policies that work against their self-interest. By their lack of information, they are asking to be manipulated, and they are.[103]

Politicians often contribute to citizen ignorance and misperception. They often avoid discussing issues, especially controversial ones, or worse, mislead by trumpeting suspect or false information. Eight out of ten Americans continued to believe Iraq had weapons of mass destruction despite none being found.[104] Nearly one-half respond that Saddam Hussein was directly involved in carrying out the 9/11 attacks with no evidence supporting such a link.[105] The Bush administration had encouraged these views, orchestrating officials' comments to assert explicitly that Iraq had weapons of mass destruction and to suggest implicitly that Iraq was linked to al-Qaeda. Even when no weapons of mass destruction were found during the war and when no significant link to al-Qaeda was found by the 9/11 Commission, the administration was reluctant to correct the record.[106]

It is hard work to stay informed. It takes time and energy. With work and family, average men and women have little time for politics. But failure to stay informed means that politicians can often ignore what the public wants.

Ideology

Average Americans hold opinions on a variety of different issues. These opinions may be consistent with each other and reflect a broader framework or worldview, what scholars call an **ideology,** or they may be inconsistent and unrelated. One might, for example, express a preference for government assistance to farmers hit by hard times, but oppose it for those out-of-work steelworkers because jobs have been outsourced to a foreign country. This might seem inconsistent because one is favoring government assistance in the first instance but not the second. Or, one might oppose any restrictions on an individual's right to free speech, but be quite strong in his or her view that government should outlaw same-sex marriage. This might seem inconsistent as one favors individual freedom in one instance but not another. However, looked at from other perspectives, neither may be inconsistent. One might believe farmers are essential to the nation's food supply and security, but steelworkers could just as easily be employed in another line of work. Or freedom of speech may be linked to Constitutional guarantees of individual liberty, whereas same-sex marriage may be viewed as a moral issue governed by religious teaching.

Most Americans lack an ideological worldview; that is, they do not have a consistent and coherent set of opinions on political issues. Nor are they consistent in evaluations of candidates for public office or political parties. Yet the major contemporary ideologies, liberalism and conservatism, are useful in thinking about public opinion and understanding the institutions of American politics and political and social conflicts in society.

Liberalism is sometimes identified by the label *left* or *left wing* and conservatism by the label *right* or *right wing*. These terms date from the French National Assembly of the early nineteenth century when liberal parties occupied the left side of the chamber and conservative parties occupied the right.

Liberalism, at least since the 1930s, embodies the notion that government can be a positive and constructive force in society, responsible for assisting individuals, businesses, and communities in dealing with social and economic problems. Franklin Roosevelt and the Democrats' New Deal policies of the 1930s were enacted to relieve the economic hardships of the Great Depression and limit the harsh consequences of an unrestrained free market economy through government regulation and control. Central to liberalism is the belief that government has a responsibility to make life better for average men and women, which necessarily means that the freedom of some, chiefly the wealthy, will be curtailed in some way.

Conservatism, on the other hand, encompasses the notion that individuals and communities are better off without government assistance. Central to conservatism is the belief that the free market should be allowed to function unencumbered by government rules

and regulations, and individuals, rather than the government, are responsible for their own well-being. Short of harming others, individuals should be allowed to do as they please. Consistent with this view, government is necessarily small, and where there is a need for government, it is best if it is at the state or local rather than the more distant federal level. While conservatism subscribes to a diminished role for government, throughout the nation's history it has been associated with the promotion of commercial and business interests that has led at times to large subsidies and other government benefits for businesses, corporations, and favored occupational groups such as farmers.

Advocating government programs to pull the nation out of the Depression, Democrats came to power in 1932 and dominated American politics through the 1960s. There was widespread agreement—indeed, a liberal consensus—that it was the government's job to ensure that all Americans enjoy a certain quality of life. Although Republicans were less enthusiastic in support of government initiatives, both parties subscribed to the notion that the government has a responsibility to reduce the disparity between rich and poor and provide at least a minimal safety net for income and health care.

The consensus began to erode, however, when liberals in the Democratic party pushed for equal rights for African Americans in the 1960s. Civil rights laws proposed by a Democratic president and enacted by liberal Democrats in Congress alienated many white Southerners, whose racial caste system dated from the nation's founding, and drove away many blue-collar ethnic groups, whose members feared increased competition for their jobs and felt the party had abandoned them in favor of blacks. Some elements of the old coalition found policies of the Republican party more attractive, and they increasingly supported conservative Republican candidates (for more on how this played out in political parties, see Chapter 7). In the 1970s, a new set of issues, unrelated to the economy and race, surfaced that added a new dimension to liberalism and conservatism. Many of these issues, such as abortion, are tied to individual rights and personal behavior. **Liberals** believe that such things are best left to individuals to decide for themselves, whereas **conservatives** would like government to impose a standard of behavior—for example, restrict or outlaw abortion and thus prod people to be more responsible about sex. Unlike the economy and race where liberals favor government action to bring about a particular outcome, with respect to abortion, contraceptive rights, and same-sex marriage liberals oppose it. And whereas conservatives object to any government interference in the economy or in pushing equality among the races, they strongly support government restric-

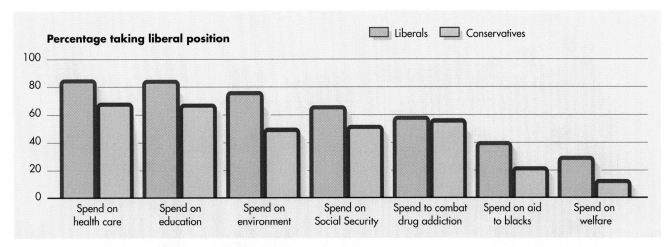

Percentage taking liberal position

☐ Liberals ☐ Conservatives

FIGURE 4.3 ■ Liberals and Conservatives Differ on Spending for Safety Net and Environmental Issues
The proportions are those who want to increase spending on each area.
SOURCE: General Social Survey, 2002 (N's = 602 to 1,301).

tions on abortion, the use of certain contraceptives, and same-sex marriage.

The emergence of such issues, referred to collectively as **the social issue**, resulted in the mobilization of Christian conservatives in the 1980s and 1990s on behalf of conservative, mostly Republican candidates, particularly in the South. In an effort to keep religious conservatives in the Republican camp, President Bush proposed laws that would spend federal money to teach sexual abstinence to teenagers and outlaw same-sex marriages and late term abortions. One commentator dubbed him the "nanny-in-chief" of the "nanny state."[107]

While these broad descriptions capture the core ideas of liberalism and conservatism, individual politicians, political parties, and most Americans reflect them imperfectly. Although Democrats are typically left of center, many take conservative positions on some issues.

President Bill Clinton endorsed a major overhaul of the nation's welfare program, limiting government assistance to families in need, typically considered a conservative position. President George W. Bush, while governing mostly from the right, confounded some conservatives by proposing an expansion of the Medicare program to include a drug benefit for seniors, usually considered a liberal position. Both presidents Clinton and Bush adopted positions from the opposite side of the ideological spectrum in an effort to attract political support from political **moderates**, those who are neither liberals nor conservatives and who hold views in between those of liberals and conservatives (Figure 4.3).

The American people tend to be conservative on some matters and liberal on others. A little more than

a third identify themselves as conservative, and a little more than a fourth identify themselves as liberal. However, more—about 40 percent—identify themselves as moderate or middle of the road.[108]

Public Opinion in Red States and Blue States

The vast majority of Americans are not ideological; that is, they do not possess an all-encompassing worldview. Nonetheless, American opinion has tended to reflect two somewhat different cultures, one more liberal and one more conservative. These divisions have strong historical roots stemming from differences between northerners and southerners going back to the time of America's founding. The Civil War (1861–1865) was a stark manifestation of these divisions. After the Civil War and continuing to this day, the more conservative agrarians in the Midwest have often found themselves in alliance with the southern agrarians against the more liberal urbanites in the East.

In the parlance of the media, the conflict is referred to as the **red states** versus the **blue states** (an updated version of the conflict between the "gray" and "blue" in the Civil War). Others have labeled the divide the "retro" states versus the "metro" ones. The red and blue labels stem from the maps employed on election night by the TV networks in 2000 and 2004 that colored those states that voted Republican for president in red and those that voted Democratic in blue. Figure 4.4 illustrates how most people in each state voted in 2000 and 2004. Presented this way, it appears that the nation is divided with majorities in New England, the upper

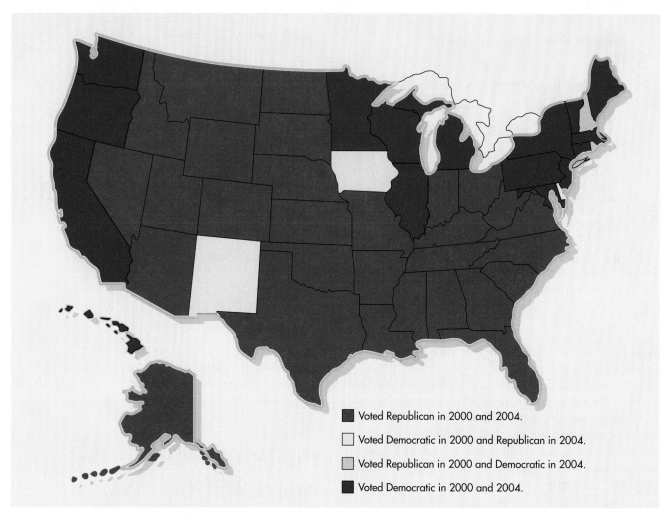

Voted Republican in 2000 and 2004.

Voted Democratic in 2000 and Republican in 2004.

Voted Republican in 2000 and Democratic in 2004.

Voted Democratic in 2000 and 2004.

FIGURE 4.4 ■ Party Strength Displays Geographic Patterns

Midwest, and the West Coast supporting the Democrats and most voters in the South, the Border and Plains states, and the Rocky Mountain West supporting the Republicans. The red states comprise most of the landmass of the United States, but are more rural and sparsely populated than the blue states, which include many of the metropolitan centers.

Red versus blue provides an interesting story line for journalists and pundits. It reduces the election outcome to a simple and intriguing explanation and one that is easily grasped by average Americans. Conservative red America has been described as religious, moralistic, patriotic, white, masculine, and less educated. Liberal blue America has been depicted as secular, relativistic, internationalist, multicultural, feminine, and college educated. Reds are seen as supporting guns, the death penalty, and the Iraq War, blues as supporting abortion and the environment. According to the stereotypes, in red America Saturday's pastime is NASCAR; Sunday's is church. In blue America, Saturday is for the farmer's market, and Sunday is for reading the *New York Times*.[109]

There are differences between red states and blue states. Religion is one difference. The red states encompass the Bible Belt, a broad area of the country where most people identify with a religion and evangelical Protestants are common. This area comprises most of the South and parts of Kansas and Missouri. In contrast, the West Coast and parts of the Southwest are much more secular. Forty-four percent of those living in red states identify themselves as born-again Christians; only 26 percent in blue states do. Many fewer people in the blue states identify with any religious organization. A much smaller margin separates church attendance patterns, because only a minority of red staters and blue staters attend church weekly, though somewhat more of red staters do.[110] These religion differences are significant, because in recent national elections, born again Christians and regular church attenders have been more likely to vote Republican than those with less religious faith.

In addition to religion differences, there are other differences that reflect more conservative values in the red states. For example, women are less active in politics and less likely to hold political office in red states. Similarly, women have lower incomes and are less likely to be managers and professionals than in the blue states. Red states impose more restrictions on abortion and incorporate more abstinence education in sex education classes (see Table 4.2).

In addition to these value differences, there are employment-related differences. Red states are more hostile to labor unions, so they have adopted laws that enable many companies to avoid unionizing their workforce. Wal-Mart, which began in Arkansas and then spread through the South, does everything in its power to keep its workers from forming or joining unions. In contrast, blue states are more hospitable to labor unions. Cities such as New York, Chicago, and San Francisco are union bastions. Another employment-related difference is that red states have fewer jobs tied to new technologies.[111]

For the 2004 election, the stereotypes were on full display. During the spring primaries, a conservative interest group ran a commercial opposing the candidacy of Howard Dean, Vermont's governor, who was running for the Democratic nomination for president. In the commercial, average people advised Dean to "take his tax-hiking, government-expanding, latte-drinking, sushi-eating, Volvo-driving, *New York Times*-reading, body-piercing, Hollywood-loving, left-wing freak show back to Vermont, where it belongs." During the fall campaign, John Kerry, the Democratic nominee from "Taxachusetts," was derided for his ability to speak French (and for his preference for Swiss cheese over Cheese Whiz?).

Based on such differences, in the aftermath of the 2004 election, one commentator declared that "the red states get redder, the blue states get bluer, and the politi-

Long before the media coined the terms "red states" and "blue states," differences in values and culture were evident between rural and urban America. One issue in the 1920s, as in the twenty-first century, was evolution. When Tennessee (and fourteen other states) banned the teaching of evolution or other theories challenging Divine creation, John Scopes, a biology teacher, tested the law. Clarence Darrow, a Chicago lawyer, defended Scopes, while William Jennings Bryan, the Nebraska senator and Democratic presidential candidate, testified for the state of Tennessee against the idea of evolution. In this photo, Darrow is appropriately on the left and Bryan on the right.

cal map of the United States takes on the coloration of the Civil War."[112] One adviser to President Bush commented, "You've got 80 percent to 90 percent of the country that look at each other like they are on separate planets."[113] Conservatives sneer at blue staters for being chardonnay-sipping elitists out of touch with average

| TABLE 4.2 | State Laws Affecting Reproductive and Homosexual Rights |

An analysis of twenty-five categories of state laws affecting reproductive and homosexual rights, ranging from laws restricting contraception and abortion to laws recognizing same-sex partnerships, found sharp differences among the states. The states with the most restrictive laws were all red states, and the states with the most permissive laws were almost all blue states. (New Mexico was the exception, although it voted Democratic in 2000 and nearly did so again in 2004.)

Most Restrictive States	Most Permissive States
Ohio and South Dakota (tied for most restrictive)	New York and New Mexico (tied for most permissive)
Indiana	New Jersey
North Dakota	Washington
Oklahoma	California
Mississippi	Vermont
Kentucky	Massachusetts
Utah	New Hampshire
Nebraska	Connecticut
Missouri	Hawaii

SOURCE: Analysis conducted by the National Gay and Lesbian Task Force and two pro-choice groups—Ipas and the SisterSong Women of Color Reproductive Health Collective. David Crary, "In Gay, Reproductive Rights Rankings, S. Dakota, Ohio Last," *Lincoln Journal Star*, June 1, 2006, 4A.

people, while liberals deride red staters for being beer-guzzling, gun-toting rednecks. However, these stereotypes are exaggerated and lack historical context.

In each state there is a mix of values and opinions, as Senator Barack Obama (D-Ill.) so eloquently stated at the Democratic National Convention. "We worship an awesome God in the blue states, and we don't like federal agents poking around our libraries in the red states. We coach Little League in the blue states and have gay friends in the red states. There are patriots who opposed the war in Iraq and patriots who supported it. We are one people, all of us pledging allegiance to the Stars and Stripes, all of us defending the United States of America."

Indeed, polling data confirm a mix of opinions and reveal surprisingly little difference between red and blue. Citizens in red states are only slightly more conservative than those in blue states. And as Figure 4.5 shows, majorities in red states are usually on the same side of various issues as majorities in blue states.

And although many in the media, based on exit polls, pointed to "moral values" as the reason for George W. Bush's victory in 2004, further analysis revealed that moral values were no more likely to be mentioned as a reason for voting Republican than in either of the two previous elections. When voters identified their main concerns in the election, they were much more likely to mention war and terrorism than moral values. Among those who did cite moral values, one-fourth to one-third voted for Kerry.

The relative absence of clear-cut divisions appears even in personal contexts. When unmarried Americans were asked whether they would be "open to marrying someone who held significantly different political views" from their own, 57 percent said they would.[114]

Like other simple story lines about politics, the characterizations of the states contain some truth but are exaggerated. They apply to a minority of the populations in the red and blue states. They apply most clearly to political activists and political junkies—the people who are the most involved and most interested in politics. These partisans in both parties are sharply divided, and increasingly so.[115]

The characterizations increasingly apply to elected officials, who themselves increasingly are polarized.[116] Most are nominated in primaries, and primaries are dominated by the more extreme members of their parties. Only 15 percent of the public votes in primary elections, and these are the most partisan voters. Republican candidates have to appease conservatives in their party, whereas Democratic candidates have to appease liberals in their party. Moreover, with little competition in most congressional districts, the more extreme and polarized views are not effectively challenged. And the campaign finance system may contribute to the polarized atmosphere by rewarding those candidates whose allegiance to a single issue or cause is most fierce.

The media also contribute to the sense that the nation is divided. The media tend to frame issues as debates and elections as contests between two sharply opposing sides. With the proliferation of cable TV channels, talk radio shows, and Internet blogs, the public can tune to those voices, and only those voices, that they agree with. This prompts the media to enlist the voices who are extreme in their positions and hostile to the opposition. The moderating effect of having three national networks, whose newscasts were not targeted toward any segment of the audience, has nearly disappeared.

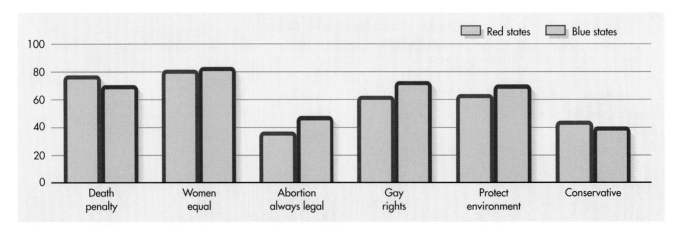

FIGURE 4.5 ■ Red- and Blue-State Voters Have Similar Opinions on Many Controversial Issues *These are proportions of voters who (1) favor the death penalty; (2) believe in equal women's role; (3) believe abortion should be legal under all conditions; (4) oppose discrimination against gays and lesbians; (5) believe we should do whatever it takes to protect the environment; and (6) see themselves as conservative.*
SOURCE: 2002 Pew National Survey reported in Fiorina, 2005.

Public Opinion toward Race

Public opinion has influenced, as well as responded to, the progress of the African American struggle for equality. Polls extending as far back as the 1940s show white America increasingly opposed to discrimination and segregation, at least in principle.[117] In fact, the change might be characterized as revolutionary. Whereas only one-third of whites accepted the idea of black and white children going to the same schools in 1942, in the 1980s more than 90 percent approved. Today nearly everyone approves. Over 80 percent respond that they have no objection to sending their children to schools where more than half of the students are black. Nearly two-thirds say they would not object to schools where most of the students are black.

The percentage of people believing that whites have a right to keep African Americans out of their neighborhoods has been cut in half since 1963.[118] Thirty-eight percent of whites were against laws forbidding interracial marriage in 1963; 85 percent were opposed in 1996.[119] Most Americans say they would vote for a black candidate for president.

Public opinion can change because individuals change or because older individuals with one set of opinions are replaced by a new generation with a different set of opinions. Changes in whites' racial opinions through the 1960s occurred for both reasons. Older whites with more stereotyped views of blacks were replaced by a younger generation who were more tolerant. At the same time, the civil rights movement promoted a reconsideration of many Americans' views about race.

With political activists and public officials generally representing the more extreme views in their party, and the media usually emphasizing those views and characterizing opposing views as un-American, it is not surprising that our political debate has become more polarized despite the fact that the average American is not extreme in either direction.

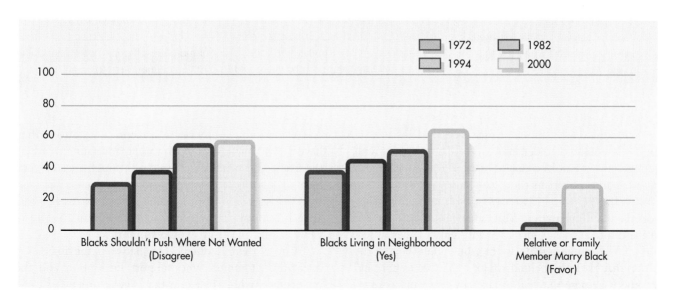

FIGURE 4.6 ■ Whites Have Grown More Accepting of Blacks

Source: General Social Survey, Selected Years (N's range from 1,130 in 1990 to 2,070 in 2000). Data from whites only.

A GOVERNMENT REBATE
AS A FAILED PANACEA

Members of Congress received an earful from irate constituents in spring, 2006. Voters were upset with the prolonged war in Iraq and seeming lack of a plan for withdrawal, concerned about the economy, irritated by reports of public officials under investigation for corruption, but most of all irate about the rise in gas prices. In fact, 75 percent said that they were "angry about the recent increases in gasoline prices." And while most of them were mad at the gas and oil companies (50 percent), 26 percent were angry with the Bush administration and another 21 percent with government in general. Only 17 percent approved of the way "George W. Bush is handling the issue of gasoline prices," and even fewer thought he had a plan to deal with the rising prices.[1]

Then Exxon Mobil announced its corporate profits for the previous year—$36.13 billion—which were the highest corporate profits in history. Its president was paid $250,000 a week.[2] A product of increasing demand throughout the world and in the United States, along with oil supplies that are not expanding fast enough to meet the demand, oil prices have skyrocketed. They were $20 a barrel when the Bush administration took over, and by spring,

2006, were over $70 a barrel. Rising oil prices translate into higher gasoline prices at the pumps.

Although the administration got blamed for the high prices, most of the increase was not of its making. The demand for energy by the Chinese and Indians has grown substantially due to economic development and improving standards of living there. More people in China and India own cars and have electricity. And few new oil deposits have been found in the past twenty years. The Bush administration has proposed drilling for oil in Alaska's Arctic National Wildlife Refuge but has been stymied by majorities in Congress, including most Democrats and some Republicans, who fear damage to the Alaskan wilderness. Regardless, even if we were to drill as much oil as geologists say is possible and do so for ten years, these deposits would only provide a six-month supply of our needs.

Of course, the Bush administration is partly responsible for the problem. The war in Iraq and subsequent sabotage of Iraqi oilfields has cut back oil production in that country and has worried the markets by threatening the stability of the Middle East. Furthermore, both Bush and Cheney were in the oil industry before holding their current offices, and both have worked

to promote the oil companies' interests. Reducing the demand for oil has not been their goal. Until recently, the administration strongly opposed conservation measures such as higher mileage standards for cars or tax incentives for producing more fuel-efficient cars. Vice President Cheney even said that conservation was simply a sign of personal virtue, not a goal of public policy.[3]

But faced with plunging popularity and increased public anxiety, Congress and the administration believed they must act. The public favored several moves, including price controls on gasoline, suspension of the taxes on gasoline, imposition of more taxes on the profits of oil companies, and even breaking up big American oil companies. Most members of Congress do not believe that any of these ideas will solve the problem. Reducing taxes on gas, for instance, would increase rather than decrease demand. Moreover, conservative Republicans would rather undergo root canals than hike taxes on oil companies, let alone break them up. And almost all politicians are loathe to increase taxes on gasoline to drive down demand and encourage consumers to trade in their cars, SUVs, and pickups for more fuel-efficient models. But doing nothing did not seem to be an option

---

Since the 1970s, most changes occurred because of the replacement of older, more prejudiced whites with younger, less prejudiced ones. Differences in socialization between those born in the 1920s and 1930s and those born in the 1950s and 1960s have led to much greater support for racial integration. More change can be expected in the future as today's teens age and replace older Americans. For example, a majority of white adults believe the reason that blacks lag behind whites in jobs, education, and income is because they fail to take advantage of opportunities available to all, whereas a large plurality of white teens believe discrimination by whites is responsible.[120]

While white Americans accept integration, they have been much slower to accept government initiatives to achieve it. For example, although racially segregated schools often are in poor central city areas and offer inferior education, busing to achieve racial balance in schools has never had much appeal to whites. Only about one-third would support it.

Why is there a discrepancy between the increasing majorities of whites who support integration and the majorities who believe that government should not make special efforts to help minorities? In some cases, unwillingness on the part of whites to endorse

By permission of Mike Luckovich and Creators Syndicate, Inc.

when constituents were clamoring for them to do something.

From this dilemma came a proposal to give consumers a $100 check as a token rebate on increased fuel prices. Fearing that Democrats might get out in front of the issue with their own proposal of an even larger rebate and expecting a wave of public support for a free $100, Bill Frist (R-Tenn.), Senate majority leader, proposed a rebate, announcing that it would be sent to 100 million Americans as part of an overall program including drilling in the Arctic refuge and repealing tax incentives benefiting energy companies. Other Republicans, including some facing tight elections in the fall, such as John

Thune (R-S.D.) and Rick Santorum (R-Pa.), joined Frist. Because of his position as majority leader and his presidential aspirations, Frist wanted to take the lead. Providing a small bonanza for every taxpaying family seemed like a good move to further these ambitions.

But the public reaction was scathing. Congressional offices received thousands of calls and e-mails lambasting the idea. Conservative talk show hosts ridiculed the plan; Rush Limbaugh said the senators were "treating us like we were a bunch of whores."[4] Just days later, the senators began to backpedal, and the House majority leader John Boehner (R-Oh.) said the measure was "insulting" and voters thought it was "stupid."[5]

Later, Frist's Republican colleagues claimed that they were never consulted. Some even argued that they had opposed it before it was announced. John Cornyn (R-Texas) probably spoke for several when he stated that "It appeared to be a nonserious response

to a serious problem."[6] By the end of the news cycle, not one senator was willing to take credit (or blame) for the idea.

In reflecting on the sequence of events, a journalist wrote, "A wonderful thing happened in Washington last week. Both political parties tried to bribe the American people past their anger over high gasoline prices, and the public response was a collective guffaw."[7] Although the public did want something done about the prices, they realized that the proposal was purely political pandering.

[1] These late April, 2006 polls are drawn from Polling Report.com/energy.htm. The questions about anger are from *USA Today*/Gallup polls, and the approval and disapproval of Bush policies is from CBS News Poll.
[2] Dorothy Wickenden, "Comment: Fuel Duel," *New Yorker*, May 22, 2006, 28.
[3] Richard Benedetto, "Cheney's Energy Plan Focuses on Production," *USA Today*, May 1, 2001. http://www.usatoday.com/news/washington/2001-05-01-cheney-usat.htm.
[4] Sheryl Gay Stolbert and Carl Hulse, "$100 Rebate: Rise and Fall of a G.O.P. Idea," *New York Times* May 5, 2006.
[5] "The Path of a Doomed Idea," *New York Times* (May 5, 2006), www.nytimes.com/imagepages/ 2006/05/05/washigton/20060505_REBATE_GRAP. Boehner later said that he didn't realize it was Frist's idea.
[6] Stolbert and Hulse, "$100 Rebate."
[7] Joe Klein, "Doing Something Hard the Smart Way," *Time* (May 15, 2006), 21.

government initiatives to end segregation reflects racist sentiments.[121] Although only 10 percent of white Americans respond that differences in jobs, housing, and income between whites and blacks are the result of biological differences,[122] 43 percent cling to the racist belief that it is lack of motivation and will power on the part of blacks.[123] Thus, anywhere from 10 to 40 percent of white Americans harbor racist beliefs in spite of their willingness to accept blacks, live in integrated neighborhoods, and have their children attend integrated schools.

However, some whites oppose government help for blacks on principle. They object to being told what

to do by government or feel government assistance for blacks is discrimination against whites. For some, government help violates their sense that individuals have a responsibility to provide for themselves.

Another reason that some white Americans are reluctant to accept government intervention is that many do not see the need. African Americans and white Americans live in very different perceptual worlds. Anywhere from 40 to 60 percent of whites believe that the average African American is as well or better off than the average white American in their schooling, job, income, and health care.[124] This is a direct contradiction to the reality that blacks lag behind whites on virtually every social and economic indicator. But misperceptions such as these lead many whites to reject any government effort to equalize the social and economic standing of the races. Whites who more accurately recognize the plight of black Americans are more likely to accept the government's role in providing equal education for black and white children and ensuring that blacks are treated equally by courts and police.[125]

Blacks, not unexpectedly, see things differently. A majority view themselves trailing whites in education, income, jobs, and health care, and of course this is the reality.[126] Moreover, 44 percent believe that they personally have been denied a job or promotion because of race.[127]

Like whites, African Americans have become somewhat less supportive of government initiatives. In 1964, 92 percent thought the federal government should ensure blacks fair treatment in jobs; by 1996, only 64 percent did. Support for government assistance in school integration has also declined. Some blacks fear that government initiatives will only antagonize whites. Others believe government aid hurts blacks by making them too dependent. Still others believe government is ineffective in bringing about an end to discrimination.

Conclusion: Is Government Responsive to Public Opinion?

In a democracy, government should be responsive to the wishes of the people. Those wishes, collectively, comprise public opinion. But is government responsive?

The most direct way to assess whether public policy is responsive to public opinion is to compare changes in policy with changes in opinion. A major study examined several hundred public opinion surveys conducted over a forty-five year period. From these surveys, the researchers culled the questions that asked about particular policies and that had been asked more than once. Public opinion had changed for more than three hundred of these questions. The researchers compared the changes in these opinions with changes in government policies. They found that when opinions changed, policies also changed for more than two-thirds of the opinions. The policy changes matched the opinion changes especially when the opinion changes were large and stable (and when the opinion changes moved in a liberal direction).

The researchers concluded that the policy changes may have caused the opinion changes about half of the time. However, the opinion changes probably caused the policy changes, or they both affected each other, the rest of the time. On important issues, when changes in public opinion were clear-cut, policy usually became consistent with opinion.[128]

Yet policy isn't as consistent with opinion now as it used to be. Twenty years ago congressional laws reflected public opinion polls about 60 percent of the time; more recently the figure is 40 percent.[129] This change may reflect the growing polarization among public officials and political activists. This change may also reflect the gerrymandering of legislative districts, which provides most members of the House of Representatives with a safe seat—either safely Republican and conservative or safely Democratic and liberal. They don't have to cater to centrist opinion in their district as much as they did in the past.[130]

Public officials also pay attention to the intensity of public opinion. Elected officials may support a minority opinion that is intensely held. President Bush continues to push tax cuts, whereas a majority of Americans prefer their tax dollars be used to reduce the deficit or fund social programs.[131] The president is responding to his core constituency that strongly favor tax cuts. A minority with intense feelings is more likely to make financial contributions, provide campaign help, and ultimately vote for a candidate who does what they want or against a candidate who does the opposite than is a majority with weaker feelings.

There are other reasons why public policy may not reflect public opinion. Interest groups, political parties, and public officials' own preferences influence policy, and they may not agree with public opinion. Some observers worry that political activists and interest groups manipulate public opinion through the increasingly intrusive media, which distort the issues and blind the public to their own self-interest.

Some observers think that politicians pay too much attention to public opinion, to the point that leaders, fearful of offending the majority of the public, do not lead but simply follow the latest polls like dieters follow faddish diets.

Even when public opinion accurately reflects the public's real attitudes, this opinion is not sacred. When a majority favors a course of action, this may not be the most desirable course to take. The Founders didn't want public opinion necessarily to become public policy. They established a federal system with separation of powers and checks and balances to ensure that the majority, in the heat of the moment, cannot work its will easily. In our system, therefore, we should not expect public policy to match public opinion always. However, the fact that governmental policy usually reflects majority opinion, especially when that opinion is large and stable, does indicate that the government generally is responsive.

Senator Frist Provided Another Diagnosis

enator Frist urged Congress to pass the law that would pressure the federal courts to intervene and overturn the state courts in the Terri Schiavo case. In doing so, he used his medical expertise to make a medical judgment. He declared that the doctors who had examined Terri Schiavo had been mistaken when they said she was in a persistent vegetative state. "I question it based on a review of the video footage which I spent an hour or so looking at last night in my office. . . . She certainly seems to respond to visual stimuli."[132] His lengthy statement referenced several medical standards.

His statement cheered conservative activists involved in the case. A conservative leader applauded Frist's action as a courageous move because he was "willing to go to the mat for one handicapped individual in Florida."[133]

But Frist's statement subjected him to ridicule from others. Doctors pointed out that relying on amateur videotapes, heavily edited, to make a diagnosis and overruling specialists who had examined her carefully in person is not good medical practice. One medical ethicist expressed surprise at his statement because after 15 years "there should be no confu-

sion about the medical data."[134] Moreover, Frist is not a neurologist and has no special expertise in the human brain. One Democratic activist jibed, "I suspect that Senator Frist has his eye more on the Iowa caucus than the Hippocratic Oath," and another one declared, "It'd be hilarious if it weren't so grotesque."[135]

Indeed, a staffer for a Republican member of Congress had circulated a memo proclaiming, "This is a great political issue."[136] Siding with the parents would not only rally pro-life forces but also demonize the courts in preparation for the anticipated vacancies on the Supreme Court and the confirmation fights that would ensue.

So, on Palm Sunday, a few days after Senator Frist's statement, Congress passed a resolution transferring jurisdiction of the case to the federal courts. For the first time, President Bush interrupted a break at his ranch and rushed back to Washington to sign the bill.

Despite Congress' efforts, the federal courts still rejected the Schindlers' appeals, and the Supreme Court again refused to hear the case. A federal appeals court judge wrote, "It is my judgment that, despite sincere and altruistic motivation, the legislative

and executive branches of our government have acted in a manner demonstrably at odds with our Founding Fathers' blueprint for the governance of a free people . . . our Constitution."[137]

The tube was removed and Terri Schiavo died from dehydration thirteen days later. The autopsy clearly indicated that her brain had been destroyed. It was discolored, scarred, shriveled to half its normal size, and damaged everywhere. The damage, according to the pathologist, "was irreversible . . . no amount of treatment or rehabilitation would have reversed it."[138] She was also blind, so she could not have responded to visual stimuli, despite the impression left by the photos and videos.

One mystery remained, however. There was no evidence about what had caused her to suffer cardiac arrest and collapse in the first place, fifteen years earlier.

Meanwhile, the public overwhelmingly opposed congressional intervention. Republicans, attempting to appeal to their base of Christian conservatives, offended many moderates by trying not only to overrule state action but to intrude in a matter between the family and their physicians, which most Americans want to keep private. The specter of the federal government moving in on such a private matter was offensive to most. Seventy percent disapproved of Congress's action, including a large majority of Republicans and a small majority of evangelical Christians.[139] Some commentators, watching the free fall of support for the president and Congress in the polls through the rest of 2005 and into 2006, saw the Schiavo case as the beginning of the fall.

One benefit did result from the hullabaloo. The case prompted millions of Americans to ponder their fate and to write living wills.

 To learn more about Terri Schiavo, go to "you are there" exercises for this chapter on the text website.

...SHE HELPED ME CONFRONT DIFFICULT ISSUES...

...SHE COMPELLED ME TO THINK ABOUT MY OWN MORTALITY...

...SHE EDUCATED ME ON THE ROLE OF COURTS AND POLITICIANS...

...SHE ENLIGHTENED ME ABOUT THE IMPORTANCE OF A LIVING WILL...

...SHE REMINDED ME ABOUT THE ENDLESS LOVE OF PARENTS...

WITHOUT EVER SAYING A WORD.

MATT HANDELSMAN
©2005
Newsday

Key Terms

public opinion

political socialization

agents of political socialization

straw polls

focus groups

push poll

exit polls

ideology

liberalism, liberals

conservatism, conservatives

the social issue

moderates

red states

blue states

Further Reading

Herbert Asher, *Polling and the Public: What Every Citizen Should Know* (Washington, D.C.: CQ Press, 2004). Asher provides an introduction to polling methodology, a discussion on the influence of polls on American politics, and advice to citizens on how to evaluate polls.

William Shakespeare, *Coriolanus*. In this most politically focused of Shakespeare's plays, a Roman politician who doesn't pander to public opinion meets a surprising fate.

Thomas Frank, *What's the Matter with Kansas? How Conservatives Won the Heart of America* (New York: Metropolitan Books, 2004). Frank explains why many blue-collar Americans in the heartland vote against their economic interests.

Susan Herbst, *Numbered Voices: How Opinion Polling Has Shaped American Politics* (Chicago: University of Chicago Press, 1993). This text is a historical review of the way public opinion has been measured and the way the evolution of measurement techniques has affected the definition of public opinion.

Lawrence R. Jacobs and Robert Y. Shapiro, *Politicians Don't Pander: Political Manipulation and the Loss of Democratic Responsiveness* (Chicago: University of Chicago Press, 2000). The authors provide an examination of how politicians use polls to craft language that will make policies that the public would likely reject acceptable to the public.

Celinda C. Lake, *Public Opinion Polling: A Handbook for Public Interest and Citizen Advocacy Groups* (Washington, D.C.: Island Press, 1987). This source includes a step-by-step treatment for lay audiences on how to conduct a public opinion poll.

Thomas E. Mann and Gary R. Orren, eds., *Media Polls and American Politics* (Washington, D.C.: Brookings Institution, 1992). Several essays focus on the influence of media-conducted polls on American political institutions and elections.

Benjamin I. Page and Robert Y. Shapiro, *The Rational Public: Fifty Years of Trends in Americans' Policy Preferences* (Chicago: University of Chicago Press, 1992). This book is an examination of the influence of public opinion on public policy using public opinion polling information generated over the past fifty years.

For Viewing

Outfoxed (2004). This documentary is a revealing but negative portrayal of the Republican bias of Fox news and how it shapes opinion.

12 Angry Men (1957). This classic film shows the power of persuasion as seen in a fictional jury room.

The Oxbow Incident (1943). The film demonstrates mob opinion at work.

 ## Electronic Resources

Many polling firms and media polls have home pages. Here is a sampling of some of the more reputable ones.

http://www.ropercenter.uconn.edu
The Roper Center website contains information on the current and past presidents' job performance and a listing of current Roper surveys.

http://www.harrisinteractive.com/harris_poll/index .asp?
The Louis Harris Center archive website links to current and past Harris surveys. Frequencies are available for all questions, and information can be downloaded and analyzed.

http://www.umich.edu/~nes/
The National Election Studies of the University of Michigan website provides access to the most recent national election study. This information can be analyzed online.

http://www.washingtonpost.com/wp-srv/politics/ polls/vault/vault.htm
This site links to polls conducted by the Washington Post.

http://www.abcnews.go.com/sections/politics/ PollVault/PollVault.html
The website links to ABC Television News surveys.

http://www.people-press.org
The Pew Center website provides recent polling information.

ThomsonNOW™

Enter ThomsonNOW™ using the access card that is available with this text or through www.thomsonedu.com/thomsonnow. ThomsonNOW™ will assist you in understanding the content in this chapter with a personalized study plan generated for your needs. A practice test will assess the areas you need to review and provide the tools to fully comprehend those concepts, including an integrated digital eBook, interactive simulations, timelines, video case studies, MicroCase exercises, and InfoTrac College Edition readers and exercises. You'll also be connected to the learning objectives, chapter outline, chapter glossary, flash cards, crossword puzzles, Internet activities, and interactive quizzes found on the companion website.

Admiral Mike Boorda and his controversial ribbons.

The Media State

    Dominance of the Media

    Concentration of the Media

    Atomization of the Media

Relationship between the Media and Politicians

    Symbiotic Relationship

    Adversarial Relationship

    Relationship between the Media and Recent Administrations

    Relationship between the Media and Congress

    Relationship between the Media and the Supreme Court

    Relationship between the Media and the Military

Bias of the Media

    Political Bias

    Commercial Bias

Impact of the Media on Politics

    Impact on the Public Agenda

    Impact on Political Parties and Elections

    Impact on Public Opinion

Conclusion: Are the Media Responsive?

YOU ARE THERE

Should You Torpedo the Admiral?

You are Evan Thomas, the Washington bureau chief of *Newsweek* magazine, and it is 1996. One of your contributors is proposing an exposé about an admiral who has worn medals he is not authorized to wear. The story could make a big splash in military, political, and publishing circles. You have to decide whether to pursue it.[1]

Admiral Mike Boorda is chief of naval operations (CNO)—the highest-ranking admiral in the United States Navy. The son of Ukrainian immigrants, he enlisted as a seventeen-year-old in 1956, and almost four decades later he reached the top. His appointment by President Bill Clinton broke several precedents. Boorda became the first CNO who had been an enlisted man, the first who had not graduated from the Naval Academy, and the first who was Jewish.

Boorda is devoted to his sailors. Every time he visits a ship or base, he holds a session to respond to the sailors' questions and complaints. He tries to show the sailors that he understands their jobs. He learned how to fly helicopters and fighter planes as well as handle ships, including battleships.

Boorda also knows how to navigate the treacherous waters of politics. He has forged ties with members of Congress and has developed skills in negotiating. Before becoming CNO, he demonstrated his talent for diplomacy by persuading UN, NATO, and U.S. commands to work together in Bosnia. (In Sarajevo, he once slipped away from UN officials and showed up in the trenches and buildings of the Serb and Muslim fighters. To their surprise, he explained, "It's the American way. We talk to each other.")

But the admiral has come under attack from traditionalists in the navy. When he implemented new policies developed by civilians in Washington, such as allowing women to serve on combat ships and fly combat planes and encouraging toleration of homosexuals (under the "don't ask, don't tell" policy, which will be explained in Chapter 14), he was upbraided for trying to make the policies work rather than attempting to resist them.

He has been criticized by retired admirals, who wield clout like an interest group, and by current officers for helping enlisted sailors with their problems. They say he is usurping the authority of ship and base commanders. And he has even been chastised for driving his own car rather than using a chauffeur as other admirals do. They say he is eroding the prestige of the admirals.

A former secretary of the navy in the Reagan administration who opposed women attending the Naval Academy and serving in combat units gave a fiery speech at the academy accusing Boorda of sacrificing navy traditions for political correctness. Excerpts were printed in the *Washington Times,* a conservative newspaper, and the *San Diego Union-Tribune,* a prominent newspaper covering navy issues. Criticisms were also printed in the *Navy Times,* a newspaper circulating throughout the navy.

After two years as CNO, Boorda has been under so much pressure that he recently told his family he will not finish the two years remaining in his term.

Amid this controversy, a Washington correspondent for the National Security News Service, which, like similar organizations with a political agenda and foundation funding, locates specialized information that it passes on to bigger media, received a tip that Boorda had worn medals he might not have been authorized to wear. The correspondent contacted a friend, David Hackworth, a retired army officer who was highly decorated and who has sharply criticized the military's "medal inflation" (as some college professors have complained about grade inflation).

After Hackworth had written a popular autobiography, he had been appointed a contributing editor of *Newsweek.* In competition with *Time* for readers, *Newsweek* had sought prominent people, such as Hackworth, who would contribute occasional articles.

Hackworth examined photos of Boorda in his uniform and concluded that the admiral should not have worn a small *V* on two ribbons from the Vietnam War. Although he was entitled to wear the ribbons, he might not have been entitled to wear the *V,* which stands for *valor* and is reserved for troops who face fire in combat. Yet later photos of Boorda show that he stopped wearing the *V.* Still, Hackworth, who is motivated by a desire to expose wrongdoing by generals and admirals, thinks he has a story. Researching regulations at the Pentagon, he confided to some officers that he is working on a story that will bring down an admiral.

Hackworth contacted the editor of *Newsweek,* informing him of the story and telling him that it could be "a real career ender" for the admiral. The editor referred the story to you, as Washington bureau chief of the magazine, and reserved a page in the next issue if you decide to run it. You met with the correspondent for the National Security News Service, who showed the photos and explained the navy's regulations to you.

You are uneasy, wary of both the correspondent for the National Security News Service and Hackworth. Neither is a regular reporter in your bureau. Neither, in fact, is an experienced

reporter. You told a fellow editor, "There's something about this story that is too good to be true. Stories are never this neat." You consulted with a senior correspondent who specializes in national defense for the magazine. He noted that the navy's regulations concerning the *V* had changed during the war, possibly reflecting the navy's confusion over its regulations, so perhaps Boorda had not worn the *V* improperly or had not done so intentionally.

Do you run Hackworth's article exposing Boorda?

Do you first seek clarification from the navy to determine whether the *V* was actually improper? Or do you question Boorda to determine whether he was honestly mistaken? If so, do you still run the article?

If you run the article, do you balance your findings of wrongdoing with information about Boorda's contributions to the navy in his forty years of service?

Or do you reject the article, because Boorda no longer wears the *V*?

You are mindful of the competition with *Time* and realize that this story would be a real scoop and could make a big splash for *Newsweek.* You also realize that the editor has reserved a page for this story, yet you do have discretion.

A *medium* transmits something. The mass media—which include newspapers, magazines, books, radio, television, movies, records, and the Internet—transmit communications to masses of people.

Although the media do not constitute a branch of government or even an organization established to influence government, such as a political party or an interest group, they have an impact on government. In addition to providing entertainment, the media provide information about government and politics. This chapter focuses on the news media—the part of the media that delivers the news about government and politics.

The Media State

The media have developed and flourished to an extent the Founders could not have envisioned. As one political scientist noted, the media have become "pervasive . . . and atmospheric, an element of the air we breathe."[2] Without exaggeration, another observer concluded, "Ancient Sparta was a military state. John Calvin's Geneva was a religious state. Mid–nineteenth-century England was Europe's first industrial state, and the contemporary United States is the world's first media state."[3]

Americans spend more time being exposed to the media than doing anything else. In a year, according to one calculation, the average full-time worker puts in 1824 hours on the job, 2737 hours in bed, and 3256 hours exposed to the media (almost 9 hours a day).[4] Ninety-eight percent of American homes have a radio, and the same percentage have a television. For years, more homes had a television than had a toilet.[5] Almost 20 percent of children younger than two have a television in their bedroom; more than 40 percent of children between four and six do; and almost 70 percent of older children do. A third of children younger than six live in homes where the television is left on all or most of the time.[6] The average child (from eight years old on) or adult watches television three hours a day.[7] By the time the average child graduates from high school, he or she has spent more time in front of the tube than in class.[8] By the time the average American dies, he or she has spent one and a half years just watching television commercials.[9]

With the evolution in digital technology, such as the Internet, companies are working "to weave media and electronic communication into nearly every waking moment of our lives."[10] Already, kids and young adults expose themselves to multiple media simultaneously. One study found that eight- to eighteen-year-olds on average pack in eight and a half hours of media in six and a half hours of time. Up to a third of them say they pay attention to more than one medium "most of the time," usually music or television while using the computer.[11]

As Internet use has shot up, it has cut into family time more than anything else. Although the average Internet user spends 30 minutes less time watching television, he or she spends 70 minutes less time interacting with family members than before.[12]

The rest of this section will examine three continuing trends in journalism: the shifting dominance of the media, the increasing concentration of the media, and the increasing atomization of the media.

Dominance of the Media

For many years newspapers were the dominant medium. Yet there were no "mass media" until the advent of broadcasting. Radio, which became popular in the 1920s, and television, which became popular in the 1950s, reached people who could not or would not read. Television especially became so central and influential in American life that one scholar speculated that the second half of the twentieth century will go down in history as "the age of television."[13]

As television grew in popularity, newspapers waned. People did not need their headlines anymore, and many people did not want their in-depth coverage either. Newspapers have struggled for readers and advertisers, and many have folded. Since 1960, more than 300 daily papers have disappeared.[14] Since 1970, the percentage of regular readers has declined (from 78 percent of adults to 42 percent).[15] The percentage of young adult regular readers has declined the most. (In 1966, 58 percent of first-year college students said "keeping up-to-date with political affairs" was an "essential" or "very important" goal. In 1998, only 26 percent held this view.)[16] Even after 9/11, which prompted a surge of interest in foreign affairs, readership continued to decline.[17]

For several decades the evening newscasts of the major networks—ABC, CBS, and NBC—replaced newspapers as the dominant medium for coverage of politics. CBS's anchor Walter Cronkite was considered "the most trusted man in America." However, the audience for the evening newscasts has declined with the rise of cable television, talk radio, and the Internet. (Since the mid-1990s, the percentage of regular viewers of the networks' evening newscasts has dropped from 60 percent to 34 percent.[18]) These other media allow people to get the news at different times and in various formats.

These trends will likely continue. Newspapers will lose more readers while television will lose its dominance and the Internet will gain new users.[19]

Today different media appeal to different groups. Seniors read newspapers and watch the major networks' evening newscasts, whereas young adults are more likely to surf the Web. The cable networks attract the least educated, and news magazines, political magazines, and the Internet attract the most educated (see Table 5.1). Conservatives tend to watch Fox television and listen to talk radio, whereas liberals tend to watch the Public Broadcasting System (PBS) and listen to National Public Radio (NPR).[20] Conservatives and liberals both scan the Web but favor different sites.

Television, in one form or another, is the most important medium for politics. It offers immediate and dramatic coverage. According to surveys, people pay more attention to it and put more faith in it than in other media. They believe they can tell more about officials and candidates from it than from other media.

TABLE 5.1	Number of Years after Introduction to Attract Fifty Million Users
Medium	**Years**
Radio	38
Television	13
Internet	4

Source: "Ticker," *Brill's Content,* March 1999, 128.

Many American families bought their first television in the 1950s.

This makes positive coverage on television essential, and negative images on television devastating, for politicians.

Yet newspapers remain important as well. They provide more thorough and thoughtful coverage. Because newspaper articles require more effort and provide more depth, they leave a longer-lasting impression. People remember the news they read in newspapers better than the news they watch on television.[21] Moreover, national newspapers such as the *New York Times* and the *Washington Post,* which blanket the country with in-depth international and national news, influence opinion leaders, who in turn influence other persons.

The Internet is becoming more important because it is attracting more users. Its any-time convenience and vast array of sites are real lures (see Figure 5.1).

Concentration of the Media

Journalism is a big business, and it has become a bigger business in recent decades. First, small media organizations owned by local families or local companies were taken over by chains (owning multiple newspapers, radio stations, *or* television stations) or conglomerates (owning multiple newspapers, radio stations, *and* television stations). Then large media organizations were taken over by chains or conglomerates. Finally,

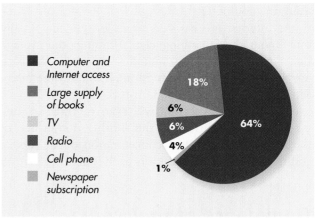

FIGURE 5.1 ■ **If You were Stranded on a Deserted Island . . .** *and could take only one of the following with you, which would you take?*

Source: Asked of 1000 households with Internet access. IPSOS Insight U.S. Express Omnibus, August 2004, cited in "Primary Sources," Atlantic Monthly, *January–February, 2005, 54.*

chains and conglomerates were bought out by larger chains and conglomerates.

Seven huge companies—Time Warner, Viacom, News Corporation, Sony, General Electric, Bertelsmann, and Disney—form the top tier of media conglomerates. Time Warner, the largest, has over eighty thousand employees and $30 billion in annual revenues. It boasts 50 percent of the online business, 20 percent of the cable television business, 18 percent of the movie business, and 16 percent of the record business in the country. It also has 160 magazines, five publishing houses, and "Looney Tunes" cartoons.[22] Twenty other companies, which are major players in one or two types of the media, form a second tier of media conglomerates.[23]

The seven huge companies are linked to each other, owning parts of each other and engaging in ventures with each other. These arrangements reduce their competition, lower their risks, increase their profits, and at the same time erect high barriers for any upstarts that try to challenge their dominance.[24]

The long-range goal of the mergers and alliances is to control the information and entertainment markets of the future. Media conglomerates want to offer all media—television stations, radio stations, newspapers, magazines, books, movies, records, and computer services—in various formats at all times of the day. Each conglomerate seeks to become the sole source of all your news and entertainment.

An early expectation for the Internet—that it would provide unlimited diversity and offer an alternative to established media—is already being dashed as powerful conglomerates are racing to swallow their competitors and influence the government to adopt policies that will lock in their advantage.[25]

This trend toward concentration of the media is certain to continue. It will provide much more convenience, at somewhat more cost, for consumers, but it will pose problems for a democracy that relies on the media to inform its citizens.

Already this trend toward concentration makes some problems apparent. The news comes from fewer sources than it used to. Although there are tens of thousands of media entities in the United States, the numbers are misleading. Chains and conglomerates own the television stations with most of the viewers, the radio stations with most of the listeners, and the newspapers and magazines with most of the readers.[26] One media analyst, referring to these chains and conglomerates, observed, "Two dozen profit-driven companies, owned and managed by billionaires operating in barely competitive markets, account for nearly the entirety of the U.S. media culture."[27]

Just ten companies publish the newspapers that reach 51 percent of the readers.[28] Six companies broadcast to 42 percent of the radio audience, and five companies broadcast to 75 percent of the television audience.[29] Six companies have more than 80 percent of the cable television market. Four companies sell almost 90 percent of all music recordings, and six companies earn more than 90 percent of all film revenues.[30] One company controls over 70 percent of live music concerts in the country.[31]

Moreover, just one wire service—the Associated Press (AP)—supplies the international and national news for most newspapers. Only four television networks—ABC, CBS, NBC, and CNN—furnish the news for most television stations.

With fewer sources of news, there is a narrower range of views—less of a marketplace of ideas—than is healthy for a democracy. Instead, a small number of powerful people provide information and opinion—essentially, define reality—for the rest of the people.

These chains and conglomerates have begun to exercise their power through political activism and censorship. During the Iraq War, Clear Channel Communications, the largest radio chain with over twelve hundred stations nationwide, organized prowar rallies in seven major cities.[32] Cumulus Media, the second largest radio chain, halted airplay of Dixie Chicks songs on its country stations after one member of the band criticized President Bush.[33] Comcast, the largest

cable company, and CNN, owned by Time Warner, rejected peace groups' attempts to buy time for antiwar ads.[34] Sinclair Broadcast Group, the largest television chain with sixty-two stations, forbade its ABC affiliates from airing *Nightline* the night Ted Koppel read the names of military personnel killed in Iraq. The company said the show would "undermine" the war effort.[35] Two weeks before the presidential election, the company ordered its stations to broadcast a film in prime time accusing John Kerry of betraying American prisoners when he returned from Vietnam and testified against the war.[36] (The company modified this directive after intense criticism prompted some advertisers to pull their commercials, some viewers to threaten a boycott, some shareholders to vow a revolt, and its stock to plummet.) These instances, although relatively minor in themselves, are ominous signs for the future. It would be naive not to expect more attempts by media chains and conglomerates to flex their muscles.

In addition, the chains and conglomerates have exercised self-censorship when news coverage has threatened corporate interests. ABC killed a story that Disney, its owner, followed employment practices that allowed the hiring of convicted pedophiles at its parks.[37] NBC broadcast a report about defective bolts used in airplanes and bridges built by GE, its owner, and by other companies, but the references to GE were removed. When the president of NBC News complained about the removal and corporate interference in their newscasts, the boss of GE poked a finger in his chest and shouted, "You work for GE!"[38]

To inform the public, other media might run a story killed by one organization, but what if a story affects the interests of many organizations? In 1996, Congress passed the Telecommunications Act, which set aside a portion of the nation's airwaves for digital television broadcasts. Although the frequencies were valued at $70 billion, the act handed them to the broadcasters free of charge. When the bill was proposed, Senator John McCain (R-Ariz.) predicted, "You will not see this story on any television or hear it on any radio broadcast because it directly affects them."[39] Indeed, during the nine months in which the bill was pending, there was little coverage of the bill or the lobbying by the broadcasters. ABC, CBS, and NBC television news shows devoted an average of just six and a half minutes to the bill and virtually none to this provision.[40] If citizens had been aware of this legislation, they might have demanded that Congress, rather than handing the broadcasters a windfall, charge market value for the frequencies and use the $70 billion to support popular governmental programs.

Another problem resulting from concentration of the media is financial pressure to reduce the quality of news coverage. News organizations are expected to match other divisions in their corporations and generate sizable profits each year. Corporate officers feel the heat from Wall Street analysts and major stockholders, such as managers of mutual funds, retirement funds, and insurance companies, who are more concerned with the value of the stock than the quality of the journalism. As a result, costs are cut—some reporters are let go, while others are shifted from time-consuming in-depth or investigative reporting to more superficial stories.[41] A reporter for a midsize newspaper in Illinois admitted, "If a story needs a real investment of time and money, we don't do it anymore." He lamented, "Who the hell cares about corruption in city government, anyway?"[42]

The Knight Ridder newspaper chain, which cut staffs and, in the opinion of its reporters produced lower-quality newspapers, increased its profits to nineteen percent per year. Nonetheless, the chain was forced by its stockholders, most of whom are large financial institutions, to put itself up for sale because it wasn't making enough profit.[43] The new owners will have to cut costs and lower quality further.

Another problem resulting from concentration of the media is a decline of local news. When a train derailed in Minot, North Dakota, and released over 200,000 gallons of ammonia, authorities tried to notify residents to avoid the area and to stay indoors. But when police called the six local commercial radio stations, nobody answered. The stations were all owned and programmed by Clear Channel, based in San Antonio, Texas.[44] By the next day, three hundred people had been hospitalized, and pets and livestock had been killed.[45]

The trend toward concentration of the media is potentially harmful for everyone but the companies and their stockholders. Already the financial value of some media conglomerates is greater than the entire economy of some foreign countries whose media monopolies we condemn as hostile to a democratic society.

Atomization of the Media

Despite the increasing concentration of the media, a contrary trend—an atomization of the media—has also developed in recent decades. Whereas concentration has led to a national media, atomization has fragmented the influence of the national media. The major newspapers and broadcast networks have lost their dominance, and other media, some not even considered news organizations, have played a significant role in politics.

This trend is partly the result of technological changes, particularly the development of cable television and the Internet. Cable television, with a multiplicity of channels, can offer more specialization in

A newsstand in Brooklyn, New York, sells sixteen Russian-language newspapers to area immigrants.

programming. It can provide **narrowcasting** to appeal to small segments of the audience in contrast to major networks' **broadcasting** to appeal to the overall audience. For example, C-SPAN covers Congress on three channels and, unlike the networks, lingers on members' speeches and committees' hearings. Other national cable networks cater to blacks and Hispanics.[46] A cable system in Los Angeles and New York caters to Jews. A cable channel in California broadcasts in Chinese, one in Hawaii broadcasts in Japanese, and one in Connecticut and Massachusetts broadcasts in Portuguese. Stations in New York also provide programs in Greek, Hindi, Korean, and Russian.

Cable television can also offer twenty-four-hour news. CNN, created as a round-the-clock news network, has a large audience. Now Fox and MSNBC are challenging it.

The Internet features additional news sites. Major newspapers post their articles on websites before the papers themselves are delivered. Online "magazines" also address politics. During the congressional impeachment of President Clinton, one online magazine—*Salon*—revealed that the Republican representative spearheading the effort (Henry Hyde of Illinois) had had an adulterous relationship. Self-styled "journalists" even post their "news" as well. Matt Drudge offers political gossip on his own website, the Drudge Report, which originated in his one-bedroom apartment.[47]

The trend toward atomization of the media is also partly the result of the populist backlash against government officials and established journalists, perceived as "Washington insiders," that characterized American

politics in the 1980s and 1990s. This is reflected in the popularity of radio talk shows. Many stations have such programs, and many people tune in.[48] Their numbers make talk radio a force in politics. Its middle-class audience acts as a national jury on governmental controversies.

The populist backlash also is reflected in the increasing attention paid to fringe media by the public.

Foreign language media are not new in America. Benjamin Franklin published a German-language newspaper to cater to the influx of German immigrants in his time.

In the 1992 presidential campaign, the *Star,* a supermarket tabloid, published allegations by Gennifer Flowers, a former nightclub singer, that she had had a twelve-year affair with Bill Clinton while he was governor of Arkansas. The major media hesitated to repeat the *Star's* story—they had nothing but scorn for the tabloids, which, they insisted, did not practice true journalism—but within days most gave in, under the pretense of debating the propriety of reporting personal matters. Flowers then appeared on *A Current Affair,* a syndicated television show, rated Clinton as a lover on a scale from 1 to 10, and sang "Stand by Your Man." Thus Flowers did not need to take her story to the major media; she got the tabloid media to tell it and pay her for it ($150,000 from the *Star* and $25,000 from *A Current Affair*).[49]

During the impeachment of President Clinton, Larry Flynt, the publisher of *Hustler* magazine, was offended by what he considered to be hypocrisy by the president's adversaries. He offered to pay for information about any affairs that Republican leaders had. Ultimately, he published an article about an affair involving the speaker of the House designate, Robert Livingston (R–La.). Although the article appeared only in his magazine, the revelation received publicity in other media and caused Livingston to resign.

Because the public pays attention to the fringe media more than it used to, politicians have begun to use these media. Instead of announcing their candidacy at a press conference, as politicians traditionally did, some have announced their candidacy on television talk shows. During the campaign, they have appeared on other television shows. Clinton played the saxophone on the *Arsenio Hall Show,* and Bush kissed the host on the *Oprah Winfrey Show.* Candidates swapped jokes with Jay Leno and David Letterman—and prayed they would not end up looking silly.

All this blurs the line between politics and entertainment. When Senator Bill Bradley (Dem–N.J.), campaigning for the Democratic nomination for president, appeared at a Houston radio station that was ranked number one among men in the area, he expected to discuss his new book. Instead, the disc jockeys had two women disrobe from the waist up to report his reaction.[50]

Politicians have to be good sports, because people who pay little attention to political news do pay attention to these shows. Almost a third of adults said they get political information from late-night comedy shows; over a third of those under thirty said these shows are their *primary* source of political news.[51] So it may not be a joke when Letterman proclaims, "The road to the White House goes through me!"

Because of the expanding role of fringe media, mainstream journalists envision a shrinking role for themselves. They no longer monopolize the market of political information; they no longer control the gates through which such information must pass.

This trend toward atomization of the media has significant implications beyond its impact on the established media and their professional journalists. Although this trend makes the news more accessible to more people, it also makes the news less factual, less reliable, and less analytical.

The proliferation of news outlets and the availability of newscasts around the clock create intense competition for news stories. The media have more space or time to fill than information to fill it. So they feel pressure to find new stories or identify new angles of old stories. In addition, they use talk shows that blend news, opinion, gossip, rumor, and speculation, because these shows are cheap to produce and, if the hosts and guests are provocative, entertaining for viewers. The media can fill their time and attract an audience. But the result is a commingling of facts and nonfacts. Then these facts and nonfacts are repeated by other organizations seeking to make sure that they are not left behind. In the rush to broadcast and publish, the media put less emphasis on assessing the accuracy of the content they disseminate than they used to. The "great new sin," a veteran reporter observed, is not being inaccurate but being boring.[52]

Interest groups exploit the competition among the media and exacerbate the problem. When Vince Foster, deputy counsel for President Clinton, apparently committed suicide in a park, a right-wing group sent a fax to news organizations linking the suicide to the Whitewater land deal (a failed real estate development on which the Clintons lost money years before reaching the White House). The group passed the rumor that Foster died at an administration "safe house" and was later moved to the park. Talk show host Rush Limbaugh reported the rumor. Other talk show hosts repeated it; some added the rumor that Foster was murdered. A few financial speculators spread the rumors as a way to manipulate the stock market, prompting newspaper business sections to repeat the rumors in articles about their effect on the stock market. Thus through announcement and repetition by the media, the rumors came to seem true to many people—yet they remained just rumors (and false ones, according to three independent counsels).[53]

The mainstream media have been uncertain how to act in such situations. They are reluctant to report rumors they are unable to verify. But they fear they will lose their audience if they fail to report stories other media report. Usually, they decide to report the stories but in a different context—under the guise of addressing the political ramifications of the accusation or the journalistic ethics of publicizing it. Nevertheless, the effect is nearly the same: The accusation winds up in the mainstream media, and the public believes it. As a result, unscrupulous groups realize they can use the fringe media to manipulate the mainstream media into publicizing bogus charges. In this way, they can drag the mainstream media down to their level. President Clinton's lawyer said it reminded him of when he lived with a bunch of guys in college: Four were neat and one was a slob; by the end of the year, all were slobs.[54]

In the 2004 presidential campaign, the "Swift Boat Veterans for Truth" ran a TV commercial charging that John Kerry had not deserved his medals from the Vietnam War. The "facts" alleged in the commercial apparently were false, but the commercial was replayed and the members of the group were interviewed over and over on Fox, MSNBC, and CNN, and the commercial was discussed ad nauseum on talk radio. Eventually, the mainstream media felt obligated to address it as well, so the misleading commercial became the major story of the campaign for a month and a major factor in the outcome of the election.[55] (However, if Kerry had responded more effectively, he might have defused its impact.)

The fringe media aggravate the problem. Their goal is entertainment and their audience is politically unsophisticated, so these media are less careful about the accuracy of the information they disseminate. Some pay for stories, possibly encouraging people to lie for the money; many sensationalize stories, possibly distorting the truth. Although the mainstream media are also commercial enterprises subject to the pressures of the marketplace, they have a tradition to uphold. Reporters at major newspapers and broadcast networks often speak of their responsibility to follow journalistic standards, whereas members of the fringe media sometimes reflect the views of radio talk show host Don Imus, who asserts, "The news isn't sacred to me. It's entertainment. . . designed to revel in the agony of others."[56]

The Internet aggravates the problem even more. Any person with a computer and a phone line can create an independent web log—a **blog**—to convey his or her information or views world wide. Blogs are an alternative to mainstream journalism, serving as "the voice of the little guy" in a world of media giants.[57] Some attract thousands or even hundreds of thousands of visitors per day. The most popular political blog—Daily Kos—has 600,000 readers each day, which is more than all but a handful of newspapers.[58]

About two hundred American soldiers in Iraq keep blogs, describing *their* war. "Sergeant Lizzie" described the result of a roadside bomb under her Humvee:

I started to scream bloody murder, and one of the other females on the convoy came over, grabbed my hand and started to calm me down. She held onto me, allowing me

to place my leg on her shoulder as it was hanging free. . . . I thought that my face had been blown off, so I made the remark that I wouldn't be pretty again LOL. Of course the medics all rushed with reassurance which was quite amusing as I know what I look like now and I don't even want to think about what I looked like then.[59]

Similar to talk radio, blogs can act like "a lens, focusing attention on an issue until it catches fire."[60] Senate Majority Leader Trent Lott (R-Miss.), at a one-hundredth birthday party for Senator Strom Thurmond (R-S. C.) in 2002, made a remark seeming to praise Thurmond's past advocacy of racial segregation. Although the mainstream media ignored the remark, the blogs kept it alive until other media addressed it. Two weeks later Lott resigned his leadership position.

Yet blogs can also perpetuate falsehoods. Blogs are free of the constraints of the mainstream media, such as objectivity and accountability. Bloggers have no editors or fact checkers—the layers of "review, revision, and correction" that the major media have.[61] And an increasing number of bloggers are partisan operatives who have been trained to engage in "guerrilla Internet

© Chris Buck

Web bloggers offer independent views and irreverent humor outside of the corporate media organizations. Here bloggers cover the Republican National Convention in 2004.

activism" while presenting themselves as average people.[62] Their fealty to the truth may be far less than their passion for the cause.

Meanwhile, the public is lost in this factual free-for-all. Most citizens are not well versed in the issues or very knowledgeable about the politicians. Without the help of professional journalists, many are not able to separate the blarney from the gospel truth when candidates and officials speak.

In sum, two opposite trends—concentration of the media and atomization of the media—are occurring. The key question is how much control the media conglomerates will exercise and how much news and how many views will emerge through other outlets. Financial pressures are bearing down, and powerful corporations are trying to dominate the media business. In the future, the huge conglomerates likely will dominate more than they do now, while independent voices from the Internet will break through on issues that have a human interest angle.

Relationship between the Media and Politicians

"Politicians live—and sometimes die—by the press. The press lives by politicians," according to a former presidential aide. "This relationship is at the center of our national life."[63]

Although this relationship was not always so close—President Herbert Hoover once refused to tell a reporter whether he enjoyed a baseball game he attended[64]—politicians and journalists now realize that they need each other. Politicians need journalists to reach the public and to receive feedback from the public. They scan the major newspapers in the morning and the network newscasts in the evening. President Lyndon Johnson watched three network newscasts on three televisions simultaneously. (Presidents Ronald Reagan, who read mostly the comics, and George W. Bush, who reads mostly the sports section, are exceptions to the rule.)[65] In turn, journalists need politicians to cover government. They seek a steady stream of fresh information to fill their news columns and newscasts.

The close relationship between the media and politicians is both a **symbiotic relationship,** meaning they use each other for their mutual advantage, and an **adversarial relationship,** meaning they fight each other.

Symbiotic Relationship

President Johnson told individual reporters, "You help me, and I'll help make you a big man in your profession." He gave exclusive interviews and, in return, expected favorable coverage.

Reporters get information from politicians in various ways. Some reporters are assigned to monitor beats. Washington beats include the White House, Congress, the Supreme Court, the State Department, the Defense Department, and some other departments and agencies. Other reporters are assigned to cover specialized subjects, such as economics, energy issues, and environmental problems, which are addressed by multiple departments or agencies.

The government has press secretaries and public information officers who provide reporters with ideas and information for stories. The number of these officials is significant; one year the Defense Department employed almost fifteen hundred people just to handle press relations.[66] The Bush White House employs over fifty.[67] The Department of Homeland Security has an entertainment liaison office to provide information to help moviemakers and, at the same time, get moviemakers to portray the department positively.[68]

The government supplies reporters with a variety of news sources, including copies of speeches, summaries of committee meetings, news releases, and news briefings about current events. Officials also grant interviews, hold press conferences, and stage "media events." The vast majority of reporters rely on these sources rather than engage in more difficult and time-consuming investigative reporting.

Interviews

Interviews show the symbiotic nature of the relationship between reporters and politicians. During the early months of the Reagan presidency, *Washington Post* writer William Greider had a series of eighteen off-the-record meetings with budget director David Stockman. Greider recounted:

> *Stockman and I were participating in a fairly routine transaction of Washington, a form of submerged communication which takes place regularly between selected members of the press and the highest officials of government. Our mutual motivation, despite our different interests, was crassly self-serving. It did not need to be spelled out between us. I would use him and he would use me. . . . I had established a valuable peephole on the inner policy debates of the new administration. And the young budget director had established a valuable connection with an important newspaper. I would get a jump on the unfolding strategies and decisions. He would be able to prod and influence the focus of our coverage, to communicate his views and positions under the cover of our "off the record" arrangement, to make known harsh assessments that a public official would not dare to voice in the more formal setting of a press conference, speech, or "on the record" interview.[69]*

Leaks

Interviews can result in **leaks**—disclosures of information that officials want to keep secret. Others in the administration, the bureaucracy, or Congress use leaks for various reasons.

Officials in the administration might leak information about a potential policy—float a trial balloon—and then gauge the reaction to it without committing themselves to it in case it is shot down. As a result of bureaucratic infighting, officials might leak to prod the president or high-ranking official into taking some action[70] or to prevent the president or high-ranking official from taking some action. When President Bush decided to appoint a Clinton administration attorney to be an antiterrorism adviser, Vice President Cheney's office leaked information to discredit the attorney and block the appointment.[71] (The attempt failed.)

Officials might leak to force public debates on matters that would otherwise be addressed behind closed doors. After Congress investigated the intelligence failures leading up to the terrorist attacks on September 11, 2001, someone leaked the information that the National Security Agency—the ultrasecret agency that engages in electronic surveillance around the world—had intercepted al-Qaeda messages on September 10 saying "Tomorrow is zero day" and "The match begins tomorrow" but had not translated the messages from Arabic until September 12.

Officials might leak to shift blame for mistakes or problems. When the Iraqi insurgency cast doubt upon our presumed victory in the Iraq War, officials apparently from the State Department leaked information suggesting that the Pentagon had rushed the country into war. Then officials apparently from the Pentagon leaked information claiming that the CIA had exaggerated the intelligence about Iraq's nuclear weapons program. Then officials apparently from the CIA leaked information indicating that the administration had distorted the intelligence about Iraq's weapons of mass destruction. Each group tried to absolve itself of the blame as the war turned sour.

Officials might leak to hurt an adversary. Diplomat Joseph Wilson was sent to Niger, which exports uranium, to investigate the possibility that Iraq had sought

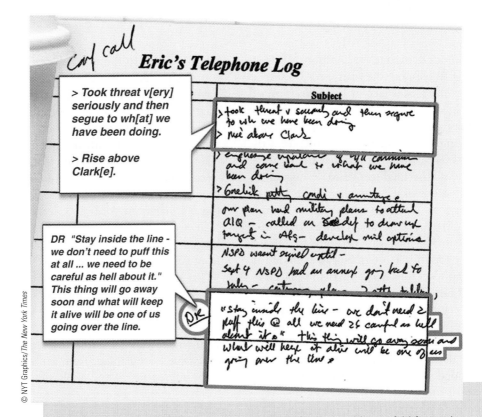

© NYT Graphics/The New York Times

After a Pentagon aide prepared Secretary of Defense Donald Rumsfeld for a television talk show addressing accusations that the Bush administration failed to do enough to combat terrorism, the aide stopped at Starbucks, where he absentmindedly left his notes. In his "Telephone Log," Eric Ruff noted, "Emphasize importance of 9/11 commission" and "Rise above Clark" (Richard Clarke, who headed the government's antiterrorism efforts and who criticized the administration for emphasizing Iraq rather than terrorism). The aide also left a map showing the route from the Pentagon to Rumsfeld's home.

After diplomat Joseph Wilson (right) challenged an administration claim that Iraq had sought uranium for nuclear weapons, administration officials leaked the identity of his wife, Valerie Plame (left), who had been a CIA undercover agent.

a type of uranium used in nuclear weapons. Wilson found no evidence to support the claim. Yet President Bush included the claim as a fact in his next State of the Union address, and others in the administration repeated it to persuade the public to support a war against Iraq. Breaking his silence, Wilson wrote an article in the *New York Times* maintaining that the administration had "twisted" the intelligence to "exaggerate" the threat. In retaliation, officials in the White House leaked the identity of Wilson's wife, Valerie Plame, who had worked for the CIA as an undercover spy. Although most reporters had the decency to refrain from reporting her identity, Robert Novak included it in his syndicated column and *Time* magazine placed it on its Web site. Unmasking Plame effectively ended her career as a spy and jeopardized the operations she had established and contacts she had made in foreign countries.[72] (In their zeal to play hardball, White House officials evidently violated laws prohibiting the disclosure of classified information and the identity of covert employees of the CIA.[73])

Officials might leak embarrassing information to help an ally or protect themselves. By leaking this information at a particular time or in a particular way, they can minimize the damage it would otherwise cause. So, officials leak embarrassing information during holidays or weekends, when the news receives less attention. They leak to small- or medium-size newspapers rather than to the *New York Times* or the *Washing-*

ton Post because these influential papers dislike giving prominent play to stories broken by less prestigious papers.[74] After President George H. Bush nominated Clarence Thomas to the Supreme Court, an official in the Bush administration leaked the fact that Thomas had experimented with marijuana in college. The official's purpose was to inoculate Thomas from the greater controversy that could have occurred if the press had discovered and revealed this fact closer to the confirmation vote.[75]

Despite the common belief that leaks are from low-level employees of the opposite party, most are from high-ranking officials of the president's party. "The ship of state," one experienced reporter noted, "is the only kind of ship that leaks mainly from the top."[76] During the Vietnam War, President Johnson himself ordered an aide to leak the charge that steel companies were "profiteering" from the war. After an executive complained, Johnson assured him that "if I find out some damn fool aide did it, I'll fire the sonuvabitch!"[77] During the Iraq war, President Bush authorized an aide to leak classified information to counter mounting criticism about the administration's use of intelligence before the war.

Presidents as far back as George Washington have been enraged by leaks. Reagan said he was "up to my keister" in leaks, and Nixon established a "plumbers" unit to wiretap aides and plug leaks once they learned who was responsible. George W. Bush, embarrassed about leaks revealing that the CIA operates secret prisons in foreign countries and the National Security Agency (NSA) wiretaps American citizens who make phone calls to foreign countries, launched the most extensive crackdown since Nixon. FBI investigations and CIA polygraph tests targeted government employees considered possible sources for the reports, and the Justice Department warned media organizations of prosecution, under a 1917 statute, for revealing secret information.[78]

Officials outside the administration might leak information about those inside the administration. Prosecutors in the independent counsel's office leaked salacious tidbits uncovered during their investigation of President Clinton. They even leaked information from grand jury testimony, which by law is supposed to remain secret.[79] The prosecutors' goal was to sway public opinion—create a presumption of guilt and generate a sense of momentum—against the president as his impeachment approached. Although the prosecutors apparently broke the law—a felony—the press paid little attention to this fact because the reporters were grateful to have the information.[80]

Leaks may serve the public by disclosing information that otherwise would not be available, but leaks would serve the public better if reporters explained the leakers' motives so the public could understand the bureaucratic or ideological conflict driving the story. Yet reporters are wary of antagonizing the leakers—their sources—for fear of not getting a story next time.

Leaks often enable reporters to break stories before their competitors can report them. Competition for these **scoops** is intense. During the 2004 presidential campaign, CBS showed a letter regarding George W. Bush's National Guard service. In its zeal for a scoop, CBS aired the story before verifying the authenticity of the letter.[81] It turned out that the letter had been forged and the network had been snookered, which proved highly embarrassing to CBS and costly to Dan Rather, who lost his anchor position.

Press Conferences

Press conferences also show the symbiotic nature of the relationship between reporters and politicians. Theodore Roosevelt, who was the first president to cultivate close ties to correspondents, started the **presidential press conference** by talking to reporters while getting shaved.[82]

Franklin Roosevelt, who was detested by newspaper publishers, realized that the press conference could help him reach the public. He held frequent informal sessions around his desk and provided a steady stream of news, which editors felt obligated to publish. This news publicized his policies at the same time that editors were ranting against them.

John Kennedy saw that the press conference could help him reach the public more directly if he allowed the networks to televise it live.[83] Then editors could not filter his remarks.

Of course, if a president wants to answer reporters, he can do so in private. If he wants to communicate with the public, he can do so in a formal speech without risking an embarrassing question. But he might opt for a televised conference if he performs well in front of the cameras or, like the youthful Kennedy, feels a need to demonstrate his competence to the watchful public.[84]

As a result, presidents and their aides transformed the conference into a carefully orchestrated media show. Now an administration schedules a conference when it wants to convey a message. Aides identify potential questions, and the president rehearses appropriate answers. (Former press secretaries brag that they predicted at least 90 percent of the questions asked—and often the reporters who asked them.[85]) During the conference, the president calls on the reporters he wants. Although he cannot ignore those from the major news organizations, he can call on others who he expects will lob soft questions. The George W. Bush administration even gave press credentials to a Republican operative posing as a real reporter so he would ask the questions the president wanted to answer.[86]

Beaming the conference to the nation results in less news than having a casual exchange around the president's desk, which used to reveal his thinking about policies and decisions. Appearing in millions of homes, the president cannot be as open and cannot allow himself to make a gaffe in front of the huge audience.

The transformation of the conference frustrates reporters and prompts them to act as prosecutors. As one press secretary observed, they play a game of "I gotcha."[87] Still, reporters value the conference. Editors consider the president's remarks news, so the conference helps reporters do their job. It also gives them a chance to bask in the limelight.

Media Events

"Media events" also show the symbiotic nature of the relationship between reporters and politicians. Staged for television, these events usually pair a photo opportunity with a speech to convey a strong impression of a politician's position on an issue.

The **photo opportunity** (often simply called a *photo op*) frames the politician against a backdrop that symbolizes the points the politician is trying to make. Photo ops for economic issues might use factories—bustling to represent success or abandoned to represent failure. The strategy is the same as that for advertisements of merchandise: Combine the product (the politician) with the symbols in the hope that the potential buyers (the voters) will link the two.[88] In the 1996 presidential campaign, Bob Dole, who was having trouble attracting young voters, arranged for a photo op at the Rock and Roll Hall of Fame rather than at, say, the Lawrence Welk Museum.

In the run-up to the 2004 presidential election, employees of the Homeland Security Department were told to provide one homeland security photo op a month as a way to link President Bush with 9/11 and the war on terrorism.[89]

Photo ops can be misleading. To persuade people that President Bush's tax cuts, which were designed primarily to benefit wealthy taxpayers, would help working Americans, the Speaker of the House, Dennis Hastert (R-Ill.), asked well-heeled lobbyists who favored the tax cuts to dress as construction workers and appear in photo ops featuring "a sea of hard hats" and signs proclaiming, "Tax Relief for Everyone." The lobbyists were urged to participate: "WE DO NEED BODIES—they must be DRESSED DOWN, appear to be REAL WORKER types, etc."[90]

After Hurricane Katrina, President Bush appeared in media events on the Gulf Coast eight times in one month to overcome the perception that his administration bungled its response to the storm. In one photo op he was shown hammering nails at a construction site.

The speech at a media event is not a classical oration or even a cogent address with a beginning, middle, and end. It is an informal talk that emphasizes a few key words or phrases or sentences—almost slogans, because television editors allot time only for a short **sound bite.** And the amount of time is less and less. In 1968, the average sound bite of a presidential contender on the evening news was about forty-two seconds, but in 1988 it was under ten seconds and since then has dropped to less than eight seconds.[91]

Speechwriters plan accordingly. "A lot of writers figure out how they are going to get the part they want onto television," a former presidential aide explained. "They think of a news lead and write around it. And if the television lights don't go on as the speaker is approaching that news lead, he skips a few paragraphs and waits until they are lit to read the key part."[92] This approach does not produce coherent speeches, but the people watching on television will not know, and the few watching in person do not matter because they are just props.

Perhaps more than any other source of news, media events illustrate the reliance of politicians on television and of television on politicians. The head of CBS News said, "I'd like just once to have the courage to go on the air and say that such and such a candidate went to six cities today to stage six media events, none of which had anything to do with governing America."[93] Yet television fosters these events, and despite occasional swipes by correspondents, networks continue to show them.

Adversarial Relationship

Although the relationship between the media and politicians is symbiotic in some ways, it is adversarial in others. Since George Washington's administration, when conflicts developed between Federalists and Jeffersonians, the media have attacked politicians and politicians have attacked the media. During John Adams's administration, Federalists passed the Sedition Act of 1798, which prohibited much criticism of the government. Federalist officials used the act to imprison Jeffersonian editors. Later, President Andrew Jackson proposed a law to allow the government to shut down "incendiary" newspapers. Even now, a former press secretary commented, "there are very few politicians who do not cherish privately the notion that there should be some regulation of the news."[94]

Henry Groskinsky, New York City

Because President Richard Nixon moved awkwardly—his gestures were out of sync with his words—he was not effective on television. He reminded some people of a marionette; one man made this doll for the president.

The conflict stems from a fundamental difference in perspectives. Politicians use the media to persuade the public to accept their policies. Politicians want the media to act as conduits, conveying their messages, exactly as they deliver them, to the public. But journalists see themselves not as conduits but as servants of the people in a democracy. They examine and question officials and policies so the public can learn more about them. According to one correspondent, "My job is not to say here's the church social with the apple pie, isn't it beautiful?"[95]

In contemporary society, information is power. The media and the government, especially the president, with the huge bureaucracy, including the intelligence agencies, at his disposal, are the two primary sources of information. To the extent that the administration controls the flow of information, it can achieve its policy goals. To the extent that the media disseminate contradictory information, they can ensure that these policy goals will be subject to public debate.

Inevitably, politicians fall short of their goals, and many blame the media for their failures. They confuse the message and the messenger, like Tsar Peter the Great, who, when notified in 1700 that the Russian army had lost a battle, promptly ordered the messenger strangled.

When President Kennedy became upset by the *New York Times*'s coverage of Vietnam, he asked the paper to transfer its correspondent out of Vietnam. (The *Times* refused.) When President Nixon became angry at major newspapers and networks, he had Vice President Spiro Agnew lash out at them. He also ordered the Department of Justice to investigate some for possible antitrust violations and the Internal Revenue Service to audit some for possible income tax violations. When aides to President George W. Bush read a *Washington Post* article questioning the truthfulness of the president's statements, they suggested that the reporter be removed from the White House beat. (The *Post* refused.[96])

However, it would be incorrect to think that the relationship between the media and politicians is usually adversarial. Normally, it is symbiotic. Although journalists like to think of themselves as adversaries who stand up to politicians, most of them rely on politicians most of the time.[97]

Yet the relationship has become more adversarial since the Vietnam War and the Watergate scandal fueled cynicism about government's performance and officials' honesty.[98] Many reporters, according to the editor of the *Des Moines Register,* "began to feel that no journalism is worth doing unless it unseats the mighty."[99] New reporters especially began to feel this way. Senator Alan Simpson (R-Wyo.) asked the

After the initial phase of the Iraq War in May 2003, President Bush used the opportunity for a dramatic photo op designed for his reelection campaign. Landing a navy jet on an aircraft carrier off the California coast, he swaggered across the deck, sporting a flight suit and backslapping the sailors. Standing under a banner that proclaimed "Mission Accomplished," he (prematurely) announced the end of major combat in Iraq.

daughter of old friends what she planned to do after graduating from journalism school. "I'm going to be one of the hunters," she replied. When he asked, "What are you going to hunt?" she answered, "People like you!"[100]

In response, politicians have restricted access for reporters out of fear that they will say something that will be used against them. In turn, reporters have complained that politicians are not accessible and that reporters cannot get the information they need to do their job. During the George W. Bush presidency, one lamented, "The idea of a truly open press conference, an unscripted political debate, a leisurely and open . . . conversation between political leaders, or even a one-on-one interview between a member of the press and an undefended politician had become almost quaint in conception."[101] (See the box "He Never Was a Straight Shooter.")

At the same time, politicians have become more sophisticated in their efforts to **spin** the media—to portray themselves and their programs in the most favorable light, regardless of the facts, and to shade the truth. In turn, reporters have become more cynical. "They don't explicitly argue or analyze what they

"When I grow up, I hope to spoil someone's bid for the Presidency."

dislike in a political program but instead sound sneering and supercilious about the whole idea of politics."[102] This prompts politicians to increase their efforts to spin the media, which prompts reporters to escalate their comments that politicians are insincere or dishonest. And so the cycle continues.

After Vice President Al Gore announced his candidacy for president in 2000 from his family's farm in Carthage, Tennessee, ABC correspondent Diane Sawyer conducted an interview reflecting these dynamics. She began, "Are you really a country boy?" He replied, "I grew up in two places. I grew up in Washington, D.C. [as the son of a senator from Tennessee], and I grew up here. My summers were here. Christmas was here." Sawyer taunted Gore, "You mucked pigpens?" Gore answered, "I cleaned out the pigpens . . . and raised cattle and planted and plowed and harvested and took in hay." Sawyer, not satisfied, challenged Gore in an attempt to show that he was a hypocrite: "I have a test for you. Ready for a pop quiz? . . . How many plants of tobacco can you have per acre? . . . What is brucellosis? . . . What are cattle prices roughly now? . . . When a fence separates two farms, how can you tell which farm owns the fence?" By announcing from his family's farm, Gore was trying to convey his rural roots; by interviewing him in this manner, Sawyer was trying to question his sincerity.[103]

The increasingly adversarial relationship is also due to other factors mentioned earlier. There are so many media, with so much space to fill, that they have a voracious appetite for news and a strong incentive to compete against each other for something "new." As a

result, they often magnify trivial things. And because the fringe media now play a more prominent role, and because their stories eventually appear in the mainstream media, all media pay more attention to politicians' personal shortcomings with sex, drugs, and alcohol and raise more questions about politicians' "character" than they ever used to.[104] In 1977, one of every two hundred stories on network newscasts was about a purported scandal; in 1997 (*before* the Monica Lewinsky affair was revealed), one of every seven stories was.[105]

After 9/11, reporters were sensitive to, and even intimidated by, the public's fear and anger from the terrorist attacks and its vocal support for the Iraq War. Consequently, reporters relaxed their stance. But they became more adversarial again when the American victory evaporated in the war's aftermath.

Yet the apparent toughness usually is "a toughness of demeanor" rather than a toughness of substantive journalism.[106] Reporters exhibit tough attitudes rather than conduct thorough investigations and careful analyses. In fact, few engage in investigative journalism.[107] Before hurricane Katrina, reporters failed to notice that the Federal Emergency Management Administration (FEMA) was headed by political hacks rather than by people experienced in disaster response. Nor did reporters question why a study found that employees' morale at FEMA was lower than that at any other federal agency.[108] Before the coal mine accidents in 2006, reporters failed to examine the impact of significant changes in mine safety regulations and enforcement by the Bush administration.[109]

When Vice President Cheney accidentally shot a fellow hunter on a Texas ranch, neither he nor his staff nor the White House reported it to the press. The next day the ranch's owner reported it to the local newspaper. Despite the media's demands for statements or interviews, the vice president refused to respond for four more days. The White House tried to shift the spotlight from the Vice President, claiming the accident was the victim's fault. Finally, Cheney agreed to an interview with Republican friendly Fox news.[1]

Comedians had a field day using the Vice President as a punch line.

Jay Leno on *The Tonight Show with Jay Leno*, NBC: "I'm surprised Dick Cheney loves to hunt so much. The five times the government tried to give him a gun, he got a deferment."

Jimmy Kimmel on *Jimmy Kimmel Live*, ABC: "Kind of a sad study out today that single women over the age of 35 are more likely to be shot by the vice president than find a husband."

Why all the jokes? Why such media clamor? This incident resembles previous incidents in which the media seemed to make a mountain out of a molehill. Vice President Dan Quayle, appearing in a grade-school class for a photo op, misspelled the word "potato." President Jimmy Carter, fishing in Georgia, shooed away a swamp rabbit approaching his boat and gnashing its teeth. This led to stories about the "killer rabbit." Although these incidents themselves were truly minor, they reflected shortcomings already perceived by reporters and people. The Quayle incident reflected doubts about the "Veep's" smarts, and the Carter incident reflected conclusions about the administration's haplessness.[2] These spontaneous and comprehensible incidents brought "all the abstractions together into one concrete image."[3]

Although Vice President Cheney's reluctance to report and acknowledge the shooting may have been due simply to his personal anguish, the merciless jokes reflected the journalists' beliefs that the vice president, and administration foreign policies for which he has been a driving force, are secretive, arrogant, and even incompetent. So the incident—a poor decision, which led to an unfortunate result, which was not acknowledged until the outcry became too great—stands in for aspects of the war on terrorism and the war in Iraq. And it represents the journalists' feelings that the vice president, though a good shot, has not been a straight shooter.

[1]Vice President Cheney's standard contract for public appearances stipulates that the temperature be set at 68 degrees; an array of diet sodas be available; and any televisions be pre-tuned to Fox News. *Wait, Wait, Don't Tell Me*, NPR, March 25, 2006.
[2]Mark Z. Barabak, "Political Blunders Crumble Careers," *Lincoln Journal Star*, February 20, 2006, A7.
[3]Psychologist Anthony Pratkanis, quoted in *Ibid*.

Relationship between the Media and Recent Administrations

Franklin Roosevelt created the model that most contemporary presidents use to communicate with the public. Newspaper publishers, who were conservative businessmen, had no use for Roosevelt and his policies. In fact, a correspondent recalled, "The publishers didn't just disagree with the New Deal. They hated it. The reporters, who liked it, had to write as though they hated it too."[110] Recognizing that he would not receive favorable coverage, Roosevelt realized that he would have to reach the public another way. He used press conferences to provide a steady stream of news about his policies. He also used radio talks, which he called **fireside chats,** to advocate his policies and reassure his listeners in the throes of the Depression. He had a fine voice and a superb ability to speak informally—he talked about his family, even his dog. He drew such an audience that he was offered as much airtime as he wanted (though he was shrewd enough to realize that too much would result in overexposure). This tactic enabled him to avoid the filters of reporters and editors and to take his case directly to the people.[111]

In addition, Roosevelt was the first president to seek systematic feedback from the people. He used public opinion polls to gauge people's views toward his policies. Thus for him, communication was a two-way process—to the people and from the people.

Reagan Administration

Ronald Reagan refined the model. As a young man, Reagan idolized Franklin Delano Roosevelt, even developing an imitation with an appropriate accent and a cigarette holder.[112] As president, Reagan duplicated Roosevelt's success in using the media. Although Reagan was fuzzy on the facts about government programs and the details about his proposals, and sometimes he made bizarre assertions (once he said trees cause most air pollution), he had an uncanny ability to convey his broad themes. Reporters dubbed him the "Great Communicator."

As Roosevelt used radio, Reagan used television. By the time he reached the White House, after a career as an actor in movies and television, Reagan had mastered the art of speaking and performing in front of live audiences and on camera.[113] Tall, handsome, and poised, he knew exactly how to use an inflection, a gesture, or a tilt of his head to keep all eyes and ears focused on him. His speeches and even his casual comments were highly effective.

His aides knew how to make his appearances especially impressive. The administration approached its relationship with the media as "political jujitsu."[114] A jujitsu fighter tries to use the adversary's force to his or her own advantage through a clever maneuver. The administration knew that the media would cover the president extensively to fill their news columns and newscasts. An aide explained the strategy: "The media, while they won't admit it, are not in the news business; they're in entertainment. We tried to create the most entertaining, visually attractive scene to fill that box [the TV screen], so that the networks would have to use it."[115]

Aides sent advance agents days or weeks ahead of the president to prepare the "stage" for media events—the specific location, backdrops, lighting, and sound equipment. A trip to Korea was designed to show "the commander in chief on the front line against communism." An advance man went to the demilitarized zone separating North and South Korea and negotiated with the army and Secret Service for the most photogenic setting. He demanded that the president be allowed to use the most exposed bunker, which meant that the army had to erect telephone poles and string thirty thousand yards of camouflage netting to hide Reagan from North Korean sharpshooters. The advance man also demanded that the army build camera platforms on a hill that remained exposed but offered the most dramatic angle to film Reagan surrounded by sandbags. Although the Secret Service wanted sandbags up to Reagan's neck, the advance man insisted that they be no more than four inches above his navel so viewers would get a clear picture of the president wearing his flak jacket and demonstrating "American strength and resolve."[116]

The Reagan administration also developed the technique of highlighting a single theme with a single message for every day and every week to emphasize whatever proposal the president was pushing at the time. The administration then offered the media information and arranged appearances reinforcing that message. Aides strictly controlled the president. They determined "the line of the day" and instructed him what to say. He refused to answer reporters' questions about other matters. When reporters asked questions inside a building, aides demanded the television lights be shut off so that the answers could not be televised; outside they ordered the helicopter's engines revved up so that the answers could not be heard. They did not want other remarks to overshadow the message of the day. The strategy was to set the agenda and to prevent the media from setting it.[117]

By alternately using and avoiding the media, President Reagan's administration managed the news more than any administration previously.

Clinton Administration

In his use of the media, Clinton emulated Roosevelt and Reagan. Like Roosevelt, he tried to leapfrog journalists to reach citizens directly.[118] Like Reagan, he tried to focus on one issue at a time to shape public opinion on that issue.

Clinton was knowledgeable about policies, perhaps the most knowledgeable president ever, and he was articulate when speaking. Unlike Roosevelt and Reagan, however, Clinton was not enthralling. He lacked discipline, talking too long and giving too many details for most listeners. He strayed from his message of the day or the week, blurring his focus. Consequently, many people said they did not know what he stood for or wanted to do. Yet Clinton was empathetic, conveying the feeling that he cared for others, so many people said they thought he understood the problems of people like them.

Clinton was especially effective one-on-one with reporters because of his knowledge and his charm. One network correspondent who was not a supporter said, "He is the most charming man I have ever met."[119]

But Clinton inspired visceral hatred from some opponents even before he set foot in the White House. Perhaps it was because he represented the excesses of the baby boom generation, having engaged in sexual affairs and drug use, or because his independent-minded wife, Hillary, reflected the nontraditional gender roles of that generation. Or perhaps it was because his election cast doubt on conservatives' expectations that Republicans had a lock on the White House and would continue the "Reagan revolution." For whichever reason, some conservative commentators, interest groups, and congressional investigators made a concerted effort from the outset of his administration to undermine his presidency. They magnified minor miscues into major

© Bettmann/Corbis

News photo of President Reagan in Korea, staged to reflect "American strength and resolve."

scandals and fed accusations and rumors, some completely unfounded, to reporters.[120] News organizations allowed themselves to be manipulated by Clinton's opponents because, due to the atomization of the media, they were competing with other organizations. They aired charges before verifying them because other organizations, including fringe media, had done so or would do so if given a chance. Also, as one reporter later acknowledged, "there's no denying that we give more coverage to stories when someone is shouting."[121] So Clinton faced a hostile press from the start.[122]

As investigations into the Whitewater land deal, revelations about the president's personal life, and concerns about his party's fundraising prompted ethical questions, they dominated the news and hindered his efforts to convey his messages and accomplish his goals. The Clintons became bitter toward the media, and reporters became cynical toward the administration. They thought Clinton did not tell the truth or at least did not leave an accurate impression; they considered him "a master of lawyerly evasion."[123] Thus they looked for falsity or hypocrisy behind his actions and statements.

George W. Bush Administration

The Bush administration has emulated the Reagan administration in trying to manage the news by alternately using and avoiding the media.

Aides establish a message for every day and e-mail talking points to administration officials, instructing them to address these ideas. The president voices the message at his appearances, and backdrops bearing the message printed as a slogan reinforce it. Administration officials who are contacted by the press repeat it. All are expected to "stay on message."

Otherwise, access to the president and White House officials is strictly limited. The president is made available for speeches to friendly audiences or for a few questions from a few reporters at the White House. Press conferences are rarely scheduled. Bush has held far fewer conferences than other modern presidents.[124] Interviews are occasionally granted, but questions must be submitted in advance. Reporters who displease the administration are punished by losing their access.[125] When veteran reporter Helen Thomas of the Associated Press displeased the president, he refused to answer her questions at press conferences for three years.[126] As a result of this process, according to President Reagan's aide for communications, "this is the most disciplined White House in history."[127]

When the president attended a meeting in Ireland, an Irish reporter who had submitted questions in advance was dissatisfied when the president answered in generalities. She interrupted him and pressed him for more specific answers. Her behavior was so unusual that it became a news story. Unlike most American reporters, she did not worry about future access to the White House.

The administration's communications strategy also entails a very active and well-financed public relations machine. The administration contracts with public relations firms and advertising agencies to produce pseudo news reports, purporting to be actual news stories, which portray the administration as vigilant and compassionate.[128] These are distributed to television stations around the country, which integrate them into their newscasts. To viewers they appear to be news rather than propaganda. In a two-and-a-half-year period, seven cabinet departments spent $1.6 billion on 343 public relations contracts for news releases and other services.[129] The administration even paid some real reporters to say positive things about the administration's policies.

President Bush is not comfortable in front of television cameras. Initially, he shunned the role of "communicator in chief." Unlike most presidents, who used public occasions to celebrate a national accomplishment or mourn a national tragedy, Bush avoided the spotlight. When aides scheduled public appearances, he bristled.[130] When he gave formal speeches or made informal remarks, he often looked awkward and sounded inarticulate. Reporters observed that he was "perhaps the least confident public performer of the modern presidency."[131] An aide to the previous president commented, "In the Clinton administration, we worried the president would open his zipper, and in the Bush administration, they worry the president will open his mouth."[132] As governor of Texas, Bush had worked behind the scenes and evidently expected to do the same as president.

The terrorist attacks thrust Bush into the public role he had avoided. Although he failed to return to the White House on September 11 to reassure Americans from the Oval Office,[133] later he visited the site of the World Trade Center and galvanized public support when he picked up a bullhorn and talked to the workers. Gradually he grew into his new role, appearing more comfortable on the national stage. Converting "grief to anger to action,"[134] he rallied the public behind the war on terrorism and the war in Afghanistan.

Bush's strength is to speak to moral clarity. The terrorist attacks allowed Bush to talk in these terms. But September 11 was "one of history's rare unnuanced days," a presidential adviser admitted.[135] On other issues, where there is less moral clarity, such as the clash between Israelis and Palestinians, Bush is less effective. His black-and-white view of the world and his "poverty of language"[136] make it difficult for him to convey any nuances in his comments. (He told one senator, "I don't do nuance."[137]) On these issues, he can seem simpleminded, and he has sent confusing and contradictory messages to the public and to foreign countries affected by our policies.

Bush's speechwriters are quite good at expressing his ideals and very effective in communicating with his supporters. They incorporate religious language to appeal to evangelical Christians.[138] In addition to references to *evil* and *evildoers*, there are terms, such as *work of mercy* and *wonder-working power,* that are recognized by the devout. When the president announced the invasion of Afghanistan, his speech included allusions to Revelation, Isaiah, Job, Matthew, and Jeremiah.[139] The president, however, did spur a backlash in the United States and abroad when he called the war on terrorism a *crusade,* thus linking it to the Crusades by European Christians against Eastern Muslims in the Middle Ages.

Although his formal speeches are good, Bush tends to stumble when he speaks without a script. At times he forgets his train of thought, makes up words, and leaves listeners bewildered.[140] But his lack of polish does not seem to hurt him in the polls. He talks like many men, in his tone and simple words—even the belligerence in his voice—and thus relates well to many voters. Sounding like a frontier sheriff in the Wild West, he declared that Osama bin Laden was "wanted, dead or alive." When Iraqi insurgents began to use roadside bombs against American soldiers, Bush threatened, "Bring 'em on." While some people are appalled by such comments, others like the swagger in his delivery.

Days after the terrorist attacks, President Bush visited the site of the World Trade Center, mounting a pile of debris and talking to the workers through a bullhorn. Bush's comments galvanized public support for the war on terrorism and boosted his standing in the polls as well.

They see his confidence in the way he points. One observer calls Bush "a master of the American vernacular, that form of expression which eschews slickness and makes a virtue of the speaker's limitations."[141]

Relationship between the Media and Congress

Members of Congress also use the media but have less impact. They hire their own full-time press secretary, who churns out press releases, distributes television tapes, and arranges interviews with reporters.[142] The Senate and House of Representatives provide recording studios for members and allow television cameras into committee rooms and C-SPAN into the chambers. Yet members still have trouble attracting the media's eye. One president can be the subject of the media's focus, but 535 members of Congress cannot. Only a handful of powerful (or, occasionally, colorful) members receive coverage from the national media. Other members get attention from their home state or district media, but those from large urban areas with numerous representatives get little publicity or scrutiny even there.[143]

Congressional committees also use the media to influence public opinion. During the Whitewater hearings, President Clinton talked with a Republican senator on the investigating committee. "They were impugning Hillary," he recalled, "and I asked this guy, 'Do you really think my wife and I did anything wrong in this Whitewater thing?' He just started laughing. He said, 'Of course you didn't do anything wrong. That's not the point. The point of this is to make people think you did something wrong.' "[144]

Relationship between the Media and the Supreme Court

Unlike presidents and members of Congress, justices of the Supreme Court shun the media. They rarely talk to reporters, and they also forbid their law clerks from talking to the press. They try to convey the impression that they are not engaged in politics and therefore should not answer reporters' questions or concern themselves with public opinion.

As a result, the media do not cover the Supreme Court nearly as much as the presidency or Congress. Few newspapers have a full-time Court reporter; no newsmagazines or television networks do. In one recent year, only twenty-seven reporters had Court press credentials, whereas an estimated seventeen hundred reporters had White House press credentials.[145]

When the media do cover the Supreme Court, they focus on the Court's rulings.[146] They seldom in-

Paul Richards/AFP/Getty Images

vestigate or peer behind the Court's curtains. They often ignore even relevant concerns, such as questions about the justices' health. The correspondent for *USA Today* violated the norm when he discovered that only 29 of the 394 clerks hired by justices on the Rehnquist Court were minorities (and that most of these were Asians). His investigation irritated other correspondents, some of whom refused to report the story for their media.[147]

Most reporters on this beat, called "Washington's most deferential press corps,"[148] reject the role of watchdog. Consequently, the justices are shielded from both the legitimate investigation and the excessive scrutiny that officials in the other branches are subjected to.

Relationship between the Media and the Military

During wartime, the military has tried to control media coverage to avoid the negative reports and the disturb-

ing photographs that typified the last years of the Vietnam War.[149] For the Afghanistan War, the administration bought the exclusive rights to the photographic images from all private satellites so that media organizations would be unable to use any. Thus American taxpayers paid private companies more than $2 million per month to prevent themselves from seeing what was happening.[150] The military also kept the journalists at arm's length from the fighting.

For the Iraq War, the military tried a new approach, embedding the journalists into fighting units. Six hundred journalists ate, slept, and traveled with the soldiers and were allowed to report live. They were prohibited from revealing sensitive information and from having anonymous interviews, which would enable the soldiers to make critical comments. Their reporting was also limited by the nature of the war. (See box, "Reporting from Iraq.")

The military's goals were to appease the media organizations and at the same time use them to show the technological prowess of our military and the

Todd Heisler, *Rocky Mountain News/Polaris*

The Bush administration has tried to prevent journalists from photographing coffins returning from the Iraq war, usually flying the coffins to military bases in the middle of the night. But a journalist observed this coffin coming home to Reno, Nevada.

"Iraq has been many things to many people: necessary war, project for democracy, quagmire without end.

"Yet for the dozens of newspaper and television reporters trying to make sense of the place, Iraq above all is a shrinking country. Village by village, block by block, the vast and challenging land that we entered in 2003 has shriveled into a medieval city-state, a grim and edgy place where the only question is how much more territory we will lose tomorrow. On some days, it seems, we are all crowded into a single room together, clutching our notebooks and watching the walls.

"What I mean, of course, is that the business of reporting in Iraq has become a terribly truncated affair, an enterprise clipped and limited by the violence all around. If the American military has its 'no-go' zones, places where it no longer sends its troops, we in the press have ours. . . . Even in areas of the capital still thought to be safe, very few reporters are still brazen enough to get out of a car, walk around and stop people at random.

"Most of us have our own store of close calls to remind us of how dangerous the streets here have become. For the newcomer, there is the video of two French reporters, kidnapped and pleading for their lives, and the list, updated regularly, of the 46 reporters killed here while doing their jobs. [Thirty-eight journalists had been kidnapped and 82 had been killed by February, 2006.]¹

"The presumption, now quaint, [is] that reporters are regarded as neutrals in armed conflicts, that they are there to record the event for history. In Iraq, this has not been true for many months. For many insurgents here, and for a fevered class of Islamic zealots, Western reporters are fair game, targets in their war.

"Here at the *New York Times,* where we have spared no expense to protect ourselves, the catalogue of hits

and near-misses is long enough to chill the hardiest war correspondent: we have been shot at, kidnapped, blindfolded, held at knifepoint, held at gunpoint, detained, threatened, beaten, and chased. . . . And that's just the intentional acts. On any given day here, car bombs explode, gun battles break out, and mortar shells fall short. . . . In the writing of this essay, . . . two rockets and three mortar shells have landed close enough to shake the walls of our house.

"In my time here, I have marked significant events here, like the drafting of a new Iraqi Constitution and the formal end of the American occupation, and I have marked a number of personal ones, too.

"Oct. 27, 2003: Attacked by a mob.

"Dec. 19, 2003: Shot at.

"May 8, 2004: Followed by a car of armed men.

"Aug. 28, 2004: Detained by the Mahdi Army. 'You are the second American spy I have captured today,' the insurgent leader boasted, leading me away.

"Stepping out of my car at the scene of a suicide bombing last fall, I stepped into what appeared to be a placid crowd, only to find that it was seething and angry, blaming the Americans, as Iraqis often do, for the death and destruction all around them. The crowd surged before I and my colleagues could get back into the car.

"'Kill them!' an old man shouted. 'Kill them!'

"We barely got away. Back at the office, we counted 17 bricks inside the car, whose every window was smashed.

"In most foreign countries where I have worked, being an American was a kind of armor; the fear of messing with an American forced even the angriest zealots to take a moment to think.

"Here, that fear has vanished, and indeed, it has become its opposite. To be an American reporter in Iraq . . . is

not just to be a target yourself, but it is to make a target of others, too. As a result, some Iraqis now shy away from meeting. . . . [One] asked me not to speak English in the hallway leading to his office. . . . [Another] asks that I meet his armed guards in front of a local mosque, who then drive me to his house. Better not to have an American reporter's car parked in front of his house.

"The real consequence of the mayhem here is that we reporters can no longer do our jobs in the way we hope to. Reporters are nothing more than watchers and listeners, and if we can't leave the house, the picture from Iraq, even with the help of fearless Iraqi stringers [assistants], almost inevitably will be blurry and incomplete.

"Some of my colleagues have given up. Most of the European reporters . . . are gone. And there are far fewer American reporters here than . . . just a few months ago."

¹Tim Rutten, "When Writing Truth Is a Crime," *Los Angeles Times,* February 25, 2006.

SOURCE: Excerpted from Dexter Filkins, "Get Me Rewrite. Now. Bullets Are Flying." *New York Times,* October 10, 2004, WK1, 1.

heroic exploits of our fighters. According to an official, it was "important for the public to be invested in this emotionally and personally," unlike the Persian Gulf War in 1991, which was covered from a distance and looked like a video arcade game.[151]

The military was so anxious for uplifting coverage that when Pat Tillman, the Arizona Cardinals defensive back who volunteered for the army after 9/11, was killed by friendly fire, the army refused to reveal the cause of death to the public or even to his parents for over a month. Instead, it issued a false press release exaggerating his actions. As its most famous volunteer, the army wanted to use him as an heroic poster boy, and President Bush wanted to use him for his reelection campaign, offering to tape a memorial for a Cardinals game just before Election Day. (The family refused.)[152]

Bias of the Media

Every night, Walter Cronkite, former anchor for *CBS Evening News,* signed off by saying, "And that's the way it is," implying that the network held a huge mirror to the world and returned a perfect reflection to its viewers, without selection or distortion. But the media do not hold a mirror. They hold a searchlight that seeks and illuminates some things instead of others.[153]

From all the events that occur in the world every day, the media can report only a handful as the news of the day. Even the fat *New York Times,* whose motto is "All the News That's Fit to Print," cannot include all the news. The media must decide what events are newsworthy. They must decide where to report these—on the front page or at the top of the newscast, or in a less prominent position. Then they must decide how to report them. When the Wright brothers invited reporters to Kitty Hawk, North Carolina, to observe the first airplane flight in 1903, none considered it newsworthy enough to cover. After the historic flight, only seven American newspapers reported it, and only two reported it on their front page.[154]

In making these decisions, it would be natural for journalists' attitudes to affect their coverage. As one acknowledged, a reporter writes "from what he hears and sees and how he filters it through the lens of his own experience. No reporter is a robot."[155]

Political Bias

Historically, the press was politically biased. The first papers, which were established by political parties, parroted the party line. Even the independent papers, which succeeded them, advocated one side or the other. The attitudes of publishers, editors, and reporters seeped—sometimes flooded—into their prose.

But the papers gradually abandoned their ardor for editorializing and adopted the practice of "objectivity" to attract and retain as many readers as possible. This means that in news stories (not in editorials or columns) they try to present the facts rather than their opinions. When the facts are in dispute, they try to present the positions of both sides. They are reluctant to evaluate these positions. Even when one side makes a false or misleading assertion, they are hesitant to notify their readers. Instead, they rely upon the other side to do so. They hope that their readers can discern which is accurate.

Although most mainstream media today follow the practice of objectivity, the public still thinks the press is biased. Many people think the press is "out to get" the groups they identify with. Executives believe the press is out to get businesses, and laborers believe it is out to get unions. Conservatives believe it is biased against conservatives, and liberals believe it is biased against liberals. Republicans believe it is biased against Republicans, and Democrats believe it is biased against Democrats.[156]

Indeed, the public is more critical today, when most media at least attempt to be objective, than in the past, when the media did not even pretend to be. Back then, citizens could subscribe to whichever local paper reflected their own biases. Now, as local newspapers and television stations have given way to national newspapers and networks and as independently owned newspapers and television stations have given way to large chains and conglomerates, people have less opportunity to follow only those media that reflect their views. People with strong views are disappointed with this more balanced coverage. So partisans on both sides criticize the same media for being biased—though in opposite directions.

To assess the presence and the direction of **political bias,** it is necessary to examine the differences in coverage by the advocacy media and the mainstream media; the differences in coverage of elections and issues; and the differences in coverage of domestic policies and international policies.

Bias in the Advocacy Media

Some media do not try to be neutral. Advocacy media intentionally tilt one way or the other and seek an audience of people who share their views. Advocacy media can be found at both ends of the political spectrum, though far more are conservative than liberal.

Because conservatives perceived a liberal bias in the mainstream media, they established their own media in the 1980s and 1990s. This vocal complex includes newspapers, such as the *Wall Street Journal* (editorial page), the *Washington Times,* and the *New York Post,* various magazines, numerous radio and television talk shows and

Internet websites, plus a network of columnists, commentators, and think tanks. These journalists, seeing themselves as part of an ideological movement, as members of the same team, are unabashedly conservative.

Their role in talk radio has been especially powerful. The rise of talk radio began in 1987 when Reagan appointees to the Federal Communications Commission (FCC) abandoned the Fairness Doctrine, which had required broadcasters to maintain editorial balance. When Congress reinstated the doctrine, President Reagan vetoed the bill, thus allowing broadcasters to cater to any audience. At the time, the daytime television audience was mostly female, and the daytime radio audience was mostly male. A gender gap emerged in political preferences as men became more conservative and women remained more liberal, and a backlash grew against feminism and affirmative action among middle-class and lower-middle-class whites. Many stations decided to capture these listeners by airing their views.

Today, more than thirteen hundred talk stations fill the airwaves, and more than a fifth of American adults consider talk radio their primary source for news.[157] The vast majority of talk shows are hosted by conservative commentators,[158] such as Rush Limbaugh, Sean Hannity, Bill O'Reilly, G. Gordon Liddy,[159] Oliver North, and numerous others. Limbaugh is given credit by Republicans for enabling the party to wrest control of Congress from the Democrats in 1994 and for helping George W. Bush win the presidency in 2000.[160] Now the Republican National Committee has a Radio Services Department that provides talking points to these hosts every day so that they will reinforce the message from the White House.[161]

The conservative advocacy media also include the Fox News Channel. Fox is the first television network to *narrowcast*—intentionally appeal to a narrow segment of the entire audience—rather than broadcast.[162] Owned by a conservative media mogul and operated by a former Republican consultant, Fox appeals to conservatives disenchanted with the mainstream media.[163] It presents a skewed lineup of commentators and guests that features prominent conservatives with strong personalities paired with relatively unknown liberals with relatively weak personalities. Fox also follows the talking points from the Republican National Committee. After years of critical coverage of President Clinton, now it offers fawning coverage of President Bush. Throughout its programming, the network blurs the distinction between news and commentary. For instance, when reporting on a proposal by President Bush to cut taxes, the network ran a line along the bottom of the screen urging, "Cut 'em already."[164] When reporting on Swiss protesters against the Iraq War, an anchor referred to the demonstrators as "hun-

dreds of knuckleheads." Another referred to France, which opposed the war, as a member of the "axis of weasels." The network then ran that phrase along the bottom of the screen when reporting about France.

Fox aired relentlessly upbeat coverage of the Iraq War. Its correspondents were urged to downplay American casualties. (In a memo from a senior executive, they were instructed: "Do not fall into the easy trap of mourning the loss of U.S. lives.") They were also told to refer to marine snipers as "sharpshooters," because the word *snipers* has a negative connotation. And all along, the network questioned the patriotism of liberals and critics of the war.[165]

Fox launched a crusade against the supposed "War on Christmas" in 2005, criticizing businesses and individuals who wished folks "Happy Holidays" instead of "Merry Christmas." It broadcast fifty-eight segments in one five-day period.[166]

A former Fox correspondent said it was common to hear producers remind them, "We have to feed the core"—that is, their conservative viewers.[167] Yet the network retains a veneer of neutrality. It claims to be "fair and balanced" and "spin free." The marketing strategy is to attract viewers by offering them conservative commentary but also the reassurance that this commentary is truth rather than opinion.[168]

The conservative media also include Christian radio networks, television organizations, and more than thirteen hundred radio and television stations.[169] These media address political issues as well as spiritual matters.

Although liberals have as many magazines and Internet websites, the only advocacy media they dominate are documentary films.[170] For example, Michael Moore's films, such as *Fahrenheit 9/11*, also offer a combination of facts, opinions, and speculation, though from the left rather than the right.

Bias in the Mainstream Media

Although the advocacy media are far more slanted, allegations of bias are leveled against the mainstream media far more often. Conservative groups and commentators, especially, claim that these media are biased toward liberal candidates and policies.[171]

Journalists for the mainstream media are not very representative of the public. They are disproportionately college-educated white males from the upper middle class. They are disproportionately urban and secular, rather than rural and religious, and they are disproportionately Democrats or independents leaning to the Democrats, rather than Republicans or independents leaning to the Republicans. Likewise, they identify themselves disproportionately as liberals rather than conservatives.[172]

Journalists who work for the most influential organizations—large newspapers, wire services, newsmagazines, and radio and television networks—are more likely to be Democrats and liberals than those who work for less prominent organizations—small newspapers and radio and television stations.[173]

Journalists in the most influential organizations are more likely than the public to support the liberal position on issues. At the same time, they support capitalism and do not think that our institutions "need overhaul."[174] Thus they are not extremely liberal.

Focusing on journalists' backgrounds and attitudes assumes that these color journalists' coverage. But several factors mitigate the effect of these traits. Most journalists chose their profession not because of a commitment to a political ideology but because of the opportunity to rub elbows with powerful people and be close to exciting events. "Each day brings new stories, new dramas in which journalists participate vicariously."[175] As a result, most journalists "care more about the politics of an issue than about the issue itself,"[176] so they are less likely to express their views about the issue.

In addition, mainstream organizations pressure journalists to muffle their views because of both a conviction that it is professional to do so and a desire to avoid the headaches that could arise otherwise—debates among their staffers, complaints from their local affiliates, complaints from their audience, perhaps even complaints from the White House or Congress. Sometimes media executives or editors pressure reporters because they have contrary views.[177]

Some organizations fear public perceptions of reporters' bias so much that they restrict reporters' private lives, forbidding any political activity, even outside the office and on their own time.[178]

For these reasons, mainstream media do not exhibit nearly as much political bias toward candidates or policies as would be expected from journalists' backgrounds and attitudes.

To measure bias, researchers use a technique called content analysis. They scrutinize newspaper and television stories to determine whether there was an unequal amount of coverage, unequal use of favorable or unfavorable statements, or unequal use of a positive or negative tone. They consider insinuating verbs ("he conceded" rather than "he said") and pejorative adjectives ("her weak response" rather than "her response"), and for television stories, they evaluate the announcers' nonverbal communication—voice inflection, eye movement, and body language.

Bias in Elections

Researchers have examined media coverage of presidential campaigns the most and have found relatively little bias. The media typically gave the two major candidates equal attention, and they usually avoided any favorable or unfavorable statements in their news stories.

They typically provided diverse views in editorials and columns, with some commentary slanting one way and other commentary slanting the opposite way. The authors of a study examining forty-six newspapers concluded that American newspapers are "fairly neutral."[179] Other studies have reached similar conclusions about various media.[180] An analysis of the data from fifty-nine studies found no significant bias in newspapers, a little (pro-Republican) bias in newsmagazines, and a little (pro-Democratic) bias on television networks.[181]

Overall, there is less bias than the public believes or the candidates feel. When candidates complain, they are usually objecting to bad news or are trying to manipulate the media. The strategy is to put reporters on the defensive so that they will go easier on the candidate or harder on the opponent in the future, just as sports coaches "work the refs" over officiating calls.

Yet the way in which the media cover campaigns can have different implications for different candidates. The media report the facts that one candidate is leading while the other is trailing, that one campaign is surging while the other is slipping. "We all respond like Pavlov's dogs to polls," an experienced correspondent explained.[182] This coverage has positive implications for those who are leading or surging—swaying undecided voters, galvanizing campaign workers, and attracting financial contributions—and negative implications for those who are trailing or slipping. Such coverage does not benefit one party over the other party in election after election, but it can benefit one party's candidate over the other party's candidate in a particular election.[183] People who support the losers consider such reporting biased. Journalists, however, consider it simply a reflection of reality.

Another habitual practice has different implications for different candidates. The press pays more attention to minor things that are easy to report—and easy to ridicule—than to substantive issues that are difficult to explain.[184] Hence the voluminous coverage about President Clinton's sexual affairs. Although reporters are willing to criticize or even ridicule candidates about minor matters, they are usually reluctant to challenge them on substantive issues. Doing so would require more knowledge about substantive policies or more nerve to draw conclusions about these policies than most reporters have.

Likewise, when covering presidential debates, the press pays more attention to style and tactics than to substantive issues—more attention to how something was said than to what was said.[185] Reporters act more like theater critics than helpful guides to confused voters. These practices do not reflect bias by reporters as much as they reflect superficiality in reporting.

There are two exceptions to the generalization that overt political bias in elections is minimal. First, the media usually give short shrift to third-party candidates.[186] Ralph Nader, who first ran for president in 2000, was well known and held views partly shared by various blocs of voters, but he received scant coverage. When he held a press conference announcing his candidacy, none of the networks and few of the newspapers even reported it. When he held enthusiastic rallies on college campuses and in large coliseums, the national media virtually ignored them. Only when the election between Gore and Bush tightened and it appeared that Nader might be a spoiler did the national media pay attention. Then they focused on his potential as a spoiler rather than on his views that had attracted the crowds.[187]

Second, newspapers traditionally print editorials and columns that express opinions. In editorials before elections, papers endorse candidates. Most owners are Republican, and many influence the editorials. Since the first survey in 1932, more papers have endorsed the Republican presidential candidate, except in the elections of 1964, 1992, and 2004, when Kerry edged Bush in endorsements—212 to 199.[188]

Bias against All Candidates and Officials

Some critics charge that a general bias exists against all candidates and officials—a negative undercurrent in reporting about government, regardless of who or what is covered. President Nixon's first vice president, Spiro Agnew, called journalists "nattering nabobs of negativism." Critics believe that this bias increased after the Vietnam War and the Watergate scandal made reporters more cynical.

There is considerable validity to this charge. Analyses of newspapers, magazines, and television networks show that the overwhelming majority of stories about government and politicians are neutral.[189] However, the rest are more often negative than positive.[190]

Emphasizing the negative distorts what candidates say. In the 1996 presidential campaign, 85 percent of the candidates' comments made a positive case for the candidates, but 85 percent of the media's coverage dwelled on the negative attacks by the candidates.[191] Emphasizing the negative also distorts what officials do. The *Washington Post* reported that Senator Robert Byrd (D-W.Va.) got the National Park Service to fund a project for his state, including the renovation of a train station—for his "personal pork barrel." "Why did the National Park Service spend $2.5 million turning a railroad station into a visitor center for a town with a population of eight?" The compelling reason—Senator Robert C. Byrd, "who glides past on Amtrak's Cardinal Limited from time to time, heading to and from his home in Sophia, a few miles south." But Byrd did not ride that train, and that train did not go to that town. Moreover, the Interior Department recom-

mended the project; it was not "slipped" into other legislation "unwanted," as the article claimed. When the reporter was questioned, he replied with disgust, "Look, everyone knows that this is the way the world works in Washington. What's the big deal?" Indeed, this is the way things work in Washington sometimes, but apparently not this time. This article, which prompted editorials in newspapers across the country, reinforced readers' cynicism. When Byrd challenged the accuracy of the article, the paper made no effort to confirm the accuracy or correct the record.[192]

Emphasizing the negative conveys the impression that the individuals involved are unworthy of the office they seek or the one they hold. It ultimately conveys the impression that the political process itself is contemptible.[193]

Bias toward Issues

The relative lack of bias in the coverage of elections (except for the negative tone against all candidates) does not necessarily mean there is no bias in the coverage of issues. Because elections are highly visible and candidates are very sensitive about the coverage, the media take more care to be neutral here than elsewhere.

Researchers have not examined the coverage of issues as much. Empirical studies of the coverage of several domestic issues, including abortion, school busing, and nuclear power, found a tilt toward the liberal positions.[194] Anecdotal reports of the coverage of other domestic issues, such as gay rights, gun control, capital punishment, the environment, and homelessness, also suggest some bias toward the left.[195]

At the same time, the media exaggerate crimes, drugs, and other urban pathologies that stereotype African Americans and, to a lesser extent, Hispanics.[196] In this respect, they do not reflect a bias toward the left.

Popular television programs, movies, and records often promote social ideas or trends characterized as liberal, such as diversity, multiculturalism, acceptance of racial minorities, acceptance of casual sex, and disparagement of traditional religion. Conservative Christians, especially, feel that their beliefs are under daily attack by the "liberal media." (However, these media also glorify violence and guns, which do not reflect liberal values.) Such entertainment might have as much or even more effect on individuals' views than the news does. But this chapter focuses on the news media, not the entertainment media, which are beyond the scope of this text.

Although debates about bias revolve around liberalism and conservatism, perhaps the questions should be pointed toward class differences. An examination of the coverage of the debate over the North American Free Trade Agreement (NAFTA), drafted to ease trade between American and Canadian and Mexican companies, showed more emphasis on the benefits of free trade than on the loss of jobs that results from the treaty. Thus the media reflected the views of business more than those of workers.[197]

Analysts now suggest that for domestic issues, the most significant bias is not liberal or conservative but upper-middle class over working class.[198] This bias usually favors the liberal positions on social issues and the conservative, or business, positions on economic issues.[199]

These views closely reflect the urban background, college education, and social class of most journalists. Most journalists are "unlikely to have any idea what it means to go without health insurance, to be unable to locate affordable housing, to have their children in underfunded and dilapidated schools, to have relatives in prison or on the front lines of the military, [or] to face the threat of severe poverty."[200]

The picture on foreign policy is different from that of domestic issues. The mainstream media toe the government line. Often this is the conservative position.[201]

During the Cold War, this meant harsh attacks on the Soviet Union and leftist Latin American regimes and their economic systems.[202] During the Persian Gulf War, this meant jingoistic coverage and unquestioning acceptance of administration claims.[203] Even during the Vietnam War, often cited as an example of journalistic rejection of governmental policies, the media offered blindly positive coverage for many years and then relatively restrained criticism near the end.[204]

This bias was apparent after the 2001 terrorist attacks. The media not only quoted the president and other officials extensively, as would be expected, but they also adopted the mindset and language of administration officials. An analysis of the editorials of twenty metropolitan newspapers showed that they echoed the president's rhetoric, magnifying our feelings of fear and portraying a conflict between values decreed by God and evil perpetrated by the terrorists and their supporters. Like the president, the newspapers emphasized urgent action over debate and national unity over dissent.[205] The television networks also followed the administration, featuring patriotic logos and melodramatic music.

Some media went further. Two newspapers fired columnists who criticized the president's delayed return to the Capitol on September 11, and cable systems yanked *Politically Incorrect*, whose host Bill Maher questioned the president's use of the word *cowardly* to refer to the terrorists.[206] CBS anchor Dan Rather, who used to pride himself on his independence, declared, "George Bush is the president. He makes the decisions and . . . wherever he wants me to line up, just tell me where." CNN's head warned the staff, "If you get on the wrong side of public opinion, you are going to get into trouble."[207] The patriotic fervor diminished media coverage and therefore public awareness of important matters, such as Arab opinion, the conflict between the Israelis and the Palestinians, and the disagreements among the countries fighting terrorism.[208]

This bias was also evident in coverage of the Iraq War. In the run-up to the war, the sources cited in television news were overwhelmingly prowar—according to one study, 71 percent were prowar, whereas only 3 percent were antiwar[209]—and the pundits on television talk shows were heavily prowar as well. Although there were snippets of doubt and clips of protests on television newscasts, there was no substantive debate.[210]

The media conveyed, without examination, officials' assertions that there was a link between Saddam Hussein and 9/11. For many people, this became a primary justification for the war. Later, the president admitted that there was no known link between the two, but only three of the nation's twelve largest newspapers reported this story on the front page, and two of the papers (the *New York Post* and the *Wall Street Journal*) did not report it at all.[211]

The media also conveyed, without examination, officials' assertions that Iraq possessed weapons of mass destruction—biological, chemical, and nuclear weapons. For many people, this, too, became a primary justification for the war. (See the box "What You Watch Affects What You Believe"). In the war, no evidence of these weapons was found (at least as of the fall of 2006).

During the war, the networks used special music, graphics, and promotions to dramatize American patriotism and evoke viewers' emotions. Fox and MSNBC used the administration's moniker for the war, "Operation Iraqi Freedom," and most networks used the administration's term *coalition forces,* thus endorsing the administration's claim that there was a broad coalition. (In fact, the war was fought by troops from the United States, with some troops from Great Britain, fewer troops from South Korea, Italy, and Poland, and token representation from other countries.) CNN, with audiences around the globe, used two news teams to cover the war. One team, beamed to the United States, was overtly prowar; the other team, beamed to the rest of the world, was more neutral.[212] And, for good measure, MSNBC removed Phil Donohue from his afternoon show out of fear that his liberal sensibilities would offend conservative viewers during wartime.[213]

Throughout the war, the American media, compared with European and Middle Eastern media, sanitized the combat. They were slow to report negative news[214] and reluctant to depict the blood and gore—the reality of war—in both words and pictures of both Americans and Iraqis.[215] (For example, the media reported that U.S. bombers were "softening up" Iraqi

WHAT YOU WATCH AFFECTS WHAT YOU BELIEVE

A majority of Americans have had serious misperceptions about important questions relating to the Iraq War, according to a study based on a series of seven polls spanning nine months. Respondents were asked whether world public opinion favored the United States's going to war, whether there was clear evidence that Saddam Hussein was working with al-Qaeda, and whether weapons of mass destruction were found during the war. (Responses to the second and third questions are shown in Figure 5.2.) Respondents were asked what their primary source of news is and how often they watch, listen to, or read this source. Respondents' misperceptions varied according to the media they followed. Those who watched Fox had the most misperceptions, whereas those who watched public television or listened to public radio had the fewest.[1] The misperceptions were not due to people's paying little attention to the news. Just the opposite: those who watched Fox more often had more misperceptions than those who watched it less often.

The results not only suggest biased or superficial coverage by some media

more than others, the results also have policy implications. Respondents' misperceptions were related to their support for the war. Those with the most misperceptions expressed the most support for the war.

Remarkably, in 2006 50 percent of Americans still believed that Iraq had weapons of mass destruction leading up to the war.[2]

[1] Researchers tried to control for the possibility that people presort themselves according to ideology by comparing the same demographic groups for each source and also by comparing similar political groups—for example, they compared people who planned to vote for Bush in 2004 and watched Fox with people who planned to vote for Bush but followed other media.
[2] Charles J. Hanley, "Half of Americans Still Believe WMD Claims, Polls Show," *Lincoln Journal Star*, August 9, 2006, 1A.

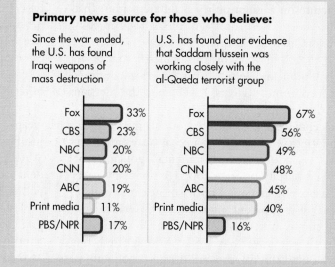

Primary news source for those who believe:

Since the war ended, the U.S. has found Iraqi weapons of mass destruction		U.S. has found clear evidence that Saddam Hussein was working closely with the al-Qaeda terrorist group	
Fox	33%	Fox	67%
CBS	23%	CBS	56%
NBC	20%	NBC	49%
CNN	20%	CNN	48%
ABC	19%	ABC	45%
Print media	11%	Print media	40%
PBS/NPR	17%	PBS/NPR	16%

FIGURE 5.2 ■ Misperceptions and Their Origins

SOURCE: Program on International Policy at the University of Maryland and Knowledge Networks. Poll of 3334 adults, conducted January–September 2003, with a margin of error of 1.7 percent (www.knowledgenetworks .com/ganp).

defenses. The Air Force commander was amused by the phrase. "We're not softening them up," he said. "We're killing them."[216]) The media sanitized the coverage because "the dirty little secret of much war 'news' is that much of the audience wants to entrance itself into emotional surrender, and news officials want to elicit precisely that surrender."[217] The media did not offer grimmer reports and starker photographs until after the collapse of Saddam's government, when the lack of real security in Iraq became apparent.

For some time, the media were cowed by the power of the administration as well as by the demands of the public. Officials insinuated that any criticism, even questioning, by reporters was unpatriotic. Officials also issued veiled threats to reporters. The White House

press secretary remarked, "People had better watch what they say."[218] Another official ominously warned a reporter that his name was on "a list," presumably of disloyal journalists who would be watched and, perhaps, dealt with.[219] The administration threatened to deny access to reporters who displeased officials. This would mean no interviews, no tips or leaks, no invitations to special events, and no seats on the plane for presidential trips. Where access is all important, this would make it difficult for reporters to do their jobs. The result was a chilling effect on reporters, editors, and executives.[220] So most media, including supposedly "liberal newspapers" such as the *New York Times* and the *Washington Post*, were little more than stenographers, writing down and passing on administration statements without serious questioning. Later, the *Post* acknowledged that its reporting before the war and early in the war was "strikingly one-sided at times."[221]

As the aftermath of the invasion revealed serious flaws in U.S. policy, many media became more critical. The *Times* apologized for its lack of scrutiny and skepticism of administration claims.[222] Its apology prompted a letter to the editor that could have been sent to most American news organizations:

> *I've followed all the stories and the "spin" to create a case for war from the beginning. . . . As a university student, I sat through it and asked questions as cabinet members made their case for war. In the sixteen months leading up to my activation to fight in Iraq as a tank platoon commander, I felt that this spin was an effort to find a magic button of support with the citizenry. . . .*
>
> *So off I went, to lead my men on this quest. We fought and died holding up the soldiers' end of the democratic bargain. I lived with many of the young men fighting and dying who had such blind faith in our system of government. They felt it was just right to do what we were doing, even though many of them could not explain or justify why.*
>
> *So on this Memorial Day weekend, as I sit and think about what I've done, the people who have been hurt, the future of this ongoing tragedy, I come to this conclusion: Shame on you.*"[223]

The mainstream media reflect the government line on foreign policy because they rely on government officials as their sources for most news.[224] They fear losing access to these officials. This means that their stories will bear officials' imprint. It also means that their stories will revolve around debates among officials—what "he said" versus what "she said." When there is little dissent within the government, as in the run-up to the Iraq war, there is little coverage of opposing views by the media, even if there are alternative views in our society.[225] Journalists seem flummoxed when they cannot frame an issue as a debate between opposing groups of officials.

Perceptions of Bias

We have seen that in the mainstream media there is minimal bias in favor of particular candidates or parties in elections, and there is some liberal bias in the coverage of social issues, some conservative bias in the coverage of economic issues, and often conservative bias in the coverage of foreign policy. Overall, however, there is far less political bias than many people believe. In particular, there is far less liberal bias than many conservatives believe.[226] Why do so many people perceive so much bias?

As noted earlier, there is some negative bias against all candidates and officials. People sense this bias against the candidates or officials on their side but don't see it against the candidates or officials on the other side. In addition, people hear aides to the candidates or officials complain about the media without realizing that the aides are simply "working the refs" rather than sincerely lodging a complaint.[227] Also, people hear the steady drumbeat from interest groups and talk shows that the media are biased against their side. Eventually, they come to believe it. They don't realize that the leaders of interest groups and hosts of talk shows are just trying to get people riled up so they will join the group, make a contribution, subscribe to a magazine, or listen to the show. One influential conservative downplayed liberal bias in an interview but at the same time was claiming liberal bias in subscription

pitches for his magazine.[228] Karl Rove, President Bush's top aide, has also dismissed the idea of liberal bias in the media.[229]

Yet many conservatives among the public assume the existence of liberal bias. Studies show that strong partisans with strong views perceive more bias than average people.[230] When strong partisans on opposite sides evaluate the same stories in the same media, both groups see bias against their side, even when the stories are balanced.[231] Certain that their side is correct, they consider coverage that is actually balanced as slanted because it gives their opponents more credence than their opponents deserve. And although these partisans say that biased coverage will not affect them, they fear it will affect others who are less aware or astute.[232]

When strong partisans evaluate coverage that is clearly biased toward their side, they see no bias or less bias than average people.[233] They consider this coverage fair, because in their eyes it reports the "truth."

Even if people's perceptions are inaccurate reflections of media coverage, their perceptions determine which newscasts they will watch. As a result of conservatives' criticism over the years, some mainstream media have become cowed. CNN has ordered producers to include more conservatives than liberals in their stories.[234] During the 2004 presidential campaign, CBS twice postponed a documentary on the faulty intelligence about Iraq's purported weapons of mass destruction. The network said that it would show the documentary after the election, when the network could not be accused of trying to affect the election's outcome.[235]

Commercial Bias

Although the public dwells on charges of political bias, **commercial bias** is far more pervasive and important in understanding media coverage of politics. As Ted Koppel, former anchor of ABC's *Nightline*, notes, "The accusation that [the] news has a political agenda misses the point. Right now, the main agenda is to give the people what they want. It is not partisanship but profitability that shapes what you see."[236]

Reasons for Commercial Bias

Traditionally, the mainstream media believed they had a "public trust" to meet journalistic standards and provide important news. Newspapers made less money than other businesses, and television news divisions consistently lost money. When *60 Minutes* first aired, the head of CBS told the creator of the show, "Make us proud."[237] The show became a hit, and in its first decade it made so much profit—more than the Chrysler Corporation did during the same years[238]—that the executives started telling the producers, "Make us money!"[239] At the same time, television newscasts

became more popular and even profitable. This transformation of the news from an economic backwater to a profit stream has had a huge impact on the mainstream media.

As private businesses, American media, except for public broadcasting, are run for a profit. The larger their audience, the more they can charge for their advertising. An increase or decrease of 1 percent in the ratings of a television news program in New York City, for example, can mean a difference of $5 million in advertising for the year.[240] NBC's news division generated 40 to 50 percent of NBC's overall profit in recent years, with its entertainment and sports divisions dividing the rest.[241] Local stations' news programs also provide 40 to 50 percent of the stations' overall profit.[242]

With chains and conglomerates taking over most media, the pressure to make a sizable profit has escalated. In the 1970s, big-city newspapers expected to make a 7 or 8 percent profit; today chains and conglomerates expect these papers to make a 20 to 30 percent profit.[243]

Corporate executives worry that financial analysts will consider them a poor investment and mutual fund managers will refuse to buy or keep their stock if their earnings fall below those available "from investments anywhere else in the financial universe, from a shirt factory in Thailand to the latest Internet start-up."[244]

The pressure to make a profit and the need to attract an audience shape the media's presentation of the news and lead to commercial bias. Sometimes this means that the media deliberately print or broadcast what their advertisers want. CBS bowed to demands by Procter & Gamble that it drop episodes of *Family Law* dealing with gun ownership, capital punishment, interfaith marriage, and abortion.[245] Sometimes the media censor themselves. In 2004, VH1 and MTV pulled clips of, and refused to run ads for, the documentary *Super Size Me*, which shows what happened to a guy who ate every meal at McDonald's for a month. They feared losing advertising from fast-food restaurants. A poll of reporters and executives found that a third admitted to avoiding stories that would embarrass an advertiser or harm the financial interests of their own organization.[246]

Usually, though, commercial bias means that the media print or broadcast what the public wants, which is to say what the public finds entertaining. (See box "Color and the Clicker.") This creates a "conflict between being an honest reporter and being a member of show business," a network correspondent confessed, "and that conflict is with me every day."[247] When Dan Rather was asked why CBS devoted time to the demolition of O. J. Simpson's house two years after his trial, Rather answered, "Fear. . . . The fear that if we

COLOR AND THE CLICKER

Television news features African Americans in "lights-and-sirens" stories about crimes and drugs and in other stories about urban pathologies, such as single parenthood, that reinforce negative stereotypes.[1] However, television news shuns African Americans in other contexts—not just in the newscasts that focus on government officials but also in the newsmagazines, such as *Dateline, 20/20, 60 Minutes,* and *48 Hours,* that air human dramas.[2] A network staff member lamented, "Can't we do a story about day-care centers and have a black day-care owner . . . ? Why can't they be regular, normal people doing regular, normal things that aren't just associated with their ethnic backgrounds? It makes me sick."[3]

A producer working on a story about a mental disability was searching for a family who had a child with that disability. "I found a great, great upper-middle-class family in Miami, but they were black. I was told . . . : 'Find another family.'" Many network staff members have had similar experiences.

"It's a subtle thing," said one. "A story involving blacks takes longer to get approved. And if it is approved, chances are that it will sit on the shelf a long time before it gets on the air. No one ever says anything. The message gets through." Sometimes it's not so subtle. Staffers were told by executives that a particular story was "not a good story for us" or that it would "not have broad appeal in the Midwest and in the South." Instead, they were told to feature "families with lots of blond-haired, blue-eyed children."[4]

One reporter observed, "They whisper it, like cancer: 'Is she white?'"

"'Yeah, she's white.'"

"'Are you sure?'"

"'Well, it says they are from Slovakian descent; I'm assuming.'"

"'Well, go out and check.'"

A producer on an evening newscast, working on a health series, found a story about a doctor who encouraged women to get mammograms. The doctor hauled her equipment to beauty parlors where she could test the women conveniently. But when the executive producer saw the piece, he exclaimed, "You didn't tell me that the doctor was black . . . that the people were black!" And he spiked the story.

This pattern is pervasive. A senior executive at a major network confessed, "It's our dirty little secret."

The reason? Research shows the demographic makeup of the audience for every program, and minute-by-minute ratings reveal which stories attract and keep an audience. Many middle-class whites do not want to watch stories about either lower-class people or racial minorities. When such stories come on, these viewers click to another channel. The networks, under pressure to boast the most viewers to generate the most profits for their corporate owners, cater to the tastes of middle-class whites— the largest segment of the audience.

What appears to be racial bias by the networks is actually commercial bias, just as we have seen that what appears to be political bias by the media is usually commercial bias. But the commercial bias here has racial implications, just as the commercial bias elsewhere has political implications. As a result, television news, which could forge understanding between the races by showing sympathetic people of all colors facing common challenges, makes little effort to do so. Instead, it accepts the subtle racism of those white viewers who will not watch the same story if it portrays black folks rather than white folks.

[1] Jeff Cohen, "Racial Tension," *Brill's Content,* October 1999, 54.
[2] The record of *60 Minutes* is not as bad as the others, perhaps because *60 Minutes* is the only one without prime-time competition. Robert Schmidt, "Airing Race," *Brill's Content,* October 2000, 145.
[3] Av Westin, "The Color of Rating," *Brill's Content,* April 2001, 84. Quotations are from this article, unless otherwise noted.
[4] Schmidt, "Airing Race," 114–115.

don't do it, somebody else will, and when they do it, they will get a few more readers, a few more listeners, a few more viewers than we do. The result is the 'Hollywoodization of the news.'"[248]

The dilemma is most marked for television. Many people who watch news on television are not interested in politics; a majority, in fact, say that newscasts devote too much time to politics.[249] Some watch newscasts because they were watching another program before the news, others because they were planning to watch another program after the news. Networks feel pressure "to hook them and keep them."[250]

Therefore, networks try to make the everyday world of news seem as exciting as the make-believe world depicted in their other programs. One network instructed its staff, "Every news story should, without any sacrifice of probity or responsibility, display the attributes of fiction, of drama. It should have structure and conflict, problem and denouement, rising action and falling action, a beginning, a middle and an end."[251] As one executive says, television news is "**infotainment.**"[252]

So television anchors and newscasters, hired as much or more for their appearance and personality as for their experience and ability, become show business stars. And show business stars become television anchors and newscasters. CNN hired comely detective Andrea Thompson from *NYPD Blue,* despite her lack of experience.

The media frenzy over anthrax prompted some families, like this one in Chicago, to buy gas masks.

Consequences of Commercial Bias

The media's commercial bias has important consequences. One is to sensationalize the news. The anthrax infections that occurred after the terrorist attacks in 2001 deserved our full attention, but the media would not let up. Even after the initial flurry of reports, they ran one overwrought piece after another. *Time* magazine featured families who bought gas masks. The *Washington Post* wrote that America is "on the verge" of "public hysteria."[253] In fact, few people panicked. In polls, large majorities expressed concern but not fear. Yet the media realized that generating fear would force people to pay attention to the news.

Another consequence of commercial bias is to feature human interest over serious news. In 2005, the three main television networks devoted a total of eighty-four minutes to Michael Jackson's trial for child molesting but only eighteen minutes to the massive genocide in Darfur, Sudan.[254] (See Table 5.2.)

The media's tendencies to sensationalize the news and to feature human interest over serious news lead to greater emphasis on scandal, sex, and crime. During President Clinton's terms, the media provided saturation coverage of the Whitewater scandal[255] and various other scandals, although a succession of special prosecutors could find nothing more damning than that the president lied about having sexual relations with a White House intern named Monica Lewinsky.[256]

The media plunged into the affair with abandon.[257] The *Los Angeles Times* assigned twenty-six reporters to examine Lewinsky's life, interviewing babysitters and kindergarten classmates.[258] The networks even interviewed one person who had eaten lunch with her three years earlier. The public was offered breathless

TABLE 5.2 Human Interest Predominates

A consequence of commercial bias is that human interest stories predominate over serious news articles.

Newspaper	Topic	Number of Page 1 Stories
USA Today	Disappearance of congressional intern Chandra Levy	8
	Disappearance of George W. Bush's military records	1
San Francisco Chronicle	Controversy over local woman mauled to death by dog	33
	Controversy of dog-handling guards terrorizing Abu Ghraib prisoners	10
New York Times	Martha Stewart getting busted for lying about stock trade	14
	Halliburton getting caught for overcharging taxpayers in Iraq	4

SOURCE: Todd Gitlin, "The Great Media Breakdown," *Mother Jones,* November/December, 2004, 59.

reports about phone sex, the president's cigar as a sex toy, and the intern's dress with a semen stain. There was tittering about the "distinguishing characteristics" of the president's genitals—and speculation about how this would be proved or disproved in court.

Although the national media cover crime extensively, the local media cover it even more fully. Local television news is, in Ralph Nader's words, "something that jerks your head up every ten seconds, whether that is shootings, robberies, sports showdowns, or dramatic weather forecasts."[259] Media consultants advise local stations how to attract the largest audience and make the most money for their chain or conglomerate.[260] The saying "If it bleeds, it leads" expresses, tongue in cheek, many stations' programming philosophy. Thus crime coverage fills one-third of local newscasts.[261] A week before the presidential election, local stations in Columbus, Ohio, devoted more than twice as much time to various crimes than to the election, although the outcome in the state, and in the nation, was in doubt.[262] One station, however, did find time for an undercover investigation of a topless car wash.

A jaded reporter put it bluntly: "It doesn't matter what kind of swill you set in front of the public. As long as it's got enough sex and violence in it, they'll slurp it up."[263] (Even so, American stations do not go as far as the Bulgarian program *The Naked Truth*, which had women disrobe as they read the news.)

Another consequence of commercial bias is to highlight conflict. Stories about conflict provide drama. Reporters, one admits, are "fight promoters" rather than consensus builders.[264] So reporters frame issues as struggles between opposite camps. After the murderous rampage at Columbine High School in Littleton,

Colorado, the media posed the question, Was the incident caused by the availability of guns in our society *or* by the glorification of violence in the media? In this moronic debate, the media prodded people to choose sides, as though the cause had to be one *or* the other rather than a combination of the two or something else entirely.

Sometimes this practice is taken to the extreme. Some stories about Holocaust survivors include bizarre statements by Holocaust deniers claiming that the Nazis didn't have a plan to exterminate European Jews or that Hitler wasn't aware of the effort or that the Germans didn't kill many Jews. The stories present these absurd statements as though they constitute an opposing opinion entitled to a public hearing.[265] With their fixation on controversy, the media allow themselves to be manipulated by ignorant or unscrupulous people. In the process, they promote confusion among people who don't know any better.

By highlighting conflict and framing issues as though they have two—and only two—sides, the media polarize the public, which makes it harder for people to accept compromises as solutions to problems and harder for politicians to forge compromises. In fact, the media belittle compromises. They portray politicians on one side as losing or "giving in" when they should have been fighting to win. Thus the media reinforce some citizens' naive belief that politicians need not and should not compromise. As one reporter admits, "the middle ground, the sensible center, is dismissed as too squishy, too dull, too likely to send the audience channel surfing."[266]

Another consequence of commercial bias is to use a **game orientation** in reporting about competing candidates, officials, or parties.[267] The assumption is that politics is a game and politicians, whether candidates campaigning for election or officials performing in office, are the players. The corollary to the assumption is that the players are self-centered and self-interested. They are seeking victory for themselves and defeat for their opponents, and they are relatively unconcerned about the consequences of their proposals or of government's policies.

With this orientation, reporters spotlight politicians' strategies and tactics, and they present new developments according to how these developments help some politicians and hinder others. Reporters slight the substance and impact of politicians' proposals and policies.

The game orientation appeals to journalists because it generates human interest. It offers new story lines as new information comes to light, much like a board game where "chance" cards inject unexpected scenarios and alter the players' moves and the game's outcomes. This orientation also appeals to journalists because it is easy and relatively free from charges of partisan or

GREGORY

"Luckily, none of the people inside appear to be celebrities."

As an actor, Ronald Reagan developed skills in speaking, gesturing, and moving his body that helped him convey a positive image to the American voters.

ideological bias. (Stories emphasize which contestants are winning, not which ones should win or what consequences might result.) If journalists seriously examined policies and proposals instead of using the game orientation, they would be less able to offer human interest and would be more vulnerable to charges of bias.

The game orientation attracts an audience, but it breeds more cynicism. It creates the impression that politics is just a game, not an essential activity for a democratic society; that politicians are just the players, not our representatives; that politicians act just in their self-interest, not in the public interest; and that politicians' goal is just to beat others, not to make good public policy.

For elections, the game orientation results in what is called **horse race coverage,** with "front-runners," "dark horses," and "also-rans." Although the race was a staple of journalism even in the nineteenth century,[268] the proportion of election coverage focusing on the race has increased in recent decades.[269]

Today, horse race coverage dominates election reporting. As much as two-thirds of the reporting by newspapers, television networks, and websites features the horse race, and much of the remaining reporting features the candidates' strategies. Far less reporting examines the candidates' positions or proposals.[270]

The quintessential reflection of horse race coverage—reporting of candidates' poll standings—has increased greatly. Not only do the media report the results of polls taken by commercial organizations, but they also conduct polls themselves.[271] Nowadays, coverage of polls takes more space than coverage of candidates' speeches, and it usually appears as the lead or next-to-lead story.[272]

Even after elections, the game orientation continues. When Clinton proposed a plan to overhaul the welfare system, all major newspapers focused on the political implications for his reelection; few even explained the plan, let alone its substantive implications.[273]

Commercial bias in the media leads to additional consequences for television specifically. One is to emphasize events, or those parts of events, that have visual interest. The networks have people whose job is to evaluate all film for visual appeal. Producers seek the events that promise the most action, camera operators shoot the parts of the events with the most action, and editors select the portions of the film with the most action.[274] Television thus focuses on disasters and protests far more than they actually occur, and it displays the interesting surface rather than the underlying substance of these events—for example, the protest rather than the cause of the anger.

Another consequence of commercial bias for television is to cover the news very briefly. A half-hour newscast has only nineteen minutes without commercials. In that time, the networks broadcast only a third as many words as the *New York Times* prints on its front page alone. Although cable television has ample time, it follows this format, too, endlessly repeating the same stories without adding new information.[275]

Television stories are short—about one minute each—because the networks think viewers' attention spans are short. Indeed, a survey found that a majority of eighteen- to thirty-four-year-olds with remote controls typically watch more than one show at once.[276] Thus networks do not allow leaders or experts to explain their thoughts about particular events or policies. Instead, networks take sound bites to illustrate what was said. Although correspondents try to explain the events or policies, they have little time to do so.

A network correspondent was asked what went through his mind when he signed off each night. "Good night, dear viewer," he said. "I only hope you read the *New York Times* in the morning."[277]

When the chairman of the board of one network, in conversation with a former Reagan aide, asked what the networks could do to provide more responsible reporting, the aide answered, "Easy, . . . just eliminate ratings for news. You claim that news is not the same as entertainment.

So why do you need ratings?" The chairman sighed, "Well, that's our big money-maker, the news."[278] A former network executive concluded, "Because television can make so much money doing its worst, it often can't afford to do its best."[279]

Overall, commercial bias in the media results in no coverage or superficial coverage of many important stories. This, more than any political bias, makes it difficult for citizens, particularly those who rely on television, to become well informed.

During the year before the September 11 terrorist attacks, al-Qaeda was mentioned only once on the networks' evening newscasts.[280] However, seven months before the airplane hijackings, a report predicting a "catastrophic attack" was issued by a government commission. A statement warning that Osama bin Laden's network was the "most immediate and serious threat" facing the country was made by the CIA director at a Senate hearing. Their dire predictions generated little interest among the media. Due to commercial bias, the media could not address these serious matters in the normal way that they cover politics. Since the terrorist attacks, the media have paid more attention to foreign affairs, yet they continue to reflect the trends that typified news coverage before 9/11.

Impact of the Media on Politics

It is difficult to measure the impact of the media on politics, because other factors also influence people's knowledge, attitudes, and behavior toward it. But there is considerable agreement that the media have a substantial impact on the public agenda, political parties and elections, and public opinion.[281]

Impact on the Public Agenda

The most important impact of the media is **setting the agenda**—influencing the process by which problems are considered important and solutions are proposed and debated.[282] The media publicize an issue, and people exposed to the media talk about the issue with their fellow citizens. When enough consider it important, they pressure officials to address it.[283]

The media's impact is most noticeable for dramatic events that occur suddenly. It is less noticeable for issues that evolve gradually. Watergate required months of coverage before making it onto the public agenda, and AIDS required the death of actor Rock Hudson before making it.[284]

Even for issues that evolve gradually, however, cumulative coverage by the media can have an impact. After years of extensive coverage, people told pollsters that drug use was the "most important problem" facing the country, and then they told pollsters that crime was.

Studies comparing people's views with the media coverage of these problems and with the actual rates of these activities show that people's views fluctuated more according to the media coverage than to the actual rates. When the media coverage increased, people considered the problems more serious, even when the actual rates of crime or drug use remained steady or decreased.[285]

The impact is usually greatest on people who are most interested in politics, because they are most likely to follow the news.[286] And the impact is usually greatest for stories that appear on the front page of the newspaper or at the top of the newscast than for those buried in the back or at the end.[287] People who don't follow the news carefully often check the beginning of the newspaper or newscast for the "important" stories.

The media's power to influence the agenda has important implications. The media play a key role in deciding which problems government addresses and which it ignores. They also play a key role in increasing or decreasing politicians' ability to govern and to get reelected.

By publicizing some issues, the media create an opportunity for politicians with the authority and ability to resolve those issues. At the same time, the media create a pitfall for those who lack the power to resolve them. The Iranian seizure of the American embassy and hostages became the prominent issue in 1980. Every night, CBS's Walter Cronkite signed off, "And that's the way it is, the ___th day of American hostages in captivity." President Carter's lack of success in persuading Iranian officials to release the hostages or in directing an American invasion to rescue them cost him dearly in his reelection bid that year.

Yet the role of the media in shaping the agenda should not be overstated. Individuals' interests prompt the media to cover some things in the first place. Individuals' experiences lead them to consider other things unimportant even when the media do cover them.[288]

Moreover, politicians play an important role in shaping the agenda. For much legislation, Congress initiates action and lets the media publicize it.[289] For many issues, the president initiates action. When President Clinton launched a campaign to reduce smoking by teenagers, the media ran many stories about the problem. They could have done so years before or after, of course, but they followed the president's lead.

For elections, candidates usually establish the agenda of *policy* issues. By emphasizing issues they think will resonate with the public and reflect favorably on themselves, candidates pressure the media to cover these rather than other issues. But the media usually establish the agenda of *nonpolicy* issues involving the candidates' personality and behavior.[290] The media are able to set the agenda for nonpolicy issues because these are more likely to catch the public's fancy.

Impact on Political Parties and Elections

The media have had an important impact on political parties and elections. In particular, they have furthered the decline of parties, encouraged new types of candidates, and influenced campaigns.

Political Parties

Political parties have declined in power, as will be addressed in Chapter 7, in large part because of the influence of the media.

In the young Republic, political parties created and controlled most newspapers. Naturally, the papers echoed the parties' views, and the journalists bowed to the parties' leaders. (The editor of one Democratic Party paper made sure a pail of fresh milk was left on the White House doorstep for President Andrew Jackson every morning, even if the editor had to deliver it himself.[291]) People got political information, however biased, from these papers.

When independent newspapers emerged as profit-making businesses, the party papers disappeared. As independent magazines, radio television networks and stations arose as well, people got political information from these media. Thus people are no longer dependent on parties for their political information; they can make up their own minds about how to vote or what to support rather than rely on parties to tell them.

In other ways as well, the media, especially television, have contributed to the decline of the parties. In place of selection of the candidates by party bosses, television allows the candidates to appeal directly to the people. If the candidates win the primaries, party officials have little choice but to nominate them. In place of management of the campaign by party bosses, television appearances require new expertise, so the candidates assemble their own campaign organizations. Television advertising requires substantial money, so the candidates solicit their own financial donors. In these ways, the media have supplanted the parties as the principal link between the people and their leaders.

Types of Candidates

Television has encouraged new types of candidates for national offices. No longer must candidates be experienced politicians who worked their way up over many years. Celebrities from other fields with name recognition can move into prominent positions without political experience. Jesse Ventura, a professional wrestler, was elected governor of Minnesota, and Arnold Schwarzenegger, an actor, was elected governor of California. In recent years, Congress has had an actor (Fred Grandy, R-Iowa—"Gopher" on *Love Boat*), a singer (Sonny Bono, R-Calif.), a professional baseball pitcher (Jim Bunning, R-Ky.), a professional basketball player (Bill Bradley, D-N.J.), two professional football players (Jack Kemp, R-N.Y., and Steve Largent, R-Ok.), and two astronauts (John Glenn, D-Ohio, and Harrison Schmitt, R-N.M.). (After one term, however, Schmitt was defeated by an opponent whose slogan was "What on Earth has he ever done?") Tom Osborne, who as the former football coach at the University of Nebraska was the best-known person in the state, got elected to Congress from a district in which he did not even live.[292]

Alternatively, unknowns with talent can achieve rapid name recognition and move into prominent positions. Jimmy Carter, who had served one term as governor of Georgia, was relatively unknown elsewhere in the country when he ran for the Democratic nomination for president in 1976. Through effective use of television, he won enough primaries that the party had to nominate him, although the leaders preferred other candidates.

At the same time that television has allowed newcomers to run, it also has imposed new requirements on candidates for national office. They must demonstrate an appealing appearance and performance on camera; they must be telegenic. President Franklin Roosevelt's body, disabled by polio and supported in a wheelchair, would not have been impressive on television. President Harry Truman's style—he was known as "Give 'em Hell Harry"—would not be impressive on television either. Although he was quite effective in whistle-stop speeches, he would come across as too "hot," too intense, if beamed into people's homes every day. A "cool," low-key style is more effective.

When Howard Dean finished third in the Iowa caucuses for the Democratic nomination for president in 2004, he gave a speech to rally his disappointed volunteers. He strained to be heard over the frenzy—shouting, "Yeah!"—but the mike, which was designed for television appearances in such situations, filtered out the background noise, making the speech sound like a rant and the shout sound like a scream. The reporters who were there could barely hear him, but on television, it appeared as though he had come unhinged. Film clips of "Dean's rant" were replayed on newscasts seven hundred times during the next week. The speech became the butt of comedians' jokes. Letterman called Dean a "hockey dad," and Leno called him "Mr. Rogers with rabies."[293] Although most networks later admitted overplaying the speech, the damage was done—and so was Dean's campaign.[294] His intense style was effective in person but not on television.

President Reagan was the quintessential politician for the television age. He was tall and trim with a handsome face and a reassuring voice. As a former actor, he could project his personality and convictions and deliver his lines and jokes better than any other politician. It is not an exaggeration to conclude, as one political scientist did, "Without a chance to display his infectious smile, his grandfatherly demeanor, and his 'nice guy' qualities to millions of Americans, Ronald Reagan, burdened by his image as a superannuated, intellectually lightweight movie actor with right-wing friends and ultraconservative leanings, might never have reached the presidency."[295]

Television has not created the public desire for politicians with an appealing personality. "When candidates shook hands firmly, kissed babies, and handed out cigars, the thrust was not on issues."[296] But television has exacerbated this emphasis on image.

The media have imposed other requirements on candidates for national offices. In recent decades, the intense scrutiny and constant criticism screen out those who are unwilling to relinquish most of their personal privacy and individual dignity. Candidates, of course, have always expected to sacrifice privacy and endure criticism, but now they are expected to sacrifice and endure even more. One columnist wonders whether public service will attract only those with the "most brazen, least sensitive personalities."[297]

Retired Admiral Bobby Ray Inman, who had held positions in both Democratic and Republican administrations, was nominated to be secretary of defense by President Clinton. During the confirmation process,

Courtesy of Franklin D. Roosevelt Library, 73-113:61

Franklin Roosevelt spent much of his life in a wheelchair, but journalists did not photograph him in it. A friend snapped this rare picture. Journalists were reluctant to photograph or write about officials' afflictions or behaviors until the Watergate scandal ushered in a new era of more personal coverage.

he came under attack by some senators and some newspapers.

One editor told him, "Bobby, you just have to get a thicker skin. We have to write a bad story about you every day. That's our job." Although he was assured by members of both parties that he would be confirmed—the New York Times reported that his nomination was "unusually well received in Washington"—Inman withdrew his nomination, saying he did not want the "daily diet" of media criticism. The newspapers then criticized him for being insecure.[298]

Campaigns

The media affect nomination and election campaigns through their news and commentary and candidates' advertisements. They help set the campaign agenda, as already explained. They also inform and persuade.

The media provide information about the candidates and the issues, and they also interpret this information.[299] The public learns about the candidates and the issues[300] but in the process is influenced by the media.

CARTOONS KILL, MEDIA AND GOVERNMENT CHILL

In a spirit of tolerance, a children's author in Denmark planned to write a book about the life of Muhammad—the founder of Islam—but she could not find an illustrator because the artists approached were afraid of retaliation if the book displeased Muslims, who believe that there should be no visual representations of Muhammad. A newspaper editor in Denmark, who had also heard that museums in England and Sweden had removed art deemed offensive to Muslims, sought cartoons about Islam to underscore the principle of free speech. He intended to provoke a reaction from Muslims.

The Danish newspaper ran a dozen cartoons equating Islam with terrorism and intolerance in fall, 2005. One cartoon showed Muhammad with a turban that was actually a ticking bomb. Another showed Muhammad at the gates of heaven, with his arms raised, telling men who look like suicide bombers, "Stop, stop, we have run out of virgins." There was little furor, even after an Egyptian newspaper reprinted them. But a Muslim cleric in Denmark assembled them and added others which were more inflammatory but which had not been printed in the newspaper, and sent the packet to other Muslim clerics.

Five months later there was a ferocious reaction throughout the Muslim world, from the Middle East to Indonesia to Nigeria, with demonstrations turning into riots. As the protests mounted, some newspapers in other countries and websites around the globe reprinted the cartoons, prompting new waves of violence. As if to confirm the cartoons' criticism, mobs attacked the embassies of Denmark and also those of Austria, Britain, France, and Norway in various countries. They stormed a United States' airbase in Afghanistan, and they burned an effigy of the Danish prime minister in Pakistan. Ultimately, almost 150 people were killed in the riots.[1]

Muslim leaders called for amputations or executions of the cartoonists and their publishers. The governments of Kuwait, Libya, Saudi Arabia, and Syria withdrew their ambassadors from Copenhagen. The governments of Saudi Arabia and Syria sponsored boycotts of Danish goods. A newspaper in Iran suggested changing the name of Danish sweetrolls. (Apparently it got the idea from Americans who changed the name of "French fries" to "freedom fries" when France refused to endorse the war in Iraq.)

Denmark was stunned. With 200,000 Muslims, the Danes considered their country a tolerant one, a safe haven for religious minorities. Yet the government had to withdraw embassy staffers and warn its citizens in Muslim countries to flee for safety.

Later it would be revealed that the demonstrations were fueled not only by religious fundamentalists, but also by the governments of Egypt, Iran, and Syria, which sought to appease Islamic radicals and to deflect growing pressure from their citizens for democratic reform. Iran also used the cartoons to rally its people against the demands by Western countries that it halt its nuclear weapons program. Yet the hairtrigger outrage was real. For many years Muslims have believed that Islamic people, their resources (oil), and their countries were being used and abused by the West.

The conflagration highlights the responsiveness of the American media and the United States government. Most American media, whether from a fear of retaliation or simply a desire not to stoke the flames any higher, refused to run the cartoons. Among large news organizations, only ABC and Fox broadcast them and only the *Austin American-Statesman* and the *Philadelphia Inquirer* printed them. (CNN, instead, showed anti-Semitic cartoons from the Arab press.) A handful of student newspapers did print them, including those at Harvard, Illinois State, Northern Illinois University, and the Universities of Illinois and Wisconsin. (The editor at the University of Illinois was fired for doing so.)

The United States government was as circumspect as most American media. Officials abhorred the cartoons while deploring the violence. They cautiously affirmed freedom of speech and press. Their low-key reaction kept the spotlight on Europe rather than on the United States, for a change. Thus the government was responsive to the demands of international diplomacy, especially to the difficulties of winning the hearts and minds of Muslim people.

Information about the candidates can have a major impact, especially at the nomination stage. In presidential elections, a party without an incumbent president running for reelection might field a dozen candidates. The media cannot cover all adequately, so they narrow the field, considering some "serious" and giving them more coverage. Once the primaries begin, they label some "winners" and others "losers," and give the "winners" more coverage.[301]

By making these judgments, the media strongly influence the electoral process at this stage.[302] Because few people have formed opinions about the candidates

Most American media were also responsive to these demands and difficulties. They were less responsive to the tradition of freedom of speech and press embodied in the First Amendment. As a constitutional theorist observed, ridicule in cartoons is a distinct form of expression, which cannot be conveyed in another, non-cartoon format. That makes cartoons powerful, as they have been for centuries. That also makes them worthy of protection, by the media as well as by the government, even when inflammatory. The media's caution may have been wise, as the government's caution was. No doubt they deflected greater outrage against American society. However, the media's refusal to show their audience what the fuss was about may also have contributed to the belief that freedom of speech and press has limits, especially when addressing religion, and that it should be balanced against the value of multiculturalism. It might even be construed as endorsement of the English government's proposal that publishing material "abusive or insulting" to religious groups be made a crime.[2]

More than anything, this tumult shows the enormous cultural gulf between the modern, secular West and Islam. Westerners cannot fathom why Muslims would riot over mere cartoons, and Muslims cannot fathom why Westerners would be so insensitive and insulting. In retaliation, an Iranian newspaper launched a contest for cartoons mocking the Holocaust, evidently expecting Jews to riot in the streets of Tel Aviv and New York. Yet Westerners are used to the "knee-jerk baiting of traditional authority," while Muslims have more respect for traditional authority and religious authority in particular.[3]

[1] And one columnist pleaded, "Lord, save us all from the irony impaired." Leonard Pitts, Jr., "Rioting Cartoons Not about Religion, But Culture," Lincoln Journal Star, February 11, 2006, B7.

[2] Ronald Dworkin, "Why God is Fair Game," New York Times, March 12, 2006, WK4. Also see Tim Rutten, "Let's Be Honest about Cartoons," Los Angeles Times, February 11, 2006, www.calendarlive.com/printedition/calendar/cl-et-rutten11feb11,0,900556.story?track-tottext

[3] Indeed, the Muslim world has no tradition of, or tolerance for, religious irony. Michael Kimmelman, "A Startling New Lesson in the Power of Imagery," New York Times, February 8, 2006.

Pakistanis burn an effigy of the Danish prime minister to condemn the publication of cartoons satirizing the Prophet Muhammed in a Danish newspaper.

this early, they are open to impressions from the media. Therefore, when the media declare some candidates winners, they help create a bandwagon effect.[303] When they declare others losers, they make it hard for these candidates to attract contributors, volunteers, and supporters.

The media can also persuade voters directly. This influence can be seen in several ways.

Televised debates do not sway most viewers because people tend to engage in **selective perception,** which is a tendency to screen out information that contradicts their beliefs. Consequently, most people conclude that their candidate performed better than the other candidate.[304] However, the debates do sway some viewers, usually those who have moderate education and some interest in politics but who are not decided or at least not strongly committed to one candidate. In 1960, the debates may have convinced enough voters to cast their ballots for Kennedy that he won the election.[305]

Media commentary about the debates can also sway viewers.[306] But this effect usually does not last long; after the media frenzy wears off, the candidate ordinarily bounces back.[307]

Newspaper endorsements of candidates apparently sway some readers, especially those with no more than a ninth-grade through twelfth-grade education. People with less education are less likely to read editorials, while those with more education have more sources of information and more defined ideologies to guide their decisions.[308] Even if endorsements sway only a small percentage of voters, they can determine the outcome of tight races.[309] Although endorsements have some effect on well-publicized races, such as those for president,[310] they have greater effect on less publicized races, such as those for state legislator or local tax assessor, because voters have little other information to guide them.

Talk radio also influences listeners. People who tune in to talk radio are more likely to turn out to vote and even to participate in campaigns.[311]

Impact on Public Opinion

Social scientists long thought that the media influenced the things people thought about but not the opinions they held about these things. Some contemporary research, however, demonstrates that the media do have a substantial impact on public opinion on matters besides elections. A comparison of the networks' newscasts with the public's policy preferences in various foreign and domestic issues shows that the media influence opinion about many issues.[312] Other research shows that the media influence opinion about particular presidents.[313]

Observers also think that the media have contributed to the public's cynicism toward politics in recent decades. The media's coverage has undermined the public's perception of the integrity of government and officials not just by reporting real shortcomings of programs and administrators but also by engaging in the practices previously addressed in this chapter. The negative bias in coverage of all candidates and officials undermines them directly, whereas the game orientation undermines them more subtly. The emphasis on conflict, though intriguing the public, at the same time polarizes and alienates the public. The practice of objectivity—reporting what he said versus what she said without evaluating the truth of either—passes along false and misleading statements and confuses the

Televised images of the abuse of Iraqi prisoners by American jailers at the Abu Ghraib prison outside Baghdad influenced public opinion in the Middle East as well as in the United States.

public.[314] So people complain, "The media? You can't believe anything they say."

Some researchers have concluded that the result of these practices is to foster **media malaise** among the public.[315] This is a feeling of cynicism and distrust, perhaps even despair, toward government and officials. Indeed, according to a 1995 survey, the public is even more cynical than journalists themselves. Seventy-seven percent of the public gave government officials a low rating for honesty and ethics, whereas only 40 percent of the journalists did.[316] Most of the public believed that politicians could "never" be trusted to do the right thing. Yet the journalists saw the American political process as "a flawed but basically decent means of reconciling different points of view and solving collective problems."[317] They apparently report in a more cynical fashion than they actually feel because of the conventions of contemporary journalism. But the public, although deploring these practices, evidently sees them as reflections of reality. Thus cynical coverage by the press leads to even more cynical attitudes in the citizenry.[318]

The cynical attitudes have important implications for politics. They probably reduce satisfaction with candidates and officials and reduce turnout in elections. At the same time, they probably increase votes for "outsiders" who present themselves as "nonpoliticians."

Thus one writer observes, "the press, which in the long run cannot survive if people lose interest in politics, is acting as if its purpose was to guarantee that people are repelled by public life."[319]

Conclusion: Are the Media Responsive?

To make a profit, the media have to be responsive to the people. They present the news they think the people want. Because they believe the majority desire entertainment, or at least diversion, rather than education, they structure the news toward this end.[320] For the majority who want entertainment, national and local television and radio provide it. For the minority who want education, the better newspapers and magazines provide it. Public radio, with its morning and evening newscasts, and public television, with its nightly newscast, also provide quality coverage. In addition, Internet websites provide news on demand. The media offer something for everyone.

When officials or citizens get upset with the media, they pointedly ask, "Who elected you?" Journalists reply that the people—their readers or listeners or viewers—"elected" them by paying attention to their news columns or newscasts.

To say that the media are responsive, however, is not to say that they perform well. Giving the people what they want most is not necessarily serving the country best. "This business of giving people what they want is a dope pusher's argument," says a former president of NBC News. "News is something people don't know they're interested in until they hear about it. The job of a journalist is to take what's important and make it interesting."[321]

Instead, the media personalize and dramatize the news. The result is to simplify the news. Superficial coverage of complex events leaves the public unable to understand these events and ultimately unable to force the government to be responsive.

The media give us the big hype—"Hey, listen to this! Here's something new you can't miss!" They reflect a crisis *du jour* mentality in which everything is important but ultimately nothing is important. Almost any political development is important for a day or a week or occasionally a month. But almost no political development is important for long. The headlines and the stories clamoring for attention go by in such a blur that after a while they all become a jumble for many people. They leave no sense of what's actually a crisis, what's only a problem, what's merely an irritant, and what's truly trivial.[322]

Thus most news coverage is episodic, presenting an event as a single, idiosyncratic occurrence, rather than thematic, presenting the event as an example of a larger pattern. For instance, a story might focus on a hungry person rather than on malnutrition as a national problem. Episodic coverage is more common because it is more entertaining—dramatic, with human interest—than thematic coverage. But episodic coverage makes it hard for people to see the connection between the problems in society and the actions of government. Then the people do not hold their leaders accountable for addressing and resolving the problems.[323]

Although the media give the people what they want, the people criticize the media. Almost two-thirds tell pollsters that the media "don't get the facts straight."[324] Actually, the media usually do get the facts straight, but the nature of their reporting confuses people rather than enlightens them. Almost three-fourths tell pollsters that the media get in the way of society's efforts to solve its problems. Only one-fourth say that the media help solve the problems.[325]

People rank the press the lowest in public esteem of any professional group except law firms.[326] People also express less support for freedom of the press. Even before the 2001 terrorist attacks, a majority said the press has too much freedom. In fact, a majority went so far as to say that the media should not be allowed to endorse or criticize political candidates, and a third

went further to say that the media should not be allowed to publish a story without government approval.[327] Thus at the same time the media are competing to give people what they want, their practices are alienating people.

The media's desperation is aggravated by a declining interest in politics and a decreasing number of people who read newspapers or watch newscasts. These declining numbers are greater than the increasing number of people who search the Web for news. Although the public is better educated now than in the 1960s, it is less likely to follow the news and less able to answer questions about the government.[328] People under thirty-five especially reflect these trends. To retain their shrinking audience, many newspapers and newscasts have revamped their formats to replace hard news with soft features. If this process continues, it will have disturbing implications. Citizens who are not aware of the news or who do not understand it cannot fulfill their role in a democracy.

The problem is circular, as one political scientist points out:

> *Americans need high-quality journalism to become sophisticated citizens, but news organizations need an audience of sophisticated citizens for the organizations to produce high-quality journalism and still generate profits. "Because most members of the public know and care relatively little about government, they neither seek nor understand high-quality political reporting and analysis. With limited demand for first-rate journalism, most news organizations cannot afford to supply it, and because they do not supply it, most Americans have no practical source of the information necessary to become politically sophisticated."[329]*

Individual journalists are aware of the shortcomings of contemporary journalism but pessimistic about their ability to improve the coverage. Because of commercial pressures, they are experiencing low morale in newsrooms across the country.[330]

Nevertheless, we should not lose sight of the fact that the American media, despite their shortcomings, provide very fast and relatively accurate reports of events. They also probe wrongdoing in society. Thus they serve as a check on government in many situations. As a former government official noted, "Think how much chicanery dies on the drawing board when someone says, 'We'd better not do that; what if the press finds out?'"[331]

Evans Pursued the Admiral

You decided to meet with Admiral Boorda to confront him with your allegations and give him an opportunity to respond. But you did not want to give him much warning, so you did not tell his office why you wanted to meet other than that you were preparing a story about the admiral.

Two hours before the meeting, Boorda's aide called for more information. Then you revealed the purpose. Later you explained, "If you go in too soon, the navy can counterattack, and the opposition gets the story."[332]

After you revealed the purpose of the meeting, Boorda's aides checked with navy officials about the ribbons. A previous secretary of the navy had questioned why admirals wore so many ribbons. When the navy investigated its 257 admirals, it found that many wore ribbons, including the *V*, who technically should not have. Apparently, the navy's practice of awarding ribbons deviated from its regulations. When Boorda was informed last year that he should not have worn the *V*, he took it off. "It was an honest mistake," he commented to an aide. He has not worn it since then.

After Boorda learned the purpose of the meeting, he went home for lunch. He typed a letter to his wife and another to the sailors. He said to the sailors:

What I am about to do is not very smart but it is right for me. You see, I have asked you to do the right thing, to care for and take care of each other and to stand up for what is good and correct. All of these things require honor, courage and commitment to our . . . core values.

I am about to be accused of wearing combat devices on two ribbons I earned during sea tours in Viet Nam. It turns out I didn't really rate them. When I found out I was wrong I immediately took them off but it was really too late. I don't expect any reporters to believe I could make an honest mistake and you may or may not believe it yourselves.

That is up to you and isn't all that important now anyway. I've made it not matter in the big scheme of things because I love our navy so much, and you who are the heart and soul of our navy, that I couldn't bear to bring dishonor to you. . . .

Finally, for those who want to tear our navy down, I guess I've given them plenty to write about for a while. But I will soon be forgotten.

You, our great navy people, will live on. I am proud of you. I am proud to have led you if only for a short time. I wish I had done it better.

Then Boorda went out to his garden and shot himself in the chest. At his funeral, Boorda was hailed as "the sailors' sailor." In Washington, however, he was criticized by some for having "thin skin." Yet as one columnist observed, "Thin skin is the only kind of skin human beings come with."[333]

Newsweek's efforts to pursue the story did not reflect political bias against the navy or the admiral or the changes he was implementing. (Other critics of Boorda did have political motives—their opposition to new policies that challenged navy traditions.) *Newsweek*'s efforts instead reflected commercial bias. The magazine was trying to attract more readers by running provocative articles by prominent writers.

Of course, *Newsweek* had not even run the article when Boorda decided to kill himself. A columnist for *Newsweek* pointed out, "It is possible [that Boorda] could have moved the story in a different direction, or talked the magazine out of publishing anything on the matter at all."[334] Evidently Boorda, who had considerable experience with the press, did not think this was likely.

No doubt *Newsweek*'s editors were as surprised as other people when Boorda killed himself. They were just trying to do their jobs. Yet their behavior reflects journalists' mind-set that public officials are not motivated by a desire to serve the public but to advance their careers or enhance their power. Moreover, journalists see public officials as insincere. With this mind-set, journalists look for wrongdoing and seek to expose it. Essentially, journalists consider officials fair game for relentless attack.[335]

 To learn more about news media, go to "you are there" exercises for this chapter on the text website.

Key Terms

narrowcasting
broadcasting
blog
symbiotic relationship
adversarial relationship
leaks
scoops
presidential press conference
photo opportunity
sound bite

spin
fireside chats
political bias
commercial bias
infotainment
game orientation
horse race coverage
setting the agenda
selective perception
media malaise

Further Reading

David Domke, *God Willing? Political Fundamentalism in the White House, the "War on Terror," and the Echoing Press* (Ann Arbor, Michigan: Pluto, 2004). An examination, with empirical analyses, of the George W. Bush administration's use of religious words and values and the media's adoption of these words and values in its coverage of the war on terrorism.

Beth J. Harpaz, *The Girls in the Van: Covering Hillary* (New York: St. Martin's Press, 2001). This book gives an account of press coverage of Hillary Clinton's Senate campaign.

Marvin Kalb, *One Scandalous Story: Clinton, Lewinsky, and Thirteen Days That Tarnished American Journalism* (New York: Free Press, 2001). As the scandal unfolded, the press abandoned its standards.

Joe McGinniss, *The Selling of the President, 1968* (New York: Simon & Schuster, 1969). An account of the often comical efforts by Richard Nixon's advisers to transform him into a media-friendly candidate.

For Viewing

All the President's Men (1976). See Robert Redford and Dustin Hoffman play Woodward and Bernstein as they investigate the Watergate scandal.

Bowling for Columbine (2002). In search of the roots of our gun violence, Michael Moore indicts local TV newscasts for creating a climate of fear.

Control Room (2004). A documentary by an Arab American, which shows how the Iraq war is covered by the Arab side. Focusing on the Arab network Al-Jazeera, the film raises questions about the nature of bias in Western and Arab media.

Fahrenheit 9/11 (2004). Michael Moore's documentary, which criticizes President Bush's handling of the war on terrorism and the war in Iraq, includes film footage that prompts viewers to ask, Why haven't we seen these things on the networks?

Good Night and Good Luck (2005). The story of legendary newscaster Edward R. Murrow and CBS News as they confronted McCarthyism in the 1950s. Nominated for an Oscar as the best picture.

Journeys with George (2002). A young journalist traveling with the Bush campaign in 2000 films the campaign from her perspective.

Outfoxed (2004). A revealing portrayal of the Republican bias of Fox news.

Electronic Resources

www.nytimes.com

The New York Times *website offers in-depth reports on international and national affairs.*

www.washingtonpost.com

The Washington Post *website provides political news from the nation's capital.*

www.sfgate.com

The San Francisco Chronicle *has been described as an "oasis of attitude" in the world of news.*

www.alternet.org

This alternative journalism site presents news and opinion not found in most other media outlets.

www.slate.com

Slate *is a "Webzine" featuring columns and wit and perhaps the best media analysis on the Web.*

www.ajr.org

A variety of stories about the media are provided by the University of Maryland College of Journalism.

www.fair.org

This watchdog site keeps an eye on the media.

www.tyndallreport.com

This site offers content analysis of news coverage.

http://english.aljazeera.net/HomePage

Here you can find news, in English, from the Arab perspective—the Al-Jazeera network.

www.daytodayiniraq.blogs.nytimes.com

Here you can find reports, in English, by Iraqi people describing their day-to-day lives during the war. This site is sponsored by the New York Times *in an effort to fill a gap in the coverage of the war by American media.*

ThomsonNOW™

Enter ThomsonNOW™ using the access card that is available with this text or through www.thomsonedu.com/thomsonnow. ThomsonNOW™ will assist you in understanding the content in this chapter with a personalized study plan generated for your needs. A practice test will assess the areas you need to review and provide the tools to fully comprehend those concepts, including an integrated digital eBook, interactive simulations, timelines, video case studies, MicroCase exercises, and InfoTrac College Edition readers and exercises. You'll also be connected to the learning objectives, chapter outline, chapter glossary, flash cards, crossword puzzles, Internet activities, and interactive quizzes found on the companion website.

CHAPTER 6

INTEREST GROUPS

A father and his son march in opposition to a congressional bill that would crack down on illegal immigrants.

David McNew/Getty Images

Group Formation

Why Interest Groups Form

Why People Join

Which People Join

Have Americans Stopped Joining?

Types of Interest Groups

Private Interest Groups

Public Interest Groups

Strategies of Interest Groups

Tactics of Interest Groups

Direct Lobbying Techniques

Indirect Lobbying Techniques: Going Public

Building Coalitions

Success of Interest Groups

Resources

Competition and Goals

Interest Groups and Democracy

Conclusion: Do Interest Groups Help Make Government Responsive?

Do You Support the "Day without Immigrants?"

You are Cardinal Roger Mahony, Archbishop of Los Angeles. Pope John Paul appointed you archbishop in 1985 and bestowed upon you the title of cardinal in 1991. You don't consider yourself a political person, although you have spoken out over the years on public issues when they involved Church doctrine. Now you have been called on to advise immigrants on how and whether they should get involved in public protests on proposed immigration legislation.

In December 2005, the House of Representatives passed the Border Protection, Antiterrorism and Illegal Immigration Control bill. Among other things, it would subject those convicted of helping illegal immigrants to five years in prison. It also calls for illegal immigrants to be deported and services withheld from them.

Although not counseling priests to disobey, the U.S. Conference of Catholic Bishops assailed the measure, calling it extremely punitive, and encouraged members of the flock to oppose it. Church officials sent lobbyists to Washington and parishioners to rallies in Chicago and Washington to push legislation to legalize the estimated eleven million undocumented workers, mostly Hispanic, in the United States and provide a pathway for them to become citizens.[1] You went even further, publicly calling on the priests

in your archdiocese to disobey the measure should it become law.

Your statements were featured on the news and you became a target of House supporters of the bill. Peter King (R-NY) and James Sensenbrenner (R-Wisc.), cosponsors of the bill, blasted you on Fox's *O'Reilly Factor*. Congressman King, who describes himself as a practicing Catholic, labeled you and others "the left wing of the Catholic Church— these are frustrated social workers."[2] News commentators Tucker Carlson and Lou Dobbs raised the question of whether the Church should maintain its tax-exempt status given its political activity on the immigration issue.

In defending yourself, you wrote on the opinion page of the *New York Times* that "Some supporters of the bill have accused the church of encouraging illegal immigration and meddling in politics."[3] You note, however, that "the mission of the Roman Catholic Church is to help people in need. It is our Gospel mandate, in which Christ instructs us to clothe the naked, feed the poor, and welcome the stranger."[4] You caution that "Providing humanitarian assistance to those in need should not be made a crime . . ." and call upon elected leaders to enact a bill that reflects the values of fairness, compassion, and opportunity.[5]

In American politics, religious groups are also interest groups.

Various religious denominations have interests that intersect with politics, as we will see more clearly in this chapter. Some religious groups, including the leadership of the Catholic Church, have been actively involved in the fight against abortion. Others support abortion, but oppose the war in Iraq. Still others focus on issues specific to the rights of religious groups, such as policy concerning prayer in the schools or religious icons in public places.

In recent years the leadership of the Catholic Church has been in unison with the Republican party over the issue of abortion, which both opposed, and the church has been a relatively conservative force in American politics. For the first time in sixteen years, George W. Bush won a majority of Catholic voters in 2004. Yet, the church also has interests more in line with more liberal political groups, such as support for fair working conditions, assistance for the poor, and so forth. The immigration issue is another issue that divides the Church leadership from the Republican party, and unlike issues such as working conditions or poverty aid, the immigration issue is now front and center on the political agenda.

The immigration issue has gained momentum since passage of the House bill, and now a bill is being considered in the Senate. Immigrant groups want to show the Senate, and the American people, how valuable immigrants are to this nation in order to fight against the rather draconian House bill. Immigrant groups, obviously, do not want a bill that would order deportation or deprive immigrants of social services. To illustrate their point, many immigrants and their supporters plan a demonstration for May 1 to show how much the nation's economy relies on immigrants. In so doing, they want to convince lawmakers to grant amnesty to illegals and make it easier for them to become citizens. Touted as a "Day without Immigrants," workers are urged to march in the streets, leaving construction sites and restaurants undermanned, crops unattended, and hotel rooms uncleaned.[6] Students were also encouraged to abandon their classrooms and join the protest.

Your parishioners are looking to you for advice on what to do. Should they leave work that day and join the protest? Or should they stay at work and support their cause in other ways?

Though you are publicly sympathetic to the cause, you are torn in rendering advice. Catholic laypeople are divided, as are most other groups in society. Some argue for amnesty and citizenship, others for tighter border control and penalties for those who cross

illegally. The Hispanic community itself is also divided.

On the one hand you want to show support for immigrants. Many of them are Catholics. If most were Swedish Lutherans living in Minnesota, the issue would not be so immediate for you. But many Hispanic immigrants are Catholics and live in Los Angeles, and you want to show solidarity with them.

At the same time, many of your other congregants take an anti-immigrant stand. Anti-immigrant feeling also runs high among some long-time residents of California. Following smaller rallies early in the year, some expressed outrage that demonstrators carried the flag of Mexico rather than the United States and displayed posters in Spanish rather than English.

Moreover, although you are sympathetic with the desire of illegal immigrants to demonstrate their contribution to the U.S. economy, you are reluctant to counsel them to walk off their jobs or for students to miss a day of school. You fear some might lose their jobs.

What do you advise? Do you instruct immigrants to take a day off and participate in the May 1st demonstrations? Or do you counsel against missing work and school?

In the United States, everything from fruits to nuts is organized. From apple growers to filbert producers, nearly every interest has an organization to represent it. These organizations touch every aspect of our lives; members of the American College of Obstetrics and Gynecology bring us into the world, and members of the National Funeral Directors Association usher us out.

Organizations that try to achieve at least some of their goals with government assistance are **interest groups.** Fruit and nut growers want government subsidies and protection from imported products; doctors and funeral directors want to limit government oversight and controls.

The effort of an interest group to influence government is called **lobbying.** Lobbying may involve direct contact between a lobbyist—or consultant or lawyer, as they prefer to be called—and a government official, or it may involve indirect action, such as attempts to sway public opinion, which in turn influences officials.

People organize and lobby because these are ways for them to enhance their influence. As one lobbyist remarked, "The modern government is huge, pervasive, intrusive into everybody's life. If you just let things take their course and don't get involved in the game, you get trampled on."[7]

The Founders feared the harmful effects of interest groups, what James Madison called factions. They did not, however, wish to limit the ability of people to organize and speak out. Rather, Madison and others tried to cure "the mischiefs of faction" through government institutions that separated powers among the three branches and between state and national governments and by providing ways for the different parts of government to check each other. Separation of powers and checks and balances make it difficult for one or more groups to override the interests of others.

Many analysts believe that these checks no longer work; they see "special interests" manipulating government for their own good, contrary to the interests of society as a whole.[8] They argue that everyone is represented in Washington but the people.

Yet others argue that special interests often represent large or important groups of citizens. The American Association of Retired People (AARP), for example, represents millions of Americans.

Do interest groups undermine the people's interests? Or do they make government more responsive by giving people greater representation in the political process? These are the difficult questions explored in this chapter.

Group Formation

Throughout most of its history, America has been a nation of joiners. As early as the 1830s, the Frenchman Alexis de Tocqueville, who traveled in America, noted the tendency of Americans to join groups: "In no country in the world has the principle of association been more successfully used or applied to a greater multitude of objects than in America."[9] Even now, Americans are more likely than citizens of other countries to belong to groups.[10] Compared with most countries, the United States is racially, religiously, and ethnically diverse. These differences give rise to different interests and views on public issues and often lead to the formation of groups that express these views.[11]

Groups also organize in the United States because they can. The freedom to speak, assemble, and petition government, guaranteed in the First Amendment to the Constitution, facilitates group formation. Without such freedom, only groups favored by government or those with members willing to risk punishment should they speak out against government are likely to exist.

Federalism also encourages the formation of groups. Because state and local governments have significant authority, groups often organize at these levels as well as the national level to promote and protect their interests.

Why Interest Groups Form

The formation of interest groups occurs in waves.[12] In some periods it is rapid and extensive, whereas at other times it is slow.

Social and economic stress often account for these surges.[13] The debates over whether colonial Americans should secede from the British Empire in the years before the Revolutionary War led to organized groups on both sides of the issue. Slavery in the decades before the Civil War led to the formation of anti- and proslavery groups. After the Civil War, rapid industrialization led to the formation of trade unions and business associations. Economic problems in agriculture spurred the development of farm groups.

The greatest surge in group formation occurred between 1900 and 1920. Stimulated by the shocks of industrialization, urbanization, immigration, and the government's response to them, the United States Chamber of Commerce, American Farm Bureau Federation, National Association for the Advancement of Colored People (NAACP), and countless others were formed.[14]

The 1960s and 1970s witnessed another interest group explosion, this time directed primarily toward Washington. As the national government expanded in power and influence in the post–World War II period, it increasingly became the center of interest group efforts to satisfy demands for favorable public policy. Spurred by the success of civil rights and war protest movements in the 1960s, other groups representing racial minorities, women, consumers, the poor, the elderly, and the environment were organized. The number of business groups surged in the late 1970s in reaction to the success of consumer and environmental groups in pushing government to regulate business activity.[15]

Technological changes also accelerate group formation. A national network of railroads and the telegraph contributed to the surge in the early 1900s. In the 1960s and 1970s, computer-generated direct mail made it easier to raise money, recruit members, and push them to action. Between 1960 and 1980, the number of groups increased by 60 percent and the number sending representatives to Washington doubled.[16] In the 1990s, the spread of personal computers and the growth of the Internet facilitated communication between people with an endless variety of narrow interests. The Internet is particularly useful for those wishing to organize citizen groups on a low budget.[17] It is also useful for groups outside the mainstream who wish to operate anonymously. Members and sympathizers of militia groups spread throughout the country, often in remote locations and with few resources, can communicate, keep each other informed, and provide social support for extreme views.

The government is also important to group formation. Government efforts to deal with problems often prompt the organization of groups opposed to such efforts.[18] In addition, government provides direct financial assistance to some groups, particularly nonprofit organizations. Groups as diverse as the American Council of Education, the National Governors Association, and the National Council of Senior Citizens obtain a large percentage of their funds through federal grants and contracts.[19]

In 1773, a group of colonists organized to protest British taxes on tea by throwing tea into Boston Harbor. In 1989, groups organized to protest a congressional pay increase by sending tea bags to their representatives in Washington.

Group organizers also play a role in group formation. These entrepreneurs often come from established groups.[20] They gain experience and then strike out on their own. Many civil rights activists of the 1950s and early 1960s founded new organizations in the late 1960s. Some used their skills to organize groups against the war in Vietnam and later to organize groups for women's rights and environmental causes.[21] Thus, the formation of one group often opens the door to the formation of others.

Why People Join

Some people join a group because of the group's political goals or cause. But many join for economic and social reasons.[22] Some groups offer monetary benefits to members, such as discounted prices for goods and services. The large nonfarm membership of the Farm Bureau is often attributed to the cut-rate insurance policies offered through the organization.[23] In addition to discount drugs and medicines, AARP (a group representing the interests of older Americans) provides health, home, and auto insurance; a motor club; a travel service; investment counseling; and several magazines. These services attract members and generate millions of dollars for the organization. In an effort to recruit new members and reach an increasingly diverse population as well as generate additional advertising revenue from its publications, AARP distributes several versions of its mainline magazine targeted to different age groups, the latest aimed at those forty-five to fifty-five years of age.[24]

Because members pay dues, thereby providing groups with resources to accomplish their goals and to enhance their influence with government, most groups provide a mix of benefits in an effort to maximize their membership. The National Rifle Association (NRA) lobbies against gun regulation and control. Some people join for this reason. Others join to secure other NRA services: *The American Rifleman* (a monthly magazine), a hunter's information service, low-cost firearm insurance, membership in local gun clubs, and shooting competitions.[25] Still others join because they enjoy associating with fellow gun enthusiasts.

Some people join groups because they are coerced. In some states, lawyers must join the state bar association to practice law.

Which People Join

Not all people are equally likely to join groups. Those with higher incomes and education are more likely to belong. They can afford membership dues, have free time necessary to take part, and have the social and intellectual skills that facilitate group participation. They also appear more attractive to many groups and therefore are more apt to be recruited. Whites more often belong to groups than blacks, but mostly because of their higher average income and education.[26]

Have Americans Stopped Joining?

Americans used to join groups at rates much higher than citizens of other democracies. But Americans are less likely to join groups than they were a few decades ago. This current trend was documented in a widely publicized book, *Bowling Alone.*[27]

What does bowling have to do with politics? The common thread is the dwindling membership in organized groups: declining church membership and church-related activities; the falloff in labor union membership, once the most common organizational affiliation among American workers; the decreasing membership in the PTA; and significantly diminished membership in league bowling.

If declining group membership reflected only a loss of revenue from the pizza and beer consumed by bowling leagues, only the owners of bowling alleys would care. However, the decline in league bowling and other group memberships parallels the loss of close personal relationships that foster discussion of public issues and trust among citizens, which are important to a vibrant democracy. Involvement in groups teaches people how to discuss issues, agree to disagree, run meetings, and keep records. It exposes members to the workings of representative democracy and reinforces the ideals of good citizenship, such as the need to obey laws, engage in public discussion, and vote.[28]

Some people argue that the decline in membership in organized groups is not a serious problem because informal social ties provide the same opportunity to interact and discuss issues.[29] For example, people may not join bowling leagues, but they visit with others when they attend their children's soccer games. Yet being part of an organized group provides a network of associates that casual contact does not.

People today claim that they are busier than ever before and that between their work and family life they have little time for other things. Women's lives, in particular, have changed over the past generation, with most women now in the paid workforce while still carrying the largest share of household and child-raising duties. Women used to be the backbone of most local civic, religious, political, and educational groups, but working women now have far less time to devote to such volunteer activities. The entrance of women into the workforce also means that most men are doing more around the house and with their children than their fathers did. This too decreases the time available for organized groups.

Although formal membership in voluntary organizations has decreased, membership in professionally managed issue advocacy groups is increasing.[30] However, "membership" involves mostly writing an occasional check to support the organization's activities.[31] Members contribute to the cause but do not interact with other members. Although these organizations can be successful politically, the benefits of social interaction are lost. Members do not discuss and share information that helps in clarifying positions and making compromises.

Some observers argue that television has replaced membership in groups as a preferred leisure-time activity. Even busy people usually find time to watch TV. But even though TV can be educational as well as entertaining, it provides no opportunity for discussion; information flows in one direction.

Types of Interest Groups

Interest groups come in all sizes. Some have large memberships, such as the American Federation of Labor–Congress of Industrial Organizations (AFL-CIO) with nine million members. Others have small memberships, such as the Mushroom Growers Association with fourteen. Some have no members at all.

Corporations have managers and stockholders but not members in the traditional sense. They act as interest groups when they lobby government.[32] Some groups, such as the Children's Defense Fund (CDF), have no members and lobby government on behalf of others.[33] Funded from private donations, the CDF represents the interests of children.

Some interest groups are formally organized, with appointed or elected leaders, regular meetings, and dues-paying members. Others have no leaders and few prescribed rules.

Groups that solicit money from private individuals have "checkbook members" who contribute money but have no say in what the group does or how their contributions are spent. Many **political action committees** (**PACs**) and so-called 527 organizations that sponsor political advertisements, such as the Media Fund and MoveOn.org, operate in this way (see Chapter 9). They raise money through direct mail and the Internet and spend it on political ads for and against issues or political candidates. Decisions are made by the group's leaders with no accountability to anyone, other than contributors' decisions not to contribute in the future.

Thus, interest groups can be distinguished according to their membership and their organizational structure. They can also be distinguished by their goals. Some groups pursue economic goals, primarily for the benefit of their members. Others pursue political goals or causes that have consequences for all or at least consequences that are not limited to members of the group.

Private Interest Groups

Private interest groups seek economic benefits for their members or clients. Examples include business, labor, and agriculture.

Business
With the declining power of unions, business organizations are the most numerous and among the most powerful interest groups in Washington (see Figure 6.1). Politics is now essentially a confrontation between business and government.[34] Business seeks to maximize profit, whereas government, at least sometimes, works to protect workers and consumers from the unfettered effects of profit-seeking businesses through regulation of wages, safety standards, and certain kinds of monopolistic practices, among other interventions.

Today, however, there is little confrontation between business and government. Although the Republican Party has long favored business, in recent years the Democratic Party has, too.[35] Regardless of who occupies the White House or which party controls Congress, business has generally done well. This reflects in part the disincentives in a capitalist economy for politicians of any persuasion to antagonize business, which is so important to the nation's economic

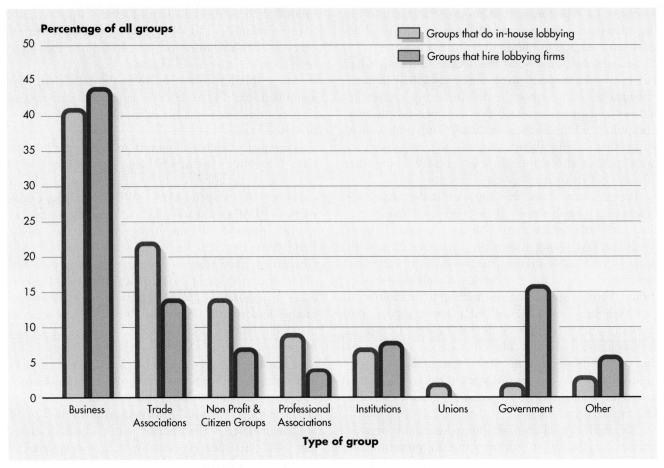

FIGURE 6.1 ■ Contemporary Interest Groups *Business interests dominate the modern interest group system. This graph categorizes 2810 groups that maintain an office in Washington, D.C., and 6601 groups that lobby there.*

SOURCE: Frank R. Baumgartner and Beth L. Leech, "Interest Niches and Policy Bandwagons: Patterns of Interest Group Involvement in National Politics," *Journal of Politics* 63 (November, 2001): 1191–1213.

Data are based on filing reports with the government. Those identified as hiring lobbying firms represent only those with no in-house lobbyists.

success.[36] If the economy falters, politicians get blamed. Rather than do something to undermine business confidence, politicians are inclined to do what business wants. Democratic support also reflects business's financial contribution to Democratic candidates; the election of moderate and conservative Democrats, such as Bill Clinton, who are generally sympathetic to business; and a general climate of opinion, fostered by the media, that favors business over labor.

During the past twenty years, business has had numerous successes in rolling back government regulation. For example, deregulation of accounting and a loosening of other financial standards led directly to the scandals of Enron and many other companies in the early years of the new century, involving the looting of employee pensions and shareholder interests by top executives (see Chapter 8). The Bush administration has also unraveled a number of environmental regulations, leaving businesses freer to pollute. In 2004,

the administration also put in place new rules reducing the obligations of businesses to pay overtime wages to their workers, a measure enthusiastically endorsed by business lobbies. In a deal struck in the House, Democrats succeeded in amending an appropriations bill to prevent the rules from taking effect, but President Bush threatened to veto the measure unless the new rules on overtime pay were restored.

Lobbying for the pharmaceutical industry illustrates the clout of the nation's most powerful industries. Indeed, there is no lobby in Washington as large, as powerful, or as well financed as the pharmaceutical industry. Battle tested in many struggles over health care issues during the past forty years, the industry spends more than $100 million a year in lobbying and campaign contributions to obtain favorable legislation. The industry is especially supportive of Republican officeholders and provides major funding for Republican candidates.[37] Given their political clout, it is no surprise that drug companies are the most profitable of any among the largest corporations in America, with around $200 billion annual profits from "take-home" prescriptions (that is, not counting drugs administered in hospitals, doctors' offices, or nursing homes.)[38]

The industry employs three thousand lobbyists, more than one-third of whom are former federal officials.[39] In the K Street corridor, home to Washington's most famous lobbying and law firms, there are 134 firms on the drug industry's payroll; many either former members of Congress or former congressional staff members and government employees. For example, one company alone, Bristol-Myers Squibb, employs fifteen firms with fifty-seven lobbyists, including several former prominent Republican and Democratic members of Congress.

The pharmaceutical industry has been especially powerful in the George W. Bush administration. One of their largest successes came with the passage of the Medicare prescription drug bill, which will subsidize prescription drug benefits for millions of senior citizens.[40] The pharmaceutical industry and health maintenance organizations spent an estimated $14 million to lobby for favorable policies. More than nine hundred lobbyists for the industry were at work, far more than the number of members of Congress! No wonder: The bill is projected to provide billions in profit for the industry. One of the chief lobbyists for the pharmaceutical industry in the debate over the Medicare drug bill in 2003 was the former health advisor to Bill Frist (R-Tenn.), the majority leader of the Senate. Another lobbyist was the former legislative director in the office of Senator Kay Bailey Hutchison (R-Tex.) a senior senator.[41]

The Medicare drug bill represented several hundred billions of dollars in sales for the drug industry, and these sales will be enhanced by restrictions put into the bill. For example, the bill forbade Medicare officials from bargaining to obtain lower prices for the millions of senior citizens who will be getting low-cost drugs; what reason could there be for such a rule other than to favor the pharmaceutical industry. Similarly, the bill forbade reimportation of drugs manufactured in the United States but sold abroad for less than here. (See the box "Interest Group Responsiveness to a National Crisis" on p. 174 for more on business efforts to win favors from Congress.)

Labor

Organized labor is a principal competitor with business but runs a distant second in influence and continues to lose ground. Although the United States has many labor unions, the AFL-CIO, a confederation of

"You can't please all the people all the time, so you might as well please the pharmaceutical lobby."

trade and industrial unions, is the most important politically. It has a staff of several hundred and some of the most skillful lobbyists in Washington. It channels money to political candidates, chiefly Democrats, through its political action committee. In the 2004 general election, it spent nearly $45 million on campaign literature, phone banks to get out the vote, television issue ads, and voter registration.[42] Furthermore, tens of thousands of union members canvassed door-to-door, particularly important in the swing states.

The fight to win the right to unionize was a bitter one. Early union efforts promoted the eight-hour working day, higher pay, the abolition of child labor, and termination of the use of convicts as labor, among other reforms. Before federal legislation giving workers the right to organize, companies often brought in strikebreakers, those willing to work without a contract. And striking workers were often attacked by police or thugs hired by owners. Hundreds or more likely thousands died during those years of organizing efforts. Some of these conflicts shocked the nation and brought about legislation that legitimatized the rights of workers to organize.

However, as the economy changed and as, in the 1950s and 1960s, the standard of living of workers increased and the reforms fought for by unions were largely adopted, unions came to be seen as less important. Membership declined and with it the political clout of unions.[43] Only 13 percent of the workforce belongs to a union, down from 20 percent in 1983 and 35 percent in 1955 (see Figure 6.2). Some of this reflects the union's own lack of effort at recruiting new members and the divisions within the labor movement

IN MEMORY OF

IDA BRAYMAN

17 YEARS OLD

who was shot & killed by an Employer Feb. 5th 1913 during the great struggle of the Garment Workers of Rochester.

Copyrighted 1913 by U. G. W. Local 14 Rochester N. Y.

Gotham Book Mart, New York

This postcard commemorates the death of a seventeen-year-old woman murdered while striking for recognition of her union, an eight-hour day, and extra pay for overtime and holidays.

over whether to use its scarce resources in organizing or serving members.[44] It also reflects the intimidating and illegal acts of employers directed toward employee efforts to unionize. From 1992 to 1997, some 125,000 employees lost their jobs for supporting a union.[45] Though these acts are illegal, they are rarely prosecuted, and in the rare case of conviction, penalties are minimal. Where employers refrain from illegal practices—namely, in the public sector (teachers and government workers)—union membership has increased. The antiunion message of business communicated through the largely antiunion media has also succeeded in convincing many people that unions are something working men and women do not need.[46] Despite this, a majority of Americans approve of unions. Most report sympathy for the side of unions in labor disputes. However, only about a third would like to see the power and influence of unions increased.[47]

Population shifts have also hurt unions. States in the South and Southwest, where antiunion sentiment is strong, have grown in population and representation in Congress. Today, 84 percent of union members reside in just twelve states.[48] Unions have therefore had a less sympathetic ear among the nation's lawmakers. Global competition and government's unwillingness to protect American workers has also hurt unions. Fearful of losing their jobs or putting an employer at a disadvantage in a competitive market, members are reluctant to strike, and without the threat of strikes, there is little reason to heed labor's demands or for employees to consider joining unions.

The decline of unions has led to lowered wages, directly because strong unions gain higher wages for their own workers, and also indirectly because having high-wage workers puts pressure on nonunion employees to keep wages high. The wage gap is wide; in 2003, unionized blue-collar workers averaged more than $30 an hour, while nonunionized workers averaged $18.[49] The weakness of unions and declining pressure on wages can be illustrated by the fact that unlike in previous economic cycles, the end of the 2001 recession brought more growth in corporate profits than in wages and benefits for workers.[50]

The decline in unions has also weakened the liberal thrust of American politics as unions lobby not only for workers rights but for progressive policies. Unions provided significant support for the civil rights movement and more recently for government-funded health care.

In an effort to expand membership, unions have reached out to the low-wage service sector and professions. Labor won a major victory in 1999 when 75,000 nursing home employees voted to be represented by the Service Employees International Union (SEIU), making it the third-largest union in the nation.[51] In 2005, SEIU and Teamsters split with the AFL-CIO over whether the principal goal of the union movement should be to expand membership or engage in political activity. The SEIU and Teamsters believe success of the union movement rests with increased membership. The division further weakened labor's influence.[52]

To try to enhance labor's influence, the AFL-CIO has enrolled a half million members in a new nonpartisan advocacy group, Working America. The goal is to bring nonunion and union members together in promoting issues of common concern. The group will draw on members to communicate with lawmakers via e-mails, letters, and phone calls.[53]

Efforts continue to organize non-blue collar employees, for example, computer specialists in areas such as Silicon Valley.[54] Doctors employed by HMOs as well as those in private practice are also organizing.[55] Graduate teaching assistants at the nation's major uni-

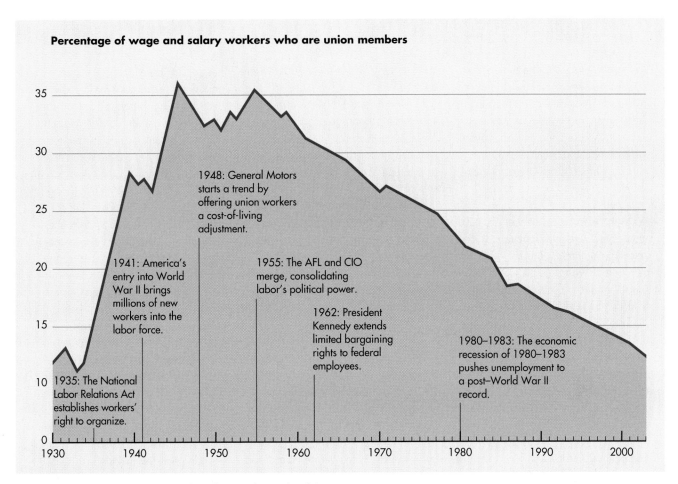

Percentage of wage and salary workers who are union members

1948: General Motors starts a trend by offering union workers a cost-of-living adjustment.

1941: America's entry into World War II brings millions of new workers into the labor force.

1955: The AFL and CIO merge, consolidating labor's political power.

1962: President Kennedy extends limited bargaining rights to federal employees.

1980–1983: The economic recession of 1980–1983 pushes unemployment to a post–World War II record.

1935: The National Labor Relations Act establishes workers' right to organize.

FIGURE 6.2 ■ Union Membership in the United States

SOURCE: U.S. Census Bureau, *Statistical Abstract of the United States,* online at www.census.gov/prod/www/statistical-abstract-02.html.

versities are unionizing over wages and working conditions.[56] Even some undergraduates are organizing.[57]

Agriculture

The American farm population is declining, but agricultural organizations are still important in agricultural policy making. Agricultural interests are represented by a number of general and specialized groups. Most support government subsidies to help farmers, although a few oppose subsidies.

The American Farm Bureau Federation, the largest of the general-interest groups, began when the federal government established the agricultural extension service to educate farmers on new farming techniques. To encourage cooperation with local agents, the government offered grants to states that organized county farm bureaus. In the early part of the twentieth century, these local bureaus gradually evolved into a national organization.

Despite its roots, the Farm Bureau is a conservative organization dominated by wealthy farmers with large landholdings. Although it opposes government aid in other sectors of the economy, it favors government

subsidies to farmers, many of whom are Farm Bureau members and involved in corporate-owned and -operated farms.

The National Farmers' Union, considerably smaller than the Farm Bureau, represents small farming interests. It supports government subsidies but wants them targeted to preserve small family farms. The American Agriculture Movement began as a protest movement in the mid-1970s and, like the Farmers' Union, addresses issues that benefit small farmers and ranchers.[58]

Along with the general-interest groups, hundreds of commodity organizations promote specific products and operate much like business trade associations. Examples include cattle, cotton, milk, tobacco, and wool producers. Large agribusiness firms such as Cargill and Archer-Daniels-Midland also have powerful lobbies in Washington.

Today, American agriculture is dominated by agribusiness and large corporate farms. The small farmer plays a minor role, although politicians often invoke the small farmer in pushing government subsidies for large corporate enterprises. Government spends more than $20 billion subsidizing crop production, or in

We like to think that in a time of national crises, we all pull together. But in fact, differences emerge even in those times. And efforts of special interests to secure benefits from government do not stop because of a national tragedy. Rather, groups refocus their appeals to take advantage of the situation.

In the wake of September 11, 2001, scores of Washington lobbyists, trade associations, interest groups, and members of Congress pleading for special interests rushed to repackage their demands in patriotic wrapping. Although not new to Washington politics, post–9/11 may represent a new low in trying to exploit a national disaster for personal and private gain. PBS television producer Bill Moyers put it this way: "It didn't take long for wartime opportunists—the mercenaries of Washington, the lobbyists, lawyers, and political fundraisers—to crawl out of their offices on K Street to grab what they can for their clients."[1]

It began with the nation's airline industry. By September 22, the government had given the airlines a sweet deal: $5 billion in cash, plus another $10 billion in loan guarantees. The airlines also won protection from lawsuits arising from the attacks, which would have cost them billions more. Former Secretary of Labor Robert Reich has pointed out that the bailout exceeded the combined value of all America's major airlines: United, American, Delta, Northwest, US Airways, America West, and Continental.[2] Of course, American taxpayers received no ownership in the airlines for their sizable investment. In the blink of an eye and with virtually no debate, Congress approved the measure for an industry in which several carriers were near bankruptcy before 9/11. (And less then three years

later, at least two of these airlines were bankrupt again).

Following on the heels of the airline bailout, the insurance industry pressed the Bush administration to shift liability for future terrorist attacks to the federal government. It also sought to have claims confined to the federal court in Manhattan rather than reviewed in state courts, where judges would more likely approve punitive damages potentially in the billions. If the White House refused, the industry warned it would cease to cover future terrorist attacks and bring the country's economy to a standstill.

The request was not a hard sell to the administration. Insurance companies spent $1.6 million to elect George Bush in 2000. The industry also had friends in Congress after donating $20 million in soft money to both Republicans and Democrats. By October 12, the White House had outlined a plan whereby taxpayers would cover all but $12 billion of the first $100 billion in future claims. Although the House of Representatives approved the bill, it died in the Democrat-controlled Senate.

Others picked up the strategy of the airline and insurance industries. Steel lobbied for direct subsidies as well as restrictions on imports of less costly foreign steel. The Democratic senator from West Virginia, Jay Rockefeller, made the case. "Without steel, we cannot guarantee our national security."[3] Carl Levin, the Democratic senator from Michigan, went a bit further. "Our weapons are made of steel." Before a group of cheering steelworkers, he shouted, "We go to war with what you make."[4] "Absolute baloney" was the response of a researcher at a Washington think tank. "One or two steel mills could provide all the steel

needed for defense."[5] Of course, Rockefeller's and Levin's views may have been tainted by the $2.7 million the steel producers contributed to Democratic candidates in 2000. The president eventually approved restrictions on steel imports at a tremendous cost to U.S. taxpayers. The move, though politically popular at home, led to protests by European countries about unfair trade. And in fact the restrictions were ultimately lifted after the World Trade Organization found that they violated free-trade agreements.

The $167 billion farm subsidy labeled the Agricultural Act of 2001 became the Farm Security Act of 2001 following 9/11. On September 24, Capitol Hill was deluged with letters from growers of twenty federally subsidized commodities with the message that "food production is vital to the national interest."[6] Like steel, the growers pumped $58 million into the 2000 elections. The measure passed the House in October, 291 to 120, and was later signed into law by the president.

Manufacturers of traffic signs, barricades, and other equipment wanted their share too. In an effort to bolster federal highway safety spending, a spokesman argued that increased spending for traffic-routing devices would help motorists flee cities faster and more safely during terrorist attacks. The American Bus Association, representing a thousand private companies providing intercity bus service, had been lobbying for $400 million to improve bus security and safety. After 9/11, the association maintained that it would help companies retain drivers who had come to fear potential terrorist attacks.

A capital gains tax cut was marketed as a national security initiative by the National Taxpayers Union.

According to the association, a reduction in capital gains taxes would "revitalize the sagging economy and bring new revenues to Washington—aiding our war against terrorism."[7] Having succeeded in winning $135 million to shore up public beaches, the American Shore and Beach Preservation Association sought additional funds arguing that "America needs to make a major commitment to its energy and water infrastructure, both for security and economic reasons."[8] Lobbyists also sought a $10 million subsidy for bison producers because, as they put it, the fear of terrorism drove patrons from the fancy restaurants that serve bison steaks and burgers.

Flight schools, operators of skydiving companies, manufacturers of small aircraft, and owners of small airports seeking compensation for business lost since the attacks also bellied up to the trough. Ethanol producers proposed blending its product with gasoline to check the nation's dependence on foreign oil. Travel agents sought $4 billion, arguing that without travel agencies, the nation's travel industry could not survive. Date growers in California petitioned the White House and Pentagon to buy dates and include them in food packages being dropped into Afghanistan. They argued that dates would be a real treat for the Afghans during Ramadan (a Muslim holy period).[9]

Of course, none of these groups were asking for anything different from what they sought before 9/11. But 9/11 offered an opportunity to provide a stronger argument for their causes. One lobbyist expressed what many were thinking: "What happened was a tragedy certainly, but there are opportunities. We're in business. This is not a charity."[10] A member of

Congress captured the view of many lawmakers and lobbyists by saying, "It's an open grab bag, so let's grab."[11]

Lobbyists are in the business of asking for things," says a researcher at the conservative Heritage Foundation. "And they adjust their message to whatever they think will sell. Right now it's national security, economic stimulus, and disaster relief, and so they link what they want to one of those—better yet all three."[12]

In earlier wars, war profiteering, making money on a war, was considered shady and unpatriotic and sometimes even illegal. Perhaps because no one is being asked to sacrifice in the war against terror except the soldiers and their families, war profiteering in this war is seen as nothing at all to be ashamed of and, indeed, practically patriotic.

[1]Bill Hogan, "Star-Spangled Lobbyists," *Mother Jones,* March-April 2002, 59–63.
[2]Alan Guebert, "Lugar's Proposal Calls Groups' Bluff," *Lincoln Journal-Star,* October 21, 2001.
[3]Hogan, "Star-Spangled Lobbyists."
[4]David E. Sanger and Joseph Kahn, "Bush's Plan to Raise Steel Tariffs Would Exempt Most Poor Nations," *New York Times,* March 4, 2002, A1, A14.
[5]Hogan, "Star-Spangled Lobbyists."
[6]Ibid.
[7]Ibid.
[8]Ibid.
[9]David E. Rosenbaum, "Since Sept. 11 Lobbyists Use New Pitches for Old Pleas," *New York Times,* December 3, 2001, B1.
[10]Ibid.
[11]Hogan, "Star-Spangled Lobbyists."
[12]Ibid.

"Pardon me, but could you tell us where the public trough is?"

some cases nonproduction, and most of those funds go to the wealthiest, largest—usually corporate—farms.[59] In most states, current farm subsidies go to 10 percent of farmers.[60]

Public Interest Groups

Public interest groups lobby for political and social causes rather than direct financial gain for their members. If they succeed, their success is shared more widely than by members of the group. The National Taxpayers Union lobbies for reduced taxes not just for its members but for everyone who pays taxes. Amnesty International lobbies for the rights of political prisoners around the world even though none of its members are prisoners.

Although nearly all groups think of themselves as pursuing the "public" interest, the label in this instance applies only to those working for other than personal or corporate interests. However, the term *public interest* is confusing in that it does not mean that a majority of the public necessarily favors the goals of these groups or that their goals are necessarily good for all or even most of the people.

Public interest groups increased dramatically in number and size during the late 1960s and early 1970s.[61] Now they number more than twenty-five hundred, with forty million members.[62] Several factors account for the surge. Americans became increasingly distrustful of government and of the so-called special interests that influence government. Public interest groups see themselves as acting on behalf of the broader citizenry. Many middle-class Americans also had the financial means to support these groups. The new technologies mentioned earlier also made it easier to reach and mobilize prospective and existing members.

Whereas many of the public interest groups established during the 1960s and 1970s were "shoestring" operations staffed by idealistic social reformers with few professional skills, many of today's public interest organizations have larger budgets and memberships and a cadre of professionals—attorneys, management consultants, direct-mail fundraisers, and communication directors—handling day-to-day operations and seeking to influence government with a variety of strategies and tactics.[63]

Multiple-Issue Groups

We can classify public interest groups as multiple- or single-issue groups. Multiple-issue groups are involved with a range of issues. Single-issue groups have a narrower focus. The following are multiple-issue groups.

Women's groups Groups advocating women's equality range from large, mass-based organizations interested in a broad array of issues to smaller groups with more specific and narrow interests.

The National Organization for Women (NOW), the largest women's group, with 250,000 members, has chapters in each state.[64] Funded chiefly by membership dues, it conducts research and lobbies at the national, state, and local levels in a number of policy areas including reproductive freedom and economic rights. With only sixteen hundred members, the Independent Women's Forum is a conservative counter to NOW.[65] It opposes government programs to achieve sexual equality, such as programs directed toward raising the performance of girls in public schools, arguing that it is boys who consistently underperform. It also opposes extending civil rights laws to cover discrimination against women's athletic programs in colleges and universities (see Chapter 15).

A few women's groups have organized specifically to elect women to office. The most successful of these is EMILY's List—EMILY stands for Early Money Is Like Yeast (it makes the "dough" rise), an organization that recruits, trains, and funds pro-choice Democratic women to run for public office. Since its founding in 1985, it has helped elect eleven women U.S. senators, sixty-one House members, and eight governors. In 2004, the group contributed nearly $11 million to candidates.[66]

The National Federation of Republican Women focuses on electing Republican women to office, but has a somewhat broader mission of supporting all Republican candidates. Like Emily, the Federation encourages, trains, and supports women candidates as well as helping get out the vote. The National Women's Political Caucus differs from these partisan groups in that it works for the election of women regardless of their party affiliation, though only those with a pro-choice position.

Religious groups Although differing in their degree of commitment, the vast majority of Americans are affiliated with a religious denomination. Many of these denominations have organizations that represent their interests in Washington. The National Council of Churches, an organization of liberal Protestant denominations, argues for civil and human rights, including abortion rights. Catholic groups are active in the antiabortion and antinuclear movements. The have also been, as noted in You Are There, outspoken on immigration. Jewish groups have lobbied for liberal causes and the nation of Israel. Muslim groups lobby for Palestinian rights and a favorable policy toward nations with Islamic populations. They also advocate for fair treatment of Muslims in the United States.[67]

Evangelical Protestant denominations—the Christian right—are the most potent religious force in American

The first wave of women's organizations campaigned for women's right to vote. Here some twenty thousand marchers parade for women's rights in New York City in 1917.

politics.[68] They oppose abortion, divorce, homosexuality, and women's rights and push their agenda through schools, newspapers, magazines, radio and television, and thousands of politically mobilized churches.[69] The Christian Coalition, one evangelical lobby group, was developed in the 1980s by a television evangelist, Pat Robertson, who sought the Republican presidential nomination in 1988.[70] The Christian Coalition is heavily involved in politics and closely linked to the Republican Party. In the early 1990s, Coalition members were a the majority in many Republican state and local party organizations.[71] Robertson and fellow television preacher Jerry Falwell were outspoken critics of President Clinton during the impeachment process, calling on him to resign and asking Christians to send money to make it happen.[72]

Very influential within the Republican primary electorate, conservative Christians helped deliver the Republican presidential nomination to George W. Bush in 2000 by mobilizing its followers in opposition to his Republican rival, John McCain. And they helped deliver the presidential election to Bush in 2004.

Still, the sway of organized conservative Christian groups may have peaked.[73] Robertson no longer heads the Christian Coalition, and the group's budget is a fraction of what it once was. Some people in the movement are disillusioned that political activity has produced so little and feel used by the Republican Party. Abortion is still legal. Creationism is excluded from the public school curriculum. The move to ban gay marriage failed in Congress. Nor are these things likely to change. Nationwide, some social attitudes are becoming more liberal. Mindful that time is against him, Falwell told would-be contributors prior to the 2004 election that they needed to push the conservative family-oriented social agenda to take advantage of Bush's popularity.[74]

There is some evidence that part of the evangelical movement is broadening its focus. In 2006, eighty-six evangelical leaders signed a major statement to fight global warming. These leaders see this as an important issue for poor people throughout the world, the ones most likely to suffer from the changes brought on by global warming. The leaders called for federal legislation, and drafted the Evangelical Climate Initiative which

Gay and lesbian rights organizations developed around 1950. At that time, homosexuals largely kept their sexual orientation private, and on the rare occasions when it came to public attention, they were characterized as deviates. Being known as a homosexual could mean loss of a job and public humiliation (as it still does in the military and in certain parts of the country).

For that reason, gays and lesbians were extremely vulnerable to blackmail and to police harassment. As an example of public attitudes toward gays in the 1950s, following a raid on a gay bar in 1954, a Miami newspaper headlined a story "Perverts Seized in Bar Raid." As late as 1965, New York's liquor authority declared that a meeting of three or more homosexuals in a bar was reason enough for the bar to lose its license.[1] Through the mid-1960s, in New York City, then as now a city of more liberal attitudes, police entrapment of homosexuals was common (police in plain clothes hung around bars waiting for a proposition and then made an arrest). Discrimination in most city hiring was abolished only in 1967 and in the fire and police departments well after that.

Through the 1960s, gays and lesbians focused primarily on how to avoid and survive persecution.[2] The first group with national scope organized to speak for the rights of homosexuals was the Mattachine Society, founded in 1950 to help raise political consciousness among gays and to fight the persecution of gays as part of the anti-Communist blacklisting in the 1950s. But the Mattachine Society was small, had branches in only a few cities, and dwindled in importance in a few years, especially when it was discovered that some leaders were communists.

Homosexuals continued to be ostracized by most of American society until 1969, widely recognized as the beginning of the modern gay rights movement thanks to a police raid at the Stonewall, a seedy bar in Greenwich Village, New York. Rumored to be owned by the Mafia and operating without a liquor license, with many underage customers, and as a dope hangout, the Stonewall, a private club, was a popular meeting place for a diverse group of gay men, "including drag queens, hippies, street people, and uptown boys slumming."[3] That summer the New York City police were engaged in a crackdown on illegal bars, focusing mostly on those frequented by gay men, Latinos, and blacks. Several gay bars had already been raided without incident before the Stonewall, but each raid heightened the anger and desperation felt in the gay community.

A small police unit entered the Stonewall at 3 A.M. and cited the employees for selling liquor without a license. The customers were asked to leave and formed a peaceful crowd

pushed for television and radio spots in states with influential legislators, information campaigns in churches, and education events at Christian colleges.[75]

On this issue, the evangelical position comes closer to that of the Interfaith Alliance and the Clergy Leadership Network, groups of mainline Protestants that counter the message and political activity of the conservative religious groups.[76] These groups put greater weight on the Christian doctrines of helping the less fortunate and working for peace than on social issues, such as abortion and gay rights, that have mobilized evangelical groups.[77]

The Freedom from Religion Foundation speaks for the estimated 14 percent of the American people who are atheists. Its goal is to make the "unbelievers'" voice loud and clear in public discourse. The organization assisted the plaintiff in a lawsuit challenging the inclusion of the words "under God" in the Pledge of Allegiance. (The U.S. Supreme Court threw the case out on a technicality.[78])

Racial and ethnic groups Groups promoting the civil rights of racial and ethnic groups have been an important part of American history. Chapter 15 discusses these groups and their role in the civil rights movement. Groups representing the interests of African Americans, such as the NAACP, the Congress for Racial Equality, and the Urban League, pressed for equal rights for black Americans and eventually won major changes in the law and ultimately in the treatment of minorities.

Hispanics and American Indians also have organized groups representing them. Though the roots of Hispanic American political groups date from the late nineteenth century, the longest-existing organization, the League of United Latin American Citizens, was founded in 1927 to combat discrimination against Mexican Americans. Another prominent group, the Mexican American Legal Defense and Educational Fund, pursues litigation challenging discriminatory practices—for example, the creation of election districts unfavorable to Hispanic voters.

Groups supporting the rights of Native Americans have focused on the improvement of the educational and income status of American Indians and for equal treatment. More recently, some have fought against school mascots that use Native American tribal names

outside. But after a police van arrived to take away those arrested, the crowd grew hostile and began to throw things—first coins, then cans and bottles, and then larger items. The police took refuge in the club, but the hostile and increasingly angry crowd pressed to break in, and the police drew their weapons.[4] Soon lighter fluid and a match were thrown inside the building and a fire started, but loss of life was avoided when more police reinforcements arrived.

The crowd, obviously feeling empowered by its attempt to finally fight back, then moved down the street shouting "gay power" and celebrating their newfound strength and solidarity (though some were injured and others had been arrested, no one was seriously hurt). The next few nights, other crowds gathered to demonstrate for gay rights, and the police were summoned on at least two occasions.

After several days, the unrest ended, and the collective sense of protest and injustice were transformed into an organization, the Gay Liberation Front. Its original founders were determined to use radical political means to fight discrimination against homosexuals. Not long after, politically moderate gays and lesbians broke from the Gay Liberation Front to form the Gay Activist Alliance. Later other groups evolved that used mainstream politics, legal challenges, and peaceful protest activities to support the cause of equality for gays and lesbians. By the early 1970s, gay pride parades, usually held in late June to commemorate the anniversary of the Stonewall raid, were common in major cities, and gay rights organizations were actively working across the land.

Changes in the status of homosexuals soon followed. In 1973, the American Psychiatric Association removed homosexuality from its list of mental disorders. Then, in the early 1980s, the tragedy of AIDS focused media attention on the gay community and brought public awareness to the issue of discrimination against gays (see Chapter 14). Entertainers and celebrities who acknowledged their homosexuality, and in some instances suffered from AIDS, raised public consciousness even more. With increasing public exposure to gay people, most people in American society began to recognize that gays are not very different from everyone else.

[1]Robert Amsel, "Back to Our Future? A Walk on the Wild Side of Stonewall," www.gayastrology.com/stonewall.shtml (excerpted from *Advocate,* September 19, 1987).
[2]The source for much of this discussion is Eric Marcus, *Making History: The Struggle for Gay and Lesbian Equal Rights, 1945–1990* (New York: HarperCollins, 1992); see also Jeffrey Schmalz, "Gay Politics Goes Mainstream," *New York Times Magazine,* October 11, 1992, 18ff.
[3]Amsel, "Back to Our Future?"
[4]An eyewitness account of all of this was provided by a *Village Voice* reporter, Howard Smith; ibid.

and, especially, symbols or demeaning images and names ("Redskins," for example). Protecting the rights of Native Americans to run casinos on their property is another interest of these groups.

Gays and lesbians Gays and lesbians are represented by the Human Rights Campaign, the Gay and Lesbian Alliance Against Defamation, and Lambda Defense Fund, among many other groups (see the box "The Origins of Gay and Lesbian Rights Groups"). Each of these groups has worked in the courts and in political and policy arenas.

One of the most important current issues is the right of homosexuals to marry. The Human Rights Campaign and other gay and lesbian advocacy groups make substantial donations to fight proposed state legislation that would define marriage as a bond exclusively between a man and a woman. These organizations are also fighting the battle in the courts. Gay and Lesbian Advocates and Defenders, a New England legal rights organization, filed a lawsuit challenging the constitutionality of Vermont's exclusion of gay and lesbian couples from the institution of civil marriage.

The state's supreme court upheld the challenge, and the state legislature ultimately extended same-sex couples all the legal benefits of marriage without granting the label. A similar lawsuit in Massachusetts ended that state's exclusion. Inspired by these decisions, local officials in a few other states began to grant marriage licenses to same-sex couples. Although these have been invalidated, it will be difficult to go back. Hoping to do so, under pressure from conservative Christian groups, the Bush administration proposed but Congress rejected a constitutional amendment banning same-sex marriages. However, eleven states approved bans on same-sex marriage and some approved bans on civil unions in the 2004 elections.

The Lambda Defense Fund also represents gay and lesbian young people who have been discriminated against or harassed in school and is working to help educate legislators, school officials, and teachers about the challenges these youth face. Although gays and lesbians have gained many legal rights and much acceptance, they are far from fully equal. Bill Clinton's public position on gay issues was mixed, but he ended the federal policy treating gays as security risks and invited gay activists to the White House. The implicit message was that gays are part of the American community, have legitimate concerns, and are accepted as full participants in political life. Despite having endorsed a constitutional amendment banning gay marriage, George W. Bush has appointed openly gay people to high-profile positions in the White House[79] and invited the Log Cabin Republicans, a gay advocacy group, to the White House for a policy briefing, reversing the 1996 decision of Republican presidential nominee Bob Dole, who returned a campaign contribution from the group. However, Republicans used the fight against gay rights to rally their political base in 2004.

Although gays can be discharged from the military and gays in most states can be fired from their jobs or evicted from their rental houses or apartments if their sexual orientation becomes known, society has grown more supportive of certain rights for gays and lesbians. Eight out of ten Americans think discrimination in jobs and housing against gays and lesbians is wrong. Gays and lesbians in the federal workforce and a dozen states are protected from job discrimination.[80]

Mary Bonauto, a lawyer with Gay and Lesbian Advocates and Defenders, brought the lawsuit that led to the legalization of civil unions in Vermont and then another that resulted in the legalization of same sex marriage in Massachusetts.

There is less consensus on issues involving gay marriage or civil recognition of gay partnerships. Gay Americans want to be free of discrimination and enjoy the rights guaranteed other Americans, including access to spousal health and death benefits provided by employers and the right to leave their surviving partners their property with the same tax advantages as married couples. But only 40 percent of the public approve civil unions that would allow those steps.[81] Even fewer support same sex marriage, even though the desire for economic equality is one justification for legitimizing same-sex marriage.

Old and young Although the population of the nation as a whole has tripled since 1900, the number of elderly has increased eightfold. Today, persons over sixty-five constitute nearly 13 percent of the population. Several groups, sometimes called the "gray lobby," represent their interests. The most prominent of these is AARP.

To counterbalance the power of the gray lobby, a number of groups such as Americans for Generational Equity and the CDF represent the interests of young people, but they are small and weak compared with the likes of AARP. Their weaknesses stem in part from the fact that children cannot vote. It also reflects that it is more politically palatable to help seniors, who have worked all their lives and are no longer able to do so, as opposed to children, whose parents are in their prime wage-earning years. Thus aid for children becomes entangled with attitudes about welfare and helping poverty-stricken adults, and advocating for children's interests is not as easy as looking out for the interests of the elderly.

Young adults have no national organization representing their interests, though they have interests in common. Young workers have interests in the minimum wage and health insurance for low-wage workers. College students have an interest in reducing tuition costs and expenses associated with a university education (see the box "Hey, Kid! Have I Got a Deal for You"). Both have interests in various age minima for activities as diverse as drinking and signing certain kinds of contracts.

Environmental groups Environmental groups are another example of multiple-issue groups. Earth Day 1970 marked the beginning of the environmental movement in the United States. Spurred by an oil spill in California, what was to be a "teach-in" on college campuses mushroomed into a day of national environmental awareness with an estimated twenty million Americans taking part. A minority movement in the 1970s, the environmental lobby today is large and active, and its values are supported by most Americans.[83]

Some environmental groups, such as the National Audubon Society, the Sierra Club, and the Natural

Tuition rates are soaring, and many students borrow money to cover the cost. In 2002–2003, over six million students borrowed $44 billion under federal student loan programs. A majority of college students now borrow money to help finance their educations.

Colleges offer one of two loan programs. Students either borrow directly from the government (the direct student loan program) or go through a private lender (the Federal Family Education Loan Program). The latter is a sweet deal for colleges and lenders but not for students.

Private lenders loan money for college to students at a fixed interest rate set by Congress above the lender's cost and conventional rates. If, however, interest rates should rise, rather than allowing the lender to lose money, the government—in other words, the American taxpayer—makes up the difference. Should students default and not repay the loan, the government covers the loss.

The direct student loan program makes $0.22 for every $100 borrowed, whereas the use of private lenders costs the government $12.80 for every $100 borrowed. One doesn't need a college education to recognize that direct loans are a better deal for American taxpayers. The direct-loan program not only saves money—indeed, the program generates income—but also costs students less by forcing private lenders to compete with the government program where interest on the borrowed money is less.

Established in 1993, the direct-loan program quickly captured a third of the student loan business and appeared on its way to dominating the market as more and more schools flocked to it. However, with billions at stake, private lenders fought back. The industry, led by Sallie Mae, the biggest player in the student loan business, attacked on two fronts. It stepped up its lobbying in Washington and began wining and dining schools.

On the lobbying front, it persuaded Congress to raise interest rates on loans and forgo a planned interest rate reduction. Students paid more, and the industry used the profits to induce schools to abandon the direct-loan program in favor of loans from private lenders. Lobbying was greased with campaign contributions to both Democrats and Republicans, particularly key members sitting on committees that oversee student loans, as well as "soft money" donations to the political parties. Said one higher education official, "In American history, this is the most outrageous giveaway ever extended by the federal government to private lenders."[1] The direct loans are unpopular with Republican conservatives, who believe that private lenders should handle the job, and Sallie Mae and the industry did not have to work too hard to convince the Bush administration that direct loans were not the way to go. Former representatives from the industry, clearly antagonistic to the direct-loan program, were appointed to oversee it. The administration ceased promoting the program to colleges and even proposed selling the loans the government already held to private lenders. That idea was abandoned when critics accused the administration of wanting to gut the program.

The second front targeted the schools themselves. Profits generated from interest charged to students were used to fund free meals, drinks, golf outings, and sailboat cruises for financial aid administrators. At Tuskegee University, Sallie Mae offered to provide free loan counseling for students and software for the financial aid office. The financial aid officer volunteered, "I have only praise for Sallie Mae. They are making sure we have what we need."

It was Sallie Mae who created "opportunity loans." Outside the federal loan program, Sallie Mae agrees to lend money to any student approved by a school. Why would Sallie Mae take on all the risk of lending to students when there is a government program that assumes the risk for them? Opportunity loans are available only if a school promises to leave the direct-loan program and push Sallie Mae's federally backed loan program to students. Colleges like opportunity funds because they keep enrollment up and tuition coming in.

Sallie Mae and others have also pushed "school as lender" schemes that generate a nice return for the schools and huge profits for the industry. Lenders make millions of dollars available to schools, which in turn lend the money to graduate students. The loans are then sold back to the lenders at a profit for the schools. In exchange, schools agree to drop out of the direct-loan program and route its undergraduate loan business exclusively to the lenders. Some argue that the arrangement is a conflict of interest because colleges stand to gain with the more loans they approve.

Under the circumstances, can colleges be expected to do what is best for their students? Sixty-two colleges and universities have dropped out of the direct-loan program since 2000, and the list is growing. Sallie Mae says it has won over $1 billion in loan business from former direct-loan schools. The shift from direct loans to private lenders is costing American taxpayers as much as $250 million a year.

How one feels about this issue depends on what one thinks the goal of a student loan program should be. Should the goals include being a profit center for lending institutions? Or should it be to provide loans at the lowest cost to students and the taxpayer? Check out which loan program your school has, and think about this issue when that first payment on your college loan comes due.

[1] Barmak Nassirian, associate executive director of the American Association of Collegiate Registrars and Admissions Officers, quoted in "Sally Mae's Romance with John Boehner," January 11, 2006, http://www.realclearpolitics.com/Commentary/com-1_11_06_FH.html

SOURCE: Adapted from "Big Money on Campus," *U.S. News and World Report,* October 27, 2003, 30–32, 35–40. Copyright 2003 *U.S. News and World Report,* L.P.

Resources Defense Council, have permanent offices in Washington with highly skilled professionals who carry out a full range of lobbying activities.[84] Groups such as Greenpeace, Earth First!, and the Sea Shepherds shun conventional lobbying approaches and are more confrontational. They seek a "green cultural revolution."

Local citizen groups have also organized in support of local environmental concerns such as the location of toxic or nuclear waste dumps. Citizens, skeptical of government and corporate claims that such facilities are safe, want them located elsewhere.[85]

The violent weather that brought hurricane Katrina and the increasing reports of melting icecaps and climate change have increased public concern with global warming. That, in turn, has brought new awareness of the political issues surrounding the environment.

Like other groups, the environmental movement has divisions within it. Some environmentalists do not want to compromise with business on any issues. Many groups rejected a Clinton administration proposal that would have allowed heavier-polluting utilities to purchase emission rights from less-polluting ones while gradually moving toward lower pollution over time.

Others argue that the key to reducing pollution is to work with industry to find solutions and accept small steps toward a better environment. They argue that when a business is persuaded to make a small, environmentally friendly change, others in the industry often follow out of fear that consumers will punish them if they don't, leading to real progress.[86]

Environmentalists have been on the defensive during the administration of George W. Bush and the conservative Congress. Conservative Republicans generally oppose environmental regulations, arguing that businesses should be allowed to regulate themselves. The election of George W. Bush saw the reversal of many Clinton era environmental regulations, such as the prohibition of road building in national forests, the use of snowmobiles in national parks, and restrictions on companies mining for gold and other minerals on public lands.[87] Many of the changes have been justified on national security grounds, though this seems a stretch for many issues. In spite of the administration's national security argument to open up the Alaskan wildlife refuge to oil exploration, environmentalists opposed it, and the measure was defeated in the Senate. Whether Bush can reopen the issue will depend on whether his popularity rebounds strongly from his dismal ratings in mid-2006.

Single-Issue Groups

Single-issue groups pursue noneconomic goals but are distinguished by their intense concern for a single issue and reluctance to compromise. The NRA is an example. Members are passionate in their opposition to gun control. Although a majority of Americans have supported gun control for years, the NRA has successfully lobbied Congress to prevent most gun control measures. The group has members in every congressional district that can be mobilized on behalf of the group's goals.

Fearful that the 2000 election of Democratic candidate Al Gore would mean gun control, the NRA waged an all-out effort to defeat him, pumping $15 million into the election campaign, making a major effort to register its members to vote, and training members in grassroots organizing. Gore's defeat in West Virginia, traditionally a Democratic state, was partially due to the anti–gun control vote there.

The NRA considered Bush a close ally, and he has proved them right. After he secured the Republican nomination, a high-ranking official boasted at an NRA gathering that a Bush win would mean direct access to the Oval Office.[88] Although this might have been an exaggeration, the Bush Justice Department, led by former Attorney General John Ashcroft, filed two briefs before the Supreme Court in cases involving gun regulation, arguing that the Second Amendment protects the right of individuals to keep and bear arms rather than a right that is tied to the nation's need to maintain an armed militia.[89] The administration's position reverses sixty years of government policy. The NRA, which featured a picture of Ashcroft on its magazine and called him "a breath of fresh air to freedom-loving gun owners," lauded the decision.[90] The Violence Policy Center, a gun control group, chided the decision, adding that the Justice Department "has shown a willingness to throw red meat at the gun lobby and put its political agenda above its institutional obligations."[91]

The NRA's latest effort is legislation prohibiting lawsuits against gun makers who manufacture and

"If you still want to belong to an organization dedicated to killing Americans, there's always the tobacco lobby."

dealers who sell guns used in crimes. Spurred on by success in suing tobacco companies, local and state governments hope to sue manufacturers and dealers to recover police and health care costs incurred as a result of gun violence.[92] It has also opposed the renewal of the decade-old ban on assault weapons and semiautomatic rifles. Possession of those weapons became legal again when Congress failed to renew the ban in 2004.

The NRA's website posts an extensive enemies list, including the CDF, the U.S. Catholic Conference, the YMCA, the Kansas City Chiefs, Hallmark Cards, Walter Cronkite, and football player, Doug Flutie.[93]

The NRA has been so successful that some politicians, especially in "red" states, who are inclined to support gun control measures have concluded that the risks to their election or reelection are so great and the probabilities of passing gun control measures are so small that it's prudent to go along with the NRA and instead save their tough stands for some other issues. Consequently, the gun control forces have had very limited success in Congress, usually only when a spasm of gun violence has inflamed the public.

Another example of single-interest groups is pro-choice and pro-life groups focused on abortion. The National Right to Life Committee seeks a constitutional amendment banning all abortions. Recognizing the unlikelihood of this, it has pushed for restrictions on abortion at the state level, such as laws requiring waiting periods and parental consent for minors. Many of these have been adopted. The antiabortion movement, including Right to Life, rallied around Republican efforts in Congress to ban late-term abortions (Right to Life groups call them partial-birth abortions) and to make it a separate offense to harm a fetus in a federal crime committed against a pregnant women. Both were approved by Congress and signed by the president. The late-term abortion ban was subsequently struck down by the courts because it had no provision to allow such abortions to save the life of the mother. The Bush White House vowed to continue to fight for the law.

While many in the pro-life movement have given up hope of outlawing abortion, they work instead to reduce the number of abortions by changes in the law that make abortion more difficult for the woman and the doctor.[94] A few continue to support violent solutions. The Army of God, a militant antiabortion group, marked the thirtieth anniversary of *Roe* v. *Wade,* the Supreme Court's 1973 decision upholding a woman's right to abortion, by celebrating the murder of Dr. Barnett Slepian, an abortion provider in Buffalo, slain in 1998. The group's website encouraged supporters to attend a march outside the clinic were Slepian worked to support the man who confessed to the killing.[95]

However, violence against abortion doctors and clinics has declined, owing in part to a judgment against an antiabortion coalition responsible for web postings of the names, addresses, and license plate numbers of doctors who perform abortions.[96] The Court agreed with pro-choice advocates that the action, dubbed the "Nuremberg Files," was designed to threaten and intimidate doctors and likely to lead to violence. The plaintiffs were awarded compensatory damages.[97]

Members of the National Abortion Rights Action League and Planned Parenthood are fervently committed to protecting a women's right to choose. Often identified with abortion rights, Planned Parenthood also advocates for access to birth control, sex education in schools, and quality reproductive health care for women. Using the theme that Americans want abortion to be safe and legal, the group uses newspaper ads, congressional testimony, a website, mailings, and local educational efforts to get the message out. In April 2004, the group mobilized more than a million people to march in the nation's capital protesting attacks on women's reproductive rights.[98]

Single-issue groups have increased in recent decades. Some people view this with alarm. When groups form around highly emotional issues and are unwilling to compromise, the system can't deal with them and the issues continue to boil,[99] consuming time and energy of policy makers at the expense of broader issues that may be more important.

On the other hand, single-issue groups have always been part of politics.[100] These groups may even be beneficial because they represent interests that may not

REUTERS/William Philpott/Landov

Pro-life demonstrators march past the Supreme Court on the anniversary of Roe v. Wade, *which legalized abortions.*

© Lynn Johnson/Aurora

Pro-choice advocates form a human corridor to protect patients and workers entering a clinic in Buffalo, New York.

win contracts for the services they provide. Halliburton and other companies lobbied the Department of Defense to obtain lucrative business contracts in Iraq. And sometimes groups turn to the courts to change things. Before civil rights groups could muster support in Congress in the 1960s, they were able to get the courts to strike down old laws requiring certain kinds of segregation and, in essence, establish a new policy. In all of these, groups worked to initiate change.

Sometimes groups wish to keep things the way they are. Abortion rights groups, for example, lobby Congress and the president to prevent the adoption of antiabortion laws. Groups favoring the status quo may also lobby administrative agencies not to change a particular policy. For example, proponents of women's equality lobbied against weakening the rules requiring equity in support for women's and men's athletics. Or groups might file lawsuits to declare a new policy illegal or unconstitutional. When pro-choice groups could not stop the passage of the ban on late-term abortions, they filed suit in court against the enforcement of the new law.

Usually it is easier to prevent rather than enact a proposed law or policy. This is so because there are many points in the policy-making process where new ideas can be killed, and thus a group intent on killing a measure only has to succeed at one of these points. Legislation can be stopped in Congress or the Oval Office. New laws can be killed in the bureaucracy when agency heads drag their feet in implementing them or implement them in a way different from Congress' intention. And should a measure become law, the courts may act to kill it.

In other words, there are many ways to stop change, but enactment of new laws requires success at each stage of the policy process. Clearly, the separation of powers and checks and balances in the American system favor the status quo.

Groups can also influence policy indirectly by influencing the choice of those who are appointed to policy-making positions in the bureaucracy and to the courts. Having a friend or ally in an important position can be important in securing policy goals.

be well represented in Congress. Fears about single-issue groups may result from the groups' own exaggerated claims of influence, their heavy media coverage, and in the case of some, their confrontational tactics.

Strategies of Interest Groups

Interest groups use a variety of strategies to influence public policy. Sometimes they are interested in changing things. They might want a new law passed. Or they might want the president to establish a new policy by executive action or to enforce a current law more or less vigorously. After numerous miners were killed in accidents in 2005, unions lobbied to get existing mine safety laws implemented and to pass new laws providing additional protections for underground miners. Sometimes groups lobby the bureaucracy to

Tactics of Interest Groups

To carry out their strategic goals, interest groups engage in a variety of tactics. Some tactics seek to influence policy makers directly, whereas others seek to mold public opinion and influence policy makers indirectly. Some do both. Others that have little chance of succeeding using conventional techniques sometimes turn to protest. Some interest groups form broad coalitions to maximize their influence.

Earmarking, Better Than Hitting the Lottery

Do you have a project that needs funds? If so, earmarking may be the ticket, and it has a better chance of a payout than the lottery. Earmarking allows individual members of Congress to target federal funds to a specific project, usually in his or her home district. Often hundreds of earmarks are included in large, complex bills; many members of Congress have little idea what these earmarks are for or how much they cost.

In a major transportation bill in 2005, for example, there were thousands of ear marks. The Speaker of the House, Dennis Hastert (R-Ill.), was able to add to the bill earmarks such as $150,000 for a police department in his district, $2 million for a local community college building project, $250,000 for another community's airport and $200,000 for a waste-water project, $750,000 for a local medical center, and another $450,000 for a health department in yet another city.[1]

None of these allocations seems worthless. The problem with earmarks is that there is no way to judge whether the new wastewater project in Speaker Hastert's district is more or less valuable than similar projects in other districts that have a less-influential representative. It is certainly a reasonable conclusion that many projects that are funded are less important than those that aren't.

Consequently, earmarking has become a huge source of waste. In 1994, federal legislation contained 4000 earmarks costing $29 billion. By 2004, the numbers of earmarks more than

tripled, and cost had more than doubled to 14,000, worth $53 billion in 2004. That year, there were nearly 35,000 requests of the Appropriations Committee in the House to earmark funds. In 2005, one transportation bill alone had more than 6300 earmarks.

Why the surge? Following the Republican takeover of the House in 1994, then Speaker Gingrich instructed the Appropriation Committee to support projects in districts where Republicans might have a difficult time getting reelected. The practice continues today. Republican leaders in the House forward a list of those who may be in trouble, and the Committee responds with earmarks for the particular districts.

Because the leadership appeared more willing to earmark, legions of lobbyists became available to help clients secure them. The number of lobbyists registered to lobby on budget and appropriations jumped from 1500 in 1998 to over 4000 in 2005. Some firms devote themselves exclusively to winning earmarks: "earmark factories" as a staff member of Appropriations called them. The strategy is a win-win for both lobbyists and politicians. Lobbyists earn millions signing on clients with promises of an appropriation for a specific project, and members of Congress win favor with the voters back home as such projects improve local communities and provide employment.

The problem of earmarks was featured in 2005 by the so-called bridge to nowhere, a $233 million earmark

linking two small towns in Alaska. One island had 50 people, 350 deer, no stores, and no paved roads. The bridge, linking that island to a nearby town of 8000, was higher than the Brooklyn Bridge and nearly as long as the Golden Gate bridge, and it cost over $230 million. This project was one of several, totaling more than $1 billion, for Alaska due to the influence of Don Young (R-Alas.), who heads the Transportation Committee in the U.S. House of Representatives.

Pork-barrel politics goes back to the time of George Washington. It is part of a lawmaker's job to "bring home the bacon." However, never before has so much legislation been tacked on in this manner outside the normal legislative process. At a time when Congress and the president are ringing up record deficits, and when there are significant needs to repair bridges, levies, and infrastructure in many parts of the country (including hurricane-damaged New Orleans), bridges to nowhere are increasingly a mark of a dysfunctional system. And of course now there are scores of lobbyists to help the process along.

[1] Jonathan Kaplan, "Hill Leaders May Be Pressed to Give up Projects," *The Hill* (January 25, 2005): http://www.hillnews.com/thehill/export/TheHill/News/Frontpage/012506/earmark2.html

SOURCE: Janet Hook and Richard Simon, "Earmarking—A Win-Win for Lobbyists and Politicians," *LA Times*, January 29, 2006, online; Jeffrey Birnbaum, "Earmark—It's $$$, Not Body Art," *Washington Post*, February 3, 2006, A17; "Marks for Sharks," *Opinion Journal, Wall Street Journal's Opinion Page*, January 9, 2006, http://www.opinionjournal.com/diary/?id=110007785

Direct Lobbying Techniques

Direct lobbying involves personal encounters with a lobbyist, of which there are currently thirty-two thousand registered in Washington.[101] Some are volunteers; others are permanent, salaried employees of the groups they represent; and others are contract lobbyists, "hired guns" who represent any individual or group willing to pay for the service. Contract lobbyists include the

numerous Washington lawyers affiliated with the city's most prestigious law firms. Many have worked in government, allowing them to boast of contacts with and access to public officials to plead their clients' cases. Since 1972, the number of lawyers in Washington has increased eightfold. At the moment, there are approximately 81,548 lawyers in Washington, which means that one in every seven people you pass on the street is probably heading from a law office to the Capitol or some federal agency to promote the interests of a client, largely corporations or large interest groups.[102]

Some lobbying is done by corporate CEOs and some by public officials themselves. The president's cabinet and advisers lobby Congress, and although one may not think of it as lobbying, members of Congress talk to and attempt to persuade their colleagues. Average citizens may occasionally visit their elected representatives and lay out their concerns. Most law firms, corporations, and trade associations find it useful to have some lobbyists in their employ who are Republicans and some who are Democrats. This ensures access to the elected members of both parties. It also means that groups are able to continue doing business in Washington without interruption when control of government shifts from one party to another.

However, the bipartisan complexion of the K Street corridor in Washington, home to lobbyists representing the nation's largest corporations and trade groups, has diminished somewhat with the Republican control of both the White House and Congress.[103] Republican leaders want to replace corporate lobbyists who are Democrats with Republicans. The goal is not simply to ensure that lobbyists are Republican but to ensure that lobbyists are loyal first and foremost to the Republican Party.

The plan, dubbed the "K Street strategy," had its beginning with the Republican takeover of Congress in the mid-1990s. Shortly after conservatives under Speaker Newt Gingrich solidified their hold in the House, they turned their attention to the core of Washington lobbyists. In 1995, House Republican leader Tom DeLay compiled a list of the four hundred largest contributors to the parties. Lobbyists were summoned to his office one by one and shown their name in either the "friendly" or "unfriendly" column, the latter the list of those who contributed to Democrats. Friendly lobbyists were invited to help write legislation. Thus, chemical industry lobbyists help write regulations on hazardous waste, oil companies help write energy policy, and military contractors help the Pentagon write weapons contracts. DeLay later told the *Washington Post,* "If you want to play in our revolution, you have to live by our rules."

Not content with strong-arming lobbyists, DeLay later met with CEOs from several large companies. He told them that Democratic lobbyists would have to go. Not unexpectedly, most, several who were Republican, reacted negatively to the "shakedown." With Clinton in the White House and treating business very well, the Republicans overreached.

However, with the election of George W. Bush in 2000, new life was breathed into the plan. With the Republicans controlling the White House and Congress, the effort to give K Street a decidedly Republican look worked well. The near parity in giving by corporations to the political parties during the 1990s has shifted so that now corporations support two Republicans to every Democrat candidate.

Meanwhile, private corporations gain more benefits and in turn provide more campaign and lobbying resources to ensure that the party remains in power. This strategy further solidified Republican control of the government. Democrats probably cannot reverse it until they regain power in one of the houses of Congress or the presidency.

However, following the old adage that "power corrupts and absolute power corrupts absolutely," complete control of government led to increasing corruption.[104] By 2006, Tom DeLay chose (under pressure from other Republicans) to leave Congress after being indicted in Texas for criminal behavior involving evading the state's ban on corporate contributions to political campaigns. Several of DeLay's staff and close associates were also under indictment for selling access to him to corporations and other groups for millions of dollars.[105]

The K-Street arrangements would have made any turn-of-the-twentieth-century machine politician green with envy (see Chapter 7). Like the old machines, the party channeled taxpayers' dollars and other favors to clients who kick back a portion, enabling the party to win a majority and remain in power. Long ago, we reformed the conditions that supported the party machines. But these oversight mechanisms do not work very well when one party controls all mechanisms of government. However, overreaching has already had negative consequences for the Republicans and may eventually end their congressional dominance.

Making Personal Contacts

Making personal contacts in an office or informal setting is a very effective lobbying technique. Concerns and questions can be dealt with on the spot, and an appeal can be tailored to those concerns. Direct contact may not be expensive, if a lobbyist is already on the payroll.

As personal contact with members of Congress or their staffs has become more difficult, some lobbyists are turning to electronic mail. Although e-mail is no substitute for a personal visit, only lobbyists with strong personal relationships developed over years can be assured of a personal audience. For those lacking such ties, e-mail may serve as a substitute.[106]

Lobbyists know that contacting every legislator is unnecessary. Contacting key legislators—party leaders, those sitting on committees of particular interest, and staff serving those committees—is crucial.[107] Conventional wisdom suggests that only legislators who support a group's position or are known to be undecided should be contacted directly.[108] Putting undue pressure on opponents may hurt prospects for working in the future on other issues.

Successful lobbying is based on friendship. As a former chair of the House Budget Committee put it, "The most effective lobbyists here are the ones you don't think of as lobbyists." Referring to one prominent Washington lobbyist, he said, "I don't think of him as a lobbyist. He's almost a constituent, or a friend." Barbara Boxer, then a Democratic representative from California, referring to the same gentleman, described him as "a lovely, wonderful guy. In the whole time I've known him, he's never asked me to vote for anything." At a gathering, she joked that he's almost "a member of the family."[109]

Direct personal contact was the strategy of the airline industry in seeking government aid following 9/11. Senator Peter Fitzgerald (R-Ill.), the only senator to vote against the $15 billion aid package, remarked, "The airline industry made a full-court press to convince Congress that giving them billions in taxpayer cash was the only way to save the republic."[110] Twenty-seven in-house lobbyists and several hired guns from forty-two Washington firms, including former White House aides, cabinet secretaries, retired members of Congress, and former Republican National Party Chair Haley Barbour, went to work. The CEOs and board members of several airlines also pitched in. One lobbyist remarked, "It was the most high-level surgical strike that I have ever seen."[111]

Rather than pursue the usual path of congressional lawmaking, committee hearings, and floor debate—which would have delayed action, allowing opposition to form, and undercut the effort—the airlines targeted a few congressional and administration leaders. "Their tactic was to bring all their top people to meet with top people in government and to say the sky is falling."[112] The result, as Representative George Miller (D-Calif.) put it, was that "the big dog got the bone."[113]

Providing Expertise

Lobbyists are an invaluable source of information. Members of Congress and the White House are not experts. They rely on lobbyists to educate them. In the mid-1990s, Congress was considering standards for high-definition TV. A representative of the Information Technology Association of America referred to pixels. A congressman spoke up, "I'm trying to stay with you here, but one of the first times I ever took a ride on an airplane was when I came to Washington to take this seat and I remember looking out the window and thought part of the wing was falling off when we landed because the flaps came up."[114]

Some groups and associations are known for the accurate and reliable information they provide. Public Citizen, founded by Ralph Nader, is an example. In recent years, it has lobbied against the erosion of government regulations dealing with clean air and water, safe drugs, food, and the workplace. It has also worked to limit corporate gifts, such as fancy vacations, to members of Congress and to enact campaign finance reform (see Chapter 9).

Lobbyists often draft legislation. A legislator may ask a lobbyist known to be an expert in an area to draft a bill, or both may work together in drafting legislation. Sometimes interest groups will take it upon themselves to draft legislation and ask a sympathetic legislator to introduce it. General Electric drafted a tax reform measure that saved it millions in taxes. In an effort to tap the flow of federal money following 9/11, drug and biotechnology companies supplied Congress with the precise legislative language required to provide them with what they wanted.[115] Biotechnology firms wanted to be absolved of any claims from injuries caused by vaccines produced to protect people from biological terrorism. Drug companies wanted the Food and Drug Administration to waive review procedures when called on to supply drugs in an emergency.

AP Images/Oceana, Linda Spillers

Lobbyists come in all shapes, sizes, and . . . species. This dolphin is trying to raise awareness of an effort in Congress to remove a provision of the Marine Mammal Protection Act restricting commercial fishing practices that entangle dolphins and whales in mammoth nets.

Testifying at Hearings

Testifying at congressional hearings establishes a group's credentials as a player in a policy area and communicates to the people it represents that those on the payroll in Washington are doing their job. It also provides free publicity. Testifying has its own rules and norms. A Washington lobbyist responsible for prepping witnesses to testify, asked to name the most important piece of advice he could give, cited the Boy Scouts' motto: "Be prepared."

Effective witnesses also know to keep their testimony short and as spontaneous as possible. Arrogant witnesses usually aren't very successful either. Some witnesses are short with members because they believe committee members don't understand their business. That may be true, but members are going to be making decisions about it. Successful witnesses also do not guess at answers. They promise to supply the answer later. Finally, effective witnesses realize that a telling anecdote or illustration can accomplish more than reams of statistics.[116]

Giving Money

Lobbyists want access to policy makers, and giving money is a way to guarantee this. A longtime financial backer of Ronald Reagan said that having a dialogue with a politician is fine, "but with a little money they hear you better."[117] A Democrat commented in a similar vein, "Who do members of Congress see? They'll certainly see the one who gives the money. It's hard to say no to someone who gives you $5000."[118]

Groups, including businesses and unions, set up PACs to give money to political campaigns. The number of PACs has grown dramatically since the mid-1970s, along with the amount of money they contribute. (PACs and the role of money in politics are discussed in Chapter 9.)

Lobbying the Bureaucracy

The battle is not over when a bill is passed. Lobbyists must also influence bureaucrats who implement policy. Regulations outlawing sex discrimination in colleges and universities were drafted in the Department of Education with little specific direction from Congress. Although the legislation was passed in 1972, both women's rights groups and interests opposing them continue to lobby over the interpretation of the regulations. The most controversial issue today is how to define equality between men's and women's athletics. Should schools have an equal number of men's and women's teams? Equal numbers of male and female athletes? Equal expenditures on men's and women's athletics? Men and women athletes in proportion to men and women in the student body? These different concepts of equality lead to different conclusions about whether a school is providing equal opportunity for women's athletics.

Bureaucrats are the targets of direct lobbying just like members of Congress. Ken Lay, former CEO of Enron, used the direct approach when he telephoned Curtis Hébert, appointed by President George W. Bush to chair the Federal Energy Commission, to let him know that Enron would continue to support him in his new job if he changed his views on electricity deregulation.[119] Lay also had access to the parties responsible for drafting the Bush administration's recommendation for the nation's energy policy. The final report included much of what Lay advocated, including finding ways to give the federal government, where Enron had substantial clout, more power over electricity transmission.[120]

Interest groups also influence who gets appointed to bureaucratic positions. By influencing the appointments to an agency, an industry or group can improve its prospects for favorable treatment by that agency. For example, the auto industry opposed a number of President Clinton's nominees to head the National Highway Traffic Safety Administration. It felt the nominees were not sympathetic enough to the interests and concerns of the auto industry and too concerned with consumers and safety. Senator Don Nickles (R-Okla.), an ally of antiabortion groups, held up the nomination of Clinton's nominee to head the Food and Drug Administration until he was convinced she would not solicit a manufacturer for RU-486, an abortion pill.[121] Later, the Food and Drug Administration, dominated by George W. Bush appointees, rejected recommendations of its professional staff to allow over-the-counter sales of RU-486.

Public Citizen and the Natural Resources Defense Council opposed President George W. Bush's choice to head the White House Office of Information and Regulatory Affairs out of concern that he would water down Clinton-era health and environmental safeguards. The nominee, a Harvard professor, promised to enforce current laws, even if he disagreed with them, and was confirmed.[122] Pharmaceutical manufacturers effectively vetoed Dr. Alastair Wood, a drug safety expert and early favorite of the Bush administration to head the Food and Drug Administration; drug company CEOs called the White House complaining that Wood was "too aggressive on drug safety issues."[123]

Litigating in Court

Like bureaucrats, judges also make policy. Although interest groups do not lobby judges the way they do legislators and bureaucrats, some achieve their goals by getting involved in cases and persuading the courts to rule in their favor. Although most groups do not litigate cases, some use litigation as their primary tactic, particularly those that lack influence with Congress and the executive branch.

Litigation has been a favorite strategy of civil rights organizations. Throughout the early part of the twentieth century, when Congress and the White House were unsympathetic to the rights of black Americans, civil rights groups fought segregation in the courts and won a series of victories, eventually leading to fuller integration (Chapter 15 provides more information on this issue). In more recent years, civil rights groups have used the courts to legitimize affirmative action, with a mixed, though largely positive, record of success.[124]

Several civil liberties organizations are pursuing court action challenging President Bush's holding suspected terrorists without giving them the right to consult an attorney and trying them in secrecy or in military tribunals.[125] The American Civil Liberties Union maintains that the president is making law when he has no constitutional power to do so; lawmaking is granted by the Constitution exclusively to Congress. Hence, in the view of the ACLU, the president's actions violate the constitutionally established separation of powers.

Environmental groups and public interest lobbies have also turned to the courts. The Natural Resources Defense Council, along with Greenpeace, Physicians for Social Responsibility, and the Alaska Public Interest Research Group, filed suit against Bush's missile defense plan, asserting that it violates federal environmental laws.[126]

In addition to filing civil suits, groups can represent defendants in criminal cases or file "friend of the court" briefs, written arguments asking the court to decide a case a particular way.[127] Some groups use the courts to try to force their opponents to negotiate with them.

Environmental groups frequently challenge developers who threaten the environment in order to delay a project, raise the costs incurred by the developers, and motivate them to negotiate with the environmental interests. The next time a project is opposed, developers may be more willing to make concessions beforehand to avoid lengthy and costly litigation.

Groups also try to influence the courts indirectly by lobbying the Senate to support or oppose judicial nominees. As we will see in Chapter 13, the appointment process is becoming increasingly politicized, with many groups fighting to make sure that new judges will be sympathetic to their causes, or at least neutral.

Indirect Lobbying Techniques: Going Public

Traditionally, lobbyists for the most part employed direct lobbying techniques—providing information, advice, and occasionally pressure. More recently, interest groups have been going public—mobilizing their activists and molding and activating public opinion. A study of 175 lobbying groups found that most were doing more lobbying than in previous years, but that in recent years they were devoting more activity in mobilizing activists and working to shape public opinion."[128] The goal of "going public" is to mobilize the grass roots to contact policy makers and generate publicity.

Protest is another form of going public used by groups. The proimmigration lobby groups referred to in You Are There in this chapter used protest quite effectively in shaping the climate within which immigration would be discussed by Congress.

Mobilizing the Grass Roots

The constituency of an interest group—a group's members, those whom the group serves, friends and allies of the group, or simply those who can be mobilized whether or not they have a connection to the group—can help in promoting the cause or voting for a candidate. The NRA is effective in mobilizing its members. The NRA, like many mass-membership organizations, can generate thousands of letters or calls to members of Congress in a short period of time. Calls from irate NRA members led one senator to remark, "I'd rather be a deer in hunting season than run afoul of the NRA crowd."[129]

Conservative Christian minister Jerry Falwell activated his "gospel grapevine" to flood the White House and Congress in opposition to President Clinton's plan to lift the ban on homosexuals in the military. Warning of a new radical homosexual rights agenda, Falwell urged viewers of his *Old Time Gospel Hour* to call and register their opinions.

Senator John McCain (R-Ariz.), a sponsor of antitobacco legislation, was swamped with letters from members of the National Smokers Alliance, an organization funded by the tobacco companies.[130] Senator Tom Harkin (D-Iowa) was surprised to receive hundreds of letters opposing his antitobacco position, strangely enough from only one small region in his state. The mystery was solved when Harkin learned that all the letters came from employees of a Kraft food plant, owned by RJ Reynolds, the tobacco company.[131]

Appeals to write or phone policy makers often exaggerate the severity of the concern and the strength of the opposition. To move members, groups suggest that a monstrous adversary or a catastrophic defeat is confronting group members.

How to mobilize To be effective, letters and phone calls must appear spontaneous and sincere. Groups often provide sample letters to aid constituents, but these are not as convincing as those written in a constituent's own words. Campaigns producing postcards with preprinted messages or facilitating online petitions or identical messages are seldom effective. While members of Congress often enlist organizations to mobilize constituents in support of legislation, many members are turned off by the flood of mail and calls they receive. As one lobbyist put it, "Members of Congress hate it when you call in the dogs."[132]

Grassroots lobbying was the hallmark of the successful effort to defeat President Clinton's health care reform proposal in 1994. Cigarette companies, drug manufacturers, health insurance agents, physicians, and hospital administrators mobilized their employees, clients, and friends to contact their representatives urging them to kill the measure.[133] Pressure of this kind can provide members of Congress in both parties with a reason to buck the president. As one lobbyist put it, "If done well, a member of Congress summoned to the Oval Office can turn to the president and say, 'I can't go with you on this, Mr. President, because I promised the people in my district.'"[134]

The nature of grassroots lobbying has changed in the past decade. Almost all groups, particularly those with resources, use it as part of an overall lobbying strategy. With e-mail and faxes, it is easy to inform supporters to communicate with elected officials. In 2004, House and Senate Offices received 201 million messages; 90 percent were email.[135] Many groups have websites that not only provide information but also invite browsers to send e-mail messages to public officials. Some sites provide the message; others suggest talking points. Electronic communication saves time and money in recruiting letter writers and checking on follow through. Because e-mails and letters often come from constituents, members of Congress pay some attention to them. Of course, a flood of e-mails with basically the same message is no more persuasive than mass postcard campaigns.

Third-party involvement Dozens of public relations firms assist groups in mobilizing their constituency, if there is one, or manufacturing the appearance of one, if there is not. Washington firms in the business of producing "citizen movements" on demand advertise specialties such as development of third-party allies, grassroots mobilization and recruitment, and grasstops lobbying.[136] (*Grasstops lobbying* involves identifying the person or persons that a member of Congress cannot say no to—a chief donor, campaign manager, political counselor, or adviser—and persuading them to persuade the member to go along with the group.) In many respects, grassroots lobbying resembles a presidential election campaign because it involves a number of specialists: a pollster to assess citizen opinion, a media consultant to produce and test-market television ads, a communications ad-

viser to enlist journalists to write stories and editorials, think tanks to provide supporting research, a recruiter to enlist local and community leaders, a Washington lobbyist to push the idea with members of Congress, and a legal expert to draft legislation. The grassroots industry spends nearly $1 billion a year putting a "public look" on private interests.[137]

The strategy of massaging constituents and marshaling public opinion has become the method of choice for business lobbies and corporations. Relying on influential lobbyists with connections to party leaders and influential congressional committee chairs no longer works. Power is too dispersed. Today, you "send in the armies, ships, tanks, aircraft, infantry, Democrats and Republicans, grassroots specialists, and people with special relationships to members."[138]

Technology and mobilization The Internet is becoming indispensable in attempts to activate individuals with no connection other than their position for or against a candidate or a cause. MoveOn.org, a left-leaning website with an e-mail list of 1.8 million, can with the click of a mouse send hundreds of thousands of messages hurtling toward Washington. Citizens opposed to electronic voting were invited to sign a petition to the president and members of Congress admonishing them to require a paper ballot backup in the 2004 election. Citizens could sign a petition demanding that Congress censure the president for lying to the American people about Iraq's weapons of mass destruction. In the 2004 campaign, the founders of MoveOn.org, husband and wife Wes Boyd and Joan Blakes, electronically solicited millions of dollars to air anti-Bush commercials in key battleground states.[139]

As part of a campaign to cut taxes on capital gains and dividends, the U.S. Chamber of Commerce paid for an ad on Google that would appear when anyone typed *dividend* in the search field. Organizations of all stripes, including the Chamber of Commerce, routinely purchases databases and sift through them for likely supporters.[140]

Blogging, attractive because it reaches those between the ages of eighteen and twenty-nine, is used by many interest groups. The National Association of Manufacturers.Shopfloor.org combines a personal voice with a loose tone and humor, "the essentials of the blogging spirit."[141]

Another example of what some refer to as Internet democracy was the so-called Virtual March on Washington, staged by Win without War, a coalition of antiwar groups including MoveOn.org. On February 25, 2003, hundreds of thousand of antiwar messages flooded congressional offices, their timing coordinated electronically to avoid tying up the telephone lines.[142]

The founders of MoveOn.org, Wes Boyd and Joan Blakes, run the organization from their Berkeley, California home.

Grass roots and democracy Does grassroots lobbying enhance democracy or undermine it? Insiders are convinced that their efforts mobilize real people with genuine and sincere interests, whether they are members, employees, or simply isolated individuals identified by polling and research. Senator Carl Levin (D-Mich.) has a different view. "When public relations firms are paid to generate calls, it creates a distorted picture of public opinion. When a member gets fifty phone calls, what he doesn't know is that 950 other people were contacted and said no way."[143]

Mobilizing the vote Groups also work hard to get their members and supporters to the polls on election day. Electing a sympathetic member to Congress, not to mention a president, is more effective in the long run than relying on a continuing effort to mobilize constituents. Many groups worked hard to get their supporters to the polls in the recent presidential elections because of the anticipated closeness of the results.[144] In 2000, labor unions in closely contested states made an effort to reach all of their current and retired members by phone or through the mail. The AFL-CIO had a website capable of producing fliers comparing the candidates on the major issues. The flier, with a personal message from the local union official, could be printed and mailed within a day. At get-out-the-vote rallies, NRA president Charlton Heston called the 2000 election "the most important since the Civil War." If Gore won, he continued, his Supreme Court will "hammer your gun rights into oblivion." As one journalist concluded, in an election where there are no great crises or burning issues, how do you get people to vote? The answer, "Scare the hell out of them."[145]

Molding Public and Elite Opinion

Groups use public relations techniques to shape public opinion as well as the opinions of policy makers. Ads in newspapers and magazines and on radio and television supply information, foster an image, or promote a particular policy; sometimes they do all three. Tobacco companies spent a record $40 million to defeat antitobacco legislation in 1998. Lockheed Martin, a defense contractor, tried to persuade Congress to purchase the company's F-22 fighter jet with an ad appearing in several publications widely read by members. The ad featured a postcard on a black background. On the card, dated June 18, 2007, a wife and mother writes home telling her husband and son not to worry because "those F-22s upstairs" are "ruling the sky." Across the bottom of the ad is the caption "One day in the future, someone you love may be depending on the F-22." According to the company, the ad was an attempt to give a human dimension to an issue that is often shrouded in Pentagon jargon and mind-numbing statistics. But Senator Dale Bumpers (D-Ark.) accused the firm of pandering to the emotions of lawmakers.[146]

On occasion, groups will fabricate information. ExxonMobil is alleged to have distorted the debate on global warming by generating bogus reports and funding scientists who supported the corporation's point of view but who were not experts in the field of climatology and whose research was not reviewed by scholars in the field.[147] Conclusions by the Environmental Protection Agency in June 2002 that global warming is a significant problem discredit ExxonMobil's view that it is not. Of course, by themselves ads are unlikely to move policy makers to action or shift public opinion dramatically in the short run. They are most effective in combination with other tactics. The EPA's experts and recommendations were undermined by the Bush administration's rejection of their conclusions.

Groups may stage events such as rallies or pickets to attract media coverage to their cause. During the apartheid era in South Africa (when blacks and whites were strictly segregated), opponents of segregation won considerable attention by organizing picketing and protesting outside the South African embassy in Washington, D.C. The action was especially effective because members of Congress, community leaders, and other celebrities participated. Arrests of members of Congress for trespassing kept the issue in the spotlight.

Framing the terms of a debate can be crucial in winning public support. People and groups arguing in favor of tort reform (limiting damages the courts can award to individuals injured in auto accidents, air disasters, unsuccessful surgeries, and other mishaps) focus on the few outrageously large settlements for seemingly minor injuries. Those arguing against reform focus on the poor widows left penniless after being permanently injured by the careless and willful behavior of large corporations.[148]

Lifetime, the television network targeted toward women, has played a significant role in raising a number of issues relevant to women through its issue-oriented programming. A movie featuring Academy Award-winning actress Mira Sorvino dealt with sex trafficking. Others have focused on DNA testing in rape cases, stalking, and spouse abuse. Following the airing of a documentary *Terror in the Home,* the National Domestic Violence Hotline had a 7000 percent increase in calls. *Video Voyeur: The Susan Wilson Story,* a movie depicting the spying of a creepy high-tech neighbor, led to the Video Voyeurism Protection Act of 2004.[149]

Hoping to influence public opinion, interest groups also rate members of Congress. Groups choose votes crucial to their concerns or votes reflecting a liberal or conservative orientation. They count how many times a member has voted with the group's interests, calculate a score, and publicize it to their members. The ultimate objective is to defeat candidates who consistently vote against them. Such ratings have little impact unless the group uses other tactics to target opponents.

Protest and Civil Disobedience

Groups that lack access or hold unpopular positions can protest. As noted in You Are There, in 2006 millions of immigrants and their supporters took to the streets all over America. They protested immigration legislation being considered in Congress that called for deportation of illegal immigrants and other severe sanctions. Another huge mass protest took place in 1999, when representatives from more than five hundred groups joined forces in protesting the World Trade Organization (WTO) at its meeting in Seattle.[150] The WTO represents 135 countries with authority to force countries to change their labor, environmental, and human rights laws that restrict trade among countries. In addition to high-profile labor unions and environmental groups, the demonstration drew less well-known organizations such as the Ruckus Society, a group that provides training in nonviolent protest, and the Raging Grannies, a human rights organization. The Sierra Club and the Steelworkers held a Seattle tea party with the slogan "No Globalization without Representation." Following their Boston forebears, they tossed steel imported from China, hormone-treated beef, and other goods they view as tainted by WTO decisions into the sea.[151] Taking a page from Vietnam War protests, the groups staged a number of activities, including teach-ins, concerts, and mock trials of corporations. Hundreds of protesters formed a human chain around Seattle's exhibition center, the

site of the meeting, demanding that the WTO cancel the debt owed by the world's poorest nations. The protest ended in violence, and several hundred protesters were arrested and jailed.

Peaceful but illegal protest activity, in which those involved allow themselves to be arrested and punished, is known as **civil disobedience.** Greenpeace, the environmental and peace group, practices civil disobedience. The organization got its start in 1971 when a group of environmentalists and peace activists sent two boats named *Greenpeace* to Amchitka Island near Alaska to protest a U.S. underground nuclear weapon test. Although the boats failed to reach the island, the publicity generated by the affair led Washington to cancel the test. Later protests included members placing themselves in the path of a harpoon to protect endangered whales and parachuting over coal-powered plants to protest acid rain. The goal of such encounters is to generate publicity in the hope of energizing the general public.

Although protests against the Iraqi war have not reached the levels of the Vietnam era, small protests against the war are held in many locales nearly every day. Anti-Iraqi war protest gained national publicity in 2005 when Cindy Sheehan, whose son died in Iraq, camped outside of President Bush's home in Crawford, Texas during his vacation there and demanded to see him. Over a period of days, thousands gathered in a peaceful protest.

Once protest organizations get a hearing—that is, once they find someone in government who is willing to listen—they often shift to an inside strategy, working with those in power rather than against them. They drop the "yelling and screaming" for more conventional

Cindy Sheehan, whose son Casey was killed in the Iraq war, camped outside President Bush's ranch to draw attention to her call for the return of American troops.

lobbying techniques. Moreover, it is increasingly difficult to draw media coverage to another story of protesters willing to risk life and limb in the interest of preserving or preventing something, and it is publicity that makes such activities effective. The first time, protests are front-page news. The second time, they are buried inside, if they are covered at all.

Benefits and Costs of Protest

Protest can generate awareness of an issue, but to be successful it must influence mass or elite opinion. Often it is the first step in a long struggle that takes years to resolve. Sometimes it leads to hostility against the protesters. Antiwar protests by college students in the 1960s and 1970s angered not only government officials, who targeted the leaders for harassment, but also many ordinary citizens. In the early years of the women's movement, the media derisively labeled many female protesters "bra burners," annoyed by their insistence that the undergarment was an unnecessary accoutrement imposed on women by men (and it is unclear whether a bra was ever burned!).

Extended protests are difficult because they demand great skill on the part of leaders and sacrifices from followers. Continued participation, essential to success, robs those involved of a normal life. It can mean jail, physical harm, or even death and requires discipline to refrain from violence, even as leaders and followers are targeted for violence.

The civil rights movement provides the best example of successful protest in twentieth-century America. By peacefully demonstrating against legalized segregation in the South, black and some white protesters drew the nation's attention to the discrepancy between the American values of equality and democracy and the southern laws that kept blacks separated from whites in every aspect of life. Protesters used tactics such as sit-ins, marches, and boycotts. Confrontations with authorities often won protesters national attention and public support, which eventually led to change. (See the box "Organizing Protest: The Montgomery Bus Boycott.")

All tactics can be effective; however, some lend themselves to particular groups more than others. Business groups with great financial resources can pay skillful lobbyists and donate to political campaigns. Labor unions with large memberships can help candidates canvass and get out the vote. Some groups can enlist the public because of the "goodness" of their cause. Where individuals and groups are excluded and prevented from participating, they can protest.

Violence

Occasionally groups turn to violence to achieve their goals. In the late nineteenth century and well into the

Culver Pictures

In 1920, a horse-drawn cart loaded with dynamite exploded on Wall Street, killing forty people. No one was ever charged with the murders, which were thought to be the work of anarchists. Although anarchists were against capitalism and big business, most of the victims were clerks and secretaries, not Wall Street bankers.

twentieth, the Ku Klux Klan targeted African Americans and their supporters for death and destruction. In the early twentieth century, company-financed strikebreakers attacked and killed workers seeking to unionize. In the period following the legalization of abortion, "pro-life" antiabortion activists burned abortion clinics and murdered abortion providers. In 1995, right-wing militants blew up the Alfred P. Murrah Federal Building in Oklahoma City, killing 168. Violence is the tactic of people with extreme views who are willing to take extreme measures, even murder, to achieve group or personal goals.

Building Coalitions

Coalitions consist of two or more interest groups that have joined together to achieve a particular goal. Coalitions can be large or small, and they can focus on many issues or just one. Groups can join together to use direct or indirect tactics.

For example, Kingsford charcoal, 7-Eleven stores, and several amusement parks and lawn and garden

ORGANIZING PROTEST: THE MONTGOMERY BUS BOYCOTT

The 1955 Montgomery, Alabama, bus boycott was the first successful civil rights protest, and it brought its twenty-six-year-old leader, Dr. Martin Luther King, Jr., to national prominence. Montgomery, like most southern cities, required blacks to sit in the back of public buses, reserving the front seats for whites. The dividing line between the two was a "no man's land" where blacks could sit if there were no whites. If whites needed the seats, blacks had to give them up and move to the back.

One afternoon, Rosa Parks, a seamstress at a local department store and a leader in the local chapter of the NAACP, boarded the bus to go home. The bus was filled, and when a white man boarded, the driver called on the four blacks behind the whites to move to the back. Three got up and moved, but Parks, tired from a long day and of the injustice of always having to move for white people, said she did not have to move because she was in "no man's land." Under a law that gave him the authority to enforce segregation, the bus driver arrested her.

That evening, a group of black women professors at the black state college in Montgomery, led by Jo Ann Robinson, drafted a letter of protest.

They called on blacks to stay off the buses on Monday to protest the arrest. They worked through the night making thirty-five thousand copies of their letter to distribute to Montgomery's black residents. Fearful for their jobs and concerned that the state would cut funds to the black college if it became known that they had used state facilities to produce the letter, they worked quickly and quietly.

The following day, black leaders met and agreed to the boycott. More leaflets were drafted, calling on blacks to stay off the buses on Monday. On Sunday, black ministers encouraged their members to support the boycott, and on Monday, 90 percent of the blacks walked to work, rode in black-owned taxis, or shared rides in private cars. The boycott inspired confidence and pride in the black community and

AP/Wide World Photos

Rosa Parks is fingerprinted in Montgomery, Alabama, after her arrest for refusing to give up her seat on the bus to a white man. Her refusal triggered a boycott of city buses that became the first successful civil disobedience in the civil rights movement and made Parks a hero to black and white Americans alike.

centers joined the Daylight Saving Time Coalition to lobby Congress to extend daylight saving time. All wanted additional evening daylight hours for the users of their products and services: Kingsford for barbecuers, 7-Eleven stores for those who prefer to drive or stop for a snack during daylight, amusement parks to attract customers who will stay longer, and lawn and garden centers so that people would have more time to work in their yards. Extending the daylight hours would mean more sales and higher profits for all.

Large coalitions formed around the health care reform issue during Clinton's administration. The AFL-CIO, American Airlines, Chrysler Corporation, the American College of Physicians, the League of Women Voters, and others supported health care reform, whereas the American Conservative Union, United Seniors Union, Citizens for a Sound Economy, and National Taxpayers Union joined a coalition against it.[152] Following the 2000 election, a coalition of corporations and business groups pressured Congress and the White House to rescind regulations issued by the Clinton administration to protect workers from repetitive-motion injuries.

In the wake of 9/11, conservative and environmental groups have joined in pushing for alternative-fuel vehicles. Set America Free advocates a combina-

signaled a subtle change in the opinions of blacks toward race relations. This was obvious when, as nervous white police looked on, hundreds of blacks jammed the courthouse to see that Rosa Parks was safely released after her formal conviction. And it was obvious later that evening at a mass rally when Martin Luther King, Jr., cried out, "There comes a time when people get tired of being trampled over by the iron feet of oppression. There comes a time when people get tired of being pushed out of the glittering sunlight of life's July, and left standing amidst the piercing chill of an Alpine November." After noting that the glory of American democracy is the right to protest, King appealed to the strong religious faith of the crowd: "If we are wrong, God Almighty is wrong. . . . If we are wrong, Jesus of Nazareth was merely a utopian dreamer. . . . If we are wrong, justice is a lie." These words and this speech established King as a charismatic leader for the civil rights movement.

In light of its initial success, the boycott was extended. Each successive day was a trial for blacks and their leaders. Thousands had to find a way to get to work, and leaders struggled to keep a massive carpool going. However, each evening's rally built up

morale for the next day's boycott. Later the rallies became prayer services, as the black community prayed for strength to keep on walking, for courage to remain nonviolent, and for divine guidance for their oppressors.

The city bus line was losing money. City leaders urged more whites to ride the buses to make up lost revenue, but few did. Recognizing that the boycott could not go on forever, black leaders agreed to end it if the rules regarding the seating of blacks in "no man's land" were relaxed. Erroneously thinking that they were on the verge of breaking the boycott, the city leaders refused. Police began to harass carpoolers and to issue bogus tickets for trumped-up violations.

Then the city leaders issued an ultimatum: settle or face arrest. A white grand jury indicted more than one hundred boycott leaders for the alleged crime of organizing the protest. In the spirit of nonviolence, the black leaders, including King, surrendered.

The decision to arrest the leaders proved to be the turning point of the boycott. The editor of the local white paper said it was "the dumbest act that has ever been done in Montgomery." With the mass arrests, the boycott finally received national atten-

tion. Reporters from all over the world streamed into Montgomery to cover the story. The publicity brought public and financial support. The arrests caused the boycott to become a national event and made its leader, Martin Luther King, Jr., a national figure. A year later, the U.S. Supreme Court declared Alabama's local and state laws requiring segregation in buses unconstitutional, and only after the city complied with the Court's order was the boycott ended.

When in 2005 Rosa Parks died at the age of ninety-two, she was lauded as one of the key figures in the civil rights movement. Fifty thousand people filed through the U.S. Capitol Rotunda, where she lay in state, the first woman and second African American to be honored in this way. Four thousand people, including members of Congress and many celebrities, attended her funeral, and thousands more lined the streets to witness her casket pulled by in a horse-drawn carriage to the cemetery.

SOURCES: Taylor Branch, *Parting the Waters: America in the King Years* (New York: Simon & Schuster, 1988), ch. 4 and 5; Juan Williams, *Eyes on the Prize* (New York: Viking, 1987).

tion of manufacturer and consumer tax credits as well as federal research funding to help U.S. companies rush to market vehicles that run on energy other than gasoline.[153]

Opposition to presidential appointments can also be a cause for coalition building. For example, several liberal groups such as Planned Parenthood, People for the American Way, AFL–CIO, and NAACP launched an unsuccessful nationwide advertising campaign opposing Samuel A. Alito, George W. Bush's nomination to the Supreme Court.

Large coalitions demonstrate broad support for an issue, important in persuading lawmakers. They can

also take advantage of each group's strength. One group may be adept at grassroots lobbying, another at public relations. One may have lots of money, another a lot of members.[154]

The growth of coalitions in recent years reflects a number of changes in policy making.[155] Issues are increasingly complex, and legislation to deal with them typically affects a variety of interests, making coalitions an effective strategy. Changes in technology make it easier for groups to communicate with one another. The number of interest groups is also larger than it used to be, especially the number of public interest groups. Many such groups have limited resources, and coalitions help them stretch their lobbying efforts. Sometimes groups find it beneficial to be connected with groups they normally oppose, so business groups with image problems sometimes seek to associate themselves with consumer groups.[156] Coalitions help political parties garner majorities at the various stages of the legislative process.

Coalitions vary in their duration—some are short term, and others are permanent. Coalitions involved with the health care issue remained intact only until the Clinton plan was dead. Coalitions supporting and opposing NAFTA ceased to exist when Congress approved the measure.

On the other hand, the Leadership Conference on Civil Rights is a permanent coalition of 180 civil rights, ethnic, religious, and other groups. They work to pass civil rights legislation, fight the watering down of civil rights laws, and ensure that judicial appointees are in favor of civil rights. Unlike short-term coalitions, permanent alliances need to be sensitive as to how their actions affect coalition members. Some issues may be avoided because they are likely to drive some coalition members away. When, however, a coalition such as the Leadership Conference is united, it can be formidable.

Coordination among PACs in channeling money to political candidates is a form of coalition. Business PACs, for example, take their lead from the Business Industry Political Action Committee. Information is shared on candidates' issue positions, likelihood of winning, and need for funding.

Success of Interest Groups

Although no interest group gets everything it wants from government, some are more successful than others. Politics is not a game of chance, where luck determines winners and losers. Knowing what to do and how to do it—strategy and tactics—are important, as are resources, competition, and goals.

Resources

Although large size does not guarantee success, large groups have advantages. They can get attention by claiming to speak for large numbers of people or by threatening to mobilize large numbers of people if their demands are ignored. Part of the airlines' success in securing a government bailout was the thousands of employees spread throughout the nation who were threatened with layoffs.

Location is also important. Because organized labor is concentrated in the Northeast, it has less influence in other parts of the country, diminishing its influence

in Congress. The Chamber of Commerce, on the other hand, has members throughout the country, enhancing its influence.

Well-educated members are an advantage, because they are more likely than those with less education to communicate with public officials and contribute to lobbying efforts.

Group cohesion and intensity are also advantages. Public officials are unlikely to respond to a group if it cannot agree on what it wants or if it does not appear to feel very strongly about its position. In recent years, the NAACP has suffered from disagreements among its leaders. Some members believe that the organization should be more accommodating and work within the system. Others feel that it should be more aggressive and confrontational. Some are pushing to work with more radical groups like Louis Farrakhan's Nation of Islam, and others want to limit the group to working with moderate and mainstream civil rights organizations. Conflicts such as these undermine cohesion and diminish the likelihood of success.

A large market share is another advantage. **Market share** refers to the number of members in a group compared with its potential membership. For years, the American Medical Association enrolled a substantial majority (70 percent or more) of the nation's doctors and wielded a lot of clout. As its market share declined, so did its influence.

Knowledge is a major resource. Policy experts are more apt to get the attention of public officials. Knowing how things get done in Washington is also important, which is why many groups employ former members of Congress and people who held positions in the executive branch as lobbyists.

Few members of Congress return to their roots once their political careers are over. Most move into high-paying positions with the dozens of law firms in Washington that lobby the government. When Bob Dole resigned from the Senate in 1995 to run for president, he indicated that if he lost the presidency, he would have no place to go but back to his hometown of Russell, Kansas. If he had done that, he would have been quite unusual. Indeed, Dole went to work for a firm that includes several former senators and members of the executive branch. The firm refers to Dole and the others as our "rock stars." Dole's job is to "make rain," which means recruiting clients who will bring in millions of dollars for his firm's 168 other lawyers and lobbyists.[157] Since 1998, more 250 members of Congress and 275 former White House aides have registered as lobbyists.[158]

Public image is another important resource. A negative public image often troubles new, change-oriented groups, such as the animal rights movement. Many of the country's traditional interest groups, big business, and organized labor also suffer from a poor image, being viewed as too powerful and self-serving. A poll revealed that only 37 percent of Americans trusted union leaders to tell the truth and 43 percent trusted business leaders to do so—and this poll was taken before the stream of revelations about corporate misdeeds in spring 2002.[159]

Obviously money is very important. It is the key to mounting a complete lobbying effort, retaining skilled lobbyists, purchasing advertising, mobilizing the grass roots through mailings and other contacts, and, very importantly, gaining access to elected officials through campaign contributions. Money is not the only resource, of course, and money does not always win, but clearly money is crucial. We will discuss more about the role of money in political activity in Chapter 8.

Few groups are blessed with all resources, but the more resources a group has, the better are its chances of getting what it wants from the government.

Competition and Goals

Success also depends on group competition and goals. Whether an athletic contest, a chess tournament, or politics, many participants are successful because they face weak opponents. Supporters of gun control have public opinion on their side, but their main lobbying group, the National Council to Control Handguns, has a membership and budget that are only a fraction of the NRA's. Used-car dealers successfully lobbied against the "lemon law," which would have required them to tell customers of any defects in cars. Few lobbyists represented the other side. Such mismatches often occur on highly technical issues where one side has more expertise or the public has little interest (or both). Some corporations have no opponents at all in lobbying for government contracts, regulatory waivers, and government subsidies.[160] Such benefits cost taxpayers billions of dollars, but they are never mobilized in opposition. The accountancy profession's opposition to regulations that would have made corporations' financial dealings more transparent had few opponents until Enron's financial dishonesty and auditor Arthur Andersen's complicity in it were revealed.

When a group competes with other groups of nearly equal resources, the outcome is often a compromise or a stalemate. The Clean Air Act was not rewritten for years because the auto industry, which wanted a weaker law, and the environmental lobby, which wanted a tougher one, were about equal in strength. The increased clout of environmental forces finally led to a strengthening of the law in 1990.

Groups that work to preserve the status quo are generally more successful than groups promoting change; it is usually easier to prevent government action than it

is to bring it about. Separation of powers among the Congress, executive branch, and the courts; checks and balances between and among the branches; and division of authority between the states and national government provide interest groups with numerous points in the political process to exercise influence. Groups wishing to change policy have to persuade officials throughout the political process to go along; groups opposed to change only have to persuade officials at one point in the process. Groups promoting change must win over the House, Senate, White House, bureaucracy, and courts; groups against change need convince only one of them.

Groups are more likely to be successful in securing very narrow and specific benefits than they are in promoting broad policy changes. For example, corporations are concerned with broad policy issues, but they are more likely to be successful in obtaining exemptions from major policy initiatives than they are in winning or losing on the policy itself. The tax code is riddled with exemptions for specific corporations; the beneficiaries are rarely identified by name. The 1986 changes in the tax code contained an exemption for Phillips Petroleum, identified in the bill as a "corporation incorporated on June 13, 1917, which has its principal place of business in Bartlesville, Oklahoma."[161] Phillips was not concerned about the basic tax changes because it would not be affected by them but very interested in getting a special deal for itself. Such exemptions are unlikely to receive media attention or become controversial. In this way, politicians are able to satisfy a major interest group without risking hostile public reaction.

Interest Groups and Democracy

Recall from Chapter 1 that the idea that groups represent our interests to government is sometimes called the pluralist model of democracy. Now that we have described in more detail the roles and tactics of groups in our political system, we can see more clearly the limitations of the idea of pluralist democracy.

Of course, thousands of lobbyists work in Washington, and they are not all working for the same handful of interests. Groups such as the AARP, the National Council of State Legislatures, and farmers', teachers', and trade unions represent significant segments of the population.

Rather than a clique of elites running the government, on many issues we have interest groups sufficiently powerful to exercise a de facto veto on issues affecting them. This suggests a system stymied by a kind of "hyperpluralism," with so many organized interests competing to influence policy that it is difficult to find common ground to work out solutions to problems. The close ties many groups have to congressional committees and subcommittees considering legislation allow them to stop policy ideas they dislike. And modern technology heightens their impact. A witness to congressional hearings on tax reform reported that lobbyists used cell phones to produce floods of protest by phone or fax the instant anyone even *mentioned* something they opposed.[162]

So many powerful groups with clout exist that attempts to alter the status quo or change national priorities are extremely difficult. Presidents Carter, Reagan, and Clinton found this out when they tried to make major changes in energy, budget, and health care policy, respectively. The Clinton White House tried to work with over eleven hundred interest groups on health care reform, to no avail.[163] Efforts to bring about major changes in national domestic priorities are extremely difficult. It is telling that one of the most sweeping recent changes in entrenched policy was the overhaul of the welfare system, a reform whose impact will be felt primarily by the poorest and least politically active Americans who do not have many strong interest groups representing them.

If competition is between well-organized groups with intensely held issue positions—such as on abortion and gun control—it may be difficult or impossible to reach a policy outcome that satisfies anyone. On the other hand, if the competition is between one side with massive resources and another side that is barely organized, public preferences are likely to be ignored, as in the awarding of tax benefits to special industries and companies. Moreover, at the same time that we have gridlock on many important domestic issues, ranging from energy to global warming to health insurance, it is relatively easy for special interests to get legislation benefiting them, whether through earmarks or other bills, that is largely hidden from the public and even from most legislators. Our system of checks and balances does not work so well when groups with massive resources are opposed by groups with very few and when the public is not paying much attention.

Even fairly active groups with large resources and many members may not represent group members. Effective power in a group or organization, no matter what its size, can and sometimes does gravitate to a few in leadership positions.[164] In fact, interest groups create their own elites by establishing permanent organizations with paid staff and leadership. This arrangement creates the potential for an issue gap between leaders and the rank and file. As the professional staff spend more time with decision makers and develop ties to public officials, they may come to see group interests differently from the rank-and-file membership. For example, the CEO of the AARP, one of the most powerful interest groups in the country, lobbied hard to gain passage of a prescription drug bill for seniors that many AARP members regarded as a sellout of the their interests. When this happens, membership in an interest group is no longer a guarantee that one's views will be accurately represented to decision makers.

This raises the prospect that the views of average men and women are not communicated to public officials by virtue of their memberships in interest groups, thus diminishing their influence. Most citizens do not have the time to monitor the actions of the president, 535 members of Congress organized into almost two hundred committees and subcommittees, and more than one hundred federal agencies. The leaders of interest groups do, and this gives them considerable power. The possibility that they may act independently of and at odds with the membership which are only rarely engaged by politics suggests a hybrid interpretation of American democracy. This emphasizes the potential clout of individual citizens through group memberships and the actual influence of elites, interest group leaders, who may or may not reflect the views of average men and women. Theories suggesting a small group of clubby, conspiring power elites no doubt miss the mark. These theories are useful because they remind us that tremendous inequalities of resources exist, enabling some individuals and groups to influence government more than others. Interest groups do not represent everyone, especially the poor, the working class, and the politically disinterested.

Conclusion: Do Interest Groups Help Make Government Responsive?

Indeed they do. The nation is simply too large and diverse to expect that citizens and their myriad concerns will be represented by elected officials alone. Interest groups represent the views and opinions of members, constituents, clients, and individuals who can be mobilized on behalf of an issue—or some combination thereof—and communicate them to elected officials.

However, interest groups do not represent all interests or all interests equally. In 1960, E. E. Schattschneider described the pressure system, the totality of interest groups in Washington, as small in terms of members and biased toward business and the wealthy. By his count, no more than fifteen hundred groups existed, and more than 50 percent represented either corporations or trade or business associations.[165] Few groups represented consumers, taxpayers, the environment, women, or minorities.

Although environmental, women's, and consumer groups are more powerful than in 1960, business interests still dominate the pressure system, and the imbalance between business and nonbusiness interests is greater today than it was in 1960. Nearly two-thirds of the groups in Washington at last count represented either corporations or trade associations. Groups representing nonbusiness interests were less than 10 percent and were only 5 percent of those that lobby. Labor traditionally formed a strong, albeit not equal, counterbalance to business, but the organizational strength and clout of labor has declined. Moreover, the Democratic Party, also traditionally aligned with labor, has shifted its policies somewhat as it seeks to appeal to the big donors who finance its campaigns and the middle-class voters who are now its core constituency.

For those who argue that America is a pluralist society where all interests are represented, Schattschneider's observation from 1960 remains valid today: "The flaw in the pluralist heaven is that the angelic chorus sings with an upper class accent."[166]

Another political analyst has commented that "more and more of the weight of influence in Washington comes from interest groups, not voters."[167] And interest groups by and large reflect the interests of business.

How is it that interest groups have greater influence in Washington than do voters? After all, America is a democracy, and elected officials have to stand for election. Voters determine who wins. One answer is the growing and continuing disparity in wealth that allows those with money to provide candidates of both political parties greater and greater resources. Those resources enable officeholders to stay in power and, more important, to define the agenda—the issues that become the focus of attention. Consequently, average people increasingly believe that the political arena does not deliver much for them.[168]

This is not to say that the interests of working- and middle-class Americans never carry the day. Consider the successes of Ralph Nader and his fellow crusaders for average Americans against the giants of corporate America. It was Nader, more than any other person, who is responsible for seat beats, padded dashboards, air bags, and other safety features in cars. Because of him, baby foods are safer, drinking water is purer, and dental X-rays less threatening. He is also the one to thank for the Freedom of Information Act, which exposes government actions and ensures greater accountability.[169]

It is also true that working- and middle-class Americans, or at least some of them, benefit from policies favoring business. Business provides jobs. Still, a system in which business interests must compete on a more equal basis with the interests of nonbusiness groups is likely to be more sensitive to the needs of average men and women. How can we preserve the constitutional rights of interest groups to form and petition government and still keep government responsive to the needs of citizens? Recognizing and correcting imbalances in the political power of interests in society is not simple or easy. One would not expect interests currently enjoying an advantage to give it up. Reformers have for decades battled to limit financial contributions of interest groups to candidates (a topic discussed in greater detail in Chapter 9). None have been very effective in restoring balance to American politics.

Father Mahony Advises against Workers Staying Away from Work and Students Staying Away from School

In his Easter Sunday sermon, Father Mahony advised his congregation against taking a day off. "Go to work. Go to School," he said. "And then join thousands of us at a major rally afterward."[170]

Despite this advice, the protest drew an estimated 250,000 in Los Angeles. Later in the day, the number swelled to 400,000. Attendance in LA public schools, mostly Hispanic, was down 27 percent. Most marchers dressed in white to signify peace and solidarity. Like an undulating carpet, punctuated with the occasional red, white, and blue of the American flag, the crowd stretched for miles. Jubilant and largely peaceful, marchers sang the National Anthem in English. Some chanted "U.S.A."; some shouted "Si se puede," which is Spanish for "Yes, it can be done." Some, no doubt feeling empowered, carried signs in Spanish that translated "Today we march, tomorrow we vote."[171]

Similar demonstrations were held throughout the country in Chicago, New York, Phoenix, and hundreds of smaller communities. In Chicago, Latinos were joined by those of Irish, Polish, Asian, and African descent.

Nationwide, more than one million people marched in support of immigrants, legal and illegal, and against efforts of the national government to make entering the country illegally and helping illegal residents a felony.

Because of the protest, those industries heavily reliant on immigrant labor suffered. Many firms involved in meat-packing, masonry, the restaurant business, and landscaping simply shut down. Truck traffic at the twin ports of LA and Long Beach—the nation's largest port complex—was off 90 percent.[172] The boycott illustrated that without a reservoir of immigrant workers, many jobs would not get done and the costs of goods and services would increase.

But others were much more negative. Counterprotestors, far fewer in number, expressed their feelings: "Illegals, Go Home, Your Rights Are There."[173] Cochair of Defend Colorado Now, an organization pressing for a constitutional amendment barring immigrants from receiving some social services, observed, "the illegals are organized by a massive well-funded campaign. There is no equivalent organizations of Americans marching

to enforce our laws."[174] A founder of the Minutemen Project, a volunteer group that patrols the U.S.-Mexican border, characterized the march as a "mobocracy."[175] The White House also had reservations. "The president is not a fan of boycotts" stated the President's Secretary Scott McClellan. "People have the right to peacefully express their views, but the president wants to see comprehensive reform pass the Congress."[176]

As for Father Mahony, he was steadfast in his vow to disobey any law making it a crime to help illegal immigrants and worked along with members of his church to register immigrant voters for the November elections. Meanwhile, these nationwide protests provided a context for the Senate eliminating the automatic deportation provisions of the House bill and providing a mechanism for long-time illegal aliens to start on the path toward citizenship.

 To learn more about interest groups, go to "you are there" exercises for this chapter on the text website.

Key Terms

interest groups	public interest groups
lobbying	single-issue groups
political action	civil disobedience
committees (PACs)	coalitions
private interest groups	market share

Further Reading

Jeffrey H. Birnbaum, *The Lobbyists: How Influence Peddlers Get Their Way in Washington* (New York: Times Books, 1993). Birnbaum presents an insightful study of lobbyists' activities surrounding major issues considered by Congress in the 1989–1990 session.

Osha Gray Davidson, *The NRA and the Battle for Gun Control* (Ames: University of Iowa Press, 1998). How the battles over gun control are fought in Congress becomes clear in this useful account.

Liza Featherstone, *Selling Women Short: the Landmark Battle for Workers' Rights at Wal-Mart* (New York: Basic Books, 2005). A journalist examines the largest employment discrimination case ever brought against a corporation. The plaintiffs represent 1.6 million female employees of Wal-Mart.

Katherine Neckerman, ed., *Social Inequality* (New York: Russell Sage Foundation, 2004). This book of readings addresses the causes and consequences of income inequality in the United States.

MoveOn.org, *Fifty Ways to Love Your Country: How to Find Your Political Voice and Be a Catalyst for Change* (Makawao, Hawaii: Inner Ocean, 2004). MoveOn.org is a citizen's group dedicated to empowering the average person. Though the tips in the book are mostly written by liberal activists, they are just as relevant to conservatives looking to get involved in their community and society.

Michael Pertschuk, *Giant Killers* (New York: Norton, 1986). Low-budget lobbies can sometimes defeat the big guys through superior organization, tactics, and luck.

E. E. Schattschneider, *The Semi-Sovereign People* (New York: Holt, 1975). This classic work explains how interest group politics benefit business and corporate interests by limiting the involvement of citizens in the political process.

For Viewing

This is an eclectic group of films showing, in some cases, groups at work and, in other cases, the conditions that gave rise to group advocacy.

Bowling for Columbine (2002). Michael Moore asks provocative questions about the causes of gun violence in American society.

The Children's Hour (1962). This film is dated but still interesting for showing the stigma faced by gays and lesbians in that era and the inability of people to discuss the issue of homosexuality publicly.

Eyes on the Prize (1987, 1990). This acclaimed fourteen-part documentary on the civil rights movement was originally presented as a two-series broadcast on PBS.

The Murder of Emmett Till (2003). The murder of a fourteen-year-old black boy in Mississippi in 1954 won national attention and was one of the sparks that ignited the modern civil rights movement.

Norma Rae (1979). A woman faces a dangerous uphill battle promoting unionization in the workplace.

On the Waterfront (1954). The hero of this award-winning film (Marlon Brando) fights corruption in the longshoreman's union in the 1950s.

Salt of the Earth (1954). Based on a true event, this film portrays the struggle of Mexican American workers striving for parity with white workers in a zinc-mining company. The film was banned by Congress for its "leftist" sympathies in a time of intense anticommunism.

Stonewall (1995). This film is a partly fictional account of the Stonewall raids that launched the gay rights movement.

Matewan (1987). This film features the struggle of unions in the coal-mining regions and the efforts by management to crush them.

 ## Electronic Resources

www.csuchico.ed/~kcfount
This website lists interest groups that lobby in Washington, arranged by the focus of the group (religion, older Americans, tax reform, women, and so on) and with an indication of each group's prominence.

www.atr.org/pdffiles/021004K-Street_trade.pdf
This website reports the results of the K Street Project (many interest groups have headquarters on or near K Street in Washington, D.C.) and identifies numerous lobbies and lobbyists along with their party affiliation, Washington contacts, and political contributions.

Most of the organizations discussed in the chapter have their own home pages. Here is a sampling:

www.aflcio.org/home.html
The home page of the largest union in America, the AFL-CIO, contains official union documents and press releases, news on issues important to the labor movement, a link to information on high corporate executive salaries in the United States, and links to other labor-related groups.

www.nam.org
The National Association of Manufacturers' web page contains material similar to that on the AFL-CIO page but from a business perspective.

www.fb.com
The Farm Bureau's web page contains similar information from the perspective of the more prosperous and conservative sector of agriculture, along with updates on the weather and a menu where you can register your favorite summertime activities.

www.moveon.org
MoveOn.org is an organization that promotes a liberal agenda. It was deeply involved in the Democratic presidential campaign in 2004.

www.cc.org
The Christian Coalition is a conservative grassroots political organization for people of faith interested in promoting issues associated with the Christian right.

www.thirdwavefoundation.org
The Third Wave Foundation is the only national activist philanthropic organization for young women. The organization supports and involves young women in a broad range of movements, including campaigning for a living wage, environmental protection, and reproductive rights.

www.aarp.org
AARP maintains an excellent website. It allows you to learn about AARP's position and congressional testimony on issues affecting the elderly and to review the myriad of benefits offered by the organization, along with much more.

www.apsanet.org
Use the American Political Science Association's home page to find out about the organization to which your professor might belong.

ThomsonNOW

Enter ThomsonNOW™ using the access card that is available with this text or through www.thomsonedu.com/ thomsonnow. ThomsonNOW™ will assist you in understanding the content in this chapter with a personalized study plan generated for your needs. A practice test will assess the areas you need to review and provide the tools to fully comprehend those concepts, including an integrated digital eBook, interactive simulations, timelines, video case studies, MicroCase exercises, and InfoTrac College Edition readers and exercises. You'll also be connected to the learning objectives, chapter outline, chapter glossary, flash cards, crossword puzzles, Internet activities, and interactive quizzes found on the companion website.

CHAPTER 7

POLITICAL PARTIES

Howard Dean, chair of the Democratic National Committee

Political Parties and Popular Control of Government

The American Party System
Two Parties
Fragmentation
Moderation
Minor Parties in American Politics

The Rise of American Political Parties
The Founders and Political Parties
Birth of Political Parties
Development of Mass Parties

Party Realignments
Rise of the Republicans and the Golden Age of Parties
Progressive Politics and the Weakening of Parties
Rise of the Democratic Party
Party Identification Today

Decline of Parties
Diminution of Party Functions
Erosion of Popular Support for Parties

Resurgence of Parties
Continuing Importance of Political Parties
Party Influence on Policy Making

Party Organization
National Party Organization
State and Local Party Organizations

Parties and Voting
Party Identification
Candidate Evaluations
Issues
Parties, Candidates, and Issues

Conclusion: Do Political Parties Make Government More Responsive?

YOU ARE THERE

Do You Follow a 50-State Strategy?

You are Howard Dean, Chair of the Democratic National Committee (DNC), the Democratic party organization at the national level. Elected to the position following the 2004 election, you won out over six others for the job. As an outsider who was unknown nationally until your 2004 presidential race, your election to the party chair on a voice vote without opposition was something of a surprise.

Casting aside your progressive message of the presidential campaign, you won by moving to the middle and on the strength of your campaign in which you cultivated the support of hundreds of party insiders. Your two-month drive to win the office had many elements of a presidential contest: advance teams, consultants, cocktail parties, and even a touch of negative advertising. Your key commitment was to raise funds to put Democratic party organizers into every state, even states where Democrats have not been competitive in recent years. You challenged fellow Democrats to contest every seat ceding none to Republicans.

In your address to the DNC following your election, you presented your vision of a Democratic return to power in Washington. You called for the elimination of the "fiscal recklessness" of the Bush administration and a restoration of the balanced budgets characteristic of the Clinton years.[1] Linking Bush to corporate accounting scandals, you noted the President's budget "brings Enron-style accounting to the nation" and demonstrates "once again what all Americans are beginning to see: you can't trust Republicans with your money."[2] You called on Democrats to "begin fighting for what they really believe in."[3] After four years of Republican control in Washington, party activists wanted a forceful voice and formidable organizer. In you, they think they have both.

Although your position as party chair is low profile, you are still an important spokesperson and party figure. What you say and do can affect the party's electoral fortunes. Almost since taking the job, you have been controversial, incurring the anger of several Democratic senators with your references to the opposition. Red state Nebraska Democratic Senator Ben Nelson, facing a difficult re-election bid and in need of all the Republican voters he can muster, cautioned you against alienating these voters with personal insults such as your comment that many "of them have not made an honest living in their lives."[4]

The upcoming 2006 midterm elections, just five months away, will be your first real test as party chair. Your goal is to return the Democrats to the majority in both the House and Senate, which are controlled by the Republicans. This will require a net gain of fifteen House and six Senate seats; a very difficult task. In the House, for example, there are relatively few competitive seats because of the way congressional district boundaries have been drawn during the past twenty years (see Chapter 9 for a discussion of districting).

To succeed in gaining seats you will need to raise large sums and allocate them to those running campaigns where additional revenues could lead to victory. This strategic use of the funds based on winnability of seats in 2006 seems to conflict with your earlier commitment to build up Democratic organizations in all states, even those that vote solidly Republican. That too is a strategic move, but the payoff is likely to be in the future, not in the 2006 elections. You argue that the Democratic strategies of the past have not worked, leaving the party uncompetitive in many states.

Several party leaders, including Harry Reid, Democratic leader in the Senate, and Nancy Pelosi, Democratic leader in the House have raised questions about your fifty-state pledge, suggesting that it will squander a golden opportunity.[5] As the congressional elections loom, President Bush's popularity is low, the Iraq War drags on, and gas prices remain high; there's also a perception that Congress isn't serving as a check on the president. The party's leaders in Congress call on you to put the money where it will do the most good to recapture the House and Senate this election year.[6] Rahm Emanuel (D-Ill.) has been especially outspoken. The chair of the Democratic Congressional Campaign Committee, he has been traveling the country lining up strong candidates to run for key seats. He has recruited war veterans, women, and several other nontraditional candidates to run in districts with winnable seats. Focusing on twenty-one key races where the Democrats think they can topple Republican incumbents or take Republican seats with no incumbent, he argues that the money the DNC raises should be targeted to those seats, setting aside money that can be used in the final days of the campaign to turn the tide. "My big thing is, come August, September, October, this is a resources game," Emanuel argued.[7] You and he have recently had a stormy meeting about this.

You won friends among state party leaders with your pledge to make Democrats competitive in all fifty states, and you have had some early successes, winning four special elections to the Mississippi state house and three in New Hampshire, contesting many more seats in the Plains states than two years ago, and revitalizing the Democratic organization in many other states. In Nebraska, for example, the DNC spent only $12,000 in the 2004 presidential race, but is now spending $120,000 to pay three full-time organizers.[8]

But these successes will mean little if the party does not do well in November. You are already at a huge financial disadvantage compared with the Republicans, with $9 million in your war chest in the spring compared with the Republicans' $48 million.[9] Your decisions on how to allocate your scarce resources could make a huge difference in this fall's elections.

You must balance the demands of the party's officeholders who hope to win in November, a short-term but important goal, and the demands of party activists who hope to build strong party organizations that will help the party win in November but also in the future. So what do you do? Do you route additional resources to the party's candidates and renege on your promise to the state parties, or do you direct money to the state organizations and run the risk of alienating the party's office holders?

George Washington warned against the "baneful" effects of parties and described them as the people's worst enemies. More recently, a respected political scientist, E. E. Schattschneider, argued that "political parties created democracy and that democracy was impossible without them."[10] The public echoes these contradictory views. Many believe that parties create conflict where none exists, yet most identify with one of the two major parties.[11]

These same feelings exist among candidates for office. They often bypass political parties by establishing their own personal campaign organizations and raising their own campaign funds. If elected, they sometimes do not follow the party line. At the same time, candidates for national and state offices are nominated in the name of political parties. They rely on parties for assistance, and they have little chance of winning unless they are Democrats or Republicans. They also vote most of the time with their party leaders.

This chapter examines American political parties to see why they are important and why many people believe that if they become less important and less effective, government will be less accountable to the people.

Political Parties and Popular Control of Government

Political parties are a major link between people and government. They provide a way for the public to have a say in who serves in government and what policies government chooses. They seek to control government by recruiting, nominating, and electing members to public office. They consist of three interrelated components: (1) citizens who see themselves as belonging to

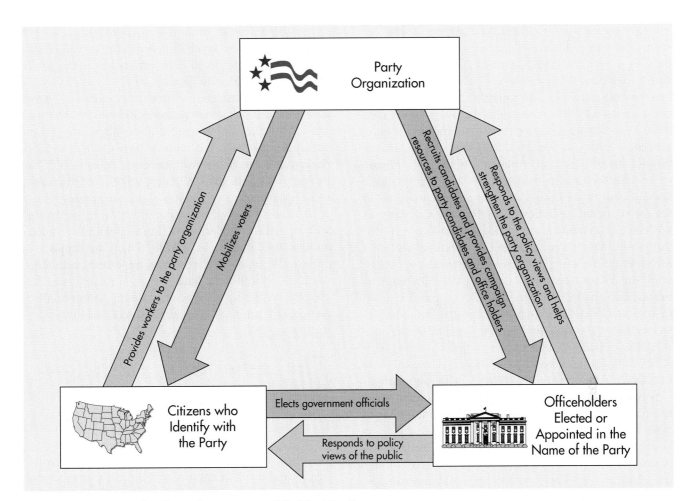

FIGURE 7.1 ■ The Three Components of Political Parties

the party, (2) officeholders who are elected or appointed in the name of the party, and (3) the activists who run the party organization and oversee party activities at the national, state, and local levels (see Figure 7.1).[12]

Americans, especially young adults, are cynical about political parties and believe the country would be better off without them. Many Americans hold them responsible for the government's inability to solve the nation's problems and feel that differences between the parties are meaningless squabbles designed to secure political advantage. Many feel that political parties create differences where none exist rather than reflecting real and legitimate differences in approaches to solving the nation's problems.

In some respects, these views are understandable. Against an absolute standard of virtue, political parties fall short. Some party leaders lack principles; they pander to special interests, and act in their own rather than the interests of the nation as a whole. Yet, the private world of corporations and labor unions also reveal leaders without principles who steal billions from shareholders and members to feather their own nests. Although such behavior is deplorable, few believe that

the nation would be better off without business and labor. Instead, there are efforts to punish wrongdoers and make corporate executives and union bosses more accountable.

The same approach should be applied to political parties. They need reform and improvement. But it is clear that government would be less accountable to average Americans without them. If political parties should suddenly disappear, the conflicts over how to use the nation's limited resources would still exist, narrow special interests would have a free hand, and the interests of average men and women would suffer.

Many citizens feel an attachment to a political party. For some, this develops early in life as they observe and model their parents. For others, it stems from an important event or the accumulation of life's experiences. When called on to vote, many simply vote their party attachment. For those with little or no knowledge of candidates or issues, who pay little attention to political campaigns, this makes sense. Even for those who pay attention, campaigns may not clarify differences between the candidates and parties very well, if at all, and issues are often complex, making it difficult for average voters to know which issue position is best for them. Because political parties have a history that reflects a fairly consistent approach to public policy issues, they provide voters with a valuable cue in sorting through confusing campaigns and complex issues.

Since the 1930s, the Democratic Party has leaned more toward a progressive politics that emphasizes using government to cushion life's hardships and regulating business in an effort to minimize its negative impact on individuals and the environment. Examples include Social Security, Medicare, and the Superfund to clean up environment pollution. The Republican Party is more likely to oppose such programs. More recently, the parties have taken opposing positions on issues of life style and morality, such as abortion and gay rights, with the Democrats opting to keep the government out of such matters and the Republican party seeking to regulate them. The Democratic party, for example, would allow abortion under most conditions, and the Republican party would make it illegal.

Most voters recognize these differences. Thus, knowing that a candidate belongs to a party is a clue, although an imperfect one, to the candidate's stand on a broad range of issues such as Social Security, the environment, abortion, and gay rights. Voters can take some solace in knowing that they do not need to study each candidate's position on such issues, a difficult and time-consuming task, but simply know which party a candidate is associated with. Thus, the party label serves as a general guideline on where a candidate stands. When citizens choose between competing parties for control of government, they have a general understanding of what their choice will mean for the policy direction of the nation. Without the party label, citizens have the monumental task of finding out the candidates' positions on issues. Should they succeed at this, they remain clueless as to how a candidate, once elected, will join with others in forming a coalition to govern. Without political parties, voting and its impact on government policy become a lottery that average people may win, but the chances are much greater that they will lose.

Political parties also provide a counterweight to special interests. One might think of politics as a teeter-totter. When parties are up, special interests are down, and vice versa.

Although special-interest groups represent citizens, by definition they represent a narrower group than political parties. Parties represent a broad spectrum of people and offer the average person a chance to combat the power and influence of special interests. Warren Buffett or Bill Gates or Oprah Winfrey or the president of any large corporation can gain immediate access to any political decision maker should they want it. Most Americans cannot. Alone, average citizens lack influ-ence to counter the influence of the wealthy, the well connected, and the special interests. Average Americans need to join together if they are to have any power. Political parties are the best means to do so.

While the existence of competitive political parties is no guarantee that average men and women will prevail in directing the course of government, the people will most assuredly fail without them.[13] The dean of American political scientists recently commented, "we can be pretty sure that a country wholly without competitive parties is a country without democracy."[14]

Parties also play an important role in organizing and operating government; they formulate policy options and ultimately decide which to support or oppose. When political parties represent individuals from widely different backgrounds and interests, they also aid society by aggregating and mediating conflicts and contributing to political and social stability.

The American Party System

There is considerable variation among the political parties of the world. The number of parties that contest for office in a particular country, the degree to which power among officeholders and the party organization is centralized in a single office or bureaucracy, and the degree to which parties are ideologically extreme are attributes of the **party system.** The American party system is somewhat unique among the nations of the world.

Two Parties

Only two political parties win seats in Congress and only two compete effectively for the presidency. Thus, the American party system is a **two-party system.** Long-standing two-party systems are extremely rare among the nations of the world.

In Western Europe, **multiparty systems** are the rule. Italy has nine national parties and several regional parties; Germany has five national parties. Great Britain, although predominantly a two-party system, has several significant minor parties. Multiparty systems are also found in Canada, which has three parties, and Israel, which has more than twenty.

Why two parties in the United States? The most common explanation is the nature of American elections.[15] Officeholders are elected from **single-member districts** with **winner take all.** This means that only one individual is elected from a district or state, the individual who receives the most votes. This contrasts with **proportional representation** (PR), in which officeholders are elected from multimember districts and the number of seats awarded to each party in each district is equal to the percentage of the total vote the party receives in the district. Thus in PR systems, representation in the national legislature is roughly proportional to the popular vote each party receives nationwide.

In single-member-district, winner-take-all elections, only the major parties have much chance of winning legislative seats. With little hope of winning office, minor parties tend to die or merge with one of the major parties. However, where seats are awarded in proportion to the vote, even a modest showing in an election—15 percent or less—may win a seat in the national assembly. In PR systems, even parties representing only a small proportion of the electorate have a voice in the legislature, enabling them to speak in support of their policy positions and providing a base for mounting a campaign in the next election.

Although the nature of elections influences the number of parties, the number of parties also influences the conduct of elections. Where there are only two parties, they have strong incentives to conduct elections in a way that undermines the development and growth of other parties.[16] For example, Democrats and Republicans long supported laws that made it difficult for other parties to get their candidates placed on election ballots, requiring them to secure tens of thousands of signatures in order to qualify. The courts eventually invalidated these laws.

Fragmentation

The federal system, with its fragmentation of power among local, state, and national governments, leads to fragmentation within parties. State and local parties have their own resources and power bases separate from those of the national party, and the interests of state and local parties are often at odds with them.

Control of each political party is also often fragmented at each level of government. At the national level, control of the party is shared between the president and members of his party in Congress. Control of the opposition party is shared between the party's members in the House and the Senate.

The national party organization may also have a role, especially for the party that lacks control of the White House. For the party controlling the presidency, the national party organization usually is subservient to the president, in fact, if not on the organizational charts.

Each level and tier of the party has its own interests and stake in manipulating and using the party for its own ends. This is reflected in the difficult time that presidents can have in winning support for their policies among their own party members in Congress. For example, Democrats in Congress broke with President Clinton on the Clinton-negotiated North American Free Trade Agreement (NAFTA). Two of the top three Democratic leaders in each chamber led the opposition. Clinton succeeded on the strength of Republican support. Several recent Bush initiatives ran into Republican opposition. For example, some party members, alarmed at the rising federal deficit, split with the president on his budget in the run-up to the 2004 election. Several Republican members in Congress took a position opposite the President on immigration. In the Senate in 2006, the immigration bill the president preferred only passed because of support from Democrats.

On some issues, members of Congress go their own way. To be reelected, they only need to satisfy a plurality of the voters in their district or state, not the president or the party. When President Clinton considered a gas tax increase to reduce the deficit, Senator Herbert Kohl (D-Wisc.) told him that the increase could be no more than 4.3 cents per gallon. Clinton had to accept Kohl's figure because the bill's outcome was in doubt and the president needed Kohl's vote. Kohl won election in his own right and was only obligated to the people of Wisconsin, not the president or the party. Similarly, President Bush and Republican leaders in Congress bowed to demands of Republicans in Congress from rural states to provide greater financial aid to rural hospitals as the price for their support for his prescription drug bill. Unwillingness to follow the president or party reflects dispersed power within American government and American parties.

However, party members are not entirely free agents. The pull of party is strong, and members normally support the legislative program of a president of their party.[17]

Moderation

Major American political parties tend toward moderation at least in their appeals to voters in national elections. The reason is that most voters cluster at or near the middle in their preferences for dealing with the nation's problems (see Figure 7.2). To win their votes, parties direct their campaigns to the middle. Historically, American political parties have been more interested in winning public office than in maintaining ideological purity and have been willing to sacrifice ideological principle in order to win. Although parties avoid the extremes in their campaign appeals, both the Democratic and Republican parties have their elements—left of center in the Democratic Party and right of center in the Republican Party—that pull them toward the extremes. In recent decades, these tendencies

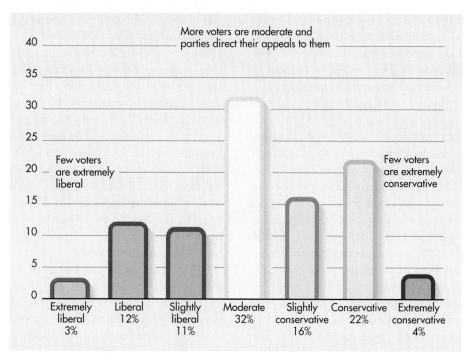

FIGURE 7.2 ■ Where the Voters Are
The labels indicate how the voters characterize themselves today. In recent years more have characterized themselves as conservative than as liberal, but most have characterized themselves as moderate. Thus, the parties usually aim their campaigns at the middle.
SOURCE: Data from General Social Survey, 2004.

have been stronger in the Republican Party, as conservatives have wrested control of the party from moderates. Elected officeholders also tend to be more extreme than their rank-and-file supporters in the electorate, creating a tension between the personal predilections of officeholders and the preferences of voters.[18]

The desire to win leads parties to nominate moderate candidates for the presidency and for ideological candidates, when they are nominated, to obscure their issue positions or move to the middle. Ronald Reagan, when running for reelection, embraced a conciliatory stance toward the Soviet Union in contrast to his earlier antagonistic posture. Bill Clinton became a "new kind" of Democrat, embracing many of the Republicans' ideas. The implication was that unlike those in the past who catered to minorities and special interests, he would deal with the problems of all Americans. As soon as his nomination as the Republican presidential candidate was secure in 2000, George W. Bush beat a hasty retreat from his conservative rhetoric in the South Carolina primary. Thereafter, calling himself a "compassionate conservative," he avoided discussing issues such as abortion that would identify him with the right and focused on more centrist issues such as education, health care, and Social Security. Once in office, Bush moved back to the right to reward his ideologically conservative base by, among

other things, appointing conservative John Ashcroft attorney general, backing tax cuts for the rich, slashing programs for the poor, and moving to undo as much government regulation as he could.

In the run-up to the 2004 election, Bush's position on gay marriage was an effort to satisfy his very conservative base. At the same time, he tried to reestablish his image as a "compassionate conservative" from the 2000 campaign by emphasizing elements of his policies that have broader appeal, such as the "No Child Left Behind" education program that increased child tax credits and his prescription drug plan for seniors.[19]

Minor Parties in American Politics

Sometimes called "third parties," minor parties are as varied as the causes they represent. Some are one-issue parties, like the American Know-Nothing Party (1856), which ran on a platform opposing immigrants and Catholics, and the Prohibition Party (1869 to the present), which campaigns to ban the sale of alcoholic beverages.

Other parties advocate radical change. Economic protest parties, such as the Populists in 1892, occasionally appear when economic conditions are bad and disappear when the economy improves. Since the 1920s, the Communist Party USA has espoused the adoption of a communist system, but generally has received little notice, let alone votes.

Some parties are simply candidates who failed to receive their party's nomination and decided to go it alone. In 1968, Alabama's segregationist governor, George Wallace, split from the Democratic Party to run for president as the candidate of the conservative American Independent Party. Though he had significant public support, the small number of votes he garnered did not influence the election's outcome.

Ross Perot's third-party candidacy in 1992 had no association with either party. He simply decided to run. His willingness to use his personal fortune to fund his campaign, including buying large blocks of expensive television time, made him a highly visible alternative to the major-party candidates. Perot would have floundered quickly and with little notice if not for his capacity to buy hours of national TV time. Although he polled 19 percent of the vote, quite extraordinary for a minor party, his candidacy did not influence the election outcome either, as he siphoned support away from both national parties.

Ralph Nader, the consumer advocate, ran in 2000 and again in 2004. In 2000, he was the nominee of the Green Party, an offshoot of the antinuclear and environmental movements. He claimed that both major parties were pawns of corporate America, and he called for checks on big business. He received just 3 percent of the votes, well below the historical average for minor-party candidates. However, his votes in

Florida were enough to deny Al Gore victory there and, consequently, victory nationally.[20] Nader received 97,000 votes in Florida. Most Nader voters preferred Gore over Bush, so if Nader hadn't been on the ballot many of them would have voted for Gore, certainly enough of them to overcome Bush's 537-vote margin in Florida. (Of course, in an election this close, other factors could have altered the outcome as well.)

Barriers to Minor Party Success

Minor parties face many obstacles in trying to establish themselves. State laws, for example, present impediments to minor-party and independent candidates seeking to get on the ballot, and federal laws make it difficult to secure public funding for third-party presidential candidates.

There are also psychological barriers. Minor-party and independent candidates confront the long-standing loyalty that most Americans feel toward the major parties. Even when voters prefer third-party or independent candidates, most are reluctant to vote for them because they do not think the minor party candidate can win. And the major parties encourage that view, reminding voters not to "waste their vote" by voting for a candidate who cannot win. Major parties also remind voters that a vote for a third-party candidate may contribute to the victory of their least preferred candidate. Pointing to the 2000 election, Democrats used this argument against Nader in the 2004 election. This time Nader received less than 1 percent of the votes and was not a factor in any state (even though some large donors to Bush also

Minor parties have trouble gaining traction because representatives of the major parties remind voters that candidates of the minor parties can't win.

financed Nader's campaign in an attempt to make it viable enough to siphon votes from the campaign of Democratic candidate John Kerry.[21])

Because voters don't think third-party candidates can win, such candidates also have difficulty raising funds and attracting media attention. Financial contributors are loath to donate to a candidate who is unlikely to win. Limited media coverage weakens the attractiveness and the fundraising capacity of third-party candidates.[22]

Practical barriers to third-party and independent candidates also exist. It is difficult for third parties to recruit qualified and experienced candidates, most of whom recognize that they are most likely to win if they run as major-party candidates.

Third parties also suffer from having their ideas co-opted by the major parties. Major parties are quick to back ideas that have voter appeal. Once a major party adopts an idea, the need for a third-party alternative is eliminated. Perot's strong stand on the need to eliminate the budget deficit in the 1992 campaign was at least partly responsible for the major parties' renewed efforts to deal with it.

Finally, third-party and independent candidates have done well in elections only at times when the nation has faced significant social and economic problems that the parties failed to deal with. Low support for third-party candidates in 2000 no doubt reflected a strong economy and a nation at peace.

Because third-party and independent candidates cannot win the presidency, their movements rarely extend beyond the defeat of their candidate. Perot was able to overcome this by spending his own money. His "United We Stand America" movement from the 1992 campaign became the Reform Party in 1996. But without Perot's financial support, Pat Buchanan, the party's nominee in 2000, received less than 1 percent of the popular vote.

Despite the difficulties third parties face, many Americans say they want to see an alternative to the major parties. That support seems rather fanciful, however. Over half of all Americans have indicated in various polls that the nation needs a third party, but few have ever voted for a third-party candidate.

The Rise of American Political Parties

Most Americans think of the Democratic and Republican parties as more or less permanent fixtures, and indeed they have been around a long time. The Democratic Party evolved from the Jacksonian Democrats in 1832, and the Republican Party was founded in 1854.

The Founders and Political Parties

Despite their eventual establishment, the Founders had little use for political parties. Many saw them as a threat and hoped to check their development in the new nation. They hoped instead, perhaps unrealistically, to govern by consensus and realized that political parties would make this impossible. There was also concern that parties would pursue narrow self-interests at the expense of the common good. As independent thinkers, others feared that parties would impose a mindless uniformity, cutting off the capacity of individuals to think for themselves.[23]

In *Federalist Paper* 10, James Madison wrote of political parties and interest groups pursuing selfish interests. John Adams dreaded what he considered the greatest political evil, the formation of rival political parties.

Given the Founders' misgivings, it is not surprising that the Constitution does not mention political parties. Nevertheless, it created a government in which parties, or something like them, were inevitable. When the Founders established popular elections as the mechanism for selecting political leaders, an agency

The factors that led to the formation of the first political parties were already vying with each other in George Washington's administration. Thomas Jefferson (standing at left) and Alexander Hamilton (second from right) are pictured here with Washington (far right).

© The Granger Collection, New York

for organizing and mobilizing supporters became a necessity. Despite their fears, Jefferson and Madison founded America's first political party.

Birth of Political Parties

With George Washington's unanimous election to the presidency in 1788, it appeared that the nation could be governed by consensus. But differences of opinion soon arose. Alexander Hamilton, Washington's secretary of the treasury, supported a strong national government. He and his supporters in Congress, who called themselves Federalists, were opposed by Thomas Jefferson, secretary of state, who feared a strong central government. The conflict led Jefferson to challenge John Adams for the presidency in 1796. Jefferson lost but set about recruiting political operatives in each of the states to mobilize support on his behalf. Newspapers were established to get out the message. On the strength of his new national party, Jefferson ran for the presidency in 1800 and won. His success conveyed the value of a political party for winning elections.

By Jefferson's second term, more than 90 percent of members of Congress were either Federalists or Jeffersonians (later called Jeffersonian Republicans) and consistently voted in support of their party's position.[24]

Development of Mass Parties

From 1815 to 1824, the so-called Era of Good Feeling, Jeffersonian Republicans, with little competition, won all presidential elections and majorities in the House and Senate. However, the party split in 1824. In the first year that an official popular vote was recorded, Andrew Jackson polled slightly over 150,000 votes, but John Quincy Adams, polling only 100,000 votes, was elected president by the House of Representatives when neither candidate received a majority in the Electoral College.

Jackson ran again in 1828, and won, in an election in which over a million votes were cast, a fivefold increase over 1824. Opponents of Jackson deplored his reaching out and mobilizing the masses. He was called a "barbarian," and his election in 1828 was derided as "the howl of raving democracy."[25] Jackson's popular appeal and the organizational effort of his party brought large numbers to the polls for the first time. Building on the efforts of Jefferson, Jackson introduced the idea of a political party with a large and loyal following among rank-and-file voters.

Jackson, like Jefferson, saw the strength of American democracy in the common person. His administration ushered in a number of changes that fostered participation in government by average Americans. Property ownership was lifted as a qualification for voting, and the franchise was extended to all adult white males. Popular elections rather than state legislatures became the mechanism for selecting the Electoral College, and party conventions, with representatives from every state and locality, became the mode for nominating presidential candidates. The closed and narrow congressional caucus (the party's elected members in Congress) that was used to nominate presidential candidates prior to

In 1828, opponents of Andrew Jackson called him a jackass (left). Political cartoonists and journalists began to use the donkey to symbolize Jackson and the Democratic Party. In the 1870s, cartoonist Thomas Nast popularized the donkey as a symbol of the party and originated the elephant as a symbol of the Republican Party. His 1874 cartoon (right) showed the Democratic donkey dressed as a lion frightening the other animals of the jungle, including the Republican elephant.

1828 gave way to the open, broader, and more participatory national presidential nominating convention.

Reflecting increased participation in politics as well as the growth in the size of the nation, the electorate continued to increase, doubling again by 1840.[26]

Party Realignments

American parties and the American party system have changed many times since the Jacksonian era. This is reflected in the death of existing parties, the birth of new ones, and shifts in the competitive balance between the parties. Some parties have increased their following, whereas others have declined in support. There have been periods when one party has dominated American politics, winning elections to the presidency and majorities in Congress over several years, and periods when neither party has dominated, with control of government divided between the parties or shifting back and forth between them.

Massive shifts in party loyalty among the voters that usher in a period of party dominance are called **realignments.** There have been several party realignments in American history, giving rise to the five party systems identified in Figure 7.3. These realignments often produced a dominant majority party for a time and followed major upheavals in American society, such as the Civil War and the Great Depression, when a majority of voters turned to one of the parties in search of an answer to the crisis.

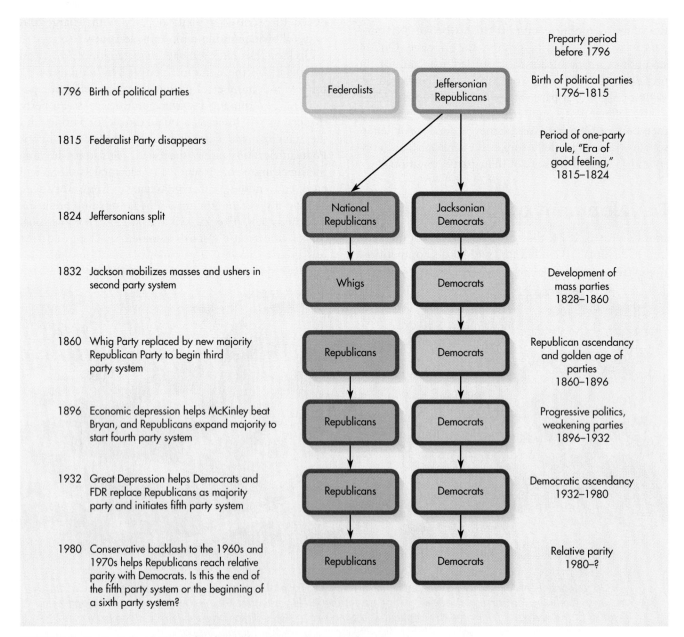

FIGURE 7.3 ■ Evolution of Political Parties in the United States

In addition to realignments, the strength and role of political parties in American politics has changed. Parties grew to be very powerful in the late nineteenth century and have declined somewhat in influence since then.

Rise of the Republicans and the Golden Age of Parties

The issue of slavery, compromised in the Constitutional Convention, began to assert itself anew in the 1840s. Abolitionists and proslavery factions split the Whig Party, the principal opposition to the Democrats during the period. By 1860, the Whigs had disappeared, and a new Republican Party (not directly related to the Jeffersonians of an earlier era) emerged. The Republicans (also known as the Grand Old Party, or GOP), reflecting abolitionist sentiment, nominated Abraham Lincoln for president. Northern Democrats who opposed slavery joined with Republicans in establishing a new dominant political party. In the decade following the Civil War (1861–1865), Republicans usually won the presidency and controlled Congress. After 1876, elections were close, and the parties were evenly matched in Congress.

Parties reached the high point of their influence in American politics after the Civil War. Local and state party leaders had exclusive control over nominations for political offices. Voters were mobilized in elections by powerful local party organizations that could dispense favors in exchange for support. Political participation and voting among those eligible also peaked in this period.

Political Machines

The era of **machine politics**, powerful party organizations that could deliver the votes, flourished during this period, with some lasting until the middle of the twentieth century. At the head of the machine was a boss, who also often served as mayor and directed city government in a way to maintain control of the city and the organization. (See the box "A Day in the Life of a Machine Politician.")

The machine relied on the votes of the poor and working class, many of whom had only recently immigrated from Europe. Most accounts of machine politics are negative, dwelling on graft and corruption. However, the machine provided a number of valuable services.

The Welfare Function of Parties

Such services provided a welfare system for immigrants and poor people. Party organizations would provide food, clothing, jobs, or housing to people who needed it. The party workers were a kind of welcome wagon to new immigrants, meeting them on the dock as they came off the ship and helping them settle into their new community and nation.

With no national welfare system or other assistance programs, parties were crucial in providing support for poor families and helping them integrate into their new community and country. Tip O'Neill (D-Mass.) told the story of a former mayor of Boston, James Curley, a leader in the Democratic organization in Boston early in the twentieth century, who one winter called Filene's, a local department store, told the owner he needed five thousand sweaters, and reminded the owner that it was time to reassess Filene's property tax assessment. Of course, Curley got the sweaters, which went to poor people in Boston, many of whom were immigrants.

It wasn't a spirit of altruism that led party machines to do favors. They did favors because they expected favors in return. The Boston machine provided poor people with sweaters in return for their votes and loyalty. The party and its elected officials gave Filene's a break on taxes in return for some goods and services that could be used to help the poor and, in many instances, enrich party leaders. As New York's machine boss George Washington Plunkitt once said, "If a family is burned out, I don't ask whether they are Republicans or Democrats. . . . I just get quarters for them, buy clothes for them if their clothes were burned up and fix them up 'til they get things runnin' again. It's philanthropy, but it's politics too—mighty good politics. Who can tell me how many votes one of these fires brings me?"[27]

Thus in the absence of Social Security, welfare, food programs, and other government safety nets, party organizations provided a helping hand for newcomers to find jobs and housing. In return, immigrants developed loyalties to the parties. Some became leaders in the organization. On election day, thousands of party workers went house to house to take voters to the polls. Naturally, turnout was very high because people felt a personal loyalty to the political party that provided for them. In 1896 voter turnout was estimated at 90 percent of those eligible to vote, particularly astonishing in an age when transportation to the polls was difficult in many parts of the country.

Political Patronage

Party leaders, once in office, openly awarded government jobs and other benefits, so-called **political patronage,** to their supporters. An army of city employees whose jobs depended on the political success of the machine would dutifully bring family and friends to the polls on election day. One of the last of the big-city bosses, Mayor Richard J. Daley, head of the Chicago machine during the 1960s and 1970s, controlled

George Washington Plunkitt was a ward leader in the infamous Tammany Hall machine, the Democratic Party organization that governed New York City for seven decades in the late nineteenth and early twentieth centuries. Although Plunkitt was on the city payroll, he did not have a free ride. The demands of his job were exhausting. Providing needed services to his constituents, he had opportunities to build support for the party. Today, government programs available to all citizens provide these services regardless of whether or not they support a political party with their votes. Although parties no longer provide the services Plunkitt delivered to his constituents, they reward their benefactors just the same, with tax breaks, government contracts, and laws that enrich some at the expense of others. Entries from

Plunkitt's diary illustrate the difficult tasks he faced each day.

- 2:00 A.M. Aroused from sleep by a bartender who asked me to go to the police station and bail out a saloon keeper who had been arrested for violating the excise law. Furnished bail and returned to bed at three o'clock.
- 6:00 A.M. Awakened by fire engines. Hastened to the scene of the fire . . . found several tenants who had been burned out, took them to a hotel, supplied them with clothes, fed them, and arranged temporary quarters for them.
- 8:30 A.M. Went to the police court to secure the discharge of six "drunks," my constituents, by a timely word to the judge. Paid the fines of two.

- 9:00 A.M. Appeared in the municipal district court to direct one of my district captains to act as counsel for a widow about to be dispossessed. . . . Paid the rent of a poor family and gave them a dollar for food.
- 11:00 A.M. At home again. "Fixed" the troubles of four men waiting for me: one discharged by the Metropolitan Railway for neglect of duty; another wanted a job on the road; the third on the subway; and the fourth was looking for work with a gas company.
- 3:00 P.M. Attended the funeral of an Italian. Hurried back for the funeral of a Hebrew constituent. Went conspicuously to the front both in the Catholic church and the synagogue.
- 7:00 P.M. Went to district headquarters to preside over a meeting of

thirty-five thousand public jobs and, indirectly through public contracts, ten thousand private ones.[28]

In addition to informing people about politics, nominating and campaigning for candidates for office, and working to enact policy, political parties also performed an important welfare function. Ability to deliver such services made political parties quite powerful social and community organizations.

Political Corruption

The flip side of the golden age of parties was political corruption. Parties provided jobs, food, and other incentives in exchange for votes. Businesses gained government contracts through political payoffs. Although many people benefited from the arrangements, which helped generations of newcomers assimilate into the nation, others saw them as a perversion of the democratic process.

Progressive Politics and the Weakening of Parties

The election of 1896 ushered in new alignment. Midwest farmers hard hit by poor economic conditions turned to the Democrats and William Jennings Bryan. Southerners, still feeling the sting of civil war and out-

rage at Lincoln and the Republicans, joined Bryan in his crusade against the banks and corporations of the Northeast that were financially squeezing ranchers and farmers. A fundamentalist Christian, Bryan also played on a growing concern with the rising number of Catholic immigrants flooding the nation's largest cities. His appeal, however, did not attract enough voters to win the election against the Republican candidate, William McKinley. And, in fact, voters shifted to the Republican party, ushering in a period of Republican dominance.

During the early part of the twentieth century, the **Progressive movement** gained strength, chiefly among middle-class Americans concerned with the corruption of big-city political machines. The movement championed a number of changes designed to wrest power from political machines and the lower-class immigrants they served. These reforms did reduce corruption in politics, but they also seriously weakened the power of political parties.

Changes included voter registration, the secret ballot, primary elections, and the introduction of merit systems. Voter registration made it difficult for parties to stuff ballot boxes with fraudulent votes, and the secret ballot prevented the party from knowing how citizens actually voted. Most devastating of all, the party lost control of nominations for public office. No longer

election district captains, submitted lists of all the voters in their districts and told who were in need, who were in trouble, who might be won over [to Tammany] and how.

- 8:00 P.M. Went to a church fair. Took chances on everything, bought ice cream for the young girls and the children, kissed the little ones, flattered their mothers, and took the fathers out for something down at the corner.
- 9:00 P.M. At the clubhouse again. Spent $10 for a church excursion. Bought tickets for a baseball game. Listened to the complaints of a dozen pushcart peddlers who said they were being persecuted by the police. Promised to go to police headquarters in the morning and see about it.
- 10:30 P.M. Attended a Hebrew wedding reception and dance. Had

previously sent a handsome wedding present to the bride.
- 12:00 A.M. In bed.

SOURCE: Alistair Cooke, *Alistair Cooke's America* (New York: Knopf, 1973), 290–291; adapted from William L. Riordon, *Plunkitt of Tammany Hall* (New York Dutton, 1963), 91–93.

George Washington Plunkitt holds forth in his unofficial office, a bootblack stand at the New York County Court House.

able to tap someone in the private confines of a smoked-filled room, nominations became the responsibility of voters in primary elections. Adopted initially in Wisconsin in 1903, the direct primary, as it was called, spread to virtually every state in the Union. The introduction of merit systems based government hiring on competence rather than party affiliation. Merit systems greatly reduced patronage in the awarding of jobs and contracts and thus robbed the parties of resources needed to maintain the organization.

Although the Progressives never captured the presidency, these ideas did win favor with large numbers of Americans and were enacted into law in every state. Political parties were weakened, with reduced capacity to mobilize voters and use government to meet the needs of those who supported them. Adoption of the reforms did not, however, bring an end to political organization and influence. But the nature of politics changed as well-established, native-born, middle-class economic interests increased their influence.

Despite the relative weakening of the power of new immigrant groups, the sheer numbers of new Americans continued to give them political clout, especially in the large cities of the Northeast and Midwest. In the 1920s, Republican support in the nation's cities declined as the party failed to respond to the plight of poor immigrants residing there. The Repub-

lican majority in Congress limited the growth of the immigrant population by enacting quotas for immigrants from Southern and Eastern Europe, at that time the largest source of immigrants. The number of immigrants dropped sharply from more than 1.2 million in 1910 to less than 150,000 by 1920.

Rise of the Democratic Party

The plight of immigrants set the stage for a new realignment. When the country was rocked by the worldwide economic Great Depression in the 1930s, poor people, immigrants, black Americans, and working people turned to the Democrats. The election of Franklin Delano Roosevelt in 1932 marked the beginning of a new era in American politics.

Roosevelt's **New Deal coalition,** composed of city dwellers, blue-collar workers, Catholic and Jewish immigrants, blacks, and southerners, elected him to an unprecedented four terms. Elements of the coalition were held together in the 1930s and 1940s, initially because of their common economic plight, then because of mobilization for World War II, and throughout by Roosevelt's personality and political skill.

After Roosevelt's death in 1945, the coalition began to unravel. The uneasy alliance between, on the

Until the 1890s, there was no pretense of secrecy in voting. Each party's ballot was a different color. Voters chose their party's ballot, like this Republican ballot for the 1888 election in Indiana, and placed it in a clear glass-sided ballot box. Vote buying in the 1888 election and the growing strength of party reform movements led to adoption of the secret ballot for the next presidential election.

World War II through the early 1990s, they had much less success in winning the presidency. Democrats have won the White House only three times since Lyndon Johnson's victory in 1964.

The Republicans won the presidency in 1952 and 1956 by nominating a popular war hero, General Dwight Eisenhower. Although the Democrats regained the White House in 1960, the civil rights movement, which saw the South move away from the party in 1964, and the Vietnam War, which split the party, cost the party victories in 1968 and 1972.[29] The Democrats have been successful by nominating southerners, first Georgia governor Jimmy Carter in 1976, then Bill Clinton, governor of Arkansas, in 1992 and 1996. In between, Democratic candidates lost to the very popular Ronald Reagan and his successor and former vice president George H. W. Bush. Al Gore, the Democratic nominee in 2000, Clinton's vice president and former Tennessee senator, won the popular vote but lost in the Electoral College when the Supreme Court ended a recount effort in Florida that resulted in George W. Bush's winning the presidency. Bush succeeded in winning both the popular and electoral vote in 2004.

Party Identification Today

Party identification is a psychological link that individuals feel toward a party; no formal or organization membership is implied.[30] A majority of Americans identify with a political party. In 2006, 34 percent identified as Democrats, 30 percent as Republicans, and the rest as independents or supporters of another party.[31] Chapter 4 discussed how individuals develop party identification early in childhood. But party identification can also develop or change as a person's life situation changes, for example moving to a new job or community or in response to changes in national political or economic conditions, periodically producing a realignment.

Realignments of the past have been characterized by compelling issues that fractured the major parties.[32] Before 1860, it was slavery. It divided the Democrats and destroyed the Whigs. In 1932, it was the economy. It pushed many Republicans and new voters to the Democratic party. Political pundits have been awaiting another realignment for decades. Kevin Phillips wrote of an emerging Republican majority in 1969.[33] That majority has yet to evolve, at least not on the scale Phillips envisioned or as Republicans hoped.

But some shifts in party identification have occurred since the New Deal. These include, most prominently (1) a party realignment in the South, which has moved from solidly Democratic to predominantly Republican; (2) declining allegiance of some elements of the New Deal coalition; (3) the growth of

one hand, traditional Southern Democrats, conservative and eager to maintain racial segregation and traditional racial norms, and on the other, more liberal northern urban dwellers, blacks, and working people, began to fray. Consequently, even though the Democrats continued to dominate Congress from the end of

Democratic loyalty among some formerly Republican groups; (4) the changing partisan effect of religion; (5) the uncertain partisanship of Latinos and Asians, "new" groups in the electorate; and (6) the growing ideological division between the parties. (Table 7.1 outlines the partisan identities of a variety of demographic groups.)

Southern Realignment

In the 1960s, race moved large numbers of white Southerners to shift to the Republican party. This change is the main reason that polls have shown a decline in Democratic loyalties nationwide.

After the Civil War (1861–1865) and until 1964, the GOP took pride in being the "party of Lincoln," the party that ended slavery. Until the New Deal era, most African Americans voted Republican, and the Southern Democratic Party was the party of whites, supporting racist policies. But these positions have reversed with the party realignment in the south.

Roosevelt's administration worked only cautiously to improve the status of African Americans, though some progress was made. But after World War II, Roosevelt's Democratic successor, Harry Truman, ordered the racial integration in the military. This move drew intense criticism in the South. Then, in 1948, the Democratic platform proposed new civil rights legislation. That led Strom Thurmond, a Democratic governor of South Carolina, and some other southern convention delegates to bolt the Democratic Party. They formed a breakaway third party, the States' Rights Party, commonly called the Dixiecrats. On the Dixiecrat label, Thurman ran for president against Truman, and carried four Southern states. Although the Dixiecrats returned to the Democratic Party by 1952, southern discomfort with the Democrats grew in the 1950s when northern Democrats supported modest civil rights legislation. But at that time, so did many Republicans.

The movement of southern conservatives to the Republican Party gained momentum when Democratic president Lyndon Johnson supported and the Democratic-controlled Congress passed the landmark Civil Rights Act of 1964. This legislation, also supported by many Republicans, including the Republican leadership, gave African Americans the right to be served in restaurants, stay in motels, go to movie theaters, and make use of any facility serving the public. The bill was strongly opposed throughout the white South because it undermined traditional white supremacy and segregation in the region. At the time he signed the bill, Johnson commented that the act would deliver the South to the Republicans for the next fifty years. And sure enough, Barry Goldwater, the Republican presidential nominee running against

TABLE 7.1 Characteristics of Republicans, Independents, and Democrats

	Republicans	Independents	Democrats
Total	30	36	34
Age 18–25	9	19	7
26–30	7	8	12
31–50	38	35	34
51–65	29	26	28
Over 65	16	13	18
Less than high school	5	10	11
High school graduate	24	31	31
Some college	34	34	28
College graduate	36	24	30
Men	49	53	38
Women	51	47	62
Married	64	46	46
Widowed, divorced, separated	18	23	30
Never married	16	23	23
White	91	70	58
Hispanic	4	7	8
African American	1	15	29
Native American	0	1	1
Asian American	3	3	1
Mixed race	1	4	3
Protestant	61	52	55
Catholic	25	24	24
Jewish	2	2	6
None	11	19	14
Attend religious services every week	38	34	34
Under $15,000	9	17	17
$15,000–$35,000	14	21	22
$35,000–$50,000	13	13	15
$50,000–$85,000	31	23	23
Over $85,000	33	26	24
Family member belongs to union	14	18	20
Family member in military	67	63	68
Employment			
Working	67	72	61
Retired	17	12	22
Unemployed	1	5	5
Homemaker	11	5	7
Conservative	83	48	31
Moderate	5	10	8
Liberal	10	38	56

Source: National Election Studies, 2004.

Johnson in 1964, denounced the Civil Rights Act as an affront to "states' rights." Although Goldwater himself seemed not to have a racial motive, and he believed strongly in states' rights in areas that had nothing to do with race, some of his advisers and other Republican leaders in the South used his opposition to appeal to the segregationist vote. His speech opposing the Civil Rights Act, delivered a couple of weeks before the election, was widely disseminated in the South,[34] and his support for "states' rights" was read as code for letting the South maintain its segregated racial system. He did better in the Deep South than any other Republican presidential candidate had up to that time.

Later, Richard Nixon institutionalized the Republican's "southern strategy," continuing to appeal to white voters in the South using racial code words such as "states' rights," "law and order," and "welfare," with the implication that *states' rights* meant shutting out African Americans and that *law and order* meant quelling African American criminals and rioters. After taping a campaign ad stressing "law and order in our schools," he said to his aides, "Yep, this hits it right on the nose. . . . It's all about law and order and the damn Negro–Puerto Rican groups out there."[35] This southern strategy was further enhanced by Ronald Reagan, who opened his presidential campaign by making a states' rights speech in Philadelphia, Mississippi, where three civil rights workers had been brutally murdered by local citizens with assistance and cover-up provided by local law enforcement officials, one of the most notorious crimes of the civil rights era (see Chapter 15). Reagan also talked about "welfare queens"—a thinly veiled refer-

ence to black women who presumably were living the high life while on welfare.

The most famous political ad of the 1988 presidential campaign was a TV commercial sponsored by the Republicans. It linked the Democratic presidential candidate, Michael Dukakis, to a black felon, Willie Horton, whom Dukakis, as governor of Massachusetts, had in accordance with the state's policy, allowed to go on a weekend furlough. While on that furlough, Horton raped a white woman. When the ad began to run, George H. W. Bush, the Republican candidate, began to rise in the polls. The link between the Democrats and black criminals was apparently deliberate. The ad and the reaction to it were so powerful that after the election, people who were questioned about what they recalled about the campaign mentioned "Bush, Dukakis, and Willie Horton."[36]

The Republicans' racial strategy was normally conducted carefully and only with code words. Rarely did public officials openly use racial epithets or praise segregation, as politicians of both parties did for generations before the Civil Rights Act. But in 2002, Trent Lott, the Republican Senate majority leader from Mississippi, disregarded these norms when on the occasion of the hundredth birthday of Strom Thurmond, the Dixiecrat candidate for president in 1948 who later switched to the Republican Party, he declared that his state was proud to have voted for Strom Thurmond's ticket. "And if the rest of the country had followed our lead," he continued, "we wouldn't have had all these problems over the years either." Lott later apologized, but the public condemnation, including a

Strom Thurmond broke with the Democratic party to run for president in 1948 on the Dixiecrat segregation ticket. Later he became a Republican. In 2002, Senate leader and fellow Republican Trent Lott (center) congratulates him on his 100th birthday.

The glowering face of criminal Willie Horton, featured in a Republican TV commercial linking the criminal to the Democratic candidate, Michael Dukakis, became one of the most memorable images of the 1988 presidential campaign.

rebuke by George W. Bush, caused him to resign his leadership position.

The southern strategy has been very successful for the Republicans. Since 1968, Republicans have carried the South in all presidential elections, except when southerner Jimmy Carter was the Democratic candidate in 1976. Even then, a majority of white southerners voted for the Republican, Gerald Ford. White southerners have increasingly voted Republican in congressional and state races too. Since 1994, they have cast the majority of their votes for Republicans.

Currently, eight of twelve southern governors are Republican, as are a vast majority of southern senators. The GOP is less advantaged in the House, but still holds over half the seats of southern states. Of course, black southerners consistently support Democrats and are the backbone of the Southern Democratic Party.[37]

This realignment certainly does not mean that all or even most southern white Republicans are racist or that all or most southern Republican officials are. It does, however, mean that since 1964 the Republicans have strategically used a conservative and sometimes implicitly racist approach to race-related issues to build their dominance in the region, just as the Democrats did for generations before them.

The shift of conservative white southerners to the Republican Party not only makes the South more Republican but also makes the Republican Party more conservative and the party system more ideological.

Conservative southern Republicans are more conservative, on the whole, than the Democrats they replaced, and they are, on the whole, more conservative than northern Republicans. Their conservative voice has shifted the balance of power in the South and among Republican officials in a conservative direction. At the same time, the Democratic Party became more liberal as the number of conservative Democrats shrank. Moreover, with African Americans as full participants in the political processes of the South, Southern Democratic public officials tend to be more liberal than the earlier generation of Southern Democratic elected officials, who were elected largely (or in some cases only) by a white electorate.

Declining Democratic Loyalty Among Elements of the New Deal Coalition

Although a realignment has occurred in the South, the same cannot be said for the nation as a whole. Yet changing issues and circumstances and the fading memory of the Depression have led to some realignment.

Blue-collar white ethnic minorities, many of them Catholic, were at the heart of Roosevelt's Democratic coalition.[38] But in the last quarter of the twentieth century, these groups found the Democrats much less attractive.[39] With the success of the New Deal and the economic security it provided, blue-collar workers felt free to focus on other issues, such as the Vietnam War, crime, race, and so-called family values.

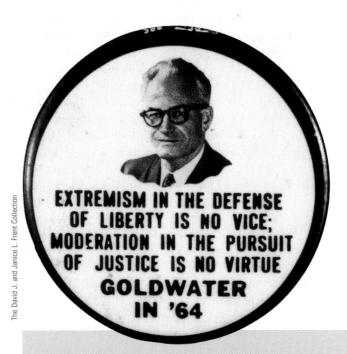

Arizona Senator Barry Goldwater captured the Republican nomination for president in 1964. His acceptance speech, quoted on this campaign pin, reflected the new dominance of the conservatives over the moderates in the party.

Ronald Reagan captured many blue-collar votes. However, the GOP was unable to establish a lasting and permanent link with them. When economic times turned bad for blue-collar workers, they again turned to the Democrats, supporting Clinton in 1992 and 1996.

Growing Democratic Support among Former Republican Groups

Whereas blue-collar workers are less Democratic today than they used to be, other groups are more Democratic in their leanings. From the 1930s through the 1970s, the more affluent, better-educated, and white-collar workers voted predominantly Republican. But the relationship between income and party allegiance has weakened considerably and in some instances reversed. Many well-educated professionals (lawyers, doctors, scientists, and academics) have found a new home in the Democratic Party, where they are supportive of Democratic initiatives to make health care more affordable, preserve the environment, and guarantee abortion rights.[40] In 2000, Al Gore did quite well in the nation's most affluent communities, winning better than 70 percent of the vote in some.[41] Other white-collar workers are also somewhat less Republican than before, especially public service workers. Many of them are sympathetic to Democratic Party efforts to retain, if not expand, the government's role in providing services and dealing with the nation's problems.

If anything, women were, traditionally, slightly more politically conservative than men. Now women are increasingly voting Democratic. Though stay-at-home moms are somewhat more likely to be Republican, working women and unmarried women are disproportionately Democrats.[42] Women seem to be attracted to the Democrats not because of their stand on women's issues such as abortion rights but rather because of their support for human service initiatives such as education, Social Security, and health insurance. Women are disproportionately the caregivers in our society, and they like the idea that government will give families a hand when needed. Women are also less likely than men to support war and military spending.[43]

Religion as a Factor Shaping Party Identity

Religion helped shape the New Deal coalition in that Catholics and Jews, many of them immigrants or children of immigrants, tended to be Democrats. Protestants tended to be Republicans. As cultural and social issues gained strength relative to economic ones, this cleavage has declined and a new religious cleavage has emerged. Today, the cleavage is between those who are very religious and those who are not. Church attendance is more highly correlated with partisanship than is either income or education. Among weekly churchgoers, Bush won 80 percent of the vote in 2000. Among those who never attend, Gore won 60 percent.[44] Although the number of nonreligious Americans appears to be growing, most Americans still claim to be quite religious.

The link between religiosity and partisanship is probably rooted in Republicans' positions against homosexuality and abortion and in favor of prayer in schools and other public places, along with similar issues that are sometimes lumped together under the banner "traditional values." Many of the very religious regret and oppose the drift toward a more secular society. They believe that American society is becoming less moral, and they see political activism as a way to combat the slide.

Uncertain Partisanship of New Demographic Groups

Latinos and Asians are growing portions of the electorate. Although both Latinos and Asians have lived in the United States for generations, many current residents are from families of recent immigrants (with the important exception of "old" Latino populations in the Southwest, some of whom predated Anglo settlement in America). As relative newcomers, they have not been part of the party histories we have described, and both parties are working to win their loyalties.

Both Latinos and Asians are divided among specific ethnic groups. Cuban Americans and Mexican Americans, for example, are both "Hispanic" but have very different histories and cultures. Latinos, except for Cuban Americans, have traditionally voted Democratic. Asians, again fragmented among many different groups, from Chinese to Pakistani, have been Republican but have become more Democratic in recent elections.

Both parties are reaching out to these groups and hope to win them over. The Bush administration has made a concerted effort to woo Hispanic voters. Bush has given his weekly radio address in Spanish, has developed a high-profile friendly relationship with the president of Mexico, and opposed the conservative base of his party by proposing that some long-time illegal immigrants be allowed to work toward citizenship rather than be deported. Given the growth of the Latino population, especially in the Southwest, winning the allegiance of significant numbers of Hispanics is crucial to the Republicans' remaining competitive in states such as California and Texas.

Ideological Parties

The party system that grew out of the Great Depression produced two parties that were each quite ideologically heterogeneous. Although the Democrats were, on balance, more liberal than the Republicans, the Democratic Party included southern conservatives as well as northern liberals. The Republican party included liberals also, though they were called "moderate Republicans." As a result of the southern Republican realignment, each party is now more ideologically homogeneous. The Republican party consists mostly of conservatives, whereas the Democratic party consists mostly of liberals (although most Democrats do not call themselves liberals). Independents are generally ideologically between Republicans and Democrats. Even though Republicans tend to be conservative, the Republican Party represents an uneasy coalition of traditional conservatives, motivated primarily by a desire to minimize government intervention in business activity, and new conservatives, motivated primarily by a desire to institutionalize their religious and moral values. Called the *Religious Right*, these new conservatives look to government to check personal behaviors they find objectionable, such as abortion and same-sex marriage. The Republican factions originally united in their hate for communism and their support for Ronald Reagan. But the disintegration of the Soviet Union and the departure of Reagan left them with less in common.[45]

In many state party organizations (discussed later in the chapter), the Religious Right has considerable influence in recruiting candidates to run for office and shaping the policy direction of the party in the state.

The Republican Party has tried to pull blue-collar workers away from their traditional home in the Democratic Party. As president, Ronald Reagan was especially effective in luring these voters.

© Andy Levin/Photo Researchers, Inc.

Since the 1992 Republican National Convention, the right has avoided open confrontation with the shrinking group of moderate Republican officeholders, and national party leaders have stressed issues such as lower taxes and smaller government, on which both agree. Candidates from the right, except in rural areas and the South, often avoid broadcasting positions that alienate moderates. Instead, they spread the word quietly through the churches. However, in 2004, they highlighted their position on same-sex marriage more than their position on abortion because most voters opposed same-sex marriage (unlike abortion). Indeed, they used the specter of same-sex marriage as a rallying cry to get like-minded voters to the polls.

The Democrats are divided in different ways. Some want to emphasize their liberal roots by appealing to working men and women and denouncing Republican support for big business and wealthy taxpayers. Others want the party to appeal to moderates who want lower taxes, less government, and more local control.[46] Bill Clinton directed his appeal toward the middle, angering many liberal Democrats in Congress. Clinton, who opened his second inaugural address with the statement, "The era of big government is over," thought it political suicide for him and the party to continue pushing a liberal agenda. As one of his aides put it, "We can't define ourselves as the party of government."[47] The party needs both its liberal base and the moderate middle to be successful. Both Al Gore and John Kerry sought to appeal to moderates in their presidential campaigns, and they were also vocal in their opposition to the Republican strategies of massive tax cuts for the wealthy.

Realignment today In the early 2000s, it appeared that the country might have completed a realignment with the Republicans as the dominant party. Although the Democratic candidate for president received more popular votes in the 2000 election, the Republican party controlled the presidency, the House, the Senate, and the majority of state houses. The terrorist attacks of 9/11 enabled the party to solidify its control over the government by appealing to the citizens' patriotism and promising an aggressive war on terrorism. But by 2006, it seemed unlikely that this dominance would be permanent or semipermanent. The Republicans overreached, passing legislation mostly benefiting their constituency of big businesses and wealthy supporters. This legislative agenda included tax cuts for the wealthy and deregulation in many areas, including energy, the environment, and consumer matters. The Republicans also made frequent appeals to their constituency of religious conservatives, with heated rhetoric about gay marriage and abortion. They pursued an aggressive foreign policy, using the "war on terrorism" to launch a preemptive attack on Iraq. But as the war dragged on, as the repeated tax cuts contributed to the largest deficits in American history, and as the administration appeared to abandon fiscal responsibility, the Republicans provided the Democrats an opportunity to regain competitiveness in Congress and the statehouses as well as in the White House in 2008.

Decline of Parties

Although political parties are alive and well, their role has shrunk since their heyday in the late nineteenth and early twentieth centuries. Parties were strong then because they played a myriad of essential roles unduplicated by other agencies and individuals: they provided welfare, jobs, and information; nominated candidates and got them elected; and organized governance. One reason for their diminished role is that other groups have stepped in to fill many of the roles that parties formerly played.

Diminution of Party Functions

Welfare

The welfare function that parties played in helping new immigrants and other poor people obtain food, housing, and jobs and assimilate into American culture has been largely superseded by many government pro-grams put in place in the twentieth century, ranging from Social Security to Medicare to food stamps. When economic hardship strikes, individuals can now obtain assistance from the government, so they do not need parties to provide it. Those who are hungry can apply for food stamps, and laid-off workers can apply for unemployment compensation. Schools also play a role in providing assistance to immigrant children (and sometimes their parents) who need to learn English and become familiar with American ways.

The ability of political parties to provide jobs has also been restricted. The adoption of merit hiring in government service (for more on that, see Chapter 12) means that once elected to office, party leaders cannot hire their supporters through patronage. Of course, some patronage jobs do exist, such as agency heads and a small number of other positions, but it is risky to put unqualified people in high-profile jobs. This point was brought chillingly home by the incompetence of the Federal Emergency Management Agency in the aftermath of the Katrina hurricane in 2005. FEMA head Mike Brown, who had no experience in emergency management, was a friend of the president's 2000 campaign manager; the top ranks of the agency seemed to have little grasp of the magnitude of the problems caused by Katrina or what to do about it. Of course, the adoption of merit-based hiring has been, on balance, a good thing. We want government employees to be qualified, not just friends and supporters of those

James Nielsen/AFP/Getty Images

Although the party that wins the presidency no longer controls most government jobs, it still controls the top jobs—several thousands—to which the president usually appoints party members. President Bush appointed political operatives rather than experienced managers to the top jobs at FEMA. When hurricane Katrina hit the Gulf Coast, their incompetence in coordinating evacuation and providing relief was apparent.

In the days before primary elections, delegates to the party's presidential nominating convention selected the party's presidential nominee. Delegates to the 1924 Democratic convention, shown here, required 103 ballots over two weeks to nominate John Davis for president. He had trouble persuading voters in the general election as well, garnering only 28 percent of the vote and losing to Republican Calvin Coolidge.

elected to office. Merit appointment also reduces the opportunities for corruption and kickbacks. And merit appointment is fairer as a way of selecting those to be hired. It's not just who you know but also what you can do that is supposed to matter in merit systems.

Information

Parties also lost control over information. In the mass media age, most people get their news from newspapers and television. Most national news media strive for balance (see Chapter 8); none are controlled by political parties.

Nominations and Campaigns

Most significant, perhaps, is that parties have lost control over their ability to select nominees for office. As we noted earlier, the introduction of primary elections turned nominations over to whomever the party's electorate chose. The national parties still hold nominating conventions, but the parties' nominees have been chosen long before the convention through presidential primaries held in most states. The winner of these contests almost invariably becomes the party's nominee. Conventions are, in some ways, superfluous, but they continue to serve the function of publicizing the nominees and rallying party supporters.

Parties also play a diminished role in actually electing their candidates. Parties certainly play some role: they help finance campaigns, provide advisers and strategists, and help publicize candidates. National party leaders will often campaign for newcomers or fellow party members in tight races. However, candidates now hire their own campaign managers, pollsters, media experts, computer gurus, event organizers, and all the other essential components of a modern campaign. They still seek advice from party leaders and often hire experts who have worked for other successful party members, but it is the candidate's choices that prevail and the candidate's funds that pay for the campaign team.

Governing

Financing campaigns and media advertising costs money. Although parties raise tens of millions of dollars for their candidates, others also provide funding. Corporations give to both parties, though in larger amounts to Republicans. Labor unions give primarily to Democrats. Special interests ranging from progun lobbies to environmental groups give to candidates of both parties. By providing financing, corporations, unions, and special-interest groups create obligations on the part of elected officeholders that are fulfilled by pushing legislation that their benefactors find desirable.

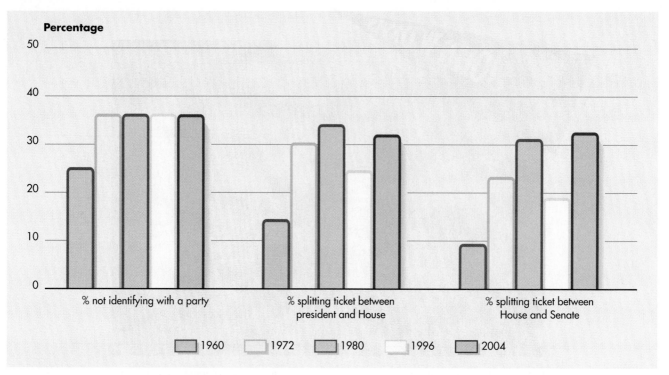

Percentage

Legend: 1960, 1972, 1980, 1996, 2004

Categories: % not identifying with a party, % splitting ticket between president and House, % splitting ticket between House and Senate

FIGURE 7.4 ■ Erosion of Support for Parties

SOURCE: National Election Studies, Center for Political Studies, University of Michigan, 1960–2004 (www.umich.edu/nes).

Erosion of Popular Support for Parties

Because parties do not play the roles they used to, people understandably believe that parties are less important then they used to be. The term **dealignment** has often been used to refer to diminished relevance of parties.

Increase in Independents and Split-Ticket Voters

There are several indicators of dealignment. One is a decline in the strength of party allegiance in the general population. The proportion of the public calling themselves Independents has risen from less than 15 percent in 1960 to more than 40 percent in 2000.[48] The proportion identifying themselves as either strong Democrats or strong Republicans has fallen, though not by much.[49] The tendency for younger rather than older Americans to identify as Independent means that the electorate may become even more independent as older Americans die. On the other hand, a highly partisan environment may diminish the number of Independents, forcing people to take sides. (Just as plausibly, however, it could drive more people to the center if they become disgusted with bitter partisan battles.)

Split-ticket voting is another indication of dealignment. It refers to voting for a member of one party for one office and another party for a different office, for example, voting for the Republican presidential candidate but a Democratic House candidate. Ticket splitting is much more common than in the 1950s (see Figure 7.4).[50] Voters who split their ticket indicate that personalities, issues, or something other than partisanship drives their vote.

Disinterest in Parties

Another sign of dealignment is disinterest in parties. The number of Americans who say there is nothing they like or dislike about either the Democratic or Republican Party has increased.[51] Parties are simply not reaching many voters.[52] Another indication of disinterest is low turnout in elections (see Chapter 8).

The failure of Americans to identify with political parties, the increasing incidence of split-ticket voting, and low voter turnout are all signs of loosening party ties.[53] And as party ties grow weaker, the capacity of Americans to hold government accountable diminishes and the influence of special-interest groups increases.[54]

Resurgence of Parties

We have painted a rather bleak picture of the decline of American parties during the past century. Parties are weaker than they were a century ago. Yet it is clear from the news that we hear every day that parties are far from dead. They still perform vital functions. And in fact, they have been experiencing something of a resurgence over the past twenty years. Partisanship in the national government has increased in the past decade, and the near parity between the parties in electoral strength and the closeness of the 2004 presidential election have re-engaged many formerly apathetic voters.

Continuing Importance of Political Parties

Although parties no longer provide much welfare, public officials have become mediators between the public and the bureaucracy. Each year, hundreds of thousands of people ask their state legislator, member of Congress, or local council member to intervene on their behalf with the bureaucracy: to find out what happened to a missing Social Security check, to intervene to cut the time to process a visa application, or even to get a government job. Elected officials are quite interested in providing these services, and their success becomes part of the record that they, and their party, run on.

Information

Parties no longer have party newspapers, but they have become increasingly involved in providing information to their supporters on the Web, through direct mail, and on radio and television. During congressional and presidential campaigns, party supporters can expect to receive weekly or sometimes even more frequent communication from the national, state, and local party organizations and congressional campaign committees. Most of this is focused on soliciting donations, but these letters and messages also provide information about issues and candidates, portraying the party in a favorable light and denigrating the opposition.

Nominations

Parties do not control nominations for national offices anymore and usually have little clout at the state level. But for many state and local offices, party leaders take the lead in encouraging qualified individuals to run for office and then provide them with an unofficial or official party endorsement and support. Party leaders often encourage and support promising candidates to run for Congress, too. Once these candidates are nominated in primaries, the parties provide support in various ways. The amount of support depends on the office and the strength of the party in the state or community. The national campaign organizations will provide candidates they believe have a chance to win with significant financial assistance, access to a variety of services (media consultants, for example), and opportunities to participate in seminars and workshops to get advice about running a successful campaign. Although the party does

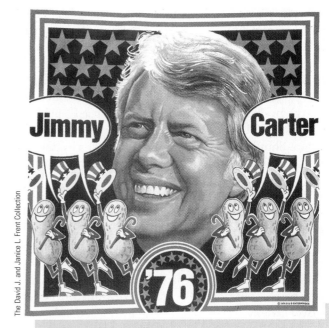

The David J. and Janice L. Frent Collection

Party officials no longer determine their nominee for president; party voters in primary elections do. In 1976 Democratic officials were reluctant to endorse Jimmy Carter, who was relatively inexperienced, but Democratic voters in the primaries liked his decency. Carter received enough support from them that the party had to nominate him. Although he won the general election (thus vindicating the voters in the primaries), he was unable to govern effectively (thus vindicating party officials). Consequently, in 1980 he lost his reelection bid.

not have a monopoly on these resources anymore, the national campaign organizations are increasingly well financed and have much to offer candidates.

Governance

Parties are increasingly important in governance. Parties have important organizational and leadership functions in Congress. The majority in each chamber controls the agenda—it decides what issues will be debated and voted on. The majority also controls what happens in committees, where the work of Congress is done. The party also links the president with the members of his party in Congress. The president's party supports his policies substantially more often than the opposition. In 2005, Republicans in the Senate and House supported George W. Bush 91 and 80 percent of the time, respectively, whereas Senate Democrats supported him 60 percent of the time and House Democrats, a scant 30 percent.[55]

Thus important legislation is often a contest between the Republican and Democratic visions of the right policy choice. Although most Americans deplore the heightened party wrangling now occurring, the clear partisan divisions make it easier to hold elected officials responsible. Voting for one party rather than the other has definite policy consequences. Assuming that voters know the general positions of the parties when they cast their votes, legislative voting along party lines increases the prospects for popular control of government. For example, given that the Republican Party's official position is pro-life and the Democratic Party's position is pro-choice, a vote for a Republican candidate will typically mean support for a pro-life position. Should the Republicans win a majority, there is every likelihood that they would attempt to enact a pro-life policy into law, as indeed they have. They might not succeed immediately, but if they have a strong enough majority and hold it for long enough, eventually it might happen.

When parties take clear and opposing positions on major issues, voters clearly perceive the positions of the parties, and elected party members seek to enact the party's position, it is called **responsible party government.**

Great Britain is often cited as an example of responsible party government. Political parties are heavily involved in developing, articulating, and implementing public policy. If elected party members defect too often from the party's position, party leaders can deny them the right to stand for reelection as the party's candidates.

American political parties do not always conform to this model. They do not always offer clear and contrasting policy positions. Even when they do, party leaders have only limited authority to force their elected members to accept the party's position. However, in recent years, Democrats and Republicans have been more likely to accept their party's positions due to the increased ideological homogeneity of the parties.

In a system of separation of powers like that of the United States, it is possible to have one party controlling the presidency and another controlling one or both houses of Congress, making responsible party government difficult. When this occurs, stalemate is often the result. Such an outcome is likely to mean that the American people are evenly divided, making it difficult for government to resolve the issue.

Party Influence on Policy Making

Party differences are reflected in partisan voting in Congress, which has increased dramatically since the 1980s.[56] To a large degree, this results from the realignment in the South. The days of white conservative Democrats who voted with the Republicans almost as often as with their own party are almost over.[57] As white conservatives have moved into the Republican Party, districts with conservative white majorities are much more likely to elect Republicans than conserva-

tive Democrats. Districts with large numbers of black voters are more likely than before to elect African American or moderate or liberal white Democrats. Thus voting patterns of representatives from the South now divide along party lines as they do in the North.[58]

Partisan voting also reflects Republican control of both houses of Congress. A number of conservative Republicans committed to a very conservative agenda were elected in 1994. Eager to retain control of Congress, moderate incumbent Republicans embraced their conservative program to show voters that the party could enact legislation and govern effectively.[59] Moderate Democrats, on the other hand, did not support the GOP's agenda, and the gap between the parties increased.

Moderate Republicans have come under intense pressure from the White House to support George W. Bush and his party's conservative agenda. Senator Olympia Snow of Maine and other moderates in the Senate are routinely summoned to the White House and lobbied by both the president and the vice president. Although presidents have always pressured members of Congress, the tactics of the administration and its allies are designed to make individuals who deviate from the party uncomfortable. For her unwillingness to support a Bush tax cut higher than $350 billion, Snow was trashed by the *Wall Street Journal* and identified on the website "Republican in Name Only," sponsored by the conservative Club for Growth.[60]

Party line voting in recent decades has been increasing and is likely to remain high. Each party has a distinct vision it is trying to implement. During the Bush administration, on issues in which majorities in each party opposed each other, House Republicans' support for the party's position averaged better than 90 percent. Democrats were somewhat less unified, supporting their party's position in the mid–80 percent range. Party support in the Senate was similar (see Figure 7.5)[61] Only the war on terror managed to bring the parties together—fleetingly, as it turned out (see the box "Party Responsiveness to a National Crisis").

It is hard to imagine a higher rate of partisanship within our existing system of separation of powers. Lower levels await a president who is committed to trying to build bridges across partisan lines and a minority party willing to work with such a president.

Party Organization

Political parties consist of the partisans among the public and the party's officeholders. Less visible is the third component of political parties, the party activists who manage the party organization. Described as hollow shells in the 1950s and 1960s, the national party organizations are stronger today than they have been since the early twentieth century. Behind their success is a steady

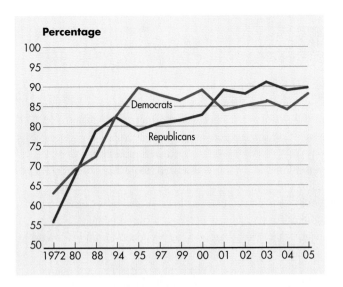

FIGURE 7.5 ■ **Party Unity in Congressional Voting**

Source: *CQ Weekly*, January 3, 2004, 48.

flow of cash from corporations, interest groups, and unions.

The major levels of party organization—national, state, and local—coincide with political units responsible for administering elections. Within local parties, there are further subdivisions. The precinct is usually the smallest unit. Several precincts compose a ward or district; several wards compose a city or county. Each lower-level organization feeds into the next higher level.

Although party organization seems hierarchical (organized from the top down), it is not. Party organization is a layered structure with each layer linked to, but independent of, the others. Higher levels cannot dictate to or impose penalties on lower levels to ensure compliance. Party organization is only loosely connected with the party in government, in contrast with the British system, where party leaders in Parliament maintain a tight grip on the party organization.

National Party Organization

The **national party chair** heads each national party organization, called the **national committee.** The president appoints the chair of his party; this task falls to the national committee of the opposition party. The national party chair is a low-profile position, and the person who serves is generally not very visible to the public, though occasionally there are exceptions. If you know that Howard Dean is the DNC chairman and Ken Mehlman the Republican National Committee (RNC) Chairman, you are well informed indeed. The primary function of party chairs these days is to raise money, but they also speak out on party and public issues.[62] When a party does not control the presidency, the party chair is often the spokesperson for the party.

Although the national committees are the primary governing institutions of the Democratic and Republican parties, they seldom meet, and it is the national chair and the permanent staff who are the de facto national organization. The national committees do choose the site of their party's national convention and establish the formula for determining how many delegates each state receives.

National committee members are selected from each state using a variety of methods established by each state party. Whereas states are represented equally on the RNC, the DNC awards states additional seats based on population and support for Democratic candidates in elections. The DNC also includes the party's leaders in Congress, the leaders of several state and local Democratic organizations, and representatives from elements of the party that are often underrepresented on the committee, including blacks, Hispanics, and young adults.

Both parties also have House and Senate campaign committees, which have grown in influence owing to their ability to raise and distribute campaign funds to their party's candidates for Congress.[63] The National Republican Senatorial Committee and the National Republican Congressional Committee together raised more than $100 million for the 2002 congressional elections, and their counterpart Democratic committees raised nearly $60 million.[64] New campaign finance laws have not stemmed fund-raising, which attained even higher levels in 2004 and 2006 (see Chapter 9).[65]

The increasing capacity of the national party organizations to offer candidates assistance in their campaigns may be responsible for the rising level of party voting in Congress. Members of Congress no doubt do feel beholden to the national party and perhaps a commitment to support party positions. At the same time, members are less beholden to state and local parties. Thus national party organizations are growing in influence at the expense of state and local parties.[66] The national parties are even communicating directly with voters via the Internet. The close link between the national party organizations and the parties in Congress moves us closer to the responsible party government model.

State and Local Party Organizations

Party organizations also exist at the state and local levels. There are chairs and committees to direct the activities of the party activists at these levels, too. In some communities, parties may be so weak and unimportant that there is little party organization. Because of this, someone who wants to become active in the party organization has only to show up at party meetings and be willing to work. Earlier, we discussed the historical political machines in large urban areas.

In his 2000 election campaign, George W. Bush urged an end to the bitter partisan conflicts that characterized the Clinton years. He promised a fresh approach, seeking cooperation and building consensus with Democrats in Congress. Bush had worked cooperatively with the Democrats when he was governor of Texas. But Texas is not Washington. The Democratic Party in Texas is generally quite conservative, and as in all states, the day-to-day workings of the legislature and state government are not covered by a national media driven to feature the conflicts that divide the parties.

Thus few believed it possible that a bipartisan spirit would take hold in Washington. The parties have major disagreements about policy, disagreements that reflect differences of opinion in the public, ranging from health care to the Middle East. Moreover, Democrats were unlikely to forget the treatment of Bill Clinton by Republicans in Congress during his presidency. Many conservative Republicans hated Clinton in a way that went beyond partisanship. In addition to his policies, many objected to his personal life. Investigations of his financial dealings before becoming president dogged his presidency, and the Monica Lewinsky scandal and the impeachment effort drove the division even deeper. Talk radio, which mostly reflected conservative Republican views, filled the airways with Bill and Hillary Clinton's real and alleged wrongdoings.

The 2000 election was extremely partisan, and the outcome, decided by the U.S. Supreme Court, was a bitter pill for the Democrats to swallow, for their candidate had won the popular vote. Many Democrats, including some in Congress, believed that Gore did win the election, and were it not for Republican-appointed justices on the Supreme Court, Gore would be sitting in the White House instead of Bush. However, the Democrats accepted the verdict and hoped that indeed the new president would be a conciliator.

In spite of Bush's early efforts to establish personal relations with congressional leaders of both parties, the tone quickly turned sour. Despite his lack of any mandate from the voters, he decided to govern from the right rather than the center. His appointments and much of his legislative agenda were directed toward pleasing his conservative base rather than reflecting his moderate tone in the campaign and the closeness of the election. And the Republican leadership in Congress seemed to give up on the idea, if they ever had it, of moving toward the center, now that the party controlled both the presidency and the House.

Then came the terrorist attacks of September 11, 2001. Suddenly, "United We Stand" became the theme. In a moment, the usual political calculations were swept aside. The Senate voted 98–0 authorizing the president to use "all necessary and appropriate force" against those involved in the attack. The House followed 420–1. Singing the "Battle Hymn of the Republic," Democrats and Republicans joined hands in the Capitol. Commentators spoke of an end to partisanship and division in American society, of a new era with the nation pulling and working together. Despite Bush's tainted election and an evenly divided Congress, bipartisanship had arrived. Democrats rallied to support the president. Of course, this response was bolstered by the president's overwhelming popular support, as his approval ratings soared to over 90 percent.

But politics is politics, and real differences about policy do not disappear because of a national disaster. The president saw an opportunity to push his domestic agenda in the guise of fighting terrorism (see "You Are There" in Chapter 4), and Democrats began to complain about that. Standing outside the Capitol on September 25, 2001, House Democrats admonished the president that wartime deference would not extend beyond proposals to combat terrorism. The terrorist-induced infusion of bipartisanship lasted exactly forty-three days, by one count, from September 11 to October 24.

Yet that judgment was more superficial than real. For months Democrats seemed afraid to challenge the president on a whole range of policy alternatives. They were fearful that the public would think they were "soft on terrorism," and the Republicans were quick to bandy those charges, even against a decorated Vietnam veteran, Senator Max Cleland (D-Ga.), who lost three limbs in that war. Most Democrats willingly signed on to support the USA PATRIOT Act, which gave investigatory agencies more power than

---

Today, these organizations are generally weak, though some, as in Chicago, retain some power.

Parties and Voting

Just how important are political parties in shaping the votes of individual citizens? For sixty years, political scientists have argued over the relative importance of parties, issues, and personalities in choosing among competing candidates. Political scientist Stanley Kelley has argued that voters go through a simple process in deciding how to vote. They add up the things they like about each candidate and party, and they vote for the candidate with the highest number of "likes." If there is a tie, they vote on the basis of their party identification, if

ever before to snoop into people's private lives, detain the accused without the usual due process procedures, and in general tip the balance between freedom and security heavily toward the latter. Democrats were hesitant to criticize the administration for the conduct of the war on terrorism even when it seemed to go badly, for failing to pursue al-Qaeda in Afghanistan, and for undertaking a military invasion of Iraq. Most Democrats were reluctant to criticize the president's plans to attack Iraq, even though the evidence linking Iraq and 9/11 was nonexistent. Indeed, most Democrats signed on to give the president authority to attack Iraq.

Growing public disenchantment as the Iraqi War began to drag on seemed to give the Democratic leaders renewed courage to speak out again, not just on the war but on domestic issues too. After all, bipartisanship had been pretty much a one-way street, with Democrats supporting the Bush program and little reciprocity from the Republicans moving toward the Democrats. Indeed, showing Republican disdain for bipartisanship, Dick Armey, the former House Republican majority leader, described bipartisanship as "another name for date rape." The Democrats began to realize that they had been victimized.[1]

Democratic activists among the rank and file were increasingly unhappy with the Democratic leadership's failure to provide alternatives to the president. The candidacy of Howard Dean for president galvanized many rank-and-file Democrats who were angry that their representatives in Congress had appeared cowed not by terrorists

but by George W. Bush. Dean's statement that he was running from "the Democratic wing of the Democratic party"[2] won thunderous applause at campaign rallies and galvanized many Democrats to turn out to vote in the primaries. Democratic turnout in the early 2004 primaries was at near-record highs, and anger toward the president grew among Democratic activists.

We are in a period of intense partisanship. Partisan voting in Congress was near all-time highs in 2003. By mid-2004, almost all Americans had made up their minds about their choice in the November presidential election, far earlier than normal. People either loved the president or despised him. Few were in between. One Democratic leader from California remarked that "the other team has a player we all hate, and we're going to take it out on that team in the field."[3] A Republican countered, "Hey, you're picking on my brother here. . . . Back off or I'll punch you in the nose." Vice President Cheney broke with Senate decorum and publicly used a strong vulgarity in cursing a Democratic senator on the Senate floor. A pollster reported that "we've become two warring nations" as incivility spread from Washington to the rest of the country.[4]

Another pollster measured this partisan intensity. Adding the proportion of Democrats who strongly disapproved of Bush to the percentage of Republicans who strongly approve of him, he calculated an "intensity rate" of 137 percent. This rate is significantly higher than that of Bill Clinton (92 percent), himself a polarizing figure,

and nearly double the rate for Clinton's predecessor, George H. W. Bush.[5]

The short run of bipartisanship should not be a surprise. Disagreements are inevitable in a democratic society, and it is through political parties that they are resolved. Bipartisanship has serious defects. When individuals are afraid or unwilling to challenge the prevailing view, the nation is likely to fall victim to bad decisions. Looking back, it appears that the USA PATRIOT Act was an extreme reaction to 9/11 and that the war in Iraq was a diversion from the central objective of rooting out terrorism. If the Democrats had been less hesitant to challenge the president as these policies were worked out, and if the Republicans had not eagerly grabbed the "soft on terrorism" charge against Democrats critical of President Bush, it is possible that compromise solutions would have been better, had wider support, and created a less hateful environment for the election of 2004 and Bush's second term. Bipartisanship plays well in campaign speeches, but it is partisanship that serves the interests of a diverse nation.

[1]Paul Glastris, "Perverse Polarity," *Washington Monthly*, June 2004, 23.
[2]A phrase credited to the late Paul Wellstone, Democratic senator from Minnesota.
[3]Miles Benson, "Campaign Incites '2 Warring Nations,' *Harrisburg Patriot-News*, July 11, 2004.
[4]Ibid.
[5]Ibid.

SOURCES: Helen Dewar, "United They Stand," *Washington Post National Weekly Edition*, November 26, 2001, 14; Karen Foerstel, "Congress and the President: A Recalibration of Power," *CQ Weekly*, September 29, 2001, 2248–2251; David S. Broder, "Fighting over the Economy" *Washington Post National Weekly Edition*, November 5, 2001, 4.

they have one. If they do not, they abstain. On the basis of this simple idea, Kelley explains more than 85 percent of the variation among voters in voting choice.[67]

To be sure, the following elements are involved:

1. the party of the candidate, which has a great effect on how the voter views everything else about a candidate,

2. the candidate's personality, style, and appearance, and

3. the issue stands of the candidate and the party.

Despite considerable disagreement as to exactly how each of these is weighted in voters' minds, political scientists have come to some general conclusions.

Party Identification

Party identification is probably the most important factor influencing a person's vote: Democrats tend to vote for Democrats and Republicans for Republicans. This is true for the president, members of Congress, the state legislature, city council, and local sheriff. Moreover, party influences how a voter perceives a candidate, his or her personality and issue positions. For some people, party identification is their only source of information about candidates, and they vote on that basis alone.

Though partisan loyalties are not as strong as in the early twentieth century, they are still a powerful predictor of the vote. Even though there are more Independents today and more people who vote contrary to their partisan loyalties than there used to be, if you are guessing how a person will vote, the best single bit of information to have is the person's party identification.

In 2000, for example, among those who went to the polls, 86 percent of all Democrats voted for Gore and 91 percent of all Republicans voted for Bush.[68] These percentages were similar in the 1998 and 2002 off-year elections. Similarly, a CNN poll in the spring of 2004 showed that 97 percent of Democrats and Republicans intended to vote for their party's nominee.[69]

How do people get to be Republicans and Democrats? Socioeconomic class is an important element. The lower one's income, the more likely he or she is to be a Democrat. But this general rule is circumvented by ethnic and religious ties (*ethnic* here refers to differences in national origin and race) and is reflected in different levels of party support in voting.

For example, Jews are much more likely to vote Democratic than other whites of similar income. On the whole, they have a higher-than-average income, yet in both 2000 and 2004, around three-fourths of Jewish voters voted Democratic. As a group, they were exceeded in their Democratic allegiance only by blacks.[70]

Catholics used to be predominantly Democratic. They still are, but not as consistently. Though a majority of Catholics voted for Reagan in 1980 and 1984, they returned to the Democratic fold in the 1990s. They favored Clinton by significant margins but gave Gore only a small plurality. In 2004, they gave a small plurality to Bush over Kerry.

African Americans are probably the most distinctive group politically. About 90 percent voted Democratic in 2000 and again in 2004; this is a higher proportion than Democrats who voted for Clinton.

Hispanics—who, like blacks, also have lower-than-average incomes—are not as universally Democratic as blacks and have voted Republican in significant numbers. Nevertheless, almost three-quarters voted Democratic in recent congressional elections and from slightly over half to around two-thirds for recent Democratic presidential candidates. Bush was more popular with Hispanics than several other recent Republican candidates. Among Hispanics, Cuban Americans are much more likely to be Republican than either Mexican Americans or Puerto Ricans. Many are refugees or descendants of refugees from Castro's Cuba and are intensely anticommunist.

The voting behavior of Asian Americans has been much less thoroughly studied than that of other groups (because until recently they were a small group). In 1992 and 1996, their voting patterns resembled those of whites, with a small plurality in favor of the Republican candidates, but in 2000 and 2004, a strong majority of Asian Americans voted Democratic.

White Protestants generally give a majority of their vote to the Republican Party and have done so for decades. Evangelical Protestants (such as Southern Baptists and members of the Assembly of God) are much more likely to vote Republican than mainline Protestants (such as Episcopalians or Presbyterians). However, as with other groups, income differences and the degree of commitment to the faith can influence how Protestants vote.

Ethnicity and religion are important in determining the vote because they reflect many other factors that influence political behavior—class, historical treatment by society, and basic culture and values. Jews are predominantly Democratic, for example, because as a persecuted minority throughout much of their history they have learned to identify with the party that traditionally has supported the underdog, even when their own economic circumstances move them into the

"This year I'm not getting involved in any complicated issues. I'm just voting my straight ethnic prejudices."

middle or upper class. Catholics were sometimes discriminated against too; this discrimination and their working-class status propelled them to the party of Roosevelt. As Catholics have moved into the middle class and as intolerance toward Catholics has diminished, Catholics, like Protestants, have tended to vote according to their income.

Candidate Evaluations

Candidates' personalities and styles have had more impact since television has become voters' major source of information about elections. Reagan's popularity in 1984 is an example of the influence of a candidate and his personality. The perceived competence and integrity of candidates are other facets of candidate evaluation. Voters are less likely to support candidates who do not seem capable of handling the job, regardless of their issue positions. Jimmy Carter suffered in 1980 because of negative evaluations of his competence and leadership among voters.

Clinton's popularity puzzled some observers. Many voters did not like his evasions and his adulterous behavior, but they voted for him anyway. During the impeachment debates, many journalists expressed amazement that Clinton's popularity remained high. The public, more than journalists, seemed to be able to separate his public and private roles. The public continued to support him because they felt he was doing a good job as president, not because they admired him personally.

Personality was important in the 2004 campaign. John Kerry seemed unable to connect with people and uncomfortable on the campaign trail. At times, he appeared to be going through the motions, playing a role. In answering questions, he often provided lengthy and detailed responses. George Bush, on the other hand, seemed more at ease, comfortable working the crowd. His responses were often truncated and general. However, both candidates' performances in the first debate raised questions about the accuracy of these characterizations. Kerry appeared calm and at ease, his answers crisp and concise. Bush seemed impatient and snarly. Regardless, the image of Kerry as an effete, somewhat snobbish, Boston patrician who was out of touch with average Americans dogged him throughout the campaign.

Issues

Issues are a third factor influencing the vote. Although Americans are probably more likely to vote on issues now than they were in the 1950s, issues influence only

© David Scull

Republicans have allied themselves with conservative Christians, especially church-going Protestant evangelicals. George W. Bush uses their language.

some of the voters some of the time. In 1984 and 1988, for example, voters' issue positions overall were closer to the positions of Mondale and Dukakis than to Reagan and Bush, yet the latter won. In 2000, voters saw themselves as much closer to Gore than Bush on the issues.[71]

To cast an **issue vote,** voters quite obviously must have a position on an issue. In recent elections, more than 80 percent of the public had a position on issues such as government spending, military spending, and women's rights.[72] An issue vote also requires the candidates to differ with respect to their issue positions and for the voters to recognize this difference. A substantial minority of voters are able to detect some differences among the issue positions of presidential candidates.[73] Lastly, voters must cast their vote for the candidate that reflects their position on the issue or at least the candidate that is closest to their issue position.

In every election since 1972, more than 70 percent of those who met these conditions cast issue votes.[74] Issues with the highest proportion of issue voting were those that typically divided Republicans and Democrats, such as government spending, military spending, and government aid to the unemployed and minorities. However, because many in the electorate were unable to define both their own and the candidates' positions on each issue, the proportion of the total electorate that can be said to cast an "issue vote" is usually less than 40 percent, and for some issues it is much less.[75] Abortion is another issue on which voters cast issue-related votes. In 1996, for example, about 60 percent of the voters cast issue-related votes on abortion. Of those voters (who had a position and also knew the candidates' position), 15 percent of those who opposed abortion under any conditions voted for Clinton, a supporter of abortion rights, compared with 81 percent of those who believed that abortion should be a matter of personal choice.[76]

Issue voting may be mostly an evaluation of the current incumbents. If voters like the way incumbents, or the incumbent's party, have handled the job in general or in certain areas—the economy or foreign policy, for example—they will vote accordingly, even without much knowledge about the specifics of the issues.

Voting on the basis of past performance is called **retrospective voting.** There is good evidence that many people do this, especially according to economic conditions.[77] Voters support incumbents if national income is growing in the months preceding the election. Since World War II, the incumbent party has won a presidential election only once when the growth rate was less than 3 percent (Eisenhower in 1956) and lost only twice when it was more than 3 percent (Ford in 1976 and Gore in 2000). Unemployment and inflation seem to have less consistent effects on voting, and economic conditions two or three years before the election have little impact on voting.[78]

Table 7.2 shows the relationship of the presidential vote in 2004 to perceptions of approval and disapproval of President Bush's handling of the economy. Ninety-six percent of those who strongly approved of his handling of the economy voted for him; only 3 percent voted for John Kerry. Only 13 percent of those who strongly disapproved his handling voted for him, while 84 percent voted for Kerry.

The first President Bush was defeated in 1992 when the economy stagnated; on the other hand,

Clinton's reelection in 1996 was assisted by the booming economy. In fact, political scientists believe that economic growth in the months before the election is one of the best predictors of election results. For that reason, many were perplexed by the close 2000 election and sought to explain it in terms of Gore's poor campaign. Other pundits, though, thought perhaps that the economy had been so good for so long that people took good times for granted.[79]

Parties, Candidates, and Issues

All three factors—parties, candidates, and issues—clearly matter. Party loyalties are especially important because they help shape our views about issues and candidates. However, if issues and candidates did not matter, the Democrats would have won every presidential election since the New Deal. Republican victories suggest that they often have had more attractive candidates (as in 1952, 1956, 1980, and 1984) or issue positions (in 1972 and in some respects in 1980). However, the Democrats' partisan advantage shrank throughout the 1980s. Although there are still more registered Democrats than Republicans in the United States, the margin is slight, and the number of Independents is large enough to tilt the outcome.

Party loyalty, candidate evaluations, and issues are important factors in congressional elections just as in presidential ones. Voting in congressional elections is discussed in Chapter 9.

Conclusion: Do Political Parties Make Government More Responsive?

Although the Founders initially opposed the idea of political parties, some later turned to parties when they began to have serious differences of opinion about public policies. They recognized that their ideas could prevail if they aligned with others who agreed with them and together elected a majority in government. Then, as now, parties were a vehicle to organize a stable majority.

Parties are also a way for average Americans to influence government policy. Making government more accountable to voters is the major contribution of political parties to democratic government. Political parties provide an easily identifiable majority, at least in two-party systems, that voters can blame when things go wrong and reward when things go right and in the process turn public policy in the direction they prefer.

TABLE 7.2	Position on President Bush's Handling of the Economy Strongly Predicts Voting in 2004	
President's Handling of the Economy	**Vote for President**	
	Bush	**Kerry**
Approve Strongly	96	3
Approve Not Strongly	83	14
Disapprove Not Strongly	30	65
Disapprove Strongly	13	84

SOURCE: National Election Studies, 2004.

Although American political parties may not always perform exactly as described, Americans have an interest in maintaining strong and viable political parties. Without them, voters would be confronted with a hopelessly confusing array of candidates and have no idea of how a vote for any one of them will influence government policy. Without parties, the media, campaign consultants, lobbying groups, big donors, and self-financed wealthy candidates would play an even larger role in politics than they do now.

There is no doubt that parties are weaker than they were a century ago. They have, however, experienced a resurgence in the past two or three decades in several important ways. The movement of voters toward independence and the erosion of party attachments appear to have reached an end. The proportion of voters claiming partisan allegiance has grown slightly after steady declines since the 1960s. Split-ticket voting peaked in 1992 but has since declined (see Figure 7.4).

Party loyalty among officeholders is also stronger. Party cohesion in Congress has increased. With the demise of the Southern Democratic conservatives, the Democratic Party is much more homogeneous. Many members of both parties are more dependent on the national party committees for campaign support than they were a decade ago. Both of these trends have contributed to the increase in party voting and support for the president by his own party.

Finally, national party organizations have become much more powerful. Their activities are fueled by their ability to raise and spend large amounts of money. New campaign finance laws might channel the flow, but they are unlikely to reduce it significantly (for more on this topic, see Chapter 9).

Although parties still compete for influence with interest groups, pollsters, campaign consultants, and the media, it is often funds raised by the national parties that buy the polling, campaign consultation, and media time. Both presidential and congressional candidates need the national party organizations to aid in raising revenue and providing other services.

Each component of American political parties— partisans in the electorate, officeholders, and party organization—has shown significant signs of revitalization. Each party has its core of supporters, seeking to achieve the party's goals, but neither has come up with a program that has appeal and energizes a wide cross section of the American people. This, of course, is the role that Schattschneider saw for political parties and that led him to reflect on the inevitability and necessity of parties for American democracy.

oward Dean and the Democratic National Committee (DNC) continued to distribute funds to build state organizations. They hired local organizers and media specialists and held party caucuses in areas where it had been a generation since the party had shown so much activity. At the same time, they accelerated their fund raising to support these activities and raised millions more to funnel to the Democratic Senatorial Campaign Committee and the Democratic Congressional Campaign Committee. Though there continued to be tensions between the DNC and the leaders of the Senate and House campaign committees, Charles Schumer (D-NY) and Rahm Emanuel (D-Ill), their combined efforts raised more money than Democrats had ever raised in off-year elections, and much of it was targeted to key districts in areas that the Democrats had not won in many years.

As the election day polls closed in the eastern time zone, it became clear that the Democrats' strategies were working. Democrats picked up three new House seats in Republican strongholds in Indiana, another two in Ohio,

and five in Pennsylvania, where Democrats now held a strong majority of the state's nineteen congressional seats. Across the nation, Democrats picked up twenty-eight House seats, including in eighteen largely rural districts held by Republicans, districts that in 2004 gave Republicans solid majorities. Democrats also won congressional elections in formerly Republican suburbs. The next day, Americans learned that the Democrats had picked up six seats to capture the Senate majority, too, with key victories in once solidly Republican Ohio and Virginia, in Missouri, and perhaps most surprisingly, in Montana, where Jon Tester bested three-term Senator Conrad Burns.

It was not only the Democratic strategies that led to their gains; the Republicans fumbled their chances in an overall environment of arrogance and privilege. A combination of an unpopular war, incompetent handling of the Katrina hurricane damage, a continuous string of financial and moral scandals, and reckless spending that antagonized the financial conservatives in the party gave the Democrats a huge opening. With that opening,

the Democratic strategy to build their organization and engage the Republicans in some of their strongest areas proved successful. The Republicans, as always, had more money to spend, but they were forced to deploy their resources across more districts than typical. Districts that in the summer they counted on to be solidly Republican suddenly were "in play." President Bush, for example, in the weekend before the election, flew to the third district of Nebraska, one of the most rural in the nation, and a district where the Democrats had worked to rebuild their party organization, to help the Republican candidate hold the seat for Republicans. Though the Republicans held that seat, and many others, in the aftermath of the election the Republicans were evaluating their own campaign strategy and its failures, while Howard Dean and his colleagues were ebullient.

To learn more about this topic, go to "you are there" exercises for this chapter on the text website.

Key Terms

party system	political patronage
two-party system	New Deal coalition
multiparty system	party identification
single-member districts	dealignment
winner take all	split-ticket voting
proportional representation	responsible party government
realignment	national party chair
machine politics	national committee
Progressive movement	issue vote
retrospective voting	

Further Reading

David Brooks, ed., *Backward and Forward: The New Conservative Writing* (New York: Vintage, 1996). This is a collection of combative, often funny essays from the political right. The authors lampoon various liberal beliefs, showing that conservatism is as much about personality as about ideology.

James Carville, *We're Right, They're Wrong: A Handbook for Spirited Progressives* (New York: Random House, 1996). In this book, President Clinton's chief campaign adviser and one of Washington's most prominent Democratic strategists responds to the Republicans' platform during the 1992 and 1996 elections. Carville includes such features as the Republicans' "Biggest Lies" and "Most Expensive Boondoggles."

Congressional Quarterly, *National Party Conventions, 1831–1996* (Washington, D.C.: CQ Press, 1997). All you ever wanted to know about each party's national nominating conventions, including lists of keynote speakers, platforms, delegate selection rules, and nominees.

David J. Gillespie, *Politics at the Periphery: Third Parties in Two-Party America* (Columbia: University of South Carolina Press, 1993). This work provides both a historical review of the roles played by third parties in American politics and a look at the impact of recent third parties on election outcomes.

Stanley B. Greenberg, *Middle-Class Dreams: The Politics and Power of the New American Majority* (New York: Times Books, 1990). President Clinton's adviser looks at the radical shape of American politics today and contends that both political parties have betrayed the middle class.

Edwin O'Connor, *The Last Hurrah* (New York: Bantam, 1957). A warm, intimate novel set in Boston in the 1950s that contrasts the old-style party election campaigns with new media-oriented ones.

William L. Riordon, *Plunkitt of Tammany Hall* (New York: Dutton, 1963). This book preserves a series of witty talks given by a ward boss of New York City's Democratic Party machine. A slice of Americana, the book discusses "honest graft" and other aspects of "practical politics" and in the process demonstrates why political machines flourished.

Mike Royko, *Boss: Richard J. Daley of Chicago* (New York: New American Library, 1971). This is an intriguing account of how the Chicago political machine operated under Mayor Richard J. Daley, who served from 1955 until his death in 1976.

Larry Sabato and Bruce Larson, *The Party's Just Begun*, 2nd edition. (New York: Longman, 2001). Sabato and Larson provide an overview of the American party system, explaining why we need it, what it does, and how we can make it work better.

Ruy Teixeira and Joel Rogers, *Why the White Working Class Still Matters* (New York: Basic Books, 2000). These authors explain why it is necessary to gain the support of the white working class in order to put together a strong party coalition and what each party can do to succeed at it.

For Viewing

The Last Hurrah (1958). This is the film version of the novel of the same name listed in Further Reading.

Tanner: A Political Fable (1988). Filmmaker Robert Altman and Pulitzer Prize-winning cartoonist Garry Trudeau are creators of this mock-documentary television miniseries that profiles a fictitious presidential candidate on the campaign trail and sheds a revelatory light on America's political process and landscape.

Last Man Standing—Politics Texas Style (2004). The film profiles a race for the Texas state legislature and reviews many of the forces at work in national politics in multicultural and urban Texas of the future that leans democratic and ascendant Republicans of the suburbs and in politically active churches.

 **Electronic Resources**

www.whitehouse.gov
The White House

www.rnc.org
Republican National Committee

www.democrats.org
Democratic National Committee

www.nrsc.org
National Republican Senatorial Committee

www.dscc.org
Democratic Senatorial Campaign Committee

www.nrcc.org
National Republican Congressional Committee

www.dccc.org
Democratic Congressional Campaign Committee

www.gop.gov
Republican House Conference

www.townhall.com
Conservative News and Information

www.epn.org
Liberal News and Information

www.politicalindex.com/sect8.htm
Link to the minor parties involved in U.S. politics

www.greenparty.org
Green Party, USA

ThomsonNOW

Enter ThomsonNOW™ using the access card that is available with this text or through www.thomsonedu.com/thomsonnow. ThomsonNOW™ will assist you in understanding the content in this chapter with a personalized study plan generated for your needs. A practice test will assess the areas you need to review and provide the tools to fully comprehend those concepts, including an integrated digital eBook, interactive simulations, timelines, video case studies, MicroCase exercises, and InfoTrac College Edition readers and exercises. You'll also be connected to the learning objectives, chapter outline, chapter glossary, flash cards, crossword puzzles, Internet activities, and interactive quizzes found on the companion website.

Karl Rove has been the chief political strategist for President Bush and the Republican Party.

The American Electorate

Early Limits on Voting Rights

Blacks and the Right to Vote

The Voting Rights Act and Redistricting

Women and the Right to Vote

Young People and the Right to Vote

Felons and the Right to Vote

Electoral Reform and New Threats
to Voting Rights

Voter Turnout

Political Activism in the Nineteenth
Century

Progressive Reforms

Recent Turnout

Who Does Not Vote?

Why Turnout Is Low

Presidential Nominating Campaigns

Who Runs for President and Why?

How a Candidate Wins the Nomination

Presidential Caucuses and Conventions

Presidential Primaries

Reforming the Nomination Process

The National Conventions

Independent and Third-Party Nominees

The General Election Campaign

Campaign Organization

Campaign Strategies

Campaign Communication

Campaign Funding

The Electoral College

The 2000 Election: A Perfect Storm

Voting Patterns in the 2004 Election

The Permanent Campaign

Congressional Campaigns

Incumbents: Unsafe at Any Margin?

Challengers

Campaigns

Voting for Congress

**Conclusion: Do Elections Make
Government Responsive?**

YOU ARE THERE

Should You Run on the War?

You are Karl Rove, deputy chief of staff to President George W. Bush. It is spring 2006, and you must work out a strategy so that the Republicans can be successful in the 2006 midterm elections. Being successful means retaining majorities in both the House and Senate, majorities that could be threatened by the increased unpopularity of the war in Iraq and the other problems that have beset the president in his second term.

Your title of deputy chief of staff does not fully reveal your importance to the Bush administration. You also head the Office of Political Affairs and the Office of Strategic Initiatives in the White House. Mostly, these positions reflect the fact that you are the chief advisor to the president on political strategies. Indeed, more than one person has referred to you as "Bush's Brain,"[1] reflecting your importance as a political strategist throughout the president's career.

Considered a political genius by many in the press and political community, you have been part of the political careers of George W. Bush and his father George H.W. Bush for more than thirty years. As head of your own political consulting firm, you worked on dozens of campaigns. Although your early efforts on behalf of the Bushes failed—the son lost his 1978 election campaign to the House of Representatives, and the father lost his campaign for the White House in 1980—your later

efforts succeeded. You formulated the strategies that got George W. Bush elected governor of Texas in 1994 and 1998 and then president in 2000 and 2004.

When George W. Bush was elected president, you moved to Washington to become his full-time advisor. In that role, you made sure that the political considerations were an important part of every decision. You have been particularly skillful in making sure that the war on terrorism stays in the minds of the public. Public events and political speeches continue to focus on the "war." And announcements of terror threats seem to come at politically propitious moments, such as during the 2004 campaign, when the Democrats had good news that was getting media attention.[2]

In your role as a strategist, you have a knack for turning your opponents' greatest strength into a perceived weakness in the voters' minds. In 2004, Senator John Kerry challenged President Bush for the presidency. Kerry was a Vietnam veteran who had won medals for valor. Democrats thought that Kerry's background would protect him from any doubts that he would be a strong military leader. Democrats also thought that Kerry's background would contrast dramatically with the president's. George W. Bush had escaped the draft and the war by joining the National Guard.

© The State/Dist. by Newspaper Enterprise Association, Inc.

(At this time, Guard personnel were not used in any wars, so the Guard was a haven for those trying to avoid the war.) At the outset of the campaign, Kerry played up his experience to assure voters that he and the Democratic party were committed to America's strength and security.

Your strategy was to attack Kerry on this very point—his greatest strength. In speeches and through the media, Republican sound bites were designed to cast doubt on the validity of Kerry's (and the military's) version of Kerry's actions and wounds that won him medals in Vietnam while commanding a small "Swift Boat." Ads by the "Swift Boat Veterans for Truth" (see Chapter 9) questioned Kerry's actions and wounds and cast suspicion on his medals. At the same time, they turned attention away from Bush's avoidance of active service in the war. Kerry's initial reluctance to respond—he thought the ads were preposterous, and he thought the voters would ignore them—may have cost him the victory in the election.

You wonder if the same kind of strategic thinking is needed in 2006. That is, the war in Iraq has become an albatross around Bush's neck and consequently is being seen by Republican leaders as well as the media as a negative drag on Republican candidates in this important midyear election. But perhaps there is a way to turn this to the Republicans' advantage.

George W. Bush won reelection in 2004 with 51 percent of the vote, more than anything else because of voters' perceptions that he would keep the nation safe from terrorist attacks, bring the war in Iraq to a successful conclusion, and show strong leadership.[3] Within a few days after the horrifying 9/11 attack, Bush's public support rose to more than 90 percent, and it stayed near there for months, longer than any president since Roosevelt.[4]

The president used this public support to advance his conservative agenda. And you and other Republicans challenged Democrats who tried to pursue their own agenda by questioning their loyalty and commitment to fight the terrorists. Even routine legislative matters, seemingly unrelated to the war on terror, such as subsidies for airlines or crops, became entangled with 9/11 patriotic fervor

(as we saw in Chapter 6). Democratic candidates who challenged Bush were labeled as soft on terrorism—a tactic that worked very effectively (see box "Government Responsiveness in a Time of Crisis").

As Democrats were cowed by Bush's popularity, he, you, and other Republican leaders kept up a constant refrain that only the Republicans would keep America safe. For example, you said, "Conservatives saw the savagery of 9/11 in the attacks and prepared for war; liberals saw the savagery of the 9/11 attacks and wanted to prepare indictments and offer therapy and understanding for our attackers."[5] Although every Democratic senator voted for the invasion of Afghanistan, your comments were effective in putting them on the defensive. And so it went for nearly two years after the attacks.

As the war in Iraq became increasingly unpopular, Bush's popularity had dramatically declined by the time of the 2004 election. Nonetheless, most Americans felt he would do a better job in protecting them from terrorism. He was reelected and the Republicans retained control of both houses of Congress. You were again lauded as a political genius.

Now in 2006, the Democrats need to capture fifteen seats to win the House.[6] That's not many, but given redistricting that has made most districts safe for incumbents, it is an uphill challenge. In the Senate, Democrats need to win six new seats. Several of your incumbents are in trouble, but so are several Democratic incumbents. So, it will be an uphill struggle for the Democrats there, too. You hope that your strategy could enable several Republicans in marginal districts to eke

Americans have fought and died in wars to preserve the rights of citizens to choose their leaders through democratic elections. Some have even died here at home, trying to exercise these rights. Despite this, most Americans take these important rights for granted; about half do not bother to vote even in presidential elections, and fewer still participate in other ways.

Moreover, the process by which we choose our leaders, especially the president, has been sharply criticized in recent years. Critics charge that election campaigns are meaningless and offer little information to

out a victory and thus hold on to both the House and Senate.

Democrats have found several appealing candidates, several of them Iraqi war veterans, to run against vulnerable Republican incumbents. They are threatening many heretofore safe Republican districts.[7] Polls show that more registered voters indicate that they will vote for the Democratic candidate in the fall than the Republican one.[8] Should the Democrats win control of even one house of Congress, in addition to an angry public, you will be faced with an opposition majority unwilling to look favorably on any new Republican policy initiatives. Democratic majors might also open investigations into Bush's handling of the war, domestic spying, and lucrative Iraq contracts gained by big Republican donors.

Although the core Democratic electorate has turned against the war, Democratic officeholders are far from united. Most say the president should never have dragged the country into the war, but others say the problem is that the administration was incompetent in the way it fought the war. Some think our troops should be withdrawn now, but others think our troops should remain for the time being. Thus, division among the Democrats offers you a possibility for the 2006 elections. You could continue to argue that opposition to the Iraq war is equivalent to support for the terrorists and paint the Democrats as the party that wants to run from the enemy. If you make Iraq the issue, and portray anti-Iraq War sentiment as pro-terrorism, you can count on most of your party uniting behind the president. Although the vast majority of Democrats are unlikely to be persuaded by your argument, it might attract enough Independents to your Republican core to carry the day.

But there are drawbacks to this strategy. It worked in 2004, but the president's popularity was higher and public confidence much higher then. Since the president was reelected, things have not been going so well. Now less than 40 percent think Bush is doing a good job, and the ratings keep sliding.[9] Only 30 percent approve of his handling of the Iraqi war, and a majority now believes the country should not have gotten involved in the first place.[10] Even the troops in Iraq are disillusioned; more than 70 percent think the United States should exit within the year.[11]

The administration's poor response to the devastation of hurricane Katrina in New Orleans and the Mississippi Gulf Coast has also eroded the president's reputation as a strong leader and protector of the country's well-being. And his major domestic initiative since reelection, privatizing part of Social Security, has sunk like a stone. Corruption scandals led to the indictment of the House majority leader, Tom DeLay, and another Republican representative. Other Republican officials are under investigation. Many Republican candidates are trying to disassociate themselves from the administration and its policies. And many members of your conservative base are also becoming antagonistic. Some are unhappy that instead of cutting government spending, you are growing it substantially; others are upset with Bush's immigration proposal that, in their view, is not tough enough on those who enter the country illegally; still others believe Bush has botched the Iraqi War by not sending enough troops to get the job done.[12] Although it is highly unlikely that many conservative Republicans would vote for Democratic candidates in the fall, many are threatening not to vote at all.

Thus, a second possible strategy would be to emphasize wooing back these social conservatives. To do that, you could focus on hot-button issues such as gay rights, abortion, and flag burning by developing legislative bills to be discussed and voted on. Although it is unlikely that a flag-burning amendment or one banning gay marriage would pass both houses of Congress, it would give Republicans a chance to show their support and force Democrats to oppose them. Though this strategy would not win many Democrats or Independents, it would energize your base and make sure they will turn out in the fall elections.

Or do you stay out of the midterm election campaigns, hoping that Republican candidates can win by focusing on local issues? This has been the traditional approach. Generally, presidents do not have much impact on midterm elections, though George W. Bush did campaign hard, and fairly successfully, in 2002, the first midterm election of his administration. The common wisdom, documented by historical experience, is that midterm elections are largely focused on local issues and personalities.

So, what do you do? Do you turn your attention to Iraq and try to portray the Democrats as sympathizers with the terrorists? This worked in the 2002 and 2004 elections, but in 2006 risks elevating an unpopular war led by your administration to the most salient issue. Do you focus on Bush's desire to implement a conservative social agenda? Or do you stay out of the midterm election campaigns, hoping that Republican candidates can win by focusing on local issues?

the voters, that candidates pander to the most ill-informed and mean-spirited citizens, and that public relations and campaign spending, not positions on issues or strength of character, determine the winners. Then in 2000, and again in 2004, it also became apparent that some voters' votes were not counted even when they went to the polls, largely due to defects in the election process itself.

In this chapter, we analyze why voting is important to a democracy and why, despite its importance, so few do it. Then we examine political campaigns and elections to see how they affect the kinds of leaders and policies we have. We will see that the lack of participation by many reinforces the government's responsiveness to those who do participate, especially those who are well organized.

The American Electorate

During the more than two centuries since the Constitution was written, two important developments have altered the right to vote, termed **suffrage.** First, suffrage gradually was extended to include almost all citizens aged eighteen or over. This expansion occurred largely through federal action: constitutional amendments, congressional acts, and Supreme Court decisions. Second, recently, serious issues of lack of access to the ballot have occurred. These limitations are largely being imposed by several states under the guise of ensuring that only eligible voters vote.

Early Limits on Voting Rights

Although the Declaration of Independence states that "all men are created equal," at the time of the Constitution and shortly thereafter, the central political right of voting was denied to most Americans. States decided who would be granted suffrage. In some, only an estimated 10 percent of the white males could vote, whereas in others 80 percent could.[13]

Controversial property qualifications for voting existed in many states. Some argued that only those with an economic stake in society should have a say in political life. But critics of the property requirement repeated a story of Tom Paine's:

> You require that a man shall have $60 worth of property, or he shall not vote. Very well . . . here is a man who today owns a jackass, and the jackass is worth $60. Today the man is a voter and he goes to the polls and deposits his vote. Tomorrow the jackass dies. The next day the man comes to vote without his jackass and he cannot vote at all. Now tell me, which was the voter, the man or the jackass?[14]

Because the Constitution gave states the power to regulate suffrage, the elimination of property requirements was a gradual process. By the 1820s, most were gone, although some lingered to midcentury.

In some states, religious tests also were applied. A voter had to be a member of the "established" church or could not be a member of certain religions (such as Roman Catholicism or Judaism). However, religious tests disappeared even more quickly than property qualifications.

By the time of the Civil War, state action had expanded the rights of white men. However, neither slaves, Indians, nor free southern blacks could vote, although northern blacks could in a few states.[15] Women's voting rights were confined to local elections in a few states.[16]

Blacks and the Right to Vote

The Civil War began the long, slow, and often violent process of expanding the rights of blacks to full citizenship. Between 1865 and 1870, three amendments were passed to give political rights to former slaves and other blacks. One, the Fifteenth Amendment, prohibited the denial of voting rights on the basis of race and thus gave the right to vote to black men.

For a short time following the ratification of this amendment, a northern military presence in the South and close monitoring of southern politics enabled blacks to vote and hold office in the South, where 90 percent of all blacks lived. During this **Reconstruction** period, two southern blacks were elected to the Senate and fourteen were elected to the House of Representatives between 1869 and 1876. One state, South Carolina, even had a black majority in its legislature.

Blacks comprised a majority of the population in South Carolina in 1866, and elected a black majority to the state legislature. The black legislators worked for civil rights, black male suffrage, and state constitutional reform. Radical is the name given to Republicans at that time.

In most places blacks did not dominate politics or even receive a proportional share of offices; whites saw blacks' political activities as a threat to their own dominance. White southerners began to prevent blacks from voting through intimidation that ranged from mob violence and lynchings to economic sanctions against blacks who attempted to vote.

Northerners tolerated these methods, both violent and nonviolent. The northern public and political leaders had lost interest in the fate of blacks or had simply grown tired of the struggle. In 1876, a compromise ended Reconstruction. In the wake of the disputed 1876 presidential election, southern Democrats agreed to support Republican Rutherford B. Hayes for president in return for an end to the northern military presence in the South and a hands-off policy toward activities there.

By the end of the nineteenth century, blacks were effectively disfranchised in all of the South. The last southern black member of Congress served to 1901. Another would not be elected until 1972.

Southern constitutions and laws legitimized the loss of black voting rights. **Literacy tests** were often required, supposedly to make sure voters could read and write and thus evaluate political information. Most blacks, who had been denied education, were illiterate. Many whites also were illiterate, but fewer were barred from voting. Local election registrars exercised nearly complete discretion in deciding who had to take the test and how to administer and evaluate it. Educated blacks often were asked for legal interpretations of obscure constitutional provisions, which few could provide.

Some laws had exemptions that whites were allowed to take advantage of. An "understanding clause" exempted those who could not read and write but who could explain sections of the federal or state constitution to the satisfaction of the examiner, and a "good moral character clause" exempted those with such character. Again, local election registrars exercised discretion in deciding who understood the Constitution and who had good character. Finally, the **grandfather clause** exempted those whose grandfathers had the right to vote before 1867—that is, before blacks could legally vote in the South.

The **poll tax** also deprived blacks of voting rights. The tax, though only a couple of dollars, was often a sizable portion of working people's monthly income. In some states, individuals had to pay not only for the present election, but also for every past election in which they were eligible to vote but did not.

In the **white primary,** blacks were barred from voting in primary elections, where party nominees were chosen. Because the Democrats always won the general elections, the real contests were in the Democratic primaries. The states justified excluding blacks on the grounds that political parties were private rather than government organizations and thus could discriminate just as private clubs or individuals could.

Less formal means were also used to exclude blacks from voting. Registrars often closed their offices when blacks tried to register, or whites threatened blacks with the loss of jobs or housing if they tried to vote. Polling places were sometimes located far from black neighborhoods or were moved at the last minute without notifying potential voters. If these means failed, whites threatened or practiced violence. In one election in Mobile, Alabama, whites wheeled a cannon to a polling place and aimed it at about one thousand blacks lined up to vote.

The treatment of blacks by the southern establishment was summarized on the floor of the Senate by South Carolina Senator Benjamin ("Pitchfork Ben") Tillman, who served from 1895 to 1918. As he put it, "We took the government away. We stuffed ballot boxes. We shot them. We are not ashamed of it."[17]

Over time, the Supreme Court and Congress outlawed the "legal" barriers to black voting in the South. The Court invalidated the grandfather clause in 1915 and the white primary in 1944. Through the Twenty-fourth Amendment, Congress abolished the poll tax for federal elections in 1964, and the Court invalidated the tax for state elections in 1966.[18] But threats of physical violence and economic reprisals still kept most southern blacks from voting. Although many blacks in the urban areas of the rim South (such as Florida, North Carolina, Tennessee, and Texas) could and did vote, those in the rural South and most in the Deep South could not; in 1960, black voter registration ranged from 5 to 40 percent in southern states.[19] (See the box titled "Blacks and Hispanics in Office.")

The Voting Rights Act and Redistricting

Despite our shameful history of depriving African Americans the right to vote, today black voting rates approach those of whites. In the Deep South, much of this dramatic change was brought about by the 1965 passage of the **Voting Rights Act (VRA),** which made it illegal to interfere with anyone's right to vote. The act abolished the use of literacy tests, and, most important, it sent federal voter registrars into counties where less than 50 percent of the voting age population (black and white) was registered. The premise of this requirement was that if so few had registered, there must be serious barriers to registration. Registrars were sent to all of Alabama, Mississippi, South Carolina, and Louisiana, substantial parts of North Carolina, and scattered counties in six other states.[20]

Blacks line up to vote in Peachtree, Alabama, after enactment of the Voting Rights Act of 1965.

Any changes in election procedures had to be approved by the Department of Justice or the U.S. District Court for the District of Columbia. States or counties had to show a clean record of not discriminating for ten years before they could escape this supervision. Those who sought to deter blacks from voting through intimidation now had to face the force of the federal government.

Though black registration had been increasing in the rim South due to voter registration and education projects, the impact of the VRA in the Deep South was dramatic.[21] Within a year after federal registrars were sent, hundreds of thousands of southern blacks were registered, radically changing the nature of southern politics. In the most extreme case, Mississippi registration of blacks zoomed from 7 to 41 percent. In Alabama, the black electorate doubled in four years.

Due to these increases, not only have dozens of blacks been elected, but white politicians must now court black voters to get elected. Even the late George Wallace, the segregationist Alabama governor who had opposed the civil rights movement in the 1960s, eagerly sought black votes in the 1970s and 1980s.

The VRA was renewed and expanded in 1970, 1975, 1982, and again in 2006, despite some grumbling by white Republican conservatives about the continuing federal scrutiny of voting rights in the South. It now covers more states and other minorities, such as Hispanics, Asians, Native Americans, and Inuits (called Eskimos in the past), and thus serves as a basic protection for mi-

nority voting rights. For example, states must provide bilingual ballots in counties in which 5 percent or more of the population does not speak English.

The VRA dramatically changed the face of the electorate in the South and then later in other parts of the nation. Given the success of the VRA and faced with an expanded black electorate, some white officials in areas of large black populations used new means to diminish the political clout of African Americans. Their technique was **gerrymandering.** (See the box titled "Racial Gerrymandering.") Through devices that political scientists call **"cracking, stacking, and packing,"** districts were drawn to minimize black representation, depending on the size and configuration of the black and white populations. *Cracking* divides significant, concentrated black populations into two or more districts so that none will have a black majority; *stacking* combines a large black population with an even greater white population; and *packing* puts a huge black population into one district rather than two, where blacks might otherwise approach a majority in each.

Initially, the Supreme Court was reluctant to find these practices illegal without specific proof that their intent was to discriminate against black voters.[22] But in 1982, congressional revision of the VRA required states with large minority populations to draw boundaries in ways to increase the probabilities that minorities will win seats. The focus of the voting rights legislation then turned from protecting the right of suffrage

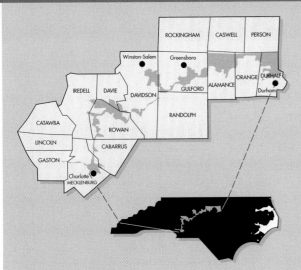

The practice of drawing strangely shaped districts to fulfill political objectives, called *gerrymandering*, is hardly new in American politics. The name originated in 1812 when the Massachusetts legislature carved out a district that historian John Fiske said had a "dragon-like contour." When painter Gilbert Stuart saw the misshapen district, he drew in a head, wings, and claws and exclaimed, "That will do for a salamander!" Editor Benjamin Russell replied, "Better say Gerrymander," after Elbridge Gerry, then governor of Massachusetts.[1] Since then, gerrymandering has been widely used by politicians to benefit their own political parties, and today is used not only to try to create districts with majority minorities, but also to protect legislative incumbents by drawing districts that include their fellow partisans and minimize the number of the opposite party.

This North Carolina district (the twelfth), shown on the maps, was drawn by its state legislature after the

1990 census to create a black majority district, and voters elected an African American in 1992. North Carolina, which is about 20 percent African American, had not elected a black representative to Congress since 1898. The state's seats, now twelve, went to whites because the black population was (and remains) relatively scattered. After redistricting in 1992, voters elected two African Americans from the twelve districts.

This Twelfth District snaked through parts of ten counties and seven of the former congressional districts as it followed Interstate 85. The district was 160 miles long and, in places, no wider than the highway corridor and, in other places, not quite this wide—the northbound and southbound lanes were in different districts. One legislator famously remarked, "if you drove down the interstate with both car doors open, you'd kill most of the people in the district." The bizarre shape was the result of the legislature's efforts to create the majority-minority district while also protecting white incumbents in other districts. Despite its strange shape, the district had some homogeneity: it was an urban district, drawing from the black populations of Charlotte, Winston-Salem, Greensboro, and Durham.

The majority of the Supreme Court, declaring the districting illegal, called the district "so irregular" and "so bizarre" that it can be understood "only as an effort to segregate the races for purposes of voting, without regard for traditional districting principles and without sufficiently compelling justification."[2] North Carolina tried redrawing its districts twice more before the Court was satisfied.

Though the redistricting was at first seen as primarily a way for African American populations to elect one of their own, Republicans supported these gerrymanders, too, for their own purposes. By concentrating black, largely Democratic, voters in a few districts, this left other districts with Republican majorities. Though the congressional and state legislative representation in the southern states was becoming more heavily Republican, these racial gerrymanders accelerated the growth of Republican representation.

[1]*Guide to Congress*, 2d ed. (Washington, D.C.: Congressional Quarterly Inc., 1976), 563; *Congressional Quarterly*, "The Race to Capitol Hill," February 29, 1992, 103–105.
[2]125 L.Ed.2d 525–526, 1993.

SOURCES: Charles Mahtesian, "Blacks' Political Hopes Boosted by Newly Redrawn Districts," *Congressional Quarterly Weekly Report*, April 25, 1992, 1087; Bruce E. Cain, "Voting Rights and Democratic Theory toward a Color-Blind Society?" *Brookings Review* (Winter 1992), 46–50; Carol M. Swain, "The Voting Rights Act: Some Unintended Consequences," *Brookings Review* (Winter 1992), 51; Douglas Amy, *Real Choices/New Voices: The Case for Proportional Representation Elections in the United States* (New York: Columbia University Press, 1993); John Gruhl and Susan Welch, "Representation and Race Conscious Districting," paper presented at the American Political Science Association meeting, August 2002.

to trying to ensure that voting rights result in the election of African American and other minority officeholders. With this new statute as an indication of congressional intent, the Court then did strike down districting in North Carolina as inappropriately diluting black voting power.[23]

After the 1990 census, eleven new **majority-minority districts** were created for blacks and six for

Hispanics. All but one were actually won by blacks and Hispanics in the 1992 election. Partly as a result of this redistricting, blacks were elected to Congress for the first time since Reconstruction in Alabama, Florida, North Carolina, South Carolina, and Virginia. Hispanics were elected for the first time ever in Illinois and New Jersey. In all, thirty-nine blacks and nineteen Hispanics were elected to Congress, a dramatic increase

Before the Voting Rights Act (VRA) in 1965, few African Americans held major public office. Only a handful were members of Congress, and few were state legislators, mayors of major cities, or other important political officers. Following the VRA, southern blacks began to have the political clout to elect members of their own race to office for the first time, and northern blacks began to increase their influence, winning races in districts where blacks were not always majorities. Progress, slow to be sure, has occurred; in 1970, there were only 179 blacks holding state and national legislative seats; by 2001, the number had more than tripled, to 633. Only two African Americans have won a governor's seat in modern times, Virginia's Douglas Wilder and, in 2006, Massachusetts' Deval Patrick. In 2004, with blacks as both major party candidates, Barack Obama (D. Ill.) won to become the only current African American member of the U.S. Senate and only the third to hold a Senate seat in the modern era.

Richard Hatcher, who became mayor of Gary, Indiana, in 1968, was the first African American mayor of a major U.S. city. By 2004, 530 African Americans served as black mayors in northern and southern cities, more than forty of them in cities of fifty thousand and more and many in communities where blacks are far less than half the population. Nationally, the number of black officeholders has increased from an estimated 1200 in 1969 to more than 9000 in 2001. Although this is far from proportional representation, it is a dramatic increase.

Hispanics, too, have improved their representation in political office. From a total of little more than 3000 Hispanic public officials in 1985, their numbers by 2004 had grown to more than 4600, including more than 200 state-elected legislators and executives.

In sum, though progress is slow, African Americans and Hispanics, like other ethnic groups, are achieving political power through elections. As a sign of their increased numbers and influence, both Hispanic and black elected officials are forming their own organizations to share ideas and plans.

SOURCE: *Statistical Abstract of the United States 2003* (Washington, D.C.: Government Printing Office, 2001), Tables 408 and 417; website of the National Council of Black Mayors, Inc, www.blackmayors.org.

Los Angeles mayor Antonio Villaraigosa

from the twenty-five blacks and ten Hispanics serving before the 1992 election.[24]

However, after this post-1990 redistricting, which used extensive gerrymandering to create the majority-minority districts, some white voters challenged their legality. In a series of cases, the Supreme Court then ruled that racial gerrymandering, the drawing of district lines specifically to concentrate racial minorities to try to ensure the election of minority representatives, is as constitutionally suspect as the drawing of district lines to diffuse minority electoral strength.[25]

To the surprise of many, despite the consequent redrawing of several majority-minority districts after the 1994 election, the African American incumbents were still able to win reelection in 1996 and after.

Creating majority-minority districts has affected the partisan composition of some southern states. Black voters were redistricted from solid Democratic districts to create new majority black districts. This left their old districts with Republican majorities and helped Republicans get their first victories in eighteen congressional districts in the 1994 elections.

Women's contributions to the war effort during World War I helped lead to the ratification of the women's suffrage amendment in 1920. Here Broadway chorus women train as Home Guards during the war.

Women and the Right to Vote

When property ownership defined the right to vote, women property owners could vote in some places. When property requirements were removed, suffrage came to be seen as only a male right. Women's right to vote was reintroduced in the 1820s in Tennessee school board elections.[26] From that time on, women had the vote in some places, usually only at the local level or for particular kinds of elections.

The national movement for women's suffrage did not gain momentum until after the Civil War. Before and during that war, many women helped lead the campaign to abolish slavery and establish full political rights for blacks. When black men got the right to vote after the Civil War, some women saw the paradox in their working to enfranchise these men when they themselves lacked the right to vote. Led by Susan B. Anthony, Elizabeth Cady Stanton, and others, they lobbied Congress and the state legislatures for voting rights for women.

The first suffrage bill was introduced in Congress in 1868 and each year thereafter until 1893. Most members were strong in their condemnation of women as potential voters. One senator claimed that if women could hold political views different from their husbands, it would make "every home a hell on earth."[27]

When Wyoming applied to join the Union in 1889, it had already granted women the right to vote.

Congress initially tried to bar Wyoming from the Union for that reason, but then relented when the Wyoming territorial legislature declared, "We will remain out of the Union one hundred years rather than come in without the women." Still, by 1910, women had complete suffrage rights in only four western states.

Powerful interests opposed suffrage for women. Liquor interests feared that women voters would press for prohibition because many women had been active in the temperance (antiliquor) movement. Other businesses feared that suffrage would lead to reforms to improve working conditions for women and children. Southern whites feared that it would lead to voting by black women and then by black men. Political bosses feared that women would favor political reform. The Catholic Church opposed it as contrary to the proper role of women. According to some people, suffrage was a revolt against nature. Pregnant women might lose their babies, nursing mothers their milk, and women might grow beards or be raped at the polls (then frequently located in saloons or barber shops).[28] Others argued less hysterically that women should be protected from the unsavory practices of politics and should confine themselves to their traditional duties.

About 1910, however, the women's suffrage movement was reenergized, in part by ideas and tactics borrowed from the British women's suffrage movement. A new generation of leaders, including Alice Paul and Carrie Chapman Catt, began to lobby more vigorously, reach out to the working class, and engage in protest marches and picketing, all new features of American politics. In 1917, the National Women's Party organized around-the-clock picketing of the White House; their arrest and subsequent torture through beatings and forced feedings embarrassed the administration and won the movement some support. These incidents, plus contributions by women to the war effort during World War I, led to the adoption of the Nineteenth Amendment guaranteeing women the right to vote in 1920. Although only 37 percent of eligible women voted in the 1920 presidential election, as the habit of voting spread, women's voting rates equaled those of men. (See the box "Women in Office.")

Young People and the Right to Vote

Federal constitutional and legislative changes extended the franchise to young adults. Before 1971, almost all states required a voting age of nineteen or more. The service of eighteen-year-olds in the Vietnam War brought protests that if these men were old enough to die for their country, they were old enough to vote. Yielding to these arguments and to the general recognition that young people were better educated than in the past, Congress adopted and the states ratified the Twenty-sixth Amendment giving eighteen-year-olds the right to vote. As we will see, however, young people are a lot less likely to vote than other groups.

Felons and the Right to Vote

The restriction of felons' rights to vote is an exception to the general liberalization of the right to vote. (Felons are those convicted of serious crimes). Most states bar convicted felons from voting while in prison or on probation, but four states, including Florida and three other southern states with large black populations,[29] bar felons from voting forever. In some states, these laws stem from Reconstruction era laws targeted to reduce the voting power of blacks. Since 2004, three states have reinstituted voting rights to felons after they serve their time.

In Florida, an estimated 525,000 people, most of them poor and black, were barred from voting in 2000 because of committing a prior felony.[30] Nationally, more than five million people are prevented from voting by felony convictions, including one in seven black men (in Alabama, one in three black men are barred).[31] Nationally, 40 percent of those barred from voting are black.[32] Analyses of the impacts of these laws suggest they have had a significant effect in put-

ting conservative Republicans in office in states with large black populations.[33]

Some might argue that we should not worry about the voting rights of felons. Loss of voting rights might be seen as part of their punishment. However, most felons barred from voting have served their time and returned to society. Many times they were convicted as young people and have been law-abiding citizens for years or even decades since. Moreover, this particular punishment does not really seem to fit the crime.

In sum, only convicted felons, the mentally incapable, noncitizens, and those not meeting minimal residence requirements are legally barred from voting now. Voting has become an essential right of citizenship, except for felons, rather than a privilege just for those qualified by birth or property.

Electoral Reform and New Threats to Voting Rights

In recent elections, new threats to voting rights, especially voting rights of African Americans, have occurred. The most widely publicized problems were in the 2000 and 2004 elections. Months after the 2000 presidential election that saw Al Gore win the popular vote but George W. Bush win the electoral vote and the presidency, half of the electorate thought that the outcome was unfair or downright crooked. (See the section titled "The 2000 Election: A Perfect Storm".) Many African Americans, who believed they were systematically disfranchised by the way the election was run in Florida, were especially outraged. One of ten votes in largely African American precincts in Florida were thrown out as invalid, compared with one of thirty-seven in white precincts, significantly reducing the Democratic vote and changing the outcome of the presidential election.[34]

Voter Reform Legislation

The 2000 election revealed a number of problems with our electoral system. (The problems had existed for a long time, but in a close election they become more crucial.) Many areas had voting equipment that not only was old, but also did not work well, resulting in many votes not being counted. Most of these were punch-card systems where voters use a penlike stylus to punch holes in the ballot in places reflecting their candidate choices. As we saw in Florida, sometimes the holes were not completely made, casting doubt on the voters' intentions. Many states had unclear laws governing procedures for recounts and challenges to voter eligibility.

To deal with some of these issues, Congress passed electoral reform legislation in 2002. This new legisla-

Even before women were given the right to vote nationally, they held political office. Women officeholders in colonial America were rare but not unknown. In 1715, for example, the Pennsylvania Assembly appointed a woman as tax collector.[1]

Elizabeth Cady Stanton, probably the first woman candidate for Congress, received twenty-four votes when she ran in 1866.[2] It was not until 1916 that the first woman member of Congress, Jeannette Rankin (R-Mont.), was actually elected. In 1872, Victoria Claflin Woodhull ran for president on the Equal Rights Party ticket teamed with abolitionist Frederick Douglass for vice president.

More than one-hundred thousand women now hold elective office, but many of these offices are minor. Inroads by women into major national offices

"Nothing against Rudy, I just feel that a woman would be instinctively better on dairy issues."

have been slow. Geraldine Ferraro's 1984 vice presidential candidacy was historic, but not victorious. In recent years, women have only gradually increased their membership in Congress. But in the 1992 elections, women candidates won striking increases in national legislative offices. Women have continued to gain seats and, after 2006, numbered at least 16 percent of the House and 16 percent of the Senate. More than two-thirds of the women in each house are Democrats.[3] Nancy Pelosi (D-Cal.), as the first woman (and Italian American) Speaker of the House, is now third in the line of presidential succession.

Real progress has also been made in state and local governments. Women hold 12 percent of the governors (Democrats) and 28 percent of the lieutenant governors. In 1969, only 4 percent of the state legislators were women; today 23 percent are. However, the rates of increase have slowed in recent years with only a 2 percent growth in the past decade.[4] The proportion ranges widely, from not quite 9 percent in South Carolina to one-third or more in Maryland, Delaware, Arizona, Nevada, Vermont and Washington. Women are also making inroads in local political offices.[5]

Does it make a difference in terms of policy to have women officeholders rather than men? Behavioral studies of women members of Congress and other legislative bodies indicate that they are, on the whole, more liberal than men.[6] Women tend to give issues relating to women, children, and the family higher priority than do male leg-

islators.[7] Women are also less likely to be involved in corrupt activities.

As more and more women are getting graduate and professional education and working outside the home, and as the public increases its support for women in politics, the trend toward more women in public office will continue. In the run up to the 2008 election, one of the most publicized issues is whether Hillary Clinton will run and if she could win. Mid-2006 polls show that slightly over half the electorate say that they definitely would vote for her or "would consider" it, with more than 40 percent saying they definitely would not.[8] Most think she is a strong leader, but many do not trust her. At the same time, 96 percent of Americans say they would vote for a qualified woman for president.

[1] Joseph J. Kelley, *Pennsylvania: The Colonial Years* (Garden City, N.Y.: Doubleday, 1980), 143.
[2] Elisabeth Griffin, *In Her Own Right* (New York: Oxford University Press, 1983).
[3] Data are from Center for the American Woman and Politics, National Information Bank on Women in Public Office, Rutgers University, www.rci.rutgers.edu/cawp/pdf/elective.pdf.
[4] Kira Sanbonmatsu, *Democrats, Republicans, and the Politics of Women's Place* (Ann Arbor: University of Michigan Press, 2002).
[5] Data are from the Center for American Women and Politics, Rutgers University, 2006, www.cawp.rutgers.edu/Facts.html#leg.
[6] Susan Welch, "Are Women More Liberal Than Men in the U.S. Congress?" *Legislative Studies Quarterly* 10 (1985), 125–134.
[7] Sue Thomas and Susan Welch, "The Impact of Gender on Activities and Priorities of State Legislators," *Western Political Quarterly* 44 (1991), 445–456.
[8] "Sen. Clinton for President?" A Washington Post-ABC News Poll, reported in the July 17–23, 2006 *Washington Post National Weekly Review*, p. 13. The poll was based on telephone interviews with 1103 randomly chosen people; half were asked each question.

tion offered states funding to buy new, modern voting equipment; mandated statewide registration lists; and required states to train poll workers, post a list of voters' rights in each polling place, and allow voters whose names do not appear on the precinct lists to cast a provisional ballot, which can be accepted or challenged later.

This legislation did bring about some positive changes. Though most of the money to purchase the machines was not provided by the federal government, many areas did buy new electronic machines that work like ATMs, responding to touches on the screen.[35] And many states enacted new standards for counts and recounts.

Not All Changes Were Positive

There were widespread concerns about the electronic voting machines, and some states used the new legislation concerning voting lists to try to reduce the electorate rather than increase it (we will discuss this below when we discuss voter turnout).

Most technical experts, and many others, are fearful that some of the new electronic machines are open to fraud. One information-security expert argues that one particular system was "so deficient in security it could be compromised by a bright teenager intent on hacking an election."[36] The reason is that in most of the new machines there is no paper backup. Your vote for X could be counted as a vote for Y and you would never know it. The fact that the CEO of the company that manufactures the most popular electronic machine (an estimated seventy-five thousand are in use) is a strong Republican supporter and a Bush Pioneer heightened the fears by both technical specialists and conspiracy theorists that the machines were rigged in some areas. Many of these machines were used in Ohio, and the CEO, in an embarrassing Republican fundraising letter, promised to "deliver Ohio to Bush."[37] In fact, Ohio did go for Bush and there were significant voting machine problems, but Bush's margin, more than one hundred thousand, preempted most discussions of whether the election was stolen in this way.

To deal with concerns about the potential for electronic systems to be rigged, California has required precincts to offer voters a choice of a paper ballot or an electronic one, and a proposed law to require paper backup for all these machines is on the ballot in California and being considered by other states.[38]

Voter Turnout

Paradoxically, as the *right* to vote has expanded, the proportion of eligible citizens *actually* voting has contracted.

Political Activism in the Nineteenth Century

In 1896, an estimated 750,000 people—5 percent of all voters—took train excursions to visit presidential candidate William McKinley at his Ohio home during the campaign.[39] This amazing figure is but one indication of the high level of intense political interest and activity in the late nineteenth century.

In those days, politics was an active, not a spectator, sport. People voted at high rates, as much as 80 percent in the 1840 presidential election,[40] and they were very partisan. They thought Independents were corrupt and ready to sell their votes to the highest bidder. In colonial America, voters usually voted by voice. By the mid-nineteenth century, most states used paper ballots. Elaborate and well-organized parties printed and distributed the ballots. Voters, after being coached by party leaders, simply dropped their party's ballot into the box. **Split-ticket voting,** that is, voting for candidates from different parties for different offices, and secrecy in making one's choice were impossible.

Progressive Reforms

The **Progressive reforms** of the late nineteenth and early twentieth centuries brought radical changes to election politics. Progressive reformers, largely professional and upper middle class, sought to eliminate corruption from politics and voting. But they also meant to eliminate the influence of the lower classes, many of them recent immigrants. These two goals went hand in hand because the lower classes were seen as the cause of corruption in politics.

The Progressive movement was responsible for several reforms: primary elections, voter registration laws, secret ballots, nonpartisan ballots (without party labels), and the denial of voting rights for aliens, which removed a major constituency of the urban party machines. The movement also introduced the merit system for public employment to reduce favoritism and payoffs in hiring.

The reforms, adopted by some states at the end of the nineteenth century and by others much later, were largely effective in cleaning up politics. But the reformers also achieved, to a very large extent, their goal of eliminating the lower classes from politics. Taking away most of the reason for the existence of the political parties—choosing candidates and printing and distributing ballots—caused the party organization to decline, which, in turn, produced a decline in political interest and activity on the part of the electorate. Without strong parties to mobilize voters, only the most interested and motivated participated. The new restrictions on voting meant that voters had to invest more time, energy, and thought in voting. They had to think about the election months in advance and travel to city hall to register. As a consequence, politics began to be a spectator activity. Voter turnout declined sharply after the turn of the century.

Turnout figures from the nineteenth century are not entirely reliable and not exactly comparable with today's figures. In the days before voter registration, many aliens could vote, and some people voted twice. In some instances, more people voted in a state election than lived there! Nevertheless, it is generally agreed that turnout was very high in the nineteenth century and that it has diminished substantially; it dropped from more than 77 percent from 1840 to 1896 to 54 percent in the 1920 to 1932 era, when the Progressive reforms were largely in place. During the New Deal era, when the Democratic Party mobilized new groups of voters, turnout rose again, but it has never achieved the same levels as in the nineteenth century.

Recent Turnout

Between 1964 and 2000, turnout in presidential elections slowly declined from 62 percent to 52 percent, but that proportion increased significantly in 2004 to 58 percent.[42]

The turnout for off-year congressional elections is even lower. It has not exceeded 45 percent since World War II, and in 2002 it was 42 percent.[43] Youth voting is abysmal in off-year elections; in 2002, for example, though 61 percent of the over sixty-five age group turned out, only 15 percent of eighteen- to twenty-year-olds did. Turnout in primary elections is far lower still, sometimes as low as 10 percent.

Although nations count their turnouts differently, it is clear that Americans vote in much lower proportions than citizens of other Western democracies. Only Switzerland, which relatively recently gave women the right to vote (in 1971), approximates our low-turnout levels.

Within the United States, turnout varies greatly among the states. In the 2000 presidential election, for example, 76 percent of Minnesota's citizens voted, but only 46 percent of Hawaii's did.[44] Turnout tends to be lower in the South and higher in the northern Plains and Mountain states.[45]

Not only are voting rates low, but even fewer participate actively in political campaigns. For example, in a recent year, about one-quarter of the population said that they worked for a party or candidate. About an equal proportion claimed that they contributed money to a party or a candidate. Smaller proportions attended political meetings or actually belonged to a political club.

Unlike voting, rates of participation in campaigns have not declined over the past twenty years. This suggests that people are about as political as they always have been, but that something about elections themselves has decreased voter turnout. Indeed, more people give money to candidates and parties than they used to, probably because, unlike twenty years ago,

candidates and parties now use mass mailings and the Internet to solicit funds from supporters.[46] Hundreds of thousands of potential donors can be reached in a very short time.

The differences in turnouts among states suggest that not only are there certain kinds of people who are unwilling to vote, but there are also certain kinds of laws and political traditions that depress voter turnout.

Who Does Not Vote?

Before we can explain why some people do not vote, we need to see who the nonvoters are. The most important thing to remember is that voting is related to education, income, and occupation—that is, to socioeconomic class. For example, if you are a college graduate, the chances are about 70 percent that you will vote; if you have less than a high school education, the chances are less than half that.[47] Differences between higher- and lower-income people are also quite large and growing. Although voting among all groups of Americans has declined in the past forty years, the proportion of college-educated persons who participated fell by less than 10 percent, while that of high school–educated persons dropped by nearly 20 percent. Education apparently is linked to voting because those with more years of education are more interested in, and knowledgeable about, politics.

Though many people take it for granted that those in the working class vote at lower rates than those in the middle and upper classes, in the United States these differences are far wider than in other nations[48]

"Granny" Haddock, at 89, spent a year walking across America and urging electoral reform.

AP Images/Jim Cole

Often young people complain that senior citizens have more political clout than they do. There are a number of reasons for that, but it starts with the ballot box and the low turnout of young people.

Many young people do not register to vote. If they do, the registration place may be in their hometowns, far away from their college or other current residence. Often voter registration officials in college towns do not want students to vote, fearing that they will challenge local norms and ways of doing things, and do everything possible to deter them. During the 2004 election season, a county district attorney threatened to prosecute students from Prairie View A&M University if they tried to register. When students filed suit, the attorney apologized. A Fox station in Tucson, Arizona, quoted a local election official that University of Arizona students who lived in dorms and tried to register might be committing a crime.[1] More typically, election officials make it difficult for students to vote by not putting polling places on campus and not trying to get students registered.

Many young voters are disaffected by politics.[2] Most candidates for national office are older and much more inclined to target their campaign messages toward middle-aged and older voters who turn out in far greater numbers than young voters.[3] One twenty-something said about the 2000 presidential race: "I feel like if you are not sixty-five-years old and don't have arthritis, these candidates have nothing to say to you."[4]

Some credit young people with recognizing, better than older people, that the political system is broken and registering their judgment on what they see as a meaningless process.[5] Others argue that young people are mostly ignored, and when they are not, they will turn out at the polls in percentages as high as any other demographic group. For example, Representative Tammy Baldwin (D-Wisc.), four-term incumbent from the congressional district that is the home of the University of Wisconsin and several other colleges and the first openly gay candidate to win election to the House, got so many student voters to the polls that her election was called

a "youthquake." The turnout was so high that some polling places ran out of ballots, and students waited in line up to two hours for more ballots.[6]

Baldwin found that getting out the youth vote is pretty much like turning out the vote among any other age group—grassroots organization and outreach. Baldwin's campaign organization established a presence in every residence hall and dormitory, complete with captains and floor leaders. She devoted a large portion of her campaign funds to reach students through ads on MTV and *Ally McBeal*. Of the three thousand precinct walkers she recruited, more than half were students.[7] To overcome the "voting is for old people" syndrome, her campaign platforms directly target student issues, including the cost of health care, the draft, and rising tuition and fees.

Although the 10 percent student composition of her constituency is not typical, Baldwin has shown that young people will participate in large numbers if targeted. In fact, the Democratic National Committee asked her to help prepare a "tool kit" for mobilizing the youth vote.

Representative Tammy Baldwin (D-WI) courts the student vote on the campus of the University of Wisconsin–Madison.

In addition to these traditional means of getting out the vote, during 2004, college campuses experienced new attempts to interest students in the election and get them to register. In addition to Rock the Vote, other action groups formed to keep young people in the campaign after Dean's departure, including Declare Yourself, the Hip-Hop Summit Action Network, Get Out Her Vote (targeted to young women on campus), Music for America, and the World Wrestling Entertainment's Smack-Down Your Vote. Some of these organizations sponsored rock concerts at popular campus venues, and the parties recruited celebrities popular with young people like Arnold Schwarzenegger (for the Republicans) and Michael Moore and Howard Dean (for the Democrats) to visit campuses.

The turnout of young people increased substantially in 2004; for example, the proportion of those voting among eighteen- to twenty-year-olds went from twenty-eight in 2000 to forty-one in 2004, an increase larger than any other group.[8] Presumably much of that was due to these "get out the vote" efforts. Perhaps, as one observer noted, those who are trying to get young people to the polls should take a lesson from the "Just Say No" antidrug campaign. "The campaign only started to have an impact when it dropped that slogan and just tried to scare the shit out of people. Maybe we should stop trying to make voting cool. We should just show kids what happens when they don't. In other words, we need to get them to watch the news."[9]

[1]These examples are from editorial, "Barriers to Student Voting," New York Times, September 28, 2004, 26.
[2]Thomas E. Patterson, The Vanishing Voter (New York: Knopf, 2002), 87–88.
[3]Amy Goldstein and Richard Morin, "The Squeaky Wheel Gets the Grease," Washington Post National Weekly Edition, October 28–November 3, 34.
[4]Steven Hill and Rashad Robinson, "Demography vs. Democracy: Young People Feel Left Out of the Political Process," Los Angeles Times, November 5, 2002. Posted by the Youth Vote Coalition (www.youthvote.org/news/newsdetail.cfm?newsid56). The survey cited was conducted by Harvard University.
[5]Hill and Robinson, "Demography vs. Democracy: Young People Feel Left Out of the Political Process," 2.
[6]Heidi Pauken, "The Students' Rep," American Prospect 14 (2003), A23.
[7]Ibid., A22.
[8]Statistical Abstract of the United States, 2006, Table 405.
[9]Ann Marie Cox, "Pimping the Vote," In These Times, May 13, 2004 (www.inthesetimes.com/site /main/article /pimping_the_vote), online article.

OTHER SOURCES: Phone interview with Representative Tammy Baldwin, September 1, 2004; Young Chang, "T-Shirt's Sassy Slogan Riles Some Voters," Seattle Times, March 2, 2004. Special thanks to Jerilyn Goodman.

and far greater than in nineteenth-century America. So there appears to be something unique about the contemporary American political system that inhibits voting participation of all citizens, but particularly those whose income and educational level are below the average.

Just as there is a strong class basis to voting, there is also a strong class basis for participation in campaign activities.[49] Those with more education and income are more likely to participate. Those with some college education actually increased their participation over the past twenty years, whereas those with less than a high school education decreased theirs. Thus, the class bias in participation, as in voting alone, has increased.[50]

Voting is also much more common among older people than younger people. (See the box "Rock the Vote or Mock the Vote?") Young people are volunteering in their communities in record numbers.[51] So why the low voting rates? Young people's initial tendency to vote is positively influenced by their parents' education and political engagement and by their own high school experiences and that of going on to college. Later in life, getting married, establishing a stable residence, and becoming active in the community are important to continuing their voting habits.[52]

Thus, low turnouts may reflect many who grew up in homes where there was a low interest in government and the news; they did not learn that politics are important.[53] Then, too, like many of their elders, some young people cannot discern significant differences between the two major political parties, or they believe that candidates do not address issues of primary concern to young people.

Low voter turnout is also a product of the high degree of mobility of young adults; they change their residences frequently and do not have time or do not take time to figure out how and where to register. Many young people are preoccupied with major life changes—going to college, leaving home, beginning their first full-time job, getting married, and starting a family.

In other kinds of political participation, even taking education into account, men usually participate slightly more than women, whites somewhat more than blacks, older people more than younger people, and southerners more than northerners. But these differences change over time. Young people participated more than their elders, and blacks more than whites, during the late 1960s and early 1970s.[54] The civil rights and anti–Vietnam War movements drew many young and black people into political activity.

Why Turnout Is Low

There are a number of other possible reasons more Americans, especially low-income and young Americans, do not vote.

Satisfaction among Nonvoters

One reason sometimes given for low rates of voter turnout is that nonvoters are satisfied; failing to vote is a passive form of consent to what government is doing.[55] This argument falls flat on two counts. First, voter turnout has decreased in an era when public trust in government has decreased, not increased. Levels of trust and voter turnout both started declining after 1964. Second, voter turnout is lower precisely among those groups of citizens who have the least reason to be content, not those who have the most reason to be so. If staying at home on Election Day were an indication of satisfaction, one would expect turnout to be lower among the well off, not among the working class and the poor.

Voters Are "Turned Off" by Political Campaigns

About one-third of a nonvoting group in the 1990 election, when asked why they did not vote, gave reasons suggesting they were disgusted with politics.[56] In explaining low turnout, analysts often point to the hateful advertising, attacks on other candidates, candidates who do not tell the truth about their positions, incessant polling, and lack of thoughtful media coverage.[57]

These analyses surely contain some grains of truth, but how many? After all, people who are most likely to pay attention to the media, watch the ads, hear about the polls, and follow the campaigns are the most likely to vote, not the least. It is possible that the increasingly media-oriented campaigns have decreased overall turnout during the past generation (and we will have more to say about these campaigns later in the chapter). In fact, turnout is inversely related to media spending; the more the candidates spend, the lower the turnout. Moreover, voters who watch negative political ads are less likely to vote or to feel their vote counts.[58] But negative advertising does not affect turnout much, if at all,[59] and negative advertising and other media attention cannot explain the class bias in nonvoting.

In addition to the *quality* of the campaigns, some people think turnout has declined because our elections are so frequent, campaigns last so long, and so many offices are contested that the public becomes bored, confused, or cynical.[60] At the presidential level, the sheer quantity of coverage, much of it focused repetitively on "who's winning," may simply bore people. Moreover,

the continual public opinion polling and the widely publicized results may lead some to believe they don't need to vote. To the extent that people feel their votes do not count, the close election in 2000 may change some minds.

At the local level, voters elect so many officeholders, all the way down to weed and mosquito control commissioners, that many have no idea for whom or what they are voting. This proliferation of elective offices, thought by some to promote democracy and popular control, may promote only voter confusion and alienation. The problem is compounded because elections for different offices are held at different times. For example, most states have decided to hold elections for governor in non-presidential election years. This decision probably reduces presidential election turnout by 7 percent and may reduce by one-third the number of those who vote for governor in those states.[61]

Primary elections also affect turnout. One estimate is that holding primary campaigns diminishes the general election turnout by 5 percent.[62]

By contrast, in Britain the time between calling an election (by the current government) and the actual election is only a month. On May 9, 2001, Prime Minister Tony Blair called the election, and on June 7, 2001, it was held. All campaigning was done during that time. There are no primaries. Moreover, as in most other parliamentary democracies, British citizens vote only for their representative in Parliament and (at one other time) for their local representative. Voters are not faced with choices for a myriad of offices they barely recognize.

Lack of Social Rootedness

Turnout is low partially because of what one analyst has called lack of "social rootedness."[63] Middle age, marriage, and residential stability lead to rootedness in one's community. Americans move around, marry late, and get divorced more than those in other nations. Mobility alone may reduce voting by as much as 9 percent. However, American turnout is still low, even taking into account these factors.

Americans living abroad, whether in the armed forces or for private reasons, have special barriers to registering and voting. In a bizarre development, in 2004, the Pentagon discouraged citizens living abroad from voting by shutting down a state-of-the-art website designed to make it easy for those citizens to register and obtain ballots.[64]

Barriers to Registration

Many people do not vote because they have not registered to vote. Most other democracies have nonpersonal systems of voter registration. That is, the state or parties are responsible for registering voters. Voter registrars go door-to-door to register voters, or voters are registered automatically when they pay taxes or receive public services. Usually, these registrar offices are nonpartisan and consider it their duty to register voters. Consequently, almost everyone is registered to vote.

The United States puts the responsibility for registration on the individual and handles voter registration through state and local agencies usually run by partisan elected officials. These conditions are a major impediment to voting. Only about 70 percent of U.S. citizens are registered.[65] Our voting turnout is embarrassingly low compared with other democracies, and this is an important reason.

About one-quarter of nonvoters surveyed in 1990 indicated they did not vote because it was too difficult. As one commentator put it, "The United States is the only major democracy where government assumes no responsibility for helping citizens cope with voter registration procedures."[66] Difficult registration procedures have a special impact on low-income Americans, who were 17 percent less likely to vote in states with difficult registration procedures than in other states.[67]

Given that states are laboratories—some things are tried in one state, other approaches tried in another—we know that some registration procedures encourage people to register and vote and others do not. One estimate is that voter turnout would be 9 percent higher if all states' procedures were similar to those of states that try to facilitate voter registration.[68]

Some states make it more convenient to register by having registration periods lasting up to Election Day (most states require registration at least twenty-five days before the election). This innovation increases registration rates.[69] Registration is also facilitated by having registration offices in neighborhoods rather than just one central county office, registration by mail, registration offices open at convenient hours, and a policy of not purging voters from the registration lists who fail to vote.

In other jurisdictions, voter registrars do not provide these options, *plus* they actually try to hinder groups working to increase registration. Some states do not allow volunteers to register voters outside the registration office.[70] Florida passed a law that seemed to discourage voter registration by organized groups. The law imposed fines of $250 for every voter registration form filed more than ten days after it is collected, even if a hurricane passes through in the meantime, and a fine of $5000 for every form that is not submitted. The Florida League of Voters, which has conducted nonpartisan voter registration drives for nearly seventy years, is suing to block the new rules, saying that its entire budget could be put at risk if a natural disaster or car accident or another such event delayed submission of forms.[71] In Ohio, the secretary of state (also a candidate for governor) issued rules making it a crime for volunteers collecting registration forms to give them personally to their supervisors for checking rather than taking them personally to the election office.[72]

Some states regularly purge the registration lists of voters who fail to vote. They are fearful that people have moved, reregistered, and will vote twice. Sometimes less high-minded motives are at work, and this tactic is used to disfranchise lower income and minority voters or use the purging process to reduce the other party's voters.[73] Sometimes private companies are hired to purge voter lists and are paid according to how many they purge.

This practice means that sometimes voters who think they are registered find they are not when they arrive at their polling places. Florida, in trying to update its voter lists, purged twenty-two thousand black voters (largely Democratic) from the voter registration lists, but only sixty-one Hispanics (who, in Florida, are more likely than blacks to be Republicans). Florida officials admitted a mistake, and claimed it was accidental. Others point out that state officials had known the process was tainted.[74]

To increase registration, a national law allows people to register at public offices, such as welfare offices and the Department of Motor Vehicles (for this reason it is called the **motor voter law**). Similar plans had increased registration in the twenty-nine states that had these policies before the federal government did.[75] The law led to the greatest

Courtesy of the Smithsonian Institute

In this chapter, there are seven photos, each marked with a blue band along the top, that illustrate American campaign tactics throughout the years. This illustration shows the 1840 Whig gimmick that prompted the phrase "keep the ball rolling."

expansion of voter registration in American history; five million new voters registered,[76] but it has not increased actual turnout.[77]

Postregistration Laws Can Influence Turnout

States could also encourage voting for those who are already registered. For example, some states mail sample ballots and information about where to vote to registered voters. Others open the polls very early and keep them open until 9 P.M. or later. Still others allow voters to vote with absentee ballots, even if they are not planning to be absent from their home on Election Day.

These practices make a significant difference in how many people turn out to vote, and the effect is particularly great for those who have less education or who are younger.[78] Some of the mystery is taken from the voting process when voters learn what the ballot looks like and where they go to vote, and their convenience is increased if they can vote before their family, job, or classes need their attention in the morning or after the dinner hour in the evening.

Absentee balloting makes voting something that can be done at the voter's convenience. One observer remarked, "The concept of Election Day is history. Now it's just the final day to vote."[79] Though this is clearly an overstatement, almost all Oregon voters vote before Election Day, perhaps a harbinger of the future for other states. Indeed, half the states, including most of those west of the Mississippi, provide for unrestricted absentee voting. Twenty states, most of them in the west and south and including many of those who also provide unrestricted absentee voting, allow voters to cast votes in the county clerk's office two to three weeks before the election.[80] For example, in Iowa, voting started forty days before Election Day, and 140,000 ballots had been requested by then.[81] To reach these voters, parties must begin television advertising and flyer mailing much earlier.

Other states make it harder to vote. Several states are considering requiring an official identification. The states with the highest barriers to voting tend to be states with the largest minority populations. Some estimates are that one out of four Ohio voters in 2004 experienced problems on voting day, including having to go to more than one polling place, having to wait more than twenty minutes to vote, or leaving the polls before voting. Nearly half of Ohio's African American population experienced one of those problems.[82] African Americans were also more likely to be asked for identification and to feel intimidated at the polls.

Failures of Parties to Mobilize Voters

Traditionally, political parties mobilized voters to turn out. In the 1980s and 1990s, the effectiveness of parties doing this declined. They spent more time raising funds than mobilizing voters.[83] The failure of parties to mobilize voters is another reason for low voter turnout, especially among the working class and poor. Because of their low income, a majority of nonvoters are Democrats. If mobilized, they would probably vote for Democrats, but not to the degree many Republicans fear. In many elections, the preferences of nonvoters have simply reflected the preferences of voters.[84]

In 2004, both parties returned to their traditional mobilization function, a development that was likely responsible for the upswing in voting. Both put much emphasis on registering voters and getting them to the polls. Both parties used increasingly sophisticated technology to link information about each party supporter with neighborhood information. Each party communicated with its core supporters via e-mail and frequently urged them to register and vote.

Both parties have developed sophisticated databases recording individuals' residential location, gender, education, race, homeowner status, and many other variables. They gather data not just from public sources such as voter registration rolls and driver's license registrations, but also from consumer data from stores ranging from book vendors to auto dealerships. So, for example, we know that Republicans are more likely to drink bourbon and Democrats gin, Democrats buy Volvos and Republicans Fords and Chevys.[85]

The Republicans have an even larger and more sophisticated database than the Democrats and are more likely to be able to cross-reference political and personal information. One goal of Howard Dean, the chair of the Democratic party, is to build better databases as well as better infrastructure for the party.

The parties use these databases to communicate and to target where they might best be able to mobilize potential voters to go to the polls and vote their way.[86] The Republicans credit their sophisticated databases with gains among targeted electorates in 2004, such as Hispanics.

Nonparty organizations such as Americans Coming Together (ACT), MoveOn.org, evangelical religious groups, and others also sometimes work to increase registration and voting. Though some of these organizations are nonpartisan, many were focused on getting out either the Democratic or Republican vote. In 2006, immigrant rights groups are working hard to convert street protests to voter registration among new immigrants.

In the past, Republicans have been most fearful of general get-out-the-vote efforts, because the Republicans have no interest in mobilizing lower- and lower-middle class voters. But now, with sophisticated databases, each party can target its own potential electorate for their efforts.[87] However, Republicans are still more likely to oppose legislation making it easier for members of the general electorate to vote. States with the highest turnout tend to have active and liberal Democratic parties, giving voters a choice and thus a motive to vote.

Lack of Strong Labor Unions

Working class citizens are much less likely to vote than white collar and professional workers. Yet, among working people, union members are much more likely to vote than are others. This reflects the mobilization efforts of the unions. If union membership were larger, these mobilization efforts would likely expand the working class electorate. Most other democracies have much stronger labor unions than in the United States and consequently higher rates of turnout among blue-collar workers.

Partisan Efforts to Discourage Voting

In the aftermath of the 2004 election, there were many instances of partisan attempts to deter registration and voting. Most of the examples that have come to light have been Republican efforts to deter Democrats, though undoubtedly there are reverse examples. In Nevada, the Republican National Committee employed a private company to register voters; it discarded those filled out by Democrats. In Wisconsin, Republicans tried to challenge thousands of registrants

in heavily Democratic Milwaukee, and in one county in Ohio, some voters received an advisory on fake Board of Elections letterhead warning them that if they registered through the Kerry campaign or the NAACP they couldn't vote.[88]

Voting as a Rational Calculation of Costs and Benefits

Nonvoting may also be the result of a rational calculation of the costs and benefits of voting. When 35 percent of Americans think voting on *American Idol* is more important than voting for the president, obviously many voters do not think that the stakes in elections are great.[89] Economist Anthony Downs argues that people vote when they believe the perceived benefits of voting are greater than the costs.[90] If a voter sees a difference between the parties or candidates and favors one party's position over the other, that voter has a reason to vote and can expect some benefit from doing so. For that reason, people who are highly partisan vote more than those less attached to a party, and people with a strong sense of political efficacy, the belief they can influence government, vote more than others.

Voters who see no difference between the candidates or parties, however, may believe that voting is not worth the effort it takes and that it is more rational to abstain. In fact, 40 percent of nonvoters in 1990 gave only the excuse that they were "too busy," suggesting a large degree of apathy.[91] Nevertheless,

In the nineteenth century, politics involved most people, and political parades and festivities were common. Here a torchlight parade honors Grover Cleveland in Buffalo in the late 1880s.

many people will vote even if they think there is no difference between the candidates because they have a sense of civic duty, a belief that their responsibilities as citizens include voting. In fact, more voters give this as an explanation for voting than any other reason, including the opportunity to influence policy.[92]

Downs assumes that the costs of voting are minimal, but, in reality, for many people the time, expense, and possible embarrassment of trying to register are greater than the perceived benefits of voting. This is especially true for lower-income people who perceive that neither party is attentive to their interests. Moreover, they are especially vulnerable to a climate where voters are being challenged at the polls over their right to vote. That is why it is crucial that either the state or the parties provide services to help voters gain information about voting and even (in the case of parties) provide assistance in getting to the polls. The frequency, length, and media orientation of campaigns may lower the perceived benefits of voting for people of all incomes by trivializing the election and emphasizing the negative.

Some analysts believe that voter turnout in the United States will not increase substantially until one of the political parties works to mobilize the traditional nonvoters through policies that appeal to them. For example, Roosevelt's New Deal mobilized thousands of new voters. If voters believe they have a reason to vote, then their calculation of the benefits of voting increases relative to the costs.

Presidential Nominating Campaigns

Many Americans believe in the Horatio Alger myth, which states that with hard work anyone can achieve great success. This myth has its parallel in politics, where it is sometimes said that any child can grow up to be president. In fact, only a few run for that office, and even fewer are elected.

Who Runs for President and Why?

In deciding whether to run for president, individuals consider such things as the costs and risks of running and the probabilities of winning.[93] Most people have little chance of being president: they are unknown to the public; they do not have the financial resources or contacts to raise the money needed for a national campaign; they have jobs they could not leave to run a serious campaign; and their friends would probably ridicule them for even thinking of such a thing.

But a few people are in a different position. Take, for instance, a hypothetical U.S. senator from Massachusetts or a governor of Texas. By their vote-gathering ability in a large state, they have demonstrated some possibility that they could win. Their decision to run might hinge on considerations such as whether they think they could raise the money necessary to run a campaign, whether they are willing to sacrifice a good portion of their private life and their privacy for a few years, whether they have an embarrassing skeleton in the closet that would be discovered and lead to humiliation, and whether they would lose the office they currently hold if they ran and lost.

These calculations are real. Most candidates for president are, in fact, senators or governors.[94] In recent decades, governors (George W. Bush, Bill Clinton, Ronald Reagan, and Jimmy Carter) have been more successful than senators (George McGovern, Robert Dole, and John Kerry). Vice presidents also frequently run, but until George H. Bush's victory in 1988, they were not successful in the 20th century.

Why do candidates run? An obvious reason is to gain the power and prestige of the presidency. But they may have other goals as well, such as to gain support for a particular policy or set of ideas. Ronald Reagan, for example, clearly wanted to be president in part to spread his conservative ideology. Jesse Jackson wanted to be president in part to help those at the bottom of the social ladder. (See the box titled "Can an African American Be Elected President?" for views on electing an African American president one day.) Eugene McCarthy ran in 1968 to challenge Lyndon Johnson's Vietnam policy.

Sometimes candidates run to gain name recognition and publicity for the next election. Many successful candidates in recent years have run before. George H. Bush lost the nomination in 1980 before being elected in 1988; Ronald Reagan lost in 1976 before his victory in 1980; Richard Nixon lost in 1960 before winning in 1968.

Sometimes candidates run for the presidency to be considered for the vice presidency, probably viewing it as an eventual stepping-stone to the presidency. But only occasionally, such as when Reagan chose Bush in 1980 or Kennedy chose Johnson in 1960, do presidential candidates choose one of their defeated opponents to run as a vice presidential candidate.

How a Candidate Wins the Nomination

The nominating process is crucial in deciding who eventually gets elected. Boss Tweed once said, "I don't care who does the electing, so long as I get to do the nominating."[95] American presidential candidates are nominated through a process that includes the general public, the financial supporters of each party, and other party leaders.

Over time, voters and fundraisers have gained more power at the expense of party leaders. Presidential candidates try to win a majority of delegates at their party's national nominating convention in the summer preceding the November election. Delegates to those conventions are elected in state caucuses, conventions, and primaries. Candidates must campaign to win the support of those who attend caucuses and conventions and of primary voters.

Normally, candidates formally announce their candidacies in the year preceding the presidential election year. Their aim then is to persist and survive the long primary and caucus season that begins in January of election year and continues until only one candidate is left. Candidates use a number of methods to try to maximize their chances of survival. They carefully choose the primaries they will enter and to which they will devote their resources. Candidates must enter

Soliciting votes by giving speeches and making appearances was once considered beneath the dignity of the presidential office. William Jennings Bryan was the first presidential candidate to break this tradition. In 1896, he traveled more than eighteen thousand miles and made more than six hundred speeches in an effort to win voters. One observer noted that he was "begging for the presidency as a tramp might beg for a pie." Although Bryan lost the election to William McKinley, his approach to campaigning became the standard. This photo illustrates how the term stump speech, used to refer to candidates' boilerplate campaign speeches, may have developed.

Courtesy of the Smithsonian Institute

enough primaries so they are seen as national, not regional, candidates, but they cannot possibly devote time and resources to every primary or caucus. Especially important are the early events—the Iowa caucus and the New Hampshire primary—and the larger state primaries.

Candidates try hard to raise substantial amounts of money early. A large war chest can mark a candidate as unbeatable. George W. Bush started strong in the 2000 primaries because he had raised millions more than all his opponents combined. Candidates also try to survive by establishing themselves as *the* candidate for a particular policy or other constituency. In 2000, Gary Bauer and Steve Forbes each tried to combat their better-known opponents by trying to win the loyalties of the new Christian Right within the Republican Party. They were unsuccessful in enlisting enough of these voters to offset Bush's head start. In 2004, Richard Gephardt tried to appeal to the union vote and Al Sharpton tried to rally African Americans to his cause, but neither was very successful.

To compete successfully, candidates also need considerable media coverage. They must convince reporters that they are serious candidates with a real chance of winning. Journalists and candidates establish expectations for how well each candidate should do based on poll results, the quality of a candidate's campaign organization, the amount of money and time spent in the campaign, and the political complexion of the state. If a candidate performs below expectations, even though garnering the most votes, this may be interpreted by the press as a weakness and hurt the campaign. On the other hand, a strong showing when expectations are low can mean a boost to a candidate's campaign.

Consequently, candidates try to lower media expectations. It is not enough to win a primary; you have to win by at least as much as the media claims you should, or you will be seen as a loser. In the Republican race in 1988, Pat Robertson's organizers tried to counter media predictions for the Iowa caucuses by urging supporters to tell pollsters that they were not going to attend the caucuses. Because pollsters do not count people who do not plan to vote, this tactic could result in an artificially low prediction—and then a surprisingly high vote.[96] (Robertson did poorly anyway.)

Sometimes even losers are portrayed as winners if they do better than expected. For example, in 1968 in the New Hampshire primary, antiwar candidate Senator Eugene McCarthy won 40 percent of the vote against President Johnson, who had become increasingly unpopular because of the Vietnam War. Although McCarthy did not win, he did much better than expected, and the press interpreted the vote as a repudiation of Johnson's leadership. Bill Clinton finished sec-

Will the American presidency continue to be held only by white, non-Jewish males? Can an African American or a woman ever be elected?

These questions sound familiar. In 1960, some doubted that a Catholic could ever be elected president. At that time, only 71 percent of all voters said they would vote for a Catholic for president.[1] The only previous major-party Catholic candidate, Alfred Smith, had been soundly defeated by Herbert Hoover in 1928. But in 1960, John F. Kennedy was elected, and that barrier was broken. In 2004, John Kerry's Catholicism did not seem to be an issue except for very conservative members of his own church, who disdained his position on abortion and gay rights. The candidacy of Joseph Lieberman, an orthodox Jew, for vice president on the 2000 Democratic ticket was widely applauded.

But not being white has been a bigger barrier than religious diversity. Among campaigns during the past twenty years, race was probably most important in the 1988 campaign. It surfaced when the Republicans succeeded in tying Democratic candidate Michael Dukakis to Willie Horton, an African American convict who raped a woman while on furlough from prison. It also came up when Jesse Jackson's prominence in the Democratic Party was highlighted and made to seem somehow illegitimate and frightening. A campaign letter from the California Republican Party asked, "Why is it so urgent you decide now? Here are two [reasons]." Below the letter were two photos, one of Bush and Reagan, the other of

Jackson and Dukakis. "If [Dukakis] is elected to the White House," it continued, "Jesse Jackson is sure to be swept into power on his coattails."[2]

This is not to say that all of those who voted against Jackson in the primaries or against the Democrats in the general election were racists. Jackson had no experience holding office and is identified with the most liberal wing of the Democratic party.

In the 1990s, many voters, both Democratic and Republican, unsuccessfully tried to persuade Colin Powell to run for president. As a former chair of the Joint Chiefs of Staff, he did not have partisan experience but did have credibility as a potential candidate with individuals across the political spectrum. More recently Barack Obama, the sole African American U.S. Senator, is being urged to run by many Democrats who believe his message of common American values is a needed antidote to the poisonous partisanship dominant today.

As the figure shows, only 6 to 7 percent of the public say they would not vote for a black or a woman who was their party's nominee, and a slightly lower proportion say they would not vote for a Jew. Although 6 to 7 percent is enough to make a difference in a close race, many more people today say they would vote for a black, Jew, or woman than said they would vote for a Catholic in 1960. John Kennedy's victory suggests that 6 or 7 percent is not an insurmountable barrier.

[1]Barry Sussman, "A Black or Woman Does Better Today Than a Catholic in '60," *Washington Post National Weekly Edition*, November 21, 1983, 42.
[2]"Though This Be Meanness, Yet There Is a Method in It," *Washington Post National Weekly Edition*, October 10, 1988, 26.

SOURCE: www.cbsnews.com/htdocs/pdf/020306woman.pdf; Gallup Poll data from www.atheists.org/flash.line/atheism9.htm.

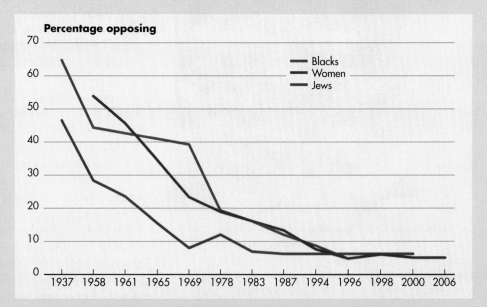

The question asked was, "If your party nominated a generally well-qualified man for president and he happened to be a black [Jew], would you vote for him?" or "If your party nominated a woman for president, would you vote for her if she were qualified for the job?" No questions were asked about African Americans until 1958. The 1961 data for blacks are from 1963. The 1994 and 1996 data are from the NORC's General Social Surveys. No data are available after 1996 for blacks and after 2000 for Jews.

ond in the New Hampshire primary in 1992, but because the top vote getter (Paul E. Tsongas) was from neighboring Massachusetts, Clinton's second place finish was considered a victory. Coming far from behind, he pronounced himself "the comeback kid," a designation that became the story of the primary. Said one journalist, "Clinton's New Hampshire abracadabra remains . . . the furriest, plumpest rabbit any politician has ever pulled out of the battered New Hampshire hat."[97] In the modern era of primary elections, Clinton is the only president not to have won the New Hampshire primary.

In sum, the primary season is a game among the media, the candidates, and the voters, with the candidates trying to raise voter enthusiasm and lower media expectations simultaneously. One commentator has called the political reporters, consultants, and pollsters "the expectorate," the group who decides whether the candidate has done well enough.[98]

The common wisdom about presidential primaries is that the key ingredient is "momentum." That is, a candidate needs to win early, or at least do better than expected, to gain momentum, and then keep winning to maintain momentum. The "expectorate" needs to pronounce him a winner. In 1976, Jimmy Carter, then an unknown governor from Georgia, won the Iowa caucuses, which attracted tremendous media attention and, in turn, led to further primary wins and eventually the nomination. John Kerry, by winning Iowa and then New Hampshire in the 2004 Democratic primaries, gained so much momentum that he knocked the other candidates out of the race very quickly, in what was originally billed as a tightly contested race.

Early in the primary season, candidates try to find the position, slogan, or idea that will appeal to the most voters. In 1984, Ronald Reagan presented himself as the candidate embodying traditional America. As one of his staff aides wrote in a campaign memo, "Paint RR as the personification of all that is right with, or heroized by, America."[99] George W. Bush capitalized on the sentiment that Bill Clinton's standard of personal morality was low, portraying himself as someone who would bring morality back to the White House.

Candidates must avoid making a big mistake or, worse yet, being caught covering up a mistake or untruth. Edmund Muskie's front-running candidacy ground to a halt in 1972 when he cried at a public appearance while denouncing a newspaper attack on his wife. Gary Hart's 1988 candidacy collapsed when the media discovered that his marriage did not prevent him from having an affair with other women. He compounded the damage by lying. The Muskie incident was taken by the media and public to indicate that he could not handle the stress of a campaign or, by inference, the presidency. The Hart incident raised questions about his character and honesty. In contrast, during the primary campaign, Clinton admitted his marriage was not perfect, but did not flaunt ongoing affairs. (The Monica Lewinsky scandal occurred after he was in the White House and was already a popular president.)

Incumbent presidents seeking renomination do not have the same problems as their challengers. Incumbents usually have token or no opposition in the primaries. No incumbent who sought renomination was denied it in the twentieth century.

In addition to these general strategies, candidates must deal specifically with the particular demands of caucuses, conventions, and primaries.

Presidential Caucuses and Conventions

Some states employ caucuses and conventions to select delegates to attend presidential nominating conventions. In 1992, one or both parties in sixteen states selected delegates in caucuses.

The Iowa caucuses, except for their timing and newsworthiness, are similar to those in other states. Iowa, as the first state to hold its caucuses, normally gets the most attention. Thousands of representatives of the media cover these caucuses, which have gained importance beyond what one would normally expect for a small state. Although only a handful of delegates to the national convention are at stake, a win with the nation's political pros watching can establish a candidate as a serious contender and attract further media attention and financial donations necessary to continue the campaign.

Senator John Kerry makes a point to a reporter during the 2004 campaign.

© Stephen Crowley *The New York Times*

Presidential Primaries

Delegates to presidential nominating conventions are also selected in direct primaries, sometimes called **presidential preference primaries.** In these elections, governed by state laws and national party rules, voters indicate a preference for a presidential candidate, for delegates committed to a candidate, or both. Some states have preference primaries, but delegates are actually selected in conventions. These primaries are often called "beauty contests" because they are meaningless in terms of winning delegates, though they can be important in showing popular support. Like other primaries, presidential primaries can be open or closed.

Until 1968, presidential preference primaries usually played an insignificant role in presidential nominations. Only a handful of states employed primaries to select delegates. The conventional wisdom was that primary victories could not guarantee nomination, but a loss would spell sure defeat.

The insignificance of most primaries was illustrated in 1968 by Vice President Hubert Humphrey's ability to win the party's nomination without winning a single primary. Humphrey was able to win the nomination because a majority of the delegates to the convention in 1968 were selected through party caucuses and conventions, where party leaders supportive of Humphrey had considerable influence.

Humphrey's nomination severely divided the Democratic Party. Many constituencies within the party, particularly those opposed to the Vietnam War, were hostile to Humphrey and believed that the nomination was controlled by party elites out of touch with the preferences of rank-and-file Democrats.

Delegate Selection Reform

In response, the Democratic Party changed delegate selection procedures to make delegates more representative of Democratic voters. One change established quotas for blacks, women, and young people to reflect the groups' percentages in each state's population. These reforms significantly increased minority and female representation in the 1972 convention and, quite unexpectedly, made the primary the preferred method of nomination. Criteria of openness and representativeness could be more easily satisfied through primary selection. In recent years, more than 70 percent of the Democratic delegates were chosen in primaries.

The Democrats have replaced quotas for minorities with guidelines urging minority involvement in party affairs. However, the quota remains that half the delegates must be women.

The Democratic Party reforms diminished the participation of party and elected officials. Critics felt that this weakened the party and increased the probability of nominating a candidate who could not work with

Wendell Willkie, Republican presidential candidate in 1940, rides into Elmwood, Indiana. In the days before television, motorcades allowed large numbers of people to see the candidates and were a way for the candidates to generate enthusiasm among the voters.

party leaders. To fix this problem and help ensure that the party's nominee would be someone who could work with other elected officials within the party, since 1984 15 to 20 percent of the delegates have been "superdelegates" appointed from among members of Congress and other party and public officials.

The Republican Party has not felt as much pressure to reform its delegate selection procedures. Republicans have tried to eliminate discrimination and increase participation in the selection process.

Reforming the Nomination Process

Each election year political observers discuss changing the presidential nomination process. They correctly complain that primaries tend to weaken political parties and have very low, unrepresentative turnouts. Moreover, the current system gives disproportionate influence to two small states, Iowa and New Hampshire, that come first in the process. Voters in most other states do not get to see most candidates; they have already been weeded out by the time the April, May, and June primaries occur. Moreover, some charge that the media has too much influence in the current system. The press exaggerates the victories of the winners and makes the losers seem weaker than they actually are.

There are two advantages of giving disproportionate influence to small states that select their delegates early. Only in these first small states do candidates come in contact with voters on a very personal basis. In large states, the primaries are strictly media events. One estimate was that candidates in contested races might spend as much as one thousand days, collectively, in Iowa, far beyond what any candidate could do in later primaries. In the 1996 campaign, one of every five New Hampshire voters had met a presidential candidate. In large states, most voters go through their entire lives without ever meeting a presidential candidate.[100] This personal attention is illustrated in this anecdote from the 1988 Iowa caucus where Democratic presidential candidate Bruce Babbitt reported that one caucus participant, a tropical fish hobbyist, said he would deliver his vote to Babbitt if he could tell him the "pH and sediment density of the Congo River at its mouth." Babbitt assigned a staffer to look into the question.[101]

Having small states at the beginning of the primary season also allows candidates to test their popularity without spending millions of dollars. Those who are successful could then attract funds for the larger, more expensive races. This system gives little-known candidates a better chance than most alternative arrangements would give.

Several large states—California, New York, Texas, Florida, and Illinois—have moved their primaries earlier

The train "whistle-stop" campaign was a staple of many presidential races. Here President Harry Truman gives a speech from the back of a train in 1948.

into the primary season to increase their influence on the nominating process. And, on **Super Tuesday,** most southern states hold their primaries simultaneously. Nonetheless, the impact of the Iowa caucuses and New Hampshire primaries remain. They are still a launching point for candidates who want to demonstrate their appeal to voters and donors alike.

Some observers are glad that we no longer have the "smoke-filled rooms," where party bosses chose nominees. Nevertheless, the primary system has weakened political parties, and the small primary electorate is unrepresentative of the general public. Indeed, these voters might be less representative of the public than the party bosses who met in smoke-filled rooms. And they know less about the nominees than the party bosses did. But the days when party leaders could anoint the nominees are probably gone forever.

The National Conventions

Once selected, delegates attend their party's national nominating convention in the summer before the November election. Changes in party rules have reduced the convention's role from an arena where powerful party leaders came together and determined the party's nominee to a body that ratifies a choice based on the outcome of the primaries and caucuses. That is, the conventions now routinely nominate whichever candidate wins the most primaries.

In the "old" days, often many ballots were necessary before a winner emerged. In 1924, it took the Democrats 103 ballots to nominate John W. Davis. Now nominees are selected on the first ballot. In most election years, some experts predict a close nomination race, which would force the decision to be made at the convention. But, in fact, the recent national party conventions served the purposes they have served for more than fifty years: to endorse the nominee and his choice for vice president, to construct a party platform, to whip up enthusiasm for the ticket among party loyalists, and to present the party favorably to the national viewing audience. Thus even without the nomination job, national conventions give meaning to the notion of a national party.

Before 1972, delegates were predominantly white and male. After 1972, the percentage of delegates who were black, women, and under thirty increased substantially. In 2004, 50 percent of the Democratic and 43 percent of the Republican delegates were women; 18 percent of the Democratic and 6 percent of the Republican delegates were black. (Only 2 percent of Republican voters are black and 28 percent of Democratic voters are.) Similarly, Democratic delegates are much more likely to be Latino and very slightly more likely to be Asian than are Republican delegates.[102]

I'd love to join you for pancakes, Mr. Kerry, but Dick Cheney is here mowing the lawn and John Edwards is on his way over to give me a foot massage.

Compared to the population, delegates to national party conventions are well educated and well off financially. Delegates also tend to be more ideologically extreme than each party's rank and file. Democratic delegates are generally more liberal and Republican delegates more conservative than their party's supporters and the public in general (see Figure 8.1).

The Activities of the Convention

National party conventions are full of color and portray at least a semblance of excitement. They are a montage of balloons, placards, and demonstrations. Candidates and their lieutenants scurry in search of uncommitted delegates. Behind-the-scenes negotiators try to work out differences among factions of the party. Journalists are everywhere covering everything from the trivial to the momentous. The keynote address reviews the party's glorious past, speaks to a promising future, and levels attacks, usually relatively gentle, on the opposition. Each candidate is placed in nomination by a party notable who reviews the candidate's background and experience. The roll call of the states ratifies the party's choice, and on the last night delegates cheer the acceptance speeches of the presidential and vice presidential nominees. Those who contested the nomination often join the nominees on the platform at the end in a display of party unity.

Aside from these very visible aspects, each convention has three central committees, which, at times, can be important. The *credentials committee* reviews any challenges that may arise regarding the right of specific delegates to participate. The *rules committee* formulates convention and party rules, such as those governing delegate selection. The *platform committee* drafts the party's platform. The contents of the platform can generate conflict, but haven't done so in recent years. For example, in 1968 the Democrats fought bitterly over a platform provision calling for an end to the

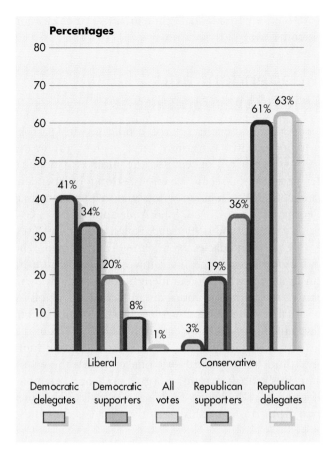

Percentages

41%	34%			
		20%	19%	36%
		8%	3%	61% 63%
		1%		

Liberal | Conservative

Democratic delegates | Democratic supporters | All votes | Republican supporters | Republican delegates

FIGURE 8.1 ■ National Convention Delegates Are More Ideologically Extreme Than Rank-and-File Members

SOURCE: Data are from delegate and public surveys reported in *New York Times*, August 29, 2004, 13.

Vietnam War. The failure of the party's nominee, Hubert Humphrey, to support the provision led many antiwar Democrats to sit out the election. After supporting the Equal Rights Amendment for years, the Republicans split over it and did not endorse it in their 1980s platforms. The abortion issue has spurred quarrels at some recent Republican conventions.

Apart from being important symbols of the direction the party wants to take, do platforms mean anything? Surprisingly, amid the platitudes, more than half of the platforms contain pledges regarding proposed future actions, and most of those pledges are fulfilled.[103] Platforms do provide observant voters with information about what the party will do if elected.

Overall, the function of the conventions might best be summarized by the comment, "Conventions are now like bar mitzvahs. They are rites of passage. But rites of passage are very important in society. The guy is changing from a politician and a candidate to one of the two people who are going to be president for sure; it gives them a certain majesty."[104]

The Media and the Convention

Before 1932, nominees did not attend the convention. Acceptance of the nomination took place sometime afterward in a special ceremony. Franklin D. Roosevelt broke with tradition in 1932 and presented his acceptance speech to the convention and to a nationwide radio audience; he did not want to lose an opportunity to deliver his message to the American people. The Republicans did not follow his example until 1944. Since then, both parties' conventions have closed with the acceptance speeches of the presidential and vice presidential nominees.

With the beginning of radio coverage in 1924 and television coverage in 1940, the conventions have become media events. In 2004, there were six times as many media representatives as delegates at the conventions.[105] The parties try to put on a show they hope will attract voters to their candidates. Polls usually show the party's candidate doing better during and after the party's convention, called the "convention bounce," though the effect does not last long.

Major addresses, such as the acceptance speech, are planned for peak viewing hours. Any potentially disruptive credential and platform proceedings (and there have been few in recent years) are scheduled for non–prime-time hours. Conventions have become tightly organized and highly orchestrated affairs where little is left to chance. The stakes are too high.

In the past, party leaders did not, or could not, exercise as much control, however. When there are deep divisions in the party, it may be impossible to prevent them from surfacing at the convention during prime time. The classic late–twentieth-century example is the 1968 Democratic Convention. It was filled with conflict—conflict inside the convention between the supporters of Hubert Humphrey and opponents of the Johnson policies on the Vietnam War and conflict outside the convention on the streets of Chicago between antiwar demonstrators and the Chicago police. Television covered both events, associating the division in the convention with the turmoil outside, and dimmed Humphrey's chances of winning the election.

In recent years, with the nomination settled well in advance of the convention and few vociferous floor fights over platforms, the conventions have been less dramatic and suspenseful. Consequently, the major networks are no longer showing them "gavel to gavel," leaving that coverage to public television or specialty cable networks such as CNN and C-SPAN. The major networks showed only a few prime-time events of each 2004 national convention: the keynote speech; an occasional speech by a party luminary, such as President Clinton at the Democratic convention and Arnold Schwarzenegger, governor of California, at the Republican one; the vice presidential acceptance speech; and the presidential acceptance speech. This limited coverage is the logical outcome of the successful attempt of party leaders to control the conventions. If there's no controversy, there's no media attention.

Selecting a Vice Presidential Nominee

Selection of a vice presidential candidate normally is done by the party's presidential nominee and then merely ratified at the convention, although in 1956, Democratic presidential nominee Adlai Stevenson broke with tradition and left the decision to the convention.

Presidential candidates usually select a vice presidential nominee who can balance the ticket. What exactly does "balance" mean? A careful analysis of vice presidential choices of both parties since 1940 revealed that presidential candidates tend to balance the ticket in terms of age—choosing a running mate from a different age cohort, as John Kerry did with John Edwards.[106] Those with little Washington experience usually balance the ticket by choosing a Washington insider as a running mate (as, in 1992, outsider Clinton did by choosing Gore and, as in 2000, outsider George W. Bush did by choosing Richard Cheney). However, Washington insiders tend to choose other insiders, as when Robert Dole chose insider Jack Kemp in 1996 and insider John Kerry chose insider John Edwards in 2004. Although common wisdom also suggests that presidential candidates balance the ticket in terms of region (e.g., John F. Kennedy from Massachusetts chose Texan Lyndon Johnson in 1960) or ideology (e.g., the more liberal Michael Dukakis chose the more conservative Lloyd Bentsen in 1988), this happens only occasionally.[107] In 2004, both presidential candidates had running mates whose ideologies were similar to their own.

Gender traditionally has not been part of a ticket-balancing effort, but since Walter Mondale's historic choice of Geraldine Ferraro in 1984, women are sometimes among those given consideration.

The most important factor, however, is choosing a vice presidential running mate from a large state—the larger, the better.[108] Presidential candidates believe that choosing a vice presidential candidate from a large state will help win that state in the November election. In fact, this is not true; the added advantage of a vice presidential candidate in his or her home state is less than 1 percent, and the bigger the state, the less the advantage.[109] About one-third of the vice presidential candidates since 1960, including John Edwards, did not even carry their home state.[110] Both Bush and Kerry ignored the large-state potential in choosing their running mates. In his 2004 debate with John Edwards, Richard Cheney even joked about his home state's miniscule contribution to the Electoral College totals (Wyoming has 3 votes out of the total 535).

Do vice presidential choices affect the election outcome? In most cases, no.

Independent and Third-Party Nominees

Independent and third-party candidates are part of every presidential campaign. Most of these candidates are invisible to all except for the most avid political devotee. But in recent elections, strong Independent candidates have emerged with some frequency, such as George Wallace in 1968, John Anderson in 1980, Ross Perot in 1992 and 1996, and Ralph Nader in 2000. The Perot candidacies were visible both because he had money to finance his campaigns and because he ran in an era when voters identified less strongly with parties and expressed more dissatisfaction with politics as usual. Though many people thought Perot might have an impact on the election, he did not. Nader did have an effect in 2000, however. His nearly one hundred thousand votes in Florida far exceeded the razor-slim Bush final margin, to give just one example. Though Pat Buchanan took some conservative votes away from Bush, too, his totals were far less than those of Nader's.

It is not easy for Independent candidates to get on the ballot. State laws control access to the ballot, and Democratic and Republican legislators and governors make those laws. Thus, the candidates of the Democratic and Republican Parties are automatically placed on the ballot in all fifty states, but Independent candidates must demonstrate significant support to get on the ballot through petitions signed by voters. In 2004, Nader tried and failed to get on the ballots in several states, though he was successful in Florida, Minnesota, and Wisconsin, among the swing states. In Pennsylvania, his supporters submitted petitions with the required number of signatures. However, the judge hearing the appeal against Nader commented that the Nader supporters "shock[ed] the conscience of the court. . . . In addition to Mickey Mouse, Fred Flintstone, John Kerry, and . . . Ralph Nader, there were thousands of names created at random." Therefore, Nader was not allowed on the Pennsylvania ballot.[111]

The General Election Campaign

We take it for granted that the election campaign is what determines who wins, and it does have a modest effect.[112] But consider this: only twice since 1952 has the candidate who was ahead in the polls in July, before the national conventions, lost the election. Those years were 1988 when Dukakis led and 2000 when Al Gore led (and since Gore won the popular vote, perhaps his case is only a partial exception to the rule).[113] This suggests that although campaigns can make a difference, a lot of other factors determine who is elected.

Campaign Organization

Staffing the campaign organization is crucial, not only to hire talented people, but also to get those with considerable national campaign experience and a variety of perspectives. In 1984 and 1988, the Republicans had the advantage in national campaign experience, but in the 1990s, the advantage shifted to the Democrats. In 2004, both teams had considerable experience, given many of Kerry's advisors were old Clinton advisors, though the Republican team was much more cohesive.

The candidate's own personal organization is only one part of the overall campaign organization. The national party organization and state parties also have some responsibilities, including the very important

... before the greatest audience ever ...
MORE THAN 70,000,000 VOTERS!

These Tips Tell How Your Behavior Can Win Democratic Votes From Our TV Audience ...

 Get into your place well *ahead* of time. The Hall can't look good across the nation with its bare seats showing, latecomers drifting in.

 Stay in your place till *after* you're told we're off the air. Impatient delegates scuttling out of a littered Hall don't make a good picture.

 Pay no attention to the cameras — then they'll pay more attention to *you*. You'll really get wiped out fast if you insist on playing lens-mugger, hand-waver, TVbitionist.

 Don't keep poking signs, banners, balloons up where they intercept cameras, speakers, candidates, all-Party displays.

 Show your enthusiasm and enjoy it. But don't interrupt speakers incessantly, don't be a point-killer. Save your punching power for the real final round.

 Remember — there's nothing phony about having good TV manners. It's just good sense. It's good for you, good for the Party.

We're Playing To The World's Greatest Audience—SHOW WHAT A GREAT PARTY WE ARE!

In the 1950s, at the dawn of the television age, Democratic Party leaders instruct their delegates how to behave on camera.

functions of registering potential party voters and getting them to the polls, as well as trying to make sure that the presidential candidate's local appearances will help the party's congressional and state candidates. Party organizations are also crucial in raising funds after the conventions, when direct fundraising by candidates is no longer legal (see Chapter 9).

Campaign Strategies

Developing a strategy is an important element of a presidential campaign. But every strategy is surrounded by uncertainty, and even political pros cannot always predict the impact of a particular strategy.

Candidates seek to do three things: mobilize those who are already loyal to them and their party, persuade independent voters that they are the best candidate, and try to convert the opposition. Most candidates emphasize mobilizing their own voters. Democrats have to work harder at this than Republicans because Democratic voters often do not vote and are more likely to vote for the other party than are Republicans.

Both parties must try to persuade independent voters because Independents are the swing voters; their votes determine the outcome. In 1964, when Johnson trounced Republican Goldwater, 80 percent of Republicans voted for Goldwater. In 2006, a large majority of Independents turned against the Republicans they had supported in 2004, and this switch led to the Democrats retaking the House and Senate majorities.

The crucial strategic question is where to allocate resources of time and money: where to campaign, where to buy media time and how much to buy, and where to spend money helping local organizations.

Allocating Resources among States

Candidates must always remember that they have to win a majority of the Electoral College vote (see "The Electoral College" section later in this chapter). The most populous states, with the largest number of electoral votes, are vital. Prime targets are those large states that could go to either party, such as, in 2004, Ohio, Pennsylvania, and of course Florida. In recent years, candidates have been increasingly sophisticated about where to use their limited resources. Thus in the 2004 presidential campaign, there was little advertising or activity in several of the largest states—California, Illinois, New York, and Texas—because the first three were considered sure Kerry states and the last a sure Bush state. Instead, the campaign focused mostly on the so-called **battleground states** (or **swing states**), where the results were in doubt: not just the large states of Ohio, Pennsylvania, and Florida, but medium-sized states such as Wisconsin and Iowa and even smaller states such as New Mexico with its five electoral votes and New Hampshire with four. As one indicator of attention, President Bush visited Pennsylvania eighteen times during the campaign, and Senator Kerry visited it twenty-two times. Ohio was John Kerry's most frequent stop (with twenty-six visits), and it was second for George W. Bush (with seventeen visits). Relatives of the candidates, entertainers, and party luminaries who campaigned for the candidates also focused on these swing states.

In focusing on swing states, candidates are attempting to expand their existing bases of support. Most of the Rocky Mountain states have been solidly Republican in their presidential loyalties. Republicans must build on this base and their strength in the South by carrying some of the large eastern or Midwestern industrial states to win.

Democrats have a strategic problem given the solid Rocky Mountain and Southern Republican bloc. Between the end of Reconstruction (in 1877) and 1948, the South was solidly Democratic. Since 1976, the Democrats have consistently lost the South, as we discussed in Chapter 7. Some strategists have urged the Democrats to win back the South by choosing more conservative candidates. Others argued for a strategy to win without the South, aiming for the industrial states of the East and Midwest along with California and a few other states of the West. This was Clinton's winning strategy, although he did win three southern states in each election. (This strategy was also used successfully by the Republicans between the 1870s and the 1920s, when they were able to capture the White House regularly without ever winning a southern state.)

Creating Images

Largely through the media, candidates try to create a favorable image and portray the opponent in an unfavorable way. The George H. Bush campaign was remarkably successful at creating a negative image for Dukakis in 1988; Dukakis was unsuccessful in either creating a positive image for himself or reinforcing Bush's negative image.

In 1992, the Bush campaign struggled to create both a positive image for the president and a negative image for Clinton. Bush could not find a focus for redefining himself, and his efforts to define a negative image for Clinton had limited success. The Clinton team had learned from the Dukakis debacle. They answered every attack Bush made, but, at the same time, they stayed focused on their own campaign message.

In 2000, George W. Bush used his warm personality to establish a positive image despite the concerns many voters had about his abilities. Voters were comfortable with Gore's abilities, but had reservations about his personality. Moreover, after eight years of Clintonian evasions and lies about personal issues, Gore's exaggerations may have seemed too much like those of Clinton.

In 2004, Bush tried to define himself as a resolute war leader and define Kerry as a "flip-flopper" with no principled positions. Kerry, in turn, painted Bush as an arrogant person unwilling to listen to criticisms or admit failures.

Issues can also be the basis for an appeal to voters. Democrats traditionally have used the "pocketbook" issues, arguing that economic times are better with Democratic presidents. In 2004, though, the Iraq War and the war on terrorism were the predominant issues of the campaign. Though Kerry sought to turn attention to domestic issues, the campaign was fought largely on the issue of who would be the stronger leader in a dangerous world. And the results indicated that those voters concerned about this issue voted strongly for Bush. By 2006, though, the unpopular war turned the key issues to a plus for Democrats.

Issue appeals are usually general, and often candidates do not offer a clear-cut choice even on the most important controversies of the time. For example, the 1968 presidential election offered voters little choice on Vietnam policy, because the positions of candidates Nixon and Humphrey appeared very similar.[114] Voters who wanted to end the war by withdrawing and others who wanted to escalate the war had no real choice of candidates. In 2004, the situation was similar with neither candidate offering an option to withdraw from Iraq, though Kerry appeared more willing to declare Iraq a failed venture.

Ideally, the major campaign themes and strategies have been put into place by the end of the summer, but these themes and strategies are revised and updated on a daily, sometimes hourly, basis as the campaign progresses. Decisions are made not only by the candidate and the campaign manager, but also by a staff of key advisers that includes media experts and pollsters. Sophisticated polling techniques are used to produce daily reports on shifts in public opinion across the nation and in particular regions. Campaign trips are modified or scratched as the candidate's organization sees new opportunities. And media events can be planned to complement the paid advertising the candidate runs.

Campaign Communication

Candidates use multiple ways of communicating with their supporters and with the millions of swing voters who might vote either way. Campaign advertising, appearances on television, candidate debates, mass mailings, and electronic communication are all part of campaign communication. They inform, they help set the

When the nation is at war or is threatened by an external enemy, there is almost always a "rally 'round the flag" effect. For the moment, anyway, citizens put aside partisan differences to provide a common front to a threatening enemy. The Gulf War in 1991 led President George H. Bush's public opinion ratings to skyrocket as the public supported the war. As we have seen, however, no president has had a bigger and more prolonged rally than George W. Bush after the events of 9/11.

It is not surprising, then, that the events of 9/11 affected the 2002 congressional campaigns. Candidates of both parties attempted to wrap themselves in the flag and identify with the war on terrorism. Republicans were effusive in their praise of President Bush. Some Republicans encouraged the view that questions about the success of the war or the way we were fighting it were dangerous to our fighting troops, if not downright treasonous. The president implied that congressional Democrats were not interested in the security of America when they did not pass a resolution quickly enough giving him a free hand to invade Iraq.

Though most Democrats seemed afraid to challenge the president on his handling of the war, Republicans used the war in attempts to unseat Democratic House and Senate incumbents in the 2002 election. Senator Tom Harkin's (D-Iowa) unsuccessful opponent, House Republican Greg Ganske, pointed out that Harkin had opposed a constitutional amendment to ban flag burning. Said Ganske, "America has a renewed sense of patriotism and a renewed appreciation for our American flag. Not everyone agrees."[1] An Iowa Republican leader accused Harkin of "trying to make America's war on terrorism a partisan issue."[2]

The Republican opponent of Senator Tim Johnson (D-S.D.) accused Johnson of voting consistently against the B-2 bomber and national missile defense system (again, before 9/11). The attack backfired, and Johnson won when his supporters ran an ad showing his son, an army sergeant, fighting in Afghanistan. Saxby Chambliss, the Republican opponent of Senator Max Cleland (D-Ga.), accused Cleland of breaking his oath to defend America by voting in favor of a chemical weapons treaty. This accusation offended even some Republicans who knew that Senator Cleland, a Vietnam veteran, had lost both legs and an arm in that war. Nonetheless, with George W. Bush's support, Chambliss won.

Real opposition to the war did not develop until the United States invaded Iraq in 2003. The seemingly quick military success turned into a prolonged civil conflict. By 2004, the protracted military action in Iraq led to significant opposition and renewed determination of the Democrats to oust the president. That opposition failed, but the protracted and bloody Iraqi civil war coupled with increased U.S. casualties gave ammunition to the war's opponents as time went on. By 2006, the Republicans were on the defensive on the war issue and charges that opposition to the war was unpatriotic no longer worked. Iraq was a key issue in the Democratic success in the mid term elections.

Patriotic rallying 'round the flag can, over time, turn to public hostility against wars that America does not win, as Presidents Johnson and Truman learned to their sorrow. This seems especially true when the president politicizes the war, as Bush did in 2002 and 2003. But even if he had not, the fears of an Iraqi quagmire would have stimulated opposition.

[1]Helen Dewar, "War on Terror Colors the Battle for Congress," *Washington Post*, July 5, 2002, A1.
[2]Ibid.

---

campaign agenda, and they help persuade voters.[115] In Chapter 5, we discussed these effects generally; here we discuss some effects related specifically to campaigns.

Media Advertising

Paid advertisements allow candidates to focus on points most favorable to their cause or to portray their opponents in the most negative light. In 2004, the presidential candidates and associated groups spent more than $1 billion on advertising in an attempt to sway public opinion.[116] Most advertising is done through television, though radio and the Internet also reach significant audiences.[117]

Television ads were first used in the 1952 campaign. One, linking the Democratic Truman administration to the unpopular Korean War, showed two soldiers in combat talking about the futility of war. Then one of the soldiers is hit and dies. The other one exposes himself to the enemy and is also killed. The announcer's voice says, "Vote Republican."[118] Today's ads are shorter and less melodramatic, but still appeal to emotions. One classic example was the 1984 Reagan ad, depicting his policies as putting the country on the road to greatness again ("It's morning in America").[119] Many of these historic ads are available for viewing online at www.movingimage.us.

There is both an art and a science to campaign ads. Most political ads are quite short, thirty or sixty seconds in length. Campaigns are sophisticated in where they place ads. Selections of television shows and media markets are important. For example, in 2004, President Bush ran many of his ads on crime shows such as *Law and Order* and *NYPD Blue* because he thought there would be an audience of conservative men sympathetic to Republican appeals watching those shows. The Kerry campaign ran more ads on shows with more appeal to women, such as *Judge Judy* and *Oprah,* and to younger and older men, such as the *Late Show with David Letterman.*[120]

Kerry also advertised more on shows with African American stars. Both campaigns spent a lot to advertise on morning news shows and popular daytime shows such as *Dr. Phil.*[121]

Both campaigns focused on the battleground states and wasted little of their advertising budget on states already thought to be sure for one candidate.[122] But within the battleground states, the Bush campaign focused more on the rural and outer suburban areas than did the Kerry campaign.

Campaigns also have to decide what combination to run of positive ads, touting their own programs; negative ads, attacking their opponents; and response ads, responding to opponents' charges. Today, media ads can be added and deleted as polls reflect their impact. Negative ads were more prominent in the 2004 election than in the recent past. At least in the early stages, the Bush campaign ran far more negative ads than the Kerry campaign.

About three-fourths of Bush's ads through the early summer were negative ads, whereas only about one-fourth of Kerry's ads were.[123] The proportions for both candidates rose as Election Day drew nearer.

This high level of negativity is unusual for an incumbent, but probably reflected his low approval ratings. Strong front-runners tend to stay positive.[124] The 2004 election was so close that both sides made liberal use of negative ads. However, many ads were run not by the candidates themselves, but by advocacy groups.

Negative ads do provide some helpful information about issues, supplementing media news coverage, which focuses heavily on personalities, conflicts, and the "horse race" aspect of campaigns.[125] Negative ads tend to reinforce previous inclinations. So, if you believed in 2004 that the president had made a mess of Iraq, then you are more likely to believe an ad charging him with that; if you thought Kerry was a flip-flopper, you were more open to negative ads on that point. Republicans and Independents find negative ads more believable than Democrats do, perhaps because Republicans and Independents are more cynical about politics and government to begin with.

Many negative ads contain some grain of truth, though not always. Kerry did vote for many tax increases, but not as many as the Republicans charged. Hundreds of thousands of jobs were lost during the Bush administration, but not as many as the Democrats claimed. The war in Iraq had not cost $200 million by September 2004 as the Democrats claimed, but it did by December. Still, there is little evidence, for example, that negative ads increase voter cynicism or depress turnout significantly.

However, many negative ads are simply false, such as charges that Kerry would raise the gas tax by fifty cents or that he claimed that all U.S. troops were responsible for the misconduct of a few at Abu Ghraib prison. Among the most discussed negative ads in 2004 were those of the Swift Boat Veterans for Truth. The group attacked Kerry's war record. (Kerry, as a young naval lieutenant, commanded a "swift boat" in the Vietnam War and won medals for heroism as well as for his wounds.) The Swift Boat veterans did not serve with Kerry, and several were angry with him for returning from Vietnam and opposing the war. The Kerry campaign was slow to respond to these August ads and lost ground in the polls during this period despite the fact that independent reexaminations of the record found nothing to substantiate the Swift Boat veterans' ad claims.

After the Swift Boat fiasco, Kerry began responding immediately to other negative ads. Technology allows opposition candidate's ads to be evaluated continuously and new ads prepared immediately to counter attacks that might be having an impact. For example, one day in October, the Kerry campaign learned that President Bush had just charged that Kerry would "weaken America and make the world more dangerous." Within three hours, the Kerry campaign had made an ad accusing Bush of "desperately attacking" Kerry. By late afternoon, the script and video were sent to reporters.[126] Often new response ads are targeted as much to the media as to the public and are only run a few times. The Bush campaign had a similar instant-response operation.

After the first debate, the Bush campaign immediately ran an ad focusing on Kerry's comment about a "global test," and implied that Kerry would not defend the United States without allies' approval. The Kerry campaign immediately struck back stating "George Bush lost the debate. Now he's lying about it" and repeated Kerry's statement about the president always having the right to make a preemptive strike. The Kerry ad ran only in a few cities and on the cable networks where the Bush ad ran.[127]

The Kerry campaign ran some negative ads of its own, raising fears that the Republicans would undermine Social Security with a privatization plan (which Bush then endorsed after the election). Some campaign advisers believe negative ads are very effective, even though most people say they do not like them.[128] One campaign advisor said, "People won't pay any attention [to positive ads]. Better to knock your opponent's head off."[129] And polls show that negative ads can sometimes have a dramatic short-term effect on a candidate's standing. The Bush campaign outspent the Gore campaign near the end of the 2000 campaign and might have shifted the balance in a few key states.

Historians tell us that negative campaigning is as American as apple pie. When Thomas Jefferson faced John Adams in 1796, a Federalist editorial called Jefferson "mean spirited, low-lived . . . the son of a half-breed Indian squaw" and prophesized that if he were elected, "[m]urder, robbery, rape, adultery and incest will be openly taught and practiced."[130] When Andrew Jackson ran for president in 1832, his mother was called a prostitute, his father a mulatto (someone of mixed races, black and white), his wife a profligate woman, and himself a bigamist.[131] A British observer of American elections in 1888 described them as a "tempest of invective and calumny . . . imagine all the accusations brought against all the candidates for the 670 seats in the English Parliament concentrated on one man, and read . . . daily for three months."[132]

Checks do exist on negative campaigns.[133] One check is the press, which could point out errors of fact. In recent campaigns, many in the press have tried to do this, but often end up simply giving more attention to the negative messages.[134] In 2004, fact-checkers were more active and many papers ran critiques of the truthfulness of ads (and statements in debates). The voters, who might become outraged, are another check. The third check is the candidate under attack, who in most cases will strike back. Both candidates were aggressive in countering negative ads in 2004.

Campaigns are expensive because they rely so heavily on the media to get the candidate's message to the voters. As one observer argued, "Today's presidential campaign is essentially a mass-media campaign. It is not that the mass media entirely determine what happens. . . . [b]ut it is no exaggeration to say that, for the large majority of voters, the campaign has little reality apart from the media version."[135]

Television Appearances and Media Events

Increasingly, candidates are getting free publicity by appearing on various television shows. In earlier elections, candidates appeared only on "serious" shows, such as the Sunday morning talk shows where candidates would be interviewed by one or more members of the press. Now it is increasingly common for candidates to appear in more informal, sometimes humorous, settings such as late night talk shows or comedy shows. The candidates hope to use these settings to show voters that they are approachable and down to earth. It also gives candidates a chance to poke fun at their own foibles and thus possibly defuse opponents' attacks.

National television appearances might be the only sight that voters in a majority of states ever get of the candidates. Given the increasing sophistication of the campaigns, most television and radio ads never appear in states that are solid for one candidate or another. Although voters in battleground states might consider it a blessing to not have to listen to campaign ads, voters in nonbattleground states may feel less connected to the campaign.

Candidates also try to use the media to their advantage by staging media events that allow them to be photographed doing and saying noncontroversial things in front of enthusiastic crowds and patriotic

© Brooks Kraft/Corbis

In 2004, George W. Bush campaigned on his role as commander in chief and was often photographed with the military.

symbols. Candidates spend most of their time going from media market to media market, hoping to get both national and local coverage.[136] Vice presidential candidates often appear in the smaller media markets, while the presidential contenders hit the major metro areas. In 1988, George H. Bush almost literally wrapped himself in the flag, frequently "pledging allegiance," until negative media reaction led his advisers to realize that they were overdoing it.

Televised Debates

Candidates also use televised debates as part of their media campaigns. In 1960, Kennedy challenged Nixon to debate during their presidential campaigns. Nixon did not want to debate because as vice president he was already known and ahead in the polls. He remembered his first election to the House of Representatives when he challenged the incumbent to debate and, on the basis of his performance, won the election. Afterward he said the incumbent was a "damn fool" to debate. Nevertheless, Nixon did agree to debate, and when the two contenders squared off, presidential debates were televised to millions of homes across the country for the first time.

Nixon dutifully answered reporters' questions and rebutted Kennedy's assertions. But Kennedy came to project an image. He sought to demonstrate his vigor, to compensate for his youth and inexperience. He also sought to contrast his attractive appearance and personality with Nixon's. So he quickly answered reporters' specific questions and then directly addressed viewers about his general goals.

Kennedy's strategy worked. He appealed to people and convinced them that his youth and inexperience would not pose problems. While Kennedy remained calm, Nixon became very nervous. He smiled at inappropriate moments, his eyes darted back and forth, he had a five-o'clock shadow that gave him a somewhat sinister look, and beads of sweat rolled down his face.

According to public opinion polls, people who saw the debates thought that Kennedy performed better in three of the four. (The only debate in which they thought Nixon performed better was the one in which the candidates were not in the same studio side-by-side. They were in separate cities, and with this arrangement Nixon was less nervous.) Yet people who heard the debates on radio did not think Kennedy performed as well. They were not influenced by the visual contrast between the candidates. Clearly, television made the difference.

No more presidential debates were held for sixteen years. The candidates who were ahead did not want to risk their lead. But in 1976, President Ford decided to debate Carter, and in 1980, President Carter decided

Families all across the country gathered in front of their TVs to watch the first televised presidential debates in 1960, featuring Senator John F. Kennedy and Vice President Richard Nixon.

to debate Reagan. Both incumbents were in trouble, and they thought they needed to debate to win. Although President Reagan was far ahead in 1984, he decided to debate Mondale because he did not want to seem afraid. By agreeing to debate, he solidified the precedent begun anew in 1976. In 2000, the low expectation by the media for Bush's performance, coupled with his congenial, personal style, helped him hold his own or even win the debates in the view of many, even though the debates revealed his limited grasp of issues and his misstatements. Gore's mannerisms seemed stiff and even phony to many, particularly in the first debate. And the press, in an attempt to be fair, mentioned more about Gore's body language than it did Bush's misstatements of fact.

Because candidates have different strengths, each campaign wants a debate format that builds on its candidate's strengths. The "debate about debates" has become as predictable a part of campaigns as the debates themselves. Representatives of candidates debate the number of debates, the formats, the topics to be covered, the size of the audience, even the size and shape of the podia. The 2004 debates were governed by a thirty-two-page set of rules agreed to by the candidates' representatives.

In 2004, those negotiating for Bush argued that the first debate should be about foreign policy, ostensibly Bush's strength. He thought he could easily show Kerry to have an uncertain grasp and a vacillating policy. Instead, Kerry looked assured and confident and attacked Bush's foreign policy mistakes throughout the debate. When cameras focused on Bush listening to Kerry, he looked surly and angry at being attacked. And when Bush had chances to respond, he was not able to consistently offer a coherent and articulate defense of his policies. Consequently, though Kerry had been trailing in the polls before the debate, his performance in this first debate narrowed the gap.

Postdebate analyses focused on the fact that Bush had been so confident before the debate that he did not prepare much. Moreover, Bush was not used to direct criticism of his policies. Within the White House, criticism was not welcomed, and on the campaign trail, Bush usually spoke only to handpicked Republican supporters, whose tough questions tended to be about whether he liked broccoli or what he felt about his legacy.[137] Thus he did not have much recent experience facing criticism nor with presenting a serious counterargument to it. The ridicule and dismissiveness that he used in his campaign stump speeches did not work well when faced with a real-life opponent making real-life arguments on stage.

The President prepared more for the second and third debates and looked more confident and pleasant.

However, most people thought that Kerry bested Bush in those debates, too, but only by a small margin.[138]

E-Campaigning

Increasingly, candidates are relying on electronic communication to keep supporters informed about the campaign and the issues, to raise money, and to solicit volunteer activity. The contemporary candidacy would not be complete without an Internet address to provide information on policies, report recent speeches, offer opportunities to send messages to the candidates, and encourage browsers to volunteer. Some sites offer opportunities to register to vote. Candidates also use websites to do negative campaigning, discrediting opponents.

With the touch of a button, e-mail allows campaigns to communicate with hundreds of thousands of people, making them feel like insiders and encouraging their continued support and allegiance (see the box titled "You've Got Mail"). These e-mail messages supplement the use of direct postal mailings, which are more expensive and less responsive to breaking events. An e-mail can be prepared and sent in a few hours, a direct mailing takes days or longer. In the 2004 election, the Kerry campaign had more than two million supporters on its e-mail lists, and the Republicans reportedly had as many as six million.

Podcasts to download are an even newer feature of e-campaigning, and the parties are also examining Internet social networks such as Friendster and Facebook to try to access groups of potential supporters.[139] In the 2006 elections, YouTube became a way for millions of Internet users to play and replay candidate mistakes. Senator George Allen's (R-Va.) comment calling an Indian American "macacca" was captured on camera and replayed to another 100,000 people. This no doubt contributed to his narrow defeat.

Blogs also have become a campaign tool. Candidates and their supporters can air their views and attack opponents through blogs, some of which are read by millions. Daily Kos, whose contributors are mostly liberal, left, and Democrats, had nearly five million hits in one month in 2005.[140] Each blog site reaches a specialized group of people. Although talk radio is dominated by conservative Republicans, the most popular political blogs are those on the liberal side.

Campaign Funding

Success in raising money is one of the keys to a successful political campaign. Although some of the money for presidential campaigns comes from public funds, much is raised privately. In Chapter 9 we will discuss campaign funding and its impact on politics.

In an attempt to assess and compare the frequency, content, and effectiveness of candidates' electronic mailings, one of the authors of this book enrolled on the e-mail lists of both candidates during the 2004 presidential election. Enrolling was easy; it only required going to the websites and filling out a simple form.

Table 8.1 summarizes the scope of the e-mailing over a seventy-day period from the conclusion of the Democratic convention through the Republican convention and all four debates.

There were both similarities and differences in the candidates' uses of e-mail. Both wrote more than once every other day (the Democrats more than the Republicans), exhorted their supporters to register to vote, then later in the period to volunteer to help register others to vote. Both asked their supporters to volunteer for other tasks, including hosting house parties during the conventions and the debates and participating in trying to spin the message after the debates. Several times the Kerry e-mails asked supporters to

sign petitions protesting some Republican act, such as the ties between the ostensibly independent group organizing the anti-Kerry Swift Boat ads and the Republican party. Both occasionally used family members and other celebrities to send messages; Laura Bush and the Bush daughters and Arnold Schwarzenegger for the Republicans and Teresa Heinz Kerry, John Edwards, and Hillary Clinton for the Democrats.

But there were also striking differences in the way the two campaigns used their electronic messages; this reflected the different context of the campaigns. The Bush campaign was well funded by corporate contributors; the Democrats relied more heavily on small donors. Hence more than 40 percent of the Kerry e-mails asked for money, whereas only about 10 percent of the Republican messages did.

Kerry needed to become better known, even to Democratic activists, so he sent a string of e-mails early in this time period outlining his views on various issues. The president was already well known to his closest supporters and did not lay out his plat-

TABLE 8.1	Content of Candidates' and Parties' E-Mails, 2004 Presidential Election

Number of:	Republicans	Democrats
E-mails sent	43	51
Requests for financial donations	5	21
Requests to volunteer to canvass, make calls, sign petitions write to newspapers, host a party	17	28
Information about the issues of the campaign	5	10
Appeals to register and vote	3	8
Negative, nonpolicy attacks on opposition	9	10
Other	15	3

SOURCE: Based on research by author Susan Welch for seventy days of the campaign.

The Electoral College

All planning for the campaign has to take into account the peculiar American institution of the **Electoral College.** In the United States, we do not have a direct election of the president. Although Al Gore had more than five hundred thousand more votes than George W. Bush in 2000, he lost the election. The Electoral College is another feature of the American constitutional system that limits democracy.[141]

The Way the System Works

What counts is the popular vote in each state, because that vote determines which candidate will receive the state's electoral votes. Each state has as many electors as its total representation in Congress (House plus Senate) (see Figure 4.4 in Chapter 4). The smallest states (and the District of Columbia) have three, whereas the largest state—California—has fifty-five. Voters choose electors of the Electoral College. The election is not decided until these elec-

tors gather in each state capitol in December after the presidential election to cast their votes for president and vice president.

With the exception of Maine and Nebraska, which divide some of their Electoral College votes according to who wins in each congressional district, all of each state's electoral votes go to the candidate winning the most votes in that state. If one candidate wins a majority (270) of the electors voting across the United States, then the election is decided. If the electoral vote is tied, or if no candidate wins a majority, then the election is decided in the House of Representatives, where each state has one vote and a majority is necessary to win. This has not happened since 1824, when John Quincy Adams was chosen. If voting in the Electoral College for the vice president does not yield a majority, the Senate chooses the vice president, with each senator having one vote. If it should get to that stage, the largest and smallest states would have equal weight, a very undemocratic procedure.

form or programs in any systematic way except to send the text of his acceptance speech from the Republican Convention. While the Kerry campaign was asking for money and volunteer activity, many of the Bush e-mails were asking supporters to go on online chats to visit with celebrities, relatives of the candidates, and campaign organizers. The Bush campaign also directed their supporters to read certain new books lauding the president and his policies. The Bush campaign was already humming and did not need additional volunteer activity or money at that time. It did want to keep its supporters engaged, so it substituted these other opportunities for campaign involvement.

The Kerry campaign had more of a sense of urgency because the campaign continually asked for money and for volunteer effort. Before the first debate, the Kerry campaign urged its supporters to participate in online polls and chat groups after the debate and gave them several web addresses to check. The Bush campaign did not do so. Then in a backhanded acknowledgement of Kerry's success in the first debate and the postdebate spin, the Republicans announced in an e-mail later in the week that "Senator Kerry demonstrated he was serious about winning an election while President Bush demonstrated he was serious about winning a war."[1] By the second debate, the Bush campaign also was urging its supporters to vote in online polls and write letters to the editor.

Several ads by both campaigns attacked the policy positions of the other. And about 20 percent of each were sharper, attacking the other candidate or organization for lies, distortions, and extremism. Half of the Kerry negative attacks were responses to the Republican-linked "Swift Boat Veterans for Truth" ads questioning his courage and patriotism (see Chapter 6). Typical was this message from Mary Beth Cahill, Kerry's campaign manager. "George Bush and his Republican friends have become so desperate that they are returning to their old tricks—whenever a campaign is going badly, they smear the record of a Vietnam veteran. They did it to John McCain in 2000, to Max Cleland in 2002, and now they are doing it to John Kerry."

The Bush campaign's negative attacks focused more on tying the Democrats to the far left wing and to unaccountable groups. Ed Gillespie, chair of the Republican National Committee wrote, "Any mention of John Kerry's votes for higher taxes and against vital weapons programs will be met with the worst kind of personal attacks. Such desperation is unbecoming of American Presidential politics. . . ."

Whether used to raise money, solicit volunteers, attack opponents, or lift the morale and fighting spirit of the candidates' core supporters, clearly e-mail has found an important place in campaign communication. It increases the candidates' abilities to have immediate communication and respond strategically to the imperatives of the developing campaigns. This technology is here to stay in political campaigns.

[1]October 2, 2004.

Strategic Implications

The campaign strategies that candidates use are shaped by the Electoral College system. In general, candidates have incentives to spend more time in the large states where the majority of the electoral votes are. However, in recent campaigns, a disproportionate amount of time is spent on the so-called swing states, states that are not safe for one candidate or the other. That is why states such as New York and California had few political ads and visits by the campaigns. Their votes were considered to be safe for John Kerry, so neither Bush nor Kerry paid attention to the state. Without an Electoral College system, both Bush and Kerry would have spent much more time in those states given their huge populations.

But the small states that tend to favor the existing system did not receive much attention either. The safe Republican states in the prairies, the South, and the Great Plains were ignored, too, by Bush as well as Kerry.

Rationale and Outcomes of the Electoral College

The Founders neither wanted nor envisioned a popular election of the president; selection of the president was placed in the hands of state elites, the electors. The Founders also agreed to enshrine the influence of small states (at that time, disproportionately Southern, slave-holding states) in the fundamental framework of the Constitution, and the Electoral College was one of the ways of doing that.[142]

The Founders assumed that the Electoral College would have considerable power, with each elector exercising independent judgment and choosing from among a large number of candidates. They did not foresee the development of political parties or the development of a political climate where the popular vote is seen as the source of legitimacy for a candidate. In practice, as state parties developed, the electors became part of the party process, pledged to party candidates. Thus electors usually rubber-stamp the choice of voters in each state rather than exercise their own judgment.

A discrepancy between the Electoral College and the popular vote outcome occurred three times in the nineteenth century (1824, 1876, and 1888). However, after more than a century of presidential elections whose outcome was known once the popular vote was tallied, and since the principle of "one person one vote" has become enshrined in law and political culture, the American public has become used to thinking of elections as an expression of the will of the people.

When the 2000 election yielded an Electoral College winner who had not won the popular vote, there were immediate calls for the elimination or reform of the Electoral College system. However, these calls went nowhere, and the Electoral College remains.

Possible Reforms

The Electoral College was designed both to temper the influence of voters by establishing an intermediate body of electors who actually choose the president and to make sure that the South had a disproportionate influence on the choice of the president.[143] It is a distinctly undemocratic mechanism that institutionalizes in the presidential election process part of the excess weight given to smaller states in the United States Senate.

Over the years, several proposed reforms have been considered. One reform would be to abolish the Electoral College altogether and leave the choice of president to the popular vote because direct election is a more understandable system. Direct election is not as simple as it seems, however, because when the election is close and there are third-party candidates who get more than a token vote, some run-off system might be necessary.

Even though one might think support for a popular election would be overwhelming given the democratic values of our society, it is not. The Electoral College is based on states, so it encourages campaigns designed to win "states." In this sense, it reinforces the federal system. People in small states support it because their electoral votes are a larger proportion of the Electoral College than their actual votes are a proportion of all votes.

On the other hand, many political and legal experts believe the Electoral College system gives greater weight to a vote cast in a large state; a one-vote margin in Pennsylvania, for example, yields twenty-one votes for the winning candidate compared to only three votes in North Dakota. Thus it is more important to get that extra vote in Pennsylvania. Therefore, candidates focus their campaigns in, and appeals to, the large states with tight races.

An even more undemocratic feature of the Electoral College is that not all states require their electors to cast their votes for the candidates who won the state vote. The **faithless elector** is one who casts his or her vote for a personal choice, even someone who was not on the ballot. Even though the intent of the Founders was to allow electors to cast their votes any way desired, today, reformers have proposed that, in our more democratic era, electors should be bound by the wishes of the voters in their states. It is true that no faithless elector has ever made a difference in the outcome of an election, but in the 2000 election, as few as three faithless electors could have made a difference.

Another target of reform is the requirement that, if the electoral vote is tied, the presidential choice is to be thrown to the House of Representatives. There is no expectation that each state's House delegation will vote for the presidential candidate that its state's voters chose; rather, states will follow the majority party in their House delegation. In this process, Alaska will carry the same clout as California. This is a very undemocratic feature of the process, and would probably cause a crisis if actually used to elect a candidate with a minority of the popular vote.

The 2000 Election: A Perfect Storm

The election of 2000 demonstrates the antidemocratic nature of the Electoral College. It was won by George W. Bush, who got fewer votes than his rival, Al Gore. In another antidemocratic twist, the election was decided by the United States Supreme Court (more on the Court's role in Chapter 13). The division in the Electoral College was very close, and the decision rested on the outcome in Florida where election mismanagement, partisan politics, and unavoidable human error came together to create chaos in a closely divided race.

Election Day exit polls of Florida voters showed Gore winning by a small margin. But after first declaring Gore the winner, the television networks declared Bush the winner, and then in the early morning hours decided it was too close to call. The election hung in the balance (the media performance on election night 2000 is discussed in Chapter 5). Bush had a tiny lead of just several hundred ballots.

Confusion reigned in the days afterward. The press and election observers reported several problems, some of them serious. Thousands of Gore votes were lost because of the strange "butterfly" ballot configuration in Palm Beach County, a heavily Democratic liberal county. The odd format, designed by the supervisor of elections in the county, made it difficult for some voters to determine which punch hole corresponded to which presidential candidate. (It was labeled the "butterfly ballot" because candidate names appeared on both sides of a row of vertical punch holes rather than only on one side, which is the standard, less-confusing format.) Even though the problem was recognized early on Election

Day by some distraught voters leaving the polling places, there was no way that local election officials felt they could fix the problem then.

More than three thousand voters punched the hole registering a vote for Patrick Buchanan, to the right of Gore's name on the ballot. This is particularly ironic because the areas of Palm Beach County casting the most votes for Buchanan were those inhabited by mostly elderly Jewish voters, the least likely group to support Buchanan, who is thought to be anti-Semitic. As one elderly Jewish woman exclaimed after mistakenly voting for Buchanan, "I would rather have had a colonoscopy than vote for that son-of-a-bitch Buchanan."[144]

Nearly three thousand voted for Gore and the socialist candidate whose punch hole was underneath Gore, apparently thinking they voted for Joseph Lieberman, Gore's vice presidential running mate, whose name was under Gore's. (Bush lost about 1600 votes from those who voted for him and Buchanan.) While some spoiled ballots are normal in every election, this erratic pattern in one county was a result of the badly designed ballot. But there was nothing the Gore campaign could do. The ballot was designed by a Democratic supervisor of elections who made the candidates' names larger so elderly voters could read them easier. But the larger typeface actually made the format harder to understand. Nevertheless, a sample ballot had been printed in the local newspapers before the election, as is required in many states. Clearly there was no intention to deceive any voters.

There was also a problem with overseas ballots. Americans overseas have the right to vote. They must ask for a ballot before the election and mail it by the day of the election, but the ballot need not be received by local officials until ten days after the election. (This time allows for mail delays.) There are strict rules about how these ballots are to be certified to avoid vote fraud: for example, the ballots have to have legible overseas postmarks showing the ballot was cast on or before Election Day, a witness was present (a Florida requirement), and the voters had to have registered in advance. But hundreds of these ballots came in without postmarks or with U.S. postmarks, from voters who were not registered, or that lacked a witness. Many military personnel must have decided to vote after the election when the outcome appeared uncertain, and some may have been persuaded to do so by partisan groups.

After the election, Gore and the Democrats pursued a conservative strategy to deal with these problems that likely cost him the election. Nothing could be done about the butterfly ballot problem save a re-vote, and nothing in Florida law allowed that. To deal with tens of thousands of incompletely punched cards throughout the state, Gore asked only for a recount in four strongly Democratic counties. Later, after the Bush campaign sued to stop the recount, Gore did challenge Bush to

have a recount in every county, but he did not file suit to accomplish it.[145] Finally, when the Florida Supreme Court mandated a recount in every county, so much time had elapsed that the U.S. Supreme Court threw up its hands and gave the election to Bush.

The biggest mistake of the Democrats was not to challenge the overseas votes, even the hundreds that were patently illegal under Florida laws. Indeed, 680 were flawed, including nearly 200 with U.S. postmarks, indicating that they had been mailed from within the country rather than from overseas; 344 were late, illegible, or missing postmarks; and even 38 reflected double voting by 19 voters.[146] Clearly, the local election judges would have thrown these out had Democratic Party representatives challenged them. But they did not out of a timid concern about not wanting to appear against voting rights of overseas armed forces personnel, even fraudulent ones. As a consequence of the illegal military ballots alone, Gore lost Florida by 537 votes when his Election Day margin was 202 votes.[147]

The Bush postelection campaign was more skillful and more aggressive. At one point the Bush campaign even organized a demonstration to intimidate election officials in Miami-Dade County to stop conducting a recount they were in the middle of. Demonstrators barged into the building, yelling and pounding on doors. Photos from that event showed that many of the "demonstrators" were staffers in conservative congressional Republican offices who had been sent to Florida to do this, though at the time the election officials recounting the ballot did not know that. The demonstration succeeded in getting the officials to halt the recount.

The Bush campaign was also more aggressive in persuading election officials how to treat overseas ballots. Republican representatives urged election officials in Democratic-majority counties to follow the law in handling overseas ballots, so illegal ballots would not be counted; in Republican counties, they urged election officials to disregard the law, so illegal ballots would be counted. (There is nothing illegal or even immoral about Republican supporters doing this, but the election officials should not have caved, and the Democratic representatives should have argued that the laws be followed.) Meanwhile, Democratic representatives, fearing a public backlash, did not try to counter Republican efforts. As a result, Florida officials accepted hundreds of overseas absentee ballots that failed to comply with state laws."[148]

In addition, the Bush campaign had strong political allies in Florida. Not only was Bush's brother the governor, but the secretary of state, who oversees the election system, was cochair of Bush's Florida campaign. Making little effort to appear nonpartisan, at every opportunity she ruled in favor of the Bush campaign and forced the Gore campaign to go to court to obtain recounts and redress.

Time also worked in favor of the Bush campaign, because it held a narrow lead throughout the post-Election Day period and because it knew that the deadline for certifying Florida's electors would put pressure on the courts to stop the recount. Thus, the Bush campaign used delaying tactics to slow and stop the recounts.

The outcome of this election will long be argued. It is likely true that a bare majority of Florida voters, in fact, favored Gore.[149] Systematic analyses have proven that the Buchanan vote was inflated by at least 2500 votes intended for Gore in Palm Beach County.[150] As one commentator noted, "No election analyst will say with a straight face that the butter-fly design didn't cost Al Gore the presidency."[151]

Of course, the overseas ballot contributed, too, by an unknown amount. That is, we know how many ballots were illegal, but we don't know for sure their distribution between Bush and Gore. Nearly two-thirds of the 2400 overseas ballots counted after November 7 were for Bush. Two independent scholars argue that the probability is about 99 percent that Gore would have won if the invalid overseas ballots were handled properly and a statewide recount was allowed under any reasonable standard for counting chads.[152]

The confusion surrounding the 2000 election outcome highlights an important aspect of our electoral process: state law and local policies determine the mechanics of presidential elections. The election brought into stark relief the problems that shoddy election procedures can create. Former president and Nobel Peace Prize winner Jimmy Carter, who, through his Carter Center, now works for peace and social justice around the world, is often invited to monitor elections in Asia and Africa and to attest to their fairness. He remarked, "I was really taken aback and embarrassed by what happened in Florida. If we were invited to go into a foreign country to monitor the election, and they had similar standards and procedures, we would refuse to participate at all."[153]

Voting Patterns in the 2004 Election

Red States and Blue States

As we discussed in Chapter 4, popular parlance often refers to the solid Republican states as "red" states and the solid Democratic states as "blue" states because TV networks use red and blue to depict them on election night maps. Figure 4.4 (in Chapter 4; p. 108) illustrates the red states and blue states as well as the results of the 2004 election.

Though the press tends to discuss the red states and blue states as if they were fixed in concrete, of course they are not. There are a core of states that, in recent years, have voted solidly Republican and a core that have voted consistently Democratic, but many states change their majorities from one election to another. However, only one state (New Hampshire) voted Republican in 2000 but Democratic in 2004, and two states (New Mexico and Iowa) voted Democratic in 2000 but Republican in 2004.

Analysts of voting in the 2004 election discovered that the crude distinction between red and blue states disguises more telling voting patterns. Most red states are in the poorer half of the states as measured by per capita income. For example, twenty-six of the twenty-eight states with the lowest per capita income voted for Bush. Given that overall the poorer you are the more likely you are to vote Democratic and given that Bush's economic policies have favored the wealthy over the poor, this seems like a paradox.

In fact, in the poorer states, such as Oklahoma and Mississippi, the wealthy are very heavily Republican, voting Republican 80 percent of the time. In these red states, there is significant class voting. In the blue states, such as Maryland, New York, Connecticut, and California, the rich and the poor, on average, vote similarly. In blue states, rich people are only slightly more likely than poor people to be Republican. Rich people in the blue states are much more likely to be Democrats than they are in the poorer, red states.[154] "Class warfare," as evidenced through the ballot box, is much more prevalent in the red, Republican-voting states.

These patterns are new in American politics. But the 2004 election was also about continuity. Incumbent presidents usually win reelection; that happened fifteen out of the twenty times incumbents ran in the past century. Incumbents, such as Bush, whose party has just captured the White House almost always win; Jimmy Carter the one exception. Most states voted the same way in 2004 as in 2000. Though much has been made in the media of the success of the Republicans in 2004 due to "values issues" such as gay marriage, more systematic analyses suggest that these were not very important. Bush's margin compared to that in 2000 was slightly higher across the states, with the exception that in the states most directly affected by the World Trade Center attack (New York, New Jersey, and Connecticut) he gained more, nearly 6 percent.[155]

The Permanent Campaign

The **permanent campaign** is a term coined by political scientists to describe the current state of American electoral politics.[156] During each election cycle, the time between the completion of one election and the beginning of the next gets shorter and shorter. By summer 2006, not even half way into Bush's second term, media reports indicated that numerous potential candidates are already on the hustings. John Edwards has visited Iowa ten times and potential Democratic rivals Evan Bayh, Tom Daschle, Mark Warner, and John Kerry several times each. On the Republican side, George Pataki, currently governor of New York, had found occasions to be in Iowa seven times, the same number as Mitt Romney, the governor of another large eastern state, Massachusetts. Several other potential Republican candidates had also visited Iowa at least five times.[157] Of course, these and other candidates are not only visiting, but assembling field operations, hiring consultants and fundraisers, and commissioning polls. No longer does the election campaign start in the election year; now it is nearly a four-year process.

Several factors are responsible for this change, some political and some technological. The political process has changed a great deal during the past twenty years. Primaries have become the chief means by which candidates get nominated, and parties have shrunk in importance in the nominating process. The necessity to win primaries in different regions of the nation means that potential candidates must start early to become known to key political figures, and ultimately to the voting public, in these states. In the "old days," candidates had to woo only party leaders, a process that, though not easy, was much less public and much less expensive than campaigning for primary victories.

Technology has also contributed to the permanent campaign. Certainly, in comparison to the turn of the twentieth century, transportation and communications technology have revolutionized campaigns. Then travel was by rail, ship, or horse, and candidates could not simply dart about the country spending the morning in New York and the afternoon in Seattle. Telephone communication was primitive, and there were no radios or televisions. The idea of potential candidates spending four years publicly campaigning for office under these conditions would have been ludicrous.

But even in comparison with only thirty years ago, the media and information technology have revolutionized campaigning and thus have contributed to the permanent campaign. Modern computer and telephone technology enable the media and private organizations to take the pulse of the public through opinion polls almost continually. As polls have become more common, they have become a source of fascination by the media (and as pollsters have discovered that the media's appetite for polls is nearly insatiable, polls have proliferated). Whereas in the 1950s polls were rarely done and poll results were rarely discussed in media coverage of elections, by the 1980s hundreds of stories about each election campaign focused on poll results. Indeed, much of the media coverage of the campaign focuses on exactly that (see Chapter 5 for more on this topic). In 2004, many news outlets carried daily polls during the last couple of months of the campaign. Thus, candidates must pay attention to how well they do in the polls, which means they must begin campaigning early to earn name recognition by the public.

And, more generally, the fact that campaigns have become media events means that candidates must begin early to establish themselves as worthy of media attention. Until candidates have organizations, fundraisers, and pollsters, the media does not take them seriously. Nor would it be very rational to do otherwise, because a modern campaign cannot succeed without these things.

All of these factors—the decline of the party organizations and the increased importance of primaries, the growth of polling, and the overwhelming role the media now play in campaigns—have contributed to the perpetual motion that modern elections have become. These trends seem irreversible. Only the rolling back of the primary system would seem to make much difference, and that change is highly unlikely.

Congressional Campaigns

Because reelection is an important objective for almost all members of Congress and *the* most important objective for many, members work at being reelected throughout their terms.[158] Most are successful, though senators are not as secure as members of the House.

Incumbents: Unsafe at Any Margin?

Most members are reelected even if they have not done that much for their home districts.[159] Indeed, one Republican member remarked, "Let's face it, you have to be a bozo to lose this job."[160] Still, incumbents believe the best way to ensure victory is to be so good at serving the home district, so successful in getting money for their districts, and so well known to the voters that no serious rival will want to run. Incumbents hope potential rivals will bide their time and wait for a better year or run for some other office.[161]

Given the advantages of office that incumbents have in name recognition and in favors they can do their constituents (for more on this point, see Chapter 10), you may wonder why they worry about losing. But worry they do. One political scientist proclaimed that members feel "unsafe at any margin."[162] No matter how big their last victory, they worry that their next campaign will bring defeat. And despite the high reelection rate of incumbents, a few do lose. This fear prompts members to spend even more of their energies preparing for the next campaign.

For the most part, this fear is misplaced. Turnover in Congress comes primarily from those who decide not to run. Even in the anti-incumbent elections of 1994, only 10 percent of House incumbents lost (all of them Democrats). In 2000, only 2 percent did, and in 2004, less than 2 percent did. In the 2004 elections, only about three dozen of the 435 seats were even competitive.

The advantages of incumbency are becoming larger. State legislative majorities in 2001 drew most House districts in ways to make sure their fellow partisans had the safest seats possible. Mostly, they protected incumbents of their own party, but in doing so created safe seats for the other party, too. The only states to have many competitive seats were where district drawing was taken out of the hands of the legislature and placed in nonpartisan hands; Iowa is the best example. This gerrymandering has significant consequences for our democracy because it is primarily through elections that we hold public officials accountable.

House members really do have to offend their constituencies to lose. Senators are somewhat more vulnerable. Most senators are also reelected, but the probabilities of defeat are higher than for the House. In the late 1970s and early 1980s, it was not uncommon for a third of the senators running to be defeated. Those proportions have decreased, but in 2000 21 percent of senators running lost. Even so, the electoral benefit of incumbency still exists for the great majority of candidates who choose to run for reelection.[163]

For example, in 2004, only nine of the thirty-three Senate seats were even seriously contested, in most cases where the incumbents had retired. But only one incumbent lost, Tom Daschle (D-S.D.), the Senate majority leader. In the other seats, the incumbent has so much money that the challenger cannot really get into the race. For example, George Voinovich (R-Ohio) raised more than $4 million whereas his Democratic opponent had less than $100,000 late in the campaign. Similarly, Harry Reid (D-Nev.) had raised more than $3 million, his opponent less than $20,000. Obviously, challengers cannot run effective races with these kinds of disadvantages.[164]

Challengers

Another reason for the uneasiness of incumbents is that as their media and public relations sophistication has grown, so has that of their challengers. Still, without the advantages of incumbents' free mailing privileges and other opportunities to become well known to constituents, challengers have a difficult time. The best advice to someone who wants to be a member of Congress is to find an open seat.

To beat an incumbent, challengers need money. The more they spend, the more likely they are to win. In recent House campaigns, a challenger needed to spend at least $1 million to have even a one in four chance of

winning—and the cost continues to rise.[165] Spending is important for challengers because they must make themselves known in a positive way, and they must suggest that something is wrong with the incumbent. Usually, challengers will charge incumbents with ignoring the district, being absent from committee hearings or floor votes, being too liberal or too conservative, or voting incorrectly on a key issue. Sometimes, of course, the incumbent has been involved in a scandal, which offers a ready target for the challenger.[166]

Sometimes challengers will try unusual tactics to make themselves known. Tom Harkin (D-Iowa) worked in a series of blue-collar jobs when running for the House to show people in his district that he understood their problems. Meanwhile, he got a lot of free publicity.

Senate challengers have a better chance than House challengers (see Figure 8.2). One reason is that Senate seats are bigger prizes and so attract stronger candidates. Then, too, in a statewide constituency there is a larger pool of challengers to draw on. Because they are often former governors or members of the House with a statewide reputation, Senate challengers are better known than House challengers.[167] One analysis of this showed that about 80 percent of voters recognized the name of the person running against their incumbent senator; less than 60 percent recognized the challenger to their House incumbent.[168]

Another reason Senate challengers have greater success is that most incumbents have not had personal contact with as high a proportion of voters as a representative due to the much greater number of people they represent. Also there is a wider range of views and demands to satisfy in their larger and more heterogeneous constituencies.[169] Senators from the largest states have about a six- or seven-point electoral disadvantage compared with senators from the smallest states. Senators from the smallest states do about as well in retaining their seats as House members from their states.[170]

Campaigns

In the nineteenth century, political parties organized congressional and presidential campaigns, and the candidates had relatively little to do. Today, however, congressional as well as presidential campaigns are candidate centered.

Congressional candidates usually hire the staff, raise the money, and organize their own campaigns. They may recruit campaign workers from local political parties; interest groups they belong to; unions, church, civic, or other voluntary organizations; or they may simply turn to friends and acquaintances.[171]

Political parties do have a significant role, however. National and local parties also recruit potential candidates. Presidents make personal appeals to fellow party members who they think can run strong races, and national campaign committees also recruit aggressively.

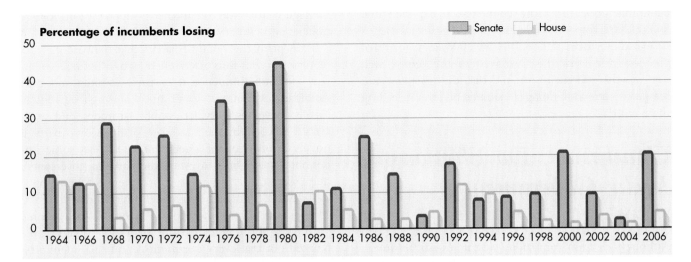

FIGURE 8.2 ■ **House Incumbents Have Had Secure Jobs in Recent Years**
In the 1980s and 1990s, more House incumbents lost in the reapportionment years (1982 and 1992); in the 1970s, most lost in 1974, the Watergate year. In the 1960s, reapportionment occurred both before the 1964 and 1966 election. Senate results do not reflect this cycle because, of course, there is no redistricting of the Senate constituencies. Each senator represents the whole state.

SOURCE: *Statistical Abstract of the United States* 2004.

Said one Democratic congressional campaign chair, "I'm not looking for liberals or conservatives. That's not my bag. I'm looking for winners."[172] Parties redouble their efforts when, as in recent elections, control of Congress is at stake. Besides, if candidates are not closely linked to parties, then, once elected, they are not as indebted to their party nor as obligated to reflect party views. Recognizing this, national parties have increasingly provided services to congressional candidates—helping them manage their campaigns, develop issues, advertise, raise money, and conduct opinion polls. National party organizations give substantial sums of money to congressional candidates.

Congressional Media Campaigns

To wage a serious campaign, the challenger or a contender for an open seat must wage a media campaign. Candidates hire media consultants and specialists in polling, advertising, and fundraising. The old-style politician who might have been effective in small groups but who cannot appear poised and articulate on television has given way to someone who can project an attractive television image. Candidates are elected on the basis of their media skills, which may not be the same skills as those needed to be a good lawmaker.

Campaign Money

The old adage says, "Half the money spent on campaigns is wasted. The trouble is, we don't know which half." This bromide helps explain why congressional campaigns are expensive. There is a kind of "campaign arms race" as each candidate tries to do what the other candidate does and a little more, escalating costs year by year.

In the next chapter, we review some of the escalating costs of running a winning House or Senate campaign.

Voting for Congress

In Chapter 7, we reviewed the impact of parties, issues, and candidates on voting choices. The same factors influence voting choices in congressional races.

Party loyalty, candidate evaluations, and issues are important factors in congressional elections just as in presidential ones.[173] Party loyalty is even more important for congressional than for presidential elections because congressional elections are less visible, so more people base their vote on party identification. Incumbency is also much more important than in presidential races. The result is that increasingly, since about 1960, voters have split their tickets in voting for presidential and congressional candidates. Ronald Reagan faced a Democratic majority in each house, whereas Bill Clinton had to deal with a Republican majority in both houses during his second term.

Normally, the party of a winning presidential candidate gains seats during a presidential election year and loses a number of seats in the midterm election. This maintains a sort of equilibrium in party control of Congress.[174] In 2006, voters delivered a rebuke to the Republicans, who lost 29 House seats and six Senate seats. This contrasted with the midterm elections of 1998 and 2002, when the president's party actually gained a few seats in the House and in 2002, the Senate too.

To some extent, midterm election results are a referendum on how well citizens think the president is doing. In 1998, Clinton was given credit for the economic good times the country was experiencing, and in 2002 voters rewarded the Republicans for Bush's strong antiterrorist stance. But by 2006, a majority of voters decided that the Iraqi war was not going well nor was the war on terror, and that the president and his party were not doing a competent job of leading the country.

Conclusion: Do Elections Make Government Responsive?

Although election campaigns are far less successful in mobilizing voters and ensuring a high turnout today than they were in the past century, in a democracy we expect elections to allow us to control government. Through them we can "throw the rascals out" and bring in new faces with better ideas, or so we think. But other than to change the party that controls government, do elections make a difference?

In the popular press, we hear a lot about "mandates." A president with a **mandate** is one who is clearly directed by the voters to take some particular course of action—reduce taxes or begin arms control talks, for example. George W. Bush won a majority in 2004. Did he have a mandate? If so, what for? The largest proportions of the public, 41 percent, were concerned about national security issues, mainly the war in Iraq and terrorism.[175] Most of those voted for Bush, but about one-third of Kerry voters thought this was the most important issue, too. So does that mean the president has a mandate to stay in Iraq until we "win," however we define a win, or is there a mandate to withdraw once elections are held? Or just to do what he thinks best?

And how about on domestic issues? More than 25 percent of voters reported that economic issues were the most important to them, and another 11 percent said domestic issues, such as health care and Social Security, were. Most voters concerned about domestic and economic issues favored Kerry, though some of Bush's supporters also thought this was most important. So Bush does not have a mandate on these issues, but as president will, of course, have to deal with them. Only about 10 percent said "cultural" issues were most important to them, and two-thirds of those voted for Bush.[176]

Did Bush have a mandate? Like most things in politics, the answer is not simple. Sometimes elections have an effect on policy, but often their effects are not clear-cut. In close elections, few would argue that there is a mandate. In 2000, voters favored the Democratic policy positions and did so in a time of peace and prosperity. A plurality gave their votes to Gore. Yet, Bush became president and acted as though his narrow Electoral College victory was a mandate in support of his foreign policies and conservative domestic policies.

It is primarily political parties that translate the mix of various issues into government action because voters' issue positions influence their party loyalties and their candidate evaluations. Over time, a rough agreement usually develops between public attitudes and policies.[177] A vote for the candidate of one's own party is usually a reflection of agreement on at least some important issues. Once in office, the party in government helps sort out the issues for which there is a broad public mandate from those for which there is not.

Elections that appear to be mandates can become "mandates for disaster." More than one observer has pointed out that every twentieth-century president who won the election by 60 percent or more of the popular vote soon encountered serious political trouble. After his landslide in 1920, Warren Harding had his Teapot Dome scandal involving government corruption. Emboldened by his 1936 triumph, Franklin D. Roosevelt tried to pack the Supreme Court and was resoundingly defeated on that issue. Lyndon Johnson won by a landslide in 1964 and was soon mired in Vietnam. Richard Nixon smashed George McGovern in 1972 but then had to resign because of Watergate. Ronald Reagan's resounding victory in 1984 (a shade less than 60 percent) was followed by the blunders of the Iran-Contra affair. Of these presidents, only Roosevelt was able to recover fully from his political misfortune. Reagan regained his personal popularity but seemed to have little influence on policy after Iran-Contra. One recent observer has argued that these disasters come because "the euphoria induced by overwhelming support at the polls evidently loosens the president's grip on reality."[178]

Elections can point out new directions for government and allow citizens to make it responsive to their needs, but the fact that many individuals do not vote means that the new directions may not reflect either the needs or wishes of the public. If election turnout falls too far, the legitimacy of elections may be threatened. People may come to believe that election results do not reflect the wishes of the majority. For this reason, the increase in turnout in 2004 should hearten all of us. If elections promote government responsiveness to those who participate in them, higher turnouts help increase responsiveness.

On the other hand, if we believe in democracy, we should be concerned about the decline in competitiveness of congressional elections. Essentially, in most states, state legislative majorities have had the capacity to determine election outcomes, including their own seats, for a decade. While the power to redistrict has always been in state legislative hands, the power and precision of new technology makes this power even greater. This is a significant challenge to responsiveness.

ove and Bush decided to make the 2006 election about Iraq and the war on terrorism. They rejected the view that the races should be left to local issues and personalities and decided to wage an aggressive national campaign. The Democrats, too, worked to make the midterm elections a referendum on the Bush administration and the war in Iraq.

The Republican's main strategy was to run supporting the war in Iraq and tying it to the war on terrorism.

But, as the summer wore on, public opinion increasingly turned against the war. The Republicans then tried to shift the focus to the war on terrorism, an issue where the Republicans continued to have popular support. But the Democrats would not let them off the hook on Iraq, and Democratic candidates all over the country made Iraq an issue. And the National Intelligence Council reported that the war in Iraq was probably increasing terrorist activities, not the reverse.

Republican candidates from the president on down grew increasingly insistent that a vote for the Democrats was a vote for the terrorists, but this charge grew increasingly ineffective. What worked like a charm in 2002 and again in 2004 had lost its power by

2006 as the majority of the public turned against the war. The Republicans received a small bump in the polls around the commemoration of the fifth anniversary of the 9/11 attacks, but the improvement was short lived. October proved to be one of the most deadly months in the war, with more than 100 Americans and thousands of Iraqis killed. The administration's promises that victory could be achieved seemed less and less realistic.

At the same time, the Republicans' messages were knocked off track by a series of scandals affecting Republican members of Congress. Two members of the House resigned because of crimes relating to financial corruption (see "You are There" Chapter 9). And, in October, another member of the House resigned suddenly after the media revealed that he had been writing sexually suggestive text messages to teenaged boys who were congressional pages. Media coverage of this story broadened to focus on the alleged cover-up of these messages by some members of the House Republican leadership. This story dominated the media in late September and early October, a time when many voters start to pay serious attention to the campaign.

When the polls closed and the media began to report the results, it soon became clear that it was a good day for the Democrats. They captured majorities in both the House and Senate. Though the 28–29 vote shift to the Democrats in the House (some races are still not decided) was not large by historical off-year standards, given that most districts were not considered to be in play at all, it was a substantial victory.

What determined the election?[179] Around 40 percent of the public considered corruption and scandals extremely important to their vote, about the same proportion who thought the economy was important, who thought the war in Iraq was important, and who thought terrorism was important. Most of those who believed corruption, the war in Iraq, or the economy were important voted Democratic. A small majority of those who thought terrorism was important voted Republican. Republicans also won a majority of voters who believed that immigration and values issues such as abortion and same-sex marriage were important.

Exit polls indicated that the Democrats picked up support compared to 2004 in every demographic group: men, women, blacks, whites, Asians, and Latinos, small town residents and denizens of large cities, the religious and the non-religious, and people of all education, age, and income groups. Republicans won 81 percent of those who approved of the war in Iraq, and Democrats won 80 percent of those who disapproved of it. Unfortunately for the Republicans, substantially more disapproved of the war than approved of it. Those who approved of the president heavily voted Republican, and those who opposed him voted for the Democrats.

Rove's strategies failed because the public had soured on the war and because the president's own popularity had dramatically declined (to below 40 per-

I WAS UNROLLING IT AND A CONGRESSMAN FELL OUT....

Luckovich for WPWWE

BY LUCKOVICH FOR THE ATLANTA JOURNAL-CONSTITUTION

cent at the time of the election). In 2002, Republican candidates were eager for the president to come to their districts to campaign for them. In 2006, Republican candidates found excuses to be away from their districts when the president arrived. One news article reported that by the waning weeks of the campaign, only one Republican candidate for Congress used the president's photo in his or her TV ads, whereas dozens of Democrats did as they tried to tie their opponents to an unpopular president.

 To learn more about this topic, go to "you are there" exercises for this chapter on the text website.

Key Terms

suffrage
Reconstruction
literacy tests
grandfather clause
poll tax
white primary
Voting Rights Act (VRA)
gerrymandering
cracking, stacking, and packing
majority-minority districts
split-ticket voting

Progressive reforms
motor voter law
presidential preference primaries
Super Tuesday
battleground states (swing states)
Electoral College
faithless elector
permanent campaign
mandate

Further Reading

Stephen Ansolabehere and Shanto Iyengar, *Going Negative* (New York: Free Press, 1996). Two political scientists report the results of their research on the impact of negative television ads on voters and voting.

Taylor Branch, *Parting the Waters: America in the King Years, 1954–63* (New York: Simon and Schuster, 1988). An excellent, readable account that illustrates the impact of political protest in changing America's race laws and, to a considerable extent, its attitudes about race.

Evan Cornog and Richard Whalen, *Hats in the Ring: An Illustrated History of American Presidential Campaigns* (New York: Random House, 2000). Here is an entertaining look at presidential campaigns, including many photos, cartoons, prints, and anecdotes along with factual information.

Robert Darcy, Susan Welch, and Janet Clark, *Women, Elections, and Representation* (Lincoln: University of Nebraska Press, 1994). An examination of the potential barriers faced by women candidates.

Kathleen Hall Jamieson, *Electing the President 2004: The Insiders' View.* (Philadelphia: University of Pennsylvania

Press, 2006). Campaign managers and consultants in both parties explain their strategies.

David A. Kaplan, *The Accidental President: How 413 Lawyers, 9 Supreme Court Justices, and 5,963,110 Floridians (Give or Take a Few) Landed George W. Bush in the White House* (New York: Morrow, 2001). A humorous look behind the scenes of the Bush and Gore organizations fighting for the 2000 election after Election Day.

Zachary Karabell, *The Last Campaign: How Harry Truman Won the 1948 Election* (New York: Knopf, 2000). The story of the Truman-Dewey 1948 campaign that some campaign experts believe was the best in the second half of the twentieth century.

Thomas E. Patterson, *The Vanishing Voter* (New York: Knopf, 2002). A political scientist blames candidates, parties, the media, and the public themselves for low turnouts and makes some suggestions for change.

Joe Trippi, *The Revolution Will Not be Televised: Democracy, the Internet, and the Overthrow of Everything* (New York: Regan Books, 2004). Howard Dean's campaign manager explains how the Internet changed campaigning.

Theodore H. White, *The Making of the President,* 4 vols.: *1960, 1964, 1968,* and *1972* (New York: Atheneum, 1961, 1965, 1969, 1973). Journalistic accounts of presidential elections from 1960 to 1972. White was the first journalist to travel with the candidates and give an inside view of campaign strategy.

For Viewing

Fahrenheit 9/11 (2004). Like it or hate it, this Michael Moore film, with its harsh critique of President Bush's handling of the war on terrorism and the war in Iraq, won both critical acclaim and a place in the campaign of 2004. The Republicans countered with several videos, probably the best being *George W. Bush: Faith in the White House.* This DVD portrays Bush as something akin to God's representative on earth and was being specifically targeted to be the counter to *Fahrenheit 9/11*. Reportedly, three hundred thousand copies were distributed to churches.

The Candidate (1972). This film starring Robert Redford features a candidate for the Senate who finds that as his chances of success increase, his ability to tell the truth as he sees it decreases.

Power (1986). Richard Gere plays a political consultant working on a major campaign. An inside look at the role of consultants in modern campaigns.

Primary (1960). A documentary that reports on John F. Kennedy and Hubert Humphrey contesting for the 1960 Democratic party nomination. This film started the trend of close film coverage of presidential candidates. You will probably be startled by the primitive technology compared with today's.

The War Room (1993). This documentary features Bill Clinton's campaign.

Journeys with George (2000). A journalist traveling with the 2000 Bush campaign provides an inside look.

Electronic Resources

Most congressional and many state candidates have websites that provide news about the candidates, issues, how to vote, and related matters.

www.democrats.org/party and www.rnc.org
Links to the Democratic National Committee and the Republican National Committee. Each of these pages contains information about the campaign organizations of the two national parties.

www.Movingimage.us
Check out historical and contemporary campaign commercials on this site.

www.washingtonpost.com
The Washington Post *covers national politics and elections more thoroughly than any other newspaper.*

www.rockthevote.com/home.php
Rock the Vote encourages young voters to register and vote and provides nonpartisan information about campaigns and issues.

www.dailykos.com
The most talked about liberal blog site.

clearcommentary.typepad.com
This site is a less visible conservative counterpart. For lists of political blogsites see abetterblogsite.com/public/item/79877.

ThomsonNOW™

Enter ThomsonNOW™ using the access card that is available with this text or through www.thomsonedu.com/thomsonnow. ThomsonNOW™ will assist you in understanding the content in this chapter with a personalized study plan generated for your needs. A practice test will assess the areas you need to review and provide the tools to fully comprehend those concepts, including an eBook, interactive simulations, timelines, video case studies, and MicroCase exercises and InfoTrac College Edition readers and exercises. You'll also be connected to the learning objectives, chapter outline, chapter glossary, flash cards, crossword puzzles, Internet activities, and interactive quizzes found on the companion website.

CHAPTER 9

MONEY AND POLITICS

High-powered lobbyist Jack Abramoff leaves court during his trial for fraud, conspiracy, and tax evasion.

Money and Politics in America's Past

Money in Nineteenth-Century American Politics

Early Reforms

Reforms of the 1970s

Fundraising in Today's Campaigns

The President as Chief Fundraiser

Members of Congress as Fundraisers

Regulating Money in Modern Campaigns

Recent Attempts at Reform: The McCain-Feingold Act

Disclosure

Regulating Campaign Spending

Contribution Limits and Ways to Avoid Them

Reforming Campaign Finance

Is Real Reform Possible?

Opposition to Reform

Ideas for Reform

The Impact of Campaign Money

Does the Campaign Finance System Deter Good Candidates?

Does Money Win Elections?

Does Money Buy Favorable Policies?

Does Our Campaign Finance System Exacerbate Class Differences?

Does Our Campaign Finance System Encourage Extortion?

Does Our Campaign Finance System Lead to Public Cynicism?

Conflicts of Interest

The Abramoff Scandal and Concierge Politics

Regulating Ethical Behavior

Democratic and Republican Corruption

Conclusion: Does the Influence of Money Make Government Less Responsive?

Should You Make a Deal?

You are Ralph Reed and it is 1999. A lifelong Republican and a key figure in the rise of conservative Christianity's influence in politics in the 1990s, you now have a decision to make about accepting a potentially lucrative contract offered by Jack Abramoff.

You became active in the Republican Party as a college student at the University of Georgia, dedicating much time and energy to the college's Young Republicans. You were also a columnist for its student newspaper, writing about political issues, but were fired for plagiarizing large parts of an article, *Gandhi: Ninny of the 20th Century*, from the magazine *Commentary*.[1] After graduation from Georgia, you landed a Washington, D.C., internship position with Jack Abramoff, who was then the chairman of the College Republicans National Committee. In that position, you worked closely with Abramoff, and Grover Norquist, the executive director of the organization. You introduced Abramoff to his future wife, and in 1983 you succeeded Norquist as executive director.[2]

About that same time, you experienced a religious conversion while in a local pub. You walked outside and called a local church where the next day you became a born again Christian. Leaving Washington, you started a new organization, Students for America, a conservative, antiabortion group that worked on behalf of Jesse Helms, a Republican then successfully running for reelection to the U.S. Senate from North Carolina. Your group also organized many protests at abortion clinics, and you were once arrested after bursting into a clinic waiting room (you signed an agreement not to return).

Your career took off in 1989, when you were asked by Pat Robertson, a nationally known radio evangelist and presidential candidate, to become the executive director of the newly formed Christian Coalition. The coalition, based on Robertson's followers but expanding to incorporate millions of conservative Christians, burst on the national scene as the voice of conservative Christianity and as an informal arm of the Republican party (see Chapter 6). The group articulated and worked to support a staunchly conservative agenda, especially on moral issues and issues threatening the traditional social order, such as women's rights and abortion rights. The coalition worked hard to support Republican candidates throughout the early 1990s, working hand in hand with evangelical churches, but also spending millions on advertising and electoral activity. Its clout and influence were undisputed, and your leadership was key to its growth. Once you were even on the cover of *Time* magazine, with the headline "The Right Hand of God."[3]

In the late 1990s, the coalition came under fire for financial irregularities when the chief financial officer of the organization went to federal authorities. You were never charged with any crimes, and you left the organization in 1997 while the investigation was still pending. Later, the organization declined significantly in its influence.

Once you left the coalition, you set up a consulting firm, Century Strategies. First, you provided consulting for Republican candidates, but most of your candidates lost. Then you began to focus on helping businesses achieve their political goals. You won several lucrative contracts, including Enron, Microsoft, and others. Your close ties with the White House and prominent congressional Republicans are a selling point of your firm. In fact, in 1998 you had e-mailed your old colleague Jack Abramoff, "I need to start humping in corporate accounts! I'm counting on you to help me with some contacts."[4] You also worked for the Republican National Committee doing voter mobilization in 2000, and you actively raised hundreds of thousands for the Bush campaign.[5] In fact, you were the Southeast regional coordinator for the Bush campaign, responsible for five states.

Now, it looks like Jack Abramoff has come through for you in a big way. He and an associate have offered your firm an opportunity for a multi-million dollar contract. The contract would be to run antigambling drives in Texas and Alabama. In Alabama you would fight a proposed state lottery and video poker bill being considered in the state legislature; in Texas you would fight a legislative bill to legalize gambling. The Alabama deal was partially to be funded from Americans for Tax Reform, an organization set up by another of your old associates, Grover Norquist.

Opposition to gambling is certainly in keeping with your own conservative beliefs, and the beliefs of many of your supporters. You know that you could mobilize churchgoers and pastors to oppose these proposed pro-gambling policies. You could work for your beliefs and make a lot of money in the process.

Your only concern is where the money comes from. Abramoff's ties with several Indian tribes running gambling casinos is fairly well known to his associates, and you know that some of the money is coming from the Mississippi Band of the Choctaw Indians, a tribe with lucrative casinos.[6] Obviously, tribes with existing casinos would benefit greatly if potential competitors are prevented from opening new casinos, so it is hardly surprising that they would support antigambling legislation (Indian tribes have a unique sovereign status within the United States and states cannot close down gambling on Indian property). Aside from potentially supporting casino gambling, which you oppose, it would be quite embarrassing to you in any future political career if, in fact, the funds were casino profits and you used them to run an antigambling crusade. Voters are sensitive to the appearance of hypocrisy. For that reason, taking the contract has a potential downside.

Do you take the job or not? Why?

Former speaker of the House of Representatives Tip O'Neill (D-Mass.) once said, "There are four parts to any campaign. The candidate, the issues . . . , the campaign organization, and the money. Without money you can forget the other three."[7] Conventional wisdom holds that "money is the mother's milk of politics." But we are not sure whether that milk is tainted or pure. On the one hand, without money, candidates or people with new political ideas could never become known in our massive and complex society. Television spreads names and ideas almost instantaneously, so having money to buy television time means that your ideas will be heard. In that sense, money contributes to open political debate.

On the other hand, money can be a corrupting influence on politics. At the least, it can buy access to decision makers. At the worst, it can buy decisions. Money allows some points of view to be trumpeted while others are forced to whisper. Some candidates or groups can afford to spend hundreds of thousands of dollars for each prime-time minute of national television or for prestigious Washington law firms to lobby; others can afford only web pages and letters. Money increases inequities in political life.

Money, then, leads to a dilemma in politics. In our largely capitalist society, we expect substantial differences in wealth and income. In most cases, we see nothing wrong when individuals of great wealth are able to buy goods and services that others cannot afford. But in politics, many people feel uneasy when high-income individuals or well-bankrolled groups are able to buy political favors. We feel so uneasy that we have outlawed certain kinds of buying of political favors, such as politicians paying voters for their votes or interest groups paying politicians and bureaucrats for their support.

But we are also uneasy about placing other limits on the influence of money. Many people feel that individuals or groups should be allowed to contribute as much money to candidates as they want and that candidates should be permitted to buy as much media time to get their point of view across as they want and can afford. This view holds that contributing money and buying media time are forms of constitutionally guaranteed freedom of speech. The opposite view says that these practices distort the democratic process.

These issues are growing more important as the cost of political campaigns increases. In 2000, candidates at all levels spent $4 billion, and that number increased in 2004: only a fraction came from public funds. So it is not surprising that political candidates scramble for money. Campaign finance laws seek to limit the amounts individuals and groups can give to candidates and establish procedures to track those donations. Journalists and other analysts also try to determine what the donors received in return for their gifts.

In this chapter, we first focus on the development of laws that regulate how money can influence politics, then turn to the role and impact of money in elections, and finally briefly examine conflicts of interest on the part of decision makers in Congress and the executive branch.

Money and Politics in America's Past

Concern about the illegitimate influence of money on politics is older than the Republic. In 1699, after asking how campaign money could be regulated, the Virginia House of Burgesses (the colony's legislature) voted to prohibit the bribing of voters.[8] In his campaign for the Virginia House of Burgesses in 1757, George Washington was accused of vote buying. He had given out twenty-eight gallons of rum, fifty gallons of rum punch, thirty-four gallons of wine, forty-six gallons of beer, and two gallons of cider. Because there were only 391 voters in his district, he had provided more than a quart and a half of beverages per voter![9]

Obviously, Washington survived these charges, and his constituents probably survived the effects of the rum and cider. But most discussions of the impact of money on politics were more sober. In his well-known analysis of controlling factions, James Madison, in *Federalist Paper* 10, recognized that "the most common and durable source of factions has been the various and unequal distribution of property." Madison went on to say that although ideally no one should be allowed to make decisions affecting his or her own self-interest, almost any subject of legislation—taxes, tariffs, debts—involves self-interest. For those making laws, "every shilling with which they overburden the inferior number is a shilling saved to their own pockets."

Madison hoped that the design of the new nation, with the power of the government divided among the branches of government and between the nation and the states, would mean that no one interest or faction would overwhelm the others. The interest of one person or group would check the interest of another.

This view of counterbalancing interests is an optimistic one and has not always worked. Over the decades, Americans have found it necessary to make additional rules to restrict the ways that people or groups with money can try to influence policy makers.

The influence of money on local politics reached a high point in the late nineteenth century. Urban machines used money to cement a complex network of businesses, voters, and political party organizations. Business payoffs to government and party officials for licenses and contracts and party payoffs to voters for their support were the norm. Graft was tolerated and even expected.

As we saw in Chapter 7, George Washington Plunkitt was a famous leader of the New York City machine known as Tammany Hall. Plunkitt, born in 1842, began life as a butcher's helper and ended up a millionaire through deals made in his role as a party leader and public official. He held a number of state and local public offices; at one point, he held four at the same time. He drew a salary for three of them simultaneously.

Plunkitt's view of graft illustrates the casual attitude about the influence of money on politics common among many of his time:

There's all the difference in the world between [honest graft and dishonest graft]. There's an honest graft, and I'm an example of how it works. I might sum up the whole thing by sayin': "I seen my opportunities and I took 'em."

Just let me explain. . . . My party's in power in the city, and it's goin' to undertake a lot of public improvements.

Well, I'm tipped off, say, that they're going to lay out a new park at a certain place. I see my opportunity and take it. I go to that place and I buy up all the land I can in the neighborhood. Then the board of this or that makes its plan public, and there is a rush to get my land, which nobody cared particular for before. Ain't it perfectly honest to charge a good price and make a profit on my investment and foresight? Of course, it is. Well, that's honest graft.

Tammany was beat in 1901 because the people were deceived into believin' that it worked dishonest graft. . . . [They supposed that] Tammany men were robbin' the city treasury or levyin' blackmail on disorderly houses, or workin' in with the gamblers and lawbreakers. . . . Why should the Tammany leaders go into such dirty business when there is so much honest graft lyin' around?

. . . I don't own a dishonest dollar. If my worst enemy was given the job of writin' my epitaph . . . he couldn't do more than write: George W. Plunkitt. He Seen His Opportunities, and He Took 'Em.

SOURCE: William L. Riordon, *Plunkitt of Tammany Hall* (1905; repr., New York: Dutton, 1963), 3–6.

Money in Nineteenth-Century American Politics

The influence of money on politics has shaped several epochs of American history. For example, from the earliest westward expansion of the nation, charges of graft and corruption surrounded the government's sale and giveaway of land. Indeed, the West was developed by giving land to speculators and railroads, sometimes in exchange for bribes. When Congress was debating whether to give federal land to the railroads, the lobbyists "camped in brigades around the Capitol building."[10]

The impact of money on political life probably reached its peak in the late nineteenth century, during the so-called Gilded Age after the Civil War. During that time, the United States grew from a small agrarian society to a large industrialized one. This industrialization produced great wealth in such fields as oil exploration and refining, the steel industry, and the railroad companies that were spanning the nation. Major components of the economy came to be controlled by companies that owned most of the country's resources in a particular area, such as steel, oil, and rubber. John D. Rockefeller's Standard Oil sold more than 80 percent of all oil products sold in the United States.[11] This was the era of "robber barons," when the owners of these giant corporations (called *trusts*) amassed huge wealth and openly bought political favors.

Business contributions to campaigns and to politicians were routine. One railroad president justified the bribing of political officials by noting, "If you have to pay money to have the right thing done, it is only just and fair to do so."[12] Mark Hanna, a Republican fundraiser in the presidential election of 1896, assessed banks at a fixed percentage of their capital and also collected substantial sums from most insurance companies and large corporations.[13] However, Cornelius Vanderbilt, one of the wealthiest men of his time, refused to contribute to election campaigns, believing that it was cheaper to buy legislators after they were elected!

Not only did lobbyists bribe politicians, but politicians bribed reporters. In the 1872 presidential campaign, the Republican Party gave money to about three hundred reporters in return for favorable coverage.[14] (See the box "Honest Graft" for more on money's role in nineteenth-century politics.)

U.S. senators bought their own seats (this was before senators were elected by the public) by bribing state legislators to select them. When one member proposed that all of those who had bribed their way into the Senate be expelled, another member observed that "we might lose a quorum" if that were done.[15]

Early Reforms

Around the turn of the twentieth century, the Progressive reformers and their allies in the press, called **muckrakers,** began to attack this overt corruption. They wanted to break up the trusts and break the financial link between business and politicians. In 1907, a law prohibited corporations and banks from making contributions to political campaigns, and a few years later, Congress mandated public reporting of campaign expenditures and set limits on campaign donations. Prohibitions against corporate giving to political campaigns were broadened over time to forbid utilities and labor unions from giving as well.

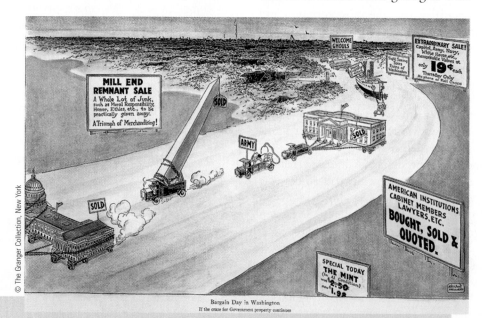

© The Granger Collection, New York

Warren G. Harding, one of the least successful presidents, could not say no to his friends. This failure led to the Teapot Dome scandal.

When Republican Teddy Roosevelt became president after the assassination of William McKinley, he fought the trusts, forced them to open their books, and filed suits to break them up. Although he accepted campaign contributions from big corporations when he ran for the presidency in 1904, he would not show them any favor. This prompted a major contributor to his campaign to complain, "We bought the son of a bitch, but he did not stay bought."[16]

The 1920s was another era of financial scandal as stock markets rose and banks sold worthless stocks and bonds. The **Teapot Dome scandal** of 1921 stimulated further attempts to limit the influence of money on electoral politics. The secretary of the interior in the Harding administration received almost $400,000 from two corporations that then were allowed to lease oil reserves in California and Wyoming (one of them was called the Teapot Dome). This led to the Federal Corrupt Practices Act (1925), which required the reporting of campaign contributions and expenditures.

Because none of these laws were enforced, each had only a momentary effect. Nevertheless, the reforms did seem to make open graft and bribery less acceptable and less common. Instead of outright bribes, political interests now sought to influence politicians through campaign contributions.

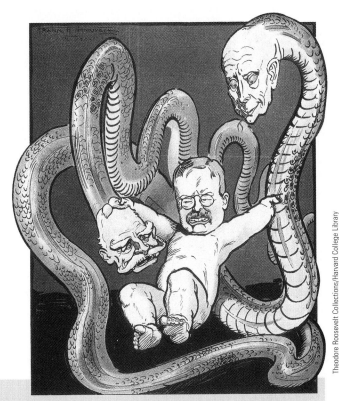

Teddy Roosevelt is portrayed as the "infant Hercules" wrestling Rockefeller's Standard Oil.

Theodore Roosevelt Collections/Harvard College Library

Reforms of the 1970s

Prompted by the increasing use of television in campaigns and the rising cost of buying television time, Congress passed a law regulating spending on advertising in 1971. The law limited the amount that candidates could donate to their own campaigns and required candidates to disclose the names and addresses of donors of more than $100.

In the course of the Watergate investigations (see Chapter 2), it became clear that corporations were not abiding by these restrictions. Several corporations secretly funded President Nixon's reelection campaign. For example, Nixon's Justice Department negotiated a settlement favorable to the ITT Corporation in a pending legal dispute soon after an ITT subsidiary gave the Republican National Committee $400,000.[17] Altogether, twenty-one individuals and fourteen corporations were indicted for illegal campaign contributions, mostly but not entirely to the Nixon reelection campaign.

In response to these scandals, Congress again attempted to regulate campaign financing. New legislation was passed in 1974. The objectives of the 1974 law were to limit spending, to make the campaign finance system more open by disclosing the names of donors, and to force candidates to be less reliant on a few big donors. Thus the law called for public financing of presidential campaigns and limited overall candidate expenditures; limited the contributions of individuals, committees, national parties, and political action groups to campaigns for federal office; required donors' identities to be disclosed; and prohibited cash contributions of more than $100. The act also established the bipartisan **Federal Election Commission** (FEC) to enforce the law. The 1974 act also imposed limits on **independent spending,** spending by groups not under the control of candidates. These limits were immediately ruled unconstitutional and no longer apply.

Because of the importance of money in campaigns, elected officials and individuals and groups who want something from the officials found ways to get around the campaign finance laws. The Supreme Court also found several provisions unconstitutional. Indeed, by the 1990s, the 1974 campaign finance law no longer had any practical effect except for the disclosure mandates.

Fundraising in Today's Campaigns

Waging a campaign is expensive. Fundraising for national elections is done by the party committees, candidates themselves, and private groups that support candidates. Winning the presidency is most expensive of all. President Bush raised $275 million and John Kerry $253 million during the primary phase of the 2004 election, and then each took public funds for the general election.[18] Kerry's sum was more money than any presidential challenger has ever raised, and Bush's was the most ever raised. And these are only the totals regulated by legislation. Money raised through other ways that we will discuss later also skyrocketed in 2004, and the total spending in the presidential campaign was estimated to be as much as $2 billion.

These numbers will likely increase. Some experts think that the 2008 presidential candidates will need to raise $100 million just to be a serious contender in the primaries.

And because most funding for such campaigns is private, candidates for office must continually look for sources to fund their campaigns. By 2006, potential presidential candidates were appearing on television and flying around the country to woo potential donors and, not less important, potential fundraisers. Without money, even the best candidates with the best ideas will go nowhere.

At least some of those who give money see donations as an opportunity for access and influence, and at least some officeholders see nothing wrong with rewarding large donors with political favors or favorable policy decisions. It is these relationships that prompt continuing calls for campaign finance reform. Yet, as soon as laws are passed, loopholes are opened by the FEC, responsible for overseeing the campaign finance laws, the courts, and candidates themselves, who are very creative in finding ways to get around the limits.

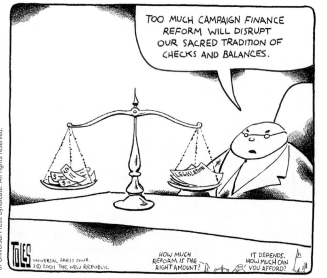

The President as Chief Fundraiser

The chief fundraiser in national politics is likely to be the president. Following the 1996 elections, the Lincoln Bedroom in the White House became a staple of editorial writers and late-night comedians. To raise soft money for the Democratic National Committee and thus for his campaign, President Bill Clinton had invited big donors to the White House to have coffee with him and, in some cases, to stay overnight. These and other revelations about fundraising practices prompted new calls for campaign finance reform and cries of outrage from Republicans. Said George W. Bush, "Will we use the White House . . . as a fundraising mechanism—in other words, you give money and you get to sleep in the Lincoln Bedroom? The answer is no."[19]

Once in office, the Bush administration just as blatantly exploited his office for partisan fundraising as the president invited big donors to dine with diplomats at an embassy and meet with cabinet officials.[20] Indeed, Bush and his organization are by far the biggest fundraisers ever among political candidates. They have used their close connections to industry to raise staggering amounts from corporate executives eager to have high-level access to the president and his team.

His top fundraising volunteers are given names of honor: the Pioneers are those who have raised $100,000 for the campaign; the Rangers, have raised $200,000; and the Super Rangers have raised $300,000. One fundraising expert provided a lively description: "Carole Bionda darted through the halls of the Capital Hilton, armed with a red-white-and-blue tote bag bulging with checks made out to Bush-Cheney '04. Three hundred executives from the nation's most influential construction firms were meeting at the hotel. . . . As the executives split up into regional caucuses, she ran from room to room, pitting South against East, West against Midwest" in a competition to see who could donate the most.[21]

In three days, Bionda raised $147,000 from the construction executives. This was easy because the Bush administration had gotten rid of regulations that would have improved working and safety conditions at construction sites, which would have cost construction companies more, and other regulations that would have denied government contracts to big polluters.

The Bush-Cheney fundraising organization set as a target $200 million in 2004, most of it expected to come via organized fundraising like this. Each Pioneer, Ranger, or Super Ranger has a number, and all donations through that person are tracked by that

Reprinted by permission of Copley News Service

number. Results are posted on the web, and competition between fundraisers is encouraged.

Large donors are given perks, such as photos with the president or the first lady, Laura Bush. After 9/11, capitalizing on the tragedy, Republican donors were given photos of George W. Bush calling Vice President Cheney on September 11, 2001.[22] Some elite donors were offered a chance to "dine with diplomats and embassy officials and discuss international affairs at one of Washington's famous embassies."[23]

More substantively, after the 2000 elections, 104 of the 246 Pioneer fundraisers received government jobs. Four were named cabinet secretaries—Tom Ridge, Don Evans, Elaine Chao, and Alphonso Jackson—and 22 received ambassadorships, including one found guilty of swindling his business partners for $1 million.[24]

For some, access is more important than jobs. More than half the 2000 Pioneers were heads of companies and another 20 percent were lobbyists.[25] Executives and lobbyists for the financial and real estate world, energy, construction, and transportation were well represented in this elite group.

Did the Bush administration deregulate specifically because it received campaign funds from big construction and other regulated industries? Probably not; conservative Republicans prefer to let business regulate itself and would favor deregulation independent of contributions. Did construction executives give money to the Bush campaign specifically to thank the administration for relaxing regulations and allowing them to make even more money? We do not know. Did they give the funds in the hope and expectation of future policies loosening regulations? Again, no one knows for sure, but that is a reasonable expectation.

It is difficult to point out the exact cause and effect of these close ties between donors and public officials. Even if all that is being bought and sold is access, access is worth something. If access did not influence policy, most people would not be trying to buy it. Even if no favors were exchanged for money and nothing illegal transpired, many Americans find these activities unethical and unbecoming a president. Indeed, the most troubling activities are the ones that are apparently legal. Unless voters elect members of Congress who agree, campaign finance activities will continue to provide material for cartoonists and comedians, embarrassment for public officials, and ultimately loss of public trust in both business and politics.

Members of Congress as Fundraisers

Members of Congress are aggressive in soliciting for donations. They fear defeat in the next election and think that raising a lot of money can protect them. Senators, for example, must raise more than $18,000 each week during all six years of their term to fund an average-cost winning reelection campaign. A senator from a populous, high-cost state needs to raise even more. Many incumbents raise millions even when they face little-known opponents.

Until the 1960s, most fundraising by members of Congress was done in their home districts because members did not want their constituents to think they were influenced by Washington lobbyists. That has changed dramatically. Today, members of Congress are heavily supported by **political action committees (PACs)** and the majority of PAC funds are raised in

Washington.[26] Members of Congress continually hold fundraisers to which dozens of lobbyists for PACs are invited. Well-known lobbyists get hundreds of invitations to congressional fundraisers every year.[27] Indeed, the number of these events is so large that a private company sells a special monthly newsletter listing all of them.

Regulating Money in Modern Campaigns

Since the early 1970s, Americans have been at least intermittently concerned about the influence of campaign money on modern politics. Laws and court decisions have dealt primarily with four questions that are at the heart of debates about campaign finance reform:

1. Should we insist on **public disclosure,** requiring that the names of donors be on the public record?

2. Should we limit candidate spending in political campaigns? How about so-called independent spending, spending by other groups in support or opposition to candidates?

3. Should we fund campaigns from public funds?

4. Should we limit the overall amount of money that individuals and groups give to candidates, called **contribution limits**?

Recent Attempts at Reform: McCain-Feingold Act

By the early 1990s, calls for reforms became deafening. Journalists, public interest groups, and ordinary citizens in public opinion polls called on Congress for new regulations to limit the flow of private funds to candidates. They worried that public confidence in government was being eroded by the close connection between wealthy special interests and elected officials. Reformers favored the public financing of the 1974 act and the disclosure provisions but wanted much tighter control over donations and spending.

In the 2000 presidential campaign, Arizona Republican John McCain, the challenger to the frontrunner, George W. Bush, in the 2000 presidential primaries, made campaign finance reform a major issue. His candidacy withered and died. Al Gore, the Democratic presidential candidate, supported campaign finance reform but did not make it one of his central issues. With the election of Bush, an opponent of campaign reform, change was seemingly postponed for several more years. But in 2002, when the Enron collapse made it all too obvious that Enron money had bought at least a decade of lax corporate regulation, campaign reform received a new impetus.

Efforts for reform were led by McCain and another Senate maverick, Russ Feingold (D-Wisc.). In 2002, after extensive negotiations and polls showing strong public support for reform, Congress passed, and the president signed, a new campaign finance law, the Bipartisan Campaign Finance Reform Act (usually referred to as the **McCain-Feingold Act** after its sponsors). The Democrats voted overwhelmingly in favor of the bill and the Republicans against it, but enough Republicans crossed party lines to pass the bill. This law had its first effect in the 2004 elections.

The primary focus of the bill was to eliminate **soft money** donations (funds given to political parties and other groups ostensibly for uses other than campaigning) to national, and in some circumstances, state, and local political parties, raise hard money contribution limits to catch up with rising costs of elections since the 1974 legislation, increase disclosure provisions for contributions to groups sponsoring political ads, and to try to further regulate use of soft money-funded advertisements by corporate and labor groups.

In general, the legislation was, at best, not much of a success. It diverted large soft money contributions from political parties, which have some measure of accountability, to small advocacy groups that have none. However, it did increase visibility of donors to those groups through disclosure provisions.

We will learn more about the limitations of this legislation as we examine the politics and impact campaign finance legislation in terms of the issues enumerated earlier.

Disclosure

The Supreme Court upheld the provisions of the 1974 campaign finance reform act that mandate disclosure of contributions. The FEC provides public reports on who has given money to whom. Through this part of the law, journalists and the public can see what private interests are contributing and who the beneficiaries of their contributions are. This is one aspect of the legislation that has been effective and relatively uncontroversial. Financers of independent groups must also be disclosed.

Regulating Campaign Spending
Spending Limits
In 1976, the Supreme Court knocked huge holes in the 1974 law when it struck down spending limits except in publicly funded presidential elections. The badly splintered Court reaffirmed this view in 2006 when it struck down very restrictive campaign spending limits in Vermont.[28] Because spending often goes

to buy advertising, the Court argued that spending restrictions violated individuals' First Amendment right of free speech. Spending in a campaign enables candidates to get their message out. Giving money is a form of expression protected by the Constitution.

Consequently, spending limits apply in presidential races only because candidates accept public funds. At the primary stage, presidential candidates may get up to $19 million in funds and are subject to a $45 million spending limit (the money comes from a voluntary checkoff of $3 on individuals' tax returns; the spending limit increases each year to take inflation into account). Candidates who do not accept public funding can spend as much as they can raise. In 2004, George W. Bush, John Kerry, and Howard Dean decided not to accept public money, so they had no spending limits at all at the primary stage.[29]

Once candidates receive their parties' nominations, public funding pays them each about $75 million for the general election campaign (also adjusted each election for inflation), and they can accept several million more from their party's national committee. At this point, fundraising is supposed to be officially over for the candidates. However, this prohibition does not limit other groups from raising and spending money to sway public opinion and thereby help their favored candidate.

Independent Spending

Independent spending by other (nonpolitical) groups is unregulated. In 1985, the Supreme Court ruled that groups, including PACs (discussed later) could spend unlimited amounts working on behalf of issues or candidates, publicly funded or not, as long as they do not give funds directly to parties or candidates.[30]

The Court assumed that this spending would be meaningfully independent. However, "independent" spending is often done by organized groups with indirect links to the candidate. Thus interest groups, through their PACs, can spend as much as they want as long as they are not actually campaigning for a candidate. Instead, they engage in "issues advocacy," usually targeted to promoting a particular candidate or party. The Court's rule to judge whether an ad is a campaign ad is whether it uses language such as "vote for" or "vote against." However, this is a meaningless criterion because only 4 percent of ads sponsored by the candidates themselves use these phrases.[31]

Thus anyone not officially part of a campaign or national party can spend as much as he or she wants. However, to be independent, a group cannot be officially linked to a candidate or party nor can it endorse a candidate or party.

Two examples illustrate how tenuous these definitions are. The Media Fund, run by a former Clinton White House adviser, ran television ads throughout

"It says here that you gave a lot of money to both parties and neither expected nor received anything in return. Very nice, but we'll have to put you in the crazy section."

the primary campaign. One featured a shot of a factory with the voice pointing out that "it's true that George W. Bush has created more jobs. Unfortunately, . . ." The camera then reveals that the factory is in China, and the voice announces that most of the new jobs were in places like China.[32] The ad did not endorse Kerry but clearly worked in his interest.

The Republicans had even more effective groups. One of the most visible was the so-called Swift Boat Veterans for Truth. Led by an ex-veteran who first opposed Kerry in the 1970s, financed largely by Bush supporters and advised by an attorney who was an official in the Bush campaign (who resigned when this tie was revealed), but technically "independent" of the Bush campaign, the group waged a scurrilous attack on Kerry's war record. (Kerry, as a young Navy lieutenant, commanded a "swift boat" in the Vietnam War and won medals for heroism as well as three Purple Hearts for his wounds.) The Swift Boat Veterans did not serve with Kerry, but were on other ships at the same time or on Kerry's ship at a different time. Several were angry at him for returning from Vietnam and subsequently opposing the war.

The original Swift Boat Veterans for Truth ad was run only in a few local spots. However, its metamorphosis from local ad to dominating news story for weeks illustrates how news is disseminated today.

The ad and the charges against John Kerry were first publicized by conservative "bloggers" who write news stories on the web. Bloggers mix fact and opinion and are not subject to the same kinds of standards as regular newspaper reporters. They made no attempt to discern the truth or falsity of any of the charges by seeking official records or interviewing people who were actually there.

Talk radio, mostly dominated by conservatives, picked up the story. Again, they had no interest in looking at the factual basis for the story.

Opinions about opinions are the staple of talk radio. Then Fox, the largely Republican television channel, began to publicize the ad and other cable news stations picked it up too. Meanwhile, some major Bush contributors donated more funds so that the ad could be run nationally and frequently.

By this time, the story was everywhere and the mainstream media—the networks and the national press—began to cover it. Although by this time the major media began investigating and presenting the facts about Kerry's war record, the story had already developed a life of its own.

Kerry and his supporters realized that they had made a strategic mistake not countering the story when it first came out. They had looked at the small local ad buys and assumed that

everyone would realize that the ad was not truthful but did not factor in how stories spread via new modes of communication. This was an incredibly naive view of both the political and information environments.

The story did continue to play among conservative audiences. The men behind the ad published a book, *Unfit for Command,* with Regnery Press, a publisher of popular conservative political books, and it enjoyed huge sales during the election season. The book reprised the points of the original Swift Boat ad and added accusations of treachery, treason, and murder conspiracies to the mix.

What was lost in all the hype was that the primary accusations in the ad were false, according to both the navy's records and the sailors' statements.

Though their claims were found to be largely untrue as documented by both official military records and the people on Kerry's ship, the ads gained national publicity for several weeks (see the box "How the Swift Boat Ad Became a National News Story") and were effective in weakening Kerry's campaign at a crucial period. They undermined a central premise of his campaign, that his service in Vietnam was an important element in his fitness to serve as president today. These ads did not endorse Bush but clearly worked in his interest.

Contribution Limits and Ways to Avoid Them

In addition to limiting candidate spending, the 1974 law also tried to limit individual and group contributions to candidates and campaigns. The Court upheld these limits, and they were raised in the McCain-Feingold Act. Individuals can now give $2,000 per candidate per election. Upward adjustments were also made in donations to national party committees ($25,000) and to state or local committees ($10,000). The overall aggregate donations permitted rose from $25,000 per year to $95,000 over a two-year election cycle (the odd-numbered year before each federal election and the election year itself). Limits on contri-

butions by PACs to candidates and parties were not changed.

Because of the legal restrictions of direct donations to candidates and campaigns, along with the prohibition of soft money to political parties, the McCain-Feingold law gave impetus to Internet fundraising, trying to attract small direct contributions from people who are not fat cats. The Democrats took an early lead in this effort, led first by Howard Dean, the Democratic front-runner in the early primary season, and then by John Kerry. The Dean campaign quickly realized the potential of the Internet to link his supporters with the campaign and with each other. Tens of thousands of his supporters were in constant contact with the campaign through e-mail and were regularly solicited for funds. Seeing the success that Dean was having through the Internet, Kerry's staff advised him to mention his web address in his Iowa victory speech. This mention resulted in an instantaneous tenfold increase in hits on Kerry's website. After he won the Super Tuesday primaries, he took in $2.6 million in a single day.[33] Enough funds were raised by both Dean and Kerry in the primary season to allow both to reject public funding for their campaigns.

By the end of the 2004 campaign, millions of citizens were on the e-mail lists of one or both parties, and tens of millions of dollars were raised from them.

This helped balance the role of the fat cats in the 2004 election.

But the fat cats had other places to play. The limits on direct contributions were negated in other ways through four huge, and largely related, loopholes: PACs, soft money, 527 groups, and independent spending.

Political Action Committees

Although the 1974 legislation and the McCain-Feingold Act limited group contributions to candidates, it did not limit individuals' contributions to groups. This loophole was originally created by a little-noticed provision of the 1974 law reaffirming the right of unions and corporations to establish PACs using voluntary contributions.

Funded from dues and "voluntary" contributions from members in the case of labor unions and "voluntary" contributions from employees in the case of businesses, PACs contributed to political campaigns of candidates seen as friendly to the interests of the organization or likely to hold powerful positions that could affect the interests of the organization. Labor unions were the first to establish PACs; businesses soon followed suit, and today many groups with interests affected by government have their own PACs. Figure 9.1 illustrates the interests of today's PACS.

Now that there were limitations on the amount of money individuals could give to campaigns, PACs became the vehicle by which individuals could channel more money to their favorite candidates. Individuals could give a limited amount directly to candidates and then give $5,000 to each of several PACs, which could in turn give it to candidates.[34] The funding activities of PACs differ greatly. Although there are more than four thousand such organizations, about one-third do not contribute to any candidates, and only four hundred or so give more than $100,000 in total.

Business and trade PACs predominate (trade PACS include groups of professionals, such as the American Veterinary Medical Association PAC; or groups of industries, such the American Wind Energy Association; and producers, such as the National Pork Producers Council Pork PAC).

PACs differ in the targets of their donations, but some patterns are clear. PACs show a distinct preference for Republicans in the presidential races and for incumbents—Republicans or Democrats—in congressional races (see Figure 9.2). PACs usually want to give to the candidate they believe will win so that they will have access to a policy maker. Enron's PAC donations are illustrative of spending patterns. It supported substantially more Republicans than Democrats but also funded Democrats on key committees, including Charles Schumer.

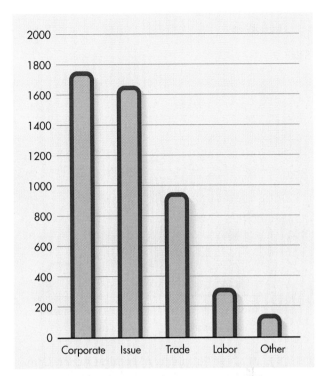

FIGURE 9.1 ■ Types of PACs Reflect Dominance of Business in American Politics
SOURCE: The data are number of PACS of each type. Data from 2004. U.S. Census Bureau, *Statistical Abstract of the United States, 2006.* (Washington, D.C.: Government Printing Office, 2006), Table 409.

Although the majority of PACs are business related and are ideologically much more sympathetic to the Republicans, PACs before 1994 gave predominantly to the Democrats because they were the majority party. When the Republicans gained control of both houses of Congress, they began receiving the majority of PAC donations.

What criteria aside from incumbency and party guide PAC donations?[35] Most PACs give money to members in districts where the PACs have a substantial interest, such as a large number of union members for a union PAC or a large factory for a corporate PAC. Enron focused much of its support on Democrats in Texas, where Enron was headquartered. And Enron's substantial support for Bush was partly due to his powerful position as Texas governor before he became president.

PACs also target contributions to members of key congressional committees. For example, PACs organized by defense contractors give disproportionately to members who serve on the Armed Services Committees, which have a big role in deciding what weapons to purchase. Unions and shipping companies involved in the maritime industry give large sums to those on the House Merchant Marine and Fisheries Committee and its Senate counterpart, the Commerce, Science, and

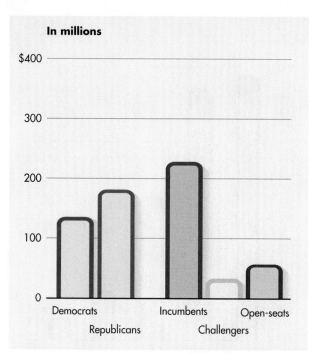

In millions

FIGURE 9.2 ■ Recipients of Political Action Committee Donations in the 2003–2004 Election Cycle
PACs give overwhelmingly to incumbents. The donations charted here were to House and Senate candidates. Open seats are those races without an incumbent.
SOURCE: U.S. Census Bureau, *Statistical Abstract of the United States, 2006.* (Washington, D.C.: Government Printing Office, 2006), table 414.

Transportation Committee.[36] Members of congressional committees that specialize in tax law (Ways and Means, Finance) and business regulations (Commerce) receive generous contributions from business PACs.[37]

Women's PACs, including EMILY's List, one of the biggest-spending PACs, are unusual in focusing most of their money on nonincumbents. Their goal is to get more women elected, which often means supporting nonincumbents with strong chances of winning.

Soft Money

Soft money provided the largest loophole in the 1974 campaign funding regulation. Soft money was exempted from limitations of the 1974 act because it was not to be used for campaigns. Instead, it is supposed to be used for such "party-building" activities as national party conventions, voter registration drives, direct mailings, polling, issue ads, and advertisements for nonfederal party candidates. Donors who wanted to give more than their legal federal maximum could give soft money to national party committees. Some of those funds were channeled to state parties, which spend under even less stringent state regulations.

In reality, most soft money was spent by independent groups for national television advertisements

for the parties' candidates. In 2004, the Democrats' ads prominently featured Kerry and the Republicans' Bush. As Robert Dole, the Republicans' 1996 presidential candidate, explained about an ad financed by soft money that spent fifty-six seconds dealing with his life and four seconds on the issues, "It never says that I'm running for President. I hope that it's fairly obvious since I'm the only one in the picture."[38]

The campaign finance reform system has evolved, in other words, in a way that makes direct campaign contribution limits irrelevant because the soft money loophole allowed people with money to spend as much as they want. Parties and candidates were raising millions, flaunting the spirit if not the letter of the campaign finance laws.

527 Groups

The McCain-Feingold Act closed part of the soft money loophole, banning soft money contributions to national political parties. However, it left a huge loophole allowing soft money contributions to various independent groups, and to a lesser extent, to state and local parties.

Because the Republicans had traditionally raised much more hard money than Democrats, whereas Democrats relied more on soft money, McCain-Feingold hurt the Democrats more than the Republicans. So the Democrats took the lead in exploiting the loophole created when McCain-Feingold banned soft money contributions to the national parties but did not ban soft money contributions to private groups.

Big donors gave to old or new so-called **527 groups,** named after the provision in the tax code authorizing them. Three of the most visible Democratic groups were MoveOn.org Voter Fund, the Media Fund, and America Coming Together (ACT), focusing on voter registration and involvement in addition to supporting Democratic candidates. The Swift Boat for Truth group was one of the most prominent Republican 527 groups in the 2004 election. These tax-exempt groups, and many others on both sides of the partisan divide, collected unregulated money from supporters of the candidates and then used that money to fund television advertisements. Neither fundraising nor expenditures of groups such as MoveOn.org are limited by the McCain-Feingold law as long as the groups are independent of the campaigns and do not endorse candidates. They can, however, bash the opposing candidate. The organizers of these 527 groups were often important party activists and donors. Thus the groups are technically independent, but in reality are closely linked to the candidates.

Reforming Campaign Finance

Is Real Reform Possible?

Campaign finance reform is a perennially vexing topic to both supporters and opponents. It's like weather, everyone talks about it, but few people are in a position to do anything about it. Most Americans find the campaign finance system distasteful and accurately believe that big interests with big money have special access. However, there is no agreement, even among the turned-off public, on what the right solutions are (see Figure 9.3).

Opposition to Reform

There are many reasons why we do not get more serious campaign finance reform. Some individuals, on both sides of the liberal-conservative divide, oppose even trying to get private money out of campaigns. They think prohibitions on private giving are a violation of free speech. Some emphasize that individuals should have the right to spend as much as they wish on the candidate of their choice. Others believe that private groups should be able to run as many advertisements as they want in support of their views.[39] Still others oppose reform because they dislike government regulation.

Some point out that it is largely impossible to regulate campaign finance if we want to allow people to give to campaigns. Campaign finance reform leads to ever more sophisticated searches for loopholes without accomplishing much.[40]

Most elected officials are not big fans of campaign finance reform either. They do not want to tie their own hands by limiting their abilities to raise funds from friendly interest groups. After all, when one party starts spending money in a close race, the impulse is for the other party to match or exceed it, a kind of campaign finance arms race. In a close contest, both sides want to do everything possible to win, and a few extra hundreds of thousands of dollars might indeed make the difference.

Powerful interest groups with money to spend also resist reform. Though reform would save them money in the short run, many big interests believe that their clout with key elected officials in getting favorable legislation is worth what they donate and much more. Major areas of business—including "pharmaceuticals, mining, oil and gas, defense, commercial banking and accounting—have basically made a decision to back the GOP."[41] Democrats, in turn, have the strong support of unions, the entertainment industry, and trial

"Some of it is soft and some of it is hard, but the main thing is that all of it is money."

lawyers. As one observer has pointed out, these divisions reflect the ideological divisions of the parties.[42] These groups are not eager to upset the status quo of campaign finance.

Ideas for Reform

Still, the unappetizing spectacle of wealthy donors, both individuals and corporations, receiving political favors from those they supported keeps the idea of reform alive. Large majorities of Americans and of donors specifically, favor some change in the current system (see Figure 9.3). Several ideas have been proposed.

Free Media Time

One proposal might avoid the pitfalls of the attempts to limit soft money by mandating that radio and TV stations grant free time to the candidates. This proposal focuses on reducing the cost of campaigns and hence the need to have so many private donors.

Why should the media be asked to donate time? Radio and television stations have free use of the public airwaves and use that gift to make considerable profit. In what Bob Dole called "a giant corporate welfare program," Congress in 1996 gave away even more airwave space to facilitate the transition to digital technology.[43] Nearly two-thirds of modern democracies do offer free access to the media.[44]

Moreover, a large part of the cost of campaigns is buying media ads. Political ads on television cost

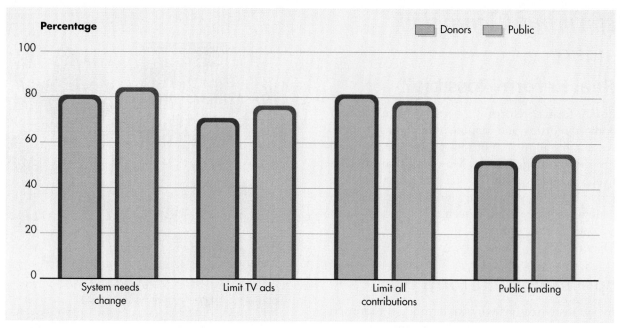

FIGURE 9.3 ■ **Opinion of Donors and the General Public on the Campaign Finance System**
Donors and the public agree that the system needs to be fixed. The bars show the percentage of respondents agreeing with various proposals suggested in a nationwide Washington Post *survey.*
SOURCE: Ruth Marcus and Charles Babcock, "Feeding the Election Machine," *Washington Post National Weekly Edition,* February 17, 1997, 10.

nearly $1 billion in the 2000 election and probably topped $1.5 billion in 2004, as the presidential campaigns bought more ads earlier in the race.[45] Nearly 10 percent of TV profit is earned through political ads, which are stations' third-largest advertising category, bigger than, for example, fast-food or movie ads.[46] A New York television station sales manager, contemplating the media ads from the 2000 Hillary Clinton–Rudy Giuliani Senate race exulted, "It's like Santa Claus came."[47]

In light of the fact that the public provides the airwaves free to broadcasters who in turn profit from campaign spending, a panel of broadcasters and reformers are asking stations to donate five minutes of free airtime each day for thirty days before the elections for political discussions among national, state, and local candidates for office. Five minutes a day sounds rather minimal, but currently the major networks broadcast each evening less than one-half minute of candidate dialogue, and local stations offer less.[48] Only twenty of the nation's thirteen hundred commercial television stations agreed to meet this standard in the 2000 election, and the proposal was opposed by the National Association of Broadcasters (NAB), fearing lost revenue.

The NAB lobbied hard and succeeded in defeating another proposal to force stations to offer political candidates their least-expensive advertising rates. This proposal passed the Senate but was killed in the House. We can expect other proposals dealing with media costs to be on the reform agenda because it is unlikely that we can stem the flow of money into campaigns without curbing the costs of the campaigns themselves.

Free or reduced-price media would dramatically reduce the costs of campaigns. Unless it was combined with public financing, it would not eliminate private gifts or affect outside groups' playing a role in campaigns.

Public Financing

A second idea is more public financing. Public funding seeks to limit the overall cost of the campaign and eliminate the need for private donations and the special access that comes with them. Currently, the presidential campaigns have such financing, but it does not begin to cover campaign costs. As noted earlier, the presidential candidates together receive $150 million for the general election, and several million more goes to primary candidates who agree not to raise private funds. However, this is a small fraction of the costs of presidential campaigns.

Some people have proposed extending public financing to congressional elections. About half the states have some public financing for their own state legislative or judicial candidates, several in conjunction with spending limits. But it seems unlikely that a major expansion of public funding for national candidates will be adopted anytime soon.[49] Opposition to government spending, public dissatisfaction with political campaigns, and the uncertainty that such a plan would really work to limit private money in politics all militate against it. And even if the official campaigns were funded, public funding does not solve the problem, if it is a problem, of independent organizations' collecting funds and promoting candidates.

Putting Distance between Officeholders and Donors

Many variants of this idea have come to the fore. One is to allow unlimited giving but keep the identity of the givers secret from the recipients. This proposal focuses on the unsavory relationship between money given and favors sought. Thus people would give as much as they want, but it would be channeled to candidates through an organization that would keep the donations anonymous. Some people, who give out of ideological and partisan conviction, would still give, but others might not give if they could not use the fact of their giving as leverage. Of course, anyone could tell a candidate that he or she gave, but the candidate would have no way of knowing who did and who did not.

A more complex idea is to combine raising congressional pay with a provision that members of Congress and the president can accept no gifts at all from anyone, including campaign donations.[50] At the same time, challengers could raise as much money as they wanted from anyone they wanted. Money would have to be immediately reported and disclosed to the public. For every $100,000 the challenger raised, the incumbent would receive a significant portion from public funds. The amount would not be the same, because part of the challenger's campaign costs would be the cost of raising money. The authors of this proposal say that the penalties would be severe (the incumbent would lose his seat if he accepted donations), and if

the challenger cheats and doesn't report, she loses her place on the ballot. If the incumbent wishes to spend his own money on the race, the government would pay the challenger an equal amount.

This proposal would combine public funding with the opportunity for challengers to raise whatever they want from whomever they want. It would strengthen public disclosure but deregulate most everything else.

The estimated cost of this proposal, if it had been applied in 2004, would be $800 million. The authors of the proposal argue that this is a lot cheaper than the current system where donors expect to get something in return for their investment: public money for tax breaks, lax regulation, and pork barrel projects.

Constitutional Amendment

Another suggestion for reform is to amend the Constitution, allowing Congress to limit free speech in the area of campaign finance. Proponents of this idea argue that prohibiting donations might limit "speech" in some respects, but the cost to democracy is much greater to allow big money to dictate public policy.

Such an amendment would prohibit groups from running any issue or attack ads during the run-up to the election (ads in favor of specific candidates are already prohibited). Assuming that part of free speech rights is the right to pay to have your speech heard, this would be a major blow to free speech and the rights guaranteed by the First Amendment to the Constitution. This would seem to have little or no chance of passage.

Public financing, media donation of time, and separating donors from public officials all may have some merits, but none of the reforms address the fundamental issue of spending by groups who have opinions about candidates and issues. And a constitutional amendment that tried to clamp down on political discussion by independent groups, no matter how seem-

caglecartoons.com

"...[T]here's plenty we can do to clean up bad neighborhoods," police and criminologists have learned.[1] City police have come to believe that the way to reduce serious crime is to severely enforce minor violations. Such a policy reassures the public, who are less likely to be confronted with street graffiti, vandalism, and turnstile jumpers, and who come to believe that the neighborhood has not been left to criminals. It deters potential criminals who come to believe that their crimes will be reported and punished. Through these means, and others, urban crime has significantly decreased in the past twenty years.

Can this strategy be used to clean up another bad neighborhood, Congress? Today, if a member of Congress fails to report a gift or campaign donation, nothing happens. Congress has an ethics committee, but it averts its eyes from most rule violations or ethical infringements. The FEC's membership is comprised mostly of officials who either oppose regulation of campaign finance or wish it weren't their job to be the regulators. Hence, federal officeholders can violate the rules that

do exist with relative impunity, short of committing a felony.

Some observers have argued, not wholly in jest, that many ethical issues surrounding Congress could be ameliorated with stricter enforcement of laws that do exist, just like on city streets. Such stricter enforcement might involve not only taking serious complaints brought to the Ethics Committee and the FEC, but FEC investigators actually hanging around congressional and K-Street offices, looking for tips about smelly deals. It might also involve higher penalties for those caught violating the rules. Those convicted of bribery might be sent away for very long terms as an example to others who might be tempted.

Of course, citizens have to demand that laws be enforced, just as they do in neighborhoods being threatened. And most citizens are not demanding that Congress live up to a higher ethical standard. That is, they say they do, but they reelect their member of Congress 98 percent of the time. As one criminologist noted, local police often are tougher with streetwalkers than with call girls, who commit similar offenses out of the public eye. "Congress is like the call girls," said one observer, "people don't feel the impact directly."[2]

[1]Quote by Jack Levin in Michael Grunwald, "Neighborhood Watch," *Washington Post National Weekly Edition* (February 20–26, 2006), p. 22.
[2]Michael Grunwald, "Neighborhood Watch," *Washington Post* (February 12, 2006), B1.

ingly partisan, would surely be further than most Americans would want to go.

Whatever the problems with the current system, we should be careful not to contrast it with an idealized version of the past. After all, over one hundred years ago, Mark Twain observed, "It could probably be shown by facts and figures that there is no distinctly native American criminal class except Congress."[51] Big interests have always had influence and access in Washington. The ways in which they exercise that influence are different now. In some ways, this influence is more open because the campaign finance reforms have made public the organizations working for special interests and the money they spend doing it.

Forty years ago, we would not have known how much each member of Congress received from each lobbying group; today we do.

The Impact of Campaign Money

We have discussed several aspects of money in elections: how much there is, who contributes it, and how they do so. Now we turn to the question of what difference campaign money makes. An obvious question is whether money influences the outcomes of elections. But we will also focus on three other kinds of potential effects of money and the way it is raised: the recruitment of good candidates, the policy decisions of elected leaders, and the cynicism of the public.

Does the Campaign Finance System Deter Good Candidates?

When John Glenn, an unsuccessful Democratic candidate in 1984, was asked whether running for president had been worthwhile despite his defeat, Glenn replied, "My family was humiliated. I got myself whipped. I gained 16 pounds. And I'm more than $2.5 million in debt. Except for that, it was wonderful."[52] In 1998, nearing the end of his career, Glenn remarked in a similar vein, "I'd rather wrestle a gorilla than ask anyone for another 50 cents."[53]

Other presidential candidates have lamented the difficulties and humiliations of having to raise money. Potential candidates often bow out early, overwhelmed by the magnitude of necessary fundraising. In 2000, George W. Bush's huge campaign war chest deterred several potential candidates from entering the race. Bush raised $94 million in the primary season and spurned federal matching funds; his next-best-financed competitor, John McCain, raised $45 million, including federal matching funds. Others, such as Elizabeth Dole, dropped out after losing early primaries, partly because of the impossibility of matching Bush's funding levels (she had raised only $5 million).[54] Bush had raised and spent more money before the first primary than Republican Bob Dole did in his entire 1996 election campaign.[55]

The necessity of raising a lot of money deters congressional candidates, too. As one leading congressional scholar noted, "Raising money is, by consensus, the most unpleasant part of a campaign. Many candidates find it demeaning to ask people for money and are uncomfortable with the implications of accepting it."[56] As one senator commented, "I never imagined how much of my personal time would be spent on fundraising. . . . I do not think a candidate for the U.S. Senate should have to sit in a motel room in Goldendale, Washington, at 6 in the morning and spend three hours on the phone talking to political action committees."[57] And once elected, many new members of Congress are surprised and chagrined to find that they must begin raising funds for their next campaign almost before they are sworn into office.

Does Money Win Elections?

Money helps win elections. It's not the only factor, of course. Many candidates have tried and failed to "buy" elections with their own money. But money certainly aids in getting the candidate's message out.

Looking first at presidential elections, the evidence is mixed as to the impact of money on winning presidential primaries. Primaries are the crucial elections that lead to each party's nomination. Some candidates are never considered serious contenders because they do not have sufficient money to mount a large campaign. In that sense, money is crucial.

In primaries, candidates of each party run against others of their party to achieve the nomination. Most primary candidates start out with little name recognition. Moreover, candidates cannot count on party loyalty to win votes. In primaries, voters choose among candidates of their own party; that is, Republican voters have to choose among Republicans rather than between a Republican and a Democrat. For both those reasons, money is crucial to increase candidate visibility.

Primary candidates who appear to be doing well generally attract money.[58] "Doing well" includes favorable media coverage that suggests the candidate is gaining popularity and momentum. Actual success in early primaries also stimulates giving. Money, in turn, allows further purchases of media ads to become known in the next primaries. However, in 2000, George Bush lost the first primary but used his huge lead in fundraising to pummel his chief opponent with hard-hitting ads in subsequent primaries.

Other things being equal, spending does influence voting in primaries. Money appears to be a necessary condition for primary victory, although it is not sufficient by itself. One analysis suggests that every 1 percent increase in spending buys 1.3 percent more votes.[59] Money is most important in multicandidate races, as is often typical early in the primary season when candidates are seeking to distinguish themselves from other little-known contenders.[60] Money is less important in two-candidate primary contests, often the situation late in the primary season when one candidate has emerged as a front-runner.

By the time presidential candidates are nominated, they have already spent a great deal of money. The name recognition achieved during the primaries and at the national conventions carries into the general election campaign. Presidential candidates receive extensive free media coverage in news stories. The amount that they spend after the convention is less likely to be as crucial. This is just as well for the health of the two-party system, because if money determined elections, the Republicans would have won every presidential election since World War II. However, of the presidential elections lost by the Democrats during that time, probably only the election of 1968 between Richard Nixon and Hubert Humphrey and possibly the Gore-Bush 2000 election were close enough that they might have turned out differently had the Democrats been able to spend more.[61] When the elections are close, as in 1968, the Republicans definitely have the advantage by having more money.[62] However, the Democrats are catching up; they have been increasingly aggressive in raising soft money and in 2004 were not significantly behind in fundraising, counting 527 groups.

In congressional races, incumbents usually start with a huge advantage. Some analysts estimate that their advantage is about 5 percent of the vote just by virtue of being incumbents.[63] Their name is recognized by many, if not most, of their constituents. And as incumbents, they are able to raise money early to finance their campaigns. In many cases, the incumbents' huge war chests deter potentially strong challengers from even entering the race.[64] Challengers know that they must raise considerable money to fund media ads even to be competitive. Thus the ability of challengers to raise and spend money is crucial to any chance of success in the election.

But incumbent fundraising and spending are also important. Fundraising is important early in the campaign to deter potential opponents. And campaign spending is important, especially for relatively new members of Congress. That is because those who have served only a few terms are less well known than more senior incumbents and thus are considered vulnerable.[65]

Of course, incumbents tend to spend the most when they have the toughest opponent. In general, as challengers spend more, so do incumbents.[66]

Most of the time, the person who spends the most to win a congressional seat wins. In 2002, for example, the biggest spender won about 80 percent of Senate races. Most of these winners were incumbents, and the link between spending and victory is also a link between incumbency and victory. The average incumbent is able to raise significantly more money than challengers. In 2002, for example, House incumbents raised about $1 million, four times what their challengers raised. The average Senate incumbent outspent his or her opponent by more than two to one.[67]

Sometimes the biggest spender loses, but the relative rarity of this occurrence only highlights the general link between spending and victory. In one of the most publicized Senate races in recent history, the 2000 open-seat contest in New York, Hillary Clinton won by a large margin over Congressman Rick Lazio, despite being outspent by more than $10 million in one of the most expensive races ever (in total, the candidates spent nearly $70 million). But Clinton was well known before she ran her first TV ad, so she did not have to spend money just to become visible.

Does Money Buy Favorable Policies?

As we have seen, donors are not a random cross section of the public. Money usually buys access, and that access is by the wealthiest segment of the population, whose views on public issues, especially economic issues, are more conservative than the larger population.

In recent years, corporate interests have pushed hard to deregulate and to lower taxes and have used substantial gifts to help gain access to rule makers. The accounting industry, for example, in the early 1990s helped fund more than three hundred congressional races, including both Democrats and Republicans, and spent $2 million for lobbyists. This clout led to Congress passing a law erasing liability for accountants and lawyers aiding and abetting securities fraud. Although President Clinton vetoed the law, his veto was overridden.[68] The law provided a disincentive for auditors to uphold strict accounting standards and removed a tool by which stockholders could hold companies accountable. Enron money bought considerable access (see the box "Buying Energy and Influence.").

If money buys access, does it also buy votes? Both anecdotal and systematic evidence suggest that money does buy votes, although only under some conditions.

Money is not likely to buy votes on issues that are highly publicized, because legislators' constituents usually have strong views on these issues and legislators feel pressured to follow them.[69] For the same reason, money is less likely to buy roll-call votes on the floor of each house than votes in committees. The former are public and recorded; the latter are not as visible to the public. Compared to their activity on the floor, in committees legislators with PAC support are more active in speaking and negotiating on behalf of the PAC's positions and offering amendments that reflect these positions.[70]

Money is also not likely to buy votes on moral issues, because legislators themselves often have firm views on these issues. These sorts of issues (abortion, gay rights, and school prayer, for example) also tend to be publicized.

But most matters that come to a vote are neither highly publicized nor moral issues. Most are relatively technical matters that constituents and legislators do not care as strongly about as PACs do. For these, members are susceptible. The deregulation of the accounting and energy industries was done when the public had no interest. "You can't buy a Congressman for $50,000. But you can buy his vote," a member admitted. "It's done on a regular basis."[71]

One survey of members found that about one-fifth admit that political contributions have affected their votes on occasion, and another one-third are not sure.[72] Analysis of voting has revealed that contributions from the AFL-CIO affected voting on the minimum wage legislation, and contributions from the trucking interests led senators to vote against deregulation of trucking.

Senators facing reelection the year in which the vote was taken were most susceptible.[73] Voting is also related to donations in such disparate areas as minimum wage legislation, gun control, and billboard regulation.[74]

One classic, well-studied example concerns used-car legislation. Auto dealers spent $675,000 in the 1980 congressional elections. This investment seemed to pay off in 1982 when Congress voted against a rule requiring dealers to inform prospective buyers of any known defects in used cars. The senators who opposed the measure received twice as much money from the auto dealers' PAC as those who voted for it. In the House, those who opposed the measure received on average of five times as much money as those who voted for it. Almost 85 percent of the representatives opposing the legislation had received PAC money.[75]

The relationship between PAC money and votes still existed even when the party and ideology of the members were taken into account. For conservatives, who might have voted against requiring auto dealers to list defects anyway, PAC contributions made only a marginal difference in their voting; but for liberals, PAC money substantially raised the probability that they would vote with the used-car dealers. " 'Of course it was money,' one House member said. . . . 'Why else would they vote for used-car dealers?' "[76]

The relationship between PAC contributions and voting should not be exaggerated, however.[77] Even on these low-visibility votes, a member's party and ideology are important. The constituency interests of members are also key factors explaining votes. For example, members with many union workers in their districts are going to vote for those interests regardless of how much or little they get in PAC contributions.[78] Members without these constituents, though, may be more swayed by PAC contributions.

More recent ties between donors and legislators concern the "buying" of special earmarks in omnibus legislation, legislation that is thousands of pages and contains hundreds of special favors for pet projects of legislators and lobbyists. We have discussed earmarking in Chapter 5, and will have more to say about it in Chapter 10.

Money can also buy influence with the executive branch. Presidential candidates tend to have widely publicized views, and their actions as president are subject to intense scrutiny and publicity. Once in office, presidents need donors less than donors need them, thus making the leverage of a campaign donation uncertain. Contributors are sometimes disappointed, as we saw with President Teddy Roosevelt earlier. However, on actions not widely visible to the public, donors can help shape policy. The Bush fundraising success is partly based on support from the oil and gas industries. Their reward has been deregulation of both accounting and financial requirements and environmental standards. The Enron scandal was only the tip of the iceberg. Contractors who received billions of dollars of contracts in Iraq and Afghanistan had donated generously to the Bush campaign. The director of the Center for Public Integrity commented that there is a "stench of political favoritism and cronyism surrounding the contracting process in both Iraq and Afghanistan."[79]

Analyses of large donors to and fundraisers for the 1992 George H. Bush campaign reveal that many were given special favors or benefits from the federal government. The Department of Labor reduced a proposed fine by nearly 90 percent against a large sugar farmer who gave $200,000 to the campaign.[80] President Clinton created a furor when on his last day in office, he pardoned the fugitive exhusband of a major campaign donor, Denise Rich. Rich had contributed generously to the Democratic Party and later to the Clinton presidential library.[81]

Large contributions to presidential campaigns often lead to appointments to public office, especially ambassadorships. The **spoils system,** the practice of rewarding jobs to supporters, has been with us since at least the time of Andrew Jackson, so it cannot be blamed on modern PACs and soft money.

Although it is impossible to prove a cause-and-effect relationship in these cases, clearly large donors who expect favorable treatment have plenty of precedents to lead them to that conclusion. As the leader of a watchdog group noted, "The point is, we're not just electing politicians. . . . We're also electing their patrons and their priorities."[82]

Does Our Campaign Finance System Widen Class Differences?

The influence of big money in presidential campaigns probably makes both parties more conservative. The biggest contributors to the Republicans in the last few presidential elections have been some of the most conservative people in that party. The big-money contributors to the Democrats are, on the whole, less liberal than the mainstream of the party.

Some Democratic House leaders were surprised when members said they could not vote against a capital

AP/World Wide Photos

Enron CEO Kenneth Lay is led away in handcuffs. In 2006 he died from a heart attack while awaiting sentencing for his financial crimes.

"No company in America did more to help George W. Bush get elected president than Enron." So reports the *Wall Street Journal*.[1] Enron's CEO, Kenneth Lay, was "the biggest sugar daddy in Bush's political career."[2] During Enron's heyday, its funds helped elect friendly lawmakers, mostly Republicans but also many Democrats; gain access at the highest levels; and buy loosened regulation and favorable tax policies. It made billions of dollars and benefited greatly from government deregulation of the energy industry. In the end, when Enron crashed, though, its substantial influence was not enough to get the government to bail it out.

This seeming contradiction illustrates well the point that money is most influential when the public is not paying attention. Most congressional legislation does not get featured on the evening news or in local papers. It is subject mostly to "inside the Beltway" battles. It is often dry, seemingly affecting only a few companies or groups of individuals. On such issues, the influence of well-organized and powerful lobbies can greatly profit the beneficiary corporations or groups.

But on well-publicized issues, those that CNN, the nightly news, and the local papers are featuring, it is more difficult for money to have the dominant influence. Thus a Bush aide spoke of the Enron affair as a "tribute to American capitalism" because the government let the company fail.[3] This point of view, of course, ignores what went on before and after Enron failed, including the enrichment of a few, the loss of millions of dollars of pension and savings of thousands of workers, the loss of public and investor confidence in the truthfulness of corporate financial statements, and later the power crisis in California, which cost California taxpayers and consumers billions.

What did Enron give, and what did it get in return? Although the full story is unlikely ever to be known, we do know that Enron gave, from 1989 to 2001, nearly $6 million to parties and candidates, three-fourths of it to Republicans.[4] Enron's generosity includes gifts from its executives and other employees, corporate soft money gifts, and gifts from Enron's PAC, funded by contributions by individual Enron employees. Fundraising for the PAC was done by high-level executives who kept track of who gave and who did not. In 1999, Kenneth Lay himself sent letters asking for contributions for the Bush campaign. One employee recalls a "menacing reference" to her husband's job and felt compelled to give even though she had not decided whether she favored Bush.[5]

Separate from corporate gifts, Lay and his wife donated more than $600,000 to the campaigns of George W. Bush, beginning when he first ran for Texas governor and including $325,000 in 2000.[6] Lay also raised millions of dollars for the Bush campaigns. Their connection was close. Bush used Enron's planes during the Republican primaries in 2000 to fly staff and even his parents. An Enron jet flew former president George H. W. Bush to his son's inauguration in January 2001, and a $100,000 donation from Lay helped fund the inaugural expenses.

But Enron also bought access to top Democrats. When Bill Clinton defeated George H. W. Bush in 1992, Lay began contributing to the Democrats. Enron gave nearly as much in soft money to Democrats as to Republicans in the 2000 election.[7] Enron may have provided funds for nearly half of all members of the House and three-fourth of the senators.[8]

What favors did Enron get from politicians? Enron profited from Democrats. In 1992, the Democratic-majority Congress approved an energy bill that set the stage for Enron's growth, and later Clinton took an interest in a large Enron project in India. In 1997, Lay met with President Clinton, Vice President Al Gore, and other administration officials to discuss the U.S. position at the Kyoto global warming conference.[9]

But Enron profited even more consistently from its Republican ties. For example, when Bush was governor, he signed an energy deregulation bill that opened lucrative markets for Enron. He established a panel that acted in secret to grant exemptions allowing power plants to exceed legal pollution limits, and Enron got several of these exemptions.[10] When Bush arrived in Washington, D.C., he rolled back efforts to crack down on American corporations' use of offshore banks (banks set up in the Caribbean, for example, to help U.S. firms—and others such as drug dealers—evade American tax and criminal laws), a move of great benefit to Enron, which reportedly had eight hundred offshore accounts. As a consequence of this and other creativity, Enron avoided paying a single penny in U.S. taxes in four of its last five years.[11]

Bush also established an energy policy task force headed by his vice president, Dick Cheney. The task force,

meeting in secret and whose membership and agenda have never been released, reportedly included Kenneth Lay and other lobbyists for the utility and energy industries, the past and present chair of the Republican Party, the secretary of energy, and other administration officials. The past Republican chair, Haley Barbour, at about the same time was lobbying utilities for large campaign contributions.[12] It is not surprising that the task force recommended a weakening of a major clean-air rule opposed by the utilities and the energy industry.

Kenneth Lay was also allowed to "interview" candidates for positions on the Federal Energy Regulatory Commission, the government agency that was Enron's regulator.[13] This seems to be a first, allowing the parties to be regulated to be involved so directly with the choice of the regulator.

Enron executives who had advance knowledge of the impending collapse of the firm sold their stock before the announcement that earnings were inflated, and they made millions (Kenneth Lay, the CEO, had made $103 million in the year before the bankruptcy; seven others made more than $5 million; and the top one hundred executives made $300 million). Lower-level Enron employees, many of whose pension plans were invested heavily in Enron, collectively lost millions, many of them their life savings. Enron had forbidden its employees to sell their Enron stock invested in company pension plans, insisting that all was well, until the stock had plummeted to 26 cents a share. Ordinary investors, likewise in the dark about the financial shenanigans, also found their stock worthless.

The consequences of Enron's criminal behavior went far beyond its shareholders. Later the public learned that Enron deliberately manipulated electricity markets, one of the major reasons for the California power crisis in 2000–2001 and the rise in prices there.

Enron's investment in public officials over a dozen years did not, in the end, save the firm from bankruptcy. But as one observer said, "Money allowed the Enron leadership to come to town. . . . Everyone says they didn't get anything. . . . But if you look back over the last five years, what they did get was no oversight."[14] Capitalism depends on a set of institutions, some private and some governmental. As one economist pointed out, "None of the checks and balances that were supposed to prevent insider abuses worked; the supposedly independent players were compromised. Arthur Andersen was told of these concerns, but . . . gave Enron a free pass . . . and the regulators were nowhere to be seen, partly because politicians with personal ties to Enron . . . took care to exempt Enron from regulation."[15]

[1]"Enron Lessons: Big Political Giving Wins Firms a Hearing, Doesn't Assure Aid," *Wall Street Journal,* January 15, 2002, 1 ff.
[2]Howard Fineman and Michael Isikoff, "Light's Out: Enron's Failed Power Play," *Newsweek,* January 21, 2002, 15.
[3]Paul Krugman, "A System Corrupted," *New York Times,* January 18, 2002, A25.
[4]Richard Stevenson and Jeff Gerth, "Web of Safeguards Failed as Enron Fell," *New York Times,* January 20, 2002, 1.
[5]Joe Stephens, "Hard Money, Strong Arms, and the 'Matrix,'" *Washington Post National Weekly Edition,* February 18, 2002, 11.
[6]Dan Morgan, "Enron's Cash Was Good for Democrats, Too," *Washington Post National Weekly Edition,* January 21, 2002, 12.
[7]Ibid.
[8]Ibid.
[9]These examples are from ibid.
[10]"Enron Lessons"; Bob Port, "Bush, Lay Friendship Is Study of Mutual Benefit," *Lincoln Journal-Star,* February 4, 2002.
[11]Molly Ivins, "Free-Range Markets: How Enron 'Aggressive Accounting Practiced' the Bank," *Fort Worth Star-Telegram,* January 29, 2002.
[12]Michael Weisskopf and Adam Zagorin, "Getting the Ear of Dick Cheney," *Time,* February 11, 2002, 15.
[13]Jonathan Alter, "Which Boot Will Drop Next?" *Newsweek,* February 4, 2002, 25.
[14]Ibid.
[15]Paul Krugman, "A System Corrupted," *New York Times,* February 18, 2002, A25.

TABLE 9.1 The Rich Are Getting Richer

Year	Bottom 90%	90–95%	95–99%	99–99.5%	99.5–99.9%	99.9–99.99	Top 13,400 Households
1970	$ 27,060	$ 80,148	$ 115,472	$ 202,792	$ 317,582	$ 722,480	$ 3,641,285
2000	$ 27,035	$ 103,860	$ 178,067	$ 384,192	$ 777,450	$ 3,049,226	$ 23,969,767
Percentage Change	-0.1%	29.6%	54.2%	89.5%	144.8%	322.0%	558.3%

Note: All income is in 2000 dollars.

Source: David Cay Johnston, *Perfectly Legal* (New York: Portfolio, 2003). Data from Thomas Piketty and Emmanuel Saez.

gains tax cut (which would benefit the wealthy) because it would anger their business contributors. Said one member, "I get elected by voters. I get financed by contributors. Voters don't care about this; contributors do."[83]

A former aid to a prominent Democratic senator remarked that he had to remind the Senator that a fundraising event was not a focus group. He went on to remark that "It's the rare politician whose perspective is not affected by his or her constant exposure to the wealthy people whose money they need to get elected."[84]

Beyond the specific policies and appointments that reflect the influence of big money, we can step back and look at the bigger picture. Public policy helps shape the distribution of income in our society through taxation, the regulation of corporations and unions, and many other ways. During the past quarter century, the rich have gotten a lot richer, and almost everyone else has struggled to maintain what they have. The wealthiest 1 percent of Americans now own 47.3 percent of all the country's wealth. In 1980, the richest 5 percent of Americans had 14.6 percent of all income; by 2001, they had 21 percent. The rest of the top 20 percent of wealthiest Americans also gained, but everyone else lost.[85]

Turning from shares of income to income that we actually spend, Table 9.1 provides an eye-opening look. Between 1970 and 2000, before the Bush administration, the average income of the bottom 90 percent of Americans fell by $25 in real terms (that is, adjusted for inflation), whereas the average income of the top 10 percent grew by tens of thousands and even more staggering amounts. The tax-cut policies of the current Bush administration have increased significantly the inequities since 2000 as higher unemployment and tax cuts directed primarily at the wealthiest Americans further skewed income.[86]

We can look at income and wealth data in different ways, using different years of comparison, but each supports the same general conclusion that the income gap is increasing. In addition, during the past twenty-five years, regulation of corporations has been weak-

ened, health insurance has decreased for millions of Americans, and other holes in our social safety net have been enlarged.

It would be inaccurate to charge the campaign finance system and the policies they have bought with all of these rising inequities. However, it would be shocking if the tens of millions of dollars flowing to the campaign coffers of our elected officials and the consequent increased access and influence of the wealthiest and most powerful interests in society did not have an impact on public policy and the distribution of wealth.

Does Our Campaign Finance System Encourage Extortion?

PAC, corporation, and union contributions to campaigns are products of mutual need. Special interests need access to and votes of members of Congress and the president, and elected officials need (or think they need) large sums of money to win elections. Thus donations are useful to officials and to the donors (see the box "Direct Contributors in the 2004 Presidential Campaign" to see to whom individual contributors donated in 2004).

Although special interests try to buy access and sometimes votes, members of Congress are not simply victims of greedy PACs and corporations. Indeed, as one observer remarked, "There may be no question that the money flowing into campaign coffers is a crime. But there is a question whether the crime is bribery of public officials or extortion of private interests."[87]

Pressure on corporations and unions is unrelenting. Some members keep lists of PACs that have given to them on their desks as an implicit indication that it is those groups that will have access. Others play one PAC off against another. Tom DeLay (R-Tex.), then the majority leader in the House, was quite open in soliciting funds and promising returns, as we saw in Chapter 6 in the discussion of the K-Street strategy. He offered lobbyists and corporate interests an open *quid pro quo:* they give, and they get to help develop

Republican strategy and interests and shape legislation that Republican leaders will support.[88] (In 2003, he went further and offered a Republican House member an endorsement for his son's race for Congress if the House member would vote with DeLay—an offer that the Ethics Committee deemed a violation of House rules.)

Not all of the fundraisers are for campaign contributions, but all involve putting the arm on lobbyists. A fundraiser titled "Salute to the President Pro Tempore" was designed to "honor the career and public service" of Ted Stevens (R-Alaska). The funds were to go to Stevens's foundation to benefit Alaska and thus were both tax exempt (campaign contributions are taxable) and not subject to the limitations of campaign finance laws. But Alaskans at the fundraiser were in short supply. The invitation list included most Washington lobbyists who were concerned about the legislation their groups have pending before the Senate Appropriations Committee, of which Stevens is the chair. And the foundation apparently consists of a former staff member in Stevens's office who is his campaign treasurer too.

In recent years, some corporations, including General Motors, Ameritech, and Monsanto, have said that they do not intend to give more political contributions. Companies such as this should favor campaign finance regulation, which could provide a defense to fundraising pressure.[89]

Does Our Campaign Finance System Lead to Money and Public Cynicism?

We have seen repeatedly that public confidence and trust in government have diminished greatly over time. Indeed, most of the public believes that most individuals in government are out to feather their own nests (see Table 9.2) and that many are crooks. Some of the reasons for this low trust have nothing to do with money. But public trust was certainly affected by the Watergate scandal in the 1970s, and it is likely that revelations about big-money lobbying activity reinforce public cynicism and lack of confidence.

American elections are funded, for the most part, by private money. It is therefore not surprising that candidates turn to people who have money to help with that funding. It is also not surprising that the current system alienates voters. Even if we believe that no votes are actually bought, the appearance of conflicts of interest that permeates the existing system and clearly disturbs the public should give pause to those interested in the health of our political system.

Walter Lippmann, a famous American journalist, once said that American attitudes about corruption alternate between "fits and starts of unsuspecting complacency and violent suspicion."[90] We think nothing is wrong, and then we think everything is wrong. So it is with our views of campaign money. For several years after the 1974 reforms, we thought things were going along pretty well. More recently, many people have become convinced that the nation is in terrible jeopardy because of the influence of money. This fear is compounded because money has helped bring about regulatory lapses, which in turn have been partly responsible for failures to check the dishonesty of many corporations, which in turn has led to eroding confidence in corporate America. So beyond leading Americans to grow cynical about government, the campaign finance system has indirectly helped lead to a loss of confidence in business, too.

Elected officials appear to be more afraid of being without campaign donations than they are that the campaign finance system will further erode confidence in the whole political system. Ideologically, Democrats are more sympathetic to limiting the influence of big money, but practically, Democratic incumbents are heavily dependent on their PAC "fixes." Thus neither party has much incentive to support campaign finance reform, despite the fact that the public is repelled by the existing system.

TABLE 9.2	Public Opinion Is Cynical about Government
Statement	**Percentage of People Agreeing That They Have a Great Deal of Confidence in . . .**
Confidence	
The military	36%
The church	26%
The presidency	23%
Congress	11%
Big business	7%
Statement	**Percentage of People who believe . . .**
Accountability	
Government is run by a few big interests	64%
Government is run for the benefit of all the people	28%

NOTE: 2% had no opinion on the first poll and 8% were unsure on the second poll.
SOURCES: Gallup poll of 1002 adults nationwide, margin of error = 3%, May 21–23, 2004; and CBS News and *New York Times* poll of 955 adults nationwide; margin of error = 3%, July 11–15, 2004; both polls online at www.pollingreport.com/institut.htm.

Direct contributors to the Democratic and Republican parties are very different, reflecting a diversity in the population that goes beyond race and gender. A group of scholars analyzed more than 1000 donors in the 1996 presidential campaign. Examining differences, they found that moderate and liberal Democrats were different from each other as well as from Republicans, and moderate and conservative Republicans were also different from each other. Below are some characteristics that distinguish among the four groups.

Of course, these are not the "fat cat" donors only, but include anyone who gave $200 to a campaign. These donors echo differences among the rank and file of each party, with Demo-crats tending to have a greater proportion of women in their base, Republicans men; Republicans having a higher proportion of support from evangelicals and mainline Protestants, and Democrats from Jews and those with no religious leanings (secular). Lawyers are more likely to be Democratic donors, and business people, Republican ones.

	Liberal Democrat	Moderate Democrat	Moderate Republican	Conservative Republican
Male	61%	76%	89%	84%
Mainline Protestant	28	37	50	41
Catholic	16	22	28	25
Evangelical	5	4	8	24
Jewish	22	22	5	2
Secular	18	10	5	2
Lawyer	32	29	12	10
Business person	18	37	56	54
View of liberals*	78	49	21	8
View of conservatives*	16	39	62	87

% indicates the percent of total donors fitting into the category; for example 61% of the liberal Democratic donors are men compared with 84% of conservative Republican donors.
* On a scale from 0 = least positive to 100 = most positive
SOURCE: "Constituencies of the Democratic and Republican Parties" by Peter Francia et al from *Social Science Quarterly* 86 (December, 2005): 761-778. Reprinted by permission of Blackwell Publishing.

Perhaps the public recognizes that a culture of greed cannot sustain itself forever. The two clearest examples of eras of rampant corruption in the American political and business systems suggest that they end unhappily. In both cases, at the end of the Gilded Age and the Roaring Twenties, they ended with the failure of thousands of banks and companies and with unemployment and despair.

Conflicts of Interest

In addition to money's influence on political campaigns and policy making, it also leads to **conflicts of interest,** situations in which officials face making decisions that directly affect their own personal livelihood or interest. The campaign contribution system we have just described presents a huge conflict of interest. Presidents and members of Congress make decisions about policies affecting people who give them campaign money. But conflicts of interest are not confined to decisions involving campaign money.

As James Madison noted, almost every decision involves potential conflicts of interest. Decisions made by presidents, bureaucrats, and members of Congress can affect their personal financial interests (including stocks, bonds, and other investments).

It is sometimes difficult to untangle the effects of personal financial interests, constituency interests, and party loyalties. For example, most people on the Agriculture Committee have agribusiness interests and represent districts with large agricultural interests. If those members vote in favor of agricultural interests, they are voting both for their own interests and those of their constituents. And they are likely to think that they are advancing the national interest at the same time. It appears that the impact of these personal interests on voting is fairly small once constituency interests are taken into account.[91]

Despite periodic attempts to limit conflicts of interest, violations of ethics codes still occur in Congress and in the executive branch. In 1981, six House members and one senator were convicted in an FBI undercover operation known as Abscam. Five were even videotaped accepting cash bribes. In 2006, Representative William Jefferson (D-La.) was also taped allegedly accepting a bribe, and police found a freezer full of bills in his office refrigerator (at the time of this writing he has not been indicted or convicted). But his alleged misdeeds were overshadowed by those of Randy "Duke" Cunningham (R-Cal.) who resigned after being sentenced to federal prison for accepting more than $2 million in bribes. Cunningham even went so far to develop a "menu" of his prices (bribes) for giving corporations the contracts they wanted. For example, he would help a business with a federal contract worth $16 million in exchange for a $140,000 gift.[92] Incidents of blatant bribery such as this are rare, but conflicts of interests are very common.

Despite rules against accepting gifts from lobbyists, lawmakers accept millions of dollars worth of gifts, often in the form of free trips to luxury resorts and other vacation areas. A 2006 report found that collectively, over a five-year period, members of Congress had accepted $50 million work of free trips that involved 23,000 trips. A significant number of trips cost more than $5000 each and some much more. The report concluded that "While some of these trips might qualify as legitimate fact-finding missions, the purpose of others was less clear."[93] Probably in the latter category were the 200 trips to Paris, 150 to Hawaii, and 140 to Italy. Congressional travelers "pondered welfare reform in Scottsdale, Arizona and the future of Social Security at a Colorado ski resort."[94]

The Abramoff Scandal and Concierge Politics

In 2005 to 2006, investigators uncovered one of the largest schemes of conflicts of interests and other misdeeds in recent memory. Jack Abramoff, the former national chairman of the College Republicans, close associate of Tom DeLay, the majority leader of the House of Representatives, and mentor to Ralph Reed, pled guilty to several felonies and implicated a wide variety of public officials, staffers, and lobbyists in his schemes.[95] Abramoff received funds from clients, such as the Indian tribes involved in the Reed case, and then distributed the money to favored groups and associates in return for access or favorable public policies, or to curry favor with powerful officials and old cronies, or as income to be kicked back for himself.

Abramoff's dealings, and ultimately crimes, should be viewed in the context of the culture that has developed in Washington. Significant conflicts of interests have always existed, but Tom DeLay's K-Street strategy, to make it clear to lobbyists that they pay to play (that is, donate money to Republican candidates in exchange for influencing legislation), has made influence buying more open (see Chapter 4 for more on the K-Street strategy). One scholar, a fellow in a conservative think tank, describes the K-Street Project as a "Tammany Hall operation."[96] Money is kicked into the machine, favors emerge. Big lobbying firms are expected to hire only Republicans at the top jobs that pay as much as $1 million a year. Once hired, "everyone is expected to contribute some of that money back into Republican campaigns."

Some former colleagues termed DeLay's role as akin to a hotel concierge, calling on favors from these wealthy donors and "arranging corporate jets, private cars, fishing trips and other expense-paid trips during congressional breaks, key votes, and party conventions, all financed by wealthy donors with interests before Congress."[97] Members getting the favors were then expected to come through with appropriate votes on pending legislation.

Abramoff, an early supporter of DeLay's bid for congressional leadership, used the close ties he had developed with DeLay and his key staffers to raise millions of dollars. Potential clients knew that he could use his clout with DeLay to get things done. After all, DeLay had publicly called him one of his "closest and dearest friends."[98]

Only a little of Abramoff's money went to the White House, as when he charged the tribes $25,000 to gain access for two of their representatives to the president.[99] Most went elsewhere. For example, $2.5 million went to the U.S. Family Network, ostensibly a grassroots organization dedicated to moral improvement, but mostly a front organization to pay the organizer of the group, a former DeLay chief of staff. (He in turn hired Tom DeLay's wife at $3200 a month for a job involving little work.) Millions more went to Americans for Tax Reform, founded by Abramoff's old colleague Grover Norquist, who then funneled some of those funds to Ralph Reed. The National Center for Public Policy Research, another Abramoff organization, provided funds to take the House Majority Leader, Tom Delay, and other officials to Scotland. Yet another organization, Capitol Campaign Strategies, run by another DeLay former staffer, received funds from the Indian tribes and kicked back significant amounts to Abramoff. And the American International Center, supposedly a "think tank," was in reality a house in Rehoboth Beach owned by the same former DeLay staffer. This front organization moved money to Abramoff and also to Ralph Reed. Another front organization, the Capital Athletic Foundation, even funneled funds to a sniper school in Israel and an orthodox Jewish school founded by Abramoff.

As of this writing, several people have pled or been found guilty in this scheme, including Abramoff, two former DeLay aides, and an executive branch employee, the former chief of staff at the General Services Agency (which is the chief purchasing agency of the government) and then the White House's chief procurement officer. Investigations continue and others may be charged. Members of Congress and the White House have hurried to disassociate themselves from Abramoff, of course.

Regulating Ethical Behavior

Congress does have an ethics committee in each house, and there are provisions for registering lobbyists. But the ethics committees are nonfunctional. When in 2004 the House Ethics Committee reprimanded Tom DeLay (R-Tex.) three times, the Speaker of the House, Dennis Hastert (R-Ill.), replaced the chair of the committee and several other Republicans with those less interested in an activist committee and more responsive to the Republican leadership.[100] The Senate committee has not investigated any of the recent scandal.

Although in light of the Abramoff and other 2005 scandals, some members pledged to put new rules in place regulating such travel, nothing was done. In fact, John Boehner (R-Ohio) was elected House majority

House Majority Leader Tom DeLay (R-Tex.) told lobbyists that they had "to pay to play."

leader, in part because he opposed any new regulation of such gifts, calling such regulation "childish."[101] Boehner himself took two hundred free trips, worth $157,000,[102] during this five-year period.[103]

However, perceived widespread congressional corruption and influence peddling were motivating factors for voters in the 2006 election, and the Republicans lost control of Congress. Whether the Democrats will take action against sleazy dealings remains to be seen.[104]

In the executive branch, decision makers operate under much less direct public and media scrutiny. Yet they, too, may be acting on matters that affect their personal economic position. Since the Carter administration, all high-level administrative officials have been required to file public financial disclosure statements to allow the public to see when they are making decisions that benefit their own financial interests. But the rules do not require officials to step aside on matters that would affect them financially.

It is also a conflict of interest to use one's government position to line up a job following a public service career. The Ethics in Government Act of 1978 tries to regulate this. The act bars former public servants from lobbying their former agencies for a year and, on matters in which they "personally and substantially" participated as public officials, for life. Current employees also are prohibited from participating in decisions affecting interests with which they are negotiating about future employment. But the act is not very stringently enforced.

Because many companies that regularly deal with government think experience in government is an asset, especially experience in the agency that regulates the company's activities, many officials take well-paying jobs in the industry they came to know while in government. Critics call this the "revolving door," referring to the movement of people from government service to the private sector and sometimes back again. Recently, most of the top executives of the Department of Homeland Security, led by Tom Ridge, its first director, have left government service to become executives, lobbyists, or board members for firms now contracting with the Homeland Security agency.[105]

The term for using access to powerful people to make money is called **influence peddling.** Former high government officials can and do use their access to former colleagues to win jobs representing clients in business or labor and then use that access to lobby for favorable policies and contracts for their new firms. Many of those lobbyists hired by K-Street firms were former Republican members of Congress, now in a position where they could solicit clients on the basis of their close relationship with DeLay and other powerful Republicans.[106]

Democratic and Republican Corruption

Conflicts of interest and influence peddling are bipartisan phenomena. Most of our examples have pinpointed Republicans because they have controlled government for the past five years, so those who want to buy influence buy it largely from them, and because conflict of interest dealings are more public than ever before. But conflict of interest accusations swirled around the Clinton White House, although no high official was convicted of illegal acts in office. But both President Clinton and First Lady Hillary Clinton were accused of conflicts of interest in the long-running investigation of the Whitewater affair (an investment scheme in which they had participated years earlier), but they were never found guilty of anything. A number of Clinton administration members, including a cabinet secretary, Mike Espy, left office under an ethical cloud relating to conflicts of interest and influence peddling.

George W. Bush came to Washington saying that the ethical standards of his administration would be higher than those of the Clinton White House, but influence peddling seemed to escalate substantially. In some cases, corporate interests have been part of secret policy-making processes inside the White House in ways never seen before. Vice President Cheney's financial interests in one of the major contractors in Iraq, Halliburton, are now the subject of investigation. Halliburton, which Cheney headed from 1995 to 2000, was given advance notice to plan for the postwar period in Iraq and received billions of dollars' worth of contracts without competitive bidding. In 2004, an audit revealed that Halliburton had billed the government for $4.3 billion in reimbursement for work that had cost the company only $1.8 billion (Halliburton's response was that conditions in Iraq made keeping up with paperwork difficult).

Conflicts of interest can never be completely eradicated from government, but presidents can make their expectations clear. George W. Bush's administration has seemed less concerned about conflicts of interest than those of his predecessors, Bill Clinton and George H. Bush. His administration seems intent on privatizing many parts of government, including military support operations, and has been unembarrassed about awarding lucrative contracts to top supporters without benefit of competitive bidding.

Some observers have pointed out that although both Democrats and Republicans have ethical lapses, the kinds of ethics problems they have are quite different. Corrupt Democrats steal. They accept bribes and improper campaign donations, divert public funds to their own pocket, and seek personal financial aggrandizement. This style of corruption is reminiscent of the "honest graft" of the big-city political machines (see the box "Honest Graft" earlier in the chapter). Although some Republicans also steal—for example, Abramoff and Cunningham, former Vice President Spiro Agnew, who pleaded no contest to charges of kickbacks, bribery, and extortion, and former representative Joseph McDade (R-Pa.), who was convicted of bribery and racketeering—most of these sorts of scandals have involved Democrats. Examples include Daniel Rostenkowski (D-Ill.), former chair of the House Ways and Means Committee, convicted of corrupt acts involving mail fraud, and Robert Torricelli (D-N.J.), censured by his Senate colleagues for accepting gifts from lobbyists.

Republican ethical failings tend to be related to the use of government for improper means. President Nixon's Watergate scandal involved trying to use the powers of government to punish his personal enemies and then lying about it. He also ordered Cambodia to be bombed and tried to keep it a secret. President Reagan tried to subvert the constitutional powers of Congress by secretly selling arms to Iran and supplying weapons to rebels in Nicaragua, both expressly against the law. The Republicans' K-Street strategy was basically an attempt to get lobbyists to buy influence on government policies and to buy government contracts in a rather overt way.

Although Democratic presidents have also been guilty of misuse of government power (for example, President Johnson lied about alleged attacks by the North Vietnamese on an American ship to justify getting the United States more deeply involved in the Vietnam War, and President Kennedy ordered the FBI to wiretap Martin Luther King, Jr.), subverting government seems more a Republican style of corruption.

Why do these differences exist? They could be coincidental, of course. But one Democrat argued that these differences were tied to the class basis of the parties: "The lower classes steal; the upper classes defraud." A prominent Republican had a different view: "Most Republicans are contemptuous of government; few Democrats are." Whatever the reason, these examples suggest that partisanship extends to more than presidential preferences.

Conclusion: Does the Influence of Money Make Government Less Responsive?

The influence of money in American politics is a perennial source of concern to those who want to live up to the democratic ideals of political equality and popular sovereignty. Our democratic values tell us that government should represent all, the poor as well as the rich, and that everyone should have an equal chance to influence government. We know that in the real world, things do not work this way. We tolerate much inequality in access because that seems to be the way the world works in the private as well as in the public sphere, because everyone is not equally interested in influencing government, and because for most people the effort of changing this pattern would be greater than the benefits gained.

Nevertheless, our reaction to the influence of money seems to be cyclical. We tolerate it; then, when stories of inside deals, influence peddling, and buying access and even votes become too frequent, we act to do something about it. But that happens rarely, and then we slip back into apathy until the next cycle comes along.[107]

In recent history, the low point of the use of money to buy access was probably during the Watergate scandals associated with the 1972 election. We then reacted strongly to those scandals by passing new laws and cleaning up our campaign finance system. But as the years went by, we found ways to get around the laws until they became nearly meaningless with the important exception that we know how much money is being given to candidates. Now it appears we are in another era of growing concern over ethical standards in government, and the 2002 campaign finance reforms and the significant Democratic successes in 2006 are indications of that.

We should not think of our times as the low point in government morality. In political campaigns, big money is certainly less influential than it was a century ago. Campaign funding disclosure legislation means that the public can at least know who is buying influence.

Nor should we conclude that ethical standards are lower in government than in the private sector. After all, some public officials are selling favors, but it is members of the private sector who are buying them. Conflicts of interest and influence peddling in government reflect the ethical standards of the larger society. Since the 1980s, the news has been filled with stories of Wall Street bankers who bought and sold illegal insider tips, savings and loan officers who looted their institutions of millions of dollars, military contractors who cheated government, and corporate leaders who falsify corporate income and plunder corporate funds for personal gain while shareholders lose their investments. One businessman lamented, "We are all embarrassed by events that make the *Wall Street Journal* read more like the *Police Gazette*,"[108] whereas several years later another remarked, "In my lifetime, American business has never been under such scrutiny, and to be blunt, much of it deserved. You pick up the paper, and you want to cry."[109]

We should also not exaggerate the amount of money involved in politics. Corporations spend much more to attract consumers than politicians spend to attract voters. We reported that the cost of the presidential campaigns in 2004 could be as much as $2 billion. This is an extremely large sum until we compare it to the $4.7 billion a year that Americans spend on laundry detergent, or the $1 billion a month that car companies spend selling their wares, or the $1 billion that the federal government spends every few hours.[110] It is not the amount of money in politics as much as its possible effects that concern us.

But the effects of money are hard to pin down. It is difficult to measure exactly the influence of money on political outcomes. Money sometimes influences votes and policies. Campaign contributions have some impact on voting in Congress. Money seems to have moved both parties toward more conservative policies. Money in politics is no doubt responsible for the increased inequality between the rich and poor. But sometimes, especially when the public is paying attention, money appears to have little impact.

We do not know exactly how presidential candidates might be influenced by huge campaign donations or whether bureaucrats are using promises of future jobs as trade-offs for current favors. We think that good candidates are hindered or deterred from running by a shortage of money or even just by the knowledge that they need to raise big money, but it is difficult to measure exactly how many. Even though money is very tangible, its influence sometimes is quite intangible.

To the extent that money has an impact, it limits the responsiveness of government to the average citizen. It causes some policy makers to be more responsive to the big interests than to the average person. This does not mean, though, that those with the most money always win. Organization and a sense of the public interest can sometimes defeat even big money.

In designing laws to regulate the use of money in political life, perhaps the best that reformers can reasonably hope for is a system in which public officials who want to be honest will not feel under pressure to

be influenced by money. Certainly, there will always be a few "bad apples," and no political system can protect us completely from them. It should be enough to design rules and structures that ensure that people of average honesty who serve in public office are rewarded for putting the public interest, rather than their private interests, first. Our current laws, especially our congressional campaign finance laws, do not always do that. The penalties we suffer are less in politicians stealing from the public till (relatively little of this occurs, certainly in comparison with the stealing that has been revealed in corporate America). They are more in the loss of public trust, an increasing alienation from government, and anger at politicians who seem to be putting their interests before the public interest. Perhaps, then, even a largely symbolic effort by our legislators to limit the influence of money on the political process is

important, because it sends the signal that they are aware of and accountable to public concerns.

Any discussion of campaign finance should include a mention of our role as citizens. It is tough to regulate this. John McCain has said, "Money is like water: it finds cracks in the wall."[111] In a democracy, it is hard to find ways of restricting the flow of private resources into political campaigns. We can be appalled by the lies in ads trashing one or the other of the candidates, and independent groups in the process are not really held accountable. That is the public's and media's responsibility. Since the ads would not appear if they were not effective, perhaps it is we, the voters, who need a higher standard of evaluation of these ads, a lower tolerance for corruption, and higher expectations for the performance of our elected officials. It is we who keep electing them.

Reed Took the Deal

Ralph Reed accepted the contract. He and an associate (a former spokesperson for Tom DeLay) mobilized hundreds of pastors and thousands of churchgoers to man phone banks under bogus organizational names such as Christian Research Network,[112] blanketed the states with antigambling advertising, and engaged in negative campaigning against the supporters of gambling to fight the proposed Alabama and Texas legislation. The more than $6 million that Reed received was only part of the total of more than $82 million that Abramoff received in lobbying fees from Indian tribes.[113] In turn, this was just one of the many money laundering projects that centered around Jack Abramoff.[114] Later, the tribes accused the lobbyists of "blatant, calculated scheme to defraud a client . . . in a series of kickbacks, misappropriated funds, and unauthorized charges."[115]

A Senate investigative report, entitled "Gimme Five," the name that Abramoff used for his scheme of taking billions from clients and funneling it to friends and favored political causes, did not accuse Reed of any wrongdoing. It did conclude that the use of these intermediary organizations to obscure the source of lobbyists' funding merited further investigation.

Ralph Reed campaigns for lieutenant governor.

Reed claimed that the report vindicated him and insisted that he did not know that the source of the funds were from casino gambling. This was contrary to e-mail evidence turned up by the Senate investigation committee, as well as a note of Abramoff's that said he told Reed of the pass-through nature of the funds.

In 2006, an Alabama Indian tribe sued Abramoff, Reed, and several other associates claiming that their own casino business was hurt by what they charged was fraud and racketeering, so the story is not going away. Reed himself now avers that "It is now clear from the benefit of hindsight that this was a piece of business I should have declined."[116]

Meanwhile, Reed moved on, embarking on an electoral career by running for Georgia's lieutenant governor in 2006. He downplayed his close ties to Abramoff.[117] However, his less prominent opponent in the Republican primary campaign hammered on those ties in an attempt to portray Reed as a hypocrite. This strategy worked, because Reed was defeated. In 2006, Abramoff began his prison term.

To learn more about this topic, go to "you are there" exercises for this chapter on the text website.

Key Terms

muckrakers
Teapot Dome scandal
Federal Election Commission
political action committees (PACs)
public disclosure
contribution limits
independent spending

McCain-Feingold Act
soft money
527 groups
spoils system
conflicts of interest
influence peddling

Further Reading

Bruce Ackerman and Ian Ayres, *Voting with Dollars* (New Haven, Conn.: Yale University Press, 2002). The authors propose a novel way of financing political campaigns through "patriot dollars," donations from the public at large, given anonymously.

Jeffrey H. Birnbaum, *The Money Men* (New York: Times Books, 2000). The real scandal in Washington isn't what's illegal; it is what is legal. This book follows the money in a very readable way.

Larry J. Sabato and Glenn Simpson, *Dirty Little Secrets: The Persistence of Corruption in American Politics* (New York: Times Books, 1996). The authors take a close look at corruption in politics.

Bradley Smith, *Unfree Speech: The Folly of Campaign Finance Reform* (Princeton, N.J.: Princeton University Press, 2001). Smith, once nominated to the FEC, argues that restricting campaign donations is unconstitutional and ineffective besides.

For Viewing

"Bigger than Enron" (2002). This *Frontline* documentary from PBS on how the failure of congressional and regulatory oversight led to corporate fraud can be viewed online at www.pbs.org/frontline.

 **Electronic Resources**

www.commoncause.org

This is the home page of Common Cause, the public interest group whose major focus is reforming the campaign finance system. Linked to the page are the group's reports tracking relevant legislation, periodic reports on campaign spending, coverage of the Enron and accounting scandals, and reports on financial ties of those voting against major regulatory legislation such as the tobacco bill.

www.pbs.org/wgbh/pages/frontline/president

The home page for the PBS Frontline special "So You Want to Buy a President" contains much useful information on how much is contributed and who the contributors are.

www.fec.gov/index.html

The Federal Election Commission does not have much regulatory power, but it does publish useful reports of campaign spending. This page describes election rules and links to FEC reports on campaign spending and on voter turnout.

http://www.fecinfo.com

This website provides information about groups receiving and giving money in election campaigns, based on FEC data. A search engine lets you see how much people you know gave to candidates and political groups.

www.politics.com

This website provides links to news stories and polls and allows you to see who in your neighborhood (or any other, by zip code) gave to which campaigns.

www.enron.com/corp

Enron's site now featuring bankruptcy news and advice for laid-off workers.

ThomsonNOW™

Enter ThomsonNOW™ using the access card that is available with this text or through www.thomsonedu.com/thomsonnow. ThomsonNOW™ will assist you in understanding the content in this chapter with a personalized study plan generated for your needs. A practice test will assess the areas you need to review and provide the tools to fully comprehend those concepts, including an integrated digital eBook, interactive simulations, timelines, video case studies, MicroCase exercises, and InfoTrac College Edition readers and exercises. You'll also be connected to the learning objectives, chapter outline, chapter glossary, flash cards, crossword puzzles, Internet activities, and interactive quizzes found on the companion website.

CHAPTER 10

CONGRESS

After the Democrats won a majority of the seats in Congress in 2006, Representative Nancy Pelosi (D-Calif.) became Speaker of the House and Senator Harry Reid (D-Nev.) became Majority Leader in the Senate. Pelosi is the first woman ever elected Speaker.

Members and Constituencies

   Members

   Constituencies

   Congress as a Representative Body

   The Advantages of Incumbency

How Congress Is Organized

   The Evolution of Congressional Organization

   Contemporary Leadership Positions

   Committees

   Staff and Support Agencies

What Congress Does

   Lawmaking

   Oversight

   Budget Making

Members on the Job

   Negotiating the Informal System

   Making Alliances

   Using the Media

   Balancing the Work

Congress and the Public

Conclusion: Is Congress Responsive?

Bipartisanship or More Partisanship?

Y ou are Pat Roberts, second-term Kansas Republican and chair of the Senate Select Committee on Intelligence. It is November 2005 and Democrats on your committee are pressuring you to reopen an investigation into how the Bush administration handled the prewar intelligence on Iraq. At the same time the White House is urging you not to do it. You are acutely aware of the mounting criticism that Congress has been neglecting one of its primary responsibilities: to oversee how executive branch officials carry out their work and to ensure that they implement legislation passed by Congress as Congress intended. Known as **oversight,** this monitoring function is provided for in our constitutional system of checks and balances to see that the laws are being faithfully executed and also to guard against Congress's powers being usurped by the executive branch. Critics charge that your committee has failed in its obligation to oversee the work of the country's multiple intelligence agencies, including the CIA.

Coming from a farm state, you spent much of your first twenty years in Congress, including sixteen in the House, specializing in agricultural, not intelligence and defense, issues. Your abolitionist great-grandfather went to Kansas with a "flatbed press, a six-gun and a Bible" and started what is now the second-oldest newspaper in the state.[1] You were the co-editor until you gave it up for politics. In 1997 after moving to the Senate, you took a seat on Armed Services and its subcommittee on emerging threats and began to study terrorism and new kinds of warfare. In 2003, just a few months before the invasion of Iraq, you became chair of the Intelligence Committee.

An ex-marine, you are a strong supporter of the military and the war in Iraq. The son of a former National Republican Party chairman, you are also a party loyalist and supporter of President Bush. But when American forces failed to find weapons of mass destruction in Iraq, you shared the widespread concern in Congress and among the public about why intelligence agencies had failed so badly.

In late 2003, a year when partisan divisions reached record heights, you agreed to an investigation into how the intelligence was gathered and how it was used to justify the war in Iraq, but only if the Democrats on the committee were willing to divide the investigation into two phases. The first phase would look at intelligence gathering and analysis by the agencies responsible for it, and the second would examine how the data was used by the president and other officials. The first phase was completed that year with a notable amount of bipartisan cooperation; and you issued a report with the ranking minority member Jay Rockefeller (D-W.Va.) concluding that the CIA and other agencies had

Pat Roberts (R-Kan.), the "funniest man in Washington," faces a serious dilemma in the Senate.

provided bad information to the White House. You called it "The most comprehensive review of intelligence since the creation of the committee in 1976."[2]

But when Democrats wanted to move to phase two and investigate how the administration had used intelligence, you refused. You tied your decision to a memo written by the Democratic committee staff that called for using the findings to attack President Bush and committee Republicans. You said the Democrats' only motivation for continuing the investigation was "nefarious"—to make a partisan attack on the president before his 2004 reelection campaign. You said that your job is to "ensure that the intelligence committee conducts its oversight in a responsible, nonpartisan manner. If we give in to the temptation to exploit our good offices for political gain, we cannot expect our intelligence professionals to entrust us with our nation's most sensitive information. In any case you believe that the main question—whether our intelligence agencies produced reasonable and accurate analysis—has been thoroughly investigated and has established that the intelligence was wrong. You said there was no point continuing the investigation to examine "how that intelligence was used by policy makers" because "there are no secrets here—nothing to review." The public could decide for themselves whether intelligence was accurately portrayed by government officials.[3] You want to

concentrate on reorganization of the intelligence agencies and offer your own plan for completely reorganizing the CIA and other intelligence agencies.[4]

You put Phase 2 "on the back burner," saying there will be no time for it until perhaps after the 2006 elections.[5] Committee Democrats were furious and continued to pester you throughout the 2004 election year. They are threatening to continue through the 2006 midterm elections. Minority Leader Harry Reid (D-Nev.) has just used a parliamentary maneuver to force the Senate into closed session for a day to discuss the issue. It was a stunt that angered Republicans, but it got the media's attention. If you do not give in, the Democrats can remind voters that you have reneged on the bipartisan agreement for a two-phased investigation and claim that you are running the committee at the bidding of the White House rather than carrying out the work of Congress. And it isn't only Democrats who believe that Congress has forgotten about the separation of powers and the system of checks and balances. Senators on both sides of the aisle believe that the Bush White House has become too involved in the legislative process and that it is working too closely with committee chairs to set agendas and procedures, depriving Congress of its independent voice. Republicans are worried, too, that by constantly deferring to the executive branch they are eroding congressional independence and setting precedents for when the Democrats control the presidency.

Many congressional experts concur that since Bush became president congress's oversight work has withered. Time and again the White House has refused to let officials testify at committee hearings, denied access to records and reports, and stonewalled on turning over subpoenaed materials.

One congress watcher called it "the battered Congress syndrome," because "The more the White House or executive branch officials defy Congress or slap Congress around, the more Congress submits. When executive officials testify, they frequently make clear that they have no intention of giving Congress what it wants."[6]

This was clear when Congress tried to exercise its oversight function prior to the war by asking the CIA for a National Intelligence Estimate of the threat Iraq presented. Few members saw anything more than an executive summary of the report, and access to it was in a secure room under guard. Even then only members of committees with oversight responsibility for intelligence and defense issues were briefed on the contents of agency assessments of Iraq's weapons of mass destruction capabilities and possible links to the al Qaeda terrorist network. When these briefings were later found to be based on information provided by a handful of unreliable Iraqi expatriots and forged documents, many Senators in both parties were livid. So were many CIA officers who knew that House and Senate intelligence committees had never seen the much more accurate assessments contained in the uncensored reports sent to the White House.[7]

In fact one of the reasons many senators want the hearings to continue is that they have come to believe that they voted to support the invasion of Iraq on what was not just faulty intelligence, but data that had been manipulated to support the war. This simply added to the intense partisan polarization in Congress. But most of your Republican colleagues do not want more hearings. They believe it's payback time, especially with the 2006 elections in sight. And what if oversight hearings do reveal deliberate manipulation of evidence by the White House or the Defense Department and it has an effect on the midterm election? You could embarrass a president you support wholeheartedly and per-

The Founders clearly intended Congress to be the dominant branch of government. They laid out its role and powers in Article I, and their discussion takes up almost half the document. Through its formal powers, Madison believed, Congress would dominate the presidency because it alone had "access to the pockets of the people." But Congress has not always been first in the hearts of the people, nor has it always been the most respected or trusted branch of government. On the other hand, most people like their own representatives and senators, at least well enough to return them to office at impressively high rates.

In this chapter, we look at the current composition of Congress and ask how representative a body it is. We describe how Congress is organized and how it carries out its constitutional responsibilities, then look at how individual members carry out their duties in Washington and their districts and what makes them so popular back home that they usually get reelected. Finally, we look at Congress's relationship to the other branches of government and to the public. To understand Congress, one must also understand the process by which members are elected, a topic covered in Chapter 8.

Members and Constituencies

Members

Alexis de Tocqueville was not impressed with the status of members of Congress, noting that they were "almost all obscure individuals, village lawyers, men in trades, or even persons belonging to the lower class." His view was shared by another European visitor, Charles Dickens, who was shocked in 1842 to find Congress full of tobacco spitters who committed "cowardly attacks upon opponents" and seemed to be guilty of "aiding and abetting every bad inclination in the popular mind."[9] However one views their behavior, members of Congress were not then, and are not now, a cross section of the American public. But they are a more diverse group than the membership of Congresses of the eighteenth and nineteenth centuries ever were or thought they should be.

Who Can Serve?

The Constitution places few formal restrictions on membership in Congress. One must be twenty-five years old to serve in the House and thirty in the Senate. One must have been a citizen for at least seven years to be elected to the House and nine years to be elected to the Senate. Members must reside in the states from which they were elected, but House members need not reside in their own districts. As a practical matter, however, it is highly unlikely that voters will elect a person to represent their district who is not from the district or who does not maintain a residence there.

Local identity is not as significant a factor in Senate races; national figures such as Robert Kennedy and Hillary Rodham Clinton, who established in-state residency within weeks or months of the election, both ran successful campaigns in New York. It is more difficult to run in another state if the state is less cosmopolitan or the candidate is not already well known, as was the case in 2004 when Maryland resident Alan Keyes ran for, and lost, a U.S. Senate seat in Illinois.

Length of Service

Every member of the House stands for election every two years, and senators serve six-year terms, with one-third of the membership standing for election every two years. Although the Articles of Confederation did set a limit on the number of terms a representative could serve, the Constitution placed no cap on how many times an individual can be elected to the House or Senate. Perhaps the Founders thought that no one would want to serve more than a few terms. In the late eighteenth and early nineteenth centuries, leaving one's home to serve in Congress was considered a great sacrifice. Washington was a muddy swamp, with debris-filled streets, farm animals running loose, and transportation so poor almost no one got home during a session. In fact, during Congress's first forty years, 41 percent of House members, on average,

In its early years, Washington, D.C., was described as "a miserable little swamp." When this photo was taken in 1882, it still retained the look and feel of a small town.

dropped out every two years, and in the early 1900s the median length of service for a representative was still only five years.[10]

But as Washington became a power center and a much more livable and accessible city, members were more receptive to longer periods of service. In the 1910s and 1920s, power in the House became less centralized, and individuals were able to build personal power bases. And as seats went uncontested in the one-party South, more legislators became career politicians, spending thirty and even forty years in Congress. These long-serving members began to dominate committee work and to control the legislative agenda. Although they by no means comprised a majority of Congress, they were probably foremost in the minds of those Americans who began to see government as increasingly unresponsive to the public.

Term Limits

During the height of public anger with government in the 1990s, there was a nationwide move to limit the number of terms that state and national legislators could serve. By 1995, over 70 percent of the survey respondents said they favored term limits.[11] Although Congress narrowly defeated term-limit legislation, in twenty-three of twenty-four states that allow ballot initiatives, voters adopted term limits for their members of Congress and state legislators.

Some supporters of term limits believed that by not having to worry constantly about getting re-elected, legislators would be free to consider the "public interest," not "special interests," and would have no desire to build personal empires. Others also saw term limits as a way to weaken the power of government by having a more rapid turnover in the membership of Congress and state legislatures.

Opponents believed that term limits would weaken Congress at the expense of the special interests and the federal bureaucracy and president. Legislators would be relative novices compared with much more experienced lobbyists and bureaucrats.

This debate subsided when in 1995, in a 5–4 vote, the Supreme Court held term limits for members of Congress unconstitutional. The majority argued that permitting individual states to have diverse qualifications for Congress would "result in a patchwork of state qualifications, undermining the uniformity and national character that the framers envisioned and sought to ensure."[12] By adding to the qualifications spelled out in the Constitution (age and citizenship), the Court ruled that states were in effect "amending" the Constitution. By definition, then, such laws would be unconstitutional because the Constitution can be amended only through the processes of adoption and ratification it specifies, not by state or congressional laws.

By the late 1990s, enthusiasm for term limits in the *state legislatures* had waned, and in 2001 Idaho became the first state to repeal them. By 2006 only sixteen of the twenty-three states that had adopted term limits still had them.[13]

Constituencies

The district a member of Congress represents is called a **constituency.** The term is used to refer to both the area within the electoral boundaries and its residents. There are two senators from each state, so each senator's constituency is the entire state and all its residents. Most states have multiple House districts, though seven states (Alaska, Delaware, Montana, North Dakota, South Dakota, Vermont, and Wyoming) have populations so small that they are allotted only a single seat in the House of Representatives. For these "at-large districts," the constituency for the House member is also the entire state. Except for those seven states, every House district must have (in accordance with the one-person, one-vote rule) roughly the same number of residents, so the number of districts in each state depends on its total population.

Except in single-district states, the geographic size of a constituency is determined by the distribution of the population within the state. In states with large urban populations, several districts may exist within a single city. The logistics of campaigning are thus very different for a representative from New York City, whose district may be as small as 12 square miles, and one from Montana, who must cover the entire state (147,042 square miles).

Reapportionment

Initially, the House of Representatives had fifty-nine members, but as the nation grew and more states joined the Union, the size of the House increased too. Since 1910, it has had 435 members, except in the 1950s, when seats were temporarily added for Alaska and Hawaii. Every ten years, in a process called **reapportionment,** the 435 seats are allocated among the states based on the latest census. Since the first Congress, the number of constituents each House member represents has grown from 30,000 to roughly 700,000 in 2006.

Within a constant 435-seat House, states with fast-growing populations gain seats, whereas those with slow-growing or declining populations lose seats. Since World War II, population movement in the United States has been toward the South, West, and Southwest and away from the Midwest and Northeast. This has been reflected in the allocation of House seats. For example, from 1950 through 2000, California gained twenty-three seats and New York lost fourteen. Illinois, Wisconsin, Pennsylvania, and Ohio lost House seats after the 2000 census, whereas Arizona, California, Colorado, Florida, Georgia, Nevada, and Texas gained seats. The census counts all residents, irrespective of legal residency or citizenship, and several of the seat-gaining states are home to millions of undocumented residents. California, for example, the state with more illegal immigrants than any other, would have shown population loss since the last census if not for immigration. Even as the state experiences a net loss of native-born population, undocu-

Reprinted with permission.

mented residents should make it possible for California to add to the size of its congressional delegation again in 2010.

Redistricting

States that gain or lose seats and states whose population shifts within the state (rural to urban or urban to suburban for example) must redraw their district boundaries, a process called **redistricting.** This is always a hot political issue. The precise boundaries of a district determines the election prospects of candidates and parties. In fact, because in most states the state legislature controls the redistricting process, districts are normally drawn to benefit the party in control of the state legislature. A district whose boundaries are devised to maximize the political advantage of a party or a racial group is known as a **gerrymander** (see also Chapter 8). Majority parties in state legislatures persist in securing political advantage by drawing bizarrely shaped districts but still complying with the Supreme Court ruling that all congressional districts be approximately equal in population.

Before 1960, states were often reluctant to redistrict their state legislative and congressional boundaries to conform to population changes within the state for fear that doing so would endanger incumbents and threaten rural areas whose populations were declining. After decades without reapportioning, some legislative districts in urban areas had nineteen times as many residents as rural districts. When state legislatures, many of which were still dominated by rural representatives, refused to reapportion themselves, the Supreme Court, in *Baker* v. *Carr* (1962), issued the first in a series of rulings forcing states to reapportion their legislative districts.[14] Two years later, the Court required congressional districts to be approximately equal in population, thus mandating the principle of "one person, one vote."[15] As a result, during the 1960s most states had to redraw district lines, some more than once. The decisions provoked strong opposition and a constitutional amendment was proposed to overturn them. But over time the principle of one person, one vote has come to be widely accepted.

Because of the important role state legislatures play in the redistricting process, the 2000 state legislative elections were crucial for both parties. In the early 1980s, Democratic-controlled state legislatures were able to help Democratic candidates in states such as California by drawing lines that concentrated Republican strength in a few areas and created districts with small Democratic majorities.[16] After the 1990 state legislative elections, which gave Republicans more clout, many states drew boundaries favoring Republicans, a factor in the Republicans' victories in 1994.

The redistricting process has been very important to underrepresented minorities, as we saw in Chapter 8.[17] However, redistricting has led to less representation in other ways. Software now available can measure voting patterns down to the block level. This allows legislators, using voter registration records that record party preferences, to draw district lines to create "safe" (noncompetitive) legislative districts for either the Republican or Democratic candidate. This is a serious problem for democratic accountability. Fair and competitive elections are the primary way the public exercises authority over government. In the run up to the 2006 election, for example, some estimates were that only thirty districts were truly competitive.

Tenure

Given that congressional seats have become ever more safe, congressional tenures have become ever longer.[18] In noncompetitive districts, members are almost certain to be reelected and thus are serving longer. The 109th Congress (2005–2006) had only 40 first-termers, down from 110 a decade earlier[19] but there were nearly 60 in the 110th (2007–2009), after Republicans lost seats in both the House and Senate they had believed were safe.

Congress as a Representative Body

What Does Representative Mean?

To take the measure of how representative Congress is, we first have to establish what "representation" means. During the Revolutionary War, John Adams said that the legislature to be created under the new government "should be an exact portrait, in miniature, of the people at large, as it should think, feel, reason, and act like them."[20] Benjamin Franklin said simply that Congress should be a mirror of the people. These statements leave unresolved what has priority in representation. Is it more important, for example, for Congress to look like a demographic cross section of the public or for the policies it advances to reflect constituent issue positions? And in what situations can elected representatives use their delegated authority to act as their conscience dictates to do what they believe is right or in the national interest, even if not supported by a majority of their constituents?

A Congress that reflects the demographic mix of the country is one where descriptive representation is high. This kind of representation is not rooted in what legislators *do* but rather on their personal characteristics—what they *are,* or *are like.*[21] The rise of identity politics has increased demands for a Congress that better reflects the country's demographic profile, and so today it is more likely than ever that a predominantly Hispanic, white, or African American congressional district will be represented by a member of the corresponding ethnicity or race. But Congress is still far from representative in this sense (see the box "Congress Is Not a Cross Section of America").

For the first century of the Republic, the possibility of having citizen-legislators who were a cross section of the general public was just a romantic notion. Only certain landed, business, or professional white men could even think about running for Congress. It was not until 1920 (with ratification of the Nineteenth Amendment, granting women the right to vote) that a majority of Americans could vote, and most of them, realistically, could not stand for office. Although federal barriers to African American male suffrage had been removed in the nineteenth century, state laws prevented most from voting until the 1960s. Today, although adults in all economic categories can meet the minimum requirements needed to stand for office, the demands of the nomination and selection process, especially campaign costs, limit the number of people who are able to run.

"Acting For" Representation

If Congress still has a way to go to *look* like the American public, does it "think, feel, reason, and act" like them? The "acting for" conceptualization of representation holds that the legislator is not just standing in for others but acting "in behalf of," "in the interest of," and "as the agent of" the members of the constituency.[22]

Part of the reason why there has been interest in having Congress look like America is that there is a relationship between a person's sex, race, ethnicity, income, and religious views and that person's position on issues. Historically, the political conditions of women and minorities have differed from those of white men to the degree that today women, African Americans, Hispanics, and Asian Americans are seen as *national* constituencies with distinct issue priorities. House members now organize around these identities so as to represent national constituencies as well as their home districts (see "Making Alliances" later in this chapter). Poor people and blue-collar workers are other groups who have sent few of their numbers to Congress and yet often have different positions from the lawyers and professionals who dominate the legislature.

The News-Gazette, Robert K. O'Daniell

In a state where African Americans are 15 percent of the population, Barack Obama (D-Ill.) received 70 percent of the vote in his first run for the Senate. He is the only African American in the Senate.

Congress is not now, and never has been, a cross section of the American population (see Table 10.1). The citizens who serve in Congress are still disproportionately white and male: white non-Hispanic males, who make up about one-third of the total population, held about 70 percent of the seats in the House of Representatives and 81 percent of the seats in the Senate in 2006.

Women, who make up 51 percent of the nation's population, are the most underrepresented demographic group. They are just 17 percent of the House membership and 16 percent of the Senate's. Three states (Iowa, Delaware, and Vermont) have never elected a woman to Congress.[1] Most states do send at least one female representative, however, and California's delegation has twenty women, including both of its senators (accounting for almost one-quarter of all women in Congress).

Hispanic, Asian, and African Americans are also below parity with their numbers in the population. But thirty-seven of the forty-one congressional districts whose populations are one-third or more African American have elected an African American to represent them.[2] Congress is also not representative of the range of religious views among the general public. Christianity and Judaism account for virtually all religious affiliations declared by members, although about 15 percent of the population claim other or no religious affiliation.

TABLE 10.1 Members of the 110th Congress: Not a Cross Section of the Public (2007–2009)*

	Population (%)	House** (%)	Senate (%)
Women	51	17	16
African American	12.3	9.2	1
Hispanic	14	5.3	3
Asian Pacific	4	0.9	2
American Indian	0.7	0.2	0
Lawyer	0.3	37	57
Blue collar	25	2	3
Millionaires	0.7	27	40
Foreign born	13	2***	0***
Median age	35	56	60
Protestant	51[†]	56	56
Catholic	25[†]	29.6	24
Jewish	2.6[†]	6	13
Mormon	1.3[†]	2.5	5
Muslim	1–2[†]	0.2	0

*Does not include undecided House races as of November 15, 2006.
**Does not include nonvoting members from Puerto Rico, Guam, Samoa, the Virgin Islands, or the District of Columbia.
***Does not include those born abroad of American parents, such as John McCain.
[†]The U.S. Census does not collect data on religion so figures for the general population are estimates. Congressional affiliations are by self-declaration and will not add up to 100 percent because ten members specified other denominations and six gave no affiliation.

SOURCE: *CQ Weekly,* November 13, 2006; *National Journal,* November 10, 2006.

Members are much better off financially than the average householder: about 30 percent are millionaires, and a number are multimillionaires.[3] They also tend to rank well above average in education; nearly all have college degrees, and a majority have graduate or professional degrees (141 masters, 224 law, 20 in medicine, and 19 doctorates, including three political scientists). Although blue-collar workers constitute nearly one-quarter

But does it make a difference? For instance, do women really represent their constituents differently from their male colleagues? There is no guarantee that any one woman (or African American or Mexican American) will represent women (or blacks or Hispanics) collectively better than, say, a white man; there is no rule that a millionaire will not look out for the interests of blue-collar workers or that a Christian or Jew will not care about the civil rights of a Muslim.

There is some evidence that first and second generation immigrants are not especially supportive of those recently arrived, or of illegal immigrants. And our demographic categories are often overly broad. Do Japanese-American, Christian senators from Hawaii really have the same perspective on the world as newly arrived immigrants from China and India or as Muslim Indonesians or Pakistanis? And has Sen. Ken Salazar (D-Col.), a man whose family emigrated

of the working population, only a dozen congressional members claim blue-collar backgrounds.[4]

The most common occupational background of congressional members has been the law. But this pattern is beginning to change as legislative careers have become more demanding. Today it is difficult for an attorney to maintain a law practice and also serve as a legislator. Ethics laws requiring financial disclosure and information about client relations have also discouraged practicing attorneys from running for congressional office. Although a majority of Senators were trained as lawyers, there are now more House members with backgrounds in business and public service than in the practice of law. But in this era of high technology, such fields as engineering and science still are barely represented in Congress. Increasingly Congress is drawing its members from professional politicians; in 2006, 72 percent of House members and eighty-eight senators had held prior elective office. Fifty-two senators had served in the House before running for the Senate.[5]

Another dent in the citizen-legislator ideal has been the presence of "dynasty" families (the Adamses, Harrisons, Lodges, Kennedys, and Bushes). In the 108th, there were three pairs of siblings and twenty-six members whose parents had also served in Congress.[6] Members of the Senate are even less a cross section of the American population than the House, but the Senate was established to represent the

The Sanchez sisters—Loretta (left) and Linda—serve in the House of Representatives as Democrats representing two districts in Southern California.

interests of the states, not to be a mirror of the people. Representation in the Senate is based on a one-state, two-vote standard, not one-person, one-vote. This structure allows for the over-representation of the interests of low-population states and the under-representation of the interests of the larger, more urban, and more ethnically and racially diverse states. Senators must still define and represent state interests in the aggregate, not just those of a specific group or district. This is less complicated for senators from low-population states that are more socially and economically homogeneous, such as Nebraska and Wyoming, than for senators from much larger and more diverse populations and economies such as New York and California.

[1]A list of all women who have served in the House can be found at www.loc/gov/thomas; those who have served in the Senate can be found at www.senate.gov/artandhistory/history/common/briefing/women_senators.htm.
[2]Gregory L Giroux, "A Touch of Gray on Capitol Hill," *CQ Weekly*, January 31, 2005, 243.
[3]These are estimates drawn from members' financial disclosure statements, which do not provide exact figures on income. Members need only report income and assets within a broad dollar range. A few members do, however, release their tax statements.
[4]"A Touch of Gray," 241.
[5]Ibid., 242.
[6]*CQ's Politics in America 2004: the 108th Congress* (Washington, D.C.: CQ Press, 2003), 1133. Eleven of the twenty-six whose mother or father served in Congress directly succeeded their parent.

from Spain and helped found Santa Fe in the 1500s (before the Mayflower arrived), really shared the same experiences as those who organize as Hispanic Americans?

There is reason to believe, however, that as women, blacks, Hispanics, and Asians increase their presence in Congress, so will the likelihood that the issues of greatest concern to them will be heard. Imagine a Congress made up not of wealthy males but of blue-collar females. It is hard to imagine that the legislation coming out of that Congress would be the same as it is today. Of course, we cannot test that speculation; nevertheless, in the 1993–1994 Congress, in which there were twenty-two new women members, Congress passed a record sixty-six bills of special importance to women. That nearly equaled the number of such bills passed in the entire previous decade.[23] This suggests that there is a relationship between *descriptive*

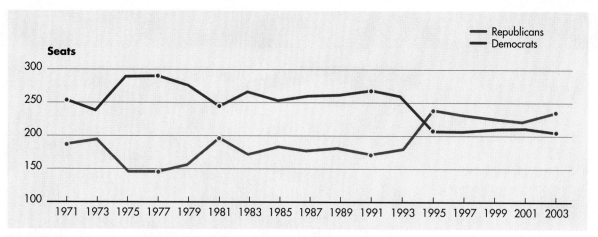

FIGURE 10.1 ■ Makeup of the House of Representatives, by Party, 1971–2003

Representation of the two major parties in the House has been much more equal since 1995 than in earlier decades but other parties have been shut out.

NOTE: Figures are for the first day of each Congress and do not include Independents or vacant seats.

SOURCE: *Congressional Quarterly Weekly Review,* April 3, 2004, 790.

and *acting for representation* and that as the Congress begins to look more like a cross section of the population, legislation may become more representative of the wishes of the broadest segment of the electorate.

One simple measure of "acting for" representation is party identification. Although only 62 percent of the public identifies with the two major parties, Republicans and Democrats hold 99.7 percent of the seats. (See Figure 10.1) There are only two Independents in Congress, one each in the House and the Senate, and they caucus with the Democrats. Due to the winner-take-all electoral system, minor party identifiers (Greens, Libertarians, the Reform Party, socialist and other labor parties), who now account for 6 to 7 percent of all voters, have no representation in Congress, except when their position on an issue overlaps with that of one of the two major parties. This compares to parliamentary systems based on proportional representation, which mandate that any party receiving a certain minimum of the votes cast—usually 1 to 5 percent, depending on the country—receive a proportionate number of seats in the legislature.

Another measure of "acting for" representation is a legislator's voting record. By casting hundreds of votes each year, members try to represent the interests of their constituencies, bring benefits to the district, and in the process win support for reelection. Members must consider what benefits their districts as a whole as well as the needs of subgroups within the district, such as party voters, socioeconomic groups, and personal supporters.[24] Overall, if districts are filled with farmers, the members must represent farmers, whether or not they know anything about farming. Representatives of districts with large universities must be sensitive to the reactions of students and pro-

fessors even if they personally think academics have pointed heads.

For members to act as their constituents would if they were making policy themselves—to pursue policies they favor and vote as they would on issues—requires that members keep in close touch with the home district. And in fact most members do spend about half of each year in their districts. On the whole, the member's issue positions are usually not far from those of his or her party or the majority of the constituency *that votes.* But members are more likely to share the issue position of constituents when the issue is important to constituents and when their opinions are strongly held. Since constituents are often uninformed, divided, or apathetic, and most votes in Congress are on bills the electorate knows little about, members can vote their personal issue preferences, with their party, or with those constituents or donors who most forcibly make their positions known.

Constituents are becoming more active in communicating with their legislators, flooding them with faxes, e-mails, poll results, and mailgrams, often at the encouragement of radio or television talk shows or interest groups mobilizing their memberships. These communicative individuals, however, are often not representative of the majority in a member's constituency and tend to hold their positions with greater intensity than the average voter. As we saw in Chapter 4, Congress is more likely to respond to those with intensely held views. And Congress itself has become more extreme in its views than the public in general. Republican members have become more conservative and Democrats more liberal. Even though 42 percent of Americans still identify as "moderates," by 2004 only 8 percent of House members were centrists and 9 percent of the Senate.[25]

The first members of Congress made $6 a day, which paid for boarding-house accommodations, firewood, candles, their meals, and a mileage allowance for travel to and from the capital.[1] Today members receive a handsome salary indexed to inflation, a generous benefits package including full medical and dental care, and money for office, staff, mailing, and travel.

Personal Benefits

Salary

Congress has indexed its salaries to inflation so that members no longer have to vote each session on salary increases. Thus, salaries have increased from $90,000 in 1989 to $165,200 in 2006. (Salaries of congressional leaders are somewhat higher.) Members are now among the top 5 percent of American wage earners.[2]

Health Care

For a modest monthly premium, members can opt for a first-class private health care plan or care at one of two military hospitals. Taxpayers spend millions more each year to keep a doctor and staff on site at the Capitol's Wellness Center, which also houses a pool and gymnasium.

Pensions

Members of Congress are required to pay Social Security taxes, but they also have 401(k) plans and a generous fed-eral pension program. They can begin collecting as early as age fifty if they have served at least twenty years. Pensions cannot be higher than 80 percent of a member's final salary, and in general, those with decades of service receive about 75 percent of their salaries. If Congress voted to convert its pension system to the same kind of cash balance plan many members have advocated for American workers, the value of their pensions would drop by as much as 60 percent.[3]

Benefits That Help Reelection Chances

Office and Clerical Support

Representatives are authorized to hire up to eighteen staff members, and they receive an allowance for office space and furniture in their home district. Senators' staff budgets vary with the population of their states. The average size of a Senator's personal staff is thirty-four full-time workers. Those who serve as committee chairs or in leadership positions have additional staff and larger expense allowances.

Travel and Mailing Allowances

Members receive an allowance for travel to and from their districts, adjusted according to their distance from Washington. They also receive mailing allowances called the franking privilege (discussed below).

Studio Access

Television and radio recording studios are provided for preparing ads and sound bites for the news.

Other Perks

Members of Congress enjoy many other prerequisites, including subsidized travel abroad; subsidized meals in the Senate and House dining rooms; free parking on Capitol Hill, on Washington streets, and at airports; free car washes; and a child care center.

A Final Benefit

Taxpayers fund life insurance policies and a death benefit equal to a year's salary for each member of Congress. And if a legislator so desires, the sergeant-at-arms will arrange for an undertaker to plan the member's final journey.

[1]*Per diem* and travel allowances for the first members were verified in 2002 when Senate custodial staff found an eighteenth-century ledger with payment accounts.
[2]Salaries of government officials can be found at www.usgovinfo.about.com. The website of the Center for Public Integrity (www.publicintegrity.org) is also excellent for tracking congressional pay and benefits.
[3]*Now with Bill Moyers*, Public Broadcasting System, July 2, 2004. www.pbs.org/now.

The Advantages of Incumbency

Because reelection is an important objective for almost all members of Congress and the most important objective for many, much of the work members do throughout their term is targeted at getting reelected. Almost all House incumbents are successful, though Senate seats are not quite as secure as House seats. Nevertheless, few members take anything for granted, and they use the many advantages of incumbency to keep themselves in office.

Before they even take the oath of office, newly elected representatives are given an introduction to the advantages of incumbency. At meetings arranged by the Democratic and Republican leadership and by the House Administrative Committee, new members learn about free mailing privileges, computers and software to help them target letters to specialized groups of constituents, facilities to make videotapes and audiotapes to send to hometown media, and other "perks" designed to keep members in touch with their constituencies and, not coincidentally, to help win reelection (see the box "Pay and Perks of Office").

Incumbents win because they are better known than nonincumbents. Voters have seen their representatives and senators on television or received mail from them, and they can give a general rating of their performance.[26] Although most voters can correctly identify their representatives and senators as liberal or conservative, only a small minority know how these legislators voted on any issue.[27] Therefore, incumbents have the advantage of name recognition without the disadvantage of having voters know how they actually cast their votes on most pieces of legislation.

Incumbents' high level of public recognition is not so surprising given that members of Congress spend much of their time and energy looking for and using opportunities to make themselves known to their constituents. Members spend half or more of their days in their district, making an average of thirty-five trips home a year—at taxpayers' expense.[28] To accommodate these trips, the House operates, as business allows, on a three-day week, Tuesday through Thursday, allowing legislators four-day weekends in the home district. The Senate operates on a five-day week but takes off every third or fourth week a month when possible to allow for longer home visits. Congress is recess during major holidays, part of the summer and prior to elections—the House and Senate often do not meet at all in August, a month designated as a "District Work Period." In 2005 Congress was in session for 139 days and the Senate for not many more.

Casework

Arguably the main advantage of incumbency is the opportunity that being in office gives representatives to perform services and do favors for their constituents. Members send constituents calendars, U.S. flags that have flown over the Capitol, and publications of the federal government. This is one of the best ways members of Congress have to make themselves known in their districts and to create a kind of patron-client relationship. You will not read about this in the Constitution, where the duties of Congress are defined. But in practice, electoral politics has meant that members must spend a great deal of their time serving the specific interests of their districts, which are not necessarily synonymous with the interests of the nation as a whole. Members take this aspect of their representational responsibilities very seriously because it is their own constituents who will reelect them—or not.

Collectively, the House and Senate receive close to two hundred million e-mail messages each year, and more than 18 million pieces of regular mail.[29] The work of answering questions and doing personal favors for constituents who write or call for help is called **constituency service** or **casework.** More

than 30 percent of senators' staffs and almost half of all representatives' staffs are located in their home state or district offices to better serve constituents.[30]

Congressional staff function as red-tape cutters for everyone from elderly citizens having difficulties with Social Security to small-town mayors trying to get federal grants for new sewer systems. They provide information to students working on term papers, people looking for federal jobs, citizens puzzled about which federal agency to ask for assistance, or residents trying to get information about a relative in the military. Typically, responsibility for mediating with federal agencies is divided among the casework staffers by issue area, allowing them to specialize and resolve constituents' problems—passports, immigration, Social Security payments, and the like—more efficiently.

Of course, not all casework is directed toward winning reelection. Some members say they enjoy their casework more than their policy roles, perhaps because the results of casework are more immediate and tangible. Individually, they may have limited power in trying to get important legislation passed, but in dealing with a constituent's problems, their power is much greater because of their clout with bureaucrats. A phone call or letter to a federal agency will bring attention to the constituent's problem. And casework does allow members to build nonpartisan and seemingly nonpolitical ties with their constituents.

Mailing Privileges

For the 110th Congress, taxpayers will provide more than a half billion dollars for office and franking expenses (mailing costs).[31] The franking privilege is a great asset of incumbency because it allows members to write their constituents without paying for postage out of pocket or using campaign funds. (The frank is a facsimile of the member's signature, and it works like metered mail, with the frank appearing where the stamp would be.) It is not free; the Postal Service records all franked mail and sends Congress a bill at the end of each year. That means that the cost of the frank goes up with each postal increase. The value of the frank has been estimated as equivalent to $350,000 in campaign contributions.

The frank helps each member increase name recognition (and newly elected members can begin using the frank immediately, even before they are sworn in). The frank cannot be used to send personal correspondence to constituents or to ask them for their vote or a campaign contribution, but members can send out newsletters that inform constituents of their work for the district or to survey constituents' issue positions. Much of the time, however, the frank is used to send constituents material they have requested, such as government forms or publications, and this too increases a member's name recognition. In 2007 the Senate received additional money to mail postcard reminders to constituents whenever a Senator holds a town meeting in their counties.[32]

Media Advantage

In addition to regular mailings, members use increasingly sophisticated production equipment and technology to make television and radio shows to send home. Constituents may see or hear stories about their representatives on local television and radio news programs produced in congressional studios by the representatives' own staff and paid for out of campaign or party funds. Members like to tape themselves at committee meetings asking questions or being referred to as "Mr. (or Madam) Chairman" (many members chair at least a subcommittee). The tape then is edited to a thirty-second sound bite and sent to local television stations. Often stations run these productions as news features without telling their viewers that they are essentially self-promotion pieces prepared by the members. Congressional staffers also write press releases about accomplishments of their bosses and fax them to local newspapers, which often print them as written.

Fundraising

Media access enhances another advantage of incumbency—the opportunity to raise funds from the hundreds of political action committees (PACs) that populate Washington. Eager to gain access to members of Congress, PACs make fundraising much easier for incumbents than challengers, as we pointed out in Chapter 9.

Committee assignments are also extremely important in fundraising. If a member wins a seat on one of the powerful "juice" committees—one that considers legislation important to big money interests or that appropriates money—the chances of attracting large campaign donations are greatly increased.

Pork Barrel Funding

Incumbents can gain the attention of or curry favor with constituents by obtaining funds for special projects, new programs, buildings, or other public works that bring jobs, benefits, and business to their districts or states. Such benefits are widely known as **pork barrel** projects. A pork feature of virtually every annual budget is money for yet another bomber, fighter plane, weapon, or military construction project the Pentagon has not requested. Universities are also

perennial winners in the pork sweepstakes; in 2003, representatives whose districts include a college or university obtained more than $3.0 billion in funding for campus projects, a figure that has since grown.

Because members consider pork barrel projects crucial to their reelection chances, there is little support in Congress for eliminating projects most know to be unwise or wasteful. (See the Government Responsiveness Box.) David Stockman, director of the Office of Management and Budget during the Reagan administration, observed, "There's no such thing as a fiscal conservative when it comes to his district."[33] Liberals and conservatives, Democrats and Republicans, protect these kinds of projects.

How Congress Is Organized

An institution with 535 voting members that must make thousands of policy decisions every year without benefit of a unified leadership is an institution not likely to work quickly or efficiently. Like all organizations, legislatures need some structure to be able to accomplish their purposes. Congress does have both a leadership system and a committee structure, but each is organized along party lines. Alongside this partisan

AP Images/Al Grillo

Senator Ted Stevens (R-Alk.), called "Uncle Ted" by his constituents because of his ability to obtain federal money for the state, secured $1.5 million to replace this bus stop outside the Anchorage Museum of History and Art.

organization exist many other groups—caucuses, coalitions, work and study groups, and task forces—whose membership cuts across party lines or reflects the division of interests within party caucuses. Some of this micro-organizing is a means of bypassing the committee system that dominates Congress's legislative and oversight functions.

The Evolution of Congressional Organization

The Constitution calls for the members of the House of Representatives to select a **Speaker of the House** to act as its presiding officer and for the vice president of the United States to serve as president (or presiding officer) of the Senate. But the Constitution does not say anything about the powers of these officials, nor does it require any further internal organization. So little about the Speaker is specified in the Constitution that it is not even required that he be a member of the House.

The first House, meeting in New York in 1789, had slow and cumbersome procedures. For its first several sessions, Congress's legislative work was accomplished by appointing ad hoc committees. By the Third Congress, there were about 350 committees, and the system had become too unwieldy. Soon permanent committees were created, each with continuing responsibilities in one area, such as taxes or trade.[34]

As parties developed, the selection of the Speaker became a partisan matter, and the Speaker became as much a party leader as a legislative manager. The seventh Speaker, Henry Clay (Whig-Ky.), who served ten of the years between 1811 and 1825, transformed the speakership from a ceremonial office to one of real leadership. To maintain party loyalty and discipline, he used his powers to appoint committee members and chairs. Under Clay's leadership, the House was the dominant branch, but its influence declined when it, like the rest of government, could not cope with the divisiveness of the slavery issue. At the time it was said that "the only people in Congress who are not carrying a revolver are those carrying two revolvers."[35] By 1856, it took 133 ballots to elect a Speaker. Many physical fights broke out on the House floor; duels were held outside.[36]

The Senate, a smaller body than the House, was less tangled in procedures, less rule-bound, and more effective in its operation. Its influence rose as visitors packed the Senate gallery to hear the great debates over slavery waged by Daniel Webster (Mass.), John C. Calhoun (S.C.), and Clay (who had moved from the House). During this era, senators were elected by state legislatures, not directly by the people. Thus they had strong local party ties and often used their influence

to get presidential appointments for home state party members. But the Senate, too, became ineffective as the nation moved toward civil war. Senators carried arms to protect themselves as debates over slavery turned to violence.

After the Civil War, with the presidency weakened by the impeachment of Andrew Johnson, strong party leadership reemerged in the House, and a period of congressional government began. Speaker Thomas Reed (R-Me.), nicknamed "The Czar" by his colleagues, assumed the authority to name members and chairs of committees and to chair the **Rules Committee,** which decided which bills were to come to the floor for debate. A major consequence of the Speaker's extensive powers was increased party discipline. Members who voted against their party might be punished by a loss of committee assignments or chairmanships.

At the same time, both the House and the Senate became more professional. The emergence of national problems and an aggressive Congress made a congressional career more prestigious. Prior to the Civil War, membership turnover was high; members of the House served an average of only one term, senators, only four years. After the war, the strengthening of parties and the growth of the one-party South, where Democrats controlled virtually all elective offices,

Although most experts believe that our largest cities are the most likely targets of terrorism, pork barrel politics has spread homeland security funds to every congressional district. Here firefighters don hazardous materials suits to protect against a chemical attack in Casper, Wyoming.

© Steve Liss/Time Magazine

made reelection easier, thus offering the possibility of a congressional career.

This desire for permanent careers in the House produced an interest in reform. Members wanted a chance at choice committee seats and did not want to be controlled by the Speaker. Resistance against the dictatorial practices of Reed and his successor, Joseph Cannon (R-Ill.), grew. Cannon, more conservative than many of his fellow Republicans, used his powers to block legislation he disliked, to punish those who opposed him, and even to refuse to recognize members who wished to speak. In 1910, there was a revolt against "Cannonism," which had become a synonym for the arbitrary wielding of the Speaker's powers.

The membership voted to remove the Speaker from the Rules Committee and to strip him of his authority to appoint committees and their chairs. The revolt weakened party influence because discipline could no longer be maintained by the Speaker's punishment of members through loss of committee assignments. And it gave committees and their chairs a great deal of independence from leadership influence.

The Senate also was undergoing a major reform. As part of the Progressive movement, pressure began to build for the direct popular election of senators. The election of senators by state legislatures had made many senators pawns of special interests—the big monopolistic corporations (called trusts) and railroads. In a day when millionaires were not as common as now, the Senate was referred to as the "Millionaires' Club."

Not surprisingly, the Senate first refused to consider a constitutional amendment providing for its direct election, although in some states popular balloting on senatorial candidates took place anyway. Finally, under the threat of a call for a constitutional convention, which many members of Congress feared might lead to other changes in the Constitution, a direct-election amendment was passed in the House and Senate in 1912 and ratified by the states a year later.

These reforms of the early twentieth century dispersed power in both the House and the Senate and weakened leadership. House members no longer feared the kind of retribution levied by Speaker Cannon on members who deviated from party positions. In the Senate, popular elections made senators responsive to the diverse interests of the electorate rather than to party leaders.

Contemporary Leadership Positions

The Speaker of the House is the only leadership position specified in the Constitution; none of the secondary leadership positions in the House and none of the current top posts in the Senate are provided for in Article I. This is because they came into being with political parties, and the Founders did not anticipate parties. There were no party organizations in Congress when it first met.

House Leadership Positions

The leaders of each party are selected by their respective members sitting in caucus—meeting as a group to conduct party business. **Party caucus** refers both to party meetings and to the party members collectively. The House Republican Caucus, for example, consists of all Republicans serving in the House, and the Democratic Caucus consists of all Democratic members, plus the lone Independent, who chooses to caucus with them. The full House must elect the Speaker of the House, of course, as specified in the Constitution, but it is a straight party line vote, so the real selection is made in the majority party's caucus. Once elected, the speaker becomes second in line to succeed to the presidency, after the vice president (provided the speaker is not foreign-born). The speaker's institutional task is to act as presiding officer and to see that legislation moves through the House.

The House party leadership positions, which have evolved through practice, include a majority leader, a minority leader, and majority and minority whips. The **majority leader** is second in command to the speaker and is officially in charge of the party's legislative agenda (since the speaker is technically an officer of the House, not of his party). The majority leader, working with the speaker, also schedules votes on bills. The **minority leader** is, as the name suggests, the leader of the minority party. **Whips** originated in the British House of Commons, where they were named after the "whipper in," the rider who keeps the hounds together in a fox hunt. This aptly describes the whips' role in Congress. Party whips try to maintain contact with party members, determine which way they are leaning on votes, and attempt to gain their support. Assisting the majority and minority whips are a number of deputy and assistant whips who keep tabs on their assigned state delegations.

Party organization in the House also includes committees that assign party members to standing committees, work out the party's stance on major policy issues, plan legislative and campaign strategies, and allocate funds to party members running for reelection.

Because the speaker is now more a party than an institutional leader, he or she is expected to use the speakership to maximize partisan advantage in committee and staff appointment and to secure the passage of measures preferred by his party. For this reason the person selected usually has been someone who has served in the House a long time, a skilled parliamen-

Vitriolic exchanges are not a new phenomenon in Congress. Shown here is a fight in the House of Representatives in 1798. After Rep. Matthew Lyon (Vt.) spit on Rep. Roger Griswold (Conn.) and the House refused to expel Lyon, Griswold attacked Lyon with a cane. Lyon defended himself with fire tongs as other members of Congress looked on—with some amusement, it seems.

tarian, and an ideological moderate who can negotiate compromises and put together legislative majorities. By tradition, the Speaker does not cast a vote on most bills before the House, participating only on "symbolic or party-defining issues."[37]

Trying to win partisan support is often difficult, but the speaker has some rewards and punishments to dispense for loyalty and disloyalty. Speakers have a say in who gets to sit on which committees, which committees will be given jurisdiction over complex bills, what bills will come to the House floor for a vote and under what rules they will be considered, and how their party's congressional campaign funds are allocated. The speaker also decides who will be recognized to speak on the floor of the House and whether motions are relevant. He or she has the authority to appoint members to conference and select committees, to control some material benefits, such as the assignment of extra office space. Speakers also have the power to name the chair of the Rules Committee and all of their party's members on the committee. Despite these formal powers, the speaker must be persuasive to be effective.

In modern times, the only speaker to attempt the level of control achieved by strong predecessors as Reed and Cannon was Newt Gingrich (R-Ga.). Before his election in 1995 Gingrich had been the in-tellectual and tactical leader of conservative House Republicans. Like other speakers who were too controlling, Gingrich met with rebellion in his own party and had to fight back a challenge to his leadership in his third year. Gingrich's demands for party discipline in support of a national legislative program (the so-called Contract with America) undercut the power of committee chairs and also left many members with too little flexibility to respond to their constituencies, which risked their chances for reelection. This is one reason that an ideological moderate with a conciliatory manner is often sought for the speaker's position.

Dennis Hastert (R-Ill.), Gingrich's successor in 1999, came to the leadership more in the mold of a traditional speaker, even though he had been elected whip as the protégé of Majority Leader Tom ("the Hammer") Delay (R-Tex.), who almost made Gingrich look like a softie. Hastert had a friendly, low-key demeanor and was seen as a mediator and persuader in contrast to the agenda-driven disciplinarians, Gingrich and Delay. In his first year, Hastert had only a five-vote margin to work with, the smallest majority in fifty years. He said then that his approach to the speakership was to "do things in regular order" and "not to throw his weight around."[38]

However, after the Republicans won the White House and regained control of the Senate in the 2000 elections, Hastert became a much more forceful leader, playing velvet-covered mallet to Delay's hammer in what some saw as a good cop-bad cop ploy. Unlike Delay, Hastert was able to push the party line and whip in the vote without making colleagues feel pressured or hit over the head.[39] By the end of Bush's first term, Hastert and Delay were the White House's go-to team; they used House rules to dominate the legislative process—even more than Gingrich had—and twisted the arms of colleagues who were slow to support bills the president wanted enacted. But Hastert was not a strong speaker in the mold of Gingrich or Cannon, both of whom tried to establish a personal power base within an independent Congress. Instead Hastert acted as a facilitator for the president's agenda and, in the eyes of his critics, as an "enabler" for Delay's strong-arm tactics.[40]

This worked well for Hastert until 2006 when Bush's poll ratings fell to historic lows. Whereas Delay was forced from office on ethics issues, Hastert was able to retain the speakership in part because he was, by contrast, such a low-key figure still little known to the public. A colleague called this "the political advantage of being boring."[41] In June 2006 Hastert became the longest-serving Republican Speaker, but his leadership was soon in jeopardy over charges of mismanagement of allegations of sexual harassment of House pages. When Nancy Pelosi (D-Ca.) became Speaker, she promised to be a leader of the House not of her party and to return partisanship to the legislative process.

Senate Leadership

The Senate has no leader comparable to the Speaker of the House. The vice president of the United States is formally the presiding officer and could attend and preside any time he chooses; part of his expense allowance is designated for Senate work. In reality the vice president attends infrequently and has relatively little power. However, when sitting as Senate president, he is allowed to cast the tie-breaking vote in those rare instances when the Senate is evenly split. Therefore whenever a head count predicts a deadlocked vote on an important bill, the vice president shows up to preside. Consistent with the Bush administration's hands-on legislative strategy, Richard Cheney has been an active presence on Capitol Hill during his tenure as vice president, making regular trips to his office just off the Senate floor and holding weekly lunches with Republican Senators.

The Senate has an elected president pro tempore, by tradition the senior member of the majority party. It is an honorific post with few duties except to preside over the Senate in the absence of the vice president. In practice, during the conduct of routine day-to-day business, presiding duties are divided among junior senators. This releases the senior member from boring work while giving the Senate's newest members a chance to learn the rules and procedures.

As in the House, both parties also elect assistant floor leaders and whips to help maintain party discipline. These are important, if not essential, positions for working one's way into the top leadership in both the House and the Senate.

The position of Senate majority leader was not created until 1911 and has often been held by individuals of no particular distinction in their parties. The office has none of the speakership's potential for control of chamber proceedings. A congressional watcher once said the majority leader "is often more a coat-check attendant than a maitre d' or chef."[42] The instances of powerful majority leaders are few, the most notable being Lyndon Johnson (D-Tex.). He assumed office at a time when the Democrats had a slim hold on the Senate, giving him an opportunity to exercise his extraordinary powers of personal persuasion to keep party members in line on key votes. Johnson's reputation was made through a combination of personality and mastery of the legislative process (he had been an aide to the House Speaker and served in the House before election to the Senate). There is nothing inherent in the office to give a majority leader the power Johnson had, and no one has had it since.

The Senate majority leader is a spokesperson for his party's legislative agenda and is supposed to help line up members' votes on key issues. But procedurally, the Senate is a free-for-all compared to the House, with "every man and woman for him- or herself."[43] Unlike the speaker, the majority leader cannot control the terms under which a bill is considered on the floor; instead rules are assigned by unanimous consent agreements, after negotiations with other Senators and a bill's floor managers. The majority leader also has little power to stop a filibuster—a procedural maneuver that allows a minority to block a bill from coming to the floor by monopolizing the session with nonstop speeches. This means that a majority leader needs to do much more than keep his own party in line to keep legislation moving through the Senate. He can influence the general atmosphere of deliberation in the Senate by adopting an approach to working with the minority party that is either conciliatory or partisan. But whether he chooses the more traditional conciliatory and clubby approach of the former leader Robert Dole (R-Kan.), or the more aggressively partisan approach of Trent Lott (R-Miss.), the majority leader must be less strident than a Speaker like Gingrich and less of an enforcer than Hastert, because those styles would never be accepted in the more egalitarian atmosphere of the Senate.

As Senate majority leader, Lyndon Johnson (left), shown here with Sen. Theodore Green (D-R.I.), "used physical persuasion in addition to intellectual and moral appeals. He was hard on other people's coat lapels." If the man he was trying to persuade was shorter than Johnson, "he was inclined to move up close and lean over the subject of his persuasive efforts." If the man was taller, Johnson "would come at him from below, somewhat like a badger." Quotes are from Eugene McCarthy, Up 'til Now (New York: Harcourt, 1987).

As Gingrich was succeeded by the more understated Hastert, Majority Leader Lott was succeeded by Bill Frist (R-Tenn.), a mild-mannered heart surgeon with a less combative style. Frist also had little political experience and had not even registered to vote until just before he ran for the Senate. As a second-term senator he also had little institutional knowledge and was badly overmatched by the White House legislative staff and by senior colleagues who knew parliamentary rules inside out. Under pressure from the administration to maintain party discipline on key votes, Frist soon became much more partisan in carrying out his leadership duties. But, ineffective both as a party leader and a legislative manager, he left the Senate after two terms to seek the presidency.

The Senate minority leader's job is similar to that of the majority leader in that its effectiveness depends on a limited package of incentives and procedural ploys to enforce party discipline. Historically the Senate's majority and minority leaders have worked closely together to conduct Senate business. But if either or both are seen as overly partisan, or more interested in personal political ambitions (such as a run for the presidency) than in running the Senate, it can weaken the collegial relationship and slow the legislative process. But both the majority and minority leaders must also articulate their parties' issue positions and try to win support for bills supported by their parties.

In fulfilling this duty they may undercut their political viability at home if their constituents are more conservative or liberal than the leadership of the national parties. Frist's successor as majority Leader, Harry Reid (D-Nev.) a Democrat from a Republican state, is more conservative (an opponent of abortion rights, for example) than the Senate party caucus. By speaking out for a more liberal Democratic membership, he could endanger his own reelection. If a Senate leader also has presidential aspirations, as Bob Dole and Bill Frist did, the balancing act is even more difficult because he must carve out issue positions that distinguish him from other senators in his party who are also seeking the nomination. Robert Dole found it so difficult to carry out all of those roles simultaneously that he resigned from the Senate during his run for the presidency.

Committees

Much of the work of Congress is done in committees. Observers of American politics take this for granted, yet the power of legislative committees is rare among Western democracies. In Britain, for example, committees cannot offer amendments that change the substance of a bill. In our Congress, the substance of a bill can be changed in committee even after its passage in both chambers.

The division of labor provided by committees and subcommittees enables Congress to consider a vast number of bills each year. If every member had to review every measure in detail, it would be impossible to deal with the current workload. Instead, most bills are killed in committee, leaving many fewer for each member to evaluate before a floor vote. Committees also help members develop specializations. Members who remain on the same committee for some time gain expertise and are less dependent on professional staff and executive agencies for background information.

Standing Committees

Today there are twenty **standing committees** in the House and sixteen in the Senate. Each deals with a different subject matter, such as finance or education or agriculture. Each has a number of subcommittees, totaling ninety-nine in the House and seventy-three in the Senate during the 109th Congress.[44] The number of committees and subcommittees fluctuates, declining during years of reform and cost-cutting and increasing during years of government growth. During the Bush administration, as government grew, with a new cabinet department and two new intelligence agencies, so did the number of congressional committees.

Nearly all legislation introduced in Congress is referred to a standing committee and then to a subcommittee. Subcommittees may hold public hearings to give interested parties a chance to speak for or against a bill. They also hold **markup** sessions to provide an opportunity for the committee to rewrite the bill. Following markup, the bill is sent to the full committee, which may also hold hearings. If approved there, it goes to the full House or Senate.

The number of seats on any committee can change from one session to another as party caucuses try to satisfy as many of their members' preferences as possible. Standing committees vary in size from nine to seventy-five members in the House and from twelve to twenty-eight in the Senate. Party ratios—the number of Democrats relative to Republicans on each committee—are determined by the majority party in the House and negotiated by the leadership of both parties in the Senate. The ratios are generally set in rough proportion to party membership in the particular chamber, but the majority party gives itself a disproportionate number of seats on several key committees to ensure control.

Committee Membership

Committees are essential not only to the legislative process but also for building a power base within Congress, attracting campaign donors, gaining the influence and name recognition needed for reelection, and perhaps even higher office. New members and members seeking committee changes express their preferences to their party's selection committee. The party tries to accommodate members' requests for assignments that will be most beneficial to their constituencies, but there is some self-selection by seniority. Historically, junior members did not ask for the most prestigious posts, but this tradition has broken down as freshmen have become bolder in their requests and even receive instruction in how to get the assignments they want. And if there are freshmen members whose reelection races are likely to be tough or whom the party leadership believes have the potential to be future leaders, those members will likely be given helpful committee assignments. For example, Barack Obama, thought to be a future Democratic star, was given a position on the influential Foreign Relations Committee in his freshman year, just as Hillary Clinton was given her first choices when she was a freshman.

The committees dealing with appropriations, taxes, and finance are always sought after because having a say in the allocation of money and how the tax burden falls on individuals and businesses gives members power and enhances their ability to help their home districts. These are sometime called "juice committees" because of the advantage they give members in squeezing interested parties for campaign contributions. Most members also want committee assignments that let them tell constituents they are working on problems of the district. Members from rural districts, for example, seek seats on committees that deal with agricultural and trade issues.

Media coverage is another criterion important in deciding committee preference. The work of some committees is more likely to be covered by television. Committees scrambled to hold attention-getting hearings on the new Department of Homeland Security and corporate fraud in 2002 and on 9/11 failures and the reorganization of intelligence agencies in 2004. Getting on the right committee is important to those who want to become nationally known. When a journalist once asked Senator Joseph Biden (D-Del.) why he was so newsworthy, Biden replied, "It's the committees, of course." Biden has served on the three committees with the greatest media exposure and this prominence has made him a credible potential candidate for the presidency in every Democratic primary season for the past twenty-five years.

The practice of filling each committee with representatives whose districts have an especially strong

Democrat Jim Webb, with his wife, celebrates his election to the Senate from Virginia. During his campaign, Webb criticized the Iraq war and wore the combat boots of his son, a marine serving in the war. Webb was one of six Democratic challengers who unseated Republican incumbents in the 2006 elections, giving the Democrats a majority in the Senate.

economic interest in its work encourages committees to be rather parochial in their outlook. It also leads to costly and wasteful legislation; if committee members' constituents benefit from programs under their jurisdiction, the members have no incentive to eliminate them or pare them back. This is one of the biggest weaknesses in the committee system.[45]

Committees are also often filled with members who have financial interests in the businesses they make policies for. Most members who sit on the banking committees own bank stock, many on agriculture committees own agribusiness stock, and those on the armed services committees hold stock in defense industries.[46] Senator Frist, an ex-surgeon who held stock in a huge hospital management company founded by his family (one that had paid multimillion dollar fines for overbilling) made it a legislative priority to help rewrite health care and medical malpractice laws. Billy Tauzin, who, as chair of the Ways and

Means Committee, shepherded Bush's Medicare drug benefit bill through Congress, immediately left Congress to take a million-dollar-a-year job as a lobbyist for pharmaceutical companies who will benefit from the legislation. And seven members of the House Appropriations committee, Republicans and Democrats, have PACs that are headed by present or former lobbyists for businesses with issues before the committee.[47]

Committee Chairs

The chair is usually the most influential member of a committee. Chairs have the authority to call meetings, set agendas, and control committee staff and funds. In addition, chairs have strong substantive knowledge of the matters that come before their committees, and this, too, is a source of influence.

Historically, the member of the majority party with the longest service on a committee became its chair by the so-called **seniority rule.** The rule was adopted to protect committee members from powerful speakers of the House, who often used their authority to award committee chairs to friends and allies. Under the ironclad seniority rule, chairs may have been senile, alcoholic, or personally disliked by every member of the committee, but if they had served the longest and their party had a majority in the House, they became chairs.

Many members believed the custom of seniority led to chairs who were dictatorial and out of step with the rest of their party. In response to those complaints, in the early 1970s both parties agreed that the seniority rule no longer had to be followed. Since then, the Committee on Committees in the Republican caucus and the Steering and Policy Committee in the Democratic caucus have recommended chairs in addition to assigning committee seats. All members of each party caucus vote on these recommendations by secret ballot, although in some cases the result is a foregone conclusion. In the House, the Speaker has power to name members to the Rules Committee and to appoint or recommend the chairs of the most powerful committees.

Some members prefer the Speaker appointment system because they believe it can prevent potentially damaging intraparty fights over who will chair important committees, just as the seniority principle did. At the same time, it reduces the likelihood of producing the kind of autocratic chairs who were common under the seniority rule.

The end of the automatic seniority rule also brought a change in the behavior of senior members. Before 1975, committee chairs were less supportive of their party than other party members in roll-call votes.[48] They could go their own way with impunity because their powerful positions were guaranteed. Since 1975, committee chairs have had to be party loyalists if they want to keep their jobs. When Arlen Specter (R-Pa.), a supporter of abortion rights, made public statements after the 2004 elections that the Bush administration should send the Senate Supreme Court nominees who were moderates if it wanted to ensure confirmation, the White House made it clear that if Specter wanted to serve as chair of the Judiciary Committee he would have to support any and all of the president's court nominees.

The same pattern holds true of those who are second, third, and fourth in seniority on each committee. Senior party members are now much less likely to deviate from their party's position. In that sense, the reforms have strengthened party influence in Congress, especially in the House, where it has led to a greater concentration of power, away from committees and to the leadership. The variation on this trend during the Bush administration has been that the White House rather than the party leadership established policy for the Republican caucus. Thus, the power of both House and Senate chairs diminished when Republicans controlled Congress.

Subcommittees

Each standing committee is divided into subcommittees with jurisdiction over part of the committee's area of responsibility. The House International Relations Committee, for example, has seven subcommittees—one each for the geographic areas of Africa, East Asia and the Pacific, the Western Hemisphere, the Middle East and South Asia, and Europe, one for oversight and a newly created subcommittee on terrorism and proliferation issues.

In the days of the seniority rule, standing committee chairs chose the subcommittee chairs and controlled subcommittees' jurisdiction, budget, and staff. Since 1974, each House subcommittee operates semi-independently of the parent committee. Similar changes took place in the Senate.

These reforms, sometimes called the "subcommittee bill of rights," allowed more members, especially newer members, to share in important decisions. In this way, they made Congress more democratic. But by diffusing power, they also made it less efficient because the very number of subcommittees contributed to government gridlock. Complex legislation might be sent to several subcommittees, each with its own interests and jurisdiction.

Under the Republican majority in the House, standing committee chairs reasserted control over their subcommittees. In 1999, new rules were adopted to streamline the legislative process and reduce the number of subcommittees. All but a few House committees were limited to five subcommittees (excluding oversight), and House members were permitted to serve on no more than four subcommittees. No restrictions were placed on the number of subcommittees in the Senate, but senators are not supposed to sit on more than five.[49]

These reforms have not ended the problem of overlapping jurisdictions. When President George W. Bush proposed establishing the cabinet-level Department of Homeland Security, for example, twelve House committees were involved in marking up the bill. And in general there is a tendency toward committee creep, with periods of committee reduction followed by periods of growth

One of the most significant rule changes under the Republican majority was the three-term limit on service as a committee chair. Opponents argue that term limits punish experience and weaken oversight as chairs are forced out just when they have become familiar with the operations of the agencies they oversee.[50] An attempt to repeal term limits for chairs was defeated in 2001, but each member is now allowed to serve six years as ranking member in addition to three terms as chair. Under Democratic leadership these rules may change for the 110th Congress.

Select, Special, Joint, and Conference Committees

There are a few other types of congressional committees. *Select* or *special committees* are typically organized on a temporary basis to investigate a specific problem or to hold hearings and issue a report on special problems that arise, such as intelligence agency failures prior to 9/11 or government response to hurricane Katrina. These committees are disbanded when their work is completed. The exceptions are the House and the Senate Select Committees on Intelligence and the Senate Select Committee on Ethics, which are in effect permanent committees.

Joint committees include members from both houses, with the chair alternating between a House and Senate member. There are four permanent joint committees, two of which study budgetary and tax policy. The other two administer institutions affiliated with Congress, such as the Library of Congress.

Conference committees, appointed whenever the Senate and the House pass different versions of the same bill, also have joint membership. Members from the committees that managed the bill in their respective chambers work out a single version for the full membership to vote on. Conference committees are dissolved after the compromise version is agreed on. Their work is discussed in greater detail in the section on lawmaking.

Task Forces

The traffic jams and turf wars surrounding much committee work have led members of Congress with strong interests in particular areas to look for ways to bypass the committee structure. Task forces and ad hoc committees have existed in the House for decades, used by Democratic and Republican leaders alike, to study major issues and draft legislation, usually to get around foot-dragging committees.[51]

Task forces achieved their greatest visibility when Gingrich was speaker, when they became a vehicle for his "adhocracy" approach of aggressively pursuing a legislative agenda and moving it through the legislative process as fast as possible. To do that, the speaker sometimes bypassed committees, handpicking members for a task force to draft bills such as a Republican version of Medicare reform. Democrats used the same strategy to bypass Ways and Means to write a welfare reform bill. But the most significant contribution of the task force has been writing bills that offer an alternative to what the relevant standing committees are likely to produce and doing it more quickly. In fact, overcoming the paralysis that results from partisan divisions in Congress or between Congress and the White House is one of the advantages of using a task force. Direct negotiations between the White House and congressional leaders can sometimes break long-standing deadlocks.

On the other hand, task forces bypass mechanisms for accountability to the public and to most rank-and-file members. Bills are written without formal hearings or the opportunity to point out any potential pitfalls and problems of the legislation. Rank-and-file members often face having to vote on a huge package of legislation about which they know only what they know little. In 2004, the House was embarrassed when it passed an appropriation bill that few had read. Someone had stuck in a provision allowing members of Congress to gain access to the personal income tax returns of private citizens. When it was reported in the press, a staff member confessed to adding it, and red-faced members removed it.

Staff and Support Agencies

Congress encompasses not only elected representatives but also a staff of more than twenty thousand, not including individuals employed in support posi-

tions such as security and maintenance. The cost of funding Congress in 2007 will be more than $4 billion.[52] Today, committee staff alone are equal in number to the entire congressional staff in 1947. But Congress cannot serve its proper role as a check on the executive branch if it does not have its own information base.

To this end, staff in support agencies carry out various research functions. The Government Accountability Office (GAO) checks on the efficiency and effectiveness of executive agencies, the Congressional Research Service (CRS) conducts studies of public issues and does specific research at the request of members, the Office of Technology Assessment provides long-range analyses of the effects of new and existing technology, and the Congressional Budget Office provides the expertise and support for Congress's budgeting job.

To research difficult problems, members can call on the seven hundred full-time congressional research staffers in the Library of Congress. These researchers have issue specializations and contacts with experts in the academic world, in all the federal agencies, and with the interest groups that lobby on behalf of these issues. No member of Congress would have the time to develop this kind of expertise, yet without it, competent legislation could not be written, and Congress would not have the background it needs to challenge facts and figures presented in communications from the executive branch.

What Congress Does

The importance of Congress is reflected in the major, explicit constitutional powers the Founders gave it: to lay and collect taxes, coin money, declare war and raise and support a military, and regulate commerce with foreign governments and among the states. Essentially, most of the named powers the Constitution gives to the national government were given to Congress. These and other powers specifically mentioned in the Constitution are called the *enumerated powers* of Congress.

Congress also has *implied powers;* that is, it is permitted to make all the laws "necessary and proper" to carry out its enumerated powers. Although the Founders did not necessarily foresee it, this tremendous grant of power covers almost every conceivable area of human activity.

Lawmaking

In each congressional session in the past decade, between three thousand and seven thousand bills and resolutions have been introduced. Less than 10 percent of these measures pass, and most die in committee. Of those passed, many are noncontroversial, including the so-called "sense of the chamber" measures, such as resolutions congratulating the winners of the Super Bowl and taking note of the death of singer Ray Charles, or very specific bills such as for the naming of a federal courthouse. In a sign of the times, even these conventionally nonpolitical resolutions became victims of partisanship in the 109th Congress when Majority Leader Frist refused to allow a vote on a congratulatory resolution offered by New Jersey's two Democratic senators. The resolution, noting the thirtieth anniversary of the "Born to Run" album, was a tip of the hat to their constituent, Bruce Springsteen. But Frist, who had sponsored his own resolutions honoring events in rock and roll and county music history, blocked the measure honoring Springsteen, for no apparent reason other than that he had campaigned for the Democratic presidential nominee in 2004.[53]

A number of the bills passed each year are private; they resolve an issue an individual or private party has with the government, such as citizenship status or a monetary claim. Our concern is with public bills, those that become laws affecting the general public.

Turning a bill into a law is like running an obstacle course. Opponents of a bill have an advantage because it is easier to defeat a bill than to pass one. Because of the need to win a majority at each stage, the end result is almost always a compromise. That does not mean a compromise of all interests but only of those that manage to play a role in shaping a particular bill. The formal steps by which a bill becomes a law are important but do not reveal the bargaining and trade-offs at every step in the process.

Submission and Referral

Bills may be introduced in either the House or the Senate, except for tax measures (which according to the Constitution must be initiated in the House) and appropriations bills (which by tradition are introduced in the House). This reflects the Founders' belief that the chamber directly elected by the people should control the purse strings.

Although the president initiates about half of all legislation passed, only members of Congress can introduce bills. Interest groups, constituents, or the president must find a congressional sponsor for a proposed bill.[54]

After a bill's introduction, it is referred to a standing committee by the speaker of the House or the presiding officer in the Senate. The content of the bill largely determines where it will go, although the speaker has some discretion, particularly over complex bills that cover more than one subject area. Many such bills are referred to more than one committee simultaneously.

Committee Action

Once the bill reaches a committee, it is assigned to the subcommittee that covers the appropriate subject area. One of the main functions of committees is to screen bills with little chance of passage. (If a committee kills a bill, there are procedures that members can use to try to get the bill to the floor, but these are used infrequently.) Bills receiving subcommittee approval go to full committee; hearings may be held at both levels.

Hearings on bills and the markup of bills are, unless otherwise specified, open to the public, although few people know about them or would have the time or opportunity to sit in. Consequently, lobbyists fill

STATE OF THE UNION

most of the hearing rooms. For critical meetings, lobbyists will hire messengers to stand in line for them, sometimes all night, and then pack the hearing room. Members who receive financial or other support from groups affected by the legislation often face intense and direct pressure to vote a particular way in committee. Sometimes lobbyists mob members as they leave the hearing room.

Scheduling and Rules

Once a House committee approves a bill, it is placed on one of four "calendars," depending on the subject matter of the bill. The Senate has just two calendars: one for private and public bills and another for treaties and nominations. Bills from each calendar are generally considered in the order in which they are reported from committee. In the House, the Rules Committee sets the terms of the debate over the bill by issuing a rule on it. The rule either limits or does not limit debate and determines whether amendments will be permitted. A rule forbidding amendments means that members have to vote yes or no on the bill; there is no chance to change it. If the committee refuses to issue a rule, the bill dies.

In earlier years, the Rules Committee was controlled by a coalition of conservative Democrats and Republicans who used their power to block liberal legislative proposals, including, for decades, meaningful civil rights proposals. Under recent Republican control the committee was dominated by the Speaker and the majority leadership. The powers inherent in the speakership allow the majority leadership to use or bend rules to force measures to the floor, where only a simple majority is necessary for passage. House members have few tactical options against a Speaker who uses his full powers to set the rules. And Hastert was willing to use the rules, not only by holding open vote counts until the leadership could round up enough votes to win passage, but by preventing amendments and other changes in the leadership-agreed-upon wording of bills. In 2003, 76 percent of all House bills were heard under restricted rules, compared with 15 percent in 1977.[55] And after Bush's reelection in 2004, Hastert announced he would let no bill come to a vote unless it had the support of a majority of House Republicans even though it might have bipartisan majority support. The practice of advancing bills only when a majority of Republican members favor them means that the leadership never had to negotiate their passage with the Democrats.

Because the Senate is a smaller body, it can operate with fewer rules and formal procedures. It does not have a rules committee. A lot of work is accomplished through the use of privately negotiated unanimous consent agreements, which allow the Senate to dispense with standard rules and define terms for the debating and amendment of a specific bill. As the Senate's workload has increased and its sense of collegiality has decreased, it has become more difficult to get opponents to accept a unanimous consent agreement. A few senators can and do delay or kill important bills.

In a closely divided Senate, where no party can have de facto control without a majority of sixty, the arm-twisting tactics that the House leadership can use to enforce party discipline cannot work for the Senate leadership. The rules do not allow for it, and senators are more high-profile figures than representatives, many with their own political aspirations; they cannot easily be dictated to, even by their own leadership.

Debate and Vote

Debate on a bill is controlled by the bill managers, usually senior members of the committee that sent the bill to the full chamber. The opposition, too, has its managers who schedule opposition speeches. "Debates" are not a series of fiery speeches of point and counterpoint. They are often boring recitations delivered to sparse audiences, some of whom are reading, conversing, or walking around. In the House after the time allotted for debate is over, usually no more than a day, the bill is reported for final action. And if a bill is brought to the floor under a rule allowing no amendments, even a day's debate can lead to no more than an up or down vote on the bill as presented.

In the Senate there is no way other than by a unanimous consent agreement to limit debate, and no restrictions on adding amendments. Opponents can add all sorts of irrelevant amendments to pending legislation. One senator held up an antibusing bill for eight months with 604 amendments.

The other major mechanism for delay in the Senate is the **filibuster.** This is a continuous speech made by one or more members to prevent the Senate from taking action on a bill. Before 1917, only unanimous consent could prevent an individual from talking. Today a **cloture** vote of three-fifths of the members closes or ends debate on an issue thirty hours after cloture is invoked. Then the measure must be brought to a vote.

The filibuster developed in the 1820s when the Senate was divided between slave and free states. Unlimited debate maintained the deadlock.[56] For over a century, the filibuster was used primarily to defeat civil rights legislation. It took a cloture vote to end seventy-three days of debate and get the 1964 Civil Rights Act to the floor for a vote.

Both liberals and conservatives use filibusters (as they do nongermane amendments). During Bill Clinton's first year in office, Republicans used the filibuster quite frequently to block proposals from the Democratic Senate majority. After Republicans took control of the Senate in 1995, Democrats returned the favor. As the senate Republican caucus has become increasingly conservative, those who are moderates and active in the Centrist Coalition have frequently broken ranks with the leadership, especially on budgetary measures and judicial nominations. Along with Democrats they have used their powers to filibuster and to place holds on nominations and certain other items of business to freeze the agenda. These are essentially passive or obstructionist tactics but have been used, with the breakdown of the deliberative process, as the only way to influence legislation other than through amendments.

Filibusters prevent domination and precipitous action by the majority. But by requiring sixty votes to end debate, they impede the majority's right to legislate and contribute to gridlock.[57] Their use by Democrats to block Bush nominees to the federal courts drew such anger from the Republican leadership that in 2005 Majority Leader Frist, calling it "minority tyranny," threatened to abolish the filibuster by getting a simple majority to support it as a rules change, a threat Sen. Trent Lott dubbed "the nuclear option." However, the filibuster is one of the most important tools the minority has to check the majority so the threat to abolish it led to a bipartisan agreement among fourteen Senators (seven Republicans and seven Democrats, the so called Gang of Fourteen) to oppose the rules change, denying Frist the majority he needed to exercise the nuclear option. In exchange for the Republicans' joining the alliance, Democrats agreed to reserve their use of the filibuster against Bush's court nominees for exceptional cases. The agreement did not apply to other uses of the filibuster.

When members finally cast their votes on major public bills, they are usually voting on the general aim of the bill without knowing its exact provisions. Rarely does any member read a bill in full. The texts of laws like the No Child Left Behind Act, the first PATRIOT Act, NAFTA, and the prescription drug benefit for seniors, run from eight hundred to more than one thousand pages. The very complex USA PATRIOT Act, which had serious implications for civil liberties, was rushed through Congress in just a few weeks with virtually no member having read it.

When a measure passes, it is sent to the other chamber for action.

Conference Committee

The Constitution requires that the House and Senate pass an identical bill before it can become law, and since this rarely happens, the two versions must be reconciled. Sometimes the chamber that passed the bill last will simply send it to the other chamber for minor modifications. But if the differences between the two versions are not minor, a **conference committee** is set up to try to resolve them. The presiding officers of each chamber, in consultation with the chairs of the standing committees that considered the bill, choose the members of the committee. Both parties are represented, but there is neither a set number of conferees nor a rule requiring an equal number of seats for each chamber.

If the leaders of both parties are strongly committed to passing a version of a bill, they may negotiate the compromise themselves and essentially impose it on the committee. They may even negotiate the final version with the president to avoid a veto. These negotiations can also be planned by the White House with intent to limit the wiggle room party leaders have to negotiate compromises.

Conference committees, or the individuals in control of them, have tremendous latitude in how they resolve the differences between the House and Senate versions of a bill. One aide to the Clinton White House described these committees as "no-man's land" because there are no formal rules governing how they operate.[58] Sometimes a bill is substantially rewritten, and occasionally a bill is killed. One senator, who didn't like the version of an energy bill passed by the Senate said, "I'll rewrite the bill."[59] And he could, through the conference committee procedure where bills can have new provisions added, others deleted, or the whole bill

© Bettmann/CORBIS

Senator Strom Thurmond, at the time a Democrat from South Carolina, is congratulated by his wife after setting a record for the longest filibuster. He talked for twenty-four hours and eighteen minutes to prevent a civil rights bill from being voted on in 1957. His effort was in vain, as the bill was adopted.

killed. Or, as President Reagan once said, "an apple and an orange could go into a conference committee and come out a pear."[60] The power of conference committees to alter bills after their passage is why they are sometimes called the "Third House" of Congress.[61]

Once the conference committee reaches an agreement, the bill goes back to each chamber, where its approval requires a majority vote. It cannot be amended at that point, so is presented to the membership on a take-it-or-leave-it basis. In the Senate, however, any individual member can challenge a provision added in conference that was not related to the original bill. In practice, both House and Senate accept most conference reports because members of both parties in each chamber have participated in working out the compromise version. However, in the years of unified government—in Clinton's first years and during most of the second Bush administration—minority parties often felt so blocked out of the negotiations that determined the final wording of a bill that they refused to sign on to conference committee reports.

Clearly, conference committees can be very influential in determining the final provisions in major legislation, yet the work they do happens almost completely out of public view. Knowing how to win a seat on a conference committee—that is, to participate in rewriting an important piece of legislation—is an essential skill for any legislator who wants to wield influence.

As should be clear from this overview of the complex legislation process, to be a successful member of Congress—to get bills passed or to keep them from being passed, to influence other members, or to rise to a position of leadership—a legislator must know how to use the inner workings of the legislative process. The conference committee is an important part of that process, as is the tactical use of a full range of parliamentary rules and procedures within the congressional system.

Presidential Action and Congressional Response

The president may sign a bill, in which case it becomes law. The president may veto it, in which case it returns to Congress with the president's objections. The president also may do nothing, and the bill will become law after ten days unless Congress adjourns during that period.

Most presidents have not used the veto lightly, but when they do, Congress does not usually override them. A two-thirds vote in each house is required to override a presidential veto. Congress voted to override only nine of former President Reagan's seventy-eight vetoes, only one of President George H. Bush's forty-six, and only two of Clinton's thirty-four. George W. Bush did not exercise his veto power until

his sixth year in office and Congress did not have the votes to override.

Lawmaking by Committee

The division of labor provided by committees and subcommittees enables Congress to consider a vast number of bills each year. If every member had to review every measure in detail, it would be impossible to deal with the current workload. Instead, most bills are killed in committee, leaving many fewer for each member to evaluate before a floor vote. Committees also help members develop specializations. Members who remain on the same committee for some time gain expertise and are less dependent on professional staff and executive agencies for information.

But committee government also has disadvantages. By splitting off into subcommittees and developing expertise in a few areas, a House member runs the danger of being more responsive to narrow interests and constituencies and less responsive to national objectives when making national policy. Over time, members of congressional subcommittees develop close relationships with lobbyists for the interest groups and staff in executive branch agencies affected by their work. Over the years, these three groups—legislators, lobbyists, and bureaucrats, sometimes called an "iron triangle"—get to know each other, often come to like and respect one another, and seek to accommodate each other's interests. The lobbyists likely provide money to help fund the legislators' campaigns. These personal relationships can result in favorable treatment of special-interest groups.

The division of authority and the specialization of individual members have often made it difficult for Congress to get things done. Most members of the majority party in the Senate and about half of those in the House chair committees or subcommittees. With their own bases of power, they have the potential to act independently from party leaders. This can make it difficult for the opposition party in Congress to mount a coherent alternative to the president and opens the possibility for members of the president's own party to block his initiatives.

Many of the reforms of the Gingrich era were aimed at stemming the flow of power to committees and their chairs and channeling it back to the leadership in hopes of ending gridlock and enforcing party government. The second Bush administration took this a step further by setting the legislative agenda in the White House and insisting that the congressional leadership enforce it. This attempt to shut down the bipartisan negotiating and compromise common to the legislative process led to Democrats being frozen out of committees and negotiations where traditionally the minority party played a role. This in turn led to an-

The Army's top brass appear before the Senate's Armed Services Committee to answer questions about abuses at the Abu Ghraib prison in Baghdad.

other kind of gridlock when Democrats and dissenting (usually centrist) Republicans, frustrated by being marginalized, resorted to obstructionist tactics (filibusters, holds on nominations, denial of unanimous consent agreements) as their only means to affect the process.

Oversight

As part of the checks-and-balances principle, it is Congress's responsibility to make sure that the bureaucracy is administering federal programs as Congress intended. This monitoring function is called **oversight** and has become more important as Congress continues to delegate authority to the executive branch. (See the You Are There box for this chapter.) For a variety of reasons, Congress is not especially well equipped, motivated, or organized to carry out its oversight function. Nevertheless, it does have several tools for this purpose.

One tool is the Government Accountability Office, created in 1921 and known as the General Accounting Office until 2004. The GAO functions as Congress's watchdog in oversight and is primarily concerned with making sure that money is used properly.

Another method of oversight, albeit not a very effective one, is committee hearings. Members can quiz representatives from agencies on the operation of their agencies, but often the hearings go into great detail about some particular problem of minor importance and neglect broader policy questions. Scheduling conflicts and the pressure of other business often mean that a member's attention is not focused on committee hearings. Nevertheless, officials in agencies view hearings as a possible source of embarrassment for their agency and spend a great deal of time preparing for

them. This is especially true when Congress decides, often for political reasons, to seek maximum media coverage for hearings.

This attempt at publicity points to one of the problems with the use of these proceedings to carry out the oversight function: hearings are often held after oversight has failed. This was painfully clear after the corporate collapses of 2002—of Enron, Global Crossing, and WorldCom, for example—when four Senate and three House committees held hearings in succession, all vying for media time. But if Congress had exercised oversight and had not weakened the regulatory clout of the Securities and Exchange Commission, these scandals might not have occurred, and some of the enormous costs to employees and investors might have been prevented. Prominent members of oversight committees, such as Joseph Lieberman (D-Conn.) and Christopher Dodd (D-Conn.), who represent a state where some of the failed businesses were headquartered and who had received large campaign contributions from them, actively worked to prevent new regulations from being adopted. Occurring after the failures, the hearings were more aftersight than oversight but served as a way for Congress both to consider remedial measures and to make it seem like it was doing something about the problem.

The incentive of committee members to place constituent protection and the interests of big campaign donors above rule enforcement is one weakness of oversight. But the fragmentation of oversight responsibility is also a problem. There were at least seven Senate committees and six House committees with some oversight responsibility for the accounting and financial practices that led to so many industry bankruptcies in

2002. And many more committees were responsible for oversight of the defense and intelligence agencies whose failures were so widely publicized after 9/11.

Congress can also exercise its oversight function through informal means.[62] One way of doing this is to request reports on topics of interest to members or committees. In a given year, the executive branch might prepare five thousand reports for Congress.[63] Moreover, the chair and staff of the committee or subcommittee relevant to the agency's mission are consulted regularly by the agency. But one can question whether any serious oversight is exercised informally. There are few electoral or other incentives for members to become involved in the drudgery of wading through thousands of pages of reports or for doing a really thorough job in any area of oversight, at least until a crisis arises or public confidence in the economy or government institutions is threatened.

The primary means for congressional oversight is its control over the federal budget. Congress can cut or add to agencies' budgets and thereby punish or reward them for their performance. Members with authority over an agency's budget can use that power to get benefits for their constituents, and by going along with the members' wishes, agencies may stand a better chance of having their budget requests approved. There is an incentive in this relationship for congressional committees to exercise oversight, but increasingly it has failed to do so. It has allowed authorizing legislation for agencies as important as the Consumer Product Safety Commission, the U.S. Commission on Civil Rights, the Corporation for Public Broadcasting, and the Federal Election and Trade Commissions, among others, to expire. The agencies continue to function because Congress waives budget rules to provide annual funding for them without oversight by authorization committees.[64]

If Congress has received low marks for gridlock in legislating, it has been absent without leave in carrying out much of its oversight function. Many members of Congress have made the charge themselves, especially with respect to oversight of intelligence operations and defense policy and appropriations. In the wake of 9/11, the Bush administration encouraged Congress to neglect oversight in these areas by arguing that the president needed a free hand to wage the war on terrorism.

Former Senator Rick Santorum (R-Pa.) explained the weakening of oversight in the Republican-controlled Congress as a party preference: "Republicans don't enjoy oversight—not nearly as much as Democrats—and so . . . we don't do as much."[65] But Representative Henry Waxman (D-N.Y.) suggested that it might be more a matter of the kind of oversight the majority preferred. He cited House Republicans' willingness to take "more than 140

hours of testimony to investigate whether the Clinton White House misused its holiday card database but less than five hours of testimony regarding how the Bush administration treated Iraqi detainees."[66] In other words, members of Congress would rather exercise oversight on presidents from the opposing party.

Budget Making

The topic of budget making may be dull, but without money government cannot function. Real priorities are reflected not in rhetoric but in the budget. An increasingly large part of the job of Congress is to pass a budget. The Constitution gave budget powers to Congress, but in the 1920s, Congress delegated its authority to prepare the annual budget to the president (through the Office of Management and Budget, or OMB). In years when the president's party does not control Congress, the congressional majority produces its own budget, with priorities distinctly different from the president's.

Congress is aided in budget review by the Congressional Budget Office (CBO), which provides expertise to Congress on matters related to both the budget and the economy. Before the establishment of the CBO, members of Congress felt they were junior partners in budget making because they had to depend on information provided by the president, his budget advisers, and the OMB. Because the CBO is responsible to both parties in Congress, it provides a less politically biased set of forecasts about the budget than the administration or the leadership of either party would.

Characteristics of Budgeting

Historically, congressional budgeting has had two basic characteristics. First, the process is usually incremental; that is, budgets for the next year are usually slightly more than budgets for the current year. Normally, Congress does not radically reallocate money from one year to the next; members assume that agencies should get about what they received the previous year. This simplifies the work of all concerned. Agencies do not have to defend, or members scrutinize, all aspects of the budget. Second, Congress tends to spend more in election years and in times of unemployment.

There are exceptions to these general rules, such as times of war or domestic crisis. The first budget submitted after 9/11, for example, requested a huge increase in defense spending. Thereafter the increases were far larger than the annual budgets show because most of the money for the wars in Afghanistan and Iraq was requested in "supplementals," special appropriations bills that authorize spending not included in

In addition to its other jobs, the Senate confirms or rejects presidential nominees to high-level positions. When President Bush appointed General Michael Hayden, left, to head the CIA, Hayden met the senators on the committee that would hold hearings on his nomination. Here he prepares to talk with Senator Patrick Leahy (D-Vt.)—as soon as the photographers leave Leahy's office.

specify funding levels, they do not actually provide the funding. **Appropriations** are acts that give federal agencies the authority to spend the money allocated to them. Both authorization and appropriations bills must pass each house, and differences must be resolved in conference.

Typically, authorizations precede appropriations, although this is not always the case. Budgetary procedures are not defined in the Constitution but are determined by House and Senate rules, which can be, and often have been, changed. The standing committees that oversee the work of the agency or program being funded usually work out the authorizations. The House Interior and Insular Affairs Committee and the Senate Energy and National Resources Committee, for example, review the authorization of the Park Service in the Department of the Interior; the agricultural committees write authorizations for the Department of Agriculture. Close ties often exist between the agency being reviewed and the authorizing committee, which can cause proposed funding levels to be set without consideration of the overall demand on federal revenues. But the real power to limit spending rests with the House and Senate Appropriations Committees.

Each of the two Appropriations Committees has subcommittees corresponding to the functional areas into which budget allocations are divided (lumped together somewhat differently in the House than the Senate). The chair of the two Appropriations committees and the ranking minority member (and the ranking majority member in the Senate as well) can sit as members of any or all of the subcommittees, adding to their power. The Appropriations Committee assigns a spending limit for each area, and the relevant subcommittee then decides how to apportion it among the agencies in its jurisdiction. The power of those who chair appropriations subcommittees is suggested by their nickname, "The Cardinals." In reviewing an agency's proposed budget, the subcommittee is not bound to fund it at the level requested in the president's budget proposal or the authorization bill. Nor do a subcommittee's funding proposals have to be accepted by the whole committee.

Although appropriations subcommittees may develop close ties with the agencies they review, the committee as a whole does not, and it may not be as generous as its subcommittees. In the bills it sends to the floor for a vote, the Appropriations Committee can increase or cut the previous year's funding levels, or it can eliminate an agency altogether.

The House and Senate also have subcommittee-free budget committees, whose membership in the House overlaps with that of Appropriations and Ways and

the fiscal year budget. There are also instances of ideological budgeting. President Reagan's domestic budget cuts and increased military spending in 1981 were clearly an exception to incrementalism. The Gingrich Contract with America approach of cutting programs wholesale was another exception.

Authorizations and Appropriations

Each year, Congress passes a budget resolution that sets a dollar amount of spending for the fiscal year, but money is not appropriated in a single piece of legislation. Since the 1970s, the budget has been divided and reviewed as separate bills, each of which focuses on a different area of expenditure, such as defense. All budget legislation goes through a process similar to but more complicated than other bills. To grasp the complexity, it is necessary to understand the distinction between budget authorizations and budget appropriations. **Authorizations** are acts that enable agencies and departments to operate, either by creating them or by authorizing their continuance. They also establish the guidelines under which the agencies operate. Although authorization bills might

MUST ALL POLITICS BE LOCAL?

I It may seem paradoxical that as the budget deficit grows, Congress spends more and more on small projects targeted to local constituencies. But the fact that members of Congress are elected by local constituencies builds a bias for local over national needs into the budget process. This preference is especially apparent in the work of the appropriations and authorization committees. Nothing shows Congress's priorities better than how it spends our money. And nothing gives senators and representatives more opportunity to prove to their states and districts that they are serving local needs than getting money earmarked for use at home.

An **earmark** is a specific amount of money designated—or set aside—at the request of a member of Congress, for a favored project, usually in his or district. The dollar amount may be included in one of the budget authorization bills, but more commonly is in the committee report attached to the bill that instructs the relevant executive branch agency how to spend the money authorized for its operations. In 2006 Congress approved 13,012 earmarks at a cost of $67 billion.[1]

Many of these earmarks, or set-asides as they are also called, qualify as what are popularly known as pork barrel projects (see section on pork barrel spending). The projects may benefit a special interest, create jobs or help the local economy in some other way, but they are not in any sense priorities, at least not outside the district. And the special interests they benefit may be big campaign contributors.

The most successful earmarkers—not surprisingly—are the most senior and most powerful members of appropriations and authorization committees, but all members have the opportunity to include earmarks in the budgets of agencies they oversee. There is little systematic oversight of agency budgets, and once an earmark

Senators Ted Stevens (R-Alk.), left, and Daniel Inouye (D-Ha.) have served on the Appropriations Committee since the 1970s. They have the power to provide numerous earmarks for their states.

makes it into a budget bill that may be hundreds of pages long there is little chance it will be seen by members. There is even less chance if the earmark is included in the committee report rather than a line in the budget bill. Virtually no one outside the subcommittees may ever see these reports. This is one reason why earmarks are so hard to monitor or to remove from a budget.

Another reason it is difficult to end the practice is because virtually everyone in Congress does it; earmarking is a beloved bipartisan tradition. Though the problem is worsening, it has continued in peacetime and wartime, when the budget is balanced and when it is in deep deficit. The practice is so common and such a necessary legislative skill that a Washington, D.C., firm offers a training seminar in how to get an earmark.[2]

Ted Stevens (R-Alaska), the former chair of the powerful Senate Appropriations committee, is a perennial earmark champion. In 2006 he got $325 million worth of earmarks for his state, drawing national attention

for $223 million in a highway appropriation bill to construct a bridge to an island in Alaska with fifty residents promptly nicknamed, "The Bridge to Nowhere". (See Chapter 6 for more on this earmark.) Citizens Against Government Waste (CAGW), which publishes an annual "Pig Book" and gives an "oinker of the month" award, estimated that about $29 billion of earmarked money was spent on close to ten thousand pork barrel projects in the 2006 election year.[3] Congress approved $13.5 million for the International Fund for Ireland and its World Toilet Summit; $1 million for water-free urinal conservation in Michigan; $235,000 for the National Wild Turkey Federation in South Carolina; $550,000 for the Museum of Glass in Tacoma, Washington; and $150,000 for a boxing club in the home state of Senate majority leader Harry Reid. This is why CAGW's spending alert system (which mimics Homeland Security's color-coded graph) registers "low" only when Congress is in recess.

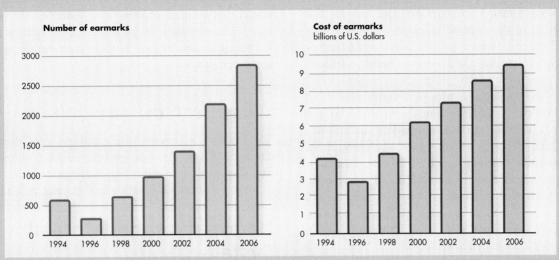

FIGURE 10.2 ■ Earmarks Have Increased Dramatically *In recent years, the number and costs of earmarks have increased dramatically. Shown here are the earmarks in defense bills.*

Source: Congressional Research Service.

The same company that offers training seminars to teach state and local officials how to get an earmark also teaches the officials how to counter criticisms for getting their "pork."[4]

Sometimes Congress seems to be crying out to be stopped because members can't help themselves. And occasionally a lone crusader such as Tom Coburn (R-Okla.) comes along to lecture colleagues on how earmarks prostitute the budget process and tries to stop them. Presidents, too, frequently take aim at earmarks, usually by demanding Congress give them the power of line-item veto, which would allow them to sign budget bills while vetoing, or deleting, individual lines, or items, within it. Congress did give Clinton the line item veto but he had barely used it when the Supreme Court ruled it an unconstitutional exercise of legislative powers by the executive branch. George W. Bush has continued the tradition of president's asking for the veto—even though he has never exercised his constitutional veto power on a budget bill—but in a new form that would allow Congress to overturn his budget deletions on a majority vote.[5] The advantage to Congress is

that any member can tell his or her constituents that they got a project or grant into the budget but it was overridden by the president. Critics say this is just another surrender of legislative power to the president.

It is important to note, though, that the public are enablers of this behavior. Although we talk as if we want an ethical, high-minded Congress whose members are always responsive first to the national interest, when fragmented into individual constituents, the public often behave quite differently. The average voter does expect his or her representative to deliver for the district. As one earmark critic says, "It is not about the size of your project. It's about the size of your politician."[6] And though many campaign donors undoubtedly do give to help reelect someone they believe in, it would surprise no one if big donors were giving to buy influence and access.

Every member can ask what their purpose is in Congress if not to be responsive to their constituents by taking their share of tax dollars back to the state or district; one has even called it his "constitutional obligation."[7] Members also can argue that earmarks comprise about 2.4 percent

of the overall budget, and that is not a high price for a road, museum, park, or research center that may mean a great deal to a locality.[8]

The conflict comes because Congress is our only national legislative body and should always weigh local demands against national needs. As Congress budgets money with one hand for earmarks, it borrows billions with the other to pay for the wars in Iraq and Afghanistan, hurricane Katrina recovery costs, and much more. But because Congress controls the purse strings there are few ways, aside from self-discipline or a voter backlash, to stop members from taking pork home to their constituents.

[1]"The Speaker's Hard Lesson in Reform," (Editorial) *New York Times,* June 25, 2006, Wk11.
[2]David Baumann, "Tempest in a Barrel," *National Journal,* February 11, 2006, 58.
[3]Citizens Against Government Waste, "Pig Book," www.cagw.org/site/PageServer?page name=reports_pigbook2006.
[4]TheCapitol.Net.
[5]Steven T. Dennis, "Item Veto Proposal Has a Real Chance," *CQ Weekly,* March 13, 2006, 642–643.
[6]Keith Ashdown of Taxpayers for Common Sense, quoted in Bill Marsh, "Pork Under Glass? Small Museums and their Patrons on Capitol Hill," *New York Times,* April 30, 2006, wk 4.
[7]Sheryl Gay Stolberg, "What's Wrong With a Healthy Helping of Pork?" *New York Times,* May 28, 2006, wk 4.
[8]Ibid.

Means, and must include representatives from the leadership of both parties. The budget committees have existed only since 1974 and were created to work with the CBO on big-picture issues such as economic forecasting and fiscal planning, including deficit management and controlling overall spending. The House Budget Committee prepares a budget proposal that sets out spending goals in the context of projected federal revenues. Budget committees are not as powerful as Appropriations and neither the House or Senate committee can enforce the spending limits they recommend.

During the budgetary process, committees hold hearings, but these have become a sideshow to the main event. The real decisions are made in private negotiations, and budgets are produced after months of direct negotiations among congressional leaders, their staff, administration aides, individual members, and the president. The rest of Congress is often left with a take-it-or-leave-it budget package laid out in separate bills for each functional area (roughly eleven), or in several omnibus appropriations bills.

Problems with the Budget Process

Almost everyone is critical of congressional budget making. One reason is that members simply cannot agree on spending for any fiscal year; it is not unusual for the new fiscal year to begin before Congress has passed all the necessary appropriations bills. Then, under time pressure, they will lump spending into several omnibus bills in order to keep government operating. These cumbersome bills are difficult to decipher and make oversight by scrutiny of agency budgets very difficult.

Another problem is that Congress does not honor its own budget resolutions, which establish the amount of total spending for each fiscal year. Congress has frequently outspent the dollar limit that it set.[67] As emergencies or unforeseen needs arise, Congress passes supplemental spending bills such as for Iraq and Afghanistan or to deal with a natural disaster like Katrina. Congress also now consistently violates the pay-as-you-go (paygo) rule that requires all new spending to be offset by a revenue source. The paygo rule, established at the end of the first Bush administration and observed throughout Clinton's presidency, was one of several key factors that made it possible to balance the budget in 2000. When George W. Bush took office, the budget was in surplus, and both he and the Congress abandoned paygo. By the end of Bush's first term, all of the supplemental spending on war and emergencies, in addition to much of the budgeted spending, came from borrowing—from the Social Security Trust Fund, private citizens, and increasingly from foreign governments.

Many members are troubled by the fact that for decades Congress has been slowly ceding budget-setting power to the executive branch. White House staff typically get involved in negotiating final dollar amounts with congressional leaders, but the Bush administration superseded the conventional congressional bargaining process here too, often working out final versions of appropriations bills with the Republican leadership before conference committees ever met.

Members on the Job

This section examines how members of Congress go about the day-to-day business of legislating, budget making, oversight, and constituency service, as well as carrying out party caucus- and campaign-related activities.

Negotiating the Informal System

To be successful, representatives and senators must not only serve their constituents and get reelected but must also know how to work with their colleagues and how to maneuver within the intricate system of parliamentary rules, customs, and traditions that govern the House and Senate.

Informal Norms

First among the many lessons every new member must learn are the customary ways of interacting with colleagues both on and off the floor of Congress.[68] These **informal norms** help keep the institution running smoothly by attempting to minimize friction and allowing competition to occur within an atmosphere of civility. As in other American institutions, the norms of Congress are changing.

The Founders' velveteen breeches, frock coats, and white wigs symbolized the drawing room gentility of their circle and helped to mask bitter rivalries. It was Thomas Jefferson, the best known of the gentlemen farmers, who in 1801 wrote the foundational rules for in-chamber conduct for members of the new Congress in an effort to contain the inevitable conflict between Federalist and Anti-Federalist, abolitionist and slave owner. His notes laid the groundwork for Congress's system of informal norms.

Throughout much of the twentieth century, the most important norm was institutional loyalty, the expectation that members would respect their fellow members and Congress itself, especially their own chamber. Personal criticism of one's colleagues was to be avoided, and mutual respect was fostered by such conventions as referring to colleagues by title, such as "the distinguished senator from New York," rather than by name.

In recent years, hostility among members seems as sharp as among those delegates to the First Congress, but scholars differ on the origins of this decline in civility. Some say it dates back decades to the time Democrats had a lock on both chambers, leaving Republicans permanently aggrieved. Some say it began with Watergate—that Nixon's enemies list and Congress's impeachment hearings poisoned the atmosphere. Others tie it to the hearings on the nominations of Robert Bork and Clarence Thomas to the Supreme Court, which were notorious for their overheated exchanges and character bashing. Still others trace the decline to Newt Gingrich's strategy as a minority tactician in the 1980s. He attacked not only the Democratic leaders but Congress as an institution (a severe departure from the institutional loyalty norm) in an attempt to sour the public on Congress so voters would be inclined to turn out incumbent Democrats. Once the Republicans captured control of the House and Gingrich became their leader, he encouraged an aggressive, combative style on the floor of the House.

The growth in partisan voting, illustrated in Figure 10.3, gives little support to the Democratic majority or Watergate explanations, though there was a small spike in 1974, the year of those investigations, but then partisanship returned to its formerly low levels. The voting data give more support to the Bork, Thomas, and especially the Gingrich explanations, since there was some increase in partisanship in 1987, at the time of the Bork hearing; in 1992 and 1993, after the Thomas hearings; and dramatically in 1995, after Gingrich became majority leader.

It was in this climate that Republicans launched the impeachment hearings against President Clinton, leaving many Democrats wanting revenge for what they felt was an outrageous diversion of time and energy from crucial business. Under Speaker Hastert's leadership, it seemed at first that there would be a trend toward more conciliation and civility in the conduct of House business. But in 2003, the Republican leadership, reinvigorated by gains in the midterm elections and determined to tighten procedural control over the House, called in the Capitol Police to break up a meeting of Democratic members. Several months later, Hastert broke House rules by holding a vote open for three hours while he rounded up the support needed to pass a Bush administration bill.

Although it is still the norm in Great Britain's House of Commons to hear members refer to one another as the "right honorable member" or "my right honorable colleague," never using personal names, today one is apt to hear much more informal and not particularly polite language when members of our Congress talk to and about one another and the institution. (See the box "Cover Your Ears, Mr. Jefferson!") And even in the House of Commons, the formal terms of address are a veneer, as Labour and Conservative members sit on opposite sides of a narrow chamber floor hooting and shouting epithets at their fellow Honourables. However, this is a long and well-loved tradition in the House of Commons and not a modern manifestation of increased hostility.

The only reassuring aspect of this intense degree of partisanship is that it is neither new nor destined to last. Congress passes through cycles of greater and lesser civility. Although they may be name calling now, they are not beating up or shooting at one another as members were in the years leading up to the Civil War. And Jefferson's ears were hardly virgin; a frequent target of gossip and character attacks, he could dish with the best and used paid agents to spread slander about his Federalist opponents.

Specialization

By specializing, a member can become an expert, and possibly influential, in a few policy areas. Given the scope of Congress's legislative authority, members cannot be knowledgeable in all areas, so House members especially specialize in subject areas important to their home districts or related to their committees. The leader of one freshmen class of legislators advised his new colleagues, "If you've got twenty things you want to do, see where everything is. You'll find that maybe ten of those are already being worked on by people and that while you may be supportive in that role, you don't need to carry the ball. . . . If you try to take the lead on everything, you'll be wasting your time and re-creating the work that's already going on."[69]

The Senate's smaller membership cannot support this degree of specialization. In addition, some senators see themselves as potential presidential candidates who need to be well versed on a variety of issues.

Reciprocity

Tied to specialization is the norm of reciprocity. Reciprocity, or "logrolling," is summarized in the statement "You support my bill, and I'll support yours." Reciprocity helps each member get the votes needed to pass legislation favored in his or her district. The traditional way in which reciprocity worked was described by the late Sam Ervin, Democratic senator from tobacco-growing North Carolina: "I got to know Milt Young [then a senator from North Dakota] very well. And I told Milt, 'Milt, I would just like you to tell me how to vote about wheat and sugar beets

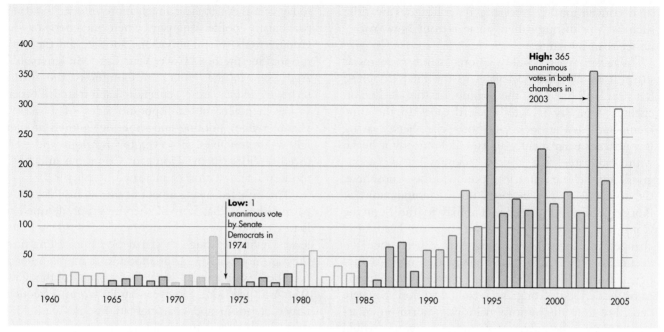

FIGURE 10.3 ■ **Partisan Voting Has Increased Significantly** *Shown here are the number of times members of one party unanimously opposed a majority of the other party on a roll call vote in the House or Senate. These increasing numbers are a sign of hardened lines and heightened partisanship.*
SOURCE: *Congressional Quarterly Weekly Review,* January 3, 2004, 15.

and things like that, if you just help me out on tobacco."[70] Reciprocity is another informal norm that is disappearing. Open meetings, media scrutiny, stronger party leadership, and more partisan voting have made it more difficult for members to "go along" on bills unpopular in their constituency or with the party leadership.

Making Alliances

Any member who wants to get legislation passed, move into the party leadership, or run for higher office needs to develop a network of allies among colleagues. Crossing ideological lines to find sponsors or votes for a bill is not uncommon. One of the most unusual alliances of recent years was between Sen. Hillary Clinton (D-N.Y.) and the Christian conservative Sen. Sam Brownback (R-Kans.), who joined forces to promote new measures to stop human trafficking, especially the selling of women and children into prostitution.

An increasingly common venue for cooperation among members, especially in the House, is the **special-interest caucus.** Caucuses are organized by members who share partisan, ideological, issue, regional, or identity interests to pool their strength in promoting shared interests and gaining passage of related legislation. Caucus size ranges from a handful to more than a hundred; almost every member belongs to at least one. The House and Senate have well over one hundred caucuses, many

organized cross-chamber. Some caucuses have a narrow focus, such as those promoting bikes, ball bearings, boating, the wine industry, or wireless technology. Some are rooted in personal experience, such as the caucuses of Vietnam veterans and cancer survivors.

Prior to the 1995 Republican-led reforms that reduced administrative spending, the most important caucuses had their own office space and budgets. Today they are run out of members' offices and are supported by their office staff and budgets, just as the smallest of the caucuses have always had to operate.

Among the most significant of the caucuses are those designed to pool the strength of women and minorities. They develop policy in key issue areas and serve national constituencies. The Caucus for Women's Issues, working across party, racial, and ethnic lines, has managed to recruit almost all women members and many male colleagues as well. With a Republican and a Democrat serving as cochairs, the caucus is regarded as one of the most bipartisan in Congress. Its legislative agenda includes supportive measures for woman-owned businesses, pay equity, and women in the military.

Hispanics, Asians, Native Americans, Asian Indians, and African Americans also have special-interest caucuses. The Black Caucus was organized in 1970 by thirteen House members determined to gain some clout. Today, all forty African Americans in the House are members. The Black Caucus declined in influence

In the past several years, members of Congress have not tried to hide their contempt for Congress or its leaders:

"[Congress] is a sick institution, and . . . has no legitimate authority. . . . [It] does not represent the constitutional government. It is, in fact, a subversion of the process of free elections."—Newt Gingrich on the MacNeil/Lehrer NewsHour, 1989.[1]

"I've never seen such amateur leadership in all the time I've been in Congress, twenty-one years."—Senate Minority Whip Harry Reid (D-Nev.), on the Senate floor, in reference to Majority Leader Bill Frist.[2]

"If you kill my dog, I'll kill your cat."—Former Republican Majority Leader Tom DeLay.[3]

"I'm glad the children of America were asleep."—House Minority Leader Nancy Pelosi, speaking to the press about Speaker Hastert's late night hold of the vote on the prescription drug bill while he searched for votes. (2004)

"F—you."—Vice President Richard Cheney to Senator Patrick Leahy (D-Vt.), on the Senate floor, July 2004.

"Only cowards cut and run, marines never do."—Rep. Jean Schmidt (R-Ohio) to Rep. John Murtha (D-Pa), who won a Bronze Star and two Purple hearts while serving as a marine in the Vietnam War, for proposing the withdrawal of troops from Iraq, 2005.

"You Guys are Pathetic! Pathetic!"—Rep. Martin Meehan (D-Mass), yelling at Rep Jean Schmidt and Republicans on the House floor for insulting Rep. Murtha, 2005.[4]

[1]Richard E. Cohen, Kirk Victor, and David Bauman, "The State of Congress," *National Journal,* January 10, 2004, 86.
[2]Sheryl Gay Stolberg, "The High Costs of Rising Incivility on Capitol Hill," *New York Times,* November 30, 2003, W-10.
[3]Cohen, Victor, and Bauman, "State of Congress," 90.
[4]Eric Schmitt, "Uproar in House as Parties Clash on Iraq Pullout," *New York Times,* November 19, 2005.

under the Republican majority. Because there are no African American Republicans in Congress and there are no African American committee chairs, with Democrats back in the majority in 2007, members of the Black Caucus will chair several key committees, and James Clymer (S.C.) will become the third-ranking Democrat serving as House Majority Whip.

Personal Friendships

In some cases, caucuses are the source of a House member's closest political allies. But with the exception of its Centrist Coalition, caucuses are not as important in the much smaller Senate. There, personal friendships might count for more than committee or caucus membership, and strong relationships of trust sometimes develop across party lines. John Kerry (D-Mass.) and John McCain (R-Ariz.) two decorated Vietnam War veterans, became friends while working together on veterans' issues. A more unusual example is the close friendship between the very liberal Senator Edward Kennedy (D-Mass.) and the very conservative Senator Orrin Hatch (R-Utah). Sometimes the chair of a committee develops both a close working relationship and personal friendship with the ranking minority member, as for example between Senators Richard Lugar (R-Ind.) and Joseph Biden (D-Del.) of Foreign Relations, or between Arlen Spector (R-Pa.) and Patrick Leahy (D-Vt.) of the Judiciary. In both houses, much of the work gets hammered out in personal conversations and exchanges away from official venues.

Political Action Committees

The most influential members of Congress now have their own PACs for raising campaign funds to disperse to colleagues. Hillary Rodham Clinton (D-N.Y.), a junior senator and former first lady, has been able to use her celebrity and connections to raise millions of dollars for her PAC, Friends of Hillary. By making donations to the reelection campaigns of colleagues, she has built a network of supporters whose chits she can cash in when looking for a committee chair, leadership position, or in a race for the presidency. Nancy Pelosi was able to beat out rivals for the Minority Leader position in 2001 due in large part to her phenomenal ability to get campaign donations for colleagues. By the time she announced that she wanted the position, dozens of fellow House members were in her political debt. Tom DeLay, the very powerful former House majority leader, also built his clout by dispensing funds.

Using the Media

Forty years ago, the workday routine in both House and Senate for resolving most issues involved bargaining with other members, lobbyists, and White House aides. Working privately, one-on-one in small groups, or in committees, members and staff discussed and debated issues, exchanged information, and planned strategies. Even though many issues are still resolved through these private channels, much has changed in the way Congress operates.

Representative John Murtha (D-Pa.) caused a furor when he publicly proposed that American troops be withdrawn from Iraq. As an ex-marine with close ties to the Pentagon, his proposal was seen as a reflection of the views of at least some high-ranking officers.

For today's members to further their goals, it is often as important to "go public," to reach beyond colleagues and to appeal directly to the larger public, as it is to engage in private negotiation.[71] **Going public** means taking an issue debate to the public through the media as Congress does when it televises floor debates and important hearings. The most media-oriented members of Congress are experts in providing short and interesting comments for the nightly network news, writing articles for major newspapers, and appearing on talk shows and as commentators on news programs.

With every congressional office wired for Internet access, members not only have a faster way to facilitate casework, but a means for self-promotion twenty-four/seven. Every district visit, town meeting, and photo-op is put up on the website immediately. Members with larger political ambitions may maintain their own listservs or blogs, but no one in Congress today has to wait for the press to come to them.

In the early days of television, networks broadcast only important congressional proceedings, such as the McCarthy hearings and testimony on investigations into the Watergate scandal and the Iran-Contra affair. In 1979, after considerable controversy and anxiety, the House began televising its proceedings. Fearful of being overshadowed by the House, in 1986 the Senate followed suit. But today exposure comes daily on C-SPAN (the Cable Satellite Public Affairs Network). Two of the three C-SPAN advertisement-free chan-

nels are available with almost all basic cable service and have almost thirty million viewers each week. Although viewership is small compared with commercial networks, the C-SPAN audience is better informed and more interested in both local and national government than the general public; nine out of ten viewers voted in the 2000 election.[72]

Local television listings provide times for daily coverage of House and Senate floor proceedings as well as for committee hearings and other official business. In addition, C-SPAN covers members of Congress on the campaign trail, attending fundraisers, giving stump speeches, and chatting with constituents. Besides its unbroken coverage of events, what sets C-SPAN apart from commercial network coverage of Congress is that there is no intermediary between the viewers and the events and people they are watching. C-SPAN does not use reporters, so televised events are free of commentary and on-the-spot analysis. This may be why C-SPAN is only one of three televisions new sources to be named as "most trusted" by Republicans, Democrats, and Independents.

The congressional leadership goes public, too. Leaders of both parties regularly call producers of television talk shows to suggest guests. They meet with the press and often have prepared statements. Before important congressional votes on key issues, the leadership plans letters to the editors of important newspapers and floor speeches designed for maximum television coverage.

Balancing the Work

Schedules

Multiple committee assignments, in combination with party caucus work, fundraising, and visits to the district, mean that members have impossible schedules (see the box "A Day in the Life of a U.S. Senator"). At times, committees cannot obtain quorums because members are tied up with other obligations. Members attend meetings with legislative staff in tow to take notes and to consult with during hearings. If they cannot attend or have to leave for floor business or another meeting, a staffer is there to take notes and brief the member later.

Use of Staff

We already noted the huge staff available to members. Staffers do most of the background work on the complex foreign and domestic issues that cross the members' desks every day, aided when deep expertise is need by the CRS staff. Through their service, staffers gain a great deal of experience and the opportunity to create a network of contacts that can help them should they decide to run for Congress, so it is not surprising that 107 members of the 109th Congress were former congressional staffers.[73]

Congress and the Public

As we have noted, one of the most frustrating things about Congress for the average citizen is the "messiness" of the legislative process. Not only is the process of crafting laws incredibly complex, but it provides many places along the way where individual legislators and interest groups, often for seemingly (or truly) selfish motives, can exact concessions from the people who want to pass the bill. Add to that the partisan bickering, with Democrats picking a proposal apart simply because a Republican introduced it or vice versa, and casual observers throw up their hands in exasperation.

It seems that the more media exposure Congress gets, the less supportive the public is of its work. Now as never before, every step—or misstep—that members of Congress take is carried to every part of the nation. Or as one observer commented, "A member's every twitch is blared to the world, thanks to C-SPAN, open meetings laws, financial-disclosure reports, and every misstep is logged in a database for the use of some future office seeker."[74] And that was more than a decade ago; today we must add Blackberries, cell phones, YouTube, and blogs. Members must be aware that every public utterance is almost certainly being monitored by someone and that if it is the least bit newsworthy will soon appear in a blog or electronic newsletter.

Media attention is valuable, because we prize open government in a democracy. But too much is not so good, because in a heterogeneous society we rely on compromise to achieve our public goals, and under the harsh glare of media, there are fewer opportunities to compromise and deliberate without fear of losing votes back home.

The public has little patience for extended partisan debates even when they reflect real policy differences among the people. Of the three branches of government, the public has been least supportive of Congress, where the processes of democracy are exposed for all to see. The conflict and gridlock, if not admirable, are not surprising either, given our complex constituencies with competing interests and worldviews. But members contribute to the poor image by belittling colleagues and the institution itself when they seek reelection by running against "Washington."

For some years, the public gave its highest level of support to the Supreme Court, the institution that is most isolated from the public. Unlike legislative debates, little of the disagreement, negotiation, and compromise of the Court has taken place in public view. When the Court meddles in politics, as it did during the 2000 presidential election vote-counting controversy in Florida, its approval ratings decline. Confidence in the presidency and approval ratings for individual presidents can fluctuate wildly, as both Bushes discovered when their approval ratings fell from near 90 percent to the low thirties. A president's support can soar when acting as a national leader (chief of state), especially in wartime, then suffer huge losses as a political leader (head of government) when his policies fail.

The public's attitudes about Congress are also conflicted. In 2004, for example, two-thirds of the public approved of their own representatives, compared with just 41 percent who approved of Congress as a whole.[75] But occasionally the public gets so down on Congress that it affects constituents' attitudes toward their own representatives. In 1994, when Republicans took control of Congress from the Democrats, there was a general mood of sweep out the old and bring in the new. Prior to the 2006 midterm elections a similar attitude prevailed, with Congress's approval ratings standing at 23 percent and some voters expressing doubts about their own members.[76]

A major factor in Congress's low approval ratings is the public's perception that most members care more about power than about the best interests of the nation and more about pleasing lobbyists who can feed their campaign coffers than serving the interests

Senator Richard Durbin is in his second term in the Senate after serving seven terms in the U.S. House and thirteen years as a legislative aide in the Illinois Senate. In the 108th Congress (2003–2004), he had the responsibility of "shaping" the weekly message for the Democratic Caucus and in the 110th became Majority whip. He sits on one of the Senate's most powerful committees, Appropriations, as well as on the Judiciary and Rules Committees. Assisting him in Washington are thirty-five staffers—legislative assistants, "legislative correspondents" who do casework, and aides assigned by the committees on which Durbin serves. As Democratic whip he is assigned additional staff to help with party work.

The days chronicled here show how the senator must divide his time among his legislative and budget-making responsibilities (committee and floor time), party caucus work, fundraising, and constituency service.

A Day in Washington

Tuesday, June 22, 2004

8:00 A.M.—Durbin meets with members of the Illinois congressional delegation over breakfast in the Senate dining room to discuss various state projects in appropriations bills.

9:00 A.M.—Meets with fellow members of the Democratic Senate leadership team.

9:47 A.M.—The Senate convenes. The Democratic leadership has decided to press the issue of Halliburton's overbilling the U.S. government. Durbin goes to the floor where Minority Leader Tom Daschle delivers the Halliburton remarks. Later in the morning, Durbin speaks in support of an amendment to require Attorney General John Ashcroft to turn over all documents relevant to the treatment of Iraqi prisoners held at Abu Ghraib. He stays for the vote on this and other amendments.

10:00 A.M.—While he is still on the Senate floor, Durbin has a scheduled meeting of the appropriations subcommittee on the District of Columbia.

10:45 A.M.—Another appropriations subcommittee, on defense, is meeting to mark up the 2005 defense budget. Durbin's legislative assistant for appropriations attends, but the senator can attend only when he is free to leave the floor.

12:00 P.M.—Meets with Sen. Ben Nighthorse Campbell (R-Colo.) regarding markup of the 2005 legislative branch appropriations bill.

12:30 P.M.—Attends the weekly Democratic Caucus luncheon.

2:00 P.M.—Scheduled meeting of the Judiciary's Terrorism, Technology and Homeland Security Subcommittee, which is considering Patriot Act II. The subcommittee is hearing testimony on the subpoena and pretrial detention powers granted by the original USA PATRIOT Act.

This is staffed by Durbin's legislative assistant for the judiciary.

2:15 P.M.—The senator slips out of his meeting to pose for the annual photo of all senators.

3:30 P.M.—With an assistant, Durbin attends a meeting of the full Appropriations Committee to mark up the 2005 defense appropriations bill.

4:30 P.M.—Meets with the chair of Dynergy, Inc., regarding the company's business operations in Illinois.

5:00 P.M.—Attends an event for the recipients of the Jefferson Awards for Public Service and gives a speech congratulating the winners.

5:30 P.M.—Meets with the director of the Centers for Disease Control and Prevention regarding the department's new goals and integrated operations.

6:30 P.M.—Attends a fundraiser for Senate Democratic Leader Tom Daschle [defeated in 2004].

7:30 P.M.—Attends a reception, dinner, and movie (The Terminal) hosted by the Motion Picture Association of America.

Senator Durbin participates in the Mexican Independence Day parade in the Little Village neighborhood of Chicago.

A Day in the District

Every Thursday night or Friday morning, Durbin flies to Illinois, returning to Washington on Monday afternoon. He also spends the Senate's monthly recess week in-state, so he is in Illinois nearly half the year. He keeps homes in both Chicago and Springfield, his hometown.

With nearly thirteen million people, Illinois is the fifth-largest state; it is more than four hundred miles long and economically diverse. It is also racially and ethnically diverse and one of the principal destinations for new immigrants. When in Illinois, the senator has nineteen staffers to assist him—ten in his Chicago office; seven in Springfield, the state capital; and two in Marion, in southern Illinois. As he travels around the state, he is accompanied by staff—outreach coordinators for the areas he visits and a press secretary. On this day, the senator is "downstate," but other days he might be in Chicago and its suburbs.

Thursday, July 1, 2004

8:40 A.M.—At Johnny's Steakhouse in Rock Island (on the Iowa border), Durbin discusses pending legislation in Congress of concern to the labor community with U.S. Rep. Lane Evans (D-Ill.) [retired 2006] and Quad Cities labor leaders.

9:45 A.M.—Departs for the Rock Island Arsenal.

10:00 A.M.—Holds a news conference to announce $33 million in new federal funding for a series of projects at the Rock Island Arsenal. He tours the arsenal's new child care facility, built with federal funding.

11:15 A.M.—Flies to Quincy, about 150 miles to the south.

12:30 P.M.—Meets with Quincy's mayor, officials from Corporate Airlines, and community leaders over lunch to discuss the airline's most recent investment in the Quincy airport.

1:30 P.M.—Holds a news conference to announce that Corporate Airlines will be relocating its maintenance facility to the Quincy airport and creating new jobs.

2:30 P.M.—In downtown Quincy, the senator meets with agricultural and labor leaders to discuss legislation (which he sponsored) that would modernize several locks and dams on the Missouri and Illinois Rivers and allow barges to transport farm products more quickly.

3:40 P.M.—Flies back to Chicago.

6:00 P.M.—Attends a fundraiser for Barack Obama, Democratic U.S. Senate candidate from Illinois (who won in 2004).

8:00 P.M.—Attends a book event to celebrate the release of Bill Clinton's *My Life* to benefit the Democratic National Committee.

SOURCES: Schedules provided by Sen. Richard J. Durbin's Chicago office; David Hawkings and Brian Nutting, eds., *CQ's Politics in America: The 108th Congress* (Washington, D.C.: CQ Press, 2003), 312–316; Michael Barone and Richard E. Cohen, *The Almanac of American Politics, 2004* (Washington, D.C.: National Journal, 2003), 531–533. Special thanks to Christina Angarola.

---

of the district. The public is not mistaken in its impression of a cozy relationship between Congress and special-interest lobbies. Eight members of the 109th Congress worked as lobbyists before running for office, and between 1998 and 2005, 50 percent of the men who left the Senate became registered lobbyists, as did more than 40 percent of the 162 who left the House.[77] Others work as "consultants" and are not required to register as lobbyists, and some members are married to, or have children working as, lobbyists. Ex–House members have had easy access to their former colleagues through their lifetime access to gym and dining facilities and the House floor—although they were prohibited from lobbying on the floor. The Jack Abramoff lobbying scandal (see Chapter 9) precipitated small rules changes including ending lifetime privileged facility access for former members of the House. (The Senate has no such restrictions.)

The 109th Congress was one of the most scandal-ridden in decades with members of both parties and hundreds of staff members accused of ethics violations for acceptance of gifts, free travel, and questionable campaign contributions from powerful lobbyists. The Republican chair of House Administration, who had close ties to Jack Abramoff, and a Democratic member of the powerful Ways and Means Committee, who was caught with thousands of dollars in his freezer—allegedly a bribe—were forced to give up their committee seats; and the thrice-censured, once-indicted Majority Leader Tom Delay resigned his leadership position and then his seat in Congress. Two of his top aides were convicted on corruption charges, also in connection with the Abramoff scandal, one of whom used his time awaiting sentencing to complete a graduate thesis on the House ethics process. The congressional newspaper, *The Hill*, called it "irony on steroids," and it encapsulates the cynicism much of the public saw in the gap between Congress's rhetoric about ethics and its conduct.[78]

By permission of Mike Luckovich and Creators Syndicate

Despite all this, the idea of Congress as a constitutionally mandated "people's house" is esteemed by the public. It is the people in Congress and the way Congress works that the public dislikes. Just over half of all voters turn out for congressional elections (less in years where the president is not being elected), and most of the public is poorly informed about what Congress does. This pattern persists even with C-SPAN coverage and even though many local papers each week print a congressional scorecard with the voting records of local legislators. Constituents are much more likely to know about ethics violations and sexual improprieties of members of Congress than they are about the legislation passed in any session. The public evaluation of Congress as accomplishing "not much" or "nothing at all" stems in part from the public's lack of awareness of what Congress has actually done. However, in the 109th Congress very little actually was done; the House was in session for only 139 days in 2005 and the Senate for little more.

Conclusion: Is Congress Responsive?

Congress is certainly responsive to individual constituents, but is it responsive to the policy demands of the national constituency? The pressures of elections and of constituency service seem to undermine Congress's ability to focus on public policy. Pressure to be in the home district meeting constituents competes with legislators' desires to do a good job at lawmaking and to work more efficiently.

The public wants Congress to be responsive to its individual needs and group interests, but then it looks down on the institution for its pork barrel politics and big spending. This is the perennial dilemma of representatives and senators: how to meet the demands of the district or state—that is to do the job members are sent to do—in order to get reelected and at the same time serve the national interest.

Pressure to raise money for reelection campaigns incurs obligations to interest groups that may not be consistent with either the members' or the constituents' views. Indeed, congressional leaders from both parties have problems articulating a clear vision in part because so many of them have become dependent on the contributions of PACs for their campaign funding. This puts them in the position of having to support some interests that are not consistent with voters' views or interests.

The procedures and organization of Congress also give individuals and small groups opportunities to block or redirect action. This is particularly true in the Senate, where procedures allow a minority of senators to engage in unlimited debate unless sixty members vote to stop it. The fragmented committee and subcommittee structure in both houses offers many venues in which action can be killed. Political parties have been strengthened in recent years, but neither party discipline nor institutional rules and norms, including ethics guidelines, have kept members from bowing to the pressure of lobbyists or outraged constituents. These factors mean that Congress continues to be more responsive to individual and group interests than to national needs.

The increasing partisanship in Congress has been one of the biggest changes since the mid-1990s. During George W. Bush's administration, the White House intervened heavily to press its policy agenda. Partisan voting hit a record high in 2003 as the legislative process became party dominated. Democrats were shut out of many important stages of the process, including the drafting of final versions of legislation in conference committees. This further heightened the partisan divisions and made the output of Congress less a product of compromise than it had been in earlier years and less responsive to the broader public. Legislation was the product of a single party and the group interests closest to its political base. As Democrats assumed control of Congress in 2007, they promised to restore bipartisanship to the legislative process.

Even in the best of times, Congress best represents those voters who identify with one of the two major parties, even though about a third of the public identify as independents or with a third party. This has complicated what was already a difficult process for the formulation of broadly responsive public policy, namely, the overweening influence of large campaign donors on voting on both sides of the aisle. It is difficult to get consistently good legislation when special interests, partisan concerns, and pork-hungry legislators dominate the lawmaking process. It is especially difficult when only the majority party is making the decisions.

Sen. Roberts Chooses Party Loyalty

In early 2006, as Sen. Roberts continued to refuse to move on to Phase 2 of his committee's investigation into Iraq intelligence failures, another oversight failure hit the newspapers. The *Washington Post* revealed that the president had authorized the National Security Agency (whose work the Intelligence Committee oversees) to wiretap domestic phone calls without getting court warrants. (See Chapter 14.) Sen. Roberts was 1 of only 8 members of Congress who had been briefed on the program; the other 527 learned about it from the newspaper. There is no way Congress can oversee executive branch activities it does not know about.

This just intensified pressure from committee Democrats to hold hearings on how the administration was using intelligence agencies and the information they gather. But in March 2006 Roberts refused to investigate the NSA program, announcing his willingness to simply rewrite current law to give the president the authority to do what he was already doing, but also to give Congress more oversight authority. He published an op-ed piece explaining his decision, calling the leak of information about the surveillance program "criminal," and flatly stating that the president's actions were "legal and constitutional."[79] And the following month, he announced he was again "postponing" Phase 2 of the hearings on Iraqi intelligence.

What bothered committee Democrats most about these decisions was that Roberts, in both cases, had worked out how to proceed by consulting with the White House rather than with congressional colleagues. A committee's schedule is supposed to be decided among committee members, not between the committee chair and the White House. The ranking member, Jay Rockefeller, told reporters that the Intelligence committee was "under the control of the White House through the chairman" to which Roberts responded that he did not much care for being portrayed as Bush's lapdog.[80]

The divisiveness on the Intelligence Committee was symptomatic of almost all oversight work by congressional committees in the 109th Congress, with the Republican majority refusing to oversee any activity of the executive branch that the White House did not want investigated. The partisan orientation of oversight work continued the trend that began during the Clinton administration, when the Republican majority investigated almost every aspect of the president's public and private life. In the decade between 1997 and 2006, of the 1015 subpoenas issued by congressional committees to provide testimony or documents for congressional hearings, 1000 were for investigations of actions taken by the Clinton administration and 15 for investigations of the Bush administration.[81]

A former Republican member of the Intelligence Committee said that "politics should stop at the door of the [Intelligence] committee . . . when you lose bipartisan oversight . . . you lose something very, very important." A former Democratic committee member concurred, calling the current state of affairs "heartbreaking," and a "disservice to the American people."[82]

Roberts was justified in his fear that Democrats would use any information on the misuse of Iraq intelligence uncovered by committee hearings to partisan advantage, but his obligation to exercise oversight of the executive branch agencies under his committee's jurisdiction was just as certain. And by not exercising oversight when the Republicans were in control of the House and Senate, he was risking what Democrats might do if they regained control in the 2006 elections. House Minority Leader Nancy Pelosi said that Democrats would leave no stone unturned: "We Win in '06, we get subpoena power." She said Democrats "would reserve the right to investigate every aspect of the Bush administration, including its rationale for the Iraq war."[83] The cost of partisanship is more partisanship.

Although as she took over the Speakership, Pelosi promised that impeachment was "off the table," increased oversight of the executive branch was a certainty.

 To learn more about this topic, go to "you are there" exercises for this chapter on the text website.

By Luckovich for the *Atlanta Journal Constitution*

Key Terms

constituency	whips
reapportionment	standing committees
redistricting	markup
gerrymander	seniority rule
constituency service	filibuster
casework	cloture
pork barrel	conference committee
Speaker of the House	oversight
earmark	authorizations
Rules Committee	appropriations
party caucus	informal norms
majority leader	special-interest caucus
minority leader	going public

Further Reading

Robert A. Caro, *Master of the Senate* (New York: Knopf, 2002). When you have some time on your hands, check out this monumental study of a master legislator at work. This is the second in a projected three-volume study that tracks the House and Senate career of former president Lyndon B. Johnson, arguably the most powerful Senate majority leader in U.S. history.

Roger H. Davidson and Walter J. Oleszek, *Congress and Its Members*, 9th ed. (Washington, D.C.: CQ Press, 2004). This classic general reference work on Congress is revised every few years.

Richard Fenno, *Home Style: House Members in Their Districts*, 2nd ed. (New York: Longman, 2003). This political science classic examines how House members interact with people in their districts and how this influences their political style and decision making.

Nolan McCarty, Keith Poole, and Howard Rosenthal, *Polarized America: The Dance of Ideology and Unequal Riches* (MIT Press, 2006). From an analysis of the past century of voting in Congress, the authors conclude that increased political polarization is linked to the widening income gap.

Norman Ornstein and Thomas E. Mann, *The Broken Branch: Problems Plaguing Our Legislative Branch* (Washington D.C.: Brookings Institution, 2006). Two of the country's leading congressional experts explain the significance of a polarized and dysfunctional Congress and suggest ways it can be reformed.

Barbara Sinclair, *Unorthodox Lawmaking: New Legislative Processes in the U. S. Congress*, 2nd ed. (Washington, D.C.: CQ Press, 2000). Sinclair examines how the legislative process is being transformed by focusing on bills that came before Congress during the Clinton administration.

For Viewing

The Congress (1989). This Ken Burns documentary traces the development of both the Capitol building and Congress as an institution, with commentary on historic leadership figures and landmark events such as the Great Compromise, the McCarthy hearings, and Watergate. It also contains clips from Frank Capra's *Mr. Smith Goes to Washington*

(1939), a classic black-and-white Hollywood film that conveys an idealistic view of how Congress works. In the same vein is Otto Preminger's *Advise and Consent* (1962), which shows the triumph of principle in the Senate.

"The Dark Side" (2006). An investigative report by PBS's *Frontline* series that examines the misuse of intelligence in the months before the invasion of Iraq. The main focus is on executive branch in-fighting, but it also covers attempts to block congressional oversight of intelligence agencies. Former Chair of the Senate Select Committee on Intelligence (Bob Graham, D-Fla.) is among many former government officials interviewed. Can be viewed online at www.pbs.org/frontline.

 **Electronic Resources**

thomas.loc.gov
"Thomas: Legislative Information on the Internet" links to texts of bills, the Congressional Record (reporting entire floor debates), and committee hearings and reports. It is also a good site for obtaining information on congressional history and individual members. It contains links to all kinds of statistics about Congress and to the home pages and e-mail addresses of members. You can also link to the latest edition of How a Bill Becomes a Law, *prepared by the House Judiciary Committee.*

www.c-span.org
The website of the cable station that covers congressional proceedings is a treasure trove of information on current affairs as well as congressional history, including a nine-hour 2006 documentary on the history of the Capitol building. It also has an archive of frequently asked questions about Congress and resources for students of American government.

www.washingtonpost.com
This is the website of the Washington Post, *whose news coverage of Congress is unrivaled.*

www.cq.com
This is the website of Congressional Quarterly, *publisher of the most authoritative weekly review of congressional affairs.*

www.publicintegrity.org
This is a good source for relationships between lobbyists and members of Congress

ThomsonNOW™

Enter ThomsonNOW™ using the access card that is available with this text or through www.thomsonedu.com/thomsonnow. ThomsonNOW™ will assist you in understanding the content in this chapter with a personalized study plan generated for your needs. A practice test will assess the areas you need to review and provide the tools to fully comprehend those concepts, including an integrated digital eBook, interactive simulations, timelines, video case studies, MicroCase exercises, and InfoTrac College Edition readers and exercises. You'll also be connected to the learning objectives, chapter outline, chapter glossary, flash cards, crossword puzzles, Internet activities, and interactive quizzes found on the companion website.

CHAPTER 11

THE PRESIDENCY

Win McNamee, Getty Images

George W. Bush has made the "imperial presidency" a reality with a vision that includes few checks on presidential power.

Development and Growth of the Presidency
   Eligibility
   Pay and Perks
   Tenure and Succession

Powers and Leadership
   Head of State
   Chief Executive
   Fiscal Leader
   Legislative Leader
   Diplomatic and Military Leader
   Party Leader
   The Ebb and Flow of Presidential Power

Presidential Staff
   Executive Office of the President
   White House Office
   Office of the Vice President

The Personal Presidency
   Going Public
   Spectacle Presidency
   The President and Public Opinion

The Presidential Reputation
   President as Persuader
   Presidential Character
   Goals and Vision

Conclusion: Is the Presidency Responsive?

YOU ARE THERE

How Should You Spend Your Political Capital?

You are George W. Bush, forty-third president of the United States. It is December 2004 and you have just been reelected to a second term. Reporters and pundits are speculating on how you will use your second term. In a pre-Christmas press conference you were asked if you think the election was a mandate that gave you the political capital to undertake new initiatives. You said "my job is to confront big challenges and lead. So I'm just going to keep doing my job."[1] But you also said the election gave you plenty of political capital—not just because you received a majority of the popular vote, but because Republicans added to their majority in Congress—and you have every intention of using it. But what should you use it for? Of all the things you want to accomplish in the next four years, to what should you give priority?

Your first term was all about foreign policy and tax cuts, with little attention to a broader domestic agenda. With post-9/11 approval ratings at 90 percent, you used your political capital to push hundreds of billions of dollars worth of tax cuts through Congress as well to win passage of laws such as the Patriot Act, which greatly expanded executive branch powers. But now your approval ratings barely break the 50 percent mark, and second terms have been political quagmires for most presidents. If they come out of the election with any kind of mandate, they need to act quickly before they are considered lame ducks and Congress loses interest in working for the goals of someone who will be gone when they run for re-election.

The threat of more terrorist attacks hangs over the country, and you have two hot wars in progress in Iraq and Afghanistan. Their costs are being paid for with borrowed money, and you have more tax cuts waiting congressional approval. The budget has been in deficit since your second year in office, so there will be no money for any big program initiative. But you have a legacy to think about and not much time to shape it. If you are going to take advantage of the momentum you have coming out of the election, you need to decide what your priorities will be and get started immediately persuading Congress and the public before your moment is gone.

On the campaign trail you promised voters that you would try to change Social Security to give them a greater say in how their retirement money is invested. You made other promises, but three factors predispose you to using some of your political capital on this issue. First, the demographic shift in the population means there will be fewer workers paying into the system to support those collecting it. At the same time the average life span has lengthened, and people collect Social Security for more years than they did in the early years of the program, meaning it is time to think about new ways of funding it.

Second, although for decades the money paid into Social Security each year has exceeded what is paid out, the government has been borrowing all of that surplus to cover its annual budget shortfalls, make the deficit look smaller, and reduce the amount of money borrowed from private individuals and foreign lenders. As the population ages and the ratio of retired people to workers increases, a way must be found to keep enough money in the system to pay the monthly stipends owed to beneficiaries.

Third, you have never liked the idea of a mandatory retirement system in which the government makes the decision on how the taxpayers' money is invested. The government is required to put the money where it is safe, not where it might get the highest rate of return. You want to change that by allowing young people just entering the system to take a certain percentage of the money that would be withheld for Social Security and invest it themselves. You think they can get a higher rate if they opt for riskier investments.

Then there is the "vision thing," the lack of which has so haunted your father's legacy. You set out to make your mark as a bold, risk-taking president. You would like to be remembered as the person who had the will and the political clout to take on one of the sacred cows of the New Deal era. If the initial stage is successful, the next generation might go a step further, maybe eventually killing off, through privatization, one of the great iconic "big government" programs. Maybe historians would think about ranking you up there with the greats or near-greats.

There are three groups of people who think it may not be such a good idea for you to take on Social Security.

First, some Republicans are leery because they will be associated with any program put forward by the leader of their party and they are not eager to run against Social Security. It has long been called the "third rail" of politics—a program that cannot be tampered with without serious political fallout. It has been an immensely successful program as measured by the number of retired and elderly people who have been lifted out of poverty since its inception. You won't be running for office again but most of Congress will; why should they bear the consequences of your risks?

This brings you to the second group of people who worry about tampering with Social Security—seniors and millions of others approaching retirement. Polls show that 56 percent of the public think you have no mandate to change Social Security, and only 40 percent favor letting younger workers invest part of their withholding tax.[2] On their side are many experts who argue that increasing the amount of income subject to the social security withholding (incomes greater than $94,200 are exempt) and making modest other reforms will ensure the soundness of the existing system. In any case no shortfall is expected for another forty-five years. Why take the political risks now? No politician who has advocated revamping Social Security or privatizing it has met with anything but failure. And advocates of major change in the system have been easy marks for the opposition, who have no difficulty in getting the attention of seniors, a serious bloc of voters. On advice from his advisers, your hero, Ronald Reagan, backed down completely from his flirtation with undoing Social Security. It was just too dangerous politically.

A third group of people who doubt your efforts will be successful are political analysts who have interpreted the election results differently than you have. Some believe the vote showed the country so evenly split that they doubt you have much political

capital to expend on any risky venture. The Electoral College vote was as close as it had been in 2000. A shift of less than 60,000 votes in Ohio could have thrown its electoral votes, and the election, to John Kerry, even with your overall popular vote majority. And because of reported election irregularities there—not enough voting machines or ballots, closed polling stations or twelve-hour waits to vote, all in heavily Democratic areas—analysts wonder if your support in that state is as strong as the final count suggested, and some even suggest that the snafus were planned by state officials eager to throw the election to you.[3] You went into the election with the polls showing voters evenly split on your presidency, and the polls show you came out of it the same way. So gambling that you can carry public opinion with you on an issue as controversial as Social Security reform is risky.

You tend to discount this kind of thinking. The important thing to remember is what John F. Kennedy said after he eked out a victory in 1960: "Mandate, schmandate. The mandate is that I'm here and you're not."[4] This is exactly how you approached your first term; lacking even a plurality of the popular vote, you seized the presidency with an intent to use all of its powers to carry out your programs. You achieved your highest poll ratings by looking bold and decisive after 9/11, so why can't the same thing work now? But you are aware that in tackling a favored domestic program there is no psychological equivalent to the "rally-round-the-flag" effect a president gets when he commits troops abroad. Also public opinion is turning against the war in Iraq; you may need all of your political capital to maintain enough support to finish the job. And if you don't achieve your goals there, perhaps nothing can salvage your legacy anyway.

In addition, under your proposal the money that would be withheld from Social Security payments to allow for private investing would further

Pharaohs, consuls, kings, queens, emperors, tsars, prime ministers, and councils of varied sizes served as executives in other governments before 1789. But no national government had a president, an elected executive with authority equal to and independent of a national legislature, until George Washington was elected president of the United States.

The Founders viewed their creation as a chief executive officer, someone who would serve as both a check on bills passed by Congress and the administrator of those enacted into law. He would also be head of state, chief diplomat, and commander of the armed forces. At its inception, the presidency was a not very powerful office in a fledgling country that had few international ties and virtually no standing army. The office's first occupants were drawn from among the Founders; a few of them, Washington and Jefferson especially, served with some reluctance. Nevertheless, they were willing to lend their reputations and abilities to the cause of stabilizing the new government, and as a result, they had the opportunity to influence the direction of its development.

Throughout the nineteenth century, except for the Civil War period, real power at the national level resided in Congress, so much so that Woodrow Wilson characterized the federal arrangement in the 1880s as "congressional government."[5] Thus between Andrew Jackson, early in the nineteenth century, and Franklin Roosevelt, in the middle of the twentieth, many who sought the presidency were "ordinary people, with very ordinary reputations."[6] There were powerful exceptions, such as Abraham Lincoln, Theodore Roosevelt, and Woodrow Wilson, and a few men of exceptional achievement before their presidencies, such as Ulysses Grant and Herbert Hoover, who fared badly in the White House.

Today the president of the United States is among the most powerful people in the world. By the 1970s, the scope of that power led one historian to write about an "imperial" presidency.[7] Yet most presidents since World War II have seemed at times almost powerless to shape events affecting the national interest. The immensely popular war hero Dwight Eisenhower (1953–1961) was unable to buck Cold War sentiment and prevent the buildup of the military-industrial complex. John Kennedy (1961–1963), who enjoyed an extraordinary success rate in a conservative Congress,

was stymied in getting civil rights legislation accepted. The domestic goals of Lyndon Johnson (1963–1968), along with his chances for reelection, were derailed by a war that took Richard Nixon (1969–1974) years to end. And Nixon, for whom the imperial presidency phrase was coined, was forced from office on obstruction of justice charges for covering up criminal activity in the Watergate scandal. Ronald Reagan (1981–1988), one of our most popular recent presidents, was so frustrated when Congress thwarted his foreign policy initiatives that he condoned illegal activities, producing the Iran-Contra scandal and a

Howard Pyle Collection/Delaware Art Museum, Wilmington/Bridgeman Art Library

Although political scientists rank Jefferson as a "near great" president, he did not consider the office, or his performance in it, very important. His instructions for an epitaph listed what he thought were his three main accomplishments in life: writing the Declaration of Independence and a Virginia law guaranteeing religious freedom and founding the University of Virginia. He did not include his two terms as president.

tarnished personal reputation. Gerald Ford (1974–1976), Jimmy Carter (1977–1980), and George H. Bush (1989–1992) failed to get reelected.

At century's end, Bill Clinton (1993–2000) discovered that instead of an imperial presidency, the country had something closer to an "impossible" or "imperiled" presidency.[8] Although he won reelection handily, most of his domestic agenda, other than economic growth and deficit reduction, was sidetracked by one congressional investigation after another. When George W. Bush entered office in 2001, he brought with him a retinue of Washington professionals and set out to restore the presidency to its former preeminence. Yet Bush also has fallen prey to the ills that beset second-term presidents, as he has watched his popularity plummet and his once popular wars drag on at an increasing cost in American and other lives.

In this chapter, we will consider the paradox of presidential power and presidential weakness. After describing the growth of the modern presidency, we look at the constitutional provisions, the qualifications for the office, and its responsibilities. We explain why a bureaucracy grew up around the presidency at the same time the president was becoming a more personal and accessible representative of the American people. Inevitably, the growth of the modern presidency has affected the balance of power between the executive and legislative branches, and that is another topic of this chapter.

Development and Growth of the Presidency

Most of the Founders believed that Congress would be the predominant branch of government and described its structure and functioning first in the Constitution. John Quincy Adams (1825–1829) reflected the relatively low status of the job when he remarked that "No man who ever held the office would congratulate another on attaining it." But over time the influence and visibility of the presidency has grown to rival and often exceed those of Congress. There have been critical periods during which the union could have failed—at the birth of the nation, the Civil War, the Great Depression, and World War II—and presidential leadership made the difference. From the beginning most Americans accepted that we need more government and executive leadership during crises and less at other times. Presidential power was traditionally supposed to return to its "normal" low profile after we resolved special problems.

This expectation may have been realistic early on, but once the nation stretched from Mexico to Canada and from the Atlantic to the Pacific, once it had a

standing army, international trade aspirations, and the ambition to dominate the hemisphere, governmental power gravitated to Washington and to the president. The image of Thomas Jefferson sitting at his desk in isolation week after week conducting the presidency by personal correspondence was a quaint memory even twenty years later when Andrew Jackson was dubbed the "people's president."[9] Jackson was the first to act assertively to fulfill the popular mandate he saw in his election—the first to veto a bill because *he* did not like it. Thirty years later, Lincoln assumed extraordinary powers during the Civil War, suspending civil liberties, overturning state laws, and boldly interpreting the Constitution to say that the Union was indivisible.

Teddy Roosevelt, who has been called the "preacher militant," used the presidency in an un-

America does not have a monarchy, but it does have political dynasties. George W. Bush, shown here with his father George H. W. Bush, who served as president, vice president, CIA director, and member of the House of Representatives, is also the grandson of a U.S. senator.

precedented way to challenge corporate power and to argue for labor reform and better living conditions for average Americans. He also saw an imperial role for the United States in world politics, especially through military expansion, and led the country toward those "entangling alliances" that George Washington had warned against. Eight years after Roosevelt left office, Wilson became the first twentieth-century president to lead us into a major foreign involvement, World War I, and he was the first president to travel to Europe while in office.

The Great Depression and World War II led to a large expansion in the role of the national government and tremendous growth in presidential power. Franklin Delano Roosevelt (FDR) was elected president in 1932 because people thought he would help them through the crisis. In his first inaugural address, he told Americans that he would ask Congress for "broad executive power" equivalent, he said, to what he might be granted if an enemy had invaded the country, to fight the Depression. The enactment of New Deal programs led to an expansion of the executive branch because new agencies had to be created and new civil servants hired. This increased the president's power by making him more important as a manager and policy maker. And after the United States entered World War II, Roosevelt assumed additional powers as a hands-on commander in chief.

Radio and television also contributed significantly to the expansion of presidential power. An integral part of national life by the 1930s, broadcasting made the news seem more immediate and compelling. It gave people a way to follow presidents and a way for presidents to "sell" their policies and provide leadership. Because it is easier to follow one person than many (as with Congress), the media helped make the presidency the focal point of national politics. With his radio broadcasts during the Great Depression, Roosevelt became a kind of national cheerleader, a one-man band of optimism, persuading the public that solutions were at hand.

Congress is not structured to provide this kind of national leadership. Its 535 members are divided into two houses and hundreds of committees and subcommittees and they come from both major political parties. It is difficult for either the majority or minority leadership to develop and articulate national policy goals or to keep its members faithful to them.

Even after the fifteen years of crisis receded, FDR's successors had little opportunity to shrink the presidency. With the United States emerging from World War II as the preeminent world power and with the onset of the Cold War, Congress was willing to cede even more leadership to the president to counter the Soviet threat. Responsibilities as chief diplomat and commander in chief of the world's largest military establishment have made the president a principal actor in world politics, a platform not afforded to any other government official or institution.

Of his postwar administration, Harry Truman said, "Being president is like riding a tiger. You have to stay on or get swallowed." And thus we have today's presidency, with everyone looking to see whether the man is riding the tiger or the tiger is swallowing the man.

Eligibility

The Constitution requires that a person meet only three conditions to be eligible to hold the presidency: one must be a "natural-born citizen," at least thirty-five years old, and have resided in the United States for at least fourteen years before taking office.

Historically, it also has helped to be a white male with roots in small-town America; a Protestant of English, German, or Scandinavian background; a resident of a state with a large population; and a good family man. In recent years, however, this profile has broadened considerably as society has become more inclusive, the electorate more diverse, and social norms more tolerant of divorce, but gender and racial barriers remain. The nature of contemporary elections also makes it necessary that a candidate be reasonably telegenic and either independently wealthy or an outstanding fundraiser.

Pay and Perks

The Constitution authorizes Congress to award the president "a Compensation," which can be neither increased nor decreased during a president's term of office. Our first seventeen presidents received an annual salary of $25,000. By the time Nixon took office, the salary was $200,000, where it stayed through the Clinton years. A majority of the public was not eager to see it go higher, even though by century's end the salary ranked 785th among the 800 highest-paid CEOs.[10] Supporters of a pay increase argued that the relatively low salary was holding down the base pay for all other top-level officials and interfering with government recruitment. Congress agreed, and doubled the salary to $400,000 in 2001. The president continues to receive $50,000 for expenses.

In addition, there are *substantial* fringe benefits. These include living quarters in one of the world's most famous mansions, a rural retreat in Maryland (Camp David), the best health care money can buy, and fleets of cars and aircraft. After leaving office, the president is entitled to a generous pension, as well as a security detail and money for an office and staff.

Tenure and Succession

Presidents serve four-year terms. The Twenty-second Amendment limits them to serving two terms (or ten years if they complete the term of an incumbent who dies or resigns). Four presidents died in office from illness (Harrison, Taylor, Harding, and Franklin Roosevelt), and four were assassinated (Garfield, McKinley, Lincoln, and Kennedy).

Presidents can be removed from office by impeachment and conviction. The House has the power of **impeachment**—that is, the authority to bring formal charges against a president (similar to an indictment in criminal proceedings) for "Treason, Bribery, or other high Crimes and Misdemeanors" (Article II, U.S. Constitution). In an impeachment inquiry, the House holds hearings to determine whether there is sufficient evidence to impeach, and if a majority votes yes, the president is impeached and the process moves to the Senate, where a trial is held with the chief justice of the United States presiding. Conviction requires a two-thirds vote of members present in the Senate and results in removal from the presidency.

The Founders established the impeachment option as part of the system of checks and balances, a final weapon against executive abuse of power. They borrowed it from British law as a means to remove a president who had abused his power—for example, violated the Constitution—or committed serious crimes, not as a means for unseating a president for partisan reasons. Thus, James Madison objected to the inclusion of the phrase "and other high crimes and misdemeanors" because he thought it was so vague

that it *could* be used for political purposes.[11] The phrase was retained, but it was precisely to guard against its partisan use that the Founders divided indictment and removal powers between the House and the Senate. If trying the charges were left to the popularly elected House, Hamilton wrote in *Federalist Paper* 65, "there will always be the greatest danger that the decision will be regulated more by the comparative strength of parties, than by the real demonstrations of innocence or guilt."

The procedure is cumbersome and meant to be; the Founders did not intend for the president, as head of state and the only nationally elected official in government, to be removed from office easily. Only three presidents have been targets of full impeachment proceedings.[12] Andrew Johnson, who came to office on Lincoln's assassination, was a southerner who was unpopular in his own party; he was impeached by the House in a dispute over Reconstruction policies in the post–Civil War South. The Senate failed to convict by a single vote. A century later, the House Judiciary Committee voted to impeach Richard Nixon on obstruction of justice and other charges stemming from the Watergate scandal, whereupon Nixon resigned as president, knowing he would lose the vote if it were brought to the full House. Once out of office, he avoided indictment on criminal charges through a full pardon granted by his successor, Gerald Ford, a move that aroused a storm of controversy at the time. In 1998 Bill Clinton became the third target of the process when the House voted to open an unrestricted inquiry into possible grounds for his impeachment. The House brought two charges against him but the Senate refused to convict.

Should a president be removed, die, resign, or become incapacitated, his replacement is provided for by the Constitution and supplemental laws. At the time the Constitution was written, it was assumed that the vice presidency would be occupied by the man who had been the runner-up in the presidential election, and the wording simply said that presidential powers "shall devolve on the Vice President." It was left to Congress to make provisions for filling the vacated vice presidency and dealing with a situation in which both the presidency and the vice presidency were vacated. When Lincoln was assassinated, there still were no provisions for replacing Vice President Andrew Johnson when he succeeded to the presidency. Had Johnson been convicted in his impeachment trial, the presidency would have gone to the president pro tempore of the Senate, who was next in the line of succession according to rules in effect at the time.

Not until 1947, two years after the death of Franklin Roosevelt had put the virtually unknown Harry Truman in the White House, did Congress pass the Presidential Succession Act. It established the order of succession of federal officeholders should both the president and the vice president be unable to serve. The list begins with the Speaker of the House, followed by the president pro tempore of the Senate, and then proceeds through the secretaries of the cabinet departments in the order in which the departments were created. The Succession Act has never been used because we have always had a vice president when something happened to the president. To ensure that this is always the case, the Constitution was amended in 1967.

That amendment, the Twenty-fifth, directs the president to name a vice president acceptable to majorities in the House and Senate if the vice presidency falls vacant. These provisions have been used twice. Nixon chose Gerald Ford to replace Spiro Agnew, who resigned after pleading no contest to charges of taking bribes when he was a public official in Maryland. After Nixon resigned and Ford became president, Ford named Nelson Rockefeller, the former governor of New York, as his vice president.

The Twenty-fifth Amendment also charges the vice president and a majority of the cabinet—or some other body named by Congress—to determine, in instances where there is doubt, whether the president is mentally or physically incapable of carrying out his duties. This provision was meant to provide for situations in which it is unclear who is or should be acting as president, such as when James Garfield was shot in July 1881. He did not die until mid-September, and during this period he was completely unable to fulfill his duties. In 1919, Woodrow Wilson had a nervous collapse in the summer and a stroke in the fall and was partially incapacitated for seven months. No one was sure about his condition, however, because his wife restricted access to him.

Under the amendment's provisions, the vice president becomes "acting president" if the president is found mentally or physically unfit to fulfill his duties. As the title suggests, the conferral of power is temporary; the president can resume office by giving Congress written notice of his recovery. If the vice president and other officials who determined the president unfit do not concur in his judgment that he has recovered, they can challenge his return to office by notifying Congress in writing. Then it falls to Congress to decide whether the president is capable of resuming his duties.

Reagan and then George W. Bush followed the spirit of this section. When each was undergoing surgery, they sent their respective vice presidents letters authorizing them to act as president while they were unconscious.

The issue of succession arose again after the terrorist attacks of 2001 when the Bush administration, just hours after the attack, activated an emergency plan established during the Eisenhower administration to provide for continuity of government in case of a nuclear attack. A shadow government of from seventy-five to one hundred senior executive branch officials (serving in a rotation system) were removed to a secret fortified location outside the capital where they lived and worked underground twenty-four hours a day. In the immediate months after the 9/11 attacks, Vice President Dick Cheney spent much of his time at undisclosed locations that the press referred to collectively as "the Bunker."

Power and Leadership

The foundation of presidential power lies in the formal duties assigned by the Constitution. It assigns the president four major areas of responsibility: administration, representing the nation, foreign policy, and military leadership. These duties are sometimes summarized by the four "chief" titles: chief executive, chief of state, chief diplomat, and commander in chief.[13] Collectively, they represent a towering set of responsibilities.

There are three other legal sources of presidential authority, two of which stem from the constitutional powers given to Congress and the courts. Congress has delegated, by law, some of its authority to the president (budget making, for example), and the federal courts have used their authority to interpret the meaning of the Constitution to validate other powers necessary for presidents to fulfill their formal duties. These are called implied or inherent powers because they are seen as natural extensions of authority granted by the Constitution. A third set of powers is informal and derived from the office itself and the person who serves. These powers expand and contract with each president and are dependent on his view of the office and his will to exercise all of its powers.

Although nineteenth-century scholars were inclined to describe our system as congressional government, today the focus is on the powers of the presidency and the expectation that whoever holds the office will be the face and voice of government. The office has grown through powers delegated by law or voluntarily ceded by Congress (foreign policy making during the Cold War and then in the war against terrorism), or assumed by default through congressional inaction. What the executive branch gained was not the simple sum of what the legislative branch lost, as if the president and Congress were contestants in a zero-sum game. Crises arose, presidential incumbents responded, and in the process they assumed powers of government never before exercised at the federal level. Indeed, several extraordinary extensions of presidential authority occurred in wartime or at a time of national crisis, including Lincoln's suspension of *habeas corpus* in the Civil War and, most recently, George W. Bush's authorization of wiretapping of domestic phone calls without court-issued warrants.

In this section, we look at how presidents use their constitutional authority, expanded powers, and national constituency to lead what some now call presidential government.[14]

Head of State

The president is the chief presiding officer or **head of government.** But in our form of republic, the head of government is also the **head of state** and the representative of the entire nation. This arrangement is not common among Western democracies, which treat the government as a separate entity, presided over by politicians and elected officials with partisan interests. The state is the embodiment of the nation itself—the people and their history, traditions, flag, and other symbols—and in most other nations, its representative (an elder statesman, a king or queen) is assumed to be above partisan politics. The unifying, nonpolitical nature of the role of head of state is the reason why some democracies choose to separate this office from that of head of government. The latter is usually filled by the leader of a political party (in Great Britain, for example, the prime minister), who is by definition partisan.

In the United States, the president serves in both roles. As head of government, he is the leader of a political party with a partisan agenda. But as head of state, the president serves as the official representative of the country and of all the people. His office symbolizes the collective unity and identity of the nation. The fusion of these two offices gives the American president a political advantage that leaders of other Western governments do not have. Members of Congress, the press, or the public who may attack him freely in his partisan role as head of government usually show more—some say too much—deference when the president is acting in his capacity as head of state. When he stands in public behind the Great Seal of the United States of America, he is not just a party leader who was elected to govern but a nonpartisan representative of all the people, entrusted with the symbols, emblems, and traditions of the country.

The president's duties as head of state include serving as the official representative of the United States at a variety of state and ceremonial occasions both at home and abroad. It could be opening the baseball season; lighting the White House Christmas tree; attending the swearing in, coronation, or funeral of a foreign head of state; or serving as official greeter when a foreign leader visits this country. The head of state is also empowered to take actions that symbolize national sentiment, such as issuing proclamations to commemorate events, or making gestures that express a humane national spirit, as in the granting of reprieves and pardons to people convicted of federal crimes. The president's role as unifier of the nation was acted out by Bill Clinton in leading the national mourning for victims of the bombing of the federal building in Oklahoma City and by George W. Bush participating in a memorial service at Washington's National Cathedral for the victims of 9/11.

As head of state, the president is required by the Constitution to report to Congress "from time to time" about the "State of the Union." There is no required form for these reports and Jefferson's practice of submitting it in writing—in the view that a personal address to Congress too closely resembled the monarch's speech that opens each session of the British Parliament—lasted for a hundred years. When Woodrow Wilson revived the practice of reporting in person, one senator labeled it a "cheap and tawdry imitation of English royalty."[15]

Today these addresses are televised and delivered in the House of Representatives before a joint session of Congress within several weeks of the opening of each congressional session. The president notes the successes of the past year, addresses problems, and outlines his policy agenda for the coming year. Part of the report deals with the mood of the country and identifies goals for maintaining or increasing national unity. These addresses are usually written from boilerplate and are rarely memorable; the "state of the union" is pronounced "strong," and Americans are reassured that they live in a great nation. An analysis of all state of the union addresses concluded that it is impossible for speechwriters to overuse "freedom" or references to the United States as "great" and "good."[16]

Even when presidents are mired in political controversy at the time of the speech—Nixon during the Watergate investigation or Clinton in 1998, delivering the State of the Union address just weeks after the revelation of allegations of personal wrongdoing—congressional leaders usually caution the membership to show respect to the person who is speaking in his constitutional role as head of state.

The chief-of-state role, then, confers political advantage and power as well as responsibilities. Through the power of pardon, the president can, on his own authority, erase the guilt and restore the civil rights of anyone convicted of a federal crime, except an impeached president. One of Lincoln's last acts, signed the day he was assassinated, was to pardon a Union Army deserter. Blanket pardons have been issued to Confederate Army veterans and Vietnam draft evaders, but most presidents have used the power to clear the names of offenders who have served their sentences. Using it to absolve government officials or persons convicted of crimes with political overtones can evoke strong public reactions. George H. Bush discovered this when he pardoned Reagan's secretary of defense and five other officials charged with or convicted of crimes related to the Iran-Contra scandal. So did Clinton, with his last-minute pardon of a fugitive commodities trader whose ex-wife was a large donor to the Democratic Party.

Hundreds of people appeal to the president for pardons every year. Although the president is not required to consult government lawyers or other law enforcement officials before granting pardons, he usually does. The overwhelming majority of requests are vetted by Department of Justice lawyers and refused.

Chief Executive

The one area where there is no doubt that the Founders expected the president to lead was in running the executive branch. The president's administrative duties are assigned by Article II's charge that "Executive power shall be invested in a President." The article has few specific provisions describing the president's administrative duties, but it does invest the president with the authority to demand written reports from his "principal officers." The Founders expected Congress to make policy and the president to administer it. But the Constitution assigns the office significant appointment and administrative powers and implies others.

Appointment

Although most of the staff in the executive branch are civil service appointees, the president nominates about three thousand people to civilian positions in the State Department and other federal agencies, two-thirds of whom do not require confirmation. Of the remaining one-third who do require formal approval by the Sen-

Teddy Roosevelt called the presidency a "bully pulpit" from which he could persuade both legislators and the public to support his programs.

Brown Brothers

At few times in American history have five ex-presidents been alive at once. This early 1990s photograph shows, from left, Richard Nixon (1969–1974), Gerald Ford (1974–1977), Jimmy Carter (1977–1981), Ronald Reagan (1981–1989), and George H.W. Bush (1989–1993).

ate, only about six hundred of the most important policy-making jobs—heads of regulatory agencies, boards and commissions, cabinet secretaries and ambassadors, and federal judges, for example—receive careful review.[17] For the highest-profile positions, such as the secretaries of state and defense, televised hearings are held prior to a confirmation vote in the Senate.

For decades, it was customary for the Senate, no matter which party controlled it, to approve the president's nominations to policy-making positions on the grounds that having won the election, he is entitled to surround himself with people who can help put his policies in place. But the highly partisan context of the Senate in the last several decades has weakened this tradition somewhat. In practice, the president's freedom to name people to some positions is limited by the custom of **senatorial courtesy.** This gives senators from the president's party a virtual veto over appointments to positions, including judicial appointments, in their states.

As the leader of his party, the president has a political (not governmental) obligation to help senators from his party get reelected. Thus he usually defers to their political needs and wishes when making federal appointments in their home states, even though doing so limits to some extent his freedom to choose.

Presidents have more latitude in nominating people to positions with national jurisdictions, such as cabinet posts and seats on regulatory boards and independent agencies. It has become customary to give preference in some appointments to people with politically useful backgrounds, such as naming a westerner secretary of the interior, a person with union

ties to be labor secretary, or a close associate of the president to be attorney general. But these considerations were never confining and, as traditions, are weakening.

The Office of Management and Budget not only proposes allocations for each department, agency, and program of the federal government but also monitors how and when executive branch agencies spend appropriated funds, their operating procedures, and the policies they develop. This gives the president an advantage over Congress, one that Reagan and George W. Bush used to great advantage. By appointing agency and department heads who oppose policies that he opposes but that Congress has funded, the president can issue directives that effectively bring policy implementation to a halt.

Removal Power

Although the power to remove appointees is not in the Constitution, presidents have it. Their power to name people they trust implies a power to remove those they find wanting, but because the power is not explicit, Congress has not always recognized it. The battle over removal powers was fought and largely won by Grover Cleveland, who on entering office in 1885 insisted on replacing many policy-making officials with his own appointees. He was challenged by the Senate, but he persevered. His persistence is credited with helping revitalize a presidency weakened by Andrew Johnson's impeachment.

In 1935, the Supreme Court refined this removal power by saying that presidents can remove appointees from purely administrative jobs but not from those with quasi-legislative and judicial responsibilities. This ruling protects many appointees, but distinguishing quasi-legislative and judicial positions from those with no policy-making authority can be subjective.[18]

There is no ambiguity, however, about a president's removal authority over people he has appointed to policy-making positions with fixed terms, such as regulatory boards and the Federal Reserve Board. Presidents *cannot* remove these people. To grant the president the power to remove federal judges would interfere with the system of checks and balances between the executive and judicial functions of government.

Of course, presidents can appoint and remove political aides and advisers on their White House staff at will; none of these appointments require Senate approval. Presidents also have wide latitude in replacing cabinet heads and some agency directors—even though these positions do require Senate confirmation—because they are seen as agents of presidential policy. This does not keep the Senate from trying at times to badger a president into firing one of his appointees, as it did repeatedly and unsuccessfully with Clinton's attorney general, Janet Reno. A president may give in for political reasons, but the Senate cannot compel him to do so.

Reorganizing Executive Branch Agencies

When the president enters office, a huge bureaucracy is already in place. Each new president has to be able to reorganize offices and agencies to fit his administrative and working style and to be consistent with the issue priorities he has set.[19] This can mean redrawing agency boundaries to promote coordination when actions overlap or duplicate each other. It may involve merging or abolishing offices or creating new ones.

Within the White House Office itself, the president has a fairly free hand to reshuffle staff and offices. But any major reorganization of government departments and agencies requires congressional approval. In the past, presidential reorganization plans went into effect absent a veto from either chamber. But approval is increasingly hard to win. Now every reorganization proposal is likely to get a thorough review in each house, and most are altered, sometimes severely.[20] When George W. Bush created the new cabinet-level Department of Homeland Security, reorganizing the jurisdictions of dozens of executive branch agencies, it required congressional approval. And because it required reassigning almost two hundred thousand federal employees, transferring funds, and authorizing new spending authority, this reorganization set up a classic turf battle, both within the bureaucracy and between the White House and Congress.

Inherent Administrative Powers

Because the Constitution charges the president with ensuring that "the laws be faithfully executed," the courts have ruled that the president has inherent power to take actions and issue orders to fulfill that duty. This gives the president the authority to issue directives or proclamations, called **executive orders,** that have the force of law and are therefore a form of legislative power residing in the executive branch. In arguing for these powers, presidents have claimed that Article II of the Constitution grants them inherent power to take whatever actions they judge to be in the nation's best interests as long as those actions are not prohibited by the Constitution or by law. The rationale is that Congress often lacks the expertise and ability to act quickly when technological or other developments require fast action and flexibility.[21] Recent examples of this use are the numerous Bush directives responding to problems created by the 9/11 attacks.[22]

The recording and numbering of executive orders did not begin until 1907, and although an effort was made to identify and retroactively number orders issued back to the Lincoln administration, it is uncertain how many have been issued over the years. Since 1946, Congress has required all executive orders, except those dealing with classified national security issues, to be published in the *Federal Register*.[23] Many of these orders have had a significant impact. Truman, for example, used an executive order to integrate the armed forces, Kennedy to end racial discrimination in public housing, and Lyndon Johnson to require affirmative action hiring by firms with federal contracts.

Presidents more commonly use executive orders to deal with organizational problems and internal procedures, but presidents also use them to implement the provisions of treaties and legislative statutes that are ambiguously stated (perhaps deliberately) by Congress. In fact, presidents have used executive orders to make policies opposed by congressional majorities. Reagan and both Bushes used this power to ban abortion counseling in federally financed clinics and financial aid to United Nations–sponsored family planning programs. Another significant use of executive orders is to manage the controversial system for classifying government documents and withholding information from the public.

Through the exercise of this inherent power of office, the presidency has acquired significant legislative authority. But executive orders are much more easily overridden than congressional acts; a president can rescind or countermand orders issued by a predecessor, as Clinton did with foreign aid restrictions on family planning and George W. Bush did with several of Clinton's environmental protection orders. Furthermore, the legality of executive orders can be challenged in federal court. Early in his presidency, George W. Bush ordered the posting of signs in union shops informing workers that they were not required to allow union dues to be withheld from their paychecks. A federal court ruled that this was a misuse of an executive order.

The president also has the power of **executive privilege,** the right of a president to refuse to make public some internal documents and private conversations. Since the 1970s, federal court rulings have argued that without such a privilege a president cannot fulfill his administrative duties because he would not be able to get full and frank advice from his aides. The courts have also ruled that the power is limited in scope rather than absolute but have not defined its limits, deferring that task to Congress. Congress has also refused to specify the limits of executive privilege, leaving it to the courts to resolve each invocation of privilege that the president and Congress cannot resolve.

In the landmark ruling ordering President Nixon to turn over tape recordings of Oval Office conversations to the Watergate special prosecutor (see "You Are There" in Chapter 2), the Supreme Court did establish that executive privilege cannot be invoked to withhold evidence material to an investigation of criminal wrongdoing. Similarly, it ruled against President Clinton when he invoked the privilege to prevent an aide from testifying before a grand jury about possible criminal wrongdoing.

However, the courts upheld Clinton's extension of executive privilege to his conversations about political strategy with his aides and to those between his aides and the first lady, who served as his political adviser and whom the courts had already recognized as serving in a quasi-official role. In 2002, President Bush took this power a step further when Congress, in its investigation of Enron's financial collapse, subpoenaed records of Vice President Cheney's meetings with executives from energy industries. The White House, claiming that executive privilege extended to the vice president, refused to turn over most of the documents, even after being ordered to do so by a federal court. On appeal, the administration's position was upheld and Congress never received most of the documents it subpoenaed, severely limiting its oversight capability.

Fiscal Leader

Another role of the president is to manage the budget. The Founders gave the House of Representatives the power to originate legislation having to do with revenue and budgets, the Senate the power to concur, dissent, or amend. All budget bills must be signed by the president, in the normal way.

For many years, the president had a negligible role in managing executive branch budgets. Federal agencies sent their budget requests directly to the House, unreviewed and unchanged by the White House. But by the end of World War I, a general awareness had developed that a larger government required better management. In the Budget and Accounting Act of 1921, Congress delegated important priority-setting and managerial responsibilities that have given presidents so inclined the opportunity to dominate budgetary politics.

The 1921 act requires the president to give Congress estimates of how much money will be needed to run the government during the next fiscal year. The president's annual budget message contains recommendations for how much money Congress should appropriate for every program funded by the national government. Formulating the message requires the White House to examine all agency budget requests and to decide which to support or reject. This exercise allows the president and his staff to begin the annual budget debate on their own terms.

Having the Office of Management and Budget (OMB) within the Executive Office of the President gives the president an edge in dealing with Congress on budget issues because its hundreds of experts work only for the president. Congress's nonpartisan budget office, the Congressional Budget Office (CBO), prepares budget reports that are regarded as substantially more reliable than those of the OMB, but the policy initiative lies with the OMB and the White House because they prepare the first budget draft. The annual budget is huge and hard to read and understand. Because the president presents it to Congress and the public, he has the opportunity to shape the debate on spending priorities.

The president's budget-writing power is one of the greatest sources of friction in relations between the executive and legislative branches. Little is possible without funding, so the stakes in the budget process are high. Presidents who are little interested in the details of domestic policy, such as Reagan and both Bushes, do not get maximum political leverage out of the budgetary powers Congress has delegated them. But a president whose strength lies in the mastery of detail may be able to use those powers, as Clinton did, to dominate budgetary politics and the debate over deficit reduction.

Presidents often cannot get the support they need to pass their draft budgets. Members of Congress have their own constituencies and careers and often serve them through pork barrel spending strongly opposed by the president (see the "Government Responsiveness" box in Chapter 10). For this reason all recent presidents, including George W. Bush, have asked Congress to give them line item veto authority; this would allow them to sign budget resolutions passed by Congress while striking from them all items (budget lines) they oppose, such as pork barrel projects. The line item veto would be an even further delegation of congressional authority to the executive branch. In addition it would give presidents much greater leverage in bargaining with Congress because they would have the power to strike or retain any special project members of Congress promise to their districts.

The delegation of budget authority to the president is partly responsible for the engorgement of the Executive Office of the President (EOP) and the growth of presidential power. But it carries political liabilities. Although Congress controls the purse strings—no money can be spent unless authorized by congressionally passed budget resolutions—the president as budget writer is held equally, and perhaps more, responsible for bad fiscal policy and budget deficits.

Legislative Leader

Part of the president's role is to work with Congress. How successful that work is depends on the leadership qualities of the president and the partisan composition in Congress. The Founders expected both Congress and the presidency to have significant policy-making powers and worked hard to balance these powers so that one branch did not dominate the other. Yet they described Congress and its powers first in the Constitution because they expected it to be the strongest branch of government.[24]

Divided Government

Presidential success in working with Congress is influenced strongly by whether Congress is controlled by the president's party or the opposition party. This explains why presidents usually take an active role in congressional campaigns. When one party controls the White House and another controls one or both houses of Congress, it is called **divided government.** The Founders made divided government possible by giving each branch its own powers and distinctive constituency and providing for different methods of election. This contrasts with parliamentary systems, in which voters elect members of the legislative branch, who in turn choose the head of government.

In the first half of the twentieth century, divided government did not occur very often. From 1900 to 1950, only four of twenty-six presidential and midterm elections resulted in divided government.[25] From 1952 to 2000, however, sixteen of twenty-five elections produced divided government. Even with Reagan's overwhelming victory in 1980, the Republicans captured only the Senate. Their dominance lasted until 1986, when the Democrats regained majority control. George H. Bush had to work with a Democratic Congress, and Clinton had a Republican-controlled Congress after 1994. In contrast, George W. Bush had a unified government for all but a few months of his first six years.

Some observers believe that divided government is at least partly responsible for the failure to solve many of the country's important problems. The term *gridlock* has often been applied to this policy stalemate. The president presents a program and Congress does not accept it, or Congress passes a bill and the president vetoes it. The result can be a lot of squabbling with few results. The especially bitter rivalry between the White House and Congress during the Clinton impeachment proceedings in 1998 brought legislative action to a standstill. But in times of national emergency, a divided Congress is not necessarily a barrier to action; witness the significant amount of legislation passed by Congress in the first months after 9/11 when the Senate briefly was controlled by the Democrats.

The impact of divided versus unified government on a president's reach can be seen in the difference between the Clinton and George W. Bush administrations. After early success when Congress was controlled by Democrats, Clinton had to modify almost all of his legislative proposals, such as welfare reform, to versions that would be accepted by Republicans after they gained control in 1995. He could not sustain any momentum in his legislative agenda because the Republican leadership tied up Congress with special investigations of the president's actions.

In contrast, when Bush worked with Republican majorities and a unified government, Democratic legislators were virtually shut out of all negotiations on final drafts of legislation and at times not allowed to bring their own bills to a vote. Bush's congressional liaisons were involved in the drafting and rewriting of administration-proposed legislation at all stages of the process. Furthermore, congressional oversight of executive agencies, especially those involved with military, foreign, environmental, and regulatory policies, came to a near halt. From the Clinton to the Bush administration, congressional limits on the president's legislative and budgetary powers all but evaporated. Thus unified government can expedite legislation but sometimes at the expense of congressional prerogatives and oversight.

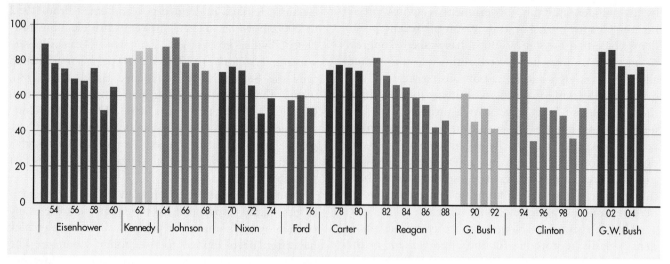

FIGURE 11.1 ■ Presidential Success on Congressional Votes

The graph indicates the percentage of the time in which the president got Congress to support his position in roll call votes. Presidents usually have the most success with Congress early in their first term.

SOURCE: *CQ Weekly,* January 9, 2006, 81.

Legislative Powers

Although conceived by the Founders as the head of the executive branch the president has many ways, in addition to his extragovernmental role as head of party, to exercise leadership over the legislative branch as well. These include agenda setting, shaping legislation, and the veto.

One way the president can wield influence over the legislative process is by setting the agenda. He is a single voice, one that commands media attention. Congress has many voices, divided among party leaders, committee leaders, and others who by their personality command attention. As the head of a political party with an issue agenda, the president has become the chief advocate of a legislative program. Whether packaged as the Square Deal, the New Deal, the Fair Deal, the New Frontier, or the Great Society, most presidents come to office with a legislative agenda. If a president is an effective salesman, he can have great influence over which bills are given priority in any session of Congress.

But a president cannot dictate what Congress spends its time on or which issues the public, media, and opinion elites talk about, especially if he gives the opposition a reason to change the subject. The Lewinsky scandal in the Clinton years, which the press, the public, and Congress found much more fascinating than policy issues, is a good example of this. And the catastrophic failure of the Iraq War policy made it almost impossible for Bush to focus public or congressional attention on any aspect of his legislative program. But if a president can clearly articulate his priorities and then stay on message and work to achieve those priorities, he can have a huge influence on what Congress—and the country—is focusing on.

Presidents can also have considerable influence over the final shape of legislation, but it depends on how active a role he wants to take and how involved he is in policy detail, as well as his knowledge of congressional operations and powers of persuasion. In all, twenty-four presidents have served in Congress and presumably understood how that institution works. Aside from their personal experience and knowledge, all presidents have advisers who serve as congressional liaisons; they lobby for the president's agenda and facilitate exchange of information with members of Congress on pending legislation.

Not all presidents who served in Congress were knowledgeable or effective. For example, Truman, Kennedy, and the first George Bush had short and undistinguished congressional careers, and Nixon used his short time in the House and Senate to build a national reputation rather than to sponsor legislation. In contrast, Gerald Ford and Lyndon Johnson rose to leadership positions through long years of congressional service. As a former Senate majority leader of legendary persuasiveness, Johnson is the classic example of the president as an inside dopester and congressional coalition builder. He knew how to approach members and was a masterful lobbyist.

Johnson was essentially a persuader and a deal maker, but sometimes White House staffers are more heavy-handed in seeking support. A Reagan aide described how the White House changed one senator's vote: "We just beat his brains out. We stood him in front of an open grave and told him he could jump in if he wanted" to oppose Reagan.[26] Such tactics can succeed but can also make a president look bad.

Reagan's leadership style in dealing with Congress involved going public to bring voter pressure to bear on members, while barely involving himself in policy detail. In contrast, Clinton, a legendary policy wonk, tried to generate congressional support for his policies by personally lobbying individual members and intermediaries such as business and union leaders and by trying to get backing in the parts of the country and from the interest groups most affected by the policies. He gave interviews to journalists whose papers and magazines reached people he wanted to influence. During his administration, the final versions of many pieces of legislation were worked out in direct negotiations between conference committee leaders and White House staffers or Clinton himself. Clinton was often criticized for having too much hands-on involvement with Congress because such a strategy invests the prestige of the office in too many issues while also risking the political capital of the president himself.

George W. Bush avoided this involvement in his first years, taking positions on far fewer issues and keeping a personal distance from Congress while relying to a great extent on Vice President Cheney to handle relationships with congressional leaders. Cheney served in the House and also worked as a legislative liaison when he was a White House staffer. Bush reportedly told one senator repeatedly, "When you're talking to Dick Cheney, you're talking to me."[27] As Bush had been a political enforcer in his father's administration, Cheney served as an enforcer for the younger Bush, using strong arm tactics when necessary to gain passage of bills on which Congress was evenly split.

No president has to rely solely on his persuasive powers to affect legislation. The Constitution has given the chief executive **veto power** over bills passed by Congress. The veto power is not listed among the president's formal powers in Article II but rather is included in Article I as a check on Congress's power to legislate.

When the president receives a bill passed by Congress, he has three options: he can sign it into law; he can veto it and send it back to Congress along with his objections; or he can take no action, in which case the bill becomes a law after ten congressional working days. An unsigned bill returned by the president can be passed into law if two-thirds of both houses vote to override the veto. But if Congress adjourns within ten working days after sending legislation to the White House and the president chooses to pocket the bill—that is, not to act on it—the legislation dies. This option, called a **pocket veto,** is a means by which the president can kill a bill without facing an override attempt in Congress.

Given the presence of White House supporters in Congress and the president's ability to go public, mobilizing two-thirds majorities in both houses to override a veto is usually very hard. As a result, presidents can try to influence the content of bills by threatening to veto them if they do not conform to presidential wishes.

Franklin Roosevelt, the longest-serving president, holds the record with 635 vetoes in fourteen years; only 9 were overridden. Presidents who use the veto too often may appear isolated or uncooperative or may seem to be exercising negative leadership. But the fact that presidents are rarely overridden reminds us of their power when they decide that they really want something.

Only eight presidents never vetoed a bill. George W. Bush did not use the veto until his sixth year, when Congress passed a bill to expand federal funding for embryonic stem cell research. His veto was upheld.

Success with Congress

Success in getting congressional support for the legislation he wants is an important indicator of the president's effectiveness with Congress, and early success can help presidents build their professional reputations. Franklin Roosevelt's ranking as one of our greatest presidents can be attributed in part to his legislative effectiveness. He was able to persuade Congress to enact much of his legislative program within the first one hundred days of his administration. Those were extraordinary times, and few presidents since have been able to match his success in Congress.

Reagan's effectiveness with Congress was greatest in his first year in office, when he got Congress to approve a major tax cut and increase military spending. Economic problems produced in part by these changes and a growing public awareness that he was uninformed about White House activities led to a drop in his effectiveness with Congress during the remainder of his administration. As Figure 11.1 shows, Reagan's congressional support fell after 1981 and was low compared with other presidents.

Congressional support for George H. W. Bush was weak throughout his term. His first-year success with Congress was the lowest of any elected president since 1953, when scores were first computed. Bush had fewer congressional Republicans to work with than any GOP president in the twentieth century, but he had low support even among them, in part because he

Teddy Roosevelt's presidency marked the emergence of the United States as a world power. Roosevelt built up the navy, as this illustration from the time portrays. He said the United States should wield "a big stick."

lacked a well-articulated legislative program. He also failed to capture the public's attention with clear themes, what he once called "the vision thing." This prevented Bush from securing more congressional support, even after the Persian Gulf War, when his popularity was very high.

Clinton tried to emulate Reagan's successful first-year strategy of asking Congress to vote on a few high-priority bills. This strategy lets presidents define their positions in relatively simple terms and seek congressional support during the postelection honeymoon period, before other influences on Congress have time to make mobilizing a majority more difficult.

With both houses of Congress controlled by Democratic majorities at the outset of his administration, Clinton did not have to deal with a divided government. Despite substantial disagreements among congressional Democrats, Clinton succeeded in getting majority support for most of his early economic proposals. His early legislative record was impressive, but it did not give him a reputation for effectiveness. It was overshadowed by the scandals that followed him into his second term and by his failure to articulate larger goals in a way that let the American people know where he wanted to lead them. In 1995 and 1999, he had the lowest success rates in Congress of any president in the second half of the century.

George W. Bush's first-year success rate of 87 percent was nearly identical to that of Clinton's first year. He achieved it by taking positions on only half as many bills as Clinton had. In addition, Bush usually

took a public stand only after Congress had drafted a bill in a form likely to pass.[28] With this strategy of doing and risking far less than his predecessor, Bush equaled Clinton's early success rate. He was also very successful in his second year, partly reflecting his post-9/11 public support. His success rate fell to a still impressive 79 percent in 2003 and hovered there well into his second term even though his public approval ratings had fallen by 50 to 60 points.

The relationship between president and Congress is a complex one. Ultimately, how persuasive a president is with Congress in getting his legislative agenda passed is an important element of whether he will be judged a successful president.

Diplomatic and Military Leader

Chief Diplomat

As head of state, the president is given ceremonial powers "to receive Ambassadors and other public Ministers." Ambassadors are individuals appointed by other nations to represent their country's interests in the United States. An ambassador must present his or her credentials to the president and have them accepted before taking up office. What appears to be a ceremonial duty has real potential for foreign policy making. Recognition is not automatic. The power to accept or reject foreign ambassadors, by extension, gives the president the power to decide which governments the United States will recognize and which will be shut out. We did not recognize the Soviet government until sixteen years after the Bolshevik Revolution of 1917 or that of the Communist government of mainland China until more than twenty-five years after it took power.

As chief diplomat, the president also appoints ambassadors and consuls to represent us abroad, subject to Senate approval. But he frequently conducts diplomacy directly with other heads of state or governments, such as at summit conferences where leaders gather to discuss economic, trade, environmental, or arms issues. The president can negotiate treaties and trade deals, although the former must be ratified by the Senate and the latter approved by both chambers, except where Congress has delegated authority to the president to negotiate trade agreements.

Some of these powers are implied in Article II of the Constitution and were acknowledged by the Supreme Court in a 1936 decision.[29] The Court said there is logic behind presidential power in foreign policy. A nation's government must be able to speak with one voice because having more than one voice could make it impossible for the government to represent its official policies and intentions to the rest of the world.

The president has an overwhelming advantage in shaping the foreign policy agenda. It is very difficult for Congress, with its 535 voices, to articulate coherent policy alternatives to the president's. Usually it is impossible even for the opposition party to unite behind an alternate policy.

The president has the advantage of being able to act decisively, whereas Congress must reach agreement and vote in order to act, and this takes time. And Congress may be reluctant to make prolonged or costly commitments against the public's wishes. When George W. Bush entered office committed to reasserting dominance over Congress in foreign policy, he unilaterally withdrew from prior treaty agreements, including those on antimissile defense and global warming, with only minimal consultation with Congress.

Members of Congress also are at a distinct disadvantage in having access to less information than the president. He can often stifle debate by citing classified or secret information from the CIA, Defense Department, State Department, and other agencies and saying, "If you knew what I knew, you would agree with me." And the president can bolster his position by making information available on a selective basis, sharing certain material with Congress (and the public) while withholding other material. In private, the president's advisers may advocate for conflicting policies, but most of these do not make it into the national debate, or at least not until after a policy has stalled or failed. Reasonable alternatives may never be mentioned in major media outlets, let alone debated by the public.

The information advantage was used to win public support for the 2003 invasion of Iraq. The president told Congress, and had his secretary of state tell the United Nations and the rest of the world, that Iraq possessed weapons of mass destruction. He also told them that Saddam Hussein was in large part responsible for the attacks of 9/11. Most of the public had no way of knowing that neither of these claims was true, or that intelligence officials did not agree with the assessment, until after the invasion when no weapons of mass destruction were found and investigations revealed that prewar intelligence had been cherry-picked by the Bush White House. Yet the claims the Bush administration made so dominated the public discussion that even into Bush's second term—and long after Bush himself had renounced his earlier claims—many Americans still believed that Saddam Hussein had played a role in 9/11.

The media did little to initiate discussion of our overall goals in either the Persian Gulf or Iraq wars, choosing instead to cover troop commitments largely as a logistical challenge and a human-interest story. Reporters' acceptance of Pentagon restrictions on news

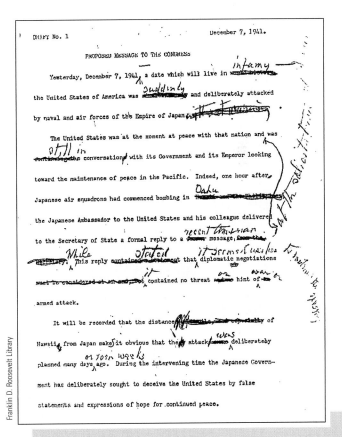

Franklin D. Roosevelt Library

As the nation's foreign policy leader, President Franklin Roosevelt edited his own speech to Congress about the Japanese attack on Pearl Harbor. He added the word infamy *that made memorable the phrase "a date which will live in infamy."*

gathering in the Gulf War also helped George H. Bush generate support for his policies by concealing information on the failures of so-called precision weaponry and on civilian casualties. His son's administration used an even more effective tactic in embedding reporters with combat units, tipping journalistic coverage to the soldiers', rather than an independent, perspective. Journalistic coverage was limited in other ways as well, such as by refusing photographers and camera crews access to soldiers' coffins being returned from Afghanistan and Iraq.

Commander in Chief

The president's military authority stems from his role as head of state and his foreign policy responsibilities. Because use of the military is sometimes necessary in the conduct of foreign policy and because the president sets foreign policy goals, the Founders made him **commander in chief.** In doing so, they were designating the president "first general" and "first admiral," as Hamilton wrote in *Federalist Paper 69*. In this way, the Constitution established the primacy of civilian over military authority; by holding the highest rank, the president can countermand the order of any military leader who is not executing defense or war policies as established by the president and his appointee, the secretary of defense.

But the Founders did not want to give the president the sole power to make war. In the words of Connecticut delegate (and later representative and senator) Roger Sherman, they believed "the Executive should be able to repel and not to commence war." The Founders, fearing that presidents, like the British kings from whom they had recently freed themselves, would be too eager to go to war gave Congress the power to declare war.[30] James Madison expressed the view of several of the Founders when he argued that "the executive is the branch of power most interested in war and most prone to it. [The Constitution] has, accordingly, with studied care, vested the question of war in the legislature."[31] The Founders therefore set up a system of checks and balances in military affairs; the president commands the troops, but Congress has the power to declare war and to decide whether to authorize funds to pay for it. Thomas Jefferson thought this arrangement would be an "effectual check to the dog of war, by transferring the power of letting him loose from the executive to the legislative body, from those who are to spend to those who are to pay."[32]

However, Congress's power to influence military policy is limited in emergency or crisis situations. When troops are deployed into combat areas Congress may hesitate to oppose the president because it fears

National Archives

As Commander in Chief, the president appoints military officers. During the Civil War, President Lincoln couldn't understand why the Union Army hadn't pressed its advantage over the Confederate army. When he visited the Antietam battlefield, he discovered that his top general, George McClellan, was both pro-Union and pro-slavery. Hoping for a stalemate in the war, McClellan tried to block Confederate advances but refused to rout Confederate troops. Lincoln replaced him.

As commander in chief, George W. Bush took America into a war with Iraq. This image is comprised of photos of the first 609 American troops killed there.

that doing so may be seen as disloyalty to the troops and by other nations as a sign of American weakness or lack of resolve. There is almost always a "rally 'round the flag" effect on the public when the president commits troops to combat. This advantage can be short-lived, however, as both George Bushes discovered. Presidents who take military action without a broad consensus need to accomplish their goals quickly or face loss of public support.

No *sitting* president has ever led troops into battle, but modern weaponry has led to more presidential involvement, especially in setting limits on the scope of battle. The decisions to wage limited wars in Korea and Vietnam, for example, were based on presidential beliefs that victories over North Korea and North Vietnam were not worth risking a nuclear holocaust. Under our Constitution, decisions on goals and containing the costs and consequences of war are for elected civilian leaders to make, not the professional military.

The development of high-tech weaponry has also given presidents more military leadership opportuni-

ties. Johnson and Nixon used sophisticated communications equipment to select targets in Vietnam. In the Persian Gulf War, Bush's White House sent orders to General Norman Schwarzkopf on everything from how to stop a blockade-running Iraqi tanker to when to end combat.[33] During the Iraq War, George W. Bush said he left the strategy entirely to the military commanders, but it was an open secret that many decisions, such as the number of combat troops committed and the types of units deployed, were made by Bush's secretary of defense, Donald Rumsfeld.[34]

War and presidential powers Despite congressional oversight of military policy, presidential power is wide ranging and sometimes extended to domestic affairs that presidents judge crucial to their national security goals. Historically, these powers have been exercised most extensively during wars endangering our national survival. During the Civil War, Lincoln suspended the use of writs of *habeas corpus,* seized control of some eastern railroads, and blockaded southern

The pivotal institution of the American government, the Presidency, has got out of control and badly needs new definition and restraint."[1] Those words were written in 1973 about the Nixon presidency, but it also sums up a now common assessment of the second Bush presidency.[2] Presidential historian Arthur Schlesinger coined the term **imperial presidency** for the Nixon administration, but he later wrote that Nixon's expansion of the office, rather than an aberration, was a culmination of the growth of the office since its creation. In fact their contemporaries wrote similar critiques about other presidents from John Adams to Lyndon Johnson.

But the Bush administration has expanded executive powers beyond any past administration. George W. Bush came into office believing that the inherent powers of the office had eroded to "an unsettling degree over the past thirty years." He said, "I have an obligation to make sure that the presidency remains robust and that the legislative branch doesn't end up running the executive branch."[3] He immediately began exploring how he could use the inherent powers of office, such as executive privilege and executive orders, to bolster the presidency against congressional and public scrutiny. In this Bush was in perfect harmony with his vice president, who was an opponent of openness in government laws and advocate of a strong and opaque presidency. He especially opposed congressional "overreaching" in foreign policy and interference with what he believed were powers reserved to the president.[4]

The national emergency precipitated by the 9/11 attacks gave the Bush administration new opportunities to claim more latitude for unilateral action as a "wartime" president. In planning a response immediately after the attacks, Vice President Cheney argued that if there was even a 1 percent chance that a person or a situation was a threat, the government had to act, a position later labeled "The One Percent Doctrine."[5]

Following Cheney's lead, Bush demanded the power to take any action he deemed necessary to protect the American people. According to then Senate Minority Leader Tom Daschle (D-S.D.), the draft resolution Bush sent to Congress three days after 9/11 asking for authority to use "all necessary and appropriate force" against al-Qaeda also asked Congress to endorse the same powers for use within the United States, but Congress refused.[6] In search of a legal basis for the actions they were already taking, Bush and Cheney requested administration lawyers for a reinterpretation of the constitutional and statutory limits on presidential exercise of powers.[7] Their unique reading of the powers assigned the president in Article II and implied by other sections of the constitution was called the New Paradigm.

Under the New Paradigm a president, using his powers as commander in chief, can take any action he deems necessary for national security reasons and take them unilaterally without oversight or restriction by Congress.[8] According to administration lawyers, the Founders, in giving Congress the power to declare war, were only making the technical point that war is made official by congressional declaration and that "unilateral presidential warmaking" is entirely consistent with the Constitution.[9]

Another key element of the New Paradigm is a very broad conception of the president's role as chief executive officer. In this reading, the constitution created a **unitary executive,** making the president sole head of the executive branch with authority to direct the work of all its employees without interference.[10]

If taken in the absolutist sense, the president could hire and fire at will, including members of the so-called independent agencies, and his directions to federal bureaucrats would supersede any directions sent them by Congress. Under the New Paradigm interpretation, the president is also within his rights to resist any congressional oversight he believes interferes with his constitutional responsibilities as he, not the federal courts, interpret them. Thus, because the Pentagon and all intelligence agencies are in the executive branch, the president has the power to collect any kind of intelligence, open mail and e-mail, look at bank accounts, seize library records, and wiretap phone calls as he sees fit.

This complements the claim to unilateral war-making powers that allow him, on his own authority, to declare any person an enemy combatant, hold them for any length of time without bringing charges or allowing access to lawyers or courts, have them interrogated under rules he sets independently of international laws and treaties the U.S. has signed, and establish tribunals outside the military justice system to try detainees. The president can do this, according to New Paradigm reasoning, without court or congressional oversight—except when the president chooses to brief members of Congress on whatever aspects of a program he chooses to reveal.

Applying the unitary executive principle to domestic policy, Bush attached statements to congressional legislation that outlined his understanding of their content and his intentions for their implementation. Known as **signing statements**, these written comments are deposited with new laws and recorded in the *Federal Register*. Other presidents have made limited use of signing statements, primarily to clarify their understanding of vague language or constitutionally ambiguous provisions in a bill should it later be contested in the courts. But Bush attached signing statements to 1 out of 10—or more than 750—laws during his first five years in office. These were not limited to foreign and military policy but included bills on "affirmative action, immigration, whistleblower protections, and safeguards against political interference in federally funded research."[11] In some instances he exempted himself from a president's constitutional obligation to provide information to congressional oversight committees. Going a step further, Bush applied the same no-need-to-comply rule to laws passed before he became president if he determined they interfered with his executive powers.

Some of Bush's signing statements were de facto declarations of his intention not to enforce, in whole or in part, the law he was signing, on the grounds that as chief executive he had final authority to instruct executive branch agencies how to carry out laws. This is a rare, if not to say bizarre, interpretation of the president's role as chief executive, which the constitution defines as to "faithfully execute" laws passed by Congress. The only power the Constitution gives a president to block congressional legislation is the veto. But vetoes can be overridden, reveal party disunity, and make public which laws the president opposes. By use of the signing statement, Bush was able, for example, to sign into law a bill forbidding the use of torture while at the same time attaching a statement—one that no one in the public would read—saying he had no intention of enforcing the legislation when he thought it interfered with his powers as commander in chief.

Under the New Paradigm, according to one Republican legal adviser, Bush has "staked out powers that are a universe beyond any other administration."[12] His use of signing statements, "is an attempt . . . to have the final word on his own constitutional powers, which eliminates the checks and balances that keep the country a democracy."[13] Yet because the security threat the country faces is very real, most members of Congress went along with most of the president's demands. In the political climate created by a direct attack on the country and significant loss of lives, the Republican leadership in Congress was reluctant to exercise its oversight of executive branch actions, and it was just as reluctant five years later. Frustrated critics in Congress charged that Bush acted as if the system of checks and balances did not exist.

Wars and crises situations are always temptations for a president who believes his office is not as strong as he wants it to be or believes it needs to be to meet a crisis. This has been strengthened by the evolution of a personal presidency and the public tendency to look first to the president to act rather than to government as a whole. The ability of the president to command the stage in these situations may in turn tempt Congress to abdicate its constitutional obligations, especially in a unified government.

Historically, when presidents have used war or other national crises to justify expansion of their powers, the separation of powers reasserted itself when the crises eased. But the powers that Bush has claimed for his office present a greater threat to maintaining three coequal branches because the "war on terrorism," as he defined it, could last into the indefinite future.

In these situations the greatest check on the president is the public because it is precisely the people, or public opinion, that the president uses to gain leverage over the other two branches. But the public, too, in these situations often forgets Benjamin Franklin's admonition: "Those who would give up essential liberty to purchase a little temporary safety, deserve neither liberty nor safety."

[1]Arthur Schlesinger, Jr. *The Imperial Presidency* (Boston: Houghton Mifflin, 1973), x.
[2]For a Libertarian assessment see George Healey and Timothy Lynch, "Power Surge: the Constitutional Record of George W. Bush, "(Washington, D.C.: Cato Institute 2006); classical conservative opposition can be read in the *National Review*, especially essays by its founder, William S. Buckley; for a liberal view within Congress see Henry Waxman's report to the Committee on Government Reform, "Secrecy in the Bush Administration" at the website of the committee's Democrats (www.democrats.reform.house.gov); for an academic treatment see Andrew Ludaveglie, *The New Imperial Presidency* (Ann Arbor: University of Michigan, 2005), ch. 7 and 8, 211–285.
[3]Quoted in Bill Straub, "A Debate Concerning the Use or Abuse of Presidential Powers," *Champaign-Urbana News-Gazette*, May 15, 2002, B5.
[4]Cheney's paper, "Congressional Overreaching in Foreign Policy," American Enterprise Institute, 1989, is cited in Paul Starobin, "Long Live the King!" *National Journal*, February 18, 2006, 25.
[5]Ron Suskind, *The One Percent Doctrine: Deep Inside America's Pursuit of Its Enemies Since 9/11* (New York: Simon & Schuster, 2006), 65.
[6]Elizabeth Drew, "Power Grab," *The New York Review of Books* 53: 11, June 22, 2006.
[7]The two principals were long-time Cheney aide, David Addington, who became Cheney's chief of staff when Lewis Libby was indicted on obstruction of justice charges in 2006, and Deputy Assistant Attorney General John Yoo, later a Law Professor at University of California Berkeley, who elaborated on his ideas in *The Powers of War and Peace: The Constitution and Foreign Affairs After 9/11* (University of Chicago Press, 2005). For others involved see Keith Perine, "Imbalance of Power," *CQ Weekly*, February 27, 2006, 545.
[8]Jane Mayer, "The Hidden Power," *The New Yorker*, July 3, 2006, 44.
[9]"Long Live the King," 26.
[10]Charlie Savage, "Bush Challenges Hundreds of Laws: President Cites Powers of his Office, *Boston Globe*, April 30, 2006, A1; "Power Grab."
[11]"Bush Challenges Hundreds of Laws,"A1.
[12]Bruce Fein, former associate deputy attorney general in the Reagan administration, quoted in "The Hidden Power," 46.
[13]Bruce Fein quoted in "Bush Challenges Hundreds of Laws," A1.

ports. He took these actions as commander in chief and without congressional authorization. The survival of the Union was at stake, and Lincoln believed that he had to take extraordinary measures. Because many in Congress agreed with him, he was able to do what he thought necessary.

Acting under his expansive definition of commander in chief, Franklin Roosevelt put one hundred thousand Americans of Japanese descent into camps during World War II. He had the government seize and operate more than sixty industries important to the war effort and vulnerable to union strikes. In addition, he created special agencies to control the consumption and price of gasoline, meat, shoes, and other goods.

Wars that do not threaten our national survival tend not to generate high levels of support for executive actions. When Truman had his secretary of commerce seize most of the nation's steel mills during the Korean War to keep them operating in the face of a possible labor strike, one of the steel companies took him to court. In 1952, the Supreme Court sided with the company by ruling that Truman had not exhausted other, legal remedies to the problem.[35] But Truman, a World War I infantry officer, exercised his power as commander in chief over General Douglas MacArthur, commander of U.S. and United Nations Forces in Korea, when he refused to carry out his orders to keep the war contained in Korea. Truman ordered MacArthur home, effectively ending his military career.

The war powers resolution The extent of the war-making power exercised by Presidents Johnson and Nixon during the undeclared war in Vietnam inspired the 1970s characterization of the presidency as "imperial" and led Congress to take action to limit the power of the president to take unilateral military action. In 1973, over Nixon's veto, Congress passed the **War Powers Resolution** to limit the president's ability to commit troops to combat. It says that the president can use troops abroad under three conditions: when Congress has declared war, when Congress has given him specific authority to do so, or when an attack on the United States or its military creates a national crisis. If a president commits troops under the third condition, he is supposed to consult with Congress beforehand, if possible, and notify it within forty-eight hours afterward. Unless Congress approves the use of troops, the president must withdraw them within sixty days, or ninety days if he needs more time to protect them. Congress can pass a concurrent resolution (not subject to presidential veto) at any time ordering the president to end the use of military force.

Every president since Nixon has believed the resolution violated his constitutional authority to protect the nation from military threats. Although presidents have not questioned Congress's constitutional authority to declare war, all have fought congressional involvement in the use of troops. As a result, enforcement of the act has proved difficult. For example, when George H. Bush sent troops to invade Panama in 1989, he did not even refer to the War Powers Resolution in the two-page letter he sent to Congress—sixty hours *after* the invasion began—justifying the invasion. He also ordered 250,000 troops to the Persian Gulf between August and November 1990 on his own authority and delayed announcing his decision to double this number until after the November elections. This kept the decision that changed our mission from defense (Operation Desert Shield) to offense (Operation Desert Storm) from coming to Congress until Bush had mobilized United States and world opinion and gained United Nations support. By the time Congress authorized using force in January 1991, the question of whether to do so was, practically speaking, already decided. The same can be said for George W. Bush's decision to invade Iraq in 2003. He reluctantly went to Congress for authorization, but the decision to invade had been made well before Congress consented.

Although the War Powers Resolution was not very effective in curtailing the president's dominance in military policy, the end of the Cold War did temporarily threaten the president's free hand in foreign policy. Without the threat of a challenging external enemy of superpower status, Congress was less willing to give the president the benefit of the doubt in major foreign policy initiatives, certainly not those involving a commitment of military forces. Clinton, the first post–Cold War president, was not able to count on congressional support even when he had committed troops, as in Bosnia and Haiti. In 2000, the Senate tried, and just narrowly failed, to use the War Powers Resolution to force Clinton to withdraw U.S. troops from the NATO contingent in Kosovo.

Party Leader

The fact that the president is the head of his party and chief advocate for its policy agenda is an important dimension of presidential power. As party leader, the president is an electoral adversary of members of the House and Senate who do not belong to his party. He can use his reputation and the weight of his office not only to challenge legislative priorities but also to try to unseat those who oppose them.

To improve the electoral chances of their party, presidents try to help recruit good candidates for House and Senate races. In addition, presidents help raise money by being the headliner at fundraising events and by staying on good terms with major contributors. They also send their aides around the country to help fellow Democrats or Republicans with their campaigns and sometimes even go themselves. Seeing presidents in person—seeing a little history in the making—is exciting, and they almost always draw a crowd and good media coverage. But the president usually tries to camouflage his role as party leader when trying to persuade people to support him or to vote for his party's candidates, because people are more likely to listen to a president when they see him as head of state.

Playing an active party role has a purpose: The more members of a president's party who sit in Congress, the more support he gets for his policies. However, a president's support, when he chooses to give it, is no guarantee of electoral success for congressional candidates, especially in off-year elections (see Table 11.1). Since 1934, the president's party has lost an average of twenty-six House and three Senate seats in off-year elections.

However, this trend no longer prevails, due to the increasing number of safe seats. District lines are drawn to protect incumbents, almost all of whom run for re-election, with a tremendous fundraising advantage. These factors help make candidates safe even when their presidential candidate loses or is unpopular at midterm. The 1998 election was the first off-year election since 1934 that the president's party had a net gain, and that feat was duplicated in 2002. In the 2006 midterm elections, the traditional pattern returned with the President's party losing seats in both chambers.

In presidential election years, the average gains for the winning presidential candidate's party in Congress are close to their losses in off-year elections: twenty in the House and three in the Senate. Again, these patterns are changing. In 1988 and 1992, the winning presidential party lost seats in Congress. In 2004, the winning presidential party gained the historical average in the Senate (three) but fell far below the historical average in the House.

The Ebb and Flow of Presidential Power

Today a person elected to the presidency is the recipient of the respect bestowed on the office itself: people stand when the president enters a room, "Hail to the Chief" is played when he appears on a dais or at ceremonial events, men and women in uniform salute him, he is surrounded by bodyguards and aides. He is almost universally regarded as the most powerful person in the world.

Though the constitutional powers of the president have not changed, over time there have been ebbs and

| TABLE 11.1 | The President's Tattered Coattails: Congressional Gains and Losses for the President's Party in Off–Year Elections |

Seats Gained or Lost by the President's Party

Year	President	House	Senate
1934	Roosevelt (D)	+9	+10
1938	Roosevelt (D)	−71	−6
1942	Roosevelt (D)	−45	−9
1946	Truman (D)	−55	−12
1950	Truman (D)	−29	−6
1954	Eisenhower (R)	−18	−1
1958	Eisenhower (R)	−47	−13
1962	Kennedy (D)	−4	+4
1966	Johnson (D)	−47	−3
1970	Nixon (R)	−12	+2
1974	Ford (R)	−48	−3
1978	Carter (D)	−11	−3
1982	Reagan (R)	−26	0
1986	Reagan (R)	−6	−8
1990	G. H. Bush (R)	−8	−1
1994	Clinton (D)	−52	−9
1998	Clinton (D)	+5	0
2002	G. W. Bush (R)	+6	+2
2006*	G. W. Bush	30	6
* Incomplete results of House races at time of publication			
Average, all off-year elections		−26	−3
Average, all presidential election years		+20	+3

SOURCES: *Congressional Quarterly Weekly Review*, various issues; Roger H. Davidson and Walter J. Oleszek, *Congress and Its Members*, 9th ed. (Washington, D.C.: CQ Press, 2004), 106.

flows in the aggressiveness with which presidents exercise their authority. Even though Congress has not declared war since 1941, presidents have used the commander-in-chief role as a pretext for expansion

Signaling the importance of Asia in U.S. foreign policy, Bill Clinton became the first president since Jimmy Carter to visit India, the world's second most populous country and an emerging nuclear power.

of executive powers (see the Government Responsiveness box). Woodrow Wilson got Congress to pass a law during World War I that permitted the arrest of anyone who spoke publicly against the war or conscription. It was used to imprison third-party presidential candidate Eugene Debs for three years, and for internment of American citizens without indictments or trials and confiscation of their property.

Some presidents have become so frustrated by limitations on their power that they try to overcome those limitations by exceeding their constitutional authority. The most famous example of illegal presidential action in the face of perceived frustration was Nixon's attempt to gather intelligence on his political opponents by invading their personal privacy with phone taps, break-ins, and unauthorized reviews of income tax returns and then obstructing justice by trying to cover up evidence of these acts.

In the last quarter of the twentieth century, however, the power of the presidency appeared to wane. The decline began in reaction to the sometimes arrogant exercise of power during the Johnson and Nixon administrations, especially with respect to the conduct of the Vietnam War and abuses of the electoral process during Nixon's reelection campaign. Reagan's personal popularity and his conception of the presidency—emphasizing the head-of-state and symbolic roles of the office over governance—restored some of the prestige

or grandeur of the presidency, but the illegalities of the Iran-Contra affair and ethics scandals involving his appointees eroded public confidence again.

The end of the Cold War also restricted the president's freedom to act unilaterally in international affairs and reduced his role as a rally figure to mobilize public opinion against foreign enemies. In domestic affairs, decades of budget deficits, the return of many responsibilities to the states, and a tendency toward downsizing national government limited how much the president could credibly promise or deliver to the American public. Under Clinton, the personal presidency seemed to be imploding as he tried to work with a congressional leadership that was diametrically opposed to him and his policies. Six years of ethics investigations, a record number of special prosecutors, sensational headlines, and constant scrutiny of the first family's personal lives all contributed to the diminution of the office.

Some historians and analysts felt that Clinton's impeachment would be similar in impact to Andrew Johnson's, which weakened the presidency for the next half-century.[36] This argument is based in large part on precedents set by federal court decisions issued during the investigation. These rulings limited a president's ability to use executive privilege to deny Congress access to records of conversations he has with his advisers and to exercise attorney-client privilege to protect such records in cases in which the advice is provided by government lawyers. The court also allowed Secret Service agents to testify before grand juries about the president's activities, including his personal conduct. But perhaps most important was the court's ruling that a sitting president can be sued for private conduct that occurred before he took office. In this last decision, judges reasoned that it was unlikely that the need to defend himself in a civil suit would divert a president's time and energy from carrying out his duties. This was a colossal misjudgment insofar as the case in the sexual harassment suit brought against Clinton was concerned. It not only consumed the time and attention of the president but also diverted much of the attention of many Washingtonians. Critics of the decision wondered whether the filing of civil suits would become one more maneuver to hamstring the presidency. However, Clinton's personal conduct probably did far more damage to his professional reputation and legacy than to the office of president.[37]

George W. Bush's ability to restore power drained from the office during the Clinton years and to add to it immeasurably illustrates the elasticity of presidential power. Bush used executive privilege to shield the office from congressional and public scrutiny and his inherent legislative authority to repeal policies of the Clinton administration. A compliant Congress went along. It is likely that Bush's early successes resulted from a convergence of his will to reassert the powers of the presidency and the opportunity handed to him by a national emergency to do so. Under President Bush we returned to concern about an overly activist president, as he wielded his expanded powers to erode civil liberties and reduce government transparency.

Presidential Staff

George Washington paid a nephew out of his own pocket to be his only full-time aide, and Jefferson had only four cabinet officers to advise him. Congress did not appropriate funds for a presidential clerk until 1857, and even then Lincoln, with a staff of four, opened and answered much of the daily mail himself. The telephone was introduced in the White House in 1879, and in the 1880s Grover Cleveland was still answering it himself. Even in the early twentieth century, Woodrow Wilson typed many of his own speeches.[38] We can think back wistfully to those days, but it was not just another time but a very different country. As just one example, Jefferson oversaw a military establishment of about 6500, whereas President Bush commands more than two million troops and sailors.

As the work of the president has expanded, staff size has exploded. Today, as presiding officer of the ex-ecutive branch, the president heads, in addition to the military, a civilian bureaucracy of fifteen cabinet departments and 2.7 million civil servants (their work is described in Chapter 12). To carry out the day-to-day duties of his office, he has a large staff of policy specialists and liaisons to Congress and federal agencies.

Executive Office of the President

The bureaucracy that surrounds the modern president had its origins in the administration of Franklin Roosevelt. Because his small staff was overwhelmed by the workload of administering New Deal agencies and programs, FDR called in a team of public administration experts to help restructure his office. Congress resisted this expansion of the office for two years but in 1939 finally passed the statute creating the Executive Office of the President (EOP), and with it the White House Office.[39] Some presidential scholars see this act as codifying changes that established "the president, rather than the parties and Congress," as "the principal agent of popular government in the United States."[40]

Lyndon B. Johnson Library

President Johnson worked continuously. When he awoke, he read newspapers, ate breakfast, and met with his staff all before getting out of bed.

President Kennedy's closest adviser was his brother Robert (right), whom he appointed attorney general.

The EOP is essentially the president's personal bureaucracy, sitting atop the executive branch and monitoring the work done in cabinet departments and agencies to see that the president's policies are carried out. Many EOP staffers are career civil servants, but the president appoints those who fill the top policy-making positions. Since FDR's administration, the EOP has been reorganized many times to reflect changing national problems and the issue priorities of individual presidents. It is not a single office but a group of offices, councils, and boards devoted to specific functional or issue areas such as national security, trade, the budget, drug abuse, the economy, and the environment.

The OMB, which has its own eight-story building, accounts for a large part of the growth in the president's bureaucracy. It is the successor agency to the Bureau of the Budget (BOB), which was created in 1921 as the primary tool for developing budget policy after Congress delegated this authority to the president. Nixon changed the name to the Office of Management and Budget to stress its function of helping the president oversee other executive branch agencies.

The EOP continued to grow in size from the 1930s to more than seventeen hundred people in George H. Bush's administration, then shrank somewhat when Clinton attempted to downsize govern-

ment. The influence of other EOP heads varies with the president's issue priorities, but the head of OMB is almost always influential.[41]

White House Office

Members of the White House staff have greater influence than most advisers because the president appoints all of them, works daily with them, and tends to trust them more than others. They are often people who helped him get elected or worked for him when he held other offices. Many presidents have counted their wives among their closest advisers, and every first lady has her own office and staff within the Office of the White House. (See the box "The First Lady: A Twofer?")

Jimmy Carter and Bill Clinton are notable among recent presidents for their degree of reliance on their wives and other longtime associates. Unlike Kennedy, Nixon, Johnson, and the first George Bush, neither Carter nor Clinton had experience in Washington, and they filled their top staff positions with old friends and political operatives from their respective home states, Georgia and Arkansas. George H. Bush was a consummate Washington insider but relied heavily on his fellow Texan and longtime friend James Baker to serve on the White House staff, in the cabinet, and as his campaign manager. Of recent presidents, Ronald Reagan, who had no close personal friends in politics, was the only one not to fill his top staff positions with long-time friends and close associates.

George W. Bush's initial appointments were notable for their insider backgrounds; three-quarters had previous Washington experience, and 43 percent had served in his father's administration. His closest advisers, Karl Rove and Karen Hughes, had worked for him in Texas, and his first chief of staff, Andrew Card, and national security adviser, Condoleezza Rice, worked in his father's administration.[42] Bush was said to be so close to Karen Hughes that she could finish his sentences.

Management of the White House staff varies with the president's personal style. Franklin Roosevelt and John Kennedy cared little for rigid lines of responsibility. They were more concerned with who could serve the president best; they gave staffers different jobs over time and fostered a competitive spirit. Lyndon Johnson's style was the archetype of aggressive, hands-on management. Known for his commitment to using all resources at his disposal to find government solutions to virtually every problem, Johnson was often accused of overworking and bullying his staff.[43]

Richard Nixon valued formal lines of authority. Nixon's chief of staff, H. R. Haldeman, saw his job this way: "Every president needs a son of a bitch, and I'm Nixon's. I'm his buffer and his bastard. I get done what he wants done and I take the heat instead of him."[44] Part of Nixon's approach was to be reclusive and keep his cards close to his vest. He demanded at least two days a week when he would see no one so he could work in seclusion; even his closest staff often did not know what he was working on.[45]

The Watergate scandal led Presidents Ford and Carter to avoid the appearance of strong staff chiefs. Reagan prided himself on delegating authority to the best people and letting them do their work without interference.[46] Serious problems developed, however, because no one had authority to make final decisions on more important matters, and Reagan was too removed from daily affairs to do so. This detached management style had its costs, most noticeably the Iran-Contra scandal.[47] To compensate for his detachment, Reagan appointed a series of strong staff chiefs whose coordination of White House operations helped restore his image.

Clinton's appointment of many staffers with little Washington experience and diverse policy positions showed his determination to immerse himself in policy details and to be the final arbiter of many competing views. He directed his first staff chief to channel all paperwork to him. However, running the White House this way made it difficult for Clinton to keep his and the nation's focus on important issues. He got so bogged down in details that his wife complained that he had become the "mechanic-in-chief."[48] In addition, a young, unruly staff and Clinton's penchant for sitting up all night with them talking issues and policy were taken by some as symptomatic of a chaotic and disorganized management style.[49] Under Clinton's second and third staff chiefs, lines of authority and communication were tightened. But his White House operation still reflected his love of policy details and an inability to maintain a schedule and stick to a few clear policy themes when communicating with the public and the media.

George W. Bush employed a near-opposite approach to management. With experience as an enforcer of political loyalties on his father's staff, and as the only president to hold a master of business administration degree, Bush set out to run his White House along corporate lines. He tried to delegate work along crisp lines of authority, kept to a tight schedule, and demanded complete team loyalty with no public dissent from administration policy.[50] The deeper he got into his term, as his policies played out, he found what most presidents find: that it is impossible to keep rivalries and dissident policy positions from emerging, even among close advisers. The most noted negative relationship among Bush's appointees was that between his Secretary of Defense Donald Rumsfeld and his first Secretary of State Colin Powell, who had disagreements over the use of intelligence and the conduct of the war in Iraq.

Bush also delegated so much policy responsibility that his first secretary of the treasury said that in cabinet and private meetings, he seemed disengaged and uninformed on issues.[51] With the parallel power base established by his vice president (see the next section) and Rove's reputation as the key political strategist (nicknamed "Bush's Brain"), Bush sometimes appeared to be a secondary figure in his own administration. Bush's press staff had to work hard to convince the public that the president was in charge of the White House, and the president himself frequently reminded the press corps that he was "the decider."

Office of the Vice President

The Office of the Vice President was made part of the EOP in 1972. Not long afterward, the vice president got his own white mansion (the former home of the chief of naval operations) when the government decided that maintaining an official residence was much less expensive than paying for the necessary security arrangements on the homes of each new vice president.[52] The vice president, paid slightly more than $202,000 in 2006, has

The president's wife has always had to walk a fine line, presiding over state social functions and being supportive of her husband without looking as though she is politically out in front of him.[1] Concern over the influence and accountability of presidential spouses is as old as the republic. The first lady is not subject to congressional approval, but neither are the members of the White House staff or the president's close advisers outside government. But as Hillary Clinton discovered, first ladies are not immune from investigation of criminal wrongdoing, and when they serve by official appointment, as she did on the health care task force, they are subject to the same rules as other public officials. One early first lady, Louisa Adams, wife of John Quincy Adams, feeling hemmed in by the limits of acceptable behavior, titled her autobiography *The Adventures of a Nobody*.[2] Barbara Bush's chief of staff described the position as "filled with banana peels and land mines."[3]

There is no mention of a presidential spouse in the Constitution, and she has no official duties and no salary. Yet a president's wife is expected to serve as what Martha Washington called "the hostess of the nation."[4] Unmarried presidents have had to borrow a stand-in: the widower Thomas Jefferson often relied on Dolley Madison, the wife of his secretary of state and future president, James Madison.

In addition to an intense schedule of state social functions, the first lady must oversee the White House domestic staff. And it has become the custom for first ladies to identify causes, usually nonpartisan, on which they will focus special effort. Jacqueline Kennedy devoted herself to historic preservation, Lady Bird Johnson to environmental issues, Betty Ford to the creative arts and welfare of the elderly, Nancy Reagan to drug abuse prevention, Barbara and Laura Bush to literacy, and Hillary Rodham Clinton to child welfare. But it was not until 1978 that Congress made formal budgetary provisions for the Office of the First Lady as an official unit within the EOP's White House office.[5] Still without salary, she is entitled to a $20,000 annual pension.

The visibility of the first lady increased enormously after the arrival of photography in the mid-nineteenth century; mass-circulation newspapers and magazines provided new means for satisfying public curiosity about the president's private life. Early in the twentieth century, first ladies began accompanying their husbands at official functions.

With the era of television campaigns, the wives of presidential candidates began to figure much more prominently in campaign strategy. But behind the scenes, wives had long been involved. Much of the work organizing and financing Warren Harding's 1920 presidential campaign was done by his wife, Florence, which explains the widely repeated comment to her husband: "I got you the presidency; now what are you going to do with it?" Even first ladies not interested in electoral politics were used to great effect in getting votes. For example, Dwight Eisenhower considered his wife a better campaigner than he was, and Jacqueline Kennedy attained a level of popularity and celebrity that surpassed her husband's.

First ladies have been loved (Dolley Madison), feared (Abigail Adams, Edith Wilson), and both loved and feared (Eleanor Roosevelt). When John Adams's opponents referred to his wife as "Mrs. President," they meant something more than her marital status. Abigail Adams was an accomplished writer with strong political opinions and not afraid to express them (for example, that women would "foment a Rebellion" if made subject to laws without representation). Her views on women's rights and other issues, coupled with the fact that her long and happy marriage to John Adams made her his principal adviser, led both sup-porters and opponents of the president to believe that she might have "undue" influence on policy decisions.

Edith Wilson served what she called a "stewardship" (but what others called "bedside government") during a seven-month period when her husband was disabled by a stroke.[6] She decoded classified diplomatic and military messages, encoded presidential responses, controlled access to her husband, and kept information about his condition from the public.

Although many first ladies have been political advisers to their husbands, no one did it quite so publicly, or from such an independent platform, as Eleanor Roosevelt. She held press conferences for women journalists shut out of the president's briefings, wrote a syndicated newspaper column read by millions, and made regular radio broadcasts. She discussed policy with her husband, peppered him with memos, and brought supporters of the causes she advocated into the White House. She served on countless committees and traveled around the world promoting racial equality, women's and social justice issues, and the war effort. After her husband's death, she served as a delegate to the United Nations, where her efforts in support of human rights and international cooperation earned her the title "First Lady of the World."

Mrs. Roosevelt's stature was attained under the exceptional circumstances of her husband's long tenure in the White House during a prolonged period of national crisis. Furthermore, after his incapacitation from polio years earlier, FDR had become dependent on Eleanor to keep his political career afloat by serving as his stand-in and surrogate campaigner. In combination with their strained marriage, this meant that Mrs. Roosevelt entered the White House as much FDR's political partner as his wife. Although some thought her too powerful, Mrs. Roosevelt always deferred to her husband in joint appearances, saying it was the job of a wife to offer no personal opinions, limit her appearances, and "lean back in an open car so voters always see *him*."[7]

Most first ladies have not been traditional wives who limited themselves to the domestic sphere. And even those who did—Bess Truman, Mamie Eisenhower, Pat Nixon, and Barbara Bush—were not without influence on their husbands. Bess Truman was uninterested in Washington politics or social life and spent as much time as possible away from the capital. But Harry Truman still called her "the Boss" and said he frequently consulted her on the content of his speeches and in making important decisions.

Since the 1960s, strong-willed women have been the norm. Claudia ("Lady Bird") Johnson helped finance her husband's congressional campaigns and in his presidential race had her own campaign train to tour the South while her husband worked on in Washington. She is said to have greeted him in the evenings with the query, "Well, what did you do for women today?" Betty Ford was an outspoken supporter of the Equal Rights Amendment and abortion rights in defiance of her husband's party's position, and she argued for a salary for her successors as first lady. Her popularity often surpassed that of her husband. Rosalynn Carter sat in on cabinet meetings, had weekly policy lunches with her husband, met with foreign heads of state to discuss policy, chaired the Commission on Mental Health Reform, and was at

times derisively referred to as "copresident." Nancy Reagan, most often seen in public gazing adoringly at her husband, often controlled access to the Oval Office and weighed in on the hiring and firing of key advisers.

The term *copresident* was revived for Hillary Clinton, a lawyer and lobbyist for child welfare causes, who was one of her husband's closest advisers and strategists throughout his career in elective office while also serving as the family's principal wage earner. Shortly after her husband's inauguration she moved the first lady's office into the West Wing to be among the policymakers. She prompted greater opposition to first lady activism than anyone since Eleanor Roosevelt. In response, she retreated into a more traditional role before the 1996 reelection campaign. But in 2000, Mrs. Clinton became the first presidential wife to run for and win elective office.

It is increasingly likely that professional couples will be occupying the White House in this century. Laura Bush, who tried to follow her mother-in-law's example, illustrates how difficult it is to keep a first lady in the background. When her husband began stumbling at the polls during his reelection campaign, she became the "secret weapon" put out front to soften his rough edges. During most of Bush's second term, his wife's approval ratings were double his own.

When wives have played active roles in getting their husbands nomi-

nated and elected, it is likely that their advice will be sought after the election. And in most long and close marriages, it is natural for husbands and wives to become confidants and to rely on one another's judgment. Yet worry persists that the special nature of a marital relationship provides opportunities for influence—of the kind Betty Ford called "pillow talk"—unavailable to others. We frequently refer to lobbyists as "getting into bed" with politicians, but wives do not have to pay to get there, and if they are successful in changing their husband's views, it is not likely that money will have had anything to do with it.

[1]Much of the material in this box is drawn from Carol Chandler Waldrop, *Presidents' Wives: The Lives of 44 American Women of Strength* (Jefferson, N.C.: McFarland, 1989); Lewis L. Gould, ed., *American First Ladies* (New York: Garland, 1996); and Kati Marton, *Hidden Power The Impact of Presidential Marriages on Our Recent History* (New York: Pantheon, 2001).
[2]Edith P. Mayo, ed., *The Smithsonian Book of First Ladies* (Washington, D.C.: Smithsonian Institution, 1996), 11, 43.
[3]Henry Louis Gates Jr., "Hating Hillary," *New Yorker*, February 26, 1996, 121.
[4]Mayo, Smithsonian Book of First Ladies, 11.
[5]Gil Troy, *Affairs of State: The Rise and Rejection of the First Couple since World War II* (New York: Free Press, 1997), 250. Troy also discusses attempts at reorganizing the first lady's office. See especially 178–188 and 248–258.
[6]Phyllis Lee Levin, *Edith and Woodrow* (New York: Scribner, 2001).
[7]Carl Sferrazza Anthony, "The First Ladies: They've Come a Long Way, Martha," *Smithsonian*, October 1992, 150.

his own budget for office and staff (housed adjacent to the White House) and an official airplane (*Air Force Two*).

Jimmy Carter's vice president, Walter Mondale, said that the vice presidency is the only elective office that is part of both the executive and legislative branches and also one that neither branch wants anything to do with.[53] That vice presidents have succeeded to office unexpectedly nine times (following eight presidential deaths and one resignation) may be responsible for the growing importance of the office.[54] Most recent vice presidents have been seasoned public servants with considerable experience and personal records of achievement. That they were willing to take the job suggests that it has become more than "standby equipment," as Nelson Rockefeller once called it.

The only formal duties the vice president has are to preside over the Senate, cast tie-breaking votes, and succeed to the presidency should it be vacated. Historically, presidents gave their vice presidents little information and few opportunities to prepare for succession. Woodrow Wilson's vice president, Thomas R. Marshall, said that holding the job was like being "a man in a cataleptic fit. He cannot speak, he cannot move. He suffers no pain. He is perfectly conscious of all that goes on. But he has no part in it." Franklin Roosevelt's first vice president, John Nance Garner, was less elegant in observing that his job was not worth a "pitcher of warm piss."

Until recent times, presidents had difficulty delegating important jobs to their vice presidents. One reason is that vice presidential candidates have often been chosen to balance a ticket geographically and ideologically, and sometimes they are electoral opponents working to build an independent political base from which to run for the presidency. This has not always made them the most loyal supporters of the president's agenda.

Historically, vice presidents were asked to deal mainly with ceremonial matters or partisan activities (such as being the attack dog during the campaign, leaving his running mate free to appear more presidential). How much work and authority vice presidents have depends on the personal relationship with the president, how needy the president is for assistance, or how generous he is about sharing power. Jimmy Carter was the first president to delegate to his vice president responsibilities for day-to-day White House operations.[55] He gave Walter Mondale, who had the Washington experience Carter lacked, a White House office, scheduled weekly lunches with him, included him in all White House advisory groups and all important meetings, and asked him to lobby Congress and read the paperwork that crossed Carter's desk. Ronald Reagan, Bill Clinton, and both George Bushes added to this new tradition.

Prior to the Bush-Cheney administration, the closest working relationship between a president and vice president was undoubtedly that between Bill Clinton and Al Gore. Gore became so influential in the Clinton White House that he was referred to as a "shadow president" and his staff as a "shadow cabinet." Divisions did not surface until Gore was running his own presidential campaign and trying to distance himself in order to establish his own identity.

Richard Cheney was already well known to George W. Bush from service in his father's administration, and he had far more administrative and Washington experience than the new president. Cheney ran Bush's transition team and chose many members of the White House staff. He came to office with the goal of "merging" the vice president's office with the president's to create a "single Executive Office" in which the vice president would serve as the president's "executive and implementer."[56] He headed the most important policy-making groups in the White House and was the author of its energy policy. He also created his own national security staff, placed his own people in key defense and state department offices, and worked closely on military policy with his old friend Donald Rumsfeld, secretary of defense (a position Cheney had once filled). Cheney had unprecedented access to the Oval Office, meeting the president every morning and sometimes several times more during the day. He was also deeply involved in the president's legislative strategy and kept a constant presence on Capitol Hill through his role as Senate president.

President George W. Bush and Vice President Dick Cheney in sync.

He went to Capitol Hill at least once a week to meet with the Republican caucus and kept a working office there. For lobbying purposes, he also kept an office in the House of Representatives; he is the only vice president in history to have had an office in that chamber.

Well into Bush's second term, many observers continued to believe that the far more experienced and policy-savvy Cheney was running a large part of the White House operation, especially because it was consistent with Bush's preference for delegating work. But outperforming the president, setting policy directions, and serving as attack dog—Cheney won the nickname "Darth Vader" for his dark critiques of the opposition—had consequences for the vice president's political standing. Midway into Bush's second term, Cheney's approval ratings stood at 18 percent.[57]

The Personal Presidency

The Founders did not anticipate that the president would one day be the leader of a national party and directly accountable to the public. They envisioned a president chosen only indirectly by the people through the intermediary of the Electoral College. Now dependent on a national electorate, no president can be successful without constant exposure to the public or without a media strategy. To paraphrase a political pundit, the president does not have to be an effective leader, but he has, at least, to play one on TV.[58]

Our earliest presidents had little contact with the general public. George Washington and Thomas Jefferson averaged only three speeches a year to the public; John Adams averaged one. Adams spent eight months of his presidency at his Massachusetts home, avoiding Congress and the need to make a decision over involvement in a war between England and France.[59]

Abraham Lincoln thought it prudent to avoid giving speeches. He told people gathered at Gettysburg the night before his famous address, "I have no speech to make. In my position it is somewhat important that I should not say foolish things. It very often happens that the only way to help it is to say nothing at all."[60]

Franklin Roosevelt's **fireside chats** were the first presidential effort to use the media to speak directly and regularly to people in their homes. They helped make him, and his office, the most important link between people and government. In a personalized style, he began, "My friends." People gathered around their radios whenever he was on, and many felt he was talking directly to them. Whereas President Herbert Hoover had received an average of forty letters a day, Roosevelt, after beginning his so-called fireside chats, received four thousand letters a day.[61] He even received some addressed not to himself by name or position but simply to "My Friend, Washington, D.C." There has been no turning back from a president's need to forge a bond with the public.

Now when a president is not heard from frequently, the media begin to speculate about what is wrong. George W. Bush took heat from the press for giving few press conferences and for spending a total of 535 days at Camp David, his ranch in Texas, and his parents' home in Maine during his first three years in office.[62] But how often and under what circumstances a president wants to address the public—or his staff wants him to—depends in part on his communication skills. Ronald Reagan, often called the "Great Communicator," although he usually read from notes, spoke in public an average of two hundred times a year. Bill Clinton, considered one of the best extemporaneous speakers ever to occupy the White House, spoke in public an amazing 550 times a year.[63]

Political scientist Theodore Lowi believes that since the New Deal era, we have had what he calls a **personal presidency**.[64] He argues that consciously or unconsciously, the American people have had a "new social contract" with the president since the 1930s. In return for getting more power and support from us than we give to other government officials, the president is supposed to make sure we get what we want from government. The personal presidency ties government directly to the people and gives us someone to rally around during times of crisis. To the extent that it serves as a focal point for national unity, the personal presidency also contributes to our ability to achieve national goals.

Polls have consistently shown that Americans consider "leadership" very important in evaluating presidents.[65] Somewhat paradoxically in light of their fear of "big government," most people want a president who can get government to "do" things. Franklin Roosevelt was the first president to use survey data to identify public needs and to use the media to tell people that he would give them what they wanted. Making himself the major link between public opinion and government often enabled him to overcome the inertia and divisions associated with a system of fragmented powers.

However, Roosevelt's actions also revealed a cost of the personal presidency: presidents with great power often seek more. Roosevelt won reelection in 1936 by a landslide, confirming popular support for his New Deal. This led him to seek more power by trying to expand the size of an unfriendly Supreme Court so that he could appoint judges who supported him. He also tried to get local and state parties to nominate congressional candidates he favored by using federal funds as an inducement. The defeat of pro-Roosevelt congressional candidates in 1938 ruined both his plans. People did not want the Court politicized, and state and local parties wanted to pick their own nominees.

Nixon and Reagan also tried to override constitutional limitations on their power after their landslide reelections in 1972 and 1984, as evidenced in the

When President Franklin Roosevelt died, most Americans felt a personal loss. Here Chief Petty Officer Graham Jackson plays "Nearer My God to Thee" as the president's body is carried to the train that returned him to Washington for burial.

Watergate and Iran-Contra scandals. George W. Bush seized on the 9/11 attacks to declare a war on terrorism and to present himself as a wartime president. He used this status to make extraordinary claims of power for the presidency and ran his reelection campaign almost entirely on his policy on fighting terrorism. The success of his presidency hinged so much on his association with this issue that a prominent foreign policy columnist said he had become "addicted to 9/11"[66] (see the box "Government Responsiveness").

The use of real or perceived popular mandates to amass power in the Oval Office illustrates how the rise of the personal presidency has fed the expansion of the office. Practitioners of the personal presidency have sought more power to deliver on all the promises they make to win votes and campaign donations. They get caught in a cycle of seeking more power to honor past promises and then make more promises for which they need ever greater power to fulfill. Inevitably, most politicians promise more than they can deliver. George H. Bush promised to send astronauts to Mars, protect the environment, be the "education president," and do many other things while cutting the budget deficit without raising taxes.

After the Reagan and Bush administrations had doubled the national debt, promising *less* from government became the tactic of the personal presidency. So while Clinton also began by making promises and saying he wanted "to do it all as quick as we can," he started his second term by announcing that "the day of big government is over."[67]

Yet Clinton had his own angle on the personal presidency, an approach that is said to have "changed the very nature of what the public expects" of presidents. While deemphasizing big government, Clinton dwelt on "little initiatives," such as his proposal to adopt uniforms in public schools. These are what one of his top advisers called "kitchen table issues," problems such as the cost of gasoline and college tuition that families deal with on a daily basis and may discuss around the kitchen table.[68] Not only was Clinton extremely adept at speaking directly to people in a conversational style, but he projected an intimate knowledge of domestic, school, and community problems that were of great concern in everyday life. In the process, he projected a clear sense of empathy for people, as his physical gestures, such as frequent hugs, showed.

Every president since the 1960s has needed and sought media exposure and has in turn had to submit to intense scrutiny by media that delve into every detail of his personal life, as well as his performance of official duties. Few people can withstand such prolonged exposure without losing public esteem. The continuous congressional and special prosecutor investigations of Bill Clinton resulted in the media's being

saturated with the most graphic private and intimate details of a president's life ever revealed. "It is entirely possible," one reporter observed, "that the Clinton era will be remembered by historians primarily as the moment when the distance between the President and the public evaporated forever."[69]

Going Public

The strategy of making a direct presidential appeal to the people to gain cooperation from Congress and Washington power brokers is known as **going public**.[70] The strategy includes giving prime-time television and radio addresses, holding press conferences, making speeches at events around the country, and using satellite technology to give interviews to local television stations, conventions, and other audiences. These techniques have become so important to the success of a president's policies that he is now sometimes referred to as the "salesman in chief." This suggests that more than a good argument, well constructed and presented, is at the root of persuasion; the packaging of the argument has become as important as the argument itself.

Much depends on the president's own communication skills, but he is not out there alone. Every president has a large communications staff, led by a press secretary, to get his message out. The goal is usually to set a message for the day or week and to keep everyone on message. George H. Bush's use of the strategy of going public in garnering support for the Persian Gulf War was very skillful. He decided to use military force soon after Iraq invaded Kuwait in August 1990. Until January, when Congress approved this option, Bush made many speeches comparing Iraq's Saddam Hussein to Hitler, condemning his use of chemical and biological weapons on his own people, and warning that Iraq would soon have nuclear weapons. Bush's efforts won more public support for using force, which in turn made congressional support more likely.

George W. Bush, widely criticized for his poor command of the language, preferred to speak more informally in venues with carefully vetted groups of political supporters, where he was highly successful. His speechwriters turned Bush's speaking limitations into a virtue by cultivating a vernacular, everyman style. Bush's speeches usually consisted of short declarative sentences, with a single point, delivered in a slow, deliberate style, stressing each syllable for effect. The average sentence length of Bush's acceptance speech at the 2000 nominating convention was less than fifteen words. This compares to the average 104 words per sentence used by William Jennings Bryan, a man considered one of the greatest political orators of the late nineteenth century.[71]

Bush needed no strategy to win popular support for the military operation against al-Qaeda's base in Afghanistan because it followed a direct attack on the United States. But in trying to rally the public behind his goal of expanding the war to Iraq, he used a tactic similar to his father's, referring to Saddam Hussein as part of an "axis of evil." When the failures of the postwar strategy for nation building began to cut into public support, the administration tried to regain that support with a single, continuously repeated message about Iraq being essential to the victory in the war on terrorism.

Staying on message was something at which George W. Bush's administration was especially skilled; the television audience tuning in to morning or evening news programs or talk shows on any given day could hear administration officials delivering the same message in virtually the same words. The pressure of running such an operation is high, and most press secretaries do not stay long in their jobs. When Bush's first press secretary turned in his resignation after two years, he said he wanted to do "something more relaxing, like dismantling live nuclear weapons."[72]

The interdependent relationship between the president and the media creates tensions on both sides and sometimes leads presidents to blame the media rather than themselves for low poll scores. For example, Nixon claimed the media hounded him from office, Reagan said they exaggerated the importance of the Iran-Contra scandal, and Clinton complained they did not give him credit for his first-year accomplishments. "I have fought more damn battles than any president has in twenty years with the possible exception of Reagan's first budget and not gotten one damn bit of credit from the knee-jerk liberal press," Clinton said. "I am sick and tired of it, and you can put that in the damn article."[73]

Spectacle Presidency

An important part of going public is being seen as well as heard. And the important part of being seen is projecting an image that conveys the president's character and style. Presidents need to "make fully realized dramatic characters out of themselves, who exist in an intimate relationship with the voting public. The character has to bear some relation to the real person . . . but it is still a genuine act of creation."[74]

If a president fails to take charge of his image (as Bill Clinton did, for example), the press or his opponents will do it for him and in ways he will not like. Teddy Roosevelt was cast as the big-game hunter and Rough Rider, FDR as the jaunty optimist, Eisenhower as the peace-loving war hero, Kennedy as the youthful and athletic man of action and intellect. Ronald Reagan and George W. Bush were very successful in portraying themselves as dramatic characters. Reagan, an actor by profession, had little difficulty projecting an image as a rugged cowboy even though he had spent most of his life in Hollywood. Bush's persona as a Texas-style "good ole boy"—he wore cowboy boots to his inaugural and made sure the press got photographs of them—was mostly invented, and his "packaging" as a war leader was even more intentional. The staging by his press staff of the flight-suited commander in chief landing by fighter jet on an aircraft carrier and then speaking in front of a "mission accomplished" sign was one of the most dramatic image-creating photo opportunities in the history of the presidency.

The advantage of such bold efforts is that the visual image lingers. But that is also the disadvantage. Bush's public relations people announced the end of the war in Iraq far too soon, and the photo op came back to haunt Bush when critics later castigated him as a reckless rather than resolute war leader.

The increasing frequency of stage-managed photo ops, featuring the president in a dramatically staged event or setting, has led one scholar to proclaim the emergence of the **spectacle presidency.** He attributes this development to the "extreme personalization" of the presidency, people's excessive expectations of the president, and "the voluminous media coverage that fixes on presidents."[75] Of course, most public appearances by presidents are not intended as spectacle, although virtually all are staged.

The observation that "all politics is theater" is sometimes intended as ridicule, but settings and character presentation do matter. Few people are aware that the retiring and reticent Calvin Coolidge gave more press conferences per year than the much better packaged Franklin Roosevelt.[76] Not many people would guess that the reluctant president William Howard Taft did more trust-busting than the much more dramatic champion of the cause, Theodore Roosevelt. And the characterization of the Kennedy administration as "Camelot" left a lasting image of a tuxedoed president hosting glamorous White House

George W. Bush cultivated an image as a tough cowboy. This image proved quite popular with many people. However, as his administration's foreign policy failures mounted, the image became a liability.

galas for classical musicians and great intellects. In fact, Kennedy preferred listening to Frank Sinatra and reading Ian Fleming's James Bond books.

The President and Public Opinion

Americans pay more attention to the president than to other public officials, and we typically link government's success to the effectiveness of his leadership. Although many factors affect public opinion about presidential effectiveness, a positive image of a president's leadership skills helps protect his ratings after serious policy failures.

Many people are predisposed to support the president and to look at his overall record rather than the short term.[77] Failure on specific issues does not always produce low scores on general performance. For example, majorities of respondents simultaneously disapproved of Reagan's handling of environmental and foreign policy issues important to them, *and* registered approval of his overall performance.

Crises called *rally events* affect presidential popularity.[78] President Clinton's approval ratings increased after the bombing of the federal building in Okla-

homa City, and George W. Bush's rose by forty points after 9/11. Public support increases significantly at such times because people do not want to undermine the president, the symbol of national unity. However, the higher levels of support produced by rally events are rarely sustained long.[79] Support for the first President Bush's policies toward Iraq after its invasion of Kuwait followed this pattern. As indicated in Figure 11.2, this increasing support helped raise Bush's general approval ratings from 54 percent in October 1990 to 89 percent in February 1991, a month after the invasion.[80] However, the effect of the Gulf War faded as Americans began focusing on domestic concerns, especially economic problems. Bush's approval rating fell to 33 percent by mid-1992, leading to his defeat by Clinton in November.[81] In a near mirror pattern, George W. Bush's support fell from an astounding 90 percent after 9/11 to around 50 percent by the time of the 2004 election, and into the low 30s by 2006.

Clinton's up-and-down scores during his first term reflected public anxiety about his leadership skills. In 1995 polls, 56 percent of Americans described Clinton as a weak president, and 80 percent expected that the Republican Congress would have more influence than

Clinton on the nation's direction.[82] But Clinton was far more adept at going public than the Republican leadership, and by the end of his first term, his approval rating was at 53 percent and Congress was in legislative retreat.

When public anger and frustration with government are widespread, winning consistently good ratings is difficult. Although short-term crises or rally events can help a president's ratings, long-term conditions will continue to influence them more decisively. Clinton's 67 percent approval rating during the impeachment investigation may have been sparked by a public backlash against the salaciousness of congressional and media commentary, but it is more likely that he got a positive bounce from public confidence in the overall state of the economy.

The more important issue is whether a president with high approval ratings can translate them into policy successes. Reagan had only qualified success in using his popularity to get Congress to enact his legislative proposals. He relied heavily on his own appointment and budgetary powers and the issuing of executive orders to accomplish much of his agenda. The problem with this approach is that it is easily reversible by a successor. Clinton, with a substantial legislative agenda and higher sustained approval ratings than Reagan or either of the Bushes had late in their terms, was not able to translate his popular support into victories in Congress.

George W. Bush had a very limited legislative agenda, but he used his high post-9/11 approval ratings to win concessions of power from Congress and to push through billions of dollars worth of tax cuts at a time when he was doubling social spending and borrowing money to fight two wars.

Presidential Reputation

Every president develops a track record of his effectiveness as a leader, what Richard Neustadt calls the president's professional reputation.[83] A president with an effective reputation has a record of getting what he wants, helping his allies, and penalizing the opposition. This reputation contributes to his continuing ability to persuade the public, Congress, and other Washingtonians. Few modern presidents were more adept at getting what they wanted from Congress than Lyndon Johnson, yet Johnson is often not ranked among the great presidents, at least not by the public. A president's professional reputation is of great importance to him while he is in office and is a commentary on his political and administrative skills. But having the ability to get what he wants is not the same as being able to do what is best for the country, and therefore presidents seen as highly effective in office are not always judged by history to have been great presidents.

President as Persuader

As presidential scholar Richard Neustadt pointed out long ago, presidents use their communication skills for more than winning popular support. They must also have the power to persuade interest group leaders; newspaper and magazine publishers, reporters, and columnists; judges who hear challenges to their policies; leaders in the business community; and a majority in Congress. These policy makers and opinion elite, whom Neustadt called Washingtonians, are, in short, the people the president needs to get his policies

The public didn't always agree with President Reagan's views or policies, but he remained popular partly because of his image as a rugged individualist.

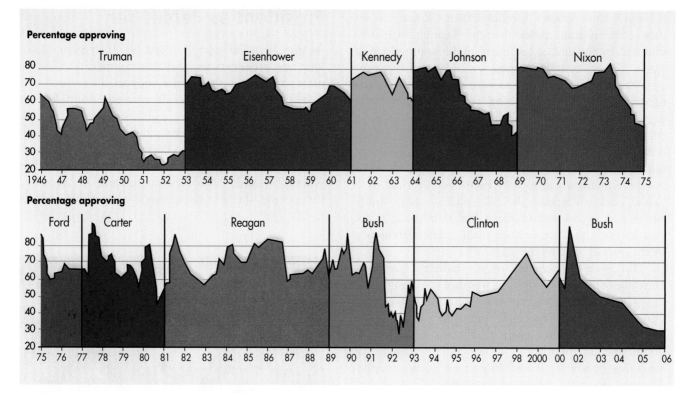

FIGURE 11.2 ■ Presidential Popularity

Since the end of World War II, presidential popularity has usually declined over time. Only three presidents—Eisenhower, Reagan, and Clinton—left office with ratings at a level comparable to that when they entered.

SOURCE: Gallup polls, reported in *Public Opinion* and updated at www.gallup.com. The question asked is, "Do you approve or disapprove of the way [name of president] is handling his job as president?" The 2006 approval rating for G. W. Bush is from CBS News/*New York Times* poll data.

enacted. Because the Washingtonians also need him to get what they want, a president can bargain and persuade.[84] Whoever his target, the president has numerous favors and penalties to dispense to enhance his persuasiveness, as party leader, budget maker, and chief executive branch employer. Presidents also use the prestige of their office as an instrument of persuasion. *Air Force One* is a favorite of all presidents for influencing anyone and everyone they want to sway with shows of the power of the office.

Neustadt believed the effective president was "one who seizes the center of the Washington bazaar and actively barters to build winning coalitions."[85] This is a conception limned from the careers of legendary persuaders and coalition builders such as FDR and Lyndon Johnson, who came up through the system of sweaty, smoke-filled rooms and face-to-face give and take. Recent presidents have been less earthy and further removed from their potential allies, and they may be as likely to use their persuasive power for fundraising as coalition building. But Neustadt wrote before the arrival of big money politics and the saturation media that give presidents uninterrupted access to the public. The Washingtonians most useful to presidents today are more likely to be K-Street lobbyists who are big campaign donors and whose powers to persuade

may be more important in getting legislation passed than the president's powers to persuade them.

George Bush's presidency may turn out to be transitional in its departure from the conventional methods of swaying Washingtonians. He has shunned the social settings—private dinner parties, embassy social events, and White House galas—most presidents have used for chatting up Washingtonians whose support they seek. Bush rarely entertained, went to bed at 9:30, and spent his time off out of town or mountain biking.

Presidential Character

Every president comes to office with a somewhat different view of the office and its reach and—depending on personality, talents, education, experience, and ideology—varying predispositions to exercise established powers or to expand them. The study of presidential character and personality is a subfield within presidential scholarship but one we only touch on in this survey chapter.[86]

How can presidential performance be measured? Neustadt has called the presidency a "choice-making machine," and presidents who can act decisively are often well regarded. Truman epitomized the decisive style and has probably benefited from the contrast with the more waffling approaches of recent presidents who are often seen as driven by polls and focus groups. "The Buck Stops Here" plaque that Truman kept on his desk illustrated both his sense of accountability and his no-nonsense rhetoric. In historical perspective, his leadership skills have looked more impressive than they did while he was in office, and this view has helped move him to the ranks of near-great presidents. (See the box "Rating the Presidents.")

It is not always immediately clear how deep an impact a president's tenure has had on the direction of the country, and assessments of presidential performance do change over time. Truman exemplifies a president who was unpopular during his tenure and in the immediate years afterward but who left a legacy of directness, personal integrity, and decisiveness on key decisions during an extremely difficult time (the national trauma of FDR's death while we were engaged in World War II).

Scholarly assessment of Eisenhower's administration has also changed significantly. Shortly after he left office, he was judged an average president, a good and honest man with strong administrative skills but one who took few chances and lacked an overall vision for the country. In retrospect, analysts regard as levelheaded and prescient both his leadership during an extremely volatile period in the nuclear arms race and his warnings about the dangers the military-industrial complex would present to the economy and our sense of national purpose.

Goals and Vision

In characterizing the role of the president, the nineteenth-century historian Henry Adams wrote that he "resembles the commander of a ship at sea. He must have a helm to grasp, a course to steer, a port to seek."[87]

That is, the incumbent must have a goal, a destination toward which he is leading the nation; he must have programs and a course of action to enable the nation to get there; and he must be willing and able to use the instruments of his office to reach that goal.

Franklin Roosevelt fit the definition of a great president as a leader "at times when certain ideas in the life of the nation had to be clarified."[88] This reminds us that an opportunity factor is involved in rising to the highest ranks of performance. The presidents FDR assessed as our best—"Washington [embodying] the idea of the federal union, Jefferson and Jackson the idea of democracy, Lincoln union and freedom"[89]—are men who served at critical times in the country's development. These are presidents whom almost all scholars rank among our greatest, and they are associated with ideas and policies that took root and affected the course of our country.

Any concept of presidential effectiveness inevitably involves vision. A president will likely be seen as effective only if he has a clear idea of where he wants to take the country. This is why Reagan is regarded by much of the public as a more effective president than George H. Bush, a man consistently described as lacking vision. To rank with the "greats," however, vision must be coupled with the political and administrative skills necessary to achieve it. In the scholarly consensus, Bush was willing and able to grab the helm but was steering to no port in particular; Reagan had a fixed destination but no firm hand on the helm and insufficient knowledge or interest to steer the ship. Like Bush, Reagan had a mediocre legislative record and an abysmal fiscal record, but in the public eye Reagan had a clear vision of what he wanted for the country. In contrast, Clinton had all the political and communication skills to steer the ship but was perceived as someone who kept changing his destination. He was unsuccessful

---

Rating the Presidents

In 2000, at C-SPAN's request, fifty-seven historians and presidential scholars rated the presidents on ten personal and professional qualities: economic management, moral authority, crisis leadership, public persuasion, relations with Congress, international relations, administrative skills, vision and agenda setting, pursuit of equal justice, and performance in the context of his time. Their overall ranking of the top ten and bottom five was arrived at by averaging those scores.

Top Ten (in rank order)

1. Abraham Lincoln
2. Franklin D. Roosevelt
3. George Washington
4. Theodore Roosevelt
5. Harry S. Truman
6. Woodrow Wilson
7. Thomas Jefferson
8. John F. Kennedy
9. Dwight D. Eisenhower
10. Lyndon B. Johnson

Bottom Five

41. William Henry Harrison
40. Warren G. Harding
39. Franklin Pierce
38. Andrew Johnson
37. James Buchanan

SOURCE: C-SPAN survey, 2000. Full results at www.americanpresidents.org.

in projecting to the public a clear and consistent vision of where the country should be headed.

In the early years of his presidency George W. Bush gave a clearer idea of what he wanted to do with the office of president than he did about where he wanted to lead the country. Early assessments were based almost entirely on how he handled the aftermath of the 9/11 attacks—both his policy response and his personal demeanor in projecting the national will. The public took his aggressive military posture as a sign of character and strong leadership and gave him high approval ratings, until disillusionment with the Iraq War set in. Up to that point Bush was very successful in turning the war against terrorism into a permanent crisis that allowed him to avoid congressional oversight of executive branch policies.

Conclusion: Is the Presidency Responsive?

The presidency has become the most consistently visible office in government as well as one of the most personalized and responsive. Americans expect leadership from the president even in these days of "less" government. The presidency is responsive in that whoever holds that office has an almost direct relationship with the public. Using the media, a skillful president can tell us what he wants and attempt to shape our opinion. Through public opinion polls and the ballot box, we tell the president what we think. In this relationship, there is a danger of overresponsiveness. To remain popular, a president may seek short-term solutions to the nation's problems and neglect long-term needs. And short-term responsiveness that caters to public opinion can siphon off the attention and resources a president should be devoting to the real needs of the nation.

Most recent presidents gradually came to understand the limits of presidential power, sometimes the hard way. Indeed, the moral of the personal presidency suggests that presidents who become popular by making exaggerated promises have trouble keeping both the promises and their popularity in this system of fragmented power. The Clinton years illustrated another danger of exercising the personal presidency in the age of tabloid media: the risk of diminishing the office when scrutiny of the occupant's private life overtakes evaluation of his public role.

One of the most interesting aspects of this unusual office is its resilience and elasticity. It can be stretched and shrunk from one administration to another or even within a single administration. Each occupant is likely to make something quite different of it than his predecessor, either by the attitude and skills he brings to it or because the times force him to do so.

Bush Spends Some Capital on Social Security

Shortly after being sworn in for his second term, President Bush mounted a campaign to change Social Security. With any legislation this controversial it has become common for presidents to go to the public first to build support for persuading Congress to accept it. Bush went on the road and over the following year traveled to dozens of towns, talking up his program in his standard venue, a kind of closed town meeting, with audiences and questions well-vetted by Bush's staff in advance of his taking the stage. In casual clothing, Bush would sit on a stool with microphone explaining the main features of his program, answering the screened questions, usually against a backdrop containing the catchwords for the publicity campaign.

But the few weeks of postelection confidence did not translate into postinaugural momentum. The Iraq War continued to go badly, and in the late summer of 2005, public attention was diverted by the colossally inadequate government response to hurricane Katrina, one of the worst natural disasters in the history of the country. Close on its heels came the introduction of the huge, and hugely complicated, drug benefit program for seniors, which had been Bush's only major legislative achievement, other than tax cuts, in the 2004 election year. Whatever the program's positive aspects, they were totally obscured by mismanaged implementation. Confidence in government receded along with Bush's approval ratings, which dipped to 30 percent levels by the end of 2005.

So, despite his commitment to selling the program to the public, Bush's proposal for Social Security reform never gained momentum with the public and never came close to passage in any of its legislative incarnations. In the venues where Bush tried to persuade the public, dissenting views had no chance to be heard. In fact, the longer he talked about it, the less support polls showed for his reform program.[90] It never had more than pockets of support in Congress and among experts and it did not help that the proposal was extremely complicated in its requirements—meaning more paperwork and bureaucracy—and would have been costly to implement. Although it promised marginally greater individual control over retirement investments, use of the earnings from those investments would still have been in government-mandated retirement accounts.

As Bush entered his sixth year in office, his Social Security reform was dead in the water, although he did continue to try to win public support long after others were aware it had no chance in Congress. Many in his own party were leery of going out on a limb to support a program being offered by a man who would never run for office again. Did they want to be martyrs to his legacy? Though second terms have been tough for almost every president since Richard Nixon (as we discussed in Chapter 9), Bush became a lame duck sooner than most. Whereas he took his reelection by a popular majority as a mandate for his style of bold, risk-taking leadership, a presidential scholar concluded that Bush had simply misread the election results: "A majority of voters said, 'We prefer you to Kerry [on national security], but please don't change anything.' But Bush heard a different voice."[91]

Bush had used public confidence in his leadership and credibility as the currency to sell his Social Security reform. But going into the 2004 election, the country had been evenly split (48–48) in its view of Bush as a uniter or a divider, and it had come out of the election the same way.[92] Worst of all, for a man selling a program on personal trust, he had developed a serious credibility problem, even among those who had voted for him. Most experts did not agree with Bush's analysis of what was wrong with Social Security, and he found Republicans in Congress distancing themselves from him in preparation for the midterm elections. It was an almost impossible situation in which to win public support for something as regime changing as altering the foundations of Social Security.

 To learn more about this topic, go to "you are there" exercises for this chapter on the text website.

Copyright © 2005. Reprinted by permission of Cagle Cartoons.

Key Terms

impeachment

head of government

head of state

executive orders

executive privilege

divided government

veto power

pocket veto

commander in chief

War Powers Resolution

imperial presidency

unitary executive

signing statements

fireside chats

personal presidency

going public

spectacle presidency

Further Reading

Anonymous [Joe Klein], *Primary Colors: A Novel of Politics* (New York: Random House, 1996). Inspired by the first Clinton presidential campaign, this is one of the most insightful and readable books on modern presidential politics and certainly the funniest.

Doris Kearns Goodwin, *Team of Rivals: the Political Genius of Abraham Lincoln* (New York: Simon and Schuster, 2005). There are countless books on Lincoln the icon and Lincoln the wartime president; this study by a presidential historian explains Lincoln the politician and chief executive by focusing on how he selected and managed a cabinet full of highly experienced and politically ambitious men.

Fred I. Greenstein, *Presidential Difference: Leadership Style From FDR to George W. Bush*, 2nd ed. (Princeton, N.J.: Princeton University Press, 2004). Brief, readable profiles that describe and compare the leadership and management styles of twelve presidents.

Richard E. Neustadt, *Presidential Power: The Politics of Leadership* (New York: John Wiley, many editions, originally published in 1960). This is a classic, one of the most cited books on the presidency. Neustadt argues that presidential power is based on the ability to persuade.

Andrew Rudalevige, *The New Imperial Presidency: Renewing Presidential Power After Watergate* (Ann Arbor: University of Michigan Press, 2005). Compare this study of the expansion of presidential power in the Bush years with the classic work that popularized the phrase "imperial presidency" to describe the Nixon presidency: Arthur Schlesinger, Jr. *The Imperial Presidency* (Boston: Houghton Mifflin, 1973).

Ron Suskind, *The Price of Loyalty: George W. Bush, the White House, and the Education of Paul O'Neill* (New York: Simon & Schuster, 2004). This is an "as told to" account of the Bush management style by Bush's first secretary of the treasury, Paul O'Neill.

Gary Wills, *James Madison* (New York: Penguin, 2001). This biography of one of the best-known Founders but one of our least-known presidents is one in a series of presidential biographies being published by Penguin in small-book format (about two hundred pages). Each is, or will be, written by a well-known American writer.

For Viewing

PBS, *The American President,* 2000. With commentary by presidential scholars, including Richard Neustadt, this ten-volume series groups presidents by shared characteristics, rather than chronologically or by party.

PBS, *The Presidents,* 1990–. These documentaries include family as well as political histories on the Lincolns and the Kennedys, Lyndon Johnson, Eisenhower, both Roosevelts, Truman, Reagan, Wilson, Grant, and Carter. These have been well reviewed for their balanced coverage and assessments. Compare these documentary treatments of presidential biographies with film treatments.

John Ford, *Young Mr. Lincoln,* 1939; Aaron Sorkin, *The American President,* 1995; Oliver Stone, *Nixon,* 2000. Stone's dark and contemporary psychological approach to presidential biography stands in stark contrast to Ford's film, one of the many idealized portrayals from Hollywood's golden era, and to Sorkin's equally romanticized treatment of a fictional president in the modern presidency that inspired the NBC series *The West Wing* (1999–2006).

PBS, *Eleanor,* 2000; Daniel Petrie, *Eleanor and Franklin,* 1976. The PBS documentary on Eleanor Roosevelt's role in her husband's presidency contains home movies, voice recordings, interviews with relatives, and news footage. Petrie's film, originally shown as a television miniseries, is a dramatic adaptation of Joseph Lash's book of the same title.

Discovery Channel, *Watergate,* 1994. This three-volume series documents the decline of the "imperial" presidency of Richard Nixon from the break-in and burglary at the Watergate complex through the conspiracy to cover up the crime and the impeachment investigation that led to the president's resignation.

PBS, *The People's President: Man, Myth and the Media.* Far from the in-depth chronicle of Watergate, this documentary on the presidency and the mass media flies by in fifty minutes, using hundreds of iconic images of presidents taken from portraits, sculpture, newsreels, ads, and excerpts from all the best-known movies and TV programs about presidents, including comments from some of the actors who played them, testimony from presidential historians, television critics, and all the living ex-presidents, some of whom read from Washington's farewell address. The point is to illustrate how a president's public image has become more important than his accomplishments or failures.

PBS, *The Jesus Factor,* 2004. This is an exploration of the role of religion in the administration of George W. Bush.

Electronic Resources

www.whitehouse.gov

The White House home page has links to the Office of the Vice President, the Office of the First Lady, the Department of Homeland Security, and all EOP offices. You can tour the White House, read presidential speeches, and e-mail the president. The link to the first lady's home page allows viewers to send e-mail, look at the work of the office, and link to biographies of each of America's first ladies.

www.millercenter.virgina.edu

The website of the University of Virginia's project on the presidency offers White House tapes from six administrations, FDR to Nixon, and a host of other resources. Use the links to Oral History and AmericanPresidents.org

www.presidents.ucsb.edu/ws

The site for the American Presidency project at the University of California—Santa Barbara allows you to access public papers of presidents from Hoover to George W. Bush, including state of the union speeches, inaugural and radio addresses, campaign debates, and more.

www.americanpresidents.org

This is C-SPAN's Peabody Award–winning website for historical coverage of the American presidency.

www.access.gpo.gov/usbudget

This site has a copy of the most recent federal budget. Reading the president's annual budget message is one way to find out the basic goals of any administration.

ThomsonNOW™

Enter ThomsonNOW™ using the access card that is available with this text or through www.thomsonedu.com/thomsonnow. ThomsonNOW™ will assist you in understanding the content in this chapter with a personalized study plan generated for your needs. A practice test will assess the areas you need to review and provide the tools to fully comprehend those concepts, including an integrated digital eBook, interactive simulations, timelines, video case studies, MicroCase exercises, and InfoTrac College Edition readers and exercises. You'll also be connected to the learning objectives, chapter outline, chapter glossary, flash cards, crossword puzzles, Internet activities, and interactive quizzes found on the companion website.

CHAPTER 12

THE BUREAUCRACY

Turf wars and failures to communicate with each other have hampered the effectiveness of U.S. intelligence-gathering bureaucracies. Intelligence agencies have also been handicapped by their lack of success in recruiting agents to do undercover work in areas such as Peshawar, Pakistan.

The Nature of Bureaucracies

Goals

Performance Standards

Openness

Growth of the Federal Bureaucracy

Why the Bureaucracy Has Grown

Controlling Growth

Agencies within the Federal Bureaucracy

What Bureaucracies Do

Administering Policy

Making Policy

Regulation

Data Collection and Analysis

Politics and Professional Standards

The Merit System

Neutral Competence

Overseeing the Bureaucracy

President

Congress

Courts

Interest Groups and Individuals

Conclusion: Is the Bureaucracy Responsive?

YOU ARE THERE

Should You Blow the Whistle on the U.S. Army Corps of Engineers?

You are Bunnatine (Bunny) Hayes Greenhouse, the highest ranking civilian in the U.S. Army Corps of Engineers (USACE). It is June 2005, and you are trying to decide what to do about what you believe are abuses of fair competition and pricing standards for awarding federal contracts.

As the Corps' top procurement officer it is your job to review all contracts for more than $10 million and decide if they satisfy federal standards. Last fall you learned from a news report that your department granted a waiver to a politically well-connected firm, Kellogg, Brown, Root (KBR) that exempted it from responding to a Pentagon audit of its billing practices. KBR is a subsidiary of Halliburton, the oil and energy giant formerly headed by Vice President Cheney. The waiver was written up and granted on a day when you were ill and away from your office. Your superiors knew you had been opposed to the terms of the original contract, had requested revisions, and that you were unlikely to approve any further special treatment for Halliburton/KBR. When you learned about the waiver you wrote to the Secretary of the Army asking for an investigation, but nothing has happened. You believe the abuses continue and that you are running out of options to stop them. Should you file a grievance, appeal again to someone farther up the line in the Pentagon, go to Congress or to the media? Any action outside normal grievance procedures will present a risk to your career.

You worked very hard to get where you are, coming from a poor family in a segregated Louisiana Delta mill town. Your father had only two years of elementary school, but your parents raised all their children to excel; your older siblings are professors and your younger brother, Elvin Hayes, was an NBA star. You left a career as a high school and college math teacher to follow your army veteran husband into a career in military procurement. You entered at the bottom of the civil service ranks and worked long hours while raising three children, supplementing your math and engineering management degrees with three senior management training courses. You received glowing personnel evaluations and by 1997 had risen into the top 1 percent of the civil service ranks, the Senior Executive Service (SES).[1] During those years, you said, "There wasn't another SES who could touch me sideways."[2] Yet now your professional judgment is being questioned by your superiors because you disagree with how they are awarding military contracts, the very thing you are there to oversee.

The problems over Iraq contracts began even before the invasion, when the Corps proposed giv-

Bunny Greenhouse blew the whistle on improper contracts for the war in Iraq. When asked why she always wears a flower with her outfit, she said, "It's my signature. My name is Greenhouse, and with a name like that I have to wear a flower everyday."

ing a no-bid contract to KBR for transport and logistical support. You objected because KBR had not satisfactorily responded to queries about billing irregularities for work done in Bosnia in 2000. But by October 2003, seven months into the war, it was clear U.S. troops would be staying in the country for some time. Without enough military personnel to perform all the services needed for troop support, much less to rebuild basic infrastructure, the Pentagon was lining up private firms as fast as possible to do this work. One contract bucked to your department for review was a no-bid, five-year $7 billion offer to Halliburton to get Iraq's oil fields operating again. Competitive bidding had been waived on the grounds that the situation in Iraq constituted an emergency.

You were not convinced that Halliburton was the only company capable of doing the job; the army had been contracting with other firms for some years, so why should 50 percent of the rebuilding contracts go to Halliburton? This was important because part of your job is to see that smaller companies and minority-owned businesses have a chance to compete for government contracts. You also said that in your twenty years of contract review

and evaluation you had never known an emergency situation to extend over a five-year period. You recommended that the contract be rewritten to terminate after one year, but your superiors sent it back to you without the change.

You also objected when officials from KBR came to USACE offices, not just to consult, but to participate in writing the contracts. You believed the cost-plus terms KBR demanded, which essentially allowed it to set costs and add on a service fee, were unwarranted and would cost taxpayers millions. On each contract you were pressured by your superiors to waive existing standards and give quick approval. After requesting revisions, you signed them with reservations because we were at war. Although you were told not to write on the contracts, you did it anyway because you knew memos had a way of getting lost and you thought it was the only way those up the administrative line would know your objections.[3]

Eventually contracts worth more than $10 billion were awarded to Halliburton/KBR for transporting fuel from Kuwait and providing a variety of support and supply services for U.S. troops. As the war progressed, many questions were raised about the quality of KBR's

work and the accuracy of its billing. Three separate government agencies raised questions about pricing and a Pentagon audit suggested KBR was overcharging for fuel and asked the company for an explanation. This is when your superiors at the Corps had taken advantage of your absence to issue a waiver that freed KBR from having to account for the alleged overbilling. When a news organization filed a Freedom of Information Request to get copies of the contracts they discovered your handwritten comments and printed them.[4]

Your superiors were already trying to get you out of USACE; they did not have the power to fire you, but the month before the KBR story broke you had been called to a meeting and threatened with demotion. You were able to delay that with your letter to the Secretary of the Army, who put a hold on it pending investigation, but you are still unable to change the way business is being done.

And there is something else at play: issues of race and gender may be complicating intraoffice professional disagreements. You were hired into your present position by Lt. General Joe Ballard, the first African-American to head the Corps of Engineers. He called you "one of the most professional people" he had ever met and hoped you would "break up the 'good old boys' network of informal contracting arrangements at the Corps" and professionalize the agency.[5] But you encountered problems with colleagues, and at least one of your deputies admitted he had difficulty having a woman as a superior. A senior USACE attorney yelled at you in staff meetings and, in front of Gen. Ballard, had used insulting language to describe you. After Ballard retired, attacks against you increased and your job reviews went from glowing to terrible. The bad reviews were left in your record even after two review panels ruled them unwarranted and ordered them upgraded. The acrimony was so strong that three years ago you filed a complaint with the Equal Opportunity Employment Office alleging race and gender discrimination. The complaint has never been investigated.

So here you are with a grievance pending and still waiting for a response from the Secretary of the Army about your request for an investigation into the contract process. What options are left to you? One is to take the problem outside the Corps and share inside information with people in a position to crack down on the abuses. As **whistleblowers,** individual bureaucrats can sometimes make a big difference by exposing wrongdoing in their workplace, be it mismanagement, fraud, or abuse of power. By their actions, some whistleblowers have helped remove dangerous products from the market, stopped discrimination and harassment on the job, and saved the taxpayers millions of dollars. It is also true that for their efforts many have been fired or demoted.

If a congressional committee would call for an investigation into Iraq War contracts, you would almost certainly be called to testify, and you would be obligated to do it. That would save you from having to take the initiative.

But the Republican-dominated Congress has all but abandoned oversight work, and they are especially touchy about challenging the administration on anything related to the war, especially in an election year.

But there is a third option: given the refusal of Republican committee chairs to launch an investigation, the Policy Committee of the Democratic congressional caucus has been holding its own series of hearings. There is another this month and they have invited you to testify. It is an opportunity to make public your criticism of how the contracts have been processed, but you would be doing so in a partisan forum—and just months before a presidential election in which everyone believes the conduct of the war will figure prominently. Your testimony would be entirely voluntary and the USACE counsel has told you your participation would be looked on unfavorably.

If you go public with your complaints about the Halliburton/KBR contracts, they can say it is just sour grapes, fallout from other office conflict. And if you air your grievances in a partisan venue such as a hearing called

by congressional Democrats, you may be handing over your career on a platter to your opponents. You are a registered Independent and not involved in party politics; as a career civil servant you are not allowed to be. You pride yourself on your professionalism and don't know why you should sit still while your competence is challenged, your authority skirted, and federal standards waived for what may be instances of political favoritism rather than national security needs. And if you do not fight back against insubordination and disrespect from colleagues you will permanently undermine your authority. If the congressional committees responsible for oversight are not going to hold hearings, then maybe appearing at the Democrats' forum—which will almost certainly be televised on C-SPAN—is the only way to get Congress's attention.

What do you do? Do you accept the slight to your authority and continue the bureaucratic infighting over the awarding and administration of no-bid contracts that may be wasting millions of taxpayer dollars, or do you blow the whistle and possibly end your career?

When George Wallace ran as a third-party candidate for president in 1968, he campaigned against "pointy-headed bureaucrats" in Washington making decisions that regulated good people's lives. Bureaucrats, according to Wallace, were out of touch with everyday citizens and their concerns. Wallace did not invent bureaucracy bashing, but he helped make it popular among candidates for federal office.

President Reagan never tired of talking about his dissatisfaction with big government and liked to say he preferred flying over Washington to being on the ground because from the air, government looked smaller. Presidential candidates Patrick Buchanan and Ross Perot ran for office by disparaging the people who run the government they wanted to lead. And not long after taking office, George W. Bush discounted a report on global warming "put out by the bureaucracy," implying that, given its source, it need not be taken seriously.

When these men refer to "Washington" they mean big government using too much money to do

unnecessary things. These critics imply that bureaucrats are not like ordinary citizens. Rather, they are busybodies committed to expanding government's size, spending taxpayers' money, and designing regulations to make life more difficult for individuals and businesses.

Bureaucratic decision making is involved in so much of our lives because government has come to serve many different purposes and interests. The federal government employs butchers, truck drivers, engineers, and three-quarters of all the holders of doctorates in mathematics working in the United States. In all, it employs 2.7 million civilians who work in one hundred agencies at more than eight hundred different occupations. (The armed forces put another 2.3 million on the federal payroll.) Federal bureaucrats do crop research and soil analysis, run hospitals and utilities, fight drug trafficking, check manufacturers' claims about their products, inspect mines, develop high-tech weapons systems, send out Social Security checks, authorize Medicare payments, administer student loan

Americans expect their public bureaucracies to be open and responsive. Andrew Jackson recognized this when he opened the civil service to people of "common" origins. By putting his frontier supporters in office, he hoped to make the bureaucracy more responsive by making it more representative. In the twentieth century, the expectation that public agencies should be open to all qualified applicants gave some groups, such as Irish, Jewish, and African Americans, more job opportunities than were open to them in the private sector because of segregation and quotas.

In the past two decades, significant progress has been made in making the federal bureaucracy more reflective of American diversity. Thirty-one percent of Americans were identified as minorities in the 2000 census, and they were 31.5 percent of the civilian federal workforce in 2004. African Americans are particularly well represented, being a substantially larger portion of the federal workforce (17.4 percent) than of the general population. American Indians and Asian Americans have a percentage of federal jobs close to their population share, whereas Hispanics remain significantly underrepresented in the federal workforce, despite an aggressive Hispanic recruitment program (7.3 percent of federal workers compared with 12.6 percent of the civilian labor force). However, the census does not distinguish between legal and illegal residency, and millions of Hispanics included in the population count would not be eligible for federal jobs. Women are represented almost in exact proportion as in the private sector, filling 44.4 percent of federal positions compared with 45.5 percent of private sector jobs, but still not at parity with their 51 percent share of the population.[1]

The relatively good news about the overall profile of the bureaucracy fades at the top of the pay scale. Women and minority men have not yet broken completely through the "glass ceiling" that has kept them out of top management positions. Even after passage of civil rights and equal opportunity legislation, barriers did not disappear because often the individuals who enforced the new regulations were opposed to the policies.

There is progress, however. Women now fill almost 26 percent of senior-grade pay positions (about one-fifth of whom are minority women), more than twice the share held fifteen years ago. And,

Federal employment has opened opportunities for African Americans. Shown here are two Bureau of Engraving and Printing employees checking the quality of $20 bills. The woman at right is holding $8000 in printing mistakes.

collectively, minorities hold 14 percent of all senior positions.

Federal court rulings and out-of-court settlements in discrimination cases account for some of the improvement in upward mobility. For example, women agents charged the FBI with denying them assignment to SWAT teams, even though experience on such teams was crucial to advancement. Only when they threatened to sue did the FBI change its promotion procedures.[2]

[1]Office of Personnel Management, *The Fact Book,* 2005 Edition, 47 (www.opm.gov/feddata/factbook/2005).
[2]Katherine C. Naff, "Through the Glass Ceiling: Prospects for the Advancement of Women in the Federal Civil Service," *Public Administration Review* 54 (1994), 513; for an account of discrimination against women in the FBI, see Rosemary Dew and Pat Pap, *No Backup: My Life as a Female FBI Special Agent* (New York: Carroll & Graf, 2003).

TABLE 12.1 **Women and Minorities as a Percentage of the Senior Federal Civil Service Workforce**

	1985	1990	2004
Women			25.8
(Non-Hispanic whites)	8	12	(21.0)
(Minority women)			(4.8)
African Americans	4	5	6.5
Hispanics	1	2	3.5
Asians and Pacific Islanders	1	1	3.2
American Indians	—	0.5	0.8

NOTE: Overall, about 1 percent of all federal employees are at this pay grade; minority percentages include men and women.

SOURCE: Office of Personnel Management, "2004 Demographic Profile of the Federal Workforce" (www. opm.gov/feddata/demograp/table2w); *The Fact Book,* 2005 Edition, 47-48 (www.opm.gov/feddata/factbook/2005).

programs, and regulate air traffic, to mention only a few responsibilities.

To some people, the federal bureaucracy has become the symbol of big government and the embodiment of everything they dislike about it. It is seen as equivalent to a fourth branch of government—powerful, uncontrollable, and with a life of its own. In fact, the federal bureaucracy has no independent legislative authority, only that delegated by Congress, and it has no budgetary powers. The bureaucracy's official role is to implement and enforce policies made by elected officials—that is, by Congress and the president. In doing this, bureaucrats do, in some instances, make new law. But departments and agencies exist at the pleasure of Congress, which can eliminate them or trim their budgets if it does not approve of their behavior. If an agency within the bureaucracy consistently supersedes its authority, it is because Congress is intentionally letting it do so or is failing to fulfill its oversight duties.

As we shall see, government bureaucrats are a lot like everyone else. They are ordinary citizens with attitudes that mirror those of their fellow citizens. Very few of these civil servants, about 16 percent, work in the Washington, D.C., metropolitan area. It may not fit your image of people pushing paper in buildings the size of the Pentagon, but the great majority of federal bureaucrats serve in offices near you; check the U.S. government listing in your telephone book and see how many branch offices of federal agencies are located in or near your hometown. (See the box "Women and Minorities in the Civil Service.")

In this chapter, we look at the evolution of the federal bureaucracy—its growth in size, function, and lawmaking powers. We describe the people who staff the bureaucracy, how they are recruited, what rules govern their work, and how Congress and the president set guidelines for the executive branch and oversee its activities. Finally, we describe ways in which the public can join in the work of monitoring the bureaucracy and have a say in the rules it makes.

The Nature of Bureaucracies

Many people automatically associate the word *bureaucracy* with the federal government. They may visualize rows of cubicles with nameless clerical workers doing monotonous work very inefficiently. Trying to cash in on this stereotype, a Virginia company once sold a "Bureaucrat" doll as "a product of no redeeming social value. Place the Bureaucrat on a stack of papers on your desk, and he will just sit on them."[6] The problem with this joke is that the parodied traits are not necessarily common among government bureaucrats, nor are they unique to bureaucrats. All organizations except the very smallest have bureaucracies: Your college or university has one, as did your local school district; every corporation, most religious denominations, and large philanthropic foundations have them, too, not to mention the Olympics, your favorite sports league, and the unions that represent the players in that league.

All these bureaucracies, public and private, share some common features. For example, all have hierarchies of authority; that is, everyone in a bureaucracy has a place in a pyramidal network of jobs, with fewer near the top and more near the bottom. Almost everyone in a bureaucracy has a boss, and except for those in the bottom tier, most have some subordinates. People advance up the hierarchy on the basis of performance or seniority, so those with more authority tend to be those with more experience and expertise.

Because of the hierarchical structure, bureaucratic behavior is not always consistent with democratic principles. Most bureaucrats are not elected, and as in any hierarchical organization, higher-level authorities can restrict the opportunity of someone lower in the pyramid to express an opinion or share expertise in the decision-making process. In their relative lack of openness, bureaucracies have the potential to restrict consumer and client access to information about their products and services and how they operate and to limit citizens' access to information about their own government. In effect, organizational tendencies, if unrestrained in a government bureaucracy, could transform "citizens" into "subordinates."[7] But our constitutional system provides checks on the power of federal bureaucrats and ways for the public to participate in decision making that few people know about or take advantage of.

Not only are government bureaucracies structurally similar to private ones, but they do the same types of work. Employees in both private and public bureaucracies perform a lot of routine tasks. Auditing expense vouchers, managing employee travel, and creating personnel systems, for example, are as routine in business firms as in public agencies. And both also have workers who are productive, honest, and efficient and others who are not. Executives in the Defense Department bought $600 toilet seats and spent more than $75 apiece for metal screws sold elsewhere for 57 cents. In the 1970s and 1980s, their private counterparts at Chrysler, Lockheed, Penn Central, and hundreds of banks and savings and loans ran their businesses into the ground, then looked to the government for bailouts or buyouts. During the 1990s, corporations such as Enron, Tyco, and WorldCom paid out hundreds of millions of dollars in stock options and bonuses to executives who, in return, also ran their businesses into the ground, lied about company earnings, and cost investors billions of dollars.

But there are some distinctions between private and public bureaucracies. Here we look at several.[8]

Goals

Businesses are supposed to make a profit; if they do not, they fail. Public agencies are supposed to promote the "public interest"; if they do not, they fail to serve the people who pay their salaries. Although people disagree over what the public interest is, it is not the same thing as making a profit, just as a government is not a business. This is why we have different words for these two kinds of organizations that exist for completely different reasons.

The goals of a public bureaucracy are defined by elected officials, who collectively determine what is in the public interest. They are sometimes accused of setting goals as if they were in a private bureaucracy—that is, making policies that will help them at the polls rather than policies that best serve the public. But in general, the goals set by these officials are supposed to accomplish tasks and provide services that private bureaucracies cannot. In some cases, such as providing for national security during wartime, they must do so irrespective of cost.

Some part of the public's varying perception of how well the bureaucracy does its job stems from a lack of agreement on the work it is given to do. One person's lazy, red tape-ridden, uncaring bureaucracy is another's responsive agency. But even when unhappy

"I'm sorry, dear, but you knew I was a bureaucrat when you married me."

with its performance, Americans still expect government to provide a vast array of services costing billions of dollars annually, from highways that accommodate high-speed cars to Social Security payments that arrive on time, from clean tap water to safe neighborhoods, from protection from foreign enemies to a cure for cancer.

Performance Standards

It is relatively easy to judge if a private organization is meeting its goals (ignoring for the moment fraudulent accounting) by asking is it profitable? We might dislike the chocolate-covered raisins that a candy company produces but would still consider the company successful if it made a profit selling them. We would not typically denigrate the company because it makes something we do not approve of. But we rightly use a different standard in judging government. Yet what is the appropriate standard for evaluating the performance of government if making a profit is not the goal?

One obvious method is to determine whether a public agency is efficient and cost-effective. That sounds logical, but any method of assigning dollar values to bureaucratic output must be partly subjective. It is usually easier to place a value on a commodity than on a government service. We can estimate what price to place on a chair or a house by computing the cost of constructing it. But placing a dollar value on such public goals as education or consumer safety is much harder. How many children have to die from swallowing pills and medications before government requires pharmaceutical manufacturers to use childproof caps on bottles? How many lives saved makes it worthwhile for government to require auto manufacturers to install air bags? How much was the life of each person killed in the World Trade Center on 9/11 worth (a calculation made in order to provide reimbursement for their families)? These are questions bureaucrats must answer. They are required to calculate how much a human life is worth and how productive an individual will be during his or her lifetime. Then they have to estimate the costs of putting the policies in place to protect lives, as well as to monitor and enforce the policies.

Private bureaucracies ask the same questions before their leaders decide whether it is profitable to install safer fuel tanks in cars or to remove a low-risk flaw from a child's toy. Although the federal bureaucrat, too, is always weighing costs against benefits, many people believe that the government should not use cost as the primary standard when lives are at risk.

Another way to evaluate performance is to measure waste that stems from inefficiency and corruption. It is not particularly difficult to calculate how much more an agency paid out because it failed to get competitive bids for equipment and supplies, hired more employees than necessary to do a job, contracted consultants to do imaginary work, or erred in calculating welfare payments or farm subsidies. Two spectacular cases of waste in government spending resulted from the Pentagon's awarding five-year, no-bid contracts to Haliburton and its subsidiaries to provide housing, food, laundry, and security services in Iraq that, prior to the 1980s, would have been provided by military personnel and from the Department of Homeland Security's (DHS's) mismanagement of rescue and recovery after hurricane Katrina. Millions in housing support was paid out to ineligible applicants and millions more wasted in purchases made on no-bid contracts.

Some kinds of government waste are harder to measure because no matter how well a program may be run, there will always be part of the public opposed to its goals. Perhaps the program is providing services a taxpayer thinks inappropriate for government, or maybe it serves relatively few people at a large cost. These were the criteria many Americans used to evaluate welfare programs. Accusations of waste and fraud were common, but as a percentage of overall expenditures, there was little client fraud in the welfare program. Most criticism stemmed from opposition to the program itself and services provided at great cost to a small clientele without appropriate results. Similar criticism comes from opponents of government health care and social insurance programs; some argue that private health insurance and pension programs are by definition more efficiently run because private businesses exist to make a profit. But in fact the administrative costs of Medicare are well below those of private health care insurers, and many private pension programs have been catastrophically underfunded and either terminated or placed in government receivership.

In a less-publicized example, a government commission called it wasteful to keep open hundreds of very small post offices that served rural communities. The commission was not alleging fraud or mismanagement but believed that the post offices cost too much for the small number of people served. To the residents of these communities, however, their post offices were a good return on their tax dollars, and paying to keep them open was more efficient than having to drive miles to a distant station.

Citizens have rarely applied this standard of waste to corporate behavior, at least not prior to our more environmentally conscious era. Historically, private corporations have been able to waste more than a government agency of comparable size without the public ever taking notice. If a business or industry makes a profit, most people think it is a job well done, without asking whether the product or service offered is in itself wasteful. Marketing a hundred different kinds of breakfast cereal in packaging twice the size of the contents may not be an efficient use of resources, but if they sell, consumers are inclined to say, "Why not?" We may not like lime green sofas with pink stripes, but we do not consider their manufacturer wasteful for making them as long as the product is profitable. In 2001, when senior managers in the federal bureaucracy got bonuses averaging $11,000, it prompted public scrutiny of their agencies' performances.[9] When CEOs of corporations that lost money got multimillion-dollar bonuses, much of the public simply said,

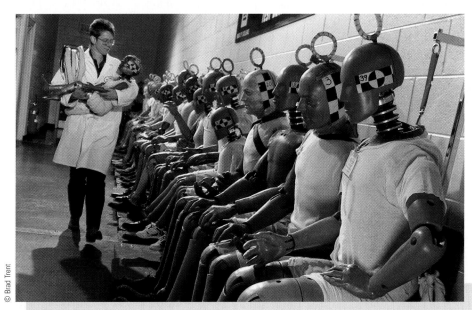

To save lives, federal regulations mandate setting standards and testing autos for safety. These dummies allow simulations of the impact of crashes.

"Whatever the market will allow." (That thinking changed when some CEOs were found to have committed criminal acts.)

We see government expenditures as *our* money, and we feel entitled to complain, especially since payment of that money (taxes) is not voluntary. Only recently has such a large percentage of the public invested in stock that they have begun paying attention to how private bureaucracies manage *investors'* money. Yet private investments are often made through public bureaucracies, such as a university's or a school district's pension fund, and when losses occur because of corruption or poor performance by the corporate bureaucracy, it may still be the public bureaucracy that takes much of the heat.

Openness

The openness of public bureaucracy is another feature distinguishing it from a private bureaucracy. Private firms operate with much more secrecy than public agencies do, even when private actions have a significant impact on the public. For example, tobacco companies' lack of openness—long assumed to be their right—cost the lives of many people. The courts ordered tobacco companies to open their files only after much scientific evidence on the dangers of tobacco had accumulated.

In contrast, the greater visibility, or openness, of public agencies helps make them more responsive. Only by having knowledge of both the process and the content of public decisions can interested groups and individuals express their preferences effectively. No one articulated this better than James Madison when he wrote, "A popular Government without popular information or the means of acquiring it, is but a Prologue to a Farce or a Tragedy or perhaps both. Knowledge will forever govern ignorance, and a people who mean to be their own Governors, must arm themselves with the power knowledge gives."[10]

To this end, Congress in 1813 established the federal depository library program, "to guarantee public access to government information by making it available free of charge" in local libraries around the country. Today there are 1250 depository libraries. But as government grew and agencies and paper proliferated, it became harder for the public to keep track of what government was doing. In 1934, Congress passed the Federal Register Act, requiring that all government rules, regulations, and laws be published in the *Federal Register* and that all rules in their final version appear in the *Code of Federal Regulations*. (Today both are available online at www.gpoaccess.gov/fr/index.html.)

Congress went further in 1946 by passing the **Administrative Procedure Act (APA),** which provides for public participation in the rule-making process. All federal agencies must disclose their rule-making procedures and publish all regulations at least thirty days in advance of their effective date to allow time for public comment. Today citizens can often post comments on proposed rules at an agency's website, but it is common for public hearings to be held on controversial rules or those with wide impact. Environmental rules frequently provoke citizen reactions, with comments sometimes numbering in the tens of thousands.

Congress increased public access to the bureaucracy in another way by passing the Freedom of Information Act in 1966. As amended in 1974, **FOIA** (pronounced "foy-ya") lets any member of the public apply to an agency for access to unclassified documents in its archives. The government also puts out a handbook telling how to take advantage of this right, and every government website is required to have a link to its FOIA office. FOIA cannot be used to gain access to internal records such as personnel files, for example, or sensitive documents on a living person. But it can be used to get your FBI file, should you have one, or the file of a person no longer living. Requests must be made according to a formal procedure, and they must cite specific documents. Agencies are not obligated to give "information," only to provide copies of the documents requested, if they have them and if they are not in an exempt category.

Efforts to make government agencies more open often run up against a desire to limit the distribution of critical or embarrassing information. It is the rare public or private bureaucracy that wants to reveal its failures. Thus an evaluation of FOIA found that agencies used many tactics to discourage people from seeking information, such as delaying responses to requests, charging high fees for copies of records (the State Department once charged $10 a page for copying records), and requiring detailed descriptions of documents requested.[11] The FBI once refused to expedite the release of information to a prisoner on death row who was afraid he would be executed before the information was available. The FBI's judgment that his situation did not show "exceptional need or urgency" was overruled by a federal court.[12]

As the chief executive, a president's views on the openness of agencies are also important. The president's policy on FOIA implementation is communicated to federal agencies by the attorney general at the beginning of each administration. Under Presidents Reagan and Bush Sr., federal agencies adopted a narrow reading of the act, making it more difficult to get information.[13] In contrast, President Carter banned classification of documents unless they were clearly related to national security, and President Clinton issued an executive order authorizing the declassification of most documents twenty-five years old or older. He also put a ten-year limit on the classified status of new documents unless a review had determined that they must remain secret.[14] The Clinton administration standard for access to government records had been to exempt a document from a FOIA request only if there was a "foreseeable harm" in its release.[15]

George W. Bush began tightening access to government documents virtually upon taking office, as part of his broader goals of strengthening the presidency and reducing both congressional and public oversight of the executive branch.[16] Vice President Cheney was a long-standing opponent of FOIA.[17] By executive order, Bush immediately established new rules for access to presidential papers, including his father's, which were due to be opened to the public. (The American Political Science Association was among the plaintiffs who sued to reverse the order.)

One month after 9/11 Bush used national security as grounds for restricting FOIA access to all government papers and reports. A memo from his first attorney general, John Ashcroft, to federal agencies reversed the openness standards established by the Clinton administration. Ashcroft assured FOIA administrators that when they "decide to withhold records, in whole or in part," the Justice Department "will defend your decisions unless they lack a sound legal basis or present an unwarranted risk of adverse impact on the

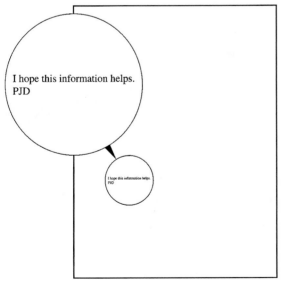

FOIA requires the release of documents, but sometimes the government will censor information within them. This comment was all that remained of an e-mail that the Bush administration censored before releasing.

ability of other agencies to protect important records."[18] Thus under the Bush standard, any FOIA request denied by an agency on any "sound legal basis" could expect Justice Department backing.

The administration ordered thousands of scientific and technical documents removed from public release, some from libraries and many from government websites such as an Environmental Protection Agency (EPA) database on chemicals used at industrial sites.[19] The government also asked scientists' professional associations to restrict what they publish.[20] Some of this censorship just created confusion. For example the Federal Aviation Administration warned pilots they were not to fly in the vicinity of nuclear power plants but at the same time told them it could not say where the plants were located because that was "sensitive security information."[21]

The justification for withdrawal of so much information from public view was a claim in a captured al-Qaeda manual that it "expected" to get most of the information it needed to plan attacks from open sources.[22] Few Americans want to make it easier for terrorists to gain access to detailed site information on nuclear waste dumps, nuclear power plants, or other utilities, or instructions on how to construct nuclear, biological, and chemical weapons. At the same time, most citizens do not want the fear of terrorism to destroy the openness and access to information essential to any democracy. And where to draw the line is the crux of the problem. Information of interest to potential terrorists is not all that the Bush administration had removed from public view. Documents on World War II, the Korean War, relations with China and other foreign policy papers that had been declassified decades ago were reclassified and removed from public view. By executive order, Bush also reversed a Clinton policy that had prohibited thousands of department and agency heads from stamping documents "secret" on their own authority. Whereas during Clinton's presidency four times as much material had been declassified as in the previous fifteen years, during Bush's first term the number of classified documents doubled and declassification dwindled to about 10 percent of what it had been at the end of the nineties.[23] The cost of classifying a document is almost four times the cost of declassification.[24] By 2004 the Bush administration was classifying an historic high of 125 documents per minute (15.6 million documents for the year)—in large part by creating vague new security classifications—at an estimated cost of $7.2 billion.[25]

Bush's narrow definition of public access rights and his penchant for secrecy drew criticism from both conservatives and liberals. The head of the nonpartisan interest group Judicial Watch concluded that the administration's attitude was simply that "the government is not to be questioned."[26] The Cato Institute, a libertarian think tank, accused the administration of being "a law unto itself,"[27] and one of Bush's strongest supporters, Representative Dan Burton (R-Ind.), said, even while granting that every president wants to protect himself from oversight, "a veil of secrecy has descended around the administration."[28] (Thomas Kean, cochair of the 9/11 Commission, said that in carrying out their investigation, "three-quarters of the classified material he reviewed . . . should not have been classified in the first place."[29])

Despite the limitations placed on FOIA, it has enabled individuals and groups to gain important and useful information. Citizens have used it to gather injury and fatality information on defective cars, to assess dangerous infant formulas, to reveal a link between aspirin and a disease known as Reye's syndrome, to learn that J. Edgar Hoover authorized the FBI to carry out a four-year investigation of women's rights groups, and to force the Internal Revenue Service (IRS) to release a 40,000-page manual on its auditing procedures.[30] Scholars have used FOIA to retrieve thousands of documents on Cold War diplomacy, to get records of medical experiments on the effect of radioactivity conducted on unwitting subjects, and to retrieve the FBI files of anthropologists kept under surveillance during the Cold War and the McCarthy era.

Public access to records that document experiments on human subjects and surveillance of private citizens is an essential check on abuse of power by federal bureaucrats. Yet some categories of information and types of deliberation among decision makers require privacy, and it is not always easy to balance individual privacy and openness of government. With the movement from paper to electronic files, new controversies arose over what should be classified. FOIA laws were written before the government began storing its records electronically so they did not define what electronic information was in the public domain. The first George Bush took his aides' e-mail tapes with him when he left office and argued that they were not public property. A federal appeals court ruled that these tapes are public records and must be preserved, and they applied the same ruling to Clinton administration requests for exemption. Because of these rulings, the second Bush administration was very cautious about exchanges of views by e-mail, and Bush himself stopped sending personal e-mail.

Another significant law mandating openness in government is the aptly named **Sunshine Act.** Adopted in 1977, it requires that most government meetings be conducted in public and that notice of such meetings must be posted in advance. Regulatory agencies, for example, must give notice of the date, time, place, and agenda of their meetings and follow certain rules to prevent unwarranted secrecy. State governments have adopted their own sunshine laws, and today it is difficult for any public body—city council or planning commission or any of their subgroups—to meet in secret to conduct official business. Results of meetings conducted in closed, unannounced sessions are open to citizen challenge.

Growth of the Federal Bureaucracy

The Founders did not discuss the federal "bureaucracy," but they did recognize the need for an administration to carry out laws and programs. They envisioned administrators with only a little power, charged with "executive details" and "mere execution" of the law. But the growing size and complexity of society and increasing demands that government do more have dramatically changed the nature of the federal bureaucracy.

George Washington's first cabinet included only three departments and the offices of attorney general and postmaster general, and all combined employed just a few hundred people. More people worked at Mount Vernon, Washington's plantation, than in the executive branch in the 1790s.[31] The Department of State had just nine employees. By 1800, the bureaucracy was still small, with only three thousand civil servants. Only the Treasury Department had much to

Early in the twentieth century, many young children worked twelve-hour days in unhealthy conditions, such as in this vegetable cannery. Eventually public demands to stop this practice led to government regulations on child labor and to the creation of bureaucratic agencies to enforce the regulations.

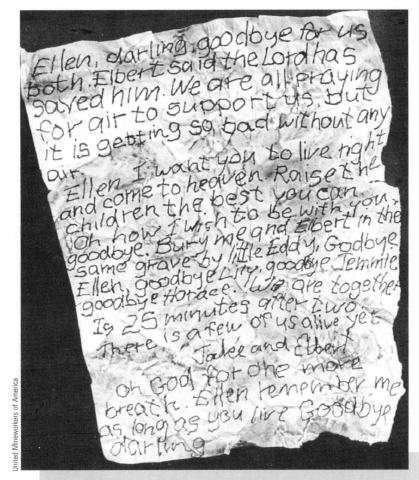

Ellen, darling, goodbye for us both. Elbert said the Lord has saved him. We are all praying for air to support us. But it is getting so bad without any air.

Ellen, I want you to live right and come to heaven. Raise the children the best you can. Oh how I wish to be with you. Goodbye. Bury me and Elbert in the same grave by little Eddy. Goodbye Ellen, goodbye Lily, goodbye Jemmie, goodbye Horace. We are together. Is 25 minutes after two. There is a few of us alive yet. Jake and Elbert. Oh God for one more breath. Ellen remember me as long as you live. Goodbye darling.

Jacob Vowell wrote this letter shortly before suffocating after a mine collapse in Fraterville, Tennessee, in 1902. Such disasters prompted government regulation of mining, which has since saved many lives. However, mining companies resist some regulations, and occasional disasters, such as the one in West Virginia in 2006, still occur.

do, collecting import and excise taxes and purchasing military supplies for an army of a few thousand. From then until 1990, the bureaucracy grew continuously, though at an uneven rate.

Why the Bureaucracy Has Grown

As we saw in Chapter 3, government, over time, responded to public wishes by creating federal agencies to assist and promote emerging economic interests of business, agriculture, and labor and more recently to provide health and economic protections for workers, consumers, retirees, and other groups.[32] One scholar explained the bureaucracy's growth by pointing to Americans' discovery that "government can protect and assist as well as punish and repress."[33] Thus at the same time we criticize government's growth, we demand education, irrigation projects, roads, airports, job training,

effective policing, consumer protection, agricultural subsidies, student loans, and many other services. Each of us might be willing to cut benefits for someone else, but most of us want to keep the benefits *we* have.

When new bureaucracies are created, the intent is to hold them to their original size, but most grow over time because once they are in place, additional responsibilities are assigned to them. After World War II, the Department of Defense did not return to its prewar size or scope because the Cold War gave us a new reason to support a massive military establishment. That era also created additional demands for health care and other services for veterans. The Administrative Procedure Act was passed in 1946 partly because the bureaucracy had grown so much in size and power during the Depression and World War II that Congress believed it needed to increase its oversight.[34] Bureaucracy usually grows during national crises. After the Cold War, when thoughts turned to downsizing the Defense Department, supporters of military spending found new justifications for expansion in the threat of global terrorism. Forty-five days after 9/11, Congress rushed to pass the USA PATRIOT Act (officially, the Uniting and Strengthening America by Providing Appropriate Tools Required to Intercept and Obstruct Terrorism Act) before members had even read it. That act increased both the power and the size of the federal bureaucracy. Implementation of government's extraordinary new power to wiretap, search e-mail, and gain access to library borrowing records and many business records, both paper and electronic, required more personnel and increased spending. Opponents, however, are more frightened by the loss of privacy and liberty than by the increased size and cost of the bureaucracy.

Bureaucrats cannot produce growth on their own. Every agency and its budget is authorized and approved by Congress and the president and continues to exist because it is valuable to enough people with enough influence to sustain it. Sometimes government grows because the president and Congress want it to be more accountable. This often results in hiring more managers, producing greater inefficiency, and ironically, more difficulty in holding agencies accountable.[35]

The growth of the bureaucracy should be seen in the perspective of the overall growth of our economy and population. For example, the number of federal bureaucrats for every one thousand people in the United States decreased from sixteen in 1953 to nine in 2006. We saw in Chapter 3 that the major growth in public employment in recent decades has been at the state and local levels. Over 37 percent of all government workers were federal employees in 1953; in 2006, fewer than 13 percent were.[36]

Controlling Growth

Once departments are established, their consolidation or elimination is rare. More commonly, departments become so large that they must subdivide (for example, the Department of Commerce and Labor was divided into separate departments of Labor and Commerce) or for offices and agencies to become so big or their work so important they are made into cabinet departments (Veterans Affairs, DHS), where they become even larger.

Yet almost every president since Lyndon Johnson has tried to streamline or downsize the bureaucracy. Richard Nixon tried to merge seven departments into four but could not gain approval, and despite many attempts to ax the Department of Education, it is stronger than it ever has been. Jimmy Carter was a committed deregulator and a micromanager who oversaw the elimination of thousands of rules and some regulators. He

unsuccessfully tried to introduce the zero-based budgeting process that would have required every agency to justify its budget every year on the basis of its success in achieving agency goals.

For all Ronald Reagan's talk against big government, it grew by over two hundred thousand employees during his administration. Although many agencies lost personnel (the biggest loser was the Department of Housing and Urban Development), others, such as Defense, Justice, and the Treasury, gained. In addition, Reagan created a new cabinet office, the Department of Veterans Affairs, from what had been an independent agency. He had entered office with a plan to wage a "war on waste," but he left office with the country another trillion dollars in debt and the Defense Department buying $600 toilet seats. The Clinton administration's initiative on "reinventing government" did have limited success; the number of government employees decreased by 1.5 percent during his years in office.

There is a general assumption that size and performance are linked. So presidents often think they can establish more efficient management plans and then cut personnel. George H. Bush, for example, came into office with a plan for "total quality management," and George W. Bush, with a business administration degree, adopted a system for grading the performance of every agency. The Office of Management and Budget (OMB), which performs much of the executive branch's internal oversight, evaluated each department or agency in five management categories: personnel, competitive bidding, financial management, e-government (using technology to improve efficiency), and whether program achievements justify a budget (similar to Carter's zero-based budgeting).[37] Those who fell short or whose work was duplicated in another department were to have their budgets slashed, with the money redirected to programs that work. Almost all agencies and departments received poor or failing marks in some categories, and the OMB even gave itself a failing grade. Under this system, some agencies did receive budget cuts. However, in 2003, the Department of Defense, which got poor marks in all five categories, received its largest one-year budget increase since the Reagan era.

Despite Bush's admiration for smaller, more efficient government, the federal bureaucracy grew by 5 percent (79,000 jobs) during his first three years in office.[38] Some of the growth was due to the war on terrorism—adding a new cabinet department and increasing defense appointments. But there was also some padding—or thickening—of the bureaucracy through the creation of new positions at the senior level in cabinet departments that have nothing to do with national security.[39] The number of people at the highest pay level more than tripled during Bush's first three years. The significance of this thickening is that it adds layers of administration to cabinet departments at a time when the efficient upward and downward flow of information within the bureaucracy has become a major issue, even a life-and-death issue, as it was in the intelligence bureaucracy in 2001. A 2004 survey showed that the new DHS had jumped from three to twenty-one layers of administration and had 146 senior administrative positions two years after its creation.[40]

Career civil servants are skeptical about the attempt of every administration to take on the bureaucracy and cut it down to size. One explanation of the perception gap is that there is a "natural antipathy" between presidents and career civil servants because the president is elected on his ability to articulate basic human values whereas "civil service is about enforcing rules and procedures and treating all citizens and issues equally." Bureaucrats are not about values in the sense that politicians use that term.[41] Reform is difficult when presidents fill political leadership positions in agencies with individuals who do not stay around long enough to learn their jobs and have little chance of really reshaping their agencies. Presidents and their appointees find that reality does not always match political slogans. And presidents find that reforming the bureaucracy is much tougher than they anticipated and soon turn to other activities with more immediate payoffs. Thus in the view of a former OMB official, reform is mostly "three yards and a cloud of dust."[42] (See the box "What Do Bureaucrats Want Anyway?")

Agencies within the Federal Bureaucracy

The Constitution says little about the organization of the executive branch other than indicating a need for the president to have a cabinet. As government's role expanded, it became clear that a single type of organization would not be appropriate for every task assigned to the bureaucracy. Cabinet departments, for example, are headed by people who serve at the president's pleasure and who are there to help carry out his policies. But other agencies must implement law without reference to an individual president's preferences. These agencies require protection from political interference, as do those established to carry out highly technical work. In this section, we review the major types of agencies in the executive branch.

Departments

Departments are organizations within the executive branch that form the president's cabinet. Their heads, called secretaries (except for the head of the Justice Department who is called the Attorney General), are appointed by the president with the consent of the Senate, and they are directly responsible to the president. There are fifteen departments; the newest is DHS (see Figure 12.1). These departments constitute the lion's share of the federal bureaucracy; the largest employer is the Defense Department, with close to 30 percent of all civil servants.

Cabinet departments exist to carry out the president's policy in specific functional areas: national security, federal law enforcement, fiscal policy, health and welfare, foreign relations, and so forth. They are staffed by career civil servants, but all top policy-making positions in each division of a department are held by presidential appointees. The fifteen cabinet departments have more than 350 such positions. Permanent staff believe that the increase in the number of appointive senior positions makes their work more difficult.

Independent Agencies

Independent agencies differ from departments in that they are usually smaller and their heads do not sit in the cabinet. Agency heads are, however, appointed by and responsible to the president. And occasionally a president does extend cabinet status to the head of an independent agency, most notably the director of the EPA. Some agencies, such as the EPA, the CIA, the Social Security Administration, the Peace Corps, and the National Aeronautics and Space Administration (NASA), are well known to the public. Others, such as the Office of Government Ethics, are relatively unknown.

Some independent agencies are responsible for highly specialized areas of policy such as space exploration (NASA) or law enforcement (FBI). The people appointed to head them usually have an appropriate professional background, not just a political profile acceptable to the president. However, if the agency deals with policy that has widespread impact, as the EPA and CIA do, political credentials are likely to be the president's first consideration in naming a director.

Independent Regulatory Boards and Commissions

Although unfamiliar to most Americans, independent agencies affect almost every aspect of our daily lives—the air we breathe, the water we drink, the interest on a bank loan, the fee at an ATM, the terms under which we buy or sell stock, labeling on food and manufactured goods and conditions in the plants where they were made, phone and mail service, and the construction of every car, train, plane, or bus we ride on.

Each independent regulatory board and commission regulates a specific area of business or the economy.

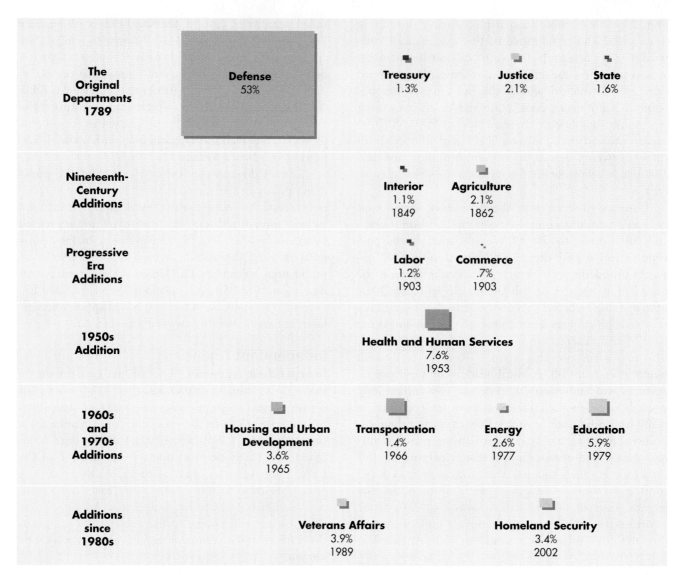

FIGURE 12.1 ■ The Development and Relative Size of Cabinet Departments

*Percentages are each department's share of the **discretionary** budget authority for fiscal 2007. The figures add to less than 100% because of non-cabinet agencies that are allocated funds (the judicial branch, the independent agencies, etc.). The modern Department of Defense (1949) replaced the Departments of War (1789) and the Navy (1798); the Justice Department (1870) replaced the Department of the Attorney General (1789); the Commerce and Labor Departments were first established in 1903 as a joint enterprise; and the Department of Health, Education and Welfare (1953) was divided in 1979 into the Department of Health and Human Services and the Department of Education.*

SOURCE: *United States Budget for Fiscal Year 2007 Historical Tables* (Washington, D.C.: Government Printing Office, 2006), Tab. 5.5, 117; *Manual of the United States Government, 2003–2004* (Washington, D.C.: Government Printing Office, 2003).

Examples include the Federal Communications Commission (FCC), which regulates the electronic media; the Securities and Exchange Commission (SEC), which makes and enforces rules regarding stocks, bonds, and securities; and the Federal Reserve System (the Fed), which sets prime interest rates and controls the amount of money in circulation. These and other regulatory agencies are designated "independent" because the work they do is supposed to be removed from politics as much as possible. Congress created the first

such commission, the Interstate Commerce Commission, in 1887 to decide such things as interstate freight rates, railroad ticket prices, routes, and conditions of service.

Each of these independent regulatory boards and commissions is directed by five to ten presidential appointees. By law, each board and commission must be balanced with members of both major political parties. Appointees serve staggered terms and cannot be removed by presidents who dislike their decisions. Because

Bureaucrats are not much different from the rest of us. They are no more likely to favor raising taxes or government spending; they have about the same confidence as other citizens in government and other institutions, such as organized religion, business, labor, and the press, and they are about as likely as other Americans to favor or oppose busing and gun control.[1]

When civil servants do differ from other citizens, they seem more open to diversity. For example, they are more likely to say they would vote for an African American or a woman as president and less likely to accept traditional gender roles. And they are somewhat *less* likely than other Americans to approve government intrusions into people's private lives. They also are less likely to approve censoring people who hold unpopular views or laws banning pornography or interracial marriage. On only one issue are they more liable to favor "big government": they are somewhat more likely to favor wiretapping.

Federal bureaucrats, like many other Americans, are critical of their own institutions. "Having endured a decade of downsizing, two decades of bureaucratic bashing, three decades of constant reform, four decades of increasing workloads, and five decades of pay and hiring freezes," the attitudes of many federal bureaucrats do not add up to a "healthy public service."[2]

Federal bureaucrats do not have a particularly high opinion of the political appointees who wander into their agencies for short periods (eighteen to twenty-four months on average) to fill leadership positions and then quickly disappear, often without ever learning very much about what the agency is all about.[3] What most bureaucrats seem to want is for Congress and the president to stop using them as guinea pigs for their management experiments and instead to provide the tools and train-ing they need to do their jobs right. Sixty percent of federal employees said that Congress "generally acts in ways that worsen the management of their organizations," and 41 percent said the same about the president. Overall, the attitude of federal employees is not "Show me the money" but "Let me do my job."[4]

At lower levels of the civil service, employees are especially apt to complain about their lack of access to training, and at most levels there is dissatisfaction over the lack of equipment, especially state-of-the-art computers, necessary to do their work properly and efficiently. Other major concerns are the impact of past reforms that have left many programs without sufficient personnel to carry out their work and the increasing number of positions within the bureaucracy that have been removed from civil service and made appointive. Some people believe that this has made the work of the bureaucracy too politicized. In addition, many of those at lower levels believe that there is too much bureaucracy—too many layers of administration between top and bottom, impeding communication and making their jobs more difficult.

Bureaucrats are very hard on themselves, both their own performance and that of their agencies, citing too many people in positions they are unqualified for, especially senior people and political appointees. They want "to eliminate the 'yes' men (and women) and give responsibility back to the employees."[5]

[1]Gregory B. Lewis, "In Search of the Machiavellian Milquetoasts: Comparing Attitudes of Bureaucrats and Ordinary People," *Public Administration Review* 50 (1990), 220–227.
[2]Paul C. Light, "What Federal Employees Want from Reform: Reform Watch Brief No. 5," Brookings Institution, March 2002, www.brookings.edu/comm/reformwatch/rw05.htm.
[3]Paul C. Light, "Fact Sheet on the Continued Thickening of Government," Brookings Institution, July 23, 2004, www.brookings.edu/views/papers/light/20040723.htm.
[4]Light, "What Federal Employees Want," 10.
[5]Ibid., 7.

Adding to their job anxieties, federal employees are sometimes on the front line of danger. A mail carrier protects herself after other postal workers were infected by anthrax spores sent through the mail in 2001.

© Stefano Paltera/Gamma Presse, Inc.

of the technical knowledge needed for decision making, appointments are supposed to be based on expertise rather than partisan considerations. Of course, it is almost impossible for politics, in the sense of an individual's values, not to have some impact on decision making. Presidents who want less government regulation appoint commissioners who share that value. Commissioners, in turn, can then make it difficult for the professionals in the agency to carry out their regulatory mission. However, the goal of having these independent commissions is to make politics secondary to professional expertise.

Government Corporations

Government corporations are businesses run by government to provide services the public needs but that no private company will provide because they are not profitable—or were not profitable at the time government began providing the service. The first government corporation, the Tennessee Valley Authority (TVA), was created when no utility company was willing to invest in the infrastructure necessary to bring electricity to what was then a very poor, undeveloped region of the country. The TVA still supplies electricity to its part of the country.

The United States Postal Service, which was originally a cabinet department, was converted to a business operation in 1971. Formerly a government monopoly, it now has competition from UPS and FedEx, for example, for some of the services it provides. In the 1960s, when railroads were no longer willing to provide passenger service, the government created the National Railroad Passenger Corporation (Amtrak). And because no private insurance company would ever bear the risk of insuring private bank deposits, the government established a corporation to protect your savings account (the Federal Deposit Insurance Corporation). Similarly, the government is now the main purveyor of terrorism insurance because after 9/11, private firms were no longer willing to assume the risk, just as after hurricane Katrina, private insurers wanted government to take even greater responsibility for insuring homeowners in coastal areas against flood damage.

Government corporations charge for their services or products but their primary objective is to provide a needed service, not to make a profit. Of course, the government is quite happy if they do or if they at least break even. When a government corporation does become profitable, its assets may be sold to private businesses and the corporation closed. This is what happened with CONRAIL, the government corporation that took over rail freight and turned it back into a profitable enterprise. The U.S. Postal Service also is

now showing a profit after decades of needing government subsidies to balance its budget. Opponents of government corporations would like to see both the Postal Service and the unprofitable Amtrak completely privatized. But the services provided are so important to the national economy that without the certainty that private businesses would guarantee their continuation, government would have difficulty justifying the sale of their assets.

What Bureaucracies Do

Having examined forms of bureaucratic organization, we now look in greater detail at the sources of the bureaucracy's authority and the responsibilities assigned to it.

After elected officials make a law, someone must carry it out. That is the primary job of the bureaucracy. Bureaucrats convert laws passed by Congress and signed by the president into rules and actions that have an actual impact on people and things. We call this process **policy implementation.** The general process of policy implementation has two major components: administering policies and making them.

Administering Policy

Public bureaucracy's oldest job is to administer the law. To "administer" is to execute, enforce, and apply the rules that have been made either by Congress or the bureaucracy itself. Thus if policy makers decide to go to war, they must empower agencies to acquire weapons, recruit and train soldiers, and devise a winning strategy. Policy making without administration is tantamount to having no policy at all.

Administration includes thousands of different kinds of activities. It involves writing checks to farmers who receive payments for growing—or not growing—crops, providing direct services to the public, evaluating how well programs are working, prosecuting those who try to defraud the government, and maintaining buildings and offices. For forest rangers, administration involves helping backpackers in the Grand Canyon or putting out a forest fire in northern Minnesota.

Making Policy

Responsibility for administering policy inevitably conferred lawmaking powers on the bureaucracy. This can be illustrated with the example of the Americans with Disabilities Act (ADA). The ADA directs employers to make a "reasonable accommodation" for a competent worker with a disability that "substantially limits" a major life activity such as seeing or walking, except when this causes "undue hardship."[43]

This seemingly straightforward law is in fact extremely complex and its impact far reaching. Although the act went into effect in 1992, the Equal Employment Opportunity Commission (EEOC), which has responsibility for its implementation, is still clarifying what specific provisions in the act mean. What is the difference between a "reasonable accommodation" and an "undue hardship"? When voters want local governments to spend less, is the $2 million that Des Plaines, Illinois, had to shell out for sidewalks and curb cuts an "undue hardship" or not?[44] Will the EEOC let colleges and universities make only some classrooms and offices accessible to students and staff in wheelchairs, or must every classroom and faculty office be accessible to people with disabilities, at a cost of millions of dollars for large universities?

Answering such questions and formulating rules to implement them is *de facto* policy making. Implementation requires disseminating the rules and negotiating interpretations with the parties who have to put them in place and enforce them. State and local counterparts of the EEOC and their clients must be informed of the rules, assisted in their attempts to use the rules, and monitored in their progress. Bills must be paid, disputes resolved, and information collected as to how successful the program is. If affected parties reject the EEOC's interpretation or the officials' implementation, the rules can be challenged in federal court. This is where almost all disputed provisions of the ADA are being decided. Bureaucrats very often do not have the last word in determining how a policy is implemented.

The passage of thousands of complex bills like the ADA accounts for the growth in policy making functions of public bureaucracies. Industrialization, population growth, urbanization, and profound changes in science, transportation, and communications have put problems of a more complex nature on government's agenda. The large number and technical nature of these problems, as well as policy differences among its members, have often limited Congress's ability to draft specific policy responses.

Congress often responds to this situation by enacting a general statement of goals and identifying actions that would help achieve them. Congress then delegates the power to an agency with the relevant expertise to draft specific rules that will achieve these goals. This **delegated legislative authority** empowers executive branch agencies to draft, as well as execute, specific policies. Just as the ADA left rule making to the EEOC, any tax reform legislation requires thousands of rules to be written by the IRS and the Treasury Department. Agency-made policy is just as binding as acts of Congress because agencies make it at the direction of Congress. In strictly numerical terms, agencies make much more policy than Congress because agencies issue many new rules and regulations for the implementation of each new law Congress passes.

Many political scientists believe that Congress abdicates its authority and acts in an irresponsible manner by refusing, because of political pressures and its heavy workload, to develop specific guidelines for agencies.[45] This leaves agencies to implement policies without much guidance from Congress beyond the wording of each bill. Sometimes, however, agency complaints about the ambiguities or lack of specificity in legislation are just excuses not to implement disliked policies. Often these lead to partisan conflicts, especially over regulatory policy. Congress can send more detailed directives to agencies. But this does not prevent the political appointees who head executive branch agencies from resisting congressional directives they dislike on the grounds that they are too complex or unrealistic to follow.

In effect, the competition between the White House and Congress was extended to the bureaucracy when Congress delegated legislative authority to agencies. This competition can intensify or subside, depending on whether the president is of the same party as congressional majorities. However, the competition has continued even in recent years under a Republican-led unified government.

Sometimes agencies are in the difficult position of having to satisfy competing demands. To figure out what Congress, the president, and others want, agency officials read congressional debates and testimony and talk to members of Congress, committee staffers, White House aides, lobbyists, and others. Although agencies also try to determine what the public wants, they are more likely to respond to well-organized and well-funded groups that closely monitor their actions. As a result, agency-made policy is often less responsive to the general public than to particular interests.

Regulation

A special kind of policy making called **regulation** produces rules, standards, or guidelines conferring benefits and imposing restrictions on business conduct and economic activity. Regulations have the force of law and are made by agencies whose directors and board members are appointed by the president and whose operating procedures are generally governed by the Administrative Procedure Act. Regulatory agencies include not only independent regulatory boards and commissions but also some independent agencies, such as the EPA, and some agencies within cabinet departments, such as the Food and Drug Administration

(FDA) in Health and Human Services and the Office of Safety and Health Administration (OSHA) in the Labor Department.

Regulatory actions include two steps: making rules and adjudicating their enforcement. Rule making is the establishment of standards that apply to a class of individuals or businesses. Adjudication occurs when agencies try individuals or firms charged with violating standards. To do this, they use procedures that are very similar to those of courts.

Most regulations derive from laws passed by Congress that direct agencies to take actions to accomplish the goals established in the legislation. Environmental legislation, for example, requires regulatory agencies to set standards for clean air, safe disposal of toxic wastes, or safe workplaces that businesses must meet. Businesses are often allowed some flexibility in the methods used to meet the standard, but failure to comply can result in fines or other legal penalties.

Consumer protection legislation directs federal regulators to set quality or safety standards for certain types of products, such as cars, toys, food, and medical equipment. This is why there are seat belts, air bags, and shatterproof windows in cars and why materials used to make children's toys or clothing cannot be flammable or toxic. Regulations may also require businesses to provide information through labeling, such as the cancer warnings on cigarette packages and lists of ingredients noting trans fats, sugar, salt, and vitamin content on packaged food.

Another form of regulation is licensing the right to own or use public properties. For example, the FCC licenses the publicly owned airwaves to people who own and operate radio and television stations.

Data Collection and Analysis

In the course of policy making and administration, the bureaucracy performs other functions. It collects data, as in the decennial census, and it makes information available to the public. Much of what we know about ourselves as a people comes from the government's collection of data on births and deaths, occupations and income, housing and health, crime, and many other things. A cursory glance at the annual *Statistical Abstract of the United States* shows that the government reports on everything from the incidence of abortions to the export of zinc and in between informs us how much celery we eat and how many DVDs we own.

Bureaucracy also keeps us informed about what government is doing, and the Internet is a valuable tool to assist in this function. Every federal agency has a website with information about its policies and programs and an e-mail link for feedback from the public. If we want to know the rules governing camping in national parks, we can call the National Park Service or go to its website. If we want to know the fate of a bill in Congress or how our representatives voted on it, we can find it posted on the Internet.

The bureaucracy engages in research, too. A prime example is the Department of Agriculture, which for nearly 140 years has conducted research on how to grow bigger and better crops, raise healthier animals, and transport and market products more effectively. Government researchers, such as those at the National Institutes of Health and the Centers for Disease Control and Prevention, do much of country's medical research, especially that related to mental health and epidemiology. Many vaccines and prescription drugs are also developed in government labs, and the Internet was invented by military bureaucrats. Every cabinet department has career civil servants—geologists, chemists, physicists, engineers, etc.—carrying out research relevant to its area of policy making, be it rocketry, soil erosion, climate change, space travel, weapons development or high-tech communications and surveillance.

Finally, in addition to its responsibilities in the four major areas just described, the bureaucracy provides continuity in governing. Presidents and members of Congress come and go, and political appointees in the bureaucracy stay an average of two years, many barely learn their jobs by the time they leave. Career civil servants have a much deeper knowledge of their agencies' work, which makes them better at it and more productive than short-term political appointees. They

Not all bureaucrats push paper. This scientist with the Food and Drug Administration (FDA) examines breast cancer protein in his lab in Bethesda, Maryland.

© Jeff Hutchens/Getty Images

keep government agencies functioning day in and day out so that all essential work continues even as elected and appointed officials come and go from office.

Politics and Professional Standards

As the part of government that implements policies made by elected officials, the bureaucracy cannot escape politics and it is subject to constant lobbying. That does not mean that civil servants have the green light to implement policy in a partisan manner. Today's civil servants are governed by laws that give priority to professional competence over political loyalty. Most Americans want fair, apolitical performance such that the quantity and quality of any government service they receive is not dependent on whether they belong to the same party as the president or their member of Congress. And most of us would prefer to have a civil engineer rather than a political crony in charge of building the dam near our town. The chances that the engineer will get the job over the crony have improved significantly since patronage was outlawed in the federal bureaucracy.

The Merit System

For decades, American public bureaucracies were staffed under the **patronage** system, which allowed elected officials to fill administrative jobs on the basis of political loyalty rather than merit. By providing

Andrew Jackson made the bureaucracy more representative of the nation's population. He also opened the doors to the White House. The guests at a White House party open to the public consumed or carried away much of a 1,400-pound cheese.

their supporters with jobs, elected officials could strengthen their political base, and many people regarded this as simply a means for government agencies to provide employment to citizens. Patronage hiring was usually referred to as the spoils system because it operated in rough accordance with the principle "to the victor belong the spoils," as the newly elected filled jobs with their own supporters. At the federal level, Andrew Jackson's presidential election in 1828 was a watershed in using the patronage system. Jackson believed that any white male citizen of average intelligence and goodwill could do a government job well. So he reversed the existing practice of naming mostly well-off people from the East Coast by appointing less well-off supporters from frontier areas.

The most obvious problem with staffing the bureaucracy with political supporters rather than by competitive recruitment is that jobs will go to people who are not competent to perform their duties. This became a major problem as government work became more technical and specialized. Furthermore, patronage could and frequently did lead to corruption, in particular to deal making between candidates and voters or individuals who controlled blocs of voters. Voters supported candidates who promised them jobs or other favors. Such corruption increasingly sullied city councils, state legislatures, and Congress during the 1800s.

Although patronage was affecting government performance, the influence wielded by the political machines that had grown powerful through its use kept Congress from acting until an unsuccessful job seeker assassinated President James Garfield in 1881. The Pendleton Act of 1883 established the **Civil Service Commission** to fill designated positions within the bureaucracy with people who had proved their competence in competitive examinations. Jobs under the commission's jurisdiction were part of the **merit system.** The new law also protected people holding merit positions from pressure to support or oppose particular candidates and from dismissal for political reasons.

Neutral Competence

The merit system established **neutral competence** as the professional standard for civil service employees. It requires that individuals filling merit positions be chosen for their expertise in executing policy and that they carry out their work in a nonpartisan or neutral manner. This standard assumes that there is no Republican or Democratic way to build a sewer, collect customs duties, or fight a war. In effect, it says that partisan politics has no place in bureaucracy. It also implies that bureaucrats should not profit personally from the decisions they make.

Woodrow Wilson, a strong advocate of neutral competence, believed that bureaucrats could learn to execute policy both expertly and responsively.[46] He saw government jobs as either political or administrative in nature and felt that by knowing which was which, we could create a bureaucracy that elected officials could control. Most current observers are less sanguine about the possibility of completely separating politics from administration.[47]

The Pendleton Act authorized the president to extend merit system coverage to additional federal jobs by executive order. In 1884, the merit system covered about 10 percent of the jobs in the federal bureaucracy and by the middle of the twentieth century rose to 90 percent. This created a rather rigid system of job classifications, pay, and rank known as the *general schedule*. It limited the president's appointment powers and also made it difficult to remove people for cause. Reforming the system was a central issue in Jimmy Carter's 1976 run for the presidency. The Civil Service Reform Act of 1978 was an attempt to modernize the personnel system and make it more competitive with the private sector. It was also a response to complaints from interest groups such as Ralph Nader's Public Interest that the Commission was concentrating on management at the expense of merit hiring, equal opportunity, and regulation.

The act got rid of the Civil Service Commission and divided its functions among several agencies. The Office of Personnel Management (OPM) today is responsible for managing a merit system for all federal employees nationwide and for working with the president to ensure that appointments to positions in exempt categories also adhere to basic standards of merit and political neutrality. Grievances and discrimination complaints are now handled by separate agencies—the Merit Systems Protection Board and the Equal Employment Opportunity Commission. The act also created a Whistleblowers Protection Agency (WBA) and an Office of Special Counsel to defend whistleblowers against retaliatory action by their agencies.

The act gave managers more opportunity to fire incompetent subordinates, and it established a more flexible classification of civil service positions. It also created the Senior Executive Service (SES) to fill the top management positions in the executive branch in the civil service. Those in the SES may be career civil servants or political appointees; they are not locked into a position but can move from agency to agency, carrying rank with them. They are also paid on the basis of performance and may receive bonuses. A number of other alternate personnel systems have been created, such as the State Department's Foreign Service and the personnel systems for the Pentagon and DHS. At least one-quarter of all positions in the federal bureaucracy are

"Sure, meritocracies are fine, but why take the chance?"

now in categories exempt from the hiring and compensation rules that govern the general schedule of civil service appointments, although all are supposed to be governed by the basic rules of merit and neutral competence. In fact there are many more political appointments in the upper levels of bureaucracy today than there were thirty years ago.

Even within the regular civil service, merit is not all that counts. The system favors veterans by adding a five-point bonus to their test scores (disabled veterans get ten points). And positioning counts as well: people already in the system are favored because they know about job openings first and may have skills identical to those in the job listing. As in the private sector, sometimes job descriptions are written to fit particular individuals.

Banning patronage from federal hiring did not end partisan political activity by federal employees, so Congress passed another law expressly defining the limits on such activities. The **Hatch Act** of 1939 prohibited federal employees from active participation in partisan campaigns, even at the state and local levels. Political activities were restricted to voting, attending rallies, and having private conversations. Under the 1939 act federal employees were not allowed to participate in party-sponsored voter registration drives, endorse party candidates, or work for or against them in any way. These prohibitions also applied to employees of state and local government who were supported by federal funds.

The Hatch Act was controversial from the beginning. Supporters argued that it protected the neutral competence of civil servants from partisan influences. Critics said it made civil servants second-class citizens by denying them the First Amendment guarantees of freedom of speech and association. In 1993, Congress changed the law to allow most federal employees to hold office within a political party, to participate in political campaigns, and to raise funds for political action committees when they are not on duty. However, all employees of law enforcement and national security agencies remain under the earlier, more stringent prohibitions.[48]

The neutral competence standard prohibits bureaucrats from gaining materially from their decisions. Civil servants are supposed to make decisions based on their professional judgment and not to advance the cause of something in which they have a financial stake. For example, bureaucrats who are stockholders in chemical companies are not supposed to be making policy about chemical waste. Even if it were possible for policy makers to put self-interest aside, holding stakes in firms they regulate automatically takes on the appearance of a conflict of interest. This in turn would allow critics of a decision to challenge the regulation in court. Furthermore, the appearance of a conflict of interest undermines public confidence in government.

To better define what constitutes a conflict of interest, Congress passed the Ethics in Government Act in 1978. The act sought to prevent former public officials with inside information from using it and their contacts to give their new employers an unfair competitive advantage. The act barred former public servants from lobbying their agencies for one year and prohibited for life lobbying on matters in which they "personally and substantially" participated as public officials. In 1989, news that former Reagan administration officials had used their government service for substantial financial gain led to the passage of a law designed to strengthen the 1978 act. These new rules had little more impact than the old ones.

President Clinton issued an executive order requiring many of his political appointees to sign a pledge that they would not lobby the agencies in which they worked for five years after leaving government and would never lobby for foreign political parties and governments. But in 2002, four of Clinton's former cabinet members and other high-level political appointees, including his trade representative and the heads of the FCC and the SEC, each held multiple seats on corporate boards. It is not unthinkable that they were hired for their government contacts, although holding such positions in itself does not violate any ethics rule.

George W. Bush appointed more corporate executives to head government agencies than any other president. Some were responsible for regulating industries whose payrolls they had just left or in which they had held stock. During the corporate accounting scandals of 2001–2002, Bush appointed Harvey Pitt to head the SEC. Pitt was a lawyer whose main work had been to defend the very Wall Street firms he was supposed to regulate as SEC head. Shortly after he took office, Pitt announced that under his direction, the SEC would be "a kinder place for accountants," a statement he undoubtedly wished he had not made after the Enron scandal broke. (Later, public outrage over his unwillingness to enforce regulations led to his resignation.)

Sometimes the range within which bureaucrats can exercise neutral competence is severely restricted by their superiors. Agencies and department heads are political, not merit, appointees, and many are specifically charged with carrying out the programs of the president who appointed them. In addition, some of the policy that bureaucrats are implementing was made by presidential directive or executive order. EPA bureaucrats gearing up to implement Clinton's executive orders on clean water and clean air in December 2000 were required to write very different rules several months later when Bush rescinded Clinton's orders and substituted radically different policies. When an agency appears to be partisan in the way it implements, or fails to implement, congressional acts, it may be because of presidential directives or orders issued by the short-term political appointee temporarily heading the agency.

Overseeing the Bureaucracy

The principal overseers of the bureaucracy are, of course, the president, who heads it and appoints its top policy makers; the Senate, which holds confirmation powers; Congress as a whole, which has authority to create, monitor, and fund agencies; and the federal courts, which often have to interpret the meaning of regulations or rule on their constitutionality. Congress has also given the public a significant, if vastly underused, role through legislation that mandates openness in government.

President

The president, constitutionally the chief executive, has primary responsibility for directing executive branch agencies and monitoring their responsiveness. He has several significant means for providing executive leadership, including budgeting, appointment and removal powers, the authority to initiate executive branch reorganizations, and, of course, his power to issue executive orders.

Congress decidedly enhanced the president's administrative powers in 1921 by delegating authority to

WHO DOES THE BUREAUCRACY SERVE?

"The government is us. Government jobs belong to the American people, not to politicians, and should be filled only with regard to public service."[1] So said the "father" of the modern civil service, Theodore Roosevelt, champion of merit hiring and neutral competence. No president has challenged these basic principles in theory or rhetoric, but some have challenged them in practice. What does it mean to serve the public? Presidents can argue that if the people elect the president and the president is the CEO of the executive branch, then isn't the bureaucracy serving the public by following the directions of the person the people choose to direct it?

The answer is yes and no. The president has hundreds of political appointees within the bureaucracy to implement his policies, but career civil servants are supposed to perform their duties free of political pressure. The thousands of scientists, mathematicians, engineers, investigators, and data analyzers who provide the information that informs policy making and implementation were hired specifically for their professional expertise, and it is their mandate as civil servants to provide that information with neutral competence. It is up to elected officials whether they choose to act on the information provided.

All administrations vet scientific reports, and on many issues there is no clear consensus in the findings. A president may cherry-pick reports for the evidence that supports his policy preferences. There are many examples of this, such as whether it is the right or wrong time to raise taxes or cut taxes, to raise the prime interest rate or hold it steady, or approve or ban a new medical procedure. In most cases a president

or members of Congress acknowledge disagreements among the experts, but they do not try to change the data. Government researchers whose findings are not followed may not be happy with the policy results, but if they are not pressured to change their findings, their neutral competence has not been challenged.

For example, President Reagan did not try to alter scientific findings about AIDS, but he did refuse to act on them. However, C. Everett Koop, his surgeon general, against administration wishes but in accordance with his own understanding of his public responsibility, undertook a mass education campaign on AIDS. The mailing of information to every American household helped reduce panic and fear about the disease, change behavior, and undoubtedly contributed to saving many lives. And, even

by going against the man who appointed him, Koop managed to keep his job.

The threat to neutral competence comes when a president, or his political appointees in federal agencies, suppress data or actually edit the content of research reports to fit policy. These attempts are most egregious when there is a consensus among experts.[2] For example, George W. Bush did not deny that global warming was occurring, but he did not accept the international scientific consensus, nor the findings of government scientists, that human behavior was a major contributing factor. In 2002 and 2003, a White House lawyer who had worked for the oil industry's largest lobby, the American Petroleum Institute, and who had no science training, edited reports on global warming by government scientists to

Jim Hansen, a government expert on climate change, was ordered by the Bush administration to stop giving speeches about global warming and explanations about how scientific findings differed from administration policy.

make their conclusions seem far less certain.[3] In 2006, Jim Hansen, an expert on climate change and the long-time head of NASA's Goddard Institute for Space Studies, complained that the administration had ordered him to stop giving speeches on global warming and not to talk about how his findings differed from administration policy.[4] One of his reports had been edited to bring the conclusions nearer the president's position. The wording changes were made by a twenty-four-year old political appointee at NASA, previously a public relations aide in Bush's presidential campaign, who had no scientific training and in fact no college degree.

Hanson's case is but one of many attempts by the Bush administration to put policy preferences above neutral competence. The scientific community has roundly criticized Bush's use of appointees to redirect agency work in ways that interfered with scientific integrity. The Union of Concerned Scientists specifically charged Bush with ordering politically motivated changes in the evidence and conclusions of reports prepared by government scientists on cli-

mate change, mercury pollution, drug safety, and the effectiveness of sex education in disease prevention.[5] One highly publicized instance was a two-year delay by Bush's appointee to head the FDA for approval of over-the-counter sales of a morning-after contraceptive, despite the scientific consensus that the drug was safe. The administration looked on it not as a contraceptive but as an abortifacient that would prevent births and encourage teenage promiscuity, and administration policy was both to oppose abortion and promote abstinence. The acting director, whose confirmation was held up pending a decision on the drug, simply denied there was a scientific consensus on the drug's safety.

Perhaps no agency head suffered more severe criticism for not exercising neutral competence than former CIA Director George Tenet. The day after the 9/11 attacks, President Bush made clear to the head of his counterterrorism unit and to others in his administration his interest in establishing a connection between Iraq and al-Qaeda.[6] The evidence of a connection was weak, but Bush thought an invasion of Iraq could be jus-

tified on the grounds that Saddam Hussein's arsenal of weapons of mass destruction presented an imminent threat. When he asked Tenet whether there was evidence to support his case to Congress and the public, Tenet told him it was a "slam dunk."[7] Postwar investigators found no evidence to support the claim that Iraq possessed stockpiles of weapons of mass destruction or even active programs to develop them.[8] Furthermore, many arms experts within the agency had questioned the validity of the evidence Bush cited in his public statements.

Tenet had been a Clinton appointee whom Bush retained when he became president; his retention and reappointment were dependent on Bush's judgment of his work. Because Bush's policy preferences on Iraq were well known inside and outside the administration, most concluded that Tenet had violated his neutral competence mandate and simply told the president what he wanted to hear. Having lost credibility in Congress and with the public, Tenet was forced to resign. Bush replaced him with Porter Goss, a political ally in Congress—albeit a former CIA employee—with instructions to purge the agency of career agents who would not subordinate their professional views to administration policy. A number of the agency's highest level, longest-serving agents resigned or were forced out. Many became sources (leaks) for a number of new books on the politicization of intelligence gathering and analysis.[9] Bush's new director lasted less than two years before being replaced by an air force general with a career in intelligence work.

Bush appointees have also ordered changes in scientific papers that are unrelated to policy but illustrate micro-managing of scientific wording to conform to a political sensibility. A discussion of the Big Bang explanation of the origins of the universe, for example, was altered to magnify its uncertainty, presumably to leave room for a biblical interpretation. In another paper a reference by NASA scientists to the death of the sun in the distant future was expunged. A spokeswoman for the agency said, "NASA is not in the habit of frightening the public with doom and gloom scenarios."[10]

Does the suppression of findings of government scientists serve the public? Does it serve the stated goal of every administration since Chester Arthur's, including Bush's, to maintain merit hiring and neutral competence as the guiding principles of the federal bureaucracy? The Bush argument has been that, as the president and the only nationally elected public official, he represents the public interest and has a popular mandate to implement his policy agenda. And following his view of the presidency as a unitary executive, it is his job to direct the work of the bureaucracy and the job of bureaucrats to follow his orders.

This is probably easier for political appointees to accept than it is for career professionals. A NASA public affairs officer, for example—a political appointee—said his job was "to make the president look good." However, his counterpart at the Goddard Institute said it was not her job nor that of the Institute's. "I'm a career civil servant and Jim Hansen is a scientist." Dr. Hansen said the mission of his agency was "to understand and protect our home planet." He claimed that constraints placed on government scientists had "already prevented the public from fully grasping recent findings about climate change. . . . Communicating with the public is essential because public concern is probably the only thing capable of overcoming special interests that have obfuscated the topic."[11] Not long after Hansen made his remarks, NASA revised its mission statement, replacing "to understand and protect our home planet," with "To pioneer the future in space exploration, scientific discovery and aeronautics research." It was a better fit with Bush's stated goal of exploring Mars.[12] Rep. Sherwood Boehlert (R-NY), chair of the House Committee on Science, said as he retired from office, "This is a town where everyone says they are for science-based decision making—until the science leads to a politically inconvenient conclusion. And then they want to go to Plan B. . . . Making science political is just a part of the current times."[13]

[1]This and other Roosevelt quotes about the merit system can be found at www.opm.gov/about_opm/tr/quotes.asp.

[2]For an overview of findings on climate change go to www.realclimate.org.

[3]Andrew Revkin, "Bush Aide Softened Greenhouse Gas Links to Global Warming," *New York Times,* June 8, 2005, 1.

[4]Andrew C. Revkin, "Climate Expert Says NASA Tried to Silence Him," *New York Times,* January 29, 2006, 1; Juliet Eilperin, "Censorship Is Alleged at NOAA: Scientists Afraid to Speak Out," *Washington Post,* February 11, 2006, A7.

[5]For reports on these issues go to the website of the Union of Concerned Scientists (www.ucsusa.org) and also the Federation of American Scientists (www.usfas.org).

[6]This was revealed by the head of the Clinton and Bush counterterrorism unit, Richard A. Clarke, who spoke with Bush on September 12, 2001, in the war room and recounted the event in *Against All Enemies* (New York: Free Press, 2004) and in public testimony before the televised 9/11 Commission hearings in 2004.

[7]Public testimony before the televised 9/11 Commission hearings, 2004.

[8]Report issued by the chief U.S. arms inspector, Charles A. Duelfer, October 2004.

[9]See, for example, James Risen, *State of War: The Secret History of the CIA and the Bush Administration* (New York: The Free Press, 2006), and Ron Suskind, *The One Percent Doctrine* (New York: Simon and Schuster, 2006). George Tenet himself was a major source for Suskind's book.

[10]Dennis Overbye, "Someday the Sun Will Go Out and the World Will End (but Don't Tell Anyone)," *New York Times,* February 14, 2006.

[11]All quotes in the paragraph from Revkin, "Climate Expert Says NASA Tried to Silence Him," 1.

[12]"What About Us?" (Editorial), *New York Times,* July 28, 2006.

[13]Claudia Dreifus, "A Conversation with Sherwood Boehlert: A Science Advocate and 'an Endangered Species,' He Bids Farewell," *New York Times,* May 9, 2006.

write the annual budget. In 1937, when Congress approved Franklin Roosevelt's executive branch reorganization, it moved the Bureau of the Budget (BOB) into the new Executive Office of the President (EOP) to help the president manage the bureaucracy. During Nixon's reorganization of the EOP, the newly created Office of Management and Budget (OMB) absorbed BOB and was given specific responsibility for overseeing executive agency performance. (It reports its findings to the public as well as the president by posting them at its website.) This constant monitoring of agencies from within the EOP gives the president more administrative control than does budget writing itself. Presidents can try to cut agency appropriations to limit agencies' range of actions or they can tie conditions to appropriations to make them take specific actions, but Congress does not have to approve White House requests. And because it has power to approve appropriations Congress has more opportunity than the president to attach strings to funding.

A president's best chance to direct the work of an agency is to put a surrogate in charge of it, that is, to appoint someone who shares his views. It is easiest to do this with cabinet departments because it is accepted that a president is entitled to appoint politically like-minded people to his own cabinet. Thus, Reagan and both Bushes filled health care–related positions in the Department of Health and Human Services with people who were against keeping abortion legal, whereas Clinton filled them with people who were pro-choice. Appointments to independent and regulatory agencies receive more scrutiny because neutral competence plays a greater role, but presidents do get most of their choices confirmed. Republican presidents tend to appoint people who favor business and Democratic presidents appoint those who lean toward the interests of consumers and organized labor. Reagan chose heads for regulatory agencies such as OSHA, the Consumer Product Safety Commission, and the EPA who agreed with his goal of reducing government regulation, whereas Clinton named a lifelong environmental activist to head the EPA.

Of course, sometimes presidential appointees, despite their being screened for issue positions, may end up—especially if they stay in a position long enough—representing long-standing agency policies and norms rather than the president's interests. Most appointees have less expertise and experience in agency operations than career civil servants, and some come to rely on career officials for information about agency history, procedures, and policy questions. But much depends on the president's leadership, how high a priority change in the agency is for him, and how closely he monitors a particular agency's activities and directions.

Administrative reform is a third means a president can use to increase his control over the bureaucracy. Generally, the more sweeping a president's recommendation for change, the more he must anticipate congressional and interest group resistance. For example, Reagan wanted to abolish the Departments of Educa-

tion and Energy and merge the Commerce and Labor Departments, but Congress would not support him. The most audacious attempt at bureaucratic control by a modern president has been George W. Bush's reorganization of the executive branch to create the new cabinet-level DHS. The plan had great scope, affecting twenty-two agencies and 177,000 employees. But what made it bold was Bush's request for exemption from worker protection laws and the authority to transfer funds and personnel from agency to agency without congressional approval. In other words, he asked Congress to cede substantial budgetary and oversight powers to the White House.

The White House can also try to influence independent agencies and commissions by lobbying and mobilizing public opinion. Attempts by presidents of both parties to influence Federal Reserve Board decisions on interest rates, for example, are legion.

Despite these powers, there are many limits on the president's executive leadership. Given the size and complexity of the federal bureaucracy, the president cannot possibly influence every important decision. Moreover, as the civil service expanded, presidents found it increasingly difficult to lead an executive branch with 90 percent of its positions filled by the merit system employees deliberately insulated from presidential control. The creation of the SES and alternative personnel systems allows for short-term and emergency appointments and easier movement within the bureaucracy. In addition, the 1978 law gave managers more opportunity to fire incompetent subordinates and authorized bonuses and a new pay scale for managers to encourage better performance. Despite the changes presidents often still feel thwarted by the constraints on removing civil servants for poor performance or because they will not do a president's

bidding. Although job security is not meant to shield public servants who do poor work, it does make firing incompetent workers difficult and time consuming. The organization of public employees into unions contributes to this, although unions also protect workers from being dismissed without grounds. The government's rate of discharging people for inefficiency, 0.01 percent a year, did not increase after the 1978 reforms, though no doubt some employees left after being threatened with dismissal or demotion. As one public employee said, "We're all like headless nails down here—once you get us in you can't get us out."[49] This attitude captures what some say is the civil service's built in bias toward job survival rather than innovation.[50]

Agencies that have strong allies in Congress, in powerful interest groups, or in the public provide another limit to presidential leadership. Presidents have more success controlling agencies that lack strong congressional allies and domestic clientele groups, such as the Treasury and State Departments, than agencies that have such allies, such as the Social Security Administration and the Agriculture and Health and Human Services Departments. However, the increasing number of political appointees in senior positions gives the president many more opportunities to exercise his influence over agency operations, even in agencies like the EPA, which has strong bipartisan support in Congress and powerful interest groups monitoring its work.

Not all presidents have the same interest in exercising executive leadership over the bureaucracy. Although all want to appoint people to policy-making positions who are committed to a similar set of goals, the will to pressure these individuals after they have been appointed varies. As discussed in Chapter 11, George W. Bush arguably has interpreted the president's role as chief executive more absolutely than any of his predecessors. He maintained that a president's powers as chief executive are not divided but unitary and that as a **unitary executive** his orders to executive branch agencies trump any directions from Congress or the courts. (See the box "Who Does the Bureaucracy Serve?")

Congress

Although the president has the edge in leadership through his appointment powers, Congress has greater scope for oversight and control. Much of the bureaucracy's power is delegated authority from Congress, and much of its work is implementing laws passed by Congress. Congress has the power to create, reorganize, or eliminate agencies and the ultimate instrument of control—the power of the purse strings. Congress not only has the power to increase or decrease the amount of money the president requests to fund an agency, it can tell an agency how it has to spend the money it allocates. Many special interest projects are funded in this way: Congress, or more often, a congressional committee, tells an agency that it must spend x number of dollars from its budget to pay for a project earmarked by a member of Congress, even though the project does not appear in the budget and the president may oppose the spending or the project itself.

Congress also has dozens of committees (supported by a staff of thousands) to which executive agencies must report. But just as an agency's outside allies can work to thwart presidential control, they can also limit congressional oversight. Agencies frequently work closely with certain congressional committees and interest groups for mutual support and outcomes favorable to all. (These relationships are sometimes called "iron triangles" or issue networks.) Agencies may adjust their actions to suit the preferences of the congressional committees that authorize their programs and appropriate their funds. For example, decisions by members of independent regulatory commissions are sensitive to the views of members of their congressional oversight committees. When the membership of the committees becomes more liberal or more conservative, so do the decisions regulators make.[51]

Iron triangles make oversight look less like monitoring the bureaucracy and more like collusion. Constituent service, by contrast, provides a motive for members of Congress to try to shape bureaucratic decision making. Members often try to influence agencies to take some action on behalf of constituents or in the interest of their districts. In fact, congressional staff who do casework often have their duties assigned according to the agencies they are responsible for contacting about constituent complaints. This can lead to inefficiencies when bureaucrats are pressured to help members of Congress satisfy constituent demands rather than use neutral competence as a decision standard. It is this kind of pressure that keeps military bases open years beyond their usefulness simply because they are good for the economy of a member's district. This pressure from Congress makes it difficult for bureaucrats to act with neutral competence.

Courts

Federal courts act as another check on the bureaucracy. Judicial decisions shape agency actions by directing agencies to follow legally correct procedures. Of course, the courts cannot intercede in an agency's decision making unless some aggrieved person or corporation files a suit against the agency. Nevertheless, in almost any controversial agency action, there will be aggrieved parties and possibly some with sufficient resources to bring a court action.

The courts interpret lawmakers' intentions by deciding what congressional majorities and the president had in mind when they made a law. This can be difficult. Sometimes, in their haste, lawmakers fail to specify crucial elements of a law, or they may be unable to reach agreement on a provision and leave it ambiguous in order to get the bill passed. Lawmakers may also write a certain amount of vagueness into a law so that agencies will be able to adapt it to unknown future conditions. How the courts read a law may augment or reduce the ability of Congress and the president to influence its implementation. In the current Supreme Court, the conservative majority has increasingly used its authority to interpret the intent of congressional acts in ways that expand the Court's own powers. We discuss these issues in Chapter 13.

Regulators and other agency policy makers appear to be quite sensitive to federal court decisions. For example, when the courts overturn the National Labor Relations Board's decisions in a pro labor direction, the board's decisions soon become more prolabor. Similarly, decisions drift the other way when courts overturn agency decisions in a probusiness direction.[52]

Interest Groups and Individuals

The public has numerous opportunities to oversee and to influence bureaucratic decision making. Most of these rights stem from laws designed to ensure openness in government.

Openness laws also extend to media access and thus provide another important check on bureaucratic abuses. But the media can also make the bureaucracy's work more difficult. Reporters like to cover conflict and bad news and are therefore usually on the lookout for stories about internal policy disputes. Newspapers and other media outlets make frequent use of FOIA to obtain documents from government agencies.

Interest groups and their lobbyists are also part of the public. Lobbyists tend to take much greater advantage of their rights of access than the general public does, and they are the source of much of the public comment on proposed rules received by agencies. Most FOIA requests still come from businesses, interest groups, lawyers, scholars, and the media. In one year, 85 percent of the requests for information submitted to the FDA came from companies that it regulates. That information enabled the companies to evaluate their strategies for influencing agency decisions that affect them. Interest groups want to make sure bureaucracies adopt rules and enforcement practices they favor. An environmental group cannot rest on its laurels just because Congress has passed a law placing new safeguards on toxic waste disposal. The group's job is not over until it makes sure the EPA writes strict rules to enforce the law. Consequently, the group must lobby the regulators as well as Congress.

If an agency seems to be sabotaging the intent of Congress, interest groups can work with friendly congressional committees to put pressure on the agency to

© Karen Kasmauski, National Geographic Society

Government agencies monitor infectious diseases around the world to protect Americans at home and also civilian and military personnel who might come in contact with such diseases abroad. This airborne evacuation team practices a rescue in West Virginia.

mend its ways. And interest groups can also try to rally public opinion to their side to pressure Congress or the president to do something about the agency. Environmental groups are especially skilled at this. Sometimes interest groups pressure an agency so effectively that the agency is said to be "captured."[53] This term is used most frequently for regulatory agencies thought to be controlled by the groups they are supposed to be regulating.

We know that interest groups can influence the bureaucracy, but can individual citizens affect policy too? It is difficult for an individual to influence public agencies when acting alone, but that does not mean there are no opportunities to do so. Perhaps one person posting a comment on a website will not change agency policy, but if all residents opposed to a decision on cleaning up a hazardous waste site in their neighborhood file comments, it can make a difference. Rules have been reversed or amended.

An individual who uses FOIA to retrieve documents that expose agency corruption or abuse can also make a difference by going public with the story. And members of the general public are increasingly taking advantage of openness laws even though the process is not easy for those who try. A lot of paperwork is involved, some costs, and often a long wait, even though government agencies employ over five thousand administrators to process the requests.

Ordinary citizens could have a greater impact if they used all the tools that Congress has given them to oversee and to influence the bureaucracy. They can even be whistleblowers by suing companies with government contracts that defraud the government (and if successful, share in the money recovered).[54] But individual whistleblowers within the bureaucracy often have the best opportunity to monitor agency practices. Some whistleblowing is unsuccessful, but some makes a real difference. One of the most famous whistleblowers was Pentagon employee Daniel Ellsberg, who in 1968 leaked thousands of documents on the conduct of the Vietnam War to the *New York Times*. Henry Kissinger claimed that Ellsberg was the most dangerous man in the world, but Ellsberg's acts helped the public understand that the Johnson and Nixon administrations' private rationale for fighting the war were not the same as the reasons they stated in public.

That same year, Ernest Fitzgerald, an Air Force cost accountant, revealed that the Lockheed C-5A transport plane vibrated so much in flight that its wings actually fell off if they were not replaced after only two hundred hours of flying time. Saying it wanted "to save expenses"—his $32,000 salary—the Air Force reacted by firing Fitzgerald. He sued to get his job back and won, but he had to wait for a court order in 1982 before the Air Force gave him responsibilities equal to his qualifications.[55]

Bureaucrats who blow the whistle on mismanagement, sexual or political harassment, or other abuses of power in their agencies are supposed to be protected from arbitrary firing. But rarely does an agency publicly thank an employee for blowing the whistle, as FBI Director Robert Mueller did when Coleen Rowley went public with that agency's mishandling of a 9/11–related investigation. Rowley, a Minneapolis-based agent involved in the case of Zacarias Moussaoui, an Algerian, under indictment as the so-called twentieth hijacker, had complained to Director Mueller that a midlevel manager had thwarted her attempt to get a search warrant to go through Moussaoui's personal belongings and the contents of his computer.[56] Rowley testified before the Senate Judiciary Committee, but even if her complaints had not become public, they would have been hard for the agency to ignore given her record. Mueller went public to commend her for her actions, but his praise was not so much an indication of changing attitudes toward whistleblowers as a measure of the trouble the agency was in with Congress and also the media attention to Rowley's case. She was one of three whistleblowers (the other two exposed fraud in the private bureaucracies of Enron and World-Com) named by *Time* magazine when it proclaimed 2002 "The Year of the Whistleblower."

Disclosure of bureaucratic failures increased after 9/11 because many individuals saw that neglected shortcomings could have serious consequences. But retaliation continued. In recent years, airport baggage screeners, border patrol agents, and the chief of the United States Park Police were disciplined or fired for reporting problems in their agencies. The most publicized case was that of Medicare's chief actuary, who was threatened with dismissal by the political appointee who headed his agency if he provided Congress with accurate numbers on the cost of the Bush administration's proposed prescription drug benefit for seniors.

In 2004, Congress responded by writing a new law with stronger protections for whistleblowers, including freedom from reprisal for those, like the Medicare actuary, who provide information to Congress. But the bill was strongly opposed by the Bush administration, which contended that it "unconstitutionally interferes with the president's ability to control and manage the government."[57]

Despite the legal protections, it is the rare person who will set aside cordial relations with colleagues and ambition for promotion in order to challenge the status quo. Most people, whether working in the private or the public sector, find it difficult to expose their employer's dirty laundry. And even if the law does protect their jobs, their careers may be effectively ruined. Rowley, who despite the public commendations, probably had little chance for promotion, retired from the FBI and in 2006 ran for Congress. About half of all whistle-blowers (like Bunnie Greenhouse in this chapter's You Are There) lose their jobs, half of those lose their homes, and half of those lose their families.[58]

Conclusion: Is the Bureaucracy Responsive?

In 2002 Congress oversaw the biggest reorganization of the federal bureaucracy in a half century when it created the DHS. The changes were prompted by failures in performance that helped make possible the terrorist attacks of September 11, 2001. Particular targets of the reform were intelligence and law enforcement agencies and customs and immigration services. A reporter noted that the bureaucratic morass in the former Immigration and Naturalization Service was encapsulated in the title of the official put in charge of the reorganization: the "assistant deputy executive associate commissioner for immigration services."[59] The failure of the reorganization either to streamline communications, as revealed in DHS's response to hurricane Katrina, or consolidate preparedness for future terrorist attacks was more evidence of the limits of reform. In fact, many observers believe that the reorganization diminished not enhanced the functions of agencies (e.g., FEMA and Immigration) incorporated into DHS.

Is the federal bureaucracy an impenetrable forest or an uncontrollable fourth branch of government, as some portray it? The turf wars, miscommunication, and fragmented authority that surfaced after 9/11 certainly indicate that at least part of the federal bureaucracy is an impenetrable forest. It is not surprising that most of the agencies that failed so badly (e.g., the CIA and the FBI) are among the least open to citizens or the media and even to congressional oversight. Those agencies continued to oppose reform even as Congress was implementing the recommendations of the 9/11 Commission to reorganize our fifteen different intelligence agencies under a single directorate to improve communication, gain more central control, and limit interagency rivalries.

But the bureaucracy as a whole is not an errant fourth branch of government. With the exception of supersecret agencies like the National Security Agency (aka No Such Agency), for which Congress has forfeited much of its oversight responsibility in the interests of national security, most of the bureaucracy is subject to presidential and congressional control, providing they are willing to exercise their powers. Indeed, one of the by-products of the Bush administration's attempts to increase presidential control of executive branch agencies at the expense of Congress is that it has reawakened some members of Congress to its oversight lapses.

Our fragmented political system means that our public agencies operate in an environment of uncertainty and competition. Bureaucrats have many bosses: a president, his appointees, Congress and its many committees and subcommittees, and the federal courts. In addition, numerous interest groups try to influence the work of federal agencies. The often contradictory demands for responsiveness and neutral competence contribute to an uncertainty of expectations, too. As a result, agencies try to protect themselves by cultivating the support of congressional committees and interest groups. Even presidents have trouble influencing agencies because of these alliances. Although some presidents, such as Franklin Roosevelt and Jimmy Carter, have occasionally rearranged the status quo, their successes in articulating a vision of national priorities are more the exception than the rule.

There is a vaguely defined but frequently articulated public suspicion that any bureaucracy is destined to be intransigent and inefficient. We have tried to show that some of that attitude stems from lack of consensus on what the work of government should be. If you do not like the work that Congress and the president have assigned to the bureaucracy, there is not much chance you will view the bureaucracy as responsive to your needs. If the dissatisfaction is more over how the bureaucracy does its work, there is hope that at least some areas of performance will meet with your approval. The public does have tools to influence how bureaucrats do their work, but it has many more ways to lobby Congress and the president to change the work they give the bureaucracy to do.

Despite people's negative feelings about the bureaucracy, the mail is delivered, bridges get inspected, social security paid, and passports are issued. It usually does what it is supposed to do. But the investigation into the INS, FBI, and CIA actions prior to September 11, 2001, made clear that these agencies had experienced catastrophic failures. Part of the problem, as subsequent investigations revealed, was that the experts within these agencies were overridden by their superiors and not allowed to exercise neutral competence. As a consequence, a number of our most experienced intelligence professionals left the government.

Paradoxically, Americans' opinion of how the government was doing its job and its overall trust in government increased substantially after the 9/11 attacks. But there was also a more serious concern for poorly functioning government agencies. The head of one government watchdog group summarized the feeling this way: "Before September 11 there was a bit of a blasé attitude of 'OK, the government screwed up again.' Now people see the consequences on their lives and see the necessity of government functioning well."[60]

Mrs. Greenhouse Blows the Whistle

Furious at her superiors for going behind her back in issuing the audit waiver for KBR, Mrs. Greenhouse agreed to testify at the June 2005 Democratic Policy Committee forum looking into charges of overbilling and fraud in Iraq War contracts. Because she was such a high-ranking bureaucrat, and because Bush's handling of the Iraq War was a central issue in the upcoming election, Greenhouse's charges grabbed headlines. It also mattered that she was one of the small number of African Americans in the Senior Executive Service and that suspicions of overbilling and outright fraud by private contractors had been swirling just under the surface of much of the reporting from Iraq. Mrs. Greenhouse told one interviewer the Halliburton/KBR agreements were "the worst activity in contracting that I'd ever seen in all of my contracting career."[61]

Three weeks after her testimony USACE informed Greenhouse that, effective August 2005, she would be demoted to a G-15 rank (placing her out of the Senior Executive Service, with a significant loss of authority and slightly less pay). Despite her years of sterling job evaluations, her boss said it was because of her "poor work habits" and had nothing

to do with her speaking out.[62] She was reminded that she did not have to take the new position but had the option of retiring with full benefits. But Greenhouse said that when she took the oath of office and said "so help me God," it meant she was going to "protect the interests of my government and my country. . . . And nobody has the right to take away my privilege to serve my government. Nobody."[63] Through her lawyers at the National Whistleblowers Center, Mrs Greenhouse wrote to the Secretary of the Army asking for a full investigation into the "integrity of the federal contracting program," and eventually the FBI took up the case.[64] Three congressional Democrats asked Defense Secretary Rumsfeld to investigate Greenhouse's demotion on the grounds that it "appears to be retaliation" for her testimony before Congress. "Retaliation against employees for providing information to Congress is illegal and entirely unacceptable," the letter said.[65]

As the war dragged on and costs mounted and reconstruction projects failed, the Pentagon and Justice Departments launched investigations into the Halliburton contracts—although at the same time Halliburton was awarded millions more in noncompetitive contracts for hurricane Katrina re-

covery work. Greenhouse returned to testify at the Democrats' hearings in September 2005, this time discussing her demotion. Also testifying were former employees of Halliburton/KBR and another USACE civil servant who had been dismissed for protesting the way contracts were awarded.[66] Finally, in July 2006 the Pentagon announced that at the end of Halliburton's five-year deal, the remaining work would be opened to competitive bidding. Mrs Greenhouse, however, was still waiting for her grievances to be resolved.

Greenhouse's former boss, Gen. Joe Ballard said, "The Corps is a tough organization. And I'll tell you, it's not easy to be a woman in this organization, and a black one at that. . . . What Bunny is caught up in is politics of the highest damn order. This is real hardball they're playing here. Bunny is a procurement officer, she's not a politician. She's not trained to do this." Ballard said he was not optimistic about her future. "I think you can put a fork in it," he said. "Her career is done."[67]

 To learn more about this topic, go to "you are there" exercises for this chapter on the text website.

Key Terms

whistleblowers
Administrative Procedure
  Act (APA)
FOIA
Sunshine Act
independent agencies
policy implementation
delegated legislative
  authority

regulation
patronage
Civil Service Commission
merit system
neutral competence
Hatch Act
unitary executive

Further Reading

C. Fred Alford, *Whistleblowers: Broken Lives and Organizational Power* (Ithaca, N.Y.: Cornell University Press, 2001). A political science professor chronicles the impact on the lives and careers of individuals who reported corruption and mismanagement in government agencies.

Jonathan Kwitny, *Acceptable Risks* (New York: Poseidon, 1992). Kwitny tells a fast-paced and well-written story of two men who prodded and fought the Food and Drug Administration to make potentially helpful medicines available to AIDS patients. It reveals the agency's rigidity but also, ultimately, its responsiveness.

Paul C. Light, *The New Public Service* (Washington, D.C.: Brookings Institution, 1999). If you are interested in a career in a public bureaucracy, this is a useful handbook written by one of the leading scholars of the U.S. Civil Service.

George Orwell, *Nineteen Eighty-Four* (New York: Harcourt, Brace, 1949). One of the most popular novels of the twentieth century gives you a look at an überbureaucracy and its intrusion into private life. It will put any complaints you might have about the federal bureaucracy into perspective.

James Risen, *State of War: The Secret History of the CIA and the Bush Administration* (New York: The Free Press, 2006). With information provided by career CIA and Pentagon officials, a *New York Times* reporter offers an inside account of how politics trumped neutral competence to manipulate intelligence on Iraq's weapons programs prior to the 2003 invasion.

Eileen Welsome, *The Plutonium Files* (New York: Dial, 1999). This is an account of secret government medical experiments that involved injection of radioactive plutonium into human subjects. The documents on which it is based were retrieved through a FOIA request.

For Viewing

An Inconvenient Truth (2006). Al Gore takes his thirty-year quest to inform the American public about global warming to movie theaters. A mixture of public lectures, personal reminiscences, and stunning graphics that summarize the scientific consensus on human contributions to the warming of the planet, with a section illustrating how scientific data have been politically manipulated.

During J. Edgar Hoover's directorship, the FBI was a national icon, a view reflected in the TV series *I Led Three Lives* (1953–1956), the movie version (equally fictional) *I Was a Communist for the FBI* (1951), and movies such as *The FBI Story* (1959)—during the making of which Hoover was on the set each day—and *Elliot Ness* (1987).

Orwell's *Nineteen Eighty-Four* was filmed and released in 1984.

October Sky (1999). Most people think of federal bureaucrats as paper pushers, but thousands are scientists and mathematicians who work in research and development. This is a true story of how one boy's interest in rocketry led to a career as a NASA bureaucrat.

 **Electronic Resources**

www.gao.gov

This is the site of the Government Accountability Office, the congressional office that monitors the performance of executive branch agencies.

www.opm.gov

At the Office of Personnel Management site you can review tables that reveal the composition of the federal workforce, demographics, occupation, pay, and many other statistics.

www.fas.org

This is the site of the Federation of American Scientists.

www.ombwatch.org

This is a site set up by interest groups and private individuals to monitor the performance of executive branch agencies. You can review agency evaluations, changes in FOIA, and other laws and rules governing openness in government.

www.openthegovernment.org

This website is devoted to tracking government policy on issues of secrecy and public access to government documents. Site managers advocate for greater openness.

www.usajobs.opm.gov

At this site you can see what jobs are open in the federal government and submit an online application.

ThomsonNOW™

Enter ThomsonNOW™ using the access card that is available with this text or through www.thomsonedu.com/thomsonnow. ThomsonNOW™ will assist you in understanding the content in this chapter with a personalized study plan generated for your needs. A practice test will assess the areas you need to review and provide the tools to fully comprehend those concepts, including an integrated digital eBook, interactive simulations, timelines, video case studies, MicroCase exercises, and InfoTrac College Edition readers and exercises. You'll also be connected to the learning objectives, chapter outline, chapter glossary, flash cards, crossword puzzles, Internet activities, and interactive quizzes found on the companion website.

To dispel the impression that Samuel Alito was insensitive to women's issues, the administration seated women immediately behind him so they would be visible when the cameras focused on him. From left, his wife and an assistant attorney general.

Judge Alito

Development of the Court's Role in Government

    Founding to the Civil War

    Civil War to the Great Depression

    Great Depression to the Present

    The Next Era

Courts

    Structure of the Courts

    Jurisdiction of the Courts

Judges

    Selection of Judges

    Tenure of Judges

    Qualifications of Judges

    Independence of Judges

Access to the Courts

    Wealth Discrimination in Access

    Interest Group Help in Access

    Proceeding through the Courts

Deciding Cases

    Interpreting Statutes

    Interpreting the Constitution

    Restraint and Activism

    Following Precedents

    Making Law

    Deciding Cases at the Supreme Court

Power of the Courts

    Use of Judicial Review

    Use of Political Checks against the Courts

Conclusion: Are the Courts Responsive?

YOU ARE THERE

Should You Be Candid?

You are Samuel Alito, a judge on a federal court of appeals for the past fifteen years and a lawyer in the Reagan administration before that. You have been nominated as a justice on the Supreme Court by President George W. Bush. As your confirmation hearings in the Senate approach, you must decide whether to be honest and forthright when answering questions posed by the senators.

When vacancies on the Court occur, the president nominates a replacement and the Senate votes to confirm or reject the nominee. As part of the confirmation process, the Senate Judiciary Committee holds hearings in which senators question the nominee about his or her views. Nominees aren't asked how they would decide particular cases—their answers would prejudge those cases—but they are asked what they think about current legal issues.

For a long time the confirmation process was minimal. The Senate did not hold confirmation hearings until 1916, and even then the nominees were not expected to attend until the 1950s.[1] In that decade, the Supreme Court's desegregation rulings were so controversial among southern senators that the nominees were quizzed about their judicial philosophy and at the same time given an earful of the senators' opinions about the Court's decisions.

The most contentious battle occurred when President Reagan nominated Robert Bork in 1987. Bork had been a law school professor and a federal court judge. In articles and speeches, he had rejected a right to privacy, which is the basis of Court decisions allowing birth control and abortion, and he had criticized Court decisions and congressional laws advancing racial equality and sexual equality. Although Bork had legal reasons for these positions—he had not advocated that whites should discriminate against blacks, for example, only that the Court should not have forbidden them from doing so—he seemed oblivious to the practical consequences of his positions. Senator Ted Kennedy (D-Mass.) gave an inflammatory speech:

> Robert Bork's America is a land in which women would be forced into back-alley abortions, blacks would sit at segregated lunch counters, rogue police could break down citizens' doors in midnight raids, school children could not be taught about evolution, writers and artists could be censored at the whim of the government, and the doors of the federal courts would be shut on the fingers of millions of citizens.

Bork's positions struck many Americans as extreme—one political cartoon, which appeared when daylight saving time ended in the fall, depicted Bork admonishing people, "Now, this fall remember to turn your clocks back thirty years."

Workers at People for the American Way headquarters in Washington, D.C., prepare information packets for their members when Justice Sandra Day O'Connor announced her retirement.

A coalition of interest groups mounted the first grassroots campaign against a judicial nomination, and the Senate denied his confirmation. This defeat, at the high-water mark of the conservative movement, signaled that moderate Americans did not want to reverse legal doctrine they considered settled (even doctrine many had opposed when it was new). Yet conservative activists were bitterly disappointed, and they vowed revenge. Two decades later, they still use this battle as a rallying cry and a continuing justification for their efforts to influence judicial appointments.

When President George H. W. Bush had his first vacancy, he chose a man who had left no trail of controversial writings and speeches. David Souter, though a former New Hampshire attorney general and then a state supreme court justice, was called the "stealth candidate" (after the bomber designed to elude radar). Souter was a private person who lived alone in a house at the end of a dirt road. He had expressed few positions and made few decisions reflecting his views on constitutional doctrine. In the hearings, he refused to reveal his views. He offered a small target and was confirmed easily.

When Bush had his second vacancy, he chose a better-known conservative, Clarence Thomas, the head of the Equal Employment Opportunity Commission and then a federal appel-

late court judge. Thomas' confirmation process became another bruising battle. The concern was over his conservative views, though the debate focused on a coworker's allegations of sexual harassment (which will be addressed in Chapter 15). Although Thomas stated his position on capital punishment—in favor—which mirrored public opinion, he refused to acknowledge his position on abortion, which we know now did not mirror public opinion. Incredibly, he said he had never thought about abortion, even though it was the major legal controversy at the time. He was confirmed by only four votes.

When Clinton had two vacancies, he was wary because Republicans had vowed to avenge Bork's defeat and Thomas's near defeat. He nominated two moderates, who had actually been recommended by Republican senators. One had frequently voted with Republican judges on a federal appellate court, and the other had previously worked with Republican lawyers on a congressional committee.[2] Their nominations sailed through.

President George W. Bush promised, or threatened (depending upon one's point of view), that he would appoint judges in the mold of Justices Antonin Scalia and Clarence Thomas, the most conservative justices on the current Supreme Court. When Chief Justice William Rehnquist died, Bush

nominated John Roberts, a federal appellate court judge. A staunch conservative, Roberts would replace the very conservative Rehnquist, so he would not alter the Court's makeup, and he was confirmed easily.

When Justice Sandra Day O'Connor retired, the political calculus became more complicated. Her retirement left only one woman on the Court, so some people called for another woman to replace her. O'Connor had been a swing justice, usually voting conservative but occasionally voting liberal, especially in cases involving sex discrimination or abortion rights. Some people called for a moderate or at least a conservative who might become another swing justice.

Bush nominated Harriet Miers, a lawyer who had served him as governor and then as president. She had never been a judge. Although many past justices—almost a third of those appointed since 1933—had not been lower court judges, Miers's lack of experience meant that she was an unknown quantity. The president assured his supporters that she was conservative and pro-life, pointing to her evangelical Christianity and her conservative church. However, right-wing commentators and interest groups worried that she was not conservative enough, so they raised a fierce ruckus within the Republican party. Ultimately, they forced Bush to back down and withdraw her nomination. As one Washington observer noted, "the dagger [was] held by the president's staunchest allies."[3]

After this debacle, the president made sure he satisfied his political base. He chose you, a clear conservative with a track record on the federal bench. The right-wing commentators and interest groups who attacked Miers's nomination were thrilled with your choice.

Although Republicans have fifty-five votes in the Senate, and a comparable advantage in the Judiciary Committee, your confirmation could be problematic. Positions you've taken and votes you've cast could raise fears among moderates as well as among liberals. If a groundswell of public opposition developed, some moderate Republican senators might join most Democratic senators against your nomination.

You will be asked about your views regarding abortion. As a lawyer in the Reagan administration, you wrote that "the Constitution does not protect a right to an abortion."[4] As a judge on the court of appeals, you urged your colleagues to uphold a law requiring a woman to notify her husband before having an abortion. When this case reached the Supreme Court, a majority led by Justice O'Connor struck down the law.[5]

As a judge, you usually favored powerful institutions over average individuals when they came in conflict. You normally favored prosecutors over criminal defendants and their rights.[6] You justified the shooting,

and killing, of an eighth-grader by a police officer because the boy was running away with a stolen purse, although he was not armed and the officer did not think he was armed.[7]

You will also be asked about your views toward presidential and congressional power. President Bush has been exercising vast power, especially in foreign affairs, and legal questions are looming. You have argued for even greater presidential power than courts now allow. On the other hand, you have argued for more reduced congressional power than that which Congress now exercises. In the Reagan administration, you maintained that Congress didn't have the power to pass the Truth in Mileage Act, which forbade car dealers from turning back the odometers in used cars. On the bench, you maintained that Congress didn't have the power to pass a law that banned individual possession of machine guns. Will your views prevent Congress from passing laws that people want?

Your views are more conservative than the views of many Americans. In your televised hearings, what strategy would make the best impression on the viewers? Should you recant any positions or votes that seem problematic? Or should you candidly acknowledge them and carefully explain them so people might be persuaded, or at least satisfied that you had legal reasons for them? Or should you avoid revealing your views as much as possible, in the hope that people won't become aware of them?

When John Roberts was questioned by committee members recently, he demonstrated his grasp of judicial doctrine but refused to indicate his views about this doctrine. He displayed grace and charm and flashed a sense of humor. No matter how confrontational senators got, Roberts retained an "invincible pleasantness."[8] He managed to convey respect for the senators while refusing to answer their questions. But you don't exude these qualities.

As administration officials escorted you from office to office to meet the senators on the committee, you seemed reserved, even cold. When the one Italian American on the committee, Senator Patrick Leahy (D-Vt.), warmly greeted you in Italian, you said, without smiling, "I don't speak Italian." When you met another senator, you remarked, "This is more human beings than I see in a month."[9]

Meanwhile, interest groups on both sides are gearing up, researching your records and sending e-mails and letters to their members. Groups favoring your nomination are trying to create the impression that you're a mainstream conservative, while groups opposing your nomination are trying to create the impression that you're an extreme conservative. (In truth, you seem in-between.) The administration is trying to convince Italian Americans that you're being smeared, so they'll rally to your defense.[10] And, of course, both sides are asking for financial contributions for the battle.

The public expresses more support for the Supreme Court than for the president or Congress.[11] The public dislikes the disagreements and debates and the negotiations and compromises among governmental officials, and it deplores the efforts of interest groups to influence governmental policies. These messy features of democratic government, which are visible in the executive

and legislative branches, are not visible in the judicial branch. Many people conclude that they do not occur.

Indeed, many people assume that courts are nonpolitical and that judges are objective. People say we have "a government of laws, not of men." But this view is a myth. At any time in our history, "it is individuals who make, enforce, and interpret the law."[12] When judges interpret the law, they are political actors and the courts are political institutions.

Thus public support for the Supreme Court and the lower courts rests partly on false assumptions about the absence of politics in this branch. There is plenty of politics, as will be seen in each of the topics covered in this chapter—the history, structure, jurisdiction, composition, operation, and impact of the courts.

Development of the Court's Role in Government

The Founders expected the judiciary to be the weakest branch of government. In the *Federalist Papers,* Alexander Hamilton wrote that Congress would have power to pass the laws and appropriate the money; the president would have power to execute the laws; but the courts would have "merely judgment"—that is, only power to resolve disputes in cases brought to them. In doing so, they would exercise "neither force nor will." They would not have any means to enforce decisions, and they would not

This portrait of William Marbury is the only portrait of a litigant owned by the Supreme Court Historical Society, testifying to the importance of the case of Marbury v. Madison.

use their own values to decide cases. Rather, they would simply apply the Constitution and laws as written. Consequently, the judiciary would be the "least dangerous" branch.[13]

This prediction was accurate for the early years of the Republic. The federal courts seemed inconsequential. The Supreme Court was held in such low esteem that some distinguished men refused to accept appointment to it; others accepted appointment but refused to attend sessions. The first chief justice thought the Court was "inauspicious,"[14] without enough "weight and dignity" to play an important role.[15] So he resigned to be governor of New York. The second chief justice resigned to be envoy to France.

When the nation's capital was moved to Washington, D.C., in 1801, new homes were built for Congress and the president but not for the Supreme Court. Planners considered the Court too insignificant for more than a small room in the Capitol. But the Court could not even keep this room. For decades, it would be shunted from one location to another, from the marshal's office to the clerk's office, from the clerk's home to the Capitol's cellar—a dark and damp chamber in which visitors joked that Lady Justice would not need to wear a blindfold because she could not see anyway—and from one committee room to another.[16] It would not get its own building until 1935.

However, the status of the Court began to change after the appointment of the fourth chief justice, John Marshall. Under his leadership, the Court began to develop "weight and dignity" and to play an important role in government.

The development of the Court's role in government can be shown by dividing the Court's history into three eras: from the founding to the Civil War, from the Civil War to the Great Depression, and from the Great Depression to the present.

Founding to the Civil War

The first major issue facing the courts, in the era from the country's founding to the Civil War, was the relationship between the nation and the states. In addressing this issue, the Supreme Court established judicial review and national supremacy.

Judicial Review

Judicial review is the authority to declare laws or actions of government officials unconstitutional. The Constitution does not mention judicial review. Although the idea was proposed at the Constitutional Convention, it was strongly opposed by some delegates who feared that it would strengthen the federal courts too much and, ultimately, weaken the state governments. The delegates who favored judicial review did not press for its inclusion because they worried that doing so might jeopardize the Constitution's ratification. Nevertheless, they expected federal judges to claim and use this authority eventually.[17]

The Supreme Court did so in the case of **Marbury v. Madison** in 1803.[18] The dispute originated in 1800, when the Federalist president, John Adams, was defeated in his bid for reelection by Thomas Jefferson and many Federalist members of Congress were defeated by Jeffersonians. With both the presidency and Congress lost, the Federalists tried to ensure continued control of the judiciary. The lame-duck president and lame-duck Congress added more judgeships, most of which were unnecessary. (Forty-two were for justices of the peace for the District of Columbia, which was sparsely populated.) They hoped to fill these positions with loyal Federalists before the new president and new Congress took over.

In addition, Adams named his secretary of state, John Marshall, to be chief justice. At the time, though, Marshall was still secretary of state and responsible for delivering the commissions to the new appointees.

But he ran out of time, failing to deliver four commissions for District of Columbia justices of the peace. He assumed that his successor would deliver them. But Jefferson, angry at the Federalists' efforts to pack the judiciary, told his secretary of state, James Madison, not to deliver the commissions.[19] Without the signed commissions, the appointees could not prove that they had in fact been appointed.[20]

William Marbury and the three other appointees petitioned the Supreme Court for a writ of *mandamus* (Latin for "we command"), an order that forces government officials to do something they have a duty to do. In this case, it would force Madison to deliver the commissions.

As chief justice, Marshall was in a position to rule on his administration's efforts to appoint these judges. Today this would be considered a conflict of interest, and he would be expected to disqualify himself. But at the time, people were not as troubled by such conflicts.

Marshall could issue the writ, but Jefferson would tell Madison to disobey it, and the Court would be powerless to enforce it. Or Marshall could decline to issue the writ, and the Court would appear powerless to issue it. Either way, the Court would reflect weakness rather than project strength.

Marshall shrewdly found a way out of the dilemma. He interpreted a provision of a congressional statute in a questionable way and then a provision of the Constitution in a questionable way as well.[21] As a result, he

Chief Justice John Marshall (right) *swears in President Andrew Jackson in 1829. Although Marshall's party, the Federalists, had dissolved, Marshall remained as chief justice, serving for thirty-four years.*

could claim that the statute violated the provision of the Constitution. Therefore, the statute was unconstitutional, and the Court could not order the administration to give the commissions. Thus, Marshall exercised judicial review. He wrote, in a statement that would be repeated by courts for years to come, "It is emphatically the province and duty of the judicial department to say what the law is."

Marshall justified judicial review this way: The Constitution is the supreme law of the land. If other laws contradict it, they are unconstitutional. Marshall continued: Judges decide cases, and to decide cases they have to apply the Constitution. To apply it, they have to say what it means. They can be trusted to say what it means because they take an oath to uphold it. On this point, some of Marshall's contemporaries disagreed with his reasoning. Other officials also have to follow the Constitution and also take an oath to uphold it, so they also could interpret it.

But Marshall was persuasive enough to convince many. A sly fox, he sacrificed the commissions—he could not have gotten them anyway—and established the power of judicial review instead. In doing so, with one hand he gave the Jeffersonians what they wanted—permission not to deliver the commissions—while with the other he gave the Federalists something much greater—judicial review. And all along he claimed he did what the Constitution required him to do.

Jefferson saw through this. He said the Constitution, in Marshall's hands, was "a thing of putty,"[22] adding that Marshall's arguments were "twistifications." But the decision did not require Jefferson to do anything, so he could not do anything but protest. Most of Jefferson's followers were satisfied with the result. They were not upset that the Court had invalidated a Federalist law, even though it had established judicial review to do so.

Of course, they were shortsighted because this decision laid the cornerstone for a strong judiciary. Thus a case that began as a "trivial squabble over a few petty political plums"[23] became perhaps the most important case the Court has ever decided.

National Supremacy

After *Marbury,* the Court did not declare any other congressional laws unconstitutional during Marshall's tenure, although it did declare numerous state laws unconstitutional.[24] These decisions solidified the authority of judicial review, and they symbolized the supremacy of the national government over the state governments.

The Court also advanced the supremacy of the national government by broadly construing congressional power. In *McCulloch* v. *Maryland,* discussed in Chapter 3, the Court interpreted the "necessary and proper clause" to allow Congress to legislate in many matters not mentioned in the Constitution and not anticipated by the Founders. Then the Court narrowly construed state power.[25]

President Andrew Jackson, who had campaigned against the eastern elites who Marshall had represented, was America's first populist president. When he named Roger Taney as chief justice, proponents of a strong national government worried that the Taney Court would undo what the Marshall Court had done. But the Taney Court did not. Although Taney did not expand national power any further, he upheld national supremacy and thus cemented Marshall's doctrine.

Yet Taney severely undermined the Court's reputation in the *Dred Scott* case.[26] Jumping into the thick of the slavery conflict, the Court declared the Missouri Compromise of 1820, which controlled slavery in the territories, unconstitutional. This was only the second case in which the Court had declared a congressional law unconstitutional, and it could not have come in a more controversial area or at a less opportune time. The slavery issue had polarized the nation, and this ruling polarized it further. Southerners had been disenchanted with the Court because of its emphasis on a strong national government; now northerners became disenchanted too. The nation moved closer to civil war, and the Court's prestige dropped so precipi-

tously that it could play only a weak role in the next two decades. President Abraham Lincoln refused to enforce one of its rulings,[27] and Congress withdrew part of its jurisdiction.[28] As a result, the Court shied away from important issues.

The Taney Court naively thought it could resolve the clash over slavery and thereby resolve the conflict between the nation and the states. But no court could achieve this. It would take the Civil War to do so.[29]

Civil War to the Great Depression

With the controversy between the nation and the states muted, the next major issue facing the courts was the relationship between the government and businesses in cases involving regulation of businesses.

After the war, industrialization proceeded at breakneck pace, bringing not only economic benefits but also many problems for society. Big corporations abused their power over their employees, their customers, and their competitors. Although legislatures passed laws to regulate these abuses, the corporations challenged the laws in court. The Supreme Court, dominated by justices who had been lawyers for corporations, reflected the views of

Although many children worked long days in unhealthy conditions, the Supreme Court declared initial laws prohibiting child labor unconstitutional. This boy worked in the coal mines in the early 1900s.

Utah State Historical Society

corporations—the *laissez-faire* attitudes of the late nineteenth and early twentieth centuries—and struck down the regulations on them.

Beginning in the 1870s, intensifying in the 1890s, and continuing in the 1900s, the Court invalidated laws that regulated child labor,[30] maximum hours of work,[31] and minimum wages for work.[32] It also discouraged employees from joining unions and unions from striking employers,[33] and it limited antitrust laws.[34] In just one decade, the Court invalidated forty-one state laws regulating railroads.[35]

In 1935 and 1936, the Court struck down twelve congressional laws,[36] nearly nullifying President Franklin Roosevelt's New Deal program to help the country recover from the Great Depression.

The Court's action precipitated another major crisis. In 1936 Roosevelt was reelected resoundingly. Confident from his victory and frustrated by his lack of opportunities to appoint new justices during his first term, he retaliated against the Court by proposing what was soon labeled a **court-packing plan.** The plan would have authorized the president to nominate and the Senate to confirm a new justice for every justice over seventy who did not retire, up to a total of fifteen. At the time, there were six justices over seventy, so Roosevelt could have appointed six new justices and assured himself a friendly Court. The plan was the dominant political issue for five months. It was debated in Congress, in newspapers, and on the radio. Public opinion was divided. Even some of Roosevelt's supporters criticized him for tampering with the Court.

Before Congress could vote on the plan, two justices who often sided with four conservative justices against New Deal legislation switched positions to side with three liberal justices for such legislation. Chief Justice Charles Evans Hughes and Justice Owen Roberts apparently thought the Court would suffer if it continued to oppose the popular president and his popular programs. Indeed, it is likely that the plan would have passed if the Court had not changed. The two justices' conversion made the court-packing plan unnecessary, and Congress scuttled it. Their switch was dubbed "the switch in time that saved nine."

Thus, the Court resolved this issue in favor of the government over businesses. Since then, it has permitted most efforts to regulate businesses.

Great Depression to the Present

With the controversy between the government and businesses subdued, the next major issue facing the courts was the relationship between the government and individuals in cases involving civil liberties and rights. Often this issue featured a conflict between the

Fred O. Seibel

Most Americans opposed court rulings invalidating New Deal legislation, but many also opposed President Roosevelt's "court-packing plan."

majority, whose views were reflected in government policy, and a minority who challenged the policy.

The courts historically paid little attention to civil liberties and rights. They usually allowed the government to ignore these rights. But this lax attitude changed when President Dwight Eisenhower, fulfilling a campaign pledge to a presidential rival, Earl Warren, appointed him chief justice. Warren led the Court more effectively than any chief since Marshall. In the 1950s and 1960s, the **Warren Court** completely overhauled doctrine involving legislative reapportionment, racial segregation, and criminal defendants' rights.[37] It also altered doctrine involving libel, obscenity, and religion. In the process, it held many laws unconstitutional. It was more activist in civil liberties and rights cases than the Court had ever been (see Figure 13.1).

The Warren Court sympathized with powerless groups and unpopular individuals—racial minorities, religious minorities, criminal defendants, and alleged subversives—when they challenged government policies. Thus, the most elite institution in our government used its power to benefit many nonelites in our society. In its sympathies, the Warren Court differed sharply from previous Courts, which typically favored the haves over the have-nots and efforts to preserve the status quo over struggles to change it.

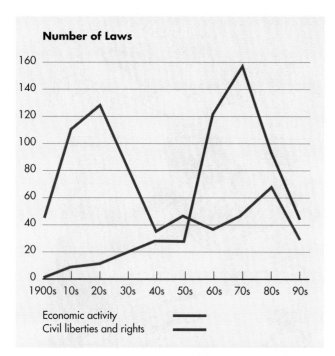

Number of Laws

FIGURE 13.1 ■ Laws Regulating Economic Activity and Restricting Civil Liberties and Rights Declared Unconstitutional by the Supreme Court since 1900

The Supreme Court was nearly as activist in striking down laws in the 1910s, 1920s, and 1930s, as it was in the 1950s, 1960s, and 1970s. But in the former years it was activist in economic cases (usually those involving government regulation of business), whereas in the latter years, it was activist in civil liberties and rights cases.

Source: Congressional Research Service, *The Constitution of the United States: Analysis and Interpretation* and its 1998 supplement (Washington, D.C.: U.S. Government Printing Office, 1996 and 1999); Kenneth Jose, *The Supreme Court Yearbook, 1998–1999* (Washington, D.C.: CQ Press, 2000); Lawrence Baum, *The Supreme Court,* 8th ed. (Washington, D.C.: CQ Press, 2004), 181.

President Ronald Reagan and his former vice president, George H. W. Bush, also wanted to reverse the Court's liberal doctrine. When Burger retired, Reagan elevated William Rehnquist, the most conservative associate justice, to be chief justice. Then Reagan and Bush appointed five more conservatives as vacancies occurred. By this time, Republican presidents had named ten justices in a row.

President Bill Clinton's election led to the first Democratic justices since 1967. Although these two moderate liberals slowed any further swing to the right, the conservative justices controlled the **Rehnquist Court** in the 1980s, 1990s, and early 2000s. But conflicts among the conservatives splintered their bloc. Some were bold, eager to sweep away liberal precedents and substitute conservative principles. Others were cautious, willing to uphold liberal precedents they would not have agreed to set in the first place and inclined to decide cases on narrow bases rather than on broad principles. In some terms, the former group dominated, but in other terms, the latter group dominated.[39] Overall, the Rehnquist Court, though markedly more conservative than the Burger Court, did not bring about a "constitutional counterrevolution" either.

Yet the Rehnquist Court did overturn some liberal doctrine. It continued to erode criminal defendants' rights. The Court also made it harder for racial mi-

The Warren Court's decisions brought about a conservative backlash in the late 1960s.[38] President Richard Nixon vowed to change the Court's direction, and after Earl Warren retired he appointed Warren Burger to be chief justice. Then Nixon and his former vice president, President Gerald Ford, appointed four more justices as vacancies occurred. They sought to slow, halt, or even reverse the Court's liberal doctrine. They expected the **Burger Court** to bring about a "constitutional counterrevolution."

But the Burger Court did not. Although it eroded some liberal doctrine in the 1970s and 1980s, particularly regarding criminal defendants' rights, it left most intact. And it initiated new liberal doctrine in two areas where the Warren Court had been silent—sexual discrimination and abortion. Although it was not as committed to civil liberties and rights as the Warren Court, the Burger Court was more committed to them than any earlier Court.

Chief Justice Earl Warren, flanked by Justices Hugo Black (left) and William O. Douglas.

TABLE 13.1	Modern Supreme Courts
Warren Court	1953–1969
Burger Court	1969–1986
Rehnquist Court	1986–2005
Roberts Court	2005–present

norities to use affirmative action and for religious minorities to practice their religion. In two less obvious areas, the Court altered doctrine in more fundamental ways. It tightened access to the courts for individuals and groups trying to challenge government policies, and it limited efforts by Congress to impose new regulations on the states. The latter development may be the most notable change by the Rehnquist Court.[40] In these ways, the Republican justices mirrored the views of the Republican presidents and members of Congress during these years.[41]

President George W. Bush, like his father and President Reagan, wants a more conservative Court. When William Rehnquist died in 2005, he appointed John Roberts to be chief justice. He then appointed another conservative, Samuel Alito. The **Roberts Court** is expected to be even more conservative than the Rehnquist Court.

In sum, throughout its history, the Court's role in government has been that of a policy maker—in relationships between the nation and the states, the government and businesses, and the government and individuals. In the first and second eras, the Court was a thoroughly conservative policy maker, protecting private property rights and limiting government regulation of businesses; in the third era, the Court was a generally liberal policy maker, permitting government regulation of businesses and supporting civil liberties and rights for individuals.

It now appears that the third era is over. Although the Rehnquist Court did not overturn most of the previous Courts' doctrine, it deemphasized individual rights, pruning them in some areas and not expanding them in others. The Roberts Court is expected to be less sympathetic to individual rights. (The rights referred to here will be discussed in Chapters 14 and 15.)

The Next Era

If the third era is over, what controversy (or controversies) will the courts address in the fourth era? We may not know for many years, until we can look back with more perspective than we have now, but it is interesting to speculate.

Might the fourth era focus on information technology, including computers, the software they use, and the data they store? And might it resolve disputes about the ways and the extent that the government and the private sector can impose restrictions on this technology? These questions would be similar to those the Court answered about freedom of speech and press, including doctrine about libel and obscenity, in the third era. Or perhaps the emphasis will be on privacy from the many intrusions of this pervasive technology. The Court barely addressed invasion of privacy in the third era.

Or might the fourth era focus on biotechnology? Advances in genetics herald a revolution promising not only cures for diseases, but the opportunity for people to live longer and better. "The next frontier," one scientist says, "is our own selves."[42] We will be able to boost our intelligence and modify our metabolism. Parents will be able to choose various characteristics of their children, such as their gender and eye color, and alter other characteristics, such as their personality and athletic ability. Women might be able to give birth in their 60s or 70s, and homosexual couples might be able to create babies with their own (modified) genes. The possibility of cloning may become a reality.

Initial legal issues might involve restrictions on experiments and techniques. Once the techniques are

Lynn Johnson/Aurora Photos

Chief Justice William Rehnquist

developed, the legal issues might involve access to these procedures. Once the procedures are available, the legal issues might involve consequences from these procedures. For instance, will enhanced people get better jobs and more promotions and pay raises than unenhanced people? If so, what actions would the executive and legislative branches take? What decisions would the courts make?

Information technology and biotechnology will experience exponential growth in the first half of the twenty-first century. Technological change, according to one scientist, "will appear to explode into infinity, at least from the limited and linear perspective of contemporary humans." This change will be "so rapid and so profound that it represents a rupture in the fabric of human history."[43] If this prediction is at all accurate, litigants and judges will be wrenched from their current preoccupations and forced to address new issues barely imagined now.

Courts

Most countries with a federal system have one national court over a system of regional courts. In contrast, the United States has a complete system of national courts side by side with complete systems of state courts, for a total of fifty-one separate systems. This arrangement makes litigation more complicated than in other countries.

Structure of the Courts

The Constitution mentions only one court—a supreme court—although it allows Congress to set up additional lower courts, which it did in the Judiciary Act of 1789. The act was a compromise between Federalists, who wanted a full system of lower courts with extensive jurisdiction (authority to hear and decide cases) in order to strengthen the national government, and Jeffersonians, who wanted only a partial system of lower courts with limited jurisdiction in order to avoid strengthening the national government. The compromise established a full system of lower courts with limited jurisdiction. The peculiar result was that there were many federal courts, but they could hear very few cases. They were authorized to hear disputes involving citizens of more than one state but not any disputes involving the U.S. Constitution or laws. The state courts were permitted to hear all these cases.

After the Civil War, Congress granted the federal courts extensive jurisdiction. It then created another level of federal courts, between the Supreme Court and the original lower courts, to complete the basic structure of the federal judiciary, which remains today.[44]

In the federal system, the **district courts** are trial courts. There are ninety-four, based on population but with at least one in each state. They have multiple judges, although a single judge or a jury decides each case.

The **courts of appeals** are intermediate appellate courts. They hear cases that have been decided by the district courts and then appealed by the losers. There are twelve, based on regions of the country known as "circuits."[45] They have numerous judges, from six to twenty-eight, although a panel of three judges decides each case.[46]

The Supreme Court is the ultimate appellate court. It hears cases that have been decided by the courts of appeals, district courts, or state supreme courts. (Although it can hear some cases—those involving a state or a diplomat—that have not been heard by the lower courts first, in practice it hears nearly all of its cases on appeal.) The group of nine justices decides its cases.

The district courts conduct trials. The courts of appeals and Supreme Court do not; they do not have juries or witnesses to testify and present evidence—just lawyers for the opposing litigants. Rather than determine guilt or innocence, these courts evaluate arguments about legal questions arising in the cases.

The state judiciaries have a structure similar to the federal judiciary. In most states, though, there are two tiers of trial courts. Normally, the lower tier is for criminal cases involving minor crimes, and the upper tier is for criminal cases involving major crimes and for civil cases. In about three-fourths of the states, there are intermediate appellate courts, and in all of the states there is a supreme court (although in a few it is known by another name).

Since 1978, the federal system has also had an unusual secret court which few Americans are aware of (see the box "Surveillance Court").

Jurisdiction of the Courts

As noted, **jurisdiction** is the authority to hear and decide cases. The federal courts can exercise jurisdiction over cases in which the subject involves the U.S. Constitution, statutes, or treaties; maritime law; or cases in which the litigants include the U.S. government, more than one state government, one state government and a citizen of another state, citizens of more than one state,[47] or a foreign government or citizen. The state courts exercise jurisdiction over the remaining cases. These include most criminal cases because the states have authority over most criminal matters and pass most criminal laws. Consequently, the state courts hear far more cases than the federal courts.

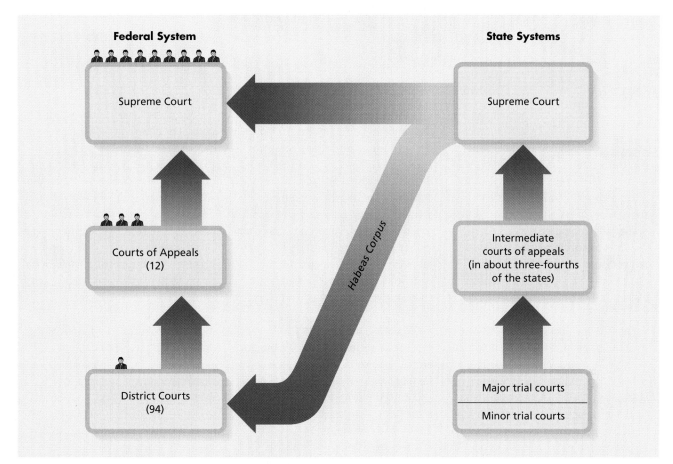

FIGURE 13.2 ■ Federal and State Court Systems
The arrows indicate the primary avenues of appeal, and the heads indicate the usual number of judges who hear cases in the federal system.

Despite this dividing line, some cases begin in the state courts and end in the federal courts. These involve state law and federal law, frequently a state statute and a federal constitutional right—for example, a criminal law and a legal question about the search and seizure (Fourth Amendment) or interrogation (Fifth Amendment) conducted by the police. For these cases, there are two paths from the state judiciary to the federal judiciary. One is for the litigant who lost at the state supreme court to appeal to the U.S. Supreme Court.

The other path, available only in a criminal case, is for the defendant who has exhausted all possible appeals in the state courts to appeal to the local federal district court through a writ of ***habeas corpus*** ("You should have the body," the first words of the writ in Latin). This order demands that the state produce the defendant and justify his or her incarceration. If the district court decides that the state courts violated the defendant's constitutional rights, it will reverse the conviction. After the district court's decision, the losing side can try to appeal to the courts of appeals and the Supreme Court (see Figure 13.2).

Judges

Selection of Judges

Benjamin Franklin proposed that judges be selected by lawyers because lawyers would pick "the ablest of the profession in order to get rid of him, and share his practice among themselves."[48] The Founders rejected this unique idea, instead deciding that the president and the Senate should share the appointment power. The Constitution stipulates that the president shall nominate judges and the Senate shall provide "advice and consent"—that is, recommend judges and then confirm or reject them.[49] There are no other requirements in the Constitution, although there is an unwritten requirement that judges be trained as lawyers.

The Founders expected these appointments to be based on merit rather than on politics. However, as soon as political parties developed, presidents and senators used politics as well as merit in making these appointments.

SURVEILLANCE COURT

Behind closed doors in a windowless room in the Justice Department, a highly secretive court meets. The court hears requests from the FBI for electronic surveillance of possible spies and terrorists and sometimes for physical searches of their homes and computers.

The **Foreign Intelligence Surveillance Court** operates like no other court in the United States. It consists of eleven district court judges handpicked by the chief justice of the Supreme Court. The members sit in panels of three judges and serve for seven years. Lawyers for the government, acting on behalf of the FBI, seek approval for electronic surveillance, much as law enforcement officers seek search warrants for routine searches from regular courts. To protect the secrecy of the surveillance, lawyers for the defense—the targets of the surveillance—do not appear in court. In fact, they are not informed, and not aware, that a case involving the defendants is being heard at all.

Congress established the court in 1978 after abuses by the Nixon administration, which itself authorized the FBI to engage in wiretapping, bugging, and other forms of electronic surveillance. The administration spied on American citizens active in the antiwar and civil rights movements, claiming

that these protesters were threats to "national security," and then tried to disrupt their organizations and harass their leaders. Yet Congress recognized that the government might need to use electronic surveillance when national security actually was at stake—from foreign agents or American citizens spying for foreign countries. Congress established the court to approve the surveillance when it was justified and to check the government when it was overzealous.

However, the court has been little more than a rubber stamp for the government. Since its inception, the court has approved almost 19,000 requests and denied just 4.[1] In recent years, the court has made "substantive modifications" to some requests.[2]

Because of the need for strict secrecy, the court's decisions are shielded from virtually all scrutiny. If the government loses, it can appeal the court's decision to the Foreign Intelligence Surveillance Court of Review, which consists of three appellate court judges, also handpicked by the chief justice. (And if the government loses here, it can appeal to the Supreme Court.) But the Court of Review has heard just one pair of cases during its existence, and it thwarted a rare attempt by the Surveillance Court to check the government.

The Surveillance Court had turned down the government's request in one pair of cases when the judges realized that the FBI had been misleading the court in seventy-five cases. When the FBI had lacked sufficient evidence to obtain approval for surveillance in ordinary criminal cases—not spying or terrorism cases—from regular courts, it had tried to circumvent the law by going to the Surveillance Court, which requires less evidence to grant surveillance because of the seriousness of spying and terrorism.[3] The furious judges admonished the FBI to discontinue this practice. But the Bush administration appealed, and the Court of Review overturned the decision, concluding that the USA PATRIOT Act had broadened the law to allow the FBI to continue this practice after all. Thus it appears that the secret Surveillance Court will be hearing many requests for surveillance, whether for spying and terrorism cases or for ordinary criminal cases, in the future as a result of 9/11.

[1]"Foreign Intelligence Surveillance Act Orders, 1979–2005," Electronic Privacy Information Center, May 2, 2006, http://www.epic.org/privacy/wiretap/stats/fisa_stats.html.
[2]In 2005, sixty-one modifications in 2074 requests. Ibid.
[3]John Podesta and Peter Swire, "Speaking Out about Wiretaps," *Washington Post National Weekly Edition*, September 9, 2002, 27; Seymour M. Hersh, "The Twentieth Man," *New Yorker*, September 30, 2002, 56–76.

Mechanics of Selection

For the lower courts, lawyers who want to become judges get politically active in their party and make financial contributions to it. When vacancies arise, they lobby political officials, bar association leaders, or interest group leaders in the hope that these elites will recommend them to the administration.

They especially focus on their senators, who play a key role through the practice of **senatorial courtesy.** This tradition allows senators in the president's party to recommend, or veto, candidates for judgeships in their state. This practice applies not only to district courts, which lie within individual states, but

also to courts of appeals, which span several states. For courts of appeals, senators informally divide the seats among the states. (This practice, of course, does not apply to the Supreme Court because it has too few seats.)

Senatorial courtesy can limit the president's choices. During President Kennedy's term, the practice was ironclad. In deference to southern senators, the president, who advocated civil rights, was forced to appoint southern judges who favored segregation. One of them characterized the Supreme Court's desegregation ruling as "one of the truly regrettable decisions of all time," and another even called blacks "niggers" and "chimpanzees" in court.[50] However, senatorial courtesy is not as ironclad now as it was then. Since the 1970s, many administrations have sought certain candidates for their ideology or diversity, so they have pressured senators to cooperate. Consequently, there is more give and take between the senators and the president than there used to be. Nevertheless, in 1999 Senator Orin Hatch (R-Utah), chair of the Judiciary Committee, blocked all of President Clinton's nominees for six months until the president agreed to nominate one of Hatch's allies for a judgeship in Utah.

For the Supreme Court, lawyers who want to become justices also try to become prominent in the legal profession. They write articles or give speeches designed to attract officials' attention. When vacancies arise, political officials, bar association leaders, and interest group leaders urge consideration of certain candidates. The administration also conducts a search for acceptable candidates. Sometimes even sitting justices make a recommendation. Chief Justice Burger, who discouraged President Nixon from choosing a woman, claiming that not one was qualified, recommended Harry Blackmun, a childhood pal and the best man at his wedding. Justice Rehnquist recommended Sandra Day O'Connor, a law school classmate whom he had dated occasionally.

Once the president has chosen a candidate, he submits the nomination to the Senate, where it goes to the Judiciary Committee for hearings. Senators question the nominee about his or her judicial philosophy, and interest groups voice their concerns. If a majority of the committee consents, the nomination goes to the whole Senate. If a majority of the Senate consents, the nomination is confirmed.

The Judiciary Committee is the battleground for controversial nominations. The committee is controlled by the party that has a majority in the Senate, so the committee reflects the views of that party. If the committee confirms the nominee, usually the whole Senate will confirm the nominee. If the committee rejects the nominee, usually the president will have to submit another one.

The mechanics of selection for all federal courts are similar, but the process of selection for the Supreme Court is more politicized at every stage because the Court is more powerful and visible. Its seats are fought over more intensely.

Criteria Used by Presidents

Although presidents want judges who demonstrate merit, they choose judges who meet various political criteria. Presidents normally nominate members of their party. In fact, they normally nominate active members who have served in public office or contributed to party candidates. In the twentieth century, presidents selected members of their party from 82 percent of the time (William Howard Taft) to 99 percent of the time (Woodrow Wilson).[51] This practice

AP Images/Pablo Martinez Monsivais

As John Roberts listened to senators' questions during his confirmation hearings to be chief justice, his face was responsive and expressive.

has become so established that senators of one party customarily defer to the president and confirm the nominees from the other party.

Some presidents want judges who hold certain ideological views. President Theodore Roosevelt sought judges who opposed business monopolies and supported labor unions, and President Franklin Roosevelt sought judges who favored his New Deal policies. President Nixon sought conservatives who would change the direction of the Warren Court and prompt white southerners to join the Republican party.

The Nixon administration was the first to recognize that it could accomplish some policy goals by selecting lower court judges as well as Supreme Court justices on the basis of ideology.[52] The Reagan administration was the first to establish systematic procedures and institutionalize this process. The George H.W. Bush administration did the same. These two administrations sought judges who held conservative views and were willing to roll back the rulings of previous courts. They had candidates fill out lengthy questionnaires and then submit to daylong interviews probing their positions. They expected candidates, for example, to oppose the right to abortion, the Supreme Court's ruling establishing the right, and the Supreme Court's reasoning in the case.[53]

President George W. Bush has followed a similar process and has screened candidates especially for their views on abortion, gay rights, and affirmative action.[54] These three Republican administrations have made the most concerted efforts to select judges according to ideology.

Some presidents want judges who provide more diversity on the courts. In the past, presidents chose westerners to balance the easterners who dominated the bench and Catholics and Jews to balance the Protestants who dominated the bench. In 1967, President Johnson chose the first black justice, Thurgood Marshall; in 1981, President Reagan chose the first woman justice, Sandra Day O'Connor. Presidents bowed to the pressure from various groups to solidify their support from these groups. Reagan, who was not an advocate of women's rights, pledged to appoint a woman to the Court to shore up his support among female voters. (After fulfilling this pledge, he felt no need to appoint many women to the lower federal courts.)

Now Hispanics want a seat on the Supreme Court. Both parties, who see support from this growing group as crucial to future electoral success, would welcome the opportunity to appoint the first Hispanic justice.

Presidents Carter and Clinton appointed numerous women and minorities to the lower federal courts. Before Carter took office, only eight women

had ever served on the federal bench.[55] Sixteen percent of Carter's appointees were women, and 21 percent were racial minorities.[56] Twenty-nine percent of Clinton's appointees were women, and 25 percent were racial minorities.[57] These two Democratic administrations, which were not as driven by ideology, made the most concerted efforts to select judges for diversity.

President George W. Bush has also made an effort, greater than previous Republican administrations, to appoint women and minorities to the lower federal courts.[58] However, he has passed over most female and all minority candidates for Supreme Court vacancies because those under consideration either were not conservative enough for the interest groups that wield power within the Republican party or too conservative for moderate senators and voters to accept.

Demands for diversity can reduce presidents' choices, but presidents can acquiesce to these demands and still find candidates with the desired party affiliation and ideological views. When Thurgood Marshall retired in 1991, President Bush felt obligated to nominate another African American for this seat, but he wanted to nominate a conservative. He chose Clarence Thomas, a court of appeals judge. Whereas Marshall had been an ardent champion of civil rights, Thomas opposes affirmative action and other policies favored by many black leaders. Whereas Marshall had been one of the most liberal justices on the Warren Court, Thomas is the most conservative justice in many years, espousing a return to some positions abandoned by the Court in the 1930s.[59] Occasionally, groups have to satisfy themselves with the symbolic benefits from having "one of their own" on the Court. Thus, many blacks get the psychological lift from having a fellow African American on the bench but not the additional satisfaction from having one who reflects their policy views. (See the box "Do Women Judges Make a Difference?")

Criteria Used by Senators

Although the Senate played a vigorous role in the appointment process in the nineteenth century, rejecting twenty-two of eighty-one presidential nominations to the Supreme Court between 1789 and 1894, it routinely accepted the president's nominations in the first half of the twentieth century, rejecting only one nomination until 1968.[60] Then it rejected two by President Johnson, two by President Nixon, and two by President Reagan.[61]

Of these six nominees, most were qualified in an objective sense.[62] Although some were accused of ethical lapses, most were rejected for ideological reasons.[63]

DO WOMEN JUDGES MAKE A DIFFERENCE?

Some people believe that there should be more women judges because women are entitled to their "fair share" of all governmental offices, including judgeships. Others believe that there should be more so women will feel that the courts represent them too. Still others believe that there should be more because women hold different views than men and therefore would make different decisions.

A study of Justice Sandra Day O'Connor, the first woman on the Supreme Court, shows that although she generally voted as a conservative, she usually voted as a liberal in sex discrimination cases. Moreover, her presence on the Court apparently sensitized her male colleagues to gender issues. Most of them voted against sex discrimination more frequently after she joined the Court.[1]

Some studies find similar results for women justices on state supreme courts. Even women justices from opposite political parties support a broad array of women's rights in cases ranging from sex discrimination to child support and property settlement.[2]

But studies that compare voting patterns on issues less directly related to gender have less clear findings. Women judges appear more liberal than men in cases involving employment discrimination and racial discrimination. Perhaps the treatment they have experienced as women has made them more sympathetic to the discrimination others have faced. On the other hand, women judges do not appear more liberal or conservative than men in cases involving obscenity or criminal rights.[3]

Studies that compare the sentencing of criminal defendants in state courts find scant differences between men and women judges.[4] However, women judges do tend to sentence convicted defendants somewhat more harshly, especially black men who are repeat offenders. Apparently women judges consider these defendants more dangerous or more prone to commit new crimes after prison. Possibly women judges are influenced by the fact that these defendants are less often married and employed than other defendants.[5]

Women judges in Harris County, Texas, which includes Houston, have applied the death penalty with "greater ferocity" than their male predecessors. This *county*, a majority of whose judges are female, has given the death penalty to more defendants than all other *states* but one.[6]

But the studies comparing men and women judges find more similarities than differences. This should not be surprising, because the two sexes were subject to the same training in law school and the same socialization in the legal profession, and they became judges in the same ways as others in their jurisdiction.

Perhaps the greatest difference women judges have made is to protect the credibility of women lawyers and witnesses. In court, some men judges and lawyers made disparaging remarks about women lawyers, suggesting that they should not be in the profession—for example, calling them "lawyerettes." Many male judges and lawyers made paternalistic or personal remarks to female lawyers and witnesses, referring to them by their first name or by such terms as "young lady," "sweetie," or "honey." Or the men, in the midst of the proceedings, commented about their perfume, clothing, or appearance. "How does an attorney establish her authority when the judge has just described her to the entire courtroom as 'a pretty little thing'?"[7] Even if the men considered their remarks harmless compliments rather than intentional tactics, their effect was to undermine the credibility of women lawyers and witnesses in the eyes of jurors. Women judges have squelched such remarks.

[1] Karen O'Connor and Jeffrey A. Segal, "Justice Sandra Day O'Connor and the Supreme Court's Reaction to Its First Female Member," in *Women, Politics, and the Constitution*, ed. Naomi B. Lynn (New York: Haworth Press, 1990), 95–104.
[2] David W. Allen and Diane E. Wall, "Role Orientations and Women State Supreme Court Justices," *Judicature* 77 (1993), 156–165.
[3] Sue Davis, Susan Haire, and Donald R. Songer, "Voting Behavior and Gender on the U.S. Courts of Appeals," *Judicature* 77 (1993), 129–133; Thomas G. Walker and Deborah J. Barrow, "The Diversification of the Federal Bench," *Journal of Politics* 47 (1985), 596–617.
[4] John Gruhl, Cassia Spohn, and Susan Welch, "Women as Policymakers: The Case of Trial Judges," *American Journal of Political Science* 25 (1981), 308–322.
[5] Darrell Steffensmeier and Chris Hebert, "Women and Men Policymakers: Does the Judge's Gender Affect the Sentencing of Criminal Defendants?" *Social Forces* 77 (1999), 1163–1196.
[6] Jeffrey Toobin, "Women in Black," *New Yorker*, October 30, 2000, 48.
[7] William Eich, "Gender Bias in the Courtroom: Some Participants Are More Equal than Others," *Judicature* 69 (1986), 339–343.

Johnson's were deemed too liberal, while Nixon's and Reagan's were deemed too conservative.

Nominations to the Supreme Court have been contentious since the 1960s partly because of the Court's activism—both liberals and conservatives have seen what the Court can do—and partly because of the divided government that has characterized our government for most years since the late 1960s. Often Republicans dominated the presidency while Democrats dominated Congress (although in the 1990s, the situation was the reverse), so both have fought over the judiciary to tip the balance. Nominations have also become contentious because of the culture wars between reformers and traditionalists, for which the abortion debate is the most obvious manifestation, and the corresponding rise of interest groups on the left and the right that scrutinize the appointments, pressuring presidents and senators on their side to nominate and vote their way.

Even nominations to the lower courts, especially to the courts of appeals, which serve as "farm teams" for future justices, have become contentious in recent decades.[64] First the Democratic Senate in the 1980s responded to the Republican presidents' (Reagan's and Bush's) efforts to choose judges according to ideology by blocking more nominations, mostly of conservatives, than senators ever had previously. Then the Republican Senate in the 1990s retaliated against the Democratic president (Clinton) by blocking many more nominations, mostly of moderates.[65] It did not matter if the nominees were well qualified; one woman who was blocked was later appointed dean of Harvard Law School. The Republican Senate followed a pace that kept about one hundred seats vacant.[66]

Once the Republican party regained control of both the presidency and the Senate in 2003, the Democratic minority in the Senate employed the filibuster, which had previously been used to block legislation rather than appointments,[67] against several conservatives nominated by President George W. Bush.[68]

This cycle of recrimination and retribution reflects the polarization of American politics today. It also demonstrates the role of interest groups. "You go out on the streets of Raleigh," Senator Jesse Helms of North Carolina said, "and ask one hundred people: 'Do you give a damn who is on the Fourth Circuit Court of Appeals?' They'll say: 'What's that?'"[69] But political activists representing interest groups on the left and the right do know and do care, deeply, because they see the connection between the judges on the lower courts and the success of the interest groups' policy goals. In elections, these political activists mobilize their party's base of voters. Thus they have influence on their party, which needs their help. They can persuade, sometimes demand, that their party's senators fight a nomination by the other party's president.[70] Then they use the controversy to enlist more members and raise more money from their supporters: "Send your contribution so that we can continue our vigilance and our efforts. . . ."

Results of Selection

Judges are drawn from the lower courts, the federal government, or large law firms. These established legal circles are dominated by white men, so most judges have been white men. Although recent presidents have appointed more minorities and women, the bench's composition changes slowly because of judges' life tenure.

Despite the efforts to provide racial and sexual diversity, no effort has been made to reflect socioeconomic diversity. Throughout history, judges have come from a narrow, elite slice of society. Most have come from upper-middle-class or upper-class families with prestige and connections as well as expectations for achievement.[71]

No Supreme Court justice since Warren Burger in 1969 has attended a public university or graduate school. Every justice since then has had a degree from one of four prestigious, private schools—Chicago, Harvard, Stanford, or Yale.[72] Most justices—at least six on the Roberts Court—have been millionaires.[73] Many lower court judges have been millionaires, too. Forty percent of Clinton's appointees were and 58 percent of Bush's appointees are.[74]

With the power to nominate judges, presidents have a tremendous opportunity to shape the courts and their decisions (see Figure 13.3).

Tenure of Judges

Once appointed, judges can serve for "good behavior," which means for life, unless they commit "high crimes and misdemeanors." These are not defined in the Constitution but are considered serious crimes or, possibly, political abuses. Congress can impeach and remove judges as it can presidents, but it has impeached only thirteen and removed only six. The standard of guilt—"high crimes and misdemeanors"—is vague, the punishment drastic, and the process time consuming, so Congress has been reluctant to impeach judges.

As an alternative, Congress in 1980 established other procedures to discipline lower court judges. Councils made up of district and appellate court judges can ask their fellow judges to resign or can prevent them from hearing cases, but they cannot actually remove them. The procedures have been used infrequently, although their existence has prompted some judges to resign before being disciplined.

Qualifications of Judges

Given the use of political criteria in selecting judges, are judges well qualified?

Political scientists who study the judiciary consider federal judges generally well qualified. This is especially true of Supreme Court justices, apparently

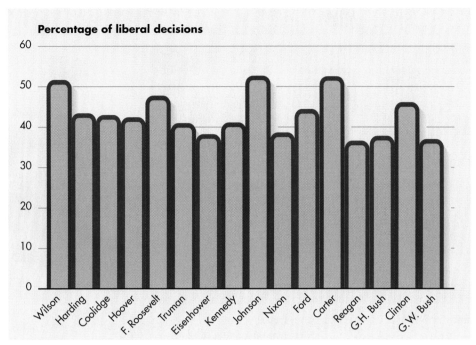

Percentage of liberal decisions

Wilson, Harding, Coolidge, Hoover, F. Roosevelt, Truman, Eisenhower, Kennedy, Johnson, Nixon, Ford, Carter, Reagan, G.H. Bush, Clinton, G.W. Bush

FIGURE 13.3 ■ **Percentage of Liberal Decisions Handed Down by District Court Appointees of Presidents Woodrow Wilson through George W. Bush**
Appointees of Democratic and Republic presidents tend to decide cases somewhat differently.
SOURCE: Robert A. Carp, Ronald Stidham, and Kenneth L. Manning, *Judicial Process in America*, 6th ed. (Washington, D.C.: CQ Press, 2004), fig. 7-1.

because presidents think they will be held responsible for the justices they nominate and do not want to be embarrassed by them. Also, because presidents have so few vacancies to fill, they can confine themselves to persons of their party and political views and even to persons of a particular region, religion, race, and sex and still locate good candidates. This is less true of lower court judges. Presidents and senators (through senatorial courtesy) jointly appoint them, so both can avoid taking full responsibility for them. These judges are also less visible, so a lack of merit is not as noticeable.

Presidents do appoint some losers. President Truman put a longtime supporter on a court of appeals who was "drunk half the time" and "no damn good." When asked why he appointed the man, Truman candidly replied, "I . . . felt I owed him a favor; that's why, and I thought as a judge he couldn't do too much harm, and he didn't."[75]

Sometimes presidents appoint qualified persons who later become incompetent. After serving for many years, they incur the illnesses and infirmities of old age, and perhaps one-tenth become unable to perform their job well.[76] Yet they hang on because they are allowed to serve for "good behavior," and they

prevent other lawyers from filling their seats on the bench. This problem has prompted proposals for a constitutional amendment setting a term limit of eighteen years[77] or a mandatory retirement age of seventy. Either of these changes would have a substantial impact because over one-third of all Supreme Court justices have served longer than twenty years and past age seventy-five. But constitutional amendments are difficult to pass, and mandatory retirement ages are out of favor now. Furthermore, some of the best judges have done some of their finest work late in their career.

Independence of Judges

Given the use of political criteria in selecting judges, can judges be independent on the bench? Can they decide cases as they think the law requires? Or do they feel pressure to decide cases as presidents or senators want them to?

Because judges are not dependent on presidents for renomination or senators for reconfirmation, they can be independent to a great extent. When President Nixon claimed executive privilege to keep the Watergate tapes secret, three of his appointees joined the other justices in ruling against him.[78] When President Clinton

As members of the Washington elite, Supreme Court justices socialize with important government officials. Although the justices are granted independence from the officials, their independence may be called into question when they interact.

Justice Antonin Scalia took a duck-hunting trip to Louisiana with Vice President Cheney and others in 2004. The trip was sponsored by an energy company. At the time, a case pending before the Court involved the vice president's energy task force, which allegedly allowed campaign contributors and energy companies to formulate the administration's energy policy. After the trip, some newspapers called for Scalia to recuse (disqualify) himself from the case, but he refused to do so—he denied having discussed the case, and he called the hunting "lousy"—and then sided with the administration in the 7–2 decision.[1] Given his views, Scalia probably would have voted this way regardless, but his participation in the case compromised his impartiality in the eyes of some people.

In the twentieth century, there were frequent contacts between justices and politicians.[2] President Franklin Roosevelt continued to play poker with Justices Robert Jackson and William Douglas after appointing them to the Court. President Truman continued to play poker with Chief Justice Vinson, who

had been his treasury secretary, after elevating him to the Court. After Truman seized private steel mills to avert a labor strike during the Korean War, the Court ruled against him.[3] Before the decision, Vinson had assured the president that the Court would rule in his favor, but the chief justice was unable to deliver the votes, and the president was embarrassed. To make amends, Justice Hugo Black, who had written the Court's opinion, invited Truman to a party with the justices at Black's home. During the party, Truman turned to Black and said, "Hugo, I don't much care for your law, but by golly, this bourbon is good!"

It is problematic when the justices discuss policies with the president rather than merely socialize with him. Justice Abe Fortas, a close confidante of President Johnson, advised him on the Vietnam War. Chief Justice Warren Burger felt so comfortable with President Nixon that he stopped at the White House unexpectedly to congratulate him for bombing Cambodia during the Vietnam War. Yet periodically cases involving the war or the protest against the war came to the Court.[4]

Social and political contacts between the justices and other officials are possible, perhaps even likely, because most justices have political backgrounds and were appointed by political officials for political purposes.

Justice Antonin Scalia (right) *and then head of the Federal Reserve Alan Greenspan socialize at the home of Secretary of Defense Donald Rumsfeld.*

Such contacts do raise questions about their independence. In recent decades, the public has become more sensitive to conflicts of interest and to appearances of conflicts of interest.

[1]*Cheney* v. *U.S. District Court,* 159 LEd.2d 459 (2004). For Scalia's justification for not recusing himself, see 158 LEd.2d 225 (2004).
[2]The rest of this box text is based substantially on Jeffrey Rosen, "The Justice Who Came to Dinner," *New York Times,* February 1, 2004, WK1.
[3]*Youngstown Sheet and Tube* v. *Sawyer,* 343 U.S. 579 (1952).
[4]Yet Burger did cast his vote against the president in the Watergate tapes case.

asserted presidential immunity from Paula Jones's lawsuit charging sexual harassment, both of his appointees joined the Republican justices in deciding against him.[79]

After surveying the Warren and Burger Court decisions involving desegregation, obscenity, abortion, and criminal defendants' rights, one scholar observed, "Few American politicians even today would care to run on a platform of desegregation, pornography, abortion, and the 'coddling' of criminals."[80]

Presidents have scoffed at the notion that their appointees become their pawns, even when they maintain a personal relationship (see the box "Rubbing Elbows with Powerful Politicians"). A study concluded that one-fourth of the justices deviated from their president's expectations.[81] Theodore Roosevelt placed

Oliver Wendell Holmes on the Court, believing that Holmes shared his views on trusts. But in an early antitrust case, Holmes voted against Roosevelt's position, prompting Roosevelt to declare, "I could carve out of a banana a judge with more backbone than that!"[82] Holmes had ample backbone; he just did not agree with Roosevelt's position in this case. Likewise, President Eisenhower placed Earl Warren on the Court, assuming that Warren was a moderate. But Warren turned out to be a liberal. Later Eisenhower said his appointment of Warren was "the biggest damn fool thing I ever did"[83] (although many legal scholars rank Warren as a great justice). President Truman concluded that "packing the Supreme Court simply can't be done. . . . I've tried it and it won't work. . . . Whenever you put a man on the Supreme Court he ceases to be your friend."[84]

Truman exaggerated, although some presidents have had trouble "packing" the courts. They have not been able to foresee the issues their appointees would face or the ways their appointees would change on the bench. (During Harry Blackmun's confirmation hearings, no senators asked about his views on abortion law, yet within six months *Roe* v. *Wade* would reach the Court, and Blackmun would author the controversial opinion.[85]) Nevertheless, presidents who have made a serious effort to find candidates with similar views usually have been able to.[86]

Access to the Courts

In our litigation-prone society, many individuals and groups want courts to resolve their disputes. Whether these individuals and groups get their "day in court" depends on their case, their wealth, and the court involved.

Courts hear two kinds of cases. **Criminal cases** are those in which governments prosecute persons for violating laws. **Civil cases** are those in which persons sue others for denying their rights and causing them harm. Criminal defendants, of course, must appear in court. Potential civil litigants, however, often cannot get access to court.

Wealth Discrimination in Access

Although the courts are supposed to be open to all, most individuals do not have enough money to hire an attorney and pay the costs necessary to pursue a case. Only corporations, wealthy individuals, or seriously injured victims suing corporations or wealthy individuals do. (Seriously injured victims with a strong case can obtain an attorney by agreeing to pay the attorney a sizable portion of what they win in their suit.) In addition, a small number of poor people supported by legal aid programs can pursue a case.

The primary expense is paying an attorney. New lawyers in law firms charge approximately $100 an hour; established partners may charge several times that.[87] Other expenses include various fees for filing the case, summoning jurors, paying witnesses, and also lost income from missed work due to numerous meetings with the attorney and hearings in court.

Even if individuals have enough money to initiate a suit, the disparity continues in court. Those with more money can develop a full case, whereas others must proceed with a skeletal case that is far less likely to persuade judges or jurors. Our legal system, according to one judge, "is divided into two separate and unequal systems of justice: one for the rich, in which the courts take limitless time to examine, ponder, consider, and deliberate over hundreds of thousands of bits of evidence and days of testimony, and hear elaborate, endless appeals and write countless learned opinions" and one for the nonrich, in which the courts provide "turnstile justice."[88] (During the week that one judge spent conducting the preliminary hearing to determine whether there was sufficient evidence to require O. J. Simpson to stand trial for murdering his exwife and her friend, other judges in Los Angeles disposed of 474 preliminary hearings for less wealthy defendants.) Consequently, many individuals are discouraged from pursuing a case in the first place.

Interest Groups Help in Access

Interest groups, with more resources than most individuals, help some individuals gain access to the courts. The groups sponsor and finance these individuals' cases. Of course, the groups do not act purely out of altruism. They choose the cases that will advance their goals. An attorney for the American Civil Liberties Union (ACLU), which takes criminal cases to prod judges to protect constitutional rights, admitted that the defendants the ACLU represents "sometimes are pretty scurvy little creatures, but what they are doesn't matter a whole hell of a lot. It's the principle that we're going to be able to use these people for that's important."

Some liberal groups—especially civil liberties organizations such as the ACLU, civil rights organizations such as the National Association for the Advancement of Colored People (NAACP), environmental groups such as the Sierra Club, and consumer and safety groups such as Ralph Nader's organizations—use litigation as a primary tactic. Other groups use it as an occasional tactic. In the 1980s and 1990s, some conservative groups began to use litigation as aggressively as these liberal groups. The Rutherford Institute arose to help persons who claimed that their religious rights were infringed, representing children who were forbidden from reading the Bible on the school bus or praying in the school cafeteria. The institute also funded Paula Jones's suit against President Clinton. Today the Alliance Defense Fund, which sponsors eighty to one hundred cases at a time, prods the courts to reflect conservative Christian values in disputes involving education, homosexuality, and embryonic stem cell research.[89]

Interest groups have become ubiquitous in the judicial process. About half of all Supreme Court cases involve a liberal or conservative interest group,[90] and many lower court cases do as well. Even so, interest groups can help only a handful of the individuals who lack the resources to finance their cases.

Interest groups' financial support can cover more than their clients' legal bills. When Paula Jones sued President Clinton for sexual harassment, Jones's team, funded by conservative groups, had her made over (from left to right) to appear more appealing.

Proceeding through the Courts

Cases normally start in a district court. Individuals who lose have a right to have their case decided by one higher court to determine whether there was a miscarriage of justice. They normally appeal to a court of appeals. Individuals who lose at this level have no further right to have their case decided by another court, but they can appeal to the Supreme Court. However, the Court can exercise almost unlimited discretion in choosing cases to review. No matter how important or urgent an issue seems, the Court does not have to hear it.

When the husband of Terri Schiavo, who was brain dead but physically alive in a persistent vegetative state, sought to have her feeding tube removed, her parents, with the help of pro-life groups, sued to take custody from her husband, then to maintain the feeding tube, and, once taken out, to reinsert it. They appealed to the Supreme Court six times. Although congressional leaders, thundering about federal judges, made her situation a political cause, the Supreme Court refused to hear the case each time it was appealed.

Litigants who appeal to the Supreme Court normally file a petition for a **writ of certiorari** (Latin for "made more certain"). The Court grants the writ—agrees to hear the case—if four of the nine justices vote to do so. The rationale for this "rule of four" is that a substantial number, though not necessarily a majority, of the justices should deem the case important enough to review. Generally, the Court agrees to review a case when the justices think an issue has not been resolved satisfactorily or consistently by the lower courts.

From over eight thousand petitions each year, the Court selects about eighty to hear, thus exercising considerable discretion.[91] The oft-spoken threat "We're going to appeal all the way to the Supreme Court" is usually just bluster. Likewise, the notion that the Court is "the court of last resort" is misleading. Most cases never get beyond the district courts or courts of appeals.

That the Supreme Court grants so few writs means that the Court has tremendous power to control its docket and therefore to determine which policies to review. It also means that the lower courts have considerable power because they serve as the court of last resort for most cases.

Deciding Cases

In deciding cases, judges need to interpret statutes and the Constitution and determine whether to follow precedents. In the process, they make law.

Interpreting Statutes

In deciding cases, judges start with statutes—laws passed by legislatures. If statutes are ambiguous, judges need to interpret them in order to apply them to their cases.

When statutes are ambiguous, judges try to ascertain the legislators' intent in passing them. They scrutinize the legislators' remarks and debates. But they often find that different members said different things, even contradictory things, and most members said nothing about the provisions in question. This gives judges considerable leeway in construing statutes.

For example, Congress passed the **Americans with Disabilities Act** to protect people from discrimination in employment and public accommodations (businesses open to the public, such as stores, restaurants, hotels, and health care facilities). The act applies to people who have a "physical impairment" that "substantially limits" any of their "major life activities." The statute does not define these terms. Thus the courts have had to do so, and in the process they have determined the scope of the act.

When a dentist refused to fill a cavity for a woman with HIV, she sued, claiming discrimination under this act. The Supreme Court agreed by a 5–4 vote.[92] The majority concluded that HIV was a physical impairment, although the woman was in the early stages and was not prevented from performing any activity yet. In concluding that HIV was a physical impairment, the majority considered what life activities it would limit and how important those activities are. The majority acknowledged that HIV would limit, for example, the important life activity of reproduction, because the disease could infect her fetus if she got pregnant. (Of course, HIV would also affect other important life activities as well.) The dissenters denied that reproduction is a major life activity, and they denied that HIV in its early stages limits reproduction. They interpreted the statute to apply to repetitive activities that are essential for daily existence rather than important activities that rarely, if ever, occur in a person's life.

When twin sisters who were severely nearsighted were denied the opportunity to become global airline pilots, they sued. This time the Court ruled the opposite by a 7–2 vote.[93] Because their condition could be corrected with glasses, they were not limited in any major life activity. Although they could not get jobs as global pilots, they could get jobs as regional pilots. The majority observed that 100 million Americans have impaired vision that requires glasses (and 28 million have impaired hearing and 50 million have high blood pressure), and they concluded that Congress could not have intended the act to apply to so many people.[94]

When a woman developed carpal tunnel syndrome on the assembly line at a manufacturing plant, she sued, claiming that the company did not make the reasonable accommodation—in this situation, give her a job that did not require repetitive manual labor—that it was required to under the act. She said her condition limited her major life activities of perform-

ing manual tasks at work and at home, including lifting, sweeping, and gardening; playing with her children; and driving long distances. The Court unanimously ruled that these are not major life activities.[95] For the act to apply, the activities must be of central importance to most people's daily lives—for example, seeing, hearing, or walking.

Thus, although the Court interpreted the act broadly when it covered persons with HIV, it interpreted the act narrowly when it refused to cover workers with less serious ailments. In these cases, the Court protected employers from having to make individual arrangements for many employees. From these rulings it should be evident that judges can make law when they interpret statutes.

Interpreting the Constitution

After interpreting statutes, judges determine whether they are constitutional. Or if the cases involve actions of government officials rather than statutes, judges determine whether the actions are constitutional. For either, they need to interpret the Constitution.

Compared to constitutions of other countries, our Constitution is short and therefore necessarily ambiguous. It speaks in broad principles rather than in narrow details. The Fifth Amendment states that persons shall not be "deprived of life, liberty, or property without due process of law." The Fourteenth Amendment states that persons shall not be denied "the equal protection of the laws." What is "due process of law"? "Equal protection of the laws"? Generally, the former means that people should be treated fairly and the latter means that they should be treated equally. But what is fairly? Equally? These are broad principles that need to be interpreted in specific cases.

Sometimes the Constitution uses relative terms. The Fourth Amendment provides that persons shall be "secure . . . against unreasonable searches and seizures." What are "unreasonable" searches and seizures? At other times the Constitution uses absolute terms. These appear more clear-cut but are not. The First Amendment provides that there shall be "no law . . . abridging the freedom of speech." Does "no law" mean literally no law? Then what about a law making it a crime to falsely shout "Fire!" in a crowded theater? Whether relative or absolute, the language needs to be interpreted in specific cases.

Occasionally, politicians, following the lead of Richard Nixon, assert that judges ought to be "strict constructionists"; that is, they ought to interpret the Constitution "strictly." This is nonsense. Judges cannot possibly interpret ambiguous language strictly. When politicians use this phrase, they are trying to persuade voters that judges from the other party are deciding cases incorrectly, as though they are departing from some clear and fixed standard.

When the language does not give sufficient guidance, some judges believe they should follow the intentions of the framers.[96] Yet these intentions are difficult to ascertain. Fifty-five delegates attended the Constitutional Convention, and many more participated in state ratifying conventions. The historical sources do not indicate what most delegates thought about most provisions.[97] And of course the delegates represented American citizens who undoubtedly had their own views.

Other judges believe they need not follow the intentions of the framers. They maintain that the Constitution was designed to be flexible and adaptable to changes in society.[98] These judges try to distill the essential meaning from the constitutional provisions and apply this meaning to contemporary situations. The Fourteenth Amendment's equal protection clause does not refer to schools, and its framers did not intend it to apply to schools. However, they did intend it to grant blacks greater equality than before, and therefore the Court applied this meaning to segregated schools. The Court then applied it to other segregated facilities, then to other racial minorities, and then to women. In short, the Court extracted the essential meaning of equality and extended it to prohibit discrimination in many situations. In this way the Court put into practice Chief Justice Marshall's statement that the Constitution is "intended to endure for ages to come."[99]

When judges interpret the Constitution, they exercise discretion. As former Chief Justice Charles Evans Hughes candidly acknowledged, "We are under a constitution, but the Constitution is what the Supreme Court says it is."[100]

Restraint and Activism

All judges exercise discretion, but not all engage in policy making to the same extent. Some, classified as restrained, are less willing to declare laws or actions of government officials unconstitutional, whereas others, classified as activist, are more willing to do so.

Restrained judges believe that the judiciary is the least democratic branch because (federal) judges are appointed for life rather than elected and re-elected. Consequently, they should defer to the other branches, whose officials are elected. That is, they should accept the laws or actions of the other branches rather than substitute their own views instead. They should be wary of "government by judiciary." "Courts are not the only agency of government that must be presumed to have the capacity to gov-

ern," Justice Harlan Stone said. "For the removal of unwise laws from the statute books, appeal lies not to the courts, but to the ballot and the processes of democratic government."[101] Restrained judges also believe that the judiciary is the least capable branch because judges are generalists who lack the expertise and resources that legislators and bureaucrats use to make policy.

Restrained judges further maintain that the power to declare laws unconstitutional is more effective if it is used sparingly. Justice Louis Brandeis concluded that "the most important thing we do is not doing."[102] That is, the most important thing judges do is declare laws constitutional and thereby build up political capital for the occasional times that they declare laws unconstitutional.

Ultimately, restrained judges contend that showing appropriate deference and following proper procedures are more important than reaching desired results. When a friend taking leave of Justice Oliver Wendell Holmes one morning said, "Well, Mr. Justice, I hope you do justice today," Holmes replied, "My job is not to do justice but to follow the law." Justice Harry Blackmun, appointed by President Nixon, reflected this view in a capital punishment case:

I yield to no one in the depth of my distaste, antipathy, and, indeed, abhorrence for the death penalty, with all its aspects of physical distress and fear and of moral judgment exercised by finite minds. That distaste is buttressed by a belief that capital punishment serves no useful purpose that can be demonstrated. For me, it violates childhood's training and life's experiences, and is not compatible with the philosophical convictions I have been able to develop. It is antagonistic to any sense of "reverence for life." Were I a legislator, I would vote against the death penalty.

But as a judge, he voted for it.[103]

Activist judges are less concerned with showing appropriate deference and following proper procedures. They seem more outraged at injustice. Chief Justice Earl Warren said that the courts' responsibility was "to see if justice truly has been done." He asked lawyers who emphasized technical procedures during oral arguments, "Yes, yes, yes, but is it right? Is it good?"[104]

Activist judges do not believe that the judiciary is the least democratic branch. Warren, who had served as governor of California, saw that the legislators, though elected, were often the captives of special interests. As a result of these attitudes, activist judges have a more flexible and more pragmatic view of separation of powers. District court judge Frank Johnson, who issued sweeping orders for Alabama's prisons and mental hospitals, replied to critics, "I didn't ask for any of these cases. In an ideal society, all of

A study of all cases in which congressional statutes were at stake (sixty-four) in the last eleven terms of the Rehnquist Court (1994–2005) reveals that the most conservative justice—Clarence Thomas—was the most activist. He voted to strike down the law in 65.6% of these cases. The next most conservative justices—Antonin Scalia and William Rehnquist—were among the most activist. The most liberal justices—John Paul Stevens, Ruther Bader Ginsburg, Steven Breyer, and David Souter—were the most restrained. (All but Rehnquist and O'Connor are on the current Roberts Court.)

Justice	% Votes to Strike Down Congressional Statute
Thomas	65.6
Kennedy	64.1
Scalia	56.3
Rehnquist	46.9
O'Connor	46.8
Souter	42.2
Stevens	39.3
Ginsburg	39.1
Breyer	28.1

SOURCE: Paul Gewirtz and Chad Golder, "So Who Are the Activists?" *New York Times*, July 6, 2005, www.nytimes.com/2005/07/06/opinion/06gewirtz.html?ei=5070&en=5b5cf694fb8.

these . . . decisions should be made by those to whom we have entrusted these responsibilities. But when governmental institutions fail to make these . . . decisions in a manner which comports with the Constitution, the federal courts have a duty to remedy the violation."[105]

Activist judges do not believe that the power to declare laws unconstitutional is more effective if it is used sparingly. Rather, they claim that the power is enhanced if it is used frequently—essentially, they urge their colleagues to "use it or lose it"—because the public gets accustomed to it.

Thus judicial restraint and judicial activism are belief systems and role concepts that people think judges should follow when they decide cases. Some judges tend to be restrained, whereas others tend to be activist; most fall somewhere in between.

Both conservatives and liberals have practiced either restraint or activism depending on the political climate at the time. In the late nineteenth and early twentieth centuries, the Court was conservative and activist, striking down regulations on business. After the switch in the 1930s, the Court was liberal and restrained, upholding regulations on business. Then in the 1950s and 1960s, the Court was liberal and activist, striking down restrictions on individual rights.

In response to the liberal activism of the Warren Court, conservative officials and commentators insisted that judges should adhere to judicial restraint. But as the number of conservative justices increased, a pattern of conservative activism by the Rehnquist Court emerged as well. Although the Rehnquist Court accepted some liberal laws, it struck down others, including laws implementing gun registration, affirmative action, legislative districts that help racial minorities elect their candidates, and governmental policies that help religious minorities practice their religion. The Court also invalidated a series of congressional laws affecting the states. In eight of the last years of the Rehnquist Court, the justices invalidated thirty-three federal laws, the highest annual average ever.[106]

In **Bush v. Gore**, which arose from the disputed presidential election of 2000, the conservative majority deliberately intervened—essentially, picked the president—although the Constitution lays out the procedures to resolve electoral deadlocks.[107] These procedures give Congress, not the courts, primary authority to choose the president. (See the box "Who Are the Activists?")

Although activism and restraint are useful concepts, we should not make too much of them. It usually is more important to know whether a judge is conservative or liberal than whether the judge purports to be restrained or activist. Political science research shows that justices' votes reflect their ideology: conservative justices vote for the conservative position, and liberal justices vote for the liberal position in most cases. Sometimes justices claim to be restrained, but usually their decision—allowing a particular law or policy to continue—produces the conservative or liberal outcome they prefer.[108] Thus some political scientists conclude that "judicial restraint" is little more than "a cloak for the justices' policy preferences."[109] That is, it enables them to proclaim their "restraint" while actually voting on the basis of their ideology—without ever admitting this to the public. We should be skeptical when we hear judges or politicians using these terms, whether touting their "restraint" to pacify the public or deriding opponents' "activism" to inflame the public.

Following Precedents

In interpreting statutes and the Constitution, judges are expected to follow precedents established by their court or higher courts in previous cases. This is the

Justice Clarence Thomas shares a laugh with his clerks in his chambers.

rule of **stare decisis** (Latin for "stand by what has been decided").

When in 1962 the Supreme Court held unconstitutional a New York law requiring public school students to recite a nondenominational prayer every day, the ruling became a precedent.[110] The following year, the Court held unconstitutional a Baltimore school board policy requiring students to recite Bible verses.[111] The Court followed the precedent it had set the year before. In 1980, the Court held unconstitutional a Tennessee law forcing public schools to post the Ten Commandments in all classrooms.[112] Although this law differed from the previous ones in that it did not require recitation, the majority concluded that it reflected the same goal—to use the public schools to promote the Christian religion—so it violated the same principle, separation of church and state. In 1992, the Court ruled that clergy cannot offer prayers at graduation ceremonies for public schools.[113] Although this situation, too, differed from the previous ones in that it did not occur every day at school, the majority reasoned that it, too, reflected the same goal and violated the same principle. Finally, in 2000, the Court ruled that schools cannot use, or allow clergy or students to use, the public address system to offer prayers before high school football games.[114] Thus, for almost four decades, the Court followed the precedent it originally set when it initially addressed this issue.

Stare decisis provides stability in the law. If different judges decided similar cases in different ways, the law would be unpredictable, even chaotic. "*Stare decisis*," Justice Brandeis said, "is usually the wise policy; because in most matters it is more important that the applicable rule of law be settled than that it be settled

right."[115] *Stare decisis* also promotes equality in the law. If different judges decided similar cases in different ways, the courts would appear discriminatory toward some litigants.

However, even when judges try to follow precedents, sometimes they have discretion in choosing which to follow. There might not be any precedents that are controlling but several that are relevant, and these might point in contrary directions. In 1996, the justices weighed government regulation of indecent programming on cable television. They had precedents that governed broadcast television, telephones, and bookstores. But as Justice Breyer observed, none of these really paralleled cable television, which looks like broadcast television but uses telephone lines rather than airwaves to transmit its signals. Thus, he was uncertain which precedents to use. Apparently, the others were uncertain also, as the nine justices split three ways and wrote six opinions while upholding one section and striking down two other sections of the law.[116]

Making Law

Many judges deny that they make law. They say that it is already there, that they merely "find" it or, occasionally, "interpret" it with their education and experience. They imply that they use a mechanical process. Justice Owen Roberts wrote for the majority that struck down a New Deal act in 1936:

> It is sometimes said that the Court assumes a power to overrule . . . the people's representatives. This is a misconception. The Constitution is the supreme law of the land. . . . All legislation must conform to the principles

it lays down. When an act of Congress is appropriately challenged in the courts as not conforming to the constitutional mandate, the judicial branch of government has only one duty—to lay . . . the Constitution . . . beside the statute . . . and to decide whether the latter squares with the former.[117]

In other words, the Constitution itself dictates the decision.

However, by now it should be apparent that judges do not use a mechanical process, that they do exercise discretion. They *do* make law—when they interpret statutes, when they interpret the Constitution, and when they determine which precedents to follow or disregard.[118]

In doing so, they reflect their own political preferences. As Justice Benjamin Cardozo said, "We may try to see things as objectively as we please. Nonetheless, we can never see them with any eyes except our own."[119] That is, judges are human beings with their own perceptions and attitudes and even prejudices. They do not, and cannot, shed these the moment they put on their robes.

But to say that judges make law is not to say that they make law as legislators do. Judges make law less directly. They make it in the process of resolving disputes brought to them. They usually make it by telling governments what they cannot do, rather than what they must do and how they must do it. And judges make law less freely. They start not with clean slates but with established principles embodied in statutes, the Constitution, and precedents. They are expected to follow these principles. If they deviate from them, they are expected to explain their reasons, and they are subjected to criticism within the legal profession.

Deciding Cases at the Supreme Court

The Supreme Court's term runs from October through June. Early in the term, the justices decide which cases to hear, and by the end of the term, they decide how to resolve those cases.

After the Court agrees to hear a case, litigants submit written arguments. These "briefs" identify the issues and marshal the evidence—statutes, constitutional provisions, and precedents—for their side. (The word *briefs* is a misnomer, as some run to more than one hundred pages.)

Often interest groups and governments, whether federal, state, or local, submit briefs to support one side. These **friend of the court briefs** present additional evidence or perspectives not included in the litigants' briefs. Major cases can prompt many briefs. A pair of affirmative action cases from the University of Michigan in 2003 had a record 102 briefs.[120]

Several weeks after receiving the briefs, the Court holds oral arguments. The justices gather in the robing room, put on their black robes, and file into the courtroom, taking their places at the half-hexagon bench. The chief justice sits in the center, with the associate justices extending out in order of seniority. The crier gavels the courtroom to attention and announces:

> *The Honorable, the Chief Justice and Associate Justices of the Supreme Court of the United States! Oyez, oyez, oyez! [Give ear, give ear, give ear!] All persons having business before the Honorable, the Supreme Court of the United States are admonished to draw near and give attention, for the Court is now sitting. God save the United States and this Honorable Court.*

The chief justice calls the case. The lawyers present their arguments, although the justices interrupt with questions whenever they want. When Thurgood Marshall, as the counsel for the NAACP before becoming a justice, argued one school desegregation case, he was interrupted 127 times. The justices ask about the facts of the case: "What happened when the defendant . . . ?" They ask about relevant precedents that appear to

Ruth Bader Ginsburg, appointed by President Clinton, was the second female justice and is the only one now. Although she tied for first place in her graduating class from Columbia Law School in 1959, she was turned down for a clerkship by Justice Felix Frankfurter and for law jobs with New York City firms. As a Jew, a woman, and a mother with young children, she had three liabilities at that time. Instead, she taught law and served as an attorney with the ACLU. In the 1970s, she argued six sex discrimination cases before the Supreme Court, winning five.

The job of a justice is unlike that of other political officials. Even after three decades of experience, Justice William Brennan often ate at his desk so he could finish his work. He was one of the most influential members of the Warren and Burger Courts.

© Lynn Johnson/Aurora

support or rebut the lawyers' arguments: "Can you distinguish this case from . . . ?" They ask about hypothetical scenarios: "What if the police officer . . . ?" These questions help the justices determine what is at stake, how a ruling would relate to existing doctrine, and how a ruling might govern future situations. They are experienced at pinning lawyers down. Chief Justice Rehnquist, who was affable toward his colleagues, was tough on the lawyers appearing before him. When asked whether the lawyers were nervous, he replied, "I assume they're all nervous—they should be."[121] Occasionally, one faints on the spot.

The chief justice allots a half hour per side. When time expires, a red light flashes on the lectern, and the chief justice halts any lawyer who continues. Rehnquist, who valued efficiency and punctuality, cut lawyers off in mid-sentence when their time was up.

The oral arguments identify and clarify the major points of the case for any justices who did not read the briefs, and they assess the potential impact of the possible rulings. The oral arguments also serve as a symbol: they give litigants a chance to be heard in open court, which encourages litigants to feel that the eventual ruling is legitimate. However, the oral arguments rarely sway the justices, except occasionally when a lawyer for one side is especially effective or ineffective.

The Court holds Friday conferences to make a tentative decision and assign the opinion. The decision affirms or reverses the lower court decision; it indicates who wins and who loses. The opinion explains why. It expresses principles of law and establishes

precedents for the future. It tells lower courts how to resolve similar cases.

A portrait of Chief Justice John Marshall presides over the conference. To ensure secrecy, no one is present but the justices. They begin with handshakes. (During his tenure, Chief Justice Marshall suggested that they begin with a drink whenever it was rainy. But even when it was sunny, Marshall sometimes announced, "Our jurisdiction extends over so large a territory that the doctrine of chances makes it certain that it must be raining somewhere."[122] Perhaps this accounts for his extraordinary success in persuading his colleagues to adopt his views.) Then the justices get down to business. The chief justice initiates the discussion of the case. He indicates what the issues are and how they ought to be decided, and he casts a vote. The associate justices follow in order of seniority. Although the conference traditionally featured give and take among the justices, discussion was perfunctory under Rehnquist, and the conference became a series of quick votes.[123]

The Court reaches a tentative decision based on these votes. If the chief justice is in the majority, he assigns the writing of the opinion to himself or another justice. If he is not in the majority, the most senior associate justice in the majority assigns it. This custom reveals the chief justice's power. Although his vote counts the same as each associate justice's vote, his authority to assign the opinion can determine what the opinion says. He knows that certain colleagues will use strong language and lay down broad principles, whereas others will use guarded language and hew closely to specific facts of the case.

Before Marshall became chief justice, each justice wrote his own opinion. But Marshall realized that one opinion from the Court would carry more weight. He often convinced the other justices to forsake their opinions for his. As a result, he wrote almost half of the more than eleven hundred opinions the Court handed down during his thirty-four years. Recent chief justices have assigned most opinions— 82 to 86 percent—but have written just slightly more than their share—12 to 14 percent.[124] Some Court watchers believe that Rehnquist downplayed his conservative views after he became chief justice to stay in the majority and retain control of the opinion.[125]

After the conference, the Court produces the opinion. This is the most time-consuming stage in the process. After Justice Brandeis died, researchers found in his files the thirty-seventh draft of an opinion he had written but still had not been satisfied with.

Because the justices are free to change their vote anytime until the decision is announced, the justice assigned the opinion tries to write it to command support of the justices in the original majority and possibly even some in the original minority. The writer circulates the draft among the others, who suggest revisions. The writer circulates more drafts. These go back and forth as the justices attempt to persuade or cajole, nudge or push their colleagues toward their position.

Unlike legislators, however, the justices don't engage in horse-trading—if you join me on this, I'll join you on that. According to one justice, there's "[n]one of that, zero. The coalitions float. Each . . . case is a new day."[126]

Sometimes the outcome changes between the tentative vote in the conference and the final vote in the decision. According to Justice Blackmun's notes, eleven times during his last three years on the Rehnquist Court, one or more justices switched sides to fashion a new majority from the original minority. In the case involving graduation prayers, Justice Anthony Kennedy was writing the **majority opinion** to allow such prayers, but he was unable to persuade himself. He abandoned the majority and joined the minority, thus making it the eventual majority.[127]

These inner workings underscore the politicking among the justices. Justice William Brennan, a liberal activist on the Warren and Burger Courts, was a gregarious and charming Irish American who was well liked by his colleagues. After drafting an opinion, he sent his clerks to other justices' clerks to learn whether their justices had any objections. Then he tried to redraft it to satisfy them. If they still had qualms, he went to their offices and tried to persuade them. If necessary, he compromised. He didn't want "to be 100 percent principled and lose by one vote," a law professor observed.[128] Brennan was so adept at persuasion that some scholars consider him "the best coalition builder ever to sit on the Supreme Court."[129] In fact, some say the Warren and Burger Courts should have been called the Brennan Court.

Justice Scalia, a conservative activist on the Rehnquist Court, is a brilliant and gregarious Italian American who, when appointed by President Reagan, was expected to dominate his colleagues and become the leader of the Court. Yet he has not fulfilled this expectation. He has been brash and imprudent, appearing to take more pleasure in insulting his colleagues than in persuading them.[130] In a case in which Justice O'Connor, also conservative but more cautious, did not want to go as far in limiting abortion rights as he did, Scalia wrote that her arguments "cannot be taken seriously."[131] In another case in which Chief Justice Rehnquist, who usually voted with Scalia, voted opposite him, Scalia wrote that his arguments were "implausible" and suggested that any lawyer who advised his client as Rehnquist urged should be "disbarred."[132] As a result, Scalia has not been as effective in forging a consensus among conservatives as Brennan was among liberals.

Leadership, by someone, is necessary with nine strong-willed individuals, each of whom has risen to the top of the legal profession and each of whom is essentially operating a one-person law firm. Sometimes the chief justice becomes the informal leader. Marshall set the standard; Warren and Rehnquist were also effective leaders. Burger, however, possessed neither the interpersonal skills nor the intellectual firepower to earn the respect of his colleagues. From all indications, new Chief Justice Roberts has the potential to become an effective leader.

If the opinion does not command the support of some justices in the original majority, they write a **concurring opinion.** This indicates that they agree with the decision but not the reasons for it. Meanwhile, the justices in the minority write a **dissenting opinion.** This indicates that they do not agree even with the decision. Both concurring and dissenting opinions weaken the force of the majority opinion. They question its validity, and they suggest that at a different time with different justices, there might be a different ruling. Chief Justice Hughes used to say that a dissenting opinion is "an appeal to the brooding spirit of the law, to the intelligence of a future day."[133]

Unlike the high courts of many other countries, which do not report any dissents, the United States Supreme Court routinely does, and the American people usually accept the existence of such disagreements about the law.[134] In recent terms, about 60 percent of the Court's cases have had dissents.[135] But too many dissents indicate a fractious Court. One-third of the Rehnquist Court's cases were decided by a 5–4 vote in 2001, possibly the highest proportion ever.[136]

Finally, the Court's print shop in its basement prints the opinions, thus preventing the leaks that might occur if the opinions were printed elsewhere. The Court then announces its decisions and distributes the opinions in public session.

Power of the Courts

Alexis de Tocqueville, the French aristocrat who traveled throughout the United States in the 1830s, observed, "Scarcely any political question arises in the United States that is not resolved, sooner or later, into a judicial question."[137] Because Americans are more inclined than others to bring suits, courts have many opportunities to wield power. The courts have been able to capitalize on these opportunities because they interpret the Constitution, which is revered by the people, and they enjoy relative (though not absolute) independence from the political pressures on the other branches.

The use of judicial review by the courts and the use of political checks against the courts reveal the extent of their power.

Use of Judicial Review

Judicial review—the authority to declare laws or actions of government officials unconstitutional—is the tool the courts use to wield power. When the courts declare a law or action unconstitutional, they not only void that law or action, but they also might put the issue on the public agenda, and they might speed up or slow down the pace of change in the government's policy.

When the Supreme Court declared Texas's abortion law unconstitutional in *Roe* v. *Wade* in 1973, the Court put the abortion issue on the public agenda.[138] It had not been a raging controversy before the decision.

The Court used judicial review as a catalyst to speed up change in the desegregation cases in the 1950s. At the time, President Eisenhower was not inclined to act, and Congress was not able to act because both houses were dominated by senior southerners who, as committee chairs, bottled up civil rights legislation. The Court broke the logjam.

The Court used judicial review as a brake to slow down change in the business regulation cases in the first third of the twentieth century. The Court delayed some policies for several decades.

Judicial review, an American contribution to government, was for years unique to this country. It is now used in numerous other countries, but not as extensively or as effectively as in the United States.

The Supreme Court alone has struck down over 150 provisions of federal laws and over 1200 provisions of state and local laws.[139] The number of laws struck down, however, is not a true measure of the importance of judicial review. Instead, the ever-present threat of review has prevented the legislatures from enacting many laws that they feared would be struck down.

By using judicial review to play a strong role in government, the Court has contradicted the Founders' expectation that the judiciary would always be the weakest branch. Usually it has been the weakest branch, but occasionally it has been stronger. Arguably, these times include some years during the early nineteenth century, when the Court established national supremacy; the late nineteenth century and early twentieth century, when the Court thwarted efforts to regulate business; and the 1950s and 1960s, when the Court extended civil liberties and rights.

Nevertheless, the extent to which the Court has played a strong role in government should not be exaggerated. The Court has not exercised judicial review over a wide range of issues; in each of its three eras, it has exercised review over one dominant issue and paid relatively little attention to other pending issues. Moreover, the one dominant issue has always involved domestic policy. Traditionally, the Court has been reluctant to intervene in foreign policy.[140]

And when the Court has addressed an issue, it has been cautious. Of the provisions of congressional laws held unconstitutional, more than half were voided more than four years after they had been passed, and more than one-fourth were voided more than twelve years after they had been passed.[141] These laws were voided after many members of Congress who had

Reproduced by special permission of *Playboy* Magazine. Copyright ©1972 by *Playboy*.

"My dissenting opinion will be brief: You're all full of crap!"

supported them had left Congress. The Court confronted Congress when it was safer to do so.

Use of Political Checks against the Courts

Although the courts enjoy relative independence from the political pressures on the other branches, they do not have absolute independence. Because they are part of the political process, they are subject to some political checks, which limit the extent to which they can wield judicial review.

Checks by the Executive

Presidents can impose the most effective check. If they dislike judges' rulings, they can appoint new judges when vacancies occur. Many appointees remain on the bench two decades after their president has left the White House.[142] President Nixon resigned in disgrace in 1974, but his appointee William Rehnquist stayed on the Court until he died in 2005.

Presidents and state and local executives, such as governors and mayors and even school officials and police officers, can refuse to enforce courts' rulings. School officials have disobeyed decisions requiring desegregation and invalidating class prayers. Police officers have ignored decisions invalidating some kinds of searches and interrogations.

Yet executives who refuse to enforce courts' rulings risk losing public support, unless the public also opposes the rulings. Even President Nixon complied when the Court ordered him to turn over the incriminating Watergate tapes.

Checks by the Legislature

Congress and the state legislatures can overturn courts' rulings by adopting constitutional amendments. They have done so four times (with the Eleventh, Fourteenth, Sixteenth, and Twenty-sixth Amendments).[143]

They can also overturn courts' rulings by passing new statutes. When courts base decisions on their interpretations of statutes, or when they make decisions in the absence of statutes, legislatures can pass new statutes, with clear language, that negate the decisions. The Supreme Court ruled in 1986 that the Air Force did not have to allow an ordained rabbi to wear his yarmulke with his uniform.[144] The next year, Congress passed a statute permitting military personnel to wear some religious apparel while in uniform. From 1967 through 1990, Congress passed statutes to negate 121 Supreme Court rulings.[145]

Legislatures can refuse to implement courts' rulings, especially when money is necessary to implement them. The legislators simply do not appropriate the money.

Although these checks are the most common, Congress has invoked others, though only rarely. It can alter the structure of the lower federal courts, it can limit the appellate jurisdiction of the Supreme Court, and it can impeach and remove judges. It can also limit the use of *habeas corpus*. In 2005 it prohibited federal courts from hearing any cases brought by alien detainees at Guantanamo Bay, Cuba.[146]

As a result of occasional checks or threatened checks, the courts have developed a strong sense of self-restraint to ensure self-preservation. This, more than the checks themselves, limits their use of judicial review.

Conclusion: Are the Courts Responsive?

The courts tend to reflect the views of the public. Studies comparing 185 Supreme Court rulings from the mid-1930s through the mid-1990s with public opinion polls on the same issues found that the rulings mirrored the polls in about 60 percent of the cases.[147] The justices reflected the views of the public about as often as elected officials did. Thus, the justices either responded to the public or, having been appointed by political officials chosen by the public, simply reflected the views of the public as political officials did.

Research shows that citizens know little about the cases (and less about the judges; more adults can identify the character names of the Three Stooges than a single justice on the Supreme Court),[148] but they do remember controversial decisions and they do recognize broad trends. A study of public opinion toward the Supreme Court from 1966 to 1984 found that the public became more negative when the Court upheld more criminal rights and struck down more congressional statutes.[149] This opinion pressured presidents and members of Congress to appoint justices with different views. Thus, these officials responded to the public, and ultimately they got the Court to respond to the public.

Although the courts are directly or indirectly responsive to the public, the Founders did not intend for them to be very responsive. The Founders gave judges life tenure so that the courts would be relatively independent of both officials and the public.

Indeed, the courts are more independent of political pressures than the other branches are. This enables them, in the words of appellate court judge Learned Hand, to stand as a bulwark against the "pressure of public panic." They can provide a "sober second thought."[150]

The courts can even protect the rights of various minorities—racial minorities, religious minorities, political dissidents, and criminal defendants—against the demands and the wrath of the majority. Chapters 14 and 15 will show how courts extended civil liberties and rights to unpopular groups and individuals who lacked clout with the executive and legislative branches and support from the public. Yet protecting the rights of these groups and individuals has historically been the exception rather than the rule. It was typical of the Warren Court era and to some extent the Burger Court era, but it was not typical of most years before and has not been typical of most years since.

The courts are part of the political process and are sensitive to others in the process, especially to the president, Congress, and the public. Although they enjoy relative independence, they are not immune to political pressure. They have therefore "learned to be a political institution and to behave accordingly" and have "seldom lagged far behind or forged far ahead" of public opinion.[151]

Alito Refuses to Be Candid

As the confirmation hearings for Samuel Alito's nomination to the Supreme Court approached, three evangelical ministers were allowed into the hearing room of the Senate Judiciary Committee to apply holy oil to the senators' seats.[152]

Meanwhile, the administration's twenty-person confirmation team launched a public relations blitz, orchestrating news conferences, opinion articles, and letters to the editor. Friends, classmates, and former law clerks were contacted for testimonies. Conservative legal scholars were enlisted to answer questions that might arise about the judge's decisions. The goal of these efforts was to influence public opinion, in particular to acknowledge that Alito was a conservative but to emphasize that he was a mainstream rather than an extreme conservative.

The rest of the team prepared Alito. A Republican consultant who guided many judicial nominees through the confirmation process instructed them that "your role in this process is that of a bridegroom at a wedding: stay out of the way, be on time, and keep your mouth shut." Therefore, "The most important rule is the 80-20 rule, which is if the senators are talking 80 percent of the time and you're talking 20 percent of the time, you're winning, and if it's 60-40 you've got a problem, and if it's 50-50, you've lost and you might as well go home."[153]

The team held mock hearings, known as "murder boards," in which administration lawyers, acting as the senators, asked Alito the questions they expected the senators to ask. They devised answers, and Alito rehearsed them. Their advice was to be closed rather than open and vague rather than specific.

At his confirmation hearings, Alito followed the team's advice. To elicit sympathetic feelings among television viewers, he told his "story"—that his father immigrated from Italy and grew up in poverty. To portray the judge as a typical suburban dad, the administration circulated photos of him coaching Little League baseball.

After telling his "story," Alito clammed up, talking no more than was necessary. When questioned by the senators, he was very careful—so careful he appeared wooden. He resisted all attempts to engage in a dialogue. "He was like a chauffeur who speaks only when spoken to, and doesn't presume to converse."[154] And his face registered few expressions.

When asked about his past statements, he soft-pedaled them, saying that he was an applicant for a job in the Reagan administration and then an advocate as a lawyer in the Reagan administration. In both positions, he was expected to make enthusiastic statements for the conservative cause. As a judge, he insisted, he would have no political agenda. Yet, despite his repeated disavowals, he refused to reveal his actual views on legal issues.

When asked about his past membership in the Concerned Alumni of Princeton, which opposed the admission of women and more minorities, he said he couldn't recall joining the organization. When asked about his failure to recluse himself as a judge in a case involving a company in which he had an investment, he said he couldn't explain why. Although he was well versed in the law, he had a short memory for these matters.

Even though the Democratic senators weren't overly aggressive, one

Republican senator, in an effort to engender more sympathy for the judge, remarked, "I am sorry that you've had to go through this. I am sorry that your family has had to sit here and listen to this."[155] Hearing these remarks, Alito's wife, who was sitting behind him, left the room in tears, and thus created more sympathy for her husband.

By the end of the hearings, Alito seemed innocuous rather than dangerous as Robert Bork had appeared. Alito seemed too decent to be an extremist, even though viewers had little clue what he would do on the bench.

The Judiciary Committee chair observed, "The hearings are really, in effect, a subtle minuet, with the nominee answering as many questions as he thinks necessary in order to be confirmed."[156] With a ten-member advantage in the Senate, the Republican candidate didn't need to answer many questions. The Democratic senators had no apparent strategy, making statements as often as asking questions and thus shifting the focus away from Alito, as the "80-20 rule" suggests they would.

They got frustrated from Alito's refusal to answer their questions, prompting them to ramble on. Senator John Kerry (D-Mass.), trying to boost his credentials among liberal Democrats for the party's presidential nomination in 2008, initiated a hapless filibuster effort, which was easily defeated, and Alito was confirmed.

The hearings were so dull that few Americans watched. Most people don't think the Court affects their lives. Their lack of interest and lack of concern that a candidate for a lifetime seat on the highest court wouldn't reveal his views on important legal issues shows that most

Americans don't care about judicial appointments, unless the nominees are out of the mainstream, as Robert Bork was, or the hearings are sensational, as Clarence Thomas's was, with the talk about pornographic movies and pubic hairs on Coke cans. Now it's obvious that future candidates will refuse to reveal their views until the public demands them to.

One disillusioned committee member proposed that the hearings be abolished because they tell us little about the nominee's views. They tell us little even about the nominee's personality. What we see is a carefully crafted persona fashioned by a public relations team. As a media consultant observed, "Every Court nominee is filtered through a machine that covers them in vanilla topping. . . . It's hard to organize against vanilla."[157]

 To learn more about this topic, go to "you are there" exercises for this chapter on the text website.

Key Terms

judicial review
Marbury v. *Madison*
court-packing plan
Warren Court
Burger Court
Rehnquist Court
Roberts Court
district courts
courts of appeals
jurisdiction
habeas corpus
Foreign Intelligence Surveillance Court
senatorial courtesy

criminal cases
civil cases
writ of *certiorari*
Americans with Disabilities Act
restrained judges
activist judges
Bush v. Gore
stare decisis
friend of the court briefs
majority opinion
concurring opinion
dissenting opinion

Further Reading

Vincent Bugliosi, *No Island of Sanity: Paula Jones* v. *Bill Clinton* (New York: Ballantine, 1998). This examination of Paula Jones's Supreme Court case is interesting and readable.

Alan M. Dershowitz, *Supreme Injustice: How the High Court Hijacked Election 2000* (New York: Oxford University Press, 2001). Analysis of the decision in *Bush* v. *Gore* and the motives of the justices by a leading legal scholar. Readers will never again assume the Court is nonpolitical.

Richard D. Kahlenberg, *Broken Contract* (Boston: Faber & Faber, 1992). This memoir by a student at Harvard Law School reveals a lot about law schools, the legal profession, and the nature of American law.

Jane Mayer and Jill Abramson, *Strange Justice: The Selling of Clarence Thomas* (Boston: Houghton Mifflin, 1994). This book explores the campaign to put Clarence Thomas on the Court and investigates the charges of sexual harassment that surfaced.

David M. O'Brien, *Storm Center*, 6th ed. (New York: Norton, 2003). This is a lively account of the Supreme Court and its very human justices.

LeRoy Phillips and Mark Curriden, *Contempt of Court* (New York: Faber & Faber, 1999). The authors tell the story of the Supreme Court's only criminal trial—of a Chattanooga sheriff for allowing a lynch mob to murder a defendant whose appeal was pending before the Supreme Court in 1906.

Bob Woodward and Scott Armstrong, *The Brethren* (New York: Simon & Schuster, 1979). This book takes a behind-the-scenes look at the politicking among Supreme Court justices for major cases during the 1970s.

For Viewing

Gideon's Trumpet (1985). A television movie based on the true story of the criminal defendant who insisted upon receiving an attorney for his defense. Eventually, he reached the Supreme Court, which used his minor case to make a landmark ruling.

Twelve Angry Men (1957). This film demonstrates the value of a jury, as one juror tries to convince the others that the case is not as clear-cut as they think.

The Ox-Bow Incident (1943). This movie based on the acclaimed novel by Walter Van Tilburg Clark examines mob justice, in the absence of legal procedures, on the frontier.

 **Electronic Resources**

www.supremecourtus.gov
This is the Supreme Court's official site, with decisions and opinions posted the day they are announced. A similar site, operated by Cornell University, is supct.law.cornell.edu/supct/index.php.

www.oyez.nwu.edu
This site, developed by Northwestern University, has biographies of all Supreme Court justices, past and present. You can hear the marshal cry, "Oyez, oyez"; listen to oral arguments in important cases; take a virtual tour of the Court; and search for Court decisions by subject, date, or citation.

www.courttv.com/library/supreme
Current legal news, recent court cases, and links to historical criminal cases from Court TV can all be found here.

www.law.umkc.edu/faculty/projects/ftrials/manson/manson.html
A law professor at the University of Missouri provides information on more than thirty famous American and international trials.

ThomsonNOW™

Enter ThomsonNOW™ using the access card that is available with this text or through www.thomsonedu.com/thomsonnow. ThomsonNOW™ will assist you in understanding the content in this chapter with a personalized study plan generated for your needs. A practice test will assess the areas you need to review and provide the tools to fully comprehend those concepts, including an integrated digital eBook, interactive simulations, timelines, video case studies, MicroCase exercises, and InfoTrac College Edition readers and exercises. You'll also be connected to the learning objectives, chapter outline, chapter glossary, flash cards, crossword puzzles, Internet activities, and interactive quizzes found on the companion website.

Detainees at Guantanamo Bay, Cuba.

©Ron Sachs/CNP/Corbis

The Constitution and the Bill of Rights
  Individual Rights in the Constitution
  The Bill of Rights
Freedom of Expression
  Freedom of Speech
  Freedom of Association
  Freedom of the Press
  Libel and Obscenity
Freedom of Religion
  Free Exercise of Religion
  Establishment of Religion
Rights of Criminal Defendants
  Search and Seizure
  Self-Incrimination
  Counsel
  Jury Trial
  Cruel and Unusual Punishment
  Rights in Theory and in Practice
Right to Privacy
  Birth Control
  Abortion
  Birth Control, Revisited
  Homosexuality
  Right to Die
Implications for Civil Liberties from the War on Terrorism
  Interrogations
  Surveillance
Conclusion: Are the Courts Responsive in Interpreting Civil Liberties?

YOU ARE THERE

Do You Challenge the President in Wartime?

You are Justice John Paul Stevens of the United States Supreme Court, which is deciding whether American courts have any jurisdiction to hear lawsuits brought by foreign men captured abroad and imprisoned at the United States Naval Base at Guantanamo Bay, Cuba.

Since the September 11, 2001, terrorist attacks, 759 men from forty-four countries have been rounded up and flown to Guantanamo Bay, where they have been detained as terrorist suspects. Most have been captured in Afghanistan or Pakistan, and most have been imprisoned for over two years. Vice President Dick Cheney called them "the worst of a very bad lot." Secretary of Defense Donald Rumsfeld called them "among the most dangerous, best-trained, vicious killers on the face of the earth."[1]

It is difficult to evaluate these claims because the Bush administration has enshrouded the captives in secrecy. It has refused to release their names or allow them to be interviewed by journalists. So far none has been charged with committing a terrorist act. About 150 have been released and returned to their countries.

Whether dangerous or not, all have been imprisoned without being charged, without being tried, without receiving counsel, and with-out gaining access to any court.[2] The administration says the remainder will be detained indefinitely.

The families of two Australian, two British, and twelve Kuwaiti captives have filed suit, asking American courts to determine the legality of their detention.[3] The plaintiffs have petitioned for a writ of **habeas corpus,** which criminal defendants use to challenge the legality of their confinement. As explained in Chapter 13, *habeas corpus* is a traditional and integral component of English and American law, mandating that government prosecutors must produce a defendant and justify his or her incarceration to the court. The U.S. Constitution stipulates that *habeas corpus* cannot be suspended unless there is a rebellion or foreign invasion. A congressional statute grants federal courts jurisdiction to hear petitions for *habeas corpus* from anyone claiming to be held in violation of the Constitution, laws, or treaties of the United States. The statute does not distinguish between American citizens and aliens, and it does not distinguish between peacetime and wartime.

The Supreme Court did rule that it does not apply to aliens who are outside of U.S. territory.[4] During World War II, American forces captured German soldiers in China and tried them before a military com-

An independent dresser as well as thinker, Justice John Paul Stevens wears bow ties, which he laboriously knots by hand. When a guest at a party poked fun at him for wearing a "clip-on" bow tie, Stevens slowly unraveled his tie and then carefully retied it without saying a word.

mission there. The Supreme Court did not allow the German soldiers to use *habeas corpus* to challenge their detention.

The Bush administration claims that this precedent should apply to the prisoners at Guantanamo Bay. The naval base consists of forty-five square miles of land and water along the southeastern coast of Cuba. It is a natural harbor where Christopher Columbus dropped anchor on one of his voyages to the Americas. The United States administered Cuba after the Spanish-American War in 1898 and granted Cuba independence four years later, retaining the right in a treaty to lease Guantanamo Bay as a naval refueling station. In 1934, the United States renegotiated the agreement to remain in effect as long as the United States wants it to. The terms specify that the United States shall have complete control and jurisdiction but that Cuba shall retain "ultimate sovereignty" over the territory. The latter provision, however, is merely symbolic. When the Castro government tried to exercise its "ultimate sovereignty" by asking the

United States to leave, the Navy refused to do so. Each year, the United States makes payment under the lease, but in protest Cuba refuses to cash the checks.

Guantanamo Bay is actually American territory. Like an American city with five thousand sailors and civilians, it has its own schools and local transportation, and it generates its own power and provides its own water. It has a golf course, a movie theater, and the only McDonald's in Cuba. But no one can enter or leave without permission of the U.S. government.

The Bush administration makes a second, more sweeping claim. It insists that the president, as commander in chief, has expanded powers during wartime that the courts cannot review or question.[5] Hence the courts cannot force the government to defend the detentions or provide any rights to the detainees. The likelihood that the detentions will continue for years or even decades makes no difference, according to the administration.

The administration also insists that international law does not apply because the detainees, as (alleged) members of al-Qaeda, do not represent an official army of an actual country, so they are "unlawful combatants." The significance of this argument is that if international law does not apply, the detainees do not have the rights normally accorded prisoners of war.

In sum, the administration maintains that the detainees have no rights—none under our Constitution or laws and none under international law. Essentially, the detainees are in a legal black hole. (Administration officials acknowledged, to each other, that they were looking for "the legal equivalent of outer space."[6]) This may be the first time that the United States has officially held anyone outside of all legal processes.[7] "The United States," remarked one legal scholar, "has cre-

ated an offshore penal colony that might as well be on the moon."[8]

Should this matter to American citizens? Some, thinking back to 9/11, might decide that a legal black hole is just fine. Others might decide that the rule of law reflects our principles and provides integrity in our procedures.

Nonetheless, the lower federal courts bowed to the president in this case, as most federal courts have in other cases involving various issues of the "war on terrorism." Now the Supreme Court is deciding this case.

You were appointed to the Supreme Court by President Gerald Ford in 1975. You were selected because of your merit rather than your ideology. As a student at Northwestern University's law school, you had the highest grades in the school's history, and as a judge on a federal appellate court in Chicago, you were well respected. A moderate Republican, you refused to move right as the party, under the dominance of southern and western conservatives, veered right. This left you as the most liberal member of the conservative Rehnquist Court. All along, you have been an independent thinker. Now, at eighty-four, you are the eldest member of the Court. You have survived prostate cancer, and you still play singles tennis three days a week.

Should the federal courts have authority to hear cases brought by the detainees and thus review policies established by the government? Or should the Supreme Court avoid this legal can of worms? Should you defer to the president's authority in wartime, or should you challenge the president's authority and risk a constitutional confrontation if the administration refuses to follow a ruling by a lower court or the Supreme Court?

How do you decide?

Americans value their "rights." Eighteenth-century Americans believed that people had "natural rights" by virtue of being human. Given by God, not by government, the rights could not be taken away by government. Contemporary Americans do not normally use this term, but they do think about their rights much as their forebears did.

Yet Americans have a split personality when considering their rights. Most people tell pollsters they believe in constitutional rights in the abstract, but many do not accept these rights in concrete situations. During the Cold War, most people said they believe in free speech, but many said communists, socialists, or atheists should not be allowed to speak in public or teach in schools.

Surveys in recent years show that Americans remain divided over their support for civil liberties. Even before the terrorist attacks, many respondents were ready to ban expression that might upset other people. One-third said they would not allow a rally that might offend community members. Two-thirds said they would not allow persons to say things in public that might offend racial groups, and over one-half said they would not allow persons to say things in public that might offend religious groups. One-fifth said they would not allow newspapers to publish without government approval of the articles.[9]

After the terrorist attacks, people's opinions reflected their fears. More respondents were skeptical about the value of the First Amendment; half said the amendment "goes too far" in guaranteeing rights (49 percent in 2002, compared with 22 percent in 2000). Two-fifths said newspapers should not be allowed to "freely criticize" the government's military strategy and performance. The same proportion said professors should not be allowed to criticize the government's military policy. Half said the government should be able to monitor religious groups for security purposes even if doing so infringes on religious freedom.[10]

By 2005, people's opinions had returned to the levels before the terrorist attacks. Twenty-three percent said the First Amendment goes too far in guaranteeing rights.[11]

Conflicts over civil liberties and rights have dominated the courts since the Great Depression. This chapter, covering civil liberties, and the next, covering civil rights, describe how the courts have interpreted these rights and tried to resolve these conflicts. We will explain the most important rights and recount the struggles by individuals and groups to achieve them. We will see how judges act as referees between litigants, brokers among competing groups, and policy makers in the process of deciding these cases.

The Constitution and the Bill of Rights

Individual Rights in the Constitution

Although the term *civil liberties* usually refers to the rights in the Bill of Rights, a few rights are granted in the body of the Constitution. The Constitution bans religious qualifications for federal office and guarantees jury trials in federal criminal cases. It bans bills of attainder, which are legislative acts rather than judicial trials pronouncing specific persons guilty of crimes, and *ex post facto* ("after the fact") laws, which are legislative acts making some behavior illegal that was not illegal when it was done. The Constitution also prohibits suspension of the writ of *habeas corpus,* except during rebellion or invasion of the country.

The Bill of Rights

Origin and Meaning

The Constitution originally did not include a bill of rights; the Founders did not think traditional liberties needed specific protections because federalism, separation of powers, and checks and balances would prevent the national government from becoming too powerful. But to win support for ratification, the Founders promised to adopt constitutional amendments to provide such rights. James Madison proposed twelve, Congress passed them, and in 1791 the states ratified ten of them, which came to be known as the **Bill of Rights.**[12] Of these, the first eight grant specific rights. (See the box "Civil Liberties in the Bill of Rights.") The Ninth Amendment says that the listing of these rights does not mean they are the only ones the people have, and the Tenth says that any powers not granted to the federal government are reserved for the state governments.

The Bill of Rights provides rights against the government. According to Justice Hugo Black, it is a list of "Thou shalt nots" directed at the government.[13] In practice, it provides rights for political, religious, or racial minorities against the majority, because government policy toward civil liberties tends to reflect the views of the majority.

As explained in Chapter 2, the Founders set up a government to protect property rights for the well-to-do minority against the presumably jealous majority. The Constitution's fragmentation of power and some specific provisions (see box "Constitutional Provisions Protecting Property" in that chapter) were designed to prevent the masses from curtailing the rights of the elites. However, as Americans became more egalitarian and as the masses gained more opportunity to participate in politics in the nineteenth and twentieth centuries, the relative importance of property rights declined while the relative importance of other rights increased. Thus, the Bill of Rights became the means to protect the fundamental rights of political, religious, and racial minorities—people who are out of the mainstream and often unpopular and powerless—when they come in conflict with the majority.

Responsibility for interpreting the Bill of Rights lies with the federal courts. Because federal judges are appointed for life, they are more independent from majority pressure than elected officials are.

Application

For many years, the Supreme Court applied the Bill of Rights only to the federal government, not to the state governments (or to the local governments, which are under the authority of the state governments). That is, the Court ruled that the Bill of Rights restricted the actions only of the federal government.[14]

In ruling this way, the Court followed the intentions of the Founders, who assumed that the states, with their capitals closer to their people, would be less likely to violate their peoples' liberties.[15] The Founders did not realize that the states would in fact be more likely to violate their peoples' liberties. Because the state governments represent smaller, more homogeneous populations, they tend to reflect majority sentiment more closely than the federal government, so they often ignored—and sometimes obliterated—the rights of political, religious, or racial minorities or of criminal defendants. When disputes arose, the state courts usually interpreted their citizens' rights narrowly.

However, in the twentieth century there was a growing sense that individual rights are important and that the state governments, as well as the federal government, should accord them. Starting in 1925[16] and continuing through 1972,[17] the Supreme Court gradually applied most provisions of the Bill of Rights to the states.[18] It applied all provisions of the First and the Fourth through the Eighth Amendments to the states except for two—the guarantee of a grand jury in criminal cases and guarantee of a jury trial in civil cases. In addition, the Court established some rights not in the Bill of Rights, and it applied these to the states, too—presumption of innocence in criminal cases, right to travel within the country, and right to privacy. Thus most provisions in the Bill of Rights, and even some not in it, now restrict the actions of both the federal and the state governments.

To see how the Court has interpreted these provisions, we will look at four major areas—freedom of expression, freedom of religion, rights of criminal defendants, and right to privacy—and also look at implications for civil liberties from the war on terrorsim. When we cover the major rulings of the Supreme Court, we will put them in italics because the law is complex and this chapter is dense.

Civil Liberties in the Bill of Rights

- First Amendment grants
  freedom of religion
  freedom of speech, assembly, and association
  freedom of the press

- Second Amendment grants
  right to keep and bear arms

- Third Amendment forbids
  quartering soldiers in houses during peacetime

- Fourth Amendment forbids
  unreasonable searches and seizures

- Fifth Amendment grants
  right to a grand jury in criminal cases
  right to due process

- Fifth Amendment forbids
  double jeopardy (more than one trial
  for the same offense)
  compulsory self-incrimination
  taking private property
  without just compensation

- Sixth Amendment grants
  right to speedy trial
  right to public trial
  right to jury trial in criminal cases
  right to cross-examine adverse witnesses
  right to present favorable witnesses
  right to counsel

- Seventh Amendment grants
  right to jury trial in civil cases

- Eighth Amendment forbids
  excessive bail and fines
  cruel and unusual punishment

Freedom of Expression

The **First Amendment** guarantees freedom of expression, which includes freedom of speech, assembly, and association, and freedom of the press.[19] The amendment also guarantees freedom of religion, which will be addressed in the next section. (Take note, in case you're asked. In 2006, Americans could name more members of *The Simpsons* cartoon family and more judges on *American Idol* than they could rights in the First Amendment.)[20]

The amendment states that "Congress shall make no law" abridging these liberties. The language is absolute, but no justices interpret it literally.[21] They cite the example of the person who falsely shouts "Fire!" in a crowded theater and causes a stampede that injures someone. Surely, they say, the amendment does not protect this expression. So the Court needs to draw a line between expression the amendment protects and that which it does not.

Freedom of Speech

Freedom of speech, Justice Black asserted, "is the heart of our government."[22] There are important theoretical justifications for freedom of speech. By creating an open atmosphere, it promotes individual autonomy and self-fulfillment. By encouraging a wide variety of opinions, it furthers the advancement of knowledge and the discovery of truth. The English philosopher John Stuart Mill, who championed freedom of speech, observed that individuals decide what is correct by comparing different views. Unpopular opinions might be true or partly true. Even if completely false, they might prompt a reevaluation of accepted opinions. By permitting citizens to form opinions and express them to others, freedom of speech helps them participate in government. It especially helps them check inefficient or corrupt government. Thus, the American philosopher John Dewey remarked that "democracy begins in conversation."[23] Finally, by channeling conflict toward persuasion, freedom of speech promotes a stable society. Governments that deny freedom of speech become inflexible. Unintentionally, they force conflict toward violence and foster rebellion.[24]

Because of our tradition and constitutional guarantee, almost all speech is allowed. However, there are some restrictions on the content of speech—what is said—and other restrictions on the manner of speech—how it is said. We will first examine the restrictions on the content of speech, focusing on seditious speech, fighting words, hate speech, and sexual speech. We will then examine the restrictions on the manner of speech.

Eugene V. Debs, the Socialist Party's candidate for president, criticized American involvement in World War I and the draft. He was convicted of violating the Espionage Act and sentenced to ten years in prison. When President Warren Harding pardoned him early, Debs commented, "It is the government that should ask me for a pardon."

Seditious Speech

Seditious speech is speech that encourages rebellion against the government.[25] The public becomes most opposed to seditious speech, and the government becomes most likely to prosecute individuals for such speech, during or shortly after war, when society is most sensitive about loyalty.

Numerous prosecutions came with World War I and the Russian Revolution, which brought the Communists to power in the Soviet Union in 1917. The Russian Revolution prompted the **Red Scare,** in which people feared conspiracies to overthrow the U.S. government. Congress passed the Espionage Act of 1917, which prohibited interfering with military recruitment, inciting insubordination in military forces, and mailing material advocating rebellion, and the Sedition Act of 1918, which prohibited "disloyal, profane, scurrilous, or abusive language about the form of government, Constitution, soldiers and sailors, flag or uniform of the armed forces." State legislatures passed similar laws. In short, our governments prohibited a wide range of speech.

During the war, the federal government prosecuted almost two thousand and convicted almost nine hundred persons under these acts, and the state governments prosecuted and convicted many others. They prosecuted individuals for saying that war is contrary to the teachings of Jesus, that World War I should not have been declared until after a referendum was held, and that the draft was unconstitutional. Officials even prosecuted an individual for remarking to women knitting clothes for the troops, "No soldier ever sees those socks."[26]

These cases gave the Supreme Court numerous opportunities to rule on seditious speech. In six major cases, the Court upheld the governments' laws and affirmed the defendants' convictions.[27] The defendants advocated socialism or communism, and some advocated the overthrow of the government to achieve their goal. Except for one—Eugene Debs, the Socialist Party's candidate for president—the defendants did not command a large audience. Even so, the Court concluded that *these defendants' speech constituted a "clear and present danger"* to the government. Justice Edward Sanford wrote, "A single revolutionary spark may kindle a fire that, smoldering for a time, may burst into a sweeping and destructive conflagration."[28] In reality, there was nothing clear or present about the danger; the defendants' speech had little effect.

Society was intolerant of dissent. When Zechariah Chafee, a Harvard Law professor and leading constitutional scholar, criticized the Court's rulings, the university's administration, prompted by the Justice Department, charged him "unfit" to be a professor. He was narrowly acquitted.[29]

More prosecutions came after World War II. In 1940, Congress passed the Smith Act, which was not as broad as the World War I acts because it did not forbid criticizing the government. But it did forbid advocating overthrow of the government by force and organizing or joining individuals who advocated overthrow.

The act was used against members of the American Communist Party after the war. The uneasy alliance between the United States and the Soviet Union during the war had given way to the Cold War between the two countries. Politicians, notably Senator Joseph McCarthy (R-Wisc.), exploited the tensions. McCarthy claimed that many government officials were Communists. (He said he had a list of 205 "known Communists" in the State Department alone.) He had little evidence (and provided no list).[30] Other Republicans also accused the Democratic administration of covering for Communists in government. They goaded it into prosecuting Communists outside government, so it would not appear "soft on communism." In 1951, the Court upheld the Smith Act and affirmed the convictions of eleven top-echelon leaders of the Communist Party.[31] These

leaders organized the party, and the party advocated overthrowing the government by force, but the leaders had not attempted to overthrow the government. (If they had, they clearly would have been guilty of crimes.) Even so, the Court majority concluded that *they constituted a clear and present danger*, and Chief Justice Fred Vinson wrote that the government does not have to "wait until the putsch is about to be executed, the plans have been laid and the signal is awaited" before it can act against the party. The minority argued that the Communist Party was not a danger. Justice William Douglas said that the party was "of little consequence. . . . Communism has been so thoroughly exposed in this country that it has been crippled as a political force. Free speech has destroyed it as an effective political party." Yet after the Court's decision, the government prosecuted and convicted almost one hundred other Communists.

However, the Cold War thawed slightly, and the Senate condemned McCarthy after he tried to bully the Army. His method was likened to witch hunts, and the tactic of making political accusations or name-calling based on little or no evidence eventually came to be known as **McCarthyism.** (However, McCarthyism began before and continued after McCarthy's tenure in the early 1950s, because other politicians and the Senate's Internal Security Committee and House's Un-American Activities Committee used similar tactics.)[32]

In the meantime, two new members, including Chief Justice Earl Warren, had joined the Supreme Court. Although the public, stoked by media speculation and traveling speakers (including one who warned parent audiences that *Mad* magazine was Communist inspired), remained fearful of communism, these developments led to a new doctrine. In a series of cases in the mid- to late 1950s and early 1960s, the Warren Court made it more difficult to convict Communists,[33] thereby incurring the wrath of the public, Congress, and President Dwight Eisenhower. In a private conversation at the White House, Eisenhower criticized the rulings. Warren asked Eisenhower what he thought the Court should have done with the Communists. Eisenhower replied, "I would kill the S.O.B.s."[34]

In addition to prosecutions under the Smith Act, the governments took other actions against the Communists. The federal government ordered them to register, and then some state governments banned them from public jobs such as teaching or private jobs such as practicing law or serving as union officers. Legislative committees held hearings to expose and humiliate them. The Court heard numerous cases involving these actions and usually ruled against the governments.

At congressional hearings, Senator Joseph McCarthy identified the supposed locations of alleged Communists and "fellow travelers."

Yet the public's fear throughout the 1950s was so consuming that the government's actions extended beyond active Communists to former Communists—some Americans had dabbled with communism during the Great Depression in the 1930s—and even to individuals who had never been Communists but who were lumped together as "Commie dupes" or "comsymps" (Communist sympathizers). Ultimately, a campaign that mandated loyalty oaths and created blacklists cost an estimated ten thousand Americans their jobs.

Although McCarthy and others of his ilk were bullies who hurt many innocent or harmless people, there actually were communist spies in the federal government, from the atomic labs at Los Alamos, New Mexico, to the State Department and the White House, according to records revealed after the collapse of the Soviet Union. Apparently most spies were discovered before the 1950s, but some were never uncovered.[35]

The Vietnam War did not prompt as much fear as World Wars I and II did. Congress did not pass any comparable laws, perhaps because many people, including "respectable" people, opposed this war and also because the Court in the 1950s and 1960s had permitted more seditious speech.

Even so, the federal government took some actions against individuals and groups. Numerous conscientious objectors were imprisoned; others felt forced to flee to Canada. Many peaceful protesters were arrested. Antiwar groups were harassed by federal grand juries, and their leaders were spied on by the U.S. Army. Some prominent opponents were prosecuted

for conspiring against the draft.[36] However, opposition to this war was so widespread that the government's actions did not silence the protesters' speech.

The Court developed new doctrine for seditious speech in 1969. A Ku Klux Klan leader said at an Ohio rally that the Klan might take "revengeance" on the president, Congress, and the Supreme Court if they continued "to suppress the white, Caucasian race." The leader was convicted under a statute similar to those upheld after World War I, but this time the statute was unanimously struck down by the Court.[37] The justices drew a distinction between advocacy and incitement. *People can advocate—enthusiastically, even heatedly—as long as they don't incite illegal action.* This doctrine protects most criticism of the government, whether at a rally, from a pulpit, or through the media, and it remains in effect today.

Thus, after many years and many cases, the Court concluded that the First Amendment protects seditious speech as much as other speech. Justice Douglas noted that "the threats were often loud but always puny."[38] Even the attorney general who prosecuted the major Communist cases later admitted that the cases were "squeezed oranges. I didn't think there was much to them."[39] Nevertheless, the Court had permitted a climate of fear to overwhelm the First Amendment for many years.

The collapse of the Soviet Union and the demise of the Cold War made communism less threatening, but this doctrine remains important. After the Oklahoma City bombing in 1995, government surveillance of right-wing militia groups increased, but prosecution of the members, under terrorism laws, was limited because most of the evidence was fiery rhetoric, which is protected speech (unless it urges immediate action to violate any laws).

After the terrorist attacks in 2001, pressure to conform—to temper criticism and to support the government's response—mounted. An organization identified forty college professors with "un-American" agendas, in an effort to prod the schools to discipline and restrain their professors. (Negative reaction prompted the organization to remove the names from its website.)[40] A tenured professor at the University of New Mexico who cracked, "Anyone who can blow up the Pentagon gets my vote," was reprimanded, and a lawsuit demanding his termination was filed.[41] During the Iraq War, pressure to conform was linked to support for our troops. Critics were branded as "unpatriotic" and "disloyal" by conservative commentators who stoked their listeners' anger.[42] Pressure to conform was muted only when the initial victory unraveled in the war's aftermath and the public criticism increased.

Although the government did not adopt comparable laws during the war on terrorism or the war in Iraq as it adopted during World Wars I and II, it did pass the USA PATRIOT Act, which has important implications for civil liberties. (See the box "The USA PATRIOT Act" later in this chapter.)

Fighting Words and Hate Speech

In some situations, fighting words and hate speech have been prohibited. **Fighting words** are ones which, when spoken face to face, prompt listeners to retaliate with a punch. The assumption is that these words are so incendiary that even reasonable listeners cannot restrain themselves. (As the characters in old westerns said just before throwing a punch or drawing their gun, "Them are fightin' words, pardner.") Therefore, governments could punish the speakers for their words rather than the listeners for their response.

The Court created this doctrine during World War II. After a man who had been distributing leaflets and denouncing religion was apprehended by police, he encountered the city marshal and called him a "damned racketeer" and "damned fascist." He was convicted for violating a state law. The Court decided that his words were fighting words (even though the marshal did not respond with a punch).[43]

Although this precedent remains on the books, it was severely undermined in the 1970s, as swearing became more common. *Courts expected people to tolerate words that would have been considered fighting words years before.*[44] Courts especially expected police to tolerate swearing and even threats, because police are trained to face emotionally charged situations when they arrest people.[45] Before the Court's rulings in 1972, arrests for swearing were common. In the District of Columbia, for example, about ten thousand people per year were arrested for swearing, usually at police (and charged with "disorderly conduct").[46]

As a result of these rulings, few words would be considered fighting words today, and they would have to be said face to face. Even then, they might not be prohibited; listeners might be expected to put up with them.

Indeed, *offensive speech in general has been allowed* since the 1970s. During the Vietnam War, a man on his way to observe a trial walked through the corridors of the Los Angeles County courthouse wearing a jacket with the words "Fuck the Draft" emblazoned on the back. A cop arrested him, and a judge convicted him. The Supreme Court reversed his conviction, as seventy-two-year-old Justice John Harlan remarked that "one man's vulgarity is another's lyric."[47] In contrast to the dissenters who called the man's expression nothing more than an "immature antic," Harlan recognized that "much linguistic expression serves a dual communicative function: it conveys not only ideas capable of relatively precise, detached explication, but otherwise inexpressible emotions as well. In fact, words are often chosen as much for their emotive as their cognitive force. . . . [The former] may often be the more important element of the overall message."

Hate speech is derogatory speech—racial, ethnic, sexual, or religious slurs—usually aimed at a group rather than at an individual. When aimed at an individual, the words impugn characteristics the individual shares with the group. Although hate speech may prompt a group or an individual to retaliate, it is discouraged because it demeans people for characteristics that are innate, such as race, ethnicity, or sexuality, or characteristics that are deeply held, such as religious faith, and as such it can cause emotional or psychological harm.

Hate speech poses problems for the First Amendment. It can be difficult to distinguish hate speech from other speech. What one person considers hate speech another may consider simply observations or valid criticisms. *Even when people agree that the words*

©Time Life Pictures/Getty Images

During the Cold War, Americans feared communism so much that some built bomb shelters in their yards, believing that taking refuge would protect their family in a nuclear attack.

constitute hate speech, it would normally violate the guarantee of free speech for governments to forbid them.[48]

Lower federal courts required the Chicago suburb of Skokie to permit the American Nazi Party to demonstrate in 1978.[49] The Nazis intentionally chose Skokie as the site for their demonstration because many Jews lived there. Forty thousand of Skokie's seventy thousand residents were Jewish. Hundreds were survivors of German concentration camps during World War II, and thousands were relatives of people who had died in the camps. The city, in anticipation of the demonstration, passed ordinances that prohibited wearing "military-style" uniforms and distributing material that "promotes and incites hatred against persons by reason of their race, national origin, or religion." These ordinances were a thinly disguised attempt to bar the Nazis' demonstration, and the courts threw them out. One court quoted Justice Oliver Wendell Holmes's statement that "if there is any principle of the Constitution that more imperatively calls for attachment than any other it is the principle of free thought—not free thought for those who agree with us but freedom for the thought we hate."[50]

Cross burning by the Ku Klux Klan presents a more difficult question. In the Klan's heyday, a cross-burning was a clear threat to the black families it was directed toward. Today a cross-burning *might* be nothing more than a rallying symbol to the Klan's members. The Supreme Court ruled that persons who burn a cross to intimidate—for example, to frighten their black neighbors—can be prosecuted, but those who burn a cross at a KKK rally in a private field hidden from other people and passing cars cannot be prosecuted.[51]

Numerous conflicts over hate speech arise in public schools because many teachers believe they should encourage their students to be tolerant. Courts generally allow schools to limit students' speech for educational purposes. But when schools go too far according to critics, they are derided for being "politically correct."

Many colleges and universities adopted hate speech codes. They worried that such speech would create a hostile and intimidating environment for the victims.[52] A student who was jeered nightly by taunts of "Faggot!" said, "When you are told you are not worth anything, it is difficult to function."[53] As a result of the codes, some students were disciplined. But colleges and universities, more than other institutions in our society, have traditionally fostered free expression and debate. And the codes, which were inherently difficult to write, were often too broad or too vague. Some were struck down by lower courts, and others were abandoned by the schools. Some were rewritten to focus on harassment and threats,

which can be prohibited, and to apply to computers. George Mason University forbade students from using computers "to harass, threaten, or abuse others." Virginia Tech disciplined a student for posting a message on the home page of a gay men's group calling for gays to be castrated and to "die a slow death."[54]

Some conservative Christians, funded by evangelical ministries and interest groups, have launched an attack on tolerance policies toward gays and lesbians. They demand that schools and workplaces revoke their policies, including speech codes and, in lower grades, dress codes prohibiting antigay T-shirts. A Georgia Tech student who was reprimanded for sending a letter that berated students who came out as gay filed suit, claiming that her faith compelled her to speak out against homosexuality.[55]

These disputes highlight the fine line between harassment and free speech. So far, the Supreme Court has not addressed campus speech codes.

Sexual Speech

In some contexts, sexual speech—that is, language or situations that fall short of the legal definition of obscenity (covered later in the chapter)—has been prohibited.

Governments can forbid nude dancing,[56] although it is expression. Through zoning, *they can restrict pornographic theaters or sex shops* from most (though not all) parts of their cities.[57]

The Federal Communications Commission (FCC) can forbid radio and television stations from broadcasting some sexual language and situations. A California radio station broadcast a monologue by comedian George Carlin. Titled "Filthy Words," it lampooned society's sensitivity to seven words that "you couldn't say on the public airwaves . . . the ones you definitely wouldn't say, ever." The seven words, according to the FCC report, included "a four-letter word for excrement" repeated seventy times in twelve minutes. A majority of the Court ruled that although the monologue was part of a serious program on contemporary attitudes toward language, it was not protected under the First Amendment because people, including children, tuning the radio could be subjected to the language in their homes.[58] Now the FCC forbids indecent material on radio and noncable television between 6 A.M. and 10 P.M. and fines any media that violate the ban. (Large fines were levied on the *Howard Stern Show,* before it moved to satellite radio, and on a New York City radio station that broadcast a tape of a couple having sex in Saint Patrick's Cathedral.)[59] Yet the Court struck down a Utah law restricting indecent material on cable television. By subscribing to and paying for cable television, its customers are accepting exposure to its programming.[60]

In summary, seditious speech, fighting words, hate speech, and sexual speech have been prohibited in the past, but most examples of such speech are allowed now because the Supreme Court broadened its interpretation of the First Amendment during the second half of the twentieth century.

We will now examine the restrictions on the manner of speech, focusing on demonstrations and symbolic speech.

Demonstrations

Protesters want people to see or hear their demonstrations, so they seek locations where people congregate and provide an audience. This means that protesters will be seen or heard by some in the crowd who do not like their message or their use of public places to disseminate it. Yet they have a right to demonstrate, although they are subject to restrictions.

Individuals are allowed to use public places, such as streets, sidewalks, parks, theaters,[61] and the grounds around public buildings,[62] *to express their views on public issues.* These places constitute the **public forum** and serve as "the poor person's printing press."

Private property is not part of the public forum, so *individuals have no right to demonstrate on private property* without the owner's permission. However, the development and proliferation of shopping malls attracted protesters who want to reach the throngs of shoppers. The Warren Court allowed the protesters to convey their views, reasoning that privately owned malls are analogous to downtown shopping districts where streets and sidewalks are part of the public forum.[63] But the Burger Court overruled the Warren Court, authorizing the malls to forbid the protesters. Thus, the Burger Court emphasized property rights over First Amendment rights.[64] During the run-up to the Iraq War, a sixty-year-old man wore a T-shirt with the slogan "Give Peace a Chance" at a mall in Albany, New York. Security guards ordered him to take off the shirt or leave the mall. When he refused, he was arrested.[65] Although his shirt was not what we think of as a demonstration, it did express his views, and the mall could forbid such expression.

Even in the public forum, individuals cannot demonstrate whenever or however they want. The streets, sidewalks, parks, and theaters in the public forum are used for purposes other than demonstrations—especially for transportation and recreation—so individuals cannot disrupt these activities. They cannot, Justice Arthur Goldberg remarked, hold "a street meeting in the middle of Times Square at the rush hour."[66]

Therefore, abortion protesters can demonstrate on public streets and public sidewalks near abortion clinics, and they can approach staffers and patients who

©Melanie Conner/The New York Times

The First Amendment prevents governments—not businesses—from restricting your speech. When Lorrie Heasley boarded a Southwest Airlines plane, she wore a T-shirt featuring President Bush, Vice President Cheney, Secretary of State Rice, and the title of the movie Meet the Fockers—except an expletive was substituted. The flight crew removed her from the plane. Although the government could not restrict this expression, the airline could.

come and go. But *protesters cannot block access* (and to ensure this, judges can order them not to come within a certain distance—for example, fifteen feet—of driveways and doorways).[67] Moreover, they cannot demonstrate at the doctor's house even if they stand on a public sidewalk. After protesters repeatedly picketed at a doctor's residence in a Milwaukee suburb, the town passed an ordinance forbidding such picketing. The Rehnquist Court ruled that protesters can march through residential neighborhoods but *cannot focus on particular houses,* because such picketing interferes with the privacy of the home.[68]

To ensure that potential demonstrations don't disrupt the normal activities of the places in the public forum, *governments can require groups to obtain a permit, which can specify the place, time, and manner of the demon-*

stration. Officials can establish restrictions to avoid disruptions. However, officials cannot use these restrictions to censor speech. They cannot allow one group to demonstrate but forbid another, no matter how much they dislike the group or its message. They cannot forbid the group even if they say they fear violence (unless the group actually threatens violence).

Symbolic Speech

Some demonstrations feature **symbolic speech,** which is the use of symbols rather than words to convey ideas. Sometimes the use of symbols has been prohibited when the use of words alone would have been permitted.

During the Vietnam War, some young men burned their draft cards to protest the war and the draft. Their action was powerful expression, and Congress tried to stifle it by passing a law prohibiting the destruction of draft cards. In the 1960s, symbolic speech was a novelty, and the justices were uncomfortable with it and unwilling to protect it. The majority said the men could simply have stated their views against the war and the draft.[69]

One year later, however, *the Court was willing to protect symbolic speech.* Junior and senior high school students in Des Moines, Iowa, including Mary Beth Tinker, wore black armbands to protest the war. When they were suspended, their families sued school officials. The Court ruled that the schools must allow the students freedom of speech, as long as the students do not disrupt the schools.[70] Public schools, Justice Abe Fortas said, "may not be enclaves of totalitarianism."

In the 1960s and 1970s, many students wore long hair or beards in violation of school policies. Some claimed they did so to protest "establishment culture." Blacks and American Indians claimed they wore Afros and braids to show racial pride. Federal courts of appeals split evenly as to whether such grooming was symbolic speech and, if so, whether it was protected speech.[71]

Some individuals treated the American flag disrespectfully to protest the Vietnam War. A Massachusetts man wore a flag patch on the seat of his pants and was arrested and sentenced to six months in jail. A Washington student taped a peace symbol on a flag and then hung the flag upside down outside his apartment. The Court reversed both convictions.[72]

When a member of the Revolutionary Communist Youth Brigade burned an American flag outside the Republican convention in 1984, the justices faced the issue of *actual desecration of the flag*—the ultimate symbolic speech. A bare majority of the Rehnquist Court *permitted* this symbolic speech.[73] Justice William Brennan wrote that the First Amendment cannot be limited just because this expression offends most people. "We do not consecrate the flag by punishing its desecration, for in doing so we dilute the freedom that this cherished emblem represents." The ruling invali-

When young men illegally burned their draft cards to protest the Vietnam War, the Supreme Court refused to protect their action as symbolic speech.

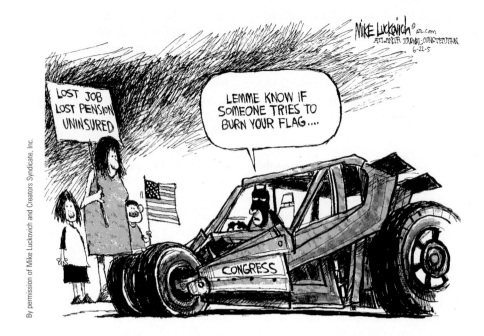

dated the laws of forty-eight states and the federal government.

In a dissent, Chief Justice William Rehnquist emotionally criticized the decision. He said the First Amendment should not apply because the flag is a unique national symbol. He recounted the history of "The Star-Spangled Banner" and the music of John Philip Sousa's "Stars and Stripes Forever," he quoted poems by Ralph Waldo Emerson and John Greenleaf Whittier that refer to the flag, and he discussed the role of the Pledge of Allegiance.

Civil liberties advocates praised the decision, but veterans' groups were outraged and many Americans were upset. President George H. W. Bush proposed a constitutional amendment to override the decision. Members of Congress, always eager to appear patriotic, lined up in support. But others, mostly Democrats, criticized the proposal for creating an unprecedented exception to the First Amendment. Eventually, instead of an amendment, Congress passed a statute prohibiting flag desecration. Apparently, a majority felt that a statute, not as permanent and not a part of the Constitution, would be an acceptable compromise between the Court's doctrine and the public's anger. Yet the justices, dividing the same way, declared the new statute unconstitutional for the same reasons they reversed the prior conviction.[74] By now, the public's anger had ebbed.[75] Even so, congressional Republican leaders periodically propose an amendment to overturn the ruling as a way to rally their conservative base. In 2006 they fell just one vote short in the Senate. With one vote more, the amendment would have been sent to the states for ratification.

Freedom of Association

Although the First Amendment does not mention *association,* the Supreme Court has interpreted the right to speak, assemble, and petition the government for a redress of grievances, all of which the amendment does list, to encompass a **freedom of association** for individuals to join with others to do these things.

This freedom implicitly entails a right not to associate as well. Therefore, groups can exclude individuals from their organization.

The right is strongest when the organization forms for "expressive association"—that is, when it speaks, assembles, and petitions the government for a redress of grievances. The right is also strong when the organization forms for "intimate association"—that is, when it is relatively personal, selective, and small, such as a social club or a country club.

Organizations formed for expressive or intimate association usually can exclude others. The Supreme Court allowed organizers of Boston's Saint Patrick's Day parade to exclude a group of gays, lesbians, and bisexuals.[76] Because the organizers were private individuals—the parade was not sponsored by the city—and because a parade is an expressive activity, the organizers did not have to allow any views contrary to their views. The Supreme Court also allowed the Boy Scouts of America to expel an assistant scoutmaster who was openly gay.[77] The Court concluded that the Boy Scouts is an expressive organization, which espouses various values, including an opposition to homosexuality.

The right is weakest when the organization forms for "commercial association"—that is, when it is designed to enhance business interests of its members and is relatively large, unselective, and impersonal. *Organizations formed for commercial association often cannot exclude others.* Their right to associate can be overridden by others' right to be free from discrimination.

For example, Minnesota and California adopted laws prohibiting sex discrimination in various organizations. The Court ruled that the Jaycees (the Junior Chamber of Commerce), which was a business organization of young men, and the Rotary Club, which was a civic organization of men, could not discriminate against women in these states because the laws forbade such discrimination.[78] The right to freedom from discrimination overrode the right to freedom of association because the organizations were formed for commercial rather than expressive or intimate association.[79]

Freedom of the Press

Freedom of the press may be as important as freedom of speech in a democracy. Indeed, it may be more important in a mass society where most people hear opposing views through the media rather than from person to person.

Prior Restraint

The core of **freedom of the press** is freedom from prior restraint—censorship. If the press violates laws prohibiting, for example, libelous or obscene material, it can be punished after publishing such materials. But freedom from prior restraint means the press can disseminate the information it considers appropriate and the public can see this information.

Mary Beth Tinker, seen here with her mother and brother, wore a black armband at school to protest the Vietnam War.

Yet freedom from prior restraint is not absolute. During the Vietnam War, the secretary of defense in the Johnson administration, Robert McNamara, ordered a thorough study of our engagement. The study, known as the Pentagon Papers, laid bare the reasons the country was embroiled—reasons not as honorable as ones the officials had fed the public—and it questioned the effectiveness of military policy. The study was so revealing that McNamara confided to a friend, "They could hang people for what's in there."[80] He classified the papers "top secret" so few persons could see them. One of the authors, Daniel Ellsberg, who was a planner in the war, originally supported the war but later turned against it. Haunted by his involvement, he photocopied the papers and passed them to the *New York Times* and *Washington Post* in the hope that their publication would sway public opinion and force the government to halt the war. (He also passed them to the television networks—ABC, CBS, and NBC—but they were afraid to use them.)[81]

The newspapers began to publish excerpts of the papers. Although the information implicated the Kennedy and Johnson administrations, President Richard Nixon was still fighting the war, and their publication infuriated him. Summoning his chief of staff and national security adviser, he demanded:

> *I have a project I want somebody to take. . . . This takes eighteen hours a day. It takes devotion and loyalty and diligence such as you've never seen. . . . I really need a son of a bitch . . . who will work his butt off and do it dishonorably. . . . And I'll direct him myself. I know how to play this game and we're going to start playing it. . . . I want somebody just as tough as I am for a change. . . . We're up against an enemy, a conspiracy. They're using any means. We're going to use any means.[82]*

This tirade set in motion the developments that would culminate in the Watergate scandal.

But first Nixon sought injunctions to restrain the newspapers from publishing more excerpts. In the *Pentagon Papers Case*, the Supreme Court refused to grant them.[83] Most justices said they would grant the injunctions if publishing the papers clearly jeopardized national security. But the information in the papers was historical; its disclosure did not hinder the current war effort.[84] Thus, *the rule—no prior restraint—remained, but some exceptions could be made.*

One exception occurred in 1979 when *The Progressive,* a monthly political magazine, planned to publish technical material about the design of hydrogen bombs. The article, "The H-Bomb Secret: How We Got It, Why We're Telling It," argued against secret classification of this material. Although the article was not a "do-it-yourself guide," it might help a medium-

AP/Wide World Photos

The press chief of the Washington Post *hails the Supreme Court's decision allowing publication of the Pentagon Papers.*

size nation develop a bomb sooner than the nation could otherwise. At the government's request, a federal judge granted an injunction prohibiting the magazine from publishing the article.[85]

The Rehnquist Court did approve prior restraint in a situation far removed from national security. When high school journalism students in St. Louis wrote newspaper articles about the impact of pregnancy and of parents' divorce on teenagers, the principal deleted the articles, and the students sued. The Court, noting that students below college level have fewer rights than adults, decided that *school officials can censor school publications*.[86]

Principals have typically exercised their authority over articles addressing school policies or social issues. A Colorado principal blocked an editorial criticizing his study hall policy while allowing another editorial praising it. A Texas principal banned an article about the class valedictorian who succeeded despite the death of her mother, the desertion of her father, and her own pregnancy. An editorial urging students to be more responsible about sex was censored by a Kentucky principal, who feared it could be interpreted as condoning sex, and a survey on AIDS was censored by a Maryland principal, who prohibited students from defining the term *safe sex*. A North Carolina high school newspaper was shut down and its adviser was fired because of three articles, including a satirical story about the "death" of

the writer after eating a cheeseburger from the school cafeteria.

Some principals have tried to restrict their students from using the Internet to criticize school officials or policies. But like the underground newspapers of the 1960s and 1970s, web pages created off campus (rather than in class) cannot be censored and their creators cannot be disciplined by administrators, unless the pages urge illegal action or make terrorist threats. A Georgia student was arrested for suggesting that the principal be shot, his daughter kidnapped, his car keyed, and its locks clogged with Superglue.

The press in the United States is freer than that in Great Britain, where freedom from prior restraint began. Britain has no First Amendment and tolerates more secrecy. The government banned radio and television interviews with all members of the outlawed Irish Republican Army and its political party, including its sole representative in Parliament.[87] The French government banned the sale of a song critical of the West during the Persian Gulf War, and it blocked the broadcasting of anti-Semitic programming by an Arab channel in 2005. The German government banned the sale of music by skinhead groups after neo-Nazi violence. The Austrian government punished a British historian for publicizing his book denying the Holocaust. (Austria is the birthplace of Hitler.)

Restrictions on Gathering News

Although prior restraint is an obvious limitation on freedom of the press, restrictions on gathering news are less obvious but no less serious. They also keep the news from the public.

The Burger Court *denied reporters the right to keep the names of their sources confidential*. In investigative reporting, reporters frequently rely on sources who demand anonymity in exchange for information. The sources might have sensitive positions in government or relations with criminals that would be jeopardized if their names were publicized. A Louisville reporter was allowed to watch persons make hashish from marijuana if he kept their names confidential. But after publication of his story, a grand jury demanded their names. When the reporter refused to reveal them, he was cited for contempt of court, and his conviction was upheld by the Supreme Court.[88] The majority said reporters' need for confidentiality is not as great as courts' need for information about crimes. So either reporters cannot guarantee anonymity to a potential source, which means they might not obtain information for an important story, or they might be cited for contempt and jailed for months.

Grand juries have demanded reporters' sources increasingly in recent years.[89] In addition, the Bush administration has tried to stanch the flow of embarrassing information to reporters. Although the president, vice president, and high officials have leaked classified information for political purposes, they were very upset by leaks from other officials revealing that the CIA was maintaining secret prisons in foreign countries and the National Security Agency (NSA) was engaging in warrantless wiretaps of American citizens. The administration launched aggressive investigations and ordered lie detector tests of agency employees. The administration also threatened reporters with criminal prosecution under the Espionage Act of 1917. The goal was to intimidate both employees and reporters and reduce future leaks.

Invasion of Privacy

The right to a free press can conflict with an individual's desire for privacy when the press publishes personal information. The Supreme Court has *permitted the press to publish factual information*. For example, although Georgia law prohibited the press from releasing the names of crime victims to spare them embarrassment, an Atlanta television station announced the name of a high school girl who was raped by six classmates and left unconscious on the lawn to die. When her father sued the station, the Court said the press needs freedom to publish information that is a matter of public record so that citizens can scrutinize the workings of the judicial system.[90]

When a man in a crowd watching President Gerald Ford noticed a woman, close by, pull out a gun, he grabbed the gun and prevented an assassination. Reporters wrote stories about this hero, including the fact

Leanne Tippell and Leslie Smart, St. Louis high school students who sued their school for suppressing their student newspaper story, meet with their attorney, Leslie Edwards (left).

© 2003 Bob Sacha

that he was a homosexual. This coverage caused him considerable embarrassment and practical problems as well, so he sued. The courts sided with the press again. The man's good deed made him newsworthy, whether he wanted to be or not.[91] Persons who become newsworthy are granted little privacy. Justice Brennan said this is a necessary evil "in a society which places a primary value on freedom of speech and of press."[92]

However, the Court has prohibited the press from sending reporters and photographers with law enforcement officers when they conduct a search or make an arrest at someone's home.[93] The Court decided that the police department's desire for good publicity and the local media's desire for interesting stories did not justify the invasion of the defendants' or residents' privacy.

Libel and Obscenity

Despite the broad protection for freedom of the press, the Supreme Court grants much less protection for libelous and obscene material. Traditionally, the justices considered such material irrelevant to the exposition of ideas and search for truth envisioned by the framers of the First Amendment. Any benefit such material might have had was outweighed by the need to protect persons' reputations and morals. For many years, the Court allowed the states to adopt libel and obscenity laws as they saw fit.

Libel

Libel consists of printed or broadcast statements that are false and that tarnish someone's reputation. Victims are entitled to sue for money to compensate them for the harm done.

The Warren Court decided that *traditional state libel laws infringed on freedom of the press too much*. The justices forced radical changes in these laws in *New York Times v. Sullivan* in 1964.[94]

The *Times* ran an ad by black clergymen criticizing Montgomery, Alabama, officials for their response to racial protests. The ad contained trivial inaccuracies. Although the ad did not name any officials, the commissioner of police claimed that it implicitly referred to him, and he sued. A local jury ordered the *Times* to pay him a half million dollars! Meanwhile, another local jury ordered the *Times* to pay another commissioner a half million dollars for the same ad. It was apparent that traditional libel laws could be used to wreak vengeance on a critical press—in this case, on a detested northern newspaper for coverage of controversial civil rights protests.

The Court, ruling against the commissioner, made it more difficult for public officials to win libel suits. It held that *officials must show not only that the statements made about them were false but also that the statements were made with "reckless disregard for the truth."* This standard gives the press some leeway to make mistakes—to print inaccurate statements—as long as the press is not careless to the point of recklessness.

This protection for the press is necessary, according to Justice Brennan, because the "central meaning of the First Amendment" is that citizens should have the right to criticize officials. This statement prompted one legal scholar to herald the decision "an occasion for dancing in the streets."[95]

In later cases, the Court *extended this ruling to public figures*—other persons who have public prominence or who thrust themselves into public controversies. These included candidates for public office[96] and activists for various causes.[97] The Court reasoned that it should be more difficult for public figures, as for public officials, to win libel suits because they also influence public policy and also are newsworthy enough to get media attention to rebut any accusations against them.[98]

In sum, the Warren Court's doctrine shifted the emphasis from protection of personal reputation to protection of press freedom.

This shift in emphasis has helped the press report the news—and consequently, helped the public learn the news—during a time when media coverage of controversial events has angered many people. Since the 1960s, individuals and groups have sued the press not primarily to gain compensation for damage to their reputation but to punish the press for its coverage. For example, a lawyer for a conservative organization that sued CBS for its depiction of the army general who commanded the U.S. military in Vietnam admitted that the organization sought the "dismantling" of the network.[99]

Obscenity

Whereas it is relatively clear what libel is and who the victim is, it is not at all clear what obscenity is and who, if anyone, the victim is. It is not even clear why the law needs to address it. Some say the law is necessary because obscenity is immoral; others say it is necessary because obscenity leads to improper behavior (although this link is uncertain). The justices themselves have disagreed.

The Warren Court decided that *state obscenity laws restricted publication of some sexual material that should be allowed*. While maintaining that *the First Amendment does not protect obscenity*, the Court narrowed the definition of obscenity in the 1950s and 1960s and thereby expanded the range of pornography that could be produced and sold.[100]

The Burger Court thought the Warren Court went too far, and it broadened the definition of ob-

scenity in the 1970s.[101] Its goal was to reduce the availability of pornography. The Burger Court *defined* **obscenity** *as sexual material that is patently offensive to the average person in the local community and that lacks any serious literary, artistic, or scientific value.* This definition revolves around the views of the average person, rather than the most tolerant or most prudish person. And it revolves around the views in the local community where the material is sold, rather than the views in Los Angeles or New York where the material often is produced and where the attitudes are more freewheeling. This definition remains in effect today. In practice, it is implemented by state legislatures and local juries when they pass obscenity statutes and decide obscenity cases.

Occasionally, local officials, especially the prosecutors aiming for higher office, get carried away. A prosecutor in Charlottesville, Virginia, announced that he would prosecute persons who sold *Playboy* magazine. A prosecutor in Albany, Georgia, prosecuted a theater manager who showed the movie *Carnal Knowledge*. The movie, which featured explicit language and occasional nudity, was nominated for an Academy Award as the best film of the year. When the theater manager appealed, the Burger Court reversed his conviction, announcing that local communities have discretion but not "unbridled discretion."[102] The movie, apparent from its nomination for an Academy Award, had serious artistic value.

A prosecutor in Cincinnati prosecuted the director of an art gallery for an exhibit of photographs by Robert Mapplethorpe. The homoerotic pictures, which the director called "tough, brutal, sometimes disgusting," included three showing penetration of a man's anus with various objects. Yet the prosecutor could not prove that the photographs lacked serious artistic value because the photographer had received praise from art critics and the pictures were displayed in an art gallery, so the jury acquitted the director.

Although the Burger Court's broader definition of obscenity should have reduced the amount of obscenity in society, it has not. Prosecutors say they actually prosecute fewer cases because people are less concerned about obscenity than they used to be, so jurors are less likely to convict.[103]

In fact, sexual material is so popular that Americans, according to estimates, spend between $8 billion and $10 billion a year on "adult entertainment"—videos and DVDs, cable and satellite porn, Internet porn, phone sex, peep shows, sexual magazines, and sexual toys. This amount approximates Hollywood's domestic box office receipts.[104] This reality, rather than legal doctrine, determines what's available.

Society is less tolerant of child pornography than adult pornography, however, partly because children are used in its production and partly because pedophiles,

Amish children head for the cornfields to avoid school officials in Iowa.

adults who molest children, are attracted to this material. Consequently, the Court has made it easier to crack down on child pornography. *Material that depicts children engaged in sexual conduct, whether obscene or not, can be prohibited,* and individuals who produce, distribute, or merely possess it can be prosecuted.[105]

The Internet poses a challenge to judicial doctrine for both obscenity and child pornography. Because the Internet enables people to get pornography in the privacy of their home without having to go to a seedy adult bookstore or theater and risk the embarrassment that might occur, perusing pornography is a common recreational use of computers. Shocked by the amount and the nature of online pornography, and worried about its availability to children, Congress passed a law prohibiting people from circulating "obscene" or "indecent" material online "in a manner available" to those under eighteen. "Indecent" material was not clearly defined. The Supreme Court, in its initial effort to apply the First Amendment to cyberspace, decided that the Internet should be nurtured rather than stifled. It upheld the portion of the law banning "obscene" material but struck down the portion banning "indecent" material.[106] This ruling meshes with existing obscenity doctrine. The portion banning "indecent" material, which reflected concerns about availability to children, was too broad and too ambiguous. It would prevent adults from getting material they should be able to

get, and it would discourage adults from communicating with each other because they wouldn't know whether the material was "indecent" and whether it was going to another adult or a child.

Congress also passed a law prohibiting people from circulating virtual child pornography, which is computer-simulated images that depict children engaged in sex. Virtual and actual child pornography can be hard to tell apart, and Congress assumed that both types lead to child abuse. But the Court invalidated the statute because virtual pornography does not involve real people, so its production harms no actual children.[107]

Freedom of Religion

Some people came to America for religious liberty, but once they arrived, many did not want to grant this liberty to others. Some communities became as intolerant as those in the Old World from which the people had fled.[108] But the colonists came with so many religious views that the diversity gradually led to grudging tolerance. By the time the Constitution and the Bill of Rights were adopted, support for religious liberty was fairly widespread.

Both the diversity and the tolerance are reflected in the two documents. Unlike the Declaration of Independence, the Constitution is a secular document. It does not mention "God," "Creator," "Providence," or "divine."[109] It does not claim to be a compact between the people and God (or, like some monarchies, between the rulers and God); rather, it is a compact among the people, as the Preamble underscores from its very start—"We the people. . . ."

The Bill of Rights grants freedom of religion in the First Amendment, which states, "Congress shall make no law respecting an establishment of religion, or prohibiting the free exercise thereof." These two clauses—the establishment clause and the free exercise clause—were intended to work in tandem to provide freedom for people's religions and, by implication, freedom from others' religions.

The Founders recoiled from Europeans' experience of continuous conflict and long wars fought over religious schisms. Consequently, Thomas Jefferson explained, the clauses were designed to build "a wall of separation between church and state."[110] Each would stay on its own side of the wall and not interfere or even interact with the other. **Separation of church and state** was a novel idea; according to one historian, although the phrase is not in the Constitution, it was the "most revolutionary" aspect of the document.[111]

When the District of Columbia was designed, a triangular configuration popular at the time was adopted. In one corner was the Capitol building for Congress, and in another was the White House for the president. In the third corner other nations would locate a church to represent the spiritual power, but the Founders did not do that because of the separation of church and state. (They could have put the Supreme Court there, but the Court was not considered important then and would not get its own building until 1935.) Instead, they located the Patent Office in the third corner to represent the spirit of innovation. They anticipated many inventions.[112] (Today the building houses the National Portrait Gallery and the Museum of American Art.)

Today some deeply religious people scorn the idea of separation of church and state. They think it devalues the importance of religion. But the Founders saw it as a means to preserve the peace that had eluded European states. In addition, they saw it as a way to protect religion itself. Without interference by government officials, whether to hinder or to help, churches would be free to determine their dogma and establish their practices as they saw fit. They would be free to flourish. Indeed, religion is stronger in the United States than in Europe, where churches endorsed and supported by the government sit mostly empty.

Despite the Founders' intention, as society became more complex and government became more pervasive, church and state came to interact, sometimes to interfere, with each other. Inevitably, the wall began to crumble, and the courts had to devise new doctrine to keep church and state as separate as possible while still accommodating the needs of each.

Free Exercise of Religion

The **free exercise clause** allows individuals to practice their religion without government coercion.

Direct Restrictions

Government has occasionally restricted free exercise of religion directly. Early in the country's history, some states prohibited Catholics or Jews from voting or holding office, and as late as 1961, Maryland prohibited nonbelievers from holding office.[113] In the 1920s, Oregon prohibited students from attending parochial schools.[114] More recently, prisons in Illinois and Texas prohibited Black Muslims and Buddhists from receiving religious publications and using prison chapels.[115] The Supreme Court *invalidated each of these restrictions.*

A suburb of Miami tried to ban the Santeria religion in 1987. Santeria blends ancient African rites and Roman Catholic rituals, but its distinguishing feature is animal sacrifice. Adherents believe that animal sacrifice is necessary to win the favor of the gods, and they practice it at initiations of new members and at births, marriages, and deaths. They kill chickens, ducks, doves, pigeons, sheep, goats, and turtles. When adherents, who had practiced their religion underground since refugees from Cuba brought it to Florida in the 1950s and 1960s, announced plans to construct a church building, cultural center, museum, and school, the city passed ordinances against ritualistic animal sacrifice, essentially forbidding adherents from practicing their religion. The Court struck down the ordinances.[116] "Although the practice of animal sacrifice may seem abhorrent to some," Justice Anthony Kennedy wrote, "religious beliefs need not be acceptable, logical, consistent, or comprehensible to others in order to merit First Amendment protection."

Indirect Restrictions

Government has also restricted free exercise of religion indirectly. As society has become more complex, some laws have inevitably interfered with religion, even when not designed to do so. The laws have usually interfered with minority religions, which do not have many members in legislatures looking out for their interests.

At first the Court distinguished between belief and action: individuals could believe what they wanted,

Alfred Smith, fired for using peyote in religious ceremonies, challenged Oregon's law prohibiting use of the drug.

but they could not act accordingly if such action was against the law. In 1878, male Mormons who believed their religion required polygamy could not marry more than one woman.[117] The Court rhetorically asked, "Suppose one believed that human sacrifices were a necessary part of religious worship?" Of course, belief without action gave little protection and scant satisfaction to the individuals involved.

In the 1960s, the Warren Court recognized this problem and broadened the protection by *granting exemptions to laws*. A Seventh-Day Adventist who worked in a textile mill in South Carolina quit when the mill shifted from a five-day to a six-day workweek that included Saturday—her Sabbath. Unable to find another job, she applied for unemployment benefits, but the state refused to provide them. To receive them, she had to be "available" for work, and the state said she was not available because she would not accept any jobs that required Saturday work. The Court ordered the state to grant an exemption to its law.[118] The Burger Court ruled that employers need to make a reasonable effort to accommodate employees' requests to fit work schedules around their Sabbath.[119]

Amish in Wisconsin withheld their children from high school, although the law required their attendance until age sixteen. The parents sent their children to elementary and junior high school to learn basic reading, writing, and arithmetic, but they complained that high school would subject their children to worldly influences that would interfere with their semi-isolated agricultural life. The Court ruled that the Amish could be exempt from the additional one to two years the law required beyond junior high school.[120]

Congress, too, has granted some exemptions. It excused the Amish from participating in the Social Security program because the Amish support their own elderly. And in every draft law, it excused conscientious objectors from participating in war.

The Court has been most reluctant to exempt individuals from paying taxes. It did not excuse either the Amish[121] or the Quakers, who as pacifists tried to withhold the portion of their income taxes that funded the military.[122] The Court worried that many other persons would try to avoid paying taxes, too.

The Rehnquist Court, which was not as sensitive to minority rights, *refused to grant such exemptions*.[123] The Native American church uses peyote, a hallucinogen derived from a cactus, in worship ceremonies. Members believe that the plant embodies their deity and that eating it is an act of communion. Although peyote is a controlled substance, Congress has authorized its use on Indian reservations, and almost half of the states have authorized its use off the reservations by church members. But when two members in Oregon, a state that did not allow its use off the reservations, were fired from their jobs and denied unemployment benefits for using the drug, the Court refused to grant an exemption.[124] A five-justice majority rejected the doctrine and precedents of the Warren and Burger Courts. Justice Antonin Scalia, a Catholic, admitted that denying such exemptions will put minority religions at a disadvantage but said that this is an "unavoidable consequence of democratic government." That is, denying minority rights is an inevitable and acceptable result of majority rule. This rationale, of course, could emasculate not only the free exercise clause but other provisions of the Bill of Rights as well.

Although Congress overturned the particular focus of the decision, restricting Native Americans' use of this drug,[125] the broad implications of the decision remained. Some adherents of minority religions were not allowed to practice the tenets of their religions. Families of deceased Jews and Laotians, who reject autopsies on religious grounds, were overruled. Muslim prisoners whose religion forbids them from eating pork were refused other meat instead. Members of the Sikh religion, who wear turbans, had been exempted from the federal law requiring construction workers to wear hard hats, but after the decision, this exemption was rescinded.[126]

Even mainstream churches worried about the implications of the ruling, and a coalition of religious groups lobbied Congress to overturn it. Congress passed an act reversing the ruling and substituting the previous doctrine. But the Rehnquist Court invalidated the act because it challenged the justices' authority and altered their interpretation of the First Amendment without going through the process required to amend the Constitution.[127]

Establishment of Religion

Two competing traditions reflecting the role of government toward religion have led to intense conflict over the **establishment clause.** Many early settlers in America wanted government to reinforce their religion, yet the framers of the Constitution were products of the Enlightenment, which emphasized the importance of reason and deemphasized the role of religion. The two individuals most responsible for the religious guarantees in the First Amendment, Jefferson and Madison, feared the divisiveness of religion. They wanted separation of church and state, advocating not only freedom *of* religion for believers but freedom *from* religion for others.[128]

Even some religious groups wanted separation of church and state. The Baptists and the evangelicals had been harassed and persecuted by the Anglicans (Episcopalians) and Congregationalists, and they feared that these larger groups would use the power of the state to promote their views and practices.[129]

The Supreme Court initially reflected the first of these traditions. In 1892, Justice David Brewer smugly declared that "this is a Christian nation."[130] But as the country became more pluralistic, the Court moved toward the second of these traditions. Since the 1960s, the Court has *generally interpreted the establishment clause to forbid government not only from designating an official church*, like the Church of England, which receives tax money and special privileges, *but also from aiding one religion over another or even from aiding religion over nonreligion.*

School Prayers

Courts have used the clause to resolve disputes about prayer in public schools. In 1962 and 1963, the Supreme Court initiated its prayer rulings. New York had students recite a nondenominational prayer at the start of every day, and Pennsylvania and Baltimore had students recite the Lord's Prayer or Bible verses. The Court, with only one justice dissenting, ruled that *these practices violated the establishment clause.*[131] Technically, the prayers were voluntary; students could leave the room. But the Court doubted that the prayers really were voluntary. It noted that nonconforming students would face tremendous pressure from teachers and peers and that leaving the room usually connotes punishment for bad behavior. The Court therefore concluded that the prayers fostered religion. According to Justice Black, "Government in this country should stay out of the business of writing and sanctioning official prayers and leave that purely religious function to the people themselves and to those the people choose to look to for religious guidance." Although schools could teach religion as a subject, they could not promote religion.

For similar reasons, the Court ruled that Kentucky *could not require public schools to post the Ten Commandments* in classrooms.[132]

Many people sharply criticized the rulings. A representative from Alabama lamented, "They put the Negroes in the schools, and now they've driven God out."[133] Students, of course, can still pray on their own at any time.

Courtesy of the National Archives

The country's religious diversity has led to demands for some exotic exemptions. Inspired by the Bible's statement that Jesus's followers "shall take up serpents" and "if they drink any deadly thing, it shall not hurt them," members of the Holiness Church of God in Jesus's Name handle snakes and drink strychnine. Some become enraptured and entranced to the point of hysteria, and occasionally some die. In 1975, the Tennessee Supreme Court forbade such practices, saying that the state has "the right to guard against the unnecessary creation of widows and orphans." However, these practices continue in some places.

© Sylvia Plachy, photographed for the *New Yorker*

Muslim students in Dearborn, Michigan, reflect our religious pluralism. The Detroit area has the second-largest concentration of Arabs outside the Middle East.

Empirical studies in the years after the rulings found that prayers and Bible readings decreased but by no means disappeared, especially in the South.[134] A Tennessee school official asserted, "I am of the opinion that 99 percent of the people in the United States feel as I do about the Supreme Court's decision—that it was an outrage. . . . The remaining 1 percent do not belong in this free world."[135]

News reports in recent years indicate that some schools, especially in the rural South, still use prayers or Bible readings in violation of the Court's rulings. These practices are reinforced by social pressure. A woman whose family had moved to Pontotoc, Mississippi, discovered that Christian prayers were being broadcast on the intercom and the Bible was being taught in a class. When she objected, rumors circulated that she was an outside agitator paid by the ACLU to force the town to change. One of her children had a teacher who told the class that he did not believe in God, while another of her children kept "getting jumped" in the bathroom. Then the woman lost her job in a convenience store after customers threatened to boycott the store.[136]

News reports also indicate that officials in Kentucky and Ohio allowed volunteers to put the Ten Commandments inside or outside public schools in violation of the Court's ruling.[137]

Although many people wanted a constitutional amendment to allow official prayers in public schools, Congress never passed one. Some people supported the rulings. Others supported the Court and did not want to challenge its authority and set a precedent for other groups on other matters. Some religious leaders doubt that the religious groups would ever agree on specific prayers. America's religious diversity means that the prayers would offend some students or par-

ents. Prayers that suit Christians might not suit Jews; those that suit Jews might not suit persons of other faiths. Recent immigrants from Asia and the Middle East, practicing Buddhism, Shintoism, Taoism, and Islam, have made the country even more pluralistic. Now, according to one researcher, America's religious diversity is greater than that of any country in recorded history.[138] Asking students in this country to say a prayer would be like "asking the members of the United Nations to stand and sing the national anthem of one country."[139] However, many local communities are not diverse, and the majority may assume that everyone, or at least all "normal" people, share their views about religion.

In lieu of an amendment, about half of the states have passed laws providing for a "moment of silence" to begin each school day. Although the laws are ostensibly for meditation, some legislators admit they are really for prayer. Yet a majority of justices indicated that they *would approve a moment of silence if students were not urged to pray.*[140]

The Rehnquist Court reaffirmed and extended the prayer rulings of the Warren Court. It held that *clergy cannot offer prayers at graduation ceremonies* for public elementary, middle, and high schools.[141] The prayers in question were brief and nonsectarian, but the majority reasoned, "What to most believers may seem nothing more than a reasonable request that the nonbeliever respect their religious practices, in a school context may appear to the nonbeliever or dissenter to be an attempt to employ the machinery of the state to enforce a religious orthodoxy." Although attendance at the ceremony was voluntary, like participation in school prayers, the majority did not consider it truly voluntary. Justice Kennedy wrote, "Everyone knows that in our society and in our culture high school

CHAPTER 14 ■ *Civil Liberties* **489**

graduation is one of life's most significant occasions. . . . Graduation is a time for family and those closest to the student to celebrate success and express mutual wishes of gratitude and respect."

Although the Court's language here was emphatic, its stance on student-led prayers has been ambiguous. In 1992, the Court refused to review a federal court of appeals ruling that allowed student-led prayers at graduation ceremonies.[142] A Texas school board permitted the senior class to decide whether to have a prayer and, if so, which student to give it. The appellate court held that this policy was not precluded by the Supreme Court's ruling because the decision was not made by officials and the prayer was not offered by a clergy member, so official coercion was not present. But in 1996, the Court also refused to review a federal court of appeals ruling from a different circuit that prohibited student led prayers at various school events.[143] The Court's reluctance to resolve this controversy means that the ruling of each court of appeals remains but applies only to schools in its circuit.

The first appellate court's holding encouraged opponents of the Supreme Court's rulings to use the same approach to circumvent these rulings as well. Several southern states passed laws allowing student-led prayers to start each school day. Some school officials, who selected the students, let them give the prayers over the intercom. Federal courts in Alabama and Mississippi invalidated these laws because school officials were involved and because all students were required or at least pressured to listen to the prayers.

The Rehnquist Court did invalidate the use of schools' public address systems by clergy or students to give prayers at high school football games.[144] Although student attendance is voluntary, the games are official school events.

The public desire for official school prayers is fueled by nostalgia for the less troubling times before the 1960s. As one writer perceived, the desire "doesn't have much to do with prayer anyway, but with a time, a place, an ethos that praying and pledging allegiance at the beginning of school each day represent."[145] For some people, buffeted by the upheavals and dislocations of our times, the reinstitutionalization of school prayers would symbolize that our society still stands for appropriate values.

The public desire for official school prayers is also fueled by occasional reports of school officials who mistakenly believe that court rulings require them to forbid all forms of religious expression. Some confused administrators have prohibited a few students from wearing religious jewelry, reading the Bible while riding the bus, and praying before eating their lunch.[146]

In another case, the Supreme Court held that the University of Missouri at Kansas City had to make its meeting rooms available to students' religious organizations on an equal basis with other organizations, even if the religious organizations used the rooms for prayer or worship.[147] Otherwise, the university would be discriminating against religion.

After this decision, Congress passed a law that *requires public high schools as well as colleges and universities to allow meetings of students' religious, philosophical, or political groups outside class hours.* The Court accepted this law in 1990.[148] Justice Sandra Day O'Connor said that high school students "are likely to understand that a school does not endorse or support student speech that it merely permits on a nondiscriminatory basis." Students have established Bible clubs in one-quarter of public high schools, according to one estimate.[149] (As a result of this act, students have also established gay-straight clubs—organizations of gay and straight students who support the rights of gays, lesbians, and bisexuals—in more than seven hundred high schools.)[150] Yet students' interest in Bible clubs has not always been the driving force. Adults eager to put prayers back into the schools have often taken the initiative. Organized networks have encouraged the clubs and provided advice, workshops, and handbooks for them.

The Rehnquist Court also held that the University of Virginia had to provide funding, from students' fees, to students' religious organizations on an equal basis with other campus organizations, even if a religious organization sought the money to print a religious newspaper.[151]

Sikhs from India were sometimes mistaken for Muslims after the 9/11 attacks. One Sikh was murdered in Arizona.

A megachurch with 12,000 members in Memphis, Tennessee, unveiled its "Statue of Liberation Through Christ" in 2006. In contrast to the Statue of Liberty, this monument holds a cross rather than a torch and, with the other arm, the Ten Commandments. She also has a tear running down her cheek because of modern secularism, legal abortions, and the absence of school prayers. According to the pastor, the purpose of the monument is to let people know that "God is in the foundation of our nation," hence the merger of church and state.

On the basis of this precedent, a federal court of appeals ruled that the University of South Alabama had to provide funding to a gay organization.

Religious Symbols

Despite its prayer rulings, the Court has been *reluctant to invalidate traditional religious symbols.* It has not questioned the motto "In God We Trust" on our coins since 1865 and paper money since 1955, or the phrase "one nation under God" in the Pledge of Allegiance since 1954.[152]

In 2002, a federal court of appeals held the phrase "under God" in the Pledge unconstitutional when recited in the public schools. The court said it promotes religion as much as if it professed that we are a nation "under Jesus" or "under Vishnu" or "under Zeus" or "under no god." It promotes Christianity and leaves out not only atheists and agnostics but believers of other deities, such as Buddhists and many Native Americans. Although the ruling was a logical extension of the prayer rulings, it was a lightning rod for the public's anger, and the Supreme Court sidestepped the issue (deciding that the student's father, an atheist, lacked authority to bring suit on the student's behalf because the student's mother, a born-again Christian, had custody of the child after their divorce).[153]

The Burger Court upheld the display of a nativity scene on government property, at least when it is part of a broader display for the holiday season.[154] Pawtucket, Rhode Island, had a crèche, Santa Claus, sleigh with reindeer, Christmas tree, and talking wishing well. The Court said that Christmas had become a secular as well as a religious holiday and that the secular decorations diluted any religious impact the nativity scene would have. A crèche by itself, however, would be impermissible.[155]

The chief justice of Alabama's supreme court had a granite marker bearing the Ten Commandments installed in Alabama's Judicial Building in the middle of the night. Lower federal courts ruled this display, which stood by itself, a violation of the establishment clause. When the chief justice defied a federal court order to remove the 5300-pound marker, he was suspended by his own court.

The Rehnquist Court addressed Ten Commandments displays in 2005 and ruled much like the Burger Court did for nativity scenes. A monument of the Ten Commandments on the Texas state capitol grounds could remain because it was just one of sixteen other monuments and twenty-one historical markers, which were secular, and because it had been there for forty years.[156] But copies of the Ten Commandments on the walls in two Kentucky courthouses could not remain because they were not part of historical displays[157] and they were posted recently for religious purposes.[158]

Evolution

Courts have also used the establishment clause to resolve disputes about teaching evolution in schools. In 1968, the Supreme Court invalidated Arkansas' forty-year-old law forbidding schools from teaching evolution.[159] Arkansas and Louisiana then passed laws requiring schools that teach evolution to also teach "creationism"—the biblical version of creation.[160] In 1987, the Court *invalidated these laws because their purpose was to advance the fundamentalist Christian view.*[161] The Kansas Board of Education tried to circumvent these rulings by deleting evolution from the state's science curriculum in 1999.

Evolution remains controversial. In 2005, at least twenty states considered antievolution proposals. A suburban Atlanta school district had disclaimers pasted onto ninth-grade biology textbooks stating, "Evolution is a theory, not a fact," and it should be "critically considered." A federal court ordered the disclaimers removed because their denigration of evolution reflected a religious view.

Critics of evolution also promoted "intelligent design"—the notion that some life is so complex that it must have been designed by an intelligent creator rather than have evolved through random chance, as the theory of evolution posits. Proponents of intelligent design tend not to believe in biblical literalism—for example, that the earth was created in six days—as creationists tend to believe.[162] The Dover, Pennsylvania, school district required teachers to discuss intelligent design in 2005. A federal court invalidated the policy because intelligent design is not a science. Although proponents address the science of evolution, they invoke a supernatural designer—that is, God[163]—whereas science deals with natural phenomena. Science, unlike intelligent design, is based on empirical evidence and testable hypotheses.

Other Policies

Conservative Christians have pushed Republican officials to adopt policies and programs reflecting their beliefs. Despite the establishment clause, the Bush administration has limited scientific research with stem cells, withheld federal money from family planning organizations and programs in the United States and abroad, given federal money to abstinence education programs, and given federal money to hundreds of church-run marriage, child care, and drug treatment programs. As a result, for example, the government gave federal money to Louisiana, which funneled it to Protestant groups to teach abstinence through Bible lessons and skits and to Catholic groups to hold prayer sessions at abortion clinics.[164] So far, the courts have not ruled that these policies and programs violate the establishment clause.

Despite ongoing tensions and frequent conflicts, the effort to separate church and state has enabled the United States to manage, and even nourish, its religious pluralism. The effort has kept many religious debates and potential religious fights out of the political arena. But today this practical arrangement is opposed by those religious conservatives who most fear the changes in modern society. They see their religion as a shield protecting their family against these changes, and they want their religion to be reinforced by the authority of the government.

Rights of Criminal Defendants

The Fourth, Fifth, Sixth, and Eighth Amendments provide numerous **due process** rights for criminal defendants. When the government prosecutes defendants, it must give them the process—that is, the procedures—they are due; it must be fair and "respect certain decencies of civilized conduct,"[165] even toward uncivilized people.

One defense attorney said that many of his clients "had been monsters—nothing less—who had done monstrous things. Although occasionally not guilty of the crime charged, nearly all my clients have been guilty of something."[166] Then why do we give them rights? We give criminal defendants rights because we give all individuals rights in court. As Justice Douglas observed, "respecting the dignity even of the least worthy . . . citizen raises the stature of all of us."[167]

But why do we give all individuals rights in court? We do so because we have established the **presumption of innocence.** This presumption is "not . . . a naive belief that most or even many defendants are innocent, or a cavalier attitude toward crime." It reflects a mistrust of the state, as it recognizes the possibility of an overzealous prosecutor or an unfair judge. It requires the state to prove the defendant's guilt, essentially saying, "We won't take your word for it."[168] Of course, when the crime rate is high or a particular crime is heinous, many people fear the state less than the criminals. Then they want to give officials more authority and defendants fewer rights. But this is the way the people eventually lose their rights.

Search and Seizure

England fostered the notion that a family's home is its castle, but Parliament made exceptions for the American colonies. It authorized writs of assistance, which allowed customs officials to conduct general searches for goods imported by the colonists without paying

What about the Second Amendment?

Individuals and interest groups opposed to gun control cite the **Second Amendment,** which provides "the right of the people to keep and bear arms." But these opponents seldom quote the rest of the amendment, which reads in its entirety, "A well regulated militia being necessary to the security of a free state, the right of the people to keep and bear arms shall not be infringed." The amendment was adopted at a time when there was no standing army to protect people from foreign invasions, Indian uprisings, or mob riots. The language links the right to bear arms with the security of the state. The language suggests that the right belongs to each state or, if to individuals, only to individuals when they are protecting their state—that is, when they are serving in the militia of their state. At the Founding, the militia was a ragtag band of civilians in each community; today the militia is the National Guard of each state. Therefore, the amendment might be a useless anachronism if it merely allows the National Guard to have weapons.

Accordingly, the federal courts have routinely upheld gun control laws when they are challenged as violations of the Second Amendment.[1] The Supreme Court has rarely reviewed these decisions, and it has never offered a definitive interpretation of the amendment.

Conservative Chief Justice Warren Burger criticized the National Rifle Association for misleading people by insisting that the Second Amendment should prevent gun control legislation. He said the amendment "has been the subject of one of the greatest pieces of fraud—I repeat the word 'fraud'—on the American public."[2]

Yet the persistent views of the American public have prompted legal scholars to take a closer look at the adoption of the Second Amendment.[3] Some have concluded that there might be a right for individuals, separate from the right for states and National Guards, to own and use guns. Their rationale is that the original notion of a militia encompassed all individuals who had political rights,

"You know, if she weren't part of a well-regulated militia, I'd be a little nervous."

such as the rights to vote and to serve on juries—that is, all white males who owned property. Today individuals who have political rights include all adult citizens (except felons in most states). Thus, the word *militia* in 1791 might mean all adult citizens today. However, this expanded view of the Second Amendment would provide a right only for individuals to own and use guns to defend their state or, possibly, their homes or themselves.[4] It would not provide a right to own and use guns for hunting or other recreational purposes because the language—"the security of a free state"—indicates that the justification for the right is just protection.[5]

Even if this expanded view of the Second Amendment becomes more common—the Bush administration is the first to advocate an expanded view—it would not bar most gun control laws or proposals. The amendment refers to a "well regulated militia," making clear that arms can be regulated, as they were even in colonial times. (George Washington proposed government inspection of private arms at least twice a year.) As Justice John Paul Stevens observed, arms have "long been subject to pervasive governmental regulation because of the dangerous nature of

the product and the public interest in having that danger controlled."[6]

So a huge gap remains between what many people think and what most judges and legal scholars have concluded.

SOURCE: Except where noted, Laurence H. Tribe, *American Constitutional Law,* 3rd ed., vol. 1 (New York: Foundation Press, 2000), 894–903.

[1] A federal district court did make headlines in 1999 when it ruled unconstitutional a federal law prohibiting a person under a restraining order from owning a gun. This was apparently the first time a court struck down a law because the court thought it infringed on the Second Amendment.

[2] Joan Biskupic, "A Second (Amendment) Look at Bearing Arms," *Washington Post National Weekly Edition,* May 15, 1995, 33.

[3] For a balanced synthesis of the conflicting views, see David C. Williams, *The Mythic Meanings of the Second Amendment* (New Haven, Conn.: Yale University Press, 2003).

[4] In the original debate over the proposed amendment, the framers apparently never discussed the use of firearms for personal protection. Garry Wills, *A Necessary Evil: A History of American Distrust* (New York: Simon & Schuster, 1999).

[5] In addition, some argue that the amendment allows the people as a whole—not a faction of the people—to use firearms to resist government tyranny. Williams, *Mythic Meanings.*

[6] *United States* v. *Thompson/Center Arms Co.,* 504 U.S. 505, 526 (1992).

taxes to the crown. The English tradition of home privacy combined with the colonists' resentment of these writs led to adoption of the Fourth Amendment, which forbids **unreasonable searches and seizures.**

In these cases, the Supreme Court has tried to walk a fine line between acknowledging officials' need for evidence and individuals' desire for privacy. This judicial doctrine is so complex that we will note just its basic principles here.

One type of seizure is the arrest of a person. Police must have evidence to believe that a person committed a crime. Another type of seizure is the confiscation of illegal contraband. *The general requirement is that police must get a search warrant from a judge* by showing evidence that a particular thing is in a particular place.

However, the Court has made numerous exceptions to this requirement that complicate the law. These exceptions account for most searches. If persons consent to a search, police can conduct a search without a warrant. If police see contraband in plain view, they can seize it; they don't have to close their eyes to it. If police have evidence to arrest someone, they can search the person and the area within the person's control. If police have reason to suspect that someone is committing a crime, but they lack evidence to arrest the suspect, they can "stop and frisk" the person—conduct a pat-down search. In some situations, if police want to search a motor vehicle, they can do so because vehicles are mobile and could be gone by the time police get a warrant. If police face an emergency situation, with a person's life in jeopardy, they can search for weapons.

Customs and border patrol officials can search persons and things coming into the country to enforce customs and immigration laws. Airport guards can search passengers and luggage to prevent hijackings and terrorism. And prison guards can search prisoners to ensure security. (See the box "When a Court Reverses a Conviction. . .")

Exclusionary Rule

To enforce search and seizure law, the Supreme Court has *established the* **exclusionary rule,** *which bars from the courts any evidence obtained in violation of the Fourth Amendment.* The rule's goal is to deter illegal conduct by police officers.

Although the Court created the rule for federal courts in 1914,[169] it did not impose the rule on state courts until 1961 in *Mapp* v. *Ohio.*[170] Until this time, police in many states had ignored search and seizure law. *Mapp* was one of the Warren Court's most controversial rulings. Many people did not think that evidence of guilt should be barred, even if search and seizure law had been violated by police.

The decision still has not been widely accepted. The Burger Court created an exception to it. In a pair of cases, the justices allowed evidence obtained illegally to be used in court because the police had acted "in good faith."[171]

Electronic Surveillance

The Fourth Amendment traditionally applied to searches involving a physical trespass and seizures producing a tangible object. Electronic surveillance, however, does not require a physical trespass or result in a tangible object.

This posed a problem for the Supreme Court when it heard its first wiretapping case in 1928. Federal prohibition agents tapped the telephone of bootleggers by installing equipment on wires in the basement of the bootleggers' apartment building. The Court's majority rigidly adhered to its traditional doctrine, saying that this was not a search and seizure, so the agents did not need a warrant.[172]

In a classic example of keeping the Constitution up-to-date with the times, the Warren Court overruled this precedent in 1967.[173] Because electronic eavesdropping might threaten privacy as much as traditional searching, *officials must get judicial authorization,* similar to a warrant, *to engage in such eavesdropping.*

Self-Incrimination

The Fifth Amendment provides that persons shall not be compelled to be witnesses against themselves—that is, to incriminate themselves. Because defendants are presumed innocent, the government must prove their guilt.

This right means that *the defendants on trial do not have to take the witness stand and answer the prosecutor's questions,* and neither the prosecutor nor the judge can call attention to their decision to exercise this right. Neither can suggest or imply that the defendants must have something to hide and must be guilty. (But if the defendants do take the stand and testify, they thereby waive their right, so the prosecutor can cross-examine them and they must answer.)

This right also means that *the prosecutors cannot introduce into evidence any statements or confessions from the defendants that were not voluntary.* However, the meaning of *voluntary* has changed over time.

For years, law enforcement officials used physical brutality—"the third degree"—to get confessions. After 1936, when the Supreme Court ruled that confessions obtained this way were invalid,[174] officials resorted to more subtle techniques. They held suspects incommunicado—preventing them from contacting relatives or lawyers and delaying them from going to court where a judge would inform them of their rights—to pressure them to confess.[175] Officials interrogated suspects for long periods of time without food or rest, in one case with alternating teams of interrogators for thirty-six hours.[176] The Court ruled that these techniques, designed to break the suspects' will, were psychological coercion, so the confessions were invalid.

The Warren Court still worried that many confessions were not truly voluntary, so it issued a landmark decision in 1966. Arizona police arrested a poor, mentally disturbed man, Ernesto Miranda, for kidnapping and raping a woman. After the woman identified him in a lineup, police interrogated him, prompting him to confess. He had not been told that he could remain silent or be represented by an attorney. In *Miranda* v. *Arizona,* the Court decided that his confession was not truly voluntary.[177] Chief Justice Warren, as a former district attorney, knew the advantage that police have in interrogation and said that suspects needed more protection. The Court ruled that *officials must advise suspects of their rights before interrogation.* These came to be known as the **Miranda rights:**

- You have the right to remain silent.

- If you talk, anything you say can be used against you.

- You have the right to be represented by an attorney.

- If you cannot afford an attorney, one will be appointed for you.

The Burger and Rehnquist Courts did not require police and prosecutors to follow *Miranda* as strictly as the Warren Court did but, contrary to expectations,

did not abandon it. In 2000, the Rehnquist Court reaffirmed *Miranda* by a 7–2 vote.[178]

Ernesto Miranda

AP/Wide World Photos

Even with the warnings, most suspects talk anyway. Some do not understand the warnings. Others think the police, who may rattle off the warnings fast or in a monotone, give them as a formality but would not follow them. Also, suspects in an interrogation are in a coercive atmosphere and face law enforcement tactics designed to exploit their weaknesses. Detectives are trained to persuade the suspects to talk despite the warnings. One said, "Before you ever get in there, the first thing an investigator usually thinks about is . . . how can I breeze through this *Miranda* thing so I don't set the guy off and tell him not to talk to me, song and dance it, sugarcoat it, whatever."[179] So detectives frequently lie and trick suspects.

Counsel

The Sixth Amendment provides the **right to counsel** in criminal cases. Initially, it permitted defendants to hire an attorney to help them prepare a defense, and later it permitted defendants to have the attorney represent them at the trial. But it was no help to most defendants because they were too poor to hire an attorney.

Consequently, the Supreme Court required federal courts to furnish an attorney to all indigent defendants as long ago as 1938.[180] But most criminal cases are state cases, and although the Court required state courts to furnish an attorney in some cases, it was reluctant to impose a broad requirement on these courts.[181]

In 1963, the Warren Court accepted the appeal of Clarence Earl Gideon. Charged with breaking into a pool hall and stealing beer, wine, and change from a vending machine, Gideon asked the judge for a lawyer. The judge refused to appoint one, leaving Gideon to defend himself. The prosecutor did not have a strong case, but Gideon was not able to point out its weaknesses. He was convicted and sentenced to five years. On appeal, the Warren Court unanimously declared that Gideon was entitled to be represented by counsel.[182] Justice Black explained that "lawyers in criminal

Courtesy of the National Archives

Clarence Earl Gideon, convinced that he was denied a fair trial because he was not given an attorney, read law books in prison so he could petition the Supreme Court for a writ of certiorari. Although he had spent much of his life in prison, he was optimistic. "I believe that each era finds an improvement in law [and] each year brings something new for the benefit of mankind. Maybe this will be one of those small steps forward."

The Supreme Court also decided that in addition to an attorney for the trial, *the courts must provide an attorney for one appeal.*[185]

Receiving counsel does not necessarily mean receiving effective counsel, however. Some assigned attorneys are inexperienced, some are incompetent, and most are overworked and have little time to prepare the best possible defense.

Some places make little effort to provide effective counsel, even in murder cases where capital punishment looms. In Illinois, at least thirty-three convicts on death row had been represented at trial by attorneys who were later disbarred or suspended.[186] In Louisiana, a defendant was represented by an attorney who was living with the prosecutor in the case. In Florida, a defendant was represented by an attorney who was a deputy sheriff at the time. In Georgia, a black defendant was represented by a white attorney who had been the Imperial Wizard of the local Ku Klux Klan for fifty years.[187] Also in Georgia, an attorney was so unversed in criminal law that when he was asked to name criminal rulings he was familiar with, he could think of only one (*Miranda*).[188] In three murder cases in one recent year in Texas, defense attorneys slept through the trials. When one of these defendants appealed his conviction on the ground that he did not receive his constitutional right to counsel, the appellate court announced that "the Constitution doesn't say the lawyer has to be awake."[189] (Stung by criticism, the appellate court sat *en banc*—that is, the entire court, rather than a three-judge panel, reheard the case—and overruled itself.) At least these attorneys were present. In Alabama, a defendant was represented by an attorney who failed to appear when his case was argued before the state supreme court. The defendant lost and was executed.[190]

In recent years, the issue of legal counsel for those defendants subject to the death penalty has received more scrutiny because new investigations and technologies have demonstrated definitively that dozens of people on death row were not guilty of the murder for which they were convicted and sentenced. Nonetheless, there is little effort to provide effective counsel for criminal defendants because few groups, other than lawyers' associations, urge adequate representation. Criminal defendants have no political power in our system, and the public has limited sympathy for their rights.[191]

Jury Trial

The Sixth Amendment also provides the **right to a jury trial** in "serious" criminal cases. The Supreme Court has defined "serious" cases as those that could result in more than six months' incarceration.[192]

courts are necessities, not luxuries." The Court finally established a broad rule: State courts must provide an attorney to indigent defendants in felony cases. Gideon proved the Court's point. Given a lawyer and retried, he was not reconvicted. The lawyer did the effective job defending him that he had not been able to do himself.

In 1972, the Burger Court expanded the rule: State courts must provide an attorney to indigent defendants in misdemeanor cases, too, except those that result in no incarceration,[183] because misdemeanor cases as well as felony cases are too complex for the defendants to defend themselves. In 2002, the Rehnquist Court expanded the rule further, declaring that state courts must provide an attorney to indigent defendants even in cases that result in no incarceration if the defendants receive probation or a suspended sentence, which could eventually result in incarceration if the defendants fail to follow the terms of such sentence.[184] Thus, *all courts must offer an attorney to indigent defendants in all cases except the most minor ones, such as traffic violations.*

The right was adopted to prevent oppression by a "corrupt or overzealous prosecutor" or a "biased . . . or eccentric judge."[193] It has also served to limit governmental use of unpopular laws or enforcement practices. Regardless of the evidence against a defendant, a jury can refuse to convict if it feels that the government overstepped its bounds.

The jury is supposed to be impartial, so persons who have made up their minds before trial should be dismissed. It is also supposed to be "a fair cross section" of the community, so no group should be systematically excluded.[194] But the jury need not be a perfect cross section and in fact need not have a single member of a particular group.[195] Most courts use voter registration lists to obtain the names of potential jurors. These lists are not truly representative because poor people do not register at the same rate as others, but courts have decided that the lists are sufficiently representative. And Congress passed and President Clinton signed the "motor voter bill," which requires drivers' license and welfare offices to offer voter registration forms. As a result, more people have registered to vote and are eligible to serve on juries.

Cruel and Unusual Punishment

The Eighth Amendment forbids **cruel and unusual punishment** but does not define it. The Supreme Court had defined it as torture or any punishment grossly disproportionate to the offense, but the Court had seldom used the provision until applying it to capital punishment in the 1970s.

Because the death penalty was used at the time the amendment was adopted and had been used ever since, it was assumed to be constitutional.[196] But the Burger Court, albeit with Chief Justice Burger and the other three Nixon appointees in dissent, held that *capital punishment as it was then being administered was cruel and unusual*.[197] The laws and procedures allowed too much discretion by those who administered the punishment and resulted in too much arbitrariness and discrimination for those who received it. The death penalty was imposed so seldom, according to Justice Potter Stewart, that it was "cruel and unusual in the same way that being struck by lightning is cruel and unusual." Yet when it was imposed, it was imposed on black defendants disproportionately to their convictions for murder.

The decision invalidated the laws of forty states and commuted the death sentences of 629 inmates. But because the Court did not hold capital punishment cruel and unusual in principle, about three-fourths of the states adopted new laws that permitted less discretion in an attempt to prove less arbitrary and discriminatory.

These changes satisfied a majority of the Court, which ruled that *capital punishment is not cruel and unusual for murder if administered fairly*.[198] But it cannot be imposed automatically for everyone convicted of murder, for the judge or jury must consider any mitigating factors that would call for a lesser punishment.[199] Also, it cannot be imposed for rape, because it is disproportionate to that offense.[200]

The new laws have reduced but not eliminated discrimination. Although past studies showed discrimination against black defendants, recent studies show discrimination against black or white defendants who murder white victims. People who affect the decision to impose the death penalty—prosecutors, defense attorneys, judges, and jurors—appear to value white lives more. Despite evidence that in Georgia those who killed whites were more than four times as likely to be given the death penalty as those who killed blacks, the Rehnquist Court, by a 5–4 vote, upheld capital punishment in the state.[201]

The new laws have not addressed an equally serious problem—inadequate representation provided to poor defendants who face the death penalty—which we discussed in conjunction with the right to counsel.

For years, most people dismissed any suggestions that innocent defendants might be put to death. They assumed that the criminal justice system used careful procedures and made no mistakes in these cases at least. However, since capital punishment was reinstated and stricter procedures were mandated in the 1970s, at least 117 inmates awaiting execution have been released because new evidence, including DNA tests, revealed their innocence.[202] This number represents one exoneration for every seven or eight executions—a disturbing frequency for the ultimate punishment.[203] Some were the victims of sloppy or biased police or overzealous prosecutors; some were the victims of mistaken witnesses; others were the victims of emotional or prejudiced jurors. Many were the victims of inadequate representation.

Due to the patterns of racial discrimination and inadequate representation, the American Bar Association called for a moratorium on the use of capital punishment in 1997. After Illinois released its thirteenth innocent inmate from death row, most after investigations by Northwestern University journalism students, its governor announced a moratorium in 2000. Three years later, when he left office, he commuted the death sentences of 167 inmates to life in prison.

In recent years, the public has become uneasy about capital punishment. Often juries have become reluctant to impose it, instead opting for life in prison.[204]

Even the Rehnquist Court, long a staunch supporter of the death penalty, reflected the public's mood. In 2002, it ruled that states cannot execute the mentally retarded.[205] Previously, it had allowed execution of the mentally retarded, including a man who had the mental capacity of a seven-year-old and still believed in Santa Claus.[206] But now, the six-justice majority observed, there was a new "national consensus" against such executions. In 2005, it ruled that states cannot execute juveniles who were younger than eighteen when they killed.[207] Previously, it had allowed execution of juveniles as young as sixteen. But Justice Kennedy noted the "evolving standards of decency" in society. Nonetheless, most states retain the death penalty for adults even though nearly all other developed countries (except Japan) have abolished it.[208]

Rights in Theory and in Practice

Overall, the Supreme Court has interpreted the Bill of Rights to provide an impressive list of rights for criminal defendants (although one of the significant changes from the Warren Court to the Burger and Rehnquist Courts was a decline in support for criminal defendants). Yet not all rights are available for all defendants in all places. Some trial court judges, prosecutors, and police do not comply with Supreme Court rulings. If defendants appeal to a higher court, they probably will get their rights, but most defendants do not have the knowledge, the resources, or the perseverance to do this.

When the rights are available, most defendants do not take advantage of them. About 90 percent of criminal defendants plead guilty, and many of them do so through a **plea bargain.** This is an agreement among the prosecutor, the defense attorney, and the defendant, with the explicit or implicit approval of the judge, to reduce the charge or the sentence in exchange for a guilty plea. A plea bargain is a compromise. For officials, it saves the time, trouble, and uncertainty of a trial. For defendants, it eliminates the fear of a harsher sentence. However, it also reduces due process rights. A guilty plea waives the defendants' rights to a jury trial, at which the defendants can present their own witnesses and cross-examine the government's witnesses and at which they cannot be forced to incriminate themselves. A guilty plea also reduces the defendants' right to counsel because it reduces their lawyers' need to prepare a defense. Consequently, most attorneys pressure their clients to forgo a trial so that the attorneys do not have to spend the time to investigate and try the case. Despite these drawbacks for due process rights, the Supreme Court allows plea bargaining, and the trial courts encourage it because the practice enables judges and attorneys to dispose of their cases quickly.[209]

Right to Privacy

Neither the Constitution nor the Bill of Rights mentions privacy. Nevertheless, the right to privacy, Justice Douglas noted, is "older than the Bill of Rights,"[210] and the framers undoubtedly assumed that people would have such a right. In fact, the framers did include amendments that reflect a concern for privacy: The First Amendment protects privacy of association; the Third, privacy of homes from quartering soldiers; the Fourth, privacy of persons and places where they live from searches and seizures; and the Fifth, privacy of knowledge or thoughts from compulsory self-incrimination. The Supreme Court would use these to establish an explicit **right to privacy.**

So far, the Court's right-to-privacy doctrine reflects a right to autonomy—what Justice Louis Brandeis called "the right to be left alone"—more than a right to keep things confidential. As noted earlier in the chapter, the Court has been reluctant to punish the press for invading people's privacy.[211]

Birth Control

The Warren Court explicitly *established a right to privacy* in *Griswold* v. *Connecticut* in 1965. In violation of an 1879 law, which prohibited distributing or using contraceptives or even disseminating information about them, Planned Parenthood and a professor at Yale University Medical School established a birth control clinic in New Haven. After authorities shut it down, the founders challenged the law, and the Court struck it down.[212] To enforce the law, the state would have had to police people's bedrooms, and the Court said the very idea of policing married couples' bedrooms was absurd. Then the Court struck down Massachusetts and New York laws that prohibited distributing contraceptives to unmarried persons.[213] "If the right of privacy means anything," Justice Brennan said, "it is the right of the individual, married or single, to be free from unwarranted governmental intrusion into matters so fundamentally affecting a person as the decision whether to bear or beget a child."[214]

Abortion

When twenty-two-year-old Norma McCorvey became pregnant in 1969, she was distraught. She had one young daughter, she had relinquished custody of two previous children, and she was divorced. She sought an abortion, but Texas prohibited abortions unless the mother's life was in danger. "No legitimate doctor in Dallas would touch me," she discovered. "I found one doctor who offered to abort me for $500. Only he didn't have a license, and I was scared to turn my body over to him. So there I was—pregnant, unmarried, unemployed, alone, and stuck."[215]

Unaware of states that permitted abortions, McCorvey put her baby up for adoption. But the state law rankled her. When she met two women attorneys who recently graduated from law school and also disliked the law, they offered to take her case to challenge the law. She adopted the name Jane Roe to conceal her identity.

In *Roe v. Wade* in 1973, the Burger Court *extended the right to privacy from birth control to abortion*.[216] Justice Harry Blackmun surveyed the writings of doctors, theologians, and philosophers over the years and found that these thinkers did not agree when life begins. Therefore, the majority on the Court concluded that judges should not assert that life begins at any particular time, whether at conception, which would make a fetus a person and abortion murder, or at birth. Without this factor in the equation, a woman's privacy, or control, of her body became paramount.

The Court ruled that *women have a **right to abortion** during the first six months of pregnancy*. States can prohibit an abortion during the last three months because the fetus becomes viable—it can live outside the womb—at this point. (However, states must allow an abortion for a woman whose life is endangered by continuing her pregnancy.) Thus, the right is broad but not absolute.

The justices, as revealed in memos discovered years later, acknowledged that their division of the nine-month term was "legislative," but they saw this as a way to balance the rights of the mother in the early

AP/Wide World Photos

Norma McCorvey—"Jane Roe" of Roe v. Wade—switched sides and joined forces with Operation Rescue's Flip Benham in 1995.

stages of pregnancy with the rights of the fetus in the later stage.[217]

Although *Roe* was not the lead story in the news when it was decided, it has had an enormous impact on American politics. The Court's ruling invalidated the abortion laws of forty-nine states[218] and increased the number of abortions performed in the country (see Figure 14.1). It put abortion on the public agenda, and it galvanized conservative groups who saw it as a symbol of loosening social restraints at a time of rampaging social problems. Disparate groups, such as Roman Catholics and evangelical Protestants (and some Orthodox Jews), rural residents and urban ethnics, who rarely saw eye to eye, coalesced around this issue and exercised leverage within the Republican Party.

The right-to-life movement pressured presidents and senators to appoint justices and lower court judges who opposed the ruling. The movement also lobbied members of Congress and state legislatures to overturn or circumvent the ruling. Although Congress refused to pass constitutional amendments banning abortions or allowing states to regulate them, Congress and state legislatures did pass statutes limiting abortions in various ways.

The Burger Court invalidated most of these statutes,[219] but it upheld a major limitation. The Medicaid program, financed jointly by the federal and state governments, had paid for abortions for poor women. As a result, the program had paid for a third of the abortions in the country each year.[220] But Congress elimi-

Courtesy of Northern Sun, www.northernsun.com

The pro-choice movement uses this symbol, referring to the history of coat-hanger abortions in the back alleys before Roe. Sarah Weddington, an attorney who challenged Texas' law in Roe, often wears this button while traveling. Recently a young flight attendant asked, "What do you have against coat hangers?"

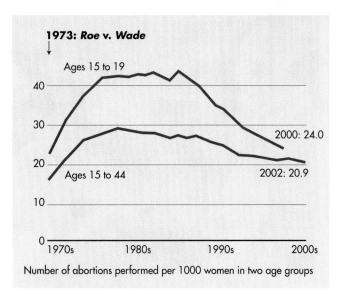

FIGURE 14.1 ■ Abortion Rate since *Roe*
The abortion rate climbed after Roe *and peaked in the 1980s. Since then it has declined steadily.*
SOURCE: *New York Times,* November 6, 2005.

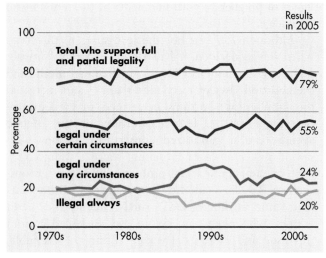

FIGURE 14.2 ■ Opinion toward the Legality of Abortions *People were asked, "Do you think abortions should be legal under any circumstances, legal only under certain circumstances, or illegal in all circumstances?"*
SOURCE: *New York Times,* November 6, 2005.

nated federal funding (except when pregnancy threatens the life of the mother or is the result of rape or incest), and thirty-three state legislatures eliminated state funding. In these states, poor women need to pay the entire cost. The Court upheld these laws, ruling that *governments have no obligation to finance abortions,* even if this means that some women cannot take advantage of their right to have them.[221]

For some women, these laws delay abortions while the women search for the money. For an estimated 20 percent of the women, these laws deny abortions because the women cannot obtain the money.[222]

Many people, including pro-choice advocates, support these bans because they dislike welfare spending. Yet according to an analysis of the states that do provide abortion funding for poor women, the states save money. For every $1 they spend on abortions, they save $4 in welfare and medical expenses in what would have been the first two years of the child's life.[223] They save much more over a longer period. Thus public distaste for welfare spending actually leads to more welfare spending in this area.

Presidents Reagan and George H. W. Bush sought justices who opposed *Roe,* and after they filled their fifth vacancy on the Court, pro-life advocates expected the Court to overturn it. Yet the Rehnquist Court did not overturn it.[224] In 1992, a bare majority reaffirmed the right to abortion.[225] At the same time, the majority *allowed more restrictions on the right—as long as the restrictions don't place an "undue burden" on the women seeking abortions.* In other words, states must permit abortions but can discourage them.[226]

Therefore, the majority upheld Pennsylvania's twenty-four-hour waiting period between the time a woman indicates her desire to have an abortion and the time a doctor can perform one. Although a twenty-four-hour waiting period is not a burden for many women, it can be for poor women who live in rural areas and must travel to cities for abortions. One Mississippi woman hitchhiked to the city and planned to sleep on outdoor furniture in the Kmart parking lot until the clinic offered to pay for her motel room.[227]

A waiting period can also affect teenagers. Some pro-life groups note the license numbers of cars driven to clinics by teenagers. After looking up the name and address of the family, they inform the parents in the hope that the parents will persuade or pressure their daughter to change her mind during the waiting period. (See the box "Teen Pregnancies and Abortions.")

The majority struck down Pennsylvania's requirement that a married woman notify her husband before having an abortion.[228] This was an undue burden because a woman who fears physical abuse from her husband would be deterred from seeking an abortion. Justice O'Connor wrote that a state "may not give to a man the kind of dominion over his wife that parents exercise over their children."

The Court upheld thirteen states' requirement that unmarried minors notify their parents and twenty-one states' requirement that unmarried minors obtain their parents' consent before having an abortion.[229] For either requirement, if a daughter does not want to tell her parents, she can seek permission from a judge. She must convince the judge that an abortion would be in her best interest or that she is mature enough to make the decision herself. If she is not mature enough, she must become a mother. These laws, Justice Thurgood Marshall wrote in dissent, force "a young woman in an already dire situation to choose between two fundamentally unacceptable alternatives: notifying a possibly dictatorial or even abusive parent or justifying her profoundly personal decision in an intimidating judicial proceeding to a black-robed stranger."[230]

Pro-life groups advocated these laws with the expectation that they would result in fewer abortions. They believed that many teenagers would go to their parents rather than face the forbidding atmosphere of a court hearing and that their parents would persuade or pressure them not to have the abortion. Some evidence indicates that the laws have had this effect.[231]

When teenagers do go to court, they routinely get waivers in some states but not in others. The Nebraska supreme court ruled that a fifteen-year-old was too immature to decide to have an abortion because, although she could discuss the consequences of keeping the baby or giving it up for adoption, discuss her philosophy of abortion, and explain the procedures involved, she was unable to explain the risks involved (even though the risks are less than those involved in giving birth).[232]

After the Rehnquist Court reaffirmed the right to abortion, pro-life groups tried to prohibit one abortion procedure known as "intact dilation and extraction" in medicine but referred to as "partial-birth abortion" in politics—a rhetorical success of antiabortion supporters. In this procedure, a doctor delivers the fetus except for the head, punctures the skull and drains the contents, and then removes the fetus from the woman. Because the procedure is gruesome, pro-life groups used it to sway undecided people in the abortion debate. Numerous states passed laws banning the procedure, but the Supreme Court struck down Nebraska's law in 2000.[233] The five-justice majority said that the law was too broad—the language might ban other methods as well—and did not provide an exception for the health of the mother.

Then Congress passed a similar law for the whole country, but it did provide an exception for the life of the mother (but not for the "health" of the mother).

In recent years, pro-life groups have quietly pressed state legislatures to enact extra stringent building codes for abortion clinics. These codes specify such things as the heights of ceilings, widths of hallways and doorways, dimensions of counseling rooms and recovery rooms, rates of air circulation, and the types and angles of jets in drinking fountains. (Although all states have construction codes for their buildings, these new laws apply only to abortion clinics.) Some codes require equipment or levels of staffing, such as a registered nurse rather than a licensed practical nurse, beyond what is normal in these clinics. Although the stated goal is health and safety, the real purpose is to drive up the clinics' expenses so they have to increase their patients' fees to the point where many women can no longer afford to have an abortion.[234] When South Car-

President Bush, surrounded by the congressional sponsors, all men, signs the Partial Birth Abortion Ban Act.

© Kevin Lamarque/Reuters/Landov

Of American teenagers aged fifteen to nineteen, about 10 percent become pregnant, and about 35 percent of these have an abortion. Our teen pregnancy rate is higher than that of every other developed country except Russia. The high rate is not because American teens are having more sex but because they are using fewer contraceptives. In European countries, contraceptives are widely encouraged and readily available.

However, our teen pregnancy rate has been falling. After peaking in 1990, it has dropped sharply. The primary reason is not abstinence; delayed onset of sexual activity accounts for just a quarter of this decline. Increasing use of contraceptives (though still less than in other countries) accounts for three-quarters of the drop.

The teen pregnancy rate of African Americans is more than twice that of whites who are not Hispanics. The rate of Latinos is almost twice that of whites who are not Hispanics.

The teen pregnancy rates also vary from region to region and state to state. The rates are highest in the South and Southwest and lowest in the North Central and Northeast regions. The conservatism of the South may discourage contraception, but it evidently does not prevent teen sex or pregnancies. On the other hand, the liberalism of the North Central and Northeast may prompt more teens to use contraception.

The American teen abortion rate is also higher than that of most other developed countries. However, the abortion *rate*, which is the number of abortions per one thousand teens, and the abortion *ratio*, which is the percentage of those teens who get pregnant who have an abortion, have both been falling. Since 1986, the abortion ratio has dropped from 46 percent to 33 percent. That is, 46 percent of teens who got pregnant in 1986 had abortions; just 33 percent did in 2000. More gave birth, perhaps because abortions

became more restricted due to state laws requiring parental notification and consent, or less available due to fewer providers or perhaps because single parenthood became less stigmatized. But the decline has occurred only among whites who are not Hispanics.

African Americans have the highest abortion ratio, at 41 percent, and Latinos have the lowest, at 28 per cent. Whites who are not Hispanics are in between, at 34 percent.

The most urban states, where abortions are more available, have the highest abortion rates.

For all racial and ethnic groups, older teens (eighteen to nineteen years old) had more pregnancies and abortions than younger teens (fifteen to seventeen years old) because the older teens are more sexually active.

SOURCE: Based on statistics for 2000 from the Alan Guttmacher Institute, 2004.

---

olina's law, which mandates twenty-seven pages of requirements just for abortion clinics, was challenged, a lower court upheld the law and the Supreme Court refused to hear the case, thus allowing the law to stand.

Despite dissatisfaction by activists on both sides of this controversy—pro-life groups are disappointed that the conservative Supreme Court has upheld the right to abortion whereas pro-choice groups are critical that it has upheld some restrictions on abortion—it is worth noting that the nonelected, nonmajoritarian Supreme Court has come closer to forging a policy reflective of public opinion than most politicians have. Polls show that the public is ambivalent. A majority believes that abortion is murder, but a two-thirds majority opposes banning it. This two-thirds majority favors letting women choose. (Over half of those who believe that abortion is murder nonetheless favor letting women choose.)[235] Thus many people support the right to abortion but are uncomfortable with it and willing to allow restrictions on it. The Court's doctrine articulates this position.[236]

But the Court's rulings are not necessarily the final word in this controversy, as they have not been the final word in some other controversies. Frustrated by

the Court's refusal to overturn *Roe,* activists in the pro-life movement (not most of the pro-life supporters) adopted more militant tactics. First they targeted abortion clinics. Organizations such as Operation Rescue engaged in civil disobedience, blockading clinics and harassing workers and patients as they came and went. Some activists sprayed chemicals inside clinics, ruining carpets and fabrics and leaving a stench that made the clinics unusable. Such incidents occurred fifty times in one year alone.[237]

Then activists targeted doctors, nurses, and other workers of the clinics. Operation Rescue ran a training camp in Florida that instructed members how to use public records to locate personal information about clinic employees, how to tail them to their homes, and how to organize demonstrations at their homes. Activists put up "Wanted" posters, with a doctor's picture, name, address, and phone number and then encouraged people to harass the doctor, the doctor's spouse, and even their children. (One thirteen-year-old was confronted in a restaurant and told that he was going to burn in hell.)[238] Letters containing powder and threatening death by anthrax were sent to over one hundred doctors and clinics.[239] Some extremists even advocated killing the doctors. One minister wrote a book—*A Time to Kill*—and marketed a bumper sticker reading "execute abortionists–murderers."[240]

In this climate, three doctors, two clinic receptionists, and one clinic volunteer were killed, and seven other doctors, employees, and volunteers were wounded.[241] Numerous clinics were firebombed.

The tactics have had their intended effect on doctors.[242] They have made the practice of providing abortions seem dangerous and undesirable. Fewer medical schools offer abortion classes, fewer hospitals provide abortion training, fewer doctors study abortion procedures, and fewer gynecologists and obstetricians, despite most being pro-choice, perform abortion operations.[243] As a result, the number of abortion providers dropped from 2908 to 1819 in the 1980s and 1990s.[244]

One pro-life leader proclaimed, "We've found the weak link is the doctor."[245] Another observed, "When you get the doctors out, you can have all the laws on the books you want and it doesn't mean a thing."[246]

Abortions remain available in most metropolitan centers but not in most rural areas. Eighty-six percent of U.S. counties, containing 32 percent of the American women aged fifteen to forty-four, have no doctor who performs abortions. Some states have only one and others have only two cities where women can obtain abortions.[247] Nevertheless, an abortion is still one of the most common surgical procedures for American women.

The future of abortion rights is unsettled. The Roberts Court is expected to be more conservative than the Rehnquist Court. This prospect has emboldened state legislatures. South Dakota, which had no doctors who perform abortions—Minnesota doctors flew in to the state's sole facility—banned abortions in 2005. In clear violation of *Roe,* the law invited the Court to overturn the landmark ruling. Yet the law spurred a debate within the pro-life movement. Some factions prefer an incremental strategy, passing numerous restrictions that might go unnoticed by most people, rather than a frontal attack that might prompt a backlash by the majority. Indeed, South Dakota's law galvanized opponents, who petitioned to put the issue on the 2006 ballot. Voters repealed the law, apparently because the law allowed no exceptions to the ban.

Birth Control, Revisited

Although the pro-life movement has been frustrated by its inability to overturn *Roe,* it has been stimulated by the conservatism of the Bush administration and the appointment of new justices to the Supreme Court. Now the movement has trained its sights on contraception in addition to abortion.[248]

Initially the pro-life movement was dominated by Catholics, whose church opposes contraceptives. The movement's leaders muted their views to avoid scaring off potential supporters. (Ninety-three percent of all Americans, and 90 percent of Catholics, supported contraceptives in 2005.)[249] The pro-life movement was joined by conservative Protestants who did not oppose birth control. Recently, however, more movement leaders, Protestants as well as Catholics, have voiced opposition to contraception. The president of the American Life League declared, "We oppose all forms of contraception."[250] Now religious interest groups, such as the Christian Coalition and Focus on the Family, address birth control. Increasing numbers of evangelical theologians oppose it and evangelical churches discuss it. A cluster of representatives and senators spearheads congressional efforts against some forms of birth control.

These groups have not only pushed Congress to suspend sale of the abortion pill (RU-486 or Mifeprex), they have also pushed the federal and state governments to adopt rules and laws making the emergency contraception—"morning after" or "Plan B"—pill more difficult to obtain. They would prevent pharmacies from selling the pill over the counter (that is, without a prescription), allow pharmacists to refuse filling prescriptions for it, and allow Catholic hospitals to refuse giving it to rape victims. (Although the medical profession insists that this is a contraceptive pill, the Catholic Church claims that it is an abortion pill.) However, the Food and Drug Administration (FDA) finally allowed sale of the pill over the counter to women eighteen and older in 2006.

In response to these groups, sympathetic members of Congress have spoken out against condoms, charging that they don't prevent pregnancy or disease to the extent people believe.

The Bush administration has shifted federal family planning policy from contraception to abstinence—from sex education, including information about birth control, to abstinence education—at least for individuals who aren't married. For 2007, the administration budgeted more than $200 million for abstinence education. The administration has also shifted federal aid to foreign countries for AIDS prevention from contraception to abstinence.[251]

President Bush, when asked whether he supports *the right* to use contraceptives, has refused to answer.[252] (His father, as a young member of Congress, was so insistent that foreign aid include contraceptives that he was nicknamed "Rubbers" by other members of the committee.)

Current opposition to contraception makes it difficult for the two sides in the abortion controversy to find common ground. Some on each side had called

John Lawrence (left) and Tyron Garner appealed their sodomy convictions to the Supreme Court, which invalidated state sodomy laws.

for greater availability of contraceptives so there would be less need for abortions. But this common ground is giving way as more who oppose abortion also oppose contraception.

What all this indicates is that for some in the pro-life movement it's not so much about abortion as it is about sex. One leader said, "We see a direct connection between the practice of contraception and the practice of abortion." They both reflect "an anti-child mindset."[253] Both serve "the selfish demands of the individual."[254] The president of the Southern Baptist Theological Seminary stated, "The effective separation of sex from procreation may be one of the most important defining marks of our age—and one of the most ominous."[255] Their goal is to reverse the sexual revolution of the 1960s, when "the pill" became commonplace, and instead to confine sex to marriage.

This debate reflects sharp cultural differences between European countries and the United States. In those countries, contraceptives are readily available, and unintended pregnancies and abortions are less frequent. There, "these things are in the open, and the only issue is to be careful. Here in the U.S., people are still arguing about whether it's O.K. to have sex."[256]

Homosexuality

For years, states prohibited adultery, fornication, and sodomy. Reflecting Christian doctrine, the statutes targeted various forms of nonmarital sex and nonprocreative sex (including masturbation and withdrawal prior to ejaculation).[257] After the "sexual revolution"

of the 1960s, many states repealed these statutes. However, most states retained their sodomy statutes, which prohibited oral or anal sex (performed by heterosexuals or homosexuals) because of the legislators' disgust toward homosexual practices and opposition to the emerging gay rights movement.[258] Although these statutes were primarily symbolic, they were occasionally enforced against homosexuals.

The Supreme Court was reluctant to extend the right to privacy to protect homosexual practices. When police delivered a summons to the residents of a house and discovered two men violating Georgia's law, police arrested them. Although prosecutors did not file charges, one of the men sued to have the courts declare the law unconstitutional. In 1986, the Rehnquist Court refused to do so.[259]

However, in 2003, the Rehnquist Court reversed itself. When a neighbor phoned a false report of an armed intruder, police responded and discovered two men violating Texas's law. The men were arrested, jailed, and fined $200. The Texas courts affirmed their conviction, but in *Lawrence* v. *Texas,* the Supreme Court overturned it and *invalidated the sodomy laws* of the thirteen states that still had them.[260] In a broad opinion, Justice Anthony Kennedy wrote, "Liberty presumes an autonomy of self that includes freedom of thought, belief, expression, and certain intimate conduct." Therefore, homosexuals are entitled to "dignity" and "respect for their private lives." In dissent, Justice Antonin Scalia accused the majority of taking sides in the "culture war." Yet a sizable shift in public opinion had occurred in the seventeen years since the 1986 ruling.[261] As more homosexuals "came out," they gained greater acceptance from straights. Most Americans say they know someone who is gay or lesbian, and a majority say they are sympathetic to the gay and lesbian communities. This shift in public opinion was reflected in the numerous states that repealed their sodomy statutes after the 1986 ruling (even though the ruling allowed the states to keep the statutes). Thus, in the *Lawrence* case, according to one law professor, "The Court legitimized and endorsed a cultural consensus."[262]

Although the majority in *Lawrence* said the ruling would not necessarily extend to same-sex marriages, the dissenters feared that establishing a right to privacy for homosexual practices would indeed lead to a right to marry for homosexual couples. Already there had been some attempts to create this right. Although most gay and lesbian groups, fearing a public backlash against the gay rights movement, had been reluctant to push for this right, some homosexual couples had filed lawsuits. In 1993, the Hawaii Supreme Court implied that same-sex couples had a right to marry, prompting the state's voters to amend their constitution to override their court.

The Hawaii ruling signaled opponents that some states might allow same-sex marriages, which would prompt homosexual couples to marry there and then return home as married couples. Under the full faith and credit clause of the Constitution, states usually must recognize the public records and judicial proceedings of other states. Although this clause might not apply to same-sex marriages,[263] opponents worried that it might apply. Congress adopted the Defense of Marriage Act, which allows states to disregard same-sex marriages performed in other states. (About forty states have passed laws to do so.) The act also forbids federal recognition of same-sex marriages and thus denies federal benefits, such as Social Security, to same-sex couples.[264]

Although marriage was a fantasy for most homosexuals, their lack of legal rights was a cause for concern and a source of anger. In the 1980s and 1990s, the AIDS epidemic swept gay communities across the United States. "Lovers, friends, and AIDS 'buddies' were spooning food, emptying bedpans, holding wracked bodies through the night. They were assuming the burdens of marriage at its hardest."[265] Yet gay partners had no legal rights. They encountered problems involving health insurance, hospital visitation, disability benefits, funeral planning, and estate settling. Gays were often unable to participate fully in these life-and-death matters due to legal impediments that did not exist for married couples. In the same decades, lesbians gave birth using donated sperm, and gays got children through adoption and surrogate mothers, yet homosexual couples realized that they did not have legal protections for their families. These developments increased the calls for legal rights commensurate with the rights of heterosexual couples.[266]

In 1999, the Vermont supreme court ruled that the state must either legalize same-sex marriages or equalize the benefits received by same-sex couples and traditional married couples. The legislature decided to equalize the benefits, such as family leave, bereavement leave, health insurance, pension benefits, and inheritance rights. To implement this policy, the legislature established "civil unions," with procedures for couples to become official partners (similar to marriage) and procedures for them to dissolve their relationship (similar to divorce). The civil unions also establish the rights to visit a partner who is in the hospital, make medical decisions for a partner who is ill, arrange the funeral and burial for a partner who dies, and receive wrongful death benefits for a partner who dies.

Although these civil unions provide most of what regular marriages provide, the unions do not apply when couples move from Vermont to other states. And they do not apply to federal benefits. By one count, 1138 federal laws apply to married couples that do not apply to unmarried couples. Some impose responsibilities; most provide rights and benefits, such as tax breaks.[267] Also, of course, the unions do not provide the symbolism that regular marriages do.

So the pressure for same-sex marriages continued. In 2004, the Massachusetts Supreme Judicial Court, hearing a suit brought by seven couples, ruled that same-sex marriages were allowed under the state's constitution. Otherwise, same-sex couples are relegated to "a different status. . . . The history of our nation has demonstrated that separate is seldom, if ever, equal."[268]

By permission of Mike Luckovich and Creators Syndicate, Inc.

Holding their twin daughters, this couple exchanges marriage vows in San Francisco before same-sex marriages were invalidated there.

In quick succession, officials in San Francisco; Portland, Oregon; and smaller cities in New York, New Jersey, and New Mexico were inspired to issue marriage licenses to same-sex couples. State courts halted the licenses but not until thousands of beaming couples had married and posed for news photos. Although the marriages were pronounced invalid, the head of the Lambda Legal Defense and Education Fund observed, "You can't put the toothpaste back in the tube."[269]

There was an immediate backlash. Polls showed that a majority of the public opposed same-sex marriages. President Bush proposed a constitutional amendment. One congressional sponsor claimed, "There is a master plan out there from those who want to destroy the institution of marriage." (However, Massachusetts, where same-sex marriage is lawful, has the nation's lowest divorce rate.)[270] Another senator, comparing the threat of gay marriage to that of terrorism, called the amendment "the ultimate homeland security." An evangelist predicted that "the family as it has been known for five millennia will crumble, presaging the fall of Western civilization itself."[271] Yet there was more fire from the pulpits than there was in the pews. Evangelical leaders expressed puzzlement and frustration that there was no loud outcry from their faithful.[272] But many people who oppose gay marriage do not feel threatened by it. Consequently, the amendment failed to pass. Nevertheless, voters in about half the states adopted such amendments to their state constitution, most by a wide margin. Conservatives continued their calls for an amendment to the U.S. Constitution.

Despite many people's objections, gay rights leaders predict that once homosexuals begin to marry and straights see that "the sky doesn't fall," people will stop opposing their marriages.[273] Indeed, the initial backlash against Massachusetts' same-sex marriages dissipated. Maine and New Jersey passed domestic-partnership laws that formally recognize same-sex partnerships and provide them some rights associated with marriage. California passed a domestic-partnership law that provides them almost all rights associated with marriage.

Yet the Supreme Court refused to hear a case challenging Florida's law that forbids gays and lesbians from adopting children.

Meanwhile, homosexuals have gained equal benefits at some workplaces. Large corporations especially have been willing to grant health care packages to same-sex couples as a way to attract and retain good workers. Some cities and states also offer these benefits.

Yet homosexuals remain vulnerable at other workplaces. In most states, employees can be fired merely for being homosexual. Although some state and local legislatures have passed laws barring discrimination in employment, housing, credit, insurance, and public accommodations, Congress rejected a bill barring discrimination in employment at the same time it passed the Defense of Marriage Act.[274]

Congress previously blocked President Clinton's pledge to issue an executive order barring discrimination against homosexuals in the military.[275] Since World War II, the military has rejected recruits who admit to being homosexual and discharged troops who are found to be homosexual. According to the military, having homosexuals in the trenches or on ships would undermine the discipline and morale essential for combat.[276] However, Western European countries, Canada, Japan, and Israel, which has a battle-tested military, all tolerate homosexuals in their services.[277]

But strident opposition from military officials and members of Congress forced President Clinton to accept a compromise, a policy called "don't ask, don't tell." The military (including the Reserves and the National Guard) is not allowed to ask questions about sexual orientation on enlistment or security questionnaires but is allowed to discharge members for statements admitting homosexuality or conduct reflecting homosexuality (or bisexuality). Such conduct is defined broadly to encompass not only sexual actions but also holding hands, dancing, or trying to marry someone of the same sex. The restrictions apply off base as well as on. They do not encompass reading gay publications, associating with gay people, frequenting gay bars or churches, or marching in gay rights parades. (These activities all reflect First Amendment rights.)

The policy has not helped much. Many commanders have seemed confused, and some have been unwilling to accept the policy; they continue to ask and discharge. In fact, more homosexuals have been discharged since the policy went into effect than before.[278] Over nine thousand have been booted since 1993.[279] In the run-up to the Iraq War, even fluent Arabic speakers, who were in very short supply, were discharged.[280] The government estimates that it has cost $200 million to recruit and train replacements for these troops.[281]

Right to Die

The Court has broadened the right to privacy to provide a limited right to die. When Nancy Cruzan's car skidded off an icy road and flipped into a ditch in 1983, doctors were able to save her life but not her brain. She never regained consciousness. She lived in a vegetative state, similar to a coma, and was fed through a tube. Twenty-five at the time of the accident, she was expected to live another thirty years. When her parents asked the doctors to remove the tube, the hospital objected, and the state of Missouri, despite paying $130,000 a year to support her, also objected. This issue, difficult enough in itself, became entangled in other issues. Pro-life groups contended that denying life support was analogous to abortion; disability groups, claiming that her condition was merely a disability, argued that withholding food and water from her would lead to withholding treatment from others with disabilities.[282] (Recall the debate recounted in Chapter 4 over removing the tube from Terri Schiavo.)

Her parents filed suit and when the battle over her life support reached the Supreme Court, the Rehnquist Court established a limited **right to die**.[283] The justices ruled that *individuals can refuse medical treatment, including food and water, even if this means they will die.* But individuals must make their decision while competent and alert. They can also act in advance, preparing a "living will" or designating another person as a proxy to make the decision if they are unable to.

After the Court's decision, Cruzan's parents returned to a Missouri court with evidence that their daughter would prefer death to being kept alive by machines. Three of Cruzan's coworkers testified that they recalled conversations in which she said she never would want to live "like a vegetable." The court granted her parents' request to remove her feeding tube. She died twelve days later.

Although the legal doctrine seems clear, difficult practical problems persist. Many people do not make their desires known in advance. Approximately ten thousand people in irreversible comas now did not announce their decision beforehand.[284] Some people who do indicate their decision beforehand waver when they face death. Some doctors, who are in the habit of prolonging life even when their patients have no chance of enjoying life, resist the patients' decision.[285]

The Rehnquist Court *refused* patients' pleas *to expand the limited right into a broader right to obtain assistance in committing suicide.*[286] The Court drew a distinction between stopping treatment and assisting suicide; individuals have a right to demand the former but not the latter. The justices seemed tentative, as is typical with an issue new to the courts. Chief Justice Rehnquist emphasized, "Our holding permits this debate to continue, as it should in a democratic society."

Oregon decided to allow assisted suicide. The law provides some safeguards. The patient must submit written requests in the presence of two witnesses, get two doctors to concur that he or she has less than six months to live, and wait fifteen days. The pro-life Bush administration challenged Oregon's law, claiming that individual states cannot allow assisted suicide. But the Supreme Court rebuffed the Bush administration and *allowed the state law to stand.*[287] So far, a modest number of terminally ill patients—thirty-eight in 2005—have taken advantage of the law.[288]

A majority of the public favors a right to assisted suicide,[289] but conservative religious groups oppose one. They insist that people, even when facing extreme pain and no hope of recovery, should not take their life. In addition, ethicists worry that patients will be pressured to give up their life because of the costs,

In Ashland, Oregon, Steve Mason suffered from terminal lung cancer and waited until he could no longer eat or sleep. Then he took the lethal drugs (on the table) prescribed by his doctor. He said, "I've lived my life with dignity. I want to go out the same way."

to their family or health care provider, of continuing it. The ethicists fear that a right will become a duty.

Meanwhile, the practice, even where officially illegal, is widely condoned, much as abortion was before *Roe*. Almost a fifth of the doctors who treat cancer patients in Michigan admitted in a survey that they have assisted suicide, and over half of two thousand doctors who treat AIDS patients in San Francisco also admitted that they have done so.[290]

Implications for Civil Liberties from the War on Terrorism

Although the Bush administration was lax about the terrorist threat before September 11, 2001, since then it has feared further attacks and has investigated and pursued possible terrorists around the world. The administration's aggressive tactics raise implications for civil liberties.

Immediately after 9/11, President Bush promised that the war on terrorism wouldn't turn into a war on Muslims, and he appeared in mosques and with Muslim groups. However, within days, the government singled out Muslims for interrogation, detention, and deportation, and it shut down Muslim charities on the assumption that they were funding terrorist cells. Eventually, it trumped up criminal charges against some Muslims, prosecuting and convicting them on the basis of little evidence.[291]

The administration also adopted systematic policies and programs to thwart radical Islamists. This section will address interrogation of detainees, surveillance of Americans and foreigners, and provisions of the USA PATRIOT Act. The "You Are There" and "Epilogue" sections discuss detention of suspected terrorists. These all pose the question, Can we wage an effective war against radical Islamists and still maintain our civil liberties?

Interrogations

Under our law, when police interrogate criminal suspects they must advise the suspects of their rights to remain silent and to have counsel, and they must stop the questioning whenever the suspects express a desire to exercise these rights. Any statements by the suspects are supposed to be voluntary rather than coerced. These strictures, of course, don't apply outside the United States or to enemy combatants captured in a war. Nevertheless, our rules for routine interrogations of criminal defendants create norms of behavior, reflecting standards of civility and decency that we have come to expect. Do no-holds-barred methods of interrogation of suspected terrorists violate these norms and standards? Might they undermine our methods of interrogation of criminal defendants?

Methods

As suspected terrorists were rounded up in Afghanistan, Pakistan, and elsewhere, they were transported to detention facilities and interrogated aggressively. The Bush administration authorized procedures it calls **"stress and duress"** and which others call "torture lite."[292] Prisoners may be locked, naked and wet, in a cold cubicle in which they cannot stand, sit, or lie. They have to kneel or squat in "stress positions." They might be bound and have a hood put over their head or dark goggles put over their eyes to keep them disoriented. Or they might be subjected to bright lights, perhaps strobe lights, and loud noise—cacophonous sounds such as babies' cries, cats' meows, and heavy metal music—to keep them awake. (Interrogators also experimented with children's songs, such as "Barney's" song, to drive them crazy. We haven't heard whether interrogators tried Barry Manilow's albums yet.) If prisoners doze, they will be awakened. (One suspect was sleep-deprived for twenty hours a day for seven weeks.[293]) They may be beaten. They may be fed irregularly. With their food, they may be drugged, perhaps with a mixture of marijuana and sodium pentothal ("truth serum") to lower their inhibitions and methamphetamines to make them talk so fast that they cannot think to lie. This "stress and duress" process, according to one government official, is "not pulling out fingernails, but it's pretty brutal."[294]

Some prisoners were shackled for twenty-four hours and left in their own excrement. When others refused to eat as a protest against their indefinite confinement, they were strapped into a chair that immobilizes their legs, arms, shoulders, and head, and they were force fed through a tube pushed up their nose and down their throat.

Other tactics use sexual humiliation and embarrassment. Some prisoners were wrapped in the Israeli flag and forced to watch homosexual pornography.[295] As the photos from the Abu Ghraib prison in Iraq showed, those prisoners were stripped and forced into various positions. At least one was stripped and led on a leash by a female guard. At Guantanamo Bay, some female interrogators rubbed their breasts against detainees and squeezed the genitals of detainees.[296] One wiped red ink, which she said was her menstrual blood, on a detainee. By violating sexual taboos, the interrogators tried to make the men feel unclean and unable to pray to their god for strength.[297]

For key suspects, interrogators have used waterboarding, which simulates drowning. The suspect is bound to a board, which is inclined so his head is lower than his feet. Then water is poured up his nose.[298]

International law forbids torture, which is generally defined as acts that intentionally inflict "severe pain or suffering, whether physical or mental."[299] International law also forbids "outrages upon personal dignity, in particular humiliating and degrading treatment."[300] Domestic law prohibits torture as well, and the Uniform Code of Military Justice commands military personnel not to engage in "cruelty" or "maltreatment" toward prisoners or to threaten or assault them.

The Bush administration claims that its tactics don't amount to torture.[301] After 9/11, it secretly redefined torture, narrowing the definition to pain

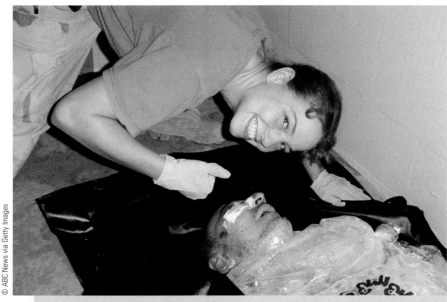

© ABC News via Getty Images

An American soldier poses with the body of an Iraqi prisoner who died during his interrogation at Abu Ghraib prison.

equivalent to that which produces the impairment of a function, the failure of an organ, or death. Under this definition, the "stress and duress" procedures, including most beatings, would not be considered torture. Of course, the administration can't unilaterally alter the definition of torture. But its definition allows the administration to insist that we don't condone or practice torture.

Many people would countenance torture, and certainly "torture lite," against terrorists if there is a "ticking time bomb" and lives could be saved. Many people may also approve such treatment if there is a less urgent situation and a possible future attack could be prevented. But, once rough treatment is used, there is a tendency for it to be extended to other enemies and other situations.

As the insurgency in Iraq proved difficult to control, American officials became frustrated. A general who had overseen the interrogations at Guantanamo Bay was sent to Baghdad to introduce similar tactics there.[302] But many arrestees in Iraq were neither terrorists nor insurgents. When attacks occurred, the American military, adopting a tactic used by the Israeli military for suicide bombings, conducted a sweep of the area, rounding up all men, roughly interrogating them, and weeding out the ones who seemed innocent.[303] Intelligence officers have estimated that 70 to 90 percent of the men who have been arrested and interrogated in Iraq have been innocent.[304] Yet they have been subjected to harsh treatment.

Another problem is that it becomes difficult for interrogators using rough methods to restrain themselves when their approach isn't producing any results.[305] We know that severe beatings have been administered to detainees (and burning cigarettes have been put in their ears).[306] As many as thirty-four prisoners may have been killed during interrogations in Afghanistan and Iraq.[307]

In response to the photos of the horrors at Abu Ghraib, Congress adopted a law that prohibits cruel treatment of our prisoners.[308] The law was proposed by Senator John McCain (R-Ariz.), who was tortured during the Vietnam War. The administration opposed the proposal, but the president was forced to sign it into law by congressional support for it. Even so, the president said, essentially, that he wouldn't feel bound by the law.[309]

Renditions

For some important prisoners, the government has arranged with countries to interrogate the prisoners for us. In a procedure called **rendition**, the CIA seizes suspects in foreign countries and whisks them away to other countries whose intelligence services have ties with the CIA. Islamic extremists have been seized not only from the Middle East, but also from countries in Africa, Asia, and Europe and taken to Egypt, Jordan, Morocco, Saudi Arabia, Syria, and Uzbekistan, all of which are known to use torture.[310] "We don't kick the [expletive] out of them," an American official said. "We send them to other countries so *they* can kick the [expletive] out of them."[311]

The transfers are made in secret, using unmarked airplanes in remote corners of airports at night. The transfers ignore legal formalities, such as extradition procedures, and have defied national laws. Six suspects were taken from Bosnia even though the Bosnian supreme court had ordered them released. The secrecy reduces court battles and minimizes the publicity that could tip off suspects' comrades or inflame public opinion, especially where the government feels threatened by rebellious groups with numerous sympathizers. An official in Indonesia, which has the world's largest Muslim population, said, "We can't be seen cooperating too closely with the United States."[312] People in Italy, Germany, and Sweden expressed outrage when they learned that the CIA had snatched suspects from their countries.

Renditions also appear to violate international agreements signed by the United States.[313]

Secret Prisons

For its most important prisoners, the government established a covert prison system run by the CIA. These "black sites," as they were known, were located in eight countries, including Afghanistan, Thailand, and several unnamed Eastern European countries. Until the *Washington Post* broke this story, these prisons were unknown to all but a handful of government officials.[314] And, of course, they were unknown to the International Red Cross, which monitors prisoners' treatment. (In September, 2006, the administration announced that these prisons were being shut down.)

Surveillance

Soon after 9/11, the government began to intercept international calls and domestic calls of American citizens without judicial approval.[315] The **National Security Agency**, which is our largest intelligence agency, conducts this program. The NSA was established in secret in 1952 to obtain intelligence of our adversaries' communications. Located at Fort Meade in Maryland, the agency was so secretive that for years the government refused to acknowledge its existence. (Washingtonians joked that "NSA" stood for No Such Agency.) Today its existence is acknowledged, and the huge agency has its own off-ramp from the Baltimore-Washington Parkway, marked "NSA Employees Only."

The agency operates at least two programs relevant here, one wiretapping international calls and another monitoring domestic calls.

Wiretapping Calls

The NSA wiretaps phone calls and e-mails between people in the United States and people in foreign countries. It uses computer searches to look for telltale words and phrases that might be used by terrorists.

When the revelations about this program broke, President Bush said, "[I]f you're talking to a member of al-Qaeda, we want to know why."[316] Vice President Cheney downplayed the revelations. "If you're calling Aunt Sadie in Paris, we're probably not really interested." A White House representative emphasized that the NSA was recording calls "from very bad people to very bad people."[317] Apparently, however, the program is more extensive than the administration admits. Thousands of ordinary Americans have had their conversations recorded or their e-mails read.[318]

The snooping occurs without judicial authorization. The Foreign Intelligence Surveillance Act requires the government to obtain authorization from the Surveillance (FISA) Court, as explained in Chapter 13. The law allows warrantless wiretapping for just three days. After 9/11, the administration sought congressional authority for warrantless wiretapping for long periods, but Congress refused to grant this authority.[319] Although it is relatively easy to get a warrant from the FISA Court, the government must have some evidence to justify its request. Because the Bush administration was conducting "a fishing expedition," it could not get a warrant.

Monitoring Calls

The NSA also monitors calls between people within the United States. (It is not clear whether the agency monitors long-distance calls only or local calls as well.) The agency has direct access to the data from at least some major communications companies. The data include the caller's and receiver's numbers and the date, time, and duration of the call.

The goal is to uncover hidden terrorists through social network analysis. Al-Qaeda is so amorphous and diffuse that it is difficult for outsiders to identify the members. By correlating calls, computers map patterns of interactions among people. If the government knows that one person is a member of al-Qaeda, the analysis might be able to identify others who are members as well.

Initial reports indicated that the monitoring program, unlike the wiretapping program, did not access the content of the calls. However, later reports indicate that the monitoring program does in fact access the content of the calls also. As a result, the government has examined the calls of "tens of thousands" of Americans without seeking judicial authorization.[320]

It is unclear whether either the wiretapping program or the monitoring program has identified any terrorists.

Most legal experts believe that the wiretapping program violates the Fourth Amendment and the FISA law. If the monitoring program accesses the content of the calls, it probably violates the Fourth Amendment and the FISA law also. If it doesn't access the content of the calls, it probably doesn't violate the Fourth Amendment, although it might violate federal laws protecting the privacy of phone records. However, our conclusions must be tentative because at the time of this edition, there were more questions than answers about this program.

For examination of other governmental measures to fight the war on terrorism, see the box "The USA PATRIOT Act."

For government policies involving interrogation and surveillance, addressed here, and detention, addressed in

THE USA PATRIOT ACT

Forty-five days after the terrorist attacks of September 11, 2001, President Bush signed the Uniting and Strengthening America by Providing Appropriate Tools Required to Intercept and Obstruct Terrorism Act—the USA PATRIOT Act. Under pressure to act decisively, Congress passed the act in a rush—with few hearings, no committee report, and little public debate—and at a time when senators were evacuated from their offices because of anthrax contamination. Yet the act has significant implications for civil liberties.

The act, which is 342 pages long, is a series of amendments expanding previous acts. (This makes it difficult for students to research.)

The act focuses on domestic intelligence gathering. It establishes the foundation for unprecedented surveillance within the United States, and it shifts the FBI's primary function from solving crimes to gathering intelligence within the United States. (The CIA and other intelligence agencies gather intelligence outside the United States.)

The act includes the following provisions:

- *Information sharing:* After revelations about illegal spying and harassment of antiwar and civil rights protesters, including Martin Luther King Jr., came to light in the 1970s, Congress erected barriers between the FBI and the CIA, preventing the agencies from sharing their information. The FBI was supposed to solve domestic crimes, and the CIA was supposed to gather foreign intelligence. And the FBI was not supposed to employ the CIA's surveillance techniques against peaceful protesters. Today such barriers could hamper efforts to nab dangerous terrorists. Because terrorist cells can operate both inside and outside our borders, each agency could obtain useful information—the FBI inside and the CIA outside—but be unaware of the other agency's information. The Patriot Act lowers these barriers.

- *"Roving wiretaps":* An old law allowed wiretaps only on particular phones—that is, on certain numbers—known to be used by criminal suspects. Today many people use multiple phones, even disposable phones; sometimes criminals do so to avoid wiretaps. The Patriot Act allows "roving wiretaps," which authorize surveillance on all phones used by particular persons, wherever they might be.[1]

- *Electronic communications and financial data:* The Patriot Act extends surveillance to devices that identify the senders and receivers of phone calls, technology that identifies Internet sites visited and key words used in search engines, and technology that identifies header information (to, from, and subject lines) in e-mail messages. Although the act does not permit surveillance of the body of email messages, a related act passed three months later does encourage Internet service providers to turn over the contents of their customers' private messages.[2] The act also extends surveillance to financial data—where people make and spend money, including what they buy online, and what they borrow and invest. FBI field supervisors, without any judicial approval, are authorized to request this data from the companies that have it. The FBI has requested such information more than 30,000 times per year. After the investigation, the information is dumped into mammoth data banks and stored indefinitely. The Bush administration reversed an established policy requiring the FBI to destroy its files on innocent Americans when it closed its investigation.[3]

- *"Sneak-and-peek searches":* Normally, law enforcement officers are expected to knock and announce themselves when executing a search warrant at someone's home or office. This practice notifies the occupants about the search so that they can contest its legality in court afterward. They can also point out any mistakes—sometimes the officers get the wrong address—and monitor the search in case the officers exceed the bounds prescribed by the warrant. In contrast, "sneak-and-peek searches" allow the officers to enter when no one is present and to conduct a search, usually taking photos (but occasionally seizing things). They do not need to notify the subject of the search until much later. Thus, they can continue to conduct their investigation without the subject's knowledge of it. Although some courts allowed these searches to a limited degree previously, the Patriot Act expands their use.

- *Tangible items:* The Patriot Act lowers the standard of proof required for the FBI to obtain court orders for tangible items such as papers, documents, records, and books. These provisions encompass bookstore and library records. FBI agents can get the records of the books bought or checked out and of the Internet sites visited on library computers. (Some 9/11 terrorists communicated via library computers.) The act forbids the bookstores and libraries from notifying their patrons that they are under investigation.

The act overrides state privacy laws passed after publicity about the FBI's "Library Awareness Program" during the Cold War. From the 1960s through the 1980s, FBI agents checked the reading habits of library patrons with Eastern European accents or those suspected of left-wing leanings.

The library provisions of the Patriot Act have been among the most controversial. The American Library Association opposes them, and some librarians have rebelled against them by posting warning signs to notify their patrons or by destroying library records at the end of each day.

The impact of these provisions is unclear. A survey of libraries revealed that at least 545 reported requests by federal or local law enforcement officers during the first year of the act's existence. But Bush's first attorney general called the librarians "hysterical" and insisted that the act's provisions had not been used at all,[4] and Bush's second attorney general also insisted, in 2005, that the act's provisions had not been used. If truthful, this could mean that local officers, rather than FBI agents, made the requests or that FBI agents made the requests without invoking the official legal procedures in the act and the librarians complied without demanding these procedures.

■ *Foreign student database:* Because some 9/11 terrorists entered the country on student visas, the Patriot Act provides for monitoring foreign college students through an electronic database. When the students apply for a visa, their data is logged into the database. Then the schools are required to forward information about the students'

classes each semester and activities on campus. When government officials investigate particular students, the schools are forbidden from disclosing to the students that their records have been checked. These provisions amend a privacy act adopted by Congress in the 1970s.

■ *Alien registration and interrogation:* Acting under authority of the Patriot Act, the U.S. Citizenship and Immigration Services (USCIS) requires male nonresident aliens who are older than sixteen and come from any of twenty-five countries, all but one of which are Arab or Muslim, to report to its offices to be fingerprinted, photographed, and interrogated. The men must report any change of address within ten days, and they must reappear annually. If they fail to appear, they can be deported. If they appear but the interrogation uncovers immigration violations, they can be detained indefinitely and then deported under other laws.

■ *Alien detentions and prosecutions:* Although the Patriot Act focuses on intelligence gathering, it contains other important provisions that enhance the government's ability to detain and prosecute aliens. Those suspected of committing a crime related to terrorism can be detained, without trial, longer than before. And those accused of providing "material support" to organizations involved in terrorism can be prosecuted more easily than before. Anyone who assists an organization involved in terrorism (as defined by the government) by soliciting money, gathering information, or providing communications, weapons, or training is guilty of providing material support, even if the person did not intend to support terrorism and even if the

assistance did not actually further terrorism. Under this provision, six Yemeni Americans from New York were indicted for traveling to Afghanistan before 9/11. They claim they went solely for religious reasons. And a college professor in Florida was prosecuted for soliciting money for a Palestinian group.

The Patriot Act puts in place a more extensive surveillance state than Americans have ever experienced. It is difficult for anyone outside the administration to evaluate the implementation and the effects of the act because this administration is unusually secretive, not only hiding its operations from potential terrorists but shielding them from congressional oversight, judicial review, and public scrutiny as well.[5]

As some provisions were about to expire in 2005, a rare alliance of civil libertarians on the left and on the right, worried about the scope of the act and of government surveillance, pushed for some revisions to the act. Yet the act, with minor changes, was renewed and made permanent. "Presented with a rare opportunity to act like a separate branch of government rather than an arm of the Bush administration," Congress "caved like an overexcited spelunker."[6]

[1]Congress initially allowed limited roving wiretaps in 1998, but the Patriot Act allows broader roving wiretaps and makes it easier to obtain them. The act also extends the life span of electronic surveillance warrants.
[2]The Homeland Security Act.
[3] The FBI issues "national security letters" to request this information and keeps a tally of the number. Barton Gellman, "The FBI Is Watching," *Washington Post National Weekly Edition*, November 14–20, 2005, 7.
[4]"Some Patriot Act Powers Have Yet to Be Used," *Lincoln Journal-Star*, September 18, 2003.
[5]Readers interested in researching the Patriot Act will find many articles in law journals, usually addressing one provision of the act. More succinct analyses by legal scholars and lawyers active in litigating issues raised by the act can be found in Cynthia Brown, ed., *Lost Liberties* (New York: New Press, 2003).
[6]"Patriot Gamesmanship," Los Angeles Times, February 17, 2006, www.latimes.com/news/opinion/editorials/la-ed-patriot17feb17,0,7116219.story?

the "You Are There" and "Epilogue," a pattern has emerged. When President Bush doesn't like the rules, he changes them unilaterally. He claims that it is necessary to protect America against terrorists. In a very expansive interpretation of presidential war powers, he justifies it by saying there's a "military necessity" to override established laws and limits. And he asserts that this will continue for as long as the conflict lasts.

At other times of crisis in our history, well-meaning political leaders, responding to peoples' fears, took bold action that affected civil liberties. During the Civil War, President Lincoln suspended the writ of *habeas corpus*. During World War II, President Roosevelt ordered the internment of Japanese Americans. (This will be covered in Chapter 15.) In response to the Russian Revolution, the executive and legislative branches launched the Red scare. In response to the Cold War, history repeated itself, as Congress pursued efforts that led to McCarthyism. In hindsight, all of these actions have been condemned as overreactions. All of them have been considered unnecessary infringements of civil liberties and rights.[321] Might some of our current efforts to ferret out terrorists be categorized in this way by later generations?

Conclusion: Are the Courts Responsive in Interpreting Civil Liberties?

The Supreme Court has interpreted the Constitution to provide valuable civil liberties. The Warren Court in the 1950s and 1960s expanded civil liberties more than any other Court in history. It applied many provisions of the Bill of Rights to the states. It substantially broadened First Amendment rights and criminal defendants' rights. It also established a right to privacy.

Observers predicted that the Burger Court would lead a constitutional counterrevolution. However, it did not. The Burger Court in the 1970s and 1980s narrowed rights in some areas, especially for criminal defendants. But the Court accepted the core of the Warren Court's doctrine and even extended the right to privacy to encompass abortions.

Nor did the Rehnquist Court produce a constitutional counterrevolution. It, too, narrowed rights in some areas, but it also accepted most of the Warren Court's doctrine and even extended the right to privacy to encompass homosexual practices.

The decisions by these Courts show the extent to which the Supreme Court is responsive to the people in civil liberties cases. The majority of the people support civil liberties in general but not necessarily in specific situations. The elites support civil liberties more than the general public. As the Court has expanded civil liberties, it has been more responsive to various minorities—political and religious minorities and unpopular groups such as criminal defendants—than to the majority. And it has been more responsive to the elites than to the masses.

When the Supreme Court has upheld civil liberties, it has fulfilled what many legal scholars consider the quintessential role of the highest court in a democracy—"to vindicate the constitutional rights of minorities, of dissidents, of the unrepresented, of the disenfranchised, of the unpopular." The other branches of government, whose officials are elected every two, four, or six years, are sensitive to the needs of "the majority, the politically powerful, the economically influential, and the socially popular."[322] So, the judicial branch should be sensitive to the needs of the others.

Because the Court was not intended to be very responsive to the majority, it was given substantial independence. Therefore, it does not have to mirror public opinion, although it cannot ignore this opinion either. It must stay within the broad limits of this opinion, or it will be pulled back. Thus, the Warren Court went too far too fast for too many people. It produced a backlash that led to the Burger and Rehnquist Courts, which were somewhat more responsive to majority opinion—and somewhat less vigilant in protecting civil liberties.

Federal Courts Can Hear Detention Suits—for Now

In *Rasul* v. *Bush,* the suit brought by families of detainees at the U.S. Naval Base at Guantanamo Bay, Cuba, the Supreme Court ruled that the federal courts do have authority to review the legality of the detention.[323] Justice Stevens wrote the opinion for the majority of six justices.

First, the majority concluded that Guantanamo Bay is essentially American territory. Next, the justices rejected the Bush administration's position that the federal courts have no authority to review and question the president's policies in wartime. Without stirring or provocative language, the majority rebuffed the president, telling him that he, too, must follow the rule of law. Therefore, the detainees are entitled to challenge their designation as "enemy combatants" by presenting evidence to the contrary before a federal judge or other neutral decision maker.

The opinion did not specify what procedures must be used. It did not even specify whether the detainees have a right to counsel or other rights.

Thus, the Court's ruling was a tentative step. Although the courts will play a role in these disputes, it may be a limited one. Despite rebuffing the president on general points, the majority acknowledged his authority to detain actual enemy combatants for the duration of the conflict. And the majority gave the administration an advantage in determining detainees' status. Although the detainees have a right to challenge their designation as enemy combatants, the administration merely has to present credible evidence against them. They then have to prove that they are not actual enemy combatants. They have to prove their innocence, which is difficult to do.

The most conservative justices on the Court—Rehnquist, Scalia,

and Thomas—dissented. They argued that the ruling is cumbersome and impractical and that it will reduce the government's authority and ultimately hamper the war effort. They did not acknowledge the advantages that the ruling gives to the government.

On the same day, the Court decided a similar case involving an American citizen who had been raised in Afghanistan and captured during the war against the Taliban government and who had been held in the United States. The Court ruled similarly, although the fact that the detainee was an American citizen prompted eight justices (all but Thomas) to declare that he was entitled to contest his detention and four justices to conclude that his detention was unlawful.[324] The ruling prompted the government to release the defendant because it did not have enough evidence to charge him. (In exchange for release, however, the government required him to renounce his citizenship and leave the country.)

The administration interpreted the rulings as narrowly as possible. The Pentagon began military hearings before military officers in the hope that these would satisfy the requirement to allow the detainees to appear before a federal judge or other neutral decision maker. The Pentagon denied the detainees an actual lawyer, although it allowed them a "personal representative" chosen by the military. The Pentagon allowed them to respond to the allegations against them. However, the officers often did not explain the evidence against them, claiming that it was classified, so they could not refute the evidence.

These hearings show that judicial decisions are not always the last word in a political controversy. Sometimes they are only the first thrust in a long battle. Court rulings on new

issues are usually tentative and ambiguous, and they reflect shifting coalitions of justices. These factors allow the officials who are supposed to comply with the rulings an opportunity to interpret them as they prefer and perhaps to circumvent them.

Nevertheless, after the hearings, numerous detainees were released. The files of many detainees, including those who were released and others who were not, were opened to the media. The files show that, although the most dangerous terrorists had been taken to the CIA's secret prisons, other suspects were housed at Guantanamo. Some, including Osama bin Laden's bodyguards, have al-Qaeda connections and are committed terrorists. Others, however, were simply in the wrong place at the wrong time.

Although the president and vice president said the prisoners were "picked up off the battlefield," according to the files only 5 percent were. Eighty-six percent were apprehended by Afghani or Pakistani warlords or tribesmen and turned over to the United States. Some were captured because they were rivals or enemies of the warlords or tribesmen; others were captured because, as purported "terrorists," they would bring a bounty from the United States (reportedly $1000 a head).[325] Others were foreigners who worked for Muslim organizations operating charities, clinics, and schools.[326] At least ten wore the wrong watch—a Casio model used by al-Qaeda bombers because of its timer, but also worn by many Arabs because it is cheap and has a compass, which enables them to point toward Mecca when they pray.[327] A thorough review of the government's files concluded, "Most, when captured, were innocent of any terrorist activity, were Taliban foot soldiers at

worst, and were often far less than that. And some, perhaps many, were guilty only of being foreigners in Afghanistan or Pakistan at the wrong time."[328] Of the men turned over by Pakistan—that is, a majority of the prisoners—the former head of the CIA's bin Laden unit concluded, they were "absolutely . . . the wrong people."[329] The U.S. military was under so much pressure to find al-Qaeda members that it accepted the persons who were delivered by the warlords and tribesmen. With too few experienced interpreters and interrogators, it couldn't separate the terrorists from the others.

The problems continued at Guantanamo. Prisoners often were classified as "terrorists" based on hearsay evidence (that is, someone heard someone else say . . .) rather than on first-hand knowledge. Prisoners also were classified as "terrorists" because of their responses during their interrogations. One

Yemeni said, "I saw bin Laden five times: three times on al Jazeera and twice on Yemeni news." In his file, the interrogator noted, "Detainee admitted to knowing Osama bin Laden."[330] Interrogators were under tremendous pressure from Washington to identify terrorists and, knowing that al-Qaeda trained its agents to lie, were reluctant to conclude that prisoners were innocent. When interrogators didn't get the answers they expected, they made the interrogations more brutal.

The indefinite detentions and harsh interrogations put the detainees under much stress. One who was shackled to the floor overnight pulled out most of his hair by morning. Many tried to hang themselves and three succeeded.[331] The human rights group Amnesty International, referring to the notorious Soviet prison for dissidents, called Guantanamo the "gulag of our times."[332] In 2006, several European leaders and

a United Nations committee urged the United States to shut down the prison.

Now Congress has passed a law that strips *habeas corpus* rights from the Guantanamo detainees. They can't appeal to the courts to challenge their detention until a military tribunal has issued a final ruling in their case. This law might override the Supreme Court's decisions addressed here. At this point, it is unclear how the courts will interpret the law.[333]

In 2006 the Court issued a second rebuke to the president in two years. A five-justice majority ruled that the administration's plan to try terrorism suspects by military commissions violated both U.S. law and international law because the commissions were not established courts and would not afford adequate rights to the suspects.[334]

Taken together, the Court's rulings on detentions and military commissions challenge the president's assertion that he alone can determine how to fight terrorism. And the rulings reflect the justices' belief that at least some constitutional standards must be followed even during wartime.

 To learn more about this topic, go to "you are there" exercises for this chapter on the text website.

Key Terms

habeas corpus
civil liberties
Bill of Rights
First Amendment
freedom of speech
seditious speech
Red Scare
McCarthyism
fighting words
hate speech
public forum
symbolic speech
freedom of association

freedom of the press
libel
obscenity
separation of church and state
free exercise clause
establishment clause
due process
presumption of innocence
Second Amendment
unreasonable searches and seizures
exclusionary rule
Miranda rights
right to counsel

right to a jury trial
cruel and unusual punishment
plea bargain
right to privacy
right to abortion
right to die

stress and duress
rendition
National Security Agency

Further Reading

Fred W. Friendly, *Minnesota Rag* (New York: Random House, 1981). Friendly provides a lively examination of the Court's first important freedom of the press case, *Near* v. *Minnesota,* in 1927.

David J. Garrow, *Liberty and Sexuality: The Right to Privacy and the Making of* Roe *v.* Wade (New York: Macmillan, 1994). This is an exhaustive account of the hard road to *Roe.*

Franz Kafka, *The Trial* (numerous editions, 1937). One of the great novels of the twentieth century shows, perhaps more dramatically than anything else written, what life without due process rights would be like.

James Kirby, *Fumble: Bear Bryant, Wally Butts, and the Great College Football Scandal* (New York: Dell, 1986). Think of this as law for football fans—the story of the libel suit against a national magazine for writing that the coach of Alabama and athletic director of Georgia fixed a football game between the two schools. The author, a lawyer, was hired by the Southeastern Conference to determine what really happened in the dispute.

Joseph Margulies, *Guantanamo and the Abuse of Presidential Power* (New York: Simon & Schuster, 2006). Written by a lawyer for Gitmo detainees, this is the best account so far of what has occurred at the detention center.

Anthony Lewis, *Gideon's Trumpet* (New York: Vintage, 1964). This is a wonderful account of Clarence Earl Gideon's suit and the Court's landmark decision.

Patricia G. Miller, *The Worst of Times* (New York: Harper-Collins, 1992). Miller presents recollections of women who had abortions before *Roe* made them legal and interviews abortionists, doctors, and police who witnessed the results.

Helen Prejean, *Dead Men Walking* (New York: Vintage, 1993). This account of capital punishment in the United States is written from the front lines.

Jonathan Rauch, *Gay Marriage: Why It Is Good for Gays, Good for Straights, and Good for America* (New York: Times Books, 2004). Presenting a conservative argument for gay marriage, the author predicts that marriage will have a greater effect on homosexuals, by imposing responsibility and conformity on them, than they will have on the institution of marriage.

Jeffrey Rosen, *The Naked Crowd: Reclaiming Security and Freedom in an Anxious Age* (New York: Random House, 2004). Rosen traces the threats to privacy posed by the combination of contemporary technology and our post–9/11 fears.

For Viewing

Atomic Café (1992). This is a collage of government propaganda films from the 1960s telling Americans that the atomic bomb is not a threat to their safety.

Fahrenheit 451 (1966). Based on a Ray Bradbury novel, this movie is set in a future time when the government bans books.

The Front (1976). This Woody Allen movie is about a poor schlub—Allen, of course—who gets embroiled in the Hollywood blacklisting during the McCarthy era.

The Thin Blue Line (1988). Documentary filmmaker Errol Morris uncovers the actual killer in the process of making a film about the death penalty.

The Way We Were (1973). This classic film addresses personal relationships during the McCarthy era and stars a younger Robert Redford and Barbra Streisand.

Electronic Resources

www.aclu.org/index.html
The American Civil Liberties Union is the foremost group dedicated to protecting civil liberties through legal and political action. Its site provides links to information and position papers on many issues covered in this chapter.

www.firstamendmentcenter.org
Broad coverage of First Amendment issues.

www.loc.gov/exhibits/religion
Information on the role of religion in the founding of the country can be found at this site, maintained by the Library of Congress.

www.perkinscoie.com
This site, maintained by a law firm, features the latest cases involving Internet legal issues.

www.lifeandliberty.gov
The Department of Justice presents arguments in favor of the Patriot Act.

www.bordc.org
This site critiques the Patriot Act.

www.naral.org
This is the site for the National Abortion Rights Action League, a pro-choice group.

www.prolifeinfo.net
This site links to pro-life groups.

www.lambdalegal.org
Lambda Legal is the oldest organization fighting for full recognition of the rights of gays, lesbians, bisexuals, and transgendered individuals.

www.nra.org
The National Rifle Association maintains this site.

ThomsonNOW™

Enter ThomsonNOW™ using the access card that is available with this text or through www.thomsonedu.com/thomsonnow. ThomsonNOW™ will assist you in understanding the content in this chapter with a personalized study plan generated for your needs. A practice test will assess the areas you need to review and provide the tools to fully comprehend those concepts, including an integrated digital eBook, interactive simulations, timelines, video case studies, MicroCase exercises, and InfoTrac College Edition readers and exercises. You'll also be connected to the learning objectives, chapter outline, chapter glossary, flash cards, crossword puzzles, Internet activities, and interactive quizzes found on the companion website.

CHAPTER 15

CIVIL RIGHTS

A three-year-old Japanese girl awaits relocation during World War II. Yukiko Llewellyn became an assistant dean of students at the University of Illinois.

National Archives

Race Discrimination

Discrimination against African Americans

Overcoming Discrimination against African Americans

Continuing Discrimination against African Americans

Improving Conditions for African Americans?

Discrimination against Hispanics

Discrimination against American Indians

Sex Discrimination

Discrimination against Women

Discrimination against Men

Affirmative Action

In Employment

In College Admissions

Conclusion: Is Government Responsive in Granting Civil Rights?

Friend or Foe?

You are Justice William Douglas, and you are facing a difficult decision during World War II. The Supreme Court is deciding the case of ***Korematsu*** v. ***United States.*** Fred Korematsu, a Japanese American, was born and raised in California. He was living in Oakland and working as a welder when Japan bombed Pearl Harbor and drew the United States into World War II. He tried to enlist in the Army but was rejected because of ulcers. A few months later, President Franklin Roosevelt, under pressure from West Coast politicians and newspapers, issued an executive order, which Congress ratified, authorizing the secretary of war to exclude persons of Japanese ancestry from the three West Coast states and part of Arizona to prevent espionage and sabotage. Under the order, all persons of Japanese ancestry, even those with American citizenship, were required to report to assembly centers—fairgrounds, racetracks, or stockyards, from which the animals had been removed just days before. From there, they were relocated, with whatever possessions they could carry, to camps in deserts and swamps farther inland for the duration of the war. Enclosed by barbed wire and patrolled by armed guards, these detention camps resembled prisoner-of-war camps.

Korematsu did not leave with the others. He had fallen in love with an Italian American woman, and they planned to marry. He had undergone plastic surgery in an attempt to appear Spanish Hawaiian instead of Japanese. But the surgery was not successful, and while walking down the street in his hometown, he was identified and arrested for violating the order. He was convicted at trial, and his conviction was upheld on appeal. Now his case has reached the Supreme Court.

The government claims that the order is justified. Since the attack on Pearl Harbor and the success of Japanese forces in the Pacific, American officials have been jittery. Although they do not expect an invasion of the West Coast, they do fear espionage and sabotage. Before the war, it appeared that many Japanese Americans supported Japan's efforts to expand its territory in Asia. Some contributed money, tinfoil, and scrap metal, and a few formed an espionage ring. Intelligence agents crushed the ring but fear renewed attempts.

Already Japanese submarines have attacked American merchant ships off the West Coast, sinking two and damaging another. Officials speculate that Japanese Americans were signaling Japanese subs. (The *Los Angeles Times* even guessed that Japanese American farmers might be guiding Japanese pilots to California targets: "Caps on Japanese Tomato Plants Point to Air Base.")[1]

Officials question the loyalty of Japanese Americans. Most, born here, are U.S. citizens, but they have been granted citizenship by Japan also because of their ancestry. And they have formed semiclosed communities and adhered to Old World cultural patterns. Thousands have sent their children to Japan for several years of schooling. The American general in charge of the evacuation expressed the prevalent attitude toward them: "There isn't such a thing as a loyal Japanese."[2] He asserted that "the very fact that no sabotage has taken place to date is a disturbing and confirming indication that such action will be taken."

Many Americans characterize Japanese Americans as rats. Some West Coast restaurants have placed signs in their windows: "This Restaurant Poisons Both Rats and Japs." Some West Coast drivers have put stickers depicting a rat with a Japanese face on their cars. A patriotic parade in New York City included a float the crowd reportedly loved—an eagle leading a squadron of American bombers toward a herd of yellow rats trying to escape.[3]

Amidst this climate, Korematsu claims that the order discriminates against him on the basis of his race and thereby violates his Fifth Amendment right to due process of law. As evidence, he notes that the order does not apply to persons of German or Italian ancestry. Although the order is general, the military commander was told not to remove the many persons of Italian descent on the West Coast. The mayor of San Francisco was Italian, and baseball star Joe DiMaggio, whose parents were aliens, was a national idol. Anyway, President Roosevelt said

Dorothea Lange, National Archives

The tar-paper barracks of the Manzanar internment camp in California held 10,000 Japanese Americans during World War II.

he was not worried about the Italians. "They are a lot of opera singers."[4]

Korematsu notes that there has been widespread discrimination against Asians on the West Coast. For decades, there has been talk of the "yellow peril." In 1913, Congress refused to allow more Japanese to become citizens and in 1924 refused to allow more to immigrate. The discrimination has resulted in segregated neighborhoods and schools and, in at least one city—Bakersfield—even the omission of their names from the telephone directory.

The hostility has fueled efforts to drive the Japanese Americans off their productive farmland. Many Japanese, brought over as cheap laborers, worked hard enough to become successful landowners. At the outbreak of the war, they grew about half of the fruits and

vegetables in California, and an acre of their land was worth more than seven times the value of an acre of other farmland in the state. Consequently, their competitors covet their land.

You are torn. You were appointed by President Roosevelt, who sought restrained justices who would uphold his New Deal programs. You are liberal, and like other liberal justices at this time, you are deferential toward presidential and congressional authority. Unlike the conservative justices, who were activist, the liberal justices have voted to support Roosevelt's New Deal programs. However, this exclusion order is nothing like the economic policies at stake in the New Deal. Moreover, you are a fierce individualist, and as your career on the bench unfolds, you will become known as an ardent champion of individual rights. What do you decide?

The term **civil rights** refers to equality of rights for persons regardless of their race, sex, or ethnic background. The Declaration of Independence proclaimed that "all men are created equal." The author, Thomas Jefferson, knew that all men were not created equal in many respects, but he meant to emphasize that they should be considered equal in rights and equal before the law. This represented a break with Great Britain, where rigid classes with unequal rights existed; nobles had more rights than commoners. The Declaration's promise did not include nonwhites or women, however. So even though colonial Americans advocated equality, they envisioned it only for white men. Others gradually gained more equality, but the Declaration's promise remains unfulfilled for some.

Race Discrimination

African Americans, Hispanics, and American Indians all have endured and continue to experience discrimination. This chapter recounts the struggle for equal rights by members of these groups.

Discrimination against African Americans

Slavery

The first Africans came to America in 1619, just twelve years after the first whites. The blacks, like many whites, initially came as indentured servants. In exchange for their passage across the ocean, they were bound to an employer, usually for four to seven years, and then freed. But later in the century, the colonies passed laws requiring blacks and their children to be slaves for life.

Once slavery was established, the slave trade flourished. In the South, slavery became the foundation of an agricultural economy, allowing the development and prosperity of huge plantations. In the North, slavery was also common. There were large plantations in Connecticut, Massachusetts, and Rhode Island that shipped agricultural products to the West Indies in exchange for molasses used to make rum. There were also slaves in the cities. In the mid-1700s, New York City had more slaves than any city in the colonies except Charleston. About 40 percent of its households owned slaves (though, unlike southern plantations, an average of only 2.4 slaves per household).[5] Gradually most northern slaves were freed, though some remained enslaved when the Revolutionary War broke out.

The British, in an attempt to disrupt American society during the war, promised freedom for the slaves. (The proclamation was a tactical rather than an ethical maneuver, as British generals themselves had slaves.) Perhaps as many as eighty thousand escaped and fought alongside the Redcoats.[6] After the war, some of these slaves fled to Canada with the Loyalists, some sailed to Caribbean islands, where they would be enslaved again, and others shipped to Sierra Leone. Most remained in America.

By the time of the Constitutional Convention, there were sharp differences between northern and southern attitudes toward slavery. In most parts of the North, slavery was condemned, but in the South it was accepted and ingrained.

As a result of the compromises between northern and southern states, the Constitution protected slavery. It allowed the importation of slaves until 1808, when Congress could bar further importation, and it required the return of escaped slaves to their owners.

Shortly after ratification of the Constitution, most northern states officially abolished slavery.[7] In 1808, Congress barred the importation of slaves but not the practice of slavery in the North, where it still existed, or in the South, where it was pervasive. Yet Thomas Jefferson, a Virginia slave owner, foresaw its demise, "whether brought on by the generous energy of our own minds" or by a "bloody process."[8]

Abolitionists called for an end to slavery. Southerners began to question the Declaration of Independence and to repudiate its notion of natural rights, attributing this idea to Jefferson's "radicalism."[9]

The Supreme Court tried to quell the antislavery sentiment in the **Dred Scott case** in 1857.[10] Dred Scott, a slave who lived in Missouri, was taken by his owner to the free state of Illinois and the free territory of Wisconsin and, after five years, was returned to Missouri. The owner died and passed title to his wife, who moved but left Scott in the care of people in Missouri.

Courtesy of the South Carolina State Museum

Southern slaveholders hired out industrious and trusted slaves to white families who had no slaves. In Charleston, the practice was formalized, with copper neck tags indicating the date and the number and occupation of the slave. One of these was a servant. The slaves had to wear the tags all the time.

Although most slave owners were white, some were black. William Ellison of South Carolina was one. Born a slave, he bought his freedom and then his family's by building and repairing cotton gins. Over time, he earned enough money to buy slaves and operate a plantation. With sixty slaves, Ellison ranked in the top 1 percent of all slaveholders, black or white.

Ellison was unusual, but he was not unique. In Charleston, South Carolina, alone, more than one hundred African Americans owned slaves in 1860. Most, however, owned fewer than four.

Although part of the slave-owning class, black slaveholders were not accepted as equals by whites. Ellison's family was granted a pew on the main floor of the local Episcopal church, but they had to be on their guard at all times. Failure to maintain the norms of black-white relations—acting deferentially—could mean instant punishment. And as the Civil War approached, whites trying to preserve the established order increasingly viewed free blacks, even slaveholders, as a threat. Harsher legislation regulated their lives. For example, they had to have a white "guardian" to vouch for their charac-

ter, and they had to carry special papers to prove their free status. Without these papers, they could be sold back into slavery.

Some black slaveholders showed little sign that they shared the concerns of black slaves. Indeed, Ellison freed none of his slaves.[1]

SOURCE: Michael Johnson and James L. Roark, *Black Masters* (New York: Norton, 1984).

[1]For an acclaimed novel exploring the moral intricacies for black slave owners, read Edward P. Jones, *The Known World* (New York: Amistad, 2003).

They opposed slavery and arranged to have Scott sue his owner for his freedom. They argued that Scott's time in a free state and a free territory made him a free man even though he was brought back to a slave state. The owner, who also opposed slavery, had authority to free Scott, but she and the people caring for him sought a major court decision to keep slavery out of the territories.

In this infamous case, Chief Justice Roger Taney stated that no blacks, whether slave or free, were citizens and that they were "so far inferior that they had no rights which the white man was bound to respect." Taney could have stopped here—if Scott was not a citizen, he could not sue in federal court at the time—but Taney continued. He declared that Congress had no power to control slavery in the territories. This meant that slavery could extend into the territories Congress already had declared free. It also raised the possibility that the states could not control slavery within their borders.[11]

By this time, slavery had become the hottest controversy in American politics, and this decision fanned the flames. It provoked vehement opposition in the North and prompted further polarization in the country, leading to the Civil War.[12] (Years later it would be cited among the worst decisions ever made by the Supreme Court.) Meanwhile, Scott received his freedom from his owner. Most other slaves were not so lucky (see the box "Black Masters"). When the Civil War began, one of every nine black people in America was free; the other eight were slaves.

The North's victory in the Civil War gave force to President Lincoln's Emancipation Proclamation ending slavery.[13] But blacks would find short-lived solace.

Reconstruction

After the war, Congress passed and the states ratified three constitutional amendments. The Thirteenth prohibited slavery. (In 1995, Mississippi became the last state to ratify the amendment, but of course the state's ratification was merely a symbolic action by then.) The Fourteenth Amendment granted citizenship to blacks, thus overruling the Dred Scott decision, and also granted "equal protection of the laws" and "due process of law." The **equal protection clause** would eventually become the primary guarantee that government would treat people equally. The Fifteenth Amendment gave black men the right to vote.

These amendments not only granted specific rights for African Americans but also transformed the relationship between the federal and state governments. Each amendment included a stipulation that "Congress shall have power to enforce" the provisions of the amendment. Congress did not trust the southern states to enforce constitutional provisions they had just fought a war against. This stipulation granted the federal government new power—whatever power was necessary to guarantee these rights. This new power stands in marked contrast to the Founders' original understanding that the federal government would have limited power. The Civil War and these amendments together thus constituted a constitutional revolution, as explained in Chapter 2.[14]

Congress also passed a series of Civil Rights Acts to reverse the "Black Codes" that southern states had enacted to deny the newly freed slaves legal rights.[15] These laws allowed blacks to buy, own, and sell property; to make contracts; to sue; and to serve as witnesses and jurors in court. They also allowed blacks to use public transportation, such as railroads and steamboats, and to patronize hotels and theaters.

Even so, freed blacks faced bleak conditions. Congress rejected proposals to break up the plantations and give former slaves "forty acres and a mule" or to provide aid to establish schools. Without land or education, they had to work for their former masters as hired hands—as "sharecroppers." Their status was not much better than it had been. Landowners designed a system to keep them dependent. Landowners allowed sharecroppers to sell half of their crop and keep the proceeds, but they paid so little, regardless of how hard the farmers worked, that the families had to borrow to tide them over the winter. The next year, they had to work for the same landowners to pay off their debts. The cycle continued, year after year. And lacking education, most sharecroppers did not keep any records, so they did not know how much they owed, and many were cheated.

During Reconstruction, the Union Army enforced the new amendments and acts. While the Army occupied the South, military commanders established procedures to register voters, including the newly freed slaves; hold elections; and ratify the Fourteenth Amendment. The commanders also started schools for children of the newly freed slaves. But in state after state, the South resisted, and eventually the North capitulated. (When the South resisted, there weren't enough Union troops in the region to maintain Reconstruction policies—just as there weren't enough U.S. troops in Iraq to maintain order.) After a decade, the two regions struck a deal to end what was left of Reconstruction. The 1876 presidential election between Republican Rutherford Hayes and Democrat Samuel Tilden was disputed in some states. To resolve the dispute, Republicans, most of whom were northerners, and Democrats, many of whom were southerners, agreed to a compromise: Hayes would be named president, and the remaining Union troops would be removed from the South.

The collapse of Reconstruction would limit the impact of the Civil War. In effect, the South would be allowed to nullify one result of the war—granting legal and political rights to blacks—in exchange for accepting two other results—preserving the Union and abolishing slavery.

In hindsight, it is not surprising that Reconstruction did not accomplish more. It was not easy to integrate four million former slaves into a southern society that was bitter in its defeat and weak economically. Northerners who expected progress to come smoothly were naive. When it did not come quickly, they grew weary and gave up. At the same time, there was a desire for healing between the two regions and lingering feelings for continuity with the past.

Public attitudes during Reconstruction thus began a recurring cycle that continues to this day: Periodically the public gets upset about the treatment of African Americans and determined to improve the conditions. But the public is naive and impatient, and when the efforts do not produce the results they expect as soon as they expect, the public becomes disillusioned with the efforts and dissatisfied with their costs. The public's lack of sophistication and patience forces the government to put the race problem on the back burner for some future generation to pick up again.[16]

Segregation

In both the South and the North, blacks came to be segregated from whites.

Segregation in the South The reconciliation between Republicans and Democrats—northerners and southerners—was effected at the expense of blacks. Removing the troops enabled the South to govern itself again, and this enabled the South to reduce blacks to near-slave status.

Before the Civil War, slavery itself had kept blacks down. Segregation would have been inconvenient when blacks and whites needed to live and work near each other. There was no residential segregation—not in rural areas, where former slaves' shacks were intermixed with plantation mansions, and not in urban areas,

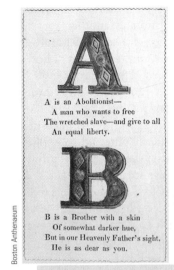
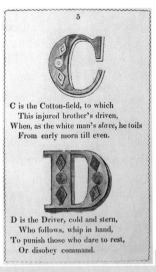

Boston Anthenaeum

Slavery became a polarizing issue years before the Civil War. The Anti-Slavery Alphabet, a children's book, was first published in 1847.

where few blocks were solidly black. But after slavery, southerners established segregation as another way to keep blacks down. Initially, they did so haphazardly—one law here, another there. By the early 1900s, however, there was a pervasive pattern of **Jim Crow laws.**[17]

Jim Crow laws segregated just about everything. Some segregated blocks within neighborhoods, others neighborhoods within cities. Laws in some small towns excluded blacks altogether. Some did so explicitly; others—"sundown towns"—established curfews that required blacks to be off the streets by 10 P.M.

Laws segregated schools, which blacks had been allowed to attend during Reconstruction, and even textbooks (black schools' texts had to be stored separately from white schools' books).

Many laws segregated public accommodations, such as hotels, restaurants, bars, theaters, and transportation. At first, the laws required the races to sit in separate sections of streetcars; then, they forced them to sit in separate cars; finally, they also required them to sit in separate sections of waiting rooms. Other laws segregated sporting events, circuses, and parks. They separated black and white checkers players in Birmingham and districts for black and white prostitutes in New Orleans. They segregated drinking fountains, restrooms, ticket windows, entrances, and exits.

They segregated the races in prisons, hospitals, and homes for the blind. They even segregated the races in death—in morgues, funeral homes, and cemeteries.

The primary harm from segregation was not that blacks were denied access to better facilities or locations, though they were, but that they were degraded. The system of Jim Crow laws was "an officially organized degradation ceremony, repeated day after day." Segregation told blacks they were inferior and did not belong in the communities where they lived.[18]

Blacks were forced to defer to whites in informal settings as well—for instance, to move off the sidewalk when a white pedestrian approached. Failure to defer could mean punishment or even death. Blacks were "humiliated by a thousand daily reminders of their subordination."[19]

Meanwhile, northern leaders, who had championed the cause of the slaves before and during the Civil War, abandoned African Americans a decade after the war. Congress declined to pass new laws, presidents refused to enforce existing laws, and the Supreme Court gutted the constitutional amendments and Civil Rights Acts.[20]

Then the Court upheld segregation itself. Louisiana passed "an Act to promote the comfort of passengers," which mandated separate accommodations in trains. New Orleans black leaders sponsored a test case challenging the act's constitutionality. Homer Adolph Plessy

sat in the white car. When the conductor ordered him to move to the black car, Plessy refused. He maintained that the act was unconstitutional under the Fourteenth Amendment. In *Plessy v. Ferguson* in 1896, the Court disagreed, claiming that the act was not a denial of equal protection because it provided equal accommodations.[21] The Court established the **separate-but-equal doctrine,** which allowed separate facilities if they were "equal." Of course, government required separate facilities only because people thought the races were not equal, but the Court brazenly commented that the act did not stamp "the colored race with a badge of inferiority" unless "the colored race chooses to put that construction on it." Only Justice John Harlan, a former Kentucky slaveholder, dissented: "Our Constitution is color-blind, and neither knows nor tolerates classes among citizens."

Three years later, the Court accepted segregation in schools.[22] A Georgia school board turned a black high school into a black elementary school without establishing a new high school for blacks or allowing them to attend the existing high schools for whites. Nevertheless, the Court said this action was not a denial of equal protection. Its ruling set a pattern in which separate but equal meant separation but not equality.

Segregation in the North Although Jim Crow laws were not as pervasive in the North as in the South, they were still quite common. In fact, "sundown towns" were more prevalent in the North, especially in the Midwest. In the 1930s, Hawthorne, California, posted a sign at its city limits: "Nigger, Don't Let The Sun Set On YOU In Hawthorne."[23] Jim Crow laws in the northern states prompted one writer to proclaim, "The North has surrendered!"[24]

Yet job opportunities were better in the North. While southern blacks were sharecropping—by 1930, 80 percent of those who farmed were still working somebody else's land[25]—northern factories were offering jobs. Between 1915 and 1940, more than a million southern blacks headed north in the "Great Migration." Although they got decent jobs, they were forced to live in black ghettos because they could not afford better housing and because they could not escape racial discrimination in the North either.

Denial of the Right to Vote

With adoption of the Fifteenth Amendment, many African Americans voted and elected fellow African Americans to office during Reconstruction, but southern states began to disfranchise them in the 1890s (as explained in Chapter 8). Thus, they were unable to elect black representatives or even pressure white officials to oppose segregation.

TABLE 15.1 Why Whites Lynched Blacks in 1907

Whites gave the following reasons for lynching blacks, who may or may not have committed the acts cited.

Reason	Number of Lynchings
Murder	5
Attempted murder	5
Manslaughter	10
Rape	9
Attempted rape	11
Burglary	3
Harboring a fugitive	1
Theft of 75 cents	1
Having a debt of $3	2
Winning a fight with a white man	1
Insulting a white man	1
Talking to white girls on the telephone	1
Being the wife or son of a rapist	2
Being the father of a boy who "jostled" white women	1
Expressing sympathy for the victim of mob violence	3

SOURCE: Adapted from Ray Stannard Baker, *Following the Color Line* (New York: Harper & Row, 1964), 176–177.

Violence

To solidify their control, whites engaged in violence against blacks. In the 1880s and 1890s, whites lynched about one hundred blacks a year. In the 1900s, vigilante "justice" continued (see Table 15.1). For example, a mob in Livermore, Kentucky, dragged a black man accused of murdering a white man into a theater. The ringleaders charged admission and hanged the man. Then they allowed the audience to shoot at the swinging body—those in the balcony could fire once; those in the better seats could empty their revolvers.[26]

Lynchings often began with a false report of a white woman being sexually assaulted by a black man. A mob would then gather and force the hapless man to endure a humiliating and excruciating ordeal. Usually they tortured him, castrating him, before they killed him. Frequently, they hacked off his fingers and ears as well.[27]

Lynchings were not the result of a few troublemakers but were a social institution in the South. The ritualized spectacles were a desperate attempt to cling to the antebellum order upset by the Civil War. At the same time, lynchings were an outgrowth of the increase in white women who worked outside the home at the turn of the century. As these women experienced greater independence, insecure men feared that the women would become too independent, perhaps even leave them for black men. Hence the ritual of castration.[28] Through lynchings, then, white men could remain in charge—at home as well as in society—while appearing to defend women's honor.

Lynchings were considered both important and entertaining. They would be photographed and, later, postcards would be sold (though after 1907 they could no longer be mailed, according to a postal regulation).

In 1919, twenty-five race riots erupted in six months. White mobs took over cities in the North and South, burning black neighborhoods and terrorizing black residents for days on end.[29]

In 1921, ten thousand whites burned down thirty-five blocks of Tulsa's black neighborhood. The incident that precipitated the riot was typical—a report of an assault by a black man on a white woman. The report was false, fabricated by the woman (and later retracted), but residents were inflamed by a racist newspaper and encouraged by the city's officials. Almost three hundred people were shot, burned alive, or tied to cars and dragged to death. Survivors reported corpses stacked like firewood on street corners and piled high in dump trucks.[30]

Sometimes the violence was intended to drive black families off their land. In addition to lynchings and burnings, bands of white farmers known as Whitecaps nailed notes, with a drawing of a coffin and a warning to leave or die, on the doors of black farmers. Then the cities or counties put the land up for auction or simply gave it to white families who owned adjacent land.[31] This process affected not just the black families at the time but their descendents for many generations. The black families lost wealth that is accumulating value for the white owners today, many of whom may be unaware of how the land changed hands.

The white supremacist Ku Klux Klan, which began during Reconstruction and started up again in 1915, played a major role in inflaming prejudice and terrorizing blacks. It was strong enough to dominate many southern towns and even the state governments of Oklahoma and Texas. It also made inroads into some northern states such as Indiana.

Federal officials contended that such violence was a state problem—presidents refused to speak out, and Congress refused to pass legislation making lynching a federal offense—yet state officials did nothing.

For at least the first third of the twentieth century, white supremacy reigned—in the southern states, the border states, and many northern states. It also pervaded the nation's capital, where President Woodrow Wilson instituted segregation in the federal government.[32] (See also the box "Passing the 'Brown Bag Test.'")

Lynching occurred not only in the South but also in northern cities such as Marion, Indiana, in 1930. The girls on the left hold pieces of the victims' clothing, torn off as "souvenirs."

two years later, they convinced the Court to invalidate laws prescribing residential segregation.[34] But the Court continued to allow most devices to disfranchise blacks and most efforts to segregate.

In 1938, the NAACP chose a thirty-year-old attorney, Thurgood Marshall, to head its litigation arm.[35] Marshall—whose mother had to pawn her engagement and wedding rings so that he could go to an out-of-state law school because his in-state school, the University of Maryland, did not admit blacks—would become a tireless and courageous advocate for equal rights. (In 1946, after defending four blacks charged with attempted murder during a riot in rural Tennessee, he would narrowly escape a lynch mob.)[36]

Over the next two decades, presidents appointed more liberals to the Supreme Court. These two developments led to the NAACP's success in the courts.

Desegregation of schools Seventeen states and the District of Columbia segregated their schools (and four other states allowed cities to segregate their schools). The states gave white students better facilities and white teachers larger salaries. Overall, they spent from two to ten times more on white schools than on black ones.[37] Few of these states had graduate schools for blacks: as late as 1950, they had fifteen engineering schools, fourteen medical schools, and five dental schools for whites and none for blacks; they had sixteen law schools for whites and five for blacks.

The NAACP's tactics were first to show that "separate but equal" really resulted in unequal schools and then to attack "separate but equal" head on, arguing that it led to unequal status.

The NAACP began by challenging segregation in graduate schools. Missouri provided no black law school but offered to reimburse blacks who went to out-of-state law schools. In 1938, the Supreme Court said the state had to provide black students a law school or admit them to the white school.[38] Texas established a black law school that was clearly inferior to the white law school at the University of Texas. In 1950, the Court said the black school had to be substantially equal to the white school.[39] Oklahoma allowed a black student to attend the white graduate school at the University of Oklahoma but designated a separate section of the classroom, library, and cafeteria for the student. The Court said this, too, was inadequate because it deprived the student of the exchange of views with fellow students necessary for education.[40] The Court did not invalidate the separate-but-equal doctrine in these decisions, but it made segregation almost impossible to implement in graduate schools.

The NAACP continued by challenging segregation in grade schools and high schools. Marshall filed suits in two southern states, one border state, one northern state, and the District of Columbia. The suit in the

Overcoming Discrimination against African Americans

African Americans fought white supremacy primarily in three arenas: the courts, the streets, and Congress. In general, they fought in the courts first and Congress last, although as they gained momentum they increasingly fought in all three arenas at once.

The Movement in the Courts

The first goal was to convince the Supreme Court to overturn the separate-but-equal doctrine of *Plessy* v. *Ferguson*.

The NAACP In response to white violence, a group of blacks and whites founded the National Association for the Advancement of Colored People, or **NAACP,** in 1909. In its first two decades, it was led by W.E.B. Du Bois, a black sociologist. In time, it became the major organization fighting for blacks' civil rights.

Frustrated by presidential and congressional inaction and its own lack of power to force action, the NAACP decided to converge on the federal courts, which were less subject to pressures from the majority. The association assembled a cadre of lawyers, mainly from Howard University Law School, a historically black school in Washington, D.C., to bring lawsuits attacking segregation and the denial of the right to vote. In 1915, they persuaded the Supreme Court to strike down the grandfather clause (which exempted persons whose ancestors could vote from the literacy test);[33]

northern state was brought against Topeka, Kansas, where Linda Brown could not attend the school just four blocks from her home because it was a white school. Instead, she had to go to a school twenty-one blocks away.[41]

When the cases reached the Supreme Court, the justices were split. Although Chief Justice Fred Vinson might have had a majority to uphold the separate-but-equal doctrine, the Court put off a decision and rescheduled oral arguments for its next term. But Vinson suffered a heart attack, and President Eisenhower appointed Earl Warren to take his place. When the Court reheard the case, the president pressured his appointee to rule in favor of segregation. Eisenhower invited Warren and the attorney for the states to the White House for dinner. When the conversation turned to the segregationists, Eisenhower said, "These are not bad people. All they are concerned about is to see that their sweet little girls are not required to sit in schools alongside some big overgrown Negroes."[42] However, Warren not only voted against segregation but used his considerable determination and charm to persuade the other justices, some of whom had supported segregation, to vote against it too. Justice Felix Frankfurter later said Vinson's heart attack was "the first indication I have ever had that there is a God."[43]

In the landmark case of **Brown v. Board of Education** in 1954, the Court ruled unanimously that school segregation violated the Fourteenth Amendment's equal protection clause.[44] In the opinion, Warren asserted that separate but equal not only resulted in unequal schools but was inherently unequal because it made black children feel inferior. In overruling the *Plessy* doctrine, the Court showed how revolutionary the equal protection clause was—or could be interpreted to be. The Court required the segregated states to change their way of life to a degree unprecedented in American history.

After overturning laws requiring segregation in schools, the Court overruled laws mandating segregation in other places, such as public parks, golf courses, swimming pools, auditoriums, courtrooms, and jails.[45]

In *Brown,* the Court had ordered the schools to desegregate "with all deliberate speed."[46] This standard was a compromise between justices who thought schools should do so immediately and those who thought communities would need to do so gradually.[47] The ambiguity of the phrase, however, allowed the communities to take many years to desegregate—far longer than any justices envisioned. The ruling prompted much deliberation but little speed.

The South engaged in massive resistance. To implement its ruling, the Court needed help from the other branches. But Congress was controlled by southerners, and President Eisenhower was reluctant to tell the states to change. In fact, the president criticized the decision. With his power and immense popularity, he could have speeded implementation by speaking out in support of the ruling, yet he offered no help for three years. When nine black students tried to attend a white high school under a desegregation plan in Little Rock, Arkansas, the governor's and state legislature's inflammatory rhetoric against desegregation encouraged local citizens to take the law into their own hands. Finally, Eisenhower acted, sending federal troops and federalizing the state's national guard to quell the riot.

President Kennedy also used federal marshals and paratroopers to stop the violence after the governor of Mississippi blocked the door to keep James Meredith

Tulsa's black neighborhood after whites burned it down in 1921.

Whites' preoccupation with skin color affected blacks even in their relationships with other blacks. In the early twentieth century, African Americans who wanted to join certain African American clubs and churches had to pass the **brown bag test.** They had to put their hand into a brown paper bag; if what was showing was lighter in color than the bag, they were eligible for membership. A social club in Nashville had a similar test. Aspiring members had to demonstrate that their blue veins could be seen through their pale skin on the inside of their wrists.

This concern for lighter skin stemmed from the slavery era, when light-skinned blacks often brought higher prices and got better jobs as household workers and skilled craftsmen rather than as field hands. In 1860, the census classified fully 30 percent of free blacks as "mulatto" (having some white ancestry), compared with only 10 percent of the slaves. After emancipation, lighter skin continued to be a social and economic advantage. Those who, as slaves, were able to learn crafts had a head start. Many blacks with darker skin used bleach, lye, or other products to lighten their color.

Although black colleges did not restrict admission to African Americans with lighter skin, in the 1930s most of their students did have lighter skin.

Sorority sisters at Fisk University, a historically black college, in 1936.

National Archives/Harmon Collection, 200(S)-HS-1-92

They were the children of doctors, dentists, lawyers, and morticians, who themselves had lighter skin and were more successful in their communities. They were predominant among African Americans who could afford to send their children to college in those years. At college, their children took up whites' pastimes, such as cotillions and tennis, in an attempt to distinguish themselves from poor blacks and to gain acceptance from whites. (But acceptance was not granted.)

As late as the 1960s, when the slogan "Black is beautiful" became popular, the homecoming queen at Howard University usually had a light complexion.

This concern for lighter skin persists. Fashion models on *Ebony*'s covers often have pale skin, and the sales of bleaching products still continue. Lighter-skinned African Americans have higher socioeconomic status, and many African Americans prefer lighter-skinned mates.

SOURCE: "For Black College Students in the 1930s, Respectability and Prestige Depended on Passing the Brown Bag Test," *Journal of Blacks in Higher Education,* January 31, 1999, 119–120; Louie E. Ross, "Mate Selection Preferences Among African American College Students," *Journal of Black Studies* 27 (1997), 554–569; St. Clair Drake and Horace R. Clayton, *Black Metropolis* (New York: Harcourt, Brace, 1945); Mark Hill, "Color Differences in the Socioeconomic Statuses of African American Men," *Social Forces* 78 (2000), 1437–1460.

---

from registering at the University of Mississippi. Kennedy again sent troops when the governor of Alabama, George Wallace, proclaiming "segregation now, segregation tomorrow, segregation forever," blocked the door to keep blacks from enrolling at the University of Alabama.

After outright defiance, some states attempted to circumvent the ruling by shutting down their public schools and providing tuition grants for students to use at new private schools, which at the time could segregate. They also provided textbooks and recreation facilities for new private schools. Some white communities offered scholarships for poor white students. These efforts hindered desegregation and hurt black education because the black communities seldom had the resources to establish their own schools.

The states also tried less blatant schemes, such as "freedom of choice" plans that allowed the students to choose the school they wanted to attend. Of course, virtually no whites chose a black school, and due to strong pressure in the communities, few blacks chose a white school. The idea was to achieve desegregation on paper, or token desegregation in practice, in order to avoid actual desegregation. But the Court rebuffed these schemes and even forbade private schools from discriminating.[48]

To black southerners, the Court's persistence raised hopes. Chief Justice Warren, according to Thurgood

AP/WideWorld Photos

Dorothy Counts, the first black student to attend one white high school in Charlotte, North Carolina, is escorted by her father in 1957.

Marshall, "allowed the poor Negro sharecropper to say, 'Kick me around Mr. Sheriff, kick me around Mr. County Judge, kick me around Supreme Court of my state, but there's one person I can rely on.'"[49]

To white southerners, however, the Court's rulings reflected a federal government, a distant authority, that was exercising too much control over their traditional practices. The rulings engendered much bitterness. Justice Hugo Black, who was from Alabama, was shunned by former friends from the state, and his son was driven from his legal practice in the state. The justice was not even sent an invitation to his fiftieth reunion at his alma mater, the University of Alabama.[50]

Despite the Court's rulings, progress was excruciatingly slow. If a school district was segregated, a group like the NAACP had to run the risks and spend the time and money to bring a suit in a federal district court. Judges in these courts reflected the views of the state or local political establishment, so the suit might not be successful. If it was, the school board would prepare a desegregation plan. Members of the school board reflected the views of the community and the pressures from the segregationists, so the plan might not be adequate. If it was, the segregationists would challenge it in a federal district court. If the plan was upheld, the segregationists would appeal to a federal court of appeals. Judges in these courts, based in Richmond and New Orleans, came from the South, but they were not as tied to the state or local political es-

tablishment, and they usually ruled against the segregationists. But then the segregationists could appeal to the Supreme Court. The segregationists knew they would lose sooner or later, but the process took several years, so they could delay the inevitable.

Thus, the segregationists tried to resist, then to evade, and finally to delay. In this they succeeded. In 1964, a decade after *Brown,* 98 percent of all black children in the South still attended all-black schools.[51]

By this time, the mood in Congress had changed. Congress passed the Civil Rights Act of 1964, which, among other things, cut off federal aid to school districts that continued to segregate. The following year, it passed the first major program providing federal aid to education. This was the carrot at the end of the stick; school districts complied to get the money.

Finally, by 1970, only 14 percent of all black children in the South still attended all-black schools. Of course, some went to mostly black schools. Even so, the change was dramatic.

Busing *Brown* and related rulings addressed **de jure segregation**—segregation enforced by law. This segregation can be attacked by striking down the law. *Brown* did not address **de facto segregation**—segregation based on residential patterns—typical of northern cities and large southern cities, where most blacks live in black neighborhoods and most whites live in white neighborhoods. Students attend their neighborhood

Busing led to riots in cities such as Boston. In 1976, protesters assault Ted Lands-mark, a lawyer who came around the corner at the wrong time.

schools, which are mostly black or mostly white. This segregation is more intractable because it does not stem primarily from a law, so it cannot be eliminated by striking down a law.

Civil rights groups proposed busing some black children to schools in white neighborhoods and some white children to schools in black neighborhoods. They hoped to improve black children's education, their self-confidence, and eventually, their college and career opportunities. They also hoped to improve black and white children's ability to get along together.

The Burger Court authorized busing within school districts—ordinarily cities. These included southern cities where there was a history of *de jure* segregation, and northern cities where there was a pattern of *de facto* segregation and evidence that school officials had located schools or assigned students in ways that perpetuated this segregation.[52]

Busing for desegregation was never extensive. In one typical year, only 4 percent of students were bused for desegregation. Far more students were bused, at public expense, to segregated public and private schools.[53]

Even so, court orders for mandatory busing ran into a wall of hostile public opinion. White parents criticized the courts sharply. Their reaction stemmed from a mixture of prejudice against black people, bias against poor persons, fear of the crime in inner-city schools, worry about the quality of inner-city schools, and desire for the convenience of neighborhood schools. They also resented the courts for telling local governments what to do. Even some black parents opposed busing because it disrupted their children's lives. Some black parents also resented the implication that their children could learn only if sitting next to white children. But other black parents favored busing because it offered the opportunity for their children to go to better schools.

Due to the opposition of white parents, busing—and publicity about it—prompted an increase in "white flight" as white families moved from public schools to private schools and from the cities to the suburbs to avoid the busing in the cities.[54] This trend overlapped other trends, especially reductions in the white birthrate and increases in the nonwhite immigration rate, that altered the racial and economic composition of our big cities. As a result, there were fewer white students to balance enrollments and fewer middle-class students to provide stability in the cities' schools.

Therefore, even extensive busing could not desegregate the school systems of most large cities, where blacks and other minorities together were more numerous than whites. Consequently, civil rights groups proposed busing some white children from the suburbs to the cities and some black children from the cities to the suburbs. This approach would provide enough of both races to achieve balance in both places.

The Burger Court rejected this proposal by a 5–4 vote in 1974.[55] It said that busing is not appropriate between school districts unless there is evidence of intentional segregation in both the city and its suburbs. Otherwise, such extensive busing would require too long a ride for students and too much coordination by administrators.

Although there was intentional segregation by many cities and their suburbs,[56] the evidence is not as clear-cut as that of the *de jure* segregation by the southern states, so it was difficult to satisfy the requirements laid down by the Court. The Court's ruling made busing between cities and suburbs very rare.

Thurgood Marshall, by then a Supreme Court justice, dissented and predicted that the ruling would allow "our great metropolitan areas to be divided up each into two cities—one white, the other black." Indeed, the ruling did contribute to this result. The ruling was the beginning of the end of the push to desegregate public schools in urban areas.

Busing could not accomplish all that civil rights groups and federal judges expected—or at least hoped—it could. Busing could not compensate for massive residential segregation. It could not overcome students' poverty or their parents' lack of involvement in their education. Consequently, studies of the performance of minority children bused to white schools showed disappointing results. In addition, busing furthered the deterioration of minority communities because it diminished the neighborhood schools that had helped define these communities and hold them together.

In 1991, the Rehnquist Court decided that school districts have no obligation to reduce *de facto* segregation, and the Court also diminished their obligation to reduce the vestiges of *de jure* segregation.[57] This ruling relieved the pressure on school districts, and by the mid-1990s most had stopped mandatory busing. When some tried other programs to balance enrollments, the Court looked askance at these methods.[58] The rulings in the 1990s reflected none of "the moral urgency of *Brown*."[59] Instead, the justices decided that desegregation is less important than minimizing judicial involvement in education and judicial authority over local governments. In these ways, the majority of the justices mirrored the views of the Republican presidents who had appointed them.

The Movement in the Streets

After the NAACP's early successes in the courts, other blacks, and some whites, took the fight to the streets. Their bold efforts gave birth to the modern civil rights movement.

The movement came to public attention in Montgomery, Alabama, in 1955, when Rosa Parks refused to move to the back of the bus. Her courage, and her arrest, roused others to boycott city buses. For their leader they chose a young Baptist minister, Dr. Martin Luther

Students sit in at a lunch counter in Jackson, Mississippi.

Firefighters turn their hoses on demonstrators in Birmingham, Alabama, in 1963.

King Jr. The boycott catapulted the movement and King to national attention (as explained in Chapter 6).

King was the first charismatic leader of the movement. He formed the Southern Christian Leadership Conference (SCLC) of black clergy and adopted the tactics of Mahatma Gandhi, who had led the movement to free India from the British. The tactics included direct action, such as demonstrations and marches, and civil disobedience—intentional and public disobedience of unjust laws. The tactics were based on nonviolence, even when confronted with violence. This strategy was designed to draw support from whites by contrasting the morality of the movement's position with the immorality of the opponents' discrimination and violence toward blacks.

For a long time, some southern whites, focusing on movement leaders and college students from other states, and fearing even infiltration by foreign communists, deluded themselves into thinking that "outside agitators" were responsible for the turmoil in their communities.[60] But the movement grew from the grass roots, and it eventually shattered this delusion.

The movement spread among black students. In 1960, four students of North Carolina A&T College sat at the lunch counter in Woolworth's, a chain of dime stores, and asked for a cup of coffee. The waitress refused to serve them, but they remained until they were arrested. On successive days, as whites waved the Confederate flag and jeered, more students sat at the lunch counter.[61] Within a year, such sit-ins occurred in more than one hundred cities.

When blacks asserted their rights, whites often reacted with violence. In 1963, King led demonstrators in Birmingham, Alabama, seeking desegregation of public facilities. Police unleashed dogs to attack the marchers. In 1964, King led demonstrators in Selma, Alabama, for voting rights. State troopers clubbed some marchers, and vigilantes beat and shot others.

In the summer of 1964, black and white college students mounted a voter registration drive in Mississippi. By the end of the summer, one thousand had been arrested, eighty beaten, thirty-five shot, and six killed.[62] When a black cotton farmer, who had tried to register to vote, was shot in the head in broad daylight by a white state legislator, the act was not even treated as a crime.[63]

Indeed, perpetrators of the violence usually were not apprehended or prosecuted. When they were, they usually were not convicted. Law enforcement was frequently in the hands of bigots, and juries were generally all white. The Supreme Court had struck down discrimination in choosing juries,[64] but discrimination continued through informal means.

During these years, whites told pollsters they disliked the civil rights movement's speed and tactics: "They're pushing too fast and too hard." At the same time, most said they favored integration more than ever. And they seemed repelled by the violence. The brutality against black demonstrators generated more support for black Americans and their cause.

The media, especially national organizations based in northern cities such as the *New York Times,* the Associated Press, and the major television networks, played a role simply by covering the conflict. The leaders of the civil rights movement staged events that captured attention, and violent racists played into their hands. As northern reporters and photographers relayed the events and violence to the nation, the movement gained public sympathy in the North. Yet the national press became as vilified as the federal government in the South. (This anger would fuel southerners' distrust of the media for many years.)[65]

Although the movement's tactics worked well against southern *de jure* segregation, they did not work as well against northern *de facto* segregation or against job discrimination in either region. By the mid-1960s, progress had stalled and dissatisfaction had grown. Young blacks from the inner city, who had not been involved in the movement, questioned two of its principles: interracialism and nonviolence. As James Farmer, head of the Congress of Racial Equality (CORE), explained, they asked, "What is this we-shall-overcome, black-and-white-together stuff? I don't know of any white folks except the guy who runs that store on 125th Street in Harlem and garnishes wages and repossesses things you buy. I'd like to go upside his head. [Or] the rent collector, who bangs on the door demanding rent that we ain't got. I'd like to go upside

his head."[66] These blacks criticized King and his tactics. In place of the integration advocated by King, some leaders began to call for "black power." This phrase, which implied black pride and self-reliance, meant different things to different people. To some it meant political power through the ballot box, and to others it meant economic power through ownership of their own businesses. To a few it meant violence in retaliation for violence by whites. The movement splintered further.

The Movement in Congress

As the civil rights movement expanded, it pressured presidents and members of Congress to act. President Kennedy, who was most concerned about the Cold War, considered civil rights a distraction. President Johnson, who was a champion of "the poor and the downtrodden and the oppressed"—a biographer calls him our second most compassionate president, after Abraham Lincoln[67]—supported civil rights but felt hamstrung by the southerners in Congress who, through the seniority system, chaired key committees and dominated both houses. As a result, the presidents considered the civil rights leaders unreasonable, because their movement alienated the southerners on whom the presidents had to rely for other legislation.

When three civil rights workers were murdered in Neshoba County, Mississippi, no one was indicted by the state. Later eighteen persons, including the sheriff (right) and deputy sheriff (left), were indicted by the federal government for the lesser charge of conspiracy. (There was no applicable federal law for murder.) Ultimately, seven persons, including the deputy, were convicted by the federal court.

AP/Wide World Photos

But once the movement demonstrated great strength, it convinced the officials to act. After two hundred thousand blacks and whites marched in Washington in 1963, President Kennedy introduced civil rights legislation. His successor, President Johnson, with consummate legislative skill, forged a coalition of northern Democrats and northern Republicans to overcome southern Democrats and pass the Civil Rights Act of 1964. After one thousand blacks and whites had been attacked and arrested in Selma, Johnson introduced and Congress passed the Voting Rights Act of 1965. Three years later, Johnson introduced and Congress passed the Civil Rights Act of 1968. Within a span of four years, Congress passed legislation prohibiting discrimination in public accommodations, employment, housing, and voting. These would become the most significant civil rights acts in history.

It is impossible to exaggerate how controversial these laws were. In 1964, the Republican nominee for president, Senator Barry Goldwater of Arizona, opposed the Civil Rights Act. He had been assured by two advisers—Phoenix attorney William Rehnquist and Yale professor Robert Bork—that it was unconstitutional.[68] The conservative Republican Ronald Reagan, preparing to run for California governor, also strongly opposed the act.[69] (Years later, as president, Reagan would appoint Rehnquist as chief justice and nominate Bork to serve as an associate justice on the Supreme Court.)

Although President Johnson believed he was doing the right thing, he realized the political ramifications. Upon signing the first of these acts, he commented that he was handing the South to the Republican Party "for the next fifty years."[70] He was prescient. In the next election, he became the first Democrat since the Civil War to lose the white vote in the southern states. In less than a decade, the South, which had been solidly Democratic since the Civil War, would go from the most Democratic region of the country to one of the most Republican regions.[71]

Desegregation of public accommodations

The **Civil Rights Act of 1964** prohibits discrimination on the basis of race, color, religion, or national origin in public accommodations. This time, in contrast to its actions after the Civil War, the Court unanimously upheld the law.[72]

The act does not cover private clubs, such as country clubs, social clubs, or fraternities and sororities, on the principle that the government should not tell people with whom they may or may not associate in private. (The Court has made private schools an exception to this principle to help enforce *Brown*.)

President Lyndon Johnson and Martin Luther King Jr., compatriots with a tense relationship.

Yoichi R. Okamoto/Courtesy LBJ Library

Desegregation of employment

The Civil Rights Act of 1964 also prohibits employment discrimination on the basis of race, color, religion, national origin, or sex and (as amended) physical disability, age, or Vietnam-era veteran status. The act covers employers with fifteen or more employees and unions.[73]

In addition to practicing blatant discrimination, some employers practiced more subtle discrimination. They required applicants to meet standards unnecessary for their jobs, a practice that hindered blacks more than whites. A high school diploma for a manual job was a common example. The Court held that the standards must relate to the jobs.[74] However, standards that hindered blacks more than whites were not necessarily unlawful. Washington, D.C., required applicants for police officer to pass an exam. Although a higher percentage of blacks failed to pass, the Court said the exam related to the job.[75]

Desegregation of housing

Although the Supreme Court had struck down laws that prescribed segregation in residential areas, whites maintained segregation by making **restrictive covenants**—agreements among neighbors not to sell their houses to blacks. In 1948, the Court ruled that courts could not enforce these covenants because doing so would involve the government in discrimination.[76]

Real estate agents also played a role in segregation by practicing **steering**—showing blacks houses in black neighborhoods and whites houses in white neighborhoods. Unscrupulous real estate agents practiced **blockbusting.** After a black family bought a house in a white neighborhood, the agents would warn white families that more blacks would move in. Because of prejudice and fear that their houses' values would decline, whites would panic and sell to the agents at low prices. Then the agents would resell to blacks at higher prices. In this way, neighborhoods that might have been desegregated were instead resegregated—from all white to all black.

Banks and savings and loans also played a role. They were reluctant to lend money to blacks who wanted to buy a house in a white neighborhood. Some engaged in **redlining**—refusing to lend money to people who wanted to buy a house in a racially changing neighborhood. The lenders worried that if the buyer could not keep up with the payments, the lender would be left with a house whose value had declined.

The government also played an important role. The Veterans Administration and the Federal Housing Authority, which guaranteed loans to some buyers, were reluctant to authorize loans to blacks who tried to buy a house in a white neighborhood but were generous to whites who fled from the big cities to buy in all-white suburbs. And the federal government, which funded low-income housing, allowed local governments to locate such housing in ghettos. In these ways, the governments helped perpetuate segregation.[77]

But the **Civil Rights Act of 1968** bans discrimination in the sale or rental of housing on the basis of race, color, religion, or national origin and (as amended) on the basis of sex, having children, or having a disability. The act covers about 80 percent of the available housing and prohibits steering, blockbusting, and redlining.

Restoration of the right to vote After years of skirmishing with the states, the Supreme Court and Congress barred measures designed to keep blacks from voting. The Voting Rights Act of 1965 permitted large numbers of blacks to vote for the first time (as explained in Chapter 8).

Continuing Discrimination against African Americans

African Americans have overcome much discrimination but still face lingering prejudice. Overt laws and blatant practices have been struck down, but subtle manifestations of old attitudes persist—and in ways far more numerous and with effects far more serious than this one chapter can convey.[78] Moreover, African Americans must cope with the legacy of generations of slavery, segregation, discrimination, and for many, the effects of poverty. And they must cope with the attitudes of whites. Although few people say they want to return to the days of legal segregation, about half reject the dream of an integrated society.[79] (See the box "How Much Is White Skin Worth?" on page 539 for a hypothetical but telling response to discrimination.)

Discrimination in Education

Segregated schools For some blacks, considerable desegregation in education has occurred. Affluent parents who pay for private schools or live in well-off neighborhoods with good public schools can send their children to integrated schools. However, for most blacks in big cities, medium cities, or areas where private schools predominate, much less desegregation has occurred.

Although *de jure* segregation of schools has been eliminated, *de facto* segregation remains. In fact, this segregation is getting worse. After progress in the mid-1960s and 1970s, the trend toward desegregation reversed itself in the 1980s and got worse in the 1990s. "For the first time since the *Brown* v. *Board* decision," according to one study, "we are going backwards"[80] (see Figure 15.1). A smaller proportion of black and Latino students attend schools that have a majority of white students than at any time since 1968.[81] One-third of black students attend schools that are 90 to 100 percent minority.[82]

The segregation is worse in the North, where it has been *de facto*, than in the South, where it had been *de jure*. The most segregated states are New York, Michigan, Illinois, and California. (The least segregated state is Kentucky.)[83] In the Northeast and Midwest, more than one-fourth of black and Latino students attend schools that are 99 to 100 percent nonwhite.[84]

The reversal is due to white flight to private schools and to the suburbs, leaving fewer white children, and due to higher nonwhite birthrates and immigration rates, bringing more nonwhite children to public schools. These changes affect the decisions of white parents, who intentionally look for schools with low numbers of racial minorities.[85] Although many say they move for better schools, few ever visit the schools in either the old neighborhood or the new one before moving, and few ever check test score results. They use racial composition as a proxy for school quality. The more racial minorities, the poorer the quality, they assume.[86]

To a lesser extent, the reversal is due to a shift in government policies and court decisions, which sent

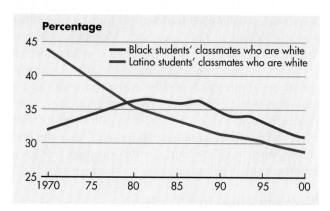

FIGURE 15.1 ■ Segregation in the Public Schools, 1970–2000 *For both black and Latino students, schools are becoming increasingly segregated. The graph for black students reflects the push for desegregation through the 1970s.* SOURCE: Ellis Cose, "A Dream Deferred," *Newsweek*, May 17, 2004, 59.

the message to school districts that desegregation is no longer an important national goal.[87]

The persistence of *de facto* segregation and the waning of society's commitment to integration have led national, state, and local officials to adopt a resigned attitude: "We still agree with the goal of school desegregation, but it's too hard, and we're tired of it, and we give up."[88]

Reforms proposed for urban schools rarely include desegregation. Officials speak of a ghetto school that is more "efficient" or one that gets more "input" from ghetto parents or offers more "choices" for ghetto children. But they seem to accept segregated education as "a permanent American reality."[89] According to one researcher, "Every district sees another way of doing *Plessy*."[90]

A writer who visited many central-city classrooms and talked with students, teachers, and administrators observed that Martin Luther King was treated as

an icon, but his vision of a nation in which black and white kids went to school together seemed to be effaced almost entirely. Dutiful references to "The Dream" were often seen in school brochures and on wall posters in February, when "Black History" was celebrated in the public schools, but the content of the dream was treated as a closed box that could not be opened without ruining the celebration.[91]

Indeed, many cities have a school named after King—a segregated school in a segregated neighborhood—"like a terrible joke on history," a fourteen-year-old, wise beyond her years, remarked.[92] In fact, if you want to find a school that's really segregated, look for the schools named after champions of integration—Jackie Robinson, Rosa Parks, and Thurgood Marshall.[93]

Some minorities have gotten so frustrated that they themselves have questioned the goal of school desegregation. Instead, they have voiced greater concern about improving the quality and safety of their schools and neighborhoods.[94] However, one education analyst counters, "For African Americans to have equal opportunity, higher test scores will not suffice. It is foolhardy to think black children can be taught, no matter how well, in isolation and then have the skills and confidence as adults to succeed in a white world where they have no experience."[95]

Despite the segregation in most metropolitan areas, there are in fact examples of successful desegregation plans that mix city and suburban students in Louisville, Milwaukee, and St. Louis. These plans have continued even after the court orders that required them have been lifted.[96]

Unequal schools In areas where the schools are segregated, the quality varies enormously—from "the golden to the godawful," in the words of a Missouri judge.[97] And of course, blacks and Latinos are more likely to be in the "godawful" ones.

By virtually every measure of school quality—school funding, class size, teacher credentials, teacher salaries, breadth of curriculum, number of computers, opportunities for gifted students—these children attend worse schools[98] (see Figure 15.2).

Schools are financed largely by property taxes paid by homeowners and businesses. Wealthy cities collect more in property taxes than poor ones. In modern America, this means that suburban school districts have more to spend per pupil than central city school districts. Even though many suburbs tax their residents at a lower rate than cities do, the suburbs still bring in more revenue because their property is valued at a higher level. Thus, these suburbs ask their residents to sacrifice less but still provide their children with an education that costs more.[99]

In about three-fourths of the states, school districts with the highest percentage of black and Latino children receive less funding than the districts with the fewest.[100] Nationwide, the difference amounts to $25,000 less per *classroom* per year for school districts with the most black and Latino children. In Illinois, the difference totals $47,000 less per classroom, and in New York it totals $50,000 less.[101] And these are the official figures; they don't count the money that affluent parents, on their own or through PTAs, contribute to hire additional teachers to reduce class sizes or to provide art and music instruction, or to buy books for the library or equipment for the gym and playground.

Spending-per-pupil figures do not take into account the fact that the needs of poor children, after

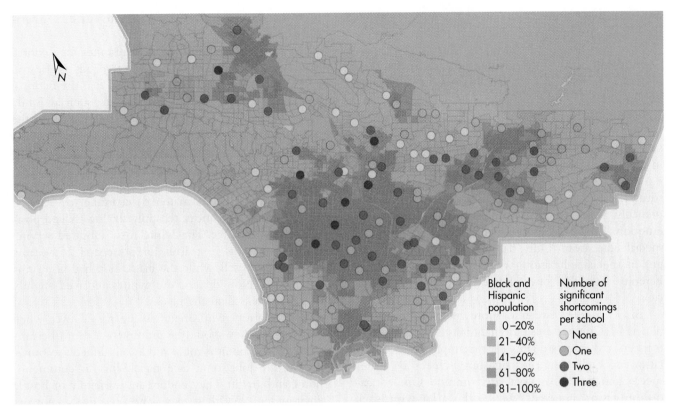

FIGURE 15.2 ■ **Shortcomings among Schools in Los Angeles County**

In Los Angeles County, schools in black and Hispanic neighborhoods have far more shortcomings than schools in white and Asian neighborhoods. A light dot represents a high school with no significant shortcomings. A darker dot represents a high school that has a significant shortcoming involving its teachers (less than 80 percent are certified), its curriculum (less than two-thirds of the courses prepare students for a four-year college), or its facilities (the students attend school in shifts because the buildings are too crowded, so they have a shorter school year). The more shortcomings, the darker the dot. Not a single school that is 90 percent or more white and Asian has a significant shortcoming.

SOURCE: *Atlantic Monthly,* July-August 2004, 64.

years of neglect and with scores of problems at home and in the neighborhood, are greater than the needs of other children. Schools for poor children would require *more* funding to provide their students an equal education.

So many inner-city schools are bleak institutions, filthy and in disrepair. A 30-year veteran of seven District of Columbia schools said all should be condemned. Of her current school, she said, "I have to cover books, computers, and student work stations with plastic to catch the falling plaster and water from the leaking roof. In the school cafeteria, 55-gallon garbage cans are strategically placed to catch the water from gaping holes in the ceiling."[102] In some Los Angeles schools, the children count the rats.[103]

Most inner-city schools are overcrowded. Some don't even have enough chairs for their students. They lack up-to-date texts and paper and pencils. They lack books for literature classes, chemicals for chemistry classes, and computers for computer classes. (Teachers *talk* about using computers.)[104]

Most inner-city schools can't attract enough good teachers. A New York City principal said he is forced to take the "tenth-best" teachers. "I thank God they're still breathing."[105] Even then, the schools can't fill all of their positions, so they must employ armies of substitute teachers to get through the year.

Despite the pattern of unequal funding, cash alone would not solve the problems of inner-city schools. Cultural and economic factors in these communities also restrict the quality of education available in these schools. But cash would help. And, unlike the cultural and economic factors, which will take generations to change, the funding shortfall could be fixed soon.

Some states have equalized funding, but moves to do so in other states have encountered fierce opposition. An alternative to equalized funding would be supplementary funding by states for schools in inner cities. But people's priorities run in other directions. In 1999, the Pennsylvania legislature approved $160 million of public financing for new stadiums for the Eagles and Phillies and another $160 million of public financing for new stadiums for the Steelers and Pirates, while the schools in Philadelphia and Pittsburgh languished.[106]

Second-generation discrimination Even where desegregation of schools has been achieved, segregation within schools exists. This "second-generation discrimination" isolates many black and Latino students by placing them in separate programs or classes from white students. Black children are less likely to be put in programs for gifted students.[107] Black boys, who are 8.6 percent of public school students nationwide, constitute 20 percent of all students who are classified as mentally retarded, 21 percent of those classified as emotionally disturbed, and 15 percent of those put in special education. (Only half as many black girls are put in special education, which suggests that neither heredity nor the boys' home environment is the cause.)[108]

Black children are also more likely to be disciplined.[109] Cultural misunderstandings between white teachers and black students—for example, misinterpretation of body language signaling respect or disrespect—and "racial paranoia" are common. One education professor observed, "We see this a lot with black boys who are cute until about the fourth grade, and then teachers start to fear them."[110] Black boys constitute 23 percent of students who are suspended and 22 percent of those who are expelled.[111] When students are suspended, they fall behind in class and are more likely to quit school.

Discrimination in Employment

Although the Civil Rights Act of 1964 and affirmative action (discussed later in the chapter) have prompted more employers to hire and promote African Americans, discrimination remains.

Researchers sent out fictional résumés for fictional applicants in response to help-wanted ads in Boston and Chicago newspapers. They found that the fictional applicants with white-sounding names, such as Emily or Greg, received significantly more responses than the fictional applicants with black-sounding names, such as Lakisha or Jamal, even though all applicants had similar credentials.[112]

Other researchers used pairs of white and black high school graduates, matched according to their job histories and demeanors, to apply for low-skilled positions in Milwaukee. The white men admitted serving eighteen months in prison for possession of cocaine with intent to sell, while the black men had no criminal record. Nonetheless, the whites received slightly more callbacks than the blacks.[113]

Many blacks who are hired are passed over when they believe they should be promoted.[114] But discrimination at this point is more subtle and difficult to prove.

On the job, some face racial slurs in comments, notes, and graffiti. They endure an unfriendly or hostile environment.[115] Others experience negative stereotypes that question their competence and value. Upper-level executives realize that it is economically advantageous to have a diverse workforce, but some middle-level white managers and lower-level white workers interact poorly with the black employees.

Discrimination in Housing

The Civil Rights Act of 1968 prohibiting discrimination in housing has fostered some desegregation of housing, but extensive segregation persists. One reason is eco-

A teacher tries to teach in the hallway of an overcrowded school in the underfunded Philadelphia school system.

You will be visited tonight by an official you have never met. He begins by telling you he is extremely embarrassed. The organization he represents has made a mistake, something that hardly ever happens.

According to the group's records, he goes on, you were to have been born black—to another set of parents, far from where you were raised.

However, the rules being what they are, this error must be rectified, and as soon as possible. So at midnight tonight, you will become black. And this will mean not simply a darker skin but the bodily and facial features associated with African ancestry. However, inside you will be the person you always were. Your knowledge and ideas will remain intact. But outwardly you will not be recognizable to anyone you now know.

Your visitor emphasizes that being born to the wrong parents was in no way your fault.

Consequently, his organization is prepared to offer you some reasonable recompense. Would you, he asks, care to name a sum of money you might consider appropriate? He adds that his group is by no means poor. It can be quite generous when the circumstances warrant, as they seem to in your case. He finishes by saying that the records show you are scheduled to live another fifty years—as a black man or woman in America.

How much financial recompense would you request?

A professor who puts this parable to white college students finds that most feel $1 million per year—$50 million total—would be appropriate. This much would protect them from, and reimburse them for, the danger and discrimination they would face if they were perceived as black. In acknowledging that white skin is worth this much, the students also are admitting that treatment of the races has not been nearly equal.

SOURCE: Andrew Hacker, *Two Nations: Black and White, Separate, Hostile, Unequal* (New York: Scribner, 1992), 31–32.

nomic. Most blacks do not have enough money to buy homes in white neighborhoods. This problem is aggravated by local zoning laws designed to establish a certain type of community. Often these laws require large lots and large houses, which command high prices.

Another reason is continuing discrimination. Occasional violence and social pressure discourage blacks who try to move into white neighborhoods. Actual discrimination by homeowners, real estate agents, lenders, and insurers also stymies them. A study of twenty metropolitan areas, using white and minority testers responding to house and apartment ads, found that blacks who try to buy a house face discrimination

17 percent of the time, and those who try to rent an apartment do so 22 percent of the time. (These figures from 2002 are about 25 percent lower than the results from 1989, which was the last time the government had conducted this research.)[116] If callers sound black, landlords may claim that the apartment has already been rented. Most Americans can identify a telephone caller as black or white.[117]

When blacks do buy a house, they are more likely to be charged a higher interest rate for their mortgage loan. Even blacks who earn $100,000 a year are charged higher rates than whites who make less than $40,000, although the blacks should pose less risk for the lenders.[118] Blacks tend to have less wealth and more credit problems than whites, and they receive less assistance and less information about interest rates from the lenders.[119]

Although residential segregation remains pervasive in metropolitan areas, it is declining. The 2000 census shows that the fast-growing suburban areas in the West and South are much more likely to have integrated neighborhoods than a decade earlier, though the stagnant "rust belt" cities in the East and Midwest are integrating slower.[120] Even middle-class blacks who escape the ghetto often end up in black neighborhoods in the suburbs of these cities.[121]

Segregation does not continue because blacks "want to live among their own kind," as some whites insist. Surveys show that only about 15 percent want to live in segregated neighborhoods, and most of them cite their fear of white hostility as the reason. Eighty-five percent would prefer mixed neighborhoods. Many say the optimal level would be half black and half white. But the optimal level for most blacks is unacceptable to most whites. Whites tend to move out when the concentration of blacks reaches 8 to 10 percent.[122] These contrasting attitudes make integration an elusive goal, given that blacks make up 13 percent of the population and a much larger percentage of some cities.

These patterns and attitudes are all the more troublesome because residential segregation, of course, leads to school segregation.

Discrimination in Other Ways

African Americans face discrimination from police officers. The practice of **racial profiling,** which is based on the assumption that minorities, especially males, are more likely to commit crimes, especially those involving drugs, targets minorities for stops and searches. Without evidence, officers stop minority drivers and search them and their vehicles.[123] Sometimes officers stop minority pedestrians and passengers in airports as well. Although police departments deny profiling, statistics show clear evidence of the practice in many places. In Los Angeles, blacks are two times as likely to be stopped and four times as likely to be searched as other drivers. However, they are less likely to be found with illegal substances.[124] Interstate 95 from Florida to New York is notorious. Through Maryland, whereas 18 percent of speeders were black, 29 percent of those stopped and 71 percent of those searched were black. On the New Jersey Turnpike, 15 percent of speeders were black, but 35 percent of the drivers pulled over were black.[125]

African Americans speak of the moving violation "DWB"—*driving while black.* A Chicago journalist who was stopped at least every other time he traveled through the Midwest learned not to rent flashy Mustangs or wear his beret. Others avoid tinted windshields or expensive sunglasses—any flamboyance—to avoid the cops.[126] Former Representative J.C. Watts (R-Okla.) was pulled over by police six times in one day in his home state.[127]

Profiling might be justified if it led to the apprehension of dangerous criminals, but apparently it does not. Although African American young men evidently do commit a larger percentage of certain crimes,[128] profiling does not lead the police to many criminals. When police stop motorists, they find no greater evidence of crimes by blacks and Hispanics than by whites.[129] Meanwhile, the encounters often humiliate those who are stopped and spark animosity toward the police in these communities (as the movie *Crash* so clearly depicted).

Some states and many counties and cities have taken steps to reduce profiling, such as recording data on every stop to see whether the police, or individual officers, are prone to profile. Yet the cops on the beat, who feel that profiling is useful, are reluctant to change their habits.

Other discrimination from police officers is less common but more serious. Sometimes officers arrest black citizens without legal cause, and occasionally they use excessive force against them. Numerous examples attest to improper beatings.[130] Sometimes officers lie while testifying against black suspects in court. As a result, even prominent African Americans say their "worst fear" is to go before the criminal justice system.[131] It is little wonder, then, that black jurors hearing the O.J. Simpson trial and black citizens following it put less faith in the police testimony than white observers did.

Cautious parents teach their children how to avoid sending the wrong signals to police. Some parents urge their children not to wear street fashions and not to use cell phones, which from a distance might be mistaken as weapons. Some schools offer survival workshops for police encounters. Minority officers instruct the students what to do when they get stopped: Don't reach for an ID unless the officer asks for one; don't mumble or talk loudly; don't antagonize by asking for a badge number or threatening to file a complaint.[132]

Most blacks, even professionals, face insults because of their race. Black women tell of being mistaken for hotel chambermaids. A family therapist, invited to speak at a professional conference, was stopped in the hallway by a white attendee who asked where the restrooms were. When the therapist appeared taken aback, the attendee said she thought the woman worked at the hotel. Although the therapist was wearing her official name tag and presenter's ribbon, the attendee did not look past her black face.[133] Black women also tell of waiting for friends in hotel lobbies and being mistaken for prostitutes by white men and police officers. A distinguished black political scientist was mistaken for a butler in his own home. Black doctors tell of dressing up to go shopping to avoid being regarded as shoplifters. But dressing up is no guarantee. A black lawyer, a senior partner in a large law firm, arrived at work early one morning, before the doors were unlocked. As he reached for his key, a young white lawyer, a junior associate in the firm, arrived at the same time, blocked his entrance, and asked, repeatedly and demandingly, "May I help you?" The white associate had taken the black partner for an intruder.[134] Although in these encounters the insults were unintentional, the stings hurt just the same.

The accumulation of such incidents, which more than eight in ten blacks say they occasionally experience, has created a "black middle-class rage" among many.[135]

African American communities often have tense relationships with local police departments. After hurricane Katrina, Leonard Thomas's family was living in its flooded home when a SWAT team burst in, believing that the family was squatting in another's home.

Overall, discrimination against African Americans continues. Whites speak of "past discrimination"—sometimes referring to slavery, sometimes to official segregation—but this phrase is misleading. Of course, there is a lot less discrimination now due to the civil rights movement, Supreme Court decisions, and congressional acts. However, there is nothing "past" about much "past discrimination."[136] The effects linger, and the discrimination itself persists.

Even when blacks point out the discrimination, some whites insist that little discrimination is left. These whites apparently assume that they know more than blacks do about what it is like to be black. Indeed, the perceptual gap between blacks and whites about the existence of discrimination is a real barrier to improved race relations. Whites who believe nothing is wrong do not favor actions to fix what they see as a nonexistent problem.

Improving Conditions for African Americans?

Despite continuing discrimination, African Americans have taken long strides toward achieving equal rights. These strides have led to much better living conditions for them and to a healthier racial climate in society.

Since the 1960s, blacks' lives have improved in most ways that can be measured.[137] Blacks have a lower poverty rate and a longer life expectancy than before. They have completed more years of education, with larger numbers attending college and graduate school. They have attained higher occupational levels—for example, tripling their proportion of the country's professionals[138]—and higher income levels. Many—well over half—have reached the middle class.[139] Almost half own their own homes,[140] and a third have moved to the suburbs.[141]

During the years that blacks' lives have improved, whites' racial attitudes have also improved. Although answers to pollsters' questions cannot be accepted as perfect reflections of people's views, especially on emotional matters such as racial attitudes, the answers can be considered general indicators of these views. Polls encompassing a wide variety of racial questions show that whites' views have changed significantly (even assuming that some whites gave more socially acceptable answers than they really felt).[142]

Whites and blacks both report more social contact with members of the other race since the 1960s, and both report more approval of interracial dating and marriage. The acceptance of interracial dating and marriage is especially significant because these practices were the ultimate taboos in segregated society.

Interracial couples represented the clearest breach and their potential offspring the greatest threat to continued segregation.

According to one survey, four of every ten Americans said they had dated someone of another race, and almost three of every ten said it had been a "serious" relationship.[143] According to the 2000 census, 6.7 percent of all marriages—up from 4.4 percent in the 1990 census—are interracial. (And many cohabitations, which aren't included in the census, are interracial as well.) Thirteen percent of marriages involving blacks are interracial; a third of those involving Hispanics and Asians are also.[144]

Some whites, of course, remain blatant racists. Due to socioeconomic reasons, these whites are more likely to have contacts with blacks—to live and work in proximity to them—than are tolerant whites, who are more educated and more prosperous. Even so, blatant racist behavior occurs less frequently and is condemned more quickly than before.

Although the push for civil rights opened many doors, some blacks were not in a position to pass through. About a quarter of the black population lives in poverty—two and one-half times the rate among the white population—and about a tenth, the poorest of the poor, exists in a state of economic and social "disintegration."[145] This "underclass" is trapped in a cycle of self-perpetuating problems from which it is extremely difficult to escape. These people are isolated from the rest of society and demoralized about their prospects for improvement.

The problems of the lower class and the underclass were exacerbated by economic changes that began in the 1970s and hit the poor the hardest. Good-paying manufacturing jobs in the cities—the traditional path out of poverty for immigrant groups—disappeared. Chicago lost over three hundred thousand jobs, New York over five hundred thousand.[146] Many jobs were eliminated by automation, while many others were moved to foreign countries or to the suburbs. Although service jobs increased, most were outside the cities, required more education, or paid lower wages than the manufacturing jobs had.

As a result, many black men, especially, lost their jobs and their ability to support a family. This led to pressure on intact families and also to a decrease in the number of "marriageable" black men and an increase in the number of households headed by black women.[147] The percentage of such households rose from about 20 percent of all black families in 1960 to 45 percent in 2000.[148] And 60 percent of black children live in such households. These families are among the poorest in the country (see Chapter 17).

Meanwhile, much of the black middle class fled the inner cities to the suburbs. Their migration left the ghettos with fewer healthy businesses, strong schools, or other institutions to provide stability and fewer role models to portray mainstream behavior.[149] By 1996, one Chicago ghetto with sixty-six thousand people had just one supermarket and one bank but forty-eight state-licensed lottery agents and ninety-nine state-licensed liquor stores and bars.[150] The combination of chronic unemployment in the inner cities and middle-class migration from the inner cities created an environment that offers ample opportunity and some incentive to use drugs, commit crimes, and engage in other types of antisocial behavior.

The development of crack, a cheap form of cocaine, in the mid-1980s aggravated these conditions. It led to more drug use and drug trafficking and, because of steady demand by users and huge profits for dealers, much more violence. As a result, crack overwhelmed whole neighborhoods.[151] The spread of AIDS, rampant among intravenous drug users, further aggravated these conditions.

Now, about 44 percent of federal and state prisoners are black, although only 13 percent of the U.S. population is black.[152] Almost 10 percent of black men between 25 and 29 are in prison.[153] According to one study in Washington, D.C., one-fourth of black males born in the 1960s were charged with drug dealing between the ages of eighteen and twenty-four.[154] (This is partly due to greater enforcement of drug laws against black offenders than white offenders.) Their behavior exacerbated the problem of too few marriageable men and too many female-headed households.

It is commonly recognized that the plight of young black men is worse than that of any other group in society. Although increasing numbers of black men are attending college, more receive their GED (high school equivalence degree) in prison than graduate from college.[155] A black man in Harlem has less chance of living past forty than a man in Bangladesh.[156]

These problems affect even middle-class blacks who escaped to the suburbs. While returning from the city to see their relatives or old friends or to get a haircut, they may be in the wrong place at the wrong time. They may wear the wrong color shirt, wrong logo hat, or the wrong brand of shoes and get caught up in gang violence. A father asks, "How many cultures can you say that when a guy turns twenty-five, he actually celebrates because he didn't think he would make it?"[157]

After widespread riots in the 1960s, the Kerner Commission, appointed by President Johnson to examine the cause of the riots, concluded, "What white Americans have never fully understood—but what the Negro can never forget—is that white society is deeply implicated in the ghetto. White institutions created it, white institutions maintain it, and white society condones it." After the riots, however, governments did little to improve the conditions that precipitated the riots. Now the conditions in the ghettos are worse.

After the riots in Los Angeles following the trial of police officers who beat Rodney King in 1992, there was more talk about improving the conditions in the ghetto. But a columnist who had heard such talk before commented, "My guess is that when all is said and done, a great deal more will be said than done. The truth is we don't know any quick fixes for our urban ills and we lack the patience and resources for slow fixes."[158]

These problems are all the more difficult to resolve because the cities have lost political power as they have lost population due to white flight and black migration. Since 1992, more voters (including many blacks) have lived in the suburbs than in the cities. Suburban voters do not urge action on urban problems. Sometimes, in fact, they resist action if it means an increase in their taxes or a decrease in their services.

For the black lower class, and especially for the black underclass, it is apparent that civil rights are not enough. As one black leader said, "What good is a seat in the front of the bus if you don't have the money for the fare?"[159]

But most blacks do not fall in the lower class or underclass, and most do not dwell in the inner cities. It would be a serious mistake to hold the stereotypical view that the majority reside in the inner cities and that a majority of them live in dysfunctional families filled with crackheads and prone to violence. Although black men lag behind, black women especially have vastly improved lives—academically, professionally, and financially—over the span of one generation.[160]

Discrimination against Hispanics

Hispanics, also called Latinos, are people in the United States who have a Spanish-speaking background. Although they are frequently considered a separate race, they can be of any race. Some are brown skinned, others black skinned, and still others white skinned. Many are an amalgam of European, African, and American Indian ancestry that makes it impossible to classify them by race. Thus, Hispanics should be regarded as an ethnic group and a statistical category rather than a distinct "race."

The first Hispanics came to America from Spain in the 1500s. They settled in the Southwest, and when the United States took this land from Mexico in 1848, they became U.S. citizens. Other Latinos came to America more recently.

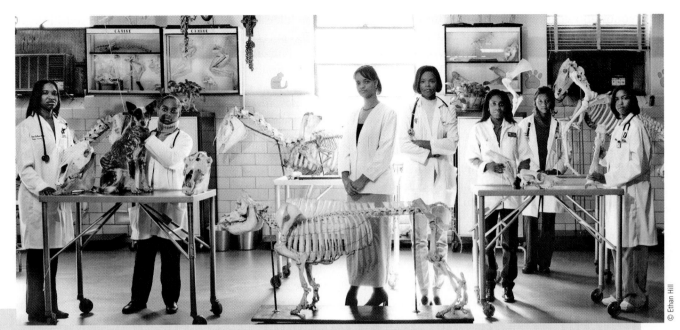

Black women are making great progress. They are more likely than black men to graduate from college and professional schools. At Tuskegee University, they dominate the veterinary school.

About 60 percent of Hispanics trace their ancestry to Mexico.[161] They are heavily concentrated in the Southwest but are increasingly spreading throughout the United States, including the Midwest and the South. About 10 percent are from Puerto Rico, which is a commonwealth—a self-governing territory—of the United States. As members of the commonwealth, they are U.S. citizens. Most live in New York, Boston, Chicago, and other cities in the North. Another 4 percent are from Cuba. Following the establishment of a Communist government in Cuba in 1959, many fled to the United States and settled in South Florida. A significant number are from various islands in the Caribbean and countries in Central America, where the emigrants left turmoil and oppression. A smaller number are from countries in South America or from Spain.

Despite the diversity of their origins, Latinos are especially concentrated in six states. More than half live in California and Texas, where they make up one-third of the population. Already they outnumber Anglos in Los Angeles (47 percent to 29 percent) and Houston (37 percent to 31 percent).[162] Many of the rest live in Florida, New Jersey, New York, and Illinois, but there are growing pockets elsewhere.

Latinos have overtaken blacks as the largest minority in the United States. They represent 15 percent of our population. (This number includes legal and illegal residents.) Now the United States has the seventh-largest Latino population in the world, and within the United States, this group, fueled by high immigration rates and birthrates, is the fastest-growing minority (slightly faster growing than Asians).

Latinos never endured slavery, but they have faced discrimination. Although numerous Latinos are Caucasian, many Puerto Ricans and Cubans have African ancestry, and many Mexicans have some Indian ancestry, so they have darker skin than non-Hispanic whites. Like blacks, Hispanics have faced discrimination in education, employment, housing, and voting.[163]

Latinos also encounter discrimination due to continuing immigration. Illegal immigrants pouring in from Mexico exacerbate hostility and discrimination against Latinos. In recent years, the flood of illegal immigration has produced a wave of anti-immigration sentiment throughout the United States. (However, the most strident opposition has come from rural counties in red states where there are few immigrants.)[164]

This sentiment affects the Latinos who are legal residents and even citizens. U.S. Border Patrol and local law enforcement officials, who cannot tell the difference between legal residents and illegal residents, often stop Latinos for questioning not only at the border but inland as well. (Agents stopped the mayor of Pomona, California, more than one hundred miles from the border and ordered him to produce papers to prove that he is a legal resident.) Because illegal residents can't get driver's licenses and most don't have driver's insurance, local law enforcement officials also stop Latino drivers to check for these things. Even when the officials are well intentioned, their conduct is considered harassment by law-abiding legal residents.

Latinos also encounter discrimination from police, as African Americans do. Police use racial profiling, suspecting them of crimes involving drugs as well as illegal immigration. In Illinois, Latinos constitute 8 percent of the population but 30 percent of individuals stopped by police.[165]

Latino immigrants who are farmworkers face additional problems. Agriculture has long avoided regulations imposed on other businesses. For decades, the minimum wage law did not apply to farmworkers. Still today, farmworkers are denied the opportunity for overtime pay and the right to organize. In many states, they are excluded from workers' compensation and unemployment benefits programs. Their lack of governmental protection, coupled with their economic desperation, makes them vulnerable to unscrupulous employers. The Department of Justice has investigated more than one hundred cases of involuntary servitude—slavery—and has prosecuted a half dozen from South Florida in recent years.[166]

Discrimination in Education

For years, Latino children in some areas were not allowed to attend schools at all. In other areas, they were segregated into "Mexican" schools whose quality was not comparable with that of Anglo schools.[167] In the 1940s, Mexican American organizations asked the federal courts to rule that Mexican Americans were "white" so they could not be segregated from non-Hispanic whites. The courts agreed. But this strategy backfired when the Supreme Court declared segrega-tion illegal. Many school districts achieved "integra-tion" by combining Hispanics with blacks, leaving non-Hispanic whites in their own schools.[168]

Although *de jure* segregation has been struck down,[169] *de facto* segregation exists in cities where Latinos are concentrated due to residential segregation and white flight to private schools and to the suburbs. Many Latinos attend schools with more than 90 percent minorities, and most attend schools with more than 50 percent minorities.[170]

Even where Latinos go to desegregated schools, they are often segregated within the schools. They face second-generation discrimination, though not as much as blacks.[171]

Predominantly Latino schools, like predominantly black schools, are not as well funded as other schools because they are located in poor communities that do not get as much revenue from property taxes. In San Antonio, Mexican American families were concentrated in the poorest districts, whereas wealthy families were concentrated in a section that was incorporated as a separate district, although it was surrounded on four sides by the rest of the city. Its property taxes financed its schools only. When Mexican American parents sued, the Burger Court ruled that the Fourteenth Amendment's equal protection clause does not require states to equalize funding between school districts.[172] The case highlighted this problem, prompting some states to equalize funding but allowing other states to maintain the status quo.

Latinos' primary problem in education, however, is the language barrier. Many are unable to speak English,

Hispanic immigrants take strenuous jobs, such as roofing, that many Americans don't want.

causing them to fail in school and drop out of school at higher rates than other students, even African Americans. One-third of Latinos leave school at some point; one-fourth drop out in high school.[173]

Bilingual education was established to help such students. These classes use the students' native language to teach them English and also substantive subjects such as math. The goal is to transition from their native language to English. In 1968, Congress encouraged bilingual education by providing funding, and in 1974 the Supreme Court, in a case brought by Chinese parents in San Francisco, held that schools must teach students in a language they can understand.[174] This can be their native language, or it can be English if they have been taught English. These federal actions prompted states to establish bilingual education programs. More than 150 languages, from Chinese to Yapese, have been offered. Because almost three-fourths of the students who do not speak English are Hispanic, Spanish has been the most common.[175]

Yet bilingual programs have not worked as well in practice as they have promised in theory. They are expensive because they require more teachers and smaller classes. They are impractical because many schools cannot find enough teachers in the necessary languages. California, where half of all students in bilingual programs lived, fell twenty-one thousand teachers short in one year.[176] Schools were unable to offer bilingual education to two-thirds of the students who were eligible.[177]

Bilingual programs have been controversial. Although Latino groups have advocated these programs as a way to preserve Latino culture, Latino parents want their children to learn English and to learn it well. A survey of Latinos in forty cities found that more than 90 percent thought U.S. citizens and residents should learn English.[178] A survey of Cuban Americans in south Florida found that 98 percent thought it was important for their children to read and write "perfect English."[179] And their children apparently agree. More than four-fifths of immigrant children in South Florida and more than two-thirds of

Cuban Americans are more likely than other Latinos to be middle class.

© Stephanie Maze/CORBIS

those in San Diego prefer English to their familial language.[180] Latino parents and children worry that bilingual programs will delay their mastery of English. Seventy-five percent of recent immigrants, including 56 percent of Mexican immigrants, oppose these programs.[181]

For symbolic reasons, many Anglos also oppose these programs. Bilingualism prompts concerns, even fears, about the continuing dominance of Anglo culture in American society.

For all of these reasons, California citizens voted to abolish bilingual programs in 1998. Now non-English-speaking students receive intensive immersion in English for one year and then move into regular classes. Initial research indicates that Spanish-speaking students are improving in their ability to read English and to understand other subjects taught in English.[182]

Despite the decline in bilingual programs and widespread perceptions of many Americans, current immigrants are learning English just as previous waves of European immigrants learned it. Among Spanish speakers in the United States, 90 percent speak English (though 18 percent say they do not speak it well).[183] Although about half of those who arrived as teenagers or adults do not speak English proficiently, almost all of those who arrived as young children or who are in the second generation do speak English proficiently.[184] Cuban Americans are learning it as fast or faster than any group in history.[185] Mexican Americans are learning it as they live longer in the United States. Although many of those who come for work and plan to return

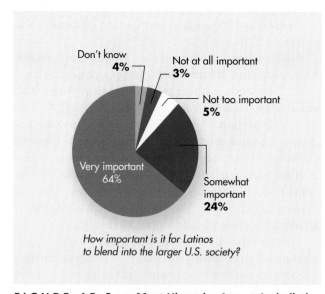

How important is it for Latinos to blend into the larger U.S. society?

Don't know **4%**
Not at all important **3%**
Not too important **5%**
Very important **64%**
Somewhat important **24%**

FIGURE 15.3 ■ Most Hispanics Accept Assimilation

SOURCE: *Time*, August 22, 2005, 56. Poll conducted by phone, with interviews in English and Spanish. *N* = 503. Margin of error = ±5 percentage points.

to Mexico do not speak English, most of those who plan to remain in the United States learn to speak more English, and almost all of their children learn to speak fluent English.[186]

The drive to learn English is so strong that only a third of Latinos born in the United States are bilingual. Most cannot speak Spanish.[187]

It is true that some immigrant communities, especially Cubans in South Florida and Mexicans in parts of the Southwest, are so large that people can survive without learning English. But most feel pressure to learn English to function in the broader society and for their children to succeed in school. Indeed, 89 percent believe that those who immigrate must learn English to succeed in the United States.[188] (For further evidence of their inclination to assimilate, see Figure 15.3 and the box "Latinos Choose Anglo Names.")

Combating Discrimination against Hispanics

In the 1960s, Latino advocacy groups tried to imitate African American groups by using protests and other forms of direct action. The Chicano movement attempted to forge a powerful bloc from the diverse population of Hispanics. César Chávez successfully led a coalition of labor, civil rights, and religious groups to obtain better working conditions for migrant farmworkers in California. But few other visible national leaders or organizations emerged.

Although their birthrates and immigration rates have expanded their numbers, Latinos remain more diverse and less cohesive than blacks. Most do not even consider themselves part of a common group.[189] They identify strongly with their national origin and have little contact with Hispanics of other national origins. Therefore, most do not call themselves "Hispanics" or "Latinos" but rather "Mexican Americans," "Puerto Ricans," or "Cuban Americans."[190] Also, they have different legal statuses. Puerto Ricans are American citizens by birth, but many other Latinos are not citizens. And they lack a shared, defining experience in their background, such as slavery for blacks, to unite them.

They do not even agree on a collective label for themselves. Traditionalists often use *Hispanic*, whereas activists usually say *Latino*. Those who derive from the Iberian peninsula, which includes Spain and Portugal, tend to favor *Hispanic*. They believe that *Latino* excludes those who are not from Latin America. Those who derive from south of the border increasingly favor *Latino*, as many in California used to prefer *Chicano*.[191] (Because of their lack of agreement, our text uses the terms *Latino* and *Hispanic* interchangeably.)

Where Hispanics are highly concentrated, however, they are increasingly powerful at the local and state levels of government. Rather than focusing primarily on immigration issues, bilingual education, and affirmative action, they are addressing broader concerns, such as improving health care and reducing school class size. Yet Latino politicians have not shaped a common agenda, perhaps because Latino people do not share a common agenda.[192]

They are potentially powerful at the national level as well. When Congress considered harsh measures toward illegal immigrants in 2006, hundreds of thousands of Latinos rallied against the measures (as Chapter 5's "You Are There" explained). Many families include legal and illegal residents—children who were born here living with parents who are illegal, or nuclear families who are legal residents living with grandparents or aunts and uncles who are illegal—so congressional threats of deportation sparked real fears in families. Politicians' comments that immigrants are taking jobs from citizens and not contributing anything to society ignited their anger. Latino teens defied their parents and school officials, leaving their schools for the rallies. In their passion, some observers saw the stirrings of political activism among young Latinos.

With their huge numbers, Latinos are a coveted bloc of voters. Yet many are not citizens, and many of those who are citizens do not register and vote. Although the Latino and African American populations are nearly the same size, six million fewer Latinos are registered to vote.[193] Nevertheless, the Latino voters are numerous enough to be courted. Although most, except Cuban Americans, are Democrats, the Republicans believe they need to attract more if their party hopes to win national elections in the future. The Bush administration has adopted a strategy to entice them. President Bush appointed a Cuban American as secretary of the Department of Housing and Urban Development and a Mexican American as attorney general. He proposed immigration reform that would allow more immigrants into the United States to work and that would grant legal status to some illegal immigrants here now. And he sprinkles Spanish into his speeches before Hispanic or mixed audiences.

Meanwhile, Latino individuals are moving up society's ladder. More attend college and become managers and professionals. At least those who speak educated English appear to be following the pattern of earlier generations of immigrants from Southern and Eastern Europe—arriving poor, facing discrimination, but eventually working their way up. Along the way, they are also assimilating through high rates of marriage to non-Latinos.

Discrimination against American Indians

More than two million American Indians live in the United States. Although some native Americans are Eskimos and Aleuts from Alaska, most are Indians, representing more than 550 tribes with different histories, customs, and languages. Proud of their tribal heritage, most prefer to be known by their tribal name, such as Cheyenne or Sioux, than by the collective terms Indians or Native Americans.[194] (Although some books use the term Native Americans, the most recent survey of these people shows a clear preference for the term Indians over Native Americans, so our text, when referring to these people collectively, will usually use the term Indians.) Most live in the western half of the country, and half live on reservations (see Figure 15.4).

American Indians have endured treatment quite different from what African Americans and Hispanics have encountered.

Government Policy toward American Indians

Government policy toward Indians has ranged from forced separation at one extreme to forced assimilation at the other. Either way, the policy has reflected discrimination toward the Indians.

Separation Initially, the policy was separation. For many years, people believed that the North American continent was so vast that most of its interior would remain wilderness populated by Indians who would have ample room to live and hunt. The Constitution reflects this belief. It grants Congress authority to "regulate commerce with foreign nations, and among the several states, and with the Indian tribes." In early cases, Chief Justice John Marshall described the tribes as "dependent domestic nations."[195] They were within U.S. borders but outside its political process.

Early treaties reinforced separation by establishing boundaries between Indians and non-Indians. The government thought these boundaries were necessary for its growth, the Indians for their survival. The

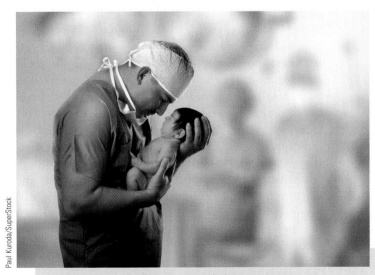

Latinos are gradually improving their status as more go to college and graduate school and become professionals, such as this doctor.

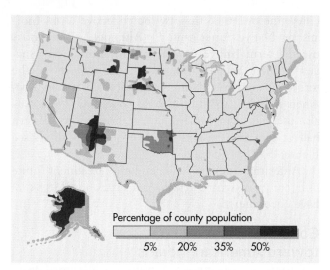

FIGURE 15.4 ■ American Indians in the United States

SOURCE: Eric Schmitt, "U.S. Now More Diverse, Ethnically and Racially," *New York Times*, April 1, 2001, sec. 1, 20.

Percentage of county population

5%   20%   35%   50%

boundaries were intended to minimize conflict. White hunters or settlers who ventured across the boundaries could be punished as the Indians saw fit.

But as the country grew, it became increasingly difficult to contain the settlers within the boundaries. Mounting pressure to push the Indians farther west led to the Indian Removal Act of 1830, which authorized removal of tribes east of the Mississippi River and relocation on reservations west of the river. At the time, people considered the Great Plains to be the great American desert, unfit for habitation by whites but suitable for Indians. The removal of most Indians was mandatory and was supervised by the cavalry.

Assimilation and citizenship As more settlers moved west, the vision of a separate Indian country far beyond white civilization faded. In the 1880s, the government switched its policy to assimilation. Prompted by Christian churches, officials sought to "civilize" the Indians—to integrate them into American society, whether they wanted to be integrated or not. In place of their traditional means of subsistence, rendered useless once the tribes were removed from their historical homelands, the government subdivided reservation land into small tracts and allotted these tracts to tribe members in the hope that they would turn to farming as white and black settlers had. Bureau of Indian Affairs (BIA) agents, who supervised the reservations, tried to root out Indian ways and replace them with white dress and hairstyles, the English language, and the Christian religion. Government boarding schools separated Indian children from their families to instill these new practices.

Since the adoption of the Constitution, Native Americans were not considered citizens but members of separate nations. Treaties made exceptions for those who married whites and for those who left their tribes and abandoned their tribal customs. But in 1890, after government policy had switched to assimilation, Congress permitted some who remained with their tribes on reservations to become citizens. Sometimes a formal ceremony marked citizenship. In one, the Indian shot his last arrow and then took hold of the handles of a plow to demonstrate his assimilation.[196] After World War I, Congress granted citizenship to those who served in the military during the war, and finally, in 1924, Congress extended it to all those born in the United States.

Citizenship enabled Indians to vote and hold office, though some states effectively barred them from the polls for decades. Arizona denied them the right to vote until 1948, Utah until 1956.[197]

Tribal restoration By the 1930s, the government recognized the negative consequences of coerced assimilation. Most Indians could speak English, but they were poorly educated in other respects. And with their traditional means of earning a living gone, most were poverty-stricken. The policy had led to the destruction of native culture without much assimilation into white society. Consequently, in 1934 Congress implemented a new policy of tribal restoration that recognized Indians as distinct persons and tribes as autonomous entities encouraged to govern themselves once again. Traditional cultural and religious practices were accepted, and

"I love the way you make those yams. You'll have to give me the recipe before your culture is obliterated from the face of the earth."

Dilos Lonewolf became Tom Torlino, during his transformation at a boarding school in Carlisle, Pennsylvania. Indians were shorn of their hair and clothes and trained to adopt white ways.

Indian children, no longer forced to attend boarding schools, were taught some Indian languages.

Reflecting the policy of tribal restoration and the efforts of other minorities in the 1960s and 1970s, Indian interest groups became active. Indian law firms filed lawsuits, seeking to protect not only tribal independence and traditional ways but also land, mineral, and water resources.

The diversity and the dispersion of the tribes—they are divided by culture and by geography, often located in the remotest and poorest parts of the country—make it difficult for them to present a united front. Nevertheless, they have been able to wrest some autonomy from the government. In particular, they have gained more authority over the educational and social programs administered by the BIA for the tribes.[198]

In recent years, Indians have fought for the return of some tribal land and for an accounting of the money owed them for the use of their individual land held in trust by the government. In the early nineteenth century, the government took tribal land and put it in trust for the Indians. But then the government divided the land, classified large tracts as "surplus," and offered the tracts to white settlers. In return, it paid individual Indians a pittance. In this way, the Indians lost two-thirds of their territory. The government held the remaining land in trust for the Indians, leasing it to ranchers, loggers, and miners. The government collected the rents and royalties for the Indians. But the BIA did not bother to keep accurate records or even to preserve its records.

A class-action lawsuit, dubbed "the Indian Enron case," seeks a reckoning of the accounts and a payment to the Indians who are owed money.[199]

After a Supreme Court ruling and a congressional law in the 1980s underscored tribal sovereignty on tribal land, tribes could establish gambling casinos on reservations, even if their state did not allow casinos.[200] Almost three hundred tribes have done so, although less than a dozen have found a bonanza—mostly small tribes in populous states where the casinos attract numerous customers.[201] Many of the casinos are bankrolled by unknown investors who keep most of the profits. A Malaysian businessman owns one, a South African developer another. For many casinos, little money trickles down to tribal members.[202]

With casino revenue, the tribes have begun to buy into the political process, as other groups have done. Threatened by gambling interests in Las Vegas and Atlantic City, which fear that tribal casinos will lure away potential customers, the tribes have formed their own lobby, the National Indian Gaming Association, and made their own contributions to politicians. These contributions reportedly total more than the contributions by individual corporations such as General Motors, Boeing, or AT&T.[203]

Now more Indians share the views of one activist who says, "You have a federal government, state governments, and tribal governments—three sovereigns in one country. This is the civil rights movement of Native Americans."[204]

Indians feel renewed cultural pride in ancient traditions but also the lure of modern technology.

Indeed, Native Americans enjoy renewed pride. This has led most tribes to establish programs to preserve their language. The goal may simply be to preserve their culture, or it may also be to avoid total assimilation.[205]

In the last four censuses, from 1970 through 2000, many more Americans identified themselves as Native Americans than birth and death records indicate.[206] According to the 2000 census, Native Americans have doubled, from two million to four million people.[207] If the censuses were accurate, Native Americans would be the fastest-growing minority group in the country. Evidently, many people, including those with only distant (or imagined) Indian ancestry, who did not wish to identify themselves as Native Americans in 1960, chose to do so in later decades. Attracted by natives' tribal culture, their spiritual life, or their personal adornments, some people engaged in "ethnic shopping."[208]

Nevertheless, Indians remain at the bottom of America's racial and ethnic ladder. They are the least educated and most unemployed group, the poorest and sickest group, with the highest alcoholism rates and lowest life expectancy, of any people in the country.

Sex Discrimination

Discrimination against Women

For many generations, people believed that natural differences between the sexes required them to occupy separate spheres of life. Men would dominate the public domain of work and government, and women would dominate the private domain of the home. Both domains were important, and men were considered superior in one and women were considered superior in the other. Unlike racial minorities, women were not held in disdain in all aspects of life.

Thomas Jefferson, the most egalitarian of the Founders, reflected this widespread view when he said, "Were our state a pure democracy there would still be excluded from our deliberations women, who, to prevent deprivation of morals and ambiguity of issues, should not mix promiscuously in gatherings of men."[209] That is, women are more moral than men, so they would be corrupted by politics, but they are also more irrational, so they would confuse the issues. For both reasons, they should not participate in politics.

So, most women were denied the right to vote, and married women were denied other rights—to manage income they received from jobs, to manage property they acquired before marriage, to enter into contracts, or to sue. Some states eventually granted these rights, but when disputes arose within families, male judges hesitated to tell other men how to treat their wives.

Even women's citizenship was tied to their husbands' citizenship. If a foreign woman married an American man, she automatically became a United States citizen. But if an American woman married a foreign man, she automatically lost her United States citizenship. (Women's citizenship would not become independent of their husbands' citizenship until 1922, shortly after women gained the right to vote.)

Women were also barred from schools and jobs. Before the Civil War, they were not admitted to public high schools. Because they were being prepared for motherhood, education was considered unnecessary, even dangerous. According to the *Encyclopaedia Britannica* in 1800, women had smaller brains than men.[210] Education would fatigue them and possibly ruin their reproductive organs. Similarly, before the Civil War, women were not encouraged to hold jobs. Those who did were shunted into jobs that were seen as extensions of the domestic domain, such as producing textiles, clothes, and shoes in sex-segregated factories.[211]

This traditional conception of gender roles created problems for those women who did not fit the mold. After the Civil War, Myra Bradwell ran a private school, founded a weekly newspaper, and worked for various civic organizations. She was active in the women's suffrage movement and instrumental in persuading the Illinois legislature to expand women's legal rights. After studying law, however, she was denied a license to practice law solely because she was a woman. The Supreme Court upheld the Illinois policy in 1873.[212] Justice Joseph Bradley declared:

Law, as well as nature itself, has always recognized a wide difference in the respective spheres and destinies of man and woman. Man is, or should be, the woman's protector and defender. The natural and proper timidity and delicacy which belongs to the female sex evidently unfits it for many of the occupations of civil life. . . . The constitution of the family organization . . . indicates the domestic sphere as that which properly belongs to the domain and functions of womanhood. The harmony . . . of interests and views which belong, or should belong, to the family institution is repugnant to the idea of a woman adopting a distinct and independent career from that of her husband. . . . The paramount destiny and mission of woman are to fulfill the noble and benign offices of wife and mother. This is the law of the Creator. And the rules of civil society must be adapted to the general constitution of things, and cannot be based upon exceptional cases.

Sometimes it was difficult to distinguish between this separate-but-equal view and discriminatory treatment. In the 1860s and 1870s, the doctors who practiced scientific medicine formed the American Medical Association (AMA) to drive out other people who offered medical services. These people included not only hucksters and quacks but also women who served as midwives or abortionists. Although abortions had been widely available, the AMA, drawing on popular fears about the women's suffrage movement, convinced male state legislators that abortions were "a threat to social order and to male authority." The woman who seeks an abortion, the AMA explained, "becomes unmindful of the course marked out for her by Providence, she overlooks the duties imposed on her by the marriage contract. She yields to the pleasure—but shrinks from the pains and responsibilities of maternity. . . . Let not the husband of such a wife flatter himself that he possesses her affection."[213]

Sometimes the discriminatory treatment was even more blatant. The Mississippi Supreme Court acknowledged a husband's right to beat his wife.[214] Using the "rule of thumb," the court held that a husband could not beat his wife with a weapon thicker than his thumb.

The Women's Movement

Early feminists were determined to remedy these inequities. Many had gained political and organizational experience in the abolitionist movement. It was not considered "unladylike" for women to campaign for abolition of slavery because that movement was associated with religious groups. Yet the women were not allowed to participate fully in the major antislavery society. They formed their own antislavery society, but when they attended a convention of these groups, they were not allowed to sit with the male delegates.

Angry at such treatment, the women held a meeting to discuss the "social, civil, and religious rights of women." In 1848, this Women's Rights Convention adopted a declaration of rights based on the Declaration of Independence proclaiming, "We hold these truths to be self-evident: that all men and women are created equal." The convention also passed a resolution calling for women's suffrage.

After the Civil War, the women who had worked in the abolitionist movement expected that women, as well as blacks, would get legal rights and voting rights. When the Fourteenth and Fifteenth Amendments did not include women, they felt betrayed, and they disassociated themselves from the black movement. They formed their own organizations to campaign for women's suffrage. This movement, led by Susan B. Anthony and Elizabeth Cady Stanton, succeeded in 1920, when the Nineteenth Amendment gave women the right to vote.

Then dissension developed within the movement. Many groups felt that the Nineteenth Amendment was just the first step in the struggle for equal rights. They proposed the Equal Rights Amendment to remedy remaining inequities. Other groups felt that the battle had been won. They opposed the Equal Rights Amendment, arguing that it would overturn labor laws recently enacted to protect women. Due to this dissension and the conservatism in the country at the time, the movement became dormant.[215]

The movement reemerged in the 1960s. As a result of the civil rights movement, many women recognized their own inferior status. Female writers sensitized other women. Betty Friedan published *The Feminine Mystique,* which grew out of a questionnaire she circulated at her fifteenth college reunion. The book addressed the malaise that afflicted college-educated women who were socialized into the feminine role but finding it unsatisfying.[216] Friedan observed that women reared the children, shopped for groceries, cooked the meals, and cleaned the house, while secretly wondering, "Is this all?" Friedan's manifesto became the best-selling nonfiction paperback in 1964. Its popularity spurred Friedan and other upper-middle-class, professional women to form the National Organization for Women (NOW) in 1966. They resolved "to bring women into full participation in the mainstream of American society *now.*"

Other women, also middle class but veterans of the civil rights and antiwar movements, had developed a taste for political action. They formed other organizations. Where NOW fought primarily for women's political and economic rights, the other organizations fought broadly for women's liberation in all spheres of life. Together these organizations pushed the issue of discrimination against women back onto the public agenda.

Nevertheless, they were not taken seriously for some years. In 1970, *Time* magazine reported, "No one knows how many shirts lay wrinkling in laundry baskets last week as thousands of women across the country turned out for the first big demonstration of the women's liberation movement. They took over [New York City's Fifth Avenue], providing not only protest but some of the best sidewalk ogling in years."[217]

Although the movement tried to broaden its base beyond upper-middle-class and college-educated women, it was unable to do so. The movement generated an image of privileged women who looked on other women with disdain. *Housewife* became a derisive term. Traditional women viewed the movement as antimotherhood and antifamily and, when it became more radical in the 1970s, prolesbian. This image gave "women's liberation" a bad name, even though most women agreed with most goals of the movement.[218] This image persists. More Americans believe that extraterrestrials have visited the earth than think that the word *feminist* is a compliment.[219] (It is unclear, however, whether this says more about Americans' attitudes toward gender equality or their penchant for paranoid conspiracy theories.)

The Movement in Congress and the Courts

Congress initially did not take the women's movement seriously either. When the House debated a bill forbidding racial discrimination in employment, eighty-one-year-old Representative Howard Smith (D-Va.) proposed an amendment to add sex discrimination to the bill. A foe of equal rights for blacks, Smith thought his proposal so ludicrous and so radical that it would help defeat the entire bill. Indeed, during their debate on the amendment, members of Congress laughed so hard that they could barely hear each other speak.[220] But the joke was on them, because the amendment, and then the entire bill—the Civil Rights Act of 1964—passed.

Congress later adopted legislation to forbid sex discrimination in credit and education.

Congress also passed the **Equal Rights Amendment (ERA).** The amendment simply declared, "Equality of rights under the law shall not be denied or abridged by the United States or by any state on account of sex." Introduced in 1923 and every year thereafter, Congress passed the amendment in 1972.

During World War II, women were urged into the labor force to replace men called to war. "Rosie the Riveter" became the symbol of the women who were contributing to the war effort. Following the war, they were told that it was patriotic to go home and give their jobs to returning veterans. The 1955 magazine cover on the right depicts the stereotypical women's role in this postwar era before the modern women's movement.

It appeared that the amendment would zip through the states. Both parties endorsed it, and a majority of the public supported it. But after about half of the states ratified it, the amendment stalled. Observers noted that it would make women subject to the draft and possibly to combat duty. Opponents charged that it would result in unisex restrooms and homosexual rights. Legal scholars denied that it would lead to these latter consequences, but after the judicial activism of recent decades, some people distrusted the courts to interpret the amendment.

The main problem, however, proved to be the symbolism of the amendment. For many women, the ERA represented an attack on the traditional values of motherhood, the family, and the home. Early feminists had emphasized equal employment so much that they gave some women the impression that they opposed these values. Traditional women sensed implicit criticism for being housewives.[221] To underscore the symbolism, the women in anti-ERA groups baked bread for state legislators scheduled to vote on ratification. Because of the symbolism, even some women who favored equality opposed the amendment itself. Although many young women supported it, fewer middle-age and elderly women did; and although many working women supported it, fewer housewives did. Women's organizations had not created an effective grassroots campaign to sway traditional women. The disaffection of these women allowed male legislators to vote according to their traditional male attitudes. They did not need to worry about a backlash from their female constituents.[222]

In 1980, the Republican Party became the first party not to endorse the ERA since 1940, and President Reagan became the first president not to support the amendment since Truman.

When the deadline for ratification set by Congress expired in 1982, the ERA fell three states short of approval by the necessary three-fourths—thirty-eight—of the states. As with the Nineteenth Amendment, the Southern states were most likely to oppose ratification.

But women began to win their rights in court. Courts historically upheld laws that limited women's participation in the public domain and occasionally even laws that diminished their standing in the private domain. As late as 1970, the Ohio supreme court ruled that a wife is a husband's servant with "no legally recognized feelings or rights."[223]

The Burger Court finally reversed this pattern. In 1971, for the first time, the Court struck down a law that discriminated against women,[224] heralding a long series of rulings that invalidated a variety of such laws. The Court used the congressional statutes and broadened the Fourteenth Amendment's equal protection clause to apply to women as well as to racial minorities.

Charles E. Steinheimer/Time Life Pictures/Getty Images

In addition to "Rosie the Riveter," there was "Rosalita." During World War II, when aircraft factories needed more workers, the government overlooked the influx of illegal aliens.

The change was especially apparent in a pair of cases involving the selection of jurors. For the pool of potential jurors, some states drew the names of men, but not women, from voter registration or other lists. These states allowed women to serve only if they voluntarily signed up at the courthouse. Consequently, few women served. In 1961, the Court let Florida use these procedures because the "woman is still regarded as the center of home and family life."[225] In 1975, however, the Court forbade Louisiana from using similar procedures,[226] thus overturning a precedent only fourteen years old.

The Court's rulings rejected the traditional stereotypes that men are the breadwinners and women the child rearers in society. The Court invalidated Utah's law that required divorced fathers to support their daughters until eighteen but their sons until twenty-one.[227] The state assumed that the daughters would get married and be supported by their husbands, whereas the sons would need to get educated for their careers. But the Court noted, "No longer is the female destined solely for the home."

Employment The Civil Rights Act of 1964 forbids discrimination on the basis of both sex and race in hiring, promoting, and firing. It prohibits discrimination on the basis of sex, except where sex is a "bona fide occupational qualification" for the job. Sex is considered a legitimate qualification for very few jobs, such as restroom attendants, lingerie salesclerks, models, or actors. It is not considered a legitimate qualification for jobs men traditionally held, such as those that entail heavy physical labor, unpleasant working conditions, late-night hours, overtime, or travel. Employers can no longer reserve these jobs for male applicants.

However, discrimination in hiring, promoting, and firing persists, even forty years after the act. A major study examined the records in lawsuits alleging sex discrimination in one recent year. A surprising and staggering number, they required employers to pay out at least $263 million to the female plaintiffs in that year alone.[228] Testimony by midlevel managers revealed that higher executives instructed them, "We do not employ women," or, "The day I hire a woman will be a cold day in hell." In dozens of cases, the managers were told to throw women's applications into the trash.[229]

The same result occurs when male managers decide according to their "gut instinct" that a man is more qualified. Their "gut instinct" may be biased without them ever realizing it. These instances are difficult, if not impossible, to identify and quantify.

The discrimination occurs up and down the ladder, against women applying to be CEOs as well as those applying to be janitors. Huge lawsuits have been brought against Merrill Lynch and Wal-Mart in recent years. But the discrimination appears most prevalent for traditional male, blue-collar jobs. Some men don't want to work with women; they don't want to break up the "good-ol'-boys' clubhouse."[230] Mysteriously, a woman's application disappears; or the letter telling her when to come for the interview gets lost in the mail; or her examination is invalidated for some reason.[231]

Although many women work as waiters, expensive restaurants have a history of hiring only men. These men, then, earn the big tips. In New York and Philadelphia, 25 percent of the 75 most elite and expensive restaurants had no women waiters.[232] In Miami, a famous restaurant that had hired 108 male waiters but no female waiters defended its discrimination by saying its male waiters offered diners a "classier" experience.[233]

Some companies that fill their positions through hiring agencies instruct the agencies to send them only men for traditional male jobs and only women for traditional female jobs.[234]

Discrimination in firing, especially for pregnancy, continues as well, despite the **Pregnancy Discrimination Act** of 1978, which forbids firing or demoting women when they become pregnant or after they return from maternity leave.[235] Some women have been fired as soon as they mentioned being pregnant, others as soon as their body showed it. Many have seen their performance evaluations drop as soon as their bellies showed, even though their actual performance did not decline.[236] Other women, such as a lawyer for a large

firm, have been demoted after giving birth. "When I returned from maternity leave, I was given the work of a paralegal and I wanted to say, 'Look, I had a baby, not a lobotomy.'"[237]

The cases examined in these studies probably represent the tip of the iceberg. To sue an employer for sex discrimination is to embark on an expensive and exhausting legal battle that will take several years of one's life. It requires a strong-willed woman who has experienced discriminatory behavior egregious enough for her to persuade a lawyer to take the case and then a company to settle or a judge or jury to find for her. Although there are some frivolous lawsuits in our legal system, there undoubtedly is more discriminatory behavior in our workplaces than is ever brought to court.

The **Equal Pay Act** of 1963 requires that women and men receive equal pay for equal work. The act makes exceptions for merit, productivity, and seniority.

As a result of the act, the gap between what women and men earn has slowly shrunk. In the 1960s, working women earned just 59 cents for every dollar men earned.[238] Today, working women earn 77 cents for every dollar men earn.[239] Among workers with the same job and experience, however, working women earn 89 cents for every dollar men earn—an improvement, but far short of real equality.[240]

One reason for the gap is old-fashioned sex discrimination. Despite the Equal Pay Act, some male employers with ingrained attitudes are reluctant to hire women or to pay them equally. The act allows exceptions for merit and productivity, which usually are determined subjectively. The employer may insist, whether sincerely or not, that the man is more meritorious or productive. Legions of women believe that they need to perform better to be paid equally.[241]

Another reason for the gap is because women and men have different jobs, whether due to discrimination or to choice. Despite the Civil Rights Act of 1964 and the societal changes—the blurring lines between genders—many women have traditional women's jobs and most men have traditional men's jobs. And traditional women's jobs pay less.

Historically, women were shunted into a small number of jobs. Even by 2000, two-thirds of working women were crowded into just twenty-one of the occupations identified by the Department of Labor.[242] These "pink-collar" jobs include secretaries (98 percent are women), household workers (97 percent), child care workers (97 percent), nurses (93 percent), bank tellers (90 percent), librarians (83 percent), elementary school teachers (83 percent), and health technicians (81 percent). In contrast, few women are carpenters (1 percent), firefighters (2 percent), mechanics (4 percent), or truck drivers (5 percent).[243]

Although the Equal Pay Act mandates equal pay for equal work, it does not require equal pay for comparable work—usually called **comparable worth**. According to a study in Washington state, maintenance carpenters and secretaries performed comparable jobs in terms of the education, the skill, or other qualifications required, but the carpenters, mostly men, made about $600 a month more than the secretaries, mostly women. In general, "men's jobs" paid about 20 percent more than comparable "women's jobs." Yet courts rejected demands by public employees that government employers boost the pay for the jobs held mostly by women. Nonetheless, some state and city governments implemented comparable worth plans for their employees after prodding by labor unions and women's groups. Private companies, however, did not, because doing so would require them to pay many female employees more.

Although the push for comparable worth has stalled, in recent years grassroots campaigns organized by labor unions and church groups have called for laws mandating a **living wage**.[244] These laws would require employers to pay more than the federal minimum wage, to pay whatever is necessary so a full-time worker does not fall below the poverty line. The ethical principle underlying a living wage is that no one who works full time should have to live in poverty (as full-time workers paid the minimum wage now do). Some proposals would apply only to government employees and to the employees of the companies that do business with the government. Other proposals would apply to all employees within a city or state. Still other proposals would apply just to the employees of "big-box stores" (for example, Wal-Mart and Home Depot). Most proposals would exempt small businesses with less than twenty-five workers. So far, some cities (Baltimore, San Francisco, and Santa Fe) and one state (Nevada) have adopted such laws.[245] If many cities and states did, living wage laws would have a significant impact on women and minorities, because women and minorities hold a disproportionate number of the lowest paying jobs. In addition, living wage laws would have a ripple effect; they would prompt employers to raise the pay of those workers just above the lowest level.

Another reason for the gap between what women and men earn is because women have children, which for various reasons affects their pay. The gap is largely between married women and married men. Single women and single men between the ages of twenty-one and thirty-five receive nearly equal pay. When the women get married and have children, their pay lags. Some interrupt their career until their children start school. Others continue to work but shift from the fast track to the so-called mommy track, working fewer hours due to child care and household responsibilities.[246] Still others fall victims to stereotypes—that mothers aren't serious about careers, that they aren't dependable because their children will get sick, and that they will work part-time or quit sooner or later anyway.[247] Through such stereotypes, managers move mothers to the "mommy track" in their own mind, whether the mothers want that track or not.

For whichever reasons, the difference in pay makes a difference in life. Early in her career, it means that a woman might not be able to pay off her credit card debts or college loans as quickly. She might not be able to have as nice a car or an apartment as her male counterpart. Later in her career, she might not be able to have as nice a house or as exotic vacations. Then, if her husband divorces her or dies before her, she might not be able to have as comfortable a retirement. The accumulated shortfall in her retirement savings, from her lower paychecks, means that she might struggle in her old age.[248]

Mothers with young children confront more obstacles than unequal pay. Male employers think women should be responsible for raising children but do little to accommodate the demands of child rearing. Most companies do not provide paid maternity leave, on-site day care, or flexible schedules. The United States lags far behind many other countries, ninety-eight of which grant partly paid maternity leaves for at least three months.[249]

"I feel like a man trapped in a woman's salary."

Generally speaking, do you prefer a male or female boss?

Male boss
34%

Female boss
9%

No preference
55%

I would feel comfortable dating a woman who earns significantly more than me

Strongly agree
55%

Somewhat agree
24%

Somewhat disagree
8%

Strongly disagree
7%

FIGURE 15.5 ■ Acceptance of Women in the Workplace

A majority of men don't care whether their boss is a woman or a man or whether the woman they date has a higher salary than they do. Shown here are the responses of 1302 men polled by telephone in 2004 to the following questions.
SOURCE: *Time*, August 23, 2004, 38.

Only California provides partly paid family leaves (55 percent of a worker's wages for up to six weeks).

Congress passed and President Clinton signed a bill requiring employers to grant unpaid maternity and paternity leaves. Companies must allow unpaid leaves for up to three months for workers with newborn or recently adopted children or with seriously ill family members. The act applies to companies that have fifty employees and to workers who work twenty-five hours a week for a year.[250] This covers about half of American workers.

But relatively few workers take advantage of these leaves. Most workers cannot afford to take unpaid leaves. Moreover, many managers don't support such measures, and some coworkers resent the additional burdens, so employees are reluctant to ask for leaves. At a time when companies have laid off workers to cut costs, "If you look like you are not career oriented, you can lose your job."[251]

Mothers and fathers with young children often face unreasonable time demands from employers accustomed to hiring married men who have a wife at home to rear the children, maintain the house, and run the errands. Now employers are putting the same demands on married women, especially those with professional jobs. Neither spouse has the time to do what the housewife did. In many families, the woman usually tries to do these tasks at night and on weekends, but both spouses frequently feel stretched thin and stressed out.

Consequently, among men with children, those who have a wife at home rise up the career ladder faster than those who have a wife working outside the home. The latter men apparently put in less "face time" at work. Executives who reach the higher rungs are "almost always" men who have a wife at home.[252]

An executive of a Fortune 500 company admitted that his company still prefers to hire men who are married to a housewife.[253]

As a result of time demands, about half of all employees—male and female, single and married—say work and family responsibilities interfere with each other. Two-thirds of employees who are parents say they don't have enough time with their children.[254]

So even though women have gained greater acceptance in the workplace (see Figure 15.5), they—and their spouses—have not yet overcome the expectations that developed long before they were ever allowed in the workplace. And these expectations are exacerbated by Americans' glorification of work and, with new communications technology, some Americans' perverse celebration of a "24/7 workweek." "We glorify an all-work, all-the-time lifestyle," notes one commentator, "and then weep crocodile tears for kids whose parents are never home."[255]

In addition to their difficulties in getting hired, promoted, and paid equally, some women also face sexual harassment (see the box "Sexual Harassment at Work").

Credit The Equal Credit Opportunity Act of 1974 forbids discrimination on the basis of sex or marital status in credit transactions. Historically, banks, savings and loans, credit card companies, and retail stores discriminated against women. Typically, these businesses determine how much money people can borrow according to how much they earn. Yet the lenders refused loans to single women, regardless of income, because they assumed that the women would work only until they got married and became pregnant. Likewise, the lenders did not count a wife's income as part of a couple's total income, again because they assumed that

The Supreme Court has ruled that sexual harassment is a form of job discrimination prohibited by the Civil Rights Act of 1964,[1] and Congress has passed a law allowing victims to sue employers and collect money for distress, illness, or loss of their job due to such behavior. Although sexual harassment can be directed toward either sex,[2] it is usually directed toward women.

Courts recognize two types of **sexual harassment.** The most obvious is *quid pro quo,* in which a supervisor makes unwanted sexual advances and either promises good consequences (for example, a promotion or pay raise) if the employee goes along or threatens bad consequences (for example, an undesirable reassignment) if the employee refuses. The less obvious type is creating a hostile environment that interferes with the employee's ability to perform the job. To prove that a hostile environment existed, the employee must demonstrate that the offensive conduct was severe or persistent.

Paula Jones's suit against President Clinton, who as Arkansas' governor allegedly asked her for oral sex, was dismissed because the sexual advance was considered neither severe enough nor, as a single incident, persistent enough to constitute a hostile environment. If it happened, the judge said, it was "boorish and offensive" but not technically harassment.

Despite many men's fears, occasional innocuous comments, jokes, or requests for dates would not be classified as harassment. Justice Antonin Scalia emphasized that the law did not create "a general civility code."[3]

Yet confusion persists because several outlandish examples have received widespread publicity. A library employee filed a complaint against a coworker who had posted a *New Yorker* cartoon in his cubicle.[4] A graduate teaching assistant filed a complaint against another who had placed a photograph of his wife, wearing a bikini, on his desk in their office at the University of Nebraska. If sexual harassment were defined this broadly, it would interfere with freedom of speech. (Anyone can file a complaint, as anyone can bring a lawsuit, but of course this doesn't mean that a bureaucratic agency or court agrees with the person filing the complaint or bringing the lawsuit. Yet the publicity gives many people this impression.)

Confusion also persists because some employers, who can be held responsible for sexual harassment by their employees,[5] have adopted "zero tolerance" policies to insulate them from potential lawsuits. These policies are stricter than the law, and they have led to the firing of a few men who would not have been convicted under the law. For example, a male executive told a female coworker about the plot of the *Seinfeld* show the night before. Seinfeld had told his friends about a woman he met but whose name he could not remember except that it rhymed with a female body part. The coworker complained of sexual harassment, and Miller Brewing Company fired the executive, despite his nineteen years with the company. (When the executive sued the company, however, a mostly female jury awarded him millions of dollars for being wrongfully dismissed.)

Women in traditional female jobs, such as secretary, are more likely to be subjected to *quid pro quo* harassment from supervisors, whereas women in traditional male jobs, especially blue-collar jobs, are more likely to be subjected to hostile-environment harassment from coworkers. Examples abound of male laborers posting sexual pictures or writing sexual messages in women's lockers or restrooms or leaving plastic penises in their toolboxes; taunting the women with sexual questions and comments or addressing them as "Bitch," "Slut," or "Whore" instead of by name; and grabbing their breasts, buttocks, or genitals. Worse for new workers, however, is having supervisors or coworkers who will not train them or help them, or coworkers who will sabotage their work, making them appear slow and shoddy, to drive them off the job. Some coworkers have even sabotaged the women's machinery or equipment—for example, male firefighters have disabled their female colleagues' life-saving equipment—and thus endangered the women's lives.

The dynamics of sexual harassment don't revolve around sex as much as they reflect abuse of power. A supervisor or coworker makes a woman feel vulnerable and thus exercises psychological dominance over her. He wants her to leave the workplace or, at least, to suffer inferior status if she remains there.

Consultants have found that a very small percentage of men harass women, but these men do it a lot. Perhaps three to five men out of one hundred create problems, but these men might affect fifty women. They typically feel bitter toward women or threatened by them. Some also have been bullies toward men as well.[6]

Surveys and stories from women indicate that many more have been sexually harassed than have sued. Relatively few have filed formal complaints, let alone brought lawsuits, because they need their jobs.

[1] *Mentor Savings Bank* v. *Vinson*, 91 L.Ed.2d 49 (1986).
[2] *Oncale* v. *Sundowner Offshore Services*, 140 L.Ed.2d 201 (1998).
[3] *Oncale* v. *Sundowner Offshore Services.*
[4] Henry Louis Gates Jr., "Men Behaving Badly," *New Yorker*, August 18, 1997, 5.
[5] *Faragher* v. *Boca Raton*, 141 L.Ed.2d 662 (1998); *Burlington Industries* v. *Ellerth*, 141 L.Ed.2d 633 (1998).
[6] Kirsten Downey Grimsley, "Confronting Hard-Core Harassers," *Washington Post National Weekly Edition*, January 27, 1997, 6.

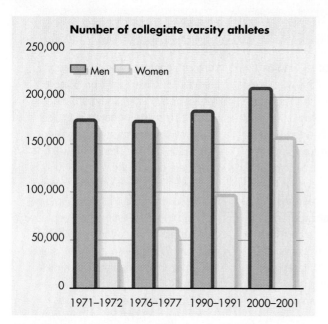

Number of collegiate varsity athletes

FIGURE 15.6 ■ **Participation in Varsity Sports since Passage of Title IX**

Both men's and women's participation in varsity sports has increased since passage of Title IX in 1972. Although many colleges have dropped some men's teams to make room for women's teams, more schools offer more sports than in the 1970s, so more men overall are participating, as well as a great many more women.

SOURCE: Welch Suggs, "Title IX at 30," *Chronicle of Higher Education*, June 21, 2002, 39.

the wife's employment was temporary. Only if women were professionals or in their forties would lenders count their income the same as men's. When businesses lent money to a married couple, they put the transactions in the husband's name. If the wife became divorced or widowed, she had no credit record and little chance to obtain credit.

The Equal Credit Opportunity Act requires lenders to lend to single women and to count the wife's income as part of a couple's total income. It restricts lenders from asking women whether they intend to bear children. The act also requires lenders to put accounts in the names of both spouses if they request it.

Education The Education Amendments of 1972 (to the Civil Rights Act of 1964) forbid discrimination on the basis of sex in schools and colleges that receive federal aid. The amendments were prompted by discrimination against women by undergraduate and graduate colleges, especially in admissions and financial aid.

The language of the amendments, often referred to as **Title IX,** is so broad that the Department of Education, which administers them, has established rules that cover more aspects of education than their congressional supporters expected.[256] The department has

used the amendments to prod institutions into employing and promoting more female teachers and administrators, opening vocational training classes to women and home economics classes to men, and offering equal athletic programs to women. If institutions do not comply, the government can cut off their federal aid.

The amendments have affected athletic programs especially. Before the amendments, schools provided far fewer sports for females than for males, and they spent far fewer dollars—for scholarships, coaches, and facilities—on women's sports. Now the department interprets the amendments to require a school either to have approximately the same percentage of female athletes as female undergraduates, to continually expand opportunities for female athletes, or to fully accommodate the interests and abilities of female students. (This last would occur if a school's female students were satisfied that it offered sufficient opportunities for them, given their interests and abilities, even if the opportunities were not equal to those for men.)

Very few colleges meet the first requirement. To comply, most are trying to meet the second requirement by expanding the number of women's sports. But they worry that they will have to fulfill the first requirement eventually. And they fear that they will have to cap the squad size of their football team, which has the most players and costs the most money, to do so. This would lessen the imbalance in the numbers of male and female athletes, and it would free more money for women's teams.

Some colleges have resisted the enforcement of Title IX, partly because athletic departments are struggling to balance their budget and partly because the act threatens deeply ingrained cultural values that are reflected in men's athletics. Administrators and boosters fear that women's sports will take money from men's sports and thereby weaken the primacy of men's athletics.

When Brown University tried to eliminate women's volleyball and gymnastics (at the same time it dropped men's golf and water polo), members of the women's teams sued. More than sixty schools filed briefs supporting Brown's decisions and criticizing the department's interpretations of Title IX. Lower courts ruled against Brown, and in 1997, the Supreme Court refused to hear the case, leaving the lower courts' rulings intact. Thus, the department's interpretations remain.

Already Title IX has had a major impact. Colleges have increased their women's teams—almost twice as many as in the early 1980s—and their female athletes—fully ten times as many as before (see Figure 15.6).[257] Women now make up 42 percent of all college athletes and receive 42 percent of the scholarship money (though their teams have lower coaches' salaries and operating expenses).[258]

Colleges with successful football or basketball programs have increased their women's teams the most because these sports generate revenue that funds women's sports. Colleges with no football program have also increased their women's teams. Colleges with football programs that do not generate a profit (and most do not) lag behind. They pour money into football but lack revenue from television or bowl contracts to fund women's sports.[259]

To reduce the gender imbalance, many colleges have eliminated low-profile men's teams, especially wrestling, gymnastics, tennis, and track. Marquette University eliminated men's wrestling even though the team was financed mostly by private donations.[260]

Title IX has also had a major impact on high schools, which have increased their girls' teams. Before Title IX, 1 of every 27 girls played on a high school team; now 1 of every 2.5 girls does.[261]

But supporters have a broader goal in mind as well. "If girls are socialized the way boys are to take part in sports," the editor of a women's sports magazine says, and "if boys and girls grow up with the idea that girls are strong and capable, it will change the way girls and women are viewed—by themselves and by society."[262]

Overall, Congress and the courts have moved steadily toward legal equality for the sexes. Women have accomplished through congressional and judicial action much of what they would have accomplished with the ERA. It is an indication of the success of the movement that young women today take their equality for granted and focus on their personal lives rather than on the need for further progress. However, challenges remain. Besides the noncompliance with congressional laws, as noted above, the demands on working parents are overwhelming. The workplace needs reform. "The failure of the workplace to make accommodations for working parents is one of the biggest unmet demands of American voters."[263] The family also needs reform. After work, most wives come home to face their "second shift." According to one survey, 40 percent feel that their husbands create more work around the house than they perform.[264]

Discrimination against Men

Although most sex discrimination has been directed at women, some has been directed at men. The traditional conception of gender roles has created problems for men who do not fit the standard mold.

When the Burger Court rejected stereotypes that led to discrimination against women, it also rejected some that led to discrimination against men. It invali-

© Bettmann/CORBIS

Men resisted the expansion of women's athletics. The Boston Marathon was traditionally a race for men only. When the first woman tried to participate in 1967, a marathon official assaulted her.

dated Mississippi's law barring men from a state university's nursing school.[265] It also invalidated Alabama's law allowing only women to seek alimony upon divorce.[266] Thus, the Court rejected stereotypes that only women become nurses and only women are dependent on their spouses.

On the other hand, the Burger Court upheld some laws that were designed to protect women but that discriminate against men. It affirmed laws prohibiting statutory rape—intercourse with a minor, with consent—by males but not by females.[267] It also affirmed a law mandating draft registration for males but not for females.[268] It rationalized that registration eventually could lead to the draft and the draft eventually could lead to combat, and it insisted that most women are not capable of combat. Thus, the Court accepted the stereotypes that only men initiate sex with underage partners and only men can fight in war.

In the absence of a draft, the most significant discrimination against men may occur in divorce cases, where the norm is to grant custody of children to mothers and require payment of support by fathers. Although courts give fathers visitation rights, they permit mothers to move miles away, making visitation difficult and sporadic. And although governments have taken steps to enforce support payments, they have done little to enforce visitation rights. This practice reflects the stereotype that fathers are capable of financing their children's upbringing but not of bringing them up themselves. The Supreme Court has ignored this problem.

Although most single parents are women, an increasing number are men, such as this father of an eleven-year-old in Dallas.

© Brent Humphreys

Affirmative Action

Assume there is a track meet, and a black runner and a white runner start together. But the officials force the black runner to carry heavy weights, and he falls behind. Eventually, the officials realize that this is unfair, and they take the weights off. Of course, the black runner is still behind. Would this be fair? Assume instead that the officials not only take the weights off but also allow him to catch up. Would this be fairer? Or would it seem unfair to the white runner, who insists that the weights were not his fault?[271]

This scenario captures the dilemma of civil rights policy today. Although most race and sex discrimination has been repudiated by the courts and legislatures, the effects of past discrimination survive. Now the question is whether civil rights policy should ignore race and sex or take race and sex into account to compensate for the effects of past discrimination. That is, should the policy require nondiscrimination only or **affirmative action** as well?

Affirmative action applies to employers for hiring and promoting minorities and women, colleges and universities for admitting minorities and women, and governments for reserving a portion of their contracts for businesses owned by minorities and women. We will examine the first two of these.

In Employment

The Civil Rights Act of 1964, which bars discrimination in employment, does not mention affirmative action, but it does authorize the bureaucracy to make rules to end discrimination. In 1969, the Department of Labor called for affirmative action by companies doing business with the federal government. Later, the Equal Employment Opportunities Commission called for affirmative action by governments and the Office of Education by colleges as well. Presidents from Nixon through Carter supported it with executive orders, and the Supreme Court sanctioned it in a series of cases.[272] Many state and local governments also adopted it.

Affirmative action requires positive steps to ensure that qualified minorities and women receive a fair share of the jobs at each level. Just what the positive steps and the fair share should be are the subject of considerable controversy.

If the number of minorities and women that work in a company that has government contracts or in a government agency, whether federal, state, or local, is less than the number in the local labor force, the company or agency must agree to recruit more or, in serious cases, draw up an affirmative action plan. The plan must include goals to hire or promote more minorities or women and a timetable to reach these goals. If

Other discrimination against men may occur in cases of unintended pregnancy. Women may choose abortion, adoption, or raising the child. Men have no choice. The Supreme Court invalidated laws requiring a husband's consent before his wife's abortion, because the woman carries the fetus so she is most affected by the decision.[269] But consider a different situation. A twenty-five-year-old man repeatedly told his girlfriend that he didn't want to have a child, but she assured him that she couldn't get pregnant because of a physical condition. After unprotected sex, however, she got pregnant. She did want to have the child, so the man, now her exboyfriend, is required by a Michigan court to pay $500 a month in child support. With help from the National Center for Men, he has filed a lawsuit, nicknamed *Roe* v. *Wade for Men*.[270] According to traditional notions of morality, fashioned before the right to abortion, if you engage in intercourse, you risk becoming a parent and shouldering those responsibilities. But the right to abortion changes the calculus. It frees women from the unintended consequences of pregnancy. Is there a need for a comparable right for men? Should men have the right to opt out of financial obligations? Should this man, who evidently was deceived, be saddled with eighteen years of child support? Or is the unfairness to him overridden by the child's need for financial support from two parents?

the company or agency does not reach them, it must show that it made an effort to do so. If the company cannot satisfy the government, it can be denied future contracts (though in reality these companies are seldom penalized).

Although the requirements for affirmative action plans speak of "goals," critics charge that they mandate quotas and that quotas amount to "reverse discrimination" and result in lower standards.[273] The terms do blur; if employers are pressured to meet goals, they might interpret *goals* to mean *quotas*. But only after a finding of deliberate and systematic discrimination does affirmative action entail actual quotas.[274]

Furthermore, the courts scrutinize the plans to make sure that they do not prevent all white men from being hired and promoted and that they are temporary (usually until the percentage of minority employees reaches the percentage of minority workers in the community).

Because of the belief that affirmative action should not pose much burden on innocent individuals, the Court has struck down affirmative action in laying off workers—that is, struck down protection for minorities and women when employers pare their workforce for economic reasons. Instead, the Court has accepted the traditional practice, based on seniority, that the last hired is the first fired.[275]

In addition to these limits on affirmative action, the Rehnquist Court made it more difficult for governments to adopt affirmative action for themselves or to require it for companies.[276] Governments must show clear evidence of some particular past discrimination by the government or company or industry, rather than simply point to the pervasive historical discrimination in society as their justification for affirmative action.

Affirmative action has definitely helped minorities and women. White men dominate public and private institutions, and as the personnel director of a Fortune 500 company observed, "People tend to hire people like themselves."[277] Thus affirmative action has prodded them to hire more minorities and women. Private companies that have government contracts, and are therefore subject to affirmative action, have shown more improvement in hiring minorities and women than other companies. And state and local governments, also subject to affirmative action, have shown more improvement in hiring than have private companies. Companies and governments subject to affirmative action have shown even greater progress in promoting minorities and women, who had previously been confined to low-level positions.[278]

The state of Alabama, for example, made dramatic gains. After a court found that the state troopers had never employed any blacks, it ordered them to hire one new black for every new white until the force reached 25 percent black. The force became the most integrated force in the country. Faced with the threat of similar orders, other departments of the government quickly hired more blacks at all levels.

Although affirmative action is a target of political controversy, private businesses use it and champion it under the name of "diversity." They have found new pools of untapped talent in overlooked groups, enabling them to reach new markets. Hiring more minority and female workers has led to insights that enable the corporations to sell products to more minority and female consumers.[279]

Affirmative action, whether mandated by governments or practiced by businesses, has helped some blacks move up a rung—from the lower middle class to the middle class or from the middle class to the upper middle class.[280] But affirmative action has not pulled blacks out of the underclass. Many, from families mired in poverty, lack the education and skills necessary to compete for available jobs.[281] And affirmative action cannot create new jobs or better jobs, so it is not as helpful to minorities or women as a flourishing economy is.

In short, affirmative action should not be given more credit or more blame than it deserves. It has boosted some minorities and women, but it cannot help many others. It has displaced some white men, but it has not affected most others.

Yet 13 percent of white men think they lost a job or promotion because of their race, and 10 percent think they did because of their sex.[282] Many others claim they "heard about" another white man who did. Yet affirmative action is not as pervasive as many people assume.[283] Many people subconsciously view affirmative action as they do handicapped parking. When looking for a parking space in a crowded lot, numerous drivers see a handicapped space and think, "If it weren't for that space, I could park here." Of course, if the space wasn't reserved for handicapped drivers, only one other driver could park there.[284] So it is with affirmative action. Many white men think they would get a particular job if it weren't for affirmative action, but only one would. Meanwhile, the rest feel victimized by the policy.

For both sides in the controversy, affirmative action has become a symbol. For civil rights leaders, it represents fairness and real progress toward equality. For critics, it represents unfairness and an attack on individuality and merit. It is important to debate these values, but it is also important to recognize that affirmative action is neither the key public policy for racial and sexual equality nor the big stumbling block for individual achievement, as supporters and detractors seem to assume.

Indeed, some supporters say affirmative action reaches so few individuals that it is an attempt to achieve "racial justice on the cheap," without facing up to the greater problem of the underclass.[285]

In College Admissions

Affirmative action also applies to college and university admissions. Colleges and universities began to use affirmative action in the 1970s. Some schools used limited programs that gave a boost to minority applicants, and other schools used extensive programs that reserved seats—essentially, they set quotas—for minority applicants. The medical school of the University of California at Davis reserved sixteen seats in its class of one hundred students for minorities. In *University of California* v. *Bakke,* the Burger Court upheld the use of race as a factor in admissions but struck down the use of quotas (unless the school had a history of intentional discrimination).

The Supreme Court would not rule on this issue again until 2003. In the meantime, voters in California and Washington and the governor of Florida mandated an end to the use of race in admissions to public universities.

The moves against affirmative action prompted concerns that minority enrollments would plunge. Some state legislatures and universities decided not to let this happen. The Texas legislature passed a law guaranteeing admission to its state universities for all high school graduates in the top 10 percent of their class. The University of California Board of Regents guaranteed admission to at least one of the UC campuses for those in the top 4 percent.

These programs use geography instead of race; in particular, they use residential segregation, which has stymied the efforts to desegregate the schools from grade schools through high schools, as a way to diversify the universities. Minority students who performed well in their segregated schools can still get admitted to the universities, even if their schools provided a less competitive education than predominantly white schools provide.

Although the programs in both states have increased the numbers of minorities above the levels they would have had without the programs, the numbers are lower than they had been with affirmative action.[286] Asians have been the prime beneficiaries of the demise of affirmative action.[287]

The Rehnquist Court revisited the *Bakke* ruling in 2003. In a pair of cases from the University of Michigan, one directed at undergraduate admissions and one directed at law school admissions, five justices upheld affirmative action but only as part of a "holistic review" that gives "individualized consideration" to each application. Schools cannot use formulas that add

© Reprinted with permission by Copley News Service.

points for minority status; they must use a more labor-intensive review.[288] The decision to uphold affirmative action came as a surprise, because the Rehnquist Court had narrowed the practice in employment cases.

Some justices may have been influenced by friend of the court briefs. A record number of these—102—were prepared, most supporting affirmative action. They were filed not only by universities but also by dozens of Fortune 500 companies. One was filed by twenty-one retired generals and admirals, including three former superintendents of the military academies. This brief recalled the Vietnam War, when there were few minority officers and there was much tension between the black troops and their white officers. Since then, affirmative action has produced an integrated officer corps and consequently, a more effective military, according to the retired brass. Justice Sandra Day O'Connor, who provided the crucial fifth vote, acknowledged that selective universities—the ones that use affirmative action—train the leaders of our society and that an integrated leadership helps govern a diverse people.

Just as some white men believe that affirmative action cost them a job or promotion, some white students believe it cost them, or will cost them, a seat in the college or university of their choice. But 60 percent of colleges admit nearly all students who apply; only 20 percent are selective enough to use affirmative action.[289] Students who apply to elite schools are more likely to lose a seat because other applicants' parents are alumni of these schools. Typically, a fifth of Harvard's students are given preferential treatment because their parents attended the school. Harvard's "legacies" are more than twice as likely to be admitted as blacks or Latinos. A similar advantage exists at other selective schools, including public schools such as the Universities of California and Virginia.[290] This advantage encourages the alumni to continue donating to their school.

Affirmative action may be more widespread in graduate and professional schools.[291] For some beneficiaries of affirmative action, recent social science research has found a mismatch between some students' abilities and law schools' demands. These students have attended law schools that are too difficult for them, making it less likely that they will graduate, pass the bar exam, and join the legal profession.[292] These findings are controversial, but if confirmed suggest that some schools may need to adjust the scope of their affirmative action programs.

Conclusion: Is Government Responsive in Granting Civil Rights?

When summarizing civil rights progress for minorities and women, an apt analogy is a glass that is half full but also half empty. The same idea is expressed in a website's title—the Half Changed World.

Blacks and women have taken long strides toward equality since the time when people would say, "A Negro's place is in the cotton field" or "A woman's place is in the home." The civil rights movement and the women's movement initiated the changes. They protested inequality and put the issue on the public agenda. As the movements grew and garnered support, they pressured the government. Finally, a century after they began to agitate for change, the government responded.

Within the government, the Supreme Court exercised decisive leadership. Historically, the Court had been both activist and restrained toward blacks—whichever stance was necessary to deny their rights—and restrained toward women. But in the 1950s and 1960s, the Warren Court was activist in striking down racial segregation, and in the 1970s and 1980s, the Burger Court was activist in striking down sexual discrimination. Each may go down in history as that Court's major achievement. But the Court's rulings themselves did not guarantee the rights. Because the Court lacks the means to enforce its decisions, the president and Congress had to help overcome public resistance.

Thus, the areas of racial and sexual discrimination show the power, and the limits of the power, of the courts. The Supreme Court exercised power because it articulated emerging views in society—that racial segregation and sexual discrimination by law are wrong. But the Court could not accomplish the changes by itself. And the Court could not diminish racial segregation and inequality any further. It made little progress toward overcoming residential segregation, which leads to school segregation and school inequality, or toward ameliorating the poverty that renders many blacks unable to take advantage of their rights.

The changes in racial and sexual policies over the years illustrate the responsiveness of the government. In its subjugation of blacks until the 1950s and its treatment of women until the 1970s, the government was responding to the majority view. When blacks and women organized to protest their status, the government began responding to them and to shifts in the majority view that their protests prompted.

In pressuring the government to respond, African Americans have benefited from being numerous, visible, and—with their common legacy of slavery, segregation, and discrimination—relatively cohesive. Their concentration in large northern cities and some southern states has helped them exercise political power. Their long legacy, though, has fostered the ghetto, with its debilitating conditions, and denied them the resources to make faster progress.

Thus, there are two black Americas—a middle class that has benefited tremendously from the civil rights movement and the changes in our society and a lower class, especially the underclass, that has been left behind to fend for itself.[293]

Latinos, whose movement is younger, have also taken strides toward equality. With increased immigration, they have become more numerous, and in coming years they will become even more numerous, giving them a large voting bloc. Their concentration in some western and southwestern states has enabled them to influence state and local governments. Their diversity and lack of cohesiveness, however, have hindered their ability to influence the national government.

American Indians are the smallest, most isolated, and least organized minority, so they have had the poorest success in pressuring the government.

As minority groups grow—together they are expected to make up half of the U.S. population by

2050—they will be able to exert pressure on government more effectively. But they will increasingly come into conflict with each other, especially when economic conditions are stagnant so jobs and government services are scarce. Already there are tensions. Some blacks resent the faster progress of Latinos and Asians. These blacks say African Americans were here before most Hispanics and all Asians, they suffered more and struggled longer, and so they should reap the rewards sooner. On the other hand, Latino leaders resent the reluctance of black groups to help them with their issues.[294] There have been conflicts, even riots. Blacks have rioted in Miami from frustration with the Cuban-dominated leadership. Latinos have rioted in Washington, D.C., out of anger with the black power structure. Continuing illegal immigration could exacerbate the tensions by pitting new immigrants against poor blacks in competition for jobs.

Nonminority women were never subjugated as much as minority men and women, so they have had less to overcome. Moreover, women are a majority, they vote as frequently as men, and they have well-organized and well-funded interest groups. Consequently, they have made the greatest strides toward equality.

Exclusion of Japanese Is Upheld

In *Korematsu* v. *United States,* the Supreme Court, by a 6–3 vote, upheld the order excluding 120,000 Japanese Americans from the West Coast.[295] Although Justice Douglas voted against the order in conference, he switched to the majority just before the decision was announced.[296]

The majority held that the government could take precautions to prevent espionage and sabotage during wartime, and it noted that the president and Congress were in agreement that the order was necessary. Thus, the majority was restrained, deferring to the other branches. These justices did not question officials' fear of espionage or sabotage by Japanese Americans. In contrast, the minority was activist, challenging the other branches. These justices disputed officials' suspicions of disloyalty and suggested that pervasive prejudice against Japanese Americans had led to the order.

The minority raised the specter that the Court's ruling would set a dangerous precedent. "A military order, however unconstitutional, is not apt to last longer than the military emergency," Justice Robert Jackson wrote. "But once a judicial opinion rationalizes such an order . . . the Court for all time has validated the principle of racial discrimination . . . and of transplanting American citizens. The principle then lies about like a loaded weapon ready for the hand of any authority that can bring forward a plausible claim of an urgent need."

In December, 1944—two and a half years after beginning the evacuation and one day before hearing the Court's decision—the military ordered the release of "loyal" Japanese Americans. (Apparently it anticipated, or at least feared, a decision invalidating the order.)

Upon their release, the Japanese Americans discovered that the government had failed to keep its promise to protect their property. Many of their possessions, stored in warehouses, had been vandalized or stolen. Some of their homes had been taken over by strangers, and some of their land had been seized for unpaid taxes.

"They did me a great wrong," Korematsu said. But he returned to live in the same town where he was arrested. "I love this country and I belong here." He got married and became a draftsman. But he was not celebrated by his fellow Japanese Americans. At the internment camp, in fact, he had been shunned. Most Japanese Americans, who were anxious to demonstrate their loyalty, had acquiesced to the evacuation order. They had considered Korematsu's actions counterproductive to their goals. After the war, they still didn't want to complain, and many didn't talk about their experience. Korematsu's own daughter didn't learn about her father's case until high school.[297]

Near the end of his career, Justice Douglas expressed regret that he and others in the majority had gone along with the government. The case "was ever on my conscience."[298]

Douglas did not live long enough to learn that the War Department had presented false information to the Court. The department had altered some reports and destroyed others demonstrating the loyalty of the Japanese Americans.[299] In fact, from Pearl Harbor until the end of the war, the government had no record of any incident of espionage or sabotage by a Japanese American citizen or alien in the United States.[300]

With help from the lawyer who discovered the false information, Korematsu reopened his case through a rarely used procedure available only when the original trial was tainted with prosecutorial misconduct and fraud. In 1983, a federal judge reversed his conviction.[301]

In 1988, Congress passed a law offering a public apology for the internment and $20,000 compensation to each surviving internee.[302]

After the September 11 terrorist attacks, there was renewed talk about the Japanese relocation: Should legal immigrants from countries with links to terrorist groups be rounded up and put in internment camps? A majority of Americans rejected this proposal, but nearly a third said they might accept it.[303] In 2003, Fred Korematsu filed a friend-of-the court brief on behalf of the detainees at Guantanamo Bay.

 To learn more about this topic, go to "you are there" exercises for this chapter on the text website.

Fred Korematsu

Key Terms

Korematsu v. United States

civil rights

Dred Scott case

equal protection clause

Jim Crow laws

Plessy v. Ferguson

separate-but-equal doctrine

NAACP

brown-bag test

Brown v. Board of Education

de jure segregation

de facto segregation

Civil Rights Act of 1964

restrictive covenants

steering

blockbusting

redlining

Civil Rights Act of 1968

racial profiling

bilingual education

Equal Rights Amendment (ERA)

Pregnancy Discrimination Act

Equal Pay Act

comparable worth

living wage

sexual harassment

Title IX

affirmative action

Further Reading

Edward Ball, *Slaves in the Family* (New York: Farrar, Straus & Giroux, 1998). The descendant of a plantation owner searches for the descendants of his family's slaves.

Jennifer Baumgardner and Amy Richards, *Manifesta: Young Women, Feminism, and the Future* (New York: Farrar, Straus & Giroux, 2000). The authors have created a primer on feminism for the members of Generation X.

Taylor Branch, *Parting the Waters: America in the King Years, 1954–63* (New York: Simon & Schuster, 1988). Branch provides a readable account of Martin Luther King Jr. and the first decade of the civil rights movement. *Pillar of Fire* (1999) continues the saga through 1965, and *At Canaan's Edge* (2006) takes the story to the end of King's life in 1968.

Seth Cagin and Philip Dray, *We Are Not Afraid: The Story of Goodman, Schwerner, and Chaney and the Civil Rights Campaign for Mississippi* (New York: Macmillan, 1988). This book documents an American crime committed in the steamy summer of 1964.

Cynthia Carr, *Our Town: A Heartland Lynching, a Haunted Town, and the Hidden History of White America* (New York: Crown, 2005). A journalist, whose family is from Marion, Indiana, discovers her grandfather in the crowd of onlookers at the lynching pictured in this text. She explores her roots, the lynching, and the KKK in the town—then and now.

Veronica Chambers, *Having It All? Black Women and Success* (New York: Doubleday, 2003). This social and cultural history examines the portrayal of black women in the media, entertainment, and business worlds.

Ian Frazier, *On the Rez* (New York: Farrar, Straus & Giroux, 2000). Frazier provides a firsthand guide to life on Indian reservations.

David Halberstam, *The Children* (New York: Random House, 1998). A focus on the lives of eight students who attended college in Nashville and helped launch the civil rights movement reveals how a small group of courageous students helped transform the country.

Peter Irons, *Justice at War* (New York: Oxford University Press, 1983). The story of Fred Korematsu and other cases involving the Japanese American relocation is recounted by the attorney who uncovered the government's false information.

Randall Kennedy, *Nigger: The Strange Career of a Troublesome Word* (New York: Pantheon, 2002). An African American law professor traces the history of this most explosive word.

Gary May, *The Informant: The FBI, the Ku Klux Klan, and the Murder of Viola Liuzzo* (New Haven, Connecticut: Yale University Press, 2005). This book explores the murky role of an FBI informant who participated in KKK assaults of civil rights demonstrators to protect his cover—or because he felt like it?

Gregory Howard Williams, *Life on the Color Line: The True Story of a White Boy Who Discovered He Was Black* (New York: Dutton, 1995). The life of a ten-year-old boy changed dramatically the day he learned that his father was black.

For Viewing

Crash (2005). The winner of the Best Picture Academy Award, this movie about race relations in Los Angeles addresses, head-on, stereotypes of whites, blacks, Latinos, Asians, Jews, and Arabs. The movie features terrific acting and poignant scenes, as multiple characters interact and collide like car crashes.

Eyes on the Prize (1987). This is a documentary series about the civil rights movement. *Freedom on My Mind* (1994). This documentary is based on the recollections of civil rights veterans.

Not for Ourselves Alone: The Story of Elizabeth Cady Stanton and Susan B. Anthony (1999). A Ken Burns documentary tells the story of these two remarkable women.

The Intolerable Burden (2003). A black family enrolled eight of their children in an all-white school in Mississippi in 1965 under the school district's "freedom of choice" plan. They weren't expected to do that, as this documentary shows.

The Untold Story of Emmett Louis Till (2005). The Mississippi murder of a black boy from the North in 1954 was a spark that ignited the civil rights movement, and this documentary helped persuade prosecutors to reopen the case.

The Native Americans (1994). A five-part documentary devotes each part to different native peoples of the various regions of the United States.

To Kill a Mockingbird (1962) and *In the Heat of the Night* (1967). These two Hollywood blockbusters show the racial climate in the southern states in the 1950s and 1960s. Starring Gregory Peck and Sidney Poitier, respectively.

Electronic Resources

www.naacp.org
The website of the NAACP, the largest and oldest civil rights organization, has links to discussions of policy issues and information about the organization and its mission.

www.census.gov/statab/www
Updated annually, the Statistical Abstract of the United States *provides information about the state of the American people, their incomes, family structures, occupations, and many other characteristics. It includes detailed information about individual ethnic and racial groups as well as men and women.*

www.americanwest.com/pages/indians.htm
This site provides information about Native Americans and their cultures and links to various tribal home pages.

oyez.nwu.edu
You can read important civil rights cases online here, accessed by name or topic.

wwwsecure.law.cornell.edu/topics/civil_rights.html
This page provides much useful information regarding civil rights.

www.yforum.com
Are there questions about blacks or whites, or Latinos or Asians, that you have never understood? Post your questions and have people from those communities respond.

www.leofranklynchers.com/leofranklynchers.html
This website addresses the lynching of a Jew in Georgia in 1915 and documents the identity of some of those responsible.

ThomsonNOW™

Enter ThomsonNOW™ using the access card that is available with this text or through www.thomsonedu.com/thomsonnow. ThomsonNOW™ will assist you in understanding the content in this chapter with a personalized study plan generated for your needs. A practice test will assess the areas you need to review and provide the tools to fully comprehend those concepts, including an integrated digital eBook, interactive simulations, timelines, video case studies, MicroCase exercises, and InfoTrac College Edition readers and exercises. You'll also be connected to the learning objectives, chapter outline, chapter glossary, flash cards, crossword puzzles, Internet activities, and interactive quizzes found on the companion website.

CHAPTER 16

ECONOMIC POLICY

Andrew Holbrooke/Corbis

The American economy is part of the larger global economy. American automobile companies make cars in China. At the same time, foreign companies make products in the United States. Seventeen percent of all workers in Indiana, for example, are employed by foreign companies.

Democracy and Capitalism

Government and the Economy

Economic Problems

Economic Tools

Economic Policy and the Election Cycle

Current Issues

Tax Reform

Deficit and Debt

The U.S. in the Global Economy

Immigration

Income Distribution

Conclusion: Is Our Economic Policy Responsive?

Should You Play the Trifecta?

ou are Patty Murray, senior senator from Washington and assistant floor leader for the Democrats in the Senate. It is August 2006, and the midterm election is just three months away. After a near-historic do-nothing session, and facing public approval ratings at a near all-time low, Congress is trying to pass some legislation to take to voters before hitting the campaign trail over the summer break. One victory most Republicans would love to give their base of conservative Republicans is permanent repeal of the estate tax. This move is strongly opposed by the Democratic minority, which has been able to block a vote on estate tax repeal by threatening a filibuster (see Chapter 10).

If the Republicans want to pass an estate tax bill before the election, the leadership has to find a bill that will persuade almost all Republicans and win over four to six Democrats in order to reach the sixty votes needed to shut off a filibuster. After several false starts, Majority Leader Frist decided to combine the proposal for estate tax reduction with a proposal to increase the minimum wage. Although most of the Republican membership does not favor increasing the minimum wage, Frist knows that for most Democrats, an increase in the minimum wage is a high priority. So, he has crafted a bill combining the reduction in the estate tax (to win Republican support), an increase in the

minimum wage (to win the support of Democrats), and for good measure tax breaks for the middle class and small businesses. Because this new bill combines the three provisions in one, it has been dubbed the Trifecta. Frist is hoping this combination contains enough goodies to form a winning coalition.[1]

Republicans believe this is a win-win issue for them. If enough Democrats vote with them, Republicans will get the credit for exempting 99.5 of all estates from taxation, and at the same time passage would give a boost to the moderate House Republicans who feel they need to be able to say they supported a minimum wage hike to stay competitive in what looks like an anti-incumbent year. But if the bill is killed, Republicans can still blame Democrats both for "taxing the dead" and voting against a wage hike for the poor.

One of the reasons the estate tax has so few active supporters is its depiction as a tax on the dead and a double billing on wealth that had been taxed during a person's lifetime. But the dead cannot be taxed, spouses of the deceased are exempt from the tax, and family-owned farms and businesses already have a higher exemption than other estates. The loss is to heirs who in many cases did not contribute to earning the wealth. That is because today very little inherited wealth comes from family farms and mom-and-pop businesses; it comes from

Sen. Patty Murray (D-Wash)

stocks, bonds, and nonfarm estate. In addition much of the money in huge estates has been sheltered and never subjected to tax. Nevertheless, the Republicans have been hitting your party over the head for fifteen years for favoring a "death tax."

You personally favor both estate tax reform and increasing the minimum wage. This should make it easy for you to vote yes, but three months before a national election in which your party has a chance to regain control of one or both houses you have to think about more than how this legislation will play at home. You are part of the Democratic leadership, most of whom strongly oppose the Trifecta bill, arguing that it is a "cynical" attempt to win enough votes to pass tax breaks for the richest by linking them to a small increase in the minimum wage for the poorest.

Now in your third term, you first ran for the Senate in 1992 on bread-and-butter issues just like these. The daughter of a disabled veteran, you were a stay-at-home mom after college, only later returning to the workforce as a teacher. You served on the local school board and made increased funding for education one of your major issues. After a state legislator said that you would never be able to make a difference because you were only a mom in tennis shoes, you ramped up your political ambitions. You said "Almost every woman I've ever met in politics got into it because she was mad about something."[2] You

turned the put-down to advantage by running for the Senate as the "mom in sneakers" and winning over voters as a person in touch with the problems of everyday life. The problems of women and children and low- and middle-income families have been your special concern. You also have taken a special interest in the plight of rural families and disappearing family farms.

When you first ran in 1992 you sympathized with the Republicans' argument that the estate tax had ruined some family farms and mom-and-pop businesses.[3] Because your state still has a number of family farms and orchards, as well as many small high-tech start-ups, you sponsored legislation to raise the estate tax exemption limit for farmers and small businesses and worked for partial or total repeal of the tax, just as you had promised in your campaign. Before the 2000 election, despite heavy opposition from your own party, you voted for a Republican bill that is now phasing out the tax over a ten-year period.

But that law has a "sunset" provision—an expiration date—that will nullify the tax cut in 2011 if Congress does not reauthorize it. In their many attempts at permanent repeal, Republicans—aware that you straddle the fence between your personal position and that of your party's—have often targeted you, adding little extras for your constituents to sweeten the pot. Just two months ago they added a big tax break for the timber industry, knowing that you and the junior senator from Washington, Maria Cantwell, are big supporters of the logging companies in your state. But every time permanent repeal has come up for a vote you have stuck with your party, arguing that even though you still support estate tax reform, the country could not afford the loss of revenue when we were running such high budget deficits.

But there are a number of reasons to vote for this bill. It is a compromise. It doesn't eliminate the estate tax, but rather it establishes a much higher

threshold so that an individual would pay no tax on $5 million or less of inheritance ($10 million for a couple). These additional reductions in the estate tax would cover all of the smaller businesses and farms you wanted to protect, but it will not be quite as expensive as the permanent repeal you have voted against. The minimum wage hike is also a compromise because it would phase in the increase over a three-year period, and even then still be at a lower level than the $7.65 the Democrats would like to have today.

Washington has thousands of low-wage, tip workers in places like Starbucks and other coffeehouses and restaurants. It is also the headquarters of Microsoft, which over the years has made a lot of Washingtonians multimillionaires. They have been among your bedrock supporters, helping you carry Seattle with nearly two-thirds of the vote. Why not do something for all of them in one fell swoop?

But on the other hand, there are compelling reasons to vote against the bill. In 2000, when you voted to phase out the estate tax, the budget was in surplus. Now conditions are very different: the costs of the wars in Iraq and Afghanistan, increased social spending, and billions in lost revenue from tax cuts for the wealthy have sent the federal budget into deficit. If the Trifecta passes, the loss of revenue in the first decade will be three-quarters of a trillion dollars. The tax cuts in the Trifecta bill would be fully phased in at about the time that Baby Boomer retirements will require significant new revenue for Social Security and Medicare payments.

Your views on the minimum wage hike are equally torn. You think it is just plain unfair that minimum wages haven't been increased for a decade, a period during which Congress raised its own salaries by almost $32,000. About five million Americans work for the minimum wage, as many as 40 percent of whom are the principal wage earners in their households. Still, the bill's passage may not mean much to Washington's hourly workers because yours is one of twenty-two states that have set the minimum wage higher than the federal standard.

Aside from your stance on the substance of the bill, there are the partisan political issues. You know that if you vote against the Trifecta, Republicans will make the most of what they call the Democrats' "block and blame" strategy.[4] They will charge the Democrats with trying to prevent the Republicans from getting credit for increasing the minimum wage. But you know that there is still time before the election for the Democrats to ask for a vote on a stand-alone bill to raise the minimum wage. That will be opposed by most

Republicans and be a clearer statement to voters on the difference in the parties' positions on wage hikes.

But above all, can you seriously consider voting for a bill your party overwhelmingly opposes just before an election? The party has been good to you; giving you strategically important committee assignments and, when you were still a junior member of the Senate with only a few years' prior legislative experience in your state's senate, a role in the Senate's minority leadership. They showed enough confidence in you to name you to head their 1998 Senate election campaign and in 2005 to be assistant floor leader, the Democrat's

third highest leadership position. The party would give a pass to anyone who needed to vote for the bill to avoid losing ground in their districts. But however you vote, it will not affect you immediately because you are not up for reelection until 2010. And even when the Republicans targeted you in 2004, you were reelected with 55 percent of the vote. You are still popular at home but in these times, when almost no one trusts a politician, and after years of promising your constituents support for both estate tax reform and a minimum wage increase, can you oppose both with a single vote? How do you vote?

Americans pride themselves on their free-market economy. Yet when economic problems occur, they want government to do something. But how much should government do? Americans disagree over the answer to that question. Only a few people believe government should not be involved at all. Most agree that government has to levy taxes in order to pay for national security and the infrastructure (roads, bridges, rails, waterways) that make interstate commerce possible. Most also believe that businesses should not be free to use publicly owned resources for private profit without government regulation and that government should prevent a concentration of economic power that stymies competition, fixes prices, and endangers consumer and worker safety. Despite broad consensus on points such as these, there is much honest disagreement about how far government in a free market economy should go in regulating to stimulate or slow growth or to alter the distribution of wealth.

Democracy and Capitalism

Our Constitution specifies only a little about the nature of our economic system. It emphasizes private property rights and gives government monetary, taxation, and regulatory powers. By contrast, the governments of most countries, whether democracies or dictatorships, have constitutions that link their political system to a form of economic organization and give government major responsibilities for achieving economic goals.

The role of government in the economy largely determines the kind of economic system a country has. An economy in which individuals and corpora-

tions own its capital goods or productive capacity— businesses, factories, and farms—is called a **capitalist economy,** or sometimes a free market, free enterprise economy. In a pure capitalist economy, prices, profits, working conditions, and wages would be totally determined by private sector decisions rather than by the government. Manufacturers would sell goods at what the market could bear, pay workers as little as possible, and manufacture products as cheaply as possible, concerned with health and safety only to the extent dictated by individual morality and the necessity to maintain consumer loyalty.

The idea that a capitalist economy would promote prosperity was popularized in 1776 by the British economist Adam Smith in *The Wealth of Nations*.[5] In his view, as each person seeks to maximize his or her own economic well-being, the collective well-being is enhanced. Businesses become more efficient, sell more at lower costs, hire more workers, and hence promote the economic well-being of the workers as well as the owners. Smith spoke of the "invisible hand" of the marketplace bringing about these positive outcomes.

In practice, there are no pure capitalist systems, and there never have been. Even Adam Smith believed there was some role for government intervention in a capitalist system, such as to ensure conditions for fair competition in the marketplace. Our own system is a mixture of private enterprise and government ownership combined with considerable government intervention through taxation and regulation. The United States government owns power-generating dams, some railroads, and 27 percent of all land, and it acts as an insurer of individual and corporate assets. It has loaned money to corporations to save them from bankruptcy,

and it has bailed out large banks in danger of failing. In other modern societies, such as Great Britain, France, Sweden, Germany, and the former communist nations of Eastern Europe, it is not unusual for government to own airlines, television networks, and telephone systems.

In fact, virtually all countries have economies that are a mix of private and government ownership. **Mixed economies** are distinguished from one another by the degree of government ownership and intervention in the economy through taxing, spending, and regulation of both business and consumption. Budget policies, for example, can make the rich richer and the poor poorer, or it can make the poor better off at the expense of the rich. Most Western democracies have fairly elaborate social welfare systems that redistribute some wealth from the rich to the poor in order to provide them with a minimal standard of living. In the United States, we do less of this than do most other industrialized nations.

Capitalist systems are not inevitably democratic. The most democratic systems in the world have mixed economies (such as Sweden, Britain, and Denmark), but many capitalist systems have been undemocratic. The United States itself was capitalist well before it was a democracy, if the definition of democracy includes universal suffrage. Most African American men could not vote until after the Civil War, and those who continued to live in southern states governed by Jim Crow laws were disfranchised until the Voting Rights Act in 1965. Women, who alone form a majority of the population, could not vote until the Constitution was amended in 1920.

Some argue that evolution toward democracy is inevitable in capitalism because the economic power that individuals gain as workers and consumers will, over time, lead to their political empowerment. But how much time? The opening of the Chinese economy a quarter century ago has not made that country more democratic, and the record in the republics formed from the former Soviet Union, including Russia, is very uneven. In most of these countries there is an inequitable distribution of wealth and little freedom for workers to organize.

For the United States greater democracy has gone hand-in-hand with increased regulation of the economy. In nineteenth-century America, government involvement in the economy was much less than it is today. Initially, we moved toward a more active economic role for government because of abuses by big business in the late nineteenth century: child labor was widely used, workers were paid a pittance, filthy and unsafe working conditions (as suggested by the term *sweatshop*) led to thousands of workers' deaths from industrial accidents, food and drugs were often unsafe, and the markets for some products came to be dominated by a few large producers who controlled prices and wages. Public anger led to increased government regulation of wages, working conditions, content of food and drugs, and more. And government responded because, as suffrage expanded, elected officials had to answer to an increasingly broader segment of the public.

There is an undeniable tension between capitalism and democracy. The capitalist marketplace rewards and encourages inequities that, if unchecked, threaten democratic beliefs about individual equality. For example, capitalist systems place no upper limits on the accumulation of wealth, even though wealth can be used to buy greater access to decision makers. The potential for greater exercise of influence by the wealthy weakens the concept of one person, one vote.

Wherever one believes the balance of power resides or should reside—with economic decision makers in the private sector or elected officials in government—governments and economies are inevitably intertwined. No government can exist without an economy, and even though economic systems existed long before there were governments, no modern economy could exist without government.

How power is dispersed among public and private decision makers and the people determines the nature of government. In systems where most power is concentrated in the government and in those where it is concentrated primarily in the hands of the corporate elite, democracy will suffer. Gravitation of political power to an unaccountable government will undermine democracy. Extreme maldistribution of wealth will also produce inequality of access and the loss of any meaningful practice of political equality. This is why in democratic capitalist systems, some government regulation of economic activity is essential and why most end up with mixed economies.

Government and the Economy

Economic cycles of boom and bust have been one of the constants of human history. Good times with rising living standards are followed by bad times when harvests are poor, economic activity slows, investment income declines, people go hungry, unemployment is rife, and living standards decline. Until modern times, governments did little to regulate these cycles, although some tried to ease the consequences of the bad times by distributing grain to people who were starving or by providing temporary shelters for the homeless. In the United States, it was not until the 1930s that government tried, through economic policies, to prevent these cycles from occurring.

The idea that government intervention could ease the boom-and-bust cycle of the economy was revolutionary. Classical economists had argued that the market would adjust itself without government action. But as governments became larger and more powerful, people expected government at least to try to alleviate economic problems. Since the Great Depression, government has almost always been linked in the public mind to poor performance by the economy, whether or not government's policies contributed much to the failures. And whether or not the public is willing to credit public policies for a robust economy, the president and Congress will certainly try to take credit for it.

Government can have an impact on some of the economic problems of greatest concern to the average citizen—unemployment, interest rates and inflation, the high cost of food and gasoline, fair employment practices, minimum wage, and barriers to trade. But it cannot do as much as many people have come to expect because much of the decision-making power lies in the private sector and outside our borders.

Economic Problems

One of the familiar economic problems that modern government is expected to do something about is unemployment. Even in a "full employment" economy, several percent of the labor force will be out of work—people who quit their jobs to look for something better, those just entering the workforce, those unable to work, and those who do not want to work for one reason or another. But most Western countries experience periods when there are many people unemployed because the economy does not create enough jobs.

A **depression** is a period of prolonged high unemployment. During the Great Depression (1929–1939), over one-quarter of the American working population

When gasoline prices rose in 2004, motorists may have thought they were paying an arm and a leg but, adjusted for inflation, gasoline was cheaper than during the 1970s crisis and consumption was basically unaffected.

was without jobs. A second recurring economic problem is **inflation**—a condition of increasing prices during which wages and salaries do not keep pace with the price of goods. As the dollar declines in value, there is little incentive to save and great incentive to borrow. In the late 1950s and early 1960s, inflation in the United States was quite low, as little as 2 or 3 percent a year, but the Vietnam War and the high cost of imported oil during the early 1970s stimulated a sharp rise in inflation. It was not until the 1990s that inflation returned to pre–Vietnam War levels.

Though some economists believe moderate inflation is not a bad thing,[6] many people feel threatened by it. It erodes the value of savings and gives people an incentive to consume rather than save. Bankers hate inflation because the dollar paid back to them in the future is going to be worth less than the dollar they lend today. Inflation drives interest rates up as banks charge higher and higher interest to compensate for the declining value of the dollar. Credit becomes more expensive, which makes it difficult for businesses and industries to expand. And, of course, inflation is bad because people think it is bad—they worry about it getting out of control.

A third economic problem is stagnant production—that is, the failure of the economy as a whole to produce increasing amounts of goods and services. Two or more consecutive quarters (a quarter is three months) of falling production are termed a **recession.** During the peak of the recession in 1981–1982, over 10 percent of the American workforce was unem-

Gasoline prices soared in 2006 due to increased demand for gasoline from developing countries and decreased supply of oil because of war and unrest in the Middle East.

ployed, and many others had only part-time work or had simply quit looking for work. In 2001, the United States went into a milder recession with unemployment rising by "only" 2 percent.

Productivity, one measure of the country's economic health, is the ratio of the total hours worked by everyone in the labor force to the dollar value of goods and services they produce (the gross domestic product, or GDP). When businesses and industries discover new ways to produce goods and services using less labor, or when a healthier, better-educated, more mobile and efficient labor force can produce more product in less time, productivity rises. To achieve improvement in the overall standard of living without increasing inflation, productivity must steadily rise. Productivity is also a measure of competitiveness; businesses must become increasingly more efficient to be competitive at home and abroad. For decades the United States has had the highest productivity rates in the world, but the rate of growth is slowing, in part because much of the gain from the introduction of computers, Internet access, and businesses streamlining, including reduction of their labor forces, has been realized.

The sum of inflation and unemployment, known as the "misery index," is an economic indicator that is especially important for anyone holding or running for office. As the number of people looking for work and the prices people have to pay for basic goods and services rise, the misery index goes up; the higher the index, the more likely people will be thinking about

the economy when they enter polling booths. Because depression, inflation, and recession all affect people's standard of living, most people expect government to take action to stimulate or slow the economy. But the public does not agree on which are the most appropriate or effective responses.

The ultimate goal in any economy is to have low unemployment, low inflation, and increasing productivity while total economic output grows steadily. Achieving all of this simultaneously is rare, however. There has long been a consensus among economists that unemployment and inflation are inversely related and that if unemployment falls below about 6 percent, wages and prices will begin to rise. Historically, inflation had been at its lowest when unemployment was high and production sagging. Conversely, increasing employment often brought high levels of inflation. Typically, this meant some trade-off among these three goals. At least that was the assumption before 1995, when the U.S. economy entered a period of economic growth with rising productivity, the lowest unemployment (3.9 percent) in a quarter-century, and a low, stable inflation rate (around 2 percent).

Economic Tools

Government has three primary tools to help achieve its economic goals: the fiscal, monetary, and regulatory powers granted by the Constitution. The president and his top economic advisors can also use their informal powers of persuasion to influence the behavior of business and consumers.

Fiscal Policy

The size of the annual budget tells us the federal government's share of the domestic economy and indicates the potential for fiscal policy to affect the nation's economy. The federal budget also reflects the country's political goals and values, because who is taxed, at what rates, and what government spends the money on reflect national priorities. Government spending is often discussed within the larger debate over fundamental political values, and disagreements on taxation have always been linked to the debate over the proper size and role of government in both a democracy and a free market economy.

Government decisions on how much money it will spend and how much tax it will levy determine **fiscal policy.** Increased spending stimulates the economy and increases employment; lower government spending helps slow the economy and decreases inflation. How great an impact government has depends on how much it spends in relation to the size of the economy. The United States spends a smaller percentage of its GDP on government than other Western industrial countries. For the past forty years, federal government spending has hovered near 20 percent of GDP, and state and local government spending accounts for another 10 percent. Thus, 70 percent of the GDP is accounted for by private spending.

Taxes are generally pegged to spending, so that government takes in enough revenue each year to cover its outlays. But tax policy is also used to help regulate economic cycles. Tax cuts leave more money in the hands of the consumer, thus stimulating private spending and reducing unemployment. Increased taxes take more money out of the hands of the consumer, slow the economy, and thus reduce inflation.

Government's ability to regulate economic activity through spending and taxation is limited, in part because it accounts for less than one-third of all economic activity. And sometimes the economy responds too quickly to increases or reductions in spending and taxation, other times not quickly enough. Moreover, our economy is linked to the global market and thus is affected by conditions over which we have little control, such as energy prices or demands for products or labor.

Who makes fiscal policy? In the United States, laws regarding taxation and spending require approval by Congress and the president. In making his recommendations to Congress about taxes, spending, and

© Bettmann/Corbis

In Germany in 1923, inflation was so high that a basket of money barely sufficed to buy a bag of groceries. This hyperinflation was caused by the German government's printing ever more money to pay penalties it was assessed by the victors of World War I. The government finally ended the inflation by issuing new currency, one unit of which was equal to one trillion of the old. This made the lifetime savings of many people worthless and contributed to the unrest that eventually toppled the democratic government and installed the Nazi government.

other economic matters, the president has the assistance, among others, of three key people: the secretary of the treasury; the head of the Office of Management and Budget (OMB), who is responsible for preparing the annual budget message; and the chair of the Council of Economic Advisers, a group of economists within the White House Office who are specialists in fiscal policy matters. Sometimes, of course, these three advisers to the president are at odds with each other or with the president's political aides, or are uncertain their advice is sound. Indeed, President Harry Truman once said he was in search of a one-armed economist so that the person could never make a recommendation and then say "on the other hand."[7] Economics, like political science, is an inexact science!

Congress has its own fiscal specialists on committees such as Appropriations and Budget and members also rely heavily on the director of the nonpartisan Congressional Budget Office (CBO).

That government can have a substantial impact on the economy through its fiscal policy has been accepted wisdom since the British economist John Maynard Keynes published *A General Theory of Employment, Interest and Money.*[8] In 1935, Keynes argued that government could stimulate the economy by increasing spending in a time of high unemployment. This would put more money into the economy, thus stimulating the demand for goods and services and, in turn, causing factories to produce more and hire more workers. Therefore, even if government had to borrow to increase spending, the deficit could be justified because eventually higher employment rates would increase tax revenue.

Keynesian economics ran counter to the conventional wisdom of the time. At the outset of the Great Depression in 1929, President Hoover believed that if the government went into debt, it would make the Depression worse, not better. His opponent in the 1932 election, Franklin D. Roosevelt, also ran on a pledge of a balanced federal budget. It was only after Roosevelt was elected that he adopted the Keynesian idea that the government could stimulate the economy by spending money, borrowing it if it had to, and in this way help the nation get out of the Depression.

Keynesian thinking dominated fiscal policy for several decades. Well into the 1960s, economists were optimistic that government could successfully regulate the economy to maintain high levels of employment and reasonable inflation. But by the 1970s, this confidence disappeared because of simultaneous high unemployment and high inflation. No government policies coped well with **stagflation,** the word coined to describe this combination of economic stagnation and inflation. Stagflation dealt a blow to Keynesian economics, which predicts that high unemployment and inflation cannot exist simultaneously (because, histori-

cally, higher levels of unemployment had driven prices down). The arrival of stagflation signaled a new era in the development of the American economy and led to increasing dissatisfaction with existing fiscal policy.

In 1981, the Reagan administration came to the White House with a new policy, **supply-side economics,** that promised to reduce inflation, lower taxes, and balance the budget simultaneously. The basic premise of this theory is that as government lowers taxes, more money is freed for private investment. Therefore, when the economy is sluggish, supply-siders advocate tax cuts to stimulate growth. They believe people will save some of the money they would have paid in taxes, thus making more money available to lend to businesses for expansion and modernization. Taxpayers would also be left with more money to spend on consumption, and to satisfy the increased demand, businesses would hire more workers. With increased employment, there would be more people paying taxes and fewer collecting unemployment compensation. So, according to supply-side economics, it is possible both to promote economic growth and to balance the budget by lowering the tax rate.

These ideas appeal to conservatives because they offer an economic rationale for smaller budgets and thus smaller government. They also have broad appeal to Republicans who, since the Great Depression, have drawn substantial electoral support from the wealthiest Americans. Whereas Keynesian economics has been used to endorse across-the-board tax cuts to stimulate consumer spending, the supply-side approach puts more emphasis on tax cuts for the highest income groups as a means of encouraging private investment.

Keynesians and supply-siders have fundamentally different views on government regulation of the economy. Keynesians believe that government intervention can be effective both in steering the economy and in cushioning the blow to consumers of a sluggish or overheated economy. Supply-siders believe that taxing and spending for these purposes are inappropriate and inefficient uses of government powers. They believe it is better to leave as many decisions on spending and investing, and as much money as possible, in the hands of consumers.

Supply-side economics, as implemented by Reagan's economic team and continued by George H. Bush's administration (despite Bush having labeled it "voodoo economics"), led to disillusionment with the policy. It created record-smashing budget deficits. Dramatically increased spending for the military combined with small cuts in spending for social programs and the loss of billions of dollars in tax revenues left the country with $2.5 trillion of new debt. Nevertheless George W. Bush followed a similar policy of using huge tax cuts for the wealthy to stimulate economic growth. Savings rates among the wealthy did not increase, however, and, although the economy did grow at a faster rate for a few years, revenues as a percentage of GDP were lower than at any time since World War II. And unlike Reagan, Bush increased both military *and* social spending. The result was $3 trillion of new debt in Bush's first six years in office.

Monetary Policy

Whereas fiscal policy affects the economy through spending and taxation decisions, **monetary policy** attempts to regulate the economy through control of short-term interest rates and the supply of money. Monetary policy is made by the Federal Reserve Board (the Fed), composed of a board of governors, twelve Federal Reserve Banks located in major cities around the country, and the Federal Open Market Committee (FOMC).[9] The FOMC meets several times a year to determine monetary policy. Since 1978, its primary mandate from Congress has been to achieve price stability and full employment (full employment is considered achieved when the unemployment rate falls somewhere between 5 and 6.5 percent).

The Federal Reserve Board is largely, but not completely, independent of the president. Fed members are appointed by the president, with Senate consent, but their terms are fourteen years. The terms are staggered in such a way that, barring resignations, the maximum number any president could appoint in a four-year term is two. The Fed chair serves only a four-year term, although reappointment is possible and often happens. The relatively short-term appointment opens the door to influence by Congress and the president, especially when the chair wants to be reappointed.

The Fed is *the* bank for the federal government; it distributes our currency, supervises and regulates some national banks, and acts as clearinghouse for many of the checks written on those banks. But from the standpoint of the overall health of the economy, its most important work is using its monetary powers to maintain a balance between demand for and supply of currency.[10]

In the nineteenth century when government spending was low and fiscal policy was not yet a major factor in the economy, "tight" money was often the main issue in elections. Today, when most people are more focused on the federal budget, you may think monetary policy is too dry a subject to bother with, but when you realize that it actually determines both interest rates and the availability of money you will quickly see why it is important to your well-being and why it can have a dramatic impact. In 1982, when the Fed tightened the money supply, forcing interest rates, unemployment, and bankruptcies up, one man entered the offices of the Fed and tried to kill its chair.[11] Other groups drew up "wanted" posters for the board members. And still others, thrown out of work or off their farms, committed suicide. When interest rates are low, as they have been in recent years, the average person focuses less on what the Fed is doing.

The Fed controls the supply of money in several ways. It can buy and sell hundreds of millions of dollars of treasury notes and bonds. When it buys, it pumps money into other banks; when it sells, it depletes the money reserves of the banks and thus takes money out of the economy. The Fed also changes the interest rates it charges banks to borrow its money. Low interest rates stimulate borrowing and put more money into the economy. As a last resort, the Fed can increase or decrease the amount of reserves (cash on hand) it requires banks to have. If the reserve requirement is increased, banks take money out of circulation to build up their reserves. If the reserve requirement is decreased, banks take money out of their reserves and lend it to customers, which increases the money supply.

When the Fed makes money scarce, interest rates go up, and businesses and industries find it harder to borrow money for expansion. As a result, production and inflation may slow. When the Fed allows more money into the economy, interest rates go down, making it easier for businesses to borrow for expansion. The Fed's influence grew in the 1980s as huge budget deficits limited the options available to the president and Congress to stimulate or slow the economy through taxing and spending. With little flexibility left in fiscal policy, monetary policy was the principal means for fine-tuning the economy. Today Wall Street and business continue to look on monetary policy as the primary means for stimulating growth and productivity as well as for slowing the economy when it becomes overheated. This is the view favored by *monetarists,* who believe that if government has to intervene in the economy, it should do so through monetary, not fiscal, policy.

Monetary policy is made primarily to protect the value of currency and ultimately to protect investors. Fiscal policy is geared more toward protecting the average consumer against unemployment and the effects of inflation (rather than toward *preventing* inflation). Although many people are both investors and consumers, and while fiscal and monetary policy should be complementary and not at odds, at times they may seem to be at cross-purposes.

In addition to the difference in the priorities of fiscal and monetary policy makers, accountability is also an issue. One factor that helps the Fed maintain its independence is that it does not depend on Congress for funding; its operating costs come out of the more than $20 billion in annual interest earned on its holdings of U.S. government securities. The Fed can do more with its money than pay its own operating costs.

On its own authority, it can extend billions of dollars in credits and loans to businesses, other banks, and even to foreign countries. During the 1995 financial crisis in Mexico, the Clinton administration wanted to make a loan quickly to avoid the crisis spreading to other countries, but it found the treasury without enough money and Congress unwilling to approve the loan. So Clinton went to the Fed, which used its own funds to loan Mexico $50 billion—something it can do *without* congressional approval. In this case, the initiative came from the White House, but it is part of the Fed's responsibilities to make independent decisions on loans and credits. Because it can act independently, it can act quickly, and it can have a significant impact on the economy without the public ever being aware of its actions. After 9/11, for example, the Fed, fearing a possible economic meltdown, freed up currency and extended billions of dollars in credits and loans to businesses.

Of all federal agencies, the Fed is the most independent as well as the most powerful. Adding to its independence is its ability to escape openness-in-government rules that apply to other federal agencies. The Fed chair is required by law to give testimony to Congress twice a year on monetary policy, but Alan Greenspan (1974–2005), nicknamed "the Maestro" and the most visible head the Fed has ever had, averaged a dozen appearances before congressional committees and fifteen public speeches each year. His comments on the state of the economy could cause the stock market to soar or plummet. Some considered the Fed under his leadership far more open than it was in the past because of the frequency of these public appearances and his pronouncements on Fed policy, but Greenspan also used his power to protect the agency from oversight. On his own authority, in reaction to a House Banking Committee demand to see transcripts of a Fed meeting, he ordered some Fed proceedings not to be taped and ruled that the only transcripts of Fed meetings that will ever be available to archives, and hence to the public, will be versions edited by Fed staff.[12] It is not likely that any other agency head could exercise this kind of power with respect to Congress.

If greater power to regulate the economy *has* gravitated toward monetary policy makers, it has passed into the hands of men and women who are not directly accountable to voters and who most Americans cannot identify. Despite the general lack of knowledge about the Fed, its chair is one of the most powerful people in the country; some call him the second most powerful person in the "free world." Not all Fed chairs want such a high political profile, but Greenspan was an adept Washingtonian and socializer (along with his wife, NBC reporter Andrea Mitchell), who was known for his ability to cultivate members of Con-

gress and the cabinet.[13] His successor, Ben Bernanke, is a low-key former academic whose goal appears to be to stay out of the spotlight and to achieve maximum transparency and clarity in public pronouncements.

Regulating Business

Regulation is government's third formal economic management power. Government's constitutional and statutory authority to regulate interstate commerce, make trade policy, provide for the common welfare, and ensure equal opportunity provides broad legal ground for regulating economic activity. Government regulates the banking industry, the stock market, hiring practices, industrial pollution, food and product safety, and, through licensing and special concessions, mediates competing claims for use of public property such as the airwaves, airspace, mineral resources, and timberland. And the federal government's stewardship of millions of acres of wilderness, forest, and grazing areas and wetlands has an impact on climate and agricultural production. The extent of regulation can be noted by the fact that the Food and Drug Administration, for example, has regulatory authority over a quarter of the United States economy.[14]

One reason for much regulation has been called the **tragedy of the commons.**[15] The *commons* refers to the air we breathe and the water we drink, which belong to us all. The *tragedy* is that some individuals may seek to exploit them for their own uses to the detriment of the common good. To maximize their profits, farmers pump as much irrigation water as they need from rivers or aquifers, even in water-short areas, and industries spew toxic chemicals into the air or bury them in the soil. They are acting in accordance with the profit motive. Indeed, most individuals who exploit the commons gain economically and thus have considerable incentive to do so. But when many people exploit the commons, the community as a whole suffers.

Consider the case of Los Angeles and General Motors (GM). Los Angeles once had a low-pollution

"No, I didn't. I never said there should be <u>no</u> government regulation."

electric railway system. In the 1930s, GM bought the system and then destroyed it, because GM wanted to sell cars, trucks, and buses. The company replaced the electric system with noisy, polluting diesel buses, so uncomfortable and unreliable that Los Angelenos were given a great incentive to rely on private autos.

In 1949, after buying and destroying electric railway systems in more than one hundred cities, GM was fined a paltry five thousand dollars by the government for illegally conspiring to replace municipal services with its own. Meanwhile, the company made millions of dollars. Due in large part to reliance on cars, smog in Los Angeles became a major health hazard. Some studies claimed that children who grew up in Los Angeles lost up to 50 percent of their lung capacity from breathing in the polluted air.[16] Obviously, it is absurd to charge GM with creating the entire automobile culture of Los Angeles, but clearly its drive for private profits did not contribute to the common good.

When GM or any other entity, such as a chemical company that disposes of its toxic wastes in an unsafe way, imposes a cost on the public, it has created an **externality.** Externalities are costs or benefits that are not reflected in market prices. Environmental degradation is a negative externality because the social costs, the burdens imposed on society, are not reflected in the cost of the goods whose production caused the damage. For example, when a coal-burning utility emits sulfur dioxide into the air, the company is essentially disposing of a by-product at no cost by simply burning it off and releasing it into the air. This places an unfair burden on the public, both in terms of the health risks and the costs of environmental cleanup.

This emission also leads to inefficiency in the marketplace because the utility is not made to bear the true cost of generating electricity. If companies are allowed to externalize costs in this way, they will produce more of a product than is economically or environmentally sound. But if they have to absorb or internalize the cost of emitting pollutants and add it to the price consumers pay for the service or product, then utilities and manufacturers have "an incentive to reduce production to acceptable levels or to develop alternative technologies."[17] It also prevents consumers from making decisions about purchasing or use that are based on real costs. Instead, costs that are hidden—deferred payments that taxpayers will make much later for environmental cleanup or health care—encourage consumption.

To make the market more efficient and to get companies to stop producing goods and services whose real costs are not reflected in the prices charged for those goods and services (for example, to get a petrochemical plant to stop releasing toxins into the air), the government can regulate, in this case set standards for how much of the pollutant can be emitted and set the recovery costs through penalties and fines from violators. Alternatively, it can impose taxes on emissions or discharges and charge for pollution up front.

Regulatory policies are bitterly contested, and proponents of deregulation are among political candidates' biggest donors. In Chapter 9 we saw the link between campaign donations and deregulation of the financial industry and the far-flung consequences of that deregulation. There will always be disagreement over which economic behavior should be regulated, how much, and which are the appropriate tools. But the debate must weigh regulation's impact on market efficiency and economic growth against its contribution to public health and safety and confidence in the market.

Persuasion, or Jawboning

The government, and the president in particular, has an informal means for affecting the economy—trying to persuade businesses or individual consumers to behave in a certain way. *Jawboning,* or persuasion, can make a difference because psychological factors affect economic behavior. For example, economists recognize the importance of consumer confidence—that is, the degree of optimism individuals have about the economy. Confidence is rooted in the real performance of the economy, but sometimes there is a lag between the economy's performance and consumers' perception of its health.

A president can try to persuade businesses to expand or consumers to spend, for example, by expressing his confidence in the country's economic direction. Lyndon Johnson was extremely skillful in persuading business and labor leaders to accept his economic policies, and Kennedy and Reagan were remarkably adept at persuading both business and the public. In contrast, Carter's calls for sacrifice to address economic problems like the energy crisis seemed to decrease consumer confidence, and George H. Bush's inability to convince the public that the country was coming out of recession in 1992 contributed to his defeat by Clinton. His son was similarly unsuccessful in his attempt, before the 2006 election, to convince edgy consumers and Wall Street investors that the economy was strong. Despite a very respectable growth rate, low inflation and unemployment, rising productivity, and significant income increases for the top 5 percent, Bush's jawboning on the strength of the economy could not offset pessimism over flat wages, high gas prices, and out-of-control Iraqi War costs.

Perhaps the most impressive feats of jawboning in recent years have come from Fed chairs. However, when the economy is in a prolonged period of expansion, as it was during the 1990s, and consumer confidence is very high, the Fed chair's persuasive powers are not as strong. At those times the economy seems to run on its own momentum. In 1999, when Greenspan tried to cool what he saw as a dangerously overheated economy by accusing investors in the stock market of "irrational exuberance" and threatening new interest rate hikes, his comments produced only a short-term flurry of activity, and the stock market continued to climb.[18]

Economic Policy and the Election Cycle

Democrats and Republicans differ in their use of fiscal and regulatory policies to influence economic growth, employment, cost of living and disposable income, and consumer and environmental safety, and these policy differences are major issues in most elections. Historically, Republicans have been more tolerant of high unemployment than Democrats have been, but less tolerant than Democrats of high inflation rates. Democrats are more supportive of government regulation for consumer and environmental protection and to correct inequities in the marketplace, whereas Republicans have been more supportive of tax cuts and deregulation of business. These positions reflect the priorities of the people from whom each party is most likely to draw votes and financial support. The general orientations still hold, but parties have modified their approaches as the economy has changed and become more subject to global influences. Republicans were long considered more committed to fiscal prudence and balanced budgets than to spending on health and safety and income support. But in the Reagan and both Bush administrations, when military spending was given priority over fiscal prudence, deficits ballooned. Today, balancing the budget is an issue that works better as an election issue for Democrats than Republicans.

Despite their issue differences, Republicans and Democrats have many similarities in their approach to budgeting. The shift in spending that occurs when control of Congress changes hands shows that both parties adhere to the old adage "To the victor go the spoils." In the early 1990s, when Democrats were in the majority, on average $34 million more per year was spent in Democratic congressional districts than in Republican congressional districts. After Republicans assumed control in 1995, spending shifted from urban and poor rural areas to suburban and farm counties until by 2001, $612 million more was being spent in Republican congressional districts than in Democratic congressional districts. Although spending increased in all districts during these years, it rose by 52 percent in Republican districts compared with 34 percent in Democratic districts.[19]

There is little difference between parties, either in Congress or the White House, in their willingness to adjust economic policy during election years.[20] Cuts in government spending and increases in taxes reduce real personal income, so budget cuts and tax increases are unlikely in election years. The prediction of multiyear budget deficits did not stop Congress from proposing additional tax cuts or making existing tax breaks permanent before the 2002, 2004, and 2006 elections. In 2004 Democrats and Republicans vied for the leading role in providing a prescription drug benefit to seniors, who not only vote in large numbers, but also are represented by one of the country's most powerful interest groups, the AARP (formerly the American Association of Retired Persons). Before the 2006 midterm elections, Republicans sponsored a bill to raise the federal minimum wage, a measure they had opposed for a decade when sponsored by Democrats. (See this chapter's "You Are There"). And congressional spending on earmarks and pork-barrel projects almost always increases by billions of dollars in election years.

Monetary policy is also subject to election year pressures. During a campaign when the economy is the central issue, there is enormous potential for politicization of the Fed despite its independence. In the summer before the 1992 election, following a jump in the unemployment rate, the Fed lowered its prime lending rate (in an attempt to increase borrowing and thus consumer and business spending). President Bush had publicly demanded such a reduction just several days earlier. His secretary of the treasury was accused of pressuring the Fed's chair (Greenspan) to lower rates even further as a condition of his renomination for another term.[21] Although Bush denied placing any condition on Greenspan's renomination, he reportedly blamed Greenspan for acting too late and dooming his reelection in 1992.

The Fed chair does not have to listen to the president. It is not uncommon for a Fed chair appointed by a Democrat to be retained by a Republican (Paul Volcker, for example), or one appointed by a Republican to be retained by a Democrat (Alan Greenspan, for example).

Partisan differences between presidents and Fed chairs can be exacerbated by the fact that fiscal and monetary policy makers have different goals. To see how this works, we can look at the fiscal policy of the Clinton administration and the monetary policy of the Fed under Greenspan's chairmanship. Clinton came into office with the goal of "growing" the economy and increasing the real wages of workers. Primarily a politician, his eye was on the earning and buying power of the average voter. As protector of the currency, Greenspan did not want to see Clinton achieve his goals through a too-rapid expansion of the money supply or by wage increases that were too precipitous. Primarily a banker, Greenspan's eye was on investors.

During Clinton's first two years in office, the growth rate soared, 5.5 million new jobs were created, and inflation stayed at or below 3 percent. But as the unemployment rate fell toward 6 percent and then below it, the Fed began imposing a series of interest rate hikes.

Greenspan also started jawboning, trying to slow the economy and offset a rise in inflation. Although it is arguable whether the impact of monetary policy can be felt so quickly, by early 1995 the rate of growth did slow and unemployment rose for the first time in two years.

To a large extent, the concerns of the Fed and the Clinton administration should have overlapped. In an era of flat wages, workers did not want higher prices, and Clinton certainly would not have wanted to take the rap for high inflation and a devalued dollar. On the other hand, most workers would rather have a job and higher prices than have no job and stable prices, especially in an era of decreased spending for welfare. And though no politician may claim to favor it, the devalued dollar can lead to more exports, and more exports can mean more jobs.

Greenspan treated George W. Bush substantially better than he did Bill Clinton. His conservative leanings led him to pull his punches in public comments on Bush's tax cuts. Having advised Clinton throughout his administration of the need to hold down spending and end budget deficits, Greenspan was very receptive to the huge tax cuts passed in Bush's administration. The explanation for this double standard, according to longtime Fed watchers, lay in Greenspan's politics: he was not so much an opponent of deficit spending as he was of spending for social programs—education, health, and welfare. Because higher amounts of social spending are more likely in a Democratic than Republican administration, Greenspan urged Clinton to avoid deficit spending then later accepted Bush's increased spending on tax cuts and defense without comment. Although in private Greenspan told Bush's first treasury secretary Paul O'Neill that the tax cuts should have had a trigger mechanism that would have reversed them if the budget fell into deficit, he never said so publicly. Instead, in keeping with his opposition to social spending, Greenspan called for "program readjustments" in Social Security.[22] In 2004, after Bush reappointed him to a fifth (and last) term—and after it was apparent Bush had increased social spending far more than Clinton had—Greenspan became more openly critical of the tax cuts and budget deficits.

The economy has an impact on the vote, although it is not as simple as one might suspect. Those who have studied the impact of economic hard times on individual vote choices have reported that how people feel they are doing compared to a year or two before does have a mild influence on their presidential and congressional voting choices. If they feel things are improving, they are somewhat more likely to favor the incumbent; if they believe their financial situation is eroding, they are somewhat more likely to vote against the incumbent.

Voters are more concerned, however, with the state of the overall economy than with their own family's situation. But they do not seem to respond decisively to changes in unemployment or inflation levels. The 1994 congressional election provided evidence for this. With the economy strong and unemployment low, voters might have been expected to support incumbents but they were strongly anti-status quo, expressing deep pessimism over the country's future.[23] But in 1998, after four years of economic boom, the president's party did gain seats in Congress midterm for only the second time in the twentieth century.

Some observers believe the 1990s run of prosperity changed, if only temporarily, the economy's impact at the polls. Whereas in the past, a prolonged period of low unemployment, low inflation, and rising wages would have helped incumbents, it did not give Vice President Al Gore much of a lift in his 2000 presidential campaign. He had to emphasize other issues such as "family values," income inequality, and health care to catch up to Bush in the polls. The reason, some argue, is that people were doing so well that they took continued growth and near full employment for granted. Though people blame the government for bad times, when good times come they attribute it to their own hard work or prudent investments. If voters adopt the view that most of the credit for economic good times lies outside the White House and Congress, then incumbents will gain little at the polls in times of prosperity.[24] Gore did win the popular vote in 2000, but it was far closer than it would have been had economic conditions been the deciding factor in how people cast their ballots.

In leaner times, the economy is more likely to be a campaign issue. Incumbents can easily become scapegoats, deserved or not. Much depends on where voters place the economy in the constellation of issues that concern them and who they hold accountable. Private investment and the stock market received most of the credit for the boom of the 1990s and apparently absorbed all of the blame for the crash of 2002. In that year's congressional elections, voters did not punish elected officials for the deregulation of the financial industry that led directly to corporate fraud and business failure. Republicans gained seats in both the House and Senate.

Nor did a so-so economy hurt George W. Bush's bid for reelection. During wartime, domestic policy and the economy can take a backseat, and this worked to Bush's advantage in 2004. Going into the election the economy was only in marginally better shape than in 2002 from the standpoint of job creation. Bush barely escaped being the first president since Herbert Hoover to have a net loss of jobs on his watch; his fiscal policy eradicated the budget surplus and created massive deficits. Those who thought the economy was the most important issue voted overwhelmingly for Senator John Kerry. Yet Bush was reelected with 51 percent of the vote because people put their concern about terrorism and the war in Iraq ahead of their anxiety about poor economic and fiscal performance. And his party again gained seats in the House and Senate.

Before the 2006 election Republicans were in the reverse situation; the economy was in better shape, but Iraq was the major issue on voters' minds, this time as a negative rather than a positive. No matter how much Bush talked up economic growth (avoiding fiscal policy and budget deficits), 70 percent of the public thought the country was on the wrong track.[25] Forty percent of voters said the economy was a factor in their vote and the Democrats picked up enough seats to regain control of Congress.

Current Issues

In this section we discuss some of the major economic issues the country has faced during the administration of George W. Bush: tax reform, budget deficits and debt, income distribution, globalization, and immigration.

Tax Reform

Tax policy is always on the agenda. Though debates over income tax may seem arcane, and sometimes are, tax policy says a lot about who the winners and losers in society are. There are many reasons for trying to revise or reform the tax code: to simplify it, to achieve greater fairness, to increase revenue to pay for new spending or to balance the budget or to decrease revenue as a way of downsizing government or of stimulating the economy in periods of sluggish growth. Reagan's tax cuts of the early 1980s were intended to stimulate the economy and to decrease government spending in favor of private investment. Clinton's tax legislation targeted fairness and deficit reduction. George W. Bush focused on cutting taxes for the rich to encourage investment and removing the lowest income groups (who pay a tiny proportion of overall taxes) from the tax rolls. None of these tax policies—Reagan's, Clinton's, or Bush's—made the system simpler.

Americans think they are highly taxed, but compared with citizens in other developed countries, they are not. Twenty-seven percent of all tax filers pay no federal income tax, and as share of household income,

"Can't we put in something about rich white guys don't have to pay taxes?"

income tax for most has been falling since the 1990s.[26] In 2001, a household with a median income of $64,600 paid about 7 percent of it in *income* taxes, the lowest amount since 1957.[27] Overall, in 2001, federal personal income, payroll, and other taxes (such as taxes on alcohol, gasoline, and cigarettes) took an average of 16.3 percent of the income of the middle fifth of American taxpayers.[28] This is the lowest percentage since the CBO began publishing such data.[29] Of course, most households also pay some combination of state income tax, sales, excise, and local taxes in addition to federal income and payroll taxes. The average taxpayer must work from January 1 until about mid-April each year to cover all these tax obligations.[30]

Americans' collective tax burden is equal to about 28 percent of GDP; the only other industrialized nation that has as low a tax burden is Japan. The average for European nations is 37 percent; Swedes set the curve with combined tax payments equal to 51 percent of GDP.[31]

Tax Fairness

In tax language, "fairness" means spreading the tax burden among households according to their ability to pay. A tax structure based on the principle of wealthy and middle-income households paying higher percentages of their income in taxes than poorer households is called a **progressive tax.** A tax that requires the poor to pay proportionately more than those in middle- and upper-income brackets is a **regressive tax.**

Experts do not agree on the degree of progressivity of current income tax law. If the Bush tax cuts are looked at in dollar savings or share of tax benefits, current rates look more regressive than in the 1990s. The average saving for the top 1 percent of earners was $56,000 and for the middle fifth $699.[32] About 22 percent of the cuts extended in 2006 will go to people earning $1 million; those earning between $40,000 and $50,000 a year got a 1 percent share.[33] However when Bush's tax cuts are looked at in terms of dollars paid in taxes and distribution of tax burden, they look more progressive. The wealthiest Americans pay the largest share of income tax revenue because they have the largest share of the country's wealth (Fig. 16.2). The top 1 percent of earners accounted for 34 percent of all income taxes paid in 2002; the bottom half paid about 3 percent.[34] Seventy-five percent of those earning less than $10,000, and 41 percent of those earning $10,000–$21,000 paid no income tax at all.[35]

Payroll taxes, however, are regressive. The reason that payroll taxes disproportionately hit lower- and middle-income taxpayers is that each year a ceiling is set on how much income is subject to Social Security tax (in 2006 the tax was assessed on the first $94,200 of earnings). Interest and dividend income is not taxed either, and this is primarily earned by wealthier Americans. Social Security and Medicare taxes take, on average, about 9 percent of income (but much less for the wealthy) and account for more than a third of all federal revenue (see Figure 16.1). However, because of the increasing life span, the majority of workers on retirement get benefits well in excess of what they have had withheld in payroll taxes.

There is a second kind of fairness in tax policy that is little discussed except by tax specialists. This is economic or tax neutrality, tax policy that does not single out for favor certain kinds of economic activity over others. Our current tax code is definitely not economically neutral, as evidenced in our complex scheme of tax breaks and deductions (discussed below). It favors home ownership over renting, raising children over having none, oil exploration over the development of solar energy and wind power, and—in what some economists think is the most worrisome preference of all—it favors consumption over saving. Supporters of greater tax neutrality say that it is inefficient to have a tax system that determines "where investment flows or who spends how much on what." Their priority in reform is to structure a tax system so that it does not favor one form of economic activity over another.[36]

Tax Simplification

President Franklin D. Roosevelt once said that our tax code "might as well have been written in a foreign language," and the laws are dozens of times more complex now. Since 1986 there have been 15,000 amendments to the tax code.[37] It offers 17,500 pages of explanation for filling out more than 650 different forms. According to the IRS, in 2003 it took the average taxpayer thirteen hours and thirty-five minutes to

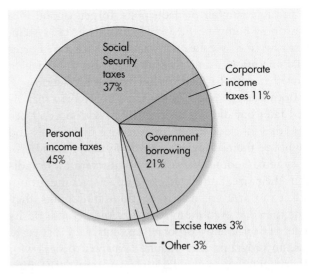

FIGURE 16.1 ■ Estimated Federal Revenue Sources, 2007† ($2.4 trillion)
*Customs duties; fines; penalties, Federal Reserve earnings, gift and estate taxes.
†Does not include revenue from business activities such as park fees. This is subtracted from spending.
SOURCE: Derived from figures in the *Budget of the United States Government, Fiscal Year 2007* (Washington, D.C.: Government Printing Office, 2006). Note that these are all OMB estimates and differ from those made by the Congressional Budget Office.

complete Form 1040; it is thus not surprising that more than half of all filers hire professionals to do their returns.[38] The rules are so Byzantine that a 2003 Treasury Department survey of IRS walk-in services found 43 percent of the questions received no answer or were answered incorrectly.[39]

Why is the tax code so complex when most policy makers claim to want to simplify it? The complexity occurs because tax policy is used to achieve a variety of social goals and to reward various constituencies with what some call tax "candy." These are more commonly known as exemptions and deductions. A deduction is the amount taxpayers have spent for some item, such as mortgage interest or business equipment, that they are allowed by law to subtract from their income before figuring their tax liability. Congress values families so it provides tax credits for child care; Congress wants to encourage business growth so it gives credits and deductions for investment. It thinks that charitable giving is a good thing, so there are deductions for gifts to charity. Congress wants to encourage Americans to become home owners, so it provides a deduction for home mortgage interest and so on and on with thousands of deductions for activities or objects that the majority of Congress values. (See Figure 16.3.)

Though each of these is wanted and lobbied heavily for by interest groups, together they create a tax code that is difficult to understand and one that favors wealthier Americans who are able to take advantage of the greatest number of deductions. To get a good idea of just how complex these breaks make our tax system, go to the IRS website (www.irs.gov), click on "Forms and Publications," and scroll through the vast array of forms that must be filed when claiming deductions.

Both Reagan and Clinton tried tax reform that altered rates but did not change the basic code, and because they did not significantly reduce deductions and loopholes, their changes offered no simplification of the system. George W. Bush's tax cuts were more radical in their size, but by targeting upper-income groups with a vast array of new deductions and credits, they made the code even more complex. And because Bush's estate, personal, and corporate tax cuts were passed as phase-in programs, they require taxpayers to deal with different numbers and rules each year until 2010. Furthermore, Congress regularly approves "extenders" or special, limited-time tax breaks for business groups or other special categories of taxpayers. Each year Congress has to either suspend or renew them. All of this piecemeal legislating adds thousands of pages to the tax code.

Then, too, sometimes influential members of Congress add special deductions for favored corporations or interests. Every budget bill contains hundreds of these special exemptions. Tax legislation is so voluminous other members may not even realize that they are voting for a special deal for an individual corporation or a small class of them. These giveaways are seldom debated, and each of them makes the tax code more complicated and less equitable.

There are four nominal personal income tax rates (not counting zero) ranging from 10 to 35 percent. The corporate tax rate is 34 percent. Sometimes people talk about these rates as if they do, in fact, reflect the share of income paid to the government. However, because of credits, exemptions, and deductions, individuals and corporations pay the nominal rate only on their net, not their gross incomes. According to the 2003 tax returns released by President Bush and Vice President Cheney, George and Laura Bush had $822,126 in taxable income and an effective tax rate of 27.7 percent; Dick and Lynn Cheney had taxable income of $1,900,339 and an effective tax rate of 12.7 percent.[40] Other people whose gross income puts them in the highest tax bracket have even lower effective rates than Bush and Cheney because of the skill of their accountants and lawyers in sheltering their income.

The same generalization applies to corporations. Many pay no tax at all, and others pay effective rates from 5 percent to 33 percent, depending on how they are able to use tax law to shelter or exempt profits.[41] The overall amount of taxes corporations are paying however is on the rise because of record profits and because the Bush administration raised some types of corporate taxes to offset the cuts for individuals.

How taxable income is computed and what write-offs are available to which people is the most complex part of the tax code. No reform that deals only with rates and ignores deductions can simplify the code or make it fairer. Sixty percent of Americans favor a progressive tax system, but the public also appears to favor a simpler, more straightforward system. This is the attraction of single rate or form-free reform proposals.

Flat Tax

One of the most frequently proposed tax reforms would abolish our present tax code and replace it with a **flat tax**—that is, a single rate for all income groups. One version of the flat tax proposed by a former member of the congressional leadership calls for a single rate of 17 percent for all Americans and the elimination of all deductions except for one large standard deduction of about $35,000 for a family of four. Its supporters argue that it would simplify the tax code, cut millions from the federal budget for IRS administration, and reduce the present U.S. 1040 form to a single-page or a postcard-sized form.

Flat tax advocates believe that a progressive tax policy punishes people for earning more and creating wealth. They argue that fairness can be better achieved by requiring all Americans to pay the same proportion of their income to the government.

Though the proposed tax rate is flat in theory, in practice it could be modestly progressive. There would be a *de facto* zero tax rate for an estimated ten million

DOONESBURY

By G.B. Trudeau

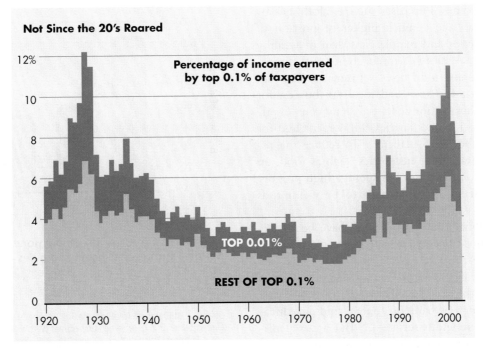

Not Since the 20's Roared

Percentage of income earned
by top 0.1% of taxpayers

TOP 0.01%

REST OF TOP 0.1%

FIGURE 16.2 ■ **The Richest 0.1% of Taxpayers Are Gaining an Ever Increasing Share of the Nation's Income**

The figure shows that not since the Roaring Twenties has the distribution of income to the very wealthy been so lopsided. There are now four times as many households with inflation-adjusted net worth of $10 million as there were twenty years ago.

Source: *New York Times*, June 5, 2005, p. 17, Figure "Not Since the 20's Roared."

of the poorest Americans. For example, using a flat rate of 17 percent, those making less than $35,000 would pay nothing; those making $135,000 would pay $17,000 (17 percent on $135,000 minus the $35,000 deduction), an effective rate of about 12.5 percent, and those making $1,035,000 would pay $170,000, or 17 percent of $1 million, an effective rate of 16.4 percent. Megamillionaires would pay close to the 17 percent rate. Middle-income taxpayers, those making $50,000 to $75,000, would pay effective rates of 5 percent to 9 percent.

The flat tax would disadvantage some low-income families, however. Most of the lowest income households are not subject to income tax now. Some would be worse off with a flat rate because they would lose the earned income tax credit they can claim under our current system (a reverse tax payment made to the working poor).

Moreover, many wealthy households would likely pay even less than their current effective tax rate and, depending on where the flat rate is set, the middle class could end up paying more. Under the existing system, every taxpayer receives a standard deduction and a personal exemption amounting to more than $22,000 for a family of four, *without* itemizing any deductions. For those middle-class families able to deduct their home mortgage interest, health insurance and medical expenses, and IRA contributions, and claim education

and child-care credits, their deductions under the current system might be greater than the single large deduction allowed under some flat rate plans. And everyone would still have to pay Social Security and Medicare taxes, as well as state and local taxes.

Even if a flat tax were adopted, it is nearly impossible to imagine that Congress or the president would refrain from adding exemptions and deductions to the basic rate. All the special interests that now have a place in a tax code that is nominally progressive will also want a place in a code that is nominally flat. And exemptions and deductions would soon make a flat tax more regressive, that is lower income people would pay more than those with higher incomes.

National Sales Tax

Another proposal is to replace the personal income tax with a national sales, or consumption, tax. Under this tax regime, our current tax code would be abolished and taxes would be levied on what we buy, not on what we earn. All but five states currently levy sales taxes, usually ranging from 4 to 7 percent, but often more for luxury items. A national sales tax would work the same way, with consumers paying as they spend, ending the need to file a tax return.

Sales tax can be very regressive because poor people spend a higher proportion of their income than the well-off, who can afford to invest a significant portion of their incomes. Purchases such as clothing, appliances, and cars take a much higher proportion of the incomes of poor and middle class than of wealthy families. A national sales tax could compound the regressivity of state and local taxes. Citizens for Tax Justice estimates that the state and local tax burden for the richest families, nationwide, is 7.9 percent of income; for middle-income families, 9.8 percent; and for the poorest families, 12.5 percent.[42] To reduce the regressivity of the tax, basic necessities, such as food, on which the lowest-income groups spend a high proportion of their earnings, would have to be exempt, as they are now in many states.

Various national sales tax proposals have been submitted to Congress but so far have not made it out of committee. One proposal would abolish income, Social Security, Medicare, corporate, and estate taxes and replace them with a 23 percent tax on retail sales and many services, such as banking (but excluding education, health, and religious services).[43] But as a replacement for all major sources of current revenue, a 23 percent sales tax would be unlikely to produce the revenue needed. Such a tax might well need to be more than 50 percent of the purchase price or cost of service to recover all of the revenue eliminated by abolishing other taxes.[44] It would have to generate enough revenue to cover Social Security payments at a time when millions of baby boomers will be retiring. By one estimate if the bottom 80 percent of taxpayers had to pay a tax on every purchase as well as many services, they could pay as much as 51 percent more than they now have withheld for income tax.[45]

One solution to the regressivity of a sales tax would be to adopt the approach taken in Great Britain and other European countries, where a value-added tax (VAT) is added to the purchase price of most goods and services. In return citizens receive a vast array of government-funded social services, including health care, which reduces every household's out-of-pocket expenses. Another approach, which would shift more of the burden to the well-off, would be to combine a national sales tax with an income tax on the highest earners.[46]

Many politicians talk about tax reform but few propose any significant changes because identifying oneself with any specific scheme is considered a "career killer."[47] At the outset of his second term, Bush said he was committed to reforming the tax code and was open to consideration of both flat and national sales tax proposals. But he also said that certain deductions, such as for home mortgage and charitable contributions, were untouchable and that he hoped to eliminate tax on capital gains and dividend income. But as his second term wore on and his popularity diminished, he stopped discussing sweeping tax reform and concentrated on making his tax cuts permanent.

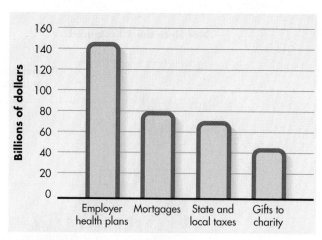

FIGURE 16.3 ■ **Tax Deductions Mostly Benefit Middle- and Higher-Income Families** *Billions of tax revenue dollars are lost through deductions, largely benefiting middle- and upper-class families. The figure shows total cost, in billions, of 2007 deductions for each category.*
SOURCE: "Estimates of Total Income Tax Expenditures," *Budget of the United States 2007: Analytic Perspectives* (Washington, D.C.: Government Printing Office, 2006), Table 19-1, 288–289.

Like Bush, many Democrats would like to see the tax code simplified, but their primary objective is to keep the tax structure progressive. Therefore Democrats have not been principal advocates for the flat tax or a national sales tax; instead they recommend undoing Bush's tax cuts and making incremental changes in the rate structure or number of deductions.

Radical tax reform has not been a winning issue for any recent politician, and in this time, when spending far outpaces revenue, it is even more chancy to kill the bird in hand. As Democrats and Republicans struggle for control of Congress neither party has shown interest in alienating constituents. A former Republican Senator who helped pass Reagan's 1986 tax reforms says, "Every person who's going to lose a deduction regards their deduction as having come with the Bill of Rights, or even Moses."[48]

Americans have to want a simpler, fairer tax code enough to give up their tax candy. Americans could also help close the revenue gap by honestly reporting all income and not taking advantage of loopholes and tax shelters. This would not make the tax code simpler or fairer but it could close the revenue gap. For fiscal 2005 the IRS estimates that it lost $315 billion through underreporting of income, mostly on individual tax returns. If collected, the revenue would have been nearly enough to cover that year's budget deficit.[49] Despite this, Congress has cut the IRS budget and thus reduced the number of auditors it hires.

Deficit and Debt

Another perennial economic issue is whether government should be allowed to spend more than it takes in. Should the government be required, as many states are, to balance its budget? If not, at what point does indebtedness become a drag on the economy?

When economists and politicians talk about the debt and deficit, they throw around numbers in the billions and trillions. The public becomes rather blasé in hearing these numbers. It is useful to consider how big a trillion is. One trillion has twelve zeroes to the right of the 1. It represents a million million dollars. Put another way, if you laid one trillion one-dollar bills end to end, you could make a chain that stretches from earth to the moon and back again two hundred times before you ran out of dollar bills. For a final example, if you started counting at the rate of one number per second, it would take you thirty thousand years to count to a trillion.

A **budget deficit** occurs when federal spending exceeds federal revenues. The accumulation of money owed by the government from all budget deficits over time is the **national debt.** In the first quarter of fiscal 2006, the national debt stood at $8.3 trillion and was rising rapidly because of record-setting deficits.

A balanced budget is generally regarded as sound policy in ordinary times. But the importance of a balanced budget fades during war and other hard times such as recession or depression. The United States has weathered extraordinary periods of overspending—the Revolutionary, Civil, and Second World Wars all left the country with huge debts that it managed to pay down. During the twelve years of the Reagan and George H. Bush administrations (1981–1992), $2.4 trillion dollars was added to the national debt. George W. Bush added almost $3 trillion in six years.

How Do We Get Such Huge Deficits?

One reason there is often a serious gap between revenues and expenditures is that the president's budget message is rooted in political as well as economic considerations and based as much on wishful thinking as on the figures produced by career accountants and budgeters at the OMB. Even for the professionals, of course, predicting revenue is not a science. To estimate accurately what revenues are likely to be and what outlays will be needed, budget writers have to project future rates of economic growth, inflation, unemployment, and productivity. With economic growth comes greater revenue from taxes. With economic slowdown, factories are idle, workers are laid off, tax revenues fall, and more money is needed for unemployment insurance, welfare support, crime control, and even mental health care. It is even harder for budget writers to foresee changes in external events, such as war, that may produce more spending than projected. Projecting growth, outlays, and revenues more than a few years out is very difficult, and even small errors in predictions make an astoundingly large difference. For example, underestimating unemployment by 1 percent can mean a multibillion-dollar error in budgeting because unemployment reduces revenue and increases expenditures.

Presidents are inclined to accept the rosiest projections because they all come to office with taxing and spending policies they want to put in place. Achieving those goals is usually seen as politically more important than balancing the budget. So they usually use the estimates of economic growth, inflation, and unemployment that work best to justify their economic policies: this is where the wishful thinking comes in. The head of the OMB is a political appointee; he or she is there to see that budget figures represent the president's agenda. David Stockman, Reagan's first budget director, described, in what has become a classic statement on budgetary politics, how such estimates were made for the first budget he prepared. To justify a huge tax reduction and show a balanced budget, significant economic growth and low inflation had to be projected. The administration's initial figures included a 2 percent projected inflation rate, a figure far below the existing rate. The chair of the Council of Economic Advisers, Murray Weidenbaum, said, "Nobody is going to predict 2 percent inflation on my watch. We'll be the laughingstock of the world."[50] So Stockman and Weidenbaum bargained over what the forecasts would be; Weidenbaum selected an inflation figure he could live with, and Stockman raised the economic growth projections. Of course, both were horribly wrong, and that is why the real deficit was a hundred times bigger than projected.

In preparing its first multiyear budget forecast, George W. Bush's staff was able to come up with much more optimistic projections than the CBO by not factoring in the long-term costs of his tax cuts and by using lower estimates of increases in mandatory spending for Medicare. The CBO, because it serves both parties and the political agenda of neither, is not compelled to accept the most or the least rosy estimates of economic performance, and thus its projections are usually more reliable than those of the White House. Although Bush's OMB predicted a return to a balanced budget in 2005, the CBO saw deficits running into 2006 and well beyond if the tax cuts were made permanent. And, in fact, the CBO forecast was much more accurate. (The 2004 budget deficit was the third highest, as a percentage of GDP, since World War II).[51]

In order to make the tax cuts more politically palatable, provisions were added to terminate the cuts after a decade. This also meant that the OMB did not have to calculate the long-term revenue losses from the tax cuts, further blurring the true state of the budget. Although the administration projected $1 trillion in surpluses over the next decade, all of that surplus was from Social Security taxes, money that is

off-budget and supposedly reserved for future payments to retirees. Minus the Social Security offset, Bush's budget projections would have shown a significant deficit.[52] One economist said, "No company, other than Enron, would think of counting its pension funds as surplus operating funds."[53]

This is a sleight of hand used by all presidents. Their annual budget message always contains two deficit estimates, one for the unified budget deficit that shows the gap between outlays and revenues as reduced by the amount of the Social Security surplus, and a second on-budget deficit without that offset. The difference in deficit size can be several hundred billions of dollars, but the larger number is rarely mentioned.[54] U.S. Treasury Department experts calculate that our true budget deficit is two to eight times the publicly debated one, depending on the accounting method used (Figure 16.4).

Deficit hawks and critics of budget writing claim that the presidential budget figures are disingenuous. And even the Treasury Department's astronomical deficit estimates do not allow for crises—war, recession, or natural disaster. Costs incurred by these events, such as hurricane Katrina or the 9/11 attacks, are typically paid for by supplemental budget requests that pile up more debt.

Are Deficits and Debt a Problem?

Despite the widespread conviction that moderate deficits are sometimes needed to stimulate the economy, most experts agree that the huge recurring deficits of the 1980s and the early 1990s impaired the country's long-term health and that today's even larger deficits are in danger of doing the same. When government borrowing reaches a high level, it crowds out private bor-

rowing and, therefore, private investment. And the intense competition for investment dollars drives up interest rates. Consumers add to the competition for money. In 2004 Americans held trillions of dollars in credit-card, mortgage, car loans, and other debts.[55]

With government and consumers competing for money, government has to turn to foreign sources to borrow funds since domestic sources are depleted. Collectively, our indebtedness to foreign governments and individual investors (Japanese, Chinese, and Europeans, principally) was equivalent to roughly 37 percent of our GDP in 2005. To cover his massive budget deficits Bush borrowed more money from foreign sources in five years than did all other presidents combined.[56]

The outflow of dollars in interest payments made by our government to foreign investors contributes to our trade deficit, weakens the dollar, and makes us even more vulnerable to the uncertainties of international markets. If foreign investors decided that our fiscal irresponsibility makes investment here risky and withdrew their investments in government bonds, then interest rates would rise sharply and our economy could be thrown into a serious recession.

The amount of the national debt owned by government agencies is also a potential time bomb. The Social Security Trust Fund, for example, is required by law to invest its surplus (money paid in each year by workers and employers in excess of what is needed to meet outlays to Social Security recipients) in government securities. Just as you, a private investor, might loan the government money by buying a treasury bond, so does the Social Security Trust Fund. The interest paid on these securities stays in the Trust Fund along with the bonds. The government uses the cash received from the Trust Fund purchase of securities,

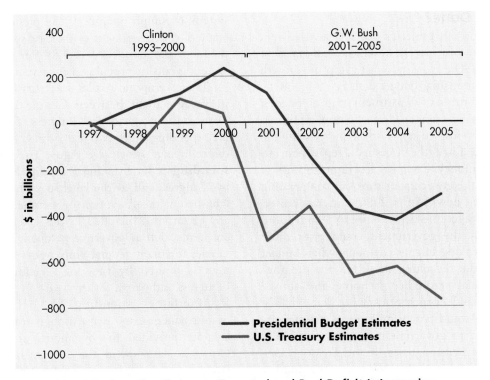

FIGURE 16.4 ■ Gap Between Reported and Real Deficit Is Increasing
The four years of surpluses in the latter years of the Clinton administration and the first year of the George W. Bush administration before the combination of the recession, the 2001 tax cuts, and increases in military spending sent the budget back into deficit in 2002. It is projected to stay there indefinitely. The figure also shows that the gap is widening between what is reported in the president's budget and what the real deficit is, setting aside Social Security surpluses.

SOURCE: OMB Historical Tables, Financial Report of the U.S. Government. Treasury estimates from an introduction to the Financial Report of the U.S. Government by Rep. Jim Cooper (D-Tenn.). www.pbs.org/now/shows/234/Government-Financial-Report.pdf.

just as it uses the cash you spend to buy a bond, to offset the budget deficit. It means less money must be borrowed from banks and other institutions at higher interest rates. When the securities held by the Trust Fund mature, the government must find the money to pay them off or the Trust Fund would not have enough reserves to pay monthly benefits to retirees (whose payments into the system were used to pay benefits to an earlier generation). There is little chance the government would default on Social Security payments, but finding the cash to pay off notes held by the Trust Fund could mean tax increases of significant magnitude or a serious reduction in promised benefits.

The size of the debt also matters because part of every tax dollar must be earmarked for interest payments to creditors here and abroad. This leaves less money in the budget to meet urgent needs in education, health care, research, the military, and the infrastructure improvements necessary to economic growth. Both the economy and the public suffer from the government's reduced fiscal flexibility. In the single year between 1998 and 1999 as the

budget went into surplus, money spent on net interest payments on the debt dropped by $13 billion; if the budget had stayed in surplus in the decade from 1998 to 2009, as then projected, annual interest payments would have declined from $243 billion to $71 billion instead of being on the increase, as they are now. Even to Bill Gates, a savings of $172 billion is a lot. In terms of policy needs, $172 billion could provide a significant amount of health care insurance for children or need-based aid for college students, to give only two examples.

Although Clinton's last budget contained a plan for paying off all of the publicly held debt by 2013, economists disagree about how urgent it is to pay it down. Those who support reducing debt level point to the amount of money tied up in annual interest payments. Those who believe there is no urgency in paying off the debt include some conservatives who believe cutting taxes is important for continued economic growth and some liberals who believe it is more important to spend on education, training future workers, and improving the infrastructure necessary for economic growth and increased productivity.

What Can Be Done?

With budget shortfalls projected for at least the next decade, the debate over paying down the national debt is a distant dream. The effort now is to stop the growth of the debt by eliminating budget deficits.

Because the Treasury Department cannot borrow beyond limits set by Congress, one obvious option is for Congress to refuse to approve an increase in the debt ceiling and force the Treasury Department to stop borrowing money. Congress has done this a few times, but when the government runs out of operating funds, it must shut down. So in 2006 Congress bowed down again and raised the debt ceiling to $9.6 trillion.

Hypothetically, the government could print more money or stop making interest payments when budget shortfalls occur. But defaulting would destroy the government's financial credibility at home and abroad with the banks and corporations who help finance the debt, and it would betray millions of private citizens who invest in government bonds individually or through their pension plans. If the Treasury Department simply printed more money, the market would be flooded with dollars, setting off an inflationary spiral.

For years, many saw the solution to recurring deficits as amending the Constitution to require a balanced budget. The most recent call for a constitutional convention to pass such an amendment won support in thirty-two states in 1990, just two short of the minimum needed. But changing the Constitution is usually regarded as a last-ditch alternative, and shepherding an amendment through to ratification can take years. Therefore, many in Congress look to legislative action as a quicker and surer route to deficit reduction.

Congress *has* tried to discipline itself by passing budget enforcement laws intended to prevent deficit spending. The Balanced Budget and Emergency Deficit Control Act of 1985, more commonly referred to by its cosponsors' names—the Gramm-Rudman-Hollings (GRH) Act—was supposed to trigger automatic cuts in most programs if annual goals for deficit reduction were not met. All it produced were accounting tricks. The deficit was artificially reduced by selling off public land and public enterprises (it is like selling your house to pay off a vacation) and by gimmicks such as delaying military pay raises for a day. Spending items were put into an "off-budget category" and not counted in the estimate of the deficit.

As deficits and debt continued to soar, Congress adopted much tougher rules that set caps on spending and barred any bill that increased spending without offsetting spending cuts or new revenue to support it. If a program had a net cost—that is, if new spending was not matched by a revenue increase—the funds were sequestered. This provision is called the pay-as-you-go

system, or simply **paygo.** If the president or Congress wanted to pass a tax cut or increase spending on an entitlement program, they had to pair it with offsetting spending cuts or provide a new revenue source.

These temporary rules were first adopted in 1990 in an agreement between George H. Bush and the Democratic majority in Congress. They divided federal spending into two categories: discretionary and direct or mandatory (see Figure 16.5). **Discretionary spending** is set by annual appropriations bills passed by Congress and, as the label suggests, amounts are established at the discretion of members of Congress in any given year. Included in this category of spending are items such as government operating expenses and salaries for many federal employees. Spending on each item is limited by the dollar ceilings, or caps, that Congress authorizes for the year.

Mandatory spending, in contrast, is mandated by permanent laws. Even though some of these outlays are provided for by annual appropriation bills, Congress *must* spend the money because there are laws that order it to do so. Examples of mandatory spending are payments made for Medicare and Medicaid, various government subsidies such as farm price supports, interest on the national debt, and unemployment insurance. In 2007, discretionary spending is expected to account for 38 percent of all budgetary outlays, and mandatory spending for the remainder.

As its name implies, mandatory spending is harder for Congress to control than discretionary spending. Yet mandatory spending is not uncontrollable in every instance. In considering the president's budget, Congress cannot simply refuse to fund Medicaid, for example, nor can it decide to drastically lower its funding level. But it can amend the law that created Medicaid to change eligibility, or it can repeal the law and remove any need for appropriations. Most mandatory spending then, while not controllable through the budgetary process alone, can be altered by legislation. This is what happened with federal welfare programs in 1995; the laws that made welfare spending mandatory were rewritten and most of the program responsibilities devolved to the states. An expenditure such as interest on the national debt, however, is truly mandatory and can be reduced only by paying down the debt.

In 1993, against the wishes of many Democrats, Clinton supported renewal of the spending caps and the paygo principle and a few years later committed to achieving a balanced budget by 2002. Continued economic growth and low unemployment that produced greater-than-anticipated federal revenues, in combination with spending caps and paygo rules produced a balanced budget three years ahead of schedule. However, the budget surpluses were achieved through the usual accounting device of offsetting rev-

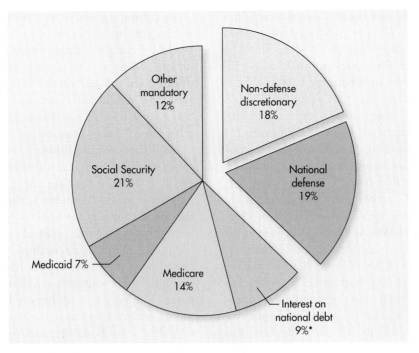

FIGURE 16.5 ■ Estimated Federal Spending, 2007

*The budget projects spending of $2.77 trillion. Overall spending will be higher because war and disaster recovery costs are not included in this budget. Neither is interest paid on government securities held by the Social Security Trust Fund.

SOURCE: *Budget of the United States Government, Fiscal Year 2007* (Washington, D.C.: U.S. Government Printing Office, 2006), Table 5-11, 386.

enue shortfalls in the regular budget with the surplus in Social Security. Fiscal 2001 was the only year with a genuine surplus and Clinton's last budget actually proposed spending 9 percent *less* than it expected to receive in revenues.

Once the budget went into surplus, however, Congress immediately began modifying the rules that had constrained spending. It has been raising caps annually since 1999, and the paygo rule was all but discarded.[57] Moderate Republicans and Democrats fought to restore paygo and caps to the 2005 budget as the only way to stop rising deficits, but the administration resisted.[58]

After reductions in discretionary spending under Reagan and Clinton, George W. Bush increased it by an amazing 36 percent during his first term, the largest increase since FDR's presidency.[59] At the same time, his tax cuts reduced federal revenues by twice the amount of Reagan's. By 2004, tax revenues as a proportion of GDP were at the lowest level since World War II.[60] Anyone who favors lower taxes and smaller government would relish the decline in revenues were it not for the fact that government spending is running near 20 percent of GDP and tax revenues at only 17 percent.

The current level of spending on defense, wars and nation building in Iraq and Afghanistan, and on Social Security and Medicare, coupled with the estate and personal and corporate income tax cuts means there is no immediate prospect that deficits will disappear or that the national debt will stop growing. Because there are no nonpartisan forecasts that economic growth alone can produce the additional revenue needed to balance the budget, there are few alternatives to increased deficits except higher taxes or drastic spending cuts.[61]

The U.S. in the Global Economy

We may still talk about an American economy, but today no border can contain financial and intellectual activities. The revolution in technology—computers, telecommunications, and transportation—brought us to this new era. Money can be electronically transferred to foreign banks instantaneously, and capital can be moved to wherever skilled labor is cheapest. The most highly paid workers—scientists, systems planners and analysts, lawyers, and entertainers, for example—are very mobile, and telecommunications makes it easy to transmit their ideas. Workers at all skill levels are all part of the global labor pool.

The international dispersion of economic activity—investment, research and development, production, and distribution—through the networking of companies across national borders is called **globalization.** By definition, globalization means that business is not as nation centered today as it was in the mid-twentieth century. The days when the board chairman of General Motors could say, "What is good for GM is good for the country and what is good for the country is good for GM" are over. Businesses do not make decisions on relocating to another country based on how their departure will affect the local economy. Those with new ideas do not worry (unless restricted by national security laws) about whether the company to which they sell their invention, new software, or design idea is an American-based or a foreign company as long as they get the highest possible price for their services or product. Thus corporations are continuously scouting for those locations where labor costs are cheapest and regulation is least burdensome. To trade unions and environmental and consumer groups, it means that U.S. corporations are becoming less dependent on and less responsive to American workers and consumers. It also means that corporations may be moving beyond the reach of regulatory policies that were adopted to safeguard workers' and consumers' rights and to protect the public against environmental abuses or other negative consequences of business activity.

The transition of the United States economy from one that is geographically based to one without borders may be as significant as the structural changes of the nineteenth and twentieth centuries from agriculture to manufacturing and from manufacturing to a predominantly service economy. Joseph Schumpeter, the famous twentieth-century economist, called such transitions "creative destruction" because they can produce great dislocation, including severe job loss and changes in the wage and salary structure, before the newer, stronger economy emerges.[62]

Those who see globalization as an irreversible but positive development believe governments have no option but to shape policies to encourage international flows of labor and investment. They argue that any government that tries to "shackle" business and labor with "unnecessary burdens" will just encourage business to leave the United States for wherever they can operate cheaper and be free of regulation. It is the least globalized countries, they argue, that are most likely to adopt policies that interfere with markets and lead to stagnation, inflation, and diminished competitiveness. Those who accept globalization with open arms see it as a race to the top for the world's workers and consumers rather than a race to the bottom, and when one looks at the upward mobility of Chinese and Indian workers this makes sense.[63]

Critics of our response to globalization believe that our government "is defining 'national interest' primarily in terms of advancing the global reach of our multinational enterprises" on the assumption that the benefits will eventually trickle down. But multinationals use the "cost-cutting technique as a competitive weapon without regard to domestic consequences. The practice works for companies and investors, but not so well for a nation." Many of the world's workers, including some of our own, will end up not being able to afford to buy what the world can make. Thus we could easily become, as Warren Buffet has commented, a "sharecropping nation" rather than an "ownership society."[64]

Whether the optimistic or pessimistic view is closer to our future, it is still true that American workers have more votes than the CEOs of multinational corporations. Furthermore, without a strong economy, the reach of our government would be severely shortened. This means that politically it is almost impossible for government to do nothing. Congress has already passed legislation allowing individuals to claim tax deductions for computers purchased for use as educational and job tools. It imposed a surcharge on telephone service that has paid for the wiring of virtually all public schools and libraries for Internet service and made it possible for all children, regardless of income group, to have access to new technology.

But these are nickel-and-dime efforts that do not meet the challenges of globalization. We will have to spend more on research and development and the training of scientists and engineers. Because we do not train enough scientists and engineers, thirty-eight percent of the scientists and engineers working in the U.S. today are foreign-born.[65] Yet given its great system of higher education, the United States should be better prepared than most countries to train workers for a high-tech, service-oriented economy. But clearly a huge remedial effort is needed to keep American students competitive with those from China and India. Based on entrance exam scores, only 21 percent of students who applied to colleges and universities in 2006 were prepared for college-level work.[66] It is also necessary to make higher education affordable for all. Declining college enrollments among children from low- and lower-middle-income families is a serious problem for our future economic competitiveness.

Using tax incentives to discourage the movement of business activity abroad is not very realistic on either political or economic grounds; the savings from tax breaks would be tiny compared to the savings from cheaper labor, which are estimated to range as high as 50 percent.[67]

Immigration

Debates over immigration policy often coincide with concern with the national economy. One of the most recent rounds, for example, occurred during the 1980s and early 1990s, as the arrival of millions of new Americans coincided with slow economic growth,

HOW MUCH PROTECTION CAN GOVERNMENT OFFER WORKERS?

The foreign policy pundit Thomas Friedman describes the consequences of globalization for American workers as a "flattening of the world" which has cost us much of our competitive edge. It was made possible by the falling away of political barriers (the opening of the so-called Iron Curtain countries), the development of Internet browsers, and the laying of fiber-optic cable that led to global interconnectivity. The rest, Friedman writes, is explained by innovations that facilitate collaboration (outsourcing, offshoring, insourcing, opensourcing, chain-supplying, and wireless technology). These developments have leveled the playing field for the world's labor force.[1]

Transferring jobs abroad for competitive advantage is called **outsourcing** or **offshoring.** Businesses have long outsourced part of the work they could not do in-house because they did not have the right personnel or equipment, but most outsourcing was domestic, subcontracted to companies also located in the United States. Today jobs move by the millions from country to country in search of the best labor for the cheapest wage as companies look for an edge against competitors and to increase profits for shareholders. The jobs are not headed to any one place. Many U.S. manufacturing jobs went first to Mexico and then on to a more highly educated and even cheaper labor force in China, where there is no chance for independent unions to organize.

Many manufacturing and higher-skilled jobs have gone to India, and now India is outsourcing to China. Whereas 80 percent of U.S. jobs are now in the service sector, China and India are on the way to becoming manufacturing giants. The competition is good in that it forces us to become

more efficient and brings greater prosperity to the citizens of other countries, who are future consumers of the goods and services we produce. But it has had an impact on the kinds of jobs available to Americans and the wages paid: 20 to 25 percent of the growth in wage inequality in the United States has been attributed to labor competition in a global market.[2]

No one is certain how many American jobs have been sent offshore because most of the data are self-reports from businesses, and they are not always forthright in providing numbers. But the jobs of many are vulnerable to offshoring—financial analysts, medical technicians, paralegals, mathematicians, and computer technologists.[3] Of course, there are limits to how far this offshoring can go because many jobs require face-to-face contact.[4]

Nevertheless, economic restructuring is occurring faster than the ability of many workers to keep pace in education and training; for most there are no comparable replacement jobs because the economy is not producing them fast enough. More than half of laid-off workers who found new jobs in 2004 took big pay cuts.[5] An estimated 13 percent of men between the ages of thirty and fifty-five, most with only a high school education but who held well-paying jobs, have dropped out of the labor force because of their inability to find new jobs or their unwillingness to accept jobs that pay much less.[6]

Even if an American economy has been supplanted by a global economy, there is little evidence to suggest that Americans have started to think of themselves as global citizens who are at the mercy of global markets. Nor is there indication that Americans have adjusted their expectations to match the limits of government's reach in the

global economy. But because our positioning in the world economy has changed, so has government's ability to affect economic change. Experts do not agree about what government should or can do to foster job growth or assist workers displaced during economic transitions. Some say government should stay out of the way, taxing and regulating business as little as possible, and wait for new job growth. Others believe government must do more to protect jobs and domestic producers.[7]

Being part of a global economy means that capital and jobs flow into the country just as they migrate out. Millions of Americans now have foreign employers, in part because state governments have used tax policy to attract them. Toyota, which has surpassed Ford as the world's second largest auto maker, has established plants across the United States. More than 200 foreign parts makers followed Toyota and Subaru into Indiana, investing $29 billion and creating 140,000 jobs. Today 17 percent of Indiana's workers are employed by foreign companies.[8]

One of the most important actions government can take is to adopt fiscal policies that will end the cycle of huge budget deficits financed by foreign creditors with whom we continue to lose leverage. There is also widespread agreement that rising health care costs will continue to discourage job creation until government steps in to assume more of the burden. Many American businesses argue that they cannot provide health benefits to their workers and remain competitive with foreign companies whose governments fund health care.

Something government can do little about is where the profits from outsourcing go. Most of the benefits realized from offshoring are going to share-holders and to the consumers who buy the cheaper products.[9] Workers whose wages have fallen now pay less for clothing and manufactured goods thanks to the cheap imports, but all of the world's low-paid workers are also subsidizing cheap goods for the well-off.

Although most economists argue that over the long term the movement of jobs around the globe will lift all boats, in the short term many American workers are struggling to stay afloat. Our government can continue doing little to address job and income issues and allow the market to set the terms of competition, the level of employment, and the distribution of wealth. But this is not the option any other modern industrial country has chosen.

"Well that does it Charlie—we've outsourced everything."

[1]Thomas L. Friedman, *"The World Is Flat: A Brief History of the Twenty-first Century"* (New York: Farrar, Straus and Giroux, 2005).
[2]David E. Sanger, "Look Who's Carping Most about Capitalism," *New York Times,* April 6, 1997, E5. This estimate has been accepted by the former chair of the Council of Economic Advisers, Laura D. Tyson.

[3]Lael Brainard and Robert E. Litan, "'Offshoring' Service Jobs: Ban or Boon and What to Do?" *Brookings Policy Brief #132,* April 2004, 2.
[4]Daniel Gross, "Why 'Outsourcing' May Lose Its Power as a Scare Word," *New York Times,* August 13, 2006, BU5, citing findings of the McKinsey Global Institute.
[5]Louis Uchitelle, "It's Not New Jobs. It's All the Jobs." *New York Times,* August 29, 2004, 3, 6.
[6]Louis Uchitelle and David Leonhardt, "Men Not Working, and Not Wanting Just Any," *New York Times,* July 31, 2006, 1.

[7]One proponent of protectionist policies is Sen. Byron Dorgan (D-ND). He makes his argument in *Take This Job and Ship It: How Corporate Greed and Brain-dead Politics Are Selling Out America* (New York: Thomas Dunne Books/St. Martin's Press, 2006).
[8]Micheline Maynard and Jeremy W. Peters, "2 Asian Automakers Plan Ventures in 2 States Left by U.S. Carmakers," *The New York Times,* March 14, 2006
[9]"'Offshoring' Service Jobs: Ban or Boon and What to Do?" 4.

serious unemployment, and huge budget deficits. Congress and state governments responded with laws restricting the benefits and services available to both legal and illegal immigrants. Since 2000, in a sign of new anxiety over national security and the country's economic future, the debate has focused on illegal immigration. Although the ability of foreigners to enter the country without documentation is an obvious security concern, the thrust of the debate has been on whether immigration is helping or hurting the economy.

In 2006 between 11 and 12 million people were living illegally in the United States; most came from Mexico on visas and overstayed them or entered the country, without papers, over the border between California and Texas. One in every seven American workers is an immigrant, and undocumented workers now account for about 5 percent of the nation's work force.[68] Does their presence benefit the economy or hurt it? Experts (of course) disagree.

No one disputes that the population growth from immigration stimulates the economy by increasing the demand for goods and services. The debate is over whether that benefit is offset by the cost of providing services to immigrants and whether the influx of so many workers is contributing to the stagnation of wages (no one argues it is the sole cause).

Between 2000 and 2004 an estimated 850,000 people entered the country each year without documents, in addition to an almost equal number who were admitted under immigration law. During the same period outsourcing took about 1.4 million jobs out of the country and domestic job growth was near zero. One of the country's leading immigration scholars, George J. Borjas (himself a Cuban immigrant), argues that what appears obvious is true: an increased supply of labor drives down wages for native workers. Borjas estimates that between 1980 and 2000—even before the big influx of undocumented workers—immigration was responsible for a 4 percent decline in the wages of native workers (about $1700 a year) and a heftier 7.4 percent for low-skill workers, reflecting the greater competition in those job categories.[69]

Most who enter the country illegally are poorly educated and much more likely than native-borns to be high school drop-outs (one out of every four high school drop-outs in the labor force is Mexican).[70] With no legal claims on, or protections from, employers, undocumented workers are likely to work for lower wages than Americans and for few or no benefits. According to a survey by the Pew Hispanic Center almost all undocumented workers from Mexico had been employed before emigrating.[71] They come to the United States because the wages are higher than in their native countries and because there are more opportunities for their children.

They also come because they are recruited by American employers who distribute flyers in Mexican towns promising workers jobs and housing if they can get to a specific place at a specific time. Although the state and federal government have stepped up enforcement of the border to stop or deport workers who enter illegally, there has been virtually no prosecution of the employers who recruit them. In 2004 Immigration and Customs Enforcement cited just three businesses for employing illegal workers.[72]

Borjas's claims about the impact on wages of labor supply is supported by a U.S. Labor Department study of the earnings of janitors (11 percent of whom are illegal immigrants). Between 1983 and 2002, as undocumented workers entered that labor pool in large numbers, wages (in real dollars) fell by 3 percent. A 1997 study by the National Academy of Science (NAS) also found a negative, but small, impact on wages but at the same time concluded that immigration was producing a small net gain for the economy of $1 billion to $10 billion a year (negligible in our multitrillion dollar economy). In California, where competition for low-wage laborers was fierce, businesses turned to nonunionized immigrants, driving native workers out of unskilled positions and slashing the going wage rates. In Pittsburgh the asbestos workers union saw the going wage drop from $31 to $19 per hour and safety conditions deteriorate under competition from nonunionized immigrants willing to work for as little as $11 or $12 an hour.

Although the majority of immigrants need more services than native residents and have fewer resources to pay for them, the NAS study concluded that, on average, adult immigrants paid more in taxes over a lifetime than they received in benefits, but if only adults were counted. When their children are factored in, immigrant families receive more in benefits than they pay in taxes. If true, research that shows significant educational and wage gains by second generation Americans would tend to offset its significance.[73] These optimistic findings, however, have been questioned by Borjas because the second generation respondents in

With globalization, American companies must compete not only with each other, but with foreign companies as well. Foreign factories can make some products, such as these jeans packed for shipment from China, cheaper than American companies, which pay higher wages, can. Although American consumers benefit from lower prices, American workers sometimes lose their jobs as a result.

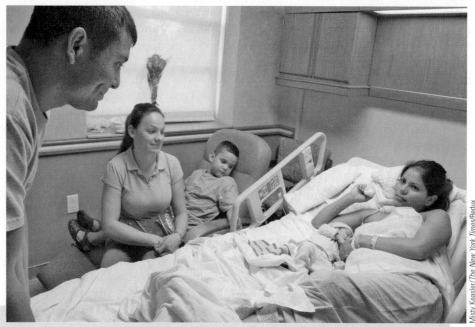

An illegal immigrant recovers from childbirth in a Fort Worth, Texas, hospital. Border states incur significant expenses for emergency health care for immigrants. Although the federal government reimburses them, the states claim that they spend more than they receive.

Misty Keasler/The New York Times/Redux

the studies were chosen at random and therefore were not necessarily the children of the first generation respondents.[74] This means we do not have convincing evidence that the children of low-skill, poorly educated immigrants do gain a wage advantage over their parents.

We do know that illegal immigration drives up health costs. For example, a Dallas hospital, over half of whose maternity cases are women in the country illegally, is reimbursed by Washington for maternity care because the newborns are automatically citizens and eligible for Medicaid. (They are called "anchor" babies because they give their parents a foothold in the country). However, the states and localities pick up much of the cost for education, health care, and other social services, as well as for law enforcement because most of the taxes paid by undocumented workers go to the federal government in the form of income and Social Security taxes. (See "You Are There" in Chapter 3.) One Texas county estimated that 14 percent of its health care budget went to treating residents without legal residency, and California claims that in 2005 it spent $1 billion more on medical care for illegal immigrants than it received in federal reimbursements.[75] In either case taxpayers spend billions annually to fund these services at a time when 46 million citizens are without health insurance.

In addition public school systems are obligated to educate children without respect to residency status. The costs are huge because of numbers alone, but also

it is expensive to provide remedial education and instruction in the students' native languages. This puts extraordinary pressure on school systems that are already turning out a high percentage of native-born students who are unprepared to do college-level work.

Despite these burdens, many economists argue that immigration is the country's economic salvation because it accounts for almost all of our population growth thereby contributing to economic growth as well. And undocumented workers have been responsible for rejuvenating local economies as they have begun spreading out across the country, following friends and relatives searching for good schools. Although it has led to cultural tension in small towns, some locals give the newcomers credit for reviving their dying towns.

But opponents of uncontrolled growth are concerned about the long-term impact of large population increases. If legal and illegal immigration continue at current rates, the U.S. population will surpass 500 million by 2050 according to Census Bureau estimates. Opponents of this expansion, including environmentalists, believe it is already having an impact on the environment and the quality of life, especially by adding to urban congestion and threatening land and resource conservation.

On the surface these problems do not seem radically different from the problems of economic integration this country has always faced. But there are some reasons to think that they could be different because there is a question of whether an older economy can continue to absorb and integrate newcomers as it did one hundred years ago. At the turn of the twentieth century 90 percent of Americans did not have high school diplomas and could make their way in an agricultural and manufacturing economy. If economic projections are correct that most new jobs will require a minimum of two years of college, then it will be progressively more difficult to absorb unskilled workers.

Whether one sees immigration as an economic benefit or liability depends in part on whether one looks at the macroeconomic picture or some smaller segment of it, such as wage growth or costs to state governments for providing medical care, education, and other social services. The economic benefits of immigration go disproportionately to the well off (such as employers of low-paid unskilled labor), and the costs fall disproportionately on the poor (competition for low-wage jobs and for social services), a fact that could worsen the growing income gap between rich and poor. In this way immigration is comparable to the impact of globalization; in the short term (and possibly the long-term too), those on the bottom rung of the economic ladder may see few of the benefits.

The poor in the home countries of immigrants do see some benefit, however, because immigrants send billions of dollars out of the country to support the relatives they left behind.[76] Mexican immigrants are estimated to remit $30 billion annually to their families, making it the second-largest source of foreign revenue for that country. Many other immigrants from Central America, China, India, Africa, and elsewhere do the same, adding to the trade deficit.

What can the federal government do besides monitor the borders and employment practices? One solution that has been proposed by groups that cut across the political spectrum is to establish a guest worker program in combination with a hike in the minimum wage, with the condition that employers who hire guest workers must pay the minimum wage. This would lead to a more orderly and controlled flow of workers into the country, reduce their exploitation by employers, and make jobs more attractive to native workers. Some who favor this approach say that Americans have always done the risky, dirty, and unpleasant jobs that today attract illegal immigrants and that they will compete for them again if they pay decent wages and provide safe working conditions.[77]

Most Americans agree that we have the right and obligation to control our borders and have the final say on who is able to enter, especially who is allowed to take up permanent residence. But some reformers argue that if immigration is good for the economy then we need not only a guest worker program for those with low skills, but a change in the law that allows us to re-

serve a much higher percentage of the residency visas issued each year for those with high-priority, high-skill jobs. This would be a logical way to link immigration more closely to economic development.

Income Distribution

One of the most contested areas of fiscal policy is the extent to which it should be used to redistribute wealth among income groups. The principal argument is whether government should help those at the lower end of the income spectrum through progressive taxation (placing a lower tax burden on middle- and lower-income families than on the wealthy) or through spending policies that provide heavily subsidized services to those who otherwise could not afford them.

Since the passage of civil rights and affirmative action laws, our society has become progressively more democratic in terms of equality before the law and equal opportunity in the marketplace. However, the distribution of wealth is more unequal than at anytime since the 1920s. Those who believe private property is the preeminent right in a capitalist society tend to oppose the use of tax and spending policy to diminish that inequality. Those who believe that a society of haves and have-nots, with relatively few in the middle,

Immigration from Mexico has spurred the creation of new restaurants and suppliers, such as the Milpa de Oro tortilla factory in Booneville, North Carolina. But these jobs usually provide few fringe benefits or advancement opportunities.

Library of Congress

Photo by Bill Ganzel, from *Dust Bowl Descent*, University of Nebraska Press

The American postwar economy lifted millions of families into middle-class status. At left is thirty-two-year-old Florence Thompson and her three daughters in 1936 after drought and the Depression drove them from Oklahoma to look for a better future in California. The family was living in a migrant labor camp and surviving on vegetables dug up from fields and birds killed by the children. Publication of the photo prompted the government to send twenty thousand pounds of food to the camp. At right is the same family forty-three years later in Modesto, California, where Mrs. Thompson's children eventually were able to buy her a home. But before her death in 1983, they had to solicit contributions to pay for her medical care.

is inherently unstable and a threat to democracy are more supportive of taxing and spending to prevent extreme maldistribution of income.

What has caused income distribution to become so unbalanced? In the immediate post–World War II era, family income grew more than 3 percent a year,[78] and in 1966, a fifty-year-old man could look back over a ten-year period in the workforce and see that his income had risen over 30 percent. But beginning in the mid-1970s and extending to the mid-1990s, times were hard for blue-collar workers as their income stagnated. Indeed, at the end of the 1980s, a man could look back over a decade to find his income had risen only 10 percent,[79] in contrast to the significant growth that his father had seen two decades earlier (women's income follows a different trajectory because of increased job opportunities).

By the 1980s, in real terms, blue-collar workers were earning less than their parents did at a comparable age, and growth in living standards had nearly stopped. There were fewer well-paying jobs for them than there had been twenty years earlier because heavy industries that traditionally paid high wages to

unionized workers fell on hard times. Wage concessions were made by workers worried about job security, and the unionized segment of the labor force dropped from 47 percent, where it had been in the postwar years, to 13 percent.[80] The decline of unions meant that workers lost both economic power and political clout since unions were an important part of the political coalition supporting civil rights, health and education reform, and other progressive policies closely tied to equality and well-being.

During the 1990s, the United States experienced a remarkable nine years of low unemployment, economic growth, and low inflation. It appeared that the country had completed the difficult transition to a service sector economy. But the recovery was a song in two keys. From the standpoint of a job hunter, the economy looked good; jobs were plentiful, but income inequality increased dramatically and working people lost benefits.

By 1995, of all men between the ages of twenty-five and thirty-four, 32 percent earned "less than the amount necessary to keep a family of four above the poverty line." Families needed two wage earners to maintain the old standard of living.[81] To the millions of uninsured Americans in low-paying jobs, a million immigrants, many of them poorly educated, were being added to the labor pool each year.

In 2000, families' net worth fell for the first time in fifty-five years.[82] Except for the most highly educated, the *lifetime* earnings of men have been declining for thirty years, while the inequality in lifetime earnings between low- and high-skill workers continued to increase over the same period.[83] Education is the key to getting ahead in this economy, but aid for lower-income students is declining while tuition costs are rising in both public and private universities. The percentage of household income required to send a child to a four-year state school rose far faster for the poorest fifth of Americans than for middle- and upper-income groups. Yet in the competition for students, many universities no longer consider need as the primary factor in awarding grants and scholarships, and the share of grants going to middle- and upper-income students is increasing. Two-thirds of all college students are in debt, with those at private colleges carrying an average debt load of $20,000 in 2006.[84]

As real wages stagnated and the average income of the poorest fifth fell, by 2005 the average corporate executive was earning more in one day than the average American worker earned in a year. With average annual salaries at $10.9 million per year, a CEO earned 262 times more than the average employee.[85] In many cases, CEO compensation was set by a Board of Directors appointed by the CEO, and amounts were unrelated to the economic performance of the company.

The wealth gap is far greater than income alone suggests, because those in the highest brackets have money to save, invest in the stock market, and buy homes. This made it possible for those already well off to take advantage of the real estate and stock booms of the 1990s in ways unavailable to those with little capital. The concentration of wealth and privilege (especially access to higher education in elite institutions) has become so pronounced that one observer refers to the formation of an "overclass."[86] Many people in the lower income groups no longer feel it possible that they can achieve the American dream (see Figure 16.6).

In addition to the rising cost of higher education, health insurance and mortgages take increasingly larger shares of disposable income. The declining competitiveness of many U.S. businesses has made it impossible for them to offer the same level of health and pension benefits as to earlier generations of workers. Many households have assumed huge debt burdens to buy larger homes and to provide health care and college educations for their children.[87] In 2006, Americans had debt equal to 132 percent of disposable income; a collective debt of more than $8 trillion that rivaled the national debt. Americans are spending over

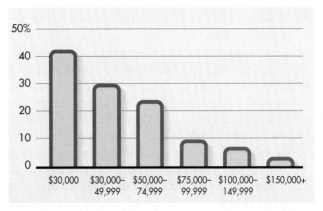

FIGURE 16.6 ■ The American Dream Seems Out of Reach for Those Who Are Poor
The following question was posed: Will you reach the American dream in your lifetime? The percentages graphed indicate the respondents saying "no."
NOTE: Data is from a *New York Times* poll conducted March 2005 with 1794 adults. Sampling error is around 3 percent.
SOURCE: Reported in *The New York Times*, May 15, 2005, p. 1ff.

19 percent of their income on interest payments, or more than twice as much as the government does servicing its debt.

The first real growth in income since the 1990s came in 2005, with a 1 percent increase, all of which went to 23 million households headed by someone sixty-five or older. These are households likely to have more income from investments than hourly wages. Median income in the other 91 million households median dropped by half a percent.[88] In fact, virtually all wage growth since 1973 has gone to the top 20 or 30 percent of earners. In 1973 the median wage for male workers was $15.24; in 2004, adjusted for inflation, it was $15.26.[89] Even with the economic growth spurt in 2004 and 2005, job creation was modest and wages did not keep pace with productivity growth or with inflation. The president's own economic report for 2006 said that average annual earnings of college graduates fell by 5 percent from 2000 to 2004. During the same period the pay gap between college and high school graduates also began to shrink, in part because college graduates were doing jobs that in earlier years had required only a high school diploma.

Politicians of all stripes quote data in a way that adds greatest support to their positions, so the income increases that went lopsidedly to a single demographic group are also used as evidence of a strengthening economy. But we need to look behind simple averages in order to get a clear picture of what economic statistics tell about the health of the economy. Here is a common illustration: nine men—firefighters, factory workers and police officers—with an average income of $50,000 are sitting in a neighborhood bar talking when Bill Gates walks through the door. The average income of the ten men in the room is now $45 billion. When an example is that extreme, it is easy to see the problem of income averaging. But it is always necessary to look beyond growth rates, GDP, and average and median income to see how aggregate wealth in real dollars is distributed across all income groups, both before and after taxes, to understand the health of the economy.

This brings us back to the beginning of the chapter and the relationship between capitalism and democracy. The past thirty years of increasing maldistribution of wealth has been paralleled by the rising influence of money in politics and an increase in legislation that benefits the well off. The ability of those with money to buy access and influence makes it increasingly difficult to sustain basic principles of capitalism and democracy, including equal opportunity in the marketplace and the one person–one vote standard.

Conclusion: Is Our Economic Policy Responsive?

The health of any economy depends on many factors, only some of which government can influence and none of which it can completely control. Private spending accounts for close to 70 percent of our economy, so economic policies of the private sector and the consumption and saving habits of Americans play an enormous role in the state of the economy. In the global economy, private investment flows with ease across borders, the labor pool is international, and the United States is a net importer and the world's largest debtor and energy consumer. In that context, it is far more difficult than in the past to protect the national economy against inflation and job loss. But government still has tools to help prevent or limit the impact of recession and depression, promote equal opportunity in the marketplace, guarantee minimum wages and safety conditions, and legislate against anticompetitive business practices such as monopolies, price-fixing, and stock market fraud.

How we weather cycles of economic boom and bust depends to a great extent on fiscal and monetary policies. We expect fiscal policy, that is, taxing and spending, to be more directly responsive to the public because it is created by elected officials. Monetary policy—setting interest rates and controlling the supply of money—is made by individuals shielded to some extent from the short-term wishes of both the public and elected officials, except perhaps in crisis situations. The fact that fiscal policy is made in a somewhat more open and democratic process does not necessarily make it more responsible. Fiscal policy is, and has to be, more responsive to the voters, whereas monetary policy mak-ers are freer to respond to macroeconomic conditions—*as they see them*.

Some argue that Congress is too responsive to the public's desire to have everything: lower taxes, social spending on programs that benefit them and their families, and massive military spending. Eager to give voters and big campaign donors what they want, fiscal policy makers have not been especially good stewards of the American economy over the past several decades. The public is equally culpable because we have not held our elected officials accountable for their budgetary mismanagement.

During the 1990s a Republican Congress and a Democratic president cooperated to bring spending more in line with revenues. But for most of the past quarter century economic policy makers have focused on the short term, preferring politically popular tax cuts over balancing the budget or investing in programs to improve our nation's infrastructure, promote research, or to upgrade human capital through education and training to prepare workers to compete in the global economy. Moreover, government has been content to let income inequalities grow and has even exacerbated them with tax cuts that benefit the wealthiest Americans and policies that favor corporate profits over income growth for the average household.

The country remains divided over how government should respond to growing income disparity. Despite our mixed economy, we have a very individualistic, capitalistic ethic. The idea that individuals, not government, should provide services and that government should be small influences a wide range of public policies. The belief that individuals are poor because of their own failings limits our sense of responsibility to provide support for low-income families. The idea that private business is inherently self-regulating makes it difficult to enact higher standards for worker health and safety. The belief that private profit is not only the most important goal of business, but perhaps the only one, means that those fighting to protect the environment from abuse by both industry and consumers must either defeat or find compromise with powerful lobbies.

The Clinton administration argued that a responsive government is one that uses fiscal policy both to foster economic growth and to regulate the distribution of income generated by that growth. George W. Bush and the Republican-controlled Congress argued that the country's economic difficulties stemmed precisely from this overresponsive, interventionist, Keynesian approach. In their view, the most responsive government is one that leaves an unfettered market to "grow" the economy and distribute its wealth. This is the essence of the long-standing debate in American politics over the proper relationship of government to the economy.

Murray Says No to the Trifecta

espite her support for raising the federal minimum wage and opposition to the estate tax, Senator Murray voted against the so-called Trifecta bill that would have raised the former and lowered the latter. Said Murray, "While there were provisions that I did support in the bill, I could not vote for a Republican plan that plunges our nation further into debt while reducing the wages of our nation's workers. This bill would have hurt all Americans."[90]

The measure was stopped, as so many bills have been in the years of unified government, by the technicality in Senate rules that requires sixty yea votes to bring a bill to the floor for a straight up or down vote. This is the only means Democrats have had of defeating a bill in the Republican-controlled Senate, other than convincing six or more Republicans to vote against a bill supported by their own party. Frist got a few Democrats to cross over to support the Trifecta, but not enough to offset defections from his party.

Why did Murray decide to vote against a bill that combined two issues that she champions? Murray found a way to justify voting against the minimum wage hike. Washington's state-mandated minimum wage of $7.63 was already in effect and indexed to inflation so Murray requested an analysis from the state's Department of Labor on how passage of the Trifecta might affect the state's hourly workers. The report concluded that Washington's tip

workers—coffee house and restaurant workers, for example—would actually see a decline in their wages if the bill were passed because of a provision that would have allowed employers to count tips as part of the hourly compensation they had to pay their workers.[91] Murray released the findings, making little of the fact that Washington's legislature could have overridden the Trifecta provision on tips.

Murray also argued, along with the majority of Democrats, that it was "cynical" to couple a wage increase for the poorest with more tax cuts for the wealthiest just before an election and to do so after a decade of refusing to support the increase.[92] In 2006 corporate profits were at a forty-year high and the buying power of the minimum wage was at a fifty-year low.[93] Furthermore, a survey of small business owners showed that 86 percent thought a hike in the minimum wage would have no economic impact on them.[94] Murray believed workers were entitled to a higher minimum wage without having to give away something to the wealthy to get it, especially to the same group of people who had received most of the benefits from previous Bush tax cuts.

The estate tax provision would have exempted 99.5 percent of estates from any tax, and cost almost three quarters of a trillion dollars in the first decade. Murray has always been a budget hawk and could not justify eliminating hundreds of bil-

lions in projected estate tax revenue at a time when we don't know where we will get the money to pay our bills. The budget deficits the Bush administration has accrued may run into the distant future, especially with continuing wars in Iraq and Afghanistan, which from the outset have been paid for with borrowed money. The administration has depended almost entirely on economic growth to produce new revenue to close the budget gap, something many economists believe is unrealistic.

In her vote against further estate tax reduction Murray had support from some of the state's wealthiest citizens. Bill Gates Sr., president of the Seattle-based Gates Foundation, has repeatedly opposed all reductions in the tax, agreeing with multibillionaire Warren Buffet, the Foundation's new partner in philanthropy, who says that those born to wealth are simply "members of the lucky sperm club."[95] But most important, Murray could not abandon the party on the Trifecta, whose passage would have given Republicans more bragging rights just before a crucial election. Senate Democrats have groomed her for leadership from her first days in office. With the House Speakership in Pelosi's future, might Majority Leader be in Murray's?

 To learn more about this topic, go to "you are there" exercises for this chapter on the text website.

Key Terms

capitalist economy
mixed economy
depression
inflation
recession
productivity

fiscal policy
Keynesian economics
stagflation
supply-side economics
monetary policy
tragedy of the commons
externality

progressive tax
regressive tax
flat tax
budget deficit
national debt
paygo
discretionary spending

mandatory spending
globalization
outsourcing (offshoring)

Further Reading

Barbara Ehrenreich, *Nickel and Dimed: On (Not) Getting by in America* (New York: Henry Holt, 2001). A journalist tries to live a decent life on minimum wage jobs, finds that it is nearly impossible, and learns that economic catastrophe is only one bad luck event away.

William Greider, *Secrets of the Temple: How the Federal Reserve Runs the Country* (New York: Simon & Schuster, 1989). It is hard to imagine a book about the Federal Reserve Board being interesting, but this one is. It reveals the human face behind this most technical institution.

Friedrich von Hayek, *The Road to Serfdom,* 50th anniversary ed. (Chicago: University of Chicago Press, 1994). The seminal statement of anti-Keynesian economics written by an Austrian economist and later championed by Milton Friedman and the University of Chicago school. Von Hayek argues that too much government intervention in the economy is dangerous and could turn people into slaves.

Robert L. Heilbroner and Lester C. Thurow, *Economics Explained: Everything You Need to Know about How the Economy Works and Where It's Going* (New York: Simon & Schuster, 1998). This text is a readable discussion of major economic concepts and issues.

David Cay Johnston, *Perfectly Legal: The Covert Campaign to Rig Our Tax System to Benefit the Super Rich—and Cheat Everyone Else* (New York: Portfolio, 2003). This text describes why the rich are getting richer and the middle and working classes are losing out.

Anka Kamenetz, *Generation Debt: Why Now Is a Terrible Time to Be Young* (New York: Riverhead/Penguin, 2006). Speaking on behalf of her own twenty-something generation, this *Village Voice* reporter complains that structural changes in the economy are making it impossible for young Americans to move up the economic ladder at the same pace as earlier generations. Read and identify but don't look for solutions.

Kevin P. Phillips, *Wealth and Democracy: A Political History of the American Rich* (New York: Broadway Books, 2002). A former Republican political operative explains why he is fed up with the economic policies of both major parties for doing so little to stop influence buying by the wealthy and growing income inequality. The main focus is on the negative impact on democracy of a maldistribution of wealth.

Amartya Kumar Sen, *Development as Freedom* (New York: Oxford University Press, 2001). A Nobel laureate in economics and one of the world's leading authorities on development explains the relationship between income and well-being and between economic development and democracy.

David A. Stockman, *The Triumph of Politics: How the Reagan Revolution Failed* (New York: Harper & Row, 1986). Reagan's budget director tells all.

Louis Uchitelle, *The Disposable American: Layoffs and their Consequences* (New York: Knopf, 2006). A *New York Times* business reporter takes up the case for Americans who have lost their jobs because of "offshoring" and downsizing. He argues that government has not done nearly enough to protect American jobs or to help those displaced by competition from the international labor pool.

Steven R. Weisman, *The Great Tax Wars: Lincoln to Wilson, the Fierce Battles over Money and Power That Transformed the Nation* (New York: Simon & Schuster, 2002). A history of the long political battle to establish a permanent income tax. Among its many interesting facts: in 1939, only 7 percent of the labor force earned enough to pay income tax.

For Viewing

Farmingville (2004 entry at the Sundance Film Festival). This film documents the hostility of a Long Island community toward migrant farm workers from Mexico and Central America.

The Fountainhead (1949). A screen treatment of Ayn Rand's blockbuster novel. It is not often that a novel becomes a major tract in the wars between economic schools of thought. Rand's brand of libertarian capitalism inspired millions, including former Fed chair Alan Greenspan. The film stars Gary Cooper.

The Hudsucker Proxy (1994). This comedy by the Coen brothers is about a company that installed a moron as president in order to drive the company into the ground and carry out a stock scam.

Roger and Me (1989). Documentary filmmaker Michael Moore shadowed General Motors's CEO, Roger Smith, hoping to get him to visit his hometown, Flint, Michigan, so he could see firsthand how GM's factory closings led to the city's economic decline. This film made many of the ten-best lists for 1989.

Wall Street (1987). This film captured public disenchantment with the "Me Decade" obsession with personal enrichment at all costs.

Electronic Resources

www.oecd.org
The website of the Organization for Economic Cooperation and Development, whose membership comprises the world's most developed industrial democracies, offers comparative data on tax structure, economic growth, distribution of wealth, and cost of living in these countries.

www.wsj.com
The Wall Street Journal *probably has the best coverage of economic news of any U.S. newspaper. However, if you want to see the web edition, you must subscribe.*

www.whitehouse.gov/fsbr/esbr.html
This site is an "Economic Statistics Briefing Room," with links to national economic statistics, GDP, income, unemployment, prices, and interest, in addition to international economic statistics.

www.omb.gov
The website of the Office of Management and Budget has links to all U.S. budget documents and supplemental appropriations.

www.whitehouse.gov/cea
Even the Council of Economic Advisers has its own webpage, with numerous links to economic statistics, budgets of the United States, and other useful information.

www.federalreserve.gov
This is the website of the Federal Reserve System with links to the regional banks. The site offers a history of the Fed, a description of the work of its constituent parts, testimony and reports to Congress, consumer information, and publications free to the public.

www.irs.gov
The website of the Internal Revenue Service offers a history of the agency and its work and provides help with personal income taxes. Users can download forms and publications and get information on the reform of the IRS passed by Congress in 1998.

www.cbpp.org
At the website of the Center for Budget and Policy Priorities, you can find reports on taxing and spending policy with a different perspective from that at government agencies.

ThomsonNOW™

Enter ThomsonNOW™ using the access card that is available with this text or through www.thomsonedu.com/thomsonnow. ThomsonNOW™ will assist you in understanding the content in this chapter with a personalized study plan generated for your needs. A practice test will assess the areas you need to review and provide the tools to fully comprehend those concepts, including an integrated digital eBook, interactive simulations, timelines, video case studies, MicroCase exercises, and InfoTrac College Edition readers and exercises. You'll also be connected to the learning objectives, chapter outline, chapter glossary, flash cards, crossword puzzles, Internet activities, and interactive quizzes found on the companion website.

CHAPTER 17

SOCIAL WELFARE AND HEALTH POLICY

Sister Roseanne Cook, a medical doctor, checks the heartbeat of her patient in Pine Apple, Alabama. Forty-six million Americans are uninsured, and federal health care programs are limited.

AP Images/Haraz Ghanbari

The Political and Legal Bases of Social Welfare Policies

The Evolution of Social Welfare Policies

Income Support Programs

Retirees and Their Dependents

The Poor

Farmers

Veterans

The Impact of Income Support Programs

Health Care Programs

Health Care for Seniors

Health Care for the Poor and Disabled

Health Care for Veterans

Subsidized Services

Education

Housing

Agriculture

Tax Subsidies

Corporations

Families and Homeowners

Current Issues

Health Care

Social Security

Reforming Aid to the Poor

Conclusion: Are Social Welfare Programs Responsive?

YOU ARE THERE

Should a Conservative Say Yes to Mandatory Health Insurance?

You are Mitt Romney, Republican governor of Massachusetts, a state that has become synonymous with liberal politics. It is April 2006 and you must decide whether to sign or veto a pay-or-play health insurance proposal passed by the Democratic-controlled state legislature. Under its terms all uninsured citizens of Massachusetts will either get a health insurance policy by 2008 or pay a penalty.

You are well aware that health care is in crisis in the United States, with skyrocketing costs and forty-six million people uninsured, at least a half million of whom are in your state. You favor broadening health insurance coverage but not raising taxes to do it, as this bill does.

Like other governors, you know that you must come to grips with rising health care costs. Spending for **Medicaid,** the program that pays for health care for the poor and disabled, is beginning to dominate state budgets and continues to rise dramatically.[1] This year Massachusetts will spend about $1 billion providing health care to the uninsured. There has been no movement in the Republican-controlled Congress toward establishing national health insurance; the Bush administration, like most Republicans, thinks the answer to bringing down costs lies in encouraging competition in the private health insurance market. Bush is also committed to cutting federal spending on

public programs such as Medicaid and **Medicare** (the health care program for elderly), and beyond that has tossed the ball to state governments, saying Medicaid must "continue to modernize through State-level reforms."[2]

The bill before you would provide a number of options for obtaining private health insurance for those who are not covered by their employers. It would establish Commonwealth Care to provide a sliding scale of subsidies to help those whose earnings are at the poverty level or up to three times the poverty level purchase policies (in 2005 the poverty threshold for a family of four was a little less than $20,000), and it would fully insure all those whose earnings fall below the poverty level. The insured would have to make copayments for some services. Help would also be provided to higher earners to find the lowest-cost policies available.

The law also contains penalties for individuals and employers who do not participate. Those refusing to purchase coverage would first lose their personal state income tax exemption and then face higher penalties, including half the amount of the lowest-cost health policy available. All of the penalty money would go into a pool to pay for policies for the uninsured. Employers who do not provide health insurance would be assessed an annual fee per employee and be liable

Massachusetts Governor Mitt Romney

for part of the fees the state pays when their employees use public health care. All of this money, too, would go into the pool to purchase coverage for the uninsured. Thus employers could not be "free riders," expecting their employees' health needs to be taken care of at taxpayer expense.

Wal-Mart has become the most egregious and visible example of shifting benefits costs to taxpayers; with over $312 billion in sales in 2005 it offered health insurance to less than half its employees, many of whom ended up on Medicaid. State policy makers are not amused, and more than a dozen states have passed laws trying to force Wal-Mart and other large corporations to spend a set fraction of their earnings on employee benefits. These laws may prove unconstitutional, but the bill you are being asked to sign gets around this with its free-rider surcharge that applies to all employers.

But these fees are the parts of the bill that most trouble you. You support the expanded coverage but you are opposed to taxing businesses to help raise the money to pay for the new services. You believe higher taxes on businesses will hurt economic growth and job creation.

You are odd-man out in a state many people call "Taxachusetts" precisely because you, like most members of your party, are opposed to raising

taxes to pay for new government programs. Trained at Harvard Business School, you decided to stay on in Boston to join a management consulting and investment firm. This firm helped get many new businesses off the ground.

You lost your first political race to Senator Edward Kennedy, a Massachusetts institution, and barely won the governorship in 2002 after stepping into the race at the last minute when the Republican party's candidate dropped out. Your political success since has been attributed to your reputation as a good fiscal manager. You made your name by taking over the organizing committee for the Salt Lake Olympics when it was in shambles, raising hundreds of millions of dollars and turning it into one of the most successful Olympic games ever held in the United States. Your success as governor is based on the same skills; you took a $3 billion deficit in the state budget and turned it into a $1 billion surplus without raising taxes. This is the last year of your term and you have decided not to run for reelection. You want to finish what you came into office to do: straighten out the financial mess, promote economic growth, and reform education to prepare Massachusetts children for the global economy.

Though you strongly oppose this fee on businesses, there are other reasons to oppose the bill. Everyone thinks you decided not to run for reelection because you are planning a run for the presidency in 2008. You have had what most political analysts believe is a very successful term, but opposition to your presidential aspirations is forming. You call yourself "a red speck in a blue state," but some of the party's bedrock conservatives have labeled you a RINO (Republican in name only) because of statements you made during your campaign.[3] Political necessity dictated that in your run for governor you avoid the most conservative positions on those social issues that Massachusans feel strongly about, such as abortion and gay rights. You took the middle road

promising not to upset the status quo even though, as a devout Mormon, you have supported the positions of your Church on social issues. If you support mandatory government-funded health insurance it could be another strike against you with the conservative base of the party.

On the other hand, 2008 looks like it may be a year when a Republican with crossover appeal might have the best chance of winning the general election. You also have a lot of reasons to support the bill. You are concerned about the threat of health care costs to the state's well-being, job expansion, and budgets. Fewer and fewer employers are able to offer health benefits to their workers; costs of health care have been a factor in many companies moving overseas where there are millions of people either living in countries where government provides universal coverage or living in less developed countries and willing to work without health care.

You have some insight into health care costs' impact on the declining auto industry in the United States. Your father, George Romney, headed one of three auto giants before he became governor of Michigan and a 1968 presidential candidate. You do not want to see in Massachusetts the kind of job losses and economic stagnation Michigan is experiencing from the downsizing and declining competitiveness of the auto industry. You know that lifting the burden of health costs could be a boon to business, but you do not want to raise business taxes or be seen as an advocate of government expansionism.

However if you do run for president, universal health insurance could be your breakout issue. If it proves effective and popular it might give you credentials no one else in the Republican primaries will have in 2008. For certain, if you were running for governor again support for this bill would be a plus, but you can't be sure it will play the same way in the Republican presidential primaries. Your party has not

In almost all areas of American politics, it is those who vote, give the most to candidates, belong to the most influential interest groups, and are politically active in other ways who have the greatest impact on government policies. It *should be* no surprise, then, that these are the same people who benefit most from social welfare policies. All the same, it probably *will be* a surprise because the term social welfare usually brings to mind images of welfare mothers, elderly people in nursing homes, and indigents receiving surplus food and living in shelters or public housing, not images of the wealthy farmers, shareholders, and CEOs who benefit from billions of dollars in tax subsidies every year.[4]

Americans tend to view welfare as largesse for the other guy, and their own benefits—scholarships and guaranteed loans for students; price supports and credit assistance to farmers; preferred mortgage rates to veterans; retirement benefits and medical care for seniors; billions in annual tax deductions for savings plans, home ownership, education, private health care, and charitable giving—as their tax dollars at work or even as an entitlement. Although federal social welfare programs aid almost all groups—rich, poor, and almost everyone in between—more social welfare spending is targeted at the well-off than at the poor.

In this chapter, we will discuss the political and legal bases for social welfare policies, briefly review how they have evolved, and then describe programs and tax policies adopted to serve the needs of specific groups of Americans.

The Political and Legal Bases of Social Welfare Policies

Imagine for a minute that you are a farmer in a chronically drought-stricken African country. If your cattle die or your crops fail, the chances of malnutrition and even starvation are fairly high. There is no crop insurance, no agricultural extension service, no income support or food vouchers, no public health service, and perhaps no schools to teach your children skills other than farming. Governments often do not have the reach, the resources, or sometimes even the will to provide a safety net.

This is what capitalism without a social welfare program would be like. It is closer to what our system was like in the early 1930s when American farmers fled the Dust Bowl states trying to find work to allow them to feed their children. Religious and other private charities and state and local governments provided some services, but all their resources combined could not cope with the dislocation and needs created by the Great Depression. The federal government's response to the Depression was the beginning of large-scale federal welfare and social insurance programs.

We use the term *social welfare policy* to refer broadly to direct or indirect government subsidies for individuals and families who are often grouped by category such as "the poor," "the disabled," and "the elderly." Direct subsidies are payments government makes to individuals by checks, vouchers, or credits. Social Security payments, price support payments, cash assistance to the poor, and food vouchers are direct subsidies. Indirect subsidies are goods or services provided by the government to the public or to a specified group at below market value—for example, public education, health care, and public housing. If you are enrolled at a state college or university or a community college, chances are that your tuition and fees cover no more than half of real costs, possibly less—taxpayers pick up the difference.

Why does government do it? And should it be doing it? Whether it should be providing so many benefits is a philosophical question on which there will never be agreement. But there are many motivations for adopting such a wide variety of support programs. A political system like ours is predicated on equality of opportunity. The sick, the poor, the disabled, and the systemically discriminated against need assistance to put them on anything close to an equal footing. This support in turn helps foster economic growth because every country's development is dependent on a healthy, educated population.

As government has grown and become involved in all segments of society, we have come to rely on its help to cushion life's blows for the least well-off. At the same time, we give even more support to the middle class and the rich because policy makers could not get elected if they were not responsive to the expectations of their most powerful supporters and constituents.

Few people in any industrialized country today think they should be left completely at the mercy of natural or market forces. They look to social welfare policies to take the worst risks out of living in a capitalist system, offering protection for the ill, disabled, elderly poor, and unemployed. At the same time our government also provides a sturdy safety net for businesses.

Where does the authority come from to do all this? According to the Preamble to the Constitution, promotion of the "general Welfare" was one purpose for creation of the Union. Article I assigns the responsibility of providing for the general welfare to Congress, but the scope of the formal powers granted to Congress is a topic of continuing debate. Congress's authority to enact social welfare programs stems from powers implied by the "general welfare" phrase and from its formal power to tax. Government's taxing authority allows it to accumulate the resources needed to provide social services as well as a means for taking income from some people and redistributing it to others. Sometimes redistribution is from the rich to the poor and sometimes from the less well-off to the wealthy.

The Evolution of Social Welfare Policies

At the time the Constitution was written, no level of government was involved in providing aid to families and individuals. Local governments were responsible for the poor but gave little aid. Orphaned or destitute children were apprenticed to better-off families, where they worked as servants. Local authorities established workhouses for the able-bodied poor and in some places gave minimal assistance to the old or sick.[5] Churches and other private charities helped the "deserving" poor and unfortunate. Those thought to be undeserving were treated harshly. These attitudes reflected the belief that individuals bore the primary responsibility for their own fate.

While government took little responsibility for the well-being of individuals, it *was* involved in the economic development of the country and the creation of jobs. In at least one case (the Homestead Act, passed

Dorothea Lange snapped this historic photo of a homeless Oklahoma family during the Great Depression. Most major federal welfare programs were adopted in the 1930s.

during the Civil War), this resulted in direct benefits to families and individuals: to encourage settlement of the western states, the government gave away 246 million acres of land, in 160-acre allotments, to 1.5 million homesteaders. If settlers stayed on the land for five years and developed it, they received title free and clear.

Government also encouraged development through its immigration policies, although it did little to help new residents after their arrival. The great waves of immigration at the end of the nineteenth century and the beginning of the twentieth generated a desperate need for health care, housing, and education in the big cities, but that demand was met primarily with services from private charities or settlement houses, such as Chicago's Hull House, or from local political party organizations. Settlement houses taught literacy and work skills and provided lessons in hygiene and rudimentary health care for infants and children. The big cities' political machines, such as New York's Tammany Hall, helped new arrivals find housing and jobs and traded those favors for votes.

The idea that government should provide extensive public services such as education, hospitals, and asylums developed in the nineteenth century. But the concept of paying individuals benefits is a twentieth-century idea. Gradually, the belief grew that government has a responsibility to help at least some of those at the bottom of the ladder. These changed attitudes led to the enactment of state laws, beginning in 1911, to establish aid programs for poor children and their mothers. Fifteen years later, most states had such laws, freeing many children from apprenticeships and poorhouses.

Most of our major federal social welfare programs were developed in the 1930s as part of the New Deal's response to the Great Depression. These programs provided support to farmers, poor families, and the elderly poor. During the 1960s' War on Poverty, old programs were expanded, and major new ones to assist with health care—Medicare and Medicaid—were added.

Over the decades, the United States has amassed a large number of social welfare programs (see Figure 17.1), but that does not make us a "welfare state." Welfare states have a coordinated set of income support programs to ensure access to basic necessities in a uniform way, not just for those in need but for the population as a whole. These are governments that accept the premise that jobs, health care, education, and the basic material necessities of life are entitlements or human rights, and some may even have that principle incorporated into their constitutions. In contrast, our social welfare programs are largely uncoordinated efforts designed to solve the particular problems of specific groups (for example, college students, the poor, farmers, the elderly) on a piecemeal basis. We shall look at some of these programs by category: income support programs, health care and other subsidized services, and tax subsidies.

Income Support Programs

Today the federal government has programs providing income support to retirees and their dependents, the disabled and their dependents, farmers, poor families, and the unemployed, in addition to pension plans for its civilian and military personnel.

Retirees and Their Dependents

The earliest and the most comprehensive of income support programs is the Old Age Survivors Disability and Health Insurance Program, adopted in 1935 to ensure that the elderly would not live in poverty after retirement. President Roosevelt and the other New Dealers who initiated the program would be astounded at its current magnitude. **Social Security** has evolved into a government-managed retirement fund for American workers from all income groups, a life insurance program for surviving dependents and spouses, and an income support program for people with disabilities. Participation is not voluntary, and over the decades, the program has grown to cover 96 percent of all workers. Social Security covers so many Americans that each of us is issued a Social Security identification number at birth.

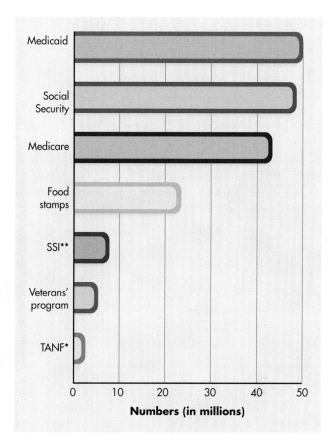

FIGURE 17.1 ■ Direct Federal Aid

More than 80 million Americans receive direct federal aid. This figure does not include indirect subsidies or tax subsidies. (The numbers in this figure add up to more than 80 million because some people benefit from more than one federal program.)

*Temporary Assistance for Needy Families, the program that replaced Aid to Families with Dependent Children. This program is what most people think of when they think of "welfare."

**Supplemental Security Income, the aid program for the needy elderly and disabled.

Source: *Budget of the United States, Fiscal Year 2007*, 238, 289; Appendix, 173, 452, 1102.

Social Security is financed through a payroll tax on employees and employers. The employee's contribution, slightly over 6.2 percent (7.65 percent, including Medicare) of the first $94,200 of earnings (periodically adjusted upward), is withheld from wages; employers contribute an equal amount. Self-employed workers must pay both the workers' and employers' share and send payments to the IRS with their annual income tax return. Social Security taxes are credited to a special off-budget trust fund and invested in government securities until they are needed to cover benefit payments. In other words, Social Security benefits are not paid out of the general revenue funds that come from personal and corporate income or excise taxes. They are paid entirely from contributions made to the trust fund by employers, their employees, and the self-employed, plus the accrued interest.

This poster was used in 1936 and 1937 when Social Security was new.

With help from Social Security, these gyrating geriatrics, rehearsing in Northampton, Massachusetts, can continue to rock on.

Social Security taxes will produce more than 36 percent of federal revenues in 2007, and payments to beneficiaries will account for just over 21 percent of federal spending. It is the single largest expenditure in the federal budget, although spending on national security is now close behind. Lower-income workers are hardest hit by these taxes because all their earnings are subject to the tax. Americans who earn more than the $94,200 subject to the tax pay a smaller proportion of their income into Social Security.

Lower-income retirees receive more benefits relative to their earnings than do wealthier participants. But 60 percent of Social Security payments do go to individuals living above the poverty line.[6] For this reason, and also to shore up the trust fund, middle- and upper-income beneficiaries are required to pay taxes on 85 percent of their Social Security income at the same rate at which the rest of their income is taxed.

The size of the monthly stipend received by beneficiaries is determined by how many years they worked, how much they earned, and whether they are alone or have dependents. The age of eligibility for full benefits rises in small increments with one's birth year.

Currently, a retiree born in 1939 can qualify for full benefits at age sixty-five years and four months and can request payments as early as age sixty-two at a lower amount. For each year up to age seventy that retirement is postponed, the monthly stipend increases.

Social Security is categorized as social insurance rather than a welfare program because it covers people in all income groups and because only those who have paid into the program, or their survivors, can collect benefits. Since people do not have to show financial need to participate, everyone can accept it without the public stigma of being on welfare. This aspect of the program increases its political popularity. Yet it is a mistake to think that all beneficiaries get back only what they and their employers paid into the program through payroll deductions, plus accumulated interest. This is true for some short-lived people. But given our longer life span, Social Security pays most of its recipients more than they paid in, something no private insurance program would do. In 1935, a sixty-five-year-old was expected to collect benefits for twelve and a half years; by 2006, that had increased to seventeen and a half years.

Social Security has grown from about 220,000 recipients in 1940 to 49 million in 2006. Ninety percent of Americans sixty-five years of age or older are currently receiving Social Security benefits. They and their dependents receive the largest share of benefits paid; the disabled and their dependents account for most of the rest. The average monthly benefit to a retired worker has risen from a mere $13 in 1940, when many fewer people were covered and withholding was much less, to $1,007 in 2006.[7] Due to annual cost of living adjustments, the monthly stipend increases by a small amount each year.

Gradually, over the years, Social Security payments have become a principal part of retirement income. In 1950, they accounted for only 3 percent of retirees' income but by 2006, 41 percent. For 43 percent of unmarried or widowed retirees, social security accounts for 90 percent of income. It forms a larger part of elderly women's income because women earn less over the life course and have fewer private pensions, savings, or other investments.[8] Without Social Security, almost half of our senior citizens would be poor, but for those sixty-five and older the poverty rate fell to an historic low of 9.8 percent in 2004 (see Figure 17.2).[9] (In contrast, the poverty rate has been rising for children). To the extent that continued payments from the fund keep people above the poverty line, they are doing what Social Security was intended to do.

Social Security has stayed afloat because of ever-increasing numbers of people paying in at steadily rising rates. The taxes withheld from the paychecks of today's workers provide the payouts to current retirees just as they supported the generation before them. The aging of the population and the declining ratio of workers to retirees does present a threat to the long-term solvency of the system. (We return to this in the "Current Issues" section.)

The Poor

Federal income support programs for the poor began as part of the original Social Security legislation, which established a national program of unemployment insurance, along with the social security program. Unemployment insurance was introduced in order to combat the effects of the Great Depression, when nearly a quarter of the workforce was unemployed and state and local programs did not have the resources to meet demand. Except for Social Security itself, which is funded and managed entirely at the federal level, income support programs for the poor have been run jointly by federal, state, and local governments, and sometimes state programs predated federal ones.

Eligibility

A major difference between beneficiaries of an inclusive program such as Social Security and one that exclusively targets the poor is that qualification for participation requires a **means test.** Participants must periodically demonstrate eligibility by showing that they are poor—they must have both limited income and few assets.

The definition of who is poor is revised each year by the Census Bureau, which makes adjustments to account for changes in inflation and the cost of living. It does not set a single income level but many, depending on age and household composition. In 2005, for example, a single person under sixty-five years of age was considered poor if his or her income was below $10,860; the comparable figure for a family of four was $19,806. Not everyone agrees with the Census Bureau's poverty estimates because they do not take into account many "in-kind" benefits poor people receive, such as food and housing subsidies and medical care. If these were added to income, critics of the threshold say, the poverty rate would be reduced by about 4 percent. Others argue that the Census Bureau *understates* the amount of poverty by using 1960s standards that focused on the price of food and underestimated the cost of housing, fuel, education, and health care. A common alternative estimate of living costs for a family of four is $30,000 to $34,000.[10]

The Elderly and the Disabled

One of the first grant-in-aid programs established under Social Security authority, **Supplemental Security Income (SSI),** provides income support for the blind and people with disabilities and for the elderly not covered by Social Security or whose Social Security benefits are not large enough to lift them out of poverty. For 20 percent of seniors, Social Security is their only income, which may be insufficient to meet their basic living costs. Other SSI recipients are workers or survivors of workers who were not covered by the Social Security program (something unlikely to happen much in the future given the expansion of Social Security to virtually all jobs). Although created by Social Security legislation and run by the same agency, SSI is funded from general tax revenues, not Social Security payroll taxes, and many recipients receive a supplement from the state government as well.

In 2006, just over seven million Americans received SSI; about one-third were Social Security recipients whose benefits were too low to meet basic needs, and most of the remainder were people under age sixty-five with disabilities.[11] SSI payments are generally quite small, ranging from $603 per month for an individual to $904 for a couple.[12]

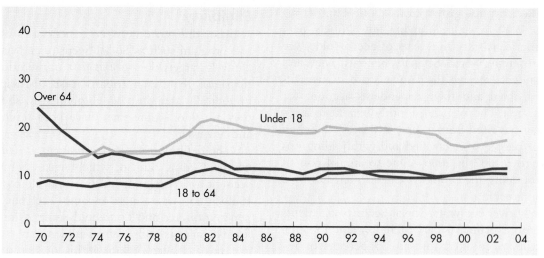

FIGURE 17.2 ■ Profile of the Poor

The number of children living in poverty has been increasing, but the number of older Americans in poverty has fallen. Children are more likely to be poor than any other age group.

SOURCE: U.S. Census Bureau, "Poverty Thresholds 2005" (www.census.gov). The poverty threshold for a single person under age sixty-five in 2005 was $10,860; for a family of four, it was $19,806.

To qualify for SSI, an individual cannot have more than $2,000 or a couple more than $3,000 in assets (cash or stocks and bonds; personal home and car do not count). SSI recipients are automatically eligible under federal standards for food stamps and health insurance (discussed later), but states have considerable leeway to change eligibility standards.

Poor Families

Aid to Families with Dependent Children (AFDC) was another grant-in-aid program that grew out of Social Security legislation. The purpose was to strengthen maternal and child welfare services being provided by the states. Coverage was soon extended to mothers as well as their dependent children and later to both fathers and mothers with dependent children. Because AFDC was a joint federal-state program administered at the state level, eligibility and benefits varied from state to state.

Despite the success that AFDC had in providing food and shelter to dependent children, critics argued that it fostered dependency instead of encouraging independence and hard work. For example, although the number of AFDC recipients was fairly stable from the mid-1970s to the late 1980s, it shot up in the recession of the late 1980s and early 1990s. In contrast to the common stereotype, however, the increase in welfare recipients was not tied to the size of welfare stipends, which in real terms (adjusted for inflation) began a steady decline in the 1970s.

The largest growth in number of recipients came when economic times were hard; but when the economy improved, the rolls did not always fall back to their previous level. Part of the reason is that even in years

when the economy was growing, many of the new jobs being created did not pay enough to meet basic living costs. Welfare rolls also grew because of the increase in the number of births to unmarried women without job skills who were often still children themselves; about 80 percent of these unwed mothers went on welfare at some point. It is extremely difficult for a single parent with no job skills to support children, especially without child-care support, so many turned to AFDC.

The number of births to single women continues to be high: 68 percent of all African American, 43 percent of all Hispanic, and 28 percent of all white births are to unmarried women, but the number of unmarried teenage women giving birth has been declining since 1990.[13]

Our society made it very difficult for women to choose low-paid work over welfare. Workers were often worse off because of child-care costs and the loss of medical benefits that came with AFDC but not with most low-paying jobs. Nevertheless, the majority of AFDC recipients collected benefits for a relatively short time.[14] They found a job or married someone who earned more than poverty wages (or both). But nearly one-quarter of the women who went on AFDC stayed for ten years or more, and another 20 percent stayed for six to nine years. Though most AFDC recipients were white, long-term recipients were more likely to be black or Hispanic unmarried teenage mothers with no high school diploma.

AFDC became the main target for critics of cash assistance to the poor. Its cost was much lower than other income support programs, but to its critics it appeared to be rewarding the wrong kind of behavior and getting no results. They saw AFDC as discouraging work, encouraging out-of-wedlock births, and allowing fathers to take no responsibility for their children. Although a consensus grew that the welfare system needed to be reformed, there were strong differences over how to do it.

In 1993, President Clinton took office promising to end welfare "as we know it." In the 1994 elections, the Republican's "Contract with America" promised even more dramatic reform. After heated debate, in 1996 Congress passed, and President Clinton signed, a welfare reform bill that abolished AFDC and with it the concept of welfare as an entitlement to all those who met federal guidelines. Instead, in the **Temporary Aid to Needy Families (TANF)** program, states were mandated to set up their own welfare systems under loose federal guidelines to be funded by block grants from the federal government.

TANF is a results-oriented program that sets time limits on eligibility and requires participants to move "from welfare to work," the signature slogan of the reform bill. States receiving TANF funds were to have, at minimum, 30 percent of the people on their welfare rolls working at least thirty hours a week during the program's initial five years. "Work" included job training, community service, and continuing education. TANF recipients are required to hold jobs within two years of entering the program, and working families can receive assistance for a lifetime maximum of five years. States were allowed to exempt up to 20 percent of the people receiving assistance from this requirement (for example, people who are physically or mentally unable to hold a job or parents with young children and no child care).

Initially, people who feared the impact of TANF on children and welfare recipients unable to find employment severely criticized the program. In response, some modifications were made to allow recipients to receive child care, transportation, and other non-cash assistance beyond the two-year cutoff. These modifications were designed to help those who took low-paying jobs and who needed such additional assistance to keep their families intact.[15] However, states have the authority to enact more stringent limits.

In the early years after the reform, some states increased spending dramatically because they offered job training and other assistance to help people move from welfare to work. Welfare rolls fell by as much as two-thirds in midwestern states and with it spending by the states. But in most states, 70 percent or more of welfare recipients still need training and other assistance if they are to find jobs. Part of the decrease in spending can be attributed to Congress's giving states considerable flexibility in how they use a certain portion of block grant money, allowing them to create "rainy day funds." States can reserve for later use money they are entitled to receive for TANF, or they can divert it to other purposes.[16]

The Working Poor

As criticism of paying welfare benefits to the chronically unemployed grew, more emphasis was placed on rewarding the working poor. This led to increases in the **earned income tax credit (EITC)**, which has been in place since 1975. The EITC is a negative income tax, which gives both single and married individuals, with and without dependent children, credits against their tax liability. The credit can be used to reduce taxes owed, but for families whose income is so low that they have no income tax liability, the credit is returned as a direct payment from the government. Claims for the credit are filed on a form attached to one's annual income tax report. In 2003, more than nineteen million families and individuals—about one of every seven tax returns filed—claimed the credit. An estimated five million families were lifted above the official poverty threshold by an EITC payment.[17]

This approach to poverty rewards work and allows poor families to receive government aid without becoming a client of the welfare bureaucracy. President Reagan called the EITC the "best antipoverty, best profamily, best job creation measure to come out of Congress." That both the Clinton and Bush administrations were able to expand EITC is a measure of its bipartisan support. But it is still a frequent target of budget cutters.

The working poor can also qualify for help with the cost of job training and, in many states, for help with child care. Welfare reform authorized states to give assistance to any family earning up to 85 percent of the state's median income.

Food Subsidies

Another major supplement to the income of the poor comes from the Department of Agriculture's **food stamp** program. Until 2004, food stamps were paper coupons that served as vouchers redeemable in grocery stores for food. Now this food subsidy is issued in the form of an electronic credit accessed by a debit card. The credit may be used only to purchase unprepared food and cannot be used for dining out or for liquor or tobacco.[18] The average food stamp allotment per poor household ranges from about $160 to $350 a month, depending on the state.

The food stamp program began as a temporary measure of support during the last years of the Great Depression but was revived and made permanent as part of Lyndon Johnson's War on Poverty. Its coverage expanded during the early 1970s in response to an investigation that revealed that tens of thousands of Americans suffered from malnourishment, resulting in retarded growth, anemia, protein deficiencies, high rates of infant mortality, scurvy and rickets (from insufficient vitamin C, vitamin D, and milk), and an impaired ability to learn. In the first years of the program, malnutrition among the poor decreased, as did the incidence of diseases caused by poor nutrition.

Even though the food stamp program was pared back during the 1980s, one of every ten Americans was receiving the coupons in the years just before the 1996 welfare reforms. One of the objectives of those reforms was to reduce the size of the program by eliminating fraud and abuse. To that end, Congress established fines for states that make too many errors in determining eligibility for the program. Most states now require recertification of eligibility every three or four months. The 1996 law also made most legal immigrants ineligible for food stamp assistance. The new restrictions on eligibility caused participation to decline for seven years. But this led the Department of Agriculture (DoA) to call for increased participation because food stamps have always been seen as a constructive means for reducing food surpluses (which are warehoused by the DoA), as well as for fighting hunger. In 2002 coverage was restored to legal immigrants who have been in the country at least five years, and greater participation by the working poor was encouraged. The rising poverty rate has also led to a steady increase in food stamp recipients, who numbered twenty-three million in 2004. This is still only 60 percent of those eligible to participate.[19]

The government provides an additional food subsidy to pregnant women and preschool children through the Special Supplemental Nutritional Program for Women, Infants, and Children. Because poorly nourished mothers have more sickly babies and because poorly nourished children do not learn as well as children with adequate diets, the government now provides support for mothers-to-be and new mothers who cannot afford to buy the kinds or amounts of foods necessary for good nutrition for themselves and their infants. These women and children are also eligible for a pre-preschool program that provides family services from before birth until the infants become eligible for Head Start (discussed later in this chapter) at age three.[20]

Farmers

Direct federal aid has accounted for almost half of total farm income since the 1980s, and it has been as high as 70 percent in some farm states. **Farm subsidies** are a means by which government underwrites part of the cost of agriculture; they include direct payments to farmers or agribusinesses to reduce the economic risks of growing food and other crops. More than 90 percent of subsidies are paid out in price supports; the government guarantees set prices—usually more than the market commands—for crops such as corn, wheat, rice, cotton, and soybeans, to name the most heavily subsidized. If the market price falls below the guaranteed level, the government pays the difference while also purchasing and storing tons of surplus crops each year. Some of that surplus goes to federal programs such as food stamps and subsidized school lunches.

The government also pays farmers to withhold land from production, either to promote conservation or to reduce the production of crops or farm products (cheese, butter, dried milk) that the government holds in surplus. Collectively, these farm support programs have made agriculture the most subsidized industry in the United States.

Like Social Security, income support for farmers was motivated by the urgent needs and dire living conditions of one segment of the American population. Because food self-sufficiency is regarded by many as essential to national security and because many farmers were being forced off the land, providing federal aid took on a special urgency. All of the rhetorical justification for continuing the program still focuses on family farms, but in fact small farmers have been going out of business by the tens of thousands since the 1970s. By 1997, there were only two million farms left in the United States, and about half of these were hobby farms, having less than $10,000 in gross sales.[21] Thus farm aid has evolved into an income support program not for poor or marginal family farms but for all farming enterprises, including the largest and most profitable.

Unlike Social Security, where even the top payments are modest and all participants get some minimum payments, farm aid provides staggeringly large sums to the wealthiest farmers whereas 60 percent of farmers receive no subsidies at all.[22] In 2000, of 1.6 million individuals receiving farm aid, about 57,500 got more than $100,000; at least 154 got more than $1 million. $17 million went to farms operated by government agencies, and millions more to university farms.[23]

The media have had some fun calling attention to well-off subsidy recipients, like an heir to the Rockefeller fortune, basketball star Scottie Pippen, and the billionaire Ted Turner, founder of CNN and TNT, but they are not exceptions. At least twenty Fortune 500 companies received checks from federal programs in 2000, as did eleven members of Congress. They included the Speaker of the House, the ranking Democrat on the House Agriculture Committee, and the chair of the Senate Finance Committee, Charles Grassley. Grassley, who claims to be primarily a farmer and not to live in Washington, D.C., "except Monday through Fridays," has received payments as large as $110,936—mailed to his Washington residence. The senator's claim to be living and farming in Iowa may stretch credulity, but his explanation that all but $20,000 of his payments went to meet equipment and operating expenses is believable.[24] The operating costs of large farms are staggering, and a good share of government aid is used to defray these expenses. The question is whether taxpayers' money should make the difference between agribusinesses' and corporate farms' staying in or going out of business.

Richard Lugar (R-Ind.), another Agriculture Committee member who receives subsidy payments for a corn and soybean farm and who says he could not grow these crops without subsidies, is still critical of the program. Subsidies, he says, "distort markets by encouraging overproduction to drive prices lower in a self-perpetuating cycle."[25] And a House colleague warned that with the current level of subsidies "we are in danger of systematically turning farmers into dependent serfs of the federal government."[26]

Farm subsidies are constant targets of budget cutters and free-marketers, but political support for their retention is formidable. After anti-big government Republicans took control of Congress, some of them made a halfhearted attempt to phase out income supports for certain crops over a seven-year period. Instead the conservative Congress and administration quadrupled payments. And Congress has continued to increase subsidies right through recession, tax cuts, budget deficits, and rising farm income. Between 2002 and 2004 farm income doubled, yet farm subsidies still rose 40 percent.[27]

President Bush, who has advocated cutting subsidies on rice and cotton, nevertheless signed into law the largest ever farm subsidy bill in 2002, describing farm and ranch families as embodying "some of the best values of our nation: hard work and risk taking."[28] This is the crux of the problem for anyone voting against farm subsidies: agriculture and the "family farm" hold a special place in the American identity—they represent the country's breadbasket, its Corn and Bible Belts, conjuring up images of waving fields of grain, pioneers, and an "authentic" America that politicians love to be associated with. But the money is not going to these farmers, and, not surprisingly, current programs are not well regarded by the small family farmers whom politicians like to claim they are saving. By 2001, fully 73 percent of rural Nebraskans polled believed that caps should be set on the amount of subsidies any individual can receive.[29]

Are subsidies a problem or a solution? Opponents argue that subsidies raise land prices and make it difficult for young farmers to make it, and some say that subsidies have contributed to the death of the family farm by making it profitable to consolidate land into corporate farms. They argue that crop subsidies keep marginal land in production, resulting in overproduction and lower prices. Corn is one of many examples. From 2000 to 2004 the average farmer lost up to $128 an acre raising corn, but they continue to plant more

By permission of Chip Bok and Creators Syndicate Inc.

corn because during those same four years taxpayers covered their losses with $25 billion in subsidies.[30] Industrial farms producing these single, heavily subsidized commodities average 14,000 acres, about the size of Manhattan. Critics of current policy argue that we are working at cross purposes by encouraging this kind of agribusiness when we should be trying to help small and medium-sized farms shift to whole foods—fruits and vegetables—that would be better for farmers, taxpayers, and the nation's health.[31]

Farm subsidies are a good example of why government continues to grow. Both liberals and conservatives want to be seen supporting income subsidies for "family farmers," and both, including the conservatives who decry big government, vote for what they believe is beneficial to their constituents and campaign donors. In that sense they are also an example of how government welfare policies often end up responding to the lobbying influence of the well-off.

If farm subsidies are to be reformed, the pressure will probably come from abroad. Continued spending on price supports for agricultural commodities conflicts with the U.S. commitment to free trade and its obligations as a member of the World Trade Organization (see Chapter 18). The United States is a party to international trade agreements that, to ensure fair competition among the world's farm exporters, limit how much a government can pay in price supports. If the WTO rules against the United States in grievances filed by other member countries, payments to farmers would have to be cut if we want to be in compliance with international obligations. Until that happens, farm subsidies will continue to reduce, if not eliminate, risk taking primarily for the wealthiest farm industries, not for the average family farmer. This is why some in rural America call it "farming the government, not farming the land."[32]

Veterans

Through the Department of Veterans Affairs, the federal government provides income support to veterans with disabilities. To qualify for a disability pension, a veteran must be able to prove that the disability was acquired while on active duty. The level of support, whether full or partial, depends on the severity of the disability. In 2007, some 3.7 million veterans will receive about $39 billion in tax-free disability payments.[33]

The government also funds a retirement program for career servicemen and servicewomen at a cost of close to $34 billion annually.[34] Obviously, we need a pension plan for military personnel, but the plan's eligibility standards have many critics. Because so many career service personnel retire at an early age, they are able to hold down full-time jobs while drawing full military pensions. As a result, most military pensions are paid to individuals with above-average incomes who will also be eligible to receive Social Security.

The Impact of Income Support Programs

Income support programs for the elderly, disabled, and dependent children played a major role in reducing poverty rates in the United States from their highs in the 1930s. Due in part to the Great Society programs of the 1960s, the proportion of families in poverty dropped from 21 percent in 1959 to 10 percent in 1973, the lowest point ever achieved in the United States.[35] It then increased steadily, reaching a high of 14 percent in 1993, before the booming economy of the 1990s sent it downward. On the rise again, it stood at 13 percent in 2005 (thirty-seven million people). One of every three poor persons is a child, and fifteen million people live in extreme poverty (below one-half of the poverty line).[36]

Income support programs for the poor and disabled draw much more attention from budget cutters than do support programs for the middle- and upper-income beneficiaries. Yet the majority of income support payouts do go, by far, to those enrolled in social insurance programs and to the owners of industrial farms rather than to the poor and unemployed.

Health Care Programs

In the United States, government aid for health care is a social benefit for some people in all income groups but not for all people. Nonetheless, health care is by far the most costly indirect government subsidy. Half of all federal, state, and local spending on means-tested programs is for medical care.[37] Through Medicare,

Medicaid, and Veterans Affairs, the government is the largest health care provider in the country.

The federal government has been involved in some aspects of health care for decades, but before 1965, there was no general federal support for individual health care. In 1965, after years of debate over government's responsibility, concern about the problems of millions of Americans who could not afford adequate health care prompted President Johnson to propose and Congress to pass two programs, Medicare (for the elderly) and Medicaid (for low-income people).

Health Care for Seniors

Medicare is a public health insurance program that funds many medical expenses for the elderly and disabled. It includes hospital insurance, and additional voluntary coverage helps pay for physicians' services, outpatient hospital services, and some other costs.

Hospital insurance is paid for by the Medicare payroll tax, and the elective portion is financed through general revenues and monthly premiums paid by participants. Everyone eligible for Social Security benefits is eligible for Medicare, and over 90 percent of Social Security recipients buy the optional insurance. In 2007, the program will cover more than forty million people at a cost of $390 billion.

There are many factors that explain the improved health profile of the elderly over the past forty years, including scientific breakthroughs in the treatment of some diseases, but Medicare is responsible for many of the gains. Compared with the period before 1965, more seniors are able to see doctors now, and the elderly have more but shorter hospital stays. There have been declines in death rates from diseases affecting the elderly, such as heart attacks and strokes, and a decrease in the number of days of restricted activity that older people experience.[38]

Despite these substantial accomplishments, Medicare has not been a complete success. It is expensive, and many of those who need it have trouble paying their portion of the costs. There has been extensive fraud in the program, especially overbilling by doctors and HMOs.

The maximum fees the government has set for services are lower than some doctors have been willing to accept, and as a consequence, they refuse to treat Medicare patients. Patients themselves have been criticized for driving up costs by making unnecessary doctor or hospital visits and having unrealistic expectations about what medical care can do to resolve their health problems. Experts of all political persuasions continue to predict that the Medicare program will go broke within the next few decades unless changes are made or a national health care system is put in place, but it is hard to imagine that the government would let such a popular and essential program fail. A similar cost problem afflicts the other major federal health care program, Medicaid.

Health Care for the Poor and Disabled

Medicaid is a federal-state program that pays for medical care for disabled and unemployed people as well as some of the working poor who do not have coverage and cannot afford to buy it. States set their own Medicaid eligibility standards, within federal guidelines. Nationwide, 11 percent of Americans receive health coverage through Medicaid, with some variation among states.[39] Medicaid pays for one-third of all births, two-thirds of nursing home stays, and provides nearly half of the public funds for AIDS patients.[40]

Medicaid, which will cover about fifty million people in 2007, has now surpassed Medicare as the second most expensive entitlement program (after Social Security). The federal government continues to shift more of the responsibility for funding and setting program standards to state governments. On average, states spend 22 percent of their budgets on Medicaid, and its rapid growth is crowding out spending for education and other needs.[41]

Even with Medicare, Medicaid, and private health insurance provided through the workplace, more than forty-six million Americans remain without health insurance, two-thirds from wage-earning families whose income is above the poverty line.

To ensure greater coverage of children, in 1997 the government created the State Children's Health Insurance Program (SCHIP). Working through existing state programs, it set a goal of insuring all children whose parents do not qualify for Medicaid and who cannot afford private insurance. About six million children have received coverage under this program. However, the states determine eligibility, and eligibility standards vary widely. With medical costs soaring, at least eleven states have begun making it harder for children to qualify and other states have established their own comprehensive programs (see "You Are There" for this chapter).

Health Care for Veterans

In addition to Medicare, Medicaid, and SCHIPS, the government also funds a national system of hospitals, outpatient clinics, nursing homes, and psychiatric clinics, run by the Department of Defense and Veterans Affairs (VA), that provide health care to five million veterans. (The VA also maintains a national system of

Like most individuals in middle-class families, this young man gets good medical treatment for chronic illnesses such as asthma. However, the uninsured and the poverty stricken are much more likely to die from lack of treatment of such diseases.

cemeteries for veterans and their families.) The wars in Afghanistan and Iraq are creating a new generation of combat veterans and an increased need for health care and rehabilitation. In recent years, the VA has become a model for reform of private healthcare.

Subsidized Services

Other subsidized services reach a broad swath of the American public. Virtually everyone who relies on a municipal bus system or intercity trains or who drives on a highway, for example, benefits from federally subsidized mass transit and support for highway construction. Similarly, all Americans benefit from government subsidies for food, education, and housing, but middle- and upper-income families reap the bulk of the housing and education benefits, as they do from tax deductions.

Education

Elementary and secondary education in the United States is primarily in the hands of local governmental units and funded largely through state and local taxes. Because the No Child Left Behind program's testing mandate has imposed significant new costs on public schools, the federal government has increased the level of aid to elementary schools, although not by nearly as much as is needed to cover the cost of the new mandates.

The federal government is a major funder of higher education through grants and guaranteed loans to undergraduates and fellowships and low-interest loans to graduate students. Almost every American college student is aware of Pell grants, but the grand-

In these times of an all-volunteer army and limited wars whose daily, or even weekly, casualties are counted in double digits, it is easy to lose sight of times when the United States was engaged in world wars, dependent on a universal male draft, and absorbing casualties that ran to thousands per day. In 1944, even after victory in Europe, the war continued in Asia where 5000 or more lives were lost in single battles for control of South Pacific islands. Needing to continue drafting tens of thousands even as it planned for the reintegration of twelve million who had already served, lawmakers wanted vets to know they would be treated better than their WWI predecessors.

World War I "doughboys" had received a tiny cash payment on mustering out but were promised a small annuity to be paid near retirement age. This was too long a wait for those who fell on hard times in the early years of the Great Depression. But in 1932, when they marched on Washington to demand early payment of their "bonuses," their demonstration was violently suppressed by U.S. Army units under the command of General Douglas MacArthur. The spectacle of our military assaulting its veterans was a black mark on the national conscience.

Nevertheless, the following year when Franklin Roosevelt took office he rejected the idea that citizen soldiers were entitled to benefits not available to all.[1] Even after we entered World War II, a comprehensive assistance package was opposed by all the powerful leaders in Congress. Some believed providing cash assistance would encourage soldiers not to look for jobs, whereas others, like Roosevelt, were opposed to singling out for benefits only one group of people who con-

tributed to the war effort. But some kind of bonus for vets was supported by an overwhelming majority of the American public. In the end, the compromise bill—called the Bill of Rights for GI Joe and Jane—was written by a member of the American Legion. Its congressional sponsors were relatively unknown Republicans and conservative Southern Democrats, some of whom supported the bill primarily as a way to prevent class warfare. Among the principal players was one woman, Edith Nourse Rogers, a liberal Republican from Massachusetts and the ranking minority member of the Veterans Affairs Committee, who had helped create the Women's Army Corps. She went on to become the first woman to chair a major House committee.

When the GI Bill—officially titled the Serviceman's Readjustment Act—was signed into law in 1944, just two weeks after D-Day, neither President Roosevelt nor Congress thought they were passing a transformative piece of legislation. They just wanted to help millions of veterans reintegrate into civilian life and the labor force. But today the bill is often called the "greatest piece of legislation Congress ever passed," a "Marshall Plan for America," and "a magic carpet to the middle class." No one foresaw the consequences of the bill's three major benefits: a living stipend and tuition vouchers for college, low-interest mortgages for purchase of a first home, and loans for starting new businesses. These measures set off a chain reaction that helped shape modern America. To understand how one bill could have such an impact, one has to keep in mind what the economic situation of the average GI was like when we entered World War II.

In 1940, the average soldier was twenty-six, had only one year of high

school, and came from a family for whom college was financially out of reach.[2] Had these young men and women not served in the war and received the GI benefit, most could never have gone back to school.

Many educators and college presidents opposed the voucher program, arguing that they would have to lower their standards and admit students with poor educational backgrounds. But veterans returned to school in record numbers, more than a million in 1946 alone, when they accounted for almost half of all college enrollments in the United States. In 1950, almost a quarter of all college students were veterans.[3] The GI Bill thus stimulated a tremendous growth in higher education, creating the need to hire more faculty and build new facilities, eventually giving rise to a new system of state colleges in many states.

In the first years after the war, however, most veterans chose private schools, since at the time vouchers provided enough to cover tuition in the Ivy League. By 1946, the influx of veterans almost doubled Harvard's enrollment, and they "hogged the honor rolls,"[4] there and throughout the Ivy League. With college educations, many working-class families moved into the middle class, making it possible for them to afford to send their children to college and continue the families' upward mobility. With federally guaranteed mortgages, many vets were also able to leave rental housing in the cities for homes in the outlying areas. So many new homeowners entered the market that it prompted the building of housing developments such as Levittown and began the suburbanization of America. This in turn fostered the building of highways and schools and the whole infrastructure necessary to support new towns.

more productive citizens for the remainder of their lives. It gave education vouchers to eight million veterans. It doubled home ownership, from one in three before the war to two in three afterward. According to a 1986 government study, "each dollar invested in the bill yielded $5 to $12 in tax revenues."[5] The GI Bill was such a success that it was renewed in 1956 with scaled-back benefits for those who had served in Korea and later for Vietnam vets. Overall, the bill's single most important contribution may have been in its extraordinary expansion of higher education because it "signaled the shift to the knowledge society." For this reason, its passage may in the future be seen "as one of the most important events of the twentieth century."[6]

A federal law passed during World War II, the GI Bill of Rights, transformed American society by granting each veteran educational benefits and loans to buy homes and start businesses. Returning veterans flooded America's universities by the millions, changing the face of higher education. The facilities at Indiana University, like those of so many other schools, were soon overtaxed, forcing relocation of student registration to its field house.

The bill did not work equally well for everyone, in part because African Americans did not have the same choices as whites in using their benefits. Because housing was segregated in most new suburban areas, including Levittown, the route out of the city to affordable housing was less possible for blacks than for whites. Although black vets got the same educational benefits, they did not have the range of choices in schools, given segregation in some universities and the use of a quota system in others. But thousands did get to college, among them many of those who would become leaders of the modern civil rights movement.

The GI Bill's significance stemmed from providing benefits that made it possible for young veterans to become

[1]Suzanne Mettler, *Soldiers to Citizens: The G.I. Bill and the Making of the Greatest Generation* (New York: Oxford University Press, 2005), 19.
[2]Doris Kearns Goodwin, on "Remembering the GI Bill," *NewsHour with Jim Lehrer*, PBS, July 4, 2000.
[3]Michael J. Bennett, *When Dreams Come True: The GI Bill and the Making of Modern America* (Washington, D.C.: Brassey's, 1996), 18.
[4]Ibid., 19.
[5]Spencer Michaels, on "Remembering the GI Bill," *NewsHour with Jim Lehrer*, PBS, July 4, 2000.
[6]Peter Drucker, *Post-Capitalist Society* (New York: HarperBusiness, 1993), 3.

daddy of all student support programs, and the most successful in terms of overall impact on the country, is the GI Bill of Rights (see the Government Responsiveness box "The GI Bill of Rights").

Government also funds an early-learning program for children from poor households. Head Start provides preschool education, with the objective of teaching children from poor families skills they will need to succeed in primary school. It also encourages parents to become involved in their children's education and to read to them at home. Head Start has been a widely supported program from its inception in the 1960s; studies show that preschoolers with Head Start experience do better in school than other poor children without preschooling.[42] However, its 2007 funding of $6.8 billion is a cut in real dollars and will accommodate fewer than one million children, a small percentage of those eligible.[43]

Housing

The federal government has many programs to support home ownership and has several agencies that help veterans, farmers, and low-income families obtain

This 55,000-ton pile of raw sugar is part of the surplus that costs taxpayers $1.4 million a month to store. Sugar subsidy programs cost American consumers $2 billion annually.

government spends a relatively small amount each year to pay for shelters for the homeless and to provide vouchers to defray housing costs for poor families.

Agriculture

The government has established separate loan agencies to help farmers buy homes, retain land, or expand operations. Like farm subsidy programs, which were designed to help the average farm family hang on to their farms, these programs provide more help to the well-off than to struggling family farmers. Moreover, though termed "loans," billions of these funds are written off as bad debt.

Agriculture support also includes subsidized land and water. Ranchers are subsidized by a Bureau of Land Management policy that allows them to graze their cattle on 270 million acres of public land at one-eighth the cost per animal that a private landowner would charge. Despite many attempts to revise these fees upward, ranchers believe they are entitled to use of these public lands, even though some land is eroding from overgrazing.

The federal government also offers ranchers and farmers billions of dollars in subsidized water. Most water project costs are never repaid. For example, the water brought to California by the $8.8 billion California Central Valley Irrigation Project created wealth for huge corporate as well as family farms. But of the $36,000-per-acre cost of irrigation, only $527 per acre is returned to the government.

Because of federal subsidies, water is cheap, and farmers grow water-intensive crops even in naturally arid areas. Most of the water used by California farmers is for pasturing cows and sheep and for growing crops that can be grown more economically elsewhere, such as alfalfa, cotton, and rice, which normally are grown only in very wet climates. These crops use far more water than the grapes, nuts, oranges, strawberries, and tomatoes we associate with California farming.[46]

mortgage loans at subsidized rates. However, most spending is to help middle-class Americans, not those at lower income levels struggling to find housing.

The Federal Housing Finance Board, which supervises twelve Federal Home Loan Banks (the best known of which go by their nicknames, Fannie Mae and Freddie Mac), makes it easier for lower- and middle-income families to obtain mortgages. They do not issue mortgages but buy them from other lenders, freeing those lenders to issue more mortgages. Through these banks, the government underwrites more than three-fourths of all mortgages on single-family homes.[44]

One of the Bush administration's priorities is fostering what it calls "an ownership society." Home ownership has been encouraged, even in the face of record debt held by consumers. The Fed helped this policy along by keeping interest rates low during a period of massive government and consumer borrowing. With this support, house sales, especially those of larger homes with bigger mortgages, increased significantly.[45] In comparison with its underwriting of home loan banks, the

Tax Subsidies

In addition to direct payments, such as farm subsidies and Social Security benefits, and indirect subsidies, such as those for education and Medicare, a third type of federal subsidy is provided through tax breaks. The biggest government subsidies for the well-off take this form, distinguishing them from the direct payment programs that characterize aid to the poor. The cost of these programs is counted in lost revenues rather than cash outlays. A tax subsidy permits some people and corporations to pay much less in taxes

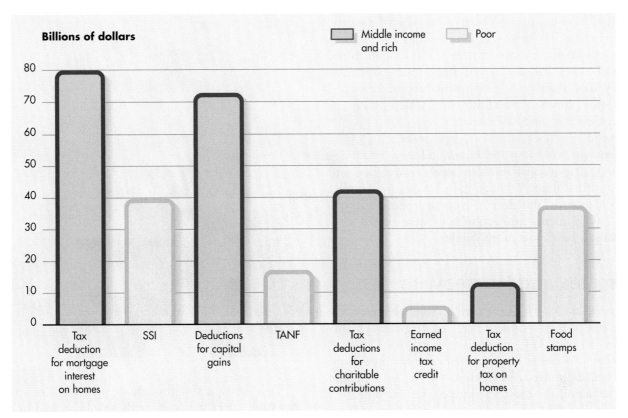

Billions of dollars

Middle income and rich ▢ Poor ▢

FIGURE 17.3 ■ The Cost of Federal Programs for the Poor and Tax Breaks for the Middle Income and Rich

SOURCE: Office of Management and Budget, *Budget of the United States, Fiscal Year 2007* (Washington, D.C.: Government Printing Office, 2006), 296–298, *Analytical Perspectives*, tab. 19-3.

than they would if the nominal rate for their income bracket was applied.

Corporations

The biggest winners in the tax-subsidies-for-the-well-off category are corporations. The usual reason cited for extending so many tax incentives to business is to encourage economic and job growth that will benefit the population at large. Although some tax breaks do lead to the creation of jobs, many do not, or at least not domestically.

The vast array of current tax breaks for business are seen by their critics as a form of welfare. **Corporate welfare** has been defined as "any action by local, state, or federal government that gives a corporation or an entire industry a benefit not offered to others." The benefit can be in the form of services, low-interest loans, grants, concessions of land, or tax exemptions, deferrals, or lowered rates.[47] Mining and logging companies, for example, lease federal land at bargain-basement prices. Tax write-offs for capital gains cost taxpayers more than income support to the elderly poor and disabled, and deductions for charitable contributions cost the Treasury more than it spends on food stamps (see Figure 17.3).

It would be easy to go on at length listing costs of various business tax breaks, but they only count as welfare if taxpayers get nothing in return for the subsidies. In many instance this seems to be the case. During the 1990s, when AT&T, Bechtel Corp., Boeing, General Electric, and McDonnell Douglas Corp. were awarded 40 percent of all loans and grants made by the Export-Import Bank, employment by those firms dropped by 38 percent. During a period in the late 1980s and early 1990s, when General Electric was buying up other companies, including RCA, it received several billion dollars in tax breaks while reducing its workforce by 165,000.[48] And while Enron was receiving government subsidies for developing oil fields, it was bilking shareholders and California's utility customers out of billions of dollars.

Tax breaks to encourage job creation are among the most controversial. Legislation setting a far lower tax rate on foreign than domestic earnings of corporations was intended to encourage the reinvestment of those savings to create jobs in the United States. All they led to was a tax giveaway that encouraged investment abroad. One estimate is that state, local, and federal tax breaks offered to attract businesses to relocate cost taxpayers from $44,000 to $29 million per job created.[49] Policy makers continue to subscribe to the argument that tax breaks for corporations will produce new jobs despite the fact that most job growth in the United States has long come from small businesses. (They have their own government support agency— the Small Business Administration, which writes or sells off millions in loans each year.)

Another major cost of corporate welfare is cleanup of toxic emissions into the air and industrial waste deposited in municipal sewage systems, waterways, and toxic waste dumps. Although corporations are required to bear more of the cleanup costs than they were before environmental protection laws were passed, taxpayers still bear most of the burden.[50]

Families and Homeowners

Corporations may be the biggest winners of tax subsidies, but the government has not neglected mainstream America. It is "working families" that Congress most likes to cite as the beneficiaries of tax breaks and tax cuts, and indeed, some are not trivial. In 2007, the tax deduction for mortgage interest, for example, will cost the U.S. Treasury five times as much as payments to TANF recipients. Families also receive tax credits for child care, adoption costs, school and college tuition, out-of-pocket health care costs, and tax deferrals for private savings plans.

Direct aid for the poor often produces outrage; even health care and income support (Medicare and Social Security) for the middle class have their critics. But subsidized services (mortgage underwriting, college scholarships, and grazing rights, for example) and tax breaks for the middle class and the well-off are subjected to much less scrutiny, perhaps because these benefits are more hidden and different in kind than benefits for senior citizens and the poor. It may also be because the most well-off, through their campaign contributions, have a greater say in the content of public debates.

Current Issues

Health Care

In 2004, 16 percent of the nation's economy, the highest share on record, was spent on health care: $6280 a person.[51] About half of that was paid for by various government programs. After the Medicare drug benefit for seniors went into full effect in 2006, the government also was paying for half of all prescription drugs sold in the country.

A stumped senior ponders the Medicare drug plan.

Justin Sullivan/Getty Images

The irony is that though we spend twice as much per capita than the country that ranks second to us in health spending, we have less to show for it. We rank below all other countries in the industrial world in infant mortality and life expectancy. And, according to a study by the *Journal of the American Medical Association*, the richest one-third of Americans are sicker than the poorest one-third in England, even though Britain spends only about 40 percent as much per person on health care as the United States.[52]

Big spending has not made us careful or efficient either: the Institute of Medicine of the National Academy of Sciences has estimated that up to 98,000 Americans die needlessly each year because of medical errors in the nation's hospitals and that medication errors harm 1.5 million people and kill several thousand each year.[53] Nor has spending given us comprehensive coverage; forty-six million Americans remain uninsured. About eighteen thousand adults between the ages of twenty-five and sixty-four die every year for lack of health coverage, and the economy loses $65 to $130 billion in productivity and other costs.[54]

The Irrationality of the Existing System
For years, policy makers have heaped scorn on nations with national health care systems, arguing that care in those countries was poorer and rationed. We've already seen that the outcomes in our health care system are inferior to those in many other nations. It is also clear that, though we pretend otherwise, in reality we too have a rationing system for medical care; it is rationed by ability to pay. If you can afford it or if you have the

right insurance, you can have the most expensive treatment, even if it will prolong your life only a few days or make you only marginally better off or not better off at all. If you do not have the money or insurance coverage, you may die at an early age even though you have a treatable condition.

Medical care is also not equally accessible to all racial and ethnic groups. Analysts have concluded that neither income nor educational differences explain the poorer health of African Americans compared with the United States population overall; they conclude that racial discrimination plays a large part in explaining why blacks receive less and poorer-quality health care than others.[55]

Medical care is also not well rationed over the life cycle; we spend a very large proportion of health care resources on people in the last year of their lives. Thirty percent of all Medicare costs are incurred for last-year care, much of it for the last month of treatment!

Other nations also ration medical care, but they do it in a different way. In Canada, which has a government-funded national health care system, more is spent on preventive medicine. Expensive tests are reserved for those with a high probability of benefiting from them. People sometimes have to wait for elective surgery, imposing an inconvenience but ensuring that facilities will be used more efficiently. In several European countries, rationing is done by a kind of triage process that determines who should have first priority for expensive procedures. For example, except in life-threatening circumstances, priority for an elective hip replacement would be given to a middle-aged working person over an elderly person.

The high cost and lack of access that are characteristic of our medical system have many other negative effects. Health insurance and medical bills stress household budgets and limit the ability of families to save, especially for college educations. Health premiums are rising faster than inflation; the average cost of private health insurance for a family of four in 2006 was more than $11,000. Although families are spending proportionately less on food and clothing than they did thirty years ago, they are spending much more on housing and health care.[56] For families who cannot afford health insurance, a major illness can lead to bankruptcy. By comparison, a patient in Sweden never has to spend more than $118 a year out of pocket for visits to the doctor, and the state pays all medical costs above $236 a year. In Belgium, where the "right to health" is an article in the constitution, a three-day treatment for a cancer patient costs only $2000, and the patient pays only $36.[57]

Health care costs are a burden on corporations as well as families. After corporate income taxes, employee benefits are the largest structural cost to business. In 2002, General Motors spent $4.5 billion on health care for its employees.[58] By one estimate, if we had government-funded national health insurance plan similar to those in Canada and Europe, U.S. automakers could save at least $1300 per vehicle.[59] High health costs drive employers to relocate abroad where the cost of labor is low, as in developing countries, or where the government picks up the costs of health care, as in Canada, Europe, and Japan.

Why High Costs?

Our system of medical care is a costly mixture of private and public. Two decades ago, government rejected publicly financed universal health care coverage in favor of encouraging private, for-profit health maintenance organizations (HMOs). HMOs are groups of doctors who agree to provide full health care for a fixed monthly charge. HMOs were seen as the way to keep down health costs. This has not worked. Health care as a proportion of our gross domestic product has jumped from about 11 percent to 16 percent in twenty-years and is still increasing.[60]

Waste and inefficiency account for 10 to 20 percent of health care costs.[61] Administration takes 25 percent, largely because we have so many different providers, both private and public. Each has its own rules and system for managing paperwork.[62]

Another major contribution to escalating costs are new drugs and new medical technology that make it possible to do more for more people.[63] In 2003, for example, drug costs rose more than 9 percent, but only one-third of the rise came from price increases. The rest came from "more people . . . using more drugs in more expensive combinations."[64]

The aging population is another reason for higher costs. One out of six people can now expect to live to the age of one hundred. The elderly have more health problems than younger people, so as their numbers increase, the demand for medical services rises. The growing reliance on high technology such as CT scanners, MRI, dialysis, and laser equipment, intensive care units, and other sophisticated medical tools costs billions of dollars. High technology has made possible organ transplants and other procedures unheard of a few years ago available today, but at a huge cost.

Hospitals all want the most sophisticated equipment, which drives up overall costs and results in duplication and underutilization. Many Americans have become obsessed with state-of-the-art technology and do not want to drive long distances to have access to it. If one hospital has a sophisticated machine, others nearby also want it, even if there are not enough patients in the vicinity to justify the extra machines. The

"Kids, your mother and I have spent so much money on health insurance this year that instead of vacation we're all going to go in for elective surgery."

resulting competition for patients encourages marketing to persuade doctors to use the equipment so that it can be paid for. The public—as patients, insurance buyers, and taxpayers—picks up the bill.

High-technology medicine also creates new demands for medical procedures even though higher spending for more treatments does not produce significantly better results than lower spending and fewer treatments.[65] When better procedures become available, more people want them, so even if the new procedures are cheaper than the old, the total cost is higher. Surgery for cataracts, an eye disease affecting many elderly, is an example. Until two decades ago, surgery was painful and often ineffective. Now new techniques and materials allow plastic lenses to be inserted into the eye surgically, greatly improving vision. As a consequence, many more people receive the surgery, at a greatly increased overall cost, even though the individual procedures cost less.[66]

The financial and even legal pressure to perform many unnecessary procedures also drives up costs. One-quarter to one-third of all medical procedures are unneeded or are actually harmful.[67] A patient's likelihood of surgery for common problems may vary more with where she lives than the condition itself. Although there are wide variations in cost for the same procedure, depending on the city of region of country, evidence suggests that spending, by itself, has no overall effect on quality of care.[68]

In 2004, almost eight thousand U.S. doctors (about 1 percent of all practicing physicians) published a letter in the *Journal of the American Medical Association* arguing that private sector solutions have failed and calling for the elimination of for-profit hospitals and

HMOs. The physicians who signed the letter advocate a government-financed health insurance system covering every American. They said it would save billions.[69]

The Bush administration reforms have focused on privatization, encouraging people on Medicare and Medicaid to enroll in HMOs and private drug insurance programs. Bush has increased tax credits for the purchase of private health insurance and created new deductions for medical savings accounts. But tax credits will not do anything to address rising costs, nor will they improve access and decrease costs for low-income families who do not have the money to buy insurance or open medical savings accounts.

The fact that government insurance programs cover many of the people most likely to be sick—the elderly and the poor—and private health insurers cover those at least risk—the young, the well, and the well-off—means that it is very hard to hold down costs of publicly funded programs. To compensate, state governments, which bear a large share of the costs, are tightening access to Medicaid and the federal government is limiting the amount it will reimburse doctors and hospitals for services provided to patients enrolled in Medicare and Medicaid.

Bush proposed cutting by as much as 20 to 30 percent payments to hospitals for complex treatments and new technologies provided to patients not ill enough to need them.[70] In addition Congress gave states the authority to require premiums or higher copayments from those enrolled in Medicaid, a policy the Congressional Budget Office predicts will leave thousands more without health coverage. This is of special concern to the one-sixth of Medicaid recipients who are eligible for coverage because of mental or physical disabilities and who could be left without the therapy, rehabilitation, personal care services, or other necessities they need to cope with daily life.[71]

With runaway budget deficits and public spending on health now rising faster than private spending, government has to take some action to contain costs. But Congress has shown little interest in major reform. It continues to approach health care much like all other social welfare issues: with changes and benefits targeted at specific groups. There is no commitment to an overall policy on health care and no consensus on who is responsible for providing it.

Greater privatization as the principal means for holding down costs makes little sense when the administrative costs of HMOs are higher than those for Medicare. The reason administrative costs are so much higher for private insurance plans is that, in the attempt to be as profitable as possible, they are highly selective. They spend a great deal of money sorting policy applicants to find those at least risk for health problems. Medicare covers everyone sixty-five and older who has paid into the program, just as the VA hospitals are open to all who have service-related health problems. An inclusive program would do more than cut administrative costs; with comprehensive coverage of all children we could treat or prevent the onset in adulthood of diseases that will impose untold costs in productivity and treatment further down the road.

This points to what is perhaps the most irrational aspect of the current approach to health care: the vast underspending on prevention. The incidence of those health problems predicted to be the greatest burden on the health care system in coming years—obesity, diabetes, AIDS, for example—could all be reduced through preventive health care.

The lack of attention paid to preventive care is compounded by government programs that encourage the very behavior that contributes to these preventable diseases: subsidies for tobacco that ends up in cigarettes; for corn, that allow agribusiness to churn out the cheap fructose-laden foods and sodas that are available in every vending machine; and for grain farmers to produce huge surpluses instead of growing more fruits and vegetables. Instead of a commitment to preventive care and to policies that promote it, government has agreed to subsidize medical services. Though the fear of "socialized" medicine has been an obstacle to thorough health care reform for decades, the irrationality and cost of the existing system is changing the opinions of some powerful interests, including corporations saddled with the high costs of health insurance benefits.

Social Security

As a retirement program for everyone, Social Security continues to be politically popular among all groups, save the very young, because it alleviates some of the economic risks of growing old. It is a great public policy success story, but the program does have problems. The aging of the population in combination with the heavy borrowing from the trust fund to pay current expenses has left the program in need of reform. Its popularity, however, makes a frank discussion of basic changes in the fundamental nature of the program politically risky, as Bush discovered when he tried to sell his partial privatization program in 2005. (See "You Are There" in Chapter 11) There is also serious disagreement over how much trouble the system is in and whether it needs another rules adjustment, such as it received in the 1970s and 1980s, or a radical overhaul.

There is agreement on the two major problems facing the Social Security system. One is that the ratio of active workers to retirees is decreasing. Even though immigration keeps us from zero growth, there will be only 2.2 active workers for each Social Security benefi-

ciary in 2031, compared with 3.3 in 2006. This reduction in the ratio of active to retired workers is because the number of people over age sixty-five is growing and is expected to almost double from thirty-seven million in 2006 to seventy-one million in 2031.[72]

The second problem is the fact that presidents and Congress continue to use Social Security trust fund surpluses to offset budget deficits. In 2007, the fund will collect over $300 billion more than it needs to make payments to current retirees. The years of overcollection were by design, in anticipation of the drain on the trust fund that will occur as the baby boom generation (those born between 1946 and 1964) reaches retirement age. Reforms passed in the 1980s increased payroll tax rates and the amount of income taxed and forced virtually all U.S. workers into the program. The intention was to lock down this surplus so that as the population aged and the number of younger workers paying into the program declined, the surplus would be there to cover payouts to the growing number of retirees. But during years when general revenue funds are insufficient to cover government spending, budget makers in the White House and Congress borrow from the Social Security trust fund to reduce deficits.

When the years of overpayments end and the money in the trust fund is needed to pay benefits, the government will have to repay what it has borrowed from the fund. Although the government will surely find a way to make good on its commitment to retirees, millions of Americans are skeptical; one poll showed that young people were more likely to believe in flying saucers than in the viability of the Social Security system.[73]

Some advocates of privatizing the system want to spread doubt and even panic about its stability and repeatedly predict that the Social Security trust fund will go broke "in the next few years" unless changes are made. However, the program's trustees say that Social Security will be financially able to make full payments to all beneficiaries until 2018 and payments of about three-fourths of the current benefit level from then until 2042 even if no changes are made in the program.

Those who are opposed to the idea of a government-managed retirement system tend to favor restructuring Social Security. The most significant and persistent of these proposals involve some degree of privatization of the payroll withholding tax. The Bush administration favored this approach, although it refused to call it privatization because that word does not play well in polls. As discussed in Chapter 11's "You are There," the Bush proposal would have allowed people who want to invest some of the money now withheld from their paychecks for Social Security in stocks, bonds, or funds of their choosing to set up their own retirement accounts.

But reductions in contributions in even small percentages would put the fund in an even more tenuous financial position as the number of beneficiaries explodes over the next few decades. However, supporters of this approach believe that those who invest on their own will be able to get a much higher rate of return than the government does on its investment of money in the trust fund, which invests solely in low-risk, low-interest government securities.

There are two formidable obstacles to the partial privatization plan. If the stock market falters or if bad investment decisions are made, millions of seniors may end up having insufficient retirement income. Most people have no special expertise in investment strategies, and whereas putting the money in stocks and bonds or mutual funds will provide a windfall in commissions for investment firms, there is no guarantee that the money will earn a higher rate of return for the investor or even that it will not be lost. The stock market and mutual funds were rocked by fraud and corruption from 2001 to 2004, and private pension plans have been failing at an alarming rate, leaving taxpayers to pay part of the bill for bankrupt companies. When retirement arrives for individuals who have lost the money invested or earned a lower return than Social Security could have provided, would they have the right to turn to the government to supplement their lower Social Security benefits, and if so, where would government get the money?

The larger and more immediate problem is where the trust fund will get the money to pay benefits to baby boomer retirees if younger workers are allowed to take up to a third of their contributions into the private market. Some Bush advisers say the answer is to borrow the money that would be needed—anywhere from $800 billion to $2 trillion—to pay retiree benefits.[74] With 40 percent of the national debt already held by foreigners and no ready domestic sources with the amount of money needed, the question is where the government would find enough lenders to fund Social Security and to cover the rest of the shortfall in spending. Critics in Bush's own party say the borrowing scheme is unrealistic and that partial privatization cannot happen without raising taxes, reducing benefits, or both.

Reducing benefits would present another set of problems because 52 percent of the workforce has no private pension coverage to supplement Social Security benefits and 31 percent of Americans have no retirement savings other than what they have paid into Social Security.[75]

For more than two million of these retirees, Social Security payments are already insufficient to meet the cost of living, so a further reduction could cause an even greater number to look to supplemental payments from the SSI program. And because SSI is funded by general revenues, not the trust fund, any large jump in the number of beneficiaries would further increase budget deficits.

In lieu of big structural changes in the system, small changes similar to those made in the 1980s are being phased in; one is a gradual raising of the retirement age—something that makes sense given how much longer people are living and working. There are

"My pension has been renegotiated, and in lieu of a monthly check I'll receive a crateful of seasonal fruit."

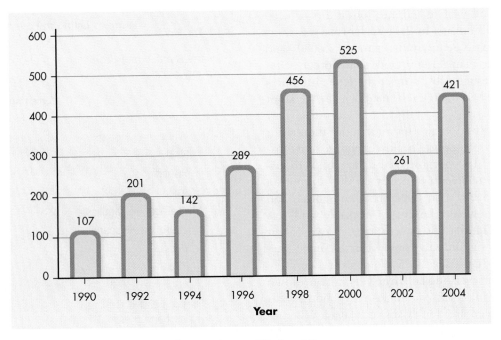

FIGURE 17.4 ■ Ratio of CEOs' Pay to Workers' Pay

The pay of the average corporate CEO is now almost 400 times that of the average worker, but only the first $94,200 of earnings are subject to Social Security tax. Some Social Security reformers want to build up the trust fund by making all of the earnings of those making more than $100,000 subject to Social Security tax.

SOURCE: Institute for Policy Studies and United for a Fair Economy. CEO compensation based on *Business Week* annual compensation surveys; pay of average worker based on Bureau of Labor statistics data.

also periodic increases in the share of earnings subject to payroll tax. Many argue that an individual's whole salary should be taxed, a change that would significantly increase the trust fund (see Figure 17.4). Other tweaking that has been tried is reducing the automatic annual cost-of-living increases recipients receive. Another possibility, not yet considered, is to reverse the income tax cut for the highest income earners instead of making it permanent as the Bush administration wants. The extra revenue would go a long way toward ending budget deficits and the need to borrow from the Social Security trust fund.

Reforming Aid to the Poor

Most analysts agree that the TANF program was a success from the standpoint of getting people off welfare and into the labor force. The new time limits and work requirements forced many states to reorient their efforts toward helping clients develop job and life skills instead of passive assistance to see that they had food and shelter. By 2005, the number of people on welfare rolls had dropped by 60 percent.

TANF has shown that, at least in good economic times, welfare rolls can be reduced and more people employed. For people healthy and skilled enough to hold down jobs and lucky enough to find them, "wel-

fare to work" has been successful in ending dependency on cash assistance. However, perhaps fewer than half of all mothers who left welfare found full-time jobs; others found only part-time work. Based on state reports, average earnings are about $8 an hour, or $16,000 a year, and that is for those lucky enough to find full-time work.[76] Lack of suitable skills for today's economy is a significant impediment to getting a job that pays a living wage, as are the mental or physical disabilities, learning disabilities, and substance abuse problems plaguing a sizable proportion of those on welfare. Any one of these conditions makes finding and keeping a job difficult, and many unemployed have more than one of these problems.[77]

When TANF was reauthorized in 2005, the Bush White House demanded that the program be amended to increase the work requirement to forty hours a week, sixteen of which could be in education and skills training, but only for a period of three months. Opponents in Congress and in state government argue that this is unrealistic given the job market and the decline in funding available for child care. The pressure to meet the welfare-to-work requirement is especially difficult for states where job growth has lagged, such as Michigan. In California, too, which is a settlement site for hundreds of thousands of immigrants, there are not enough low-skills jobs to place all of the people it needs to move off welfare and into jobs if it is to keep its federal TANF dollars. In 2006 California was short over 60,000 jobs, Pennsylvania almost 23,000, and Michigan more than 11,000, and many other states did not have enough jobs to meet the federal requirement of having half their TANF recipients in the labor force.[78]

The reauthorization also set aside more money for Bush's initiative to support "healthy marriage and family formation."[79] The purpose of the program is to encourage welfare recipients to marry on the assumption that children do better in two-parent households and that child care would be more workable and less costly.[80] It is a fact that the poverty rates in two-parent households are significantly lower than in single-parent households (see Table 17.1). Women earn on average 75 cents for every dollar earned by a man (down from 76 cents in 2003), so single-parent households headed by women are doubly disadvantaged. Whether taxpayer-funded programs can convince parents to marry is another issue.

The Bush administration continued the process of devolution to the states begun by Clinton. The most significant tool in this process is the **superwaiver**, blanket exemptions that free states from federal poverty program standards and requirements so they have much greater latitude to set standards and eligibility for a wide range of poverty programs, including TANF (with the exception of the work requirement), food stamps, child care, employment and job-training services, and public housing.[81] States have long been able to obtain waivers from federal agencies freeing them from requirements for a specific program, but superwaivers allow exemptions on all federally mandated poverty programs.

The superwaiver encapsulates the Bush approach to welfare reform in that it signals an intent to withdraw the federal government from such programs as far as possible. Many members of Congress are very critical of superwaivers because they believe they concentrate authority for program decisions in the executive branch. Governors can go to a cabinet secretary (Health and Human Services, for example) or an agency head and get a superwaiver that could allow them to escape congressionally mandated standards for providing income, educational, and health services to the poor and disabled.[82]

Impact of Reform

The number of families on welfare rolls fell by 60 percent in the decade between TANF's passage and 2005. During those same years the percentage of never-married mothers in the labor force jumped from 49 to 63 percent.[83] It is difficult to know if the drop occurred because of TANF or because of the rapidly growing

| TABLE 17.1 | Families Living in Poverty |

Poverty is much more common in female-headed and minority families.

	Percentage in Poverty
All families	11
White, non-Hispanic	7
Black	24
Hispanic*	21
Asian	8
Married-couple families	5
White, non-Hispanic	5
Black	8
Hispanic*	16
Asian	8
Female-headed families, no husband present	31
White, non-Hispanic	22
Black	40
Hispanic*	39
Asian	13

*Hispanics can be of any race.

Source: U.S. Census Bureau, "Historical Poverty Tables," tab. 2 (www.census.gov); 2006 *Statistical Abstract of the United States*, tab. 699.

economy that led employers to hire people who would not be hired if there were more workers available.

However, in most states the decline in welfare enrollments began three years before TANF went into effect in part due to a booming economy that created twenty-three million jobs during the Clinton administration. By some estimates the strong economy accounted for 35 to 45 percent of the decline in caseloads and the reforms themselves for 25 to 35 percent. A third factor, which may have reduced the number of households on welfare by another 20 or 30 percent, was the expansion of the EITC.[84] Some of the decline may also be attributed to the complexity of the rules and pressure from caseworkers trying to meet their welfare-to-work quotas.

There have been blips in the pattern of declining caseloads. In 2003, after several years of net job losses in the private sector and a rising poverty rate, welfare enrollments did increase before falling again as the economy improved. It remains to be seen if the first round of reductions in welfare rolls can be improved on or if one welfare researcher was correct when he said the huge drop in welfare rolls in the 1990s was "a once-in-a-hundred-years coming together of policies that pushed people off of welfare and pulled people into jobs."[85]

TABLE 17.2 — Distribution of Household Income in the United States, 1980–2001

Income distribution in the United States is becoming more lopsided.

Percentage of Households	Percentage of Income Earned		
	1980	1990	2001
Lowest 20%	4.3	3.9	3.5
Next lowest 20%	10.3	9.6	8.7
Middle 20%	16.9	15.9	14.6
Next highest 20%	24.9	24.0	23.0
Highest 20%	43.7	46.6	50.1
Top 5%	15.8	18.6	22.4

SOURCE: U.S. Census Bureau, Income Inequality Table, IE-3, www.census.gov/hhes/www/income/histinc/ie3.html/.

Why Welfare Reform?

There will never be agreement among welfare reformers on what kinds of reforms are necessary because there is no basic agreement on why people are poor. Those who think that poverty is the fault of the poor because they are deficient in character or effort are far less likely to support government help for the poor than are those who believe that poverty is a product of the economic system, bad luck, and parentage (the wealth of your parents determines a lot about your own opportunities to get ahead).

Although the cost to taxpayers is a frequently stated goal of reform and was one of the forces driving the 1996 welfare reform, it was probably not the primary objective. Income support for the poor pales in comparison to income support and indirect subsidies to millions of far better-off Americans. In 2006 we were spending more on interest payments to service the national debt than we were spending on welfare for the poor. It is likely that playing to the distaste people have for "welfare" and the idea that some recipients are getting something for nothing were at least as important a motivation for reform as saving money.

Improving program performance and getting results for the individual are far more compelling reasons than cost reduction for trying to reform welfare. This would be better for the individual clients and also for the economy and society as a whole. In America, we like to think that everyone can have a chance to achieve to the best of his or her ability and that parents can have a reasonable hope that their children's lives will be better than their own. Moreover, democracies function better when there are no permanent classes of haves and have-nots (see Table 17.2). People who must worry about how to feed and house their families are not going to be full participants in the po-

litical process. By helping sustain an underclass, we undermine the political system itself.

Conclusion: Are Social Welfare Programs Responsive?

Looking at our vast array of social welfare benefits, it would be easy to conclude that government is not only responsive to the American public but hyperresponsive. Through income support programs, subsidized services, and tax breaks, social welfare provides something for everyone while reflecting government's greater responsiveness to individuals and groups who wield political influence. The poor, although comprising more than 12 percent of the population, do not have the influence, organization, or access to win public support for programs benefiting them. In hard times, when support is most needed, programs for the poor often take the brunt of budget cuts. But not all Americans view politics solely in terms of what they get, and some have learned that the growth of an underclass harms everyone.

Most taxpayers define themselves as middle income, and they support services for themselves and others like them. Benefits to the upper classes are tolerated to a large extent because they often take the form of technical or specially tailored tax breaks that most of the public has never heard of. When they do catch the public's attention, often because of abuse—such as offshore tax shelters or business deductions for stock options given to CEOs—they can trigger resentment and reform.

The making of social welfare policy also illustrates our government's lack of an overarching policy or philosophy about its responsibilities for ensuring basic human services. Instead, it responds in piecemeal fashion to crises or to pressure from the most influential interest groups and lobbyists and gives far too little attention to long-term planning. Though Americans worry about the viability of the country's health care system, Congress is too often preoccupied with responding to short-term demands such as holding down drug costs or capping jury awards in malpractice suits.

Finally, it is clear that Congress has established a massive tangle of support programs to protect individuals and businesses from the risks of the same marketplace whose self-regulating properties it loves to praise. Two of the central questions about social welfare policies today have to be whether government assumes too much risk for individuals and for business and whether it assumes more risk for the powerful than for the weak.

Romney Says Yes and No

Governor Romney signed the bill that will require all citizens of Massachusetts to have health insurance coverage by the end of 2008 or pay penalties for refusing. But Romney vetoed eight sections of the bill, including those that established new fees and surcharges on those businesses that do not provide coverage and another that extended dental coverage to those enrolled in Medicaid. A photo-op signing ceremony was staged at Faneuil Hall, with Sen. Kennedy, who helped arrange the federal portion of the financing, and other state leaders. Romney called it "An achievement that comes around once in a generation, and it proves that government can reach across the aisle for the common good." The first line of his press release took care to point out that it was a private, market-based reform.[86]

But Romney had it both ways. He took full credit for passage of a universal coverage health bill that originated in the legislature while vetoing the portions that raised taxes on businesses. The bill had passed the Senate unanimously and the House with only two no votes; thus it was certain the portions of the bill Romney vetoed would be reinstated when it went back to the legislature. And they were. This left Romney able to go out on the campaign trail with the claim he made when signing the bill: "Massachusetts is leading the way with health insurance for everyone, without a government takeover and without raising taxes."[87] That is, without Romney having agreed to a tax increase.

It will take several years to know whether Massachusetts' approach to health care reform works. Projected state expenditures on the program were predicated on health care costs rising no more than 10 percent a year over the next several years and on federal subsidies remaining stable.[88] Either or both of these assumptions might prove faulty.

The projected first-year cost was $1.2 billion, but the state was already paying $1 billion for health insurance programs for only part of the population. With universal coverage, the bill has a good chance of stabilizing premium costs by putting the healthy uninsured people into a common insurance risk pool with those at highest health risk, most of whom had been covered by publicly funded programs. It is the first ever pay-or-play health insurance program for individuals and thus far the most comprehensive effort made to come to grips with the impact of rising health costs. Massachusetts is also the first state to accept the reality that universal access to health care is essential for a competitive economy and a healthy productive labor force.

 To learn more about this topic, go to "you are there" exercises for this chapter on the text website.

Key Terms

Medicaid
Medicare
Social Security
means test
Supplemental Security Income (SSI)
Temporary Aid to Needy Families (TANF)
earned income tax credit (EITC)
food stamps
farm subsidies
corporate welfare
superwaiver

Further Reading

Jason DeParle, *American Dream: Three Women, Ten Kids, and a Nation's Drive to End Welfare* (New York: Viking, 2004). A veteran *New York Times* reporter whose beat is the inner city followed three single welfare mothers for a decade and set down their stories within a short history of welfare policy.

David Cutler, *Your Money or Your Life: Strong Medicine for America's Health Care System* (New York: Oxford University, 2004). A Harvard economist and former health policy adviser to the Clinton administration explains why Clinton's attempt at major health care reform failed and how it should be done.

Barbara Ehrenreich, *Nickel and Dimed: On (Not) Getting By in America* (New York: Metropolitan Books, 2001). Ehrenreich, a well-known writer and women's rights activist (and a biologist by training), tells about her experience doing blue-collar work to find out what it would be like for a woman to try to support herself at minimum-wage jobs. She found that many who worked full time, some holding several jobs, still could not afford both food and housing.

Ronald Jager, *The Fate of Family Farming: Variations on an American Idea* (Hanover, N.H.: University Press of New England, 2004). A philosophy professor who grew up on a family farm discusses the link between agriculture and democracy and looks at how four different types of family farms have adapted to high-tech agriculture, global markets, and government subsidies.

Laurence J. Kotlikoff and Scott Burns, *The Coming Generational Storm* (Cambridge, Mass.: MIT Press, 2004). Boston University economists give a worst-case scenario of the economic burden facing the next generation from accumulated budget deficits and indebtedness to government entitlement and insurance programs.

For Viewing

Dark Days (2000). An award-winning documentary at the Sundance Film Festival, this film looks at the lives of homeless people who live in the train tunnels beneath Manhattan.

The Farmer's Wife (1998). This PBS documentary watched by millions explores what one farm couple had to do to survive economically and the impact on family life. The first hour can be viewed online at www.pbs.org/frontline. Compare this documentary treatment of a real farm family to two commercial films released in 1984 inspired by the despair in farming communities during the wave of farm foreclosures in the 1970s and 1980s: *The River*, with Sissy Spacek and Mel Gibson, and *Country*, with Jessica Lange and Sam Shepard.

Harvest of Shame (1960). This CBS documentary, narrated by Edward R. Morrow, at the time one of the country's most respected newscasters, generated public awareness of malnutrition and poverty among migrant workers in the United States and helped build support for the war on poverty.

The Hospital (1971). Chaos in a hospital—or as it was once billed, "Madness, Murder, and Malpractice"—was never so entertaining as in this Oscar-winning black comedy.

America's War on Poverty (1995). This is a History Channel series on the 1960s legislative program to eradicate poverty in America.

 Electronic Resources

www.aphsa.org
This page of the American Public Human Services Association has information on and analyses of all welfare programs. It is a useful site for tracking the progress of welfare reform.

www.ncsl.org
As part of its responsibility to state legislative bodies, the National Conference of State Legislatures provides assessments of changes in federal welfare law. In addition, this is a source of information on the welfare and Medicaid programs of individual states.

www.socialsecurity.gov
Like all other government agencies, the Social Security Administration has its own website, providing a broad array of information on its history and programs. Here employers can find out how to com-ply with laws governing Social Security taxation, and parents of disabled children can learn how to avoid losing SSI benefits.

www.hhs.gov
This page links to the agencies of the Department of Health and Human Services, including the Food and Nutrition Service, the Administration for Children and Families, and the Centers for Disease Control and Prevention.

www.ewg.org
This website is maintained by the Environmental Working Group to make public farm subsidy disbursements. If you want to know who gets how much, this is the place to look.

ThomsonNOW™

Enter ThomsonNOW™ using the access card that is available with this text or through www.thomsonedu.com/thomsonnow. ThomsonNOW™ will assist you in understanding the content in this chapter with a personalized study plan generated for your needs. A practice test will assess the areas you need to review and provide the tools to fully comprehend those concepts, including an integrated digital eBook, interactive simulations, timelines, video case studies, MicroCase exercises, and InfoTrac College Edition readers and exercises. You'll also be connected to the learning objectives, chapter outline, chapter glossary, flash cards, crossword puzzles, Internet activities, and interactive quizzes found on the companion website.

AP Images/Ian Waldie/Pool

Iraq has more oil than any country in the world except Saudi Arabia. After the United States attacked Iraq, the American troops tried, without success, to protect the oil wells and pipelines from sabotage to ensure the continued flow of oil.

Foreign Policy Goals

Making Foreign Policy in a Democracy

The President and His Inner Circle

Specialists

Congress

Interest Groups and Lobbyists

Public Opinion

Changing Approaches to U.S. Foreign Policy

Isolationism

Containment

Détente

Cold War Revival and Death

Merchant Diplomacy and Multilateralism

Regime Change and Preemptive War

Redefining Security in the Global Age

Physical Security

Economic Security

Conclusion: Is Our Foreign Policy Responsive?

YOU ARE THERE

Should You Attack the President's War Policy?

You are John Murtha, sixteen-term Democratic congressman from rural western Pennsylvania. It is November 2005 and you are increasingly troubled by the way the war is going in Iraq. You need to make a decision about whether to continue to voice your concerns behind the scenes or to go public, criticizing the president as commander in chief. Between active duty and the reserves you spent thirty-seven years in the Marines. You enlisted as a private during the Korean War and left in 1990 as a colonel. During your active service in Vietnam you were awarded two Purple Hearts, a Bronze Star, and a Distinguished Service award. You were the first Vietnam veteran elected to the House and during your thirty-two years there, military and veteran affairs have been your area of specialization. You have maintained your contacts, from enlisted men and women and field commanders, up to the top Pentagon brass.

You supported the invasion of Iraq, but looking at the rising death toll, the huge dollar cost driving up deficits, and no end in sight, you have come to the conclusion that "We're the target; we're part of the problem," and that it is time to reevaluate our strategy.[1]

What really bothers you is the administration's unwillingness to make any major adjustments in policy or to admit it entered the war unprepared and on false premises.

You were especially offended when Secretary of Defense Donald Rumsfeld said last December, "As you know, you go to war with the Army you have. They're not the Army you might want or wish to have at a later time." You have spent your career trying to get the best of everything for the troops—equipment, training, medical care—and have been arguing for some time that our forces in Iraq were undermanned and underequipped. On your trips to Iraq you found "44,000 troops without body armor and shortages of up-armored Humvees and jammers."[2]

But you are worried about more than underequipped troops; you say that the spending in Iraq is "a gross misallocation of resources," that our annual spending there dwarfs "the combined budgets of all other programs . . . to fight terrorism."[3] The cost of the war has risen from $4 billion a month in 2003 to $8 billion a month; that is $267 million a day, or $11 million an hour.[4] You believe this spending has left active duty and reserve units not deployed to Iraq at their lowest point of readiness since World War II. You say it is pointless to continue debating our role in the Middle East and North Korea without a military capable of carrying out strategic requirements.[5]

You believe the cost would be worth it if we were doing what we should be doing: striking where the leadership and strength of al-Qaeda

The Iraqi insurgency against the American presence has evolved into a virtual civil war between two rival Muslim sects.

are and winning the ideological struggle for the hearts and minds of the Muslim world. These you believe are the two "central fronts" in the war against terrorism. Instead we are trapped in the "ultimate" asymmetrical war, having overwhelming military, economic, and logistical power but losing against forces better able to marshal their geographic, linguistic, religious, and cultural resources.

Still you think we *could* have won if the president had committed to an all-out effort. Though the president talks about the war as if it were an all-out effort to save civilization, he did not mobilize the country or call for a draft; he did not send nearly as many troops as the Chairman of the Joint Chiefs said we needed when the war was being planned, and he has pushed through tax cuts four years in a row, the only tax cuts ever passed during a prolonged war. So the rhetoric has not matched the reality.

As Iraqi war casualties mounted, you began making weekly trips to nearby Walter Reed Hospital to visit the wounded, spending a lot of time in the rehabilitation wards with amputees and those severely maimed. This had a big impact on getting you to where you are

now. One of your House colleagues, a fellow Catholic, says you are going through "a long night of the soul."[6]

Even though you are the ranking member on the Defense Appropriations subcommittee, you refuse to use Congress's main check on presidential war-making powers—the purse strings—to bring about change. No president can fight a war without funding, but you will not consider cutting appropriations because you think only the troops will suffer. This leaves only a few options: you can continue working behind the scenes, quietly making your views known in the Pentagon and White House, or you can go public with your criticism of current war policy.

There are many reasons to try to bring about change quietly, and you "like to do things behind the scenes," avoiding public confrontations. Unlike some colleagues, you are not fond of the spotlight and do not seek that kind of publicity. Moreover, with the kind of contacts you have in Washington there are certainly avenues open to make your views known at the highest levels.[7] You have long been considered one of the Pentagon's best friends in Congress. But you think of your former mentor, the late House Speaker Tip

O'Neill, who told President Johnson in 1967 that Vietnam was a lost cause. Maybe it is your turn to deliver a similar message to President Bush about Iraq.[8] But Tip O'Neill was a career politician speaking to another career politician; you are a career military man, used to respecting the chain of command, especially in wartime. You have always supported the troops. So the idea of *publicly* challenging the commander in chief's policy while troops are engaged in combat weighs on you heavily. There are also political costs of going public. If you went public, you could become persona non grata in the Pentagon; your network of contacts may dry up, and old friends may turn away from you. Furthermore, you would have to brace yourself for the storm of negative attacks that will surely come from the White House and the Republicans in Congress.

But there are also good reasons to go public. In private conversations with high-ranking military officials, you have been getting a different account of how the war is going than you hear from the White House and Defense Department. You know that the public is not hearing the truth about the war, at least the truth as seen by the some of the military's top officers. You also know that, ultimately, it is Congress that sends troops to war and therefore it is your obligation "to speak out for them." Speaking out might rally more public support for policy change and thus may actually accomplish something.

What do you do: continue to privately convey your unhappiness with current war policy or go public?

The foreign policy of the United States has a substantial impact on the world, yet we are not all-powerful. We are one of many nations; decisions about war and peace and about trade and diplomacy are made by people in all nations. In this sense, public expectations about what we can achieve have often been unrealistically high.

Yet we are the world's most powerful nation in terms of both military and economic strength. Thus our power, and how we use it, has a tremendous impact on people throughout the world.

In the 1990s, many of the resources that had been devoted to competition with the former Soviet Union were redirected toward other goals. We suffered from a sense of uncertainty because the Cold War with Soviet bloc countries, which had defined much of our foreign policy since the late 1940s, was over. The nature of international cooperation and competition changed, and we were forced to rethink the means we use to pursue our foreign policy objectives. During the unprecedented period of peace and prosperity at the end of the century, we were more inward looking and less willing to devote as much of our energies and resources to foreign policy as we had in the past. As we shifted from a world divided between East and West to one increasingly linked by the forces of globalization, much of the world left behind the great power struggles of the Cold War and immersed itself in trade rivalries and economic competition.

At the outset of the twenty-first century, as the sole remaining superpower, we settled into a kind of triumphalism grounded in a belief that the Western ideals of democracy, capitalism, and free trade had become the world's agenda. One pundit even called it "The End of History."[9] In this atmosphere of unrivaled military power, the United States experienced the first attack on its territory since the Japanese bombed Pearl Harbor in 1941 and the first attack on the continental United States since the War of 1812.

In this chapter, we examine past and present foreign policy goals, how foreign policy decisions are made, and how foreign policy concerns have changed over time. Then we discuss why the challenges policy makers face in an era of globalization and new security threats require adjustments in how we pursue our foreign policy goals.

Foreign Policy Goals

The goals any nation has and the means it uses to pursue them are influenced by its traditions, core values, ideology, and geopolitical situation (that is, the advantages and limitations imposed by geographical location, size, and wealth relative to other nations). Foreign policies are the strategies adopted and actions taken by a government to achieve its goals in its relationships with other nations. These actions range from informal negotiations to waging war, from writing position papers to initiating trade boycotts. They may require economic, political, cultural, or military resources.

The art of foreign policy making includes choosing means suitable to the objective sought. Due to our size and great wealth, huge diplomatic corps, military forces, and intelligence establishment, we have the fullest possible range of foreign policy instruments at our disposal. Sometimes the possession of so many means of pursuing foreign policy objectives affects the setting of goals; that is, the more a country is able to do, the more it may try to do.

Our primary foreign policy goal, like that of every other nation, is to protect our physical security. Until the era of long-range bombers and ballistic missiles, achieving this goal meant preventing land invasions, and in this we have been successful. Our success was due largely to our separation from the other major powers by two oceans and being bounded on the north and south by two friendly countries. In the nuclear era, when we could be attacked by air by long-range bombers and intercontinental ballistic missiles launched by land or sea, we had to develop an air as well as a ground defense.

In today's era of terrorist attacks—with conventional weaponry or biological, chemical, or nuclear weapons of mass destruction—physical security must be defended against both external and internal attacks. Since September 11, 2001, greater emphasis has been placed on how to prevent terrorist attacks from within and how to stop the proliferation of weapons of mass destruction (WMD). As we will discuss later, how we provide for our physical security in an age of high technology and globalization is undergoing serious rethinking.

A second goal is to help protect the physical security of our neighbors and major democratic allies. Since World War II, we have committed ourselves, through the North Atlantic Treaty Organization (NATO), to join in the defense of Canada and Western, Southern, and now even some Eastern European nations. We also have treaty commitments to Japan, South Korea, and the nations of South and Central America and a bilateral agreement on defense with Taiwan.

A third goal is to protect our economic security. Although the United States is blessed with many natural resources, we must purchase such essential resources as oil, manganese, and tin elsewhere. Safeguarding access to these resources may include stabilizing the governments of producing nations or protecting the sea lanes in which goods are shipped.

Some Americans think humanitarian aid should be a goal of U.S. foreign policy, but others, especially policy makers, prefer to focus on U.S. self-interest, despite dire needs around the globe. Here malnourished Sudanese children wait for aid from international relief agencies.

AP/Wide World Photos

In the 1780s, Thomas Jefferson said he hoped Spain would hold on to its territory in South America until "our population can be sufficiently advanced to gain it from them piece by piece."[10] Since the beginning of the nineteenth century, we have warned off foreign powers from meddling in the affairs of any country in the Americas, and there is still a tendency to see Latin America as "our turf." Since World War II, our sphere of interest has extended around the world. We have sought to influence security arrangements on all continents. Even after the post–Cold War base closures, we still have more military bases and more troops outside our borders than any other country.

We also try to spread our influence by promoting democracy, capitalism, and Western cultural values. Our State Department maintains a system of public libraries around the world to disseminate information on our government, economy, and popular culture and also funds thousands of cultural and academic exchanges between American and foreign artists and scholars each year. More proactively, we fund (to the tune of almost $2 billion in 2006) a good deal of both open and covert democracy promotion through political parties and front organizations in other countries. The Orange Revolution that brought down the Ukraine's authoritarian government after it tampered with election results was achieved with financial support from the United States. At optimum we offer our political and economic systems as models of development and at minimum try to foster a favorable attitude toward the United States that will make it easier for us to achieve our foreign policy goals. But these efforts can be undercut by foreign policy actions that seem to conflict with the values and ideals we promote; the Iraq War, for example, has made it very difficult to promote or sustain favorable attitudes toward the United States, even among our allies.

Our specific foreign policy objectives, such as protecting access to oil in the Middle East, drying up funding sources for terrorist operations, removing trade barriers and increasing U.S. exports, are almost always related to achieving one or more of these four general goals.

Making Foreign Policy in a Democracy

Alexis de Tocqueville was one of the first to remark that it is difficult to have a coherent foreign policy in a democracy. His sentiments have been echoed thousands of times since. Why, when there has been basic agreement on the broad goals of our foreign policy, has the United States had such difficulty articulating a coherent and consistent set of objectives?

Our economic well-being is equally dependent on selling our goods abroad, which in turn depends on how cheaply we can manufacture or grow products desired in other parts of the world and how willing our trading partners are to buy them.

Economic self-interest is almost always a factor in foreign policy, even in dealings with our closest allies, because they do not always want to import U.S. goods that compete with their own. Thus trade missions and participation in the international organizations that govern trade relations are crucial to achieving our foreign policy goals, even though most of the public paid scant attention to them before the 1990s. Today the electronic flow of capital into and out of the country is also essential to our economic viability, so ensuring the privacy of information transfers, including financial transactions and securing computer systems against hackers, is becoming as important to national security as protecting sea lanes.

A fourth overlapping goal is to extend our sphere of influence. Historically, this has meant keeping foreign powers out of the Caribbean and Latin America.

Some of the confusion in foreign policy making arises because we elect new leaders every four or eight years. Inconsistencies within a single administration can also be partly explained by the sheer number of organizations and individuals who in some way influence the process of making and implementing foreign policy: the president, members of Congress, heads of relevant cabinet departments and independent agencies, foreign service officers, chiefs of the armed services, White House staff and other political advisers, interest groups, lobbyists, the media, and the public. Leaders and citizens from other countries may also have some influence when they are crucial to the successful pursuit of an objective. (For example, when he made the decision to invade Iraq, President Bush told the Saudi Arabian ambassador, Prince Bandar—whose country he would need to use as a staging area—before he informed his own secretary of state.) Which groups and individuals have an impact on policy varies greatly with the issue and the decision-making style of the president.

Historically, inconsistencies in our foreign policy were rarely caused by differences among policy makers over fundamental goals but rather over specific actions that should be taken. But between the end of the communist threat and the September 11 attacks, there was disagreement even over the fundamentals. There was confusion about what constituted the primary threats to national security and exactly who and what we should be protecting ourselves from. The direct attack on U.S. soil on 9/11 crystallized our foreign policy focus and Americans united behind the goal of destroying al-Qaeda's terrorist network, just as they had agreed on containing Soviet influence during the Cold War. But once again disagreement emerged on how much intervention in the internal affairs of another country is justifiable, what form that intervention should take, and to what extent fundamental principles of government should be compromised in the name of national security.

Here we look at some of the groups and individuals who influence the foreign policy-making process and how division and conflict among them can affect the content and execution of U.S. policy.

The President and His Inner Circle

As head of state and commander in chief of the armed forces, the president is in control of the nation's diplomatic and military establishments. In addition, as the nexus of the vast diplomatic and military communications and intelligence networks, he has the most complete and privileged access to information of anyone in the policy-making network. In times of crisis, with-

out immediately available alternative sources of reliable information, members of Congress and the public have historically almost always relied on the president's sources. The Clinton years of divided government were a partial exception to this rule; with no overt foreign policy crises, presidential decisions, even those made in response to attacks on U.S. facilities and forces abroad, were constantly challenged by an especially contentious Congress.

Given the central role of the president in foreign policy making and the fact that most presidents enter office with very little foreign policy expertise, it is important to know who advises him. No firm rules dictate whom the president must consult on foreign policy, but usually he gives at least a perfunctory hearing to people who head departments and agencies involved with making or implementing policy. The government officials best positioned to advise the president on foreign policy include the secretaries of defense and state, the national security adviser, and the head of the National Intelligence Agency (NIA). The president also frequently consults others, including the Joint Chiefs of Staff and influential members of Congress.

These individuals represent a wide range of experience and bring different perspectives to the analysis of foreign policy issues. The secretary of state is usually concerned with the nation's diplomatic relations and

"Of course, it would be a different story entirely if we could extract crude oil from stem cells."

Osama bin Laden continues to frustrate American policy makers. He remains popular among Muslims, especially in Pakistan where it is thought he is hiding.

the use of diplomatic channels to implement the president's policies. The secretary of defense (a civilian) is primarily concerned with military and security issues and the use of the military to pursue foreign policy goals. The National Security advisor heads the National Security Council, a team of security specialists working within the Executive Office of the President. They are essentially political advisors whose job is to vet all security-related information coming into the White House and make recommendations to the president.

Members of the Joint Chiefs of Staff are military professionals who give advice to the president on both the readiness of their service arms and the appropriateness of their use in specific situations. Members of Congress may be consulted because they are political allies of the president, because they are in leadership positions crucial for mobilizing support on an issue, or because they have developed expertise in military or foreign policy issues through their committee assignments.

The president may also consult his wife or friends and advisers outside government, not because of their policy expertise but because he trusts in their good judgment and wants the perspective of people close to him who have no organizational interests or policy agenda to advance.

Who the president draws into his inner circle of advisers depends in large part on his experience and decision-making style. President Kennedy, who had almost no foreign policy experience, assembled a committee of cabinet heads and close advisers to help him construct his response to the Soviets during the Cuban Missile Crisis. But during the Persian Gulf crisis, the first Presi-

dent Bush reportedly made the decision to send troops to Saudi Arabia relying almost exclusively on his own judgment and that of a few close advisers.

If a president comes to office with a foreign policy agenda and expects to make his political reputation and leave his mark on history in this policy area, as Richard Nixon and the first George Bush did, he will surround himself with like-minded people and replace those who disagree with him or ignore their advice. Bush Sr. appointed both members of the foreign policy establishment who had held high positions in previous administrations and several associates from his tenure as the Central Intelligence Agency (CIA), director, an organizational tie that made many in Congress uncomfortable.

Ex-governors such as Carter, Reagan, Clinton, and George W. Bush can compensate for their lack of foreign policy experience when they become president by surrounding themselves with experts. Nevertheless, Carter and Reagan chose foreign policy advisers with limited experience and had difficulty maintaining unity among them. In contrast, Clinton appointed an experienced team of advisers, including a number from the Carter administration, but was himself more focused on domestic policy and less decided on foreign policy goals early in his presidency.

George W. Bush came to office with even less international experience than Clinton and a pronounced disinterest in international politics. He chose his entire first-tier foreign policy advisers, and part of the second tier, from those who had served in his father's and earlier Republican administrations. Arguably they were, collectively, the most experienced group of foreign policy advisers assembled by any president since the end of World War II. But some came with predetermined worldviews and their own policy agendas. Donald Rumsfeld wanted to transform the military and brought with him neoconservatives associated with his long-time colleague Richard Cheney. This subset of advisers had a list of objectives, including the overthrow of Saddam Hussein, that it had publicized in the 1990s.[11] Their influence, exercised through the Department of Defense and the vice-president's office, dwarfed advice received from the State Department and the president's own National Security Council. Bush's administration is the only one in American history in which foreign policy is as closely—perhaps more closely associated—with the vice-president than the president.

Specialists

Much further removed from the president are the career specialists in the federal bureaucracy who are not political appointees: the staff of intelligence agencies, area specialists in the State and Defense Departments, and almost all members of the Foreign Service. Although they must implement the president's policy as directed, when giving advice their job is to exercise neutral competence, not to serve a political agenda. However, their briefings may simply be ignored if they do not support policy choices preferred by their superiors. Turf battles between advisers and their agencies can result in incomplete or inaccurate information reaching the highest levels. Agency separation, competition, and even antagonism led to many of the failures and misuses of intelligence prior to and after the September 11 attacks.

Foreign Service Officers

The principal office for carrying out the president's foreign policy, the State Department, has eleven-thousand Foreign Service officers who are experts on every policy area and region of the globe. Ambassadors, the president's personally appointed emissaries to other countries, are often career professionals, but in some of the largest and most important embassies and in some of the smaller but very desirable posts, the ambassador may be a political appointee chosen from among the president's friends or campaign contributors.

The work of Foreign Service officers is divided by function—cultural and military attachés, trade representatives, aid specialists, and consular and political officers, for example. It is common in the most strategically important countries for one or more of these individuals to be an undercover CIA officer. Political officers in

Washington and in our embassies and consulates abroad write daily summaries of important political and economic events in the countries to which they are assigned. This information is used to provide daily briefings for higher-level officials, but almost none of it ever reaches the president's desk, and only a small portion of it can be read even by the secretary of state.

We should not assume that these experts present neutral information that is somehow mechanically cranked out as public policy. Even if the experts do their best to provide the most accurate information and most comprehensive policy alternatives possible, top policy makers see the information through their own perceptual and ideological lenses. Our Vietnam policies failed in part because many of our best Asia experts had been purged from the State Department during the McCarthy era. The Reagan administration ignored advisers who cautioned against its covert policies in Nicaragua and Iran and replaced State Department experts who disagreed with its Central America policies. The second Bush administration ignored both intelligence reports and advice from experts in the State Department in its rush to war in Iraq. High

Tony Cenicola/New York Times/Redux

The United States is offering millions of dollars for information leading to the capture of Osama bin Laden. The reward is printed on matchbooks and posters. However, many villagers are sympathetic to him, and they are aware that anyone who turns him in will not be safe.

turnover in specialist positions has at times put us at a disadvantage relative to our adversaries and allies.

Almost all of the policy-making positions within the foreign policy establishment are held by political appointees who usually stay only a few years. And even career specialists can be ignored or downgraded when their recommendations do not support the preferred policies of a particular administration.

Intelligence Agents

One of the important components in formulating foreign and military policy is economic, military, and diplomatic information gathered by operatives of the government's fifteen intelligence agencies. The best known of these is the CIA, but several cabinet departments (Treasury, State, and Energy) also have intelligence-gathering offices, and Justice has the FBI. The Pentagon has its own Defense Intelligence Agency (DIA), and each of the service arms (Army, Navy, Air Force, Marines) also has an intelligence office. There are separate agencies for high-tech intelligence gathering, such as satellite reconnaissance and aerial mapping. The National Security Agency is so secret its employees cannot be photographed; its funding is part of the "black budget," unknown to the public and to much of Congress (hence its nickname, No Such Agency).

Though novels written about intelligence work focus on undercover agents, and our agencies have many of those, in fact most of the work done by intelligence agencies, including the CIA, involves routine fact collecting, research, and report writing rather than covert operations. The exception are the agencies specializing in electronic and satellite surveillance. Fully 60 percent of the data used to prepare the president's daily intelligence briefing is reported to come from NSA intercepts.[12]

In 2005 all fifteen intelligence operations were put under the supervision of a sixteenth, the NIA, whose head briefs the president daily. The consolidation was undertaken to correct the rivalry and turf wars between agencies that contributed to inefficiencies in data sharing and analysis so criticized after 9/11.[13] It is also meant to discourage policy makers from "analysis shopping," choosing whichever agency's data best supports their policy preferences.[14] How successful the NIA will be in fixing these problems remains to be seen.

Congress

The leading members of congressional committees on foreign affairs and armed services and of the oversight committees for intelligence agencies play a larger role in foreign policy than the average member plays. But Congress as a whole has specific constitutional authority to act as a check on the president's policies through its power to declare and fund wars and the requirement for Senate ratification of treaties and confirmation of ambassadorial and high-level State and Defense Department and intelligence agency officials. Because Congress appropriates all money for carrying out foreign policy, the president is limited in the scope of the actions he can take without congressional approval.

Rivalry between the White House and Congress in foreign policy making intensifies or diminishes with the issue in question. Nowhere is conflict greater than over the use of the military to achieve foreign policy goals. Politicians and scholars have been arguing for more than two hundred years about how Congress's constitutional authority to "declare war" limits the president's authority as commander in chief. The Founders, believing it too dangerous to give war powers to the president alone, were also unwilling to accept wording that would have given Congress the power to "make war." Instead, they gave Congress the power to "declare war," leaving the president, according to James Madison's notes on the debate, "the power to repel sudden attacks."[15] This left Congress and the president to struggle over what constitutes an attack on the United States and when a military intervention is a war.

There have been more than two hundred occasions when the president has sent troops into combat situations without congressional approval. In fact, Congress has exercised its power to declare war only five times, and on only one of those occasions, the War of 1812, did it conduct a debate before issuing the declaration. Yet the two undeclared wars in Korea and Vietnam alone produced almost one hundred thousand American deaths, more than the combined losses of all of our declared wars, except World War II and the Civil War.[16]

The War Powers Resolution, which was intended to curb what Congress believes is presidential usurpation of its authority, has been opposed by every president since Lyndon Johnson. No prior approval was sought for sending troops to Lebanon, Grenada, or Panama, and both Presidents Bush sought it for their actions in Iraq only under pressure. During the Clinton administration, Democrats tried to strengthen the act and Republicans to repeal it; neither effort was successful. As one supporter of the act commented, "Every president finds Congress inconvenient, but we're a democracy, not a monarchy."[17]

In his dealings with Congress over use of the military George W. Bush paid little attention to the War Powers Resolution, concentrating instead on establishing a new interpretation of the president's powers as commander in chief. As part of their attempt to argue that the presidency is a unitary executive with complete authority to direct the work of all executive

Cubans in Miami celebrate upon hearing that Cuban leader Fidel Castro was ill and had ceded power to his brother. Cuban Americans' bitterness toward Castro has influenced American policy toward Cuba.

branch agencies, Justice Department attorneys claimed virtually unchecked powers for the commander in chief in committing and directing the armed forces in combat and in all domestic actions a president judges necessary to achieving military goals. (This issue is discussed in greater detail in Chapter 11.)

Whatever their differences with Congress, presidents in the postwar era have usually proclaimed their desire to have a "bipartisan" foreign policy; that is, they want support from both parties in order to present a united front to the world. Presidents will often try to frame policies in a national security context as a way to pressure Congress into accepting their position, but Congress's role is not simply to rubber-stamp executive branch policies. Presidents especially need bipartisan support when treaties are to be ratified because it is rare for one party to have the necessary two-thirds majority in the Senate or for members of each party to be united in their ranks.

Presidents like to say that in facing the rest of the world, Americans are all on the same side. But this view is too simplistic. Americans come from all over the world and once here look out on the rest of the world from very different vantage points. Party positions, too, differ on these as on most other issues, as shown in roll call votes.[18] Democrats tend to favor lower levels of military spending and higher levels of foreign aid than Republicans and to support interest group demands for worker and environmental protection restrictions on trade agreements, the funding of international agencies, and working multilaterally to achieve goals. Republicans are more likely to support unrestricted trade and military intervention to protect U.S. economic interests and to oppose family planning aid to poor countries and working through the United Nations. They are also more likely than Democrats to oppose placing U.S. troops under foreign command as part of multilateral forces.[19]

Differences between the two major parties on foreign policy are usually apparent in the national platform each party issues in presidential election years. Even so, it often seems that the opposition party has no coherent alternative to the president's policy. This is probably because under normal circumstances, most members of Congress spend their time on the domestic issues that are so important to their constituents (especially at election time). In times of crisis, as when U.S. troops are committed to combat, the opposition party usually rallies in support of administration policy so that the country can present a united front to the world.

Once these troops are actually engaged in battle, those who continue to oppose the president's actions can find themselves in the position of appearing to give higher priority to their policy preferences than to the safety of U.S. troops. At this point, it is very difficult for the opposition party to oppose the president's policy effectively. There are notable exceptions, such as bipartisan criticism of Johnson's and Nixon's Vietnam policies, but this dissent came late in the course of the fighting, when public opinion was turning against the war and administration policies did not seem to be working. Even then, Congress approved virtually all expenditures requested to wage the war.

And even as criticism of George W. Bush's handling of the Iraq war mounted, very few Republicans or Democrats voted against supplemental funding to pay the costs. Most members are fearful that their vote will be seen not as opposition to policy but as a refusal to support U.S. troops, and the president's party loyalists are eager to paint a dissenting vote that way. (See the "You Are There" for this chapter.)

In Congress, members of the opposition party are more likely to state policy alternatives on an *ad hoc* basis, acting as individuals, not for the party. The public may be confused when it hears a half dozen or more policy alternatives presented by members of the same party, and it may even conclude that they are "lone rangers" trying to gain political advantage in a situation that seems to call for national unity.

Interest Groups and Lobbyists

A multiplicity of interest groups are concerned with foreign policy issues: international businesses; public interest groups, such as those that lobby on environmental and human rights issues; veterans' organizations; farmers who grow crops for export; labor unions; and ethnic groups interested in their ancestral lands, such as African, Jewish, Muslim, Arab, Irish, Cuban, Mexican, and Polish Americans.

In general, it is harder for interest groups to affect foreign policy than to influence domestic policy. Part of the reason for this is that the president and the executive branch have greater weight than Congress in day-to-day foreign policy decision making. But interest group activity has always been effective in some policy areas, especially those related to containing communism and regulating trade and foreign investment. For example, electronics industries lobby against national security restrictions that keep them from exporting computer equipment and software that have military applications. Farm and business organizations lobby on behalf of import quotas and tariffs to protect their domestically produced goods and against trade restrictions and embargoes that prevent them from selling their products abroad.

Americans have a long history of trying to win favorable U.S. policy for their countries of birth or ancestry. Some have even undertaken private action in support of home countries: Irish Americans have sold guns to the Irish Republican Army and Jewish Americans to Jews in Palestine trying to establish an independent state (in the territory that became Israel). Cuban Americans have trained a military force on U.S. soil to overthrow the Castro government in Cuba (even though it is illegal to do so under U.S. law). Mexican Americans have

mobilized millions for street demonstrations supporting legal residency for Mexican nationals who entered the country without permission. Arab and Muslim Americans, seeing the effectiveness of these lobbies, are only now seriously organizing to try to influence foreign policy toward Middle Eastern countries.

Perhaps no other nationality group has had as much success in setting the foreign policy agenda for their homeland as Cuban Americans. The strength of their lobby is due in part to a predisposition in Congress for their policy preference and in part to the concentration of their population in one state with a large number of electoral votes (Florida). The Cuban American lobby has been the driving force behind preferential treatment for Cuban immigrants (special terms of entry and financial help from the government) and the maintenance of an economic embargo against the Castro government. In recent years, however, the Cuba lobby has seen its influence decline. U.S. farm and business lobbies, afraid of losing export and investment opportunities on the island to Canada and Europe, succeeded in getting Congress to lift the sanctions on food exports and lighten travel restrictions. As indication of how important an electoral force Cuban Americans are in Florida, Bush toughened sanctions on travel and humanitarian aid before the 2004 election. He did not, however, interfere with agricultural trade deals.

During the past quarter century, three factors have opened up the foreign policy decision-making process to greater influence by interest groups. The first is the growing importance of campaign spending and the rise of political action committees (PACs). Both the president and members of Congress depend on large campaign contributions from interest groups and are thus more vulnerable to their demands.

Second, the personal presidency, in combination with the rise of identity politics, has increased the need of presidents to serve a multitude of constituencies and interests. Under pressure from African American interest groups, Clinton gave U.S. policy toward Africa a prominence it had never had previously. His twelve-day trip to six African nations in 1998 was the first by a U.S. president in twenty years and the most extensive ever. Women's and religious interest groups have also become important lobbies, affecting policies on foreign aid, family planning, abortion, immigration, and women's rights. Women's groups found an advocate in Madeleine Albright, the first woman to serve as secretary of state; she identified the promotion of women's rights and ending the trafficking of women and children as among the Clinton administration's priority issues.

Third, the globalization of economic activity has intensified interest groups' efforts to influence trade policy because of their concern about its impact on wages, job opportunities, child labor, worker safety, and the environment. This has led to new and very vocal alliances among trade unions and environmental and human rights groups who oppose some aspects of current trade policy. During a conference of the world's top trade officials in Seattle in 1999, thousands of protesters took to the streets and managed to shut down parts of the city and interrupt the proceedings at this and at each succeeding summit meeting. They have launched similarly high-profile attacks on international monetary policy, driving economic summit organizers to move the meetings to ever more remote locations.

Lobbyists for Foreign Governments

Some former members of Congress and high-level political appointees have become registered agents (lobbyists) for foreign governments after leaving office. Some who are public officials one day are private citizens the next and public officials again a few years later.[20] Rules about what constitutes a conflict of interest in such cases are unclear. For example, Henry Kissinger, former secretary of state; Brent Scowcroft, former national security adviser; and Lawrence Eagleburger, former undersecretary of state, formed a consulting business. They advised some of the world's largest corporations about foreign affairs and how international developments might affect the world economic climate in general and their corporations in particular. At the same time, Kissinger and his associates provided advice to the U.S. government through their service on various influential advisory boards.

Think Tanks

Experts outside government who are associated with various think tanks are also sometimes influential in foreign policy making. Primarily located in Washington, close to decision makers and the national media, these institutions—such as the Institute for Policy Studies on the left of the political spectrum, the Libertarian Cato Foundation and the conservative Heritage Foundation on the right, and the Brookings Institution, the American Enterprise Institute, and the Council on Foreign Relations in the middle—conduct and publish research on policy issues. By writing articles for national newspapers and journals and being interviewed on news and public affairs programs, experts in these institutions "wage perpetual war against each other" trying to determine the course of American foreign policy.[21]

Public Opinion

Overall, the views of the public on foreign policy are not that different from those of elected policy makers. When they do vary, public opinion has little direct effect except on high-profile issues that could make a difference at the polls. One reason is that much of our foreign policy is made incrementally over a long period of time and out of public view. Public opinion also has little short-term impact on decisions made in "crisis" situations or in secrecy for national security reasons.

Another factor limiting the public's ability to influence foreign policy decisions is that only a minority of Americans know much about even the most publicly discussed issues, and many have no opinion about them. The public has always been more interested in domestic issues that impinge directly on daily life, such as the availability of jobs and the cost of consumer goods. Although there is growing awareness of the impact of foreign policy, especially trade issues, on daily life, it is difficult for the public to be well informed on the technical problems involved in trade and tariff negotiations.

People who rely on television as their main news source, as a majority of Americans do, see only a few minutes of foreign coverage each day. Responding to their viewers' primary interest in domestic issues,

In World War I, government rhetoric and propaganda shaped public opinion by portraying German opponents as bloodthirsty gorillas. This army enlistment poster was printed in 1917.

network television news programs cut back international coverage substantially during the 1990s. After 9/11, when viewers began expressing more interest in foreign policy and information about other countries, especially those with Muslim populations, television news increased coverage of international affairs. But in polls taken one month after the attacks, Americans were saying again that their primary concerns were jobs and the economy.

In general, the public is more likely to concede its ignorance on a wider range of issues in foreign policy than in domestic policy and to accept the judgments of decision makers. Therefore, on most issues, it is easier for the president to influence public opinion on foreign affairs through use of the media than it is for public opinion to change the president's foreign policy. President Bush's consistent linking of al-Qaeda and Iraq was hugely successful in convincing the public that Iraq had had a role in the 9/11 attacks. Three years later, well after the president and secretary of defense conceded publicly that there was no evidence for such a link, 40 percent of Americans continued to believe that Saddam Hussein had been "personally involved" in the attacks.[22] That belief appeared to be an important factor in Bush's reelection in 2004, a campaign in which national security was the main issue. Only after public opinion turned against the war in Iraq did the public show signs of separating it from the 9/11 attacks; by late 2006, 41 percent of those surveyed said Iraq was not a part of the war on terrorism.[23]

Sometimes public opinion resists attempts to change it. Even as the Bush administration discounted our ties to our traditional allies when they refused to support the invasion of Iraq—countries Rumsfeld referred to as "old Europe"—66 percent of the public continued to believe our partnership with Western European on security and diplomatic matters should remain as close it has always been.[24] Deeply held opinions like these are more resistant to administration pressure.

In the long term, the public always has the option of voting out of office those who disagree with majority views on foreign policy issues. However, it is difficult to use the vote to mandate that a president take a specific action, since, as we saw in Chapter 8, people vote on the basis of many different issues.

Trade policy provides a good illustration of the limits on the ability of public opinion to change the president's position on a foreign policy issue. Interest group opposition to the North American Free Trade Agreement (NAFTA), which eliminated trade barriers between Mexico, Canada, and the United States, was so strong that it led most Democrats, who were then the majority in Congress, to openly oppose their own party's president on this issue. One member said, "All of the traditional groups we count on to reelect us [Democrats] are against NAFTA."[25] Despite this opposition from his own party's leadership and from traditional Democratic constituencies, Clinton never wavered in his support for NAFTA because increasing trade was the cornerstone of both his domestic and his foreign policies.

Ultimately, without some public support, foreign policy objectives that require substantial commitments of time and resources will prove unsuccessful. The necessity of public support for large-scale undertakings is evident in attempts to manipulate public access to information. This is most common during wartime, when the government can justify press censorship on national security grounds. Withholding negative information (for example, high casualty rates, slow progress, civilian losses) can help keep public support high. The Persian Gulf War was fought with keen attention to public opinion. The short air war preceding the ground attack was calculated not only to minimize military casualties and the length of the ground war but also to maintain public support for the president's policies. Moreover, the restricted press coverage, which did not allow casualties to be shown, enhanced that support.

In the Iraq War, the Defense Department embedded reporters with the troops, partly on the assumption that living with the troops in combat zones and being under fire with them would be a bonding experience that would produce less-distanced, more sympathetic coverage. The Defense Department also prohibited the photographing of soldiers' coffins as they were returned to the United States for burial. They said it was to protect family privacy, but it was also a way to divert public attention from the rising body count. In addition, official casualty counts issued by the Department of Defense included only troops wounded in combat, not those who were wounded in the line of duty but outside of combat, and no tally at all was kept of Iraqi civilian deaths. This policy understated the actual casualty count by thousands.

A few years into the war the Defense Department was forced to change its policy on reporting both American and Iraqi casualties because interest groups and international agencies were posting their counts on websites for all the world to see. Similarly, the public learned about prisoner abuse in the Abu Ghraib prison camp—which the International Red Cross and government officials had known about months earlier—because digital photos taken by troops at the site were e-mailed to friends and relatives and were circulating on the Internet.

In general, because of the revolution in information technology, it is becoming harder for the president, or the president and Congress together, to appeal for public support based on a claim of privileged information. The press, interest groups, and the general public now have many more sources of information on foreign policy issues than they had a decade ago. More Americans are in e-mail contact with people in other countries and have access to the websites of foreign newspapers, governments, and think tanks, as well as to declassified documents in electronic archives. In fact, private firms here and abroad, including some run by former Soviet intelligence operatives, will even sell satellite reconnaissance photography to order and Internet sites such as Earth Google regularly show high-altitude shots of secret locales such as North Korea's suspected nuclear test sites.[26]

Changing Approaches to U.S. Foreign Policy

Isolationism

Historically, noninvolvement with other nations outside the Americas was a principal goal of our foreign policy. This policy is called **isolationism.** In the nineteenth and early twentieth centuries, Americans generally stayed aloof from European conflicts and turned inward, busy with domestic expansion and development.

One important exception was our continuing military and political involvement in Latin America, which was justified by the **Monroe Doctrine** of 1823. In articulating this doctrine, President James Monroe warned European powers that were not already in Latin America to stay out. This was a brazen move because we were a minor power challenging the major powers of the time.

As European powers withdrew from the region in the late nineteenth and early twentieth centuries, the United States began to play an increasingly active and at times interventionist role. With little regard for national sovereignty, we sent troops to protect U.S. citizens or business interests and to replace existing governments with those more sympathetic to our wishes. Paradoxically, the Monroe Doctrine derived primarily from isolationist, not interventionist, sentiment. By keeping foreign powers on their side of the ocean and out of our hemisphere, we believed we would be less likely to be drawn into conflicts abroad.

During this time, Americans did not think it appropriate to intervene in the problems of Europe or to keep a large standing army at home. This attitude was an offshoot of the predominant mood in domestic affairs: preoccupation with economic growth and fear of a strong central government. Isolationism was also a realistic position in the sense that the United States was not yet a world power. Another source of isolationist sentiment was the belief that the United States was unique and that the more entangling alliances it entered into with foreign countries, the more likely it would "be corrupted and its unique nature . . . subverted."[27]

© Sovfoto

Millions of Russian civilians and soldiers were killed in World War II. In this photo, grieving Soviets search for their loved ones after Nazi murder squads massacred a village in the Crimea in 1942.

This isolationist sentiment lapsed briefly in 1917–1919, when America entered World War I on the side of the British and French against Germany, but rapidly revived at its close. Despite the wishes of President Woodrow Wilson, the U.S. Senate refused to join the League of Nations, the ill-fated precursor to the United Nations. Although we have no public opinion polls from these early years, 70 percent of Americans polled in 1937 thought, in hindsight, it had been a mistake to enter World War I.

Yet the United States was never truly isolationist in its actions. Throughout the whole early isolationist era, we frequently intervened diplomatically and militarily in the Caribbean and Central America and consistently sought to expand U.S. commercial and cultural influence throughout the world. Even President McKinley, who was labeled an "imperialist" by Democrats for his military adventures in the Caribbean and the Philippines, was easily reelected. And his successor, Theodore Roosevelt, is better characterized as an interventionist than an isolationist. Polls from the post–World War I era show that Americans overwhelmingly favored joining an international peacekeeping body like the League of Nations. And historians have pointed out that there were enough votes in the Senate to ratify participation in the League had President Wilson been willing to accept amendments to the treaty agreement.[28]

Americans have almost always been willing to participate in world affairs to defend our national interests. But we are often slow to recognize just what is at stake. In 1939, we refused to join Britain in its war to stop Nazi Germany's attempted conquest of Europe. It was not until the December 1941 Japanese attack on Pearl Harbor, Hawaii, that the public was willing to support entry into World War II. When Germany and Italy then declared war on the United States, we fought in Europe alongside Britain, the Soviet Union, and remnant armies from the occupied nations of Europe.

Containment

The Allied victory in 1945 brought a split between the Soviet Union and its Western allies. The Soviet Union lost at least twenty million people in the war (the United States lost four hundred thousand). Given these losses in a German invasion that was only one of many invasions of Russian territory over the centuries, the Soviet government was determined, especially as a protection against Germany, to have friendly neighbors in Europe, just as we wanted them in Latin America. To ensure this, the Soviet Union was willing to use any means, including intervention, to secure Communist governments in the ring of nations surrounding it—Poland, Czechoslovakia, Romania, Hun-

Reprinted from *Better Dead Than Red* by Michael Barson (Hyperion)

During the Cold War, communism generated real fear among Americans, as this poster for a 1962 Hollywood documentary shows. Soviet Premier Nikita Khrushchev had proclaimed, "We'll bury you!"

gary, and Bulgaria. Our wish for free elections in these nations was seen by the Soviet Union as an attempt to isolate it. The Russians believed we wanted to surround them with anti-Soviet governments, thus making their sacrifices in World War II futile. Many of our policy makers saw the subversion of Eastern European governments as the beginning of a Soviet effort to conquer Europe.

As the only major power not decimated by the war, the United States was unable to return to its isolationist prewar stance. In 1947, the Truman administration formulated a policy to limit the spread of communism by meeting any action taken by the Soviet

Union to spread its influence with counterforce or a countermove by the United States. Known as **containment** (also called the Truman Doctrine), this policy led U.S. decision makers to see most of the world's conflicts in terms of rivalry between the Soviet Union and the United States. The Soviet coup d'état in Czechoslovakia in 1948 and the rise to power of the Chinese Communist government of Mao Zedong in 1949 fueled U.S. fears that the Communists would try to expand the area under their control as far as possible. Consequently, when Communist North Korea attacked South Korea in 1950, we intervened as the nucleus of a United Nations force, believing we had to stop the spread of communism in Korea before the Soviets undertook further expansion.

Just as isolationism began as a defensive posture to keep European conflicts out of the Americas, containment was aimed at limiting the Russians to their post–World War II reach and out of our sphere of influence. Instead of trying to roll back Soviet power, containment was designed to keep it from expanding to a point that changed the global power balance or dragged the United States into unwanted conflicts. The chief instruments of containment policy were economic and military aid to developing countries, cultural exchanges, covert activity, alliance building, nuclear deterrence, and as in Korea and Vietnam, limited wars fought with conventional weaponry.

Containment philosophy was at work in the Marshall Plan, which provided economic relief to the nations of Western Europe in 1947 (aid was offered to some Eastern European governments, but they refused it). In addition, the United States entered into military alliances with friendly nations in Europe and Asia to stop the spread of Soviet influence or even to roll it back. The most important of these was the **North Atlantic Treaty Organization,** which in 1949 joined the United States, Canada, and their Western European allies in a mutual defense pact against Soviet aggression in Europe. Building these military alliances to compete with the Soviet Union and its Eastern European allies was a response to the **Cold War** era that we had now entered. We were not in a military battle (or hot war) with the Russians, but the deep hostility between the two nations threatened to turn any conflict into a major armed confrontation.

Nuclear Deterrence

The nuclear era began in 1945, when the United States dropped atomic bombs on the Japanese cities of Hiroshima and Nagasaki. Although the debate on the necessity and ethics of dropping these bombs still continues, Japan surrendered, bringing the war in the Pacific to an end and making an invasion of the island by the Allies unnecessary.

At the close of the war, the United States was the only nuclear power. The Soviet Union exploded its first bomb in 1949, but it did not have an operational warhead until the mid-1950s and for a while thereafter had no intercontinental bombers or missiles to deliver the bombs. Despite our nuclear superiority, we found our power limited. Nuclear weapons were of little use in the pursuit of most foreign policy objectives because the threat of inflicting mass destruction to achieve a nonvital objective was not credible to opponents. Hence during the period of nuclear superiority, the United States saw its Chinese Nationalist allies lose to Communists in China, its French allies lose to Ho Chi Minh in Indochina (Vietnam), and an anti-Communist uprising in Hungary in 1956 crushed by Soviet tanks.

In 1955, the Soviet Union and its Eastern European satellites formed the Warsaw Pact, a military alliance to counter NATO. People began to see all international relations as part of the bipolar competition between a Western bloc of countries united under the U.S. nuclear umbrella and an Eastern bloc of nations operating under the protection of the Soviet nuclear umbrella.

American nuclear dominance began to erode in the late 1950s. *Sputnik,* the Soviet satellite that was the first to orbit Earth, showed that the Soviet Union had successfully built large rockets capable of firing missiles that could reach the United States. The fear of Soviet rocketry advances led to a program to build and deploy nuclear-tipped intercontinental ballistic missiles (ICBMs) to supplement our bomber force.

Even with Soviet advances, American nuclear superiority was maintained for another decade. Yet everyone agreed that neither side could attack the other without the certain knowledge that both the attacker and the attacked would suffer enormous damage. No sane leader would risk so much damage by striking first.[29] This capability is called **mutual assured destruction,** referred to by the fitting acronym **MAD.**

Despite public frustration with the Cold War—being neither totally at war nor at peace—successive administrations found that "rolling back" communism in the nuclear age was not possible without the kind of risk and commitment of resources most Americans were unwilling to assume. Although the Kennedy administration did risk nuclear war over Soviet placement of nuclear weapons in Cuba, ninety miles from our shores, we stood by and avoided such risks when the Soviet Union invaded Hungary in 1956, Czechoslovakia in 1968, and Afghanistan in 1979. And the Soviet Union stood down when we tried to overthrow Castro in 1961, when we forced the removal of Russian missiles from the island in 1962, and avoided confrontation when we sent military forces to oppose a Russian-backed nationalist movement in Vietnam.

One of the basic premises of containment was that all Communist nations were controlled by the Soviet Union. But as the 1950s progressed, it became clear that this was not true. Both Albania and Yugoslavia spurned Moscow's control. The Chinese became increasingly independent and in the early 1960s broke with the Soviet Union, declaring that "there are many paths to socialism." Despite this, we continued to define most international events in terms of Communists versus anti-Communists, no matter how poorly the characterization fit. This conviction formed the basis of the **domino theory,** the proposition that if one country fell to Communist rule, it would set off a chain reaction in neighboring countries, just as a long line of dominoes standing on end will fall in sequence when the first one is toppled. If U.S. intervention could prevent the first country to come under attack from falling, others would stand firm. This rationale led us into Vietnam, our longest war to date.

Vietnam

Early period If one were ranking the landmark events of the twentieth century, surely World War II would rank at the top. We live in a completely different world than would have existed had Hitler not been defeated. Fighting alongside Britain and the Soviet Union, the United States achieved its greatest military victory and forged the alliance with Western Europe that led to our most important treaty relationship. Yet the Vietnam War has had a far greater impact

The Vietnamese guerrillas dug a vast complex of tunnels west of Saigon, the capital of South Vietnam and the hub of American bases in the country. The tunnels led to underground rooms used as kitchens, hospitals, and factories. The guerrillas hid in the tunnels and sneaked out to launch their attacks.

on U.S. military policy since its end in 1975. We will try to explain why.

When we became involved in Vietnam, it was still part of the French colonial territory of Indochina. After the defeat of the Japanese occupying forces in World War II, the Indochinese Communist Party, led by Ho Chi Minh, engaged the returning French forces in a war for independence. Ho appealed several times to the United States—a critic of both British and French colonial policies—for support in this effort but was rebuffed. As the war in Indochina dragged on, the Cold War settled in, and containment became the organizing concept in American foreign policy. By 1954, when Ho's troops defeated the French in a major battle, the United States was underwriting 80 percent of the cost of the French effort in Vietnam. But after considerable deliberation, the Eisenhower administration refused to provide troops or air support to save the French because Eisenhower believed this could bog us down in a long war requiring many troops, certainly a prescient view.

At a conference in Geneva in 1954, a temporary boundary was established separating the territory of Ho's government in the North from that of the French- and U.S.-backed government in the South until elections could be held to choose leaders for all of Vietnam. The new prime minister in the South, Ngo Dinh Diem, was a staunch anti-Communist Catholic with influential friends in the U.S. Catholic community and Congress. Diem's government refused to participate in the elections scheduled for 1956, and the United States backed him because it feared that Ho's Communist government would win the election. The temporary partition between the North and South continued, and after the assassination of Diem in 1963, it soon became clear that the South Vietnamese government would collapse without more U.S. intervention.

Armed intervention In 1964, President Johnson won congressional approval for massive intervention in Vietnam. In an August television address to the American public, Johnson claimed that two U.S. destroyers had been attacked by North Vietnamese torpedo boats while on routine patrol in international waters near the Gulf of Tonkin. He announced his intention to retaliate by bombing sites in North Vietnam. The next day, after presenting misleading information about the role of the U.S. destroyers in initiating the attack, he asked Congress to endorse the Gulf of Tonkin Resolution authorizing him "to take all necessary measures to repel any armed attack against the forces of the U.S. and to prevent further aggression."

Johnson said the resolution was like "grandma's nightshirt. It covers everything."[30] He and President

Nixon used the Tonkin Resolution to justify each act of escalation in the war. This deception laid the groundwork for the gradual erosion of congressional support for the war effort.

In early 1965, Johnson sent in U.S. troops in the belief that the war would be over "in a matter of months." After all, the United States had sophisticated equipment and training and complete air superiority. But three years later, after a half million U.S. troops had been committed to combat, the Vietcong—North Vietnam's southern allies—were able to launch a major offensive that demonstrated that all our military efforts had not made one square foot of Vietnam truly secure. When the Joint Chiefs of Staff requested more than two hundred thousand additional troops, a stunned President Johnson decided to undertake a review of Vietnam policy. Even the Joint Chiefs were not sure how many years and troops it might take to win. As public opposition to the war grew, Johnson called for peace talks and announced that he would not run for reelection in 1968. The talks began in May 1968 and dragged on through the administration of Johnson's successor, Richard Nixon.

President Nixon wanted to leave Vietnam without appearing to have lost the war. To accomplish this, he tried "Vietnamizing" the war by forcing the South Vietnamese government to give more responsibility to its own army. He authorized the massive bombing of Hanoi and began withdrawing U.S. troops.

Nixon's most controversial war policy was his decision to expand the war into neighboring Cambodia, supposedly to destroy a huge underground headquarters of the North Vietnamese army near the Vietnamese border. In addition to igniting the largest public protests of the war, the invasion finally led to significant congressional opposition. The Gulf of Tonkin Resolution was repealed, and a resolution was passed prohibiting the president from using budgeted funds to wage a ground war in Cambodia. Nixon had planned to withdraw the troops from Cambodia anyway and did so quickly. But bombing in Cambodia continued until 1973, when Congress forbade the use of funds for this purpose. This was the only time Congress actually blocked presidential policies in the war.

In 1973, the United States and North Vietnam signed a peace agreement. We might have reached the same agreement in 1969, but President Nixon had believed this would jeopardize his reelection chances in 1972 and perhaps other foreign policy goals, too.[31] The victory of the Vietcong and North Vietnamese finally occurred in 1975 as the South Vietnamese army disintegrated in the face of a Communist attack.

Lessons from Vietnam Much of our thinking about the use of the military today is still informed by the

Jack Kightlinger/Lyndon Baines Johnson Library

President Johnson listens in anguish to a tape sent by his son-in-law (Charles Robb, then an officer in Vietnam and later a U.S. senator from Virginia), talking about the men lost in battle in Vietnam.

lessons of policy failures in Vietnam.[32] Even though at its peak in 1968–1969 our military force in Vietnam exceeded half a million, had sophisticated equipment and training, and had complete air superiority, we were eventually defeated. Why did we fail?

■ *We did not have clear goals.* Policy makers never agreed on whether we were fighting China, the Soviet Union, North Vietnam, or rebels in the South (the Vietcong). It was not clear what or whom we were trying to defend or what Vietnam was supposed to look like after the North was defeated.

■ *We did not understand the political aspects of the war.* Supporting a series of unpopular South Vietnamese governments, we were at first oblivious to the vast indigenous opposition to the South Vietnamese government from Communists, other nationalists, and Buddhists. Our inability to construct an effective policy for "winning the hearts and minds" of the domestic opposition to the South Vietnamese government appears to have been a fatal weakness of policy makers from Eisenhower through Nixon.

In 1995, on the twentieth anniversary of the war's end, Robert McNamara, secretary of defense in the Kennedy and Johnson administrations and a

This photo of a naked South Vietnamese girl screaming after a napalm attack by "friendly" forces became one of the most famous photographs of the war and a major incitement to antiwar protest. The girl, Kim Phue, survived, despite enduring pain and long-term treatment for her wounds. Now living in Canada, she is pictured at right with her son, Huan (his name means "prospects"). She notes, "I know my picture did something to help stop the war. I have to show [my son] what happened to his mom, to her country, and that there should never be war again."

principal architect of early Vietnam policy, wrote a book publicly stating for the first time that by 1967 he had come to the conclusion that the war was a mistake and could not be won. Principal among his eleven reasons for the loss were the incompetence of the South Vietnamese government and armed forces and American underestimation of the North Vietnamese.[33] President Johnson's refusal to accept this conclusion led McNamara to leave—or be made to leave—the cabinet in 1968. But as revealed by the release of the tapes of Johnson's phone calls, at the very time he was making large troop commitments, Johnson was saying, "I don't see any way of winning."[34]

■ *We did not understand the nature of guerrilla warfare.* For much of the war, we did not fight against a standing army dressed in the uniform of an enemy force. It was often impossible for our troops to tell soldier from civilian or enemy from ally. Although we inflicted heavy casualties on the Vietcong and North Vietnamese forces, we killed thousands of civilians in the process. Our opponents were able to demonstrate to the people of the South that their government and its ally, the United States, could not protect them or their villages. In fact, the Vietcong were able to dominate much of the rural South. Our policies—to "destroy villages in order to save them" and to take people from their own villages to "strategic hamlets," where presumably they were safe from the Vietcong—were bitterly resented by many South Vietnamese.

■ *We were impatient with the war and were unwilling to devote unending resources to winning it.* We knew

from the British experience in defeating Communist guerrillas in Malaysia that we would need at least ten soldiers to the guerrillas' one and that we might need ten years to win the war, but no leader dared tell the public that we must commit ourselves for that long. We were unwilling to invest the resources or time needed to defeat a guerrilla enemy. Since the goals were unclear, few wanted to risk use of the ultimate weaponry that could have destroyed the North. Although this stance was rational, it did not seem to lead to the obvious question of whether our objectives were worth the effort we were making.

■ *We did not have public support.* Although public opinion was generally supportive during the first years of the war, support eroded as it became clear that we were bogged down in an interminable and indecisive conflict. Only about 20 percent of the public favored an immediate withdrawal in 1965, but by mid-1969, support for withdrawal began to increase and reached 50 percent within the next year. By 1971, public support for withdrawal grew to overwhelming proportions.[35]

The United States persisted in Vietnam for nearly eleven years because most policy makers believed in standing firm against what they saw as Communist aggression and because no president wanted to be responsible for losing a war. But Vietnam shattered the belief in containment and U.S. illusions that it could serve as the world's police force. Many Americans believed that both our aims and tactics in Vietnam were immoral. Others believed that our aims were just but unachievable. Still others thought that we should have stayed until we won. All these sentiments led to a good deal of public self-examination.

The failure of our Vietnam policy produced the **Vietnam syndrome,** an attitude among the public and officials of uncertainty about our foreign policy goals and our ability to achieve them through military means. Decision makers became more reluctant to commit troops to combat situations or to threaten military action to pursue containment goals. Some people regarded this new caution as a positive development that would keep us from becoming involved in new military entanglements we could not win. But many others believed that this national self-doubt tied the hands of decision makers and prevented them from using the full range of our capabilities to pursue national interests abroad.

These differences persist among policy makers today. Colin Powell, former chairman of the Joint Chiefs of Staff and George W. Bush's first secretary of state, did two tours of duty in Vietnam. His experience there was the basis of what is now called the *Powell doctrine:* never commit U.S. forces to combat abroad without clear goals and an exit plan. It led to Powell's initial opposition both to committing troops to the Persian Gulf War in 1991 and to unilateral military action against Iraq in 2003.

Détente

Richard Nixon came to office after public opinion had begun to turn against the war, and he immediately began looking for ways to shape international relations in the post–Vietnam War era. As a man whose career was built on making political hay out of his staunch anticommunism, President Nixon was well placed to make diplomatic overtures to the Soviet Union without fear of being attacked by any but the most die-hard Cold Warriors. Thus Nixon and his national security adviser and later secretary of state, Henry Kissinger, developed a policy called **détente,** which was designed to deescalate Cold War rhetoric and to promote the notion that relations with the Soviet Union could be conducted in ways other than confrontation.

With a policy of détente, we could reward the Soviet Union for "good behavior" on the international scene and at the same time reduce our own military expenditures, slow the arms race, and perhaps step back from the brink of war. The détente doctrine recognized that although the Soviet Union would remain our adversary, it, too, had legitimate interests in the world. Détente also recognized the growing military strength of the Soviet Union and the fact that it was in our interests to pursue bilateral agreements, such as on arms control, that would try to limit this strength. Among the most notable achievements of the détente policy were the treaty agreements limiting the number of defensive antiballistic missile (ABM) launchers that each side could possess and freezing the number of offensive missiles in each side's stockpile.

During this era of new diplomacy with the Soviet Union, President Nixon also sent out feelers to see whether China was interested in reestablishing diplomatic ties. Even though it was home to one-fifth of the world's population, China had been shut out of the mainstream diplomatic community, largely due to U.S. pressure, since the Communist victory in 1949. After two years of negotiations through third parties, the first cultural exchange (a visit by the U.S. Ping-Pong team) was arranged in 1971. By the time of President Nixon's visit in 1972, many nations had resumed diplomatic relations with China, and it had regained its seat in the United Nations Security Council. Full diplomatic recognition by the United States, however, did not come until the Carter administration.

The resumption of diplomatic relations between China and the United States was one of the most remarkable achievements of Nixon's and Kissinger's attempts to break the Cold War stalemate. Nonetheless, it was consistent with their balance-of-power approach to foreign policy. By making this effort during a period of hostility in relations between the Soviet Union and China, Nixon was probably hoping to gain leverage in dealings with the Soviet Union (what some referred to as "playing the China card").

The Nixon-Kissinger visits to China were all the more remarkable because they occurred while U.S. troops were still fighting in Vietnam. It had been the specter of a Sino-Soviet-led Communist bloc and a near paranoid fear of "yellow hordes" (in the racist parlance of the time) advancing throughout Asia that led us to fight in Korea and Vietnam. Within a few short years, China's image was recast from dreaded enemy to friendly ally, and Cold War fears of world Communist domination were greatly diminished.

The doctrine of détente complemented the mood of isolationism and weariness that grew in the wake of the Vietnam War. Public and elite opinion after the war was divided. Isolationist, go-it-alone sentiment peaked immediately after the war but then declined.

A new spirit of cooperative internationalism characterized the early Carter administration.[36] Carter and his advisers saw the world as far more complex than Cold War rhetoric suggested. They believed that problems of global poverty, inequitable distribution of wealth, abuse of human rights, and regional competitiveness were substantial threats to world order and that the United States should work with other nations to solve these problems.

In 1979, Carter signed a new agreement with the Soviet Union placing limits on offensive missiles. But the Soviets' stunning invasion of Afghanistan that same

One of the first major achievements of the Nixon-Kissinger policy of détente was to reestablish normal relations with the People's Republic of China, governed by the Communist Party since 1949. Here Nixon attends a state banquet in Beijing with then premier Zhou Enlai.

year ended the chance of gaining Senate approval for the treaty. Public and elite opinion shifted, and Cold War views, never completely abandoned, became much more respectable again.

Cold War Revival and Death

The Reagan administration took office in 1981 determined to challenge the Soviet Union in every way possible. During his first term, Reagan totally renounced the Nixon-Kissinger principle of détente and labeled the Soviet Union an "evil empire." He and his advisers continued to view the world largely in light of a U.S.-Soviet competition. They painted a simple picture of an aggressive, reckless, and brutal Soviet Union and a peace-loving and virtuous United States. Despite the rhetoric, however, the administration did not risk direct confrontation.

Reagan's approach differed from containment because it was more ideologically than strategically driven; he sought not just to contain the Soviets but to undo the status quo. One method Reagan endorsed was stepping up the arms race and, by forcing them to keep pace, drive the Soviets into economic ruin. The centerpiece of this policy was his plan to build an antimissile defense system, the Strategic Defense Initiative (SDI), derisively known as Star Wars. The plan was based on a laser technology that did not yet exist but that was supposed to intercept and destroy nuclear-tipped ballistic missiles before they reached their targets in the United States. Its projected cost was tens of billions of dollars.

Reagan's SDI and military buildup programs increased military spending to record peacetime levels.

Though the election of Reagan put a Cold Warrior in the White House, the public was not willing to buy Cold War arguments wholeheartedly. By Reagan's second term, a dramatic drop in public support for increased military spending and growing public pressure for progress on arms control helped push the administration toward a less belligerent stance. Violent rhetoric was toned down, and conciliatory gestures multiplied.[37] Common wisdom was that President Reagan wanted to reach some agreement with the Soviets in order to be remembered as a peacemaking president.

The moderation in Reagan's rhetoric was also a response to changes in the Soviet Union. In 1985, Mikhail Gorbachev, the new general secretary of the Communist Party of the Soviet Union, called for "new thinking" and began to shake up Soviet society as it had not been shaken since the Russian Revolution in 1917.[38] Faced with a stagnating economy and an antireform Soviet leadership, Gorbachev encouraged competition in the economy, criticism of corruption and inefficiencies by government agencies, and free elections of some government legislative bodies.

In addition to his domestic reforms, Gorbachev challenged the status quo in the international community with his policy of *glasnost,* or opening to the outside world. He encouraged foreign investment and requested foreign aid to help rebuild the Soviet economy; he made it easier for Soviet citizens to emigrate, pulled Soviet troops out of Afghanistan, and reduced aid to Soviet-backed governments in Nicaragua and Cuba.

Gorbachev also took the initiative in resuming arms control negotiations with President Reagan. In 1987, the two men reached an agreement on intermediate-range nuclear forces. To ensure compliance, the United States sent inspectors or monitors to the Soviet Union, and the Soviets sent them to Western Europe and the United States to observe production facilities and the dismantling and removal of the missiles.

During the first two years of George H. Bush's administration, the Soviet empire in Eastern Europe disintegrated with such rapidity that all policy makers were caught off-guard. The Soviet-dominated governments were dismantled, Communist parties changed their names, opposition parties formed, and free multiparty elections were held.

In late 1989, demonstrators assaulted the most visible symbol of the Cold War, the Berlin Wall (built by the Soviets in 1961 to divide Soviet-occupied East Berlin from NATO-occupied West Berlin), and began tearing it down. A year later, the reunification of Germany marked the end of the post–World War II power alliance in Europe.

Then, in 1991, after a brief, unsuccessful coup against him, Gorbachev resigned as head of the Communist Party and stripped the party of its role in government. Facing massive restructuring problems, he made major foreign policy concessions to Western governments in order to obtain economic aid. Among them was an agreement to remove Soviet military forces from Cuba, the last vestige of Cold War competition in the Western Hemisphere.

With no strong center left in Moscow, the non Russian states of the Soviet Union declared their independence. Gorbachev was left with no country to lead, his power supplanted by the presidents of the fifteen newly independent republics. As the Soviet Union passed from the scene, all nations had to adjust to a realignment of the world order.

Early in the 1990s, the first President Bush spoke of a "new world order," although no one was quite certain what it meant in terms of concrete foreign policies, other than the absence of U.S.-Soviet military competition. In the new order, foreign policies would presumably be less dependent on military capabilities. Still, some Americans feared that as the world's sole remaining military superpower, the United States would feel freer to use its military advantage in pursuit of its foreign policy goals. However, without the Soviet threat to justify expenditures, the United States began to shrink its military. There was also strong public pressure to avoid new foreign entanglements. With the Cold War over, Americans seemed weary of trying to understand and change the world. They were more impressed by the failures of foreign aid, military intervention, and diplomacy than by foreign policy successes, more weighed down by problems at home than by those in other countries. Bush Sr. found that he could justify intervention in the Persian Gulf, and later in the civil war in Somalia, only through cost sharing and participation in an international force under UN auspices.

Merchant Diplomacy and Multilateralism

Bill Clinton took office as the first president born after World War II and one of twelve never to have served in the military. He was a self-described child of the Cold War, an opponent of the Vietnam War, and more shaped by the skepticism of that era than by memories of the Allied victory in World War II. In his campaign, he reminded voters that we had not defeated the Soviet Union in battle but that it had collapsed from within due to "economic, political, and spiritual failure." The lesson, Clinton said, was clear: "Given the problems we face at home, we must first take care of our own people and their needs." He believed that the best foreign policy is to have a strong economy.[39]

With this as his theme, Clinton signaled a change in approach to foreign policy. Befitting the end of the Cold War, greater emphasis would be given to economic than to military instruments of foreign policy, and more attention would be paid to using our economic strength to achieve political goals, such as promotion of democracy and human rights, which Clinton said we had neglected in our pursuit of strategic interests.

Clinton was an exception among modern Democratic presidents in that he was openly committed to free trade. **Free trade** is a policy of minimum intervention by governments in trade relations. Its advocates, or free traders, believe that government regulation of trade, for economic or political reasons, reduces the efficiency of the world economy, thus preventing countries from maximizing their income.[40] Free trade, like capitalism, is relative; all countries place some restrictions on trade to protect domestic labor and business interests. In fact, forms of protection historically, and today, apply to as much as 40 percent of all trade.

Protectionism is government intervention to protect domestic producers and their employees against competition from foreign producers of manufactured and agricultural goods. Protectionist policies can take the form of a ban on goods from abroad, quotas on imports, or taxes (tariffs) on imports to make them more expensive and therefore less competitive in the United States. We have used protectionist policies to help American farmers and the manufacturers of automobiles, textiles, steel, clothing, computer chips, and other goods.

When Clinton came to office many Americans, especially those who worked in manufacturing and agriculture, still expected the president, especially a Democrat, to take action to protect their jobs. But believing globalization was not reversible and that the shift at home to a high-tech, service economy was unstoppable, Clinton believed jobs and capital should gravitate wherever market forces took them as long as all countries played by a common set of rules. He argued "that open markets and rules-based trade are the best engine we know to lift living standards, reduce environmental destruction and build shared prosperity."[41] In other words, increasing trade with China, India, and African countries would create jobs in the United States and raise living standards in poorer countries while costing the American taxpayer virtually nothing in aid. At the same time eradicating trade barriers for those countries would create a huge new pool of customers for American goods and services.

Of course Clinton was no pure free-trader; no American president has been, in large part because pressure from interest groups to retain certain protections, such as agricultural subsidies, is too great. But he moved his party away from advocacy of protectionism and made it seem that free trade was fixed as a cornerstone of American foreign policy, regardless of which party held the presidency.

Clinton's foreign policy was so rooted in the pursuit of national economic interests that almost all issues were discussed in terms of their value to U.S. trade relations. (Clinton's second-term national security adviser was an international trade lawyer.) This led some observers to label his foreign policy "merchant diplomacy."[42] Deemphasizing military in favor of economic diplomacy suited the public mood, which, although not one of withdrawal from world affairs, was leery of new political entanglements.

Despite the deemphasis on military force, there were many occasions during Clinton's administration when its use was deemed necessary. But unlike previous presidents, Clinton was reluctant to rely on the unilateral use of force. When he ordered troops to Haiti in 1994 to oust a military dictatorship and restore the elected president, it was only after gaining UN backing. It marked the first time an American president had sought prior international approval for a military intervention in the Caribbean. To some, it was a radical departure from, or even an end to, the Monroe Doctrine.[43] But it was compatible with Clinton's view of the post–Cold War world as a community of nations becoming increasingly linked through the forces of globalization and in which every country should assume part of the burden for maintaining international peace and security. Avoiding costly military entanglements also helped end the huge budget deficits run up by the military spending and tax cuts of the Reagan era.

The difficulty with a multilateral approach to achieving foreign policy goals is that the national interests (and therefore the motivation for intervening) that each country has at stake in any international dispute vary. This can paralyze the policy process and make military cooperation to resolve a conflict impossible to achieve. Reluctance to act alone kept the United States on the sidelines when its intervention might have saved hundreds of thousands of lives. Clinton did not intervene to stop ethnic cleansing in the breakaway republics of Yugoslavia until thousands had died. When we did get involved, it was as part of a NATO force, with shared costs and troop commitments, but one could argue that it was with greater legitimacy and a more effective force than the United States could have provided by acting on its own in Europe.

The most glaring failure of multilateralism during Clinton's administration was the decision to follow the UN's lead in not intervening to stop the genocide in Rwanda, a conflict that cost an estimated eight hundred thousand lives. Both Clinton and the intervention-shy UN leadership later admitted this was a drastic failure of preventive diplomacy and international peacekeeping.

Regime Change and Preemptive War

When he campaigned for the presidency, George W. Bush advocated a foreign policy that was even less interventionist than Clinton's had been. He opposed any long-term or open-ended commitment of U.S. troops to international combat units or peacekeeping missions. He said that we had to be "humble" about our role in the world and that we should not be engaged in nation building in countries where our troops were committed. Selecting Colin Powell, the former chair of the Joint Chiefs of Staff and a man famously reluctant to commit U.S. troops to combat, as his secretary of state suggested that Bush might follow a very cautious approach to American military involvement around the world.

Bush's early actions also indicated a shrinking back from diplomatic engagement, and he soon established himself as someone who preferred going it alone. The United States did not withdraw from international organizations, but Bush's rhetoric suggested that he would only *consult* with other countries, not deal with them as equals. He announced his opposition to a number of treaty arrangements. He withdrew U.S. involvement in the Kyoto agreements on global warming, which Clinton had signed, because he thought it placed unreasonable burdens on American businesses and too few on those in poorer countries. He refused to renew the ABM treaty because it would keep him from pursuing the development of the space-based antimissile defense system Reagan had begun, and he refused to agree to U.S. participation in an international court to try war crimes and human rights abuses because he thought it would make American peacekeeping troops subject to false accusations.

These early actions contributed to the view that Bush's foreign policy approach would shift the U.S. stance from multilateralism to unilateralism. The terrorist attacks of September 11, 2001, reinforced certain aspects of this approach but changed others. Bush did organize a multinational force before taking military action in Afghanistan, suggesting an accommodation with multilateralism. But laying claim to Reagan's "evil empire" terminology, he labeled three nations—Iraq, Iran, and North Korea—an "axis of evil" and agents of state-sponsored terrorism. The conviction that an international ring of state-sponsored terrorists

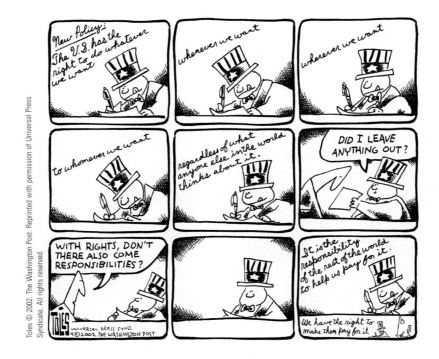

was lying in wait to launch other attacks led to a major redefinition of U.S. defense policy. Whereas historically the United States had maintained a posture of defensive response, striking only after being attacked, the Bush national security team endorsed a strategy of **preemption,** or striking first.[44] In a much-quoted speech delivered at West Point after 9/11, Bush said, "The war on terrorism will not be won on the defensive. . . .We must take the battle to the enemy, disrupt its plans, and confront the worst threats before they emerge." Reinforcing this point, Vice President Cheney added, "We have enemies with nothing to defend. . . . For that reason, this struggle will not end with a treaty or accommodation of terrorists [but] with complete and utter destruction" of terrorist networks.[45]

Preemption is not a new idea in U.S. foreign policy; it has always been there as an option in defense policy. John Kennedy, for example, asked General Maxwell Taylor to write a paper outlining a strategy for a nuclear first strike against the Soviet Union.[46] It is unlikely that any president would fail to strike first in a situation where it was certain it would prevent a lethal attack on the United States. The distinctive aspect of the Bush position is his use of preemption, not as one option, but as a guiding principle in defense policy.

Bush put his policy into effect shortly after announcing it by calling for a preemptive strike against Iraq. If the administration had argued that it had proof that an attack on the United States was imminent, probably few analysts would have seen preemption as a policy shift. But Bush's Iraq policy was based not on known capabilities or actual plans but on assumed *intent.* And it was unclear whether it was to be a unique

operation or just the first in a series of strikes against the "axis of evil." Many members of Congress argued that invoking the policy to send thousands of combat troops to invade a sovereign nation encroached on Congress's constitutional prerogative to declare war.

After less than two years in office, Bush's approach to foreign policy had been drastically revised from a passive unilateralism to an interventionist unilateralism. For reasons of both principle and cost (human and economic), many in Congress expressed a reluctance to accept preemption as a principle of foreign policy, if not rejecting it as a necessary option in specific situations. Opponents of preemptive war believe that attacking a country to prevent the possibility that it *might* one day attack us sets a frightening precedent for international rules of engagement, legitimizing preemptive military or nuclear strikes by other countries against their enemies.

Bush did put together a "coalition of the willing" to participate in the invasion of Iraq, but of the more than thirty countries signing on, only Great Britain contributed any serious contingent of combat troops. Troops and civilian personnel from other countries served mainly in support and humanitarian roles and sometimes numbered only a handful. And Great Britain's contribution of nearly thirty thousand troops for the invasion was immediately reduced to eight thousand after U.S. troops reached Baghdad and therefore were gone when the major fighting began. And whereas the coalition partners Bush Sr. put together to fight the first Gulf War paid for virtually all of the war's cost, we paid most of Bush Jr's coalition partners (other than Great Britain and Australia) to participate.

Although Clinton's multilateralism slowed U.S. response to crises where lives could have been saved had we acted more quickly, it was an approach that rationed the use of U.S. military force and spending, maintaining the bulk of strength for response to vital national security threats. It was also an approach that tried to augment our worldview by factoring our allies' assessments of foreign policy crises into our own analyses. Multilateralism slows response time, but it can prevent precipitous entry into situations we do not fully understand. Bush's preemptive unilateralism, or token multilateralism, pushed U.S. military strength to its limits, leaving no ready reserve for responding to other substantial threats. In its execution, unilateralism led the Bush administration back to multilateralism because alone we did not have the economic and military resources to stabilize and reconstruct Iraq and carry on the war in Afghanistan. By 2005 NATO troops were the bulk of the military presence in Afghanistan.

Bush's commitment to spreading democracy was a corollary of his policy of preemptive war. Waging a war not just to disarm a country but to overthrow its government inevitably led to nation building. Bush justified the imposition of a new government on Iraq by saying that in establishing a model for democratic government there he was laying the groundwork for regime change across the Middle East. By fostering the creation of governments more in our own image, he argued, we would be helping to ensure our physical and economic security. Bush suggested he would follow a similar policy toward other countries in the

"axis of evil," and subsequent mission statements of his State Department listed democracy promotion as a fundamental goal of U.S. foreign policy. (See the "Government Responsiveness" box)

Bush's policies unleashed a wave of anti-Americanism throughout Europe and parts of Asia as well as the Middle East. After 9/11, world opinion was almost entirely sympathetic, but the U.S. decision to launch a war of choice and overthrow the government of a sovereign country triggered fear and hatred in many

TABLE 18.1	Global Attitudes toward the U.S. Have Become Less Favorable in the Iraqi War Era	
	1999 – 2000	**2006**
Great Britain	83	56
France	62	39
Germany	78	37
Spain	50	23
Russia	37	43
Indonesia	75	30
Turkey	52	12
Jordan	25*	15
Pakistan	23	27

*The figure is from 2002.
SOURCE: Pew Global Attitudes Project, June 13, 2006, "America's Image Slips, But Allies Share U.S. Concerns on Iran and Hamas," pewglobal.org/reports. In March and April, 2006, 17,000 people were surveyed in fifteen nations. The margin of error in each nation is 3–4 percent.

"They may seem slow and peaceful, but don't underestimate their anti-American rage."

IDEALS AND NATIONAL INTEREST IN MIDDLE EAST FOREIGN POLICY

Responsiveness to the public in foreign policy is difficult to define, but almost everyone will agree that government's first obligation is to protect the physical and economic security of the country. Many Americans want the United States's relations with other nations to be consistent with our fundamental values and political ideals, as well. After this it gets complicated because people do not agree on what makes us secure, how we achieve security, or which policies or instruments of foreign policy in any given situation best reflect our values.

George W. Bush brought a new wrinkle to the debate over finding the proper balance between the national interest, democratic values, and human rights in foreign policy. After the 9/11 attacks, Bush divided the world into good and evil forces, between those who shared our civilization's values, or supported our efforts to preserve them, and those who were enemies of "civilization." This led Bush to conclude that the only way we could be secure is if other people in the world shared our political values—democracy and freedom, he said, were divine gifts to which all people were entitled. "Our freedom is best protected by ensuring that others are free. Our prosperity depends on the prosperity of others and our security relies on a global effort to secure the rights of all."[1]

Bush's basic premise implies that our ideals and national self-interest go hand in hand. In positing democracy as a divine gift he was also saying that all people want to live in democratic systems and therefore if we "bring" it to them, even by force, we will be acting in both their interests and our own. He made the Middle East his test case and in doing so set himself apart from predecessors he saw as too willing to

tolerant dictatorships in the name of national interest. So now it is fair to ask, in comparison to his predecessors, how responsive has his foreign policy been to American ideals and political values.

The United States has been actively trying to influence politics and shape governments in the Middle East for almost sixty years. After World War II broke up the empires of the colonial powers—Britain, France and Germany—that dominated the area, the United States moved in. The main objectives of successive administrations were to keep the area stable, out of Soviet control, and the oil supply lines open. For the most part this meant staying on good terms with monarchs and dictators, training their armies, and sending billions of dollars in military aid.

When the rare regime change was attempted it was not in support of democracy. A 1953 CIA-backed coup overthrew the elected government of Iran (which was considering nationalization of oil resources) and restored the monarchy, putting on the throne a family hand-picked decades earlier by the British. The Shah of Iran's rule, which featured secular pro-Western polices and a brutal secret police we trained and equipped, created such dissent in Iran that it fomented the Islamic revolution of 1979, which replaced the Shah with an even more oppressive Shia Muslim theocracy. We have not had normal diplomatic relations with Iran since.

To counter the unfriendly Shia regime in Iran, the Reagan administration established close ties with neighboring Iraq's dictator, Saddam Hussein, a secular Sunni Muslim, trained and equipped his army, and supported him through a war with Iran that we hoped would bring down the virulently

anti-American theocracy. The war produced nothing but hundreds of thousands of deaths, some of them caused by Saddam's use of chemical weapons (obtained with the help of the United States) against Iraqi dissidents as well as Iranians.

In 1991 when Saddam invaded neighboring Kuwait, threatening oil exports from that country, the first Bush administration put together an international force under UN auspices to drive Saddam's army back into Iraq. After achieving our goals of reinstating a friendly Kuwaiti monarchy and ensuring access to its oil fields, we withdrew rather than moving on to Baghdad and removing Saddam (whom Bush Sr. had equated with Hitler) from power. U.S. decision makers, aware that Saddam's dictatorship was what held together Iraq's conflictive Kurds, Shia, and Sunni Muslims under one government, preferred the status quo and political stability over regime change. Even when the majority Shia Muslims rebelled against Saddam, we left them to die at Saddam's hand.

Our policy in Afghanistan reaped a similar backlash. When the Soviet Union invaded Afghanistan in 1979, overthrowing the monarchy and establishing a communist government, we declined to intervene militarily. But we did send covert advisers and arms to Muslim rebels to fight the Soviet army. After the Russians were driven out, the strongest faction among the rebels, the Taliban, took over the government and established a fundamentalist Muslim government hostile to the United States. Soon the country became a sanctuary for al-Qaeda and our weapons were turned against us.

In Saudi Arabia, Jordan, Pakistan, and Egypt, national interest rather than ideals has also led us to support monarchies and military dictatorships that suppress opposition and resist elections. Our closest Arab ally, Saudi Arabia, has funded a worldwide system of schools that train students in *Wahhabism*, a branch of Muslim teaching subscribed to by many Islamist fundamentalists, that preaches virulent anti-Semitism.

Even with Israel, our most stalwart ally in the Middle East and the one with whom we share by far the closest political and cultural ties, our alliance was driven primarily by national interest. Israel was created in 1948, but it was not until its display of military prowess in the 1967 Six Day War against neighboring Arab countries that we began to see it as a valuable ally against Soviet intrusion into the Middle East.

Despite our commonality of interests with Israel, we have been unable, in thirty years of trying, to negotiate a settlement of the land dispute between the Israelis and Palestinians. The significant achievement of Jimmy Carter in negotiating a peace agreement between Israel and Egypt ended in the assassination of Anwar Sadat, the Egyptian president who signed the accords. It also fueled the growth of the Islamic Brotherhood, perpetrators of the assassination plot, and to the esteem of one of its members, Dr. Ayman al-Zawahiri, now better known as the brains behind al-Qaeda. There were two more breakthroughs during the Clinton years, the Oslo Accords, which led to the first *intifada*, or uprising, of Palestinians opposed to a peace settlement; and the two-state agreement brokered personally by Clinton in 2000, which was within a hair's breath of agreement before it fell apart. Clinton's first Israeli partner in negotiations, Prime Minister Yitzhak Rabin, was assassinated by an Israeli religious zealot. Ehud Barak, his

successor in the negotiations, lost his job to an opponent of the agreement.

However much we have in common with the Israelis, our national interests differ: ours is regional stability and access to oil and theirs is survival. Many Israelis felt withdrawal from occupied territories or sharing control of Jerusalem would endanger their security (and some religious fundamentalists felt it morally wrong to give away land that, in their view, was theirs by Biblical right.) No matter how close the tie, we cannot define the national interest for Israelis.

George W. Bush sought to change business as usual in the Middle East with his program of "Democracy and Economic Freedom in the Muslim World."[2] With this policy, he tried to align foreign policy goals with American values. He refused to deal with the Palestinian leader Yasir Arafat, made known his support was for Israel and his willingness to use force if Israel is attacked (the first American president to make that pledge). And when he invaded Iraq to overthrow Saddam, he expected it to be the tipping point for the emergence of a "new Middle East" of friendly democratic governments.

However, what Bush labeled the equal pursuit of ideals and national interest compromised our national security, diminished our moral authority, and increased regional instablity. Bush's refusal to deal with Yasir Arafat stalled the peace process for several years. There were new rounds of suicide bombings by Palestinians, followed by Israeli incursions into Palestinian-controlled territory and the building of a wall separating those territories from Israel. The elections Bush called for to replace the obstinate Arafat brought to power Hamas, a militant Islamic faction

that refuses to recognize Israel's right to exist. The democratic process did not produce leaders who believed in the peaceful resolution of differences with Israel or who shared American or Israeli democratic values.

The intervention in Afghanistan in 2002, a military response to 9/11, ended Taliban rule and created a new government chosen by popular election. But the small number of troops we committed to the operation was insufficient to protect freedoms for anyone living outside a few key cities or to put in place a government that had control of the country. Where warlords resumed control of their old territories, many of the same restrictions, including those on women, were restored. Furthermore, free of the Taliban's religious restrictions, many farmers returned to growing poppies as their main crop, and by 2006 Afghanistan was the source of 90 percent of the world's heroin supply. And in the midst of the country's political instability and on top of our commitments elsewhere, we had created a demand for nation building that we were not able to man or fund.

The overthrow of Saddam Hussein in 2003 unleashed the kind of religious and ethnic conflict that Bush Sr. had feared when he decided to end the Gulf War short of regime change. Iraqis elected a new government but one without the power to provide security or guarantee the freedoms promised by the new constitution. The nation fell into sectarian warfare, attracted outside jihadists, and spawned a new generation of terrorists in a nation where there had been few outside of Saddam's government before the invasion.

While advocating democracy for Palestine, Iraq, and Afghanistan, Bush maintained strong ties to monarchies and dictatorships in the region—Saudi Arabia, Pakistan, Egypt, and Jordan—for the same reason his predecessors had: because they all believed it served our national interest to do so. While Bush refused, on principle, to talk with less accommodating dictatorships such as Iran and Syria, these two otherwise enemies made common cause in supporting an attack on Israel by radical Shia elements in Lebanon (Hezbollah). And Iran took pleasure in its ability to ignore Bush's demand that it end its program for developing nuclear technology. Moreover, in fighting a war to promote democracy, the Bush administration endorsed actions never before sanctioned by our government: torturing those suspected of being enemy combatants and holding them for years without charges being filed or the right to see evidence against them. When Bill Clinton, through NATO and the UN, involved the United States in nation building in the Balkans, Haiti, and Somalia, Bush called it "misplaced idealism."[3] Bush's own approach to foreign policy has been a combination of brutal realism (pursuing national interest at the expense of international law) and very poorly executed idealism (the promotion of democracy through regime change). Unwilling to commit enough troops to stop the violence in Iraq, the Bush policy made the U.S. look feckless in the eyes of the world. So much money was borrowed to pay for the wars that our indebtedness to foreign creditors jeopardized our economic security. Although Bush talked about pursuing his democracy agenda with a preemptive attack on Iran or North Korea, the wars in Iraq and Afghanistan left the armed forces with virtually no battle ready troops other than those already deployed. American credibility sank to all time low and anti-Americanism to an all time high, undermining the efforts of our diplomats.

Critics say that Bush's policy was no different from that of his predecessors, that his program of regime change and refusal to carry on business as usual with dictators was just national interest dressed up to look like high principle. But taking his stated purpose at face value, did the pursuit of ideals achieve more than the pursuit of raw self-interest?

[1]U.S. State Department, "Fiscal Yr 2004–2009 Department of State and USAID Strategic Plan" (www.state.gov).
[2]Ibid., 3.
[3]Steven R. Weisman, "Democracy Push by Bush Attracts Doubters in Party," *New York Times*, March 17, 2006.

AP Images/Oded Balilty

The United States's thirty-year effort to mediate the Israeli-Palestinian conflict is crucial to our overall goals in the Middle East. The fierce resistance of these Israeli settlers to their government's attempt to remove them from the occupied territories in conjunction with the peace process shows how difficult it is for the Israeli government to change the status quo, let alone for an outside power such as the United States.

parts of the world. Even among our closest allies, including Britain, Canada, Germany, and Australia, public opinion was against the war. International criticism increased after revelations about rendition (sending prisoners to other countries where laws do not prevent use of torture), secret CIA prisons for holding suspected terrorists, and the use of torture in American-run prisons in Iraq and Afghanistan. Animosity deepened when Bush claimed he did not have to abide by all terms of the Geneva Convention on prisoners of war. By 2006 anti-Americanism was at an historic peak. (See Table 18.1.)

Negative public opinion can have serious consequences if it encourages people to pressure their governments to refuse to help the United States achieve its objectives. When Bush had to go to NATO to ask that more troops be sent to Afghanistan and to ask allies to share the burden for reconstructing Iraq, he found himself working against public sentiment in those countries. It is a consequence of living in an intensely interdependent world that the leaders of activist governments must court world, as well as domestic, opinion.

"I miss the Commies."

Redefining Security in the Global Age

The international environment is always in a state of flux. Power shifts from region to region and country to country, and the basis of power itself changes. In some eras a country's diplomatic skills are paramount, in others military resources determine a nation's relative strength in the international hierarchy; and at yet other times it is economic strength that gives a country leverage. Today the United States has different links to the international community than it did in the eighteenth and nineteenth centuries, or in the mid- to late twentieth century when we may have reached our zenith of international influence.

Sometimes paradigmatic shifts in the international power structure force profound changes in how a country pursues its foreign policy goals. We saw this after World War I and the Russian Revolution, again after World War II, and with the breakup of the Soviet empire and the end of a bipolar balance of power. At the beginning of the twenty-first century, the emergence of non-state actors as global security threats and the rise of new economic giants to challenge the dominance of the old western industrial powers brought about other shifts. These changes in the structure of the international community require a reassessment of how we pursue both physical and economic security. In this section we look at some of these changes.

Physical Security

In our global economy international exchanges of people and goods are ubiquitous, and there are many new points of vulnerability, including the computer systems on which international business and finance and national security systems are now completely dependent. Globalization means that foreign problems left unattended find their way to our door, not only armed conflicts but also financial and environmental crises and epidemic diseases that can spread rapidly from one country to another.

World Health

During the Clinton administration the State Department declared health, education, and environmental protection in developing countries as primary U.S. foreign policy goals, linking them to U.S. national security. Almost everyone can see the worldwide AIDS epidemic as an urgent humanitarian problem, but many in Congress were stunned by Clinton's characterization of the AIDS epidemic in Africa as a national security concern. Today it is widely accepted that it is, and the Bush administration has given the AIDS epidemic higher priority than his predecessor did.

Eight thousand people die of AIDS and 14,000 more are infected every day. Of nearly forty million people infected with the human immunodeficiency virus (HIV) worldwide, two-thirds are in Africa. It is spreading most rapidly among women and from them to their newborns. The United Nations estimates that in six sub-Saharan nations, the average child born in 2004 will not live to forty years of age.[47] Local economies have been decimated and millions of children orphaned. Adding to the potential for instability is the rising incidence of AIDS in the armies of some African nations; one in four South African soldiers is reportedly infected with HIV/AIDS.[48]

A 2002 CIA report reinforced the view of the AIDS epidemic as an international security problem; it identified five "major regional or global players," including China and Russia, whose political and economic stability are endangered by surging rates of HIV and AIDS.[49] Money to teach AIDS prevention and pay for health care is now an important aspect of foreign aid. However, Bush has attached strings to the huge increase he has proposed in funding to fight AIDS. No money is to be released to any government whose performance or policies are not consistent with our foreign policy objectives. Thus far this has meant that most of the promised $15 billion has not been released. America's main effort against the spread of AIDS and treatment of those infected is being waged by private entities such as the Gates Foundation and Bill Clinton's Global Initiatives.

Containing diseases like AIDS, drug-resistant tuberculosis, and bird flu that can spread rapidly from one country to another, and treating the ill, have become essential to protecting national security in a very interdependent world.

Nuclear Proliferation

A few years ago, it was hard to imagine that we might look back at the Cold War as a simpler and even safer time, yet today's world is more complex than it was in the days of MAD. Nuclear proliferation makes defense against a nuclear strike exceedingly difficult because it is no longer sufficient just to monitor national defense establishments. It is less certain from where or from whom a strike might come. The CIA's failure to predict India's nuclear tests, despite years of surveillance of its arms program, is not reassuring regarding our ability to determine when other countries, let alone nonstate actors, have gained access to nuclear, chemical, and biological weapons or missile technology.

Both the Clinton and the Bush administrations declared that unsecured nuclear material and its possible access by terrorist groups constituted the primary threat to world peace and the country's most difficult security challenge: how can we stop terrorist groups, acting alone or in concert with a state hostile to the United States, from gaining access to missile technology and to the materials needed to make biological, chemical, or nuclear weapons. During the Cold War, only five nations (the United States, the Soviet Union, Britain, France, and China) produced and stockpiled nuclear weapons. The MAD strategy was rooted in, and dependent on, the conviction that the fairly small number of people who were in a position to make decisions about the use of nuclear weapons were sane and rational and had something to lose if their countries were destroyed and that the threat of mutual destruction would keep any leader from launching a first strike.

But now, many states are trying to gain a nuclear capability, and the materials and technology to make nuclear weapons have proliferated across the globe. When India and Pakistan conducted tests in 1998, the number of nuclear-ready countries increased to seven. Now there are at least nine nations—and perhaps as many as forty more nations—that have the capacity to produce warheads. The head of Pakistan's nuclear program has admitted selling materials and parts to China and Iran and perhaps other countries as well (perhaps with tacit official consent, since he received only token punishment).

And large reservoirs of enriched uranium and plutonium needed to make nuclear weapons lie unsecured and undocumented at sites in Russia and other parts of the former Soviet Union. Substantial black market trafficking in these materials is well documented.[50] Once the material is acquired, the technology necessary to build a simple uranium bomb like the one dropped on Hiroshima in 1945 is available to "anyone with a personal computer."[51] Although it is not as simple to assemble an operational bomb as that quote suggests, the likelihood that nuclear weapons will fall into the hands of terrorist groups continues to grow.

Defense Policy

Our defense policy has evolved in rough correspondence with the changing approaches to foreign policy discussed in the previous section. We began as a nation that feared standing armies and foreign involvements but have developed the largest conventional armed forces in the world. We moved on to acquire a nuclear arsenal capable of destroying the earth many times over. Each policy outlived its effectiveness as new threats emerged.

For more than forty years we thought our military strength was our most important asset in our effort to keep the world "free." Relying on the strategy of MAD, we built up an arsenal of nuclear-tipped missiles and bombers capable of delivering nuclear warheads. But we neglected other aspects of our military capability, including the capacity to fight limited wars with conventional weaponry. Yet conventional fighting forces have always been more important than nuclear weapons in pursuing containment and other foreign policy goals.

South Koreans burn a North Korean flag in protest of their neighbor's nuclear weapons program. Despite world pressure to abandon the program, North Korea conducted an underground test of a nuclear weapon in 2006.

The Vietnam War demonstrated what a drain on our economic and military resources a limited war could be, and after our defeat there, the Carter and Reagan administrations placed greater emphasis on improving combat readiness and building a new arsenal of high-tech weaponry. The Reagan administration vowed to crush the Soviets economically by forcing them into a spending war in a race to acquire an ABM system. The arms race added to the Soviets' economic woes but also endangered our own economic security by contributing to huge budget deficits and robbing the civilian economy of many of our best scientists and engineers.

The end of the Cold War removed the need to prepare for a major nuclear confrontation with the Soviet Union. The arsenal of warheads, ICBMs, and nuclear bombers was drastically cut, and many domestic and foreign bases closed. After the Persian Gulf War, the size of the military was cut by a third, and base closings continued. We also reached tentative agreement with Russia to reduce our stockpile of 10,400 operable nuclear weapons to 2000. By the turn of the century, military spending was at its lowest level—3 percent of gross domestic product (GDP)—since before World War II.

By the beginning of the Clinton administration it was clear that the major security threats—terrorism, nuclear proliferation, environmental degradation, and political instability caused by poverty and disease—were not being addressed by old defense strategies and that military training and spending had to be re-

assessed. Early in the Bush administration, military planners called for a shift to give the military a "richer set of military options."[52]

Today, the primary objective of military reform is to make our armed forces more mobile, capable of a quick response, and armed with lighter, more flexible high-tech weaponry. A major showdown over this change came at the outset of Secretary of Defense Donald Rumsfeld's tenure. Rumsfeld wanted to kill new heavy-weapons programs and use the funds to outfit a mobile light infantry more suitable to counterterrorism. He won despite opposition by some of the Army's top leadership.

In 2001, in response to the 9/11 attacks, the Pentagon began to prepare the armed forces for **asymmetrical warfare**—conflict between combatants of very unequal strength. In this type of warfare, the weaker antagonist, knowing that direct military confrontation would lead to certain defeat, identifies and attacks a weak spot in the armor of the stronger opponent. Al-Qaeda found a security vulnerability in one of our strengths—the openness and access of American society—and used it to its advantage in organizing the attack, training the operatives, and eventually gaining control of commercial airliners to use as weapons against American citizens.

Transforming the military to fight this new kind of warfare requires a break with old strategies, weaponry, training, traditions, and career paths established in the armed forces over a period of decades. It has not been easy for civilian leaders to win acceptance among military professionals who have prepared for everything from guerrilla and limited warfare to all-out nuclear confrontation and some of whom believe we have not seen the last of traditional ground warfare. Rumsfeld forced out those who resisted, including the Army's chief of staff and others who opposed an Iraq invasion plan that was based on the new thinking—fewer troops, with lighter-weight, more mobile equipment. The top leaders argued that Rumsfeld was asking for fewer troops than needed to carry out the mission, especially for stabilizing Iraq after Saddam Hussein's overthrow. In addition, many of the lightweight, unarmored vehicles that troops had to use to patrol postinvasion Iraq and to transport supplies became death traps. Three years into the war, despite all evidence to the contrary, Rumsfeld insisted that the war plan had succeeded.

Rumsfeld also built on the policy of outsourcing military functions that dates back to the 1980s. The armed services bolster service personnel with military contractors—private citizens—to help train recruits and do other combat-related work. In Bosnia in 1996, one of every ten Americans in the peacekeeping force was a civilian under contract to the Pentagon.[53] The numbers are at least as high in Iraq, where low-paid infantry officers can be assigned to protect civilian employees earning three to four times as much and who are not subject to the same rules, discipline, or chain of command as regular military personnel.

There are two reasons for outsourcing—one is the assumption that private companies can provide logistical and support services more cheaply than the military. But many, if not all, privatized services have proven to be more, not less costly, and the contracting process has been riddled with fraud. (See the "You Are There" in Chapter 12.) The second reason is that both civilian and military leaders have opted to stay with an all-volunteer force rather than reinstating the draft, which Nixon abolished in 1971 to quell anti-Vietnam War protests. By outsourcing much of the work troops would have done, the military can get by with far fewer personnel.

The conversion to all-volunteer armed services more than thirty years ago produced enough enlistees to meet the military's combat needs until the wars in Afghanistan and Iraq required a large-scale commitment of troops for a prolonged period. Now with National Guard and army reserves accounting for more than 40 percent of all troops in Iraq, and Congress and the administration unwilling to support the draft, the Defense Department is more dependent than ever on privatization.

Defense Spending

Although Rumsfeld tried to shift planning and training away from preparing for large conventional ground warfare, he had virtually no impact on how defense dollars are spent. Despite administration claims that the greatest threats to national security come from terrorists planning to attack our chemical plants, public utilities, transportation facilities, nuclear storage sites, or to smuggle in WMD through our ports or air cargo, we still spend ten times as much (more than a half trillion dollars in 2007) preparing for conventional warfare abroad than on homeland security.

Before spending on defense can be redirected to homeland security, the grip that arms manufacturers, military leaders, and their congressional allies have on the defense budget will have to be loosened. This iron triangle is the military-industrial-political complex President Eisenhower spoke of as he left office in 1961. Recognizing the potential for profit-hungry defense industries and pork-hungry congressional allies to drive military spending, determining the kind of weaponry purchased, and encouraging the use of military force to achieve objectives, Eisenhower warned: "The conjunction of an immense military establishment and a large arms industry is new in the American experience," and "we must not fail to comprehend its grave implications. . . . The potential for the disastrous rise of misplaced power exists and will persist. We must never let the weight of this combination endanger our liberties or democratic processes."

Sen. John McCain (R-Ariz.) is one of many who thinks Eisenhower's "fear became a reality long ago. He was worried that priorities are set by what benefits corporations as opposed to what benefits the country."[54]

Trying to change military spending priorities is like trying to turn around an ocean liner on a dime. This is perhaps the largest challenge we face in formulating effective national security policy. But if protecting our physical security depends on stopping terrorist attacks on our own soil, a drastic reordering of military spending must happen soon.

Building Alliances

One lesson learned since we began defending against groups of loosely allied terrorists who are scattered across Europe, the Middle East, North Africa, and South and Southeast Asia is that trying to pursue them on our own is impossible. Our principal military allies are still Canada, Great Britain, and the nations of Western Europe with whom we share cultural heritage, commitment to democratic government, and common membership in NATO.

Since its beginnings in 1949, NATO has acquired a much broader strategic focus than its original purpose of deterring Soviet aggression in Europe. Despite the unity of purpose among the founding members, there were always internal differences.

In the post-Cold War years, NATO members have collaborated on ending ethnic warfare in the former Yugoslavia and addressing separatist movements in the successor states of the Soviet Union. By 2004, NATO's original dozen members had expanded to twenty-six, encompassing most of the countries of Eastern as well as Western Europe and Turkey. The cultural cohesiveness and dominant purpose—deterring nuclear war and expansion of the Soviet Union—are gone, and many members are at odds with the United States's strategy for fighting terrorism. Leaders were under enormous pressure from their citizens, especially Muslims, to refuse collaboration with the United States in the invasion of Iraq. Several members did send small contingents to do support work, but only Great Britain sent combat troops. NATO members, however, do provide the largest contingent of troops fighting al-Qaeda and the Taliban in Afghanistan. And some countries that refused public support to the Bush administration—France and Germany for example—provided a good deal of support behind the scenes for the apprehension of suspected terrorists. How NATO will evolve remains to be seen, but its original singularity of purpose no longer exists.

The United States has treaty and bilateral security relationships with many other countries including China, Japan, South Korea, and the nations of Latin America, but none as close as the original working relationship in NATO. Moreover, the Bush administration definition of the threat of terrorism and the strategies for dealing with it have left little political wiggle room for the leaders of other countries who might want to be part of a multilateral effort. They can either join the United States on its terms or go their own way. This same kind of preemptive approach to defining policy has alienated delegates to regional and international agencies as well. American prestige in international organizations it cofounded, such as the UN, has never been so low, and Bush's successor will have to mend these relationships because guaranteeing our security demands a multilateral approach.

Economic Security

Although some still see the world as unipolar in terms of military power, in the economic sphere the competition is intense. Although the public eye is focused on Iraq and terrorism, much of our foreign policy establishment is involved with economic affairs. We are always looking for new markets for exports to close the trade gap and create more jobs at home and to limit our vulnerability to foreign creditors. Much of this economic diplomacy is carried out by the State Department or representatives to international financial institutions such as the International Monetary Fund and the World Bank. But other cabinet departments, Commerce and Treasury especially, devote increasing amounts of time to the pursuit of international economic goals, and American ambassadors now receive training in how to promote American businesses.[55]

Trade

Trade problems loom large in our foreign policy. At the end of World War II, the United States was the world's greatest trading power; half of all world trade passed through our ports. Today that figure has fallen to 14 percent, and we have lost much of the power we once had to regulate the flow of trade.[56] This is especially significant because trade now accounts for about a quarter of our GDP and one-third of our economic growth.[57]

We import far more goods from other countries than they import from us, creating a trade deficit. For years this deficit has been climbing, reaching a new high with virtually each successive quarter of financial reporting; it amounted to roughly one-quarter of a trillion dollars in 2006. We have not had a trade surplus since 1975. Between that shortfall and the deficit created by our government spending hundreds of billions more than it receives in revenues each year we have become the world's largest debtor nation. We need to borrow a great deal of money; by one estimate we need an inflow of at least $3 billion per day to keep our economy afloat. In 2005 foreign investors spent more than $1 trillion on Treasury bonds, equities in American companies, and other securities. Much of that money came from China and the Middle East.[58]

Our huge trade deficit has greatly weakened the dollar. Although that should improve our trade imbalance (because it makes American goods cheaper to buy abroad), it has not. Americans continue to buy massive quantities of imported goods because they are so much cheaper than American-produced goods, and American investors continue to take their money abroad looking for cheaper labor and less government regulation. (See Chapter 16 for a discussion of outsourcing.) Despite the demand for cheap, foreign goods, American workers and producers still make it difficult for our trade negotiators and financiers by lobbying for restrictions (import quotas, tariffs, and surcharges) to protect domestic goods from foreign competition. But the ability of our, or any, government to adopt protectionist measures and have them stick is limited by membership in the **World Trade Organization** (WTO). The WTO, headquartered in Geneva, Switzerland, was founded in 1995 to remove barriers to free trade and to mediate trade disputes between member countries. WTO policies are set primarily by consensus of its member countries, represented by their trade ministers. All members belong to the general council, which is empowered to resolve trade disputes. However, there is an appellate body, and countries can be sanctioned for not abiding by WTO decisions.[59]

The near-universal membership of the WTO includes many smaller and poorer countries that do not have the legal infrastructure or the political freedoms that exist in the United States. This has created concern among U.S. interest groups that membership in the WTO will cause a rollback in regulatory standards to the lowest level existing in any member country. Unions worry they will lose well-paying jobs with benefits to nonunionized workers in poorer countries who will work for low wages, no benefits, and few safety protections and who in some cases lack the freedom to unionize. And environmental activists fear that none of the regulations applied to food production and distribution in the United States will be enforced for foodstuffs imported from countries without a commitment to environmental protection. They claim that globalization and free trade are hastening the relocation of industry to countries where there are no limitations on toxic emissions into the air and

Carol Guzy/The Washington Post. Reprinted with permission.

A demonstrator refuses to give way to a police horse during protests against economic policies toward developing nations.

water or regulation of the dumping and storing of hazardous waste. Human rights groups claim that free trade is adding to the already widespread abuse of child labor, unequal pay for women, and the exploitation of prison labor. They oppose the removal of barriers to trade and investment in countries controlled by dictatorships, fearing that by helping build up these economies, we will strengthen their governments and contribute to even greater human rights abuses.

Protecting American workers and industries sounds patriotic. Supporters of protectionism argue that these policies protect new industries until they can get established and support old industries essential to our defense and basic self-sufficiency. But protectionist policies usually result in higher consumer prices because of the elimination of competition from foreign labor and the products they produce. Free traders, who include all presidents since Ronald Reagan, argue that it is cheaper to compensate displaced domestic workers and retrain them for other jobs than it is to pay the higher cost for protected goods and labor. They also claim that in addition to increasing prices, protectionism also discourages industry efficiency, just as the lack of domestic competition does. Finally, critics of protectionism say that imposing quotas or tariffs on other nations' goods just leads them to respond in kind, limiting our export markets. Retaliatory measures can spiral into a trade war, and trade wars have the potential to expand into military competition to protect market access.

Despite these dangers, and our treaty obligations not to adopt protectionist measures, demand for their adoption continues because job retention and creation are major issues in all industrialized countries. George W. Bush elevated free trade to a "moral principle," but this did not keep him from imposing quotas or tariffs on steel, textiles, beef, and other goods to satisfy the demands of a number of interest groups.[60] Such actions may temporarily relieve domestic political pressure, but most of Bush's measures ended up in international arbitration. And despite great interest group pressure, presidents Clinton and Bush advocated for and signed into law agreements (NAFTA and CAFTA), which established the United States, Mexico and the states of Central America as a free trade area.

The strongest free trade area is the **European Union (EU).** Formerly called the European Economic Community or European Common Market, the EU was formed in 1957 to foster political and economic integration in Europe. In 1992, the EU removed all internal economic barriers and customs posts for member nations, and in 2002 it began phasing in a common currency (the euro). The membership of the EU has expanded to twenty-five from its original six members, with four more awaiting entry. The EU, with a single trade policy, a single agricultural policy, and a single market of 440 million people, is the world's biggest trading bloc. Despite the near complete focus on the war on terrorism, trade will continue to be a—if not *the*—central foreign policy issue for most Americans because of what it means for job security and the cost of goods.

Promoting Prosperity Abroad

The words in the State Department's mission statement—"our prosperity depends on the prosperity of others"—has become a mantra of our foreign policy, if not yet a national conviction.[61] About one half of the world's people live on less than $2 a day. The fear is that globalization will exacerbate this already lopsided division of the world's wealth, leaving behind anyone without educational or technological resources. If we want to change this we have to strike down trade barriers that make it difficult for poor countries to export to the United States. Despite the free trade rhetoric, American and European protectionist policies on agricultural products are some of the most economically damaging policies farmers in the poorest countries face. As one World Bank official noted, "The average cow is supported by three times the level of income of a poor person in Africa."[62] We also have to change the kind of aid we provide and the way we provide it.

The majority of our foreign aid has been in the form of military assistance, which is very good for U.S. arms manufacturers but not for development in the donee countries (The United States is the world's largest arms dealer.) Aid can also take the form of grants, technical assistance, or guaranteed loans, for example. Loans and credits to help bail out countries suffering from recession or financial collapse became a common form of foreign aid in the 1980s and 1990s. Though Congress and the public have been reluctant to help pay for the political and financial failings of other countries, especially when they are strong trade competitors, in the global economy we are all swimming in the same financial sea, and a regional economic crisis can quickly become a world crisis. If it foments political instability, such an economic crisis may even lead to larger security crises. The technology that has allowed money to move almost instantaneously from one country to another has also, as former Federal Reserve Board chair Alan Greenspan warned, "enhanced the ability of the system to rapidly transmit problems in one part of the globe to another."[63] To prevent or minimize the impact on our economy, we have to help pay for other governments' mistakes—just as they may have to help pay for ours.

Historically the primary object of foreign aid has been to promote development and stability, but indirectly it is a means for influencing the direction of other countries' development, expanding export markets for U.S. goods, and spreading our sphere of influence. During the Cold War era, when we were trying to woo countries from the Soviet sphere of influence, we targeted aid to countries that were politically important but not necessarily democratic or stable. Aid money ended up in the bank accounts of corrupt leaders—as in Haiti, Zaire, and Panama, for example—or was spent on showy construction projects that did little to further development. Most of the money earmarked for economic assistance has been channeled through the State Departments' Agency for International Development, USAID, and 80 percent of its contracts and grants were used to purchase American goods.[64] Not much of this aid trickled down to the poorest people, and when it did, it was in the form of food staples that may keep people alive but did little to keep them healthy or to improve their economic status. Such failures led to congressional and public disillusionment with the effectiveness of foreign aid, both as a tool of foreign policy and as a spur to economic development.

That is why, relative to other industrial countries, the United States is not a large aid donor; our foreign aid budget is dwarfed (as a percentage of GDP) by those of Japan and Western Europe. Some people wonder why we bother at all to aid governments with poor human rights records, that have made little effort to improve the lot of the average person, and that are sometimes militantly anti-American in their foreign policy rhetoric. The reason is, aside from humanitarian impulses, that it is not good that half of the world's population is unable to buy the agricultural and industrial goods we export. For many years, the world's largest economies have been one another's principal trading partners. With their populations stabilizing, their economies and ours may not be able to continue to grow unless there is growth in developing economies that creates new markets for our goods and services.

Today it is less likely that aid money will find its way into the hands of a corrupt leader because of safeguards that make receipt of aid conditional on local government policies. The Bush administration proposed increasing aid to the poorest countries by 50 percent but only if they commit to democracy, free trade, open markets, and deregulation.[65] Also, to avoid the corruption in state bureaucracies, aid programs are now often funded and administered through humanitarian agencies and other nongovernmental organizations.

Effective foreign assistance enhances the chance of success for other policy. For example the financial support and military aid the United States gave to victims of the 2004 tsunami in the Indian Ocean, many of whom were Muslim, worked on both humanitarian and political levels. In Indonesia, a county that is very important to us in fighting Islamist terrorism, the number of Indonesians who looked on the United States favorably increased substantially after direct contact with soldiers and other aid workers. Aid can be seen as an investment that will pay off in stability and friendly governments, that in turn will translate into more exports and reduced military spending for us.

Conclusion: Is Our Foreign Policy Responsive?

As the head of the world's largest military and economic power and a partner in major military and trade alliances, the president has a constituency larger than the American public. He is often called on to be responsive to the needs of other people or countries—victims of famines, civil wars, natural disasters, and human rights abuses or countries in need of military and economic assistance.

But is the direction of our foreign policy responsive to public opinion, and should it be, given how poorly informed most Americans are on specific issues? Public attitudes can constrain the general policy directions of the president and Congress, but presidents can do a lot to shape these attitudes. Over the long term, as in Vietnam, the administration must be somewhat responsive to public sentiment that intensely opposes administration policy. But it is far harder for the public to have a short-term impact on military policy. Because everyone agrees on the general goal of protecting the nation from external attack, the public is far less inclined to be critical of military policy than it is of other areas of foreign policy. But this free rein has led to excessive secrecy, inefficiencies, and extravagant spending that are surely not in the public interest.

After 9/11, there was no need to convince the public that a threat existed, and the public gave the president unprecedented support for military action against al-Qaeda. As long as the public believed in a connection between Iraq and the 9/11 attacks, there was substantial backing for President Bush's preemptive war policy. But when evidence for such a connection failed to materialize and the war turned into an occupation characterized by urban warfare and sectarian conflict, public support waned. Nevertheless it is difficult for a government to respond to public opinion shifts once troops are engaged in combat. The commitment has been made, and responsiveness to public mood has to wait.

In other areas of foreign policy, the public has more opportunity for influence than in the past, even on more technical issues such as trade, immigration, and human rights. The rise of powerful lobbies and the voting blocs of "hyphenated" Americans, for example, can have a significant impact on policy decisions. The information revolution also has given the public a much greater opportunity to be informed on the whole range of foreign policy issues, even, on occasion, on classified war policy. Without the dissemination of photographs showing prisoner abuse at the Abu Ghraib prison in Iraq, public pressure might never have been brought to bear to end the practices.

Because of our greater connectedness to all parts of the world through the Internet and because of globalization in general, Americans are far more aware of the relationships between foreign policy and their everyday lives and standard of living. In the day-to-day world of diplomacy, Foreign Service officers work tirelessly to promote American agricultural and other exports and American business interests in general. The State Department's own description of its work cites creating jobs and opening markets as central to its mission. Representing American policy as a vehicle for the promotion of individual economic interests is in itself an indication of how necessary policy makers feel it is to at least have the appearance of being responsive to the public.

Murtha Goes Public

urtha discussed his dilemma with Minority Leader Nancy Pelosi, knowing she, too, wanted to take on the president's war policy. After meeting with the Democratic Caucus to describe the policy recommendation he wanted to put before the House, it was decided Murtha alone would introduce his resolution. The rest of the party would "keep their distance while their own Marine charged up the Hill."[66]

At a press conference on November 17, 2005, Murtha said, "The war in Iraq is not going as advertised. It is a flawed policy wrapped in illusion." He spoke of his visits to the severely wounded saying, "This war needs to be personalized. . . . Our military has done everything that has been asked of them, the U.S. can not accomplish anything further in Iraq militarily. It is time to bring them home."[67] He released the text of the resolution he said he would submit to the House. It gave eight reasons why it was time to change direction in Iraq and proposed three actions: no new troops would be deployed to Iraq and those already there would be withdrawn "at the earliest practicable date"; a quick strike force would be deployed in a neighboring country; and the stabilization of Iraq would be pursued by diplomatic means.

The next day, as Murtha walked on to the House floor to debate his resolution, Democrats cheered and Republicans went on the attack. A junior Republican member was sent to the podium to call Murtha a coward and to remind the decorated veteran that Marines "never cut and run." Democrats stormed into the aisles with raised fists demanding an apology and removal of the insult from the daily record. They screamed, "You're pathetic, you're pathetic" at the Republican name callers; one of their number crossed to the Republi-

can side to mix it up with those attacking Murtha but the Majority Leader arrived and restored order.[68]

Murtha's resolution was never allowed to come to a vote because Republicans controlled how bills and resolutions work their way through the House. They substituted Murtha's page-long proposal for withdrawal of troops at "the earliest practicable date" with a twenty-one-word, one sentence resolution calling for "immediate termination" of the U.S. presence in Iraq.[69] Of course this was not what Murtha was proposing, and, as Republicans knew, virtually no one would vote for a measure that said U.S. troops should just get on a plane and go home. Although the Democratic caucus claimed it would vote however Murtha directed, a yes vote would have been an albatross for most members to carry into the election. There was no chance Murtha would ask them to support the Republican version because he would be voting no himself. The Resolution went down on a 403-3 vote.

But the fight was only beginning. The administration brought out its big guns to attack Murtha. The vice-president called him a politician who had lost his "memory or his backbone." Bush's press secretary called Murtha's position "a surrender to terrorists" and said he found it "baffling that [Murtha] is endorsing the policy positions of Michael Moore and the extreme liberal wing of the Democratic Party."[70] And, predictably, Murtha was swift-boated; within a few days of his press conference, conservative blogs were questioning whether he really earned the two Purple Hearts he was awarded for service in Vietnam.

The White House decided to embrace the war as a central issue in the midterm elections and had a seventy-

four-page Pentagon briefing book sent to Republican congressional offices to help them make the case that withdrawal from Iraq "would mean thousands of troops would have died for nothing, would give extremists a launching pad from which to build an Islamo-fascist empire, and would hand the United States its most humiliating defeat since Vietnam."[71]

Murtha struck back at his critics, singling out Cheney, "I like guys who get five deferments, have never been there and . . . send other people to war," and then won't listen to those who have been there.[72] Murtha was so discouraged by the administration's refusal to reconsider its Iraq policy that he said if he were young he would avoid military service. The chairman of the Joint Chiefs of Staff accused Murtha of "damaging the morale of the troops."[73]

On and on it went for months. For the most part Murtha hung out there alone, although a few other decorated combat veterans like Charles Rangel (D-NY) joined in the attack on Cheney. Minority Leader Pelosi was one of the few to commit to Murtha's plan for withdrawal, but she refused to call for the Democratic caucus to take a position because "a vote on the war is an individual vote."[74] Senate Minority Leader Harry Reid, looking for Senate gains for Democrats in November, and Hillary Clinton, with an eye on a possible presidential run in 2008, agreed with Cheney that immediate withdrawal would be "a big mistake."[75] Joe Biden (D-Del.), the ranking Democrat on the Senate Foreign Affairs committee also declined to endorse a withdrawal resolution, saying "political posturing" wouldn't help; things were going sufficiently well in Iraq, he said, that the United States would be able to start drawing troops out in 2006 and wind things down in

"Who ever thought patriotism would be so complicated?"

2007. The head of the House Democratic campaign committee simply said the Democrats would develop their own Iraq War strategy "when the time is right."[76]

Democrats were split over how to handle the Iraq issue. Almost all thought the administration's policy was a colossal failure, but it was such a failure that options to improve the situation were limited. And of course, they did not want to be painted by the Republicans as pursuing a policy of "cut and run." It was not until six months after Murtha's call for withdrawal, and much closer to the midterm elections, that the Democratic Party leadership signed a letter to the president calling for an exit strategy; several members introduced new resolutions calling for withdrawal. But Sen. Clinton continued to hang back, leading Murtha to attack her for not speaking out more forcefully.[77] For being out there and taking the brickbats—that is, for services rendered—and perhaps because he felt let down by the lack of fighting spirit from some of his colleagues, Murtha wrote a letter to members of the Democratic Caucus saying that if their party regained control of the House, he wanted to be considered for Majority Leader.[78]

The abuse Murtha took for criticizing Iraqi war policy illustrates the upper hand a president has in wartime. The White House felt certain it could get away with accusing a thrice-decorated veteran and military hawk of being an unpatriotic coward simply because he had the temerity to criticize war policy. Equally telling was Bush's ability to harness his party to his ends, getting House members to insult a distinguished member of their own chamber in defense of the authority of the *executive branch*. Using the "we're at war" rationale, Bush was also able to intimidate most Democrats from doing little more than coming to Murtha's personal defense. And Bush was able to do it all with lower approval ratings than any other wartime president and in the face of majority opinion opposed to the war.

Under attack from one Republican president, Murtha quoted another, Theodore Roosevelt, who said in 1918, "to announce that there must be no criticism of the president, or that we are to stand by the president, right or wrong, is not only unpatriotic and servile, but is morally treasonable to the American public."[79]

Key Terms

isolationism
Monroe Doctrine
containment
North Atlantic Treaty Organization (NATO)
Cold War
mutual assured destruction (MAD)
domino theory
Vietnam syndrome
détente
free trade
protectionism
preemption
asymmetrical warfare
World Trade Organization (WTO)
European Union (EU)

Further Reading

Louis Fisher, *Presidential War Power* (Lawrence: University of Kansas Press, 1995). A staff member of the Congressional Research Service reviews presidential use of the military from the first days of the Republic to the present and concludes that congressional war-making powers have been usurped by the executive branch.

Thomas L. Friedman, *The World Is Flat: A Brief History of the Twenty-first Century* (New York: Farrar, Straus & Giroux, 2005). An account by the country's best-know foreign affairs columnist of how globalization has leveled the playing field for workers and entrepreneurs around the world. Within this optimistic assessment of what is ahead for the world economy, there is advice about what Americans must do to stay competitive.

James Mann, *The Rise of the Vulcans: Bush's War Cabinet* (New York: Viking, 2003). This study of key members of George W. Bush's cabinet and national security staff explains how they came to be so influential in setting the direction of foreign policy.

Robert S. McNamara, *In Retrospect: The Tragedy and Lessons of Vietnam* (New York: Times Books, 1995). The former secretary of defense and a principal architect of Vietnam War policy gives eleven reasons why he thinks the Vietnam War was a mistake, rejecting the domino theory and placing a preponderance of blame on the incompetence of South Vietnamese forces and U.S. underestimation of the North Vietnamese.

Joseph Nye, *The Paradox of American Power: Why the World's Only Superpower Can't Go It Alone* (New York: Oxford University Press, 2002). A political science professor and former Clinton Defense Department official explains why he believes that unilateralism cannot work in the era of globalization.

David Remnick, *Lenin's Tomb: The Last Days of the Soviet Empire* (New York: Random House, 1993). This is a critically acclaimed account of the demise of the Soviet Union.

Thomas Ricks, *Fiasco: The Military Adventure in Iraq* (New York: Penguin, 2006) Written by the *Washington Post's* Pulitzer Prize-winning senior Pentagon correspondent, this is the most acclaimed account to date of mistakes in planning for the post-war period in Iraq. It is based almost entirely on inside sources.

Neil Sheehan, *A Bright Shining Lie* (New York: Random House, 1988). The Vietnam War is seen through its effect on a young American officer.

Lawrence Wright, *The Looming Tower: Al Qaeda and the Path to 9/11* (New York: Alfred A. Knopf, 2006). This is perhaps *the* best account of how the failure of the FBI and CIA to share information contributed to the successful attacks on the World Trade Center. Grippingly told by a *New Yorker* staff writer based on his interviews with the FBI's principal Arabic-speaking agent and other principals involved in investigations of pre-9/11 al-Qaeda attacks.

For Viewing

Ambush in Mogadishu (1998). This PBS *Frontline* documentary on the incident that came to be known as Blackhawk Down—the killing of eighteen American soldiers in Somalia—won the Edward R. Murrow journalism prize. It contains gripping footage of the shootout between Marines and Somalia warlord gangs and shows how a humanitarian mission can draw American troops into conflict. View it online at www.pbs.org/wgbh/ pages/frontline/shows/ambush, and compare it with the popular commercial film on the same event, *Blackhawk Down*, 2001.

The Best Years of Our Lives (1946). Winner of seven Academy Awards including Best Picture, this film was one of first to deal seriously with the problems war veterans have reacclimating to civilian life. It emphasizes the solidarity among World War II vets of different ages and backgrounds by focusing on three from the same town who meet on the return journey at war's end—one from the working class, a second from the middle class, and the third a wealthy banker. The middle-class teen was played by a nonactor and real-life double amputee veteran. Compare this to a film about the reintegration of a Vietnam War vet such as *Coming Home* (1978) or *Born on the Fourth of July* (1989), and note what a difference forty years and public perception of the Vietnam War made in film treatments of the issue of returning vets. *Coming Home* starred noted antiwar activist Jane Fonda.

The Fog of War (2003). This is less a documentary than an arty filmic treatment of interviews with former defense secretary and Vietnam war planner Robert McNamara on the foreign policy of the Kennedy and Johnson administrations.

Hearts and Minds (1975). This is a polemic against the Vietnam War, reissued in 2004. When the government attempts to mold public opinion in support of a controversial foreign policy goal or an unpopular war, it usually produces a counterreaction in the world of art and film. Compare *Hearts and Minds* as both film and argument with *Fahrenheit 9/11,* Michael Moore's 2004 polemic against the Iraq war.

Is Wal-Mart Good for America? (2004). This *Frontline* documentary looks at the impact of Wal-Mart's merchandising strategy on America's trade imbalance and the decline of its manufacturing sector. It can be viewed online at www.pbs.org/wgbh/pages/frontline/shows/walmart.

Tinker, Tailor, Soldier, Spy (1979) and its sequel, *Smiley's People* (1982). The story of the archrivalry between the world-weary head of Britain's MI-5 and the brilliant mastermind of Russian intelligence is drawn from the novels by John Le Carré, himself a former British intelligence officer. There is no better portrait of the dedicated but jaded combatants in the spy wars between the free world and the Iron Curtain countries.

The Trials of Henry Kissinger (2002). Based on Christopher Hitchens's shoot-to-kill book on one of the most controversial national security advisers and secretaries of state in the postwar era, this documentary raises questions about the effectiveness and the morality of Kissinger's realist, balance of power approach to foreign policy during the Nixon administration.

Rumsfeld's War (2004). This PBS *Frontline* documentary examines former Secretary of Defense Donald Rumsfeld's battle with the Pentagon hierarchy—the "war" of the title—to make over the U.S. military into a smaller, more mobile force equipped with lighter weapons. It explores the split this caused among Pentagon brass and its effects on planning and strategy in the Iraq War. It can be viewed online at www.pbs.org/wgbh/pages/frontline/shows/pentagon.

Dr. Strangelove, or How I Learned to Stop Worrying and Love the Bomb (1964). This classic black-and-white film from the Cold War era takes the fear of nuclear war with the Soviet Union and the MAD strategy that dominated nuclear weapons programs and works them into comic hysteria.

The War Behind Closed Doors (2003). This PBS *Frontline* documentary looks at the policy differences among Bush's top advisers about the wisdom of invading Iraq. It can be viewed online at www.pbs.org/wgbh/pages/frontline/shows/iraq.

Why We Fight (2005) and (1943–1944). Compare these documentaries of the same name. The first was a series of short films made by legendary director Frank Capra during World War II for the Office of War Information (reissued on DVD in a four-disc set in 2005). Their purpose was to mobilize public support behind Allied troops, led by General Dwight Eisenhower. The 2005 *Why We Fight*, made by documentary filmmaker Eugene Jarecki, explores American perceptions of why we went to war in Iraq in 2003 and asks whether it is time to take another look at President Dwight Eisenhower's 1961 conjecture that there is a relationship between having a huge military establishment and the inclination to use it.

Electronic Resources

usinfo.state.gov
This site has the United States Information Agency's daily briefings and news on a variety of international issues from the official U.S. government perspective. It includes links to several foreign-language sources and a searchable database from archived material.

www.state.gov
The home page of the State Department contains links to information on the department itself and on a variety of international issues, organized by region and by issue.

www.economist.com
The home page of The Economist, *an international magazine that specializes in in-depth articles on important international and political issues and provides a foreign perspective on the news.*

www.cwihp.si.edu
The Cold War International History Project at the Smithsonian's Woodrow Wilson Center makes available new information and

perspectives on the history of the Cold War, especially findings from previously inaccessible sources from former Communist countries.

www.loc.gov/rr/international/portals.html
Portals to the World, a site managed by the Library of Congress, offers maps, in-depth information, and annotated Internet resources for selected countries of Europe, Africa, North and South America, and Asia.

www.gwu.edu/nsarchiv
This site, maintained by an independent research institute at George Washington University, makes available declassified international affairs and national security documents obtained under the Freedom of Information Act.

ThomsonNOW™

Enter ThomsonNOW™ using the access card that is available with this text or through www.thomsonedu.com/thomsonnow. ThomsonNOW™ will assist you in understanding the content in this chapter with a personalized study plan generated for your needs. A practice test will assess the areas you need to review and provide the tools to fully comprehend those concepts, including an integrated digital eBook, interactive simulations, timelines, video case studies, MicroCase exercises, and InfoTrac College Edition readers and exercises. You'll also be connected to the learning objectives, chapter outline, chapter glossary, flash cards, crossword puzzles, Internet activities, and interactive quizzes found on the companion website.

THE DECLARATION OF INDEPENDENCE*

In Congress, July 4, 1776.

A Declaration by the Representatives of the United States of America, in General Congress assembled.

When in the Course of human Events, it becomes necessary for one People to dissolve the Political Bonds which have connected them with another, and to assume among the Powers of the Earth, the separate and equal Station to which the Laws of Nature and of Nature's God entitle them, a decent Respect to the Opinions of Mankind requires that they should declare the causes which impel them to the Separation.

We hold these Truths to be self-evident, that all Men are created equal, that they are endowed by their Creator with certain unalienable Rights, that among these are Life, Liberty, and the Pursuit of Happiness—That to secure these Rights, Governments are instituted among Men, deriving their just Powers from the Consent of the Governed, that whenever any Form of Government becomes destructive of these Ends, it is the Right of the People to alter or to abolish it, and to institute new Government, laying its Foundation on such Principles, and organizing its Powers in such Forms, as to them shall seem most likely to effect their Safety and Happiness. Prudence, indeed, will dictate that Governments long established should not be changed for light and transient Causes; and accordingly all Experience hath shewn, that Mankind are more disposed to suffer, while Evils are sufferable, than to right themselves by abolishing the Forms to which they are accustomed. But when a long Train of Abuses and Usurpations, pursuing invariably the same Object, evinces a Design to reduce them under absolute Despotism, it is their Right, it is their Duty, to throw off such Government, and to provide new Guards for their future Security. Such has been the patient Sufferance of these Colonies; and such is now the Necessity which constrains them to alter their former Systems of Government. The History of the present King of Great Britain is a History of repeated Injuries and Usurpations, all having in direct Object the Establishment of an absolute Tyranny over these States. To prove this, let facts be submitted to a candid World.

He has refused his Assent to Laws, the most wholesome and necessary for the public Good.

He has forbidden his Governors to pass Laws of immediate and pressing Importance, unless suspended in their Operation till his Assent should be obtained; and when so suspended, he has utterly neglected to attend to them.

He has refused to pass other Laws for the Accommodation of large Districts of People, unless those People would relinquish the Right of Representation in the Legislature, a Right inestimable to them, and formidable to Tyrants only.

He has called together Legislative Bodies at Places unusual, uncomfortable, and distant from the Depository of their Public Records, for the sole Purpose of fatiguing them into Compliance with his Measures.

He has dissolved Representative Houses repeatedly, for opposing with manly Firmness his Invasions on the Rights of the People.

He has refused for a long Time, after such Dissolutions, to cause others to be elected; whereby the Legislative Powers, incapable of Annihilation, have returned to the People at large for their exercise; the State remaining in the mean time exposed to all the Dangers of Invasion from without, and Convulsions within.

He has endeavoured to prevent the Population of these States; for that Purpose obstructing the Laws for Naturalization of Foreigners; refusing to pass others to encourage their Migration hither, and raising the Conditions of new Appropriations of Lands.

He has obstructed the Administration of Justice, by refusing his Assent to Laws for establishing Judiciary Powers.

He has made Judges dependent on his Will alone, for the Tenure of their offices, and the Amount and payments of their Salaries.

He has erected a Multitude of new Offices, and sent hither Swarms of Officers to harass our People, and eat out their Substance.

He has kept among us, in times of Peace, Standing Armies, without the consent of our Legislatures.

He has affected to render the Military independent of, and superior to the Civil Power.

He has combined with others to subject us to a Jurisdiction foreign to our Constitution, and unacknowledged by our Laws; giving his Assent to their Acts of pretended Legislation:

For quartering large Bodies of Armed Troops among us:

For protecting them, by a mock Trial, from Punishment for any Murders which they should commit on the Inhabitants of these States:

---

*The spelling, capitalization, and punctuation of the original have been retained here.

For cutting off our Trade with all Parts of the World:

For imposing Taxes on us without our Consent:

For depriving us, in many cases, of the Benefits of Trial by Jury:

For transporting us beyond Seas to be tried for pretended Offences:

For abolishing the free System of English Laws in a neighbouring Province, establishing therein an arbitrary Government, and enlarging its Boundaries, so as to render it at once an Example and fit Instrument for introducing the same absolute Rule into these Colonies:

For taking away our Charters, abolishing our most valuable Laws, and altering fundamentally the Forms of our Governments:

For suspending our own Legislatures, and declaring themselves invested with Power to legislate for us in all Cases whatsoever.

He has abdicated Government here, by declaring us out of his Protection and waging War against us.

He has plundered our Seas, ravaged our Coasts, burnt our towns, and destroyed the Lives of our People.

He is, at this Time, transporting large Armies of foreign Mercenaries to compleat the works of Death, Desolation, and Tyranny, already begun with circumstances of Cruelty and Perfidy, scarcely parallelled in the most barbarous Ages, and totally unworthy the Head of a civilized Nation.

He has constrained our fellow Citizens taken Captive on the high Seas to bear Arms against their Country, to become the Executioners of their Friends and Brethren, or to fall themselves by their Hands.

He has excited domestic Insurrections amongst us, and has endeavoured to bring on the Inhabitants of our Frontiers, the merciless Indian Savages, whose known Rule of Warfare is an undistinguished Destruction, of all Ages, Sexes and Conditions.

In every state of these Oppressions we have Petitioned for Redress in the most humble Terms: Our repeated Petitions have been answered only by repeated Injury. A Prince, whose Character is thus marked by every act which may define a Tyrant, is unfit to be the Ruler of a free People.

Nor have we been wanting in Attentions to our British Brethren. We have warned them from Time to Time of Attempts by their Legislature to extend an unwarrantable Jurisdiction over us. We have reminded them of the Circumstances of our Emigration and Settlement here. We have appealed to their native Justice and Magnanimity, and we have conjured them by the Ties of our common Kindred to disavow these Usurpations, which would inevitably interrupt our Connections and Correspondence. They too have been deaf to the Voice of Justice and of Consanguinity. We must, therefore, acquiesce in the Necessity, which denounces our Separation, and hold them, as we hold the rest of Mankind, Enemies in War, in Peace Friends.

We, therefore, the Representatives of the UNITED STATES OF AMERICA, in General Congress Assembled, appealing to the Supreme Judge of the World for the Rectitude of our Intentions, do, in the Name, and by Authority of the good People of these Colonies, solemnly Publish and Declare, That these United Colonies are, and of Right ought to be, Free and Independent States; that they are absolved from all Allegiance to the British Crown, and that all political Connection between them and the State of Great Britain, is and ought to be totally dissolved; and that as Free and Independent States, they have full Power to levy War, conclude Peace, contract Alliances, establish Commerce, and to do all other Acts and Things which Independent States may of right do. And for the support of this declaration, with a firm Reliance on the Protection of divine Providence, we mutually pledge to each other our Lives, our Fortunes, and our sacred Honor.

CONSTITUTION OF THE UNITED STATES OF AMERICA*

We the people of the United States, in Order to form a more perfect Union, establish Justice, insure domestic Tranquility, provide for the common defence, promote the general Welfare, and secure the Blessings of Liberty to ourselves and our posterity, do ordain and establish this Constitution for the United States of America.

Article I

Section 1. All legislative Powers herein granted shall be vested in a Congress of the United States, which shall consist of a Senate and House of Representatives.

Section 2. The House of Representatives shall be composed of Members chosen every second Year by the People of the several States, and the Electors in each State shall have the Qualifications requisite for Electors of the most numerous Branch of the State Legislature.

No person shall be a Representative who shall not have attained to the Age of twenty-five Years, and been seven Years a Citizen of the United States, and who shall not, when elected, be an Inhabitant of that State in which he shall be chosen.

Representatives and direct [Taxes][1] shall be apportioned among the several States which may be included within this Union, according to their respective Numbers [which shall be determined by adding to the whole Number of free Persons, including those bound to Service for a Term of Years, and excluding Indians not taxed, three fifths of all other Persons].[2] The actual Enumeration shall be made within three Years after the first Meeting of the Congress of the United States, and within every subsequent Term of ten Years, in such Manner as they shall by Law direct. The Number of Representatives shall not exceed one for every thirty Thousand, but each State shall have at Least one Representative; and until such enumeration shall be made, the State of New Hampshire shall be entitled to chuse three, Massachusetts eight, Rhode Island and Providence Plantations one, Connecticut five, New-York six, New Jersey four, Pennsylvania eight, Delaware one, Maryland six, Virginia ten, North Carolina five, South Carolina five, and Georgia three.

When vacancies happen in the Representation from any State, the Executive Authority thereof shall issue Writs of Election to fill such Vacancies.

The House of Representatives shall chuse their Speaker and other Officers; and shall have the sole Power of Impeachment.

Section 3. The Senate of the United States shall be composed of two Senators from each State [chosen by the Legislature thereof],[3] for six Years; and each Senator shall have one Vote.

Immediately after they shall be assembled in Consequence of the first Election, they shall be divided as equally as may be into three Classes. The Seats of the Senators of the first Class shall be vacated at the Expiration of the second year, of the second Class at the Expiration of the fourth Year, and of the third Class at the Expiration of the sixth Year, so that one third may be chosen every second Year [and if Vacancies happen by Resignation, or otherwise, during the Recess of the Legislature of any State, the Executive thereof may make temporary Appointments until the next Meeting of the Legislature, which shall then fill such Vacancies.][4]

No Person shall be a Senator who shall not have attained to the Age of thirty Years, and been nine Years a Citizen of the United States, and who shall not, when elected, be an Inhabitant of that State for which he shall be chosen.

The Vice President of the United States shall be President of the Senate, but shall have no Vote, unless they be equally divided.

The Senate shall chuse their other Officers, and also a President pro tempore, in the Absence of the Vice President, or when he shall exercise the Office of President of the United States.

The Senate shall have the sole Power to try all Impeachments. When sitting for that Purpose, they shall be on Oath or Affirmation. When the President of the United States is tried, the Chief Justice shall preside: And no Person shall be convicted without the Concurrence of two thirds of the Members present.

Judgment in Cases of Impeachment shall not extend further than to removal from Office, and disqualification to hold and enjoy any Office of honor, Trust or Profit under the United States; but the Party convicted shall nevertheless be liable and subject to Indictment, Trial, Judgment and Punishment, according to Law.

---

*The spelling, capitalization, and punctuation of the original have been retained here. Brackets indicate passages that have been altered by amendments to the Constitution.
1. Modified by the Sixteenth Amendment.
2. Modified by the Fourteenth Amendment.

3. Repealed by the Seventeenth Amendment.
4. Modified by the Seventeenth Amendment.

Section 4. The Times, Places and Manner of holding Elections for Senators and Representatives, shall be prescribed in each State by the Legislature thereof; but the Congress may at any time by Law make or alter such Regulations, except as to the Places of chusing Senators.

[The Congress shall assemble at least once in every Year, and such Meeting shall be on the first Monday in December, unless they shall by Law appoint a different Day.][5]

Section 5. Each House shall be the Judge of the Elections, Returns and Qualifications of its own Members, and a Majority of each shall constitute a Quorum to do Business; but a smaller Number may adjourn from day to day, and may be authorized to compel the Attendance of absent Members, in such Manner, and under such Penalties as each House may provide.

Each House may determine the Rules of its Proceedings, punish its Members for disorderly Behaviour, and, with the Concurrence of two thirds, expel a Member.

Each House shall keep a Journal of its Proceedings, and from time to time publish the same, excepting such Parts as may in their Judgment require Secrecy; and the Yeas and Nays of the Members of either House on any question shall, at the Desire of one fifth of those present, be entered on the Journal.

Neither House, during the Session of Congress, shall, without the Consent of the other, adjourn for more than three days, nor to any other Place than that in which the two Houses shall be sitting.

Section 6. The Senators and Representatives shall receive a Compensation for their Services, to be ascertained by Law, and paid out of the Treasury of the United States. They shall in all Cases, except Treason, Felony and Breach of the Peace, be privileged from Arrest during their Attendance at the Session of their respective Houses, and in going to and returning from the same; and for any Speech or Debate in either House, they shall not be questioned in any other Place.

No Senator or Representative shall, during the Time for which he was elected, be appointed to any civil Office under the Authority of the United States, which shall have been created, or the Emoluments whereof shall have been encreased during such time; and no Person holding any Office under the United States, shall be a Member of either House during his Continuance in Office.

Section 7. All Bills for raising Revenue shall originate in the House of Representatives; but the Senate may propose or concur with Amendments as on other Bills.

Every Bill which shall have passed the House of Representatives and the Senate, shall, before it become a Law, be presented to the President of the United States; If he approves he shall sign it, but if not he shall return it, with his objections to that House in which it shall have originated, who shall enter the Objections at large on their Journal, and proceed to reconsider it. If after such Reconsideration two thirds of that House shall agree to pass the Bill, it shall be sent, together with the Objections, to the other House, by which it shall likewise be reconsidered, and if approved by two thirds of that House, it shall become a Law. But in all such Cases the Votes of both Houses shall be determined by yeas and Nays, and the Names of the Persons voting for and against the Bill shall be entered on the Journal of each House respectively. If any Bill shall not be returned by the President within ten Days (Sundays excepted) after it shall have been presented to him, the Same shall be a Law, in like Manner as if he had signed it, unless the Congress by their Adjournment prevent its Return, in which Case it shall not be a Law.

Every Order, Resolution, or Vote to which the Concurrence of the Senate and House of Representatives may be necessary (except on a question of Adjournment) shall be presented to the President of the United States; and before the Same shall take Effect, shall be approved by him, or being disapproved by him, shall be repassed by two thirds of the Senate and House of Representatives, according to the Rules and Limitations prescribed in the Case of a Bill.

Section 8. The Congress shall have Power To lay and collect Taxes, Duties, Imposts and Excises, to pay the Debts and provide for the common Defence and general Welfare of the United States; but all Duties, Imposts and Excises shall be uniform throughout the United States;

To borrow Money on the credit of the United States;

To regulate Commerce with foreign Nations, and among the several States, and with the Indian Tribes;

To establish a uniform Rule of Naturalization, and uniform Laws on the subject of Bankruptcies throughout the United States;

To coin Money, regulate the Value thereof, and of foreign Coin, and fix the Standard of Weights and Measures;

To provide for the Punishment of counterfeiting the Securities and current Coin of the United States.

To establish Post Offices and post Roads;

To promote the Progress of Science and useful Arts, by securing for limited Times to Authors and Inventors the exclusive Right to their respective Writings and Discoveries;

To constitute Tribunals inferior to the supreme Court;

To define and punish Piracies and Felonies committed on the high Seas, and Offences against the Law of Nations;

To declare War, grant Letters of Marque and Reprisal, and make Rules concerning Captures on Land and Water;

To raise and support Armies, but no Appropriation of Money to that Use shall be for a longer Term than two Years;

To provide and maintain a Navy;

To make Rules for the Government and Regulation of the land and naval Forces;

To provide for calling forth the Militia to execute the Laws of the Union, suppress Insurrections and repel Invasions;

To provide for organizing, arming, and disciplining the Militia, and for governing such Part of them as may be employed in the Service of the United States, reserving to the

---

5. Changed by the Twentieth Amendment.

States respectively, the Appointment of the Officers, and the Authority of training the Militia according to the discipline prescribed by Congress;

To exercise exclusive Legislation in all Cases whatsoever, over such District (not exceeding ten Miles square) as may, by Cession of particular States, and the Acceptance of Congress, become the Seat of the Government of the United States, and to exercise like Authority over all Places purchased by the Consent of the Legislature of the State in which the Same shall be, for the Erection of forts, Magazines, Arsenals, dock-Yards, and other needful Buildings;—And

To make all Laws which shall be necessary and proper for carrying into Execution the foregoing Powers, and all other Powers vested by this Constitution in the Government of the United States, or in any Department or Officer thereof.

Section 9. The Migration or Importation of such Persons as any of the States now existing shall think proper to admit, shall not be prohibited by the Congress prior to the Year one thousand eight hundred and eight, but a Tax or duty may be imposed on such Importation, not exceeding ten dollars for each Person.

The Privilege of the Writ of Habeas Corpus shall not be suspended, unless when in Cases of Rebellion or Invasion the public Safety may require it.

No Bill of Attainder or ex post facto Law shall be passed.

[No Capitation, or other direct, Tax shall be laid, unless in Proportion to the Census or Enumeration herein before directed to be taken.][6]

No Tax or Duty shall be laid on Articles exported from any State.

No Preference shall be given by any Regulation of Commerce or Revenue to the Ports of one State over those of another; nor shall Vessels bound to, or from, one State, be obliged to enter, clear, or pay Duties in another.

No Money shall be drawn from the Treasury, but in Consequence of Appropriations made by Law; and a regular Statement and Account of the Receipts and Expenditures of all public Money shall be published from time to time.

No Title of Nobility shall be granted by the United States; and no Person holding any Office or Profit or Trust under them, shall, without the Consent of the Congress, accept of any present, Emolument, Office, or Title, of any kind whatever, from any King, Prince, or foreign State.

Section 10. No state shall enter into any Treaty, Alliance, or Confederation; grant Letters of Marque and Reprisal; coin Money; emit Bills of Credit; make any Thing but gold and silver Coin a Tender in Payment of Debts; pass any Bill of Attainder, ex post facto Law, or Law impairing the Obligation of Contracts, or grant any Title of Nobility.

No State shall, without the Consent of the Congress, lay any Imposts or Duties on Imports or Exports, except what may be absolutely necessary for executing its inspection Laws; and the net Produce of all Duties and Imposts, laid by any State on Imports or Exports, shall be for the Use of the Treasury of the United States; and all such Laws shall be subject to the Revision and Controul of the Congress.

No State shall, without the Consent of Congress, lay any duty of Tonnage, keep Troops, or Ships of War in time of Peace, enter into any Agreement or Compact with another State, or with a foreign Power or engage in War, unless actually invaded, or in such imminent Danger as will not admit of delay.

Article II

Section 1. The executive Power shall be vested in a President of the United States of America. He shall hold his Office during the Term of four Years, and, together with the Vice President, chosen for the Same Term, be elected, as follows.

Each State shall appoint, in such Manner as the Legislature thereof may direct, a Number of Electors, equal to the whole Number of Senators and Representatives to which the State may be entitled in the Congress; but no Senator or Representative, or Person holding an Office of Trust or Profit under the United States, shall be appointed an Elector.

[The Electors shall meet in their respective States, and vote by Ballot for two Persons of whom one at least shall not be an Inhabitant of the same State with themselves. And they shall make a List of all the Persons voted for, and of the Number of Votes for each; which List they shall sign and certify, and transmit sealed to the Seat of the Government of the United States, directed to the President of the Senate. The President of the Senate shall, in the Presence of the Senate and House of Representatives, open all the Certificates, and the Votes shall then be counted. The Person having the greatest Number of Votes shall be the President, if such Number be a Majority of the whole Number of Electors appointed; and if there be more than one who have such Majority, and have an equal Number of Votes, then the House of Representatives shall immediately chuse by Ballot one of them for President; and if no Person have a Majority, then from the five highest on the List the said House shall in like Manner chuse the President. But in chusing the President, the Votes shall be taken by States, the Representation from each State having one Vote; A quorum for this Purpose shall consist of a Member or Members from two thirds of the States, and a Majority of all the states shall be necessary to a Choice. In every Case, after the Choice of the President, the Person having the greatest Number of Votes of the Electors shall be the Vice President. But if there should remain two or more who have equal Votes, the Senate shall chuse from them by Ballot the Vice President.][7]

The Congress may determine the Time of chusing the Electors, and the Day on which they shall give their Votes; which Day shall be the same throughout the United States.

No person except a natural born Citizen, or a Citizen of the United States, at the time of the Adoption of this Constitution, shall be eligible to the Office of President; neither shall

---

6. Modified by the Sixteenth Amendment.

7. Changed by the Twelfth Amendment.

any Person be eligible to that Office who shall not have attained to the Age of thirty five Years, and been fourteen Years a Resident within the United States.

[In Case of the Removal of the President from Office, or of his Death, Resignation, or Inability to discharge the Powers and Duties of the said Office, the same shall devolve on the Vice President, and the Congress may by Law provide for the Case of Removal, Death, Resignation or Inability, both of the President and Vice President, declaring what Officer shall then act as President, and such Officer shall act accordingly, until the Disability be removed, or a President shall be elected.][8]

The President shall, at stated Times, receive for his Services, a Compensation, which shall neither be increased nor diminished during the Period for which he shall have been elected, and he shall not receive within that Period any other Emolument from the United States, or any of them.

Before he enter on the Execution of his Office, he shall take the following Oath or Affirmation:—"I do solemnly swear (or affirm) that I will faithfully execute the Office of President of the United States, and will to the best of my Ability, preserve, protect and defend the constitution of the United States."

Section 2. The President shall be Commander in Chief of the Army and Navy of the United States, and of the Militia of the several States, when called into the actual Service of the United States; he may require the Opinion, in writing, of the principal Officer in each of the executive Departments, upon any Subject relating to the Duties of their respective Offices, and he shall have Power to grant Reprieves and Pardons for Offences against the United States, except in Cases of Impeachment.

He shall have Power, by and with the Advice and Consent of the Senate, to make Treaties, provided two thirds of the Senators present concur; and he shall nominate, and by and with the Advice and Consent of the Senate, shall appoint Ambassadors, other public Ministers and Consuls, Judges of the supreme Court, and all other Officers of the United States, whose Appointments are not herein otherwise provided for, and which shall be established by Law; but the Congress may by Law vest the Appointment of such inferior Officers, as they think proper, in the President alone, in the Courts of Law, or in the Heads of Departments.

The President shall have Power to fill up all Vacancies that may happen during the Recess of the Senate, by granting Commissions which shall expire at the end of their next Session.

Section 3. He shall from time to time give to the Congress Information of the State of the Union, and recommend to their Consideration such Measures as he shall judge necessary and expedient; he may, on extraordinary Occasions, convene both Houses, or either of them, and in Case of Disagreement between them, with Respect to the Time of Adjournment, he may adjourn them to such Time as he shall think proper; he shall receive Ambassadors and other public Ministers; he shall take Care that the Laws be faithfully executed, and shall Commission all the Officers of the United States.

Section 4. The President, Vice President and all civil Officers of the United States, shall be removed from Office on Impeachment for, and Conviction of, Treason, Bribery, or other high Crimes and Misdemeanors.

Article III

Section 1. The judicial Power of the United States, shall be vested in one supreme Court, and in such inferior Courts as the Congress may from time to time ordain and establish. The Judges, both of the supreme and inferior Courts, shall hold their Offices during good Behaviour, and shall, at stated Times, receive for their Services, a Compensation, which shall not be diminished during their Continuance in Office.

Section 2. The judicial Power shall extend to all Cases, in Law and Equity, arising under this Constitution, the Laws of the United States, and Treaties made, or which shall be made, under their Authority;—to all Cases affecting Ambassadors, other public Ministers and Consuls;—to all Cases of admiralty and maritime Jurisdiction;—to Controversies to which the United States shall be a Party;—to Controversies between two or more States;—[between a State and Citizens of another State;][9]—between Citizens of different States,—between Citizens of the same State claiming Lands under Grants of different States, [and between a state, or the Citizens thereof, and foreign States, Citizens or Subjects.][10]

In all cases affecting Ambassadors, other public Ministers and Consuls, and those in which a State shall be Party, the supreme Court shall have original Jurisdiction. In all the other Cases before mentioned, the supreme Court shall have appellate Jurisdiction, both as to Law and Fact, with such Exceptions, and under such Regulations as the Congress shall make.

The Trial of all Crimes, except in Cases of Impeachment, shall be by Jury; and such Trial shall be held in the State where the said Crimes shall have been committed; but when not committed within any State, the Trial shall be at such Place or Places as the Congress may by Law have directed.

Section 3. Treason against the United States, shall consist only in levying War against them, or in adhering to their Enemies, giving them Aid and Comfort. No Person shall be convicted of Treason unless on the Testimony of two Witnesses to the same overt Act, or on Confession in open Court.

The Congress shall have Power to declare the Punishment of Treason, but no Attainder of Treason shall work Corruption of Blood, or Forfeiture except during the Life of the Person attainted.

8. Modified by the Twenty-fifth Amendment.

9. Modified by the Eleventh Amendment.
10. Modified by the Eleventh Amendment.

Article IV

Section 1. Full Faith and Credit shall be given in each State to the public Acts, Records, and judicial Proceedings of every other State. And the Congress may by general Laws prescribe the Manner in which such Acts, Records and Proceedings shall be proved, and the Effect thereof.

Section 2. The Citizens of each State shall be entitled to all Privileges and Immunities of Citizens in the several States.

A Person charged in any State with Treason, Felony, or other Crime, who shall flee from Justice, and be found in another State, shall on Demand of the executive Authority of the State from which he fled, be delivered up, to be removed to the State having Jurisdiction of the Crime.

[No Person held to Service or Labour in one State under the Laws thereof, escaping into another, shall, in Consequence of any Law or Regulation therein, be discharged from such Service or Labour, but shall be delivered up on Claim of the Party to whom such Service or Labour may be due.][11]

Section 3. New States may be admitted by the Congress into this Union; but no new State shall be formed or erected within the Jurisdiction of any other State; nor any State be formed by the Junction of two or more States, or Parts of States, without the Consent of the Legislatures of the States concerned as well as of the Congress.

The Congress shall have Power to dispose of and make all needful Rules and Regulations respecting the Territory or other Property belonging to the United States; and nothing in this Constitution shall be so construed as to Prejudice any Claims of the United States, or of any particular State.

Section 4. The United States shall guarantee to every State in this Union a Republican Form of Government, and shall protect each of them against Invasion, and on Application of the Legislature, or of the Executive (when the Legislature cannot be convened) against domestic Violence.

Article V

The Congress, whenever two thirds of both Houses shall deem it necessary, shall propose Amendments to this Constitution, or on the Application of the Legislatures of two thirds of the several States, shall call a Convention for proposing Amendments, which, in either Case, shall be valid to all Intents and Purposes, as Part of this Constitution, when ratified by the Legislatures of three fourths of the several States, or by Conventions in three fourths thereof, as the one or the other Mode of Ratification may be proposed by the Congress; Provided that no Amendment which may be made prior to the Year One thousand eight hundred and eight shall in any Manner affect the first and fourth Clauses in the Ninth Section of the first Article; and that no State, without its Consent, shall be deprived of its equal Suffrage in the Senate.

Article VI

All Debts contracted and Engagements entered into, before the Adoption of this Constitution, shall be as valid against the United States under this Constitution, as under the Confederation.

This Constitution, and the laws of the United States which shall be made in Pursuance thereof; and all Treaties made, or which shall be made, under the Authority of the United States, shall be the supreme Law of the Land; and the Judges in every State shall be bound thereby, any Thing in the Constitution or Laws of any State to the Contrary notwithstanding.

The Senators and Representatives before mentioned, and the Members of the several State Legislatures, and all executive and judicial Officers, both of the United States and of the several States, shall be bound by Oath or Affirmation, to support this Constitution; but no religious Test shall ever be required as a Qualification to any Office or public Trust under the United States.

Article VII

The Ratification of the Conventions of nine States, shall be sufficient for the Establishment of this constitution between the States so ratifying the Same.

Done in Convention by the Unanimous Consent of the States present the Seventeenth Day of September in the Year of our Lord one thousand seven hundred and Eighty seven and of the Independence of the United States of America the Twelfth. IN WITNESS whereof we have hereunto subscribed our Names.

Go. WASHINGTON
Presid't. and deputy from Virginia

Attest
William Jackson
Secretary

Delaware
Geo. Read
Gunning Bedford jun
John Dickinson
Richard Basset
Jaco. Broon

Massachusetts
Nathaniel Gorham
Rufus King

Connecticut
Wm. Saml. Johnson
Roger Sherman

New York
Alexander Hamilton

New Jersey
Wh. Livingston
David Brearley

Wm. Paterson
Jona. Dayton

Pennsylvania
B. Franklin
Thomas Mifflin
Robt. Morris
Geo. Clymer
Thos. FitzSimons
Jared Ingersoll
James Wilson
Gouv Morris

Virginia
John Blair
James Madison Jr.

North Carolina
Wm. Blount
Richd. Dobbs Spaight
Hu Williamson

---

11. Repealed by the Thirteenth Amendment.

South Carolina

J. Rutledge
Charles Cotesworth Pinckney
Charles Pinckney
Pierce Butler

Georgia

William Few
Abr. Baldwin

New Hampshire

John Langdon
Nicholas Gilman

Maryland

James McHenry
Dan of St Thos. Jenifer
Danl. Carroll

Amendment I[12]

Congress shall make no law respecting an establishment of religion, or prohibiting the free exercise thereof; or abridging the freedom of speech, or of the press; or the right of the people peaceably to assemble, and to petition the Government for a redress of grievances.

Amendment II

A well regulated militia, being necessary to the security of a free State, the right of the people to keep and bear arms, shall not be infringed.

Amendment III

No Soldier shall, in time of peace be quartered in any house, without the consent of the owner, nor in time of war, but in a manner to be prescribed by law.

Amendment IV

The right of the people to be secure in their persons, houses, papers, and effects, against unreasonable searches and seizures, shall not be violated, and no warrants shall issue, but upon probable cause, supported by oath or affirmation, and particularly describing the place to be searched, and the persons or things to be seized.

Amendment V

No person shall be held to answer for a capital, or otherwise infamous crime, unless on a presentment or indictment of a Grand Jury, except in cases arising in the land or naval forces, or in the militia, when in actual service in time of war or public danger; nor shall any person be subject for the same offence to be twice put in jeopardy of life or limb; nor shall be compelled in any criminal case to be a witness against himself, nor be deprived of life, liberty, or property, without due process of law; nor shall private property be taken for public use, without just compensation.

Amendment VI

In all criminal prosecutions, the accused shall enjoy the right to a speedy and public trial, by an impartial jury of the State and district wherein the crime shall have been committed, which district shall have been previously ascertained by law, and to be informed of the nature and cause of the accusation; to be confronted with the witnesses against him; to have compulsory process for obtaining witnesses in his favor, and to have the assistance of counsel for his defence.

Amendment VII

In Suits at common law, where the value in controversy shall exceed twenty dollars, the right of trial by jury shall be preserved, and no fact tried by a jury, shall be otherwise reexamined in any Court of the United States, than according to the rules of the common law.

Amendment VIII

Excessive bail shall not be required, nor excessive fines imposed, nor cruel and unusual punishments inflicted.

Amendment IX

The enumeration in the Constitution, of certain rights, shall not be construed to deny or disparage others retained by the people.

Amendment X

The powers not delegated to the United States by the Constitution, nor prohibited by it to the States, are reserved to the States respectively, or to the people.

Amendment XI
(Ratified February 7, 1795)

The Judicial power of the United States shall not be construed to extend to any suit in law or equity, commenced or prosecuted against one of the United States by Citizens of another State, or by Citizens or Subjects of any Foreign State.

Amendment XII
(Ratified June 15, 1804)

The Electors shall meet in their respective states, and vote by ballot for President and Vice-President, one of whom, at least, shall not be an inhabitant of the same state with themselves; they shall name in their ballots the person voted for as President, and in distinct ballots the person voted for as Vice President, and they shall make distinct lists of all persons voted for as President, and of all persons voted for as Vice-President, and of the number of votes for each, which lists they shall sign and certify, and transmit sealed to the seat of the government of the United States, directed to the President of the Senate;—The President of the Senate shall, in the presence of the Senate and House of Representatives, open all the certificates and the votes shall then be counted;—The person having the greatest number of votes for President, shall be the President, if such number be a ma-

12. The first ten amendments were passed by Congress on September 25, 1789, and were ratified on December 15, 1791.

jority of the whole number of Electors appointed; and if no person have such majority, then from the persons having the highest numbers not exceeding three on the list of those voted for as President, the House of Representatives shall choose immediately, by ballot, the President. But in choosing the President, the votes shall be taken by states, the representation from each state having one vote; a quorum for this purpose shall consist of a member or members from two-thirds of the states, and a majority of all the states shall be necessary to a choice. [And if the House of Representatives shall not choose a President whenever the right of choice shall devolve upon them, before the fourth day of March next following, then the Vice-President shall act as President, as in the case of the death or other constitutional disability of the President.][13]— The person having the greatest number of votes as Vice-President, shall be the Vice-President, if such number be a majority of the whole number of Electors appointed, and if no person have a majority, then from the two highest numbers on the list, the Senate shall choose the Vice-President; a quorum for the purpose shall consist of two-thirds of the whole number of Senators, and a majority of the whole number shall be necessary to a choice. But no person constitutionally ineligible to the office of President shall be eligible to that of Vice-President of the United States.

Amendment XIII
(Ratified on December 6, 1865)

Section 1. Neither slavery nor involuntary servitude, except as a punishment for crime whereof the party shall have been duly convicted, shall exist within the United States, or any place subject to their jurisdiction.

Section 2. Congress shall have power to enforce this article by appropriate legislation.

Amendment XIV
(Ratified on July 9, 1868)

Section 1. All persons born or naturalized in the United States, and subject to the jurisdiction thereof, are citizens of the United States and of the State wherein they reside. No State shall make or enforce any law which shall abridge the privileges or immunities of citizens of the United States; nor shall any State deprive any person of life, liberty, or property, without due process of law; nor deny to any person within its jurisdiction the equal protection of the laws.

Section 2. Representatives shall be apportioned among the several States according to their respective numbers, counting the whole number of persons in each State, excluding Indians not taxed. But when the right to vote at any election for the choice of electors for President and Vice President of the United States, Representatives in Congress, the

Executive and Judicial officers of a State, or the members of the Legislature thereof, is denied to any of the male inhabitants of such State, being [twenty-one][14] years of age, and citizens of the United States, or in any way abridged, except for participation in rebellion, or other crime, the basis of representation therein shall be reduced in the proportion which the number of such male citizens shall bear to the whole number of male citizens twenty-one years of age in such State.

Section 3. No person shall be a Senator or Representative in Congress, or elector of President and Vice President, or hold any office, civil or military, under the United States, or under any State, who having previously taken an oath, as a member of Congress, or as an officer of the United States, or as a member of any State legislature, or as an executive or judicial officer of any State, to support the Constitution of the United States, shall have engaged in insurrection or rebellion against the same, or given aid or comfort to the enemies thereof. But Congress may by a vote of two-thirds of each House, remove such disability.

Section 4. The validity of the public debt of the United States, authorized by law, including debts incurred for payment of pensions and bounties for services in suppressing insurrection or rebellion, shall not be questioned. But neither the United States nor any State shall assume or pay any debt or obligation incurred in aid of insurrection or rebellion against the United States, or any claim for the loss or emancipation of any slave, but all such debts, obligations and claims shall be held illegal and void.

Section 5. The Congress shall have power to enforce, by appropriate legislation, the provisions of this article.

Amendment XV
(Ratified on February 3, 1870)

Section 1. The right of citizens of the United States to vote shall not be denied or abridged by the United States or by any State on account of race, color, or previous condition of servitude.

Section 2. The Congress shall have power to enforce this article by appropriate legislation.

Amendment XVI
(Ratified on February 3, 1913)

The Congress shall have power to lay and collect taxes on incomes, from whatever source derived, without apportionment among the several States, and without regard to any census or enumeration.

13. Changed by the Twentieth Amendment.

14. Changed by the Twenty-sixth Amendment.

Amendment XVII
(Ratified on April 8, 1913)

The Senate of the United States shall be composed of two Senators from each State, elected by the people thereof, for six years; and each Senator shall have one vote. The electors in each State shall have the qualifications requisite for electors of the most numerous branch of the State legislatures.

When vacancies happen in the representation of any State in the Senate, the executive authority of such State shall issue writs of election to fill such vacancies: *Provided,* That the legislature of any State may empower the executive thereof to make temporary appointments until the people fill the vacancies by election as the legislature may direct.

This amendment shall not be so construed as to affect the election or term of any Senator chosen before it becomes valid as part of the Constitution.

Amendment XVIII
(Ratified on January 16, 1919)

Section 1. After one year from the ratification of this article the manufacture, sale, or transportation of intoxicating liquors within, the importation thereof into, or the exportation thereof from the United States and all territory subject to the jurisdiction thereof for beverage purposes is hereby prohibited.

Section 2. The Congress and the several States shall have concurrent power to enforce this article by appropriate legislation.

Section 3. This article shall be inoperative unless it shall have been ratified as an amendment to the Constitution by the legislatures of the several States, as provided in the Constitution, within seven years from the date of the submission hereof to the States by the Congress.[15]

Amendment XIX
(Ratified on August 18, 1920)

The right of citizens of the United States to vote shall not be denied or abridged by the United States or by any State on account of sex.

Congress shall have power to enforce this article by appropriate legislation.

Amendment XX
(Ratified on January 23, 1933)

Section 1. The terms of the President and Vice President shall end at noon on the 20th day of January, and the terms of Senators and Representatives at noon on the 3rd day of January, of the years in which such terms would have ended if this article had not been ratified, and the terms of their successors shall then begin.

Section 2. The Congress shall assemble at least once in every year, and such meeting shall begin at noon on the 3rd day of January, unless they shall by law appoint a different day.

Section 3. If, at the time fixed for the beginning of the term of the President, the President elect shall have died, the Vice President elect shall become President. If a President shall not have been chosen before the time fixed for the beginning of his term, or if the President elect shall have failed to qualify, then the Vice President elect shall act as President until a President shall have qualified; and the Congress may by law provide for the case wherein neither a President elect nor a Vice President elect shall have qualified, declaring who shall then act as President, or the manner in which one who is to act shall be selected, and such person shall act accordingly until a President or Vice President shall have qualified.

Section 4. The Congress may by law provide for the case of the death of any of the persons from whom the House of Representatives may choose a President whenever the rights of choice shall have devolved upon them, and for the case of the death of any of the persons from whom the Senate may choose a Vice President whenever the right of choice shall have devolved upon them.

Section 5. Sections 1 and 2 shall take effect on the 15th day of October following the ratification of this article.

Section 6. This article shall be inoperative unless it shall have been ratified as an amendment to the Constitution by the legislatures of three-fourths of the several States within seven years from the date of its submission.

Amendment XXI
(Ratified on December 5, 1933)

Section 1. The eighteenth article of amendment to the Constitution of the United States is hereby repealed.

Section 2. The transportation or importation into any State, Territory, or possession of the United States for delivery or use therein of intoxicating liquors, in violation of the laws thereof, is hereby prohibited.

Section 3. This article shall be inoperative unless it shall have been ratified as an amendment to the Constitution by conventions in the several States, as provided in the Constitution, within seven years from the date of the submission hereof to the States by the Congress.

Amendment XXII
(Ratified on February 27, 1951)

No person shall be elected to the office of the President more than twice, and no person who has held the office of President, or acted as President, for more than two years of a term to which some other person was elected President shall be

---

15. The Eighteenth Amendment was repealed by the Twenty-first Amendment.

elected to the office of the President more than once. But this Article shall not apply to any person holding the office of President when this Article was proposed by the Congress, and shall not prevent any person who may be holding the office of President, or acting as President, during the term within which this Article becomes operative from holding the office of President or acting as President during the remainder of such term.

Amendment XXIII
(Ratified on March 29, 1961)

Section 1. The District constituting the seat of Government of the United States shall appoint in such manner as the Congress may direct:

A number of electors of President and Vice President equal to the whole number of Senators and Representatives in Congress to which the District would be entitled if it were a State, but in no event more than the least populous State; they shall be in addition to those appointed by the States, but they shall be considered, for the purposes of the election of President and Vice President, to be electors appointed by a State; and they shall meet in the District and perform such duties as provided by the twelfth article of amendment.

Section 2. The Congress shall have power to enforce this article by appropriate legislation.

Amendment XXIV
(Ratified on January 23, 1964)

Section 1. The right of citizens of the United States to vote in any primary or other election for President or Vice President, for electors for President or Vice President, or for Senator or Representative in Congress, shall not be denied or abridged by the United States or any State by reason of failure to pay any poll tax or other tax.

Section 2. The Congress shall have power to enforce this article by appropriate legislation.

Amendment XXV
(Ratified on February 10, 1967)

Section 1. In case of the removal of the President from office or of his death or resignation, the Vice President shall become President.

Section 2. Whenever there is a vacancy in the office of the Vice President, the President shall nominate a Vice President who shall take office upon confirmation by a majority vote of both Houses of Congress.

Section 3. Whenever the President transmits to the President pro tempore of the Senate and the Speaker of the House of Representatives his written declaration that he is unable to discharge the powers and duties of his office, and until he transmits to them a written declaration to the contrary, such powers and duties shall be discharged by the Vice President as Acting President.

Section 4. Whenever the Vice President and a majority of either the principal officers of the executive departments or of such other body as Congress may by law provide, transmit to the President pro tempore of the Senate and the Speaker of the House of Representatives their written declaration that the President is unable to discharge the powers and duties of his office, the Vice President shall immediately assume the powers and duties of the offices as Acting President.

Thereafter, when the President transmits to the President pro tempore of the Senate and the Speaker of the House of Representatives his written declaration that no inability exists, he shall resume the powers and duties of his office unless the Vice President and a majority of either the principal officers of the executive department or of such other body as Congress may by law provide, transmit within four days to the President pro tempore of the Senate and the Speaker of the House of Representatives their written declaration that the President is unable to discharge the powers and duties of his office. Thereupon Congress shall decide the issue, assembling within forty-eight hours for that purpose if not in session. If the Congress, within twenty-one days after receipt of the latter written declaration, or, if Congress is not in session, within twenty-one days after Congress is required to assemble, determines by two-thirds vote of both Houses that the President is unable to discharge the powers and duties of his office, the Vice President shall continue to discharge the same as Acting President; otherwise; the President shall resume the powers and duties of his office.

Amendment XXVI
(Ratified on July 1, 1971)

Section 1. The right of citizens of the United States, who are eighteen years of age or older, to vote shall not be denied or abridged by the United States or by any State on account of age.

Section 2. The Congress shall have the power to enforce this article by appropriate legislation.

Amendment XXVII
(Ratified on May 7, 1992)

No law, varying the compensation for the services of the Senators and Representatives, shall take effect, until an election of Representatives shall have intervened.

Among the numerous advantages promised by a well-constructed Union, none deserves to be more accurately developed than its tendency to break and control the violence of faction. The friend of popular governments never finds himself so much alarmed for their character and fate as when he contemplates their propensity to this dangerous vice. He will not fail, therefore, to set a due value on any plan which, without violating the principles to which he is attached, provides a proper cure for it. The instability, injustice, and confusion introduced into the public councils have, in truth, been the mortal diseases under which popular governments have everywhere perished, as they continue to be the favorite and fruitful topics from which the adversaries to liberty derive their most specious declamations. The valuable improvements made by the American constitutions on the popular models, both ancient and modern, cannot certainly be too much admired; but it would be an unwarrantable partiality to contend that they have as effectually obviated the danger on this side, as was wished and expected. Complaints are everywhere heard from our most considerate and virtuous citizens, equally the friends of public and private faith and of public and personal liberty, that our governments are too unstable, that the public good is disregarded in the conflicts of rival parties, and that measures are too often decided, not according to the rules of justice and the rights of the minor party, but by the superior force of an interested and overbearing majority. However anxiously we may wish that these complaints had no foundation, the evidence of known facts will not permit us to deny that they are in some degree true. It will be found, indeed, on a candid review of our situation, that some of the distresses under which we labor have been erroneously charged on the operation of our governments; but it will be found, at the same time, that other causes will not alone account for many of our heaviest misfortunes; and, particularly, for that prevailing and increasing distrust of public engagements and alarm for private rights which are echoed from one end of the continent to the other. These must be chiefly, if not wholly, effects of the unsteadiness and injustice with which a factious spirit has tainted our public administration.

By a faction I understand a number of citizens, whether amounting to a majority or minority of the whole, who are united and actuated by some common impulse of passion, or of interest, adverse to the rights of other citizens, or the permanent and aggregate interests of the community.

There are two methods of curing the mischiefs of faction: the one, by removing its causes; the other, by controlling its effects.

There are again two methods of removing the causes of faction: the one, by destroying the liberty which is essential to its existence; the other, by giving to every citizen the same opinions, the same passions, and the same interests.

It could never be more truly said than of the first remedy that it was worse than the disease. Liberty is to faction what air is to fire, an aliment without which it instantly expires. But it could not be a less folly to abolish liberty, which is essential to political life, because it nourishes faction than it would be to wish the annihilation of air, which is essential to animal life, because it imparts to fire its destructive agency.

The second expedient is as impracticable as the first would be unwise. As long as the reason of man continues fallible, and his is at liberty to exercise it, different opinions will be formed. As long as the connection subsists between his reason and his self-love, his opinions and his passions will have a reciprocal influence on each other; and the former will be objects to which the latter will attach themselves. The diversity in the faculties of men, from which the rights of property originate, is not less an insuperable obstacle to a uniformity of interests. The protection of these faculties is the first object of government. From the protection of different and unequal faculties of acquiring property, the possession of different degrees and kinds of property immediately results; and from the influence of these on the sentiments and views of the respective proprietors ensues a division of the society into different interests and parties.

The latent causes of faction are thus sown in the nature of man; and we see them everywhere brought into different degrees of activity, according to the different circumstances of civil society. A zeal for different opinions concerning religion, concerning government, and many other points, as well of speculation as of practice; an attachment to different leaders ambitiously contending for pre-eminence and power; or to persons of other descriptions whose fortunes have been interesting to the human passions, have, in turn, divided mankind into parties, inflamed them with mutual animosity, and rendered them much more disposed to vex and oppress each other than to cooperate for their common good. So strong is this propensity of mankind to fall into mutual animosities that where no substantial occasion presents itself the most frivolous and fanciful distinctions have been sufficient to kindle their unfriendly passions and excite their most violent conflicts. But the most common and durable source of factions has been the various and unequal distribution of property. Those who hold and those who are without property have ever formed distinct interests in society. Those who are creditors, and those who are debtors, fall under a like discrimination. A landed interest, a manufacturing interest, a mercantile interest, a moneyed interest, with many lesser interests, grow up of necessity in civilized nations, and divide them into different classes, actuated by different sentiments and views. The regulation of these various and interfering interests forms the principal task of modern legislation and involves the spirit of party and faction in the necessary and ordinary operations of government.

No man is allowed to be a judge in his own cause, because his interest would certainly bias his judgment, and, not improbably, corrupt his integrity. With equal, nay with greater reason, a body of men are unfit to be both judges and parties at the same time; yet what are many of the most important acts of legislation but so many judicial determinations, not indeed concerning the rights of single persons, but concerning the rights of large bodies of citizens? And what are the different classes of legislators but advocates and parties to the causes which they determine? Is a law proposed concerning private debts? It is a question to which the creditors are parties on one side and the debtors on the other. Justice ought to hold the balance between them. Yet the parties are, and must be, themselves the judges; and the most numerous party, or in other words, the most powerful faction must be expected to prevail. Shall domestic manufacturers be encouraged, and in what degree, by restrictions on foreign manufacturers? are questions which would be differently decided by the landed and the manufacturing classes, and probably by neither with a sole regard to justice and the public good. The apportionment of taxes on the various descriptions of property is an act which seems to require the most exact impartiality; yet there is, perhaps, no legislative act in which greater opportunity and temptation are given to a predominant party to trample on the rules of justice. Every shilling with which they overburden the inferior number is a shilling saved to their own pockets. It is in vain to say that enlightened statesmen will be able to adjust these clashing interests and render them all subservient to the public good. Enlightened statesmen will not always be at the helm. Nor, in many cases, can such an adjustment be made at all without taking into view indirect and remote considerations, which will rarely prevail over the immediate interest which one party may find in disregarding the rights of another or the good of the whole.

The inference to which we are brought is that the *causes* of faction cannot be removed and that relief is only to be sought in the means of controlling its *effects*.

If a faction consists of less than a majority, relief is supplied by the republican principle, which enables the majority to defeat its sinister views by regular vote. It may clog the administration, it may convulse the society; but it will be unable to execute and mask its violence under the forms of the Constitution. When a majority is included in a faction, the form of popular government, on the other hand, enables it to sacrifice to its ruling passion or interest both the public good and the rights of other citizens. To secure the public good and private rights against the danger of such a faction, and at the same time to preserve the spirit and the form of popular government, is then the great object to which our inquiries are directed. Let me add that it is the great desideratum by which alone this form of government can be rescued from the opprobrium under which it has so long labored and be recommended to the esteem and adoption of mankind.

By what means is this object attainable? Evidently by one of two only. Either the existence of the same passion or interest in a majority at the same time must be prevented, or the majority, having such coexistent passion or interest, must be rendered, by their number and local situation, unable to concert and carry into effect schemes of oppression. If the impulse and the opportunity be suffered to coincide, we well know that neither moral nor religious motives can be relied on as an adequate control. They are not found to be such on the injustice and violence of individuals, and lose their efficacy in proportion to the number combined together, that is, in proportion as their efficacy becomes needful.

From this view of the subject it may be concluded that a pure democracy, by which I mean a society consisting of a small number of citizens, who assemble and administer the government in person, can admit of no cure for the mischiefs of faction. A common passion or interest will, in almost every case, be felt by a majority of the whole; a communication and concert results from the form of government itself; and there is nothing to check the inducements to sacrifice the weaker party or an obnoxious individual. Hence it is that such democracies have ever been spectacles of turbulence and contention; have ever been found incompatible with personal security or the rights of property; and have in general been as short in their lives as they have been violent in their deaths. Theoretic politicians, who have patronized this species of government, have erroneously supposed that by reducing mankind to a perfect equality in their political rights, they would at the same time be perfectly equalized and assimilated in their possessions, their opinions, and their passions.

A republic, by which I mean a government in which the scheme of representation takes place, opens a different prospect and promises the cure for which we are seeking. Let us examine the points in which it varies from pure democracy, and we shall comprehend both the nature of the cure and the efficacy which it must derive from the Union.

The two great points of difference between a democracy and a republic are: first, the delegation of the government, in the latter, to a small number of citizens elected by the rest; secondly, the greater number of citizens and greater sphere of country over which the latter may be extended.

The effect of the first difference is, on the one hand, to refine and enlarge the public views by passing them through the medium of a chosen body of citizens, whose wisdom may best discern the true interest of their country and whose patriotism and love of justice will be least likely to sacrifice it to temporary or partial considerations. Under such a regulation it may well happen that the public voice, pronounced by the representatives of the people, will be more consonant to the public good than if pronounced by the people themselves, convened for the purpose. On the other hand, the effect may be inverted. Men of factious tempers, of local prejudices, or of sinister designs, may, by intrigue, by corruption, or by other means, first obtain the suffrages, and then betray the interests of the people. The question resulting is, whether small or extensive republics are most favorable to the election of proper guardians of the public weal; and it is clearly decided in favor of the latter by two obvious considerations.

In the first place it is to be remarked that however small the republic may be the representatives must be raised to a certain number in order to guard against the cabals of a few; and that however large it may be they must be limited to a certain number in order to guard against the confusion of a multitude. Hence, the number of representatives in the two cases not being in proportion to that of the constituents, and being proportionally greatest in the small republic, it follows that if the proportion of fit characters be not less in the large than in the small republic, the former will present a greater option, and consequently a greater probability of a fit choice.

In the next place, as each representative will be chosen by a greater number of citizens in the large than in the small republic, it will be more difficult for unworthy candidates to practice with success the vicious arts by which elections are too often carried; and the suffrages of the people being more free, will be more likely to center on men who possess the most attractive merit and the most diffusive and established characters.

It must be confessed that in this, as in most other cases, there is a mean, on both sides of which inconveniencies will be found to lie. By enlarging too much the number of electors, you render the representative too little acquainted with all their local circumstances and lesser interests; as by reducing it too much, you render him unduly attached to these, and too little fit to comprehend and pursue great and national objects. The federal Constitution forms a happy combination in this respect; the great and aggregate interests being referred to the national, the local and particular to the State legislatures.

The other point of difference is the greater number of citizens and extent of territory which may be brought within the compass of republican than of democratic government; and it is this circumstance principally which renders factious combinations less to be dreaded in the former than in the latter. The smaller the society, the fewer probably will be the distinct parties and interests composing it; the fewer the distinct parties and interests, the more frequently will a majority be found of the same party; and the smaller the number of individuals composing a majority, and the smaller the compass within which they are placed, the more easily will they concert and execute their plans of oppression. Extend the sphere and you take in a greater variety of parties and interests; you make it less probable that a majority of the whole will have a common motive to invade the rights of other citizens; or if such a common motive exists, it will be more difficult for all who feel it to discover their own strength and to act in unison with each other. Besides other impediments, it may be remarked that, where there is a consciousness of unjust or dishonorable purposes, communication is always checked by distrust in proportion to the number whose concurrence is necessary.

Hence, it clearly appears that the same advantage which a republic has over a democracy in controlling the effects of faction is enjoyed by a large over a small republic—is enjoyed by the Union over the States composing it. Does this advantage consist in the substitution of representatives whose enlightened views and virtuous sentiments render them superior to local prejudices and to schemes of injustice? It will not be denied that the representation of the Union will be most likely to possess these requisite endowments. Does it consist in the greater security afforded by a greater variety of parties, against the event of any one party being able to outnumber and oppress the rest? In an equal degree does the increased variety of parties comprised within the Union increase this security. Does it, in fine, consist in the greater obstacles opposed to the concert and accomplishment of the secret wishes of an unjust and interested majority? Here again the extent of the Union gives it the most palpable advantage.

The influence of factious leaders may kindle a flame within their particular States but will be unable to spread a general conflagration through the other States. A religious sect may degenerate into a political faction in a part of the Confederacy; but the variety of sects dispersed over the entire face of it must secure the national councils against any danger from that source. A rage for paper money, for an abolition of debts, for an equal division of property, or for any other improper or wicked project, will be less apt to pervade the whole body of the Union than a particular member of it, in the same proportion as such a malady is more likely to taint a particular county or district than an entire State.

In the extent and proper structure of the Union, therefore, we behold a republican remedy for the diseases most incident to republican government. And according to the degree of pleasure and pride we feel in being republicans ought to be our zeal in cherishing the spirit and supporting the character of federalists.

To what expedient, then, shall we finally resort, for maintaining in practice the necessary partition of power among the several departments as laid down in the Constitution? The only answer that can be given is that as all these exterior provisions are found to be inadequate the defect must be supplied, by so contriving the interior structure of the government as that its several constituent parts may, by their mutual relations, be the means of keeping each other in their proper places. Without presuming to undertake a full development of this important idea I will hazard a few general observations which may perhaps place it in a clearer light, and enable us to form a more correct judgment of the principles and structure of the government planned by the convention.

In order to lay a due foundation for that separate and distinct exercise of the different powers of government, which to a certain extent is admitted on all hands to be essential to the preservation of liberty, it is evident that each department should have a will of its own; and consequently should be so constituted that the members of each should have as little agency as possible in the appointment of the members of the others. Were this principle rigorously adhered to, it would require that all the appointments for the supreme executive, legislative, and judiciary magistracies should be drawn from the same fountain of authority, the people, through channels having no communication whatever with one another. Perhaps such a plan of constructing the several departments would be less difficult in practice than it may in contemplation appear. Some difficulties, however, and some additional expense would attend the execution of it. Some deviations, therefore, from the principle must be admitted. In the constitution of the judiciary department in particular, it might be inexpedient to insist rigorously on the principle: first, because peculiar qualifications being essential in the members, the primary consideration ought to be to select that mode of choice which best secures these qualifications; second, because the permanent tenure by which the appointments are held in that department must soon destroy all sense of dependence on the authority conferring them.

It is equally evident that the members of each department should be as little dependent as possible on those of the others for the emoluments annexed to their offices. Were the executive magistrate, or the judges, not independent of the legislature in this particular, their independence in every other would be merely nominal.

But the great security against a gradual concentration of the several powers in the same department consists in giving to those who administer each department the necessary constitutional means and personal motives to resist encroachments of the others. The provision for defense must in this, as in all other cases, be made commensurate to the danger of attack. Ambition must be made to counteract ambition. The interest of the man must be connected with the constitutional rights of the place. It may be a reflection on human nature that such devices should be necessary to control the abuses of government. But what is government itself but the greatest of all reflections on human nature? If men were angels, no government would be necessary. If angels were to govern men, neither external nor internal controls on government would be necessary. In framing a government which is to be administered by men over men, the great difficulty lies in this: you must first enable the government to control the governed; and in the next place oblige it to control itself. A dependence on the people is, no doubt, the primary control on the government; but experience has taught mankind the necessity of auxiliary precautions.

This policy of supplying, by opposite and rival interests, the defect of better motives, might be traced through the whole system of human affairs, private as well as public. We see it particularly displayed in all the subordinate distributions of power, where the constant aim is to divide and arrange the several offices in such a manner as that each may be a check on the other—that the private interest of every individual may be a sentinel over the public rights. These inventions of prudence cannot be less requisite in the distribution of the supreme powers of the State.

But it is not possible to give to each department an equal power of self-defense. In republican government, the legislative authority necessarily predominates. The remedy for this inconveniency is to divide the legislature into different branches; and to render them, by different modes of election and different principles of action, as little connected with each other as the nature of their common functions and their common dependence on the society will admit. It may even be necessary to guard against dangerous encroachments by still further precautions. As the weight of the legislative authority requires that it should be thus divided, the weakness of the executive may require, on the other hand, that it should be fortified. An absolute negative on the legislature appears, at first view, to be the natural defense with which the executive magistrate should be armed. But perhaps it would be neither altogether safe nor alone sufficient. On ordinary occasions it might not be exerted with the requisite firmness, and on extraordinary occasions it might be perfidiously abused. May not this defect of an absolute negative be supplied by some qualified connection between this weaker department and the weaker branch of the stronger department, by which the latter may be led to support the constitutional rights of the former, without being too much detached from the rights of its own department?

If the principles on which these observations are found be just, as I persuade myself they are, and they be applied as a criterion to the several State constitutions, and the federal Constitution, it will be found that if the latter does not perfectly correspond with them, the former are infinitely less able to bear such a test.

There are, moreover, two considerations particularly applicable to the federal system of America, which place that system in a very interesting point of view.

First. In a single republic, all the power surrendered by the people is submitted to the administration of a single government; and the usurpations are guarded against by a division of the government into distinct and separate departments. In the compound republic of America, the power surrendered by the people is first divided between two distinct governments, and then the portion allotted to each subdivided among distinct and separate departments. Hence a double security arises to the rights of the people. The different governments will control each other, at the same time that each will be controlled by itself.

Second. It is of great importance in a republic not only to guard the society against the oppression of its rulers, but to guard one part of the society against the injustice of the other part. Different interests necessarily exist in different classes of citizens. If a majority be united by a common interest, the rights of the minority will be insecure. There are but two methods of providing against this evil: the one by creating a will in the community independent of the majority—that is, of the society itself; the other, by comprehending in the society so many separate descriptions of citizens as will render an unjust combination of a majority of the whole very improbable, if not impracticable. The first method prevails in all governments possessing an hereditary or self-appointed authority. This, at best, is but a precarious security; because a power independent of the society may as well espouse the unjust views of the major as the rightful interests of the minor party, and may possibly be turned against both parties. The second method will be exemplified in the federal republic of the United States. Whilst all authority in it will be derived from and dependent on the society, the society itself will be broken into so many parts, interests and classes of citizens, that the rights of individuals, or of the minority, will be in little danger from interested combinations of the majority. In a free government the security for civil rights must be the same as that for religious rights. It consists in the one

case in the multiplicity of interests, and in the other in the multiplicity of sects. The degree of security in both cases will depend on the number of interests and sects; and this may be presumed to depend on the extent of country and number of people comprehended under the same government. This view of the subject must particularly recommend a proper federal system to all the sincere and considerate friends of republican government, since it shows that in exact proportion as the territory of the Union may be formed into more circumscribed Confederacies, or States, oppressive combinations of a majority will be facilitated; the best security, under the republican forms, for the rights of every class of citizen, will be diminished; and consequently the stability and independence of some member of the government, the only other security, must be proportionally increased. Justice is the end of government. It is the end of civil society. It ever has been and ever will be pursued until it be obtained, or until liberty be lost in the pursuit. In a society under the forms of which the stronger faction can readily unite and oppress the weaker, anarchy may as truly be said to reign as in a state of nature, where the weaker individual is not secured against the violence of the stronger; and as, in the latter state, even the stronger individuals are prompted, by the uncertainty of their condition, to submit to a government which may protect the weak as well as themselves; so, in the former state, will the more powerful factions or parties be gradually induced, by a like motive, to wish for a government which will protect all parties, the weaker as well as the more powerful. It can be little doubted that if the State of Rhode Island was separated from the Confederacy and left to itself, the insecurity of rights under the popular form of government within such narrow limits would be displayed by such reiterated oppressions of factious majorities that some power altogether independent of the people would soon be called for by the voice of the very factions whose misrule had proved the necessity of it. In the extended republic of the United States, and among the great variety of interests, parties, and sects which it embraces, a coalition of a majority of the whole society could seldom take place on any other principles than those of justice and the general good; whilst there being thus less danger to a minor from the will of a major party, there must be less pretext, also, to provide for the security of the former, by introducing into the government a will not dependent on the latter, or, in other words, a will independent of the society itself. It is no less certain than it is important, notwithstanding the contrary opinions which have been entertained, that the larger the society, provided it lie within a practicable sphere, the more duly capable it will be of self-government. And happily for the *republican cause,* the practicable sphere may be carried to a very great extent by a judicious modification and mixture of the *federal principle.*

ABRAHAM LINCOLN'S GETTYSBURG ADDRESS

Four score and seven years ago our fathers brought forth on this continent a new nation, conceived in liberty and dedicated to the proposition that all men are created equal. Now we are engaged in a great Civil War, testing whether that nation or any nation so conceived and so dedicated can long endure. We are met on a great battlefield of that war. We have come to dedicate a portion of that field as a final resting place for those who here gave their lives that that nation might live. It is altogether fitting and proper that we should do this. But in a larger sense, we cannot dedicate—we cannot consecrate—we cannot hallow this ground. The brave men, living and dead, who struggled here have consecrated it far above our poor power to add or detract. The world will little note nor long remember what we say here, but it can never forget what they did here. It is for us the living, rather, to be dedicated here to the unfinished work which they who fought here have thus far so nobly advanced. It is rather for us to be here dedicated to the great task remaining before us—that from these honored dead we take increased devotion to that cause for which they gave the last full measure of devotion—that we here highly resolve that these dead shall not have died in vain, that this nation, under God, shall have a new birth of freedom, and that government of the people, by the people, for the people shall not perish from the earth.

NOTES

Chapter 1

[1]John B. Anderson and Ray Martinez III, "Voters' Ed," *New York Times*, April 6, 2006, A25. Anderson is a former Republican congressman and was an independent candidate for president in 1980.

[2]Michael X. Delli Carpini and Scott Keeter, *What Americans Know About Politics and Why It Matters* (New Haven: Yale University Press, 1996), 1–21. For an overview of the relationship between education and democracy see Edward L. Glaser, Giacomo Ponzetto, and Andrei Shleifer, "Why Does Democracy Need Education?" National Bureau of Economic Research, Working Paper 12123, March, 2006. (www.nber.org/papers/w12128)

[3]Molly Andolina, "Back to the Future: Generation X and the 2000 Election," in Stephen J. Wayne and Clyde Wilcox, eds. *The Election of the Century* (Armonk, N.Y.: M. E. Sharp, 2002), 95.

[4]John R. Hibbing and Elizabeth Theiss-Morse, *Stealth Democracy: Americans' Beliefs about How Government Should Work* (New York: Cambridge University Press, 2002), 111.

[5]See John Hibbing and Beth Theiss-Morse, *Congress as Public Enemy: Public Attitudes toward American Political Institutions* (Cambridge: Cambridge University Press, 1995); John Hibbing and Beth Theiss-Morse, "Civics Is Not Enough: Teaching Barbarics in K–12," *PS*, March 1996, 57–62.

[6]Hibbing and Theiss-Morse, *Congress*.

[7]*Federalist Paper 2*.

[8]Gore Vidal, "Coached by Camelot," *New Yorker*, December 1, 1997, 88.

[9]Walt Whitman, Preface to *Leaves of Grass* (1855), in *Leaves of Grass and Selected Prose*, ed. Lawrence Buell (New York: Random House, 1981), 449.

[10]Edward Countryman, *Americans: A Collision of Histories* (New York: Hill & Wang, 1996).

[11]John Sugden, *Tecumseh: A Life* (New York: Holt, 1998).

[12]U.S. Immigration and Naturalization Service, *2000 Statistical Yearbook of the Immigration and Naturalization Service* (Washington, D.C.: Government Printing Office, 2000). These are estimates; the government collects detention and return figures but has not collected emigration data since 1957.

[13]Rachel L. Swarns, "Republican Split on Immigration Reflects Nation's Struggle," *New York Times*, March 29, 2006, 1; U.S. Census Bureau, "The Foreign-Born Population in the United States: 2003" (report issued August 2004) (www.census.gov).

[14]*2004 Yearbook of Immigration Statistics* (Washington, D.C.: Department of Homeland Security, 2004), tab. 3 (uscis.gov).

[15]James Q. Wilson, "The History and Future of Democracy," lecture delivered at the Ronald Reagan Presidential Library, November 15, 1999.

[16]"Religion and the Founding of the American Republic. Part I: America as a Religious Refuge: The Seventeenth Century," Library of Congress exhibit (lcweb.loc.gov/exhibits/religion).

[17]Nicholas von Hoffman, "God Was Present at the Founding," *Civilization* (April-May 1998), 39–42.

[18]Michael J. Sandel, *Democracy's Discontent: America in Search of a Public Philosophy* (Cambridge, Mass.: Belknap Press, 1997), 56–57.

[19]Sarah Mondale and Sarah B. Patton, eds., *School: The Story of American Public Education* (Boston: Beacon Press, 2001), 36.

[20]Elizabeth Becker, "All White, All Christian, and Divided by Diversity," *New York Times*, June 10, 2001, sec. 4, 7. Becker was writing about her hometown.

[21]Census Bureau, *U.S. Statistical Abstract, 2006*, tab. 69, 58. These numbers are derived from self-reports because the Census Bureau does not collect data on religious affiliation. The number of Muslims in the United States is variously stated as from 1 to 8 million. The higher estimates are from Muslim clergy.

[22]*U. S. Statistical Abstract 2006*, tab 34.

[23]On identity politics, see Walter Benn Michaels, *Our America: Nativism, Modernism, and Pluralism* (Durham, N.C.: Duke University Press, 1997).

[24]Rachel L. Swarns, "Hispanics Resist Racial Grouping by Census," *New York Times*, October 24, 2004, 1.

[25]ABC Evening News with Peter Jennings, February 21, 2005.

[26]Alan Mairson, "Muslims in America," *National Geographic*, February 2003.

[27]U.S. Census Bureau, *General Social and Economic Characteristics: U.S. Summary* (Washington, D.C.: Government Printing Office, 1990), pt. 1, tab. 12.

[28]Census Bureau, *Statistical Abstract, 2005*, table 54.

[29]Gregory Rodriguez, "Mongrel America," *Atlantic Monthly*, January-February, 2003, 96.

[30]Michael Lind, "The Beige and the Black," *New York Times Magazine*, August 16, 1998, 38; Randall Kennedy, *Interracial Intimacies* (New York: Pantheon, 2003).

[31]The origins of governmental systems are discussed by John Jay in *Federalist Paper 2*.

[32]Garry Wills, *Lincoln at Gettysburg: The Words That Remade America* (New York: Simon & Schuster, 1992), 145.

[33]Carl F. Kaestle, "Introduction," in *School*, ed. Mondale and Patton, 13.

[34]Ibid., 16.

[35]Brian Friel, "Don't Know Much about History," *National Journal*, August 2, 2003, 2500-2501.

[36]"The Educated Citizen," in *School*, ed. Mondale and Patton, 22.

[37]Ibid.

[38]Adam Cohen, "According to Webster: One Man's Attempt to Define 'America,'" *New York Times*, February 12, 2006, Sec. 4, 13.

[39]Noah Webster quoted in Jack Lynch, "Dr. Johnson's Revolution," *New York Times*, July 2, 2005.

[40]Robert Reinhold, "Resentment against New Immigrants," *New York Times*, October 26, 1986, 6E.

[41]Michael Thompson, Richard Ellis, and Aaron Wildavsky, *Cultural Theory* (Boulder, Colo.: Westview, 1990), 216.

[42]For a discussion of the Declaration of Independence's origins in pragmatism versus the political philosophy of the Founders, see Pauline Maier, *American Scripture: Making the Declaration of Independence* (New York: Knopf, 1997).

[43]Wilfred M. McClay, "Communitarianism and the Federal Idea," in *Community and Political Thought Today*, ed. Peter Augustine Lawler and Dale McConkey (Westport, Conn.: Praeger, 1998), 102.

[44]President Johnson quoted in Tim Funk, "Civil Rights Act of 1964 Paved Way for Prosperity," *Champaign-Urbana News Gazette*, July 11, 2004, B1.

[45]Alexis de Tocqueville, *Democracy in America* (New York: Knopf, 1945; originally published 1835).

[46]Quoted in Anthony Lewis, "Hail and Farewell," *New York Times*, December 15, 2001, A31.

[47]This discussion draws on Sidney Verba and Norman Nie, *Participation in America* (New York: Harper & Row, 1972), and Stephen Earl Bennett and Linda L. M. Bennett, "Political Participation," in *Annual Review of Political Science*, ed. Samuel Long (Norwood, N.J.: Ablex, 1986).

[48]E. J. Dionne Jr., *Why Americans Hate Politics* (New York: Simon & Schuster, 1991).

[49]Robert D. Putnam, *Bowling Alone: The Collapse and Revival of American Community* (New York: Simon & Schuster, 2000).

[50]Robert A. Dahl, *A Preface to Democratic Theory* (Chicago: University of Chicago Press, 1956), 142.

[51]These ideas are at the core of rival bodies of theory in political science. See especially Robert A. Dahl's classic *Who Governs? Democracy and Power in an American City* (New Haven, Conn.: Yale University Press, 1961) on pluralism; C. Wright Mills, *The Power Elite* (New York: Oxford University Press, 1956); and Michael Parenti, *Democracy for the Few*, 7th ed. (Belmont, Calif.: Wadsworth, 2001), on permanent losers.

[52]See Arthur F. Bentley, *The Process of Government* (Chicago: University of Chicago Press, 1908), and David Truman, *The Governmental Process* (New York: Knopf, 1951).

[53]Theda Skocpol, *Diminished Democracy: From Membership to Management in American Civic Life* (Norman: Oklahoma University Press, 2003).

[54]Russell Baker, "That Insolent Weld," *New York Times*, August 26, 1997, A19. *Champaign-Urbana News-Gazette*, August 29, 1997, A4.

[55]Joseph Schumpeter, *Capitalism, Socialism, and Democracy* (New York: Harper Bros., 1950).

[56]E. E. Schattschneider, *The Semisovereign People* (New York: Holt, Rinehart and Winston, 1960), 141.

[57]Alan Wolfe, "Couch Potato Politics," *New York Times*, March 15, 1998, sec. 4, 17.

[58]League of Conservative Voters poll, March 2002.

[59]Unless otherwise identified, poll results are from *What Americans Know About Politics and Why It Matters*, 62–104.

[60]Ibid.

[61]2004 Knight Foundation Survey of high school students, administrators, and faculty on first amendment freedoms. Results of the survey can be found at knightfdn.org by linking to the First Amendment survey pages.

[62]Ibid.

[63]Stephen Macedo, et al., *Democracy at Risk: How Political Choices Undermine Citizen Participation,*

and What We Can Do About It (Washington, D.C.: Brookings Institution, 2005), 20. This report was commissioned by the American Political Science Association.

Chapter 2

1. Nixon hoped he might be considered an American Disraeli. Benjamin Disraeli was a British prime minister in the nineteenth century known for his progressive ideas. Nixon admired Robert Blake's biography of Disraeli, and mentioning this to Attorney General Elliot Richardson in 1971, Richardson replied, "The similarities are great, Mr. President, but what a pity that Blake could not quote Disraeli's conversations." That Nixon did not destroy the tapes even after they became a liability can apparently be attributed to this reason. Sidney Blumenthal, "The Longest Campaign," New Yorker, August 8, 1994, 37.

2. United States v. Reynolds, 345 U.S. 1 (1953). Years later it was discovered that the administration invoked executive privilege to protect the air force from embarrassment over a plane crash that resulted from poor maintenance and pilot error. "Morning Edition," National Public Radio, September 9, 2005.

3. The Indians, of course, had their own governments, and the Spanish may have established Saint Augustine, Florida, and Santa Fe, New Mexico, before the English established Jamestown. The Spanish settlements were extensions of Spanish colonization of Mexico and were governed by Spanish officials in Mexico City.

4. This is not to suggest that the Pilgrims believed in democracy. Apparently, they were motivated to draft the compact by threats from some on the Mayflower that when the ship landed they would "use their owne libertie; for none had power to command them." Thus the compact was designed to bind them to the laws of the colony. Richard Shenkman, "I Love Paul Revere, Whether He Rode or Not" (New York: HarperCollins, 1991), 141–142.

5. David Hawke, A Transaction of Free Men (New York: Scribner, 1964), 209.

6. William H. Riker, Federalism (Boston: Little, Brown, 1964), 18–20.

7. For an account of the foreign affairs problems under the Articles of Confederation, see Frederick W. Marks III, Independence on Trial: Foreign Affairs and the Making of the Constitution (Baton Rouge: Louisiana State University Press, 1973).

8. Louis Fisher, President and Congress (New York: Free Press, 1972), 14.

9. The government under the Articles, however, could boast one major accomplishment: the Northwest Ordinance, adopted in 1787, provided for the government and future statehood of the land west of Pennsylvania (land that would become most of the Great Lakes states). The law also banned slavery in this territory.

10. Gordon S. Wood, "The Origins of the Constitution," This Constitution: A Bicentennial Chronicle, Summer 1987, 10–11.

11. Eric Black, Our Constitution (Boulder, Colo.: Westview Press, 1988), 6.

12. For development of this idea, see Kenneth M. Dolbeare and Linda J. Medcalf, "The Political Economy of the Constitution," This Constitution: A Bicentennial Chronicle, Spring 1987, 4–10.

13. Black, Our Constitution, 59.

14. The Constitution would, however, retain numerous positive aspects of the Articles. See Donald S. Lutz, "The Articles of Confederation as the Background to the Federal Republic," Publius 20 (Winter 1990), 55–70.

15. Robert McCloskey, The American Supreme Court (Chicago: University of Chicago Press, 1960), 29.

16. Fred Barbash, "James Madison: A Man for the '80s," Washington Post National Weekly Edition, March 30, 1987, 23.

17. Robert A. Dahl, A Preface to Democratic Theory (Chicago: University of Chicago Press, 1956), 5. Yet according to a poll in 1987, the bicentennial of the Constitution, only 1 percent of the public identified Madison as the one who played the biggest role in creating the Constitution. Most—31 percent—said Thomas Jefferson, who was a diplomat in France during the convention. Black, Our Constitution, 15.

18. Some argue that Hamilton, rather than Madison, was the driving force behind the Constitution, especially if his efforts after ratification—as an influential member of Washington's cabinet and later—are taken into account. Kenneth M. Dolbeare and Linda Medcalf, "The Dark Side of the Constitution," in The Case Against the Constitution: From the Antifederalists to the Present, ed. Kenneth M. Dolbeare and John F. Manley (Armonk, N.Y.: Sharpe, 1987), 120–141.

19. Robert A. Dahl, How Democratic Is the American Constitution? (New Haven, Conn.: Yale University Press, 2001), 7.

20. Gouverneur Morris, of Pennsylvania. Dahl, How Democratic, 11–12.

21. Dahl, How Democratic, 11–12.

22. Ibid., 14.

23. Paul Finkelman, "Slavery at the Philadelphia Convention," This Constitution: A Bicentennial Chronicle (1987), 25–30.

24. Ibid., 29.

25. Ibid., 18.

26. Quoted in Thomas G. West, Vindicating the Founders: Race, Sex, Class, and Justice in the Origins of America (Lanham, Md.: Rowman & Littlefield, 1997), 15.

27. Theodore J. Lowi, American Government (Hinsdale, Ill.: Dryden, 1976), 97.

28. Quoted in C. Herman Pritchett, Constitutional Law of the Federal System (Englewood Cliffs, N.J.: Prentice Hall, 1984), xi.

29. Quoted in Richard Hofstadter, The American Political Tradition (New York: Random House, 1948), 13.

30. Quoted in Richard Hofstadter, The American Political Tradition (New York: Vintage, 1948), 6–7.

31. Federalist Paper 51.

32. Federalist Paper 47.

33. Max Farrand, The Framing of the Constitution of the United States (New Haven, Conn.: Yale University Press, 1913).

34. Charles O. Jones, The Presidency in a Separated System (Washington, D.C.: Brookings Institution, 1994), 14.

35. Charles O. Jones, Separate but Equal Branches (Chatham, N.J.: Chatham House, 1995), 12.

36. Federalist Paper 51.

37. Jones, Presidency in a Separated System, 16, thus modifying Neustadt's classic definition of "a government of separated institutions sharing powers." Richard E. Neustadt, Presidential Power and the Modern Presidents (New York: Macmillan, 1990), 29.

38. For elaboration, see Dahl, How Democratic Is the American Constitution? 24–25.

39. Ibid.

40. Seymour Martin Lipset, "Why No Socialism in the United States?" in Sources of Contemporary Radicalism, ed. Seweryn Bialer and Sophis Sluzar (Boulder, Colo.: Westview Press, 1977), 86.

41. These were not the only reasons people migrated to America, of course, but these were the primary ones. For development of this idea, see John W. Kingdon, America the Unusual (Boston: Bedford St. Martin's, 1999), 58–63. After the Revolutionary War, many Americans who were sympathetic to England and more comfortable with authority moved to Canada. At the same time, some Canadians who were more individualistic moved to the United States, thus reinforcing the original migration pattern.

42. For elaboration, see West, Vindicating the Founders, 43–54.

43. Donald S. Lutz, "The Relative Influence of European Writers on Later Eighteenth-Century American Political Thought," American Political Science Review 78 (1984), 139–197.

44. Alpheus T. Mason and Richard H. Leach, In Quest of Freedom: American Political Thought and Practice, 2nd ed. (Englewood Cliffs, N.J.: Prentice Hall, 1973), 51.

45. For development of this idea, see Martin Landau, "A Self-Correcting System: The Constitution of the United States," This Constitution: A Bicentennial Chronicle (Summer 1986), 4–10.

46. John P. Roche, "The Founding Fathers: A Reform Caucus in Action," American Political Science Review 56 (1962), 799–816.

47. Benjamin F. Wright Jr., "The Origins of the Separation of Powers in America," in Origins of American Political Thought, ed. John P. Roche (New York: Harper & Row, 1967), 139–162.

48. John R. Roche, "The Founding Fathers: A Reform Caucus in Action," American Political Science Review 55 (December, 1961), 805.

49. James MacGregor Burns, The Vineyard of Liberty (New York: Knopf, 1982), 33.

50. Bernard Bailyn, Voyagers to the West (New York: Knopf, 1982), 20.

51. The Boston Tea Party, contrary to myth, was not prompted by higher taxes on British tea. Parliament lowered the taxes to give the British East India Company, facing bankruptcy, an advantage in the colonial market. This threatened American shippers who smuggled tea from Holland and controlled about three-fourths of the market. The shippers resented Parliament's attempt to manipulate the economy from thousands of miles away. Shenkman, "I Love Paul Revere," 155.

52. Federalist Paper 10.

53. Black, Our Constitution, 21.

54. For elaboration, see Dolbeare and Medcalf, "Dark Side of the Constitution."

55. Calvin C. Jillson and Cecil L. Eubanks, "The Political Structure of Constitution Making," American Journal of Political Science 29 (1984), 435–458.

56. Jonathan Elliot, The Debates in the Several State Conventions on the Adoption of the Federal Constitution as Recommended by the General Convention at Philadelphia, in 1787, 2nd ed., 5 vols. (Philadelphia, 1896), 2: 102.

57. On Anti-Federalist thinking, see William B. Allen and Gordon Lloyd, eds., The Essential Antifederalist, 2nd ed. (Lanham, Md.: University Press of America, 2002); John F. Manley and Kenneth M. Dolbeare, The Case against the Constitution (Armonk, N.Y.: Sharpe, 1987).

58. Richard S. Randall, American Constitutional Development, vol. 1, The Powers of Government (New York: Longman, 2002), 54.

[59]"A Fundamental Contentment," *This Constitution: A Bicentennial Chronicle* (Fall 1984), 44.

[60]Quoted in Charles Warren, *The Making of the Constitution* (Boston: Little, Brown, 1928), xiv. Jefferson made this observation from afar, as he was serving as ambassador to France at the time of the Constitutional Convention.

[61]Keith Perine, "Congress Shows Little Enthusiasm for Bush's Marriage Amendment," *CQ Weekly* (February 28, 2004), 533.

[62]Alan P. Grimes, *Democracy and the Amendments to the Constitution* (Lexington, Mass.: Lexington Books, 1978). Grimes also shows how the adoption of new amendments reflects the rise of new power blocs in society.

[63]This discussion borrows heavily from George P. Fletcher, *Our Secret Constitution: How Lincoln Redefined American Democracy* (New York: Oxford University Press, 2001); Bruce Ackerman, *We the People,* vol. 2, *Transformations* (Cambridge, Mass.: Belknap Press, 1998); and Garry Wills, *Lincoln at Gettysburg* (New York: Simon & Schuster, 1992). For a complementary view, see Charles Black, *A New Birth of Freedom: Human Rights, Named and Unnamed* (New York: Grosset/Putnam, 1997). For a somewhat different view about the impact of the New Deal, see G. Edward White, *The Constitution and the New Deal* (Cambridge, Mass.: Harvard University Press, 2001).

[64]Historian James McPherson, quoted in Fletcher, *Our Secret Constitution,* 57; Ackerman, *We the People,* 10.

[65]Many of Lincoln's prejudicial comments came in response to more blatant racist remarks by his opponents. Lincoln abandoned his support for black emigration before he was elected to a second term as president. For a critical perspective on Lincoln's racial views, see Lerone Bennett Jr., *Forced into Glory: Abraham Lincoln's White Dream* (Chicago: Johnson, 2000). For a positive perspective, see William Lee Miller, *Lincoln's Virtues: An Ethical Biography* (New York: Knopf, 2002).

[66]Fletcher, *Our Secret Constitution,* 24.

[67]John Hope Franklin, *From Slavery to Freedom,* 3rd ed. (New York: Vintage, 1969), 283.

[68]The proclamation also prompted European workers, who were attracted to the idea of laborers around the world gaining more freedom, to rally to the Union's cause. Ibid., 283.

[69]These paragraphs rely on the interpretations of Wills, *Lincoln at Gettysburg,* and Fletcher, *Our Secret Constitution.*

[70]Fletcher, *Our Secret Constitution,* 53.

[71]A precursor of this view was the era of Jacksonian democracy in the 1830s.

[72]A contemporary celebration of the nation as an entity can be seen in the poetry of Walt Whitman.

[73]Wills, *Lincoln at Gettysburg,* 38. Wills insists that this was not a coincidence, and he debunks the notion that Lincoln hastily dashed off his remarks while on his way to the town or to the speech itself (27–31).

[74]Fletcher, *Our Secret Constitution,* 35, 4. Others might nominate Lincoln's second inaugural address, in which he offered reconciliation to the South, or Martin Luther King Jr.'s "I Have a Dream" speech.

[75]The *Dred Scott* case is explained in Chapters 13 and 15.

[76]The equal protection clause is covered fully in Chapter 15, and the due process clause is covered fully in Chapter 14.

[77]Fletcher, *Our Secret Constitution,* 25.

[78]In this vein, Congress first experimented with an income tax during the war. It would return to this tax in the decades after the war.

[79]There was a debate about the validity of the Thirteenth Amendment and especially the Fourteenth, much as there had been about the validity of the Constitutional Convention and the Constitution for bypassing the procedures for amendment established by the Articles of Confederation. Congress conditioned the slave states' reentry into the Union upon their ratification of the Fourteenth Amendment. Otherwise, not enough states would have ratified the amendment. Yet one legal scholar argues that Congress served as a quasi constitutional convention in which members, like Lincoln before them, sensed that they were reinventing rather than following the Constitution. Their actions would have been thwarted if the public had opposed them. Ackerman, *We the People,* ch. 6–8.

[80]For example, the abolitionist movement and the Fifteenth Amendment would fuel the drive for women's suffrage, as explained in Chapter 15.

[81]This section borrows heavily from Ackerman, *We the People,* and Theodore J. Lowi, *The Personal President* (Ithaca, N.Y.: Cornell University Press, 1985).

[82]We never had a pure laissez-faire approach— there always was some governmental regulation—but this is the term most associated with the attitudes of the time.

[83]At least one legal scholar dismisses the notion that the Court's "old men" were reactionaries or fools. Although today people consider them mistaken, at the time they were following established doctrine. Ackerman, *We the People.*

[84]Elaboration of and sources for these statements can be found in Chapter 13.

[85]The Court said he did affect the market slightly because he did not buy the twelve acres' worth of wheat that he would have needed if he had obeyed the order. The Court's main point, however, was that Congress has the authority to pass such laws. *Wickard* v. *Filburn,* 317 U.S. 111 (1942).

[86]Lowi, *Personal President,* 49. Writers during the Depression and in the decades after it also recognized this as a revolution. Ernest K. Lindley, *The Roosevelt Revolution, First Phase* (New York: Viking, 1933); Mario Einaudi, *The Roosevelt Revolution* (New York: Harcourt, Brace & World, 1959).

[87]Karl Vick, "A President Who Woke Up Washington," *Washington Post National Weekly Edition,* April 28, 1997, 8.

[88]Ibid., 9.

[89]Lowi, *Personal President,* 44.

[90]Ibid., xi.

[91]This era also saw a shift to a more presidency-centered government that persists to a significant degree today. Lowi, *Personal President.*

[92]President Ronald Reagan in the 1980s and congressional Republicans in the early 1990s mounted major challenges to the changes initiated by the Depression and the New Deal. President George W. Bush has also mounted significant challenges. These will be addressed in later chapters. In addition, some conservative judges and legal scholars support the "Constitution in exile" movement, which claims that the changes in legal doctrine during and after the 1930s have been illegitimate.

[93]Of course, the process was evolutionary; the changes did not spring solely from these two crises. Moreover, some might maintain that the Supreme Court under the leadership of Chief

Justice Earl Warren in the 1950s and 1960s also remade the Constitution because of its rulings expanding the Bill of Rights. Yet the changes brought about by the Warren Court probably had less impact overall than those wrought by Reconstruction or the New Deal.

[94]For a discussion of the role played by the philosophy of pragmatism in resolving these conflicts, see Fletcher, *Our Secret Constitution,* ch. 11.

[95]Henry Steele Commager, *Living Ideas in America* (New York: Harper & Row, 1951), 109.

[96]West, *Vindicating the Founders,* xi.

[97]Parts of the Constitution have been copied by some Latin America countries, Liberia (founded by Americans), and the Philippines (formerly an American territory).

[98]"South Africa Looks at U.S. Constitution," *Lincoln Journal Star,* October 7, 1990; David Remnick, "'We, the People,' from the Russian," *Washington Post National Weekly Edition,* September 10, 1990, 11.

[99]European countries, Australia, Canada, Costa Rica, Israel, Japan, and New Zealand.

[100]Dahl, *How Democratic . . . ?* tabs. 1 and 2, 164–165. Dahl counts only countries that have "strong" federalism, bicameralism, and judicial review.

[101]Jones, *Presidency in a Separated System,* xiii.

[102]Dahl, *How Democratic . . . ?* 115.

[103]Jones, *Presidency in a Separated System,* 3.

[104]Kingdon, *America the Unusual,* 7–22. Exceptions include education and regulation of civil rights and the environment. They also include a massive national defense establishment and an extensive criminal justice system. In these aspects, our government is bigger than in many other advanced industrialized countries.

[105]Richard Morin, "Happy Days Are Here Again," *Washington Post National Weekly Edition,* August 25, 1997, 35.

[106]About 25 percent split their ticket between candidates for president and representative. In addition, others split their vote between candidates for president and senator or between candidates for representative and senator. For an examination of the research about divided government, see Morris Fiorina, *Divided Government,* 2nd ed. (Boston: Allyn & Bacon, 1996), 153.

[107]Lewis Lapham, "Get Me Rewrite!" *New York Times Book Review,* February 4, 1996, 11.

[108]418 U.S. 683 (1974).

[109]For a contemporary analysis of executive privilege, see Mark J. Rozell, *Executive Privilege,* 2nd ed. (Lawrence: University of Kansas, 2002).

[110]Jeffrey Toobin, *A Vast Conspiracy* (New York: Touchstone, 1999), 333–334.

[111]Jeb Stuart Magruder. "Ex-Aide: Nixon Ordered Watergate Break-In," *Lincoln Journal Star,* July 27, 2003.

[112]Tip O'Neill with William Novak, *Man of the House* (New York: Random House, 1987). The tapes did contain some useful advice for future presidents. Unfortunately, this advice, on tapes not released until 1999, came too late for President Clinton: "Frankly, we shouldn't have had those interns. They're a pain in the ass." "Verbatim," *Time,* October 18, 1999, 35.

[113]Bob Woodward and Carl Bernstein, *The Final Days* (New York: Simon & Schuster, 1976), 343, 403–404, 423.

[114]"Tapes Confirm Nixon Approved Hush Money," *Lincoln Journal Star,* June 5, 1991. For a survey of presidents' efforts to record their conversations, see William Doyle, *Inside the Oval Office: White House Tapes from FDR to Clinton* (New York: Kodansha, 1999).

Chapter 3

[1]Background on Napolitano's political career and Arizona's economy from Michael Barone and Richard E. Cohen, *Almanac of American Politics 2006* (Washington D.C.: National Journal, 2005), 86–93 and Governor Napolitano's website (www.azgovernor.gov).

[2]Arizona-Mexico Commission, "Labor Shortages and Illegal Immigration: Arizona's Three-Pronged Strategy," 7–9. (www.azmc.org)

[3]Janet Napolitano, "Message of the Week," August 17, 2005, 1. (http://azgovernor.gov/dms/)

[4]William H. Riker, *The Development of American Federalism* (Boston: Kluwer Academic, 1987), 6.

[5]The delegate was George Read of Delaware. See William H. Riker, *Democracy in America,* 2nd ed. (New York: Macmillan, 1965).

[6]*Federalist Paper* 39.

[7]Vernon L. Parrington, *Main Currents in American Thought* (New York: Harcourt, Brace, 1927).

[8]David Truman, "Federalism and the Party System," in *Federalism: Mature and Emergent,* ed. Arthur W. MacMahon (New York: Russell & Russell, 1962), 123.

[9]See Madison's discussion of this in *Federalist Paper* 39.

[10]See Forrest McDonald, *States' Rights and the Union: Imperium in Imperio, 1776–1876* (Lawrence: University Press of Kansas, 2000).

[11]A 1976 Supreme Court decision (*National League of Cities* v. *Usery,* 426 U.S. 833) used the Tenth Amendment as a reason to forbid the federal government to extend minimum wage and hour laws to state and local government employees. (This decision was partly overruled in 1985 in *Garcia* v. *San Antonio Metropolitan Transit Authority,* 469 U.S. 528.)

[12]Political scientist Howard Gillman, quoted in Linda Greenhouse, "At the Court, Dissent over States' Rights Is Now War," *New York Times,* June 10, 2002, sec. 4, 3.

[13]Part of this discussion is drawn from Richard Leach, *American Federalism* (New York: Norton, 1970), ch. 1. See also Christopher Hamilton and Donald Wells, *Federalism, Power and Political Economy: A New Theory of Federalism's Impact on American Life* (Englewood Cliffs, N.J.: Prentice Hall, 1990).

[14]*McCulloch* v. *Maryland,* 4 Wheat. 316 (1819).

[15]*Niles' Register,* May 13, 1819.

[16]Richard Neustadt, *The American Presidency,* episode 5, PBS, April 2000. (See "For Viewing" section)

[17]Daniel Elazar, *The American Partnership* (Chicago: University of Chicago Press, 1962).

[18]Alfred Kelly and Winfred Harbeson, *The American Constitution: Its Origins and Development* (New York: Norton, 1976).

[19]Garry Wills, "War between the States and Washington," *New York Times Magazine* (July 5, 1998), 26.

[20]Alice Rivlin, *Reviving the American Dream: The Economy, the States, and the Federal Government* (Washington, D.C.: Brookings Institution, 1992).

[21]Timothy Conlan, *From Federalism to Devolution: Twenty-Five Years of Intergovernmental Reform* (Washington, D.C.: Brookings Institution, 1998), 6.

[22]On Nixon's managerial approach to federalism, see Lawrence D. Brown, *New Policies, New Politics: Government's Response to Government's Growth* (Washington, D.C.: Brookings Institution, 1983). The comparative discussion of Lyndon Johnson's, Richard Nixon's, and Ronald Reagan's federalism policies draws on Conlan, *From New Federalism to Devolution,* ch. 1, 6, and 13.

[23]Conlan, *From New Federalism to Devolution,* 109.

[24]See, for example, William J. Clinton, "Federalism," Executive Order 13132, *Federal Register* 54, no. 163 (August 10, 1999): 43255–43259. Clinton discussed his views on state activism and federalism in general with the historian Gary Wills in "The War between the States and Washington."

[25]Grover Norquist, arguably the most powerful lobbyist in Washington quoted in Philip Gourevitch, "Fight on the Right," *The New Yorker,* April 12, 2004, 37.

[26]Jia Lynn Yang, "States: Battling Cleanup," *National Journal,* August 9, 2003, 2544.

[27]*U.S. Budget for Fiscal Year 2007, Historical Tables* 15.1 (Washington, D.C.: U.S. Government Printing Office, 2006), 309.

[28]Ibid., 15.2, 311.

[29]David Dagan, "Personal Politics" (Special Report), Center for Public Integrity Special Report, September 24, 2004 (www.publicintegrity.org), 1.

[30]For a review of the politics surrounding the law, its provisions, and limitations, see Conlan, *From New Federalism to Devolution,* ch. 13.

[31]"2006 State Homeland Security Directors Survey" (Issue Brief of the NGA Center for Best Practices), April 3, 2006. (www.nga.org/center)

[32]Pam Belluck, "Mandate for ID Meets Resistance From States," *New York Times,* May 6, 2006.

[33]"Lobbyists, Yes. The People, Maybe" (Editorial), *New York Times,* July 10, 2006, A16.

[34]Letter from the National Governors' Association to President George W. Bush, February 3, 2006 (www.nga.org).

[35]Enid F. Beaumont and Harold Hovey, "State, Local, and Federal Development Policies: New Federalism Patterns, Chaos, or What?" *Public Administration Review* 45 (1985), 327–332; Barry Rubin and C. Kurt Zorn, "Sensible State and Local Development," *Public Administration Review* 45 (1985), 333–339.

[36]Robert Pear, "U.S. Report Faults States' Medicaid Tactics," *New York Times,* June 28, 2005.

[37]John Tierney, "New York Wants Its Money Back, or at Least Some of It," *New York Times,* June 27, 2004, sect. 4, 4.

[38]A discussion of state-tribal relations can be found at the National Conference of State Legislatures' website (www.ncsl.org).

[39]David Broder, "Take Back the Initiative," *Washington Post National Weekly Edition,* April 10, 2000, 6; John Maggs, "Ballot Boxing," *National Journal,* July 1, 2000, 2147.

[40]"That Flurry of Ballot Questions" (Editorial), *New York Times,* November 5, 2005.

[41]Wills, "War between the States . . . and Washington," 27.

[42]Dagan, "Personal Politics," 1. (www.publicintegrity.org)

[43]B. Drummond Ayres Jr., "Louisiana Apathy: The Ebb and Flow," *New York Times,* November 18, 2001, A20.

[44]Katherine Sullivan, "In Defense of Federal Power," *New York Times Magazine,* August 18, 1996, 36.

[45]Broder, "Take Back the Initiative," 6.

[46]James W. Brosnan, "Not Taxing Internet Sales Hurts," *Champaign-Urbana News-Gazette,* February 21, 2000, A6.

[47]Rep. Barney Frank (D-Mass.), quoted in Michael Grunwald, "Everybody Talks about States' Rights," *Washington Post National Weekly Edition,* November 1, 1999, 29. Frank was referring to Republicans only, but the quote fits Democrats as well.

[48]Sheryl Gay Stolberg, "As Congress Stalls, States Pursue Cloning Debate," *New York Times,* May 26, 2002, 1, 19.

[49]Stephen Labaton, "Washington's Deregulatory Mood Finds Its Opposite in Vexed States," *New York Times,* January 13, 2002, 1.

[50]Kirsten Downley Grimsley, "Where Congress Fears to Tread," *Washington Post National Weekly Edition,* August 21, 2000, 18.

[51]Ibid., 19.

[52]Linda Greenhouse, "In Roberts Hearing, Specter Assails Court," *New York Times,* September 15, 2005, 1.

[53]Dan Carney, "Latest Supreme Court Rulings Reinforce the Federalist Trend," *Congressional Quarterly,* June 26, 1999, 1528; Linda Greenhouse, "High Court Faces Moment of Truth in Federalism Cases," *New York Times,* March 28, 1999, 20.

[54]*U.S. Budget for Fiscal Year 2007, Historical Tables,* Table 15.1, 309.

[55]Neela Banerjee, "Christian Conservatives Turn to Statehouses," *New York Times,* December 13, 2004. 1.

[56]John D. Donahue, "The Disunited States," *Atlantic Monthly,* May 1997, 20.

[57]NBC News/*Wall Street Journal* poll, December 2001; both CBS and Gallup polls in June 2002 showed declining approval levels for Congress and the Supreme Court. Data for 2006 from Pew Research Center survey cited by David Brooks, "The Age of Skepticism," *New York Times,* December 1, 2005, A33.

[58]Paul Davenport, "Napolitano Calls Summit on Immigration Law," June 8, 2005. (www.azcentral.com)

[59]Randal C. Archibold, "Arizona County Uses New Law to Look for Illegal Immigrants," *New York Times,* May 10, 2006.

[60]Ralph Blumenthal, "Citing Violence, 2 Border States Declare a Crisis," *New York Times,* August 17, 2005, A14.

[61]Napolitano, "Message of the Week," August 17, 2005, 1.

[62]Katie Kelley, "A Deal in Colorado on Benefits for Illegal Immigrants," *New York Times,* July 12, 2006, 18. Data from the National Conference of State Legislators.

[63]John M. Broder, "Governors of Border States Have Hope, and Questions," *New York Times,* May 17, 2006, 1.

[64]"Napolitano Leads Western Governors to Comprehensive Immigration Plan." News release from Arizona Governor's office, February 28, 2006. (www.azgovernor.gov)

[65]Ibid.; "Western Governors' Association Proposed Policy Resolution 06-1," 1–5. (www.wga.org)

Chapter 4

[1]The first poll is a Fox News poll taken March 1–2, 2005, the second and third are ABC News and *Washington Post* polls taken in mid-March, and the last is an ABC News poll taken March 20, 2005. These are summarized on www.religioustolerance.org/schiavo7.htm.

[2]"Opinions of the American Public," found on Religious Tolerance.org, based on ABC news polls taken March 20, 2005. www.religioustolerance.org/schiavo7.htm

[3]Peggy Noonan, *Wall Street Journal* (March 18, 2005), opinion page.

[4]Information about Senator Frist's background is drawn largely from Michael Barone with Richard Cohen and Grant Ujifusa, *Almanac of American Politics, 2004.* Washington, D.C.: National Journal, 1478–1481.

[5]Ibid., 1479.

[6]Richard Morin, "The Ups and Downs of Political Poll-Taking," *Washington Post National Weekly Edition,* October 5, 1992, 37.

[7]Timothy E. Cook, "The Bear Market in Political Socialization and the Costs of Misunderstood Psychological Theories," *American Political Science Review* 79 (1985), 1079–1093.

[8]S. W. Moore et al., "The Civic Awareness of Five- and Six-Year-Olds," *Western Political Quarterly* 29 (1976), 418.

[9]R. W. Connell, *The Child's Construction of Politics* (Carlton, Australia: Melbourne University Press, 1971).

[10]Fred I. Greenstein, *Children and Politics* (New Haven, Conn.: Yale University Press, 1965), 122; see also Fred I. Greenstein, "The Benevolent Leader Re-visited: Children's Images of Political Leaders in Three Democracies," *American Political Science Review* 69 (1975), 1317–1398; Robert D. Hess and Judith V. Torney, *The Development of Political Attitudes in Children* (Chicago: Aldine, 1967).

[11]Amy Carter and Ryan Teten, "Assessing Changing Views of the President: Ravishing Greenstein's Children and Politics," *Presidential Studies Quarterly* 32 (2002), 453–462.

[12]Greenstein, *Children and Politics.*

[13]Hess and Torney, *The Development of Political Attitudes in Children;* Connell, *The Child's Construction of Politics.*

[14]Greenstein, *Children and Politics;* Greenstein, "The Benevolent Leader Revisited: Children's Images of Political Leaders in Three Democracies"; and Hess and Torney, *The Development of Political Attitudes in Children.*

[15]Connell, *The Child's Construction of Politics.*

[16]Carter, "Assessing Changing Views."

[17]F. Christopher Arterton, "The Impact of Watergate on Children's Attitudes toward the President," *Political Science Quarterly* 89 (1974), 269–288; see also P. Frederick Hartwig and Charles Tidmarch, "Children and Political Reality: Changing Images of the President," paper presented at the 1974 Annual Meeting of the Southern Political Science Association; J. Dennis and C. Webster, "Children's Images of the President and Government in 1962 and 1974," *American Politics Quarterly* 4 (1975), 386–405; Robert Hawkins, Suzanne Pingree, and D. Roberts, "Watergate and Political Socialization," *American Politics Quarterly* 4 (1975), 406–436.

[18]Gallup Organization, "Public Trust in Federal Government Remains High," January 8, 1999.

[19]Michael Delli Carpini, *Stability and Change in American Politics: The Coming of Age of the Generation of the 1960s* (New York: New York University Press, 1986), 86–89.

[20]Richard M. Merelman, *Political Socialization and Educational Climates* (New York: Holt, Rinehart and Winston, 1971), 54; more recently, the percentage of liberals among college freshmen and the public is about the same.

[21]Roberta Sigel and Marilyn Hoskin, *The Political Involvement of Adolescents* (New Brunswick, N.J.: Rutgers University Press, 1981).

[22]John R. Hibbing and Elizabeth Theiss-Morse, *Congress as Public Enemy: Public Attitudes toward American Political Institutions* (Cambridge: Cambridge University Press, 1995). It is plausible to assume that the content of early political socialization influences what is learned later, but the assumption has not been adequately tested. Thus we might expect the positive opinions toward government and politics developed early in childhood to condition the impact of traumatic events later in life; David Easton and Jack Dennis, *Children in the Political System: Origins of Regime Legitimacy* (New York: McGraw-Hill, 1969); Robert Weissberg, *Political Learning, Political Choice, and Democratic Citizenship* (Englewood Cliffs, N.J.: Prentice Hall, 1974). See also Donald Searing, Joel Schwartz, and Alden Line, "The Structuring Principle: Political Socialization and Belief System," *American Political Science Review* 67 (1973), 414–432.

[23]Jack Citrin, "Comment: The Political Relevance of Trust in Government," *Washington Post National Weekly Edition* 68, September 1974, 973–1001; Jack Citrin and Donald Green, "Presidential Leadership and the Resurgence of Trust in Government," *British Journal of Political Science* 16 (1986), 431–453.

[24]John Alford, Carolyn Funk, and John Hibbing, "Are Political Orientations Genetically Transmitted," *American Political Science Review* 99 (May, 2005), 153–168. How do scientists determine hereditary traits from those environmentally determined? Much of this research looks at identical twins, who share the exact same genetic traits, and compares them with nonidentical twins, who do not.

[25]Christopher Achen, "Parental Socialization and Rational Party Identification," *Political Behavior* 24 (June, 2002), 151–170.

[26]Dean Jaros, Herbert Hirsch, and Frederic J. Fleron Jr., "The Malevolent Leader: Political Socialization in an American Subculture," *American Political Science Review* 62 (1968), 564–575.

[27]Kent Tedin, "The Influence of Parents on the Political Attitudes of Adolescents," *American Political Science Review* 68 (1974), 1579–1592.

[28]M. Kent Jennings, *Generations and Politics* (Princeton, N.J.: Princeton University Press, 1981).

[29]Kathleen Dolan, "Attitudes, Behaviors, and the Influence of the Family: A Re-examination of the Role of Family Structure," *Political Behavior* 17 (1995), 251–264.

[30]On the impact of the public schools and teachers on political socialization, particularly with respect to loyalty and patriotism, see Hess and Torney, *The Development of Political Attitudes in Children.*

[31]Gabriel A. Almond and Sidney Verba, *The Civic Culture: Political Attitudes and Democracy in Five Nations, an Analytic Study* (Boston: Little, Brown, 1965); John R. Hibbing and Elizabeth Theiss-Morse, "Civics Is Not Enough: Teaching Barbarics in K–12," *PS: Political Science and Politics* (1996), 12; Norman H. Nie, Jane Junn, and Kenneth Stehlik-Barry, *Education and Democratic Citizenship in America* (Chicago: University of Chicago Press, 1996).

[32]Nie, et al., *Education and Democratic Citizenship in America.*

[33]Hibbing and Theiss-Morse, *Congress as Public Enemy: Public Attitudes toward American Political Institutions.*

[34]Richard G. Niemi and Jane Junn, *Civil Education: What Makes Students Learn* (New Haven, Conn.: Yale University Press, 1998). See also Richard G. Niemi and Julia Smith, "Enrollments in High School Government Classes: Are We Shortchanging Both Citizenship and Political Science Training?" *PS: Political Science and Politics* 34 (2001), 281–288. Honors and advanced placement (AP) programs, along with active learning, can improve student understanding and achievement in American history.

[35]Stephen Bennett, Staci Rhine, and Richard Flickinger, "Reading's Impact on Democratic Citizenship in America," *Political Behavior* 22 (2000), 167–195.

[36]Nie, et al., *Education and Democratic Citizenship in America.*

[37]Alfonso Damico, M. Margaret Conway, and Sandra Bowman Damico, "Patterns of Political Trust and Mistrust: Three Moments in the Lives of Democratic Citizens," *Polity* 32 (2000), 377–400.

[38]Joel Westheimer and Joseph Kahne, "Educating the 'Good' Citizen: Political Choices and Pedagogical Goals," *PS: Political Science and Politics* 2 (2004), 241–247.

[39]Richard M. Merelman, "Democratic Politics and the Culture of American Education," *American Political Science Review* 74 (1980), 319–332; Hibbing and Theiss-Morse, "Civics Is Not Enough: Teaching Barbarics in K–12"; Nie, et al., *Education and Democratic Citizenship in America.*

[40]Material for this section is drawn from Everett C. Ladd and Seymour M. Lipset, *The Divided Academy: Professors and Politics* (New York: McGraw-Hill, 1975); Charles Kesler, "The Movement of Student Opinion," *National Review,* November 23, 1979, 29; Ernest L. Boyer, *College: The Undergraduate Experience in America* (New York: Harper & Row, 1987); "Fact File: Attitudes and Characteristics of This Year's Freshman," *Chronicle of Higher Education,* January 11, 1989, A33–A34; General Social Survey, *National Opinion Research Center,* 1984, 87. During the early 1970s, more college freshmen identified themselves as liberal compared with the public at large.

[41]David Horowitz, *The Professors: The 101 Most Dangerous Academics in America* (Regnery Publishing, 2006).

[42]Rebecca Trounson, "Poll Says College Freshmen Lean Left," www.commondreams.org/headlines02/0128-01.htm.

[43]Alexander W. Astin, William S. Korn, and Linda Sax, *The American Freshman: Thirty Year Trends* (Los Angeles: Higher Education Research Institute, Graduate School of Education and Information, 1997).

[44]Thomas Bartlett, "Evaluating Student Attitudes Is More Difficult This Year," *Chronicle of Higher Education,* February 1, 2002, A35–A38. See also Linda Sax, Alexander W. Astin, and William S. Korn, *The American Freshman: National Norms for Fall 1998* (Los Angeles: Higher Education Research Institute, Graduate School of Education and Information Studies, 1998).

[45]"College Freshman More Politically Liberal Than in the Past, UCLA Survey Reveals," 2001 CIRP Press Release: CIRP Freshman Survey, January 28, 2001.

[46]Linda Sax, Alexander W. Astin, William S. Korn, and Kathryn M. Mahoney, *The American Freshman: National Norms for Fall 1999* (Los Angeles: Higher Education Research Institute, Graduate School of Education and Information Studies, 1999).

[47]"Attitudes and Characteristics of Freshmen," *Chronicle of Higher Education,* August 27, 2004, 19.

[48]"The American Freshman: National Norms for Fall 2005," News release of the Higher Education Research Institute, Spring 2006.

[49]M. Kent Jennings and Richard G. Niemi, *The Political Character of Adolescence: the Influence of Families and Schools* (Princeton, N.J.: Princeton University Press, 1974), 243. The stability of political attitudes over the lifetime is demonstrated in Duane Alwin and Jon Krosnick, "Aging, Cohorts, and the Stability of Sociopolitical Attitudes Over the Life Span," *American Journal of Sociology* 97, 169–195.

[50]Maxwell McCombs and Donald Shaw, "The Agenda Setting Function of the Media," *Public Opinion Quarterly* 36 (1972), 176–187.

[51]Benjamin I. Page, Robert Y. Shapiro, and Glenn R. Dempsey, "What Moves Public Opinion?" *American Political Science Review* 81 (1987), 23–44.

[52]Herbert F. Weisberg, "Marital Differences in American Voting," *Public Opinion Quarterly* 51 (1987), 335–343.

[53]Michael A. Fletcher, "On Campus, a Patriotic Surge," *Washington Post National Weekly Edition,* December 10, 2001, 31.

[54]Philip E. Converse, Aage R. Clausen, and Warren E. Miller, "Electoral Myth and Reality: The 1964 Election," *American Political Science Review* 59 (1965), 321–326.

[55]John P. Robinson, "The Press as Kingmaker: What Surveys Show from the Last Five Campaigns," *Journalism Quarterly* 49 (1974), 592.

[56]See jacob@jacbian.org; also Nick Anderson, "Kerry Wins the Paper Endorsement Derby, for What It's Worth," *Los Angeles Times,* October 29, 2004, A5. Two hundred twelve newspapers endorsed Kerry, 199 recommended Bush. Newspapers endorsing Kerry had a circulation of twenty-two million, Bush sixteen million.

[57]Susan Herbst, *Numbered Voices: How Opinion Polling Has Shaped American Politics* (Chicago: University of Chicago Press, 1993); Benjamin Ginsberg, "How Polling Changes Public Opinion" in *Manipulating Public Opinion: Essays on Public Opinion as a Dependent Variable,* ed. Michael Margolis and Gary A. Mauser (Pacific Grove, Calif.: Brooks/Cole, 1989).

[58]For a review of the history of polling, see Bernard Hennessy, *Public Opinion,* 4th ed. (Monterey, Calif.: Brooks/Cole, 1983), 42–44, 46–50. See also Charles W. Roll and Albert H. Cantril, *Polls: Their Use and Misuse in Politics* (New York: Basic Books, 1972), 3–6.

[59]Peverill Squire, "Why the 1936 Literary Digest Poll Failed," *Public Opinion Quarterly* 52 (1988), 125–133; see also Don Cahalan, "The Digest Poll Rides Again," *Public Opinion Quarterly* 53 (1989), 107–113.

[60]Hennessy, *Public Opinion,* 4th ed., 46.

[61]"Consulting the Oracle," *U.S. News and World Report,* December 4, 1995, 52–55; Joshua Green, "The Other War Room," *Washington Monthly,* April 2002, 11–16.

[62]Green, "The Other War Room."

[63]Joe Klien, *The Natural* (New York: Doubleday, 2002), 7.

[64]John E. Harris, "Presidency by Poll," *Washington Post National Weekly Edition,* January 8, 2001, 9–10.

[65]Green, "The Other War Room."

[66]Harris, "Presidency by Poll."

[67]Steven Mufson and John E. Harris, "Clinton's Global Growth," *Washington Post National Weekly Edition,* January 22, 2001, 8–9.

[68]Green, "The Other War Room."

[69]Ibid., 11.

[70]Ibid., 12.

[71]Lawrence R. Jacobs and Robert Y. Shapiro, *Politicians Don't Pander: Political Manipulation and the Loss of Democratic Responsiveness* (Chicago: University of Chicago Press, 2000).

[72]Deborah Tannen, "Let Them Eat Words," *American Prospect,* September, 2003, 29–31.

[73]Richard Morin, "Surveying the Surveyors," *Washington Post National Weekly Edition,* March 2, 1992, 37.

[74]David Broder, "Push Polls Plunge Politics to a New Low," *Lincoln Journal Star,* October 9, 1994, 5E.

[75]Bill Kovack and Tom Rosensteil, "Campaign Lite," *Washington Monthly,* January–February 2001, 31–38.

[76]Claudia Deane, "And Why Haven't You Been Polled?" *Washington Post National Weekly Edition,* January 18, 1999, 34; Richard Morin, "The Election Post Mortem," *Washington Post National Weekly Edition,* September 30, 1996, 37.

[77]Real Clear Politics, www.realclearpolitics.com/ polls.html; see also "Pre-Election Polls Largely Accurate," *The Pew Research Center for the People and the Press,* November 23, 2004, www.people-press.org/commentary/display.php3?AnalysisID5 102.

[78]"All Things Considered," National Public Radio, October 30, 1992.

[79]Richard Morin, "Voters Are Hung Up on Polling," *Washington Post National Weekly Edition* (November 1–7, 2004), 12.

[80]Ibid.

[81]Ibid.

[82]Richard Morin and Claudia Deane, "Why the Florida Exit Polls Were Wrong," *Washington Post,* November 8, 2000.

[83]Diana Owen, "Media Mayhem: Performance of the Press in Election 2000," in *Overtime! The Election 2000 Thriller,* ed. Larry J. Sabato (New York: Longman, 2002), 144.

[84]Steve Freeman, *Polling Bias or Corrupted Count.* Philadelphia: American Statistical Association, Philadelphia Chapter, October 14, 2005. (Freeman is a faculty member at the University of Pennsylvania).

[85]*New Yorker,* March 20, 1999, 18.

[86]Richard Morin, "When the Method Becomes the Message," *Washington Post National Weekly Edition,* December 19, 1994, 33.

[87]Richard Morin, "Tuned Out, Tuned Off," *Washington Post National Weekly Edition,* February 5, 1996, 6–8.

[88]Ibid., 8.

[89]Ibid., 8.

[90]Richard Morin, "They Know Only What They Don't Like," *Washington Post National Weekly Edition,* October 3, 1994, 37.

[91]National Election Study, 2004.

[92]Ibid.

[93]Center for Political Studies, 1986 National Election Study, University of Michigan, "Wapner Top Judge in Recognition Poll," *Lincoln Journal Star,* June 23, 1989, 1.

[94]Michael Delli Carpini and Scott Keeter, "Stability and Change in the U.S. Public's Knowledge of Politics," *Public Opinion Quarterly,* (1991), 583–612.

[95]Richard Morin, "We Love It—What We Know of It," *Washington Post National Weekly Edition,* September 22, 1997, 35.

[96]Morin, "They Know Only What They Don't Like," 35.

[97]Ibid.

[98]Richard Morin, "Foreign Aid: Mired in Misunderstanding," *Washington Post National Weekly Edition,* March 20, 1995, 37.

[99]Richard Morin, "What Informed Public Opinion?" *Washington Post National Weekly Edition,* April 10, 1995, 36.

[100]Vladimer Orlando Key, *The Responsible Electorate* (Cambridge, Mass.: Harvard University Press, 1966); Norman H. Nie, Sidney Verba, and John R. Petrocik, *The Changing American Voter* (Cambridge, Mass.: Harvard University Press, 1976), ch. 18; Samuel L. Popkin, *The Reasoning Voter: Communication and Persuasion in Presidential Campaigns* (Chicago: University of Chicago Press, 1994).

[101]Gallup Organization, poll conducted April 6, 2004.

[102]Popkin, *The Reasoning Voter: Communication and Persuasion in Presidential Campaigns.*

[103]Morin, "Tuned Out, Turned Off," 8.

[104]Gallup Organization, poll conducted June 16, 2003.

[105] *Newsweek,* poll conducted September 2–3, 2004.

[106]Harold Meyerson, "Fact-Free News," *Washington Post National Weekly,* October 10–26, 2003, 26.

[107]Andrew Sullivan, article found on www.andrewsullivan.com/main_article.php? artnum520040126.

[108]General Social Survey, 2002.

[109]Jonathan Rauch, "Bipolar Disorder," *Atlantic Monthly* (January–February 2005), 102.

[110]John Sperling, *The Great Divide: Retro and Metro America* (USA: PoliPoint Press, 2004), 212.

[111]Ibid., 165, 178, 192.

[112]E. J. Dionne Jr., "One Nation Deeply Divided," *Washington Post,* November 7, 2004, A31, quoted in Morris P. Fiorina with Samuel J. Abrams and Jeremy C. Pope, *Culture War? The Myth of the Polarized America* (New York: Pearson Longman, 2005), 6.

[113]Matthew Dowd, quoted in Fiorina, Ibid., 6.

[114]Conducted by the Gallup Organization for the online dating service Match.com during July 2004. Cited in Jonathan Rauch, "Bipolar Disorder," *Atlantic Monthly,* January–February, 2005, 105.

[115]Various studies are summarized in Rauch, "Bipolar Disorder," 102–110.

[116]Editorial, "A Polarized Nation?" *Washington Post,* November 14, 2004, 6. Several of these ideas were summarized nicely in this article.

[117]This section draws heavily on Howard Schuman, Charlotte Steeh, and Lawrence Bobo, *Racial Attitudes in America* (Cambridge, Mass.: Harvard University Press, 1985); Howard Schuman, Charlotte Steeh, Lawrence Bobo, and Maria Krysan, *Racial Attitudes in America,* rev. ed. (1997); data summaries are drawn from the General Social Surveys of the National Opinion Research Center, University of Chicago, and National Elections Studies of CPS, University of Michigan; see also Lee Sigelman and Susan Welch, *Black Americans' Views of Racial Inequality* (Cambridge, Mass.: Cambridge University Press, 1991).

[118]General Social Survey, 1996; Richard Morin, "Polling in Black and White: Sometimes the Answers Depend on Who's Asking the Questions," *Washington Post National Weekly Edition,* October 30, 1989, 37.

[119]General Social Survey, 1996; "Whites Retain Negative Views of Minorities, a Survey Finds," *New York Times,* January 10, 1991, C19; Mary R. Jackman, "General and Applied Tolerance: Does Education Increase Commitment to

Racial Inequality?" *American Journal of Political Science* 25 (1981), 256–269; Donald Kinder and David Sears, "Prejudice and Politics: Symbolic Racism versus Racial Threats to the Good Life," *Journal of Personality and Social Psychology* 40 (1981), 414–431.

[120]Richard Morin, "We've Moved Forward, but We Haven't," *Washington Post National Weekly Edition,* October 5, 1998, 34.

[121]"Whites Retain Negative Views of Minorities, a Survey Finds," C19.

[122]General Social Survey, 1998; see also Donald Kinder and Lynn Saunders, *Divided by Color: Racial Politics and Democratic Ideals* (Chicago: University of Chicago Press, 1996); Howard Schuman and Lawrence Bobo, "Survey-Based Experiments on White Attitudes toward Residential Integration." *American Journal of Sociology* 94 (1988), 519–526; see also Schuman et al., *Racial Attitudes in America,* rev. ed.

[123]General Social Survey, 1998.

[124]Richard Morin, "It's Not as It Seems," *Washington Post National Weekly Edition,* July 16, 2001, 34.

[125]Ibid.

[126]Morin, "It's Not as It Seems"; ABC/ *Washington Post* poll, 1981 and 1986.

[127]General Social Survey, 1998.

[128]Benjamin I. Page and Robert Y. Shapiro, "Effects of Public Opinion on Policy," *American Political Science Review* 77 (1983), 175–190.

[129]Morin, "Voters Are Hung Up on Polling."

[130]Lawrence Jacobs and Robert Y. Shapiro, *Politicians Don't Pander* (Chicago: University of Chicago Press, 2000).

[131]Ibid.

[132]Charles Babington, "Viewing Videotape, Frist Disputes Florida Doctors' Diagnosis," *Washington Post,* March 19, 2005, 16.

[133]Ibid.

[134]Ibid.

[135]Ibid.

[136]Leonard Pitts Jr., "A Family Tragedy and GOP Hypocrisy," *Lincoln Journal Star,* March 26, 2005, 7B.

[137]Andrew Cohen, "Terri Schiavo and the Constitution," CBS News website, March 31, 2005. www.cbsnews.com/stories/2005/03/31/opinion/courtwatch/main684181.shtml.

[138]David Brown and Shailagh Murray, "Schiavo Autopsy Released: Brain Damage was Irreversible," *Washington Post,* June 16, 2005, 1.

[139]Herold Meyerson, "Target of Opportunism," *Washington Post National Weekly Edition,* March 28–April 3, 2005, 26.

Chapter 5

[1]The source for information in this vignette is Nick Kotz, "Breaking Point," *Washingtonian,* December 1996, 94–121.

[2]James David Barber, *The Pulse of Politics* (New York: Norton, 1980), 9.

[3]Kevin Phillips, "A Matter of Privilege," *Harper's,* January 1977, 95.

[4]Richard Harwood, "So Many Media, So Little Time," *Washington Post National Weekly Edition,* September 7, 1992, 28.

[5]Edwin Diamond, *The Tin Kazoo* (Cambridge, Mass.: MIT Press, 1975), 13.

[6]Study by Kaiser Family Foundation, cited in Lauran Neergaard, "Parents Encouraging TV Use among Young Kids, Study Says," *Lincoln Journal Star,* May 25, 2006, 4A, and in Ruth Marcus, "Is Decency Going Down the Tubes?" *Washington Post National Weekly Edition,* June 26–

July 9, 2006, 26.

[7]Lindsey Tanner, "Studies Suggest Watching TV Harms Children Academically," *Lincoln Journal Star,* July 5, 2005, 6A.

[8]Doris A. Graber, *Mass Media and American Politics* (Washington, D.C.: Congressional Quarterly Press, 1980), 2.

[9]William Lutz, *Doublespeak* (New York: Harper & Row, 1989), 73–74.

[10]Robert W. McChesney and John Nichols, "It's the Media, Stupid," in *Voices of Dissent,* 5th ed., ed. William F. Grover and Joseph G. Peschek (New York: Longman, 2004), 116–120.

[11]According to the Kaiser Family Foundation. Claudia Wallis, "The Multitasking Generation," *Time,* March 27, 2006, 50–51.

[12]Rob McGann, "Internet Edges Out Family Time More than TV Time," ClickZ, January 5, 2005, www.clickz.com/stats/sectors/demographics/article.php/3455061.

[13]Shanto Iyengar, *Is Anyone Responsible? How Television Frames Political Issues* (Chicago: University of Chicago Press, 1991), 1.

[14]James Rainey, "More News Outlets, Fewer Stories: New Media 'Paradox,'" *Los Angeles Times,* March 13, 2006, www.latimes.com/news/nationworld/nation/la-nanews13mar13,0,2018145.story?

[15]Elizabeth Gleick, "Read All about It," *Time,* October 21, 1998, 66; Dana Millbank, "A Bias for Mainstream News," *Washington Post National Weekly Edition,* March 28–April 3, 2005, 23. See also Tom Rosenstiel, *The State of the News Media, 2004* (Washington, D.C.: Project for Excellence in Journalism, 2004).

[16]"Ticker," 128.

[17]Scott Althaus, "American News Consumption during Times of National Crisis," *PS,* September 2002, 517–521.

[18]Millbank, "A Bias for Mainstream News."

[19]Michael J. Wolf and Geoffrey Sands, "Fearless Predictions," *Brill's Content,* July–August 1999, 110. For a discussion of the future impact of the Internet on media concentration and diversity, see Robert W. McChesney, *The Problem of the Media* (New York: Monthly Review Press, 2004), 211–217.

[20]Eve Gerber, "Divided We Watch," *Brill's Content,* February 2001, 110–111.

[21]Thomas E. Patterson, *The Mass Media Election* (New York: Praeger, 1980), 58–60, 62–63.

[22]Donald Kaul, "Effects of Merger between AOL, Time Warner Will Be Inescapable," *Lincoln Journal Star,* January 18, 2000; Ken Auletta, "Leviathan," *New Yorker,* October 29, 2001, 50.

[23]McChesney, *Problem of the Media,* 182–183.

[24]McChesney and Nichols, "It's the Media," 120. Antitrust laws provide few restrictions on these activities. McChesney, *Problem of the Media,* 235–240.

[25]For examination of this development, see Lawrence Lessing, *The Future of Ideas* (New York: Random House, 2001). For an alternative view, see McChesney, *Problem of the Media,* 205–209.

[26]Benjamin M. Compaine, *Who Owns the Media?* (White Plains, N.Y.: Knowledge Industry Publications, 1979), 11, 76–77; Michael Parenti, *Inventing Reality* (New York: St. Martin's Press, 1986), 27; Paul Farhi, "You Can't Tell a Book by Its Cover," *Washington Post National Weekly Edition,* December 5, 1988, 21; Andrews, "A New Tune for Radio."

[27]Robert McChesney, "AOL–Time Warner Merger Is Dangerous and Undemocratic,"

Lincoln Journal Star, January 17, 2000.

[28]Rosenstiel, *State of the News Media,* 9.

[29]Daren Fonda, "National Prosperous Radio," *Time,* March 24, 2003, 50; Marc Fisher, "Sounds All Too Familiar," *Washington Post National Weekly Edition,* May 26, 2003, 23.

[30]McChesney, *Problem of the Media,* 178.

[31]Ibid., 188.

[32]Mary Lynn F. Jones, "No News Is Good News," *American Prospect,* May 2003, 39.

[33]"Clear Channel Growth the Result of 1996 Deregulation," *Lincoln Journal Star,* October 5, 2003.

[34]David Gram, "Opponents of War Have Trouble Getting Message Out," *Lincoln Journal Star,* February 25, 2003.

[35]"Broadcaster: *Nightline* Won't Air on Its Stations," *Lincoln Journal Star,* April 30, 2004.

[36]money.cnn.com/2004/10/11/news/newsmakers/sinclair_kerry/index.htm?cnn5yes

[37]Elizabeth Lesly Stevens, "Mouse.Ke.Fear," *Brill's Content,* December 1998–January 1999, 95. For other examples, see Jane Mayer, "Bad News," *New Yorker,* August 14, 2000, 30–36.

[38]Jim Hightower, *There's Nothing in the Middle of the Road but Yellow Stripes and Dead Armadillos* (New York: HarperCollins, 1997), 121.

[39]Rifka Rosenwein, "Why Media Mergers Matter," *Brill's Content,* December 1999– January 2000, 94.

[40]Dean Alger, *Megamedia: How Giant Corporations Dominate Mass Media, Distort Competition, and Endanger Democracy* (Lanham, Md.: Rowman & Littlefield, 1998). ABC did address it once—at 4 A.M.

[41]The Project for Excellence in Journalism, affiliated with Columbia University's Graduate School of Journalism, concluded after a five-year study that newscasts by stations owned by smaller companies were significantly higher in quality than newscasts by stations owned by larger companies. "Does Ownership Matter in Local Television News?" February 17, 2003 (www.journalism.org).

[42]Neil Hickey, "Money Lust," *Columbia Journalism Review,* July–August 1998, 28.

[43]"All Things Considered," NPR, December 16, 2005.

[44]*Now, with Bill Moyers,* PBS, April 11, 2003.

[45]Ted Turner, "Break Up This Band!" *Washington Monthly,* July–August, 2004, 35.

[46]In response, ABC made all of its prime-time programming available in Spanish in 2005.

[47]Howard Kurtz, "Welcome to Spin City," *Washington Post National Weekly Edition,* March 16, 1998, 6. See also Roger Parloff, "If This Ain't Libel . . . ," *Brill's Content,* Fall 2001, 95–113.

[48]Times Mirror Center for the People and the Press, *The Vocal Minority in American Politics* (Washington, D.C.: Times Mirror Center for the People and the Press, 1993).

[49]In addition, she received $50,000 for a book elaborating on her story, $250,000 for posing nude for *Penthouse* magazine, and about $20,000 for appearing on German and Spanish television shows. "Flowers Says She Made Half Million from Story," *Lincoln Journal Star,* March 21, 1998.

[50]Ernest Tollerson, "Politicians Try to Balance Risk against Rewards of Reaching Talk-Radio Audiences," *New York Times,* March 31, 1996, 12.

[51]McChesney, *Problem of the Media,* 96; Paul Taylor, "The New Political Theater," *Mother Jones,* November–December 2000, 30–33.

52David Halberstam, "Preface," in Bill Kovach and Tom Rosenstiel, *Warp Speed: America in the Age of Mixed Media* (New York: Century Foundation Press, 1999), x.

53Tom Rosenstiel, *The Beat Goes On: President Clinton's First Year with the Media* (New York: Twentieth Century Fund, 1994), 35. For an extensive examination of this incident, see Dan E. Moldea, *A Washington Tragedy* (New York: Regnery, 1998). A similar pattern occurred when a conservative magazine, *Insight,* charged that the Clinton administration was "selling" burial plots in Arlington National Cemetery to "dozens of big-time political donors or friends of the Clintons." Because the cemetery is reserved for military veterans, anonymous officials were quoted as saying this was "corruption of the worst kind." The charge was repeated on talk radio and then aired in Congress when some members demanded an investigation. Within forty-eight hours, it was reported in the mainstream media. Yet there was no truth to it. Howard Kurtz, "The Story That Wouldn't Stay Buried," *Washington Post National Weekly Edition,* December 1, 1997, 12.

54Kurtz, "Welcome to Spin City," 6.

55None of the "Swift Boat Veterans for Truth" served with Kerry on his boat. The charges were disputed by Kerry's crewmates and contradicted by navy records. Evidently the "Swift Boat Veterans for Truth" were motivated by their anger toward Kerry's antiwar stance after he returned from Vietnam, which became the subject of the group's second commercial. Todd Gitlin, "Swifter Than Truth," *American Prospect,* November, 2004, 29–30.

56Quoted in Richard Corliss, "Look Who's Talking," *Time,* January 23, 1995, 25.

57Lev Grossman, "Meet Joe Blog," *Time,* June 21, 2004, 66.

58Matt Bai, "Can Bloggers Get Real?" *New York Times Magazine,* May 28, 2006, 13.

59Elizabeth LeBel, "Life in This Girl's Army," www.sgtlizzie.blogspot.com, cited in Jonathan Finer, "The New Ernie Pyles: Sgtlizzie and 67cshdocs," www.washingtonpost.com/wp-dyn/content/article/2005/08/11/AR2005081102168.

60Ibid.

61Richard A. Posner, "Bad News," *New York Times Book Review,* July 31, 2005, 10–11. Posner, however, argues that the number of bloggers provides a fact-correcting mechanism in the blogosphere.

62Garance Franke-Ruta, "Blog Rolled," *American Prospect,* April, 2005, 40.

63Dom Bonafede, "Press Paying More Heed to Substance in Covering 1984 Presidential Election," *National Journal,* October 13, 1984, 1923.

64Seth Mnookin, "Advice to Ari," *Brill's Content,* March 2001, 97.

65Ken Auletta, "Fortress Bush," *New Yorker,* January 19, 2004, 53.

66Charles Peters, *How Washington Really Works* (Reading, Mass.: Addison-Wesley, 1980), 18.

67Auletta, "Fortress Bush," 54.

68Matthew Brzezinski, *Fortress America: On the Front Lines of Homeland Security—an Inside Look at the Coming Surveillance State* (New York: Bantam, 2004).

69William Greider, "Reporters and Their Sources," *Washington Monthly,* October 1982, 13–15.

70See, for example, Jeffrey Toobin, *A Vast Conspiracy: The Real Story of the Sex Scandal That Nearly Brought Down a President* (New York: Simon & Schuster, 1999), 310.

71Murray Waas, "Why Novak Called Rove," *National Journal,* December 17, 2005, 3874–3878.

72When a spy's identity becomes public, foreign governments try to retrace the spy's movements and determine his or her contacts to see how the CIA operated in their country.

73Reporters, however, are not liable for reporting information that officials disclosed. Following their journalistic standards, they refused to reveal the identity of their sources.

74Howard Kurtz, "Lying Down on This Job Was Just Fine," *Washington Post National Weekly Edition,* April 19, 1999, 13.

75Ann Devroy, "The Republicans, It Turns Out, Are a Veritable Fount of Leaks," *Washington Post National Weekly Edition,* November 18, 1991, 23.

76Daniel Schorr, "A Fact of Political Life," *Washington Post National Weekly Edition,* October 28, 1991, 32.

77Howard Kurtz, "How Sources and Reporters Play the Game of Leaks," *Washington Post National Weekly Edition,* March 15, 1993, 25.

78Dan Eggen, "Bush's Plumbers," *Washington Post National Weekly Edition,* March 13–19, 2006, 11.

79Steven Brill, "Pressgate," *Brill's Content,* July–August 1998, 123–151; Steven Brill, "At Last, a Leakless Investigation," *Brill's Content,* December 1998–January 1999, 31–34.

80Brill, "Pressgate," 149.

81Nancy Franklin, "Rather Knot," *New Yorker,* October 4, 2004, 108–109.

82Samuel Kernell, *Going Public: New Strategies of Presidential Leadership* (Washington, D.C.: Congressional Quarterly Press, 1986), 59. Woodrow Wilson also tried to cultivate correspondents and host frequent sessions, but he did not have the knack for this activity and so scaled back the sessions. Kernell, *Going Public,* 60–61. He did perceive that "some men of brilliant ability were in the group, but I soon discovered that the interest of the majority was in the personal and the trivial rather than in principles and policies." James Bennet, "The Flack Pack," *Washington Monthly,* November 1991, 27.

83Dwight Eisenhower was actually the first president to let the networks televise his press conferences, but he did not do so to reach the public. When he wanted to reach the public, he made a formal speech. The networks found his conferences so untelegenic that they stopped covering the entire session each time. Kernell, *Going Public,* 68.

84Ibid., 104.

85Bennet, "The Flack Pack," 19.

86Frank Rich, "The Armstrong Williams NewsHour," *New York Times,* June 26, 2005, WK13.

87Dom Bonafede, " 'Mr. President,' " *National Journal,* October 29, 1988, 2756.

88Charles Hagen, "The Photo Op: Making Icons or Playing Politics?" *New York Times,* February 9, 1992, H28.

89Frank Rich, "Operation Iraqi Infoganda," *New York Times,* March 28, 2004, AR21.

90"The Man behind the Curtain Award," *Mother Jones,* September–October 2002, 67.

91Kiku Adatto, cited in Howard Kurtz, "Networks Adapt to Changed Campaign Role," *Washington Post,* June 21, 1992, A-19. See also Diana Owen, "Media Mayhem: Performance of the Press in Election 2000," in *Overtime! The Election 2000 Thriller,* ed. Larry J. Sabato (New York: Longman, 2002), 123–156.

92Lance Morrow, "The Decline and Fall of Oratory," *Time,* August 18, 1980, 78.

93David Halberstam, "How Television Failed the American Voter," *Parade,* January 11, 1981, 8.

94George E. Reedy, *The Twilight of the Presidency* (New York: New American Library, 1970), 112.

95Sam Donaldson, quoted in Thomas Griffith, "Winging It on Television," *Time,* March 14, 1983, 71.

96Auletta, "Fortress Bush," 61–62.

97W. Lance Bennett, *News: The Politics of Illusion,* 2nd ed. (White Plains, N.Y.: Longman, 1988).

98Larry J. Sabato, *Feeding Frenzy: How Attack Journalism Has Transformed American Politics* (New York: Free Press, 1991).

99Deborah Tannen, *The Argument Culture* (New York: Ballantine, 1998), 81.

100Ibid., 55.

101Orville Schell, "Preface" to Michael Massing, *Now They Tell Us: the American Press and Iraq* (New York: New York Review of Books, 2004), xiv.

102Fallows, *Breaking the News,* 62–63.

103Joan Konner, "Diane 'Got' Gore. But What Did We Get?" *Brill's Content,* September 1999, 59–60.

104See Sabato, *Feeding Frenzy,* for additional reasons for this increase.

105"Ticker," *Brill's Content,* July–August 1998, 152, citing the Project for Excellence in Journalism, "Changing Definitions of News: A Look at the Mainstream Press over 20 Years," March 6, 1998.

106Fallows, *Breaking the News,* 196.

107An examination of 224 incidents of criminal or unethical behavior by Reagan administration appointees found that only 13 percent were uncovered by reporters. Most were discovered through investigations by executive agencies or congressional committees, which then released the information to the press. Only incidents reflecting personal peccadilloes of government officials, such as sexual offenses, were exposed first by reporters. John David Rausch Jr., "The Pathology of Politics: Government, Press, and Scandal," *Extensions* (University of Oklahoma), Fall 1990, 11–12. For the Whitewater scandal, reporters got most of their tips from a Republican Party operation run by officials from Republican presidential campaigns. Regarding sexual matters, reporters got most of their tips from prosecutors for the independent counsel, lawyers for Paula Jones, or a book agent for Linda Tripp. See Brill, "Pressgate," 134.

108Except for a reporter at a small paper in North Carolina. Charles Peters, "Tilting at Windmills," *Washington Monthly,* October/November, 2005, 15.

109Charles Peters, "Tilting at Windmills," *Washington Monthly,* March, 2006, 8. Only a reporter for a Charleston, West Virginia, newspaper sounded an alarm.

110William Rivers, "The Correspondents after 25 Years," *Columbia Journalism Review* 1 (Spring 1962), 5.

111Coolidge, in his reelection campaign, was actually the first president to use radio as a means of addressing the public directly.

112James David Barber, *Presidential Character* (Englewood Cliffs, N.J.: Prentice Hall, 1992), 238.

113Reagan got his start in show business as a radio sportscaster in Des Moines, Iowa, announcing major league baseball games "live." Of course, he was not actually at the games: he got the barest details—who was at bat, whether the pitch was a strike or a ball or a hit—from the wireless and made up the rest to create a commentary that convinced listeners that he was watching in person.

[114]Hedrick Smith, *The Power Game* (New York: Random House, 1988), 403.

[115]Timothy J. Russert, "For '92, the Networks Have to Do Better," *New York Times,* March 4, 1990, E23.

[116]Smith, *Power Game,* 420.

[117]Steven K. Weisman, "The President and the Press," *New York Times Magazine,* October 14, 1984, 71–72; Dick Kirschten, "Communications Reshuffling Intended to Help Reagan Do What He Does Best," *National Journal,* January 28, 1984, 154.

[118]Sidney Blumenthal, "The Syndicated Presidency," *New Yorker,* April 5, 1993, 45.

[119]Brit Hume, of NBC News.

[120]For an extensive examination of this phenomenon, see Toobin, *Vast Conspiracy.*

[121]John F. Harris, "Bush's Lucky Break," *Washington Post National Weekly Edition,* May 14, 2001, 23.

[122]For examination of coverage during Clinton's early days in office, see William Glaberson, "The Capitol Press vs. the President: Fair Coverage or Unreined Adversity?" *New York Times,* June 17, 1993, A11; Christopher Georges, "Bad News Bearers," *Washington Monthly,* July–August 1993, 28–34; and Toobin, *Vast Conspiracy,* 247–248.

[123]Howard Kurtz, "Assessing—and Controlling—the Damage to the Presidency," *Washington Post National Weekly Edition,* February 2, 1998, 21.

[124]Auletta, "Fortress Bush," 60.

[125]Auletta, "Fortress Bush," 54, 57, 64.

[126]*All Things Considered,* NPR, March 21, 2006.

[127]Ibid., 55.

[128]David Barstow and Robin Stein, "Is it News or Public Relations? Under Bush, Lines Are Blurry," *New York Times,* March 13, 2005, YT1. The Clinton administration also used these, though less extensively.

[129]According to a report by the Government Accountability Office (GAO). Christopher Lee, "Report: White House Spent $1.6 Billion on PR," *Lincoln Journal Star,* February 19, 2006, 3A.

[130]John F. Harris, "On the World Stage, Bush Shuns the Spotlight," *Washington Post National Weekly Edition,* April 23, 2001, 11; Ronald Brownstein, "Bush Forced into Role He May Not Want: Communicator," *Lincoln Journal Star,* September 15, 2001.

[131]John F. Harris and Dan Balz, "A Well-Oiled Machine," *Washington Post National Weekly Edition,* May 14, 2001, 6.

[132]James Carville, quoted in John F. Harris, "Bush's Lucky Break," *Washington Post National Weekly Edition,* May 14, 2001, 23.

[133]Aides claimed that *Air Force One* was a target, but it was revealed that this claim was an exaggeration to parry the criticism that Bush received. Eric Pooley and Karen Tumulty, "Bush in the Crucible," *Time,* September 24, 2001, 49.

[134]Calvin Woodward, "Warrior Bush: It Doesn't Come Naturally," *Lincoln Journal Star,* October 6, 2002.

[135]Michael Duffy, "Marching Alone," *Time,* September 9, 2002, 42.

[136]Presidential historian Henry Graff, cited in Ron Fourier, "President Stumbles with Mideast Rhetoric," *Lincoln Journal Star,* April 20, 2002.

[137]Joe Klein, "Why the 'War President' Is Under Fire," *Time,* February 23, 2004, 17.

[138]For an empirical examination, see David Domke, *God Willing? Political Fundamentalism in the White House, the War on Terror, and the Echoing Press* (Ann Arbor, Michigan: Pluto,

2004). Domke also examines the intolerance of dissent reflected in speeches and remarks issued by the administration.

[139]David Greenberg, "Fathers and Sons," *New Yorker,* July 12 and 19, 2004, 97.

[140]David L. Greene, "Bush Often Great Miscommunicator," *Lincoln Journal Star,* October 6, 2002.

[141]Philip Gourevitch, "Bushspeak," *New Yorker,* September 13, 2004, 38.

[142]Stephen Hess, *Live from Capitol Hill!* (Washington, D.C.: Brookings Institution, 1991), 62; Timothy E. Cook, *Making Laws and Making News: Media Strategies in the U.S. House of Representatives* (Washington, D.C.: Brookings Institution, 1989), 2.

[143]Hess, *Live from Capitol Hill!* 102.

[144]Joe Klein, *The Natural* (New York: Doubleday, 2002), 109.

[145]Robert Schmidt, "May It Please the Court," *Brill's Content,* October 1999, 74.

[146]For analysis, see Rorie L. Spill and Zoe M. Oxley, "Philosopher Kings or Political Actors? How the Media Portray the Supreme Court," *Judicature,* July–August 2003, 22–29.

[147]Schmidt, "May It Please the Court," 73.

[148]Ibid.

[149]During the invasion of Grenada in 1983, the military excluded all journalists, even turning away at gunpoint those who reached the island on their own. During the invasion of Panama in 1989 and the Persian Gulf War in 1990, the military created press pools with some journalists who were escorted to selected sites and who reported the news for media organizations in the pools. Censorship also reduced coverage.

[150]Michael Tomasky, "Breaking the Code: Or, Can the Press Be Saved from Itself?" in Cynthia Brown, ed., *Lost Liberties* (New York: New Press, 2003), 151–152.

[151]Auletta, "Fortress Bush," 62.

[152]Tillman was killed in Afghanistan at the time of the Iraq War. Frank Rich, "The Mysterious Death of Pat Tillman," *New York Times,* November 6, 2005, WK12.

[153]Edward Jay Epstein, *News from Nowhere* (New York: Random House, 1973), 13.

[154]Graber, *Mass Media and American Politics,* 62.

[155]Milton Coleman, "When the Candidate Is Black Like Me," *Washington Post National Weekly Edition,* April 23, 1984, 9.

[156]Roper Organization, "A Big Concern about the Media: Intruding on Grieving Families," *Washington Post National Weekly Edition,* June 6, 1984. See also Cappella and Jamieson, *Spiral of Cynicism,* 210.

[157]McChesney, *Problem of the Media,* 116.

[158]Karen Tumulty, "I Want My Al TV," *Time,* June 30, 2003, 59. A new liberal network, Air America Radio, which reaches some of these cities, began in 2004. Even the Sunday talk shows of the major television networks lean right. Significantly more guests are conservative or Republican than liberal or Democrat, and the journalists who question them are more conservative than liberal, according to a study of the shows from 1997 through 2005. Paul Waldman, "John Fund Again? It's Not Your Imagination—the Sunday Shows Really Do Lean Right," *Washington Monthly,* March, 2006, 9–13.

[159]Liddy, who was convicted in the Watergate scandal, instructed listeners where to aim when shooting agents of the Bureau of Alcohol, Tobacco, and Firearms to kill them.

[160]Tony Blankley, "Radio Show Goes On," *Washington Times,* October 10, 2002. An empiri-

cal study reinforces this conclusion. David C. Barker, *Rushed to Judgment* (New York: Columbia University, 2002).

[161]McChesney, *Problem of the Media,* 117.

[162]For a history of the origins of Fox News, see David Carr, *Crazy Like a Fox* (New York: Portfolio, 2004).

[163]For analysis, see Ken Auletta, "Vox Fox," *New Yorker,* May 26, 2003, 58.

[164]Geneva Overholser, "It's Time for News Networks to Take Sides," *Lincoln Journal Star,* August 26, 2001.

[165]Robert S. Boynton, "How to Make a Guerrilla Documentary," *New York Times Magazine,* July 11, 2004, 22. See also the documentary *Outfoxed* (2004).

[166]Nicholas D. Kristof, "A Challenge for Bill O'Reilly," *New York Times,* December 18, 2005, WK13. The crusade coincided with publication of a book on this subject by a Fox broadcaster.

[167]Auletta, "Vox Fox," 63–64.

[168]Overholser, "It's Time"; David Plotz, "Fox News Channel," *Slate,* November 22, 2000 (slate.msn.com).

[169]Jeff Cohen and Jonah Goldberg, "Face-Off: Beyond Belief," *Brill's Content,* December 1999–January 2000, 54.

[170]For examination, see Tommy Nguyen, "The Reel Liberal Majority," *Washington Post National Weekly Edition,* August 2–8, 2004, 14.

[171]Edith Efron, *The News Twisters* (Los Angeles: Nash, 1971); L. B. Bozell and B. H. Baker, "And That's the Way It Isn't," *Journalism Quarterly* 67 (1990), 1139; Bernard Goldberg, *Bias* (New York: Regnery, 2002); Alterman, *What Liberal Media?*

[172] S. Robert Lichter, Stanley Rothman, and Linda S. Lichter, *The Media Elite* (Bethesda, Md.: Adler & Adler, 1986), 21–25. See also Hess, *Live from Capitol Hill!* app. A, 110–130.

[173]John Johnstone, Edward Slawski, and William Bowman, *The Newspeople* (Urbana: University of Illinois Press, 1976), 225–226.

[174]Stanley Rothman and S. Robert Lichter, "Media and Business Elites: Two Classes in Conflict?" *Public Interest* 69 (1982), 111–125; S. Robert Lichter and Stanley Rothman, "Media and Business Elites," *Public Opinion,* October-November 1981, 44.

[175]Stephen Hess, *The Washington Reporters* (Washington, D.C.: Brookings Institution, 1981), 89; see also Lichter et al., *Media Elite,* 127–128.

[176]James Fallows, "The Stoning of Donald Regan," *Washington Monthly,* June 1984, 57. Most individual reporters also probably care more about their career than ideology, but this could lead to bias. In 1976, one media analyst ran into an old friend, an NBC correspondent. When the analyst asked how she was doing, she answered, "Not so great. My candidate lost." That is, the candidate she had covered during the presidential primaries lost his bid for the nomination. Because reporters often follow "their" presidential candidate into office, she lost her chance to become NBC's White House correspondent. Graeme Browning, "Too Close for Comfort?" *National Journal,* October 3, 1992, 2243.

[177]One Pittsburgh publisher interjects his views into news stories. Kimberly Conniff, "All the Views Fit to Print," *Brill's Content,* March 2001, 105.

[178]Howard Kurtz, *Media Circus* (New York: Random House, 1994), 48.

[179]Russell J. Dalton, Paul A. Beck, and Robert Huckfeldt, "Partisan Cues and the Media

Information Flows in the 1992 Presidential Election," *American Political Science Review* 92 (March 1998), 118.

[180]C. Richard Hofstetter, *Bias in the News* (Columbus: Ohio State University Press, 1976); Graber, *Mass Media and Politics,* 167–168; Michael J. Robinson, "Just How Liberal Is the News?" *Public Opinion,* February–March 1983, 55–60; Maura Clancy and Michael J. Robinson, "General Election Coverage: Part I," *Public Opinion,* December 1984–January 1985, 49–54, 59; Michael J. Robinson, "The Media Campaign, '84: Part II," *Public Opinion,* February–March 1985, 43–48.

[181]Dave D'Alessio and Mike Allen, "Media Bias in Presidential Elections: A Meta-Analysis," *Journal of Communication* 50 (2000), 133–156. Some studies did find some bias against incumbents, front-runners, and emerging challengers. For these candidates, the media apparently took their watchdog role seriously. Clancy and Robinson, "General Election Coverage"; Robinson, "Media Campaign, '84"; Michael J. Robinson, "Where's the Beef? Media and Media Elites in 1984," in *The American Elections of 1984,* ed. Austin Ranney (Durham, N.C.: Duke University Press, 1985), 184; Michael J. Robinson, "News Media Myths and Realities: What Network News Did and Didn't Do in the 1984 General Campaign," in *Elections in America,* ed. Kay Lehman Schlozman (Boston: Allen & Unwin, 1987), 143–170; Kim Fridkin Kahn and Patrick J. Kenney, *The Spectacle of U.S. Senate Campaigns* (Princeton, N.J.: Princeton University, 1999), 126–129.

[182]Robert Shogan, *Bad News: Where the Press Goes Wrong in the Making of the President* (Chicago: Dee, 2001), 231.

[183]It helped the Democrat Carter in 1976 but hurt him in 1980. It helped the Republican Bush in 1988 but hurt him in 1992. Thomas E. Patterson, *Out of Order* (New York: Vintage, 1994), 131. It helped the Democrat Clinton in 1996, and at different stages of the campaign, it helped the Republican Bush or the Democrat Gore in 2000.

[184]Shogan, *Bad News,* 204–245; Clymer, "Better Campaign Reporting."

[185]Fewer than one in ten stories on the 2000 debates focused on policy differences; seven in ten focused on candidates' performance or strategy. Bill Kovach and Tom Rosenstiel, "Campaign Lite," *Washington Monthly,* January–February 2001, 31–32. For a perceptive analysis, see Clymer, "Better Campaign Reporting."

[186]The media, however, did pay a lot of attention to Ross Perot's presidential bid in 1992 because he said he would spend $100 million on his campaign and because polls showed he could compete with Bush and Clinton.

[187]For a recounting of his 2000 campaign, see Ralph Nader, "My Untold Story," *Brill's Content,* February 2001, 100.

[188]"Clinton Gains More Support from Big Papers," *Lincoln Journal Star,* October 25, 1992. Newspapers insist that there is little relationship between their editorial endorsements and their news coverage or even their political columns. An endorsement for one candidate does not mean more positive coverage or columns for that candidate because American media have established a tradition of autonomy in the newsroom. Dalton et al., "Partisan Cues," 118. However, some research shows that when papers endorse candidates, the papers show a small bias toward the candidates in their news stories (if the candidates are incumbents). Kim Fridkin Kahn and Patrick J. Kenney, "The Slant of the News: How Editorial Endorsements Influence Campaign Coverage and Citizen's Views of Candidates," *American Political Science Review* 96 (June 2002), 381–394.

[189]Hofstetter, *Bias in the News;* Hess, *Live from Capitol Hill!* 12–13.

[190]Robinson, "Just How Liberal . . . ?" 58; Arthur H. Miller, Edie N. Goldenberg, and Lutz Erbring, "Type-Set Politics," *American Political Science Review* 73 (January 1979), 69; Patterson, *Out of Order,* 6; Charles M. Tidmarch and John J. Pitney Jr., "Covering Congress," *Polity* 17 (Spring 1985), 463–483.

[191]Richard Morin, "The Big Picture Is out of Focus," *Washington Post National Weekly Edition,* March 6, 2000, 21.

[192]Steven Brill, "Quality Control," *Brill's Content,* July–August 1998, 19–20.

[193]Patterson, *Out of Order,* 25, 245.

[194]Stanley Rothman and S. Robert Lichter, "The Nuclear Energy Debate," *Public Opinion,* August–September 1982, 47–48; Stanley Rothman and S. Robert Lichter, "Elite Ideology and Risk Perception in Nuclear Energy Policy," *American Political Science Review* 81 (June 1987), 383–404; Lichter et al., *Media Elite,* ch. 7; Sabato, *Feeding Frenzy,* 87; and sources cited therein. But a study examining twenty years' coverage of governors and their states' unemployment and murder rates shows no bias toward Democratic or Republican governors. David Niven, "Partisan Bias in the Media?" *Social Science Quarterly* 80 (December 1999), 847–857.

[195]Goldberg, *Bias,* ch. 5; Alterman, *What Liberal Media?* ch. 7.

[196]Alterman, *What Liberal Media?* 104–117.

[197]Ibid., 118 –138. For an analysis of the coverage of the economy in the booming 1990s, see John Cassidy, "Striking It Rich: The Rise and Fall of Popular Capitalism," *New Yorker,* January 14, 2002, 63–73.

[198]Bruce Nussbaum, "The Myth of the Liberal Media," *Business Week,* November 11, 1996; Fallows, *Breaking the News,* 49.

[199]Further, the media give scant attention to labor matters, except when strikes inconvenience commuters. Mark Crispin Miller, "The Media and the Bush Dyslexicon," in Grover and Peschek, *Voices of Dissent,* 137–146. In 2001, the three main television networks used representatives of corporations as sources thirty times more often than representatives of unions. McChesney, *Problem of the Media,* 70–71.

[200]McChesney, *Problem of the Media,* 106.

[201]Robinson, "Just How Liberal . . . ?" 59.

[202]Parenti, *Inventing Reality,* ch. 7–11; Charles E. Lindblom, *Politics and Markets* (New York: Basic Books, 1977); J. Fred MacDonald, *One Nation under Television: The Rise and Decline of Network TV* (New York: Pantheon Books, 1990); Dan Nimmo and James E. Combs, *Mediated Political Realities* (White Plains, N.Y.: Longman, 1983), 135; Benjamin I. Page and R.Y. Shapiro, *The Rational Public* (Chicago: University of Chicago Press, 1992); John R. Zaller and Dennis Chiu, "Government's Little Helper: U.S. Press Coverage of Foreign Policy Crises, 1945–1991," *Political Communication* 13 (1996), 385–405.

[203]John R. MacArthur, *Second Front: Censorship and Propaganda in the Gulf War* (New York: Hill & Wang, 1992); James Bennet, "How They Missed That Story," *Washington Monthly,* December 1990, 8–16; Christopher Dickey, "Not Their Finest Hour," *Newsweek,* June 8, 1992, 66.

[204]In the 1950s and early 1960s, newspapers, magazines, and television networks sent few correspondents to Vietnam, so most accepted the government's account of the conflict. Susan Welch, "The American Press and Indochina, 1950–1956," in *Communication in International Politics,* ed. Richard L. Merritt (Urbana: University of Illinois Press, 1972), 207–231; Edward J. Epstein, "The Selection of Reality," in *What's News?,* ed. Elie Abel (San Francisco: Institute for Contemporary Studies, 1981), 124. When they did dispatch correspondents, many filed pessimistic reports, but their editors believed the government rather than the correspondents and refused to print these reports. Instead, they ran articles quoting optimistic statements by government officials. See David Halberstam, *The Powers That Be* (New York: Dell, 1980), 642–647. In 1968, the media did turn against the war, but rather than sharply criticize it, they conveyed the impression that it was futile. Daniel C. Hallin, *The "Uncensored War": The Media and Vietnam* (New York: Oxford University Press, 1986).

[205]David Domke, *God Willing? Political Fundamentalism in the White House, the "War on Terror," and the Echoing Press* (London: Pluto, 2004).

[206]"Return of Talk Show Is Healthy Sign," *Lincoln Journal Star,* October 6, 2001.

[207]Alterman, *What Liberal Media?* 202.

[208]Anthony Collings, "The BBC: How to Be Impartial in Wartime," *Chronicle of Higher Education,* December 21, 2001, B14.

[209]*Weapons of Mass Deception,* a documentary film by Danny Schechter (Cinema Libre Distribution, 2005).

[210]Alterman, *What Liberal Media?* 29; Todd Gitlin, "Showtime Iraq," *American Prospect,* November 4, 2002, 34–35.

[211]McChesney, *Problem of the Media,* 122–123.

[212]*Weapons of Mass Deception.*

[213]Bill Moyers, "Our Democracy Is in Danger of Being Paralyzed," Keynote address to the National Conference on Media Reform, November 8, 2003, www.truthout.org/docs_03/printer_111403E.shtml.

[214]James Poniewozik, "What You See vs. What They See," *Time,* April 7, 2003, 68–69. For example, that U.S. searches caused considerable damage to Iraqi homes and that these raids swept up many innocent family members. *Morning Edition,* National Public Radio, May 4, 2004. Also, that in the run-up to the war, U.S. agents had bugged the homes and offices of United Nations Security Council members who had not proclaimed support for the war. Camille T. Taiara, "Spoon-Feeding the Press," *San Francisco Bay Guardian,* March 12, 2003 (www.sfbg.com/37/24/x_mediabeat.html).

[215]Frank Rich, "The Spoils of War," *New York Times,* April 13, 2003, AR1; Paul Janensch, "Whether to Show Images of War Dead Is Media Dilemma," *Lincoln Journal Star,* March 31, 2003.

[216]Terry McCarthy, "Whatever Happened to the Republican Guard?" *Time,* May 12, 2003, 38.

[217]Todd Gitlin, "Embed or in Bed?" *American Prospect,* June 2003, 43.

[218]Schell, "Preface," vi.

[219]Massing, *Now They Tell Us,* 7.

[220]For an examination, see Massing, *Now They Tell Us.*

[221]Howard Kurtz, quoted in Todd Gitlin, "The Great Media Breakdown," *Mother Jones,*

November/December, 2004, 58.

[222]"The *Times* and Iraq," *New York Times,* May 26, 2004, A10; Daniel Okrent, "Weapons of Mass Destruction? Or Mass Distraction?" *New York Times,* May 30, 2004, WK1.

[223]Jim Thompson, "Letters to the Public Editor," *New York Times,* June 6, 2004, WK2.

[224]Reporters turn to officials because it is easy and because, ironically, they want to avoid charges of bias. They believe that their superiors and the public consider officials to be reliable, so ignoring or downplaying them might be construed as showing bias against them. Cook, *Making Laws and Making News,* 8. See also Leon V. Sigal, *Reporters and Officials* (Lexington, Mass.: Heath, 1973), 120–121; Lucy Howard, "Slanted 'Line'?" *Newsweek,* February 13, 1989, 6; Hess, *Live from Capitol Hill!* 50. Trivia buffs might wonder who has been the subject of the most cover articles in *Time* magazine—the answer is Richard Nixon (fifty-five). "Numbers," *Time,* March 9, 1998, 189.

[225]W. Lance Bennett, "Toward a Theory of Press-State Relations in the United States," *Journal of Communication* 40 (1990), 103–125.

[226]Three times as many people believe the media are "too liberal" than believe they are "too conservative" (45 percent to 15 percent). McChesney, *Problem of the Media,* 114.

[227]M. D. Watts, D. Domke, D. V. Shah, and D. P. Fan, "Elite Cues and Media Bias in Presidential Campaigns: Explaining Public Perceptions of a Liberal Press," *Communication Research* 26 (1999), 144–175.

[228]William Kristol, quoted in Alterman, *What Liberal Media?* 2–3.

[229]Elizabeth Wilner, "On the Road Again," *Washington Post National Weekly Edition,* June 6–12, 2005, 22.

[230]Robert Vallone, Lee Ross, and Mark R. Lepper, "The Hostile Media Phenomenon," *Journal of Personality and Social Psychology* 49 (1985), 577–585; Roger Giner-Sorolla and Shelly Chaiken, "The Causes of Hostile Media Judgments," *Journal of Experimental Social Psychology* 30 (1994), 165–180.

[231]Dalton et al., "Partisan Cues and the Media."

[232]W. Phillips Davison, "The Third-Person Effect in Communication," *Public Opinion Quarterly* 47 (1983), 1–15.

[233]Dave D'Alessio, "An Experimental Examination of Readers' Perceptions of Media Bias," unpublished manuscript, University of Connecticut, n.d.; Mark Peffley, James M. Avery, and Jason E. Glass, "Public Perceptions of Bias in the News Media," paper presented at the annual meeting of the Midwest Political Science Association, Chicago, April 19–22, 2001.

[234]According to a statement by a CNN producer in the documentary *Outfoxed.*

[235]And HBO postponed a documentary film, *Last Letters Home,* based on excerpts of letters from soldiers later killed in Iraq, because this powerful film might have turned viewers against the war. *All Things Considered,* NPR, November 11, 2004.

[236] Ted Koppel, "And Now, a Word for Our Demographic," *New York Times,* January 29, 2006, WK16.

[237]Goldberg, *Bias,* 92.

[238]Theodore H. White, *America in Search of Itself* (New York: Harper & Row, 1982), 186.

[239]Goldberg, *Bias,* 92.

[240]"Anchorwoman Verdict Raises Mixed Opinions," *Lincoln Journal Star,* August 9, 1983.

[241]Kovach and Rosenstiel, *Warp Speed,* 64.

[242]Hess, *Live from Capitol Hill!* 34; Rosenstiel, *State of the News Media,* 21.

[243]Molly Ivins, "Media Conglomerates Profit at Expense of News, Public," *Lincoln Journal Star,* October 26, 2001.

[244]James Fallows, "On That Chart," *Nation,* June 3, 1996, 15.

[245]Maureen Dowd, "Flintstone Futurama," *New York Times,* August 19, 2001, WK 13.

[246]"Poll: Reporters Avoid, Soften Stories," *Lincoln Journal Star,* May 1, 2000; David Owen, "The Cigarette Companies: How They Get Away with Murder, Part II," *Washington Monthly,* March 1985, 48–54. See also Daniel Hellinger and Dennis R. Judd, *The Democratic Facade,* 2nd ed. (Belmont, Calif.: Wadsworth, 1994), 59. Through the 1920s, newspapers refrained from pointing out that popular "patent medicines" were usually useless and occasionally dangerous because the purveyors bought more advertising than any other business. Mark Crispin Miller, "Free the Media," *Nation,* June 3, 1996, 10.

[247]Roger Mudd, quoted in *Television and the Presidential Elections,* ed. Martin A. Linsky (Lexington, Mass.: Heath, 1983), 48.

[248]"Q&A: Dan Rather on Fear, Money, and the News," *Brill's Content,* October 1998, 117.

[249]Barry Sussman, "News on TV: Mixed Reviews," *Washington Post National Weekly Edition,* September 3, 1984, 37.

[250]Bill Carter, "Networks Fight Public's Shrinking Attention Span," *Lincoln Journal Star,* September 30, 1990.

[251]Epstein, *News from Nowhere,* 4.

[252]William A. Henry III, "Requiem for TV's Gender Gap," *Time,* August 22, 1983, 57.

[253]Richard Morin, "The Nation's Mood? Calm," *Washington Post National Weekly Edition,* November 5, 2001, 35.

[254]According to the Tyndall Report, cited in Nicholas Kristof, "Please, Readers, Help Bill O'Reilly!" *New York Times,* February 7, 2006, A21.

[255]For an examination of how the media exaggerated the Whitewater scandal, see Gene Lyons, *Fools for Scandal* (New York: Franklin Square Press, 1996).

[256]The third and final special prosecutor concluded that there might be some evidence of wrongdoing in the law firm records of Hillary Clinton but that there was not enough evidence to justify prosecution.

[257]The pope was making a historic visit to Cuba. The networks had considered this so important that they had sent their anchors to Havana. At the same time, renewed violence in Northern Ireland threatened to scuttle the peace talks between Catholics and Protestants, and continued refusal from Iraq to cooperate with United Nations biological and chemical weapons inspectors threatened to escalate to military conflict.

[258]Eric Pooley, "Monica's World," *Time,* March 2, 1998, 40.

[259]Quoted in Fallows, *Breaking the News,* 201.

[260]Samuel G. Freedman, "Fighting to Balance Honor and Profit on the Local News," *New York Times,* September 30, 2001, sec. 2, 26.

[261]Lawrie Mifflin, "Crime Falls, but Not on TV," *New York Times,* July 6, 1997, E3. According to one researcher, crime coverage is also "the easiest, cheapest, laziest news to cover" because stations just listen to the police radio and then send a camera crew to shoot the story.

[262]Heather Maher, "Eleven O'Clock Blues," *Brill's Content,* February 2001, 99.

[263]Molly Ivins, "Don't Moan about the Media, Do Something," *Lincoln Journal Star,* November 1999.

[264]David S. Broder, "Can We Govern?" *Washington Post National Weekly Edition,* January 31, 1994, 23.

[265]Newspaper ads were placed in college papers by Holocaust deniers, claiming that there is no proof that gas chambers actually existed. The editor of one paper justified accepting the ad by saying, "There are two sides to every issue and both have a place on the pages of any open-minded paper's editorial page." Tannen, *Argument Culture,* 38. For examination of this phenomenon, see Deborah E. Lipstadt, *Denying the Holocaust: The Growing Assault on Truth and Memory* (New York: Plume, 1993).

[266]Howard Kurtz, quoted in Tannen, *Argument Culture,* 29.

[267]Patterson, *Out of Order,* 53–59.

[268]Lee Sigelman and David Bullock, "Candidates, Issues, Horse Races, and Hoopla: Presidential Campaign Coverage, 1888–1988," *American Politics Quarterly* 19 (January 1991), 5–32. So was emphasis on human interest. In 1846, the *New York Tribune* described the culinary habits of Representative William "Sausage" Sawyer (D-Ohio), who ate a sausage on the floor of the House every afternoon: "What little grease is left on his hands he wipes on his almost bald head which saves any outlay for Pomatum. His mouth sometimes serves as a finger glass, his shirtsleeves and pantaloons being called into requisition as a napkin. He uses a jackknife for a toothpick, and then he goes on the floor again to abuse the Whigs as the British party." Cook, *Making Laws and Making News,* 18–19.

[269]Patterson, *Out of Order,* 74; Marion R. Just, Ann N. Crigler, Dean E. Alger, Timothy E. Cook, Montague Kern, and Darrell M. West, *Crosstalk: Citizens, Candidates, and the Media in a Presidential Campaign* (Chicago: University of Chicago Press, 1996); Mathew Robert Kerbel, *Remote and Controlled* (Boulder, Colo.: Westview Press, 1995); Bruce Buchanan, *Electing a President* (Austin: University of Texas Press, 1991).

[270]Owen, "Media Mayhem," 127.

[271]Richard Morin, "Toward the Millennium, by the Numbers," *Washington Post National Weekly Edition,* July 7, 1997, 35.

[272]Patterson, *Out of Order,* 81–82.

[273]Fallows, *Breaking the News,* 162, 27.

[274]Epstein, *News from Nowhere,* 179, 195.

[275]Rosenstiel, *State of the News Media,* 18.

[276]John Horn, "Campaign Coverage Avoids Issues," *Lincoln Journal Star,* September 25, 1988. Another survey found that 28 percent of women and 40 percent of men change channels every time during commercial breaks. "Ticker," *Brill's Content,* September 1999, 128.

[277]John Eisendrath, "An Eyewitness Account of Local TV News," *Washington Monthly,* September 1986, 21.

[278]Michael Deaver, "Sound-Bite Campaigning: TV Made Us Do It," *Washington Post National Weekly Edition,* November 7, 1988, 34.

[279]Fred Friendly, quoted on *All Things Considered,* National Public Radio, March 4, 1998.

[280]Thomas E. Patterson, *The Vanishing Voter* (New York: Knopf, 2002), 92.

[281]The extent of the media's impact has been debated over the years. See Lawrence Bartels, "Messages Received: The Political Impact of Media Exposure," *American Political Science Review* 87 (June 1983), 267–285; John R. Zaller,

"The Myth of Massive Media Impact Revived: New Support for a Discredited Idea," in *Political Persuasion and Attitude Change*, ed. Diane Mutz, Paul Sniderman, and Richard Brody (Ann Arbor: University of Michigan Press, 1996).

[282]Donald L. Shaw and Maxwell E. McCombs, *The Emergence of American Political Issues: The Agenda-Setting Function of the Press* (Saint Paul, Minn.: West, 1977). For a review of agenda-setting research, see Everett M. Rogers and James W. Dearing, "Agenda-Setting Research: Where Has It Been, Where Is It Going?" in *Communication Yearbook 11* (Newbury Park, Calif.: Sage, 1988), 555–594.

[283]Lutz Erbring, Edie N. Goldenberg, and Arthur H. Miller, "Front-Page News and Real-World Clues: A New Look at Agenda-Setting by the Media," *American Journal of Political Science* 24 (February 1980), 16–49.

[284]Michael Bruce MacKuen and Steven Lane Coombs, *More than News* (Beverly Hills, Calif.: Sage, 1981), 140; Rogers and Dearing, "Agenda-Setting Research," 572–576; Gladys Engel Lang and Kurt Lang, *The Battle for Public Opinion* (New York: Columbia University Press, 1983), 58–59.

[285]Richard Morin, "Public Enemy No. 1: Crime," *Washington Post National Weekly Edition*, January 24, 1994, 37; Molly Ivins, "Hard Questions, Easy Answers," *Lincoln Journal Star*, July 7, 1994; Richard Morin, "A Public Paradox on the Drug War," *Washington Post National Weekly Edition*, March 23, 1998, 35.

[286]Erbring et al., "Front-Page News," 38; MacKuen and Coombs, *More than News*, 128–137.

[287]Shanto Iyengar and Donald R. Kinder, *News That Matters* (Chicago: University of Chicago Press, 1987), 42–45.

[288]Rogers and Dearing, "Agenda-Setting Research," 569; MacKuen and Coombs, *More than News*, 101; Erbring et al., "Front-Page News," 38.

[289]Rogers and Dearing, "Agenda-Setting Research," 577, citing Jack L. Walker, "Setting the Agenda in the U.S. Senate," *British Journal of Political Science* 7 (1977), 423–445. See also Cook, *Making Laws and Making News*, 116, 130–131.

[290]Michael J. Robinson and Margaret A. Sheehan, *Over the Wire and on TV* (New York: Russell Sage Foundation/Basic Books, 1983); Robinson, "Media Campaign, '84," 45–47.

[291]Thomas Griffith, "Leave Off the Label," *Time*, September 19, 1984, 63.

[292]He did own property in the district, so he did satisfy the residency requirement.

[293]Charles Krauthammer, "We Conservatives Had a Dream: His Name Was Howard Dean," *Lincoln Journal Star*, January 24, 2003.

[294]Although Dean's campaign had started declining before this speech, he would have done better in the New Hampshire primary and then could have hung on longer. The speech received so much attention because it confirmed for reporters their belief that he said inappropriate things and was "not presidential."

[295] Doris A. Graber, "Kind Pictures and Harsh Words: How Television Presents the Candidates," in *Elections in America*, ed. Kay Lehman Schlozman (Boston: Allen & Unwin, 1987), 141.

[296]Ibid., 116.

[297]Anthony Lewis, quoted in Larry J. Sabato, "Open Season: How the News Media Cover Presidential Campaigns in the Age of Attack Journalism," in *Under the Watchful Eye*, ed.

Mathew D. McCubbins (Washington, D.C.: CQ Press, 1992), 146.

[298]Tannen, *Argument Culture*, 79–83.

[299]See the excellent summary found in Stephen Ansolabehere, Roy Behr, and Shanto Iyengar, "Mass Media and Elections," *American Politics Quarterly* 19 (January 1991), 109–139.

[300]Bruce Buchanan, *Electing a President: The Markle Commission Report on Campaign '88* (Austin: University of Texas Press, 1990); Montague Kean, *30-Second Politics* (New York: Praeger, 1989); Marion Just, Lori Wallach, and Ann Crigler, "Thirty Seconds or Thirty Minutes: Political Learning in an Election," paper presented at the annual meeting of the Midwest Political Science Association, Chicago, April 1987.

[301]In the Democratic race in 1976, Jimmy Carter finished second to "uncommitted" in the Iowa caucuses. This was enough to give him twenty-three times more coverage in *Time* and *Newsweek* and five times more coverage on network television than any of his rivals. Finishing first by just 4 percent in the New Hampshire primary landed him on the covers of *Time* and *Newsweek* and brought him twenty-five times more coverage on network television than the runner-up. David Paletz and Robert Entrum, *Media—Power—Politics* (New York: Macmillan, 1981), 35ff.

[302]Ansolabehere et al., "Mass Media and Elections," 128–129; Christine F. Ridout, "The Role of Media Coverage of Iowa and New Hampshire in the 1988 Democratic Nomination," *American Politics Quarterly* 19 (January 1991), 45–46, 53–54; Marc Howard Ross, "Television News and Candidate Fortunes in Presidential Nomination Campaigns," *American Politics Quarterly* 20 (January 1992), 69–98.

[303]Henry Brady, "Chances, Utilities, and Voting in Presidential Primaries," paper delivered at the annual meeting of the Public Choice Society, Phoenix, 1984, cited in Ansolabehere et al., "Mass Media and Elections"; Bartels, *Presidential Primaries and the Dynamics of Public Choice* (Princeton, N.J.: Princeton University Press, 1988).

[304]Lee Sigelman and Carol K. Sigelman, "Judgments of the Carter-Reagan Debate," *Public Opinion Quarterly* 48 (1984), 624–628.

[305]Theodore H. White, *The Making of the President, 1960* (New York: Atheneum, 1961), 333.

[306]The clearest examples occurred in 1976 and 1984. In the 1976 debate between Gerald Ford and Jimmy Carter, Ford erroneously said that there was "no Soviet domination of Eastern Europe." People surveyed within twelve hours of the debate said they thought Ford won. But the media zeroed in on this slip, and people surveyed later said they thought Carter had won. In the first debate in 1984, Reagan appeared tired and confused. By a *modest margin*, people polled immediately after the debate said they thought Walter Mondale had won. But the media focused on Reagan's age and abilities, and by *increasingly large margins*, people polled in the days after the debate said Mondale had won. Perhaps viewers did not catch Ford's statement or, due to selective perception, notice Reagan's doddering, but the media called attention to them, which prompted many viewers to reconsider and reverse their verdict.

[307]John R. Zaller, "Monica Lewinsky's Contribution to Political Science," *PS*, June

1998, 182–189.

[308]MacKuen and Coombs, *More than News*, 222.

[309]For a review, see ibid., 147–161.

[310]Robert S. Erickson, "The Influence of Newspaper Endorsements in Presidential Elections," *American Journal of Political Science* 20 (1976), 207–233; Dalton et al., "Partisan Cues." Also see Kahn and Kenney, "Slant of the News."

[311]David Barker, "The Talk Radio Community," *Social Science Quarterly* 79 (1998), 261–272; C. Richard Hofstetter, "Political Talk Radio, Situational Involvement, and Political Mobilization," *Social Science Quarterly* 79 (1998), 273–286.

[312]Benjamin I. Page, Robert Y. Shapiro, and Glenn R. Dempsey, "What Moves Public Opinion?" *American Political Science Review* 81 (1987), 23–43. Critical news and commentaries about presidents seem to lower their popularity. Darrell M. West, "Television and Presidential Popularity in America," *British Journal of Political Science* 21 (1991), 199–214. Even television's "framing" of events, as isolated incidents or parts of patterns, affects viewers' opinions about these events. Shanto Iyengar, *Is Anyone Responsible? How Television Frames Political Issues* (Chicago: University of Chicago Press, 1991). See also Thomas E. Nelson, Rosalee A. Clawson, and Zoe M. Oxley, "Media Framing of a Civil Liberties Conflict and Its Effect on Tolerance," *American Political Science Review* 91 (1997), 567–583. For empirical examination of the impact of talk radio on listeners' opinions, see Barker, *Rushed to Judgment*.

[313]Iyengar, *Is Anyone Responsible?* ch. 6 and 8.

[314]Kathleen Hall Jamieson, quoted in Howard Kurtz, "Tuning Out the News," *Washington Post National Weekly Edition*, May 29, 1995, 6; William Raspberry, "Blow-by-Blow Coverage," *Washington Post National Weekly Edition*, November 6, 1995, 29.

[315]Michael J. Robinson, "Public Affairs Television and the Growth of Political Malaise," *American Political Science Review* 70 (1976), 409–432; Miller et al., "Type-Set Politics."

[316]"Study: Public More Cynical than Media," *Champaign-Urbana News-Gazette*, May 22, 1995.

[317]Fallows, *Breaking the News*, 202–203.

[318]See Cappella and Jamieson, *Spiral of Cynicism*.

[319]Fallows, *Breaking the News*, 247.

[320]Graber, *Mass Media*, 244; Doris Graber, *Processing News: How People Tame the Information Tide* (White Plains, N.Y.: Longman, 1984). A 1993 survey concluded that almost half of Americans over sixteen have such limited reading and math skills that they are unfit for most jobs. One task the survey included was to paraphrase a newspaper story. Many people could scan the story but not paraphrase it when they finished it. Paul Gray, "Adding Up the Under-Skilled," *Time*, September 20, 1993, 75. For a critique, claiming that the oligopolistic structure of the media makes it impossible to know if people are getting what they actually want, see McChesney, *Problem of the Media*, 198–202.

[321]Reuven Frank, quoted in Neil Hickey, "Money Lust," *Columbia Journalism Review*, July–August 1998, 35.

[322]The idea for this paragraph came from James Fallows, "Did You Have a Good Week?" *Atlantic Monthly*, December 1994, 32, 34.

[323]Iyengar, *Is Anyone Responsible?*

[324]James Poniewozik, "Don't Blame It on Jayson Blair," *Time*, June 9, 2003, 90.

[325]Times Mirror Center for the People and the Press, "The New Political Landscape" (poll),

October 1994.
[326]Patrick D. Healy, "Believe It: The Media's Credibility Headache Gets Worse," *New York Times,* May 22, 2005, WK4. At least this is an improvement. In the late 1990s, reporters ranked lower than lawyers. Joe Klein, "Dizzy Days," *New Yorker,* October 5, 1998, 45.
[327]Marta W. Aldrich, "Support for Media Freedoms Waning," *Lincoln Journal Star,* July 4, 1999.
[328]Stephen Earl Bennett, "Trends in Americans' Political Information," *American Politics Quarterly* 17 (October 1989), 422–435; Richard Zoglin, "The Tuned-Out Generation," *Time,* July 9, 1990, 64.
[329]Robert N. Entman, *Democracy without Citizens: Media and the Decay of American Politics* (New York: Oxford University Press, 1989), 17.
[330]See McChesney, *Problem of the Media,* 96–97.
[331]Peters, *How Washington Really Works,* 32.
[332]The source for the epilogue, except where noted otherwise, is Kotz, "Breaking Point."
[333]Tannen, *Argument Culture,* 82.
[334]Ibid., 74.
[335]Yet when journalists themselves come under occasional attack from other media, they do not like it any more than officials do. They are just as "thin skinned" as officials are. Issues of *Brill's Content* provide numerous examples. Another example comes from Toobin, *Vast Conspiracy,* 268. After the 1992 election, Linda Bloodworth-Thomason, a Hollywood supporter of Bill Clinton, produced a short film for the inauguration. The film included a series of sound bites from Washington journalists during the campaign, dismissing Clinton as "unelectable" and "dead meat." Although Thomason apparently regarded the film as "a harmless needle at some puffed up egos," some of the journalists regarded it as "an act of war." In Toobin's view, the controversy over the film, which poisoned the relationship between the president and the press from the beginning, reflected the thin skins of the press corps.

Chapter 6

[1]Rachel L. Swarns, "The Nation: Rift on Immigration Widens for Conservatives and Catholics," *New York Times* (March 19, 2006), online.
[2]Ibid.
[3]Ibid.
[4]Roger Mahony, "Called by God to Help," *New York Times,* March 22, 2006, online.
[5]Ibid.
[6]Gillian Flaccus, "Immigrants Walk off Jobs," *Lincoln Journal Star,* May 1, 2006, A1.
[7]Jeffrey H. Birnbaum, *The Lobbyists: How Influence Peddlers Get Their Way in Washington* (New York: Times Books, 1993), 32.
[8]Mark A. Peterson and Jack L. Walker, Jr., "Interest Group Responses to Partisan Change: The Impact of the Reagan Administration upon the National Interest Group System," in *Interest Group Politics,* 2nd ed., ed. Allan J. Cigler and Burdett A. Loomis (Washington, D.C.: CQ Press, 1987), 162.
[9]Alexis de Tocqueville, *Democracy in America* (New York: Knopf, 1945), 191. (Originally published 1835.)
[10]Gabriel Almond and Sidney Verba, *Civic Culture* (Boston: Little, Brown, 1965), 266–306.
[11]David Truman, *The Governmental Process* (New York: Knopf, 1964), 25–26.
[12]Ibid., 59.
[13]Ibid., 26–33.

[14]James Q. Wilson, *Political Organizations* (New York: Basic Books, 1973), 198.
[15]Graham K. Wilson, *Interest Groups in America* (Oxford: Oxford University Press, 1981), ch. 5; see also Graham K. Wilson, "American Business and Politics," in *Interest Group Politics,* 2nd ed., ed. Cigler and Loomis, 221–235.
[16]Kay Lehman Schlozman and John T. Tierney, "More of the State: Washington Pressure Group Activity in a Decade of Change," *Journal of Politics* 45 (1983), 335–356.
[17]Christopher H. Foreman Jr., "Grassroots Victim Organizations: Mobilizing for Personal and Public Health," in *Interest Group Politics,* 4th ed., ed. Allan J. Cigler and Burdett A. Loomis (Washington, D.C.: CQ Press, 1994), 33–53.
[18]William Brown, "Exchange Theory and the Institutional Impetus for Interest Group Formation," in *Interest Group Politics,* 6th ed., ed. Allan J. Cigler and Burdett A. Loomis (Washington, D.C.: CQ Press, 2002), 313–329; William Brown, "Benefits and Membership: A Reappraisal of Interest Group Activity," *Western Political Quarterly* 29 (1976), 258–273; Terry M. Moe, *The Organization of Interests: Incentives and the Internal Dynamics of Political Interest Groups* (Chicago: University of Chicago Press, 1980).
[19]Jack L. Walker Jr., "The Origins and Maintenance of Interest Groups in America," *American Political Science Review* 77 (1983), 398–400.
[20]Robert H. Salisbury "An Exchange Theory of Interest Groups," *Midwest Journal of Political Science* 13 (1969): 1–32.
[21]Jeffrey M. Berry, *The Interest Group Society* (Boston: Little Brown, 1984), 26–28.
[22]Ibid.
[23]Wilson, *Political Organizations,* ch. 3.
[24]Alex Kuczynski, "New AARP Magazine Courting Younger Readers," *New York Times,* January 22, 2001, C1.
[25]Clyde Brown, "Explanations of Interest Group Membership over Time," *American Politics Quarterly* 17 (1989), 32–53.
[26]Nicholas Babchuk and Ralph V. Thompson, "The Voluntary Associations of Negroes," *American Sociological Review* 27 (1962), 662–665; see also Patricia Klobus-Edwards, John N. Edwards, and David L. Klemmack, "Differences in Social Participation of Blacks and Whites," *Social Forces* 56 (1978), 1035–1052.
[27]Robert D. Putnam, *Bowling Alone* (New York: Simon & Schuster, 2000). See also Robert D. Putnam, "Bowling Alone: America's Declining Social Capital," *Journal of Democracy* 6 (1995), 65–78, and Robert J. Samuelson, "Join the Club," *Washington Post National Weekly Edition,* April 15, 1996, 5.
[28]Theda Skocpol, "The Narrowing of Civic Life," *American Prospect,* June 2004, A5–A7.
[29]Samuelson, "Join the Club."
[30]Richard Stengel, "Bowling Together," *Time,* July 22, 1996, 35.
[31]Theda Skocpol, "Associations without Members," *American Prospect,* July–August 1999, 66–73.
[32]Mark T. Hayes, "The New Group Universe," in *Interest Group Politics,* 2nd ed., ed. Cigler and Loomis, 133–145.
[33]Calvin Tomkins, "A Sense of Urgency," *New Yorker,* March 27, 1989, 48–74.
[34]Walker, "Origins and Maintenance of Interest Groups"; E. E. Schattschneider, *Semi-Sovereign People* (New York: Holt, Rinehart and Winston, 1960), 118.
[35]David S. Broder and Michael Weisskopf,

[35]"Finding New Friends on the Hill," *Washington Post National Weekly Edition,* October 3, 1994, 11.
[36]Charles E. Lindblom, "The Market as Prison," *Journal of Politics* 44 (1982), 324–336; Michael Genovese, *The Presidential Dilemma: Leadership in the American System* (New York: HarperCollins, 1995).
[37]M. Asif Ismail, "Drug Lobby Second to None," The Center for Public Integrity, http://www.publicintegrity.org/rx/report.aspx?aid=723.
[38]"Pharmaceutical Industry Ranks as Most Profitable Industry—Again," *Public Citizen,* April 18, 2002, www.citizen.org/pressroom/release.cfm?ID51088.
[39]Asif, ibid.
[40]*Democracy on Drugs: The Medicare Prescription Drug Bill: A Study in How Government Shouldn't Work.* Common Cause, May 18, 2004. www.commoncause.org/atf/cf/%7BFB3C17E2CDD1-4DF6-92BE-BD4429893665%7D/democracy_on_drugs.pdf
[41]Ibid.
[42]Steven Greenhouse, "Labor Is Forced to Reassess as Union Leaders Convene," *New York Times,* March 9, 2004, A12.
[43]Steven Greenhouse, "Union Membership Rose in '98, but Unions' Percentage of Workforce Fell," *New York Times,* January 20, 1999, A22; Paul E. Johnson, "Organized Labor in an Era of Blue-Collar Decline," in *Interest Group Politics,* 3rd ed., ed. Allan J. Cigler and Burdett A. Loomis (Washington, D.C.: CQ Press, 1991), 33–62.
[44]Harold Myerson, "Organize or Die," *American Prospect,* September 2003, 39–42.
[45]Steven Greenhouse, "Report Faults Laws for Slowing Growth of Unions," *New York Times,* October 24, 2000, A14.
[46]Steven Greenhouse, "Union Membership Slides Despite Increased Organizing," *New York Times,* March 22, 1998, A8.
[47]"Poll Indicates Unions Gaining Favor with Public," *Champaign, Illinois, News-Gazette,* August 30, 2001, C10.
[48]Thomas B. Edsall, "Working With the Union You Have," *Washington Post National Weekly Edition,* March 14–20, 2005, 15.
[49]David S. Broder, "The Price of Labor's Decline," *Washington Post,* September 9, 2004, A27. See also Lawrence Mishel, Jared Bernstein, and Sylvia Allegretto, *The State of Working America* (Washington, D.C.: Economic Policy Institute, 2004).
[50]Broder, "Price of Labor's Decline."
[51]Frank Swoboda, "A Healthy Outcome for Organized Labor," *Washington Post National Weekly Edition,* March 8, 1999, 18; Steven Greenhouse, "In Biggest Drive since 1937, Union Gains a Victory," *New York Times,* February 26, 1999, Al.
[52]Thomas B. Edsall, "Two Top Unions Split From AFL-CIO," *Washington Post,* January 26, 2005, A01.
[53]Steven Greenhouse, "Labor Federation Looks beyond Unions," *New York Times,* July 11, 2004, 18.
[54]Steven Greenhouse, "The Most Innovative Figure in Silicon Valley? Maybe This Labor Organizer," *New York Times,* November 14, 1999, 26.
[55]Steven Greenhouse, "Angered by HMOs' Treatment, More Doctors Are Joining Unions," *New York Times,* February 4, 1999, Al, A25.
[56]Steven Greenhouse, "Graduate Students Push

for Union Membership," *New York Times,* May 15, 2001, A18.

[57] Undergraduate resident hall advisers at the University of Massachusetts recently voted to affiliate with the United Auto Workers. The issue is job security. A residence hall assistant was fired for missing a staff meeting. Richard Corliss, "RAs of the World Unite!" *Time,* March 25, 2002, 56; Daniel J. Fitzgibbons, "Administration Opposes Union Bid by RAs," *University of Massachusetts, Campus Chronicle,* April 13, 2001.

[58] Allan J. Cigler and John M. Hansen, "Group Formation through Protest: The American Agriculture Movement," in *Interest Group Politics,* 1st ed., ed. Allan J. Cigler and Burdett A. Loomis (Washington, D.C.: CQ Press, 1983), 84–109; Allan J. Cigler, "Organizational Maintenance and Political Activity on the Cheap: The American Agriculture Movement," in *Interest Group Politics,* 3rd ed., ed. Allan J. Cigler and Burdett A. Loomis (Washington, D.C.: CQ Press, 1991), 81–108.

[59] Information on annual expenditures is found in U.S. Census Bureau, *Statistical Abstract of the United States, 2003* (Washington, D.C.: Government Printing Office, 2003), tab. 812.

[60] Dick Lugar, "The Farm Bill Charade," *New York Times,* January 21, 2002, A15.

[61] Andrew S. McFarland, *Common Cause: Lobbying in the Public Interest* (Chatham, N.J.: Chatham House, 1984); see also Andrew S. McFarland, *Public Interest Lobbies: Decision Making on Energy* (Washington, D.C.: American Enterprise Institute, 1976).

[62] Ronald G. Shaiko, "More Bang for the Buck: The New Era of Full-Service Public Interest Groups," in *Interest Group Politics,* 3rd ed., ed. Cigler and Loomis, 109.

[63] Ibid., 120.

[64] For a discussion of the evolution of NOW and its success in lobbying Congress, see Anne N. Costain and W. Douglas Costain, "The Women's Lobby: Impact of a Movement on Congress," in *Interest Group Politics,* ed. Cigler and Loomis.

[65] Richard Morin and Claudia Deane, "The Administration's Right-Hand Women," *Washington Post National Weekly Edition,* May 7, 2001, 12.

[66] EMILY'S List home page, www.emilyslist.org.; Jeffrey H. Birnbaum and Eric Pooley, "New Party Bosses," *Time,* April 8, 1996, 28–32.

[67] Eric M. Uslaner, "A Tower of Babel on Foreign Policy," in *Interest Group Politics,* 3rd ed., ed. Cigler and Loomis, 309.

[68] Kenneth D. Wald, *Religion and Politics* (New York: St. Martin's Press, 1985), 182–212.

[69] Sidney Blumenthal, "Christian Soldiers," *New Yorker,* July 18, 1994, 36.

[70] James L. Guth, John C. Green, Lyman A. Jellstedt, and Corwin E. Struck, "Onward Christian Soldiers: Religious Activist Groups in American Politics," in *Interest Group Politics,* 3rd ed., ed. Cigler and Loomis, 57; Charles Levendosky, "Alternative Religious Voice Finally Being Raised," *Lincoln Journal Star,* March 3, 1996, 7B.

[71] Michael Lind, "The Right Still Has Religion," *New York Times,* December 9, 2001, Section 4, 13; Blumenthal, "Christian Soldiers."

[72] "Citing 'Moral Crisis,' a Call to Oust Clinton," *New York Times,* October 23, 1998, Al, A8.

[73] Richard Parker, "On God and Democrats," *American Prospect,* March 2004, 40.

[74] Richard Berke, "Falwell Is Raising Money to Press Conservative Family Agenda," *New York Times,* December 14, 2001, Al, A9.

[75] Laurie Goodstein, "Evangelical Leaders Join Global Warming Initiative," *New York Times,* February 8, 2006, online.

[76] Levendosky, "Alternative Religious Voice."

[77] Lynette Clemetson, "Clergy Group to Counter Conservatives," *New York Times,* November 17, 2003, A15.

[78] Stephanie Simon, "Atheist Organization Jubilant over Ruling on Pledge," *San Francisco Chronicle,* July 1, 2002, A2.

[79] Elisabeth Bumiller, "On Gay Marriage, Bush May Have Said All He's Going To," *New York Times,* March 1, 2004, A15.

[80] Sheryl Gay Stolberg, "Vocal Gay Republicans Upsetting Conservatives," *New York Times,* June 1, 2003, A15.

[81] Shawn Zeller, "Marching On, but Apart," *National Journal,* January 12, 2002, 98–103.

[82] Barmak Nassirian, associate executive director of the American Association of Collegiate Registrars and Admissions Officers, quoted in "Sally Mae's Romance with John Boehner," January 11, 2006, www.realclearpolitics.com/Commentary/com-1_11_06_FH.html

[83] Christopher J. Bosso, "Adaptation and Change in the Environmental Movement," in *Interest Group Politics,* 3rd ed., ed. Cigler and Loomis, 155–156.

[84] Ibid., 162.

[85] Ibid., 169.

[86] Andrew Goldstein, "Too Green for Their Own Good?" *Time,* August 26, 2002, A58.

[87] Katharine Q. Seelye, "Bush Team Still Reversing Environmental Policies," *New York Times,* November 18, 2001, A20.

[88] John Mintz, "Would Bush Be the NRA's Point Man in the White House?" *Washington Post National Weekly Edition,* May 8, 2000, 14; Mike Doming, "NRA Promises an All-Out Assault on Al Gore's Presidential Campaign," *Lincoln Journal Star,* May 21, 2000, 2A; Thomas B. Edsall, "Targeting Al Gore with $10 Million," *Washington Post National Weekly Edition,* May 29, 2000, 11.

[89] Linda Greenhouse, "U.S., in a Shift, Tells Justices Citizens Have a Right to Guns," *New York Times,* May 8, 2002, A1.

[90] Ibid.

[91] Ibid.

[92] "Echoes of Tobacco Battle in Gun Suits," *New York Times,* February 21, 1999, 18.

[93] Bob Herbert, "The NRA Is Naming Names," *New York Times,* October 13, 2004, A21.

[94] Robin Toner, "Abortion's Opponents Claim the Middle Ground," *New York Times,* April 25, 2004, Section 4, 1.

[95] Kate Zernike, "30 Years after Abortion Ruling, New Trends but the Old Debate," *New York Times,* January 20, 2003, A1, A16.

[96] Sam Howe Verhovek, "Creators of Antiabortion Web Site Told to Pay Millions," *New York Times,* February 3, 1999, A11.

[97] Charles Lane, "Ruling Curbs Abortion Foes' Tactics: Court Says 'Wanted' Posters and Web Site Are Intimidation," *Washington Post,* May 17, 2002, A2.

[98] Alissa Rubin, "Interest Groups and Abortion Politics in the Post-Webster Era," in *Interest Group Politics,* 3rd ed., ed. Cigler and Loomis, 249–251; *Congressional Quarterly Weekly Report,* March 27, 1993, 755–757; "More than a Million March in Washington for Reproductive Rights," press release, Planned Parenthood Federation of American, April 25, 2004.

[99] David S. Broder, "Let 100 Single-Issue Groups Bloom," *Washington Post,* January 7, 1979, C1–C2; see also David S. Broder, *The Party's Over: The Failure of Politics in America* (New York: Harper & Row, 1972).

[100] Wilson, *Interest Groups in America,* ch. 4.

[101] "Some Funny Facts About D.C.," *Parade Magazine,* March 19, 2006, 25.

[102] Charles Peters, "Tilting at Windmills: Scary Facts," *The Washington Monthly,* April 2006, 5.

[103] The following paragraphs on K Street are drawn from Nicholas Confessore, "Welcome to the Machine: How the GOP Disciplined K Street and Made Bush Supreme," *Washington Monthly,* July-August 2003, 31–37.

[104] Quote attributed to Lord Acton, a nineteenth-century historian.

[105] Ruth Marcus, "DeLay Exits, Stage (Hard) Right," *Washington Post* (June 12, 2006): A21.

[106] Ed Henry, "It's the '90s: Old Dogs, New Tricks," *Roll Call Monthly,* November 1997, 1.

[107] Diana M. Evans, "Lobbying the Committee: Interest Groups and the House Public Works and Transportation Committee in the Post-Webster Era," in *Interest Group Politics,* 3rd ed., ed. Cigler and Loomis, 257–276.

[108] Berry, Interest Group Society, 188.

[109] Birnbaum, *Lobbyists,* 40.

[110] Leslie Wayne and Michael Moss, "A Nation Challenged: The Airlines; Bailout for Airlines Showed the Weight of Mighty Lobby," *New York Times,* October 10, 2001, Al, B10.

[111] Ibid., B10.

[112] Ibid., B10.

[113] Ibid., B10.

[114] Todd S. Purdum, "Go Ahead, Try to Stop K Street," *New York Times,* January 8, 2006, WK 4.

[115] Robert Pear, "Lobbyists Seek Special Spin on Federal Bioterrorism Bill," *New York Times,* December 11, 2001, A1, A18.

[116] Ernest Wittenberg and Elisabeth Wittenberg, *How to Win in Washington* (Cambridge, Mass.: Blackwell, 1989), 24.

[117] Elizabeth Drew, *Politics and Money: The New Road to Corruption* (New York: Macmillan, 1983), 78.

[118] Ibid.

[119] Lowell Bergman and Jeff Gerth, "Power Trader Tied to Bush Finds Washington All Ears," *New York Times,* May 25, 2001, A1.

[120] Ibid.

[121] Eric Schmitt, "Nomination for FDA Post Nears Approval in Senate," *New York Times,* October 21, 1998, A13.

[122] Rebecca Adams, "Harvard Professor Faces Tough Questions but Is Expected to Win Confirmation as Head of Regulatory Affairs Office," *CQ Weekly,* May 19, 2001, 1166.

[123] Sheryl Gay Stolberg, "Bush in Political Hot Spot in Picking an FDA Chief," *New York Times,* February 8, 2002, A17; Sheryl Gay Stolberg, "Deputy Is Appointed to Direct Food and Drug Agency as Impasse Continues," *New York Times,* February 26, 2002, A22.

[124] Evelyn Nieves, "Civil Rights Groups Suing Berkeley over Admissions Policy," *New York Times,* February 3, 1999, A11.

[125] William Glaberson, "Groups Gird for Long Legal Fight on New Bush Antiterror Powers," *New York Times,* November 30, 2001, Al, B7.

[126] James Dao, "Environmental Groups to File Suit over Missile Defenses," *New York Times,* August 28, 2001, A10.

[127] For more on interest group litigation at the district court level, see Lee Epstein and C. K. Rowland, "Debunking the Myth of Interest

Group Invincibility in the Courts," *American Political Science Review* 85 (1991), 205–220.

[128]Samuel Kernell, *Going Public: New Strategies of Presidential Leadership* (Washington, D.C.: CQ Press, 1986), 34.

[129]Richard Harris, "If You Love Your Grass," *New Yorker*, April 20, 1968, 57.

[130]Alison Mitchell, "A New Form of Lobbying Puts Public Face on Private Interest," *New York Times*, September 30, 1998, Al, A14.

[131]Ibid.

[132]Evans, "Lobbying the Committee," 269.

[133]Michael Weisskopf, "Letting No Grass Roots Grow under Their Feet," *Washington Post National Weekly Edition*, October 24, 1993, 20–21.

[134]Sandra G. Boodman, "Health Care's Power Player," *Washington Post National Weekly Edition*, February 14, 1994, 6.

[135]John Cochran, "A New Medium for the Message," *CQ Weekly*, March 13, 2006, 654.

[136]Ibid., 7.

[137]Ibid., 7.

[138]Ibid., 7.

[139]"MoveOn's Big Moment," *Time*, November 24, 2003, 32.

[140]Cochran, op. cit., p. 656.

[141]Cochran, op. cit., p. 655.

[142]George Packer, "Smart-Mobbing the War," *New York Times Magazine*, March 9, 2003, 46–49.

[143]Boodman, "Health Care's Power Player," 7.

[144]James Dao, "The 2000 Campaign: The Grassroots," *New York Times*, October 21, 2000, Section 1, 18.

[145]Ibid.

[146]Michael Towle, "Ad for Fighter Plan Aimed at Congress," *Lincoln Journal Star*, May 2, 1997, 7A.

[147]Greenpeace, Denial and Deception: A Chronicle of ExxonMobil's Efforts to Corrupt the Debate on Global Warming (Washington, D.C.: Greenpeace, 2002).

[148]Birnbaum, *Lobbyists*, 40.

[149]Kate Aurthur, "Lifetime's Place Is in the House (and Senate)," *New York Times*, October 16, 2005, Section 2, p 30.

[150]Steven Greenhouse, "Carnival of Derision to Greet the Princes of Global Trade," *New York Times*, November 11, 1999, A12.

[151]Ibid.

[152]Dan Balz and David S. Broder, "Take Two Lobbyists and Call Me in the Morning," *Washington Post National Weekly Edition*, October 18, 1993, 10–11.

[153]Greg Schendier, "Unlikely Bedfellows," *Washington Post National Weekly Edition*, April 11–17, 2005, 20.

[154]R. Kenneth Godwin and Barry J. Seldon, "What Corporations Really Want from Government: The Public Provision of Private Goods," in *Interest Group Politics*, 6th ed., ed. Allan J. Cigler and Burdett A. Loomis (Washington, D.C.: CQ Press, 2002), 205–224.

[155]Much of the information in this section is from Burdett A. Loomis, "Coalitions of Interests: Building Bridges in the Balkanized State," in *Interest Group Politics*, 2nd ed., ed. Cigler and Loomis, 258–274.

[156]Birnbaum, *Lobbyists*, 83.

[157]David Segal, "Bob Dole Leads the Cast of Rainmakers," *Washington Post National Weekly Edition*, September 27, 1997, 20.

[158]Purdum, op. cit.

[159]Deborah L. Acomb, "Poll Track," *National Journal*, January 5, 2002, 58.

[160]Godwin and Seldon, "What Corporations Really Want."

[161]Dan Clawson, Alan Neustadt, and Denise Scott, *Money Talks* (New York: Basic Books, 1992), 91.

[162]Robert Wright, "Hyper Democracy," *Time*, January 23, 1995, 18.

[163]David S. Broder, "Can We Govern?" *Washington Post National Weekly Edition*, January 31, 1994, 23.

[164]The modern statement of this idea began with Robert Michels, who formulated the "iron law of oligarchy" in *Political Parties: A Sociological Study of the Oligarchical Tendencies of Modern Democracy*, trans. Eden and Cedar Paul (New York: Hearst International, 1915; originally published 1911).

[165]Schattschneider, *Semi-Sovereign People*, ch. 2.

[166]Ibid., 35.

[167]Kevin Phillips, "Fat City," *Time*, September 26, 1995, 51.

[168]Christopher Jencks, "On Unequal Democracy," *American Prospect*, June 2004, A2–A4; see also Katherine Neckerman, *Social Inequality* (New York: Russell Sage Foundation, 2004).

[169]Comment "Reckless Driver," *New Yorker Magazine*, March 8, 2004, 25.

[170]Associated Press, "Some Fear Immigration Protest Backlash," *New York Times*, April 19, 2006, online.

[171]Gillian Flaccus, "Making a Point," *Lincoln Journal Star*, May 2, 2006, 1A.

[172]Ibid.

[173]Monica Davey, "Producing Smaller Numbers, But Laying Claim to Majority," *New York Times*, May 2, 2006, online.

[174]Ibid.

[175]Randall Archibold, "Immigrants Take to U.S. Streets to Show of Strength," *New York Times*, May 2, 2006, online.

[176]Flaccus, op. cit., p. 2A.

Chapter 7

[1]Anne E. Kornblut, "Democrats Elect Dean as Committee Chairman," *New York Times*, February 13, 2005, online.

[2]Ibid.

[3]Paul Krugman, "The Fighting Moderates," *New York Times*, February 15, 2005, online.

[4] Anne E. Kornblut. "Dean's Remarks Draw Fire from Both Sides of the Aisle," *New York Times*, June 10, 2005, online.

[5]Adam Nagourney, "Dean and Party Leaders in a Money Dispute," *New York Times*, May 11, 2006, online.

[6]Dan Balz and Chris Cillizza, "Democratic Leaders Question Whether Dean's Right on the Money," *Washington Post*, March 5, 2006, A04.

[7]Mike Allen and Perry Bacon, Jr., "Whose Party is It?" *Time*, (June 12, 2006), 46.

[8]Jill Lawrence, "Democrats Rebuild on the Prairie," *USA Today*, June 13, 2006. www.usatoday.com/news/washington/ 2006-06-13-nebraska_x.htm.

[9]Allen and Bacon, p. 46.

[10]E. E. Schattschneider, *Party Government* (New York: Holt, Rinehart and Winston, 1960), 1.

[11]Jack Dennis, "Trends in Public Support for the American Party System," in *Parties and Elections in an Anti-Party Age*, ed. Jeff Fishel (Bloomington: Indiana University Press, 1978).

[12]Frank J. Sorauf, *Political Parties in the American System*, 4th ed. (Boston: Little, Brown, 1980).

[13]Ibid.

[14]Robert A. Dahl, *How Democratic Is the American Constitution?* (New Haven: Yale University Press, 2003), 30.

[15]Maurice Duverger, *Political Parties* (New York: Wiley, 1963). See also Edward R. Tufte, "The Relationship between Seats and Votes in Two-Party Systems," *American Political Science Review* 67 (1973), 540–554.

[16]Theodore J. Lowi, in *The Personal President: Power Invested, Promise Unfulfilled* (Ithaca, N.Y.: Cornell University Press, 1985), notes that the two-party system survived in the United States despite the use of multimember districts in elections for Congress in the nineteenth century.

[17]*CQ Weekly*, January 12, 2002, 136; *CQ Weekly*, January 2, 2004, 53.

[18]Robert S. Erikson, Gerald C. Wright, and John P. McIver, *Statehouse Democracy: Public Opinion and Policy in the American States* (New York: Cambridge University Press, 1993), ch. 5.

[19]Frank Bruni, "Bush Signaling Readiness to Go His Own Way," *New York Times*, April 3, 2000, A1–A15.

[20]Robert G. Kaiser, "Hindsight Is 20/20," *Washington Post National Weekly Edition*, February 19, 2001, 11. Nader's support in Florida and New Hampshire prevented Gore from winning those states.

[21]"Republicans Helping Nader," NewsMax.com, July 12, 2004 (www.newsmax.com/archives/articles/2004/7/11/160540.shtml). This amounted to about $50,000 of the $1 million Nader had raised at the time.

[22]Ralph Nader, "My Untold Story," *Brill's Content*, February 2001.

[23]Richard Hofstadter, *The Idea of the Party System: The Rise of Legitimate Opposition in the United States, 1780–1840* (Berkeley: University of California Press, 1969).

[24]Lowi, Personal Presidency.

[25]James MacGregor Burns, *The Vineyard of Liberty* (New York: Knopf, 1982).

[26]In 1820, there had been around 1.2 million free white men over twenty-five years of age; by 1840, there were 3.2 million white men of over the age of twenty.

[27]William L. Riordon, *Plunkitt of Tammany Hall* (New York: E.P. Dutton, 1963), 28.

[28]Milton L. Rakove, *Don't Make No Waves, Don't Back No Losers* (Bloomington: Indiana University Press, 1975), 112.

[29]Kevin Phillips, *The Emerging Republican Majority* (New York: Doubleday, 1969).

[30]In contrast, European parties do have members, who pay dues and sign a pledge that they accept the basic principles of the party. The percentage of voters who are members ranges from 1 or 2 percent in some countries to over 40 percent in others.

[31]Gallup Poll, May 12, 2006.

[32]James L. Sundquist, *Dynamics of the Party System: Alignment and Realignment of Political Parties in the United States* (Washington, D.C.: Brookings Institution, 1973).

[33]Phillips, *Emerging Republican Majority*.

[34]Tali Mendelberg, *The Race Card* (Princeton, N.J.: Princeton University Press, 2001).

[35]Ibid., 97.

[36]Ibid., 3.

[37]Thomas F. Shaller, "Forget the South," *Washington Post National Weekly Edition*, November 24, 2003, 21.

[38]Thomas B. Edsall, "The Fissure Running through the Democratic Party," *Washington Post National Weekly Edition*, June 6, 1994, 11.

[39]John R. Petrocik and Frederick T. Steeper, "The Political Landscape in 1988," *Public Opinion,* September–October 1987, 41–44; Helmut Norpoth, "Party Realignment in the 1980s," *Public Opinion Quarterly* 51 (1987), 376–390.

[40]Edsall, "Fissure," 11.

[41]Thomas B. Edsall, "The Shifting Sands of America's Political Parties," *Washington Post National Weekly Edition,* April 9, 2001, 11.

[42]Mary Agnes Carey, "Democrats Want Women: Party Targets Single Female Voters," *CQ Weekly,* March 6, 2004, 567.

[43]Gebe Martinez and Mary Agnes Carey, "Erasing the Gender Gap Tops Republican Playbook," *CQ Weekly,* March 6, 2004, 565.

[44]Ibid.

[45]David Sarasohn, "Wall Falls on Reagan Coalition," *Lincoln Sunday Journal Star,* February 18, 1990, 1C.

[46]David Von Drehle, "The Left Invigorated," *Washington Post National Weekly Edition,* July 14, 2003, 13.

[47]Steven Roberts, "Near-Death Experience," *U.S. News and World Report,* November 6, 1996, 28.

[48]Ibid.

[49]National Election Studies, Center for Political Studies, University of Michigan, 1952–2000 (www.umich.edu/nes).

[50]Everett Carill Ladd, *Where Have All the Voters Gone?* (New York: Norton, 1982).

[51]Martin P. Wallenberg, *The Rise of Candidate-Centered Politics* (Cambridge, Mass.: Harvard University Press, 1991).

[52]Thomas E. Patterson, *The Vanishing Voter* (New York: Knopf, 2002).

[53]Walter Dean Burnham, *Critical Elections and the Mainstream of American Politics* (New York: Norton, 1970); Helmut Norpoth and Jerrold Rusk, "Partisan Dealignment in the American Electorate," *American Political Science Review* 76 (1982), 522–537; David W. Rhode, "The Fall Elections: Realignment and Dealignment," *Chronicle of Higher Education,* December 14, 1994, 131–132.

[54]John R. Petrocik, "Realignment," *Journal of Politics* 49 (1987), 347–375; George Rabinowitz, Paul-Henri Gurian, and Stuart MacDonald, "The Structure of Presidential Elections and the Process of Realignment," *American Journal of Political Science* 28 (1984), 611–635; David S. Broder, "The GOP Plays Dixie," *Washington Post National Weekly Edition,* September 12, 1988, 4; Thomas B. Edsall, "A Serious Case of White Flight," *Washington Post National Weekly Edition,* September 10, 1990, 13.

[55]*CQ Weekly,* January 9, 2006, p. 86.

[56]For a discussion of party influence on voting in Congress, see William R. Shaffer, *Party and Ideology in the United States Congress* (Lanham, Md.: University Press of America, 1980).

[57]Bruce I. Oppenheimer, "The Importance of Elections in a Strong Congressional Era," in *Do Elections Matter?* ed. Benjamin Ginsberg and Alan Stone (Armonk, N.Y.: Sharpe, 1996), 120–138.

[58]David S. Broder, "Polarization a Growing Force for Political Parties," *Lincoln Journal Star,* January 22,1995, 4B.

[59]Dan Carney, "As Hostilities Rage on the Hill, Partisan-Vote Rate Soars," *Congressional Quarterly Weekly Report,* January 27, 1996, 199–200.

[60]Mary Lunn F. Jones, "Rock and a Hard Place," *American Prospect,* June 2003, 18–19.

[61]*Congressional Quarterly Weekly Report,* December 11, 1999, 2993–2994; *CQ Weekly,* January 3, 2004, 48.

[62]Lloyd Grove, "A Good Ol' Boy Going in for the Kill," *Washington Post National Weekly Edition,* August 22, 1998, 12–13.

[63]Frank J. Sorauf, *Money in American Elections* (Glenview, Ill.: Scott, Foresman, 1988), 121–153; Paul Herrnson, *Party Campaigning in the 1980s* (Cambridge, Mass.: Harvard University Press, 1988).

[64]Federal Election Commission, Campaign Finance Reports and Data: Party Activity, 2002 (www.fec.gov).

[65]Anthony Corrado and Heitor Gouvea, "Financial Presidential Nominations under the BCRA," in *The Making of the Presidential Candidate, 2004,* ed. William G. Mayer (Lanham, Md.: Rowman & Littlefield, 2003).

[66]Xandra Kayden, "The Nationalization of the Party System," in *Parties, Interest Groups, and Campaign Finance Laws,* ed. Michael Malbin (Washington, D.C.: American Enterprise Institute, 1980).

[67]Stanley Kelley Jr., *Interpreting Elections* (Princeton, N.J.: Princeton University Press, 1983); Stanley Kelley Jr., Richard Ayres, and William G. Bower, "Registration and Voting: Putting First Things First," *American Political Science Review* 61 (1967), 359–379.

[68]Marjorie Connelly, "Who Voted," *New York Times,* November 12, 2000, 4.

[69]Gallup Poll, "Public Divide on Bush: Great Partisan Difference in Job Approval," March 10, 2004.

[70]Data from "Portrait of an Electorate," *New York Times,* November 10, 1996, 28; Lee Sigelman, "If You Prick Us, Do We Not Bleed? If You Tickle Us, Do We Not Laugh? Jews and Pocketbook Voting," paper prepared for presentation at the 1990 American Political Science Meeting; Susan Welch and Lee Sigelman, "The Politics of Hispanic Americans," *Social Science Quarterly,* 1991; New York Times, November 5, 1992, B9.

[71]Paul Abramson, John H. Aldrich, and David Rohde, *Change and Continuity in the 2000 Elections* (Washington, D.C.: CQ Press, 2003).

[72]Ibid.

[73]In recent elections, the percentages able to identify correctly general differences between the major party candidates varied between 26 and 55 percent.

[74] Abramson, Aldrich, and Rohde, *Change and Continuity, 2000.*

[75]Ibid.

[76]Paul Abramson, John H. Aldrich, and David Rohde, *Change and Continuity in the 1996 Elections* (Washington, D.C.: CQ Press, 1998).

[77]Morris Fiorina, *Retrospective Voting in American National Elections* (New Haven, Conn.: Yale University Press, 1981).

[78]Edward R. Tufte, *Political Control of the Economy* (Princeton, N.J.: Princeton University Press, 1978); Douglas Hibbs, "The Mass Public and Macroeconomic Performance," *American Journal of Political Science* 23 (1979), 705–731; John Hibbing and John Alford, "The Electoral Impact of Economic Conditions: Who Is Held Responsible," *American Journal of Political Science* 25 (1981), 423–439.

[79]Robert Kaiser, "Deeply Divided We Stand—and That's No Surprise," *Washington Post National Weekly Edition,* November 20, 2000, 22.

Chapter 8

[1]James Moore and Wayne Slater used that label to title their book, *Bush's Brain: How Karl Rove Made George W. Bush Presidential.* Hoboken, New Jersey: John Wiley and Sons, 2003.

[2]For one media reflection on this pattern, see Joshua Micah Marshall, "Toying with Terror Alerts," *Time* (July 7, 2006): online at www.time.com/time/nation/article/0,8599,1211369,00.html.

[3]Gallup Poll, October 5, 2004.

[4]Richard Morin and Dana Milbank, "Bush and GOP Enjoy Record Popularity," *Washington Post,* January 29, 2002, A01.

[5]"White House Defends Rove over 9/11 Remarks," MSNBC from an AP release, June 24, 2005, www.msnbc.msn.com/id/8324598/.

[6]Libby Copeland, "Politics by the Numbers," *Washington Post National Weekly Edition,* (June 19–25, 2006), 14; Dan Balz and Chris Cillizza, "The Races to Watch," *Washington Post National Weekly Edition,* (February 13–19, 2006), 8.

[7]Jonathan Weisman, "Can They 'Ride a Wave'?" *Washington Post National Weekly Edition,* (April 17–23, 2006), 14. See also James Dao and Adam Nagourney, "They Served, and Now They're Running," *New York Times,* (February 19, 2006), Week in Review, 1.

[8]"Election 2006," *The Gallup Poll,* March 2, 2006, online.

[9]"Presidential Job Approval in Depth," *The Gallup Poll,* March 3, 2006, online.

[10]Gallup Poll, December 15, 2005.

[11]Nicholas D. Kristoff, "The Soldiers Speak. Will President Bush Listen?" *New York Times,* February 26, 2005, online.

[12]For an explanation of the conservative case against Bush, see Richard A. Viguerie, "Fury on the Right," *Washington Post National Weekly Edition,* May 29–June 4, 2006, 20.

[13]William H. Flanigan, *Political Behavior of the American Electorate,* 2nd ed. (Boston: Allyn and Bacon, 1972), 13. See also Chilton Williamson, *American Suffrage from Property to Democracy 1760–1860* (Princeton, N.J.: Princeton University Press, 1960).

[14]James MacGregor Burns, *Vineyard of Liberty* (New York: Knopf, 1982), 363.

[15]August Meier and Elliot M. Rudwick, *From Plantation to Ghetto: An Interpretive History of American Negroes* (New York: Hill & Wang, 1966), 69.

[16]Robert Darcy, Susan Welch, and Janet Clark, *Women, Elections, and Representation* (Lincoln: University of Nebraska Press, 1994).

[17]Ralph G. Neas, "The Long Shadow of Jim Crow: Voter Intimidation and Suppression in America Today," *People for the American Way Foundation,* August 2004, or online at www.naacp.org/inc/pdf/jimcrow.pdf.

[18]Grandfather clause: *Guinn v. United States,* 238 U.S. 347 (1915); white primary: *Smith v. Allwright,* 321 U.S. 649 (1944).

[19]Data on black and white voter registration in the southern states are from the *Statistical Abstract of the United States* (Washington, D.C.: U.S. Bureau of the Census, various years).

[20]California, Florida, Michigan, New Hampshire, New York, and South Dakota.

[21]Richard J. Timpone, "Mass Mobilization or Government Intervention? The Growth of Black Registration in the South," *Journal of Politics* 57 (1995), 425–442.

[22]*City of Mobile v. Bolden,* 446 U.S. 55 (1980).

[23]*Thornburg v. Gingles,* 478 U.S. 301 (1986).

[24]Bob Benenson, "Arduous Ritual of Redistricting Ensures More Racial Diversity," *Congressional Quarterly Weekly Report,* October 24, 1992, 3385. For a very thorough review of the legal and behavioral impact of the Voting Rights Act, see

Joseph Viteritti, "Unapportioned Justice: Local Elections, Social Science, and the Evolution of the Voting Rights Act," *Cornell Journal of Law and Public Policy* (1994), 210–270.

[25] *Shaw v. Reno,* 125 L.Ed.2d 511, 113 S.Ct. 2816 (1993); *Miller v. Johnson,* 132 L.Ed.2d 762, 115 S.Ct. 2475 (1995); *Bush v. Vera,* 135 L.Ed.2d 248, 116 S.Ct. 1941 (1996).

[26] Darcy et al., *Women, Elections, and Representation.*

[27] Speech in 1867 by George Williams cited in Peter Pappas's "Re-defining the Role of Women in Industrial America" at www.peterpappas.com/journals/industry/women3.pdf.

[28] The discussion in this paragraph is drawn largely from Lois W. Banner, *Women in Modern America: A Brief History* (New York: Harcourt Brace Jovanovich, 1974), 88–90; Glenn Firebaugh and Kevin Chen, "Vote Turnout of Nineteenth Amendment Women," *American Journal of Sociology* 100 (1995), 972–996.

[29] Alabama, Florida, Virginia, and Kentucky.

[30] Nicholas Thompson, "Locking Up the Vote: Disenfranchisement of Former Felons was the Real Crime in Florida," *Washington Monthly,* (January–February 2001), 17–21; see also Amanda Ripley, "Barred from the Ballot," *Time,* January 21, 2001, 63. Data cited are from a forthcoming book by Jeff Manza and Christopher Uggen, *Locking Up the Vote* (New York: Oxford University Press, 2005).

[31] Thompson, ibid., 18.

[32] "Groups Report Progress against Laws Banning Felons from Voting," *Lincoln Journal Star,* (June 22, 2005), 4a.

[33] Thompson, ibid., 20.

[34] Tom Fiedler, "The Perfect Storm," in *Overtime!: The Election 2000 Thriller,* ed. Larry J. Sabato (New York: Longman, 2002), 11.

[35] Liz Krueger, "Budgeting for Another Florida," *New York Times,* February 8, 2004, 14.

[36] Dale Keiger, "E-lective Alarm," *Johns Hopkins Magazine,* February 2004, 50.

[37] Ibid.

[38] See report of Electiononline.org on voting law changes at www.electionline.org/site/docs/pdf/2004.Election.Preview.Final.Report.pdf.

[39] Richard Jensen, "American Election Campaigns: A Theoretical and Historical Typology," paper delivered at the 1968 Midwest Political Science Association Meeting, quoted in Walter Dean Burnham, *Critical Elections and the Mainsprings of American Politics* (New York: Norton, 1970), 73.

[40] Frances Fox Piven and Richard A. Cloward, *Why Americans Don't Vote* (New York: Pantheon Books, 1988), 30.

[41] These examples are from editorial, "Barriers to Student Voting," *New York Times,* September 28, 2004, 26.

[42] Part of the explanation for declining voting rates is that the number of citizens who are ineligible to vote has increased, which depresses voter turnout statistics. Immigrants, other noncitizens, and, in some states, convicted felons are not eligible to vote. When those individuals are removed from the calculation of proportion voting, the proportion voting is increased by about five points; and most of the turnout decline occurred in the 1960s. See Michael P. McDonald and Samuel Popkin, "The Myth of the Vanishing Voter," *American Political Science Review* 95 (2001), 963–974.

[43] *Statistical Abstract of the United States 2006,* Table 405. This self-report is probably an overestimate.

[44] *Statistical Abstract of the United States 2006,* Table 406.

[45] Daniel J. Elazar, *American Federalism: A View from the States* (New York: Crowell, 1972); *Statistical Abstract of the United States 2006,* Table 406.

[46] Norman H. Nie, Sidney Verba, Henry Brady, Kay Lehman Schlozman, and Jane Junn, "Participation in America: Continuity and Change," presented at the Midwest Political Science Association, April 1988. The standard work, though now dated, on American political participation is Sidney Verba and Norman H. Nie, *Participation in America: Political Democracy and Social Equality* (New York: Harper & Row, 1972).

[47] Piven and Cloward, *Why Americans Don't Vote,* 162; *Statistical Abstract of the United States 2001,* Table 401; Piven and Cloward, *Why Americans Still Don't Vote: And Why Politicians Want It That Way* (Boston: Beacon Press, 2001).

[48] G. Bingham Powell, "American Voter Turnout in Comparative Perspective," *American Political Science Review* 80 (1986), 30; Piven and Cloward, *Why Americans Don't Vote,* 119; Arend Lijphart, "Unequal Participation: Democracy's Unresolved Dilemma," *American Political Science Review* 91 (1997), 1–14.

[49] Brady et al., "Beyond SES: A Resource Model of Political Participation."

[50] Nie et al., "Participation in America: Continuity and Change"; Verba and Nie, *Participation in America: Political Democracy and Social Equality.*

[51] Steven Hill and Rashad Robinson, "Demography vs. Democracy: Young People Feel Left Out of the Political Process," *Los Angeles Times,* November 5, 2002, 2. Posted by the Youth Vote Coalition (www.youthvote.org/news/newsdetail.cfm?newsid56). The survey cited was conducted by Harvard University.

[52] Eric Plutzer, "Becoming a Habitual Voter: Inertia, Resources, and Growth in Young Adulthood," *American Political Science Review* 96 (2002), 41–56.

[53] Anna Greenberg, "New Generation, New Politics," *American Prospect,* October 1, 2003, A3.

[54] Paul Allen Beck and M. Kent Jennings, "Political Periods and Political Participation," *American Political Science Review* 73 (1979), 737–750; Nie et al., "Participation in America: Continuity and Change."

[55] George F. Will, "In Defense of Nonvoting," *Newsweek,* October 10, 1983, 96.

[56] Richard Morin, "The Dog Ate My Forms, and, Well, I Couldn't Find a Pen," *Washington Post National Weekly Edition,* November 5, 1990, 38.

[57] Lawrence R. Jacobs and Robert Y. Shapiro, *Politicians Don't Pander: Political Manipulation and the Loss of Democratic Responsiveness* (Chicago: University of Chicago Press, 2000).

[58] Priscilla L. Southwell, "Voter Turnout in the 1986 Congressional Elections," *American Politics Quarterly* 19 (1991), 96–108; Stephen Ansolabehere, Shanto Iyengar, Adam Simon, and Nicholas Valentino, "Does Attack Advertising Demobilize the Electorate?" *American Political Science Review* 88 (1994), 829–838.

[59] Richard Lau, Lee Sigelman, Caroline Heldman, and Paul Babbitt, "The Effects of Negative Political Advertisements," *American Political Science Review* 93 (1999), 851–875; Steven E. Finkel and John Geer, "A Spot Check: Casting Doubt on the Demobilizing Effect of Attack Advertising," *American Journal of Political Science* 42 (1998), 573–595. Research on turnout is found in Stephen Ansolabehere and Shanto Iyengar, *Going Negative* (New York: Free Press, 1996). In her book *Packaging the Presidency: A History and Criticism of Presidential Campaign Advertising* (New York: Oxford University Press, 1984), Kathleen Jamieson also argues that there are checks on misleading advertising, but later ("Is the Truth Now Irrelevant in Presidential Campaigns?"), she notes that these checks do not always work well. See Jamieson, *Dirty Politics: Deception, Distraction, and Democracy* (New York: Oxford University Press, 1992).

[60] Thomas E. Patterson, *The Vanishing Voter* (New York: Knopf, 2002); Curtis B. Gans; "The Empty Ballot Box," *Public Opinion* 1 (September–October 1978), 54–57; Curtis Gans, quoted in Jack Germond and Jules Witcover, "Listen to the Voters—and Nonvoters," *Minneapolis Star Tribune,* November 26, 1988. This effect was foreshadowed by Michael J. Robinson, "American Political Legitimacy in an Era of Electronic Journalism," in *Television as a Social Force: New Approaches to TV Criticism,* eds. Douglass Cater and Richard Adler (New York: Praeger, 1975). See also Austin Ranney, *Channels of Power: The Impact of Television on American Politics* (New York: Basic Books, 1983); and Richard Boyd, "The Effect of Election Calendars on Voter Turnout," paper presented at the Annual Meeting of the Midwest Political Science Association, April 1987, Chicago.

[61] Boyd, "The Effect of Election Calendars on Voter Turnout," 43. See Piven and Cloward, *Why Americans Don't Vote,* 196–197, for illustrations of these kinds of informal barriers, and Piven and Cloward, *Why Americans Still Don't Vote: And Why Politicians Want It That Way,* for further examples.

[62] Ibid.

[63] Ruy Texeira, *Why Americans Don't Vote: Turnout Decline in the United States 1960–1984* (Boulder, Colo.: Greenwood, 1987); Texeira, *The Disappearing American Voter* (Washington, D.C.: Brookings Institute, 1992); and Peverill Squire, Raymond Wolfinger, and David Glass, "Residential Mobility and Voter Turnout," *American Political Science Review* 81 (1987), 45–66.

[64] Jennifer Joan Lee, "Pentagon Blocks Site for Voters Outside U.S.," *International Herald Tribune,* September 20, 2004.

[65] Piven and Cloward, *Why Americans Don't Vote,* 17.

[66] For a review of these studies, see Bill Winders, "The Roller Coaster of Class Conflict: Class Segments, Mass Mobilization, and Voter Turnout in the United States, 1840–1996," *Social Forces* 77 (1999), 833–860.

[67] Ibid.

[68] Raymond E. Wolfinger and Steven J. Rosenstone, *Who Votes?* (New Haven, Conn.: Yale University Press, 1980), Table 6-1.

[69] Steven J. Rosenstone and Raymond E. Wolfinger, "The Effect of Registration Laws on Voter Turnout," *American Political Science Review* 72 (1978), 22–45; Glenn Mitchell and Christopher Wlezien, "Voter Registration Laws and Turnout, 1972–1982," paper presented at the Annual Meeting of the Midwest Political Science Association, April 1989, Chicago; Mark J. Fenster, "The Impact of Allowing Day of Registration Voting on Turnout in U.S. Elections from 1960 to 1992," *American Politics Quarterly* 22 (1994), 74–87.

[70] Kim Quaile Hill and Jan E. Leighley, "Racial Diversity, Voter Turnout, and Mobilizing Institutions in the United States," *American Politics Quarterly* 27 (1999), 275–295.

[71] "Block the Vote," *New York Times,* (May 30, 2006) editorial.

[72] "Block the Vote, Ohio Remix," *New York Times,* (June 7, 2006) editorial.

[73]Sasha Abramssky, *Moral Panic Conned: How Millions Went to Prison, Lost the Vote, and Helped Send George W. Bush to the White House.* New Press: 2006. This book is partly anecdotal but does point out the huge numbers of people disenfranchised by both laws and intimidation.

[74]See www.Tallahassee.com/mld/tallahassee/news/9202503.htm.

[75]Piven and Cloward, *Why Americans Don't Vote,* 230–231.

[76]Stephen Knack, "Does 'Motor Voter' Work?" *Journal of Politics* 57 (1995), 796–811.

[77]Michael Martinez and David Hill, "Did Motor Voter Work?" *American Political Quarterly* 27 (1999), 296–315; Piven and Cloward, *Why Americans Still Don't Vote: And Why Politicians Want It That Way.*

[78]These examples are drawn from Raymond Wolfinger, Benjamin Highton, and Megan Mullin, "How Postregistration Laws Affect the Turnout of Blacks and Latinos," paper presented at the 2003 Annual Meeting of the American Political Science Association, Philadelphia, Pennsylvania, August 28–31.

[79]Jo Becker, "Voters May Have Their Say before Election Day," *Washington Post,* August 26, 2004, A01.

[80]Texas, Minnesota, Louisiana, and Missouri are the only states west of the Mississippi not allowing unrestricted absentee voting; Florida, North Carolina, Vermont, and Maine are the only states east of the Mississippi who do. See Michael Moss, "Parties See New Promise When Ballot Is in the Mail," *New York Times,* August 22, 2004, 12; R. W. Apple, Jr., "Kerry Pins Hopes in Iowa on Big Vote from Absentees," *New York Times,* September 28, 2004, 18.

[81]Apple, Jr., ibid.

[82]Diane Feldman and Cornell Belcher, "Democracy at Risk, the 2004 Election in Ohio," report for the Democratic National Committee found online at http://a9.g.akamai.net/7/9/8082/v001/www.democrats.org/pdfs/ohvrireport/fullreport.pdf.

[83]More recent studies of turnout include Richard J. Timpone, "Structure, Behavior and Voter Turnout in the United States," *American Political Science Review* 92 (1998), 145–158; Henry Brady, Sidney Verba, and Kay Lehman Schlozman, "Beyond SES: A Resource Model of Political Participation," *American Political Science Review* 89 (1995), 271–294.

[84]Winder, "The Roller Coaster of Class Conflict: Class Segments, Mass Mobilization, and Voter Turnout in the United States, 1840–1996." For a review of this literature, see John Petrocik, "Voter Turnout and Electoral Preference," in *Elections in America,* ed. Kay Lehman Schlozman (Boston: Allen & Unwin, 1987). See also Bernard Grofman, Guillermo Owen, and Christian Collet, "Rethinking the Partisan Effects of Higher Turnout," *Public Choice* 99 (1999), 357–376.

[85]Tom Hamburger and Peter Wallsten, "Parties Are Tracking Your Habits," Los Angeles Times, July 24, 2005: www.latimes.com/news/nationworld/nation/lanarncdnc24jul24,0,535024, full.story

[86]Paul Farhi, "Politics Enters the Information Age," *Washington Post National Weekly Edition,* July 26, 2004, 13.

[87]Kim Quaile Hill, Jan Leighley, and Angela Hinton-Anderson, "Lower-Class Mobilization and Policy Linkage in the U.S. States," *American Journal of Political Science* 39 (1995), 75–86.

[88]Miles Rapoport, "The Democracy We Deserve," *Prospect* (January, 2005): A7.

[89]"Numbers," *Time,* (May 15, 2006), 17.

[90]Anthony Downs, *An Economic Theory of Democracy* (New York: Harper, 1957).

[91]Morin, "The Dog Ate My Forms, and, Well, I Couldn't Find a Pen."

[92]Kay Lehman Schlozman, Sidney Verba, and Henry Brady, "Participation's Not a Paradox: The View from American Activists," *British Journal of Political Science* 25 (1995), 1–36.

[93]The following discussion draws heavily upon John H. Aldrich, *Before the Convention: Strategies and Choices in Presidential Nomination Campaigns* (Chicago: University of Chicago Press, 1980).

[94]Ibid. See also David W. Rohde, "Risk Bearing and Progressive Ambition: The Case of Members of the United States House of Representatives," *American Journal of Political Science* 23 (1979), 1–26.

[95]Quoted in Audrey A. Haynes, Paul-Henri Gurian, Stephen M. Nichols, "The Role of Candidate Spending in Presidential Nomination Campaigns," *Journal of Politics* 59 (February 1997), 213–225.

[96]Ibid.

[97]"Political Grapevine," *Time,* February 8, 1988, 30.

[98]Hendrick Hertzberg, "This Must Be the Place," *New Yorker,* January 31, 2000, 36–39.

[99]"The Fall Campaign," *Newsweek Election Extra,* November–December 1984, 88.

[100]B. Drummond Ayres Jr., "It's Taking Care of Political Business," *New York Times,* July 18, 1999, 22.

[101]Bruce Babbitt, "Bruce Babbitt's View from the Wayside," *Washington Post National Weekly Edition,* February 24, 1988, 24. The one thousand days figure is from the *Congressional Quarterly Weekly Report,* February 1, 1992, 257.

[102]Katharine Q. Seelye and Marjorie Connelly, "Republican Delegates Leaning to Right of G.O.P. and the Nation," *New York Times,* August 29, 2004, 13.

[103]Gerald M. Pomper and Susan S. Lederman, *Elections in America: Control and Influence in Democratic Politics* (New York: Longman, 1980), ch. 7.

[104]Quote from Gerald M. Pomper in Adam Nagourney, "What Boston Can Do for Kerry," *New York Times,* July 18, 2004, 5.

[105]David Carr, "Whose Convention Is It? Reporters Outnumber Delegates 6 to 1" *New York Times,* July 27, 2004, E1.

[106]Lee Sigelman and Paul Wahlbeck, "The 'Veepstakes': Strategic Choice in Presidential Running Mate Selection," *American Political Science Review* 94 (1997), 855–864.

[107]Ibid.

[108]Ibid.

[109]Robert L. Dudley and Ronald B. Rapaport, "Vice-Presidential Candidates and the Home State Advantage: Playing Second Banana at Home and on the Road," *American Journal of Political Science* 33 (1989), 537–540.

[110]*New York Times,* July 11, 2004, 16.

[111]Associated Press, "Nader Denied Spots on Several State Ballots," October 14, 2004. Article online at www.firstamendmentcenter.org/news.aspx?id514192.

[112]Daron Shaw, "A Study of Presidential Campaign Event Effects from 1952 to 1992," *Journal of Politics* 61 (1999), 387–422.

[113]See *Congressional Quarterly,* July 23, 1988, 2015; Thomas M. Holbrook, "Campaigns, National Conditions and U.S. Presidential Elections," *American Journal of Political Science* 38 (1994), 973–998.

[114]Benjamin I. Page and Richard A. Brody, "Policy Voting and the Electoral Process: The Vietnam War Issue," *American Political Science Review* 66 (1972), 979–995.

[115]The discussion of the functions of the media relies heavily on the excellent summary found in Stephen Ansolabehere, Roy Behr, and Shanto Iyengar, "Mass Media and Elections," *American Politics Quarterly* 19 (1991), 109–139.

[116]Kathleen Hall Jamieson, "Ad Wars," *Washington Post National Weekly Edition,* October 4, 2004, 22.

[117]L. Marvin Overby and Jay Barth," Radio Advertising in American Political Campaigns," *American Politics Research* 34 (July, 2006): 451–478.

[118]Robert MacNeil, *People Machine: The Influence of Television on American Politics* (New York: Harper & Row, 1968), 182.

[119]Elisabeth Bumiller, "Selling Soup, Wine and Reagan," *Washington Post National Weekly Edition,* November 5, 1984, 6–8.

[120]Jim Rutenberg, "Seeking Voters through Habits in TV Viewing," *New York Times,* July 18, 2004, 1.

[121]Data are drawn from Rutenberg, ibid. See Thomas E. Mann, "Elections and Change in Congress," in *The New Congress,* eds. Thomas E. Mann and Norman J. Ornstein (Washington, D.C.: American Enterprise Institute for Public Policy Research, 1981), 32–54; David Mayhew, *Congress: The Electoral Connection* (New Haven, Conn.: Yale University Press, 1974); Glenn R. Parker and Roger H. Davidson, "Why Do Americans Love Their Congressmen So Much More Than Their Congress?" *Legislative Studies Quarterly* 4 (1979), 53–62.

[122]Daron Shaw, "The Methods behind the Madness: Presidential Electoral College Strategies, 1988–1996," *Journal of Politics* 61 (1999), 893–913, shows the evolution of advertising focus during these three elections.

[123]Dana Milbank and Jim VandeHei, "The Mean Season Is in Full Bloom," *Washington Post National Weekly Edition,* June 7, 2004, 13. Both campaigns agreed the figures were accurate.

[124]John Theilmann and Allen Wilhite, "Campaign Tactics and the Decision to Attack," *Journal of Politics* 60 (1998), 1050–1062.

[125]The study of negative advertising research was done by Richard Lau, Lee Sigelman, Caroline Heldman, and Paul Babbitt, "The Effects of Negative Political Advertisements," *American Political Science Review* 93 (1999), 851–875.

[126]Howard Kurtz, "The Ad-Slingers in the TV Corral," *Washington Post,* October 10, 2004, A06.

[127]Ibid.

[128]Democratic consultants are more likely to find negative advertising distasteful than Republican consultants. However, this does not necessarily translate into partisan differences in use.

[129]Paul Taylor, "Pigsty Politics," *Washington Post National Weekly Edition,* February 13, 1989, 6.

[130]Eileen Shields West, "Give 'Em Hell These Days Is a Figure of Speech," *Smithsonian* (October 1988), 149–151. The editorial was from the Connecticut Courant.

[131]Charles Paul Freund, "But Then, Truth Has Never Been Important," *Washington Post National Weekly Edition,* November 7, 1988, 29.

[132]Quoted in Freund, "But Then, Truth Has Never Been Important," 29.

[133]Ansolabehere and Iyengar, *Going Negative.*

[134]Jamieson, *Packaging the Presidency: A History and Criticism of Presidential Campaign Advertising.*

[135]Thomas E. Patterson, *The Mass Media Election: How Americans Choose Their President* (New York: Praeger, 1980), 3.

[136]Martin Schram, *The Great American Video Game: Presidential Politics in the Television Age* (New York: Morrow, 1987).

[137]Mike Allen, "Bush's Isolation from Reporters Could Be a Hindrance," *Washington Post,* October 8, 2004, A09.

[138]Daron Shaw, "A Study of Presidential Campaign Event Effects from 1952 to 1992," *Journal of Politics* 61 (May, 1999), 387–422, reports on a systematic study of campaign events and their impact on the elections.

[139]Adam Nagourney, "Internet Injects Sweeping Change into U.S. Politics," *New York Times,* (April 2, 2006), 1ff.

[140]David Perlmutter, "Political Blogs: The New Iowa?" *Chronicle of Higher Education* (May 26, 2006), B6.

[141]Robert Dahl, *How Democratic Is the American Constitution?* Yale University Press, 2001.

[142]Akhil Reed Amar, *America's Constitution: A Biography* (Random House, 2005).

[143]Ibid.

[144]Quoted in Alan M. Dershowitz, *Supreme Injustice: How the High Court Hijacked Election 2000* (New York: Oxford University Press, 2001), 25.

[145]Hendrik Hertzberg, "Up for the Count," *New Yorker,* December 18, 2000, 41.

[146]Kosuke Imai and Gary King, "Did Illegally Counted Overseas Absentee Ballots Decide the 2000 U.S. Presidential Election?" available at gking.Harvard.edu.

[147]Ibid.

[148]David Barstow and Don Van Natta Jr., "How Bush Took Florida: Mining the Overseas Absentee Vote," *New York Times,* July 15, 2001, available at www.nytimes.com/2001/07/15/ www. national/15ball.

[149]Ibid.

[150]Jonathan Wand, Kenneth Shotts, Jasjeet Sekhon, Walter R. Mebane, Jr., Michael Herron, and Henry Brady, "The Butterfly Did It: The Aberrant Vote for Buchanan in Palm Beach," *American Political Science Review* 95 (2001), 793–809. They examined the Palm Beach Buchanan vote in relation to all other counties in the United States to the absentee ballots (which did not use the butterfly format) in Palm Beach County, precinct-level data, and individual ballots.

[151]Tom Fiedler, "The Perfect Storm," in *Overtime! The Election 2000 Thriller,* ed. Larry J. Sabato (New York: Longman, 2002), 8.

[152]Imal and King, 3.

[153]Jimmy Carter, quoted from *NPR* in Kéllia Ramares's special report "House Strikes Truth from the Record," *Online Journal,* July 23, 2004. You can find the full Ramares article at www. onlinejournal.com/Special_Reports/ 072304Ramares/072304ramares.html.

[154]Andrew Gelman, Boris Shor, Joseph Bafumi, David Park, "Rich State, Poor State, Red State, Blue State: What's the Matter with Connecticut?" abstract and slides can be found at http://home.uchicago.edu/~bshor/papers. A summary can be found at http://harrisschool. uchicago.edu/about/publications/HarrisView/ spring06/shor.asp.

[155]Alan Abramowitz, "Terrorism, Gay Marriage, and Incumbency: Explaining the Republican Victory in the 2004 Presidential Election," *The Forum* 2 (Issue 4); 2004. Found online at the Berkeley Electronic Press: www.bepress.com/forum.

[156]For example, see Norman J. Ornstein and Thomas E. Mann, ed., *The Permanent Campaign and Its Future* (Washington, D.C.: American Enterprise Institute and the Brookings Institution, 2000).

[157]"Pass the Pancakes," *Newsweek,* (July 17, 2006), 17.

[158]See Thomas E. Mann, "Elections and Change in Congress," in *The New Congress;* Mayhew, *Congress: The Electoral Connection;* Parker and Davidson, "Why Do Americans Love Their Congressmen So Much More Than Their Congress?"

[159]See Paul Feldman and James Jondrow, "Congressional Elections and Local Federal Spending," *American Journal of Political Science* 28 (1984), 152; Glenn R. Parker and Suzanne Parker, "The Correlates and Effects of Attention to District by U.S. House Members," *Legislative Studies Quarterly* 10 (1985), 239.

[160]Christopher Buckley, "Hangin' with the Houseboyz," *Washington Monthly* (June 1992), 44.

[161]Linda L. Fowler and Robert D. McClure, *Political Ambition: Who Decides to Run for Congress?* (New Haven, Conn.: Yale University Press, 1989), 47. John Hibbing and Sara Brandes, "State Population and the Electoral Success of U.S. Senators," *American Journal of Political Science* 27 (1983), 808–819. See also Glenn R. Parker, "Stylistic Change in the U.S. Senate, 1959–1980," *Journal of Politics* 47 (1985), 1190–1202.

[162]Thomas E. Mann, *Unsafe at Any Margin: Interpreting Congressional Elections* (Washington, D.C.: American Enterprise Institute for Public Policy Research, 1978).

[163]"Women, Minorities Join Senate," *CQ Almanac* (1992), 8A–14A; "Wave of Diversity Spared Many Incumbents," *CQ Almanac* (1992), 15A–21A, 24A; "The Elections," *Congressional Quarterly,* November 12, 1994, 3237.

[164]These examples are drawn from David S. Broder, "What Democracy Needs: Real Races," *Washington Post,* October 31, 2004, B7.

[165]See Gary C. Jacobson, *The Politics of Congressional Elections,* 2nd ed. (Boston: Little, Brown, 1987), 51 for a discussion of financial needs in the 1980s.

[166]Ibid.

[167]Barbara Hinckley, "The American Voter in Congressional Elections," *American Political Science Review* 74 (1980), 641–650; Barbara Hinckley, "House Reelections and Senate Defeats: The Role of the Challenger," *British Journal of Political Science* 10 (1980), 441–460.

[168]John Alford and John R. Hibbing, "The Disparate Electoral Security of House and Senate Incumbents," paper presented at the Annual Meeting of the American Political Science Association, September 1989, Atlanta, 107.

[169]A good review of these arguments is found in John R. Hibbing and Sara L. Brandes, "State Population and the Electoral Success of U.S. Senators," *American Journal of Political Science* 27 (1983), 808–819. See also Eric Uslaner, "The Case of the Vanishing Liberal Senators: The House Did It," *British Journal of Political Science* 11 (1981), 105–113; Abramowitz, "A Comparison."

[170]Hibbing and Brandes, "State Population and the Electoral Success of U.S. Senators." See also Glenn R. Parker, "Stylistic Change in the U.S. Senate, 1959–1980," ibid.

[171]Edie N. Goldenberg and Michael W. Traugott, *Campaigning for Congress* (Washington, D.C.: CQ Press, 1984); Gary C. Jacobson and Samuel Kernell, *Strategy and Choice in Congressional Elections.* (New Haven, Conn.: Yale University Press, 1981).

[172]Edward Walsh, "Wanted: Candidates for Congress," *Washington Post National Weekly Edition,* November 25, 1985, 9.

[173]See Gerald C. Wright Jr. and Michael B. Berkman, "Candidates and Policy in United States Senate Elections," *American Political Science Review* 80 (1986), 567–588; Robert S. Erikson and Gerald C. Wright, "Voters, Candidates, and Issues in Congressional Elections," in Lawrence C. Dodd and Bruce I. Oppenheimer, eds., *Congress Reconsidered,* 7th ed. (Washington, D.C.: CQ Press, 2001), 67–95.

[174]See James Campbell, "Explaining Presidential Losses in Midterm Elections," *Journal of Politics* 47 (1985), 1140–1157. See also Barbara Hinckley, "Interpreting House Midterm Elections," *American Political Science Review* 61 (1967), 694–700; Samuel Kernell, "Presidential Popularity and Negative Voting," *American Political Science Review* 71 (1977), 44–66; Edward Tufte, "Determinants of the Outcomes of Midterm Congressional Elections," *American Political Science Review* 69 (1975), 812–826; Alan Abramowitz, "Economic Conditions, Presidential Popularity and Voting Behavior in Midterm Elections," *Journal of Politics* 47 (1985), 31–43.

[175]Data on voters' issue preferences on Election Day can be found in the article "41% Said National Security Issues Most Important," *Rasmussen Reports,* November 2, 2004 at www.rasmussenreports.com/Issue%20Clusters_Election%20Night. htm.

[176]Editorial, "A Polarized Nation?" *Washington Post,* November 14, 2004, 6. Several of these ideas were summarized nicely in this article.

[177]Benjamin I. Page and Robert Y. Shapiro, "Effects of Public Opinion on Policy," *American Political Science Review* 77 (1983), 175–190.

[178]Arthur Schlesinger Jr., *Wall Street Journal,* December 5, 1986. But see also Jacobs and Shapiro, *Politicians Don't Pander: Political Manipulation and the Loss of Democratic Responsiveness.*

[179]"How Voters Feel," *USA Today,* November 8, 2006, p. 2A.

Chapter 9

[1]Reported in Nina J. Easton, *Gang of Five: Leaders at the Center of the Conservative Crusade,* New York: Simon and Schuster, 2000, 131–132.

[2]In 1991, Reed received a Ph.D. from Emory University.

[3]May 15, 1995.

[4]Susan Schmidt and James V. Grimaldi, "Panel Says Abramoff Laundered Tribal Funds," *Washington Post,* June 23, 2005, A1.

[5]Peter Stone, "Reed in the Rough," *National Journal,* July 7, 2006.

[6]E-mails revealing this knowledge came to light in a later Justice Department investigation released in 2005 by the Senate Indian Affairs Subcommittee. See Susan Schmidt and James V. Grimaldi, "Panel Says Abramoff Laundered Tribal Funds," *Washington Post,* June 23, 2005, 1.

[7]Jimmy Breslin, *How the Good Guys Finally Won: Notes from an Impeachment Summer* (New York: Ballantine, 1974), 14.

[8]Robert E. Mutch, "Three Centuries of Campaign Finance Law," in *A User's Guide to Campaign Finance Reform,* ed. Gerald C. Lubenow (Lanham, Md.: Rowman & Littlefield, 2001).

[9]Congressional Quarterly, *Dollar Politics,* 3rd ed. (Washington, D.C.: CQ Press, 1982), 3.

[10]Haynes Johnson, "Turning Government Jobs into Gold," *Washington Post National Weekly Edition,* May 12, 1986, 6–7.

[11]Richard Lacayo, "Fighting the Fat Cats," *Time* July 3, 2006, 71.

[12]Quoted in Richard Hofstadter, *The American Political Tradition* (New York: Vintage, 1958), 165.

[13]Congressional Quarterly, *Dollar Politics*, 3.

[14]Larry J. Sabato, *Feeding Frenzy* (New York: Free Press, 1991).

[15]Kevin Phillips, "How Wealth Defines Power," *American Prospect*, Summer 2003, A9. The U.S. Constitution defines a quorum as a majority of senators currently in office.

[16]Digital History, *Hypertext History*, "The Progressive Era," October 30, 2004, www.digital history.uh.edu/database/hyper_titles.cfm. The history was made by steel baron Henry Frick.

[17]Elizabeth Drew, *Politics and Money* (New York: Collier, 1983), 9.

[18]Thomas B. Edsall and Chris Cillizza, "Money Will Do the Talking," *Washington Post National Weekly Edition*, March 20–26, 2006, 10.

[19]Mike Allen, "Does an Embassy Trump the Lincoln Bedroom?" *Washington Post National Weekly Edition*, May 7, 2001, 14.

[20]Ibid.

[21]Barry Yeoman, "Bush's Bagmen," *Rolling Stone*, March 10, 2004, www.rollingstone.com/politics /story/_/id/5940033. See also Thomas Byrne Edsall, Sarah Cohen, and James Grimaldi, "Pioneers Fill War Chest, Then Capitalize," *Washington Post*, May 16, 2004, A1.

[22]Mike Allen, "The Mother of All Fundraisers," *Washington Post National Weekly Edition*, May 20, 2002, 13.

[23]Mike Allen, "Does an Embassy Trump the Lincoln Bedroom?" *Washington Post National Weekly Edition*, May 7, 2001, 14.

[24]Edsall, Cohen, and Grimaldi, "Pioneers Fill War Chest," A1.

[25]Ibid.

[26]Larry Makinson and Joshua Goldstein, *Open Secrets: The Cash Constituents of Congress*, 2nd ed. (Washington, D.C.: CQ Press, 1994), 23.

[27]Amy Dockser, "Nice PAC You've Got There . . . A Pity If Anything Should Happen to It," *Washington Monthly*, January 1984, 21.

[28]*Buckley v. Valeo*, 424 U.S. 1 (1976); the Vermont case is *Randall v. Sorrell* 548 U.S. (2006).

[29]Glen Justice, "Irrelevance Stalks a Post-Watergate Invention," *New York Times*, November 16, 2003, 3.

[30]*Federal Election Commission v. National Conservative PAC*, 470 U.S. 480 (1985).

[31]David S. Broder, "Both Major Parties Abuse Soft Money Loophole," *State College* (Pa.) *Centre Daily Times*, May 30, 2000, 6A.

[32]Pauol Farhi, "A Team Effort," *Washington Post National Weekly Edition*, March 29, 2004, 12.

[33]Glen Justice, "Kerry's Campaign Finances Soar," *International Herald Tribune*, June 28, 2004, 7.

[34]See Larry J. Sabato and Glenn Simpson, *Dirty Little Secrets: The Persistence of Corruption in American Politics* (New York: Times Books, 1996); Marick Masters and Gerald Keim, "Determinants of PAC Participation among Large Corporations," *Journal of Politics* 47 (1985), 1158–1173; and J. David Gopoian, "What Makes PACs Tick?" *American Journal of Political Science* 28 (1984), 259–281.

[35]See Kevin Grier and Michael Mangy, "Comparing Interest Group PAC Contributions to House and Senate Incumbents," *Journal of Politics* 55 (1993), 615–643.

[36]J. David Gopoian, "Change and Continuity in Defense PAC Behavior," *American Politics Quarterly* 13 (1985), 297–322; Richard Morin and Charles Babcock, "Off Year, Schmoff Year,"

Washington Post National Weekly Edition, May 14, 1990, 15.

[37]Thomas Romer and James M. Snyder, "An Empirical Investigation of the Dynamics of PAC Contributions," *American Journal of Political Science* 38 (1994), 745–769.

[38]Alison Mitchell, "Time Passes, Money Flows," *New York Times*, June 16, 1996, E5.

[39]Bradley Smith, *Free Speech: The Folly of Campaign Finance Reform* (Princeton, N.J.: Princeton University Press, 2001); Russ Lewis, "Foreign to the First Amendment," *Washington Post*, July 2, 2002, A15.

[40]George Will, "Corrupt Campaign 'Reform,'" *Washington Post*, June 29, 2006, A27.

[41]Thomas Byrne Edsall, "Campaign Reform Boomerang," *American Prospect*, September 2003, 61.

[42]Ibid.

[43]Paul Taylor, "TV's Political Profits," *Mother Jones*, May-June 2000, 32.

[44]Robert Pastor, "America Observed," *Prospect* (January, 2005), A3. An earlier study of 146 countries found that the U.S. was the only country without free media, *Washington Post*, February 24, 2002, B7.

[45]David S. Broder, "Where the Money Goes," *Washington Post National Weekly Edition*, March 26, 2001, 4.

[46]Jeff Leeds, "TV Stations Balk at Free Air Time for Candidates," *Lincoln Journal Star*, May 14, 2000, 3A.

[47]Ibid.

[48]Ibid.

[49]"Public Order in the Courts," *American Prospect*, November 18, 2002, 8. See also Harold Stanley and Richard Niemi, *Vital Statistics on American Politics, 2001–02* (Washington, D.C.: CQ Press, 2002), tab. 2-3.

[50]James Carville and Paul Begala," Not One Dime," *Washington Monthly* (March, 2006), 14–15.

[51]Mark Twain, *Pudd'nhead Wilson's New Calendar*.

[52]Quoted in *New York Times*, June 13, 1998, A7.

[53]Ibid.

[54]Stanley and Niemi, *Vital Statistics on American Politics*, tab. 2-4.

[55]"Numbers," *Time*, February 28, 2000, 27.

[56]Quoted in Gary Jacobson, *Money in Congressional Elections* (New Haven, Conn.: Yale University Press, 1980), 61.

[57]David S. Broder, "The High Road to Lower Finance?" *Washington Post National Weekly Edition*, June 29, 1987, 4; see also Diane Granat, "Parties' Schools for Politicians or Grooming Troops for Election," *Congressional Quarterly Weekly Report*, May 5, 1984, 1036.

[58]Diana C. Mutz, "Effects of Horse-Race Coverage on Campaign Coffers: Strategic Contributing in Presidential Primaries," *Journal of Politics* 57 (1995), 1015–1042.

[59]Audrey A. Haynes, Paul-Henri Gurian, and Stephen M. Nichols, "The Role of Candidate Spending in Presidential Nomination Campaigns," *Journal of Politics* 59 (1997), 220. See also Gary Orren, "The Nomination Process," in *The Elections of 1984*, ed. Michael Nelson (Washington, D.C.: CQ Press, 1986), ch. 2; and Wayne Parent, Calvin Jillson, and Ronald E. Weber, "Voting Outcomes in the 1984 Democratic Primaries and Caucuses," *American Political Science Review* 81 (1987), 67–84.

[60]Haynes, Gurian, and Nichols, "Role of Candidate Spending," 223.

[61]Nelson Polsby and Aaron Wildavsky, *Presidential Elections* (New York: Scribner, 1984), 56.

[62]David Nice, "Campaign Spending and Presidential Election Results," *Polity* 19 (1987), 464–476, shows that presidential campaign spending is more productive for Republicans than for Democrats.

[63]John Alford and David Brady, "Person and Partisan Advantages in U.S. Congressional Elections, 1846–1990," in *Congress Reconsidered*, ed. Larry Dodd and Bruce Oppenheimer, 5th ed. (Washington, D.C.: Congressional Quarterly, 1993).

[64]David Epstein and Peter Zemsky, "Money Talks: Deterring Quality Challengers in Congressional Elections," *American Political Science Review* 89 (1995), 295–308.

[65]Robert S. Erickson and Thomas R. Palfrey, "Campaign Spending and Incumbency: An Alternative Simultaneous Equations Approach," *Journal of Politics* 60 (1998), 355–373; Alan Gerber, "Estimating the Effect of Campaign Spending on Senate Election Outcomes Using Instrumental Variables," *American Political Science Review* 92 (1998), 401–411.

[66]Jacobson, *Money in Congressional Elections*; Gary Jacobson, "The Effects of Campaign Spending in House Elections," *American Journal of Political Science* 34 (1990), 334–362; Christopher Kenny and Michael McBurnett, "A Dynamic Model of the Effect of Campaign Spending on Congressional Vote Choice," *American Journal of Political Science* 36 (1992), 923–937; Donald Green and Jonathan Krasno, "Salvation for the Spendthrift Incumbent," *American Journal of Political Science* 32 (1988), 884–907; Gary Jacobson, *The Politics of Congressional Elections*, 2nd ed. (Boston: Little, Brown, 1987), ch. 4; Stephen Ansolabehere and Alan Gerber, "The Mismeasure of Campaign Spending," *Journal of Politics* 56 (1994), 1106–1118; Alan Gerber, "Estimating the Effect of Campaign Spending."

[67]Federal Elections Commission, 2001–2002 database, www.fec.gov; Common Cause, report of November 6, 2002, www.commoncause.org.

[68]"Scandal Shocks Even Those Who Helped It Along," *New York Times*, February 3, 2002, 7.

[69]See Woodrow Jones and K. Robert Keiser, "Issue Visibility and the Effects of PAC Money," *Social Science Quarterly* 68 (1987), 170–176. Janet Grenzke, "PACs and the Congressional Supermarket," *American Journal of Political Science* 33 (1989), 1–24, found little effect of PAC money on a series of votes that were not obscure. Laura Langbein, "Money and Access," *Journal of Politics* 48 (1986), 1052–1064, shows that those who received more PAC money spend more time with interest group representatives.

[70]Jean Reith Schroedel, "Campaign Contributions and Legislative Outcomes," *Western Political Quarterly* 39 (1986), 371–389; Richard L. Hall and Frank Wayman, "Buying Time: Moneyed Interests and the Mobilization of Bias in Congressional Committees," *American Political Science Review* 84 (1990), 797–820.

[71]Thomas Downey (D-N.Y.), quoted in "Running with the PACs," *Time*, October 25, 1982, 20.

[72]"Congress Study Links Funds and Votes," *New York Times*, December 30, 1987, 7.

[73]John Frendreis and Richard Waterman, "PAC Contributions and Legislative Behavior: Senate Voting on Trucking Deregulation," *Social Science Quarterly* 66 (1985), 401–412. See also W. P. Welch, "Campaign Contributions and Legislative Voting," *Western Political Quarterly* 25 (1982), 478–495.

[74]Diana Evans, "Policy and Pork: The Use of Pork Barrel Projects to Build Policy Coalitions in the House of Representatives," *American Jour-*

nal of Political Science 38 (1994), 894–917; Laura Langbein, "PACs, Lobbies, and Political Conflict: The Case of Gun Control," *Public Choice* 75 (1993), 254–271; Laura Langbein and Mark Lotwis, "The Political Efficacy of Lobbying and Money: Gun Control in the House, 1986," *Legislative Studies Quarterly* 15 (1990), 413–440; Schroedel, "Campaign Contributions and Legislative Outcomes."

[75]Adam Clymer, "84 PACs Gave More to Senate Winners," *New York Times*, January 6, 1985, 13.

[76]Quoted in Drew, *Politics and Money*, 79.

[77]See Grenzke, "PACs and the Congressional Supermarket"; also see Frank Sorauf, *Money in American Elections* (Glenview, Ill.: Scott, Foresman, 1988).

[78]Grenzke, "PACs and the Congressional Supermarket"; John Wright, "Contributions, Lobbying, and Committee Voting in the U.S. House of Representatives," *American Political Science Review* 84 (1990), 417–438; Henry Chappel Jr., "Campaign Contributions and Voting on the Cargo Preference Bill," *Public Choice* 36 (1981), 301–312.

[79]John Alford and David Brady, "Person and Partisan Advantages in U.S. Congressional Elections, 1846–1990," in *Congress Reconsidered*, ed. Larry Dodd and Bruce Oppenheimer, 5th ed. (Washington, D.C.: CQ Press, 1993); Peter Slevin, "Postwar Contracting Called Uncoordinated," *Washington Post*, October 31, 2003, A23.

[80]"Study: Bush Donors Get Government Favors," *Lincoln Journal Star*, May 28, 1992.

[81]"Clinton Regrets Rich Pardon," March 31, 2002, CBSNEWS.com/stories/2002/03/31/politics/main505042.shtml; BBC News World Edition, "Rich's '$450,000' for Clinton Library," news.bbc.co.uk/hi/English/world/Americas/newid_1163000/1163917.stm. George H. W. Bush's last-minute pardon of a convicted $1.5 million heroin trafficker got much less publicity; John Monk and Gary Wright, "Why Did Bush Free Smuggler? Mystery Lingers in Charlotte Case," *Charlotte Observer*, March 27, 1993, 1A.

[82]Charles Lewis, quoted in "Book Details Candidates' Extensive Financial Alignments," *Lincoln Journal Star*, January 12, 1996, 5A.

[83]Tom Kenworthy, "The Color of Money," *Washington Post National Weekly Edition*, November 6, 1989, 13.

[84]Quoted in Daniel Franklin," Heiristrocracy," *The Washington Monthly* (May, 2005), 60.

[85]Kevin Phillips, "How Wealth Defines Power," *American Prospect*, Summer 2003, A9; U.S. Census Bureau, *Statistical Abstract of the United States, 2003* (Washington, D.C.: Government Printing Office, 2003), tab. 688.

[86]Aviva Aron-Dean and Isaac Shapiro, "New Data Show Extraordinary Jump in Income Concentration in 2004," Center on Budget and Policy Priorities, July 10, 2006; www.cbpp.org/7-10-06inc.htm.

[87]Gary Wasserman, "The Uses of Influence," *Washington Post National Weekly Edition*, January 11, 1993, 35.

[88]Juliet Eilperin, "The 'Hammer' DeLay Whips Lobbyists into Shape," *Washington Post National Weekly Edition*, October 25, 1999, 8.

[89]Jeff Leeds, "TV Stations Balk at Free Air Time for Candidates," *Lincoln Journal Star*, May 14, 2000, 3A.

[90]Walter Lippmann, "A Theory about Corruption," in Arnold J. Heidenheimer, ed. *Political Corruption* (New York: Holt, Rinehart and Winston, 1970), 294–297.

[91]Susan Welch and John Peters, "Private Interests in the U.S. Congress," *Legislative Studies Quarterly*

7 (1982), 547–555; see also John Peters and Susan Welch, "Private Interests and Public Interests," *Journal of Politics* 45 (1983), 378–396.

[92]"Congress for Sale," *USA Today* (March 7, 2006), 17A.

[93]Jeffrey Birnbaum, "Privately Funded Trips Add up on Capitol Hill," *Washington Post*, June 6, 2006, A1.

[94]Ibid.

[95]Many news media covered this scandal and the complicated interrelationships within it extensively. See for example, Karen Tumulty, "The Man Who Bought Washington," *Time*, January 16, 2006, 31–39.

[96]Norman Ornstein, a fellow at the American Enterprise Institution, as quoted in Lou DuBose, "Broken Hammer," *Salon*, http://dir.salon.com/story/news/feature/2005/04/08/scandals/index1.html.

[97]R. Jeffrey Smith and Juliet Eilperin, "Caught in an Ethical Snare," *Washington Post National Weekly Edition*, January 16–22, 2006, 14.

[98]Lou DuBose, "K Street Croupiers," *Texas Observer*, observer.bryhost.com/article.php?aid=2138.

[99]For a rundown of these confusing front organizations see Tumulty, op. cit.; DeBose, ibid.

[100]Eliza Newlin Carney, "Cleaning House (and Senate)," *National Journal*, January 28, 2006, 33.

[101]"Congress for Sale," ibid.

[102]"Congress for Sale," ibid.

[103]Birnbaum, ibid.

[104]Mike McIntire, "New House Majority Leader Keeps Old Ties to Lobbyists," *New York Times*, July 15, 2006.

[105]Frank Rich, "The Road from K Street to Yusafiya," *New York Times*, June 25, 2006, WK13.

[106]"Having It All, Then Throwing It Away," *Time*, May 25, 1987, 22.

[107]Elizabeth Drew, "Letter from Washington," *New Yorker*, May 1, 1989, 99–108; see also Dan Balz, "Tales of Power and Money," *Washington Post National Weekly Edition*, May 1, 1989, 11–12.

[108]Quoted in Drew, "Having It All," 22.

[109]Hank Paulson, CEO of Goldman Sachs, quoted in Joseph Nocera, "System Failure," *Fortune*, June 24, 2002, 62ff.

[110]Keith Bradsher, "How to Pooh-Pooh $70 Million War Chests," *New York Times*, April 30, 2000, 6.

[111]Quoted in Nancy Gibbs and Karen Tumulty, "A New Day Dawning," *Time*, April 9, 2001, 50.

[112]Susan Schmidt and James Grimaldi, "Panel Says Abramoff Laundered Tribal Funds," *Washington Post*, June 23, 2005, 1.

[113]22.

[114]Stone, op cit.

[115]Ibid. See also indianz.com/News/2006/014803.asp; Philip Shenon, "Senate Report Lists Lobbyists' Payments to Ex-Head of Christian Coalition," *New York Times*, June 23, 2006, 22.

[116]Peter Stone, "Reed in the Rough," *National Journal*, July 7, 2006.

[117]Jim Galloway, "Report Wraps up over Reed, Tribes," *Atlanta Journal-Constitution* (June 23, 2006); online cite: www.ajc.com/metro/content/metro/stories/0622abramoff.html

Chapter 10

[1]Information on Senator Roberts' background and service in Congress used for this YAT segment come from Michael Barone and Richard E. Cohen, *Almanac of American Politics 2006* (Washington, D.C.: *National Journal*, 2005), 683–686, and from the senator's website.

[2]Pat Roberts, "A Panel Above Politics," *Washington Post*, November 13, 2003, A31.

[3]Ibid.

[4]Barone and Cohen, p. 685.

[5]J. Marshall, "Congress Keeps Ducking Niger Investigation," *The Hill*, October 27, 2005 (www.thehill.com).

[6]Norman J. Ornstein, "Relationship between President, Congress Is Still Dysfunctional," *Roll Call*, April 26, 2006 (online version at www.aei.org, along with other Ornstein articles on the same subject). Another leading congressional expert whose work is frequently critical of Congress's poor performance on oversight is Thomas Mann, whose articles can be found at www.brookings.edu.

[7]Testimony from former CIA officers involved in writing the National Intelligence Estimate and providing other intelligence for the Bush administration prior to the Iraq invasion can be heard in the investigative report, "The Dark Side," aired on *Frontline* in 2006. In it former chair of the Senate Select Committee on Intelligence Bob Graham (D-Fla.) describes conditions under which senators were allowed access to intelligence reports. (The program can be viewed online at www.pbs.org/frontline.) Also see Ron Suskind, *The One Percent Doctrine* (New York: Simon and Schuster, 2006), 177–179.

[8]Quoted in Scott Shane, "Senate Panel's Partisanship Troubles Former Members," *The New York Times*, March 12, 2006, 18.

[9]James R. Chiles, "Congress Couldn't Have Been This Bad, or Could It?" *Smithsonian*, November 1995, 70–80.

[10]Susan Webb Hammond, "Life and Work on the Hill: Careers, Norms, Staff, and Informal Caucuses," in *Congress Responds to the Twentieth Century*, ed. Sunil Ahuja and Robert Dewhirst (Columbus: Ohio State University Press, 2003), 74.

[11]David S. Broder, "Dumbing Down Democracy," *Lincoln Journal Star*, April 5, 1995, 18.

[12]Quoted in Kenneth J. Cooper and Helen Dewar, "No Limits on the Term Limits Crusade," *Washington Post National Weekly Edition*, May 29, 1995, 14.

[13]A list of states that have term limits can be found at www.termlimits.org.

[14]*Baker v. Carr*, 369 U.S. 186 (1962).

[15]*Wesberry v. Sanders*, 376 U.S. 1 (1964).

[16]Bruce Cain and Janet Campagna, "Predicting Partisan Redistricting Disputes," *Legislative Studies Quarterly* 12 (1987), 265–274.

[17]See the report on *Miller v. Johnson*, 515 U.S. 900 (1995); see *New York Times*, July 2, 1995, E1, E4.

[18]"Congress of Relative Newcomers Poses Challenge to Bush, Leadership," *Congressional Quarterly Weekly Review*, January 20, 2001, 179–181.

[19]"Datafile," *Congressional Quarterly Weekly Review*, February 21, 2004, 456. "For the Record," *CQ Monthly Report*, November 13, 2006, 3068-3075.

[20]Hanna F. Pitkin, *The Concept of Representation* (Berkeley: University of California, 1967), 60.

[21]Ibid., 60–61.

[22]Pitkin, 61.

[23]Leslie Laurence, "Congress Makes Up for Neglect," *Lincoln Journal Star*, December 5, 1994, 8.

[24]Roger H. Davidson and Walter J. Oleszek, *Congress and Its Members*, 9th ed. (Washington, D.C.: CQ Press, 2004), 132–134; Richard Fenno, *Home Style: House Members in Their Districts*, 2nd ed. (New York: Longman, 2003), 232–247.

[25]Carl M. Cannon, "State of Our Disunion," *National Journal*, January 21, 2006, 23; Norman Ornstein and Barry McMillion, "One Nation, Divisible," *New York Times*, June 23, 2005.

[26]Davidson and Oleszek, 114.

[27]John Alford and John Hibbing, "The Disparate Electoral Security of House and Senate Incumbents," paper presented at the annual meeting of the American Political Science Association, Atlanta, September 1989.

[28]Fenno, *Home Style.*

[29]John Cochran, "A New Medium for the Message," *Congressional Quarterly Weekly Review,* March 13, 2006, 657.

[30]Ibid., 145.

[31]*Budget of the United States, Fiscal 2007: Appendix* (Washington, D.C.: Government Printing Office, 2006), 15–18.

[32]Ibid, 15–16.

[33]Quoted in Kenneth Shepsle, "The Failures of Congressional Budgeting," *Social Science and Modern Society* 20 (1983), 4–10. See also Howard Kurtz, "Pork Barrel Politics," *Washington Post,* January 25, 1982.

[34]Congressional Quarterly, *The Origins and Development of Congress* (Washington, D.C.: CQ Press, 1976).

[35]Historian David S. Reynolds quoting a newspaper reporter of the time in Sheryl Gay Stolberg, "What Happened to Compromise," *New York Times,* May 29, 2005, sect. 4, 4.

[36]Neil McNeil, *Forge of Democracy* (New York: McKay, 1963), 306–309.

[37]Mark Hankerson, "Participation Hits Record," *Congressional Quarterly Weekly Review,* December 11, 1999, 2979.

[38]Jackie Koszczuk, "Master of the Mechanics Has Kept the House Running," *Congressional Quarterly Weekly Review,* December 11, 1999, 2963.

[39]David Nather, "Hastert Keeps His Cool, and His Post," *Congressional Quarterly Weekly Review,* February 6, 2006, 313.

[40]Rep. Barney Frank (D-Mass.), quoted in David D. Kirkpatrick, "As Dust Settles, The Speaker of the House Emerges, Still Standing," *New York Times,* February 5, 2006, 24.

[41]Ibid.

[42]Michael Barone, Richard E. Cohen, and Charles E. Cook Jr., *Almanac of American Politics, 2002* (Washington, D.C.: National Journal, 2002), 46.

[43]Ibid.

[44]For a review of all congressional committees and subcommittees, see the special report, "CQ Guide to the Committees," *Congressional Quarterly Weekly Review,* March 13, 2006, 659–693. Every January CQ publishes a special report on committees, their memberships and agendas.

[45]Davidson and Oleszek, *Congress and Its Members,* 198.

[46]See Roger Davidson, "Subcommittee Government," in *The New Congress,* ed. Thomas E. Mann and Norman J. Ornstein (Washington, D.C.: American Enterprise Institute for Public Policy Research, 1981), 110–111. Some of this occurs because members of Congress tend to be wealthy, and the wealthy make investments in corporations. It also occurs because members' financial interests are often similar to the interests in their districts (for example, representatives from farm districts are likely to be involved in farming or agribusiness).

[47]Jonathan Weisman and Charles S. Babcock, "The Currency of Corruption," *Washington Post National Weekly Edition,* February 6, 2006, 15.

[48]Sara Brandes Crook and John Hibbing, "Congressional Reform and Party Discipline: The Effects of Changes in the Seniority System on Party Loyalty in the U.S. House of Representatives," *British Journal of Political Science* 15 (1985), 207–226.

[49]Davidson and Oleszek, *Congress and Its Members,* 204.

[50]Richard E. Cohen, "Best Seats in the House," *National Journal,* March 4, 2000, 682; Karen Foerstel, "House Offers Mixed Reviews for Committee Term Limits," *Congressional Quarterly Weekly Review,* June 22, 2002, 1653–1655.

[51]For a review of how the task force has been used, see Walter J. Oleszek, "The Use of Task Forces in the House," Congressional Research Service Report No. 96-8, 3-GOV, 1996, www.house.gov/rules/96-843.htm.

[52]*Budget of the United States, Fiscal 2007: Appendix* (Washington, D.C.: Government Printing Office, 2006), 15–38.

[53]Harlan Coben, "Rock and a Hard Place," *New York Times,* November 25, 2005.

[54]Ronald Moe and Steven Teel, "Congress as a Policy-Maker: A Necessary Reappraisal," *Political Science Quarterly* 85 (1970), 443–470.

[55]"The State of Congress," *National Journal* (Special Issue), January 10, 2004, 92.

[56]Thomas Geoghegan, "Bust the Filibuster," *Washington Post National Weekly Edition,* July 12, 1994, 25.

[57]Michael Malbin, "Leading a Filibustered Senate," in *Extensions* (Carl A. Albert Center, University of Oklahoma), Spring 1985, 3.

[58]Clinton aide Chuck Brain, quoted in Richard E. Cohen, "The Third House Rises," *National Journal,* July 28, 2001, 2395.

[59]John Podesta, "The Perils of Partisanship," www.americanprogress.org/site/pp.asp?c=biJRJ8OVF&b=12825.

[60]Paul C. Light, "Filibusters Are Only Half the Problem," *New York Times,* June 3, 2005.

[61]David J. Vogler, *The Third House: Conference Committees in the United States Congress* (Evanston, Ill.: Northwestern University Press, 1971); see also Lawrence D. Longley and Walter J. Oleszek, *Bicameral Politics* (New Haven, Conn.: Yale University Press, 1989).

[62]Morris Ogul, "Congressional Oversight: Structures and Incentives," in *Congress Reconsidered,* ed. Dodd and Oppenheimer; see also Loch Johnson, "The U.S. Congress and the CIA: Monitoring the Dark Side of Government," *Legislative Studies Quarterly* 5 (1980), 477–501.

[63]Joseph Califano, "Imperial Congress," *New York Times Magazine,* January 23, 1994, 41.

[64]Richard E. Cohen, Kirk Victor, and David Bauman, "The State of Congress," *National Journal,* January 10, 2004, 104–105.

[65]Quoted in ibid., 105.

[66]Henry A. Waxman, "Free Pass from Congress," *Washington Post,* July 6, 2004, A19.

[67]Cohen, Victor, and Bauman, "State of Congress," 96.

[68]Herbert Asher, "Learning of Legislative Norms," *American Political Science Review* 67 (1973), 499–513. Michael Berkman points out that freshmen who have had state legislative experience—who now account for more than half of all House members—adapt to the job faster than other members. See "Former State Legislators in the U.S. House of Representatives: Institutional and Policy Mastery," *Legislative Studies Quarterly* 18 (1993), 77–104.

[69]Rep. Jim DeMint (R-S.C.), quoted in Davidson and Oleszek, *Congress and Its Members,* 264.

[70]*Minot* (N.D.) *Daily News,* June 17, 1976.

[71]Samuel Kernell, *Going Public* (Washington, D.C.: CQ Press, 1986).

[72]Viewer statistics are available at C-SPAN's website (www.c-span.org). These are from July 2002 but are the most recent posted.

[73]Profile of the 109th Congress (www.cspan.org).

[74]Michael Wines, "Washington Really Is in Touch. We're the Problem," *New York Times,* October 16, 1994, 4: 2.

[75]Gallup poll, June 2004, www.gallup.com.

[76]*New York Times*/CBS poll, May, 2006.

[77]Editorial, "A Richer Life Beckons Congress," *New York Times,* August 8, 2005.

[78]Editorial, "Ethical Notes on the Reforming Class," *New York Times,* May 6, 2006.

[79]Pat Roberts, "No Investigation Needed," *USA Today,* March 10, 2006, A14.

[80]Quoted in "Senate Panel's Partisanship Troubles Former Members," 18.

[81]"Investi-Gate," *Washington Monthly,* May 29, 2006, 3.

[82]Ibid.

[83]Jeffrey Goldberg, "Central Casting," *The New Yorker,* May 29, 2006, 66.

Chapter 11

[1]Quoted in Carl M. Cannon, "Bush's Year of Living Dangerously," *National Journal,* January 7, 2006, 23–24.

[2]Nicholas Congessore, "Going for Broke May Break Bush," *New York Times,* February 6, 2005, sect. 4, 1.

[3]Robert F. Kennedy, Jr., "Was the 2004 Election Stolen?" *Rolling Stone,* www.rollingstone.com/news/story/10432334/was_the_2004_election_stolen/2.

[4]"Bush's Year of Living Dangerously," 27.

[5]Woodrow Wilson, *Congressional Government: A Study in American Politics* (New Brunswick, N.J.: Transaction, 2002). Originally published in 1885.

[6]Theodore Lowi, *The Personal President: Power Invested, Promise Unfulfilled* (Ithaca, N.Y.: Cornell University Press, 1985).

[7]Arthur M. Schlesinger Jr., *The Imperial Presidency* (Boston: Houghton Mifflin, 1973). Schlesinger has published an updated version based on the presidency of George W. Bush: *War and the American Presidency* (New York: Norton, 2004).

[8]Harold M. Barger, *The Impossible Presidency* (Glenview, Ill.: Scott, Foresman, 1984).

[9]Jefferson's management of the presidency is described in Joseph J. Ellis, *American Sphinx: The Character of Thomas Jefferson* (New York: Knopf, 1997), 186–228.

[10]David Stout, "Presidential Candidates Seem Indifferent to a Salary Rise," *New York Times,* May 30, 1999, 16; Daniel J. Parks, "Prospective Presidential Pay Raise, First in 30 Years, Would Also Ease Other Officials' Salary 'Compression,' " *Congressional Quarterly Weekly Review,* May 29, 1999, 1264.

[11]"George Mason: Forgotten Founder," *Smithsonian,* May 2000, 145.

[12]Information on all three impeachment proceedings can be found at www.historyplace.com.

[13]These terms were popularized by Clinton Rossiter in *The American Presidency* (New York: Harcourt, Brace & World, 1956), a political science classic.

[14]Lowi, *The Personal President,* xi.

[15]Francis Wilkinson, "Song of Myself," *New York Times,* January 31, 2006.

[16]Ted Widmer, "The State of the Union Is Unreal," *New York Times,* January 31, 2006.

[17]Michael Nelson, ed., *Presidency A to Z* (Washington, D.C.: CQ Press, 1998), 12.

[18]For discussion of the president's removal powers in light of a 1988 Supreme Court decision

regarding independent counsels, see John A. Rohr, "Public Administration, Executive Power, and Constitutional Confusion," and Rosemary O'Leary, "Response to John Rohr," *Public Administrative Review* 49 (1989), 108–115.

[19]Jones, *Presidency in a Separated System,* 53.

[20]Alexander Simendinger, Sydney J. Freedberg Jr., and Siobhan Gorman, "The Experiment Begins," *National Journal,* June 15, 2002, 1775–1787.

[21]Nelson, *Presidency A to Z,* 169.

[22]The Bush White House provides a link to all executive orders issued by the president at the White House home page (www.whitehouse.gov).

[23]Nelson, *Presidency A to Z,* 170.

[24]Charles O. Jones, *Separate but Equal Branches* (Chatham, N.J.: Chatham House, 1995).

[25]Morris Fiorina, *Divided Government* (New York: Macmillan, 1992), 7.

[26]Quoted in Dick Kirschten, "Reagan Warms Up for Political Hardball," *National Journal,* February 9, 1985, 328.

[27]Nicholas Lemann, "The Quiet Man," *New Yorker,* May 7, 2001, 68.

[28]"Bush Starts a Strong Record of Success with the Hill," *Congressional Quarterly Weekly Review,* January 12, 2002, 112.

[29]*United States* v. *Curtiss-Wright Export Corporation,* 299 U.S. 304 (1936).

[30]See the discussion in *Federalist Paper* 69, written by Alexander Hamilton.

[31]Quoted in "Notes and Comment," *New Yorker,* June 1, 1987, 23.

[32]Ibid.

[33]John Barry, "What Schwarzkopf's Book Leaves Out," *Newsweek,* September 28, 1992, 68.

[34]A good overview of Rumsfeld's attempts to transform the military and his role in planning and directing the war in Iraq can be found in the transcript of the PBS program *Rumsfeld's War,* broadcast October 26, 2004, available at www.pbs.org/wgbh/pages/frontline/shows/pentagon.

[35]*Youngstown Sheet and Tube Co.* v. *Sawyer,* 343 U.S. 579 (1952).

[36]See, for example, the comments of Arthur M. Schlesinger Jr. in Cannon, "Judging Clinton," 22; Steven A. Holmes, "Losers in Clinton-Starr Bouts May Be Future U.S. Presidents," *New York Times,* August 23, 1998, 18; and Adam Clymer, "The Presidency Is Still There, Not Quite the Same," *New York Times,* February 14, 1999, 4: 1.

[37]See, for example, David S. Broder and Dan Balz, "Who Wins?" *Washington Post National Weekly Edition,* January 15, 1999, 6–7, and Cannon, "Judging Clinton," 22–23.

[38]Thomas F. Cronin, *The State of the Presidency* (Boston: Little, Brown, 1975), 118.

[39]Congress's anger at Roosevelt's court-packing scheme held up the reorganization for two years; see Chapter 13.

[40]Sidney M. Milkis, "George W. Bush and the 'New' Party System," *Clio: Newsletter of Politics and History* 16:1 (Fall/Winter 2005–2006), 44.

[41]*The Presidency in a Separated System,* 56–57.

[42]For more on Bush's White House staff and method of making appointments, see G. Calvin Mackenzie, "The Real Invisible Hand: Presidential Appointees in the Administration of George W. Bush," and Martha Joynt Kumar, "Recruiting and Organizing the White House Staff," *PS: Political Science and Politics* 1 (2002), 27–40.

[43]"Hell from the Chief: Hot Tempers and Presidential Timber," *New York Times,* November 7, 1999, 4: 7.

[44]Quoted in Richard Pious, *The American Presidency* (New York: Basic Books, 1979), 244.

[45]Public Broadcasting System, *The American President,* episode 10.

[46]Ann Reilly Dowd, "What Managers Can Learn from Manager Reagan," *Fortune,* September 15, 1986, 32–41.

[47]See John H. Kessel, "The Structures of the Reagan White House," *American Journal of Political Science* 28 (1984), 231–258.

[48]Hillary Rodham Clinton, quoted in Carol Gelderman, *All the Presidents' Words: The Bully Pulpit and the Creation of the Virtual Presidency* (New York: Walker, 1997), 160.

[49]A good description of Clinton's relationship to his White House staff can be found in Joe Klein, *The Natural: The Misunderstood Presidency of Bill Clinton* (New York: Doubleday, 2002).

[50]For more on Bush's management style, see the several articles in the special section "C.E.O. U.S.A.," *New York Times Magazine,* January 14, 2001, 24–58.

[51]Ron Suskind, *The Price of Loyalty: George W. Bush, the White House, and the Education of Paul O'Neill* (New York: Simon & Schuster, 2004).

[52]*The Presidency A to Z,* 487–488.

[53]Former vice-president Walter Mondale, speech at the Carter Center in Atlanta, Georgia (C-SPAN broadcast, March 14, 2006).

[54]For a review of the backgrounds of men who have served in the vice presidency and the roles they have played, see L. Edward Purcell, *Vice Presidents* (New York: Facts on File, 2001); Michael Nelson, *A Heartbeat Away* (New York: Priority, 1988); Paul C. Light, *Vice-Presidential Power: Advice and Influence in the White House* (Baltimore: Johns Hopkins University Press, 1984); and George Sirgiovanni, "The 'Van Buren Jinx': Vice Presidents Need Not Beware," *Presidential Studies Quarterly* 18 (1988), 61–76.

[55]Purcell, *Vice Presidents,* 380.

[56]Jane Mayer, "The Hidden Power," *The New Yorker,* July 3, 2006, 50.

[57]CBS News poll, March 2006.

[58]Paul Krugman, "The Mensch Gap," *New York Times,* February 20, 2006, A. Krugman was not generalizing about the presidency but making specific remarks about George W. Bush.

[59]Jeffrey K. Tulis, *The Rhetorical Presidency* (Princeton, N.J.: Princeton University Press, 1987).

[60]Quoted in Garry Wills, *Lincoln at Gettysburg* (New York: Simon & Schuster, 1992), 31.

[61]David Halberstam, *The Powers That Be* (New York: Dell, 1980), 30.

[62]"Travels of the President," *New York Times,* August 8, 2004, 18.

[63]Michael Waldman, Clinton's former chief speechwriter, interviewed on *Morning Edition,* National Public Radio, January 1, 2002.

[64]Lowi, *The Personal President.*

[65]"Poll Shows Americans Want a Strong Leader," *Lincoln Journal Star,* June 16, 1992, 5.

[66]Thomas Friedman, "Addicted to 9/11," *New York Times,* October 14, 2004, p. A 29.

[67]"A Talk with Clinton," *Newsweek,* January 25, 1993, 37.

[68]Carl M. Cannon, "Judging Clinton," *National Journal,* January 1, 2000, 23.

[69]Klein, *The Natural,* 208.

[70]Samuel Kernell, *Going Public: New Strategies of Presidential Leadership* (Washington, D.C.: CQ Press, 1986), 15.

[71]Geoffrey Nunberg, "The Curious Fate of Populism: How Politics Turned into Prose," *New York Times,* August 15, 2004, WK7; Philip

Gourevitch, "Bushspeak," *New Yorker,* September 13, 2004, 36–43.

[72]Ari Fleischer, quoted in *Congressional Quarterly Today News,* May 19, 2003, www.cq.com.

[73]"The Presidency," *Newsweek,* December 20, 1993, 46.

[74]Nicholas Lemann, "Remember the Alamo," *New Yorker,* October 18, 2004, 153.

[75]Bruce Miroff, "The Presidency and the Public: Leadership and Spectacle," in *The Presidency and the Political System,* 5th ed., ed. Michael Nelson (Washington: CQ Press, 1998), 320.

[76]Lonnie G. Bunch III et al., *The American Presidency: A Glorious Burden* (Washington, D.C.: Smithsonian Institution, 2000), 19.

[77]George C. Edwards III, *The Public Presidency* (New York: St. Martin's Press, 1983), 253.

[78]John Mueller, *War, Presidents, and Public Opinion* (New York: Wiley, 1970).

[79]For example, see Edwards, *Public Presidency,* 239–247.

[80]*National Journal,* December 8, 1990, 2993; January 19, 1991, 185; February 16, 1991, 412.

[81]For more on the Gulf War's impact on Bush's ratings, see John A. Krosnick and Laura A. Brannon, "The Impact of the Gulf War on the Ingredients of Presidential Evaluations: Multidimensional Effects of Political Involvement," *American Political Science Review* 87 (1993), 963–975.

[82]"Opinion Outlook," *National Journal,* February 18, 1995, 452.

[83]Richard E. Neustadt, *Presidential Power: The Politics of Leadership from FDR to Carter* (New York: Wiley, 1980).

[84]Ibid.

[85]Kernell, *Going Public: New Strategies of Presidential Leadership.*

[86]A classic study on this topic is James David Barber's *Presidential Character: Predicting Performance in the White House* (Englewood Cliffs, N.J.: Prentice Hall, 1989), originally published in 1973.

[87]Quoted in Arthur M. Schlesinger Jr., "The Ultimate Approval Rating," *New York Times Magazine,* December 18, 1996, 50.

[88]Ibid.

[89]Ibid.

[90]National CNN/Gallup Polls taken in February, March, and July, 2005, showed support dropping from 44% to 29% and disapproval rising correspondingly. See www.pollingreport.com/social.htm.

[91]Lewis L. Gould quoted in "Bush's Year of Living Dangerously," p. 27.

[92]"Bush's Year of Living Dangerously," 26.

Chapter 12

[1]Neely Tucker, "A Web of Truth," *Washington Post,* October 19, 2005, C1; other biographical information is from "Mrs Bunnatine H. Greenhouse: Biography" (www.whistleblowers.org/html/greenhouse.htm).

[2]"A Web of Truth," C1.

[3]Chris Matthews interview with Stephen [sic] M. Kohn, lawyer with the National Whistleblowers Center, representing Mrs. Greenhouse. "Hardball with Chris Matthews" (MSNBC), October 29, 2004.

[4]Adam Zagorin and Timothy J. Burger, "Beyond the Call of Duty," *Time Magazine,* November 1, 2005, 64.

[5]"A Web of Truth," C1.

[6]Bruce Adams, "The Frustrations of Government Service," *Public Administration Review* 44 (1984), 5. For more discussion of public attitudes about the civil service, see Herbert Kaufman, "Fear of

Bureaucracy: A Raging Pandemic," *Public Administration Review* 41 (1981), 1.

[7]The classic early work on western bureaucracy is Max Weber's. See H. H. Gerth and C. Wright Mills, trans., from Max Weber: *Essays on Sociology* (New York: Oxford University Press, 1946), 196-239.

[8]On distinctions between public and private bureaucracies see Barry Bozeman, *All Organizations Are Public: Bridging Public and Private Organizational Theories* (San Francisco: Jossey-Bass, 1987).

[9]"Federal Executives' Bonuses Scrutinized," *Champaign-Urbana News-Gazette,* January 23, 2002, A4.

[10]From a letter to W. T. Barry, quoted in "A Citizen's Guide on Using the Freedom of Information Act and the Privacy Act of 1974 to Request Government Records," report to the U.S. House of Representatives 50 (1999), 2.

[11]Reported in Sam Archibald, "The Early Years of the Freedom of Information Act, 1955-1974," *PS: Political Science and Politics,* December 1993, 730.

[12]Debra Gersh Hernandez, "Many Promises, Little Action," *Editor and Publisher,* March 26, 1994, 15.

[13]Government Accounting Office, Freedom of Information Act: State Department Request Processing (Washington, D.C.: Government Printing Office, 1989).

[14]"President Declassifies Old Papers," *Omaha World-Herald,* April 18, 1995, 1.

[15]Clinton administration policy on compliance with FOIA can be found in Federation of American Scientists, Project on Government Secrecy, "Clinton Administration Documents on Classification Policy," 2003, www.fas.org/sgp/clinton/index.html.

[16]Linda Greenhouse, "A Penchant for Secrecy," *New York Times,* May 5, 2002, WK1.

[17]As a presidential aide in the Ford administration, Cheney encouraged President Ford to veto the 1974 bill that strengthened FOIA rights. Congress ultimately passed the bill over Ford's veto.

[18]Memo from Attorney General John Ashcroft, October 12, 2001. The text of this memo and all major Bush administration statements and documents regarding its FOIA and openness in government policies are posted at the Federation of American Scientists website, www.fas.org. Also see openthegovernment.org.

[19]Useful websites for tracking data removed from government websites include: www.ombwatch.org, openthegovernment.org, and www.fas.org.

[20]William S. Broad, "U.S. Is Tightening Rules on Keeping Scientific Secrets," *New York Times,* February 17, 2002, 1, 13.

[21]David Nather, "Pilots Need-to-Know Conundrum," *CQ Weekly,* July 18, 2005, 1966.

[22]Christopher Drew, "Efforts to Hide Sensitive Data Pit 9/11 Concerns against Safety," *New York Times,* March 5, 2005.

[23]Ellen Nakashima, "Frustration on the Left—and the Right," *Washington Post National Weekly Edition,* March 11, 2002, 29; Scott Shane, "Increase in the Number of Documents Classified by the Government," *New York Times,* July 3, 2005, 12.

[24]Eric Lichtblau, "Government by, and Secret from, the People," *New York Times,* September 5, 2004, WK5.

[25]Shane, "Increase in the Number of Documents Classified by the Government,"12; David Nather, "Classified: A Rise in State Secrets," *CQ Weekly,* July 18, 2005, 1960.

[26]Nakashima, "Frustration."

[27]Greenhouse, "Penchant for Secrecy."

[28]Interview by Bill Moyers, "Behind the Freedom of Information Act," on *Now with Bill Moyers,* PBS, April 5, 2002.

[29](Senators) Trent Lott and Ron Wyden, "Hiding the Truth in a Cloud of Black Ink," *New York Times,* August 26, 2004, A27.

[30]Evan Hendricks, Former Secrets: Government Records Made Public through the Freedom of Information Act (Washington, D.C.: Campaign for Political Rights, 1982); "Behind the Freedom of Information Act," *Now with Bill Moyers,* PBS, April 5, 2002.

[31]Joyce Appleby, "That's General Washington to You," *New York Times Book Review,* February 14, 1993, 11, a review of Richard Norton Smith, *Patriarch* (Boston: Houghton Mifflin, 1993). See also James Q. Wilson, "The Rise of the Bureaucratic State," *Public Interest* 41 (1975), 77-103.

[32]Wilson, "Rise of the Bureaucratic State."

[33]Leonard D. White, *Introduction to the Study of Public Administration,* 4th ed. (New York: Macmillan, 1955), 4.

[34]David H. Rosenbloom, "'Whose Bureaucracy Is This Anyway?' Congress's 1946 Answer," *PS: Political Science and Politics,* December 2001, 773.

[35]Paul C. Light, *Thickening Government: Federal Hierarchy and the Diffusion of Accountability* (Washington, D.C.: Brookings Institution, 1995).

[36]U.S. Census Bureau, *Statistical Abstract of the United States,* 2006 (Washington, D.C.: Government Printing Office, 2005), tab. 451.

[37]Richard E. Stevenson, "Bush Budget Links Dollars to Deeds with New Ratings," *New York Times,* February 3, 2002, 1, 23; Eric Schmitt, "Is This Any Way to Run a Nation?" *New York Times,* April 14, 2002, WK4. Agency evaluations can be viewed at the OMB website, www.omb.gov.

[38]"Federal Government Found to Have Gotten Bigger," *Champaign-Urbana News-Gazette,* January 23, 2004, A3.

[39]Paul C. Light, "Fact Sheet on the Continued Thickening of Government," Brookings Institution, July 23, 2004, www.brookings.edu/views/papers/light/20040723.htm.

[40]Ibid. Light does an "inventory" of senior positions in cabinet departments every six years.

[41]Jim Hoagland, "Dissing Government," *Washington Post National Weekly Edition,* December 8, 2003, 5.

[42]Paul C. Light, "What Federal Employees Want from Reform: Reform Watch Brief No. 5," Brookings Institution, March 2002, www.brookings.edu/comm/reformwatch/rw05.htm.

[43]For a discussion of these issues, see Peter T. Kilborn, "Big Change Likely as Law Bans Bias toward Disabled," *New York Times,* July 19, 1992, 1, 16.

[44]Jill Smolows, "Noble Aims, Mixed Results," *Time,* July 31, 1995, 54.

[45]Theodore Lowi, *The End of Liberalism* (New York: Norton, 1969).

[46]Woodrow Wilson, "The Study of Administration," *Political Science Quarterly* 56 (1941), 481-506. Originally published in 1887.

[47]See David H. Rosenbloom, "Have an Administrative Rx? Don't Forget the Politics!" *Public Administration Review* 53 (1993), 503-507.

[48]The changes in allowable political activities made possible by the Hatch Act Reform Amendments are outlined by Office of Personnel Management in its online history, "Biography of an Ideal." See the section "Hatch Act Revisited and Transformed" (www.opm.gov).

[49]Charles Peters, *How Washington Really Works* (Reading, Mass.: Addison-Wesley, 1980), 46–47.

[50]Nicolas Thompson, "Finding the Civil Service's Hidden Sex Appeal," *Washington Monthly,* November 2000, 31.

[51]Terry More, "Regulators' Performance and Presidential Administrations," American Journal of Political Science 26 (1982), 197–224; Terry More, "Control and Feedback in Economic Regulation," *American Political Science Review* 79 (1985), 1094–1116.

[52]More, "Control and Feedback."

[53]Use of the term *capture* by political scientists studying regulation seems to have originated with Samuel Huntington, "The Marasmus of the ICC," *Yale Law Journal* 61 (1952), 467–509; it was later popularized by Marver Bernstein, *Regulating Business by Independent Commission* (Princeton, N.J.: Princeton University Press, 1955).

[54]W. John Moore, "Citizen Prosecutors," *National Journal,* August 18, 1990, 2006–2010.

[55]David C. Morrison, "Extracting a Thorn, Air Force Style," *National Journal,* March 7, 1987, 567. For more on Fitzgerald's experiences, see A. Ernest Fitzgerald, *The Pentagonists: An Insider's View of Waste, Mismanagement, and Fraud in Defense Spending* (Boston: Houghton Mifflin, 1989).

[56]Steve Fainaru and Dan Eggen, "Chief among the Charges," *Washington Post National Weekly Edition,* June 10, 2002, 30.

[57]Robert Pear, "Congress Moves to Protect Federal Whistleblowers," *New York Times,* October 3, 2004, 21.

[58]Fred Alford, quoted in Barbara Ehrenreich, "All Together Now," *New York Times,* July 15, 2004, A23.

[59]Eric Schmitt, "The Rube Goldberg Agency," *New York Times,* March 24, 2002, WK5.

[60]Schmitt, "Is This Any Way to Run a Nation?"

[61]Interview with David Brancaccio, *Now* (PBS), October 14, 2005.

[62]"A Web of Truth," *Washington Post,* C1.

[63]Deborah Hastings, "Bunny Greenhouse under Attack for Revealing Corruption in Military Contracting" (www.reclaimdemocracy.org). First published by the Associated Press, August 7, 2005.

[64]Erik Eckholm, "The Billions: Top Army Official Calls for a Halliburton Inquiry," *New York Times,* October 25, 2004, 1.

[65]The letter was sent by Senators Byron L. Dorgan (D-N.D.) and Frank Lautenberg, (D-N.J.), and Rep. Henry Waxman, (D-Calif.).

[66]The dismissed civil servant had headed the Louisville office of USACE and made many of the same criticisms as Greenhouse. The testimony of all witnesses, including Mrs. Greenhouse, who appeared at the Democratic Policy Committee hearings on Iraq War contracts, 2004–2006, can be found by going to senate.democrats.gov and linking to committee reports. Transcripts from all of the hearings are online.

[67]Michael H. Cottman, "Bunny Greenhouse, a Vocal Critic of Halliburton Contract, Gets Demoted" (BlackAmericaWeb.com). First published by Associated Press, August 29, 2005.

Chapter 13

[1]For elaboration, see John Anthony Maltese, *The Selling of Supreme Court Nominees* (Baltimore: Johns Hopkins University Press, 1995).

[2]Ruth Bader Ginsburg and Stephen Breyer.

[3]David Broder, "President Pushover," *Washington Post National Weekly Edition,* November 7-13, 2005, 4.

[4]"Judging Samuel Alito," *New York Times,* January 8, 2006, WK13.

[5]*Planned Parenthood of Southeastern Pennsylvania* v. *Casey,* 120 L.Ed. 674 (1992).

[6]Amy Goldstein and Sarah Cohen, "On the Record," *Washington Post National Weekly Edition,* January 9-15, 2006, 13.

[7]Charles Peters, "Tilting at Windmills," *Washington Monthly,* March, 2006, 8.

[8]Janet Malcolm, "The Art of Testifying," New Yorker, March 13, 2006, 72.

[9]Lois Romano and Juliet Eilperin, "Lessons from Bork," *Washington Post National Weekly Edition,* February 6-12, 2006, 12.

[10]Ibid.

[11]John Hibbing and Elizabeth Theiss-Morse, *Congress as Public Enemy: Public Attitudes toward American Political Institutions* (New York: Cambridge University Press, 1995), ch. 2 and 3.

[12]John R. Schmidhauser, *Justices and Judges* (Boston: Little, Brown, 1979), 11.

[13]*Federalist Paper 78.*

[14]Henry J. Abraham, *Justices and Presidents* (New York: Oxford University Press, 1974), 74.

[15]Henry J. Abraham, *The Judicial Process,* 3rd ed. (New York: Oxford University Press, 1975), 309.

[16]Drew Pearson and Robert S. Allen, *The Nine Old Men* (New York: Doubleday/Doren, 1937), 7; Barbara A. Perry, *The Priestly Tribe*: The Supreme Court's Image in the American Mind (Westport, Conn.: Praeger, 1999), 8-9.

[17]Some state courts already used judicial review, and in *Federalist Paper* 78 Hamilton said that federal courts would have authority to void laws contrary to the Constitution.

[18]5 U.S. 137 (1803). Technically, *Marbury* was not the first use of judicial review, but it was the first clear articulation of judicial review by the Court.

[19]Jefferson was also angry at the nature of the appointees. One had led troops loyal to England during the Revolutionary War. Eric Black, *Our Constitution: The Myth That Binds Us* (Boulder, Colo.: Westview Press, 1988), 66.

[20]Debate arose over whether the four should be considered appointed. Their commissions had been signed by the president, and the seal of the United States had been affixed by Marshall, as secretary of state. Yet it was customary to require commissions to be delivered, perhaps because of less reliable record keeping by government or less reliable communications at the time.

[21]Marbury had petitioned the Court for a writ of *mandamus* under the authority of a provision of the Judiciary Act of 1789 that permitted the Court to issue such a writ. Marshall maintained that this provision broadened the Court's original jurisdiction and thus violated the Constitution. (The Constitution allows the Court to hear cases that have not been heard by any other court before-if they involve a state or a foreign ambassador. Marbury's involved neither.) Yet it was quite clear that the provision did not broaden the Court's original jurisdiction-so clear, in fact, that Marshall did not even quote the language he was declaring unconstitutional. Furthermore, even if the provision did broaden the Court's original jurisdiction, it is not certain that the provision would violate the Constitution. (The Constitution does not say that the Court shall have original jurisdiction only in cases involving a state or a foreign ambassador.) Many members of Congress who had drafted and voted for the Judiciary Act had been delegates to the Constitutional Convention, and it is unlikely that they would have initiated a law that contradicted the Consti-

tution. And Oliver Ellsworth, who had been a coauthor of the bill, then served as chief justice of the Supreme Court before Marshall. But these interpretations allowed Marshall a way out of the dilemma.

[22]Quoted in Walter F. Murphy and C. Herman Pritchett, *Courts, Judges, and Politics,* 3rd ed. (New York: Random House, 1979), 4.

[23]John A. Garraty, "The Case of the Missing Commissions," in *Quarrels That Have Shaped the Constitution,* ed. John A. Garraty (New York: Harper & Row, 1962), 13.

[24]*Fletcher v. Peck,* 10 U.S. 87 (1810); *Martin v. Hunter's Lessee,* 14 U.S. 304 (1816); *Cohens v. Virginia,* 19 U.S. 264 (1821).

[25]Especially to regulate commerce. *Gibbons* v. *Ogden,* 22 U.S. 1 (1824).

[26]*Scott v. Sandford,* 60 U.S. 393 (1857).

[27]*Ex parte Merryman,* 17 Fed. Cas. 144, no. 9487 (1861).

[28]*Ex parte McCardle,* 74 U.S. 506 (1869).

[29]For examination of the ways in which the Civil War and Reconstruction fomented a constitutional "revolution," see Bruce Ackerman, *We the People: Transformations* (Cambridge, Mass.: Harvard University Press, 1998). Ackerman offers a similar examination of the significance of the New Deal period.

[30]*Hammer v. Dagenhart,* 247 U.S. 251 (1918).

[31]*Lochner v. New York,* 198 U.S. 45 (1905).

[32]*Adkins v. Children's Hospital,* 261 U.S. 525 (1923).

[33]*Adair v. United States,* 208 U.S. 161 (1908); *In re Delis,* 158 U.S. 564 (1895).

[34]*United States* v. *E.C. Knight Co.,* 156 U.S. 1 (1895).

[35]Lawrence Baum, *The Supreme Court,* 8th ed. (Washington, D.C.: CQ Press, 2004).

[36]C. Herman Pritchett, *The American Constitution,* 2nd ed. (New York: McGraw-Hill, 1968), 166.

[37]For convenience, scholars and journalists refer to the Supreme Court by the name of the chief justice, although the Court's doctrine is determined by all of its justices.

[38]However, the Warren Court may not have been as out of step with the political branches as often believed. See Lucas A. Powe, *The Warren Court and American Politics* (Cambridge, Mass.: Harvard University Press, 2000), 160-178.

[39]One legal scholar says the most striking feature about Supreme Court decision making in the 1990s was the effort by five justices to resolve most issues as narrowly as possible, shunning sweeping pronouncements for case-by-case examination. Cass R. Sunstein, *One Case at a Time: Judicial Minimalism on the Supreme Court* (Cambridge, Mass.: Harvard University Press, 2001).

[40]For an analysis, see John T. Noonan, *Narrowing the Nation's Power* (Berkeley: University of California Press, 2002).

[41]At the same time, however, the Rehnquist Court took the first step toward new doctrine for homosexuals.

[42]Gregory Stock, quoted in Joel Garreau, "Evolution of Our Species," *Washington Post National Weekly Edition,* June 20-26, 2005, 6.

[43]Ray Kurzweil, quoted in Joel Garreau, "The Second Evolution of the Species," *Washington Post National Weekly Edition,* May 6, 2002, 11.

[44] These developments occurred in 1875 and 1891.

[45]In addition, there is the Court of Appeals for the Federal Circuit, which handles customs and patents cases.

[46]Occasionally, for important cases, the entire group of judges in one circuit will sit together, "en banc." (In the large Ninth Circuit, eleven judges will sit.)

[47]If at least $75,000 is at stake, according to congressional law.

[48]Quoted in Henry J. Abraham, "A Bench Happily Filled," *Judicature* 66 (1983), 284.

[49]For elaboration on the Senate's role, see Stephen B. Burbank, "Politics, Privilege, and Power: The Senate's Role in the Appointment of Federal Judges," *Judicature* 86 (2002), 24.

[50]Victor Navasky, *Kennedy Justice* (New York: Atheneum, 1971), 245-246.

[51]Harry P. Stumpf, *American Judicial Politics,* 2nd ed. (Upper Saddle River, N.J.: Prentice Hall, 1998), 175. After Taft nominated a Catholic to be chief justice, the speaker of the House cracked, "If Taft were Pope, he'd want to appoint some Protestants to the College of Cardinals." Henry J. Abraham, *Justices and Presidents: A Political History of Appointments to the Supreme Court,* 2nd ed. (New York: Oxford University Press, 1985), 168.

[52]Elliot E. Slotnick, "A Historical Perspective on Federal Judicial Selection," *Judicature* 86 (2002), 13.

[53]For an analysis of internal documents that established this process in the Reagan administration, see Dawn Johnsen, "Tipping the Scale," *Washington Monthly,* July–August 2002, 1-18.

[54]Robert A. Carp, Ronald Stidham, and Kenneth L. Manning, *Judicial Process in America,* 6th ed. (Washington, D.C.: CQ Press, 2004), 164.

[55]Marilyn Nejelski, *Women in the Judiciary: A Status Report* (Washington, D.C.: National Women's Political Caucus, 1984).

[56]Sheldon Goldman, "Reagan's Second-Term Judicial Appointments," *Judicature* 70 (1987), 324–339.

[57]Sheldon Goldman, Elliott E. Slotnick, Gerard Gryski, Gary Zuk, and Sara Schiavoni, "W. Bush Remaking the Judiciary: Like Father Like Son?" *Judicature* 86 (2003), 304, 308. For further examination, see Rorie L. Spill and Kathleen A. Bratton, "Clinton and Diversification of the Federal Judiciary," *Judicature,* March–April, 2001, 256.

[58]Ibid.

[59]Especially congressional power under the commerce clause.

[60]David Greenberg, "Actually, It Is Political," *Washington Post National Weekly Edition,* July 26-August 1, 2004, 23.

[61]One of President Reagan's nominees, Douglas Ginsburg, withdrew his nomination due to widespread opposition in the Senate, so officially his nomination was not denied.

[62]Nixon's nomination of G. Harold Carswell was a notable exception. At his confirmation hearing, a parade of legal scholars called him undistinguished. Even his supporters acknowledged that he was mediocre. Nixon's floor manager for the nomination, Senator Roman Hruska (R-Nebr.), blurted out in exasperation, "Even if he is mediocre, there are a lot of mediocre judges and people and lawyers. They are entitled to a little representation, aren't they, and a little chance? We can't have all Brandeises, Cardozos, and Frankfurters, and stuff like that there." Abraham, *Justices and Presidents,* 6–7.

[63]For an examination of the relationship between ethical lapses and ideological reasons, see Charles M. Cameron, Albert D. Cover, and Jeffrey A. Segal, "Senate Voting on Supreme Court Nominees: A Neoinstitutional Model," *American Political Science Review* 84 (1990), 525–534.

[64]For some time, the Senate confirmed fewer nominees to the lower courts in the fourth year of a president's term when the Senate's majority was from the other party. The senators hoped their candidate would capture the White House in the next election. They delayed confirmation so there would be numerous vacancies for their president and, through senatorial courtesy, for themselves to fill as well. Jeffrey A. Segal and Harold Spaeth, "If a Supreme Court Vacancy Occurs, Will the Senate Confirm a Reagan Nominee?" *Judicature* 69 (1986), 188–189.

[65]For an objective measure of obstruction and delay, see Sheldon Goldman, "Assessing the Senate Judicial Confirmation Process: The Index of Obstruction and Delay," *Judicature* 86 (2003), 251.

[66]Al Kamen, "Switching Sides to Court Victory," *Washington Post National Weekly Edition,* July 14, 1997, 15.

[67]Except for the Republican filibuster against Abe Fortas' nomination by President Johnson in 1968.

[68]At one point, the Democrats were filibustering ten nominees, but a compromise fashioned by moderates in both parties allowed most of these to be confirmed.

[69]Quoted in Savage, "Clinton Losing Fight for Black Judge," *Los Angeles Times,* July 7, 2000, A1.

[70]Scherer, "Judicial Confirmation Process," 240–250.

[71]Schmidhauser, *Justice and Judges,* 55–57.

[72]David Leonhardt, "Who Has a Corner Office?" *New York Times,* November 27, 2005, BU4.

[73]All except Kennedy, Thomas, and possibly Alito.

[74]Goldman et al., "W. Bush Remaking the Judiciary," 304, 308.

[75]Merle Miller, *Plain Speaking* (New York: Berkeley Putnam, 1974), 121.

[76]Harold W. Chase, *Federal Judges* (Minneapolis: University of Minnesota Press, 1972), 189.

[77]John Gruhl, "The Impact of Term Limits for Supreme Court Justices," *Judicature* 81 (1997), 66-72.

[78]The fourth, Rehnquist, disqualified himself because he had worked on the administration's policy toward executive privilege.

[79]*Jones* v. *Clinton,* 137 L.Ed.2d 945, 117 S. Ct. 1636 (1997).

[80]Martin Shapiro, "The Supreme Court: From Warren to Burger," in *The New American Political System,* ed. Anthony King (Washington, D.C.: American Enterprise Institute, 1978), 180-181.

[81]Robert Scigliano, The Supreme Court and the Presidency (New York: Free Press, 1971), 147-148.

[82]Quoted in Abraham, *Justices and Presidents,* 62.

[83]Earl Warren, *The Memoirs of Earl Warren* (Garden City, N.Y.: Doubleday, 1977), 5.

[84]Quoted in Abraham, *Justices and Presidents,* 63.

[85]Linda Greenhouse, "In the Confirmation Dance, the Past but Rarely the Prologue," *New York Times,* July 24, 2005, WK5.

[86]For elaboration, see Lee Epstein and Jeffrey A. Segal, *Advice and Consent* (New York: Oxford University Press, 2005), ch. 5.

[87]"How Much Do Lawyers Charge?" *Parade,* March 23, 1997, 14.

[88]Lois G. Forer, *Money and Justice* (New York: Norton, 1984), 9, 15, 102.

[89]Peter Slevin, "Courting Christianity," *Washington Post National Weekly Edition,* July 17-23, 2006, 29.

[90]Karen O'Connor and Lee Epstein, "The Rise of Conservative Interest Group Litigation," *Journal of Politics* 45 (1983), 481. See also Richard C. Cortner, *The Supreme Court and the Second Bill of Rights* (Madison: University of Wisconsin Press, 1981), 282.

[91]Epstein and Segal, *Advice and Consent,* 12. The Court also takes about this many to decide summarily—without oral arguments and full written opinions.

[92]The dentist agreed to fill the cavity only in a hospital, where the procedure would be far more expensive. *Bragdon* v. *Abbott,* 141 L.Ed.2d 540 (1998).

[93]*Sutton* v. *United Air Lines,* 144 L.Ed.2d 450 (1999).

[94]The Court ruled the same in a case involving a man with high blood pressure who could not get a job driving trucks. *Murphy* v. *United Parcel Service,* 144 L.Ed.2d 484 (1999).

[95]*Toyota Motor Manufacturing* v. *Williams,* 151 L.Ed.2d 615 (2001).

[96]Robert Bork, *The Tempting of America* (New York: Touchstone/Simon & Schuster, 1990).

[97]James Madison's notes from the Constitutional Convention and the Federalist Papers are considered the most authoritative sources, but relying on them is fraught with problems. Because Madison edited his notes many years after the convention, his experiences in government or lapses of memory might have colored his version of the intentions of the delegates. Because Madison, Hamilton, and Jay published the *Federalist Papers* to persuade New York to ratify the Constitution, their motive may have affected their account of the intentions of the delegates.

[98]Lawrence Tribe, *On Reading the Constitution* (Cambridge, Mass.: Harvard University Press, 1992).

[99]*Osborn* v. *U.S. Bank,* 22 U.S. 738 (1824), at 866.

[100]Abraham, *Judicial Process,* 324.

[101]*United States* v. *Butler,* 297 U.S. 1, at 94.

[102]Murphy and Pritchett, *Courts, Judges, and Politics,* 586.

[103]*Furman* v. *Georgia,* 408 U.S. 238 (1972). Blackmun did vote against the death penalty later in his career.

[104]Quoted in Alexander Bickel, *The Morality of Consent* (New Haven, Conn.: Yale University Press, 1975), 120.

[105]"Judicial Authority Moves Growing Issue," *Lincoln Journal,* April 24, 1977.

[106]Thomas M. Keck, *The Most Activist Supreme Court in History* (Chicago: University of Chicago Press, 2004).

[107]531 U.S. 98 (2000).

[108]Jeffrey A. Segal and Albert D. Cover, "Ideological Values and the Votes of U.S. Supreme Court Justices," *American Political Science Review* 83 (1989), 557–564. For different findings for state supreme court justices, see John M. Scheb II, Terry Bowen, and Gary Anderson, "Ideology, Role Orientations, and Behavior in the State Courts of Last Resort," *American Politics Quarterly* 19 (1991), 324–335.

[109]Harold Spaeth and Stuart Teger, "Activism and Restraint: A Cloak for the Justices' Policy Preferences," in *Supreme Court Activism and Restraint,* ed. Stephen P. Halpern and Clark M. Lamb (Lexington, Mass.: Lexington Books, 1982), 277.

[110]*Engel* v. *Vitale,* 370 U.S. 421 (1962).

[111]*Abington School District* v. *Schempp,* 374 U.S. 203 (1963).

[112]*Stone* v. *Graham,* 449 U.S. 39 (1980).

[113]*Lee* v. *Weisman,* 120 L.Ed.2d 467 (1992).

[114]*Santa Fe Independent School District* v. *Doe,* 147 L.Ed.2d 295 (2000).

[115]*Burnet* v. *Coronado Oil and Gas,* 285 U.S. 293 (1932), at 406.

[116]*Denver Area Educational Telecommunications Consortium* v. *Federal Communications Commission,* 116 S. Ct. 2374 (1996).

[117]*United States* v. *Butler,* 297 U. S. 1 (1936), at 79.

[118]Some might say that judges, rather than make law, mediate among various ideas that rise to the surface, killing off some and allowing others to survive. Robert Cover, "Nomos and Narrative," *Harvard Law Review* 97 (1983), 4.

[119]Quoted in Murphy and Pritchett, *Courts, Judges, and Politics,* 25.

[120]*Gratz* v. *Bollinger,* 156 L.Ed.2d 257 (2003); *Grutter* v. *Bollinger,* 156 L.Ed.2d 304 (2003).

[121]Quoted in David J. Garrow, "The Rehnquist Reins," *New York Times Magazine,* October 6, 1996, 70.

[122]Quoted in Robert Wernick, "Chief Justice Marshall Takes the Law in Hand," *Smithsonian,* November 1998, 162.

[123]Joan Biskupic, "Here Comes the Judge? Maybe Not," *Washington Post National Weekly Edition,* February 14, 2000, 30.

[124]Jeffrey A. Segal and Harold J. Spaeth, *The Supreme Court and the Attitudinal Model* (New York: Cambridge University Press, 1993), 262–264.

[125]Jeffrey Rosen, "Rehnquist's Choice," *New Yorker,* January 11, 1999, 31.

[126]Justice Breyer, quoted by Jeffrey Toobin, "Breyer's Big Idea," *New Yorker,* October 31, 2005, 43.

[127]*Morning Edition,* National Public Radio, March 5, 2004.

[128]Michael S. Serrill, "The Power of William Brennan," *Time,* July 22, 1985, 62.

[129]Ibid.

[130]David J. Garrow, "One Angry Man," *New York Times Magazine,* October 6, 1996, 68-69.

[131]*Webster* v. *Reproductive Health Services,* 492 U.S. 490 (1989).

[132]*United States* v. *Virginia,* 135 L.Ed.2d 735, 787–789 (1996).

[133]Charles Evans Hughes, *The Supreme Court of the United States* (New York: Columbia University Press, 1928), 68.

[134]Interview with Justice Ruth Bader Ginsburg, *Morning Edition,* National Public Radio, May 2, 2002. Ginsburg said that foreign jurists admit they disagree with each other but do not make it public.

[135]Craig R. Ducat, *2005 Supplement for Constitutional Interpretation,* 8th ed. (Belmont, California: Wadsworth, 2006), 3.

[136]Linda Greenhouse, "The High Court and the Triumph of Discord," *New York Times,* July 15, 2001, sec. 4, 1. Perhaps this calls into question Rehnquist's reputation as an effective leader.

[137]Alexis de Tocqueville, *Democracy in America* (1832).

[138]*Roe* v. *Wade,* 410 U.S. 113 (1973).

[139]Baum, *Supreme Court,* 170, 173.

[140]Craig R. Ducat and Robert L. Dudley, "Federal Appellate Judges and Presidential Power," paper presented at the Midwest Political Science Association meeting, April 1987.

[141]Baum, *Supreme Court,* 158.

[142]Sheldon Goldman, "How Long the Legacy?" *Judicature* 76 (1993), 295.

[143]The Eleventh Amendment overturned *Chisholm* v. *Georgia* (1793), which had permitted the federal courts to hear suits against a state by citizens of another state. The Fourteenth over-

turned the Dred Scott case, *Scott* v. *Sandford* (1857), which had held that blacks were not citizens. The Sixteenth overturned *Pollock* v. *Farmers' Loan and Trust* (1895), which had negated a congressional law authorizing a federal income tax. The Twenty-Sixth overturned *Oregon* v. *Mitchell* (1970), which had negated a congressional law allowing eighteen-year-olds to vote in state elections.

[144]*Goldman* v. *Weinberger,* 475 U.S. 503 (1986).

[145]William N. Eskridge Jr., "Overriding Supreme Court Statutory Interpretation Decisions," *Yale Law Journal* 101 (1991), 338.

[146]Detainee Treatment Act of 2005.

[147]Thomas R. Marshall, "Public Opinion and the Rehnquist Court," in *Readings in American Government and Politics,* 3rd ed. (Boston: Allyn & Bacon, 1999), 115–121.

[148]Richard Morin, "A Nation of Stooges," *Washington Post,* October 8, 1995, C5.

[149]Gregory A. Caldeira, "Neither the Purse nor the Sword," paper presented at the American Political Science Association meeting, August 1987.

[150]Quoted in Abraham, *Justices and Presidents,* 342–343.

[151]Robert G. McCloskey, *The American Supreme Court* (Chicago: University of Chicago Press, 1960), 225.

[152]Harold Meyerson, "Up Front," *American Prospect,* February, 2006, 6.

[153]Tom Korologos, "Roberts Rx: Speak Up, but Shut Up," *New York Times,* September 4, 2005, WK12.

[154]Janet Malcolm, "The Art of Testifying," *New Yorker,* March 13, 2006, 74.

[155]Lindsey Graham (R-S.C.), quoted in Malcolm, "The Art of Testifying," 75.

[156]Arlen Specter (R-Pa.), quoted in Jeffrey Toobin, "Comment: Unanswered Questions," *New Yorker,* January 23 and 30, 2006, 30.

[157]David Axelrod, quoted in James A. Barnes, "Confirming Their Frustration," *National Journal,* January 21, 2006, 54.

Chapter 14

[1]Ian James, "Importance of Gitmo Questioned," *Lincoln Journal Star,* June 26, 2004.

[2]The administration has announced that some will be tried in military tribunals. These few will be charged, will receive counsel, and will gain access to military tribunals, of course.

[3]When the Supreme Court agreed to take the case, the government released the two Britons.

[4]*Johnson* v. *Eisentrager,* 339 U.S. 763 (1950).

[5]A related argument is that the military has discretion on the battlefield, and in the war on terrorism, all American territory, including foreign bases, is part of the battlefield.

[6]Michael Isikoff and Stuart Taylor, Jr., "The Gitmo Fallout," *Newsweek,* July 17, 2006, 23.

[7]Joseph Margulies, "At Guantanamo Bay, a Year in Limbo," *Washington Post National Weekly Edition,* January 6, 2003, 22.

[8]Michael Ratner, "Moving Away from the Rule of Law," *Cardozo Law Review* 24 (2003), 1518.

[9]Richard Morin, "The High Price of Free Speech," *Washington Post National Weekly Edition,* January 8, 2001, 34.

[10]Poll for the First Amendment Center and the *American Journalism Review,* conducted by the Center for Survey Research and Analysis at the University of Connecticut, June and July 2002. Reported in Ken Paulson, "Too Free?" *American Journalism Review,* September 2002, available at www.ajr.org/Article.asp?id52621.

[11]First Amendment Center, in cooperation with the *American Journalism Review.* Survey conducted May 13–23, 2005. (*N*=1003; sampling error=3%).

[12]The states did not ratify a proposed amendment that would have required at least one representative in Congress for every fifty thousand people. That amendment would have put about five thousand members in today's Congress. The states also did not ratify, until 1992, another proposed amendment that would have prohibited a salary raise for members of Congress from taking effect until after the next election to Congress.

[13]*Reid* v. *Covert,* 354 U.S. 1 (1957).

[14]*Barron* v. *Baltimore,* 32 U.S. 243 (1833).

[15]Also, many states had their own bill of rights at the time, and other states were expected to follow.

[16]*Gitlow* v. *New York,* 268 U.S. 652 (1925). *Gitlow* is usually cited as the first because it initiated the twentieth-century trend. However, *Chicago, Burlington and Quincy R. Co.* v. *Chicago,* 166 U.S. 266 (1897), was actually the first. It applied the Fifth Amendment's just compensation clause, requiring government to pay owners "just compensation" for taking their property.

[17]*Argersinger* v. *Hamlin,* 407 U.S. 25 (1972).

[18]The Court used the Fourteenth Amendment's due process clause as justification. This clause, adopted after the Civil War to protect former slaves from their southern governments, reads, "Nor shall any state deprive any person of life, liberty, or property without due process of law." This clause applies to states and refers to "liberty." Although ambiguous, the Court interpreted it to mean that the states also have to provide the liberties in the Bill of Rights.

[19]The amendment also includes a right "to petition the government for a redress of grievances," which is incorporated in freedom of speech and assembly. The language does not explicitly include freedom of association, but the Court has interpreted the amendment to encompass this right.

[20]Anna Johnson, "Know Your First Amendment Rights? Poll Shows Many Don't," *Lincoln Journal Star,* March 1, 2006, 10A.

[21]Even Justice Black, who claimed that he interpreted it literally. To do so, he had to define some speech as "action" so that it would not be protected.

[22]*Milk Wagon Drivers Union* v. *Meadowmoor Dairies,* 312 U.S. 287 (1941).

[23]Quoted in Deborah Tannen, *The Argument Culture* (New York: Ballantine, 1998), 25.

[24]Thomas I. Emerson, *The System of Freedom of Expression* (New York: Random House/Vintage, 1971), 6–8.

[25]For a history of speech cases between the Civil War and World War I, see David M. Rabban, *Free Speech in Its Forgotten Years* (New York: Cambridge University Press, 1997).

[26]Zechariah Chafee Jr., *Free Speech in the United States* (Cambridge, Mass.: Harvard University Press, 1941), 51–52.

[27]*Schenk* v. *United States,* 249 U.S. 47 (1919); *Frohwerk* v. *United States,* 249 U.S. 204 (1919); *Debs* v. *United States,* 249 U.S. 211 (1919); *Abrams* v. *United States,* 250 U.S. 616 (1919); *Gitlow* v. *New York,* 268 U.S. 652 (1925); *Whitney* v. *California,* 274 U.S. 357 (1927).

[28]*Gitlow* v. *New York.*

[29]David Cole, "The Course of Least Resistance: Repeating History in the War on Terrorism," in *Lost Liberties,* ed. Cynthia Brown (New York: New Press, 2003), 15.

[30]Novelist Philip Roth observes, "McCarthy understood better than any American politician before him that people whose job was to legislate could do far better for themselves by performing; McCarthy understood the entertainment value of disgrace and how to feed the pleasures of paranoia. He took us back to our origins, back to the seventeenth century and the stocks. That's how the country began: moral disgrace as public entertainment." *I Married a Communist* (New York: Vintage, 1999), 284.

[31]*Dennis* v. *United States,* 341 U.S. 494 (1951).

[32]For the role of the Senate's Internal Security Committee, see Michael J. Ybarra, *Washington Gone Crazy: Senator Pat McCarran and the Great American Communist Hunt* (Hanover, New Hampshire: Steerforth, 2004).

[33]In the cases of *Yates* v. *United States,* 354 U.S. 298 (1957), and *Scales* v. *United States,* 367 U.S. 203 (1961), among others.

[34]Earl Warren, *The Memoirs of Earl Warren* (Garden City, N.Y.: Doubleday, 1977), 6.

[35]The records included some code names that have not been linked to real people. Charles Peters, "Tilting at Windmills," *Washington Monthly,* May, 2006, 8. See also Ted Morgan, *Reds: McCarthyism in Twentieth-Century America* (New York: Random House, 2003).

[36]Cole, "Course of Least Resistance," 1.

[37]*Brandenburg* v. *Ohio,* 395 U.S. 444 (1969). In more recent cases, a cross was burned at a Ku Klux Klan rally in a privately owned field and another was burned in the yard of an African American family. The Supreme Court ruled that states can ban cross burning with an intent to intimidate because this amounts to a threat. Thus it upheld the conviction in the latter case but struck down the conviction in the former case. *Virginia* v. *Black,* 155 L.Ed.2d 535 (2003).

[38]*Brandenburg* v. *Ohio.*

[39]Attorney General Tom Clark quoted in *Esquire,* November 1974.

[40]Jean E. Jackson, "ACTA Report Criticizes Professors," *Anthropology News,* March 2002, 7.

[41]Gia Fenoglio, "Is It 'Blacklisting' or Mere Criticism?" *National Journal,* January 19, 2002, 188.

[42]For some examples, see Michael Tomasky, "Dissent in America," *American Prospect,* April 2003, 22. See also Ann Coulter, *Treason: Liberal Treachery from the Cold War to the War on Terrorism* (New York: Crown Forum, 2003), and Sean Hannity, *Deliver Us from Evil* (New York: Regan Books/HarperCollins, 2004).

[43]*Chaplinsky* v. *New Hampshire,* 315 U.S. 568 (1942).

[44]*Rosenfeld* v. *New Jersey,* 408 U.S. 901 (1972).

[45]*Gooding* v. *Wilson,* 405 U.S. 518 (1972); *Lewis* v. *New Orleans,* 408 U.S. 913 (1972).

[46]C. Herman Pritchett, *The American Constitution,* 2nd ed. (New York: McGraw-Hill, 1968), 476, n. 2. However, police in some places continue to arrest for swearing. Judy Lin, "ACLU Fights Police on Profanity Arrests in Pittsburgh Area," *Lincoln Journal Star,* July 11, 2002.

[47]*Cohen* v. *California,* 403 U.S. 15 (1971).

[48]However, public schools below the college level can restrict the speech of their students— still children—for educational purposes, and private schools and businesses can restrict the speech of their students and employees at school and work because they are private entities.

[49]*Collin* v. *Smith,* 447 F.Supp. 676 (N.D. Ill., 1978); *Collin* v. *Smith,* 578 F.2d 1197 (7th Cir, 1978).

[50]*United States* v. *Schwimmer,* 279 U.S. 644 (1929).

[51]*Virginia* v. *Black,* 155 L.Ed.2d 535 (2003). Previously, the Court invalidated a St. Paul, Minnesota, ordinance prohibiting the display of a

Nazi swastika or a cross-burning on public or private land. *R.A.V. v. St. Paul,* 120 L.Ed.2d 305 (1992).

[52]For a legal analysis supporting these codes, see Richard Delgado and David H. Yun, "Pressure Valves and Bloodied Chickens: An Analysis of Paternalistic Objections to Hate Speech Regulation," *University of California Law Review,* 82 (1994), 716.

[53]Mary Jordan, "Free Speech Starts to Have Its Say," *Washington Post National Weekly Edition,* September 21–27, 1992, 31.

[54]Michael D. Shear, "A Tangled World Wide Web," *Washington Post National Weekly Edition,* October 30–November 5, 1995, p. 36.

[55]Stephanie Simon, "Christians Sue for Right Not to Tolerate Policies," *Los Angeles Times,* April 10, 2006, www.latimes.com/news/nationworld/nation/la-nachristians10apr10,0,6204444.story?

[56]*Barnes v. Glenn Theater,* 501 U.S. 560 (1991).

[57]*Young v. American Mini Theatres,* 427 U.S. 50 (1976); *Renton v. Playtime Theatres,* 475 U.S. 41 (1986).

[58]*FCC v. Pacifica Foundation,* 438 U.S. 726 (1968).

[59]Jonathan D. Salant, "FCC Wants to Up Fine for Cursing," *Lincoln Journal Star,* January 15, 2004.

[60]*Wilkinson v. Jones,* 480 U.S. 926 (1987).

[61]*Southeastern Promotions v. Conrad,* 420 U.S. 546 (1975).

[62]*Jeannette Rankin Brigade v. Chief of Capital Police,* 409 U.S. 972 (1972); *Edwards v. South Carolina,* 372 U.S. 229 (1963); *United States v. Grace,* 75 L.Ed.2d 736 (1983). The grounds around jails and military bases are off-limits due to the need for security. *Adderley v. Florida,* 385 U.S. 39 (1966); *Greer v. Spock,* 424 U.S. 828 (1976).

[63]*Amalgamated Food Employees v. Logan Valley Plaza,* 391 U.S. 308 (1968).

[64]*Lloyd v. Tanner,* 407 U.S. 551 (1972); *Hudgens v. NLRB,* 424 U.S. 507 (1976).

[65]Leonard Pitts Jr., "Intolerance Meets Its Nemesis at an Albany Mall," *Lincoln Journal Star,* March 10, 2003.

[66]*Cox v. Louisiana,* 379 U.S. 536 (1965).

[67]*Schenk v. Pro-Choice Network,* 137 L.Ed.2d 1 (1997).

[68]*Frisby v. Schultz,* 101 L.Ed.2d 420 (1988).

[69]*United States v. O'Brien,* 391 U.S. 367 (1968).

[70]*Tinker v. Des Moines School District.*

[71]The Supreme Court refused to hear any of these cases, so there was no uniform doctrine.

[72]*Smith v. Goguen,* 415 U.S. 566 (1974); *Spence v. Washington,* 418 U.S. 405 (1974).

[73]*Texas v. Johnson,* 105 L.Ed.2d 342 (1989).

[74]*United States v. Eichman,* 110 L.Ed.2d 287 (1990).

[75]However, in 1995, after Republicans became the majority in Congress, they renewed efforts to adopt a constitutional amendment but fell just three votes short in one house.

[76]*Hurley v. Irish-American Gay, Lesbian and Bisexual Group of Boston,* 515 U.S. 557 (1995).

[77]*Boy Scouts of America v. Dale,* 147 L.Ed.2d 554 (2000).

[78]*Roberts v. U.S. Jaycees,* 468 U.S. 609 (1984); *Board of Directors of Rotary International v. Rotary Club of Duarte,* 481 U.S. 537 (1987).

[79]The Court has also invalidated racial discrimination in labor unions and private schools and sexual discrimination in law firms, despite claims of freedom of association. *Railway Mail Association v. Corsi,* 326 U.S. 88 (1945); *Runyon v. Mc-*

Crary, 427 U.S. 160 (1976); *Hison v. King & Spalding,* 467 U.S. 69 (1984) 6957.

[80]Quoted in David Halbertstam, *The Best and the Brightest* (Greenwich, Conn.: Fawcett, 1969), 769.

[81]Bill Moyers, "Our Democracy Is in Danger of Being Paralyzed," Keynote Address to the National Conference on Media Reform, November 8, 2003, www.truthout.org/docs_03/printer_111403E.shtml.

[82]From Watergate tapes released in 1996. For transcripts of tapes made public in 1996 see Stanley Kutler, ed., *Abuse of Power: The New Nixon Tapes* (New York: Free Press, 1998).

[83]*New York Times v. United States,* 403 U.S. 713 (1971). In addition to seeking injunctions, the Nixon administration sent a telegram to the *New York Times* demanding that it cease publication of the excerpts, but the FBI had the wrong telex number for the newspaper, so the telegram went first to a fish company in Brooklyn. R.W. Apple, "Lessons from the Pentagon Papers," *New York Times,* June 23, 1996, E5.

[84]Actually, the Pentagon Papers did include some current information regarding ongoing negotiations and the names of CIA agents in Vietnam, but Ellsberg had not passed this information to the newspapers. However, the government and the Court were unaware of this, so the government argued that publication could affect national security, and the Court decided the case with this prospect in mind. Thus the Court's ruling was stronger than legal analysts realized at the time. Erwin N. Griswold, "No Harm Was Done," *New York Times,* June 30, 1991, E15.

[85]*United States v. Progressive,* 467 F.Supp. 990 (W.D., Wisc., 1979).

[86]*Hazelwood School District v. Kuhlmeier,* 98 L.Ed.2d 592 (1988).

[87]Then radio and television stations used actors with Irish accents to dub the comments made by IRA members. In 1994, the government lifted the ban.

[88]*Branzburg v. Hayes,* 408 U.S. 665 (1972).

[89]Jeffrey Toobin, "Name That Source," *New Yorker,* January 16, 2006, 30.

[90]*Cox Broadcasting v. Cohn,* 420 U.S. 469 (1975).

[91]This was not a Supreme Court case.

[92]*Time v. Hill,* 385 U.S. 374 (1967).

[93]*Wilson v. Layne,* 143 L.Ed.2d 818 (1999); *Hanlon v. Berger,* 143 L.Ed.2d 978 (1999).

[94]*New York Times v. Sullivan,* 376 U.S. 254.

[95]Harry Kalven, "*The New York Times* Case: A Note on 'the Central Meaning of the First Amendment,'" *Supreme Court Review* (1964): 221.

[96]*Monitor Patriot v. Roy,* 401 U.S. 265 (1971).

[97]*Associated Press v. Walker,* 388 U.S. 130 (1967); *Greenbelt Cooperative v. Bresler,* 398 U.S. 6 (1970). This set of rulings began with *Curtis Publishing v. Butts,* 388 U.S. 130 (1967).

[98]*Gertz v. Robert Welch,* 418 U.S. 323 (1974), and *Time v. Firestone,* 424 U.S. 448 (1976).

[99]Eric Press, "Westmoreland Takes on CBS," *Newsweek,* October 22, 1984, 62.

[100]*Roth v. United States,* 354 U.S. 476 (1957); *Manual Enterprises v. Day,* 370 U.S. 478 (1962); *Jacobellis v. Ohio,* 378 U.S. 184 (1964); *A Book Named "John Cleland's Memoirs of a Woman of Pleasure" v. Attorney General of Massachusetts,* 383 U.S. 413 (1966).

[101]*Miller v. California,* 413 U.S. 15 (1973).

[102]*Jenkins v. Georgia,* 418 U.S. 153 (1974).

[103]"Project: An Empirical Inquiry into the Effects of *Miller v. California* on the Control of Obscenity," *New York University Law Review* 52 (1977): 810–939.

[104]Eric Schlosser, "Empire of the Obscene," *New Yorker,* March 10, 2003, 61.

[105]*New York v. Ferber,* 458 U.S. 747 (1982). The Court left open the question of whether child pornography with serious literary or artistic value would be protected. *Osborne v. Ohio,* 495 U.S. 103 (1990).

[106]*Reno v. American Civil Liberties Union,* 138 L.Ed.2d 874 (1997).

[107]*Ashcroft v. Free Speech Coalition,* 152 L.Ed.2d 403 (2002).

[108]The Pilgrims, who had experienced religious toleration in Holland (after persecution in England), left because they wanted a place of their own, not because they could not worship as they pleased. The Dutch were so tolerant that the Pilgrims' children had begun to adopt Dutch manners and ideas. Richard Shenkman, *I Love Paul Revere, Whether He Rode or Not* (New York: HarperCollins, 1991), 20–21.

[109]The only religious reference in the Constitution occurs in the date when the document was written: "Year of our Lord one thousand seven hundred and eighty-seven." And that may have been mere convention; "year of our Lord" is the English equivalent of A.D.

[110]Apparently Roger Williams, a clergyman and the founder of Rhode Island, was the first to use this metaphor. Lloyd Burton, "The Church in America," *New Yorker,* September 29, 2003, 10. James Madison was another of the Founders who pioneered our religious freedom. For an analysis of his views, see Vincent Phillip Munoz, "James Madison's Principle of Religious Liberty," *American Political Science Review,* 97 (2003), 17–32.

[111]Gary Wills, quoted on *Thomas Jefferson,* PBS, February 18, 1997.

[112]According to Mark Pachter, Curator of the National Portrait Gallery, *Morning Edition,* NPR, June 25, 2006.

[113]*Torcaso v. Watkins,* 367 U.S. 488 (1961).

[114]*Pierce v. Society of Sisters,* 268 U.S. 510 (1925).

[115]*Cooper v. Pate,* 378 U.S. 546 (1963); *Cruz v. Beto,* 405 U.S. 319 (1972).

[116]*Church of the Lukumi Babalu Aye v. Hialeah,* 124 L.Ed.2d 472 (1993).

[117]*Reynolds v. United States,* 98 U.S. 145 (1879). Most Mormons, however, did not approve of polygamy. Even when polygamy was most popular, perhaps only 10 percent of Mormons practiced it. Shenkman, *I Love Paul Revere,* 31. Yet today reports indicate that polygamy is still flourishing among Mormons, perhaps more than ever. Lawrence Wright, "Lives of the Saints," *New Yorker,* January 21, 2002, 43.

[118]*Sherbert v. Verner,* 374 U.S. 398 (1963).

[119]Although a congressional statute mandates "reasonable accommodation," the Court interpreted it so narrowly that it essentially requires only minimal accommodation. *Trans World Airlines v. Hardison,* 432 U.S. 63 (1977). For analysis, see Gloria T. Beckley and Paul Burstein, "Religious Pluralism, Equal Opportunity, and the State," *Western Political Quarterly* 44 (1991), 185–208. For a related case, see *Thornton v. Caldor,* 86 L.Ed.2d 557 (1985).

[120]*Wisconsin v. Yoder,* 406 U.S. 205 (1972).

[121]*United States v. Lee,* 455 U.S. 252 (1982).

[122]*United States v. American Friends Service Committee,* 419 U.S. 7 (1974).

[123]*Goldman v. Weinberger,* 475 U.S. 503 (1986); *O'Lone v. Shabazz,* 482 U.S. 342 (1986).

[124]*Employment Division v. Smith,* 108 L.Ed.2d 876 (1990).

[125]American Indian Religious Freedom Act of 1994.

[126]Ruth Marcus, "One Nation, under Court Rulings," *Washington Post National Weekly Edition,* March 18, 1991, 33.

[127]*Boerne* v. *Flores,* 138 L.Ed.2d 624 (1997). Congress then passed another law that addressed just two kinds of government action—zoning and the rights of inmates at public correctional and mental institutions. The law required state and local governments to consider exceptions for religious practices. Although this was another attempt to override the Court's ruling, the Court upheld the law. *Cutter* v. *Wilkinson,* 125 S.Ct. 2113 (2005).

[128]William Lee Miller, "The Ghost of Freedoms Past," *Washington Post National Weekly Edition,* October 13, 1986, 23–24.

[129]Steven Waldman, "The Framers and the Faithful," *Washington Monthly,* April, 2006, 33–38.

[130]*Church of Holy Trinity* v. *United States,* 143 U.S. 457 (1892).

[131]*Engel* v. *Vitale,* 370 U.S. 421 (1962); *Abington School District* v. *Schempp,* 374 U.S. 203 (1963).

[132]*Stone* v. *Graham,* 449 U.S. 39 (1980). The Ten Commandments themselves have been divisive. In 1844, six people were killed in a riot in Philadelphia over which version of the Ten Commandments to post in the public schools. E. J. Dionne Jr., "Bridging the Church-State Divide," *Washington Post National Weekly Edition,* October 11, 1999, 21.

[133]George W. Andrews (D-Ala.), quoted in C. Herman Pritchett, *The American Constitution,* 3rd ed. (New York: McGraw-Hill, 1977), 406.

[134]Kenneth M. Dolbeare and Phillip E. Hammond, *The School Prayer Decisions* (Chicago: University of Chicago Press, 1971).

[135]Robert H. Birkby, "The Supreme Court and the Bible Belt," *Midwest Journal of Political Science* 10 (1966), 304–315.

[136]Julia Lieblich and Richard N. Ostling, "Despite Rulings, Prayer in School Still Sparks Debate, Still Practiced," *Lincoln Journal Star,* January 16, 2000.

[137]"Five Schools Get Ten Commandments," *Lincoln Journal Star,* August 12, 1999.

[138]J. Gordon Melton, quoted in Jon D. Hull, "The State of the Union," *Time,* January 30, 1995, 55.

[139]Peter Cushnie, "Letters," *Time,* October 15, 1984, 21.

[140]The Supreme Court invalidated Alabama's law that authorized a moment of silence "for meditation or voluntary prayer" because the wording of the law endorsed and promoted prayer. But most justices signaled approval of a moment of silence without such wording. *Wallace* v. *Jaffree,* 86 L.Ed.2d 29 (1985).

[141]*Lee* v. *Weisman,* 120 L.Ed.2d 467 (1992).

[142]*Jones* v. *Clear Creek,* 977 F.2d 965 (5th Cir., 1992).

[143]*Moore* v. *Ingebretsen,* 88 F.3d 274 (1996).

[144]*Santa Fe Independent School District* v. *Doe,* 530 U.S. 290 (2000).

[145]Anna Quindlen, "School Prayer: Substitutes for Substance," *Lincoln Journal Star,* December 8, 1994.

[146]A current guide for public school teachers, addressing practices that are permissible and those that are advisable in various situations, is Charles C. Haynes and Oliver Thomas, *Finding Common Ground* (Nashville, Tenn.: First Amendment Center, 2002).

[147]*Widmar* v. *Vincent,* 454 U.S. 263 (1981). The law requires high schools that receive federal funds to allow meetings of students' religious, philosophical, or political groups if the schools permit meetings of any "noncurriculum" groups. Schools could prohibit meetings of all noncurriculum groups. A Salt Lake City high school banned all nonacademic clubs rather than let students form an organization for homosexuals in 1996. Interviews with teachers and students two years later indicated that as a result of the ban on clubs, school spirit declined and class and racial rifts expanded. Clubs no longer brought students together, and clubs such as Polynesian Pride and the Aztec Club, for Latinos, no longer provided a link between these students and their school. "Club Ban Aimed at Gays Backfires," *Lincoln Journal Star,* December 6, 1998.

[148]*Board of Education of the Westside Community Schools* v. *Mergens,* 496 U.S. 226 (1990).

[149]David Van Biema, "Spiriting Prayer into School," *Time,* April 27, 1998, 28–31.

[150]Harriet Barovick, "Fear of a Gay School," *Time,* February 21, 2000, 52.

[151]*Rosenberger* v. *University of Virginia,* 132 L.Ed.2d 700 (1995). Yet the Rehnquist Court later ruled that states that provide scholarships for students at colleges and universities don't have to provide them for students preparing for the ministry. *Locke* v. *Davey,* 158 L.Ed.2d 21 (2004).

[152]For the nation's first celebration of Columbus Day in 1892, Francis Bellamy wrote, "I pledge allegiance to my flag and the republic for which it stands, one nation indivisible, with liberty and justice for all." For Bellamy, the key words were *indivisible,* which referred to the Civil War and emphasized the Union over the states, and *liberty and justice for all,* which emphasized a balance between freedom for individuals and equality between them. During the Cold War in the 1950s, Americans feared "godless communism." Some objected to communism as much because of the Soviet Union's official policy of atheism as because of its totalitarianism. A religious revival swept the United States as preachers such as Billy Graham warned that Americans would perish in a nuclear holocaust unless they opened their arms to Jesus Christ. Congress replaced the traditional national motto—"E Pluribus Unum" ("Out of Many, One")—with "In God We Trust," and it added this new motto to our paper money. Fraternal organizations, especially the Catholic Knights of Columbus, and religious leaders campaigned to add "under God" to the Pledge of Allegiance. The Presbyterian pastor of President Eisenhower's church in Washington urged the addition in a sermon as the president sat in a pew. With little dissent, Congress passed and the president signed a bill to do so in 1954. The legislative history of the act stated that the intent was to "acknowledge the dependence of our people and our government upon . . . the Creator . . . [and] deny the atheistic and materialistic concept of communism." The president stated that "millions of our school children will daily proclaim in every city and town . . . the dedication of our nation and our people to the Almighty." Thus the phrase was adopted expressly to endorse religion. David Greenberg, "The Pledge of Allegiance: Why We're Not One Nation 'under God,'" *Slate,* June 28, 2002, http://slate.msn.com/?id_2067499 S.

[153]*Elk Grove Unified School District* v. *Newdow,* 159 L.Ed.2d 98 (2004).

[154]*Lynch* v. *Donnelly,* 79 L.Ed.2d 604 (1984).

[155]*Allegheny County* v. *ACLU,* 106 L.Ed.2d 472 (1989).

[156]*Van Orden* v. *Perry,* 162 L.Ed. 2d 607 (2005).

[157]Initially they stood alone. As the cases proceeded through the lower courts, officials added other historical documents but never made a sincere effort to integrate them.

[158]*McCreary County* v. *ACLU,* 162 L.Ed.2d 729 (2005).

[159]*Epperson* v. *Arkansas,* 393 U.S. 97 (1968).

[160]Some groups use the more sophisticated-sounding term *creation science.* Although these groups do address the science of evolution, courts consider creationism and creation science as interchangeable.

[161]*Edwards* v. *Aguillard,* 482 U.S. 578 (1987).

[162]They do acknowledge that some evolution has occurred.

[163]However, to avoid court rulings similar to those against creationism—that it reflects a religious view—they try to avoid mention of God.

[164]Wendy Kaminer, "The God Bullies," *American Prospect,* November 18, 2002, 9.

[165]*Rochin* v. *California,* 342 U.S. 165 (1952).

[166]Seymour Wishman, *Confessions of a Criminal Lawyer* (New York: Penguin, 1981), 16.

[167]*Stein* v. *New York,* 346 U.S. 156 (1953).

[168]Wendy Kaminer, *It's All the Rage* (Reading, Mass.: Addison-Wesley, 1995), 78.

[169]*Weeks* v. *United States,* 232 U.S. 383 (1914).

[170]*Mapp* v. *Ohio,* 367 U.S. 643 (1961).

[171]This exception applies when police use a search warrant that they did not know was invalid. *United States* v. *Leon,* 82 L.Ed.2d 677 (1984); *Massachusetts* v. *Sheppard,* 82 L.Ed.2d 737 (1984). The Roberts Court has also created an exception to the exclusionary rule. When police have a search warrant but fail to knock and announce their presence before entering, as they have traditionally been required to do, any evidence seized may be used against the suspect despite the violation of the Fourth Amendment. *Hudson* v. *Michigan,* 165 L.Ed.2d 56 (2006).

[172]*Olmstead* v. *United States,* 277 U.S. 438 (1928).

[173]*Katz* v. *United States,* 389 U.S. 347 (1967).

[174]*Brown* v. *Mississippi,* 297 U.S. 278 (1936).

[175]*McNabb* v. *United States,* 318 U.S. 332 (1943); *Mallory* v. *United States,* 354 U.S. 449 (1957); *Spano* v. *New York,* 360 U.S. 315 (1959).

[176]*Ashcraft* v. *Tennessee,* 322 U.S. 143 (1944).

[177]*Miranda* v. *Arizona,* 384 U.S. 436 (1966).

[178]*Dickerson* v. *United States,* 530 U.S. 428 (2000).

[179]Jan Hoffman, "Police Tactics Chipping Away at Suspects' Rights," *New York Times,* March 29, 1998, 35.

[180]*Johnson* v. *Zerbst,* 304 U.S. 458 (1938).

[181]*Powell* v. *Alabama,* 287 U.S. 45 (1932).

[182]*Gideon* v. *Wainwright,* 372 U.S. 335 (1963).

[183]*Argersinger* v. *Hamlin,* 407 U.S. 25 (1972); *Scott* v. *Illinois,* 440 U.S. 367 (1974).

[184]*Alabama* v. *Shelton,* 152 L.Ed.2d 888 (2002).

[185]*Douglas* v. *California,* 372 U.S. 353 (1953).

[186]Wendy Cole, "Death Takes a Holiday," *Time,* February 14, 2000, 68.

[187]Jill Smolowe, "Race and the Death Penalty," *Time,* April 29, 1991, 69.

[188]Peter Applebome, "Indigent Defendants, Overworked Lawyers," *New York Times,* May 17, 1992, E18.

[189]Alan Berlow, "Texas, Take Heed," *Washington Post National Weekly Edition,* February 21, 2000, 22.

[190]Richard Carelli, "Death Rows Grow, Legal Help Shrinks," *Lincoln Journal Star,* October 7, 1995.

[191]The Burger Court did rule that the right to counsel entails the right to "effective" counsel, but the Court set such stringent standards for establishing the existence of ineffective counsel that few defendants can take advantage of this right. See *Strickland* v. *Washington,* 466 U.S. 668

[192](1984), and *United States v. Cronic,* 466 U.S. 640 (1984).

[192]*Baldwin v. New York,* 339 U.S. 66 (1970); *Blanton v. North Las Vegas,* 489 U.S. 538 (1989).

[193]*Duncan v. Louisiana,* 391 U.S. 145 (1968).

[194]*Taylor v. Louisiana,* 419 U.S. 522 (1975).

[195]*Swain v. Alabama,* 380 U.S. 202 (1965).

[196]The Court implicitly upheld the death penalty in *Wilkerson v. Utah,* 99 U.S. 130 (1878), and *In re Kemmler,* 136 U.S. 436 (1890).

[197]*Furman v. Georgia,* 408 U.S. 238 (1972).

[198]*Gregg v. Georgia,* 428 U.S. 153 (1976).

[199]*Woodson v. North Carolina,* 428 U.S. 289 (1976).

[200]*Coker v. Georgia,* 433 U.S. 584 (1977).

[201]*McCleskey v. Kemp,* 95 L.Ed.2d 262 (1987). Studies of Florida, Illinois, Mississippi, and North Carolina have found similar results. Fox Butterfield, "Blacks More Likely to Get Death Penalty, Study Says," *New York Times,* June 7, 1998, 16.

[202]Jeffrey Toobin, "Killer Instincts," *New Yorker,* January 17, 2005, 54.

[203]Leonard Pitts Jr., "Fate of 100 Innocent Men Casts Doubt on Capital Punishment," *Lincoln Journal Star,* April 13, 2002.

[204]Adam Liptak, "Juries Reject Death Penalty in Nearly All Federal Trials," *New York Times,* June 15, 2003, 12; Alex Kotlowitz, "In the Face of Death," *New York Times Magazine,* June 6, 2003, 34.

[205]*Atkins v. Virginia,* 153 L.Ed. 2d 335 (2002).

[206]*Penry v. Lynaugh,* 106 L.Ed.2d 256 (1989).

[207]*Roper v. Simmons,* 161 L.Ed.2d 1 (2005).

[208]Some Asian countries (notably China) and many Middle Eastern countries also retain it.

[209]*Brady v. United States,* 397 U.S. 742 (1970).

[210]*Griswold v. Connecticut,* 38 U.S. 479 (1965).

[211]For a rare exception, see *Time v. Hill,* 385 U.S. 374 (1967).

[212]*Griswold v. Connecticut.*

[213]*Eisenstadt v. Baird,* 405 U.S. 438 (1972); *Carey v. Population Services International,* 431 U.S. 678 (1977).

[214]*Eisenstadt v. Baird.*

[215]Lloyd Shearer, "This Woman and This Man Made History," *Parade,* 1983.

[216]*Roe v. Wade,* 410 U.S. 113 (1973).

[217]Bob Woodward, "The Abortion Papers," *Washington Post National Weekly Edition,* January 30, 1989, 24–25.

[218]All but New York's. Three other states allowed abortion on demand, though not quite as extensively as *Roe,* so the ruling also invalidated their laws. Jeffrey A. Segal and Harold J. Spaeth, *The Supreme Court and the Attitudinal Model* (New York: Cambridge University Press, 1993), 333.

[219]*Akron v. Akron Center for Reproductive Health,* 76 L.Ed.2d 687 (1983).

[220]"The Supreme Court Ignites a Fiery Abortion Debate," *Time,* July 4, 1977, 6–8.

[221]*Beal v. Doe,* 432 U.S. 438 (1977); *Maher v. Roe,* 432 U.S. 464 (1977); *Poelker v. Doe,* 432 U.S. 519 (1977); *Harris v. McRae* 448 U.S. 297 (1980).

[222]Benjamin Weiser, "The Abortion Dilemma Come to Life," *Washington Post National Weekly Edition,* December 25, 1989, 10–11.

[223]Alan Guttmacher Institute, *Facts in Brief: Abortion in the United States* (New York: Alan Guttmacher Institute, 1992); Stephanie Mencimer, "Ending Illegitimacy as We Know It," *Washington Post National Weekly Edition,* January 17, 1994, 24.

[224]*Webster v. Reproductive Health Services,* 106 L.Ed.2d 410 (1989).

[225]*Planned Parenthood of Southeastern Pennsylvania v. Casey,* 120 L.Ed.2d 674 (1992). Justice Anthony Kennedy changed his mind after the justices' conference, from essentially overturning *Roe* to reaffirming it. His was the fifth vote to reaffirm, as it would have been to overturn.

[226]Kathleen Sullivan, cited in Robin Toner and Adam Liptak, "In New Court, *Roe* May Stand, So Foes Look to Limit Its Scope," *New York Times,* July 10, 2005, YT16.

[227]William Booth, "The Difference a Day Makes," *Washington Post National Weekly Edition,* November 23, 1992, 31.

[228]*Planned Parenthood of Southeastern Pennsylvania v. Casey,* 120 L.Ed.2d 674 (1992).

[229]*Hodgson v. Minnesota,* 111 L.Ed.2d 344 (1990); *Ohio v. Akron Center for Reproductive Health,* 111 L.Ed.2d 405 (1990); *Planned Parenthood Association of Kansas City v. Ashcroft,* 462 U.S. 476 (1983). Number of states from Holly Ramer, "Never-Enforced Abortion Law to Go before Supreme Court," *Lincoln Journal Star,* November 27, 2005, 4A.

[230]*Hodgson v. Minnesota,* 111 L.Ed.2d 344 (1990).

[231]Margaret Carlson, "Abortion's Hardest Cases," *Time,* July 9, 1990, 24.

[232]Butch Mabin, "Supreme Court Says Teen Seeking Abortion Too Immature," *Lincoln Journal Star,* December 13, 1997.

[233]*Stenberg v. Carhart,* 530 U.S. 914 (2000).

[234]Barry Yeoman, "The Quiet War on Abortion," *Mother Jones,* September–October 2001, 46–51.

[235]"Survey Reveals U. S. Views on Abortion to Be Contradictory," *Lincoln Journal Star,* June 19, 2000.

[236]For an analysis of the political dynamics that produced this moderate result, see William Saleton, *Bearing Right: How Conservatives Won the Abortion War* (Berkeley: University of California Press, 2003). The title is an exaggeration.

[237]Alissa Rubin, "The Abortion Wars Are Far from Over," *Washington Post National Weekly Edition,* December 21, 1992, 25.

[238]Richard Lacayo, "One Doctor Down, How Many More?" *Time,* March 22, 1993, 47.

[239]Rebecca Mead, "Return to Sender the Usual Hate Mail," *New Yorker,* October 29, 2001, 34.

[240]Douglas Frantz, "The Rhetoric of Terror," *Time,* March 27, 1995, 48–51.

[241]Dan Sewell, "Abortion War Requires Guns, Bulletproof Vests," *Lincoln Journal Star,* January 8, 1995.

[242]"Blasts Reawaken Fear of Domestic Terrorism," *Lincoln Journal Star,* January 17, 1997.

[243]Richard Lacayo, "Abortion: The Future Is Already Here," *Time,* May 4, 1992, 29; Jack Hitt, "Who Will Do Abortions Here?" *New York Times Magazine,* January 18, 1998, 20.

[244]Jodi Enda, "The Women's View," *American Prospect,* April, 2005, 26.

[245]Randall Terry, quoted in Anthony Lewis, "Pro-Life Zealots 'Outside the Bargain,'" *Lincoln Journal Star,* March 14, 1993.

[246]Joseph Scheidler, quoted in Sandra G. Boodman, "Bringing Abortion Home," *Washington Post National Weekly Edition,* April 15, 1993, 6.

[247]Stanley K. Henshaw, "Abortion Incidence and Services in the United States, 1995–1996," *Family Planning Perspectives,* November–December 1998.

[248]Much of this section is taken from Russell Shorto, "Contra-Contraception," *New York Times Magazine,* May 7, 2006, 48–55, 68, 8.

[249]Harris Poll, Ibid., 54.

[250]Judie Brown, quoted in Ibid. 50.

[251]Ibid., 50, 68.

[252]Ibid., 51, 53.

[253]Judie Brown, quoted in Ibid., 50.

[254]As the author concludes from the leaders' statements. Ibid., 54.

[255]R. Albert Mohler, Jr., quoted in Ibid., 50.

[256]Sarah Brown of the National Campaign to Prevent Teen Pregnancy, quoted in Ibid., 83.

[257]For an elaboration of this history, see "In Changing the Law of the Land, Six Justices Turned to Its History," *New York Times,* July 20, 2003, WK7.

[258]Four states at this time revised their statutes to bar sodomy only between homosexuals: Kansas, Missouri, Oklahoma, and Texas.

[259]*Bowers v. Hardwick,* 92 L.Ed.2d 140 (1986); see also *Doe v. Commonwealth's Attorney,* 425 U.S. 901 (1976).

[260]*Lawrence and Garner v. Texas,* 539 U.S. 558 (2003).

[261]"Gays Getting More Acceptance as They're More Open, Poll Says," *Lincoln Journal Star,* April 11, 2004.

[262]Paul Gewirtz, quoted in Joe Klein, "How the Supremes Redeemed Bush," *Time,* July 7, 2003, 27.

[263]The courts apply the clause to "adversarial proceedings," such as lawsuits, including divorces.

[264]The House sponsor of the act, Robert Barr (R-Ga.), said the act was necessary because "the flames of hedonism, the flames of narcissism, the flames of self-centered morality are licking at the very foundation of our society, the family unit." At the time he was protecting the family unit, he was in his third marriage. Margaret Carlson, "The Marrying Kind," *Time,* September 16, 1996, 26.

[265]Jonathan Rauch, "Families Forged by Illness," *New York Times,* June 11, 2006, WK15.

[266]For elaboration, see David Von Drehle, "Same-Sex Unions Take Center Stage," *Washington Post National Weekly Edition,* December 1, 2003, 29.

[267]John Cloud, "1,138 Reasons Marriage Is Cool," *Time,* March 8, 2004, 32. A few go in the opposite direction, such as eligibility for Medicaid, which takes into account a spouse's income.

[268]Advisory Opinion on Senate No. 2175, Supreme Judicial Court of Massachusetts, February 3, 2004.

[269]David J. Garrow, "Toward a More Perfect Union," *New York Times Magazine,* May 9, 2004, 54.

[270]Hendrik Hertzberg, "Comment: Distraction," *New Yorker,* June 19, 2006, 30.

[271]Senator Wayne Allard (R-Colo.); Senator Rick Santorum (R-Pa.); James Dobson. Andrew Sullivan, "If at First You Don't Succeed . . . ," *Time,* July 26, 2004, 78.

[272]Alan Cooperman, "Anger without Action," *Washington Post National Weekly Edition,* June 28, 2004, 30.

[273]Garrow, "Toward a More Perfect Union," 57.

[274]The Supreme Court did invalidate a Colorado constitutional amendment prohibiting laws barring discrimination against homosexuals, saying that the amendment singled out homosexuals and denied them the opportunity enjoyed by others to seek protection from discrimination. This put the brakes on a drive to adopt similar provisions in other states. *Roemer v. Evans,* 134 L.Ed.2d 855 (1996).

[275]President Clinton also ordered the FBI to end policies that made it difficult for homosexuals to be hired.

[276]The policy was originally based on psychoanalytic theory, which considered homosexuality a mental illness. This conclusion was rejected by

the American Psychiatric Association some years later.

[277]Israel drafts every eighteen-year-old man and woman. It does consider homosexuality in the assignment of jobs. Gays who admit their orientation to their superiors confidentially are restricted from security-sensitive jobs for fear they are susceptible to blackmail. But gays who acknowledge their orientation openly could not be blackmailed, so they are treated the same as straights. Randy Shilts, "What's Fair in Love and War," *Newsweek,* February 1, 1993, 58–59; Eric Konigsberg, "Gays in Arms," *Washington Monthly,* November 1992, 10–13; "Canada Had No Problems Lifting Its Military Gay Ban," *Lincoln Journal Star,* January 31, 1993. See also Randy Shilts, *Conduct Unbecoming: Gays and Lesbians in the U.S. Military* (New York: St. Martin's Press, 1993).

[278]Ibid.; "Group Says Gays Worse Off in Military since New Policy," *Lincoln Journal Star,* February 28, 1996. Pentagon officials say many discharges result from recruits who decide that they do not like the military and who then volunteer that they are homosexual as a way of getting discharged. Dana Priest, "The Impact of the 'Don't Ask, Don't Tell' Policy," *Washington Post National Weekly Edition,* February 1, 1999, 35. As a result of the increase in discharges, the Clinton administration tried to bolster the policy by having the services discourage harassment, from threats to derogatory jokes aimed at gays, and by requiring low-ranking officers to consult with senior legal advisers before beginning an investigation into alleged homosexual conduct.

[279]"Numbers," *Time,* March 7, 2005, 25.

[280]Charles Peters, "Tilting at Windmills," *Washington Monthly,* May 2001, 4.

[281]"Numbers," *Time,* March 7, 2005, 25.

[282]Al Kamen, "When Exactly Does Life End?" *Washington Post National Weekly Edition,* September 18, 1989, 31; Alain L. Sanders, "Whose Right to Die?" *Time,* December 11, 1989, 80.

[283]*Cruzan v. Missouri Health Department,* 111 L.Ed.2d 224 (1990).

[284]Otto Friedrich, "A Limited Right to Die," *Time,* July 9, 1990, 59.

[285]Tamar Lewin, "Ignoring 'Right to Die' Directives, Medical Community Is Being Sued," *New York Times,* June 2, 1996, 1.

[286]*Washington v. Glucksberg,* 138 L.Ed.2d 772 (1997); *Vacco v. Quill,* 138 L.Ed.2d 834 (1997).

[287]*Gonzales v. Oregon,* 163 L.Ed.2d 748 (2006).

[288]"Numbers," *Time,* May 8, 2006, 26.

[289]David E. Rosenbaum, "Americans Want a Right to Die—or So They Think," *New York Times,* June 8, 1997, E3.

[290]Ibid.

[291]See, for example, Milton Viorst, "The Education of Ali al-Timimi," *Atlantic Monthly,* June, 2006, 69–78.

[292]For a very useful article, see Mark Bowden, "The Dark Art of Interrogation," *Atlantic Monthly,* October, 2003, 51–76.

[293]Adam Zagorin, "One Life Inside Gitmo," *Time,* March 13, 2006, 22.

[294]Anonymous official, quoted in Jodie Morse, "How Do We Make Him Talk?" *Time,* April 15, 2002, 92.

[295]"FBI Memos Reveal Allegations of Abuse," *Lincoln Journal Star,* February 24, 2006, 5A.

[296]Neil A. Lewis and Eric Schmitt, "Inquiry Finds Abuses at Guantanamo Bay," *New York Times,* May 1, 2005, YT23.

[297]Paisley Dodds, "Guantanamo Translator Tells of Sexual Tactics Used on Detainees," *Lincoln Journal Star,* January 28, 2005, 5A.

[298]For more information, including the role of medical personnel in devising the tactics, see Jane Mayer, "The Experiment," *New Yorker,* July 11 and 18, 2005, 60–71.

[299]According to the Geneva Conventions and the United Nations Convention Against Torture and also under treaty law, to which the United States is a party, and customary law, which is binding on all nations.

[300]From the Geneva Conventions.

[301]The administration also claims that al-Qaeda members aren't entitled to the protection of international law because as stateless fighters they are "unlawful enemy combatants" and because neither al-Qaeda nor the Taliban regime of Afghanistan were a party to the Geneva Conventions.

[302]Mayer, "The Experiment," 70.

[303]*Marketplace,* NPR, May 5, 2004.

[304]Rajiv Chandrasekaran and Scott Wilson, "Many in Prison in Error," *Lincoln Journal Star,* May 11, 2004.

[305]The phenomenon is known as "force drift." Mayer, "The Experiment," 70.

[306]According to the government's own documents. For more incidents and documents, see Mark Danner, *Torture and Truth* (New York: New York Review of Books, 2004).

[307] Ninety-eight have died, and thirty-four of these have been suspected or confirmed homicides, according to Human Rights First, a human rights group. Drew Brown, "Report: 98 Died in U.S. Custody," *Lincoln Journal Star,* February 23, 2006, 3A.

[308]The law is essentially a statement of our policy. It doesn't authorize prisoners to bring lawsuits to stop such treatment or to penalize the interrogators.

[309]In a signing statement, he said that he would interpret the law "in a manner consistent with the constitutional authority of the President to supervise the unitary executive branch and as Commander in Chief and consistent with the constitutional limitations on the judicial power."

[310]Don Van Natta Jr., "How Ally with Abuse Record Became a Surrogate U.S. Jailer," *New York Times,* May 1, 2005, YT1.

[311]Dana Priest and Barton Gellman, "U.S. Decries Abuse but Defends Interrogations; 'Stress and Duress' Tactics Used on Terrorism Suspects Held in Secret Overseas Facilities," *Washington Post,* December 26, 2002, A1.

[312]Rajiv Chandrasekaran and Peter Finn, "Interrogating Terrorist Suspects 'in a Way We Can't Do on U.S. Soil,'" *Washington Post,* March 12, 2002, A1.

[313]U.N. Convention against Torture and Other Cruel, Inhuman, or Degrading Treatment or Punishment of 1984, signed in 1994.

[314]Dana Priest, "The CIA's Secret Prisons," *Washington Post National Weekly Edition,* November 7–13, 2005, 10–11.

[315]There are assertions that the administration notified two judges on the FISA court, but it did not seek official approval.

[316]Barton Gellman, Dafna Linzer, and Carol D. Leonnig, "Spying That Yields Little," *Washington Post National Weekly Edition,* February 13–19, 2006, 6.

[317]Zev Borow, "Very Bad People," *New Yorker,* February 6, 2006, 44.

[318]Ibid.

[319]The administration asked for such authority in the resolution approving the use of force against those responsible for the attacks. Richard Lacayo, "Has Bush Gone Too Far?" *Time,* January 9, 2006, 30.

[320]Seymour M. Hersh, "National Security Dept.: Listening In," *New Yorker,* May 29, 2006, 25.

[321]Joseph J. Ellis, "Finding a Place for 9/11 in American History," *New York Times,* January 28, 2006. Available online at http://select.nytimes.com/search/restricted/article?res=FB0A13F93A5B0C7B8EDDA8089

[322]Alan M. Dershowitz, *Supreme Injustice: How the High Court Hijacked Election 2000* (New York: Oxford University Press, 2001), 189.

[323]159 L.Ed.2d 548 (2004).

[324]*Hamdi v. Rumsfeld,* 159 L.Ed.2d 578 (2004).

[325]*This American Life,* NPR, March 12, 2006.

[326]Corine Hegland, "Guantanamo's Grip," *National Journal,* February 1, 2006, 20–34.

[327]Ibid., 29.

[328]Ibid., 28.

[329]Michael Scheuer, quoted in Ibid., 31.

[330]Ibid., 30–31.

[331]"Military: Detainees Attempted Mass Hanging Protest in 2003," *Lincoln Journal Star,* January 25, 2005, 6A. By this date, the guards had logged 120 instances in which prisoners had tried to hang themselves, although the military says the majority were done in protest rather than in an attempt to commit suicide.

[332]Hegland, "Guantanamo's Grip," 23.

[333]The Detainee Treatment Act of 2005. Petitions for a writ of *habeas corpus* were filed for all detainees before this law was passed, so the courts might conclude that the law doesn't apply to these cases already in progress.

[334]*Hamdan v. Rumsfeld,* 165 L.Ed.2d 723 (2006).

Chapter 15

[1]John W. Dower, *War without Mercy* (New York: Pantheon, 1986), 112.

[2]Peter Irons, *Justice at War* (New York: Oxford University Press, 1983), 269.

[3]Dower, *War without Mercy,* 92.

[4]John Hersey, "Behind Barbed Wire," *New York Times Magazine,* September 11, 1988, 120.

[5]Exhibition "Slavery in New York," New York Historical Society, November, 2005. For more details, see Ira Berlin and Leslie M. Harris, ed., *Slavery in New York* (New York: New York Historical Society/New Press, 2006).

[6]Gary B. Nash, *The Forgotten Fifth* (Cambridge, Massachusetts: Harvard University Press, 2006). See also Simon Schama, *Rough Crossings: Britain, the Slaves, and the American Revolution* (New York: Ecco, 2006).

[7]Although New York didn't abolish slavery until 1827 and New Jersey didn't until 1865.

[8]Adam Goodheart, "Setting Them Free," *New York Times Book Review,* August 7, 2005, 1.

[9]Russell Nye, *Fettered Freedom* (Lansing: Michigan State University Press, 1963), 187, 227–229. Note that the 1860 census shows eighteen slaves in New Jersey.

[10]*Scott v. Sandford,* 60 U.S. 393 (1857).

[11]Despite the ruling, Taney considered slavery "a blot on our national character." Three decades before the case, he had freed his own slaves, whom he had inherited from his parents. When the South seceded, Taney remained with the Union. Richard Shenkman, *I Love Paul Revere, Whether He Rode or Not* (New York: Harper-Collins, 1991), 168.

[12]Slavery became so much a part of the southern economy that the paper money of some Confederate states featured pictures of slaves harvesting cotton. *Fresh Air Weekend,* NPR, August 18, 2002.

[13]The Emancipation Proclamation, issued during the Civil War in 1863, was apparently a tactical

move to discourage European countries from aiding the Confederacy. It gave the Civil War a moral purpose, making foreign intervention less likely. The proclamation could not free southern slaves at the time because the Union did not control the southern states, which had seceded.

[14]Bruce Ackerman, *We the People: Transformations* (Cambridge, Mass.: Harvard University Press, 1998); George Fletcher, "Unsound Constitution: Oklahoma City and the Founding Fathers," *New Republic,* June 23, 1997, 14–18. These conclusions make dubious the arguments that judges should be guided only by the intentions of the original Founders as they resolve contemporary cases. Ignoring the transformation that occurred as a result of the Civil War and these amendments amounts to using a highly selective and self-serving version of history.

[15]Civil Rights Act of 1866; Civil Rights Act of 1871; Civil Rights Act of 1875.

[16]See Eric Foner, *Reconstruction: America's Unfinished Revolution* (New York: Harper & Row, 1988).

[17]The name Jim Crow came from a white performer in the 1820s who had a vaudeville routine in which he blackened his face with burnt cork and mimicked black men. He sang "Wheel About and Turn About and Jump, Jim Crow." This routine led to minstrel shows in high schools and colleges, with students portraying and satirizing blacks. The shows were popular into the 1960s.

[18]Kenneth Karst, "Equality, Law, and Belonging: An Introduction," in *Before the Law,* 5th ed., ed. John J. Bonsignore et al. (Boston: Houghton Mifflin, 1994), 429.

[19]C. Vann Woodward, *The Strange Career of Jim Crow,* 2nd ed. (London: Oxford University Press, 1966), 44.

[20]*Civil Rights Cases,* 109 U.S. 3 (1883).

[21]*Plessy v. Ferguson,* 163 U.S. 537 (1896). The Court's ruling prompted states to expand their Jim Crow laws. Before *Plessy,* states segregated just trains and schools.

[22]*Cumming v. Richmond County Board of Education,* 175 U.S. 528 (1899). Then the Court enforced segregation in colleges. It upheld a criminal conviction against a private college for teaching blacks together with whites. *Berea College v. Kentucky,* 211 U.S. 45 (1908).

[23]See, generally, James W. Loewen, *Sundown Towns: A Hidden Dimension of American Racism* (New York: New Press, 2005).

[24]Woodward, *The Strange Career of Jim Crow,* 113. Before the Civil War, northern states had passed some Jim Crow laws, which foreshadowed the more pervasive laws in southern states after the war. Leon F. Litwack, *Trouble in Mind: Black Southerners in the Age of Jim Crow* (New York: Knopf, 1998).

[25]Jacqueline Jones, *The Dispossessed: America's Underclasses from the Civil War to the Present* (New York: Basic Books, 1992), 83. And they were still being cheated. One sharecropper went to the landowner at the end of the season to settle up but was told he would not receive any money that year because the landowner needed it to send his son to college. The sharecropper moved to the North. Interview with the sharecropper's son on *The Best of Discovery,* Discovery television channel, June 11, 1995.

[26]Richard Kluger, *Simple Justice* (New York: Knopf, 1976), 89–90.

[27]Philip Dray, *At the Hands of Persons Unknown* (New York: Random House, 2002).

[28]Ibid.

[29]Woodward, *The Strange Career of Jim Crow,* 114.

[30]Yet talk of the riot was banished from newspapers, textbooks, and everyday conversations. After some years, most Oklahomans were unaware of it, except those who lived through it. In the 1990s, newspaper articles prompted the state to establish a commission to investigate the riot, leading to more awareness. Jonathan Z. Larsen, "Tulsa Burning," *Civilization,* February–March 1997, 46–55; Brent Staples, "Unearthing a Riot," *New York Times Magazine,* December 19, 1999, 64–69. For an examination, see James S. Hirsch, *Riot and Remembrance: The Tulsa Race War and Its Legacy* (New York: Houghton Mifflin, 2002).

[31]"Torn from the Land," Associated Press, wire.ap.org. The website offers an investigative report with numerous stories. For an illuminating look at the lives and status of black people in the Deep South in the 1920s, see Nan Woodruff, *American Congo: The African American Freedom Struggle in the Delta* (Cambridge, Mass.: Harvard University Press, 2003).

[32]Wilson apparently opposed segregation in government but still allowed it to appease southerners who were a major portion of his Democratic Party and whose support was essential for his economic reforms.

[33]*Guinn v. United States,* 238 U.S. 347 (1915). This clause had been written into election laws to make it more difficult for freed blacks and their children to qualify to vote (their grandfathers having been illiterate slaves) while effectively exempting whites from having to submit to literacy testing.

[34]*Buchanan v. Warley,* 245 U.S. 60 (1917).

[35]In 1939, the NAACP established the NAACP Legal Defense and Educational Fund as its litigation arm. In 1957, the Internal Revenue Service, pressured by southern members of Congress, ordered the two branches of the NAACP to break their connection or lose their tax-exempt status. Since then, they have been separate organizations, and further references in this chapter to the NAACP are in fact to the NAACP Legal Defense and Educational Fund.

[36]Juan Williams, "The Case for Thurgood Marshall," *Washington Post,* February 14, 1999, W16.

[37]Kluger, *Simple Justice,* 134.

[38]*Missouri ex rel. Gaines v. Canada,* 305 U.S. 337 (1938).

[39]*Sweatt v. Painter,* 339 U.S. 629 (1950).

[40]*McLaurin v. Oklahoma State Regents,* 339 U.S. 637 (1950).

[41]Esther Brown, a white woman from a Kansas City suburb, had a black maid who lived in nearby South Park. In 1948, when Brown saw the decrepit school for black students in South Park, she complained to the board of education in the town. At a meeting, she said, "Look, I don't represent these people. One of them works for me, and I've seen the conditions of their school. I know none of you would want your children educated under such circumstances. They're not asking for integration, just a fair shake." From the audience, Brown received catcalls and demands to go back where she came from. A woman behind her tried to hit her. The school board responded by gerrymandering the black neighborhood out of the South Park school district. Kluger, *Simple Justice,* 388–389.

[42]Earl Warren, *The Memoirs of Earl Warren* (Garden City, N.Y.: Doubleday, 1977), 291.

[43]Kluger, *Simple Justice,* 656.

[44]*Brown v. Board of Education of Topeka,* 347 U.S. 483 (1954).

[45]*Holmes v. Atlanta,* 350 U.S. 879 (1955); *Baltimore v. Dawson,* 350 U.S. 877 (1955); *Schiro v. Bynum,* 375 U.S. 395 (1964); *Johnson v. Virginia,* 373 U.S. 61 (1963); *Lee v. Washington,* 390 U.S. 333 (1968).

[46]*Brown v. Board of Education II,* 349 U.S. 294 (1955).

[47]Justice Tom Clark later told a political science conference that one justice had proposed desegregating one grade a year, beginning with kindergarten or first grade, but this concrete standard was rejected because the other justices felt it would take too long. In retrospect, it might have been quicker, and easier, than the vague standard used.

[48]*Griffin v. Prince Edward County School Board,* 377 U.S. 218 (1964); *Norwood v. Harrison,* 413 U.S. 455 (1973); *Gilmore v. Montgomery,* 417 U.S. 556 (1974); *Green v. New Kent County School Board,* 391 U.S. 430 (1968).

[49]Quoted in James F. Simon, *In His Own Image* (New York: McKay, 1974), 70.

[50]*All Things Considered,* NPR, December 10, 2003.

[51]William Cohen and John Kaplan, *Bill of Rights* (Mineola, N.Y.: Foundation Press, 1976), 622.

[52]*Swann v. Charlotte-Mecklenburg Board of Education,* 402 U.S. 1 (1971); *Columbus Board of Education v. Penick,* 443 U.S. 449 (1979); *Dayton Board of Education v. Brinkman,* 443 U.S. 526 (1979); *Keyes v. School District 1, Denver,* 413 U.S. 921 (1973).

[53]Lee A. Daniels, "In Defense of Busing," *New York Times Magazine,* April 17, 1983, 36–37.

[54]White flight began after World War II as affluent families moved to the suburbs. Although white flight continued for economic reasons, it increased because of busing as well.

[55]*Milliken v. Bradley,* 418 U.S. 717 (1974).

[56]For example, some suburbs of Kansas City, Missouri, did not allow black students to attend high schools. Some black families, then, moved back to the city, aggravating both school segregation and residential segregation. James S. Kunen, "The End of Integration," *Time,* April 29, 1996, 41.

[57]*Board of Education of Oklahoma City v. Dowell,* 112 L.Ed.2d 715 (1991). The Court said that school districts could stop busing when "the vestiges of past discrimination had been eliminated to the extent practicable." See also *Freeman v. Pitts,* 118 L.Ed.2d 108 (1992).

[58]*Missouri v. Jenkins,* 132 L.Ed.2d 63 (1995).

[59]Anjetta McQueen, "Desegregation Waning," *Lincoln Journal Star,* May 16, 1999.

[60]FBI director J. Edgar Hoover ordered wiretaps that he hoped would link King with communists. When the taps failed to reveal any connection, Hoover had agents bug a hotel room, where they heard King having extramarital sex. Taylor Branch, *Pillar of Fire: America in the King Years, 1963–65* (New York: Simon & Schuster, 1998).

[61]Although this sit-in usually is cited as the first, a sit-in at a lunch counter in a drugstore in Wichita, Kansas, actually was the first—in 1958. But the Greensboro sit-in prompted the wave of sit-ins through the South.

[62]Woodward, *The Strange Career of Jim Crow,* 186.

[63]This incident occurred in 1961. Nicholas Lemann, "The Long March," *New Yorker,* February 10, 2003, 88.

[64]*Norris v. Alabama,* 294 U.S. 587 (1935); *Smith v. Texas,* 311 U.S. 128 (1940); *Avery v. Georgia,* 345 U.S. 559 (1952).

[65]An excellent collection of articles is presented in *Reporting Civil Rights: American Journalism, 1941–1973* (New York: Library of America, 2003).

[66]Henry Louis Gates Jr., "After the Revolution," *New Yorker,* April 29 and May 6, 1996.

[67]Robert A. Caro, "The Compassion of Lyndon Johnson," *New Yorker,* April 1, 2002, 56.

[68]Louis Menand, "He Knew He Was Right," *New Yorker,* March 26, 2001, 95.

[69]Lemann, "Long March," 86.

[70]Patrick Reddy, "Why It's Got to Be All or Nothing," *Washington Post National Weekly Edition,* October 18, 1999, 23.

[71]This was true for national elections. The transformation took longer for state and local elections.

[72]*Heart of Atlanta Motel v. United States,* 379 U.S. 421 (1964).

[73]For discussion of organized labor's ambivalence toward enactment and enforcement of the employment provisions of the act, see Herbert Hill, "Black Workers, Organized Labor, and Title VII of the 1964 Civil Rights Act: Legislative History and Litigation Record," in *Race in America,* ed. Herbert Hill and James E. Jones (Madison: University of Wisconsin Press, 1993), 263–341.

[74]*Griggs v. Duke Power,* 401 U.S. 424 (1971).

[75]*Washington v. Davis,* 426 U.S. 229 (1976). When the Burger Court held that standards must relate to the job, it placed the burden of proof on employers. (They had to show that their requirements were necessary.) In *Wards Cove Packing v. Atonio,* 490 U.S. 642 (1989), the Rehnquist Court shifted the burden of proof to workers. This technical change had a substantial impact; it made it hard for victims to win in court. In 1991, Congress passed new legislation to override the ruling and clarify its intent that employers should bear the burden of proof.

[76]*Shelley v. Kraemer,* 334 U.S. 1 (1948).

[77]Less directly, the numerous national and state policies that encouraged urban sprawl provided the opportunity for middle-class whites to flock to the suburbs, leaving the cities disproportionately black.

[78]For more extensive examination, see Andrew Hacker, *Two Nations: Black and White, Separate, Hostile, Unequal* (New York: Scribner, 1992).

[79]Richard Morin, "Southern Discomfort," *Washington Post National Weekly Edition,* July 15, 1996, 35.

[80]Gary Orfield, quoted in Mary Jordan, "Separating the Country from the *Brown* Decision," *Washington Post National Weekly Edition,* December 20, 1993, 33. See also Maia Davis, "Harvard Study Finds New Segregation," *Lincoln Journal Star,* January 20, 2003.

[81]Jonathan Kozol, *The Shame of the Nation: The Restoration of Apartheid Schooling in America* (New York: Crown, 2005), 19.

[82]Adam Cohen, "The Supreme Struggle," *New York Times,* January 18, 2004, E22.

[83]Kozol, *The Shame of the Nation,* 226–227.

[84]Ibid., 19.

[85]Consequently, magnet schools in minority neighborhoods often don't attract many white students. Sandy Banks, "Mixed Results for L.A.'s Magnet Schools," *Los Angeles Times,* January 20, 2006, www.latimes.com/news/local/la-me-magnet20jan20,0,6132919,fullstory?coll=la-home-headlines.

[86]Thomas M. Shapiro, *The Hidden Cost of Being African American* (New York: Oxford University, 2004), 170–179.

[87]Jordan, "Separating the Country from the *Brown* Decision."

[88]Kunen, "End of Integration," 39.

[89]Jonathan Kozol, *Savage Inequalities: Children in America's Schools* (New York: HarperPerennial, 1992), 4.

[90]Gary Orfield, quoted in ibid., 225.

[91]Ibid., 3.

[92]Ibid., 35. However, only three public schools in Alabama are named after King, a native of the state. "Numbers," *Time,* January 24, 2000, 23.

[93]Kozol, *The Shame of the Nation,* 24–25.

[94]Rob Gurwitt, "Getting off the Bus," *Governing,* May 1992, 30–36; Jervis Anderson, "Black and Blue," *New Yorker,* April 29 and May 6, 1996.

[95]Richard Rothstein, quoted in Kozol, *The Shame of the Nation,* 230.

[96]Kozol, *The Shame of the Nation,* 215–236.

[97]"That's Quite a Range," *Lincoln Journal,* January 21, 1993.

[98]Shapiro, *Hidden Cost,* 144–145.

[99]In addition, cities have numerous nonprofit institutions—colleges, museums, hospitals—that benefit the entire urban area but do not pay property taxes. According to one estimate, 30 percent of the cities' potential tax base is tax-exempt, compared with 3 percent of the suburbs'. Kozol, *Savage Inequalities,* 55. There are a few exceptions. Jordan, "On Track," 31.

[100]Kozol, *The Shame of the Nation,* 245.

[101]Ibid., 60.

[102]Charles Peters, "Tilting at Windmills," *Washington Monthly,* March, 2006, 6.

[103]Kozol, *The Shame of the Nation,* 172.

[104]Ibid., 171.

[105]Ibid., 53, 84.

[106]Steve Lopez, "Money for Stadiums but Not for Schools," *Time,* June 14, 1999, 54.

[107]Jay Mathews, "A Confirmation of Bias," *Washington Post National Weekly Edition,* March 19, 2001, 34; Robert England and Kenneth Meier, "From Desegregation to Integration: Second-Generation School Discrimination as an Institutional Impediment," *American Politics Quarterly* 13 (1985), 227–247; Charles Bullock and Joseph Stewart, "Incidence and Correlates of Second-Generation Discrimination," in *Race, Sex, and Policy Problems,* ed. Marian Palley and Michael Preston (Lexington, Mass.: Lexington Books, 1979); Stephen Wainscott and J. David Woodard, "Second Thoughts on Second-Generation Discrimination," *American Politics Quarterly* 16 (1988), 171–192.

[108]Rosa A. Smith, "Saving Black Boys," *American Prospect,* February, 2004, 49.

[109]Although lower-class students are disproportionately disciplined, and African Americans are disproportionately lower-class, African Americans are even more disproportionately disciplined than their class status would indicate.

[110]Beverly Cross, quoted in Jodie Morse, "Learning while Black," *Time,* May 27, 2002, 50.

[111]Smith, "Saving Black Boys," 49.

[112]"Employers' Replies to Racial Names," *NBER Digest,* September 2003, 1.

[113]David Wessel, "Studies Suggest Potent Race Bias in Hiring," *Wall Street Journal,* September 4, 2003, A2.

[114]Earl G. Graves, *How to Succeed in Business without Being White* (New York: Harper Business, 1997).

[115]Reed Abelson, "Anti-Bias Agency Is Short of Will and Cash," *New York Times,* July 1, 2001, BU1.

[116]"Hispanics Face More Bias in Housing," *Lincoln Journal Star,* November 8, 2002. Another study found similar discrimination in fairly progressive northern cities. "Professional Should Address Discrimination," *Lincoln Journal Star,* April 24, 2002.

[117]*All Things Considered,* NPR, August 5, 2001.

[118]According to analysis conducted by the *Charlotte Observer* of records from twenty-five of the nation's largest lenders. Binyamin Appelbaum and Ted Mellnik, "High Rates Hit More Blacks," *Lincoln Journal Star,* August 28, 2005, 5A.

[119]According to a Department of Housing and Urban Development study in 2002, cited in ibid.

[120]John Iceland and Daniel Weinberg with Erika Steinmetz, *Racial and Ethnic Residential Segregation in the United States, 1980–2000.* Washington, D.C.: United States Census, 2002, ch. 5. Available on the web at www.census.gov/hhes/www/housing/housing_patterns/pdf/censr-3.pdf.

[121]James Traub, "The Year in Ideas," *New York Times Magazine,* December 9, 2001, 94.

[122]Hacker, *Two Nations,* 35–38. For information on why blacks do not want to live in white neighborhoods, see Maria Krysan and Reynolds Farley, "The Residential Preferences of Blacks: Do They Explain Persistent Segregation?" *Social Forces* 80 (2002), 937–980.

[123]According to the Supreme Court's interpretation of Fourth Amendment search and seizure law, police can stop and frisk individuals who officers have a "reasonable suspicion" to believe are committing a crime. But officers must have more than a hunch to meet the standard of "reasonable suspicion" (though less than the "probable cause" required to obtain a search warrant). A person's race is not a valid criterion, except when the person's race and physical description match those of a particular suspect being sought.

[124]Sandy Banks, "Growing Up on a Tightrope," *Los Angeles Times,* March 3, 2006, www.latimes.com/news/local/la-me boys3mar03,0,2282338.full.story.

[125]John Lamberth, "DWB Is Not a Crime," *Washington Post National Weekly Edition,* August 24, 1998, 23.

[126]Michael A. Fletcher, "May the Driver Beware," *Washington Post National Weekly Edition,* April 8, 1996, 29.

[127]Jake Tapper, "And Then There Were None," *Washington Post National Weekly Edition,* January 13, 2003, 9.

[128]Jeffrey Goldberg, "The Color of Suspicion," *New York Times Magazine,* June 20, 1999, 53.

[129]David Cole and John Lamberth, "The Fallacy of Racial Profiling," *New York Times,* May 13, 2001, sec. 4, 13.

[130]Pierre Thomas, "Bias and the Badge," *Washington Post National Weekly Edition,* December 18, 1995, 6–9.

[131]Henry Louis Gates Jr., "Thirteen Ways of Looking at a Black Man," *New Yorker,* October 23, 1995, 59; Anderson, "Black and Blue," 64.

[132]Tammerlin Drummond, "Coping with Cops," *Time,* April 3, 2000, 72–73.

[133]Laura M. Markowitz, "Walking the Walk," *Networker,* July-August 1993, 22.

[134]William Raspberry, "The Little Things That Hurt," *Washington Post National Weekly Edition,* April 18, 1994, 29. See also Ellis Cose, *The Rage of a Privileged Class* (New York: HarperCollins, 1993).

[135]Morin and Cottman, "Invisible Slap," 6.

[136]Kozol, *Savage Inequalities,* 179–180.

[137]Stephan Thernstrom and Abigail Thernstrom, *America in Black and White: One Nation, Indivisible* (New York: Simon & Schuster, 1997), especially part 3. Some improvement began before the civil

rights movement, when southern blacks migrated to northern cities in the 1940s.

[138]Andrew Tobias, "Now the Good News about Your Money," *Parade,* April 4, 1993, 5.

[139]James Smith and Finis Welch, "Race and Poverty: A 40-Year Record," *American Economic Review* 77 (1987), 152–158.

[140]However, their rate of home ownership—48 percent—is the same as the national rate was in the 1940s. Whites' rate is 74 percent now. Deborah Kong, "Strides Made, but Still Much Disparity between Blacks, Whites," *Lincoln Journal Star,* July 22, 2002.

[141]Joel Garreau, "Candidates Take Note: It's a Mall World after All," *Washington Post National Weekly Edition,* August 10, 1992, 25.

[142]Thernstrom and Thernstrom, *America in Black and White,* 500.

[143]Francine Russo, "When Love Is Mixing It Up," *Time,* November, 2001, Bonus Section, F5.

[144]Benedict Carey, "In-laws In the Age of the Outsider," *New York Times,* December 18, 2005, WK1.

[145]Orlando Patterson, quoted in Anderson, "Black and Blue," 62.

[146]From 1967 to 1987, according to calculations by William Julius Wilson. David Remnick, "Dr. Wilson's Neighborhood," *New Yorker,* April 29 and May 6, 1996.

[147]Sociologist William Julius Wilson develops this idea extensively in *The Truly Disadvantaged* (Chicago: University of Chicago Press, 1987).

[148]U.S. Census Bureau, *Statistical Abstract of the United States, 2001* (Washington, D.C.: Government Printing Office, 2001), tab. 38.

[149]Wilson, *The Truly Disadvantaged.*

[150]Remnick, "Dr. Wilson's Neighborhood," 98.

[151]Samuel Walker, *Sense and Nonsense about Crime and Drugs,* 3rd ed. (Belmont, Calif.: Wadsworth, 1994), xviii, 3.

[152]According to the U.S. Bureau of Justice Statistics, cited in Fox Butterfield, "Despite Drop in Crime, an Increase in Inmates," *New York Times,* November 8, 2004.

[153]Ibid.

[154]Peter Reuter, "Why Can't We Make Prohibition Work Better? Some Consequences of Ignoring the Unattractive," in *Perspectives on Crime and Justice, 1996–1997 Lecture Series* (Washington, D.C.: National Institute of Justice, 1997), 30–31.

[155]Smith, "Saving Black Boys," 49.

[156]"Doctor: Harlem's Death Rate Worse than Bangladesh's," *Lincoln Journal,* January 18, 1990.

[157]Sandy Banks, "Growing Up on a Tightrope."

[158]Donald Kaul, "Only Surprise Is That Riots Didn't Happen Sooner," *Lincoln Journal,* May 19, 1992.

[159]Drummond Ayres, Jr., "Decade of Black Struggle: Gains and Unmet Goals," *New York Times,* April 2, 1978, sec. 1, 1.

[160]See Veronica Chambers, *Having It All?* (New York: Doubleday, 2003).

[161]"Inside America's Largest Minority," *Time,* August 22, 2005, 56.

[162]Harold Meyerson, "A Tale of Two Cities," *American Prospect,* June 2004, A8.

[163]According to the most recent research, in 2002, Hispanics might face somewhat more discrimination in housing than blacks. Hispanics who tried to buy a house faced discrimination 20 percent of the time, and those who tried to rent an apartment did so 25 percent of the time. "Hispanics Face More Bias in Housing."

[164]Fifty-nine percent of voters in counties in which immigrants are less than 5 percent of the population say that all illegals should be deported. Joe Klein, "Bush Is Smart on the Border—and the G.O.P. Isn't," *Time,* May 29, 2006, 25.

[165]Tammerlin Drummond, "It's Not Just in New Jersey," *Time,* June 14, 1999, 61.

[166]John Bowe, "Nobodies," *New Yorker,* April 21, 2003, 106.

[167]Guadalupe San Miguel, "Mexican American Organizations and the Changing Politics of School Desegregation in Texas, 1945–1980," *Social Science Quarterly* 63 (1982), 701–715.

[168]Ibid., 710.

[169]Even children of illegal aliens have been given the right to attend public schools by the Supreme Court. The majority assumed that most of these children, although subject to deportation, would remain in the United States, given the large number of illegal aliens who do remain here. Denying them an education would deprive them of the opportunity to fulfill their potential and would deprive society of the benefit of their contribution. *Plyler v. Doe,* 457 U.S. 202 (1982).

[170]Luis Ricardo Fraga, Kenneth J. Meier, and Robert E. England, "Hispanic Americans and Educational Policy: Structural Limits to Equal Access and Opportunities for Upward Mobility," unpublished paper, University of Oklahoma, 1985, 6.

[171]Luis Ricardo Fraga, Kenneth J. Meier, and Robert E. England, "Hispanic Americans and Educational Policy: Limits to Equal Access," *Journal of Politics* 48 (1986), 850–873.

[172]*San Antonio Independent School District v. Rodriguez,* 411 U.S. 1 (1973).

[173]Anjetta McQueen, "Dual-Language Schools Sought," *Lincoln Journal Star,* March 16, 2000.

[174]*Lau v. Nichols,* 414 U.S. 563 (1974).

[175]McQueen, "Dual-Language Schools Sought."

[176]"Bilingualism's End Means a Different Kind of Change," *Champaign-Urbana News-Gazette,* June 7, 1998.

[177]Margot Hornblower, "No Habla Español," *Time,* January 26, 1998, 63.

[178]Lynne Duke, "English Spoken Here," *Washington Post National Weekly Edition,* December 21, 1992, 37.

[179]Eloise Salholz, "Say It in English," *Newsweek,* February 20, 1989, 23.

[180]Joel Kotkin, "Can the Melting Pot Be Reheated?" *Washington Post National Weekly Edition,* July 11, 1994, 23.

[181]James Traub, "The Bilingual Barrier," *New York Times Magazine,* January 31, 1999, 34–35.

[182]Jacques Steinberg, "Test Scores Rise, Surprising Critics of Bilingual Ban," *New York Times,* August 20, 2000, Y1.

[183]U.S. Census Bureau, "Social and Economic Characteristics," *2000 Census of the Population* (http://factfinder.census.gov/servlet/QTTable?_bm5y&-geo_id5D&-qr_name5DEC_2000). Four percent of Asian language speakers do not speak English.

[184]Nancy Landale and R.S. Oropesa, "Schooling, Work, and Idleness among Mexican and Non-Latino White Adolescents," working paper, Pennsylvania State University, Population Research Institute, 1997.

[185]Thomas Boswell and James Curtis, *The Cuban American Experience* (Totowa, N.J.: Rowman & Allanheld, 1983), 191.

[186]Kevin F. McCarthy and R. Burciaga Valdez, *Current and Future Effects of Mexican Immigration in California—Executive Summary* (Santa Monica, Calif.: RAND Corp., 1985), 27.

[187]Ruben Navarrette Jr., "Hispanics See Themselves as Part of United States," *Lincoln Journal Star,* December 23, 2002.

[188]Ibid.

[189]"Survey: Hispanics Reject Cohesive Group Identity," *Lincoln Journal,* December 15, 1992.

[190]Lynne Duke, "English Spoken Here," *Washington Post National Weekly Edition,* December 21, 1992, 37.

[191]Darryl Fears, "The Power of a Label," *Washington Post National Weekly Edition,* September 1, 2003, 29.

[192]Gregory Rodriguez, "Finding a Political Voice," *Washington Post National Weekly Edition,* February 1, 1999, 22–23.

[193]Karen Tumulty, "Courting a Sleeping Giant," *Time,* June 11, 2001, 74.

[194]A 1995 Census Bureau Survey indicated that 49% of Native people preferred being called *American Indian,* 37% preferred *Native American,* 3.6% preferred "some other term," and 5% had no preference. Bureau of Labor Statistics, U.S. Census Bureau Survey, May 1995. www.census.gov/prod/2/gen/96arc/ivatuck.pdf.

[195]*Cherokee Nation v. Georgia,* 30 U.S. 1 (1831); *Worcester v. Georgia,* 31 U.S. 515 (1832).

[196]Vine Deloria Jr. and Clifford M. Lytle, *American Indians, American Justice* (Austin: University of Texas Press, 1983), 221.

[197]Ibid., 222–225.

[198]Indian Self-Determination Act (1975).

[199]Ellen Nakashima and Neely Tucker, "A Fight over Lost Lands, Money Owed," *Washington Post National Weekly Edition,* April 29, 2002, 30.

[200]According to the Indian Gaming Regulatory Act (1988), tribes can establish casinos if their reservation lies in a state that allows virtually any gambling, including charitable "Las Vegas nights."

[201]Kathleen Schmidt, "Gambling a Bonanza for Indians," *Lincoln Journal Star,* March 23, 1998.

[202]Donald L. Barlett and James B. Steele, "Wheel of Misfortune," *Time,* December 16, 2002, 44–48.

[203]Ibid., 47.

[204]W. John Moore, "Tribal Imperatives," *National Journal,* June 9, 1990, 1396.

[205]Jack Hitt, "The Newest Indian," *New York Times Magazine,* August 21, 2005, 40–41.

[206]Felicity Barringer, "Ethnic Pride Confounds the Census," *New York Times,* May 9, 1993, E3.

[207]Jack Hitt, "The Newest Indians," *New York Times Magazine,* August 21, 2005, 38.

[208]Ibid., 38–39.

[209]Quoted in Ruth B. Ginsburg, *Constitutional Aspects of Sex-Based Discrimination* (Saint Paul, Minn.: West, 1974), 2.

[210]Karen De Crow, *Sexist Justice* (New York: Vintage, 1975), 72.

[211]Nadine Taub and Elizabeth M. Schneider, "Women's Subordination and the Role of Law," in *The Politics of Law: A Progressive Critique,* rev. ed., ed. David Kairys (New York: Pantheon, 1990), 160–162.

[212]*Bradwell v. Illinois,* 83 U.S. 130 (1873).

[213]From an amicus curiae (friend of the court) brief by 281 historians filed in the Supreme Court case, *Webster v. Reproductive Health Services,* 106 L.Ed.2d 410 (1989).

[214]Donna M. Moore, "Editor's Introduction" in *Battered Women*, ed. Donna M. Moore (Beverly Hills, Calif.: Sage, 1979), 8.

[215]Barbara Sinclair Deckard, *The Women's Movement*, 2nd ed. (New York: Harper & Row, 1979), 303.

[216]In the early 1960s, a board game for girls—What Shall I Be?—offered these options: teacher, nurse, stewardess, actress, ballerina, and beauty queen. David Owen, "The Sultan of Stuff," *New Yorker*, July 19, 1999, 60.

[217]Reprinted in "Regrets, We Have a Few," *Time Special Issue: 75 Years of* Time, 1998, 192.

[218]For an examination of Betty Friedan's role in the movement and the political dynamics among the various factions in the movement, see Judith Hennessee, *Betty Friedan: Her Life* (New York: Random House, 1999). For an examination of women's views toward feminism, see Elinor Burkett, *The Right Women* (New York: Scribner, 1998).

[219]Robert Alan Goldberg, *Enemies Within* (New Haven, Conn.: Yale University Press, 2002).

[220]De Crow, *Sexist Justice*, 119.

[221]This is why Betty Friedan later felt compelled to write a book espousing the concept of motherhood: *The Second Stage* (New York: Summit, 1981).

[222]For a discussion of these points, see Jane Mansbridge, *Why We Lost the ERA* (Chicago: University of Chicago Press, 1986); Mary Frances Berry, *Why ERA Failed* (Bloomington: Indiana University Press, 1986); Janet Boles, "Building Support for the ERA: A Case of 'Too Much, Too Late,'" *PS: Political Science and Politics* 15 (1982), 575–592.

[223]Shenkman, *I Love Paul Revere*, 136–137.

[224]*Reed v. Reed*, 404 U.S. 71 (1971).

[225]*Hoyt v. Florida*, 368 U.S. 57 (1961).

[226]*Taylor v. Louisiana*, 419 U.S. 522 (1975).

[227]*Stanton v. Stanton*, 421 U.S. 7 (1975).

[228]Cases were from 2002. They were compiled by The WAGE Project (www.wageproject.org) and examined and reported in Evelyn F. Murphy, with E. J. Graff, *Getting Even: Why Women Don't Get Paid Like Men—and What to Do about It* (New York: Simon & Schuster, 2005), 40–48. This total also includes sexual harassment suits, which, of course, reflect a type of sexual discrimination.

[229]Ibid., 56.

[230]Ibid., 157.

[231]Ibid., 153.

[232]Sara Rab and Jerry A. Jacobs, "Sex Discrimination in Restaurant Hiring Practices," unpublished manuscript, Department of Sociology, University of Pennsylvania, 2003, cited in ibid., 57.

[233]Joe's Stone Crab. Murphy, *Getting Even*, 60.

[234]Ibid., 60–61.

[235]Ibid., 84–85.

[236]Ibid., 200.

[237]Ibid., 199.

[238]Ibid., 4.

[239]Amy Joyce, "Women Work Hard to Catch Up in Pay Equity with Men," *Lincoln Journal Star*, April 25, 2006, 1A.

[240]"Gender Wage Gap Still an Issue," *Champaign-Urbana News-Gazette*, April 3, 2001.

[241]Murphy, *Getting Even*, 185.

[242]Ibid., 146.

[243]U.S. Census Bureau, *Statistical Abstract of the United States, 1997* (Washington, D.C.: Government Printing Office, 1997), tab. 645.

[244]The phrase itself is not new. It was used by workers in the nineteenth century and as the title of a book by a Catholic priest in 1906. Jon Gertner, "What Is a Living Wage?" *New York Times Magazine*, January 15, 2006, 42.

[245]For discussion, see ibid., 38.

[246]Lisa McLaughlin, "In Brief," *Time*, October 9, 2000, G12.

[247]For discussion, see Murphy, *Getting Even*, 194–213.

[248]See Murphy, *Getting Even*, for numerous examples.

[249]Susan Benesch, "The Birth of a Nation," *Washington Post National Weekly Edition*, August 4, 1986, 12.

[250]The act also requires employers to continue health insurance coverage during the leave and to give the employee the same job or a comparable one upon her or his return.

[251]Lisa Genasci, "Many Workers Resist Family Benefit Offers," *Lincoln Journal Star*, June 28, 1995.

[252]Nancy R. Gibbs, "Bringing Up Father," *Time*, June 28, 1993, 55–56.

[253]In a conversation with business professors at a southwestern university not long ago. One of the participants conveyed his remark to the author of this chapter.

[254]Karen Kornbluh, "The Joy of Flex," *Washington Monthly*, December, 2005, 30.

[255]Ann Crittenden, "Parents Fighting Back," *American Prospect*, June 2003, 22.

[256]Joyce Gelb and Marian Lief Palley, *Women and Public Policies* (Princeton, N.J.: Princeton University Press, 1982), 102. The author of Title IX, Representative Patsy Mink (D.-Hawaii), had applied to medical schools but was not considered because she was a woman. Mink intended Title IX to open the doors. She said it was "never intended to mean equal numbers or equal money" in athletics. Susan Reimer, "Title IX Has Unintended Consequences," *Lincoln Journal Star*, April 9, 2000.

[257]"Women's Determination Has Evened Playing Fields," *State College* (Pa.) *Centre Daily Times*, May 1, 2004.

[258]Welch Suggs, "Uneven Progress for Women's Sports," *Chronicle of Higher Education*, April 7, 2000, A52–A56; Bill Pennington, "More Men's Teams Benched as Colleges Level the Field," *New York Times*, May 9, 2002, A1.

[259]Suggs, "Uneven Progress for Women's Sports," A52.

[260]Michele Orecklin, "Now She's Got Game," *Time*, March 3, 2003, 57.

[261]"Title IX Facts Everyone Should Know," www.womensportsfoundation.org/cgi-bin/iowa/issues/geena/record,html?record=862.

[262]Mary Duffy, quoted in E. J. Dionne Jr., "Nothing Wacky about Title IX," *Washington Post National Weekly Edition*, May 19, 1997, 26.

[263]Kornbluh, "The Joy of Flex," 30.

[264]Linda R. Hirshman, "Homeward Bound," *American Prospect*, December, 2005, 25.

[265]*Mississippi University for Women* v. *Hogan*, 458 U.S. 718 (1982).

[266]*Orr* v. *Orr*, 440 U.S. 268 (1979).

[267]*Michael M.* v. *Sonoma County*, 450 U.S. 464 (1981).

[268]*Rostker* v. *Goldberg*, 453 U.S. 57 (1981).

[269]*Planned Parenthood of Southeastern Pennsylvania v. Casey*, 120 L.Ed.2d 674 (1992).

[270]David Crary, "Man Sues for Right to Decline Fatherhood," *Lincoln Journal Star*, March 9, 2006, 7A.

[271]A simplified version of this scenario was used by President Johnson in support of affirmative action.

[272]Early decisions include *University of California Regents v. Bakke*, 438 U.S. 265 (1978); *United Steelworkers v. Weber*, 443 U.S. 193 (1979); and *Fullilove v. Klutznick*, 448 U.S. 448 (1980).

[273]Two critics include Thomas Sowell, *Preferential Policies: An International Perspective* (New York: Morrow, 1990), and Dinesh D'Souza, *Illiberal Education* (New York: Free Press, 1991).

[274]*United Steelworkers v. Weber; Sheet Metal Workers v. EEOC*, 92 L.Ed.2d 344 (1986); *Firefighters v. Cleveland*, 92 L.Ed.2d 405 (1986); *United States v. Paradise Local Union*, 94 L.Ed.2d 203 (1987).

[275]*Firefighters v. Stotts*, 467 U.S. 561 (1985); *Wygant v. Jackson Board of Education*, 90 L.Ed.2d 260 (1986).

[276]*Richmond v. Croson*, 102 L.Ed.2d 854 (1989); *Adarand Constructors v. Pena*, 132 L.Ed.2d 158 (1995). The perception that minorities are taking over is also reflected in a peculiar poll finding: The average American estimated that 32 percent of the U.S. population was black and 21 percent was Hispanic at a time when they were just 12 percent and 9 percent. Richard Nadeau, Richard G. Niemi, and Jeffrey Levine, "Innumeracy about Minority Populations," *Public Opinion Quarterly* 57 (1993), 332–347.

[277]Quoted in Robert J. Samuelson, "End Affirmative Action," *Washington Post National Weekly Edition*, March 6, 1995, 5.

[278]James E. Jones, "The Genesis and Present Status of Affirmative Action in Employment," paper presented at the annual meeting of the American Political Science Association, Washington, D.C., September, 1984; Robert Pear, *New York Times*, June 19, 1983; Nelson C. Dometrius and Lee Sigelman, "Assessing Progress toward Affirmative Action Goals in State and Local Government," *Public Administration Review* 44 (1984), 241–247; Peter Eisinger, *Black Employment in City Government* (Washington, D.C.: Joint Center for Political Studies, 1983); Milton Coleman, "Uncle Sam Has Stopped Running Interference for Blacks," *Washington Post National Weekly Edition*, December 19, 1983.

[279]This "is one of the better kept secrets of the debate." Alan Wolfe, "Affirmative Action, Inc.," *New Yorker*, November 25, 1996, 107. See also the numerous sources cited there.

[280]Gertrude Ezorsky, *Racism and Justice: The Case for Affirmative Action* (Ithaca, N.Y.: Cornell University Press, 1991), 48–49, 63–65.

[281]Wilson, *The Truly Disadvantaged*.

[282]Donald Kaul, "Privilege in Workplace Invisible to White Men Who Enjoy It," *Lincoln Journal-Star*, April 9, 1995; Richard Morin and Lynne Duke, "A Look at the Bigger Picture," *Washington Post National Weekly Edition*, March 16, 1992, 9.

[283]Eisinger, *Black Employment in City Government*.

[284]Thomas J. Kane, "Racial and Ethnic Preference in College Admissions," paper presented at the Ohio State University College of Law Conference, "Twenty Years after *Bakke*," Columbus, April 1998.

[285]Stephen Carter, quoted in David Owen, "From Race to Chase," *New Yorker*, June 3, 2002, 54.

[286]Jeffrey Rosen, "How I Learned to Love Quotas," *New York Times Magazine*, June 1, 2003, 54; Lee Hockstader, "The Texas 10 Percent Solu-

tion," *Washington Post National Weekly Edition,* November 11, 2002, 30. A major effect on the University of California system has been "cascading," with minority enrollments dropping at the most competitive UC campuses but increasing at the less competitive ones. Minorities have been cascading from the top tier to the next tiers, where their academic records more closely match those of the other students. Traub, "The Class of Prop. 209," *New York Times Magazine,* May 2, 1999, 51.

[287]Jacques Steinberg, "The New Calculus of Diversity on Campus," *New York Times,* February 2, 2003, WK3.

[288]*Gratz* v. *Bollinger,* 156 L.Ed.2d 257; *Grutter* v. *Bollinger,* 156 L.Ed.2d 304.

[289]Traub, "Class of Prop. 209."

[290]John Larew, "Why Are Droves of Unqualified, Unprepared Kids Getting into Our Top Colleges?" *Washington Monthly,* June 1991, 10–14; Theodore Cross, "Suppose There Was No Affirmative Action at the Most Prestigious Colleges and Graduate Schools," *Journal of Blacks in Higher Education,* March 31, 1994, 47, 50.

[291]For an examination of the *Bakke* ruling and its impact on graduate schools, see Susan Welch and John Gruhl, *Affirmative Action and Minority Enrollments in Medical and Law Schools* (Ann Arbor: University of Michigan Press, 1998).

[292]Richard H. Sander, "House of Cards for Black Law Students," *Los Angeles Times,* December 20, 2004, www.latimes.com/news/opinion/la-oe-sander20dec20,0,436015,print.story; Adam Liptak, "For Blacks in Law School, Can Less Be More?" *New York Times,* February 13, 2005, WK3.

[293]For further discussion, see David T. Canon, *Race, Redistricting, and Representation* (Chicago: University of Chicago Press, 1999), 23–25. Of course, there's also a small upper class of wealthy business people, entertainers, and athletes.

[294]Dick Kirschten, "Not Black-and-White," *National Journal,* March 2, 1991, 496–500.

[295]*Korematsu* v. *United States,* 323 U.S. 214 (1944).

[296]Peter Irons, "Race and the Constitution: The Case of the Japanese American Internment," *This Constitution,* Winter 1986, 23.

[297]Matt Bai, "He Said No to Internment," *New York Times Magazine,* December 25, 2005, 38.

[298]William O. Douglas, *The Court Years* (New York: Random House, 1980), 279.

[299]Irons, *Justice at War,* vii–ix, 186–218.

[300]Ibid., vii, 367; Hersey, "Behind Barbed Wire," 73.

[301]*Korematsu* v. *United States,* 584 F.Supp. 1406 (1983).

[302]In 1948, Congress passed a law providing $37 million to settle damage claims by internees, but this was less than one-tenth of the amount that the government estimates internees had lost.

[303]Tom Zeller, "In Every Mind the Memory, in Every Building a Threat," *New York Times,* September 30, 2001, WK4.

Chapter 16

[1]The politics of the legislation are discussed in David Nather, "Bills Merged in Pre-Recess Flurry," *CQ Weekly,* July 31, 2006, 2110–2113.

[2]Michael Barone and Richard E. Cohen, *Almanac of American Politics 2006* (Washington, D.C.: National Journal, 2005), 1754; other background information on Murray comes from her website (murray.senate.gov/about).

[3]Senator Patty Murray, "Statement in Favor of the Estate Tax Elimination Act (S. 1128)." Murray's website maintains an archive of press releases (www.murray.senate.gov/news).

[4]David Nather and Rachel Van Dongen, "Frist Loses Estate Tax Showdown," *CQ Weekly,* August 4, 2006, 2176.

[5]Adam Smith, *Inquiry into the Nature and Causes of the Wealth of Nations* (1776; reprinted in several editions, including Indianapolis: Bobbs-Merrill, 1961).

[6]James K. Galbraith, *Balancing Acts: Technology, Finance, and the American Future* (New York: Basic Books, 1989); Robert L. Heilbroner and Lester C. Thurow, *Five Economic Challenges* (Englewood Cliffs, N.J.: Prentice Hall, 1981), 62.

[7]Quoted in John Greenwald, "Knitting New Notions," *Time,* January 30, 1989, 46.

[8]John Maynard Keynes, *The General Theory of Employment, Interest and Money* (New York: Harcourt, Brace, 1935).

[9]The FOMC is made up of a board of governors including five Federal Reserve Bank heads.

[10]For a brief review of the Fed's work, see James L. Rowe Jr., "Holding the Purse Strings," *Washington Post National Weekly Edition,* June 28, 1999, 6–8.

[11]William Greider, *Secrets of the Temple: How the Federal Reserve Runs the Country* (New York: Simon & Schuster, 1987), 461. Grieder's analyses of the Reserve Board's anti-inflation policies in the early 1980s are revealing and compelling.

[12]Robert D. Auerbach, "That Shreddin' Fed," *Barrons,* December 10, 2001, 36. Auerbach was an economist for the House Banking Committee for eleven years.

[13]Ben Wildavsky, "Atlas Schmoozes," *National Journal,* May 17, 1997, 974–977.

[14]Gardiner Harris, "F.D.A. Approves Broader Access to Next-Day Pill," *New York Times,* August 25, 2006.

[15]See discussion in William Ophuls, *Ecology and the Politics of Scarcity; Prologue to a Political Theory of the Steady State* (San Francisco: W. H. Freeman, 1977), 145–147.

[16]NBC News Special Report on the 20th Anniversary of Earth Day, April 22, 1991.

[17]William P. Cunningham, et al., eds., *Environmental Encyclopedia,* 2nd ed.(Detroit: Gale Research, 1998), 395; Ruth A. Eblen and William R. Eblen, eds., *The Encyclopedia of the Environment* (Boston: Houghton Mifflin, 1994), 243.

[18]Louis Uchitelle, "He Didn't Say It. But He Knew It," *New York Times,* April 30, 2000, sec. 3, 1.

[19]"Spoils to GOP Victors," *Champaign-Urbana News-Gazette,* August 6, 2002, 1.

[20]Edward R. Tufte, *Political Control of the Economy* (Princeton, N.J.: Princeton University Press, 1978).

[21]Steven Greenhouse, "Brady Sought Greenspan Policy Pledge," *International Herald Tribune,* September 25, 1992, 13.

[22]Paul Krugman, "The Maestro Slips Out of Tune," *New York Times Magazine,* June 6, 2004, 80.

[23]"Poll: Citizens OK about Money, Glum on Future," *Champaign-Urbana News-Gazette,* April 12, 1995, B8.

[24]Paul Krugman, "Dynamo and Microchip," *New York Times,* February 20, 2000, sec. 4, 13.

[25]CBS/*New York Times* Poll, August, 2006.

[26]Jill Barshay, "The Uneven Field," *CQ Weekly,* February 7, 2005, 292. Data cited is from Congress's Joint Economic Committee.

[27]The government raises small amounts of revenue by taxing consumption through the levies it places on the sale or manufacture of some luxury and nonessential items such as liquor and cigarettes, as well as on a few essential products such as gasoline. These excise taxes are designed not only to raise revenue, but also to limit or discourage use of scarce or dangerous products, which is why they are sometimes called "sin taxes."

[28]Isaac Shapiro, "Overall Federal Tax Burden on Most Families—Including Middle-Income Families—at Lowest Levels in More Than Two Decades," Center on Budget and Policy Priorities Report, April 10, 2002, 2.

[29]Data are from the Center on Budget and Policy Priorities Report (www.cbpp.org), quoted in "Middle-Class Tax Blow Hits Lowest Level Since 1957," *Champaign-Urbana News-Gazette,* April 15, 2002, A8.

[30]John Cranford, "Code Words: Tax Neutrality," *CQ Weekly,* February 7, 2005, 288–290.

[31]Joseph J. Schatz, "National Sales Tax: the Pros and Cons," *CQ Weekly,* June 13, 2005, 1558.

[32]Jill Barshay, "Rich vs. Poor," *CQ Weekly,* February 7, 2005, 295.

[33]Edmund L. Andrews, "Senate Approves 2-Year Extension of Bush Tax Cuts," *New York Times,* May 12, 2006, citing data from the Tax Policy Center.

[34]U.S. Congress, Joint Economic Committee.

[35]"The Uneven Field."

[36]"Code Words: Tax Neutrality," 289. The economist quoted is Alice Rivlin, former director of the CBO and the OMB, and former vice-chair of the Fed.

[37]Roger Lowenstein, "Tax Break: Who Needs the Mortgage-Interest Deduction?" *New York Times Magazine,* March 5, 2006, 78.

[38]"Rich vs. Poor," 297.

[39]"Problems Cited at IRS Help Centers," *Champaign-Urbana News-Gazette,* September 4, 2003, 1.

[40]David Cay Johnston, "A Taxation Policy to Make John Stuart Mill Weep," *New York Times,* April 18, 2004, WK14.

[41]Jill Barshay, "Business Lobby Storms Senate to Shape Corporate Tax Bill," *CQ Weekly,* May 8, 2004, 1073.

[42]Citizens for Tax Justice, "State and Local Taxes Hit Poor and Middle Class Far Harder than the Wealthy." Report issued June 26, 1996. See the report online at www.ctj.org/html/whopays.htm.

[43]"National Sales Tax: the Pros and Cons," 1557–1559.

[44]Institute on Taxation and Economic Policy, "The Effects of Replacing Most Federal Taxes with a National Sales Tax: A State-by-State Distributional Analysis." Paper issued September 2004, 2.

[45]Ibid., 3.

[46]This is a proposal made by Yale law professor Michael J. Graetz, "To the Point of No Returns," *New York Times,* November 15, 2004, A23.

[47]Joseph L. Schatz, "The Power of the Status Quo," *CQ Weekly,* February 6, 2006, 322.

[48]Former chair of the Senate Finance Committee, Bob Packwood (R-Ore.) quoted in ibid., 323.

[49]Joseph J. Schatz, "IRS Set to Lean Harder on Wayward Taxpayers," *CQ Weekly,* April 25, 2005, 1055.

[50]David Alan Stockman, *Triumph of Politics: How the Reagan Revolution Failed* (New York: Harper & Row, 1986).

[51]Citizens for Tax Justice, "Bush Still on Track to Borrow $10 Trillion by 2014 According to Latest Official Estimates," Paper issued January 30, 2004, 1 (www.ctj.org).

[52]Robert Greenstein, "President's Budget Uses Accounting Devices and Implausible Assumptions to Hide Hundreds of Billions of Dollars in Costs," Center for Budget and Policy Priorities, February 5, 2002, 2 (www.cbpp.org).

[53]Mark Murray, John Maggs, et al., quoting Brookings' analyst William G. Gale in "The Deficit Difference," *National Journal,* February 9, 2002, 384.

[54]U.S. Treasury Department, *The Financial Report of the United States 2005* (Washington D. C.: Government Printing Office, 2006).

[55]Maggs, "Winners and Losers in the Bush Economy," *National Journal,* May 15, 2004, 1496.

[56]Rep. Jim Cooper, "Why This Report Matters to You," commentary on the Financial Report of the United States, 2005, xv (transcript is at www.pbs.org/now).

[57]Victor Allred, "PAYGO Goes by the Wayside," *Congressional Quarterly Weekly Report,* January 13, 2001, 96.

[58]Andrew Taylor, "Deal on Pay-As-You-Go Rules a Must for Budget Resolution," *Congressional Quarterly Weekly Report,* April 17, 2004, 897–900.

[59]Maggs, "Winners and Losers in the Bush Economy," 1495.

[60]Ibid., 1496.

[61]For a worst-case scenario see Laurence J. Kotlikoff and Scott Burns', *The Coming Generational Storm: What You Need to Know about America's Economic Future* (Cambridge, Mass.: MIT Press, 2004). Kotlikoff estimates the government will have a gap of $51 trillion between revenues and obligations over the coming decade.

[62]Joseph A. Schumpeter, *Business Cycles: A Theoretical, Historical, and Statistical Analysis of the Capitalist Process* (New York: McGraw-Hill) 1939.

[63]This is the view of Richard W. Fisher, president of the Federal Reserve Bank of Dallas.

[64]William Greider, "America's Truth Deficit," *New York Times,* July 18, 2005. A more complete statement of Greider's view in his *One World, Ready or Not.*

[65]Thomas L. Friedman, "*The World Is Flat: A Brief History of the Twenty-first Century* (New York: Farrar, Straus and Giroux, 2005).

[66]Diana Jean Schemo," 2-Year Colleges, Students Eager but Unready," *New York Times,* September 2, 2006

[67]Ibid., 4.

[68]Pew Hispanic Center and National Conference of State Legislatures.

[69]Bruce Stokes, "The Lost Wages of Immigration," *National Journal,* January 7, 2006, 58. Borjas also claims that immigration drives down wages at the high skill end as well because the labor supply is expanded by foreign students who stay on after receiving PhDs. See, for example, "Immigration in High-Skill Labor Markets: The Impact of Foreign Students on the Earnings of Doctorates," Working Paper 12085, National Bureau of Economic Research, March 2006.

[70]Roger Lowenstein, "The Immigration Equation," *New York Times Magazine,* July 9, 2006.

[71]"Unemployment Plays a Small Role in Spurring Mexican Migration to the U.S." Press release of the Pew Hispanic Center, December 6, 2005.

[72]Edward Porter, "The Search for Illegal Immigrants Stops at the Workplace," *New York Times,* March 5, 2006, Bu 3.

[73]Barry R. Chiswick, "Sons of Immigrants: Are They At an Earnings Disadvantage?" *American Economic Review* 67 (1977), 377–380; Geoffrey Carliner, "Wages, Earnings, and Hours of First, Second and Third Generation American Males," *Economic Inquiry* 18 (1980), 887–102.

[74]George J. Borjas, "Making It in America: Social Mobility in the Immigrant Population," Working Paper 12088, National Bureau of Economic Research, March 2006 (www.nber,org/papers/w12088).

[75]Julia Preston, "Texas Hospitals Reflect the Debate on Immigration," *New York Times,* July 18, 2006, 1.

[76]"Hispanics: A People in Motion," Pew Hispanic Center, 2005, 12–13.

[77]One advocate for this approach is former Massachusetts governor and presidential candidate Michael Dukakis. Michael Dukakis and Daniel J. B. Mitchell, "Raise Wages, Not Walls," *New York Times,* July 25, 2006

[78]John Berry, "The Legacy of Reaganomics," *Washington Post National Weekly Edition,* December 19, 1988; Spencer Rich, "Are You Really Better Off Than You Were Thirteen Years Ago?" *Washington Post National Weekly Edition,* September 8, 1986, 20; Levy, "We're Running Out of Gimmicks to Sustain Our Prosperity," *Washington Post National Weekly Edition,* December 29, 1986, 18–19.

[79]Editorial, "Two Trillion Dollars Is Missing," *New York Times,* January 8, 1989, E28.

[80]Louis Uchitelle, "For Employee Benefits, It Pays to Wear the Union Label," *New York Times,* July 16, 1995, F10.

[81]Lester C. Thurow, "Companies Merge; Families Break Up," *New York Times,* September 3, 1995, E11.

[83]"Family Wealth Down for 1st Time in 55 Years," *Champaign-Urbana News-Gazette,* March 14, 2001, A8.

[83]Stephanie Aronson, "The Rise in Lifetime Earnings Inequality among Men," Federal Reserve Board Staff Report, Finance and Economics Discussion Series, March 2002, 4 (www.federalreserve.gov).

[84]Jon Gertner, "Forgive Us Our Student Debts," *New York Times Magazine,* June 11, 2006, 60.

[85]Economic Policy Institute.

[86]Michael Lind, *The Next American Nation: The New Nationalism and the Fourth American Revolution* (New York: Free Press, 1995), 139–216.

[87]On the health care and mortgage debt burden see Elizabeth Warren and Amelia Warren Tyagi, *The Two-Income Trap: Why Middle-Class Mothers and Fathers Are Going Broke* (New York: Basic Books, 2003), 84–87 and 129–137.

[88]Rick Lyman, "Census Reports Slight Increase in '05 Incomes," *New York Times,* August 30, 2006, 1.

[89]Bruce Stokes, "The Lost-Wages of Immigration," *National Journal* January 7, 2006, 58.

[90]http://murray.senate.gov/current.html.

[91]"State Labor Department Analysis Reveals Flaw in Republican Trifecta Bill," August 4, 2006. This press release from Senator Murray's office also contains the statement by the Labor Department. (murray.senate.gove.news.cfm?id= 261339) .

[92]"Murray Votes Against Republican 'Trifecta' Bill," press release from Murray's office, August 3, 2006 (murray.senate.gove.news.cfm?id= 261267).

[93]David Nather, "Minimum Wage Boost Still a Maybe at Best," *CQ Weekly,* July 24, 2006, 2019.

[94]Ibid., 2020.

[95]Quoted in Landon Thomas, Jr., "A $31 Billion Gift Between Friends," *New York Times,* June 27, 2006.

Chapter 17

[1]Robert Pear, "House and Senate Still Far Apart on Medicaid Changes," *New York Times,* December 12, 2005.

[2]*Budget of the United States, Fiscal Year 2007* (Washington D.C.: U.S. Government Printing Office, 2006), 114.

[3]A number of Romney's issue quotes are posted at www.ontheissues.org.

[4]Donald L. Barlett and James B. Steele, "Corporate Welfare," *Time,* November 9, 1998, 35.

[5]Patricia Dunn, "The Reagan Solution for Aiding Families with Dependent Children: Reflections of an Earlier Era," in *The Attack on the Welfare State,* ed. Anthony Champagne and Edward Harpham (Prospect Heights, Ill.: Waveland, 1984), 87–110.

[6]Melinda Upp, "Relative Importance of Various Income Sources of the Aged, 1980," *Social Security Bulletin,* January 1983, 5.

[7]All of the statistics on Social Security recipients are from Social Security Administration, "Social Security Basic Facts" (www.socialsecurity.gov/pressoffice/basicfact.htm).

[8]Social Security Administration, "Social Security Information for Women" (www.ssa.gov/women).

[9]U.S. Census Bureau, "Poverty: 2004 Highlights" (www.census.gov/hhes/poverty/poverty04/pov04hi.html).

[10]Barbara Ehrenreich, who writes on working-class life, is one who believes that the poverty level is set too low. Swanee Hunt, "Number of Poor May Be Far Higher Than Government Statistics Indicate," *Champaign-Urbana News-Gazette,* December 7, 2003, B1.

[11]Social Security Administration, "Social Security Basic Facts" July 2006, 1 (www.socialsecurity.gov/pressoffice/basicfact.htm).

[12]Social Security Administration, "Social Security Highlights 2005–2006," 2 (www. socialsecurity. gov/policy/docs/quickfacts/proghighlights. index.html).

[13]U.S. Census Bureau, *Statistical Abstract of the United States, 2006* (Washington, D.C.: Government Printing Office, 2005), tab. 80 and 81.

[14]Greg J. Duncan, *Years of Poverty, Years of Plenty: The Changing Economic Fortunes of American Workers and Families* (Ann Arbor: Survey Research Center, Institute for Social Research, University of Michigan, 1984); Spencer Rich, "Who Gets Help and How," *Washington Post National Weekly Edition,* May 15, 1989, 37.

[15]Department of Health and Human Services, Temporary Assistance for Needy Families (TANF) Program, Administration for Children and Families, final rule summary (www.acf.dhhs. gov/programs/ofa/exsumcl.htm); Liz Schott, Ed Lazere, Heidi Goldberg, and Eileen Sweeney, "Highlights of the Final TANF Regulations," Center on Budget and Policy Priorities, April 29, 1999 (www.cbpp.org/4-29-99wel.htm).

[16]Ibid.

[17]Nicholas Johnson, Joseph Llobrera, and Bob Zahradnik, "A Hand Up: How State Earned Income Tax Credits Help Working Families Escape Poverty in 2003," Center on Budget and Policy Priorities, March 3, 2003 (www.cbpp.org/3-3-03sfp.htm). Seventeen states also offer the EITC against state income taxes.

[18]Robert Pear, "Electronic Cards Replace Coupons for Food Stamps," *New York Times,* June 23, 2004, 1.

[19]Food and Nutrition Service, "Food Stamp Participation Rates: 2004" (www.usda.gov).

[20] Jay Mathews, "Study Shows Early Head Start Gains," *State College* (Pa.) *Centre Daily Times,* June 5, 2002, 1.

[21]U.S. Census Bureau, *Statistical Abstract of the United States, 2001* (Washington, D.C.: Government Printing Office, 2001), tab. 801.

[22]Nicholas Kristof, "Farm Subsidies That Kill," *New York Times,* July 5, 2002, A21.

[23]John Kelly, "Lion's Share of Farm Subsidies Going to a Select Few," *State College* (Pa.) *Centre Daily Times,* September 10, 2001, 1.

[24]John Lancaster, "Our Farm-Friendly Lawmakers," *Washington Post National Weekly Edition,* September 10, 2001, 11.

[25]Quoted in ibid.

[26]Gebe Martinez, "Free-Spending Farm Bill a Triumph of Politics," *Congressional Quarterly Weekly Review,* May 4, 2002, 114. The first quote is from John Boehner (R-Ohio) and Cal Dooley (D-Calif.), the second from Patrick Toomey (R-Pa.).

[27]Timothy Egan, "Big Farms Reap Two Harvests with Aid as Bumper Crop," *New York Times,* December 26, 2004, sec. 1, 36.

[28]Press release from the office of Senator Tim Hutchinson, May 13, 2002.

[29]Elizabeth Becker, "As House Prepares Farm Bill, Questions of Who Needs Help and How Much," *New York Times,* September 9, 2001, 22.

[30]Nicholas D. Kristof, "A Gift to the World, and Ourselves," *New York Times,* December 25, 2005, Wk9.

[31]Dan Barber, "Stuck in the Middle," *New York Times,* November 23, 2005.

[32]Kristof, "Farm Subsidies That Kill."

[33]*Budget of the United States 2007, Historical Tables,* tab 5.1, 94.

[34]U.S. Census Bureau, *Statistical Abstract of the United States, 2003* (Washington, D.C.: Government Printing Office, 2004), tab. 545.

[35]Richard B. Freeman, "Labor Market Institutions and Earnings Inequality," *New England Economic Review,* May–June 1996, 158; U.S. Census Bureau, "Current Population Survey," March 1960 to 2001 (www.census.gov).

[36]U.S. Census Bureau, "2003 Poverty Tables." For an analysis of the data in these tables, see "Census Data Show Poverty Increased, Income Stagnated, and the Number of Uninsured Rose to a Record Level in 2003," Center on Budget and Policy Priorities, August 27, 2004 (www.cbpp.org/8-26-04pov.htm).

[37]Mark Murray, Marilyn Werber Serafini, and Megan Twohey, "Untested Safety Net," *National Journal,* March 10, 2001, 691.

[38]Clarke E. Cochran et al., *American Public Policy,* 6th ed. (New York: St. Martin's/Worth, 1999), 282.

[39]Rebecca Adams, "America's Unraveling Safety Net," *Congressional Quarterly Weekly Review,* May 22, 2004, 1225.

[40]Ibid., 1226; Robert Pear, "Nursing Home Inspections Miss Violations, Report Says," *New York Times,* January 16, 2006.

[41]Erin Heath, "Medicaid: The Pendulum Swings," *National Journal,* August 9, 2003, 2546.

[42]Lawrence J. Schweinhart et al., *Lifetime Effects: The High/Scope Perry Preschool Study through Age 40* (Ypsilanti, Mich.: High/Scope Press, 2004).

[43]*U.S. Budget for Fiscal Year 2007,* 117.

[44]"Greenspan Warns about Mortgage Giants' Debt," *Champaign-Urbana News-Gazette,* February 24, 2004, C8.

[45]Timothy L. O'Brien and Jennifer Lee, " Seismic Shift under the House of Fannie Mae," *New York Times,* October 3, 2004, sec. 3, 1, 9.

[46]"Nature Humbles a State of Mind," *New York Times,* February 10, 1991, E3; Marc Reisner, "The Emerald Desert," *Greenpeace,* July–August 1989, 7.

[47]Barlett and Steele, "Corporate Welfare," 38.

[48]Ibid., 87.

[49]See Donald L. Barlett and James B. Steele, "Paying a Price for Polluters," November 23, 1998, 77, and "Corporate Welfare," 39.

[50]For some sample costs of cleanup of industrial waste, see Barlett and Steele, "Paying a Price for Polluters," 72–80.

[51]Robert Pear, "Growth of National Health Spending Slows Along With Drug Sales," *New York Times,"* January 10, 2006.

[52]Paul Krugman, "Our Sick Society," *New York Times,* May 5, 2006.

[53]"Hospital-Caused Deaths" (Editorial), *New York Times,* July 5, 2006; Gardiner Harris, "Report Finds a Heavy Toll From Medication Errors," *New York Times* July 21, 2006.

[54]Institute of Medicine study, cited in Hillary Rodham Clinton, "Now Can We Talk About Health Care?" *New York Times Magazine,* April 18, 2004, 20.

[55]The findings of a study on this subject can be found in "Racial Differences in Health Care." *New England Journal of Medicine* (Aug 2005).

[56]Elizabeth Warren and Amelia Warren Tyagi, *The Two-Income Trap: Why Middle-Class Mothers and Fathers Are Going Broke* (New York: Basic Books, 2003).

[57]"Europe Mulls Private Medical Care," *Champaign-Urbana News-Gazette,* November 29, 2003, A3.

[58]Daniel Gross, "Whose Problem Is Health Care?" *New York Times,* February 8, 2004, BU6.

[59]Robert Fitch, "Big Labor's Big Secret," *New York Times,* December 28, 2005.

[60]Donald L. Barlett and James B. Steele, "The Health of Nations," *New York Times,* October 24, 2004, WKH.

[61]Steve Lohr, "Health Care Costs Are a Killer but Maybe That's a Plus," *New York Times,* September 26, 2004, WK5.

[62]Clinton, "Now Can We Talk?" 30.

[63]Lohr, "Health Care Costs Are a Killer"; Malcolm Caldwell, "High Prices," *New Yorker,* October 25, 2004, 88.

[64]Caldwell, "High Prices," 88; see also John Abramson, *Overdosed America* (New York: Harper-Collins, 2004).

[65]Gina Kolata, "More May Not Mean Better in Health Care, Studies Find," *New York Times,* July 21, 2002, sec. 1, 20.

[66]Ibid.

[67]Erik Eckholm, "Those Who Pay Health Costs Think of Drawing Lines," *New York Times,* March 28, 1993, 1.

[68]Gina Kolata, "Research Suggests More Health Care May Not Be Better," 20.

[69]Mark Sherman, "Doctors Call for National Coverage," *Lincoln Journal Star,* August 13, 2003, 1.

[70]Robert Pear, "Bush Administration Plans Medicare Changes," *New York Times,* July 17, 2006.

[71]Robert Pear, "House and Senate Still Far Apart on Medicaid Changes," *New York Times,* December 12, 2005.

[72]Social Security Administration, "Social Security Basic Facts 2006," 2 (www.socialsecurity.gov/pressoffice/basicfactalt.htm).

[73]Robert Pear, "AARP Opposes Bush Plan to Replace Social Security with Private Accounts," *New York Times,* November 12, 2004, A19.

[74]Richard W. Stevenson, "Bush's Social Security Plan Is Said to Require Vast Borrowing," *New York Times,* November 28, 2004, 1, 22.

[75]"Social Security Basic Facts, 2006," 2.

[76]Douglas J. Besharov, "End Welfare Lite as We Know It," *New York Times,* August 15, 2006.

[77]Eileen P. Sweeney, "Recent Studies Indicate That Many Parents Who Are Current or Former Welfare Recipients Have Disabilities," Center on Budget and Policy Priorities, February 29, 2000 (www.cbpp.org/2-29-00wel.pdf); Erica Goode, "Childhood Abuse and Adult Stress," *New York Times,* August 2, 2000, A22.

[78]Kevin Freking, "Many States Facing Welfare Dilemma," *Champaign-Urbana News-Gazette,* September 10, 2006, C-3.

[79]*Budget of the United States 2007,* 116.

[80]On Bush's marriage initiative and work requirements, see Bill Swindell, "Welfare Reauthorization Becomes Another Casualty in Congress's Partisan Crossfire," *Congressional Quarterly Weekly,* April 3, 2004, 805–806.

[81]Pietro S. Nivola, Jennifer L. Noyes, and Isabel V. Sawhill, "Welfare and Beyond," Policy Brief No. 29, Brookings Institution, March 2004, 2.

[82]Ibid., 3–6.

[83]Department of Health and Human Services, "Reauthorization of the Temporary Assistance for Needy Families Program,"4 (www.aphsa.org). Program renewal was part of the Deficit Reduction Act of 2005.

[84]Douglas J. Besharov, "End Welfare Lite as We Know It."

[85]Gordon Berlin, vice president of MDRC, a nonpartisan research group, quoted in Hegland, "What Works for Welfare?" 108.

[86]Press release form the office of Governor Mitt Romney, April 12, 2006.

[87]Mitt Romney, Signing message to the Massachusetts state legislature in returning House Bill No. 4479, April 12, 2006.

[88]Scott Helman and Liz Kowalczyk, "Joy, Worries on Healthcare," *Boston Globe,* April 13, 2006, 1.

Chapter 18

[1] Howard Fineman, "Politics," *Newsweek,* November 28, 2005, 28.

[2] "Murtha Responds to Rumsfeld," August 30, 2006. This press release from Murtha's office lists claims made by Rumsfeld about the War in Iraq and counters with a list of "facts" to refute them. (www.murtha.house.gov).

[3]Letter from John P. Murtha to the Democratic Caucus, December 14, 2005. (www.murtha.house.gov).

[4]"Murtha Compares Cost of War and Domestic Expenses," July 11, 2006. This press release issued by Murtha's office compares the dollar cost for various kinds of defense preparedness and for environmental and economic development needs to dollars spent per hour, day, and week in Iraq.

[5]Letter from Rep. John P. Murtha and Rep. David Obey (D-Ohio) to President George W. Bush, July 26, 2006. Text at Murtha's website (www.murtha.house.gov).

[6]Fineman, "Politics," 28.

[7]Ibid.

[8]Ibid.

[9]Francis Fukuyama, The End of History and the Last Man (New York: Free Press, 1992).

[10]Walter LaFeber, "Marking Revolution, Opposing Revolution," New York Times, July 3, 1983, sec. 4, 13.

[11]The group was known as the Project for the New Century (PNAC); it circulated its call for the overthrow of Saddam Hussein in 1995.

[12]Philip Bobbitt, "Why We Listen," New York Times, January 30, 2006.

[13]The findings of the congressional investigation into intelligence failures prior to and after 9/11 can be read at the website for the Senate Select Intelligence Committee (intelligence.senate.gov). See transcripts of the testimony of Eleanor Hill, director of the Joint Inquiry staff.

[14]For a discussion of how the Bush administration cherry-picked intelligence data to support the invasion of Iraq in 2003 see James Risen, State of War: the Secret History of the CIA and the Bush Administration (New York: Free Press, 2006).

[15]Madison's notes from Documents Illustrative of the Formation of the Union of the American States, quoted in Joan Biskupic, "Constitution's Conflicting Clauses Underscored by Iraqi Crisis," Congressional Quarterly Weekly Report, January 5, 1991, 34.

[16]Ronald D. Elving, "America's Most Frequent Fight Has Been the Undeclared War," Congressional Quarterly Weekly Report, January 5, 1991, 37.

[17]Representative Toby Roth (R-Wis.), quoted in Katharine Q. Seelye, "House Defeats Bid to Repeal 'War Powers,'" New York Times, June 11, 1995, A7.

[18]Barry B. Hughes, The Domestic Context of American Foreign Policy (San Francisco: Freeman, 1978), ch. 5.

[19]Robert Weissberg, Public Opinion and Popular Government (Englewood Cliffs, N.J.: Prentice Hall, 1976).

[20]For a discussion of the foreign policy establishment, see Walter Isaacson and Evan Thomas, The Wise Men: Six Friends and the World They Made (New York: Simon & Schuster, 1986).

[21]I. M. Destler, Leslie H. Gelb, and Anthony Lake, Our Own Worst Enemy: The Unmaking of American Foreign Policy (New York: Simon & Schuster, 1984), 115–116.

[22]Tom Zeller, "The Iraq-Qaeda Link: A Short History," New York Times, June 20, 2004, WK4.

[23]New York Times/CBS News poll, August, 2006.

[24]Andrew Kohut, "Speak Softly and Carry a Smaller Stick," New York Times, March 24, 2006. Kohut is a pollster for the Pew Foundation.

[25]Carl M. Cannon, "Judging Clinton," National Journal, January 1, 2000, 21.

[26]Robert Wright, "Private Eyes," New York Times Magazine, September 5, 1999, 50–54; William J. Broad, "North Korea's Nuclear Intentions, Out There for All to See," New York Times, October 8, 2006, wk5; and www.earth.google.com.

[27]Historian Michael Hogan, quoted in John M. Broder, "Gentler Look at the U.S. World Role," New York Times, October 31, 1999, 14.

[28]Paul Johnson, "The Myth of American Isolationism," Foreign Affairs, May-June 1995, 162.

[29]Bruce Russett, The Prisoners of Insecurity (San Francisco: Freeman, 1983).

[30]Quoted in Robert Dallek, Lyndon B. Johnson, Portrait of a President (New York: Oxford University Press, 2004), 179.

[31]See James Nathan and James Oliver, United States Foreign Policy and World Order, 2nd ed. (Boston: Little, Brown, 1981), 359–361.

[32]For one view of the impact of Vietnam on the thinking of today's high-ranking officers, see H. R. McMaster, Dereliction of Duty (New York: Harper-Collins, 1997).

[33]Robert S. McNamara, In Retrospect: The Tragedy and Lessons of Vietnam (New York: Times Books, 1995).

[34]Michael Beschloss, Reaching for Glory: Lyndon Johnson's Secret White House Tapes, 1964–1965 (New York: Simon & Schuster, 2001), 166.

[35]Weissberg, Public Opinion and Popular Government, 144–148.

[36]Ole Holsti, "The Three-Headed Eagle," International Studies Quarterly 23 (1979), 339–359; Michael Mandelbaum and William Schneider, "The New Internationalisms," in The Eagle Entangled: U.S. Foreign Policy in a Complex World, ed. Kenneth Oye, Donald Rothchild, and Robert J. Lieber (New York: Longman, 1979), 34–88.

[37]For an analysis of U.S.-Soviet relations in the Reagan era, see Alexander Dallin and Gail Lapidus, "Reagan and the Russians," and Kenneth Oye, "Constrained Confidence and the Evolution of Reagan Foreign Policy," in Eagle Resurgent? ed. Kenneth Oye, Robert Lieber, and Donald Rothchild (Boston: Little, Brown, 1987); and John Newhouse, "The Abolitionist" (pts. 1 and 2), New Yorker, January 2 and 9, 1989.

[38]See George F. Kennan, "After the Cold War," New York Times Magazine, February 5, 1989, 32ff.

[39]Bill Clinton, "A Democrat Lays Out His Plan," Harvard International Review, Summer 1992, 26.

[40]For a concise summary of the advantages and disadvantages of protectionism and free trade, see Paul Krugman, The Age of Diminished Expectations (Cambridge, Mass.: MIT Press, 1992), 101–113.

[41]Bill Clinton, quoted in Jane Perlez, "At Conference on Trade, Clinton Makes Pitch for Poor," New York Times, January 30, 2000, 6.

[42]Thomas Friedman, "What Big Stick? Just Sell," New York Times, October 2, 1995, E3.

[43]Elaine Sciolino, "Monroe's Doctrine Takes Another Knock," New York Times, August 7, 1994, E6. For a discussion of the U.S. turn to multilateralism, see Stanley Hoffmann, "The Crisis of Liberal Internationalism," Foreign Policy 98 (1995, 159–177).

[44]"National Security Strategy of the United States," September 2002. The president's annual report to Congress is posted at www.whitehouse.gov.

[45]"Bush Plans 'Strike First' Military Policy," Champaign-Urbana News-Gazette, June 10, 2002, A-3.

[46]Fred Kaplan, "JFK's First-Strike Plan," Atlantic Monthly, October 2001, 81–86.

[47]Michael Wines and Sharon LaFraniere, "Hut by Hut, AIDS Steals Life in a Southern Africa Town," New York Times, November 28, 2004, 1.

[48]Henri E. Couvin, "Stability of Africa Is Threatened as AIDS Gains Foothold in Armies," New York Times, November 24, 2002, 11.

[49]"AIDS Threatens Global Security," NewsHour with Jim Lehrer, PBS, October 1, 2002.

[50]Material in this section is drawn from Michael R. Gordon, "A Whole New World of Arms Races to Contain," New York Times, May 3, 1998, sec. 4, 1; John Kifner and Jo Thomas, "Singular Difficulty in Stopping Terrorism," New York Times, January 18, 1998, 16; Keith Easthouse, "The Stewardship Debate," Champaign-Urbana News-Gazette, June 14, 1998, B1, B4–B5; and Michael R. Gordon, "Russian Thwarting U.S. Bid to Secure a Nuclear Cache," New York Times, January 5, 1997, 1, 4.

[51]"What Does It Take to Make a Bomb?" Frontline, PBS, 1998 (www.pbs.org/wgbh/pages/frontline/shows/nukes/stuff /faqs.html).

[52]U.S. Department of Defense, Quadrennial Defense Review Report (Washington, D.C.: Government Printing Office, 2001), 17. The full report is at the Pentagon's website (www.dod.gov/pubs/qdr2001.pdf).

[53]Leslie Wayne, "America's For-Profit Secret Army," New York Times, October 13, 2002, sec. 3, 10.

[54]Interview for the documentary Why We Fight, 2005. (See the For Viewing section.)

[55]Joan Spero, an undersecretary of state, quoted in David E. Sanger, "How Washington Inc. Makes a Sale," New York Times, February 19, 1995, sec. 3, 1.

[56]"Diplomacy's New Hit Man: The Free-Market Dollar," New York Times, May 24, 1998, sec. 4, 5.

[57]Julie Kosterlitz, "Trade Crusade," National Journal, May 9, 1998, 1054–1055.

[58]Estimate by Clyde Prestowitz, former Reagan official and president of the Economic Strategy Institute, cited in Eduardo Porter, "Dubai Deal's Collapse Prompts Fears Abroad on Trade With U.S.," New York Times, March 10, 2006.

[59]For a description of WTO structure, membership, and activities, see "WTO: Special Report," Congressional Quarterly Weekly Report, November 27, 1999, 2826–2838.

[60]"National Security Strategy of the United States," 18.

[61]U.S. Department of State, "FY 2004–2009 Department of State and USAID Strategic Plan," 1 (www.state.gov).

[62]Congressional Quarterly Daily Monitor, August 28, 2002.

[63]Quoted in David E. Sanger, "Strategies in a Market Era," New York Times, January 4, 1998, sec. 4, 4.

[64]"Diplomacy: The State Department at Work," 2.

[65]David E. Sanger, "Bush Plan Ties Foreign Aid to Free Market and Civic Rule," New York Times, November 26, 2002, A12.

[66]Ibid.

[67]"War in Iraq," press release from Murtha's office, November 17, 2005 (www.murtha.house.gov).

[68]Fineman, "Politics," 29.

[69]H. Res. 571, *Congressional Record,* November 18, 2005, HR1005.

[70]"War-Backer Dem Wants Out," *New York Post,* November 18, 2005, 26.

[71]Jim Rutenberg and Adam Nagourney, "G.O.P. Decides to Embrace War as Issue," *New York Times,* June 22, 2006.

[72]Kenneth R. Bazinet, "Rangel Joins Dem Attack on Veep, War," *New York Daily News,* November 20, 2005, 26.

[73]Richard Sisk, "Top U.S. General Rips Murtha," *New York Daily News,* January 6, 2006, 34.

[74]Douglas Turner, "Pelosi Now Backs Quick Out from Iraq," *Buffalo News,* December 1, 2005. A8.

[7] "Hil Echoes Veep's Call to Keep Troops in Iraq," *New York Daily News,* November 22, 2005, 8.

[76]"Pelosi Now Backs Quick Out from Iraq," A8. The quote is from Rep. Rahm Emanuel (D-Ill.).

[77]David Selfman, "Murtha's at War with Hill," *New York Post,* August 30, 2006, 19.

[78]"Murtha Wants Promotion if Democrats Take House," *The Times Union,* June 10, 2006, A5.

[79]John Murtha, commentary read on *CBS Sunday Morning,* March 19, 2006.

527 groups Tax-exempt groups, named after the provision in the tax code, that are organized to provide politically relevant advertising, usually with the aim of helping particular candidates or parties. Technically they are supposed to be independent but in reality are often closely linked to the candidates.

Activist judges Judges who are not reluctant to overrule the other branches of government by declaring laws or actions of government officials unconstitutional.

Administrative Procedure Act (APA) Legislation passed in 1946 that provides for public participation in the rule-making process. All federal agencies must disclose their rule-making procedures and publish all regulations at least thirty days in advance of their effective date to allow time for public comment.

Affirmative action A policy in job hiring or university admissions that gives special consideration to members of historically disadvantaged groups.

Agents of political socialization Sources of information about politics; include parents, peers, schools, the media, political leaders, and the community.

Aid to Families with Dependent Children (AFDC) A program that provides income support for the poor. Replaced by TANF.

American Civil Liberties Union (ACLU) A nonpartisan organization that seeks to protect the civil liberties of all Americans.

Americans with Disabilities Act Passed to protect those with disabilities from discrimination in employment and public accommodations, such as stores, restaurants, hotels, and health care facilities.

Antifederalists Those who opposed the ratification of the U.S. Constitution.

Antitrust law Laws that prohibit **monopolies.**

Appropriations Budget legislation that specifies the amount of authorized funds that will actually be allocated for agencies and departments to spend.

Articles of Confederation The first constitution of the United States; in effect from 1781 to 1789.

Asymmetrical warfare Conflict between combatants of very unequal military strength.

Authorizations Budget legislation that provides agencies and departments with the legal authority to operate; may specify funding levels but do not actually provide the funding (the funding is provided by **appropriations**).

Baker v. Carr A 1962 Supreme Court decision giving voters the right to use the courts to rectify the malapportionment of legislative districts.

Balanced budget amendment A proposed constitutional amendment that would require balancing the federal budget.

Bandwagon effect The tendency of voters to follow the lead of the media, which declare some candidates winners and others losers, and vote for the perceived winner. The extent of this effect is unknown.

Battleground states Also known as "swing states." During a presidential election, these are states whose Electoral College votes are not safely in one candidate's pocket; candidates will spend time and more money there to try to win the state.

Bible Belt A term used to describe portions of the South and Midwest that were strongly influenced by Protestant fundamentalists.

Bilingual education Programs where students whose native language is not English receive instruction in substantive subjects such as math in their native language.

Bill of Rights The first 10 amendments to the U.S. Constitution.

Bills of attainder Legislative acts that pronounce specific persons guilty of crimes.

Black Codes Laws passed by Southern states following the **Civil War** that denied most legal rights to the newly freed slaves.

Blockbusting The practice in which realtors would frighten whites in a neighborhood where a black family had moved by telling the whites that their houses would decline in value. The whites in panic would then sell their houses to the realtors at low prices, and the realtors would resell the houses to blacks, thereby resegregating the area from white to black.

Block grants A system of giving federal funds to states and localities under which the federal government designates the purpose for which the funds are to be used but allows the states some discretion in spending.

Blog Common term for independent web log, which is an independent website created by an individual or group to disseminate opinions or information.

Blue states These are the states that voted Democratic in 2000 and 2004 and in general more liberal in outlook. They include New England, Middle Atlantic, Upper Midwest, and Pacific Coast states.

Broadcasting An attempt by a network to appeal to most of the television or radio audience.

Brown bag test An informal requirement of some African American clubs and churches in the first half of the twentieth century that prospective members have enough "white blood" so that their skin color was lighter than the color of a brown paper bag.

Brown v. Board of Education The 1954 case in which the U.S. Supreme Court overturned the **separate-but-equal doctrine** and ruled unanimously that segregated schools violated the Fourteenth Amendment.

Budget and Accounting Act of 1921 This act gives the president the power to propose a budget and led to presidential dominance in the budget process. It also created the **Bureau of the Budget,** changed to the **Office of Management and Budget** in 1970.

Budget deficit Occurs when federal spending exceeds federal revenues.

Bureau of the Budget Established in 1921 and later changed to the **Office of Management and Budget,** the BOB was designed as the president's primary means of developing federal budget policy.

Burger Court The U.S. Supreme Court under Chief Justice Warren Burger (1969–1986). Though not as activist as the **Warren Court,** the Burger Court maintained most of the rights expanded by its predecessor and issued important rulings on abortion and sexual discrimination.

Bush v. Gore U.S. Supreme Court case in 2000 where the Supreme Court set aside the Florida Supreme Court's order for a manual recount of the presidential votes cast in the state. The Court's decision meant that Bush got Florida's electoral votes, giving him a majority of all electoral votes and, thus, the election.

Capitalist economy An economic system in which the means of production are privately owned and prices, wages, working conditions, and profits are determined solely by the market.

Captured agencies Refers to the theory that regulatory agencies often end up working on behalf of the interests they are supposed to regulate.

Casework The assistance members of Congress provide to their constituents; includes answering questions and doing personal favors for those who ask for help. Also called **constituency service.**

Caucus Today, a meeting of local residents who select delegates to attend county, state, and national conventions where the delegates nominate candidates for public office. Originally, caucuses were limited to party leaders and officeholders who selected the candidates.

Central Intelligence Agency (CIA) Created after World War II, the CIA is a federal agency charged with coordinating overseas intelligence activities gathering and analysis.

Checks and balances The principle of government that holds that the powers of the various branches should overlap to avoid power becoming overly concentrated in one branch.

Civil case A case in which individuals sue others for denying their rights and causing them harm.

Civil disobedience Peaceful but illegal protest activity in which those involved allow themselves to be arrested and charged.

Civil rights The principle of equal rights for persons regardless of their race, sex, or ethnic background.

Civil Rights Act of 1964 Major civil rights legislation that prohibits discrimination on the basis of race, color, religion, or national origin in public accommodations.

Civil Rights Act of 1968 Civil rights legislation that prohibits discrimination in the sale or rental of housing on the basis of race, color, religion, or national origin; also prohibits **blockbusting, steering,** and **redlining.**

Civil Service Commission An agency established by the **Pendleton Act of 1883** to curb **patronage** in the federal bureaucracy and replace it with a merit system.

Civil War The war between the Union and the Confederacy (1861–1865), fought mainly over the question of whether the national or state governments were to exercise ultimate political power. Secession and slavery were the issues that precipitated this great conflict.

Classical democracy A system of government that emphasizes citizen participation through debating, voting, and holding office.

Closed primary A primary election where participation is limited to those who are registered with a party or declare a preference for a party.

Cloture A method of stopping a **filibuster** by limiting debate to only 20 more hours; requires a vote of three-fifths of the members of the Senate.

Coalition A network of **interest groups** with similar concerns that combine forces to pursue a common goal; may be short-lived or permanent.

Coalition building The union of **pressure groups** that share similar concerns.

Cold War The era of hostility between the United States and the Soviet Union that existed between the end of World War II and the collapse of the Soviet Union.

Commander in Chief The president's constitutional role as head of the armed forces with power to direct their use

Commercial bias A slant in news coverage to please or avoid offending advertisers.

Committee of the Whole Refers to the informal entity the House of Representatives makes itself into to debate a bill.

Commodity interest groups Associations that represent producers of specific products, such as cattle, tobacco, or milk producers.

Comparable worth The principle that comparable jobs should pay comparable wages.

Concurring opinion The opinion by one or more judges in a court case who agree with the decision but not with the reasons given by the majority for it. The concurring opinion offers an alternate legal argument for the ruling.

Confederal system A system in which the central government has only the powers given to it by the subnational governments.

Conference committee A committee composed of members of both houses of Congress that is formed to try to resolve the differences when the two houses pass different versions of the same bill.

Conflict of interest The situation when government officials make decisions that directly affect their own personal livelihoods or interests.

Conscientious objectors Persons who oppose all wars and refuse military service on the basis of religious or moral principles.

Conservative A person who believes that the domestic role of government should be minimized and that individuals are responsible for their own well-being.

Constituency Both the geographic area and the people a member of Congress represents. For a senator, the state and all its residents; for a member of the House, a congressional district and all its residents.

Constituency service The assistance members of Congress provide to residents in their districts (states, if senators); includes answering questions and doing personal favors for those who ask for help. Also called **casework.**

Constitution The body of basic rules and principles that establish the functions, limits, and nature of a government.

Constitutional Convention The gathering in Philadelphia in 1787 that wrote the U.S. Constitution; met initially to revise the **Articles of Confederation** but produced a new national **constitution** instead.

Containment A policy formulated by the Truman administration to limit the spread of communism by meeting any action taken by the Soviet Union with a countermove; led U.S. decision makers to see most conflicts in terms of U.S.- Soviet rivalry.

Contribution limits Ceilings set on the overall amount of money that individuals and groups give to candidates.

Cooperative federalism The day-to-day cooperation among federal, state, and local officials in carrying out the business of government.

Cooperative internationalism The belief that problems of global poverty, inequitable distribution of wealth, abuse of human rights, and regional competitiveness are substantial threats to world order, and that the United States should work with other nations to solve these problems.

Corporate welfare Tax breaks or financial subsidies given by government to corporations.

Court-packing plan President Franklin D. Roosevelt's attempt to expand the size of the U.S. Supreme Court in an effort to obtain a Court more likely to uphold his New Deal legislation.

Courts of appeals Intermediate courts between trial courts (**district courts** in the federal system) and the supreme court (the U.S. Supreme Court in the federal system).

Cracking, stacking, and packing Methods of drawing district boundaries that minimize black representation. With cracking, a large concentrated black population is divided among two or more districts so that blacks will not have a majority anywhere; with stacking, a large black population is combined with an even larger white population; with packing, a large black population is put into one district

rather than two so that blacks will have a majority in only one district.

Criminal case A case in which a government (national or state) prosecutes a person for violating its laws.

Cruel and unusual punishment Torture or any punishment that is grossly disproportionate to the offense; prohibited by the Eighth Amendment.

Cumulative voting A proposed reform to increase minority representation; calls for members of Congress to be elected from at-large districts that would elect several members at once. Each voter would have as many votes as the district had seats and could apportion the votes among the candidates as he or she wished, such as giving all votes to a single candidate.

Dealignment Term used to refer to the diminished relevance of political parties.

De facto **segregation** Segregation that is based on residential patterns and is not imposed by law; because it cannot be eliminated by striking down a law, it is more intractable than **de jure segregation.**

Deficit A budgetary condition in which government expenditures exceed revenues.

De jure **segregation** Segregation imposed by law; outlawed by *Brown* v. *Board of Education* and subsequent court cases.

Delegated legislative authority The power to draft, as well as execute, specific policies; granted by Congress to executive branch agencies when a problem requires technical expertise.

Democracy A system of government in which sovereignty resides in the people.

Depression A period of prolonged high unemployment.

Deregulation Ending **regulation** in a particular area.

Detente A policy designed to deescalate **Cold War** rhetoric and promote the notion that relations with the Soviet Union could be conducted in ways other than confrontation; developed by President Richard M. Nixon and Secretary of State Henry Kissinger.

Devolution The delegation of authority by the national government to lower units of government (such as at the state and local level) to make and implement policy.

Direct democracy A system of government in which citizens govern themselves directly and vote on most issues; e.g., a New England town meeting.

Direct lobbying Direct personal encounters between lobbyists and the public officials they are attempting to influence.

Direct primary An election in which voters select a party's candidates for office.

Discretionary spending Spending levels set by the federal government in annual **appropriations** bills passed by Congress; includes government operating expenses and salaries of many federal employees.

Dissenting opinion The opinion by one or more judges in a court case who do not agree with the decision of the majority. The dissenting opinion urges a different outcome.

District courts The trial courts (lower-level courts) in the federal system.

Divided government The situation when one political party controls the presidency and the other party controls one or both houses of Congress.

Dixiecrat A member of a group of southern segregationist Democrats who formed the States' Rights Party in 1948.

Domino theory The idea that if one country fell under communist rule, its neighbors would also fall to communism; contributed to the U.S. decision to intervene in Vietnam.

Dred Scott case An 1857 case in which the U.S. Supreme Court held that blacks, whether slave or free, were not citizens and that Congress had no power to restrict slavery in the territories; contributed to the polarization between North and South and ultimately to the **Civil War.**

Dual federalism The idea that the Constitution created a system in which the national government

and the states have separate grants of power with each supreme in its own sphere.

Due process The 14th Amendment guarantee that the government will follow fair and just procedures when prosecuting a criminal defendant.

Earmark A specific amount of money designated—or set aside—at the request of a member of Congress, for a favored project, usually in his or her district. The dollar amount may be included in one of the budget authorization bills, but more commonly is in the committee report attached to the bill that instructs the relevant executive branch agency how to spend the money authorized for its operations.

Earned income tax credit (EITC) A negative income tax. On filing income tax reports, persons with low incomes receive a payment from the government or a credit toward their taxes owed.

Electoral College A group of electors selected by the voters in each state and the District of Columbia; the electors officially elect the president and vice president.

Emancipation Proclamation Abraham Lincoln's 1863 proclamation that the slaves "shall be . . . forever free." At the time, applied only in the Confederate states, so had little practical impact, because the Union did not control them. However, it had an immense political impact, making clear that the Civil War was not just to preserve the Union but to abolish slavery.

Environmental Protection Agency (EPA) The regulatory agency with responsibility for pollution control; created in 1970 by President Richard M. Nixon.

Equal Credit Opportunity Act This act forbids discrimination on the basis of sex or marital status in credit transactions.

Equal Employment Opportunity Commission (EEOC) The EEOC enforces the **Civil Rights Act of 1964,** which forbids discrimination on the basis of sex or race in hiring, promotion, and firing.

Equal Pay Act A statute enacted by Congress in 1963 that mandates that women and men should receive equal pay for equal work.

Equal protection clause The Fourteenth Amendment clause that is the Constitution's primary guarantee that everyone is equal before the law.

Equal Rights Amendment (ERA) A proposed amendment to the Constitution that would prohibit government from denying equal rights on the basis of sex; passed by Congress in 1972 but failed to be ratified by a sufficient number of states.

Establishment clause The First Amendment clause that prohibits the establishment of a state religion.

European Union (EU) A union of European nations formed in 1957 to foster political and economic integration in Europe; formerly called the European Economic Community or Common Market.

Exclusionary rule A rule that prevents evidence obtained in violation of the Fourth Amendment from being used in court against the defendant.

Executive leadership The president's control over the bureaucracy in his capacity as chief executive; achieved through budgeting, appointments, administrative reform, lobbying, and mobilizing public opinion.

Executive orders Rules or regulations issued by the president that have the force of law; issued to implement constitutional provisions or statutes.

Executive privilege The authority of the president to withhold specific types of information from the courts and Congress.

Exit polls Election-day poll of voters leaving the polling places, conducted mainly by television networks and major newspapers.

Ex post facto **law** A statute that makes some behavior illegal that was not illegal when it was done.

Externality A cost or benefit of production that is not reflected in the product's market price. **Regulation** attempts to eliminate negative externalities.

Faithless elector A member of the **Electoral College** who votes on the basis of personal preference rather than the way the majority of voters in his or her state voted.

Farm subsidies Government payments to farmers for withholding land from production or to guarantee set prices for certain crops.

Federal Communication Commission (FCC) A regulatory agency that controls interstate and foreign communication via radio, television, telegraph, telephone, and cable. The FCC licenses radio and television stations.

Federal Election Campaign Act A 1974 statute that regulates campaign finance; provided for public financing of presidential campaigns, limited contributions to campaigns for federal offices, and established the **Federal Election Commission,** among other things.

Federal Election Commission Created in 1975, the commission enforces federal laws on campaign financing.

Federalism A system in which power is constitutionally divided between a central government and subnational or local governments.

Federalist Papers A series of essays in support of ratification of the U.S. Constitution; written for New York newspapers by Alexander Hamilton, James Madison, and John Jay during the debate over ratification.

Federalists Originally, those who supported the U.S. Constitution and favored its ratification; in the early years of the Republic, those who advocated a strong national government.

Federal Register A government publication that provides official notification of executive orders, agency rulings and federal statutes.

Federal Reserve Board Created by Congress in 1913, the board regulates the lending practices of banks and plays a major role in determining **monetary policy.**

Felonies Crimes considered more serious than **misdemeanors** and carrying more stringent punishment.

Fifteenth Amendment An amendment to the Constitution, ratified in 1870, that prohibits denying voting rights on the basis of race, color, or previous condition of servitude.

Fighting words Words which are so inflammatory that when spoken face to face prompt even reasonable listeners to retaliate.

Filibuster A mechanism for delay in the Senate in which one or more members engage in a continuous speech to prevent the Senate from voting on a bill.

Fireside chats Short radio addresses given by President Franklin D. Roosevelt to win support for his policies and reassure the public during the Great Depression.

First Amendment The first amendment to the United States constitution, guaranteeing freedom of expression, which includes freedom of speech, religion, assembly, association, and freedom of the press.

Fiscal policy Government's actions to regulate the economy through taxing and spending policies.

Flat tax A tax structured so that all income groups pay the same rate.

Focus groups A group of a dozen or so average men and women brought together by political consultants and pollsters to share their feelings and reactions to different things in an effort to develop a campaign strategy that will attract voters to or away from a particular candidate.

FOIA The Freedom of Information Act, passed in 1966 and amended in 1974, lets any member of the public apply to an agency for access to unclassified documents in its archives.

Food stamp program A poverty program that gives poor people electronic credits redeemable in grocery stores for food.

Foreign Intelligence Surveillance Court Created by the Foreign Intelligence Surveillance Act of 1978, this secretive court hears requests from the U.S.

government to conduct electronic surveillance, or physical searches of the home and computer, of suspected spies or terrorists.

Franking The privilege of members of Congress that allows them to send free mail to their constituents at government expense.

Freedom of association Guarantees the right of an individual to join with others to speak, assemble, and petition the government for a redress of grievances. This right allows a minority to pursue interests without being prevented from doing so by the majority.

Freedom of speech The First Amendment guarantee of a right of free expression.

Freedom of the press Freedom from censorship, so the press can disseminate the news, information, and opinion that it deems appropriate.

Free exercise clause The First Amendment clause that guarantees individuals the right to practice their religion without government intervention.

Free trade A policy of minimum intervention by government in trade relations.

Friend of the court briefs Legal arguments filed in court cases by individuals or groups who aren't litigants in the cases. These briefs often provide new information to the court and usually urge the judges to rule one way.

Frontrunners Candidates whom political pros and the media have portrayed as likely winners.

Full faith and credit A clause in the U.S. Constitution that requires the states to recognize contracts that are valid in other states.

Fundraiser An event, such as a luncheon or cocktail party, hosted by a legislator or candidate for which participants pay an entrance fee.

Game orientation The assumption in political reporting that politics is a game and that politicians are the players; leads to an emphasis on strategy at the expense of substance in news stories.

Gender gap An observable pattern of modest but consistent differences in opinion between men and women on various public policy issues.

General revenue sharing A Reagan administration policy of giving states and cities federal money to spend as they wished, subject to only a few conditions.

Gerrymander A congressional district whose boundaries are drawn so as to maximize the political advantage of a party or racial group; often such a district has a bizarre shape.

Gettysburg Address Famous 1863 speech by President Lincoln to dedicate the battlefield where many had fallen during the Civil War. Lincoln used the occasion to advance his ideal of equality and to promote the Union.

Glasnost Mikhail Gorbachev's policy of opening the Soviet Union to the outside world by encouraging foreign investment, allowing more Soviet citizens to emigrate, and permitting multiparty elections in eastern Europe.

Globalization The international dispersion of economic activity through the networking of companies across national borders.

Going public The process in which Congress or its members carry an issue debate to the public via the media; e.g., televising floor debates or media appearances by individual members.

GOP Grand Old Party or Republican Party, which formed in 1856 after the Whig Party split. The GOP was abolitionist and a supporter of the Union.

Grandfather clause A device used in the South to prevent blacks from voting; such clauses exempted those whose grandfathers had the right to vote before 1867 from having to fulfill various requirements that some people could not meet. Since no blacks could vote before 1867, they could not qualify for the exemption.

Grand jury A jury of citizens who meet in private session to evaluate accusations in a given **criminal**

case and to determine if there is enough evidence to warrant a trial.

Grants-in-aid Federal money provided to state and, occasionally, local governments for community development and to establish programs to help people such as the aged poor or the unemployed; began during the New Deal.

Grassroots lobbying The mass mobilization of members of an **interest group** to apply pressure to public officials, usually in the form of a mass mailing.

Great Compromise The decision of the **Constitutional Convention** to have a bicameral legislature in which representation in one house would be by population and in the other house, by states; also called the Connecticut Compromise.

Habeas corpus Latin for "have ye the body." A writ of habeas corpus is a means for criminal defendants who have exhausted appeals in state courts to appeal to a federal **district court.**

Hatch Act A statute enacted in 1939 that limits the political activities of federal employees in partisan campaigns.

Hate speech Racial, ethnic, sexual, or religious slurs which demean people for characteristics that are innate or beliefs that are deeply held.

Head of government The president's partisan, policy-making role as head of the executive branch and as head of his party in government, in contrast to his nonpartisan duties as head of state and representative of the country.

Head of state The president's role as a symbolic leader of the nation and representative of all the people.

Health maintenance organization (HMO) A group of doctors who agree to provide full health care for a fixed monthly charge.

Home rule The grant of considerable autonomy to a local government.

Honoraria Legal payments made to legislators who speak before **interest groups** or other groups of citizens.

Horse race coverage The way in which the media reports on the candidates' polling status and strategies, rather than covering their positions on relevant issues.

Hyperpluralism The idea that it is difficult for government to arrive at a solution to problems because **interest groups** have become so numerous and so many groups have a "veto" on issues affecting them.

ICBM Intercontinental ballistic missiles, or land-based missiles.

Identity politics The practice of organizing on the basis of sex, ethnic or racial identity, or sexual orientation to compete for public resources and influence public policy.

Ideology A highly organized and coherent set of opinions.

Impeachment The process provided for in the Constitution by which the House of Representatives can indict (impeach) a president for "Treason, Bribery, or other High Crimes and Misdemeanors." If the House votes to lodge formal charges against the president he is impeached. But a president cannot be removed from office unless two-thirds of the Senate finds him guilty of the charges.

Imperial presidency A term that came into use at the end of the 1960s to describe the growing power of the presidency.

Implied powers clause The clause in the U.S. Constitution that gives Congress the power to make all laws **"necessary and proper"** for carrying out its specific powers.

Independent A voter who is not aligned with any political party.

Independent agencies Government bureaus that are not parts of **departments.** Their heads are appointed by and responsible to the president.

Independent counsel See **Special prosecutor.**

Independent expenditures Campaign contributions made on behalf of issues or candidates, but not made directly to candidates or political parties.

Independent spending Spending on political campaigns by groups not under the control of the candidates.

Indirect democracy A system of government in which citizens elect representatives to make decisions for them.

Indirect lobbying Attempts to influence legislators through such nontraditional means as letter-writing campaigns.

Individualistic political culture One in which politics is seen as a way of getting ahead, of obtaining benefits for oneself or one's group, and in which corruption is tolerated. See also **moralistic** and **traditionalistic political cultures.**

Inflation The situation in which prices increase but wages and salaries fail to keep pace with the prices of goods.

Influence peddling Using one's access to powerful people to make money, as when former government officials use access to former colleagues to win high-paying jobs in the private sector.

Informal norms Unwritten rules designed to help keep Congress running smoothly by attempting to diminish friction and competition among the members.

Infotainment A word for television newscasts that attempt to entertain as they provide information.

Injunction A court order demanding that a person or group perform a specific act or refrain from performing a specific act.

Institutional loyalty An **informal norm** of Congress that calls for members to avoid criticizing their colleagues and to treat each other with mutual respect; this norm has eroded in recent decades.

Interest groups Organizations that try to achieve at least some of their goals with government assistance.

Investigative reporting In-depth news reporting, particularly that which exposes corruption and wrongdoing on the part of government officials and big institutions.

Isolationism A policy of noninvolvement with other nations outside the Americas; generally followed by the United States during the nineteenth and early twentieth centuries.

Issue consistency The extent to which individuals who identify themselves as **"liberal"** or **"conservative"** take issue positions that reflect their professed leanings.

Issue voting Refers to citizens who vote for candidates whose stands on specific issues are consistent with their own.

Jeffersonian Republicans (Jeffersonians) Opponents of a strong national government. They challenged the **Federalists** in the early years of the Republic.

Jim Crow laws Laws enacted in southern states that segregated schools, public accommodations, and almost all other aspects of life.

Joint resolutions Measures approved by both houses of Congress and signed by the president that have the force of law.

Judicial review The authority of the courts to declare laws or actions of government officials unconstitutional.

Junkets Trips by members of Congress to desirable locations with expenses paid by lobbyists; the trips are ostensibly made to fulfill a "speaking engagement" or conduct a "fact-finding tour."

Jurisdiction The authority of a court to hear and decide cases.

Justices of the peace Magistrates at the lowest level of some state court systems, responsible mainly for acting on minor offenses and committing cases to higher courts for trial.

Keynesian economics The argument by John Maynard Keynes that government should stimulate the economy during periods of high unemployment by increasing spending even if it must run **deficits** to do so.

Kitchen cabinet A group of informal advisers, usually longtime associates, who assist the president on public policy questions.

Know-Nothing Party An extreme right-wing party in mid-nineteenth-century America that opposed Catholics and immigrants.

Korematsu v. United States After the attack on Pearl Harbor during World War II, Fred Korematsu and many other Japanese Americans were relocated (by presidential order) to detention camps in inland states. Korematsu claimed that the order discriminated against him on the basis of his race and thereby violated his Fifth Amendment right to due process of law. On appeal, the U.S. Supreme Court upheld the order removing 120,000 Japanese Americans from the West Coast. The majority held that the government could take precautions to prevent espionage and sabotage during wartime.

Lame duck An officeholder who has diminished authority because he or she has lost an election or is near the end of the term in office.

Landslide An election won by a candidate who receives an overwhelming majority of the votes, such as more than a 10-point gap.

Leaks Disclosures of information that some government officials want kept secret.

Legislative calendar An agenda or calendar containing the names of all bills or resolutions of a particular type to be considered by committees or either legislative chamber.

Libel Printed or broadcast statements that are false and meant to tarnish someone's reputation.

Liberal A person who believes in government activism to help individuals and communities in such areas as health, education, and welfare.

Limited government A government that is strong enough to protect the people's rights but not so strong as to threaten those rights; in the view of John Locke, such a government was established through a **social contract.**

Line-Item veto A proposal that would give a president the power to veto one or more provisions of a bill while allowing the remainder of the bill to become law.

Literacy tests Examinations ostensibly carried out to ensure that voters could read and write but actually a device used in the South to disqualify blacks from voting.

Litigation Legal action.

Living wage A wage that is high enough to allow full-time workers' to mee the basic cost of living, something the minimum wage does not do.

Lobbying The efforts of **interest groups** to influence government.

Majority leader The title of both the leader of the Senate, who is chosen by the majority party and the head of the majority party in the House of Representatives who is second in command to the **Speaker.**

Majority-minority district A congressional district whose boundaries are drawn to give a minority group a majority in the district.

Majority opinion The joint opinion by a majority of the judges in a federal court case which explains why the judges ruled as they did.

Managed competition An aspect of the Clinton health care plan that involved joining employers and individuals into large groups or cooperatives to purchase health insurance.

Mandamus, writ of A court order demanding government officials or a lower court to perform a specified duty.

Mandate A term used in the media to refer to a president having clear directions from the voters to take a certain course of action; in practice, it is not always clear that a president, even one elected by a large majority, has a mandate or, if so, for what.

Mandatory spending Spending by the federal government that is required by permanent laws; e.g., payments for **Medicare.**

Marbury v. Madison The 1803 case in which the U.S. Supreme Court enunciated the doctrine of **judicial review.**

Market share The number of members of an **interest group** compared to its potential membership; having a large market share is an advantage.

Markup The process in which a congressional subcommittee rewrites a bill after holding hearings on it.

McCain-Feingold Act Also known as the Bipartisan Campaign Finance Reform Act of 2001, this legislation was created to regulate campaign financing. It limited the amount of gifts and banned soft money contributions to the national parties but not to certain types of private groups.

McCarthyism Methods of combating communism characterized by irresponsible accusations made on the basis of little or no evidence; named after Senator Joseph McCarthy of Wisconsin who used such tactics in the 1950s.

McCulloch v. Maryland An 1819 U.S. Supreme Court decision that broadly interpreted Congress's powers under the **implied powers clause.**

Means test An eligibility requirement for poverty programs under which participants must demonstrate that they have low income and few assets.

Media event An event, usually consisting of a speech and a photo opportunity, that is staged for television and is intended to convey a particular impression of a politician's position on an issue.

Media malaise A feeling of cynicism and distrust toward government and officials that is fostered by media coverage of politics.

Medicaid A federal-state medical assistance program for the poor.

Medicare A public health insurance program that pays many medical expenses of the elderly and the disabled; funded through **Social Security** taxes, general revenues, and premiums paid by recipients.

Merit system A system of filling bureaucratic jobs on the basis of competence instead of **patronage.**

Minority leader The leader of the minority party in either the House of Representatives or the Senate.

Miranda rights A means of protecting a criminal suspect's **rights against self-incrimination** during police interrogation. Before interrogation, suspects must be told that they have a right to remain silent; that anything they say can be used against them; that they have a right to an attorney; and that if they cannot afford an attorney, one will be provided for them. The rights are named after the case *Miranda v. Arizona.*

"Mischiefs of faction" A phrase used by James Madison in the *Federalist Papers* to refer to the threat to the nation's stability that factions could pose.

Misdemeanors Crimes of less seriousness than **felonies,** ordinarily punishable by fine or imprisonment in a local rather than a state institution.

Missouri Compromise of 1820 A set of laws by which Congress attempted to control slavery in the territories, maintaining the balance between slave and nonslave states.

Mixed economies Countries that incorporate elements of both capitalist and socialist practices in the workings of their economies.

Moderates Also referred to as "middle of the roaders," these are persons with centrist positions on issues that distinguish them from liberals and conservatives.

Monetary policy Actions taken by the **Federal Reserve Board** to regulate the economy through changes in short-term interest rates and the money supply.

Monopoly One or a few firms that control a large share of the market for certain goods and can therefore fix prices.

Monroe Doctrine A doctrine articulated by President James Monroe in 1823 that warned European powers not already involved in Latin America to stay out of that region.

Moralistic political culture One in which people feel obligated to take part in politics to bring about change for the better, and in which corruption is not tolerated. See also **individualistic** and **traditionalistic political cultures.**

Motor voter law A statute that allows people to register to vote at public offices such as welfare offices and drivers' license bureaus.

Muckrakers Reform-minded journalists in the early twentieth century who exposed corruption in politics and worked to break the financial link between business and politicians.

Multiparty system A type of political party system where more than two groups have a chance at winning an election.

Mutual assured destruction (MAD) The capability to absorb a nuclear attack and retaliate against the attacker with such force that it would also suffer enormous damage; believed to deter nuclear war during the **Cold War** because both sides would be so devastated that neither would risk striking first.

NAACP (National Association for the Advancement of Colored People) An organization founded in 1909 to fight for black rights; its attorneys challenged segregation in the courts and won many important court cases, most notably, *Brown v. Board of Education.*

Nader's Raiders The name given to people who work in any of the "public interest" organizations founded by consumer advocate and regulatory watchdog Ralph Nader.

Narrowcasting An attempt by a network to appeal to a small segment of the television or radio audience rather than to most of the audience.

Nation-centered federalism The view that the Constitution was written by representatives of the people and and ratified by the people. Nation-centered federalists believe that the national government is the supreme power in the federal relationship. (Hamilton articulated this view in the *Federalist Papers.*) Nation-centered federalism was the view used by northerners to justify a war to prevent the southern states from seceding in 1861. The alternative view, state-centered federalism, holds that the Constitution is a creation of the states.

National chair The head of a political **party organization,** appointed by the **national committee** of that party, usually at the direction of the party's presidential nominee.

National committee The highest level of **party organization;** chooses the site of the national convention and the formula for determining the number of delegates from each state.

National debt The total amount of money owed by the federal government; the sum of all budget **deficits** over the years.

National Organization for Women (NOW) A group formed in 1966 to fight primarily for political and economic rights for women.

National Security Agency (NSA) The U.S. government's largest intelligence service, which uses electronic surveillance to obtain the communications of possible adversaries.

NATO (North Atlantic Treaty Organization) A mutual defense pact established by the United States, Canada, and their western European allies in 1949 to protect against Soviet aggression in Europe; later expanded to include other European nations.

Natural rights Inalienable and inherent rights such as the right to own property (in the view of John Locke).

"Necessary and proper" A phrase in the **implied powers clause** of the U.S. Constitution that gives Congress the power to make all laws needed to carry out its specific powers.

Neutral competence The concept that bureaucrats should make decisions in a politically neutral manner in policymaking and should be chosen only for their expertise—not their political affiliation.

New Deal A program of President Franklin D. Roosevelt's administration in the 1930s aimed at stimulating economic recovery and aiding victims of the Great Depression; led to expansion of the national government's role.

New Deal coalition The broadly based coalition of southern conservatives, northern liberals, and ethnic and religious minorities that sustained the Democratic Party for some 40 years.

New federalism During the Nixon administration, the policy under which unrestricted or minimally restricted federal funds were provided to states and localities; during the Reagan administration, a policy of reducing federal support for the states.

News release A printed handout given by public relations workers to members of the media, offering ideas or information for new stories.

Nineteenth Amendment An amendment to the Constitution, ratified in 1920, guaranteeing women the vote.

Nullification A doctrine advocated by supporters of state-centered federalism, holding that a state could nullify laws of Congress.

Obscenity Sexual material that is patently offensive to the average person in the community and that lacks any serious literary, artistic, or scientific value.

Obstruction of justice A deliberate attempt to impede the progress of a criminal investigation or trial.

Occupational Safety and Health Administration (OSHA) An agency formed in 1970 and charged with ensuring safe and healthful working conditions for all American workers.

Office of Management and Budget (OMB) A White House agency with primary responsibility for preparing the federal budget.

Open primary A primary election that is not limited to members of a particular party; a voter may vote in either party's primary.

Outsourcing (offshoring) Companies' transfer of jobs abroad in order to increase their profit (because they pay foreign workers less).

Overlapping membership The term refers to the tendency of individuals to join more than one group. This tends to moderate a group's appeals, since its members also belong to other groups with different interests.

Oversight Congress's responsibility to make sure the bureaucracy is administering federal programs in accordance with congressional intent.

Parliamentary government A system in which voters elect only their representatives in parliament; the chief executive is chosen by parliament, as in Britain.

Party boss The head of a political "machine," a highly disciplined state or local **party organization** that controls power in its area.

Party caucus Meetings of members of political parties, often designed to select party nominees for office, or of all members of a party in the House or Senate to set policy and select their leaders.

Party convention A gathering of party delegates, on the local, state, or national level, to set policy and strategy and to select candidates for elective office.

Party identification A psychological link between individuals and a political party that leads those persons to regard themselves as members of that party.

Party in government Those who are appointed or elected to office as members of a political party.

Party in the electorate Those who identify with a political party.

Party organization The "professionals" who run a political party at the national, state, and local levels.

Party system The configuration of parties in a political system. Usually noted in conjunction with the number of parties in the system—one party system, two party system, or multiparty system.

Patronage A system in which elected officials appoint their supporters to administrative jobs; used by **political machines** to maintain themselves in power.

Paygo ("pay-as-you-go") Budgetary rules adopted by Congress that set caps on spending and bars legislation to increase spending without offsetting cuts in spending or increases in revenue.

Pendleton Act of 1883 This act created the **Civil Service Commission,** designed to protect civil servants from arbitrary dismissal for political reasons and to staff bureaucracies with people who have proven their competence by taking competitive examinations.

Pentagon Papers A top-secret study, eventually made public, of how and why the United States became embroiled in the Vietnam War; the study was commissioned by Secretary of Defense Robert McNamara during the Johnson administration.

Permanent campaign The situation in which elected officials are constantly engaged in a campaign; fundraising for the next election begins as soon as one election is concluded.

Personal presidency A concept proposed by Theodore Lowi that holds that presidents since the 1930s have amassed tremendous personal power directly from the people and, in return, are expected to make sure the people get what they want from government.

Photo op A "photo opportunity" that frames the politician against a backdrop that symbolizes the points the politician is trying to make.

Platform committee The group that drafts the policy statement of a political party's convention.

Plea bargain An agreement between the prosecutor, defense attorney, and defendant in which the prosecutor agrees to reduce the charge or sentence in exchange for the defendant's guilty plea.

Plebiscite A direct vote by all the people on a certain public measure. Theodore Lowi has spoken of the "Plebiscitary" presidency, whereby the president makes himself the focus of national government through use of the mass media.

Plessy v. Ferguson The 1896 case in which the U.S. Supreme Court upheld segregation by enunciating the **separate-but-equal doctrine.**

Pluralism The theory that American government is responsive to groups of citizens working together to promote their common interests and that enough people belong to **interest groups** to ensure that government ultimately hears everyone, even though most people do not participate actively in politics.

Pocket veto A legislative bill dies by pocket veto if a president refuses to sign it and Congress adjourns within 10 working days.

Policy implementation The process by which bureaucrats convert laws into rules and activities that have an actual impact on people and things.

Political action committee (PAC) A committee established by corporation, labor union, or **interest group** that raises money and contributes it to a political campaign.

Political bias A preference for candidates of particular parties or for certain stands on issues that affects a journalist's reporting.

Political culture A shared body of values and beliefs that shapes perceptions and attitudes toward politics and government and, in turn, influences political behavior.

Political equality The principle that every citizen of a democracy has an equal opportunity to try to influence government.

Political machines Political organizations based on **patronage** that flourished in big cities in the late nineteenth and early twentieth centuries. The machine relied on the votes of the lower classes and, in exchange, provided jobs and other services.

Political patronage Party leaders who, once in office, openly award government jobs and other benefits to their supporters.

Political socialization The process of learning about politics by being exposed to information from parents, peers, schools, the media, political leaders, and the community.

Political trust The extent to which citizens place trust in their government, its institutions, and its officials.

Politics A means by which individuals and **interest groups** compete, via political parties and other extragovernmental organizations, to shape government's impact on society's problems and goals.

Poll tax A tax that must be paid before a person can vote; used in the South to prevent blacks from voting. The Twenty-fourth Amendment prohibits poll taxes in federal elections.

Popular sovereignty Rule by the people.

Pork barrel Funding for special projects, buildings, and other public works in the district or state of a member of Congress. Members support such projects because they provide jobs for constituents and enhance the members' reelection chances, rather than because the projects are necessarily wise.

Power to persuade The president's informal power to gain support by dispensing favors and penalties and by using the prestige of the office.

Precedents In law, judicial decisions that may be used subsequently as standards in similar cases.

Precinct The basic unit of the American electoral process—in a large city perhaps only a few blocks—designed for the administration of elections. Citizens vote in precinct polling places.

Preemption Military strategy of "striking first." Endorsed by the Bush national security team after the September 11, 2001 terrorist attacks.

Pregnancy Discrimination Act A congressional act from 1978 that forbids firing or demoting employees for becoming pregnant.

Presidential preference primary A **direct primary** where voters select delegates to presidential nominating conventions; voters indicate a preference for a presidential candidate, delegates committed to a candidate, or both.

Presidential press conference A meeting at which the president answers questions from reporters.

Pressure group An organization representing specific interests that seeks some sort of government assistance or attempts to influence public policy. Also known as an **interest group.**

Presumption of innocence A fundamental principle of the U.S. criminal justice system in which the government is required to prove the defendant's guilt. The defendant is not required to establish his innocence.

Pretrial hearings Preliminary examinations of the cases of persons accused of a crime.

Prior restraint Censorship by restraining an action before it has actually occurred; e.g., forbidding publication rather than punishing the publisher after publication has occurred.

Private interest groups Interest groups that chiefly pursue economic interests that benefit their members; e.g., business organizations and labor unions.

Probable cause In law, reasonable grounds for belief that a particular person has committed a particular crime.

Productivity The ratio of total hours worked by the labor force to total goods and services produced.

Professional association A **pressure group** that promotes the interests of a professional occupation, such as medicine, law, or teaching.

Progressive Movement Reform movement designed to wrest control from political machines and the lower-class immigrants they served. These reforms reduced corruption in politics, but they also seriously weakened the power of political parties.

Progressive reforms Election reforms introduced in the early twentieth century as part of the Progressive movement; included the secret ballot, primary elections, and voter registration laws.

Progressive tax A tax structured so that those with higher incomes pay a higher percentage of their income in taxes than do those with lower incomes.

Prohibition Party A political party founded in 1869 that sought to ban the sale of liquor in the United States.

Proportional representation An election system based on election from multimember districts. The number of seats awarded to each party in each district is equal to the percentage of the total the party receives in the district. Proportional representation favors the multiparty system.

Protectionism Government intervention to protect domestic producers from foreign competition; can take the form of **tariffs**, quotas on imports, or a ban on certain imports altogether.

Public disclosure The requirement that names of campaign donors be made public.

Public forum A public place such as a street, sidewalk, or park where people have a First Amendment right to express their views on public issues.

Public interest A term generally denoting a policy goal, designed to serve the interests of society as a whole, or the largest number of people. Defining the public interest is the subject of intense debate on most issues.

Public interest groups Interest groups that chiefly pursue benefits that cannot be limited or restricted to their members.

Public opinion The collection of individual opinions toward issues or objects of general interest.

Push poll A public opinion poll presenting the respondent with biased information favoring or opposing a particular candidate. The idea is to see whether certain "information" can "push" voters away from a candidate or a neutral opinion toward the candidate favored by those doing the poll. Push polls seek to manipulate opinion.

Quorum calls A roll call of members of a legislative body to determine if enough members are present to conduct business; often used as a delaying tactic.

Racial profiling Practice that targets a particular group for attention from law enforcement based on racial stereotypes, A common occurrence is black drivers being stopped by police disproportionately.

Realignment The transition from one stable party system to another, as occurred when the **New Deal coalition** was formed.

Reapportionment The process of redistributing the 435 seats in the House of Representatives among the states based on population changes; occurs every 10 years based on the most recent census.

Recession Two or more consecutive three-month quarters of falling production.

Reciprocity An **informal norm** of Congress in which members agree to support each other's bills; also called logrolling.

Reconstruction The period after the **Civil War** when black rights were ensured by a northern military presence in the South and by close monitoring of southern politics; ended in 1877.

Reconstruction Amendments Three amendments (13th, 14th, and 15th), adopted after the Civil War from 1865 through 1870, that eliminated slavery (13), gave blacks the right to vote (15), and guaranteed due process rights for all (14).

Redistricting The process of redrawing the boundaries of congressional districts within a state after a census to take account of population shifts.

Redlining The practice in which bankers and other lenders refused to lend money to persons who wanted to buy a house in a racially changing neighborhood.

"Red Scare" Prompted by the Russian Revolution in 1917, this was a large-scale crackdown on so-called seditious activities in the United States.

Red states These are the states that voted for George Bush in 2000 and 2004 and in general more conservative in outlook. They include the states of the South, Great Plains, and Rocky Mountain West.

Reelection constituency Those individuals a member of Congress believes will vote for him or her. Differs from a geographical, loyalist, or personal constituency.

Regressive tax A tax structured so that those with lower incomes pay a larger percentage of their income in tax than do those with higher incomes.

Regulation The actions of regulatory agencies in establishing standards or guidelines conferring benefits or imposing restrictions on business conduct.

Rehnquist Court The U.S. Supreme Court under Chief Justice William Rehnquist (1986 –2005); a conservative Court, but one that did not overturn most previous rulings.

Religious tests Tests once used in some states to limit the right to vote or hold office to members of the "established church."

Rendition The process in which the CIA seizes terrorist suspects in foreign countries and takes them to other countries for interrogation. The purpose is to have other countries use methods of interrogation, often torture, that the U.S. would not use.

Republic A system of government in which citizens elect representatives to make decisions for them; an **indirect democracy.**

Responsible party government A governing system in which political parties have real issue differences, voters align according to those issue differences, and elected officials are expected to vote with their party leadership or lose their chance to run for office.

Responsiveness The extent to which government conforms to the wishes of individuals, groups, or institutions.

Restrained judges Judges who are reluctant to overrule the other branches of government by declaring laws or actions of government officials unconstitutional.

Restrictive covenants Agreements among neighbors in white residential areas not to sell their houses to blacks.

Retrospective voting Voting for or against incumbents on the basis of their past performance.

Right against self-incrimination A right granted by the Fifth Amendment, providing that persons accused of a crime shall not be compelled to be witnesses against themselves.

Right to abortion U.S. Supreme Court ruling in *Roe v. Wade* (1973) established that women have a right to terminate a pregnancy during the first six months. States can prohibit an abortion during the last three months because at that time the fetus becomes viable—it can live outside the womb.

Right to a jury trial The Sixth Amendment's guarantee of a trial by jury in any **criminal case** that could result in more than six months' incarceration.

Right to counsel The Sixth Amendment's guarantee of the right of a criminal defendant to have an attorney in any **felony or misdemeanor** case that might result in incarceration; if defendants are indigent, the court must appoint an attorney for them.

Right to die Rehnquist court ruling that individuals can refuse medical treatment, including food and water, even if this means they will die. Individuals must make their decision while competent and alert. They can also act in advance, preparing a "living will" or designating another person as a proxy to make the decision if they are unable to.

Right to privacy A right to autonomy—to be left alone—that is not specifically mentioned in the U.S. Constitution, but has been found by the U.S. Supreme Court to be implied through several amendments.

Roberts Court The current Supreme Court under the leadership of Chief Justice John Roberts (2005–).

Rules Committee The committee in the House of Representatives that sets the terms of debate on a bill.

Scientific polls Systematic, probability-based sampling techniques that attempt to gauge public sentiment based on the responses of a small, selected group of individuals.

Second Amendment "The right of the people to keep and bear arms." Some interpret this as an absolute right to own and use guns, others as only an indication that guns can be owned if one is part of a state militia.

Seditious speech Speech that encourages rebellion against the government.

Selective perception The tendency to screen out information that contradicts one's beliefs.

Senatorial courtesy The custom of giving senators of the president's party a virtual veto over appointments to jobs, including judicial appointments, in their states.

Senior Executive Service The SES was created in 1978 to attract high-ranking civil servants by offering them challenging jobs and monetary rewards for exceptional achievement.

Seniority rule The custom that the member of the majority party with the longest service on a particular congressional committee becomes its chair; applies most of the time but is occasionally violated.

Separate-but-equal doctrine The principle, enunciated by the U.S. Supreme Court in *Plessy* v. *Ferguson* in 1896, that allowed separate facilities for blacks and whites as long as the facilities were equal.

Separation of church and state Constitutional principle that is supposed to keep church and state from interfering with each other. In practice it restricts government from major efforts either to inhibit or advance religion.

Separation of powers The principle of government under which the power to make, administer, and judge the laws is split among three branches—legislative, executive, and judicial.

Setting the agenda Influencing the process by which problems are deemed important and alternative policies are proposed.

Sexual harassment A form of job discrimination prohibited by the Civil Rights Act of 1964. Sexual harassment can consist of either 1) a supervisor's demands for sexual favors in exchange for a raise or promotion or in exchange for not imposing negative consequences; or 2) the creation of a hostile environment which prevents workers from doing their job.

Sharecroppers Tenant farmers who lease land and equipment from landowners, turning over a share of their crops in lieu of rent.

Shays's Rebellion A revolt of farmers in western Massachusetts in 1786 and 1787 to protest the state legislature's refusal to grant them relief from debt; helped lead to calls for a new national **constitution.**

Shield laws Laws that protect news reporters from having to identify their sources of information.

Signing Statements Written comments a president may attach to a law after signing it and sending it to the Federal Register for publication. Historically they have been used to indicate provisions in a law the president believes the federal courts may find unconstitutional. George W. Bush used them frequently to indicate sections of laws he would refuse to implement, thus setting up a conflict between the executive and legislative branches.

Single-issue groups Interest groups that pursue a single public interest goal and are characteristically reluctant to compromise.

Single-member districts Where only one individual is elected from a particular electoral district.

Social choice An approach to political science based on the assumption that political behavior is determined by costs and benefits.

Social contract An implied agreement between the people and their government in which the people give up part of their liberty to the government in exchange for the government protecting the remainder of their liberty.

Social insurance A social welfare program such as **Social Security** that provides benefits only to those who have contributed to the program and their survivors.

Socialism An economic system in which the government owns the country's productive capacity—industrial plants and farms—and controls wages and the supply of and demand for goods; in theory, the people, rather than the government, collectively own the country's productive capacity.

Social issue An important, noneconomic issue affecting significant numbers of the populace, such as crime, racial conflict, or changing values.

Social Security A social insurance program for the elderly and the disabled.

Soft money Contributions to national party committees that do not have to be reported to the federal government (and sometimes not to the states) because they are used for voter registration drives, educating voters on the issues, and the like, rather than for a particular candidate; the national committees send the funds to the state parties, which operate under less stringent reporting regulations than the federal laws provide.

Sound bite A few key words or phrase included in a speech with the intent that television editors will use the phrase in a brief clip on the news.

Speaker of the House The leader and presiding officer of the House of Representatives; chosen by the majority party.

Special interest caucuses Groups of members of the House of Representatives and Senate who are united by some personal interest or characteristic; e.g., the Black Caucus.

Specialization An **informal norm** of Congress that holds that since members cannot be experts in every area, some deference should be given to those who are most knowledgeable about a given subject related to their committee work.

Special prosecutor A prosecutor charged with investigating and prosecuting alleged violations of federal criminal laws by the president, vice president, senior government officials, members of Congress, or the judiciary.

Spectacle presidency Term used to describe presidents who are mostly seen by the public as actors in public spectacles, stage-managed photo ops, featuring the president in a dramatically staged event or setting.

Spin What politicians do to portray themselves and their programs in the most favorable light, regardless of the facts, often shading the truth.

Split-ticket voting Voting for a member of one party for one office and another party for a different office, such as for a Republican presidential candidate but a Democratic House candidate.

Spoils system The practice of giving political supporters government jobs or other benefits.

Stagflation The combination of high inflation and economic stagnation with high unemployment that troubled the United States in the 1970s.

Standing committees Permanent congressional committees.

Stare decisis Latin for "stand by what has been decided." The rule that judges should follow **precedents** established in previous cases by their court or higher courts.

"Star Wars" The popular name for former President Reagan's proposed space-based nuclear defense system, known officially as the Strategic Defense Initiative.

State-centered federalism The view that our Constitutional system should give precedence to state sovereignty over that of the national government. State centered federalists argue that that the states created the national government and the states are superior to the federal government.

States' rights The belief that the power of the federal government should not be increased at the expense of the states' power.

Statutes Laws passed by the legislative body of a representative government.

Steering The practice in which realtors promoted segregation by showing blacks houses in black neighborhoods and whites houses in white neighborhoods.

Straw polls Unscientific polls.

Stress and duress Also called "torture lite," this term refers to a wide variety of measures that constitute rough interrogation just short of serious physical injury.

Subcommittee bill of rights Measures introduced by Democrats in the House of Representatives in 1973 and 1974 that allowed members of a committee to choose subcommittee chairs and established a fixed jurisdiction and adequate budget and staff for each subcommittee.

Subgovernment A mutually supportive group comprising an **interest group,** an executive agency, and a congressional committee or subcommittee with common policy interests that makes public policy decisions with little interference from the president or Congress as a whole and little awareness by the public. Also known as an iron triangle.

Subpoena A court order requiring someone to appear in court to give testimony under penalty of punishment.

Suffrage The right to vote.

Sunshine Act Adopted in 1977, this act requires that most government meetings be conducted in public and that notice of such meetings must be posted in advance.

Superdelegates Democratic delegates, one-fifth of the total sent to the national convention who are appointed by Democratic Party organizations, in order to retain some party control over the convention. Most are public officials, such as members of Congress.

Super Tuesday The day when most southern states hold **presidential preference primaries** simultaneously.

Superwaiver Blanket exemptions that free states from federal program standards and requirements and give them greater latitude to set standards and eligibility requirements. Has been applied to welfare programs.

Supplemental Security Income (SSI) A program that provides supplemental income for those who are blind, elderly, or disabled and living in poverty.

Supply-side economics The argument that tax revenues will increase if tax rates are reduced; on the assumption that more money will be available for business expansion and modernization. This in turn would stimulate employment and economic growth and result in higher tax revenues.

Supremacy clause A clause in the U.S. Constitution stating that treaties and laws made by the national government take precedence over state laws in cases of conflict.

Symbiotic relationship A relationship in which the parties use each other for mutual advantage.

Symbolic speech The use of symbols, rather than words, to convey ideas; e.g., wearing black armbands or burning the U.S. flag to protest government policy.

Tariff A special tax or "duty" imposed on imported or exported goods.

Tax deductions Certain expenses or payments that may be deducted from one's taxable income.

Tax exemptions Certain amounts deductible from one's annual income in calculating income tax.

Teapot Dome scandal A 1921 scandal in which President Warren Harding's secretary of the interior received large contributions from corporations that were then allowed to lease oil reserves (called the Teapot Dome); led to the Federal Corrupt Practices Act of 1925, which required reporting of campaign contributions and expenditures.

Temporary Assistance for Needy Families (TANF) A program that provides income support for the poor; successor to Aid to Families with Dependent Children (AFDC).

Tenth Amendment Constitutional amendment stating that powers not delegated to the federal government nor prohibited to the states are reserved to the states and to the people. This amendment has generally not had much impact, though a few recent Supreme Court cases have referred to it.

Third party A political party established in opposition to two dominant parties, often advocating radical change or pushing single issues.

Three-fifths Compromise The decision of the **Constitutional Convention** that each slave would count as three-fifths of a person in apportioning seats in the House of Representatives.

Ticket splitting Voting for a member of one party for a high-level office and a member of another party for a different high-level office.

Title IX Equal Opportunity in Education Act that forbids discrimination on the basis of sex in schools and colleges that receive federal aid. The amendment was prompted by discrimination against women by colleges, especially in admissions, sports programs, and financial aid.

Trade association An **interest** or **pressure group** that represents a single industry, such as builders.

Traditionalistic political culture One in which politics is left to a small elite and is viewed as a way to maintain the status quo. See **individualistic** and **moralistic political cultures.**

Tragedy of the commons The concept that although individuals benefit when they exploit goods that are common to all such as air and water, the community as a whole suffers from the resulting pollution and depletion of resources; a reason for **regulation.**

Treason The betrayal of one's country by knowingly aiding its enemies.

Truth in labeling The requirement that manufacturers, lenders, and other business entities provide certain kinds of information to consumers or employees.

Turnout The proportion of eligible citizens who vote in an election.

Two-party system A political system like that in the U.S. in which only two parties have a realistic chance of winning most government offices. This system is rare among the world's other democracies.

Unanimous consent agreements Procedures by which the Senate may dispense with standard rules and limit debate and amendments.

Underdogs Candidates for public office who are thought to have little chance of being elected.

Unfunded mandates Federal laws that require the states to do something without providing full funding for the required activity.

Unitary executive A minority interpretation of Article II of the Constitution made by lawyers in the Bush administration that claims the president has sole power to direct the work of executive branch agencies, without interference from Congress or the federal courts. This interpretation is considered at odds with the conventional understanding of the checks and balances built into our system of three branches of government.

Unitary system A system in which the national government is supreme; subnational governments are created by the national government and have only the power it allocates to them.

Unreasonable searches and seizures Searches and arrests that are conducted without a warrant or that do not fall into one of the exceptions to the warrant requirement; prohibited by the Fourth Amendment.

Unscientific polls Unsystematic samplings of popular sentiments; also known as **straw polls.**

Veto power The president's constitutional authority to refuse to sign a law passed by Congress. Vetoes may be overridden by a two-thirds vote in each house of Congress.

Vietnam syndrome An attitude of uncertainty about U.S. foreign policy goals and our ability to achieve them by military means; engendered among the public and officials as a result of the U.S. failure in Vietnam.

Voting Rights Act (VRA) A law passed by Congress in 1965 that made it illegal to interfere with anyone's right to vote. The act and its subsequent amendments have been the main vehicles for expanding and protecting minority voting rights.

War Powers Resolution A 1973 statute enacted by Congress to limit the president's ability to commit troops to combat without congressional approval.

Warren Court The U.S. Supreme Court under Chief Justice Earl Warren (1953–1969); an activist Court that expanded the rights of criminal defendants and racial and religious minorities.

Watergate scandal The attempt to break into Democratic National Committee headquarters in 1972 that ultimately led to President Richard M. Nixon's resignation for his role in attempting to cover up the break-in and other criminal and unethical actions.

Weber, Max German social scientist, author of pioneering studies on the nature of bureaucracies.

Whigs Members of the Whig Party, founded in 1834 by National Republicans and several other factions who opposed Jacksonian Democrats.

Whips Members of the House of Representatives who work to maintain party unity by keeping in contact with party members trying to ensure they vote for party-backed bills. Both the majority and the minority party have a whip and several assistant whips.

Whistleblower An individual employee who exposes mismanagement and abuse of office by government officials.

White primary A device for preventing blacks from voting in the South. Under the pretense that political parties were private clubs, blacks were barred from voting in Democratic primaries, which were the real elections because Democrats always won the general elections.

Whitewater investigation An investigation conducted by a **special prosecutor** into the activities of President Bill Clinton and Hillary Rodham Clinton in connection with an Arkansas land deal and other alleged wrongdoings.

Winner-take-all The outcome of an election where only one individual is elected from a district or state, the individual who receives the most votes. It is contrasted with multi member systems where more than one person wins seats in an election.

Wire services News-gathering organizations such as the Associated Press and United Press International that provide news stories and other editorial features to the media organizations that are their members.

World Trade Organization (WTO) Founded in 1995 to remove barriers to free trade and to mediate trade disputes between member countries. WTO policies are set primarily by consensus of its member countries, represented by their trade ministers. Its general council, to which all members belong, is empowered to resolve trade disputes.

Writ of *certiorari* An order issued by a higher court to a lower court to send up the record of a case for review; granting the writ is the usual means by which the U.S. Supreme Court agrees to hear a case.

Chapter 1

Copyright 2006 Mark Alan Stamaty. Reprinted with permission. **2** © Bettmann/Corbis **6** The Library Company of Philadelphia **9** Photography by Jeff Ridel **11** AP Images/Pablo Martinez Monsivais **12** Courtesy of Wayne Joseph **14** © Jason Tanaka Blaney Photography **16** Seymour Chwast **17** © The New Yorker Collection 1987, J. B. Handelsman from cartoonbank.com. All rights reserved. **18** © The New Yorker Collection 1981, Robert Mannkoff from cartoonbank.com. All rights reserved. **21** AP Images/St. Petersburg Times, Daniel Wallace **23**

Chapter 2

Courtesy of Winterthur Museum. **26** © Dennis Brack Ltd./Black Star **28** © Bettmann/Corbis **29** The Metropolitan Museum of Art, Bequest of Charles Allen Munn, 1924 (24-90-35) **33** © Bettmann/Corbis **35** © Joseph Sohm; ChromoSohm Inc. /Corbis **36** © The New Yorker Collection 1974, Donald Reilly from cartoonbank.com. All rights reserved. **42** © Tom Myer **43** © Underwood & Underwood/Corbis **46** © Bettmann/Corbis **47** The David J. and Janice L. Frent Collection **49** AP/Wide World Photos **50** © Paul Conrad from *The King and Us* (Los Angeles: Clymer Publications, 1974) Reprinted by permission. **53**

Chapter 3

© Omar Torres/AFP/Getty Images **56** © 2005 Zuma Press. © Robert King/Zuma/Corbis **58** © The Granger Collection, New York **61** © Underwood & Underwood/Corbis **67** AP/Wide World Photos **68** National Archives **68** Reuters/David J. Phillip/Pool/Landov **77** Tribune Media Services, Inc. All rights reserved. Printed with permission. **82** AP Images/Gregory Bull **85**

Chapter 4

© Getty Images **88** AP Images/Patti Longmire **90** © Robin Nelson/Black Star **95** © The New Yorker Collection 2002, Tom Cheney from cartoonbank.com. All rights reserved. **99** © Bettmann/Corbis **100** © Todd Yates/The Facts, Clute, Texas **101** © Bettmann/Corbis from John Sperling, The Great Divide. **109** The American Prospect, Feb. 2005. © Tom Tomorrow. **111** By permission of Mike Luckovich and Creators Syndicate, Inc. **113** © Tribune Media Services, Inc. All Rights Reserved. Reprinted with permission. **115**

Chapter 5

AP Photo/Defense Department **118** Robert Natkin Photography **122** Copyright © 2003. Reprinted by permission of Cagle Cartoons. **123** © Bettmann/Corbis **125** © Rebecca Cooney/*The New York Times* **125** © Chris Buck **127** © NYT Graphics/The *New York Times* **129** © Carol Joynt/Getty Images **130** Henry Groskinsky, New York City **132** © Brooks Kraft/Corbis **133**

© The New Yorker Collection 1996. Lee Lorenz from cartoonbank.com. All rights reserved. **134** © Bettmann/Corbis **136** © Paul Richards/AFP/Getty Images **138** © Todd Heisler, *Rocky Mountain News*/Polaris **139** © Rob Rogers reprinted by permission of United Features Syndicate. **147** © Time Life Pictures/Getty Images **150** © The New Yorker Collection 1999. Alex Gregory from Cartoonbank.com All rights reserved. **151** © Courtesy Everett Collection **152** Courtesy of Franklin D. Roosevelt Library, 73-113:61 **155** AP Images/Adnan Ali **157** © Sungsu Cho/Polaris Images **158** © 2003 Nick Anderson, Courier Journal. Reprinted with permission. **160**

Chapter 6

© David McNew/Getty Images **164** © 1989 Ken Heinen **168** © The New Yorker Collection 2006. Barbara Smaller from cartoonbank.com. All Rights Reserved. **171** Gotham Book Mart, New York **172** © The New Yorker Collection 2002. Dana Fradon from cartoonbank.com. All rights reserved. **175** © Bettmann/Corbis **177** AP/Wide World Photos **180** © The New Yorker Collection 2002. Alex Gregory from cartoonbank.com. All rights reserved. **182** REUTERS/William Philpott/Landov **183** © Lynn Johnson/Aurora **184** AP Images/Oceana, Linda Spillers **187** AP Images/Noah Berger **191** AP Images/LM Otero **192** Culver Pictures **193** AP/Wide World Photos **194** © Tribune Media Services, Inc. All rights reserved. Reprinted with permission. **199**

Chapter 7

© Alex Wong/Getty Images for Meet the Press **202** © Craig Mitchelldyer/Getty Images **209** © The Granger Collection, New York **210** © The Granger Collection, New York **211** © The Granger Collection, New York **211** Courtesy of Smithsonian Institute, neg #98-4290 **216** © AFP/Stephen Jaffe/Getty Images **218** Courtesy of Strom Thurmond Institute, Clemson University **218** AP/Wide World Photos **219** The David J. and Janice L. Frent Collection **219** © Andy Levin/Photo Researchers, Inc. **221** © James Nielsen/AFP/Getty Images **222** © Bettmann/Corbis; © The David J. and Janice L. Frent Collection **223** The David J. and Janice L. Frent Collection **225** © The New Yorker Collection 1970. Whitney Darrow, Jr. from cartoonbank.com. All rights reserved. **230** © David Scull **231**

Chapter 8

© Chip Somodevilla/Getty Images **236** © The State/Dist. by Newspaper Enterprise Association, Inc. **238** Library of Congress **240** © Bettmann/Corbis **242** Brown Brothers **245** © The New Yorker Collection 2000. Donald Reilly from cartoonbank.com. All rights reserved. **247** AP Images/Jim Cole **249** Courtesy of Tammy Baldwin for Congress **250** Courtesy of the Smithsonian Institute **253** © Bettmann/Corbis **255** Courtesy of the Smithsonian

Institute **257** © Stephen Crowley The *New York Times* **259** AP/Wide World Photos **260** © Bettmann/Corbis **261** © 2004 Jim Borgman, *Cincinnati Enquirer* **262** Courtesy of the Smithsonian Institute **265** © Brooks Kraft/Corbis **269** © Bettmann/Corbis **270** Luckovich for *WPNWE* **281**

Chapter 9

AP Images/Gerald Herbert, File Photo **284** © The Granger Collection, New York **288** Theodore Roosevelt Collections/Harvard College Library **289** Toles © 2001 The New Republic. Reprinted with permission of Universal Press Syndicate. All rights reserved. **290** Reprinted by permission of Copley News Service **291** © The New Yorker Collection. 1999. J. B. Handelsman from cartoonbank.com. All rights reserved. **293** © The New Yorker Collection. 1999. J.B. Handelsman from cartoonbank.com. All rights reserved. **297** Copyright 2006. Reprinted by permission of Cagle Cartoons. **299** Oliphant Copyright © 1990. Universal Press Syndicate. Reprinted with permission. **300** AP/World Wide Photos **304** Ziv Koren/Polaris **310** Calvin Hobbes © Watterson. Reprinted with permission of United Press Syndicate. All rights reserved. **313** © Barry Williams/Getty Images **314**

Chapter 10

© Getty Images **316** © Alex Wong/Getty Images **318** National Archives **320** Reprinted with permission. **321** The News-Gazette, Robert K. O'Daniell **323** © David McNew/Getty Images **325** AP Images/Al Grillo **329** © Steve Liss/Time Magazine **330** Library of Congress **332** © George Tames/NYT Permissions **334** AP Images **336** Reprinted by permission of Copley News Service. **339** © Bettmann/Corbis **341** © Charles Ommaney/Contact Press **343** AP Images/Gerald Herbert **345** © Joe Raedle/Getty Images **346** ©Alex Wong/Getty images **352** Courtesy of Senator Durbin **354** By permission of Mike Luckovich and Creators Syndicate **356** By Luckovich for the *Atlanta Journal Constitution* **358**

Chapter 11

Win McNamee, Getty Images **360** Howard Pyle Collection/Delaware Art Museum, Wilmington/Bridgeman Art Library **363** George Bush Presidential Library **364** Doonesbury © 1999 G. B. Trudeau. Reprinted with permission of Universal Press Syndicate. All rights reserved. **366** Brown Brothers **369** AP/Wide World Photos **370** Theodore Roosevelt Collection, Harvard College Library **376** Franklin D. Roosevelt Library **377** National Archives **378** Courtesy Joe Wezorek **379** © Reuters/Corbis **384** Lyndon B. Johnson Library **385** Hank Walker/Time Life Pictures/Getty Images **386** © Time Life Pictures/Getty Images **390** © Time Life Pictures/Getty Images **391** © Columbus Dispatch/Dist. by Newspaper Enterprise Association, Inc. **392** © Time &

INDEX

Page numbers in boldface refer to photographs and tables.

AARP, 168, 180, 198
ABC, 123, 124, **146**
ABM systems, 654, 662
Abolitionists, 213, 551
Abortion
   antiabortion groups, 285
   availability of, 502–503
   Catholic Church on, 166
   discouragement of women
      performing, 551
   fathers and, 560
   federal funding for, 500
   interest groups on, 183
   issue votes on, 232
   in judicial confirmation
      hearings, 436–437
   in liberalism and conservatism,
      106
   "partial-birth," 501, **501**
   political appointments and, 427
   political party differences on,
      206, 226
   protests against, 193, 478,
      502–503
   public opinion on legality of,
      93, **110, 500**
   rates of, **500**, 502
   regulation of sexual behavior
      and, 504
   state laws on, 63, 500–501
   Supreme Court rulings on,
      437, 453, 461, 462,
      499–502
   in unmarried minors, 500–502
Abramoff, Jack, **284**, 285–286,
   309–310, 314, 355
Abscam, 309
Absentee balloting, 254
Abstinence, promotion of,
   503–504
Abu Ghraib prison abuse, **158,**
   509, **509,** 644
Accounting industry, regulations
   of, 302
ACLU (American Civil Liberties
   Union), 189, 453
ACT (America Coming
   Together), 254, 296
Activist judges, 456–457, **457**
ADA (Americans with Disabilities
   Act), 83, 418–419, 455
Adams, Abigail, 33, 388
Adams, Charles Francis, 32
Adams, John
   on democracy, 36
   election decided in the House,
      272
   negative campaigning by, 269
   packing of the courts by, 439
   on political parties, 210
   on representativeness of
      Congress, 322

   secessionist threats under, 61
Adams, John Quincy, 211, 364
Adams, Louisa, 388
Ad hoc committees, 338
Administrative Procedure Act
   (APA), 410, 413
Adversarial relationships, between
   media and politicians, 128
Advocacy media, 141–142
AFDC (Aid to Families with
   Dependent Children),
   612–613
Affirmative action policies, 11,
   560–563
Afghanistan War
   background of, 657, 658–659
   cronyism in contract awards in,
      303
   date growers and, 175
   death of Pat Tillman in, 141
   media and, 139, 141
   NATO troops in, 656, 664
AFL-CIO, 171–172, 191
African Americans. *See also* Civil
   rights; Race discrimination;
   Slavery
   Black Caucus, 350–351
   "black middle-class rage,"
      540–541
   "brown bag test," 528
   citizenship of, 48, 522, 680
   Civil Rights Act of 1964 and,
      19, 217–218
   in civil service, 406, **406**
   cultural diversity among, 6–7
   current conditions for,
      541–542
   in election of 2000, 246, 253
   families in poverty, **628**
   in federal bureaucracy,
      404–406, **406,** 432
   foreign policy toward Africa
      and, 642
   GI Bill of Rights and, 619
   interest groups, 178
   lynchings of, 525, **525, 526**
   in the media, 149
   in the military, 217
   Montgomery bus boycott,
      194–195, **194,** 531–532
   party identification by, **217,**
      230
   in political office, 240–241,
      240, 244, 258, **258**
   political participation by, 21
   poorer health of, 623
   public opinion on plight of,
      113–114
   racial profiling of, 539–541,
      540
   Reconstruction Amendments,
      48–49, 240, 522–524

   as slave owners, 522
   in the Supreme Court, 448
   Supreme Court rulings on, 52,
      446–447
   teen pregnancy rates in, 502
   in the "underclass," 541, 561
   violence against, 193, 241, 525,
      525, 526, 532
   voting rights of, 11, 240–241,
      242, 522, 524, 526, 532
Agencies, federal, 415–418
Agenda, setting the, 153–154,
   374–375
Agents of political socialization,
   92
Agnew, Spiro, 144, 311
Agribusiness lobbies, 173
Agriculture
   farm subsidies, 614–615, 620,
      620
   government assistance after
      9/11, 174–175
   interest groups, 173, 176
   during the New Deal, 50
AIDS
   among drug users, 542
   gay community awareness, 179
   government response to, 424
   media coverage of, 153
   needle-exchange programs, 100
   as worldwide epidemic,
      660–661
Aid to Families with Dependent
   Children (AFDC), 612–613
Airlines, government bailout after
   9/11, 174, 187
Alabama
   affirmative action results in,
      561
   civil rights movement in, 532,
      532
   Montgomery bus boycott in,
      194–195, **194,** 531–532
   Ten Commandments in Judicial
      Building in, 491
Alaska Public Interest Research
   Group, 189
Alexander, Lamar, 4
Alito, Samuel
   confirmation hearings of, 195,
      434, 435, 437, 465–466
   on states' rights, 83
Alliance Defense Fund, 453
Al-Qaeda. *See also* 9/11/2001
   perception of connection with
      Hussein, 146, **146,** 425,
      644
   reporting on, prior to 9/11,
      153
AMA (American Medical
   Association), 196, 551
Ambassadors, 376–377, 639

America Coming Together
   (ACT), 254, 296
American Agriculture Movement,
   173
American Bus Association, 174
American Civil Liberties Union
   (ACLU), 189, 453
American Dream, attainability of,
   599
American Farm Bureau
   Federation, 173
American History Achievement
   Act of 2005, 4
American Independent Party, 209
American Indians. *See* Native
   Americans
American International Center,
   309
American Medical Association
   (AMA), 196, 551
American Nazi Party, 477
American Petroleum Institute,
   424
American Public Welfare
   Association, 75
The American Rifleman, 168
Americans for Generational
   Equity, 180
Americans for Tax Reform, 309
American Shore and Beach
   Preservation Association, 175
Americans with Disabilities Act
   (ADA), 83, 418–419, 455
Amicus curiae briefs, 562
Amish, 487
Amnesty International, 176
Amtrak, 418
Anderson, John, 264
Anthony, Susan B., 245, 551
Anthrax infections, 150, **150**
Anti-Federalists, 43
The Anti-Slavery Alphabet, **523**
APA (Administrative Procedure
   Act), 410, 413
Appellate courts, 444–446, **445,**
   494. *See also* Supreme Court
Appropriations, 345, 348
Appropriations Committees, 185,
   345, 346, **346**
Arafat, Yasir, 658
Aristotle, 5
Arizona, immigration issues in,
   57–58, 84–85
Armey, Dick, 229
Arms race, 652, 661–662
Arms trade, 666
Army of God, 183
Art, obscenity and, 484
Arthur Andersen, 305
Articles of Confederation, 29–31,
   29, 59
Ashcroft, John, 182, 411

Asian Americans
  in civil service, 406, **406**
  families in poverty, **628**
  Japanese-American internment,
    69, **518**, 519–520, 565
  party affiliation of, **217**, 220,
    230
Assembly on Federal Issues, 75,
  78
Assisted suicide, 507–508
Asymmetrical warfare, 662–663
Athletic programs, women's,
  558–559, **558**
Authorizations, 345, 348
"Axis of evil," 654–655, 656
Babbitt, Bruce, 261
Baker v. Carr, 322
Baldwin, Tammy, 250, **250**
Balkans, Clinton and, 382, 659,
  664
Ballot initiatives, 80
Bangladesh, formation of, 60
Banks
  establishment of a national, 66
  Federal Reserve System, 416,
    577–581
  race discrimination by, 535,
    539
Barak, Ehud, 658
Barbary pirates, 30
Barbour, Haley, 187, 305
Battleground states, 265–266
Bauer, Gary, 257
Bedford, Gunning, 34
Belknap, Jeremy, 36
Berlin Wall, 652
Bernanke, Ben, 578
Bernstein, Carl, 27–28
BIA (Bureau of Indian Affairs),
  548–549
Bias. *See* Political bias
Bible riots of 1843, **9,** 10
Biden, Joseph, 335, 668
Bilingual education, 545–546
Bill of Rights. *See also specific*
    amendments
  application to state
    governments, 472
  freedom of association,
    480–481
  freedom of religion, 485–492,
    487, 488, 489, 490, 491
  freedom of speech, 473–480,
    478, 479
  freedom of the press, 481–483
  gun control, 493
  libel and, 483–484
  obscenity laws, 477, 484–485
  origin and meaning of, 44,
    471–472
  overview of civil liberties in,
    44–45, 472
  ratification of the Constitution
    and, 43
  rights of criminal defendants,
    492–498
  USA PATRIOT Act and,
    508–514

Bills
  conference committees,
    341–342
  debate and vote on, 340–341
  markup sessions, 335
  presidential action on, 342
  scheduling and rules on, 340
  signing statements, 381
  submission and referral, 339
  veto power, 342, 375
Bills of attainder, 471
bin Laden, Osama, **638, 639**
Bipartisanship, 228–229, 641
Bird flu virus, 73
Birth control, 498, 503–505
Bison producers, 175
Black, Hugo, 452, 529
Black Americans. *See* African
    Americans
Black Caucus, 350–351
Blackmun, Harry, 447, 453, 456,
  461
"Black power," 533
Blakes, Joan, 190, **191**
BLM (Bureau of Land
    Management), 620
Blockbusting, 535
Block grants, 72, **74**
Blogs, 127–128, 271
Blue states, 107–111, **108, 110,**
  276
BOB (Bureau of the Budget),
  386, 426
Boehlert, Sherwood, 426
Boehner, John, 113, 310
Bomb shelters, **476**
Bonauto, Mary, **180**
Bookstores, USA PATRIOT Act
    and, 512
Boorda, Mike, **118,** 119–120,
  161
Border Protection, Antiterrorism
    and Illegal Immigration
    Control bill, 165
Borjas, George J., 594–596
Bork, Robert, 28, 349, 435, 534
Bowling Alone, 21, 168
Boxer, Barbara, 187
Boyd, Wes, 190, **191**
Boy Scouts of America, 480
Bradley, Bill, 126
Bradley, Joseph, 550–551
Bradwell, Myra, 550
Brandeis, Louis, 456, 458, 460
Breaux, John, 91
Brennan, William, 460, 461, 479,
  483, 484
Brewer, David, 488
Breyer, Steven, **457,** 458, 462
"Bridge to nowhere," 185
Britain. *See* Great Britain
Broadcasting, narrowcasting *vs.,*
  125
Brown, Linda, 527
Brown, Michael, 77, 222
Brownback, Sam, 350
"Brown bag test," 528
Brown v. Board of Education, 527
Bryan, William Jennings, **109,**
  214, **257,** 393

Buchanan, Pat, 264, 275–276,
  405
Budget. *See* Federal budget
Budget deficits, 586–591, **589,**
  591
Buffet, Warren, 592, 601
Bumpers, Dale, 191
"The Bunker," 367
Bureaucracy, federal, 403–432.
    See also Federal employees
  administration reform in,
    427–428
  agencies within, 415–418, **416**
  Congress and, 428
  controlling growth of, 414–415
  data collection and analysis,
    420–421
  federal courts and, 428–429
  goals of, 408
  hierarchical nature of, 407–408
  merit system in, 215, 222–223,
    421, 424
  neutral competence in,
    421–423, 424–427, **424**
  openness in, 410–412, 429
  performance standards in,
    408–410
  policy administration by, 418
  policy making by, 418–419
  presidential power to
    reorganize, 371
  public opinion of, 407
  reasons for growth of,
    413–414, **413**
  responsiveness of, 431
  waste in, 409
  whistleblowers in, 430–431
  women and minorities in, 406,
    406
Bureau of Indian Affairs (BIA),
  548–549
Bureau of Land Management
    (BLM), 620
Bureau of the Budget (BOB),
  386, 426
Burger, Warren, 28, 442, 447,
  452, 493
Burger Court, **443**
  on abortion, 499–500
  on busing of students, 530–531
  on capital punishment, 497
  on demonstrations, 478
  expectations of, 442
  on religious symbols, 491
  restrictions on gathering news,
    482–483
  on sex discrimination, 553
Burton, Dan, 412
Bus boycott, Montgomery,
  194–195, **194,** 531–532
Bush, George H. W.
  on birth control, 503
  donors to, 303
  efforts to control spending, 590
  foreign policy of, 638, 653,
    654–660
  image creation and, 266, 270
  invasion of Panama, 382
  judicial appointments of, 436,
    448, 500

Persian Gulf War, 145, 382,
    392, 644, 657
  photograph with son, **364**
  on public access to records, 412
  public opinion of, 267, 394,
    396
  relationship with Congress,
    374, 375–376
  on supply-side economics, 576
  Willie Horton political ad, 218,
    219
Bush, George W. *See also* Election
    of 2000; Election of 2004;
    Iraq War
  appointments of corporate
    executives to agencies, 423
  authority of federal courts over
    policies of, 515
  bipartisanship and, 228–229
  budget forecasts of, 587–588
  budget increases of, 591
  campaign fundraising by, 257,
    290–291, 293, 301
  campaign image of, 266, **269**
  church and state separation
    under, 107, 138, 492
  classification of documents
    under, 411–412, **411**
  as "compassionate
    conservative," 208
  "crafted talk" of, 101
  in debates with Kerry, 271
  direct public appeals by,
    392–393
  e-campaigning by, 272–273
  economic policy of, 576–577,
    581, 600
  on education, 74–75, 617
  on environmental regulations,
    182
  on ethical standards, 311
  expansion of executive
    privilege by, 54
  on farm subsidies, 615
  foreign policy advisers of,
    638–639
  on free trade, 665
  on gay and lesbian rights, 179,
    180
  global warming data
    suppression by, 191,
    424–426, **424**
  on health care, 605, 624
  Hispanic voters and, 220
  on home ownership, 620
  image comprised of photos of
    war casualties, **379**
  Imperial Presidency of,
    380–381
  income tax paid by, 584
  insurance industry support of,
    174
  judicial appointments of,
    436–437, 448
  on lawmaking process,
    342–343
  leak of identity of Wilson's CIA
    wife, 129–130, **130**
  leaks to the media and,
    130–131

management style of, 387
media relationship with, 133,
137–138, 391, 393
Middle East policy of, 658–659
on morality in the White
House, 259
on Murtha's criticism of Iraq
War, 669
in the National Guard,
237–238
negative ads, 268–269
NRA support for, 182–183
persona of, 393, **394**
pharmaceutical industry
influence on, 171
photograph with father, **364**
public opinion of, **396**
reduction of federal regulation
by, 73, 170
response to 9/11, 99, 137, **138**
response to hurricane Katrina,
76–77, **77**, 132, 222–223,
222
retrospective voting on, 232,
232
size of government under,
414–415
Social Security reform, 101,
361–363, 399, 587–588,
625–626
spreading false information
about McCain, 102
staff of, 387
state-centered federalism and,
81
support by conservative
Christians, 177, **231**
support by Republicans in
Congress, 225, 226
tax cuts of, 114, 221–222, 226
as Texas governor, 305
torture definition by, 509–510
as unitary executive, 380–381,
428
on use of polling, 100–101
Bush v. *Gore,* 228, 457
Business
campaign contribution benefits
to, 223, 302, 306–307
corporate welfare, 621–622
court decisions on, 440–441
environmental cleanup costs,
622
globalization and, 591–594
government corporations, 418
government regulation of, 50,
170, 578–579
health care costs of, 606–607,
623, 630
interest groups, 169–171, **170**
political action committees of,
295
Republican lobbyists for, 186
rights of commercial
association, 480–481
taxes paid by, 584
Busing for racial balance,
529–531, **530**
Butterfly ballots, 274–275, 276
Byrd, Robert C., 144
Cabinet, 367, 415, **416**

CAGW (Citizens Against
Government Waste), 346
Cahill, Mary Beth, 273
Calendars, congressional, 340
Calhoun, John, 66
California
abolition of bilingual education
in, 545
ballot initiatives in, 80
demographic change in,
321–322
domestic partnerships in, 506
Enron's role in power crisis of,
305
immigrants in, 595–596
Los Angeles County, 537, **537,**
542, 578–579
redistricting in, 322
shortage of jobs for welfare
mothers, 627–628
Cambodia, secret bombing of,
311
Campaign finance. *See also*
Campaign fundraising
benefits to donors, 223,
302–303, 306–307
class differences and, 303, 306,
306
conflicts of interest and,
308–311
disclosure laws, 292
donor demographics, 308, **308**
early reforms, 288–289, **289**
by Enron, 304–305
as extortion, 306–307
527 groups, 296
free media time proposals,
297–298
as free speech, 299–300
importance of money in
winning, 301–303
independent spending, 289,
293–294
McCain-Feingold Act, 292
in nineteenth-century politics,
288
opposition to reform, 297
proposal to keep donors' names
secret, 299
public cynicism and, 307–308,
307
public funds for, 293, 298–299,
298
public opinion on, **298,**
307–308, **307**
reforms of the 1970s, 289
responsiveness of government
and, 312
soft money, 292, 296
spending limits, 292–293
ways to avoid contribution
limitations, 292–296
Campaign fundraising, 289–292.
See also Campaign finance
in congressional campaigns,
279, 291–292, 302, 329
by Democratic Party, 227, 234
by political parties, 227, 234
by presidents, 257, 290–291
by Republican Party, 227
ways to avoid contribution

limitations, 292–296
Campaigns, 264–276
buying votes, 287
congressional, 277–280, **279**
e-campaigning, 271–273
economic impacts on, 581
image creation in, 266
media and, 155–158, 267–270
national conventions, 262–264,
263
organization of, 265
permanent, 276–277
spending, 278
strategies, 265–266
voters "turned off" by, 252
whistle-stop, **261**
Canada, health care in, 623
Cannon, Joseph, 331
Cantwell, Maria, 570
Capital Athletic Foundation, 309
Capital gains tax cut, 174–175,
190, 303, 306
Capitalist economy, 571–572, 607
Capital punishment. *See* Death
penalty
Cardozo, Benjamin, 459
Carlin, George, 477
Carlson, Tucker, 165
Carpal tunnel syndrome, 455
Carter, Jimmy
in debates, 270–271
downsizing efforts of, 414
on election standards in
Florida, 276
on FOIA, 410–411
foreign policy of, 651–652
Iranian seizure of Embassy
hostages, 153–154
judicial appointments of, 448
Middle East agreements, 658
nomination of, 154, **225,** 259
public opinion of, **396**
swamp rabbit incident, 135
Carter, Rosalynn, 389
Casework, 328
Catholic Church and Catholics
on birth control, 503
election of Catholic to
presidency, 258
party identification of, 219,
230–231
on political issues, 165–166,
176, 200
against women's suffrage, 245
Catholic–Protestant conflict,
9–10, **9**
Cato Institute, 412
Catt, Carrie Chapman, 245–246
Caucuses, presidential, 259
Caucus for Women's Issues, 350
CBO (Congressional Budget
Office), 338, 344, 372, 576,
587
CBS news, 124, 131, **146,** 148
CDC (Centers for Disease
Control and Prevention), 73
CDF (Children's Defense Fund),
169, 180
Censorship, 132, 481–482. *See
also* Freedom of speech
Census Bureau, 6, 13

Center for Public Integrity, 303
Centers for Disease Control and
Prevention (CDC), 73, 420
Central Intelligence Agency
(CIA)
communication with FBI, 512
foreign policy and, 640
Iraq prewar intelligence,
318–319, 358, 425
purge of career agents under
Bush, 425
secret prisons of, 660
Centrist Coalition, 341, 351
Century Strategies, 286
Certificate of Degree of Indian
Blood, 15
Chafee, Zechariah, 474
Chamber of Commerce, 190, 196
Chambliss, Saxby, 267
Chávez, César, 546
Checks and balances, 39–40, **40,**
686–687
Cheney, Richard
cursing of, 229
energy policy task force of,
305, 372
on FOIA, 411
Halliburton connections, 311,
403
hunting accident of, 135
hunting trip with Supreme
Court justice, 452
income tax paid by, 584
on Iraq War, 668
leaking information to
influence events, 129
on presidential powers, 380
role as vice president, 333, 390
Chertoff, Michael, 77
Chicanos, 546. *See also* Hispanics
Child labor laws, **440,** 441
Child pornography, 484–485
Children
child labor laws, **440,** 441
custody rules, 559
food subsidies for, 614
health care for, 617
of illegal immigrants, 595–596
impact on women's wages,
555–556
men's rights and, 559–560
political socialization of, 92–94,
95
in poverty, 612–613, **612**
public interest groups for, 180
of single women, 612
Children's Defense Fund (CDF),
169, 180
China, U.S. relations with, 651,
652
Christian Coalition, 177,
285–286
Christian conservatives
Bush's cooperation with, 107,
138, 492
after the Cold War, 221
Forbes and, 257
media and, 142, 144
in the Progressive movement,
214
public interest groups, 176–177

Christian conservatives (continued)
on state-level issues, 83
on Terri Schiavo, 91
Christian Research Network, 314
CIA. *See* Central Intelligence
Agency
Citizen education, 95–96
Citizens Against Government
Waste (CAGW), 346
Citizenship
of African Americans, 48, 522,
680
of Native Americans, 548
of women, 550
Civics courses, 95
Civil cases, 453
Civil disobedience, 192–193, 532
Civil liberties, 469–516. *See also*
Civil rights
affirmative action policies, 11,
560–563
education discrimination,
535–538, **536, 537**
employment discrimination,
538
freedom of association,
480–481
freedom of religion, 485–492,
487, 488, 489, 490, 491
freedom of speech, 473–480,
478, 479
freedom of the press, 481–483
of Guantanamo Bay detainees,
463, **468,** 469–470,
515–516
of Hispanics, 542–547
housing discrimination,
538–539
Internet use and, 485
interrogations, 508–510, **509**
libel, 483–484
of Native Americans, 547–550
obscenity laws, 477, 484–485
overview of, 472
racial profiling, 539–541, **540,**
544
renditions, 510
responsiveness of government
in, 514
rights of criminal defendants,
492–498
right to privacy, 498–508, **500**
school desegregation, 526–531,
529, 530, 534, 544
secret prisons, 510
sex discrimination, 550–560
USA PATRIOT Act and,
508–514
Civil rights, 519–565. *See also*
Civil rights movement
"black power," 533
busing of students, 529–531,
530
Civil Rights Act of 1964, 19,
217–218, 340, 529
court decisions on, **442,** 446,
527–529
definition of, 520
under Eisenhower, 52
filibusters against, 340, **341**

Japanese-American internment,
69, **518,** 519–520, **520,**
565
under Johnson, 19, 69–70,
217–218, 340, 529, 533
under Kennedy, 533
litigation by organizations for,
189
Montgomery bus boycott,
194–195, **194,** 531–532
murder of civil rights workers,
218, **533**
party realignments and, 106,
217–218
racial integration in the
military, 217
responsiveness of government
in, 563–564
Rules Committee and, 340
under Truman, 217
Voting Rights Act of 1965,
241–244, **242,** 534 (*See
also* Voting rights)
Civil Rights Act of 1964
affirmative action and, 560–562
Education Amendments of
1972, 558–559, **558**
Johnson on, 19, 217–218
passage of, 340, 552
school desegregation and, 529,
529
on sex discrimination, 553–556
southern realignment after,
106, 217–218
Civil Rights Act of 1968, 535
Civil Rights Acts, during
Reconstruction, 523
Civil rights movement
in Congress, 533–535
Montgomery bus boycott,
194–195, **194,** 531–532
murder of civil rights workers,
218, **533**
school desegregation, 526–531,
529, 530, 534, 544
spread of, 531–533, **531, 532,
533**
Civil servants. *See* Federal
employees
Civil service. *See* Bureaucracy,
federal
Civil Service Commission,
421–422
Civil Service Reform Act of
1978, 422
Civil unions, 505. *See also* Same-
sex marriages
Civil War, 46–49
Emancipation Proclamation,
46–47, 48
Gettysburg Address, 47–48, 688
as manifestation of regional
differences, 107
power of Congress after,
330–331
power of the federal
government, 49, 59
Reconstruction Amendments,
48–49, 522–523

voting rights of blacks and,
240–241, **240**
Clarke, Richard, **129**
Classified documents, 410–412,
411
Clay, Henry, 330
Clean Air Act, 197
Clear Channel Communications,
123, 124
Cleland, Max, 228, 267
Clergy Leadership Network, 178
Cleveland, Grover, **255,** 370
Climate change
bogus reports by ExxonMobil,
191
Kyoto protocols on, 82, 305,
654
political policy of George W.
Bush on, 191, 405,
424–425, **424**
support from evangelical
movement, 177
Clinton, Hillary
alliance with Brownback, 350
as First Lady, 388, 389
future presidential campaign of,
247, 271
in-state residency of, 319
political action committee of,
351
Senate race of, 302
Whitewater investigation, 311
Clinton, William J.
appeals to the middle, 221
campaign fundraising by, 290
downsizing under, 414
economic policy of, 580–581,
590–591, 600
effects of divided government
on, 373
on employee pledge not to
lobby, 423
FEMA reorganization under,
76
on FOIA, 411
foreign policy of, 653–654
hatred by Republicans, 228
health care reform proposal of,
190, 198
homosexual rights and,
179–180, 506–507
impeachment hearings, 349,
366, 384
judicial nominations of, 436
loan to Mexico by, 578
management style of, 387
Middle East agreements, 658
nomination of, 257, 259
pardon of husband of Denise
Rich by, 303
personal popularity of, 231,
392
public opinion of, 92–93,
394–395, **396**
relationship with Congress,
374, 376, 384
relationship with the media,
136–137, 393
sexual harassment suit by Paula
Jones, 385, 453, **454,** 557

sexual scandals of, 126,
150–151, 228, 259, 453,
454
state-federal relations under,
72–73
on teenage smoking, 154
use of polls by, 100
veto of accounting bill, 302
welfare reform under, 100, 107
Whitewater investigation, 138,
150, 311
Cloning, 81
Cloture, 340
CNN, 124, 145, **146,** 148
Coalition building, 193–196
Coburn, Tom, 347
Code of Federal Regulations, 410
Cold War
arms race in, 652, 661–662
containment policy, 646–651,
646
détente, 651–652
end of, 653
government spending during,
69
McCarthyism, 474–475, **475**
media coverage of, 145
revival under Reagan, 652–653
Colleges. *See also* Education
affirmative action admissions
policies, 562–563
competitiveness of students
from, 592
financial aid, 599
GI Bill of Rights, 618–619,
618
hate speech codes, 477
low political interest of students
in, 96, 250–251
political socialization and, 96,
97
student antiwar protests, 193
student interest groups,
180–181
student loan programs, 181
subsidies to, 617–619
voting location of students, 250
women's athletic programs at,
558–559, **558**
Colorado, illegal immigration
and, 84
Colorado River, water resources
in, 79
Comcast, 123–124
Commerce. *See* Trade
Commercial bias, 148–153, **150**
Committees. *See* Congressional
committees
Communism. *See also* Cold War
containment policy, 646–651
détente, 651–652
domino theory, 648
McCarthyism and, 474–475,
475
Communist Party USA, 209
Communitarianism, 18
Comparable worth, 555
Concurring opinions, 461
Confederal system, 59
Confederate states, 46–47, 48

Conference committees, 338, 341–342
Confessions, 495
Confidential tapes, in Watergate scandal, 27–28, 53–54
Conflicts of interest, 308–311
Congress, 317–358. *See also* House of Representatives; Senate
  alliances in, 350–351
  authorizations and appropriations, 345, 348
  budget making, 344–345, 348
  bureaucracy oversight and funding, 428
  campaign fundraising by members of, 291–292, 298–299, 302
  casework by, 328
  in checks and balances, 40, **40,** 463
  civil rights movement and, 533–535
  committees in, 334–338 (*See also* Congressional committees)
  conflicts of interest in, 308–309
  constituencies of, 321–322
  demographics of, 323–325, **324**
  "dynasty" families in, 325
  earmarking by, 185, 329, 346–347, **347**
  election and terms in, 37, **38,** 279–280, **279,** 298–299
  enumerated *vs.* implied powers, 338
  ethics regulation by, 310–311
  evolution of organization of, 330–331
  foreign policy and, 640–642
  incumbents, 277–279, **279, 296,** 302, 322, 327–329
  informal norms in, 348–340
  lawmaking process, 339–343 (*See also* Bills)
  leadership positions in, 331–334
  length of service, 319–321
  mailing privileges in, 328–329
  media coverage of, 138, 329, 351–352
  oversight responsibilities of, 317–319, 343–348, **343,** 358
  pay and perks of, 327
  personal friendships in, 351
  political action committee contributions to, 295–296
  power to declare war, 378–379
  presidential influence in, 373–376, **374**
  public and, 353, 356
  qualifications for, 319
  reciprocity in, 349–350
  representativeness of, 322–329, **324, 326**
  responsiveness of government and, 356–357
  role of money in, 302
  schedules of members, 353–355
  seniority in, 336
  specialization by members, 349
  staff and support agencies, 338, 353
  on state-centered federalism, 81
  trends in partisan voting in, 349, **350**
Congressional Budget Office (CBO), 338, 344, 372, 576, 587
Congressional campaigns, 277–280, **279,** 291–292, 298–299, 302
Congressional committees, 334–338
  in budget-making process, 345, 348
  chairs of, 336–337
  conference, 338, 341–342
  conflicts of interest in, 308–309
  evolution of, 330
  hearings, 188, 343, **343**
  joint, 337–338
  in lawmaking process, 339–343
  membership on, 335–336
  select, 337
  staff of, 338, 353
  standing committees, 335
  subcommittees, 335, 337
  task forces, 338
Congressional hearings, 188, 343, **343**
Congressional Research Service (CRS), 338
Congress of Racial Equality (CORE), 178, 533
Connecticut Compromise, 34
CONRAIL, 418
Conservatism, 106
Conservatives, 106–111, **107,** 221. *See also* Christian conservatives; Republican Party and Republicans
Constituencies, 321–322
Constituency service, 328
Constitution, 27–54, 674–682. *See also* Bill of Rights
  checks and balances in, 39–40, **40,** 686–687
  Constitutional Convention, 31–36
  court interpretation of, 438–440, 455–457, **457,** 462–463
  courts in, 444 (*See also* Judiciary)
  election of senators in, 37, 40, 70, 330–331
  federalism in, 37
  general welfare provision, 608
  government responsiveness and, 51–52
  individual rights in body of, 471
  on interstate relationships, 78
  motives of the Founders, 41–43
  during the New Deal, 49–51
  process for amending, 43–45
  ratification of, 43, 45
Reconstruction Amendments, 48–49, 522–523
Republic form in, 36
responsiveness of, 51–52
separation of church and state in, 486
separation of powers in, 37–39, **38, 39**
text of, 674–682
undemocratic features in, 40–41
voting rights in, 240
Constitutional Convention, 31–36
  consensus at, 33
  delegates to, 31
  federalism in, 60
  on representation, 34
  on role of federal government, 31–33, 36
  on slavery, 34–35, 40
Consumption tax, 585–586
Containment policy, 646–651
Continental Congress, 29
Contraceptives, 498, 503–505
Contract lobbyists, 185
Contract with America, 332, 613
A Conversation with America (Luntz), 101
Cook, Roseanne, **604**
Coolidge, Calvin, 393
Cooperative federalism, 73
Corbin, Margaret, 32–33
CORE (Congress of Racial Equality), 178, 533
Core values, 17–20
Cornyn, John, 113
Corporate collapses of 2002, 343–344. *See also* Enron
Corporate welfare, 621–622
Corporations. *See* Business
Corruption
  Abramoff scandal, **284,** 285–286, 309–310, 314, 355
  campaign finance and, 300
  cyclical nature of, 312
  in golden age of political parties, 214
  influence peddling, 310–311
  public opinion about, 307–308, **307**
  regulating ethical behavior, 310–311
  Tammany Hall machine, 214–215, 287
  in 109th Congress, 355
Council of Economic Advisers, 576
Counterterrorism, 75, 79. *See also* War on terrorism
Counts, Dorothy, **529**
Court-packing plan, 441, **441**
Courts. *See* Judiciary
Courts of appeals, 444
Coyotes, 58
Crack, 542
"Cracking, stacking, and packing," 242
Crafted talk, 101
Creationism, 492
Credentials committee, 262
Credit, sex discrimination in, 556–558
Criminal cases, 453
Criminal defendants, rights of, 492–498
  cruel and unusual punishment, 497–498
  due process rights, 48, 492
  exclusionary rule, 494
  interrogations, 508–511, **509**
  presumption of innocence, 492
  renditions, 510
  right to a jury trial, 496–497
  right to counsel, 495–496
  search and seizure, 494
  secret prisons, 510
  self-incrimination, 494–495
  in theory and in practice, 498
Cronkite, Walter, 141, 153
Cross burning, 477
CRS (Congressional Research Service), 338
Cruel and unusual punishment, 497–498
Cruzan, Nancy, 507
C-SPAN, 352
Cuban Americans, foreign policy and, **641,** 642
Cultural diversity. *See* Diversity
Cumulus Media, 123
Cunningham, Randy "Duke," 309
Curley, James, 213
Currency, under the Articles of Confederation, **29,** 30
Dahl, Robert, 33
Daily Kos, 127, 271
Daley, Richard J., 213–214
Danish cartoons of Muhammed, 156–157, **157**
Darrow, Clarence, **109**
Daschle, Tom, 278, 380
Date growers, 175
Daughters of Liberty, 32
Davis, John W., **223,** 262
Daylight Saving Time Coalition, 194
Day Without Immigrants, **164,** 165–166, 200
Dealignment, 224, **224**
Dean, Howard
  as DNC chairman, **202,** 203–204, 227, 234
  presidential campaign of, 109, 155, 229, 293, 294
Death penalty
  applied by women judges, 449
  Blackmun on, 456
  as cruel and unusual punishment, 497–498
  in red *vs.* blue states, **110**
"Death tax," 101. *See also* Estate tax
Debs, Eugene V., 384, **473,** 474
Debt, national, 586–591, **589, 591,** 626
Debt, private, 599

Declaration of Independence
  adoption of, 29
  core values in, 17, 18
  Gettysburg Address and, 47–48
  text of, 672–673
Deep South, 62
De facto segregation, 529–530,
  533, 535–536, **536,** 544
Defend Colorado Now, 200
Defense, under the Articles of
  Confederation, 30
Defense Department, 128, 413,
  414, **416,** 663
Defense of Marriage Act, 78, 505
Defense policy, 661–663
Defense secretary, 638
Defense spending, 663
Deficits, 586–591, **589, 591**
De jure segregation, 529–530, 535
DeLay, Tom
  Abramoff scandal and,
    309–310, **310**
  indictment of, 239
  K Street strategy and, 186, 306
  as Majority Leader, 332–333
  resignation of, 355
Delegated legislative authority,
  419
Democracy
  Andrew Jackson on, 211
  capitalism and, 571–572
  citizen education and, 95–96
  direct *vs.* indirect, 20, 36, 104,
    274
  as goal of foreign policy of
    Bush, 656, 657, 658–659
  grass roots and, 191
  interest groups and, 21–22,
    197–198
  meaning of, 19
  participation in, 20–22
  pluralist model of, 22
  power in, 22–23
  republic form, 20, 33, 36
Democratic National Committee
  (DNC), **202,** 203–204, 227,
  234
Democratic Party and Democrats
  campaign strategy for 2006,
    203–204, 234
  characteristics of Democrats,
    217
  corruption in, 311
  decline after 9/11 attacks,
    228–229
  delegate selection process,
    260–261
  donor demographics, 220, 297,
    308, **308**
  economic policies of, 580
  Enron's donations to, 305
  foreign policy tendencies, 641
  founding of, 210
  geographic patterns in recent
    elections, 107–108, **108**
  House representation by, **326**
  ideology and, 220–222
  on Iraq War, 281
  low voter turnout by, 254–255
  on Murtha's criticism of Iraq
    War, 633–634, 668–669

organization of, 226–228
party unity in congressional
  voting, **227**
political action committee
  contributions to, 295
rise of, 215–216
in the South, 216–219
youth vote increases, 250–251
Demographics of the U.S.
  in California, 321–322
  of campaign donors, 308, **308**
  of Congress, 322–325, **324**
  of Florida, 62
  immigration and ethnic
    diversity, 5–12
  party identification and, **217,**
    220
  in Utah, 62
  voter turnout and, 249–251
Demonstrations, 192, 478–479,
  478
Department of Agriculture
  (DoA), 420, 613
Department of Defense and
  Veterans Affairs (VA), 617
Department of Homeland
  Security. *See* Homeland
  Security Department
Departments, 415, **416.** *See also
  specific departments*
Depository libraries, 410
Depressions, 573–574. *See also*
  Great Depression
Desegregation
  busing for racial balance,
    529–531, **530**
  of employment, 534, 538
  of housing, 534–535, 538–539
  of public accommodations,
    531–533, **531, 532, 533,**
    534
  of schools, 526–529, **529,** 544
Détente, 651–652
Devolution, 72, 79
Dewey, John, 473
Dictionary of American English
  (Webster), 16
Diplomacy, leadership of
  president in, 376–378
Direct democracy, 20, 36, 104,
  274
Direct lobbying, 185–189
Direct primary, 215
Disabilities, people with
  health care for, 616–617
  income support for, 611–612
  state *vs.* federal rulings and, 83
  veterans, 83, 418–419, 455
Disclosure laws, 292
Discretionary budget authority,
  416
Discretionary spending, 590
Discrimination. *See also* Race
  discrimination
  in employment, 534–535, 538,
    553–556
  of homosexuals, 178, 180
  in housing, 534–535, 538–539
  Japanese-American internment,
    69, **518,** 519–520, **520,**
    565

against men, 559–560
pregnancy, 554
after Reconstruction, 49,
  522–523
second-generation, 538
sexual harassment as, 557
in sports, 558–559, **558**
against women, 550–560
Dissent
  demonstrations, 478–479, **478**
  as seditious speech, 473–476,
    475
  Theodore Roosevelt on, 669
Dissenting opinions, 461
District courts, 444, 446, **451**
District of Columbia, 486
Diversity, 5–8
  economic, 10
  identity politics and, 10–12
  immigration and, 5–9, **7, 8, 16**
  political culture and federalism,
    62–63
  religious, 9–10, 489–490
Divided government, 37, 39, 373
Divorce, 63, 558
Dixiecrats, 217, **218**
DNA testing, race concept and,
  11–12, 13–15
DNC (Democratic National
  Committee), **202,** 203–204,
  227, 234
Dobbs, Lou, 165
Dodd, Christopher, 343
Dole, Elizabeth, 301
Dole, Robert, 132, 180, 196,
  296, 333
Domestic-partnerships, 506. *See
  also* Same-sex marriages
Domino theory, 648
Donohue, Phil, 145
Douglas, William, 474, 475,
  519–520, 565
Douglass, Frederick, 247
Downs, Anthony, 255
Dred Scott decision, 440,
  521–522
Drudge, Matt, 125
Dual federalism, 65–66
Du Bois, W. E. B., 526
Due process clause, 48, 492
Dukakis, Michael, 218, 258, 265,
  266
Durbin, Richard, 354–355, **354**
Earmarking, 185, 329, 346–347,
  347
Earned income tax credit (EITC),
  585, 613, 628
Earth First!, 182
E-campaigning, 271–273
Economic policy, 569–601. *See
  also* Federal budget
  business regulation, 578–579
  capitalist economy, 571–572
  deficit and debt, 586–591, **589,
    591,** 626
  election cycle and, 580–582
  fiscal policy, 575–577, 593, 600
  foreign indebtedness, 588
  globalization and, 591–594
  immigration and, 592–597
  mixed economies, 572

monetary policy, 577–578
persuasion in, 579–580
productivity, 574
responsiveness of, 600
results of problems in, 573–574
tax reform, 582–586, **583, 585,
  586**
wealth gap, 106, 306, **306,**
  597–600, **599, 629**
Economy
  current changes in, 599–600
  illegal immigration and,
    594–597
  income distribution changes,
    106, 306, **306,** 597–600,
    599, 629
  voting based on, 232, **232**
Education. *See also* Colleges;
  Public schools
  affirmative action admissions
    policies, 562–563
  of Amish children, 487
  bilingual, 545–546
  busing for racial balance,
    529–531, **530**
  Catholic church-run schools,
    10
  censorship in public schools,
    482
  continuing discrimination in,
    535–538, **536, 537, 538**
  evolution, teaching of, **109,**
    491–492
  federal funding in, 66
  financial aid for, 599, 617
  GI Bill of Rights, 618–619,
    618
  Head Start programs, 619
  Hispanic discrimination in,
    544–546
  of illegal immigrants, 58
  importance to Founders, 15–16
  inequality of funding for,
    536–538, 544
  No Child Left Behind
    program, 74–75, 617
  political participation and, 249,
    251
  political socialization and,
    94–96
  pre-preschool programs, 614
  school desegregation, 526–531,
    529, 530, 534, 544
  school prayers, 10, 458,
    488–490
  segregation in, 524, 535–536,
    536
  sex discrimination in, 559
  subsidies to, 617–619
  Title IX athletic programs,
    558–559, **558**
  unequal schools, 536–538, **537**
Edwards, John, 264, 277
EEOC (Equal Employment
  Opportunity Commission),
  419, 560
Eighteenth Amendment, **46,** 681
Eighth Amendment, 44,
  497–498, 679

Eisenhower, Dwight D.
  appointment of Earl Warren,
    441–442, **442**, 452, 527
  character of, 397
  on civil rights, 52
  on conviction of Communists,
    474
  election of, 216
  government spending, 69
  military-industrial complex
    and, 363, 663
  public opinion of, **396**
  on school segregation, 527
EITC (earned income tax credit),
    585, 613, 628
Elderly. *See* Seniors
Election of 2000
  butterfly ballot in, 274–275,
    276
  election eve and exit polls, 102,
    103
  Florida Republican election
    officials, 275–276
  geographic distribution of votes
    in, 107–108, **108**
  impact of economy on, 581
  Nader in, 144, 209–210
  overseas ballots in, 275–276
  recounts in, 275
  role of Supreme Court in, 83,
    228, 457
  winner of popular vote in, 216,
    274–276
Election of 2004
  Electoral College strategy in,
    265–266, 273
  e-mails in, 272–273
  geographic distribution of votes
    in, 107–108, **108,** 276
  impact of economy on,
    581–582
  money raised in, 289–290
  negative ads in, 268–269
  pre-election polls in, 102
  question of mandate in, 280
  "Swift Boat Veterans for Truth"
    in, 127, 238, 268, 273,
    293–294, 296
  televised debates, 271
  voter knowledge in, 105
  voting by citizens living abroad,
    252
  voting machines in, 248
Elections. *See also* Election of
    2000; Election of 2004; Voter
    turnout; Voting; Voting rights
  of 1924, **223**
  of 1964, 217–218, **219**
  of 1968, 263, 301–302
  of 1998, 218, **219**
  of 2006, 203–204, 234,
    237–238, 281
  campaign advertising, 267–269
  candidate debates, 157–158,
    270–271, **270**
  candidate personality and, 231
  congressional campaigns,
    277–280, **279,** 298–299
  direct, 274
  Electoral College, 36, 37, 40,
    216, 265, 272–274
  horse race coverage of, 152

impact of media on, 154–158
impact of money in, 301–303
issue votes in, 231–232
media bias in, 143–144
national conventions, 262–264,
    263
nominations, 223, 256–264,
    258, 263
party identification in, 230–231
permanent campaign, 276–277
policy *vs.* nonpolicy issues in
    the media, 154
presidential eve polls, 102, 103
Progressive movement and,
    214–215, **216,** 248–249
responsiveness of government
    and, 280
run-off systems, 274
separation of powers and, 37,
    38
tampering in, 103
voting machines in, 246–248
Electoral College
  campaign strategy for,
    265–266, 273
  operation of, 272
  popular vote and, 216, 246,
    274
  possible reforms of, 274
  rationale and outcomes of,
    273–274
  reasons for, 36, 37, 40
  ties in, 272, 274
Electoral reform legislation of
    2002, 246–248
Electronic surveillance
  Bush and, 131, 358, 483, 511,
    514
  Foreign Intelligence
    Surveillance Court, 446,
    511
  Fourth Amendment rights and,
    494
  Kennedy and, 311
  monitoring calls, 511, 514
  Nixon and, 384
  roving wiretaps, 512
  "sneak-and-peek searches," 512
  in the USA PATRIOT Act,
    446, 512–513
  wiretapping calls, 511
Eleventh Amendment, 679
Ellison, William, 522
Ellsberg, Daniel, 430, 481–482
E-mail, lobbying through, 186,
    190
Emancipation Proclamation,
    46–47, 48
Emanuel, Rahm, 204, 234
EMILY's List, 176
Employment. *See* Workers' rights
"Enemy combatants," 470, 515.
    See also Guantanamo Bay,
    Cuba
Energy deregulation, 302–303,
    305. *See also* Oil and gas
    companies
England. *See* Great Britain
Enron
  appointment of Harvey Pitt to
    SEC and, 423
  avoidance of taxes, 305

House committee hearings on,
    343
  influence of, 292, 295, 302,
    304–305, 372
  scandal, 170, 197, 292,
    304–305, **305**
  subsidies to, 621
Enumerated powers, 338
Environmental interest groups,
    180, 182
Environmental Protection Agency
    (EPA)
  interest groups and, 429–430
  as policy making agency,
    419–420
  political appointments to, 427
  withholding documents from
    public, 411
Environmental regulations
  cleanup as corporate welfare,
    622
  externalities, 579
  fuel efficiency in cars, 112
  liberals *vs.* conservatives on,
    107
  reduction under Bush
    administration, 170
  by states, 74, 82, **110**
  tragedy of the commons and,
    578–579
EOP (Executive Office of the
    President), 373, 385–386,
    426
EPA. *See* Environmental
    Protection Agency
Equal Credit Opportunity Act of
    1974, 556, 558
Equal Employment Opportunity
    Commission (EEOC), 419,
    560
Equality, political. *See also* Civil
    rights
  belief in, 18–19
  for gays and lesbians, 93
  Gettysburg Address and, 47,
    688
  Reconstruction Amendments
    and, 48–49, 522–523
Equal Pay Act of 1963, 554–555
Equal protection clause, 48, 51,
    522, 527, 553
Equal Rights Amendment
    (ERA), 263, 551, 552–553
Era of Good Feeling, 211
Ervin, Sam, 349
Espionage Act of 1917, 473–474,
    473, 483
Espy, Mike, 311
Establishment clause, 488, 492
Estate tax, 101, 569–571, 601
Ethanol producers, 175
Ethics in Government Act of
    1978, 310, 423
Ethnic diversity. *See* Diversity
EU (European Union), 665–666
Europe. *See also* Great Britain
  at end of Cold War, 652–653
  European Union, 665–666
  freedom of the press in, 482
  health care in, 623
  unitary system in, 59
  after World War II, 646–648

European Americans, cultural
    diversity in, 6
European Union (EU), 665–666
Evangelical Climate Initiative,
    177–178
Evolution, **109,** 492
Exclusionary rule, 494
Executive branch. *See* Presidency
Executive Office of the President
    (EOP), 373, 385–386, 426
Executive orders, 371
Executive privilege, 28, 53–54,
    372
Exit polls, 103
Expertise, from lobbyists, 187
Ex post facto laws, 64, 471
Expressive organizations, 480
Externalities, 579
ExxonMobil, 191
Facebook, 271
Fahrenheit 9/11 (Moore), 142
Fairness Doctrine (FCC), 142
Faithless electors, 274
Falwell, Jerry, 177, 189
Families. *See also* Children
  distribution of income in, **629**
  political socialization in, 94
  in poverty, 612–613, **612, 628**
  social welfare programs for,
    612–613, **612,** 627–628
  tax subsidies to, 622
Family farmers, 614–615
Family leave, 556, 558
Farm Bureau, 168, 173
Farmer, James, 533
Farmers, during the New Deal,
    50
Farm Security Act of 2001, 174
Farm subsidies, 614–615, 620,
    620
Farrakhan, Louis, 196
FBI (Federal Bureau of
    Investigation), 512–513
FCC (Federal Communications
    Commission), 142, 416, 477
FDA (Food and Drug
    Administration), 188,
    419–420, 429, 578
FDIC (Federal Deposit Insurance
    Corporation), 418
"The Fed," 416, 577–581
Federal Aviation Administration,
    41
Federal budget. *See also*
    Economic policy;
    Government spending
  authorizations and
    appropriations, 345, 348
  congressional oversight on,
    344–345
  deficit projections in, 587–588,
    589
  discretionary authority, **416**
  discretionary *vs.* mandatory
    spending, 590–591, **591**
  earmarking in, 185, 329,
    346–347, **347**
  efforts to balance, 590–591
  increased executive powers
    under Bush, 427
  interest payments, 589
  line-item veto, 347, 373

Federal budget (continued)
  paygo rule, 348, 590
  presidential role in, 372–373
  problems with process, 348
Federal Bureau of Investigation
  (FBI), 512–513
Federal Communications
  Commission (FCC), 142,
  416, 477
Federal Corrupt Practices Act of
  1925, 289
Federal court system. *See also*
  Judiciary; Supreme Court
  access to, 453–454
  appellate courts, 444–446, **445,**
    494
  authority over presidential
    policies in wartime, 515
  independence of judges,
    451–453
  judge qualifications, 450–451
  judge tenure, 450
  jurisdiction of, 444–445
  liberal decisions in, **451**
  power of the courts, 461–463
  proceeding through, 454
  selection and term of judges,
    37, **38**
  structure of, 444, **445**
Federal Deposit Insurance
  Corporation (FDIC), 418
Federal depository library
  program, 410
Federal Election Commission,
  289
Federal Emergency Management
  Agency (FEMA)
  history of, 76
  hurricane Katrina and, 76–77,
    77, 222–223, **222**
  9/11/2001 terrorist attacks
    and, 76
  Oklahoma City federal
    building bombing and, 76
  political appointees at head of,
    134
Federal employees. *See also*
  Bureaucracy, federal
  concerns of, 417
  limits on political activities of,
    422–423
  merit system for, 421
  neutral competence of,
    421–423, 424–427
  political limitations on work of,
    424–426, **424**
  Senior Executive Service, 403,
    422, 427, 432
  unions of, 428
Federal Energy Regulatory
  Commission, 305
Federal Family Education Loan
  Program, 181
Federal government
  checks and balances in, 39–40,
    40, 686–687
  Constitutional Convention on,
    31–36
  federal aid to schools, 529
  growth of, 66–70
  implied powers clause, 64, 66

land ownership by, 75
during the New Deal, 50–51,
  69
number of employees in, 66,
  71
press relationships with, 128
Reconstruction Amendments
  and, 48–49, 522–523
school desegregation and,
  527–531, **529, 530,** 534,
  544
separation of powers in, 37–39,
  38, 39
smaller-government movement
  under Reagan, 70
supremacy clause, 64
Federal Housing Authority, 535
Federal Housing Finance Board,
  620
Federalism, 57–85
  under Bush administration,
    81–83
  confederal system, 59
  conflict in, 39–40, 73–75
  in the Constitution, 37
  cooperative, 73
  definition of, 59
  dual, 65–66
  early judicial interpretations,
    65–66
  federal-state relations, 72–73
  federal systems, 59
  government responsiveness and,
    85
  growth of national
    government, 66–70
  instrumental, 72
  in Iraq, 60
  major features in American,
    64–65
  nation-centered *vs.* state-
    centered, 65
  political costs and benefits of,
    60–61
  political culture and diversity,
    62–63
  political interpretations of, 65
  unitary systems, 59–60
The Federalist Papers, 37, 45, 65,
  438. *See also specific issues*
Federalist Paper 10, 60–61, 210,
  287, 683–685
Federalist Paper 39, 65
Federalist Paper 45, 65
Federalist Paper 47, 381
Federalist Paper 51, 686–687
Federalist Paper 65, 366
Federalist Paper 69, 378
Federalists, 43, 211
Federal Open Market Committee
  (FOMC), 577
Federal Register, 371, 381, 410
Federal Reserve System ("the
  Fed"), 416, 577–581
Feingold, Russ, 292
Felons, voting rights of, 246
FEMA (Federal Emergency
  Management Agency). *See*
  Federal Emergency
  Management Agency

The Feminine Mystique (Friedan),
  551
Ferraro, Geraldine, 247, 264
Fifteenth Amendment
  citizenship of African
    Americans, 48, 522
  exclusion of women from, 551
  text of, 680
  voting rights, 240, 524
Fifth Amendment
  Japanese-American internment
    and, 520, 565
  judicial interpretation of, 455
  right to privacy and, 498
  self-incrimination, 494–495
  text of, 679
Fighting words, 476
Filibusters, 333, 340–341, **341,**
  465
Financial disclosure statements,
  310
Fireside chats, 135, 391
First Amendment, 473–485. *See
  also* Civil liberties
  campaign financing and,
    299–300
  in cyberspace, 485
  drafting of, 44
  freedom of association,
    480–481
  freedom of religion, 485–492,
    487, 488, 489, 490, 491
  freedom of speech, 473–480,
    478, 479, 485
  freedom of the press, 481–483
  libel and, 483–484
  obscenity laws, 477, 484–485
  reprinting of Danish cartoons
    of Muhammad and,
    156–157
  right to privacy and, 498
  text of, 679
First Lady, 388–389
FISA (Foreign Intelligence
  Surveillance Act), 446, 511
Fiscal policy, 575–577, 593, 600
Fitzgerald, Ernest, 430
Fitzgerald, Peter, 187
527 groups, 296
Flag burning and desecration, 23,
  267, 479–480
Flat tax, 584–585
Florence Harding, 388
Florida
  age demographics in, 62
  election problems in, 83, 103,
    246, 253
  Schiavo case, **88,** 89–91, 115
  state lobbyists from, 75
  voter registration in, 253
Flowers, Gennifer, 126
Flynt, Larry, 126
Focus groups, 101
FOIA (Freedom of Information
  Act), 199, 410–412, **411,**
  429
FOMC (Federal Open Market
  Committee), 577
Food and Drug Administration
  (FDA), 188, 419–420, 429,
  578

Food stamps, **609,** 613–614
Forbes, Steve, 257
Ford, Betty, 389
Ford, Gerald, 54, 270–271, 366,
  367, **396**
Foreign aid, 105, 666–667
Foreign Intelligence Surveillance
  Act (FISA), 446, 511
Foreign Intelligence Surveillance
  Court, 446, 511
Foreign Intelligence Surveillance
  Court of Review, 446
Foreign policy, 633–669. *See also*
  Cold War
  alliances in, 663–664
  Congress and, 640–642
  containment, 646–651
  defense policy and, 661–663
  defense spending, 663
  détente, 651–652
  economic security and,
    664–667
  foreign aid, 105, 666–667
  Foreign Service officers,
    639–640
  global attitudes towards the
    U.S., 656, **656,** 670
  goals of, 635–636
  intelligence officers, 640
  interest groups and, 642–643
  isolationism, 645–646
  leadership of president in,
    376–378
  lobbyists for foreign
    governments, 643
  merchant diplomacy and
    multilateralism, 653–654,
    656
  in the Middle East, 657–659
    (*See also* Iraq War)
  nuclear proliferation and, 661
  presidential advisers, 637–639
  public opinion and, 643–645
  under Reagan, 652–653
  regime change and preemptive
    war, 654–660
  responsiveness of, 667
  think tanks, 643
  Vietnam War, 648–651, **650**
  world health and, 660–661
Foreign Service officers, 639–640
Foreign student database, 513
Fortas, Abe, 452, 479
Foster, Vince, 126
Founders. *See also specific founders*
  on checks and balances, 39–40,
    40, 686–687
  at the Constitutional
    Convention, 31–36
  distrust of direct democracy by,
    36, 40–41
  on the Electoral College,
    273–274
  experience of, 42
  on foreign policy roles of
    president and Congress,
    640
  hypothetical response to
    initiative process, 80
  motives of, 41–43

on political parties, 210–211, 683–685

on power of national government, 64

on the presidency, 363

problems left unresolved by, 51–52

on representativeness of Congress, 322

on separation of church and state, 486

on separation of powers, 37–39, **38, 39**

on slavery, 34–35, 42

Founding Mothers, 32–33

Fourteenth Amendment

equal protection clause, 48, 51, 522, 527

judicial interpretation of, 455–456

segregation and, 524

sex discrimination and, 551, 553

text of, 680

Fourth Amendment

electronic surveillance and, 494, 511

judicial interpretation of, 455

right to privacy and, 498

text of, 679

Fox News Channel, 142, 145–146, **146**

Frankfurter, Felix, 527

Franking expenses, 328

Franklin, Benjamin

at the Constitutional Convention, 31, 34, **36**

German-language newspaper of, **125**

on representativeness of Congress, 322

on selection of judges, 445

Freedom from Religion Foundation, 178

Freedom of association, 480–481

Freedom of Information Act (FOIA), 199, 410–412, **411,** 429

Freedom of religion, 485–492

establishment clause, 488

free exercise clause, 486–488

religious symbols, 491

school prayers and, 458, 488–490

teaching of evolution and, **109,** 491–492

Freedom of speech, 473–480

demonstrations, 478–479, **478**

fighting words and hate speech, 476–477

Internet and, 485

seditious speech and, 473–476

sexual harassment and, 557

sexual speech, 477–478

symbolic speech, 479–480, **479**

Freedom of the press, 481–483

Free exercise clause, 486–488

Free market, conservatism and, 106

Free speech. *See* Freedom of speech

Free trade, 653, 665

Friedan, Betty, 551

Friedman, Thomas, 593

Friend of the court briefs, 459

Friendster, 271

Frist, Bill

on abolishing filibusters, 341

on Democrats' plan for Iraq, 281

health care financial interests of, 336

in Schiavo case, 89–91, 115

as Senate majority leader, **90,** 334

on "sense of the chamber" measures, 339

on $100 tax rebate, 113

on Trifecta bill, 569

Front organizations, concierge politics and, 309

Fugitive Slave Act, 78

Full faith and credit clause, 78–79

Gallup, George, 98, 100

Gambling interests, 286, 309, 549

Game orientation, 151–152

Ganske, Greg, 267

GAO (Government Accountability Office), 338, 343

Garfield, James, 367

Garner, Tyron, 504

Gates, Bill, Sr., 601

Gates, Henry Louis, 14

Gay Activist Alliance, 179

Gay and Lesbian Advocates and Defenders, 179, **180**

Gay and Lesbian Alliance Against Defamation, 179

Gay Liberation Front, 179

Gay marriage. *See* Same-sex marriages

Gay rights. *See* Homosexual rights

GDP (gross domestic product), 574

General Motors, Los Angeles electric railway and, 578–579

General schedule, of job classifications, 422

A General Theory of Employment, Interest and Money (Keynes), 576

Gephardt, Richard, 257

Germany, inflation in, **575**

Gerry, Elbridge, 243

Gerrymandering. *See also* Redistricting

definition of, 322

incumbent elections and, 278

public opinion and, 114

after Voting Rights Act of 1965, 242–244, **243**

Gettysburg, battle at, 47

Gettysburg Address, 47–48, 688

GI Bill of Rights, 618–619, **618**

Gideon, Clarence Earl, 495–496, **496**

Gillespie, Ed, 273

"Gimme Five," 314

Gingrich, Newt

aggressive style of, 332, 349

earmarking instructions of, 185

Gingrich Republicans, 73, 81

K Street strategy and, 186

task forces under, 338

Gingrich Republicans, 73, 81

Ginsburg, Ruth Bader, **457, 459,** 462

Glasnost, 652

Glenn, John, 301

Globalization

foreign policy and, 643

promoting prosperity abroad, 666–667

tax breaks for job creation and, 621

of U.S. economy, 591–592

worker protection and, 593–594

world health and, 660–661

World Trade Organization, 192, 615, 664–665

Global warming. *See* Climate change

Goddard, Mary Katherine, 32

Going public, 352, 392–393

Goldberg, Arthur, 478

Goldwater, Barry, 217–218, **219,** 265, 534

"Good moral character clause," 241

GOP (Grand Old Party). *See* Republican Party

Gorbachev, Mikhail, 652–653

Gore, Al

appeals to moderates, 221

in debates with Bush, 271

declared winner by media, 103

impact of economy on campaign of, 581

NRA opposition to, 182

popular vote winner, 216, 246, 274–276

relationship with press, 134

support in affluent communities, 220

as vice president, 390

Goreham, Nathaniel, 31

Goss, Porter, 425

Government Accountability Office (GAO), 338, 343

Government corporations, 418

Government spending. *See also* Federal budget

block grants to states, 72, **74**

under Bush administration, 83

during the Cold War, 69

discretionary *vs.* mandatory, 590–591, **591**

estimated for 2007, **591**

in the New Deal, 68, **69**

pork-barrel, 185, 329, 346–347, **347**

in World War II, 69

Graduation ceremonies, prayers at, 489–490

Graft. *See* Corruption

Gramm-Rudman-Hollings (GRH) Act of 1985, 590

Grandfather clause, 241, 526

Grants-in-aid, 68, **69,** 72, 81

Grassley, Charles, 614

Grass roots mobilization, 189–191

Grasstops lobbying, 190

Great Britain

freedom of the press in, 482

in the Iraq War, 655

responsible party government in, 226

timing of primaries and elections, 252

unitary system in, 59

value added tax in, 586

Great Compromise, 34

Great Depression, 49–51, **50,** 68, 573

"Greatest Compromise," 35

"Great Society," 69

Green, Theodore, **334**

Greenhouse, Bunnatine Hayes, 403–405, **404,** 432

Green Party, 209

Greenpeace, 182, 189, 192

Greenspan, Alan, **452,** 578, 580–581, 666

Greider, William, 128

Gridlock, 373

Griswold, Roger, **332**

Griswold v. *Connecticut,* 498

Gross domestic product (GDP), 574

Guantanamo Bay, Cuba, **468**

interrogation techniques at, 509

jurisdiction of U.S. legal system in, 515–516

Korematsu brief on detainees, 565

limitations of *habeus corpus,* 463, 516

origin of prisoners at, 515–516

Supreme Court on, 469–470, 515–516

Guerrilla warfare, 650

Guest workers, 60, 85

Gulf of Tonkin Resolution of 1964, 648–649

Gulf War of 1991. *See* Persian Gulf War

Gun control, 493

Habeas corpus

appeals to federal district courts based on, 445, **445**

Guantanamo detainees and, 463, 469–470, 516

internment of Japanese Americans, 514

provision for suspension during invasion and rebellion, 471

suspension by Lincoln, 379, 382, 514

Hackworth, David, 120

Haddock, "Granny," **249**

Haig, Alexander, 54

Haley, Alex, 13

Halliburton, 311, 403–405, 432

Hamas, 658

Hamilton, Alexander
  on the Commander in Chief,
    378
  at the Constitutional
    Convention, 32, 33, 34
  Federalist Papers, 45
  Federalist party of, 211
  on impeachment, 366
  on the judiciary, 438
  on nation-centered federalism,
    65
  painting of, **210**
Hand, Learned, 464
Hanna, Mark, 288
Hansen, Jim, **424,** 425–426
Harding, Warren, 280, **288**
Harkin, Tom, 189, 278
Harlan, John, 476, 524
Harrisburg Pennsylvanian, 98
Hart, Gary, 102, 259
Hastert, Dennis
  earmarking by, 185
  as Speaker of the House, 310,
    316, 332–333, 340, 349
  strategies to promote tax cuts,
    132
Hatch, Orin, 447
Hatch Act of 1939, 422–423
Hatcher, Richard, 244
Hate speech, 476–477
Hawaii, same-sex marriages in,
    504–505
Hayden, Michael, **345**
Hayes, Rutherford B., 241, 523
Head of government, 368. *See
  also* Presidency
Head of state, 368. *See also*
  Presidency
Head Start programs, 619
Health and Human Services
  Department, 427
Health care
  administrative costs for,
    624–625
  business competitiveness and,
    593
  call for government-financed
    health insurance, 624
  coalitions for and against
    reform, 190, 194
  of Congress members, 327
  federal aid to states for, 79
  health insurance, 599,
    605–607, 623, 630
  health maintenance
    organizations, 616, 623
  for illegal immigrants, 58, 596
  irrationality of existing system,
    622–623
  Medicaid, 590, **591,** 605–606,
    609, 617
  Medicare, 107, 171, 409, **609,**
    616–617
  overall quality of, 622
  pay-or-play health insurance,
    605–607, 630
  pharmaceutical industry and,
    170–171, 623
  preventative care, 625

reasons for high cost of,
    623–625
  state costs from federal drug
    benefit program, 75
  state programs for, 82
Health insurance, 599, 605–607,
    623, 630
Health maintenance organizations
    (HMOs), 616, 623
Hébert, Curtis, 188
Helms, Jesse, 285, 450
Henry, Patrick, 32
Heston, Charlton, 191
Hezbollah, 659
Hill, Anita, 57
Hispanics
  ancestry of, 543
  assimilation of, **546,** 547
  in civil service, 406, **406**
  discrimination against,
    542–547, **546**
  distribution of, 62
  effects of immigration on, 543
  families in poverty, **628**
  interest groups, 178
  meaning of term, 12, 546
  party identification of, **217,**
    220, 230
  in political office, 244
  political participation by, 21
  teen pregnancy rates in, 502
  Voting Rights Act of 1965 and,
    244
HIV, as physical disability, 455
HMOs (health maintenance
    organizations), 616, 623
Hobbes, Thomas, 17
Ho Chi Minh, 648
Holmes, Oliver Wendell, 452,
    456, 477
Holocaust, 104, 151
Homeland Security Department
  administrative layers in, 415
  entertainment liaison in, 128
  establishment of, 337, 371
  funding provisions of, 427
  inefficiency of reforms in, 431
  photo ops for the president in,
    132
  response to hurricane Katrina,
    76–77, **77,** 132, 222–223,
    222
  share of discretionary budget,
    416
  state funding distribution from,
    79, **330**
  subsequent jobs of executives
    in, 310
  unfunded mandates from, 75
  worker protection law
    exemptions in, 427
Home rule, 79
Homestead Act, 608
Homosexual rights. *See also*
    Same-sex marriages
  in adopting children, 506
  conservative Christian attacks
    on, 477
  expressive organizations and,
    480

in the military, 180, 189,
    506–507
  public interest groups, 178–180
  in red *vs.* blue states, **109, 110**
  Supreme Court rulings on,
    504–507
  in the workplace, 506
Hoover, Herbert, **49,** 68, 128,
    576
Horse race coverage, 152
Horton, Willie, in political ad,
    218, **219,** 258
House Appropriations
    Committees, 345
House Ethics Committee, 310
House Interior and Insular Affairs
    Committee, 345
House of Representatives. *See also*
    Congress
  demographics of, 324–325,
    324, 326
  elections, 37
  in Electoral College ties, 272,
    274
  evolution of organization of,
    330–331
  impeachment of Nixon in, 28,
    53, 366
  incumbent elections in, 278,
    279
  leadership positions in,
    331–333
  pay and perks of, 327
  reapportionment, 321–322
  Rules Committee, 262, 330,
    332, 336, 340
Housing
  discrimination in, 534–535,
    538–539
  subsidies for, 619–620
  tax subsidies for
    homeownership, 622
Hughes, Charles Evans, 441, 456,
    461
Hughes, Karen, 387
Human interest stories, 150–151,
    150
Human Rights Campaign, 179
Humphrey, Hubert, 260, 263
Hussein, Saddam
  efforts to link to 9/11 terrorist
    attacks, 101, 105,
    145–146, **146,** 425, 644
  Reagan administration ties to,
    657
Hutchison, Kay Bailey, 171
ICC (Interstate Commerce
    Commission), 416
Identity politics, 10–12, 322–323
Ideology of American people,
    105–107, **107**
Illegal immigrants
  costs of, 74, 596
  "Day Without Immigrants,"
    164, 165–166, 200, 547
  economic impact of, 594
  estimated number of, 594
  lack of enforcement against
    employers of, 595
  location and timing of entry,

7–8, **7, 8**
  lowering of wages by, 594–595
  problems for state governments,
    57–58, 84–85
  statistics on, **8,** 58, 594
Illinois, local government in, 79
Immigration, 5–8. *See also* Illegal
    immigrants
  alien detentions and
    prosecutions, 513
  alien registration and
    interrogation, 513
  bureaucratic complexity, 431
  cultural diversity of immigrants,
    5–6, **16**
  "Day Without Immigrants,"
    164, 165–166, 200
  decline of Republican party
    and, 215
  food stamp programs and, 614
  impact on economy, 592–597
  influence on foreign policy,
    642
  legal restrictions on, 7–8, **7**
  party identification and, 9, 220
  political party welfare and, 213
  state governments and, 57–58,
    84–85
Impeachment
  Clinton, 349, 366, 384
  Johnson, Andrew, 384
  Nixon, 28, 53, 366
  power of, 366
  presidential power and,
    384–385
Imperial Presidency, 380–381
Implied powers clause, 64, 66,
    388
Imus, Don, 127
Incapacitation of president, 367
Income. *See also* Poverty
  African American "underclass,"
    541, 561
  changing distribution of, 106,
    306, **306,** 597–600, **599,**
    629
  of Congress members, **324,**
    327
  court access and, 453
  decreases in, 599
  Equal Pay Act of 1963,
    554–555
  of mothers leaving welfare,
    627–628
  "overclass," 599
  of the president, 365
  ratio of CEOs' pay to workers'
    pay, **627**
  voting patterns based on, **217,**
    276
Income tax, personal, 67
Incumbents
  advantages of, 327–329
  pork barrel funding and, 329
  reelection of, 277–279, **279,**
    296, 302, 322
Independent agencies, 415–418
Independents
  characteristics of, **217**
  ideology of, 221

increase in number of, 224
nomination of, 264
representation in Congress, 326
Independent spending, in
    campaigns, 289, 293–294
Independent Women's Forum,
    176
Indian Removal Act of 1830, 548
Indians. *See* Native Americans
Indirect democracy, 20, 33, 36
Individual citizens, FOIA requests
    by, 430
Individualistic political culture, 62
Individual liberty, 17–18
Individual rights, in liberalism *vs.*
    conservatism, 106. *See also*
    Civil liberties
Inflation, 573–574, **575,** 577
Influence peddling, 310–311
Informal norms, 348–340
Infotainment, 149
Initiative process, 20
Inman, Bobby Ray, 155
Inouye, Daniel, **346**
Instrumental federalism, 72
Insurance industry, government
    protection after 9/11, 174
Intelligence agencies, 640. *See also*
    Central Intelligence Agency
Intelligent design, 492
Interest groups, 165–200. *See also*
    Lobbies
    on appointments to
        government positions, 188
    campaign financing by, 223
    categories of, **170**
    Congressional relationship
        with, 355
    court access and, 453
    declining group memberships,
        168–169
    definition of, 166
    democracy and, 21–22,
        197–198
    foreign policy and, 642–643
    influence on bureaucracy,
        429–431
    judicial nominations and, 436
    in lawmaking process, 340
    political action committees,
        169, 196, 291–296, **295,**
        296, 303
    private, 169–176, **170, 173**
    public, 176–184
    reason for formation of,
        167–168
    resources of, 196–197
    responses to 9/11, 174–175
    responsiveness of government
        and, 198–199
    strategies of, 184
    term limits and, 320
    why people join, 168
Interest rates
    deficits and, 588
    election cycles and, 580–581
    home ownership and, 620
    monetary policy and, 577
Interfaith Alliance, 178
Internet
    blogs, 127–128

campaign fundraising in,
    294–295
citizen comments on proposed
    rules through, 410
e-campaigning, 271–273
electronic surveillance of, 512
federal regulations and laws on,
    23, 410
interest groups and, 167, 169,
    186, 190
news on, **121,** 122–123, 125,
    644–645
obscenity and child
    pornography on, 485
taxation of, 81
tax forms on, 584
Interracial marriages, 12, 541
Interrogations, 508–510, **509,**
    516
Interstate Commerce
    Commission (ICC), 416
Interstate compacts, 78
Interviews, 128
Intifada, 658
Invasion of privacy, 483
Iowa
    caucuses, 259, 261–262
    puritan Sunday laws in, 10
Iran
    Iran-Contra affair, 280, 311,
        363–364, 369, 639
    U.S. installation of Shah in, 657
Iraq War. *See also* Hussein,
    Saddam
    Abu Ghraib prison abuse, **158,**
        509, **509,** 644
    congressional authorization of,
        382
    congressional oversight on,
        317–319, **343,** 344, 358,
        377
    contract-awarding process in,
        303, 311, 403–405, 409,
        432
    criticism by Murtha, **352,**
        633–634, 668–669
    cut-and-run theme, 281
    efforts to link Hussein to 9/11
        terrorist attacks, 101, 105,
        145–146, **146,** 425, 644
    election strategy in 2006 and,
        238–239, 281
    federalism in, 60
    interrogation techniques in,
        509–510, **509**
    leak of identity of Wilson's CIA
        wife, 129–130, **130**
    media prowar bias in, 142,
        145–147
    media restrictions, 139–141,
        139, 644
    "Mission Accomplished" photo
        op, **133**
    as "Operation Iraqi Freedom," 145
    perception of connection with
        al-Qaeda, 146, **146,** 425,
        644
    power of the presidency
        during, 52
    preemption in, 655
    pressure to conform during,

229, 475
    prewar intelligence on,
        129–130, 317–319, 358,
        377, 425
    protests against, 192
    public opinion on, 239
    secret prisons, 660
    sectarian warfare in, 658
    soldiers' blogs, 127
    state troops in, 75
    weapons of mass destruction
        and, 101, 105, 129–130,
        130, 145
Iron triangles, 428
Irrigation projects, 620
Isolationism, 645–646
Israel, 658–659, **659**
Issue votes, 231–232
Jackson, Andrew
    civil service merit system and,
        406, 421
    election of, 211
    growth of political parties
        under, 211–212, **211**
    growth of presidency under,
        364
    judicial appointments, 440
    negative campaigning against,
        269
    swearing in, **439**
Jackson, Jesse, 256, 258
Jackson, Robert, 565
Japanese-American internment,
    69, **518,** 519–520, 565
Jawboning, 579, 581
Jaworski, Leon, 28
Jay, John, 5, 45
Jefferson, Thomas
    on amending the Constitution,
        44
    on equality of rights, 520
    on exclusion of women, 550
    on foreign policy, 636
    on in-chamber congressional
        conduct, 348
    on judicial review, 439–440
    painting of, **210**
    political party of, 211
    on the power to declare war,
        378
    on the presidency, **363,** 364
    purchase of Louisiana
        territories, 67
    secessionist threats under, 61
    on separation of church and
        state, 486, 488
    on slavery, 521
    on small government, 51, 67
    on two-house legislature, 37
Jefferson, William, 309
Jeffersonians (Jeffersonian
    Republicans), 211
Jews
    geographic distribution of, 62
    Holocaust and, 104, 151
    inadvertent votes for Buchanan
        by, 275
    party identification of, **217,**
        230–231
    plausibility of election to
        presidency, 258, **258**

Jim Crow laws, 524
Johnson, Andrew, 366, 384
Johnson, Claudia "Lady Bird,"
    389
Johnson, Frank, 456–457
Johnson, Lyndon Baines
    Civil Rights Act, 19, 69–70,
        217–218, 340, 529
    civil rights under, 533–534
    creation of health-care
        programs, 616
    grants to localities under, 72
    Great Society of, 69
    judicial appointments of, 448
    management style of, 387
    McCarthy voters and, 257
    newscasts watched by, 128
    professional reputation of, 395
    public opinion of, **396**
    schedule of, **385**
    as Senate majority leader, 333,
        334
    Vietnam War and, 311,
        648–649, **649**
    War on Poverty, 613
Johnson, Tim, 267
Joint Chiefs of Staff, 638
Joint committees, 337–338
Jones, Paula, 453, **454,** 557
Joseph, Wayne, **14**
Journalists, protection of sources
    by, 482–483
Judge selection, 445–450
Judicial nominations, **434,**
    435–437, 465–466
Judicial review, 438–440,
    462–463
Judicial Watch, 411–412
Judiciary, 435–466. *See also*
    Federal court system;
    Supreme Court
    access to courts, 453–454
    appellate courts, 444–446, **445,**
        494
    in checks and balances, 40, **40,**
        463
    from Civil War to the Great
        Depression, 440–441
    court jurisdiction, 444–445
    court structure, 444, **445**
    early interpretations of
        federalism, 65–66
    Foreign Intelligence
        Surveillance Court, 446,
        511
    from founding to the Civil War,
        438–440
    from Great Depression to the
        present, 441–443, **442**
    interpretation of Constitution
        by, 45
    judge selection, 445–450
    judge tenure, 450
    judicial review, 438–440,
        462–463
    law making by, 458–459
    military hearings, 515–516
    national supremacy in, 440
    power of the courts, 461–463
    precedents in, 457–458

Judiciary (continued)
proceeding through the courts, 454
responsiveness of, 463–464
restraint and activism in, 456–457, **457**
role in bureaucracy, 428–429
rulings on state laws, 70
state courts, 444
Judiciary Act of 1789, 444
Judiciary Committee, 447, 465
"Juice committees," 335
Juries, women in, 553
Jurisdiction of courts, 444–445
Jury trials, right to, 496–497
Katrina, hurricane
government response to, 76–77, **77**, 222–223, **222**
photo ops at, 132
racial profiling after, **540**
KBR (Kellogg, Brown, Root), 403–405, 432
Kean, Thomas, 412
Kelley, Stanley, 228–229
Kellogg, Brown, Root (KBR), 403–405, 432
Kennedy, Anthony, 461, 462, 486, 504
Kennedy, Edward (Ted), 4, 91, 435
Kennedy, John F.
as Catholic, 258
civil rights under, 533–534
management style of, 387
persona of, 393–394
on preemption, 655
press conferences of, 131
on press coverage of Vietnam, 133
public opinion of, **396**
on school desegregation, 527–528
in televised debates, 158, 270, **270**
wiretapping by, 311
Kennedy, Robert, 319, **386**
Kerner Commission, 542
Kerry, John
appeals to moderates, 221
campaign fundraising by, 290, 293, 294–295
campaign image of, 266
as Catholic, 258
e-campaigning by, 272–273
filibuster against Alito nomination, 465
media stereotype of, 109
military background of, 237–238
negative ads, 124, 268–269
nomination of, 259, **259**
personality of, 231
"Swift Boat Veterans for Truth," 127, 238, 268, 273, 293–294, 296
Keyes, Alan, 319
Keynes, John Maynard, 576
Keynesian economics, 576
Khrushchev, Nikita, **646**

King, Martin Luther, Jr., 195, 311, 531–532
King, Peter, 165
King, Rodney, 542
Kissinger, Henry, 651
Knight Ridder newspaper chain, 124
Know-Nothing Party, 9, 10, 208
Kohl, Herbert, 207
Koop, C. Everett, 424
Koppel, Ted, 148
Korea, Reagan's trip to, 136, **136**
Korean War, 267
Korematsu, Fred, 519–520, 565, **565**
Korematsu v. United States, 519–520, 565
Kosovo, War Powers Resolution and, 382
"K street strategy," 186, 306–307, 309, 311
Ku Klux Klan, 193, 475, 477, 525
Kuwait, 657
Kyle, Jon, 58
Kyoto protocols on global warming, 82, 305, 654
Laissez-faire, 49
Lambda Defense Fund, 179
Land ownership
constitutional provisions for protecting, 44
by federal government, 75
by Japanese Americans, 520
mortgage tax subsidies, 622
by Native Americans, 549
as natural right, 41, 42
violence against African Americans and, 525
westward expansion and, 42
Landsmark, Ted, **530**
Language, national, 16
Latinos, meaning of term, 546. *See also* Hispanics
Law enforcement
confessions, 495
Miranda rights, 495
racial profiling, 539–541, **540, 544**
search and seizure, 494
Lawmaking process, 339–343, 375. *See also* Bills
Lawrence, John, 504
Lawrence v. Texas, 504
Law schools, desegregation of, 526
Lay, Kenneth, 188, 304–305, **304**
Lazio, Rick, 302
Leadership Conference on Civil Rights, 196
League of United Latin American Citizens, 178
Leahy, Patrick, **336, 345,** 437
Leaks to the media, 129–131, **129**
Legislation process. *See* Bills
Legislature. *See* Congress
Lesbian rights. *See* Homosexual rights
Levin, Carl, 174, 191
Lewinsky, Monica, 150–151

Libel, 483–484
Liberalism, 106
Liberals, 106–107, **107**, 108–110, **451**. *See also* Democratic Party and Democrats
Libraries
depository, 410
Library of Congress, 338
USA PATRIOT Act and, 512–513
Library of Congress, 338
Liddy, G. Gordon, 54
Lieberman, Joseph, 258, 281, 343
Limbaugh, Rush, 113, 142
Limited government, 41
Lincoln, Abraham
on abolition of slavery, 46
Gettysburg Address, 47–48, 688
growth of presidency under, 364
nomination of, 213
on popular sovereignty, 19
on power of federal government, 67
suspension of *habeas corpus* by, 379, 382, 514
Line-item veto, 347, 373
Lippmann, Walter, 307
Literary Digest straw poll, 98
Livingston, Robert, 126
Living wage, 555
Living wills, 507
Llewellyn, Yukiko, **518**
Lobbies. *See also* Interest groups
coalition building by, 193–196
definition of, 166
direct lobbying techniques, 185–189
on federal bureaucracy, 429–430
for foreign governments, 643
foreign policy and, 642–643
indirect lobbying techniques, 189–193
pharmaceutical industry, 170–171, 187
resources of, 196–197
in state governments, 80
states and localities as, 75, 78
Lobbyists
to bureaucrats who implement policy, 188
contract, 185
earmarking and, 185
expertise from, 187
giving money, 188
grass roots mobilization by, 189–191
legislation drafted by, 187, 188
litigating in court, 188–189
mobilizing the vote, 191
molding public opinion, 191–192
personal contact by, 186–187
Republican, 186
"revolving door" phenomenon, 310, 336
testifying at hearings, 188
third-party involvement by, 190
use of, in photo ops, 132

Local governments, 75, 78, 79
Local party organizations, 227–228
Locke, John, 17, 41
Lockheed Martin, 191
Log Cabin Republicans, 180
Logrolling, 349–350
Los Angeles County
General Motors and electric railway system of, 578–579
police, 542
schools, 537, **537**
Los Angeles Times, 150
Lott, Trent, 127, 218–219, **218,** 333, 341
Louisiana
hurricane Katrina response, 76–77, **77**, 132, 222–223, **222**
perception of corruption in, 80
Lowi, Theodore, 391
Lugar, Richard, 615
Luntz, Frank, 101
Lynchings of African Americans, 525, **525, 526**
Lyon, Matthew, **332**
MacArthur, Douglas, 382
Machine politics, 213–215
MAD (mutual assured destruction), 647–648, 661
Madison, James
on checks and balances, 39, 287, 686–687
on conflicts of interest, 308
on Congressional pay raises, 45
at the Constitutional Convention, 32–36
drafting of Bill of Rights by, 44, 471
on federalism, 60–61
on human nature, 37
on impeachment, 366
on individual liberty, 18
on interest groups, 166–167
on minority rights, 19
on openness in government, 410
painting of, **61**
on political parties, 210, 683–685
on power to declare war, 378
on property protection, 42
as secretary of state, 439
on separation of church and state, 488
on separation of powers, 37
on state-centered federalism, 65
Maher, Bill, 145
Mahony, Cardinal Roger, 165–166, 200
Maine, domestic partnerships in, 506
Majority leader, House, 331
Majority-minority districts, 243–244
Majority opinions, 461
Majority rule, 19, 61
Mandamus, 439
Mandates, 280
Mandatory spending, 590

Mapp v. *Ohio,* 494
Marbury, William, **438**
Marbury v. *Madison,* **438,** 439
Marine Mammal Protection Act, **187**
Market share, in interest groups, 196
Markup sessions, 335
Marriages. *See also* Same-sex marriages
  abortion restrictions in, 500
  divorce, 63, 558
  encouragement for welfare mothers, 628
  interracial, 12, 541
  polygamy, 63, 487
Marshall, John
  as Chief Justice, **439,** 460
  on judicial review, 438–440
  on Native American tribes, 547
  on supremacy of national authority, 64, 65–66
Marshall, Thurgood, 448, 526–527, 531
Marshall Plan, 647
Maryland, national bank in, 66
Massachusetts
  gerrymandering in, 243
  pay-or-play health insurance plan, 605–607, 630
  same-sex marriages in, 78, 179, **180,** 505–506
Mass media. *See* Media
Maternity leaves, 556, 558
Mattachine Society, 178
McCain, John
  antitobacco legislation of, 189
  campaign financing reform, 292, 294, 295
  campaign tactics used against, 102, 177
  on cruel treatment of prisoners, 510
  fundraising by, 301
  on guest worker program, 58
  on influence of money, 313
  on media regulation, 124
  on military-industrial complex, 663
McCain-Feingold Act, 292, 294, 295–296
McCarthy, Eugene, 256, 257
McCarthy, Joseph, 474–475, **475**
McCarthyism, 474–475, **475**
McClellan, George, **378**
McCorvey, Norma, 498–499, **499**
McCulloch v. *Maryland,* 66, 440
McDade, Joseph, 311
McKinley, William, 214, 248
McNamara, Robert, 481, 649–650
Means tests, 611
Media. *See also* Television
  atomization of, 124–128
  bias against candidates and officials, 144
  bias toward issues, 144–147
  campaign advertising, 267–269
  candidate endorsements by, 98

censorship of, 132, 148
  in the civil rights movement, 532–533
  commercial bias in, 148–153, **150**
  committee preference and, 335
  concentration of, 122–124
  congressional use of, 279, 329, 351–352
  decreasing interest in news and, 159–160
  election bias, 143–144
  emphasizing divisions within the country, 110
  events, 269–270
  free campaign time proposals, 297–298
  fringe, 127
  game orientation in, 151–152
  going public, 352, 392–393
  growth of exposure to, 120–122, **121, 122**
  impact on political parties and elections, 154–158
  impact on public opinion, 158–159
  impact on the public agenda, 153–154
  incumbents and, 329
  Iraq War coverage, 64, **133,** 139–142, **139,** 145–147, 377–378
  local news, 151
  mainstream bias, 142–143
  muckrakers, 288
  in nominating process, 257
  "objectivity" in, 141
  party conventions and, 263–264
  political bias in, 141–148, **146**
  political socialization and, 94, 97
  press conferences, 131, 137
  race in, 149
  radio news, 121, **121,** 125, 135
  relationship with Bill Clinton, 136–137
  relationship with Congress, 138
  relationship with George W. Bush, 133, 137–138
  relationship with politicians, 128–132, **129**
  relationship with Ronald Reagan, 135–136
  relationship with the military, 139–141, **139**
  relationship with the Supreme Court, 138–139
  responsiveness of, 159–160
  sexual speech on, 477–478
  talk shows, 125, 126, 142, 158, 294
  use of polls by, 102–104
  violence in, 151
Media events, 131–132
Media Fund, 169, 293, 296
Media malaise, 159
Medicaid
  coverage of, 617
  direct payments for, **609**

for employees without health insurance, 606
  increased state costs for, 605, 617
  as mandatory spending item, 590, **591**
Medicare
  accomplishments of, 616–617
  administrative costs of, 409
  Bush on, 605
  direct payments for, **609**
  fees in, 616
  fraud by doctors and HMOs, 616
  lack of accurate cost figures, 430
  prescription drug program, 107, 171, 198, 336, 622
Mehlman, Ken, 227
Men
  discrimination against, 559–560
  young black, 542
Mentally retarded, execution of, 498
Meredith, James, 527–528
Merit system, in government hiring, 215, 222–223, 421, 424
Mexican American Legal Defense and Educational Fund, 178
Michigan, shortage of jobs for welfare mothers in, 627–628
Middle East foreign policy, 657–659, **659.** *See also specific countries*
Midwest, political culture in, 62
Miers, Harriet, 436–437
Military
  asymmetrical warfare, 662–663
  Commander in Chief of, 378–382, **378**
  defense strategy, 661–663
  draft, 559
  GI Bill of Rights, 618–619, **618**
  homosexuals in, 180, 189, 506–507
  media relationship with, 139–141, **139**
  military hearings, 515–516
  outsourcing military functions, 663
  racial integration in, 217
  rivalry between White House and Congress over, 640
  Rumsfeld's changes to, 662–663
  veterans benefits, **609,** 616, 617
Military hearings, 515–516
Military-industrial complex, 363, 663
Military spending, under Reagan, 72
Mill, John Stuart, 473
Miller, George, 187
Minimum wage increase, 569–571, 601
Minorities. *See also specific minorities*
  in Congress, 324–325, **324**

as judges, 448
  as national constituencies, 323
  redistricting and, 322
  teen pregnancy rates in, 502
Minority leader, House, 331
Minority rights, 19
Minutemen, **58,** 200
Miranda, Ernesto, 495, **495**
Miranda rights, 495
Miranda v. *Arizona,* 495
"Mischiefs of faction," 61
"Misery index," 574
Mississippi
  African American population in, 62
  civil rights movement in, **531, 533**
Missouri Compromise of 1820, 440
Mixed economies, 572
Mobility, voter turnout and, 252
Moderates, 107
Mommy track, 555
Mondale, Walter, 389–390
Monetarists, 577
Monetary policy, 577–578
Money. *See also* Economic policy; Economy
  under the Articles of Confederation, **29,** 30
  Federal Reserve System, 416, 577–581
  fiscal policy, 575–577, 593, 600
  influence over politics, 285–314 (See also Campaign finance; Campaign fundraising)
  monetary policy, 577–578
Monroe, James, 645
Monroe Doctrine, 645, 654
Montesquieu, Charles de, 41
Montgomery bus boycott, 194–195, **194,** 531–532
Moore, Michael, 142
Moral issues, influences on, 302
Moralistic political culture, 62
Morris, Gouverneur, 34
Mortgage interest deductions, 622
Motor voter law, 253–254
MoveOn.org, 169, 190, **191,** 254, 296
Moyers, Bill, 174
Moynihan, Daniel Patrick, 104
MSNBC, 145
Muckrakers, 288
Mueller, Robert, 430
Mulattoes, 13, 528
Multiculturalism. *See* Diversity
Multilateralism, 653–654, 656
Multiparty systems, 206
Multiple-issue interest groups, 176–182. *See also* Public interest groups
Murray, Patty, 569–571, 601
Murtha, John, **352,** 633–634, 668–669
Muskie, Edmund, 259
Muslims
  Barbary pirates, 30

Muslims (continued)
diversity in American, 12
after 9/11, 508
public interest groups, 176
response to Danish cartoons, 156–157, **157**
Mutual assured destruction (MAD), 647–648, 661
NAACP (National Association for the Advancement of Colored People), 178, 196, 453
NAB (National Association of Broadcasters), 298
Nader, Ralph
campaign of, 144, 209–210, 264
influence on consumer safety, 199
on local television news, 151
in Public Citizen, 187, 188
NAFTA (North American Free Trade Agreement), 100, 144–145, 207, 644, 665
The Naked Truth, 151
Napolitano, Janet, 57–58, 84–85
Narrowcasting, 125, 142
NASA (National Aeronautics and Space Administration), 415, 426
Nast, Thomas, **211**
National Abortion Rights Action League, 183
National Archives, Watergate tapes in, 54
National Association for the Advancement of Colored People (NAACP), 178, 196, 453, 526, 529
National Association of Broadcasters (NAB), 298
National Association of Manufacturers, 190
National Audubon Society, 182
National bank, 66
National Center for Public Policy Research, 309
National committees
Democratic National Committee, **202,** 203–204, 227, 234
Republican National Committee, 227, 255
National Conference of State Legislatures (NCSL), 75
National conventions, 262–264, **263**
National Council of Churches, 176
National Council to Control Handguns, 197
National debt, 586–591, **589, 591,** 626
National Farmers' Union, 173
National Federation of Republican Women, 176
National government, 59. *See also* Federal government
National Governors Association (NGA), 78
National Guard, 75–78, 84–85

National Highway Traffic Safety Administration, 188
National Indian Gaming Association, 549
National Institutes of Health, 420
National Intelligence Agency (NIA), 640
National League of Cities, 75
National Museum of the American Indian, **12**
National Organization for Women (NOW), 176, 551
National party chair, 227
National Railroad Passenger Corporation (Amtrak), 418
National Rifle Association (NRA), 168, 182–183, 189, 191, 493
National Right to Life Committee, 183
National sales tax, 585–586
National Security Agency (NSA)
congressional oversight of, 358, 431
foreign policy and, 638
secrecy of, 640
wiretapping by, 483, 510–511
National Smokers Alliance, 189
National Taxpayers Union, 174–175, 176
National Women's Party, 246
National Women's Political Caucus, 176
Nation-centered federalism, 65
Native Americans
assimilation and citizenship of, 548
Bureau of Indian Affairs, 548–549
in civil service, 406, **406**
Constitutional Convention on, 34
cultural diversity among, 5–6
discrimination against, 547–550
distribution of, **548**
DNA testing of, 14–15
freedom to exercise religion, 487, **487**
gambling interests of, 286, 309–310, 314, 549
interest groups, 178–179
National Museum of the American Indian, **12**
number of recognized tribes, 6
separation policy, 547–548
state-tribe relations, 79
tribal restoration, 548–550
voting rights of, 11, 548
Nativity scenes, 491
NATO (North Atlantic Treaty Organization), 647, 656, 663–664
Natural disasters, 76–77
Natural Resources Defense Council, 182, 188, 189
Natural rights, 41
Navy Times, 120
NBC, 123, 124, **146**
NCSL (National Conference of State Legislatures), 75

"Necessary and proper" laws, 64, 66
Negative campaign ads
against Andrew Jackson, 269
by George H. W. Bush, 218, **219, 258**
by George W. Bush, 127, 238, 268–269, 273, 293–294, 296
impacts on campaigns, 103–104
by John Adams, 269
Nelson, Ben, 203
Neustadt, Richard, 395–396
Neutral competence, 421–423, 424–427, **424**
Nevada
legalized prostitution in, 63
proposed nuclear waste storage in, 75
RNC discarding of Democrat voter registration in, 255
New Deal
coalition during, 215–216
court decisions on, 49–50, 441, 458–459
decline of coalition, 219–220
growth of federal government in, 50–51, **69**
policies of, 68, **68**
New Deal coalition, 215–216
New England. *See also specific states*
moralistic political culture in, 62
secessionist threats by, 61
New Hampshire primary, 261–262
New Jersey, domestic partnerships in, 506
New Jersey Plan, 34
New Mexico
Hispanic population in, 62
illegal immigrants in, 84
New Orleans, hurricane Katrina in, 76–77, **77,** 132, 222–223, **222**
New Paradigm, 380–381
News media. *See* Media
Newspapers, 121, 123. *See also* Media
Newsweek, 119–120, 120, 161
Newton, Isaac, 41–42
New York Herald, 98
New York Post, 141
New York Times, 133, 140, 141, 147, 165
New York Times v. *Sullivan,* 483
NGA (National Governors Association), 78
Ngo Dinh Diem, 648
NIA (National Intelligence Agency), 640
Nickles, Don, 188
Nineteenth Amendment, 246, 681
9/11/2001 terrorist attacks
Bush's call to Americans after, 99, 137, **138**
cooperative federalism after, 73

expansion of presidential powers after, 380
FEMA assistance after, 76
impact on elections, 267
interest group responses to, 174–175, 187
9/11 commission, 412, 431
pressure to conform after, 475
public opinion of Bush after, 99, 394
solidification of Republican Party after, 221, 228–229
strategy to link Iraq with, 101, 105, 145–146, **146,** 425, 644
untranslated messages from al-Qaeda, 129
Ninth Amendment, 44, 551, 679
Nixon, Richard M.
awkwardness of, **132**
civil rights under, 218
in debates with Kennedy, 270, **270**
downsizing efforts of, 414
foreign policy of, 638, 651, **652**
Imperial Presidency of, 380
judicial appointments of, 448
management style of, 72, 387
pardon of, 54, 366
Pentagon Papers and, 481–482
public opinion of, **396**
relationship with press, 133
resignation of, 54
Vietnam War, 649
vote to impeach, 28, 52, 366
Watergate scandal, 27–28, 53–54, 280, 289, 311
wiretapping by, 446
No Child Left Behind program, 74–75, 617
Nominations, presidential, 256–264
national conventions, 262–264, **263**
procedure for, 256–259
reforms in, 260–262
role of political parties in, 223, 225
state caucuses and conventions, 259
vice-presidential, 264
who runs and why, 256
Noonan, Peggy, 91
Norquist, Grover, 285, 286, 309
North American Free Trade Agreement (NAFTA), 100, 144–145, 207, 644, 665
North Atlantic Treaty Organization (NATO), 647, 656, 663–664
North Carolina
civil rights movement in, **529, 532**
gerrymandering in, 243, **243**
NOW (National Organization for Women), 176, 551
NRA (National Rifle Association), 168, 182–183, 189, 191, 493

NSA. *See* National Security Agency
Nuclear waste storage, 75
Nuclear weapons
  in Cold War arms race, 652, 654, 661–662, 662
  as deterrence, 647–648
  nuclear proliferation, 661, **662**
  Strategic Defense Initiative, 652
Obama, Barack, 110, 244, 258, **323**, 335
Obscenity laws, 477, 484–485
O'Connor, Sandra Day
  on abortion restrictions, 437, 500
  on affirmative action, 562
  as first woman on Supreme Court, 449
  nomination of, 447, 448
  on religion in schools, 490
  selecting nominee to replace, 83, 436, 437
Octoroons, 13
Offensive speech, 476
Office of Management and Budget (OMB)
  agency evaluation by, 414
  budgetary politics in, 587–588
  creation of, 344, 386, 426
  role in budget development, 372, 576
  role in fiscal policy, 576
Office of Personnel Management (OPM), 422
Office of Safety and Health Administration (OSHA), 420
Office of Technology Assessment, 338
Office of the Vice President, 387–390
Offshoring, 593–594, 621
Ohio, election problems in, 248, 253, 254, 255
Oil and gas companies. *See also* Enron
  consumer prices and corporate profits, 112–113
  deregulation of, 302–303, 305
  distortion of global warming data by, 191
  in era of "robber barons," 288
  Teapot Dome scandal, 280, **288**, 289
Oklahoma City federal building bombing, 76, 193, 394, 475
Old Age Survivors Disability and Health Insurance Program, 609. *See also* Social Security
OMB. *See* Office of Management and Budget
O'Neill, Paul, 581
O'Neill, Tip, 213, 286, 634
Operation Rescue, 502
OPM (Office of Personnel Management), 422
Oregon, "right to die" law in, 83, 507
O'Reilly Factor, 165
Osborne, Tom, 154

OSHA (Office of Safety and Health Administration), 420
Oslo Accords, 658
Outsourcing, 593–594, 621, 663
"Overclass," 599
Overseas ballots, 275–276
Oversight, congressional, 317–319, 343–348, **343**, 358
Packing votes, 242
PACs. *See* Political action committees
Pakistan, formation of, 60
Palestinians, 658, **659**
Pardons, presidential, 54, 303, 366, 369
Parks, Rosa, 194–195, **194**, 531–532
"Partial-birth abortion," 501, **501**
Participation in government, 20–22, 422–423. *See also* Voter turnout
Party caucuses, 331
Party identification, 216–222. *See also* Political parties
  "acting for" representation and, 326
  affluence and, 220
  current realignment, 106, 221–222
  decline in, 219–220, 224
  demographics of, **217**, 220
  influence on voting, 230–231
  Republican racial strategy and, 216–219, **218, 219**
Party system, 206
Pataki, George, 277
Paternity leaves, 556, 558
Paterson, William, 34
Patriot Act. *See* USA PATRIOT Act
Patriotism, 99, 146–147
Patronage jobs, 213–214, 222–223, **222**, 421
Paul, Alice, 245–246
Paygo rule, 348, 590
PBS/NPR, **146**
Pearl harbor, Japanese attack on, 99
Pell grants, 617
Pelosi, Nancy
  on DNC campaign strategy for 2004, 204
  fundraising abilities of, 351
  on Iraq war policy, 668
  as Speaker of the House, **316**, 331
Pendleton Act of 1883, 421–422
Pennsylvania, shortage of jobs for welfare mothers, 627–628
Pensions, for career servicemen and servicewomen, 616
Pentagon Papers, 481–482
People for the American Way, **436**
Permanent campaign, 276–277
Perot, Ross, 209, 210, 264, 405
Persian Gulf War
  background on, 657
  congressional authorization of, 382

direct presidential appeal for, 392
  media coverage of, 145
  public opinion and, 267, 644
Personal contacts, lobbying through, 186–187
Peyote, in Native American religion, 487, **487**
Pharmaceutical industry, 170–171, 187
Philadelphia Bible riots of 1843, **9**, 10
Phillips, Kevin, 216
Phillips Petroleum, 197
Photo opportunities, 131–132
Phue, Kim, **650**
Physicians for Social Responsibility, 189
Pirates, 30
Pitt, Harvey, 423
Plame, Valerie, 130, **130**
Plan B pill, 503
Planned Parenthood, 183
Platform committee, 262–263
Plea bargains, 498
Pledge of Allegiance, 178, 491
Plessy, Homer Adolph, 524
Plessy v. *Ferguson,* 524, 526
Plunkitt, George Washington, 213–215, **215**, 287
Pocket veto, 375
Podcasts, 271
Police. *See* Law enforcement
Policy implementation, 418
Political action committees (PACs)
  coordination among, 196
  dominance of business in, 295, **295**
  fundraising for members of Congress by, 188, 291–292
  influence on votes, 303
  of members of Congress, 351
  operation of, 169
  recipients of, 295–296, **296**
  unlimited spending in issues advocacy, 293–294
Political bias, 141–148
  in the advocacy media, 141–142
  against all candidates and officials, 144
  in elections, 143–144
  in the mainstream media, 142–143
  perceptions of, 147–148
  role of media in, 146, **146**
  toward issues, 144–147
Political culture, 12–17
  definition of, 12
  federalism and, 62–63
  geographic differences in, 62–63, **63**
  learning, 14–17
  mobility and, 62
  responsiveness of state governments and, 79–80
  significance of, 14
Politically Incorrect (Maher), 145

Political parties, 203–234. *See also specific parties*
  birth of, 211
  campaign fundraising by, 227, 234
  components of, 204–205, **205**
  congressional campaigns and, 278–279
  continuing importance of, 224–226
  decline of, 207, 222–224, **223, 224**
  development of mass parties, 211–212, **211**
  evolution of, **212**
  Founders and, 210–211, 683–685
  ideological differences in, 220–222
  impact of media on, 154
  machine politics and, 213–215
  minor, 208–210
  moderation trend in, 207–208, **208**
  national conventions, 262–264, **263**
  organization of, 226–228
  party identification, 216–222, **217**
  platforms, 262–263
  policy influence by, 226
  popular control of government and, 204–206
  president as leader of, 370, 382–383, **383**
  Progressive movement and, 214–215, 248–249
  realignments, 106, 212, 216–218, 221–222
  redistricting and, 322
  responsiveness of government and, 232–233
  rise of the Democrats, 215–216
  rise of the Republicans, 213–214
  role in governance, 225–226
  role in shaping votes, 229–232
  third parties, 208–210, 264
  two-party system, 206–207
  voter mobilization by, 254–255, **255**
Political socialization
  agents of, 94–97, **95, 97**
  of different generations, 112
  impact of, 97
  process of, 91–93
Politics, definition of, 5
Polls or polling, 97–104. *See also* Public opinion
  confusing language in, 104
  emergence of scientific polling, 98, 100
  ethical dilemmas from results of, 101–102
  exit polls, 103–104
  negative impacts on campaigns, 103–104
  push polls, 102
  straw polls, 98

Polls or polling (continued)
   use by media, 102–104
   use by politicians, 100–102
   use of telephones in, 98, 102
Poll taxes, 241
Polygamy, 63, 487
Population growth, 596
Populists, 208–209
Pork-barrel spending, 185, 329, 346–347, **347**
Pornography, 484–485
Postal Service, 409, 417, 418
Poverty
   age profile of poor, **612**
   eligibility for social welfare programs, 611
   families in, 612–613, **612, 628**
   health care and, 617
   immobility and, 10
   income distribution and, 306, **306,** 597–600, **599**
   living wage laws and, 555
   media bias and, 145
   working poor, 613
Powell, Colin, 13, 258, 387, 651, 654
Powell doctrine, 651
Power, in democracies, 22–23
PR (proportional representation), 206–207
Preemption, 65
Pregnancy Discrimination Act of 1978, 554
Prescription drugs, 107, 170–171, 187, 198, 336, 622
Presidency, 361–399
   administrative powers of, 371–372, 423, 426–428
   agenda setting by, 374–375
   appointments of, 369–370, 426–427
   areas of responsibility, 367–368
   cabinet, 367, 415, **416**
   campaign fundraising in, 290–291
   changes in powers of, 383–385
   in checks and balances, 40, **40,** 463
   as chief diplomat, 376–378
   as chief executive, 369–376
   as commander in chief, 378–382, **378, 379**
   development and growth of, 364–367
   direct public appeals in, 392–393
   election and term of, 37, **38,** 260–261 (See also Elections)
   eligibility requirements, 365
   ethical behavior regulation, 310
   Executive Office of the President, 373, 385–386, 426
   expansion under George W. Bush, 81, 380–381
   federal-state relations and, 72–73
   First Lady, 388–389
   as fiscal leader, 372–373
   foreign policy role of,

   376–378, 637–639
   as head of government and head of state, 368–369
   impeachment, 28, 53, 349, 366, 384–385
   Imperial Presidency, 380–381
   incapacitation of president, 367
   influence of donors on, 303
   judicial appointments of, 447–448, 452
   as legislative leader, 373–376, **374**
   managerial approach in, 72
   Office of the Vice President, 387–390
   openness in government and, 410–411
   as party leader, 370, 382–383, **383**
   pay and perks, 365
   personal, 390–395
   power to reorganize bureaucracy, 371
   professional reputation, 395–398
   public opinion and, 394–395, **396**
   ranking presidents, **397**
   removal power of, 370–371
   responsiveness of, 398
   role in federal budget, 372–373
   signing statements of, 381
   spectacle, 393–394, **394**
   staff, 385–390
   tenure and succession, 366–367
   unitary executive, 380–381, 428
   veto power of, 342, 375
   War Powers Resolution, 382
   in wartime, 379, 382
   White House Office, 386–387
Presidential preference primaries, 260–261. See also Primaries
Presidential press conferences, 131
Presidential Succession Act, 367
President pro tempore, Senate, 333, 367
Press. See Media
Press conferences, 131, 137
Presumption of innocence, 492
Price supports, 614
Primaries
   dates of, 261–262
   delegate selection reform, 260–261
   direct, 215
   evolution of permanent campaigns and, 277
   impact of money on, 301
   role in nominating process, 257, 259–261
   voter turnout for general election and, 252
   white, 241
Prior restraint, 481–482
Privacy, right to, 498–508
   abortion and, 498–503
   birth control and, 498, 503–504
   electronic surveillance and,

   511, 512–513
   homosexuality and, 504–507
   right of free press and, 483
   right to die laws and, 507–508
   searches and seizures, 494
   USA PATRIOT Act and, 131, 358, 483, 511–514
Private interest groups, 169–176
   agriculture, 173, 176
   business, 169–171, **170**
   labor, 171–173
Private schools, desegregation of, 534
Pro-choice movement, **499**
Productivity, 574
The Progressive, 481–482
Progressive reforms, 214–215, **216,** 248–249, 288, 331
Progressive taxes, 582–583
Prohibition Party, 208
Pro-life movement, 502–504
Proportional representation (PR), 206–207
Protectionism, 653, 665
Protest, 189, 192–193
"Psychology of localism," 61
Public Citizen, 187, 188
Public employees. See Federal employees
Public forum, 478
Public image, of interest groups, 196–197
Public interest groups, 176–184
   environmental groups, 180, 182
   gay and lesbian rights, 178–180
   for the old and young, 180
   racial and ethnic groups, 178–179
   religious groups, 176–178
   women's groups, 176, **177**
Public officials, libel laws and, 483–484
Public opinion, 89–116. See also Polls or polling
   on abortions, 93, **500**
   adult socialization and, 97
   on campaign finance system, **298**
   on Congress, 114, 353, 356
   cynicism about government, 307–308, **307**
   definition of, 90
   education and, 94–96
   family and, 94
   focus groups and, 101
   foreign policy and, 643–645
   government responsiveness and, 114, 116
   ideology and, 105–107, **107**
   impact of 9/11 on, 99
   interest group influence on, 191–192
   knowledge and information and, 104–105
   leaks and, 131
   measurement of, 97–104
   media impact on, 97, 158–159
   peers and, 96
   political socialization and, 91–93

   on presidents, 91, **92,** 239, 394–395, **396**
   on race, 111–114, **111**
   in red *vs.* blue states, 107–111, **108, 109, 110**
   on same-sex marriage, 93, **93**
   on Social Security changes, 362
   on the Supreme Court, 437–438
   in the Terri Schiavo case, 89–91
   on token tax rebate, 113
   on unions, 172
   on the Vietnam War, 650
   on women in the workplace, **556**
   world opinion on the U.S., 656, **656,** 660, 664
Public schools. See also Education
   busing for racial balance, 529–531, **530**
   continuing discrimination in, 535–538, **536, 537, 538**
   desegregation of, 526–531, **529, 530,** 534, 544
   founding of, 15–16
   gays and lesbians in, 179
   illegal immigrants in, 596
   inequality of funding for, 536–538, 544
   patriotic rituals in, 95
   religion in, 10, 458, 488–490
   segregation in, 524
   subsidized school lunches, 614
   teaching of evolution in, **109,** 492
Publius, 45
Puritan Sunday laws, 10
Push polls, 102
Quadroon, 13
Quayle, Dan, 135
Quid pro quo harassment, 557
Rabin, Yitzhak, 658
Race discrimination, 521–542. *See also* Slavery
   affirmative action policies, 11, 560–563
   against African Americans, 526–535, **529, 530, 531, 532, 533, 536**
   "brown bag test," 528
   busing and, 529–531, **530**
   civil rights movement in Congress, 533–535
   civil rights movement in the streets, 531–533, **531, 532, 533**
   continuing, 535–542
   denial of voting rights, 524
   in employment, 534, 538
   health care and, 623
   against Hispanics, 542–547, **546**
   in housing, 534–535, 538–539
   lynchings of African Americans, 525, **525, 526**
   against Native Americans, 547–550
   racial profiling by police, 539–541, **540,** 544
   Reconstruction and, 522–523
   school desegregation, 526–531,

529, 530, 534, 544
in schools, 535–538, **536, 537, 538**
second-generation, 538
segregation and, 523–524
slavery as, 521–522
violence against African Americans, 193, 241, 525, **525, 526**
worth of white skin, 539
Race issues
interest groups, 178–179
public opinion on, 111–114, **111**
in Republican Party, 217–219, **218, 219**
Racial gerrymandering, 242–244, **243**
Racial identity, DNA testing and, 11–12, 13–15
Racial profiling, 539–541, **540,** 544
Radical Republicans, 48, 51
Radio
news, 121, **121,** 125, 135
talk shows, 125, 126, 142, 158, 294
Raging Grannies, 192
Railroad magnates, 288
Rally events, 394
Randolph, Edmund, 29, 34
Rangel, Charles, 668
Rankin, Jeannette, 247
Rasul v. Bush, 515
Rather, Dan, 131, 145, 148
Reagan, Nancy, 389
Reagan, Ronald
AIDS response by, 424
blue-collar worker support for, 220
on civil rights, 534
in debate with Carter, 270–271
Equal Rights Amendment opposition by, 553
foreign policy of, 652
goals and vision of, 397
government size under, 70–73, 405, 414
Iran-Contra affair, 280, 311, 363–364, 369, 639
judicial appointments of, 50, 448
management style of, 387
media image of, 155
nomination of, 259
public opinion of, 395, **395, 396**
reason for running, 256
relationship with Congress, **374,** 375
relationship with the media, 135–136
small-government rebellion of, 70–71
on states' rights, 218
on supply-side economics, 576
veto of Fairness Doctrine in broadcasting, 142
on "welfare queens," 218
Real ID law of 2005, 75

Realignments, 106, 212, 216–219, 221–222
Reapportionment, 321–322
Recession, 573–574
Reconstruction
black legislators after the Civil War, 240–241, **240**
end of, 241, 523
Reconstruction Amendments, 48–49, 240, 522–523
voting rights of blacks during, 240–241, **240**
Redistricting, 322. *See also* Gerrymandering
Redlining, 535
Red Scare, 473
Red states, 107–111, **108, 110,** 276
Reed, Ralph, 285–286, 309, 314
Reed, Thomas, 330–331
Reform Party, 210
Regressive taxes, 582–583, 585–586
Regulation, by federal bureaucracy, 419–420
Regulatory boards, 415–418, 419–420
Rehnquist, William, 442, **443,** 460, 480, 534
Rehnquist Court
on abortion, 500–501
accomplishments of, 442–443, **443,** 457, **457**
activist judges in, **457**
on affirmative action, 562
on busing of students, 531
on capital punishment, 497–498
in election of 2000, 228, 457
on homosexual rights, 504
on prior restraint, 482
on religious symbols, 491
on right to counsel, 496
on right to die, 507
on school prayer, 489–490
on self-incrimination, 495
Reich, Robert, 174
Reid, Harry, 204, 278, 318, 334, 668
Religion. *See also* Catholic Church and Catholics; Christian conservatives; Freedom of religion; Muslims
church and state separation, 486
direct restrictions on, 486
establishment clause, 488, 492
free exercise clause, 486–488
geographic distribution of, 62
indirect restrictions on, 486–488, **487, 488**
as interest groups, 165–166
members of Congress and, 324, **324**
party identity and, 220, 221
public interest groups, 176–178
in red *vs.* blue states, 108
religious tests for voting, 240
in schools, 10, 458, 488–490

state religions, 9–10
Religious diversity, 9–10
Religious Right, 221. *See also* Christian conservatives
Religious symbols, 491
Renditions, 510
Reporters, protection of sources by, 482–483
Representativeness, 322–326, **324, 326**
Representatives. *See* House of Representatives
Reproductive rights, **109,** 183, 498, 503–505. *See also* Abortion
Republican National Committee, 227, 255
Republican Party and Republicans
campaign fundraising by, 227, 297
characteristics of Republicans, **217**
Congressional voting unity, 225, 226, **227**
corruption in, 311
"crafted talk" by, 101
delegate selection process, 261
discouraging voters of other parties, 255
donor demographics, 297, 308, **308**
earmarking by, 185
economic policies of, 580
in election of 2006, 237–238, 281
Enron's donations to, 305
Equal Rights Amendment opposition, 553
foreign policy tendencies, 641
founding of, 210
geographic patterns in recent elections, 107–108, **108**
gerrymandering and, 243–244
House representation by, **326**
ideology and, 220–222
"K street strategy," 186, 306–307, 309, 311
on Murtha's criticism of Iraq War, 633–634
organization of, 226–228
partisan voting by, 226
political action committee contributions to, 295
present realignment of, 106, 221–222
racial strategy of, 217–219, **218, 219,** 258
during Reconstruction, 48, 217
rise of, 213–214
in the South, 217–219
"talking points" sent to conservative media, 142
use of war on terrorism in partisanship, 229, 267
voter turnout and, 254–255
Republic form of government, 20, 33, 36, 59–60
Research, 420

Responsible party government, 226
Responsiveness of government
bureaucracy and, 431
in civil liberties, 514
Congress and, 356–357
Constitution and, 51–52
courts and, 463–464, 514
economic policy and, 600
elections and, 280
federalism and, 85
foreign policy and, 667
in granting civil rights, 563–564
influence of money and, 312–313
interest groups and, 198–199
media and, 146, 159–160
political parties and, 232–233
presidency and, 398
public opinion and, 114, 116
during riots from Danish cartoons of Muhammad, 156–157
social welfare programs and, 629
of state governments, 79–80
voters' influence, 23
Restrained judges, 456, **457**
Restrictive covenants, 534
Retirement, for career servicemen and servicewomen, 616
Retrospective voting, 232, **232**
Revenue sharing, 72
Revolutionary War, slavery and, 521
"Revolving door" phenomenon, 310, 336
Rhode Island, religious freedom in, 9
Rich, Denise, 303
Richardson, Bill, 84
Right to counsel, 495–496
Right to die
assisted suicide, 507–508
Oregon law on, 83, 507–508
Supreme Court rulings on, 507–508
Terri Schiavo case, **88,** 89–91, 115
Right to Life, 183
Right to privacy. *See* Privacy, right to
Right Words (Luntz), 101
Robber barons, 288
Roberts, John, 23, 83, 436, 437, **447**
Roberts, Owen, 441, 458–459
Roberts, Pat, 317–319, **318,** 358
Roberts Court, 443, **443**
Robertson, Pat, 91, 177, 257, 285
Robinson, Jo Ann, 194
Rockefeller, Jay, 174, 317–318, 358
Rockefeller, John D., 288
Rockefeller, Nelson, 367
Rock the Vote, 251

Roe v. Wade, 183, 453, 462, 499. *See also* Abortion
Roe v. Wade for Men, 560
Rogers, Edith Nourse, 618
Roman Catholic Church. *See* Catholic Church and Catholics
Romney, Mitt, 277, 605–607, **606,** 630
Roosevelt, Eleanor, 388–389
Roosevelt, Franklin
  on civil rights, 217
  expansion of role of federal government, 67–68
  faulty polling during election of, 98, 100
  fireside chats, 135, 391
  fiscal policy of, 576
  foreign policy of, **376, 377**
  goals and vision of, 397
  growth of presidency under, 365
  judicial appointments of, 448
  liberalism and, 106
  management style of, 387
  media portrayal of disability, 154, **155**
  New Deal, 49–51, 68, **68,** 215–216
  photograph of, **68**
  at the political convention, 263
  press conferences of, 131, 135
  relationship with Congress, 375
  Supreme Court and, 49–50, 70, 280, 441, 458–459
  vetoes by, 375
  World War II, 69
Roosevelt, Theodore
  as "American-American," 13
  on civil service, 424
  on dissent, 669
  election of senators, 70
  growth of presidency under, 364–365
  judicial appointments of, 448, 452
  photographs of, **67, 369**
  press conferences of, 131
  on role of federal government, 67
  trust breaking by, 289, **289**
Roots (Haley), 13
Rostenkowski, Daniel, 311
Rove, Karl
  on election of 2006, 237–239, 281
  on the media, **148**
  photograph of, **236**
  "Swift Boat Veterans for Truth," 238, 273, 293–294, 296
Rowley, Coleen, 430–431
RU-486, 188, 503
Ruckus Society, 192
"Rule of thumb," 551
Rules Committee, House, 262, 330, 332, 336, 340

Rumsfeld, Donald
  on efforts to combat terrorism, **129**
  on going to war with the Army you have, 633
  Iraq War decisions of, 379
  objectives of, 639, 662–663
  on outsourcing military functions, 663
  relationship with Powell, 387
Russia, 645, **645,** 651
Rutherford Institute, 453
Sadat, Anwar, 658
Sallie Mae, 181
Salon, 125
Same-sex marriages
  legalization in individual states, 63, **63,** 504–506
  party politics and, 221
  public opinion on, 93, **93,** 180
  recognition of, performed in other states, 78, 505
  Supreme Court rulings on homosexuality and, 504
Sample, random, 98
Sanchez, Linda, **325**
Sanchez, Loretta, **325**
San Diego Union-Tribune, 120
Sanford, Edward, 474
Santeria religion, 486
Santorum, Rick, 113, 344
Saudi Arabia, 658
Sawyer, Diane, 134
Scalia, Antonin, 452, **452, 457,** 461, 462, 487
Schattschneider, E. E., 198–199, 204
Schiavo, Terri, **88,** 89–91, 115, 454
SCHIP (State Children's Health Insurance Program), 617
Schlesinger, Arthur, 380
School desegregation, 526–531, **529, 530,** 534, 544
School prayers, 458, 488–490
Schools. *See* Education
Schumer, Charles, 234
Schumpeter, Joseph, 592
Schwarzenegger, Arnold, 154
SCLC (Southern Christian Leadership Conference), 532
Scoops, 131
Search and seizure, 494
Sea Shepherds, 182
SEC (Securities and Exchange Commission), 416
Secession, 46–47, 48, 61
Second Amendment, 44, 493, 679
Second-generation discrimination, 538
Secretary of defense, 638
Secretary of state, 637–638
Secret prisons, 510
Securities and Exchange Commission (SEC), 416
Sedition Act of 1798, 132
Sedition Act of 1918, 473–474
Seditious speech, 473–476

Segregation. *See also* Desegregation
  de jure and *de facto,* 529–530, 533, 535–536, 544
  Jim Crow laws, 524
  Montgomery bus boycott, 194–195, **194,** 531–532
  in the North, 524
  presently, in schools, 535–536, **536**
  public opinion on, 111–112, **111**
  after Reconstruction, 49, 523–524
  school desegregation, 526–531, **529, 530,** 534, 544
  separate-but-equal doctrine, 524, 526
  in the South, 523–524
  in South Africa, 191
  Supreme Court rulings on, 52, 446–447
SEIU (Service Employees International Union), 172
Seizure, 494
Select committees, 337
Selective perception, 157–158
Self-belief, 20
Self-incrimination, 494–495
Senate. *See also* Congress
  approval of Supreme Court nominations, 448–450
  demographics of, 324–325, **324**
  evolution of organization of, 330–331
  fundraising by members of, 291–292
  incumbent elections in, 278, **279**
  leadership positions in, 333–334
  pay and perks of, 327
  senators buying their seats, 288
  unequal representation of citizens in, 38–39, **39**
Senate Appropriations Committees, 345
Senate Energy and National Resources Committee, 345
Senate majority leader, 333–334, **334**
Senate minority leader, 334
Senatorial courtesy, 370, 446–447
Senators, election of, 37, 40, 70, 330–331. *See also* Senate
Senior Executive Service (SES), 403, 422, 427, 432
Seniority rule, 336
Seniors
  health care for, 616–617
  Medicare, 107, 171, 409, **609,** 616–617
  proportion of health care costs for, 623
  Social Security, 609–611 (*See also* Social Security)
  Supplemental Security Income, **609,** 611–612
Sensenbrenner, James, 165

"Sense of the chamber" measures, 339
Separate-but-equal doctrine, 524, 526
Separation of church and state, 486
Separation of powers, 37–39, **38, 39**
September 11, 2001 attacks. *See* 9/11/2001 terrorist attacks
Service Employees International Union (SEIU), 172
SES (Senior Executive Service), 403, 422, 427, 432
Set America Free, 194–195
Setting the agenda, 153–154, 374–375
Seventeenth Amendment, 37, 67
Seventh Amendment, 44, 679
Seventh-Day Adventists, 487
Sex discrimination, 550–560
  affirmative action, 560–562
  Civil Rights Act of 1964, 552
  in credit, 556–558
  in employment, 553–556
  Equal Rights Amendment, 263, 551, 552–553
  against men, 559–560
  in organizations, 481
  against women judges, **459**
  women judges on, 449
Sexual harassment
  suit by Paula Jones, 453, **454,** 557
  Thomas' confirmation hearings and, 436
  at work, 557
Sexual relations, 93, 504
Sexual speech, 477–478
Shadow government, 367
Sharecroppers, 523
Sharpton, Al, 257
Shays, Daniel, 31
Shays's Rebellion, 31
Sheehan, Cindy, **192**
Sherman, Roger, 378
Sierra Club, 182
Signing statements, 381
Simpson, Alan, 133
Simpson, O.J., 540
Sinclair Broadcast Group, 124
Single-issue interest groups, 182–184. *See also* Public interest groups
Single-member districts, 206–207
Sixteenth Amendment, 680
Sixth Amendment, 44, 495–497, 679
60 Minutes, 148
Slavery
  abolition in northern states, 521
  abolitionists, 213, 551
  under Articles of Confederation, 34
  by Barbary pirates, 30
  black masters, 522
  Civil War and, 46
  Constitutional Convention on,

34–35, 40
core values and, 18, 19
cultural diversity in, 6–7
current, 544
Dred Scott decision and, 440, 521–522
Emancipation Proclamation, 46–47, 48
by Founders, 42
laws on importation of, 35
return of escaped slaves, 35, 78
Revolutionary War and, 521
rise of Republican party and, 213
slave ship diagram, **35**
slaves hired out, **521**
Thirteenth Amendment abolition of, 48, 522
widespread establishment of, 521
Slepian, Barnett, 183
Smart, Leslie, **483**
Smith, Adam, 571
Smith, Alfred, 258, **487**
Smith, Howard, 552
Smith Act of 1940, 474
"Sneak-and-peek searches," 512
Snowe, Olympia, 226, 319
Social contract, 41
"The social issue," 107
Social rootedness, 252
Social Security
benefits from, 610–611
under Bush, 101, 362–363, 399, 587–588, 625–626
under Clinton, 100
current problems in, 625–626
direct payments for, **609**
financing of, 609–610
limit on income taxed for, 362, 627, **627**
in the New Deal, 68
raising of retirement age, 626
as regressive tax, 583
Social Security Trust Fund borrowing, 588–589, 625
Social welfare programs, 605–630
accusations of waste and fraud in, 409
under Clinton, 100, 107
for corporations, 621–622
costs of programs for poor *vs.* middle income and rich, **621**
decline in party functions and, 222–223
direct aid payment types, **609**
education subsidies, 617–619, **619**
evolution of, 608–609
for farmers, 614–615, 620, **620**
food subsidies, 613–614
health care programs, 616–617 (*See also* Medicaid; Medicare)
housing subsidies, 619–620
impact of income support programs, 616
liberals and conservatives on, 106–107, **107**
under the New Deal, 68

political and legal bases of, 607–608
of political party organizations, 213
for the poor, 611–614, **612,** 627–629
reforms of, 613, 627–629
responsiveness of, 629
for retirees and their dependents, 609–611 (*See also* Social Security)
superwaivers in, 82
veterans benefits, 616
in welfare states, 609
for working poor, 613
Soft money, 292, 296
Sound bites, 132
Sources, protection of reporters', 482–483
Souter, David, 436, **457**
South Carolina, black legislators after the Civil War, **240**
Southern Baptists, 62
Southern Christian Leadership Conference (SCLC), 532
Soviet Union, 645, **645,** 651. *See also* Cold War
Speaker of the House
committee chair appointments by, 336
evolution of role of, 330–331
Hastert as, 310, **316,** 332–333, 340, 349
Pelosi as, **316,** 331
in presidential succession, 367
Special-interest caucus, 350
Special interests. *See* Interest groups
Special Supplemental Nutritional Program for Women, Infants, and Children (WIC), 614
Spectacle presidency, 393–394, **394**
Specter, Arlen, **336,** 337
Speech, freedom of. *See* Freedom of speech
Spin, media, 133–134
Split-ticket voting, 224, **224,** 248
Spoils system, 303
Sports, women's, 558–559, **558**
SSI (Supplemental Security Income), **609,** 611–612
Stacking votes, 242
Stagflation, 576
Standing committees, 335
Stanton, Elizabeth Cady, 245, 247, 551
Star, 126
Stare decisis, 458
Star Wars (SDI), 652
State-centered federalism, 65, 81–83
State Children's Health Insurance Program (SCHIP), 617
State courts, 444, **445**
State governments
on abortion, 63, 500–501
under Articles of Confederation, 30, 31
Bill of Rights and, 472
under Bush administration,

81–82
federalism and, 37
on food safety, 81
as lobbyists, 75, 78
national-centered *vs.* state-centered federalism and, 65
number of employees in, **71**
political culture and, 62–63
recent growth of, 71, **71**
relations between states, 78–79
responsiveness of, 79–80
sales taxes, 585–586
same-sex marriages and, 63, **63,** 78, 504–506
state-local relations, 79
state religions, 9–10
supremacy clause and restriction of, 64
Tenth Amendment and, 64–65
unfunded mandates in, 74
as unitary systems, 59–60
in welfare reform, 627–628
State nominating conventions, 259
State of the Union addresses, 368–369
State party organizations, 227–228
States, equal representation in the Senate, 37–39, **39**
States' rights, as code for white supremacy, 218
States' Rights Party, 217, **218**
Statistical Abstract of the United States, 420
Statutory rape, 559
Steel industry, government assistance after 9/11, 174
Steering, by real estate agents, 535
Stem cell research, 81, 492
Stevens, John Paul, **457,** 469–470, **470,** 493, 515–516
Stevens, Ted, 307, **329,** 346, **346**
Stewart, Potter, 497
Stockman, David, 128, 329, 587
Stone, Harlan, 456
Stonewall (New York City), 178–179
Strategic Defense Initiative (SDI), 652
Straw polls, 98
Stress and duress procedures, 509
Student loan programs, 181
Students for America, 285
Stump speeches, **257**
Subcommittees, 335, 337
Subsidies
corporate, 621–622
education, 617–619, **619**
to Enron, 621
farm, 614–615, 620, **620**
food, 614
homeownership, 622
housing, 619–620
school lunch, 614
state, to businesses, 79
Succession of the presidency, 367
Suffrage, definition of, 240. *See also* Voting rights

Sugar industry, 303, **620**
Sunshine Act, 412
Superdelegates, 261
Super Size Me, 148
Super Tuesday, 262
Superwaivers, 82, 628
Supplemental Security Income (SSI), **609,** 611–612
Supply-side economics, 576
Supremacy clause, 64
Supreme Court. *See also* Judiciary
on abortion, 437, 453, 461, 462, 499–502
activist judges, 456–457, **457**
on affirmative action, 562
as appellate court, 444, **445**
on bilingual education, 545
on birth control, 498
on busing of students, 530–531
on campaign financing reform, 289, 292–293
on capital punishment, 497–498
Constitution interpretation by, 455–456
on cruel and unusual punishment, 497–498
deciding cases, 459–461
demographics of judges, 450
on demonstrations, 478
in election of 2000, 83, 228, 457
on executive privilege, 28, 53–54
on free exercise of religion, 486
in the future, 443–444
on hearing cases from Guantanamo Bay Naval Base, 469–470, 515–516
on homosexual rights, 504–507
humor in, 462
independence of judges, 451–453
interest groups and, 453
on Japanese internment, 519–520, 565
judge qualifications, 450–451
on line-item veto, 347
making law, 458–459
national supremacy in, 440
during the New Deal, 49–50, 70
precedents in, 457–458
on presidential removal powers, 370–371
on prior restraint, 482
on publication of the Pentagon Papers, 481, **482**
on reapportionment, 322
recent trend toward state immunity from federal laws, 82–83
on regulation of corporations, 440–441
relationship with the media, 138–139
on religious symbols, 491
on restrictions on gathering news, 482–483
on right to counsel, 495–496
on right to die, 507

Supreme Court (continued)
on right to die laws, 507–508
on school desegregation,
527–529
on school prayer, 489–490
on search and seizure, 494
on seditious speech, 474
on segregation, 524, 526, 527
selection of cases before, 454
selection of justices, 447–450
on self-incrimination, 495
on sex discrimination, 553
on slavery, 440, 521–522
statute interpretation by,
454–455
on term limits, 320–321
Surveillance. *See* Electronic
surveillance
Surveillance courts, 446
Swearing, 476
Sweden, unitary system in, 59
"Swift Boat Veterans for Truth,"
127, 238, 273, 293–294, 296
Swing states, 265–266
Symbiotic relationships, of media
and politicians, 128–132,
129
Symbolic speech, 479–480, **479**
Taft, William Howard, 393
Talk radio, 125, 126, 142, 158,
294
Tammany Hall machine,
214–215, 287
Taney, Roger, 440, 522
TANF (Temporary Assistance for
Needy Families), **609**, 613,
627–628
Tariffs, northern states *vs.*
southern states on, 35–36.
See also Trade
Task forces, 338
Tauzin, Billy, 336
Tax deductions and credits, 583,
586, **586**
Taxes
under the Articles of
Confederation, 30
capital gains tax cut, 174–175,
190, 303, 306
congressional access to returns,
338
in Constitutional Convention,
35–36, 64
consumption, 585–586
corporate welfare and, 621–622
cuts for the wealthy, 114,
221–222, 226
deductions and credits, 583,
586, **586**
earned income tax credit, 585,
613, 628
on e-commerce, 81
of Enron, 305
estate tax, 101, 569–571, 601
exemptions for specific
corporations, 197
family subsidies, 621–622
federal personal income, 67
fiscal policy and, 575–576
flat tax, 584–585

homeownership subsidies, 622
House origination of, 34
on the national bank by states,
66
national sales tax, 585–586
reform of, 582–586, **583, 585,
586**
relative rates of, 582
religious, 9
Shays's rebellion and, 31
simplification of, 583–584
Social Security, 609–610
sources of, **583**
state subsidies to businesses, 79
tax fairness, 582–583
token rebates on, 113
Tax neutrality, 583
Tax reform, 582–586, **583, 585,
586**
Teamsters, 172
Teapot Dome scandal, 280, **288,**
289
Technology, interest group
formation and, 167
Teen pregnancies, 500–502
Telecommunications Act of 1996,
124
Television
candidate appearances,
269–270
candidate debates, 157–158,
270–271, **270**
congressional gift of airwave
space, 297
episodic coverage on, 159
news, 121–123, **121**, 152–153,
643–644 (*See also* Media)
press conferences, 131, 137
Temporary Assistance for Needy
Families (TANF), **609**, 613,
627–628
Tenant, George, 425
Ten Commandments, display of,
491
Tennessee Valley Authority
(TVA), 418
Tenth Amendment, 44, 64–65,
66, 679
Term limits, 320–321, 337
"Terri's law," 90
Terrorism. *See* 9/11/2001
terrorist attacks; War on
terrorism
Texas, immigrants in, 596
Textbooks, political socialization
and, 95
Think tanks, 643
Third Amendment, 44, 48, 498,
679
Third parties, 208–210, 264
Thirteenth Amendment, 48, 522,
680
Thomas, Clarence
as activist judge, **457**
confirmation hearings of, 57,
130, 349, 436, 466
lack of humor of, 462
nomination of, 448
photograph of, **458**
Thomas, Evan, 119–120, 161

Thomas, Helen, 137
Thompson, Andrea, 149
Thompson, Florence, **598**
Three-fifths Compromise, 35, 40
Thune, John, 113
Thurman, Strom, 217, **218, 341**
Tilden, Samuel, 523
Tillman, Benjamin, 241
Tillman, Pat, 141
Tinker, Mary Beth, 480, **481**
Tippell, Leanne, **483**
Title IX, 558–559, **558**
Tocqueville, Alexis de, 19, 167,
461, 636
Torricelli, Robert, 104, 311
Torture, 509–510, **509**, 660
Town meetings, 20, 104
Tracking polls, 102
Trade
Constitutional Convention on,
35–36
e-commerce, 81
farm subsidies and, 615
foreign policy and, 643,
664–666
free *vs.* protectionism, 653
overturning federal laws on
interstate, 82
tariffs, northern states *vs.*
southern states on, 35–36
World Trade Organization,
192, 615, 664–665
Trade deficit, 664
Tragedy of the commons,
578–579
Transportation, need for
regulation of, 578–579
Treaties, power of president in
withdrawing from, 377
Tribal restoration, 548–550
Trifecta bill, 569–571, 601
Truman, Bess, 389
Truman, Harry S
character of, 397
containment policy of,
646–647
on economic advisors, 576
faulty polls during election of,
100
judicial appointments of, 451,
452–453
Korean War and, 267
ordering MacArthur home,
382
public opinion of, **396**
racial integration in the military
by, 217
seizure of steel mills by, 452
style of, 154–155
whistle-stop campaign of, **261**
Truman Doctrine, 647
Trusts, nineteenth-century,
288–289, **289**
Truth in Mileage Act, 437
TVA (Tennessee Valley
Authority), 418
Twain, Mark, 300
Tweed, Boss, 256–257
Twelfth Amendment, 679–680
Twentieth Amendment, 681

Twenty-fifth Amendment, 367,
682
Twenty-first Amendment, **46,**
681
Twenty-fourth Amendment, 682
Twenty-second Amendment,
681–682
Twenty-seventh Amendment, 682
Twenty-sixth Amendment, 246,
682
Twenty-third Amendment, 682
Two-party system, 206–207
"Underclass," 541, 561
"Understanding clause," 241
Unemployment insurance, 611
Unfit for Command, 294
Unfunded mandates, 74–75, 84
Unilateralism, 654, 656
Unions and unionization. *See also*
Workers' rights
Bush on, 372
court decisions on, 441
current decline of, 171–173,
173
history of unionization,
171–172, **172**
localization of, 196
political action committees of,
295
in red *vs.* blue states, 109
voter mobilization by, 255
Unitary executive, 380–381, 428,
640
Unitary systems, 59–60
United Nations, compared with
Articles of Confederation, 30
United States v. *Nixon*, 28, 33–34
"United We Stand America"
movement, 210
Universities. *See* Colleges
University of California v. *Bakke*,
562
"Unlawful combatants," 470, 515.
See also Guantanamo Bay,
Cuba
Unreasonable searches and
seizures, 494
Urban League, 178
U.S. Army Corps of Engineers
(USACE), 403–405, 432
U.S. Citizenship and Immigration
Services (USCIS), 8, 513
U.S. Family Network, 309
USACE (U.S. Army Corps of
Engineers), 403–405, 432
USA PATRIOT Act
alien registration and
detentions in, 513
bipartisan passage of, 228–229,
414
foreign students in, 513
surveillance provisions in, 446,
512–513
USA Today, 139
USCIS (U.S. Citizenship and
Immigration Services), 8,
513
USDA (U.S. Department of
Agriculture), 420, 613
Used-car legislation, 303, 437

Utah
  age demographics in, 62
  polygamy in, 63
VA (Department of Defense and
  Veterans Affairs), 617
Value-added tax (VAT), 586
Vanderbilt, Cornelius, 288
Ventura, Jesse, 154
Vermont, same-sex unions in, 78,
  179, **180,** 505
Veterans Administration, 535
Veterans benefits, 535, **609,** 616,
  617
Veto power, 342, 375
Vice presidency, 256, 264,
  387–390
Vidal, Gore, 5
Vietnam syndrome, 651
Vietnam War
  armed intervention stage of,
    648–649, **649, 650**
  1968 Democratic platform and,
    262–263
  early period of, 648
  Gulf of Tonkin Resolution,
    311, 648–649
  lessons from, 649–651
  media coverage of, 145
  opposition to, 475, 479, **479**
  political identity of college
    students during, 96
  power of the presidency
    during, 52
  purge of State Department
    prior to, 639
  "Swift Boat Veterans for Truth,"
    127, 238, 273, 293–294,
    296
  voting age lowering during,
    246
Villaraigosa, Antonio, **244**
Vinson, Fred, 474, 527
Violence
  against African Americans, 193,
    241, 525, **525, 526,** 532
  in the media, 151
  as protest, 193
Violence Policy Center, 182
Virginia Plan, 34
Virtual March on Washington,
  190
Voinovich, George, 278
Volcker, Paul, 580
Voltaire, 9
Voter mobilization, by political
  party, 254–255, **255**
Voter registration, 252–254, 497,
  532
Voter turnout
  cost and benefit calculation
    and, 255–256
  demographics of, 249–251
  mandates and, 280
  postregistration laws and, 254
  Progressive reforms and,
    248–249
  reasons for low, 252–256
  recent, 249
  registration procedures and,
    252–254

Voting. *See also* Elections; Voter
    turnout; Voting rights
  absentee balloting, 254
  age differences and, 10
  barriers to registration of,
    252–254
  for Congress, 279–280
  issue votes, 231–232
  mobilizing the vote, 191
  political activism in the
    nineteenth century, 248
  poverty and, 10
  Progressive reforms on,
    214–215, **216,** 248–249
  property ownership and, 40
  reforms by Andrew Jackson,
    211
  regional differences in, 10
  retrospective, 232, **232**
  role of parties in shaping votes,
    228–232
  slavery and, 35
  split-ticket, 224, **224,** 248
Voting age, 246
Voting machines, 246–248
Voting rights
  of African Americans, 11, 48,
    240–241, 522, 524, 526,
    532
  denial of, 241
  early limitations on, 240
  electoral reform legislation of
    2002, 246–248
  extensions of, 11
  federal regulation of, 23
  of felons, 246
  Fifteenth Amendment, 48, 240,
    494–495, 522, 524
  gerrymandering and, 242–244,
    243
  under Johnson, 69, 241–244,
    242, 534, 535
  of Native Americans, 548
  of women, 245–246, 551
  of young people, 246
Voting Rights Act (VRA) of
    1965, 241–244, **242,** 534,
    535
Vowell, Jacob, **413**
Wahabism, 658
Wallace, George
  courting black votes, 242
  on government bureaucrats,
    405
  presidential campaign of, 209,
    264
  on segregation, 528
Wall Street Journal, 141
Wal-Mart, health insurance for
    employees of, 606
War, declaration of, 23
War on terrorism. *See also* USA
    PATRIOT Act
  border control and, 58
  campaign strategy and,
    237–239, 281
  capital gains tax cut and,
    174–175
  disproportionate costs of Iraq
    War in, 633–634

expansion of presidential
    powers in, 380–381
  Guantanamo Bay detainees,
    468, 469–470, 515–516
  impact on voting, 267
  interrogations, 508–510, **509**
  referred to as "crusade," 138
  reluctance of Democrats to
    criticize, 228–229
  renditions in, 510
  secret prisons, 510
War Powers Resolution, 382, 640
War profiteering, after 9/11, 175
Warren, Earl
  as activist judge, 456
  appointment of, 441–442, **442,**
    452
  on desegregation, 528–529
  on seditious speech, 474
  on self-incrimination, 495
Warren, Mercy Otis, 32–33
Warren Court
  accomplishments of, 441–442,
    442, 443, 457
  on birth control, 498
  on demonstrations, 478
  on exclusionary rule, 494
  on libel laws, 483–484
  on obscenity, 484–485
  on right to counsel, 495–496
  on school desegregation,
    527–529
  on school prayer, 488–489
  on self-incrimination, 495
Warsaw Pact, 647
Washington, D.C. climate, **320**
Washington, George
  accusation of vote-buying by,
    287
  on Articles of Confederation,
    29
  cabinet of, 412, **416**
  at the Constitutional
    Convention, 31–32, 34,
    35
  paintings of, **26, 210**
  on two-house legislature, 37
Washington Post, 144, 150, 186
Washington Times, 120, 141
Waterboarding, 509
Watergate scandal
  campaign financing reform
    after, 289
  confidential tapes in, 27–28,
    53–54
  executive privilege and, 372
  public reaction to, 92, 312
  as use of power to punish
    personal enemies, 311
Water resources, 79, 620
Watts, J.C., 540
Waxman, Henry, 344
WBA (Whistleblowers Protection
    Agency), 422
Wealth gap
  American Dream and, **599**
  causes of, 598–599
  increasing trends in, 306, **306,**
    599–600, **629**
  responsibility of government in

reducing, 106, 597–598
The Wealth of Nations (Smith),
  571
Weapons of mass destruction
    (WMDs)
  distortion of intelligence on,
    129–130, **130,** 425
  media reports on, 145
  nuclear proliferation, 661, **662**
  public opinion on Iraq having,
    105
  strategy to link Hussein to, 101
Webster, Daniel, 330
Webster, Noah, 16
Weidenbaum, Murray, 587
Welfare programs. *See* Social
    welfare programs
Welfare states, 609
Western Governors' Association,
  85
Whig Party, **212,** 213, 216, **253**
Whips, 331, 333
Whistleblowers, 403–405, **404,**
  430, 432
Whistleblowers Protection
    Agency (WBA), 422
Whistle-stop campaigns, **261**
Whitecaps, 525
White cards, 15
White families in poverty, **628**
White House Office, 386–387
White primaries, 241
Whitewater investigation, 138,
  150, 311
Whitman, Walt, 5
WIC (Special Supplemental
    Nutritional Program for
    Women, Infants, and
    Children), 614
Wilder, Douglas, 244
Wilkie, Wendell, **260**
Wilson, Edith, 388
Wilson, James, 34
Wilson, Joseph, 129–130, **130**
Wilson, Woodrow
  on League of Nations, 646
  nervous collapse of, 367
  on neutral competence, 422
  on seditious speech, 384,
    473–474
  on the Supreme Court, 45
  Winner take all, 206–207
  Win without War, 190
  Wiretapping. *See* Electronic
    surveillance
WMDs. *See* Weapons of mass
    destruction
Women. *See also* Sex
    discrimination
  in abolitionist movement, 551
  citizenship of, 550
  in Congress, 324, **324**
  credit for, 556–558
  declining group memberships
    by, 169
  in federal bureaucracy,
    404–406, **406,** 432
  funding for sports of, 558–559,
    558

Women (continued)
  growing support of Democratic
      Party, 220
  as judges, **448,** 449, **459**
  as lawyers, 449
  as national constituencies, 323
  party identification, 220
  in political office, 247
  possibility of election to
      presidency, 258, **258**
  public interest groups for, 176
  in red *vs.* blue states, 109, **110**
  reproductive rights, **109,** 183,
      498, 503–505 (*See also*
      Abortion)
  rights movement, 551–559
  sexual harassment of, 436, 453,
      454, 557
  traditional gender roles,
      550–551
  violence against, 551
  violence against black men
      with independence of, 525

voting rights of, 245–246, 551
  during World War II, **552, 553**
Women's movement, 551–559
Women's Rights Convention of
    1848, 551
Wood, Alastair, 188
Woodhull, Victoria Claflin, 247
Woods, Tiger, 13
Woodward, Bob, 27–28
Workers' rights. *See also* Unions
    and unionization
  affirmative action, 560–562
  in blue *vs.* red states, 109
  child labor laws, **440,** 441
  court decisions on, **440,** 441
  family leaves, 556, 559
  globalization and, 592–594
  government involvement in,
      572
  illegal immigration and, 594–595
  under *laissez-faire* policies, 49
  of Latino farmworkers, 544
  during the New Deal, 49, 219

overtime regulations, 170
racial discrimination in
    employment, 534, 538
sex discrimination in
    employment, 553–556,
    556
sexual harassment at work, 557
state laws on, 82
Working America, 172
Working poor, 613
Works Progress Administration
    (WPA), **68**
World Trade Center terrorist
    attacks. *See* 9/11/2001
    terrorist attacks
World Trade Organization
    (WTO), 192, 615, 664–665
World War I
  public opinion in, **643,** 646
  seditious speech during, 384,
      473–474
  veterans' benefits, 618
  women's suffrage and, **245,** 246

World War II
  entry into, 646
  growth of federal government
      during, 69
  intolerance of dissent during
      and after, 474
  Soviet casualties in, 645–647,
      645
  women in, **552, 553**
WPA (Works Progress
    Administration), **68**
Writ of certiorari, 454, **496**
Writs of assistance, 492
WTO (World Trade
    Organization), 192, 615,
    664–665
Wyoming, women's suffrage in,
    245
Young, Don, 185
Al-Zawahiri, Ayman, 658